T0188810

Lecture Notes in Computer Science　10639

Commenced Publication in 1973
Founding and Former Series Editors:
Gerhard Goos, Juris Hartmanis, and Jan van Leeuwen

More information about this series at http://www.springer.com/series/7407

Derong Liu · Shengli Xie
Yuanqing Li · Dongbin Zhao
El-Sayed M. El-Alfy (Eds.)

Neural Information Processing

24th International Conference, ICONIP 2017
Guangzhou, China, November 14–18, 2017
Proceedings, Part VI

 Springer

Editors
Derong Liu
Guangdong University of Technology
Guangzhou
China

Shengli Xie
Guangdong University of Technology
Guangzhou
China

Yuanqing Li
South China University of Technology
Guangzhou
China

Dongbin Zhao
Institute of Automation
Chinese Academy of Sciences
Beijing
China

El-Sayed M. El-Alfy
King Fahd University of Petroleum
  and Minerals
Dhahran
Saudi Arabia

ISSN 0302-9743   ISSN 1611-3349   (electronic)
Lecture Notes in Computer Science
ISBN 978-3-319-70135-6   ISBN 978-3-319-70136-3   (eBook)
https://doi.org/10.1007/978-3-319-70136-3

Library of Congress Control Number: 2017957558

LNCS Sublibrary: SL1 – Theoretical Computer Science and General Issues

Printed on acid-free paper

This Springer imprint is published by Springer Nature
The registered company is Springer International Publishing AG
The registered company address is: Gewerbestrasse 11, 6330 Cham, Switzerland

Preface

ICONIP 2017 – the 24th International Conference on Neural Information Processing – was held in Guangzhou, China, continuing the ICONIP conference series, which started in 1994 in Seoul, South Korea. Over the past 24 years, ICONIP has been held in Australia, China, India, Japan, Korea, Malaysia, New Zealand, Qatar, Singapore, Thailand, and Turkey. ICONIP has now become a well-established, popular and high-quality conference series on neural information processing in the region and around the world. With the growing popularity of neural networks in recent years, we have witnessed an increase in the number of submissions and in the quality of papers. Guangzhou, Romanized as Canton in the past, is the capital and largest city of southern China's Guangdong Province. It is also one of the five National Central Cities at the core of the Pearl River Delta. It is a key national transportation hub and trading port. November is the best month in the year to visit Guangzhou with comfortable weather. All participants of ICONIP 2017 had a technically rewarding experience as well as a memorable stay in this great city.

A neural network is an information processing structure inspired by biological nervous systems, such as the brain. It consists of a large number of highly interconnected processing elements, called neurons. It has the capability of learning from example. The field of neural networks has evolved rapidly in recent years. It has become a fusion of a number of research areas in engineering, computer science, mathematics, artificial intelligence, operations research, systems theory, biology, and neuroscience. Neural networks have been widely applied for control, optimization, pattern recognition, image processing, signal processing, etc.

ICONIP 2017 aimed to provide a high-level international forum for scientists, researchers, educators, industrial professionals, and students worldwide to present state-of-the-art research results, address new challenges, and discuss trends in neural information processing and applications. ICONIP 2017 invited scholars in all areas of neural network theory and applications, computational neuroscience, machine learning, and others.

The conference received 856 submissions from 3,255 authors in 56 countries and regions across all six continents. Based on rigorous reviews by the Program Committee members and reviewers, 563 high-quality papers were selected for publication in the conference proceedings. We would like to express our sincere gratitude to all the reviewers for the time and effort they generously gave to the conference. We are very grateful to the Institute of Automation of the Chinese Academy of Sciences, Guangdong University of Technology, South China University of Technology, Springer's *Lecture Notes in Computer Science* (LNCS), IEEE/CAA *Journal of Automatica Sinica* (JAS), and the Asia Pacific Neural Network Society (APNNS) for their financial support. We would also like to thank the publisher, Springer, for their cooperation in publishing the proceedings in the prestigious LNCS series and for sponsoring the best paper awards at ICONIP 2017.

September 2017

Derong Liu
Shengli Xie
Yuanqing Li
Dongbin Zhao
El-Sayed M. El-Alfy

ICONIP 2017 Organization

Asia Pacific Neural Network Society

General Chair

Derong Liu   Chinese Academy of Sciences and Guangdong University
                               of Technology, China

Advisory Committee

Sabri Arik   Istanbul University, Turkey
Tamer Basar   University of Illinois, USA
Dimitri Bertsekas   Massachusetts Institute of Technology, USA
Jonathan Chan   King Mongkut's University of Technology, Thailand
C.L. Philip Chen   The University of Macau, SAR China
Kenji Doya   Okinawa Institute of Science and Technology, Japan
Minyue Fu   The University of Newcastle, Australia
Tom Gedeon   Australian National University, Australia
Akira Hirose   The University of Tokyo, Japan
Zeng-Guang Hou   Chinese Academy of Sciences, China
Nikola Kasabov   Auckland University of Technology, New Zealand
Irwin King   Chinese University of Hong Kong, SAR China
Robert Kozma   University of Memphis, USA
Soo-Young Lee   Korea Advanced Institute of Science and Technology,
                               South Korea
Frank L. Lewis   University of Texas at Arlington, USA
Chu Kiong Loo   University of Malaya, Malaysia
Baoliang Lu   Shanghai Jiao Tong University, China
Seiichi Ozawa   Kobe University, Japan
Marios Polycarpou   University of Cyprus, Cyprus
Danil Prokhorov   Toyota Technical Center, USA
DeLiang Wang   The Ohio State University, USA
Jun Wang   City University of Hong Kong, SAR China
Jin Xu   Peking University, China
Gary G. Yen   Oklahoma State University, USA
Paul J. Werbos   Retired from the National Science Foundation, USA

Program Chairs

Shengli Xie	Guangdong University of Technology, China
Yuanqing Li	South China University of Technology, China
Dongbin Zhao	Chinese Academy of Sciences, China
El-Sayed M. El-Alfy	King Fahd University of Petroleum and Minerals, Saudi Arabia

Program Co-chairs

Shukai Duan	Southwest University, China
Kazushi Ikeda	Nara Institute of Science and Technology, Japan
Weng Kin Lai	Tunku Abdul Rahman University College, Malaysia
Shiliang Sun	East China Normal University, China
Qinglai Wei	Chinese Academy of Sciences, China
Wei Xing Zheng	University of Western Sydney, Australia

Regional Chairs

Cesare Alippi	Politecnico di Milano, Italy
Tingwen Huang	Texas A&M University at Qatar, Qatar
Dianhui Wang	La Trobe University, Australia

Invited Session Chairs

Wei He	University of Science and Technology Beijing, China
Dianwei Qian	North China Electric Power University, China
Manuel Roveri	Politecnico di Milano, Italy
Dong Yue	Nanjing University of Posts and Telecommunications, China

Poster Session Chairs

Sung Bae Cho	Yonsei University, South Korea
Ping Guo	Beijing Normal University, China
Yifei Pu	Sichuan University, China
Bin Xu	Northwestern Polytechnical University, China
Zhigang Zeng	Huazhong University of Science and Technology, China

Tutorial and Workshop Chairs

Long Cheng	Chinese Academy of Sciences, China
Kaizhu Huang	Xi'an Jiaotong-Liverpool University, China
Amir Hussain	University of Stirling, UK

James Kwok	Hong Kong University of Science and Technology, SAR China
Huajin Tang	Sichuan University, China

Panel Discussion Chairs

Lei Guo	Beihang University, China
Hongyi Li	Bohai University, China
Hye Young Park	Kyungpook National University, South Korea
Lipo Wang	Nanyang Technological University, Singapore

Award Committee Chairs

Haibo He	University of Rhode Island, USA
Zhong-Ping Jiang	New York University, USA
Minho Lee	Kyungpook National University, South Korea
Andrew Leung	City University of Hong Kong, SAR China
Tieshan Li	Dalian Maritime University, China
Lidan Wang	Southwest University, China
Jun Zhang	South China University of Technology, China

Publicity Chairs

Jun Fu	Northeastern University, China
Min Han	Dalian University of Technology, China
Yanjun Liu	Liaoning University of Technology, China
Stefano Squartini	Università Politecnica delle Marche, Italy
Kay Chen Tan	National University of Singapore, Singapore
Kevin Wong	Murdoch University, Australia
Simon X. Yang	University of Guelph, Canada

Local Arrangements Chair

Renquan Lu	Guangdong University of Technology, China

Publication Chairs

Ding Wang	Chinese Academy of Sciences, China
Jian Wang	China University of Petroleum, China

Finance Chair

Xinping Guan	Shanghai Jiao Tong University, China

Registration Chair

Qinmin Yang   Zhejiang University, China

Conference Secretariat

Biao Luo   Chinese Academy of Sciences, China
Bo Zhao   Chinese Academy of Sciences, China

Contents

Pattern Recognition

Robotics and Control

Electromyogram Activation Reflects Property of Isochrony Phenomenon During Cyclic Human Arm Movement

Hiroshi Yokoyama[✉], Rie Kurai, Isao Nambu, and Yasuhiro Wada

Graduate School of Engineering, Nagaoka University of Technology,
1603-1 Kamitomioka, Nagaoka, Niigata 940-2188, Japan
h_yokoyama@stn.nagaokaut.ac.jp

Abstract. The isochrony principle is a well-known phenomenon, whereby the speed of human arm movement is regulated to increase as its planned trajectory distance increases. The isochrony principle is observed in many studies, but its relationship with the motor planning process has never been explained. To address this issue, we attempt to explain the relationship between the isochrony principle and trajectory planning based on observable physiological information. Assuming that electromyography (EMG) reflects the temporal aspect of motor commanded signals, we directly evaluated the EMG changes during cyclic arm movement to consider the physiological mechanism underlying the isochrony phenomenon. Our presented result suggested the tendency that duration-average of the EMG change is equal, regardless of the differences in the movement distance. Its tendency suggest experimental evidence that human arm trajectory is planned to ensure constant EMG changes, rather than for equalization of movement durations.

Keywords: Electromyography · Isochrony principle · Human arm trajectory

1 Introduction

The isochrony principle is a well-known phenomenon of human motor control [1,2,4], where human arm movement is planned so that its speed is increased to compensate for increased movement distance. Therefore, when we continuously hand-write two letters of similar trajectories but different sizes the durations of movement in each trajectory are approximately equal, regardless of the differences in the movement distance.

Even though this phenomenon was observed in many situations for hand movements [1–4], to date, most studies have not explained the relationship between the isochrony principle and the computational criteria of motor planning. One previous study [2] suggested that the isochrony phenomenon is observed as a secondary effect of point-to-point movement time equalization,

© Springer International Publishing AG 2017
D. Liu et al. (Eds.): ICONIP 2017, Part VI, LNCS 10639, pp. 3–10, 2017.
https://doi.org/10.1007/978-3-319-70136-3_1

based on the minimum commanded torque change criterion [5]. The computational criterion of trajectory planning assumes that movement trajectory must pass from beginning point to end point through some specified points (so-called via-points). The minimum commanded torque change criterion considers two hypotheses [5]: (1) the commanded torque reflects a temporal aspect of the motor commanded signal for human trajectory planning, and (2) the transit time of arm movement between each via-point is adjusted to ensure constant commanded torque change. These two hypotheses suggest the possibility that the commanded torque change is equalized to ensure constant commanded torque change between two similar trajectories with different size. Experimental evidence from the study supports this suggestion. However, the previous study considered the computational relationship with isochrony phenomenon based only on the kinematical information. The study did not mention how physiological mechanisms are involved in the relationship between trajectory planning process and isochrony phenomenon. If said experimental evidence were correct, the relevant property of the isochrony phenomenon would be also reflected in the observational biological signal involved in the human arm movement.

To address this issue, we attempt to explain the relationship between the isochrony principle and human motor control based on the observable physiological property. In this study, the subjects conducted two reaching tasks, figure eight and double elliptical shapes, which were applied in the previous isochrony studies [2,4]. Assuming that electromyography (EMG) reflects the temporal aspect of motor commanded signals, we measured EMGs during the arm movement trajectory of these tasks. For analysis, we evaluated EMG temporal change duration averages to consider how EMG changes are controlled to satisfy the isochrony principle.

2   Procedure and Design

2.1   Pre-task: Maximum Voluntary Contraction (MVC) Measurement

To consider the variance of measured EMG signal depending on the individuals, the EMG signals were normalized by the value of maximum activation for each channel in the analyses (see Analysis for the details). This task was conducted to evaluate the maximum value of EMG activation for each subject.

Nine healthy right-handed males participated in this experiments (mean age: 22 years old) after obtaining written informed consent. The subjects sat on a chair placed in front of a monitor, and grasped a joystick of the force sensor (IFS-67M25A25-I40, NITTA Corporation, Japan; sampling frequency: 200 Hz). After alignment of the initial hand posture (hand, elbow, and shoulder positions), the subjects conducted a task following visual and auditory stimuli. The visual stimuli guided to the direction from an upright ($0°$) position to $135°$ in eight steps of $45°$ with clockwise-order, and the stimuli presented at one direction on each trial. After the stimuli was presented, the subjects were instructed to sustain the max voluntary contraction for the corresponding direction according to the presented stimuli for 3 s using the joystick. In total, the visual stimuli were presented 24 times ($= 3 \times 8$ directions) on each session, and the subjects conducted one session this task. We then measured 11-channels surface EMGs (Trigno Wireless EMG, Delsys, INC., Massachusetts, USA; sampling frequency: 2000 Hz), which were put in the corresponding positions including anterior deltoid, medial deltoid, posterior deltoid, pectoralis major, teres major, long head of biceps brachii, long head of triceps brachii, triceps medialis, triceps lateralis, brachialis, and brachioradial.

2.2 Main-Task: Cyclic Arm Movement Task

Experimental Environment. The experimental environment is illustrated in Fig. 1. In the cyclic arm movement task, the subjects sat on a chair placed in front of a monitor (Fig. 1), and their wrists were supported by a brace mounted on an air sled to reduce the influence of friction (Fig. 1). Moreover, the infrared markers were located on three positions (hand, elbow, shoulder) to measure the arm movement trajectory while performing the task (Fig. 1). The movement trajectories in each marker were measured by the 3-dimensional motion capture system (Optotrak Certus, Northern Digital Inc., Waterloo, Canada; sampling frequency: 200 Hz).

Design of Trajectory Patterns. Two trajectory patterns were applied for the cyclic arm movement task as shown in Fig. 2. First one is an eight-shaped trajectory (so-called *figure-eight*, Fig. 2A) which has 3 different variations of the perimeter ratio between left and right loops (herein-after called large and small loops). The latter one is a double elliptical trajectory (so-called *double-ellipse*, Fig. 2B) which has 2 different variations of the perimeter ratio between large and small loops. Movement distance differs between large and small loops. Totally, five different trajectory patterns (3 figure-eight and 2 double-ellipse patterns) were designed to determine the effect of this difference on the isochrony phenomenon. The following describes how the tasks were performed for each pattern (Fig. 2).

Task Procedure. In this task, same nine healthy right-handed males participated. The task involved the continuous cyclic tracing of each shape (Fig. 2). First, target markers and cursor were shown on the monitor, and the subjects were instructed to move the cursor, which provided the visual feedback for the current position of the hand, to the beginning position (Fig. 2). The subjects were then directed to move the cursor from the beginning point to ending point in the order of large to small loops for 5 cycles upon hearing a starting beep sound. The subjects were required to finish this reaching task within 10 s after hearing the starting beep. The beep sound was presented again after 10 s from task-onset. After presenting these beeps, rest intervals were given for 5 s until presenting next task-onset. During the rest intervals, the subjects were instructed to keep the hand in a relaxed state at the beginning point position. We measured the

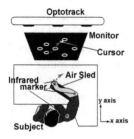

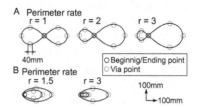

Fig. 1. Experimental settings.

Fig. 2. Trajectory shapes and target points.

hand position using the Optotrak Certus and 11-channels surface EMGs. Note that we selected the 6 channels related to the 2-link 6-muscle model (including anterior deltoid, posterior deltoid, long head of biceps brachii, long head of triceps brachii, triceps lateralis, and brachioradial) for the analyses in this study.

3   Analysis

3.1   Behavioral Data

Trajectory data were filtered by fifth-order Butterworth filter with a cutoff frequency of 15 Hz. As a threshold to determine the starting and ending point of hand movement, we applied the tangential velocity with 5% of the maximum value. This threshold was evaluated for each trial. Then, the time-intervals, satisfied that the tangential velocity is greater than this threshold, were applied to data analysis as the actual movement intervals. Further, the first and last cycle of each trial were excluded for the analysis. These cycles contained unstable movement due to start or termination of the movements. We rejected any outlier trials wherein hand trajectories missed, i.e., did not pass through, the target markers at least once from the analysis. The ratio of movement times between large and small loops was calculated as:

$$r_d = \frac{1}{3} \sum_{k=2}^{4} \frac{t_{L,k}}{t_{S,k}} \qquad (1)$$

where $t_{L,k}$ and $t_{S,k}$ were movement time for large and small loops with the number of movement cycles $k(= 2, 3, 4)$.

3.2   EMG Data

EMG data were digitally rectified, filtered with a fifth-order Butter-worth filter (cutoff frequency: 100 Hz), resampled at 200 Hz, and filtered digitally with a 30 points moving average filter. This preprocessing was applied to data for both MVC measurement task and cyclic arm movement task.

After the preprocessing, EMG data of the MVC measurement task were averaged over trials in each direction. The value of MVC was calculated as the max value of averaged EMGs for each channel. This value was used for cyclic arm movement task EMG data normalization.

The preprocessed cyclic arm movement task EMG data were normalized with the value of MVCs in each channel. In this analysis, we applied the EMGs as the biological index for motor-commanded signals, and the duration average of EMG changes were evaluated to quantify the changes of motor-related signals based on the following formula:

$$C_L = \tfrac{1}{3} \sum_{k=2}^{4} \left\{ \tfrac{1}{t_{L,k}} \int^{t_{L,k}} \sum_{n=1}^{N} \left(\tfrac{dE_{n,k}(t)}{dt} \right)^2 dt \right\} \tag{2}$$

$$C_S = \tfrac{1}{3} \sum_{k=2}^{4} \left\{ \tfrac{1}{t_{S,k}} \int^{t_{S,k}} \sum_{n=1}^{N} \left(\tfrac{dE_{n,k}(t)}{dt} \right)^2 dt \right\} \tag{3}$$

where L and S indicate large or small loops, k ($= 2, 3, 4$) is the number of cycles, and $E_{n,k}(t)$ is EMG signal of the channel n ($n = 1, 2, ..., N$) with time-samples t in cycle k. For simplification, here, we assumed that temporal aspects of the motor commanded signals could be evaluated as the accumulated value over the channel of EMGs. The ratio of EMG changes between large and small loop was calculated as $r_{emg} = C_L/C_S$. Whereas the previous study [2] applied the duration average of the commanded torque changes as an evaluation index for motor-commanded signals, this study applied the duration average of EMG changes as this index to elucidate the relationship between the isochrony principle and motor-commanded signals based on the observable physiological property.

3.3   Isochrony Coefficient

The ratio of movement durations $t_{emg} = t_L/t_S$. The ratio of EMG $r_{emg} = C_L/C_S$. Both were used to evaluate the isochrony coefficient as $I = (r - r_*)/(r - 1)$ [2,4], where r is the ratio of measured movement perimeters, and r_* is r_d or r_{emg}. This value, I, quantifies the degree of isochrony phenomenon within the range $[0, 1]$, with $I = 1$ implying perfect isochrony and $I = 0$ implying complete absence of isochrony [4]. Here, in the case of $r_* < 1$, r_* is substituted with $1/r_*$ so that I does not exceed 1.

4   Results

4.1   Movement Duration and EMG Change

Figure 3 shows both results for r_{emg} and r_d. Whereas r_d indicates the tendency that the movement duration increased relative to increasing the movement distance, r_{emg} indicates the tendency that the EMG changes were modulated to be equal over movement duration between large and small loops regardless of the differences in the movement distance. Statistically, r_d were significantly different

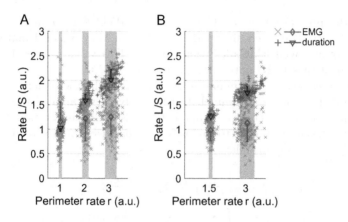

Fig. 3. Group-averaged result in r_{emg} and r_d. (A) Result in figure-eight. (B) Result in double-ellipse. Diamond and triangular symbols indicate group-averaged data, r_{emg} and r_d, respectively. X-mark (x) and cross (+) symbols are data samples in each trial over the subjects. Error bars show the standard deviation (SD) for r_{emg} and r_d. Shaded areas indicate measured perimeter movement ratio SD over the subjects.

in each perimeter movement ratio condition r (figure eight: $p < 0.001$, double ellipse: $p < 0.001$, by one-way analysis of variance (ANOVA)). However, r_{emg} has no significant difference in each perimeter movement ratio condition r (figure eight: $p = 0.1206$, double ellipse: $p = 0.199$, by one-way ANOVA). These tendencies suggest the possibility that human arm movements for large and small loop trajectories are planned to ensure constant EMG change rather than for equalization of movement durations. Moreover, we directly compared r_{emg} and r_d to each perimeter movement ratio condition r over the subjects. Statistical comparison with one-way ANOVA showed that the r_{emg} and r_d were significantly different in each condition of r without dependence on shape (Table 1).

Table 1. Statistical comparison between $r_{emg} = C_L/C_S$ and $r_d = t_L/t_S$ with one-way ANOVA. r_{emg} and r_d showed the group-averaged value for each condition of the perimeter ratio r. Asterisk (*) indicates the significant level with $p < 0.001$.

Figure eight								
$r = 1$			$r = 2$			$r = 3$		
r_{emg}	r_d	F	r_{emg}	r_d	F	r_{emg}	r_d	F
1.16	1.03	27.89*	1.21	1.58	129.22*	1.26	2.02	583.24*
Double ellipse								
$r = 1.5$			-			$r = 3$		
r_{emg}	r_d	F	-			r_{emg}	r_d	F
0.98	1.27	395.14*	-			1.13	1.76	589.72*
*: $p < 0.001$								

4.2   Isochrony Coefficient

In further consideration of the above-mentioned tendency, we evaluated the isochrony coefficients I_{emg} and I_d. Figure 4 shows the tendency that the I_{emg} were higher than I_d regardless of shape and perimeter ratio r. Moreover, we statistically compared I_{emg} and I_d in each condition of perimeter ratio r over the subjects by one-way ANOVA. We found that I_{emg} and I_d were significantly different in each condition of r without dependence on shape (Table 2).

Table 2. Statistical comparison between I_{emg} and I_d with one-way ANOVA. I_{emg} and I_d were the group-averaged isochrony coefficient with EMG data and movement duration for each condition of the perimeter rate r. Asterisk (*) indicates the significant level with $p < 0.001$.

Figure eight								
$r = 1$			$r = 2$			$r = 3$		
I_{emg}	I_d	F	r_{emg}	r_d	F	I_{emg}	I_d	F
-			0.68	0.45	146.44*	0.82	0.52	600.38*
Double ellipse								
$r = 1.5$			-			$r = 3$		
I_{emg}	I_d	F	-			I_{emg}	I_d	F
0.69	0.52	91.30*	-			0.86	0.63	533.31*

*: $p < 0.001$

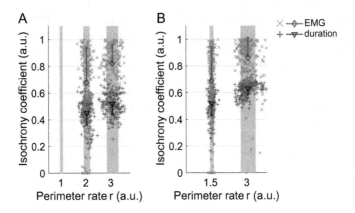

Fig. 4. Group averaged result of isochrony coefficients I_{emg} and I_d. (A) Result in figure-eight. (B) Result in double-ellipse. Diamond and triangular symbols indicate group-averaged isochrony coefficients for I_{emg} and I_d, respectively. X-mark (x) and cross symbols (+) are all data samples for the computation of isochrony coefficient, corresponding to the EMG and movement duration data, respectively. Error bars show the isochrony coefficient SD over the subjects. Shaded areas indicate the measured perimeter movement ratio SD over the subjects.

5   Conclusions

Our results suggest evidence that the isochrony phenomenon is more strongly reflected in EMG changes than movement duration. The tendency that the EMG changes are equal between large and small loops is consistent with the tendency of the commanded torque change mentioned in the previous study [2]. Compared with previous studies on the trajectory planning [1,2,4], one unique aspect of our study is that we showed the possible relationship between the isochrony principle and human motor control based on the observable physiological property.

However, our presented results still have not explained the computational relationship between EMG changes and commanded torque changes. Further, the biomechanical relationship between agonist and antagonist muscles was not considered in this study because we assumed that temporal aspects of the motor commanded signals could be evaluated as an accumulated value over the channel of EMGs. These limitations of our presented results call for important future work including an investigation as to whether EMG activations encode the computational process of joint torque for arm movement.

Acknowledgments. This research was supported by the JSPS KAKENHI (24300051, 26560303, 15K12597).

References

1. Flash, T., Meirovitch, Y., Barliya, A.: Models of human movement: trajectory planning and inverse kinematics studies. Rob. Auton. Syst. **61**(4), 330–339 (2013)
2. Saito, H., Tsubone, T., Wada, Y.: Can human isochrony be explained by a computational theory? In: 28th Annual International Conference of the IEEE Engineering in Medicine and Biology Society, EMBS 2006, pp. 4494–4497. IEEE (2006)
3. Sartori, L., Camperio, A., Bulgheroni, M., Castiello, U.: Reach-to-grasp movements in Macaca fascicularis monkeys: the isochrony principle at work. Front. Psychol. **4**, 114 (2013)
4. Viviani, P., Flash, T.: Minimum-jerk, two-thirds power law, and isochrony: converging approaches to movement planning. J. Exp. Psychol. Hum. Percept. Perform. **21**(1), 32 (1995)
5. Wada, Y., Kawato, M.: A via-point time optimization algorithm for complex sequential trajectory formation. Neural Netw. **17**(3), 353–364 (2004)

A Learning-Based Decentralized Optimal Control Method for Modular and Reconfigurable Robots with Uncertain Environment

Bo Dong[1,2], Keping Liu[1,2], Hui Li[1,2], and Yuanchun Li[1,2(✉)]

[1] Department of Control Science and Engineering,
Changchun University of Technology, Yan'an Avenue. 2055,
Changchun 130012, China
{dongbo,liukeping,lihui,liyc}@ccut.edu.cn
[2] State Key Laboratory of Management and Control for Complex Systems,
Institute of Automation, Chinese Academy of Sciences,
Zhongguancun East Road. 95, Beijing 100190, China

Abstract. This paper presents a novel decentralized control approach for modular and reconfigurable robots (MRRs) with uncertain environment contact under a learning-based optimal compensation strategy. Unlike the known optimal control methods that are merely suitable for specific classes of robotic systems without implementing dynamic compensations, in this investigation, the dynamic model of the MRR system is described as a synthesis of interconnected subsystems, in which the obtainable local dynamic information is utilized effectively to construct the feedback controller, thus making the decentralized optimal control problem of the MRR system be formulated as an optimal compensation issue of the model uncertainty. A policy iteration algorithm is employed to solve the Hamilton-Jacobi-Bellman (HJB) equation with a modified cost function, which is approximated by constructing a critic neural network, and then the approximate optimal control policy can be derived. The asymptotic stability of the closed-loop MRR system is proved by using the Lyapunov theory. At last, simulations are performed to verify the effectiveness of the proposed decentralized optimal control approach.

Keywords: Modular and reconfigurable robots · Decentralized control · Adaptive dynamic programming · Optimal control · Neural networks

1 Introduction

Modular and reconfigurable robots (MRRs) are comprised of the robot modules, which contain power supplies, processing systems, actuators and sensors. These modules are assembled to desirable configurations with standard electromechanical interfaces to satisfy the requirements of various tasks with complex working environments. Furthermore, MRRs need appropriate control systems that taking into consideration of both control precision and power consumption.

© Springer International Publishing AG 2017
D. Liu et al. (Eds.): ICONIP 2017, Part VI, LNCS 10639, pp. 11–21, 2017.
https://doi.org/10.1007/978-3-319-70136-3_2

To ensure the stability and accuracy of trajectory tracking of the robotic systems, and simultaneously taking into account the optimal realization of the composite of control performance and power consumption have attached widespread attention in the robotics community. As an effective tool to address the optimal control problems in nonlinear systems, the adaptive dynamic programming (ADP) methodology has been considered as one of the key directions for the researches on designing discrete-time, continuous-time and data driven-based intelligent systems. In the past few years, numerous studies have been carried out on analytical description of robot manipulator systems under the ADP-based optimal control [1–4]. However, these methods are concentrated on centralized control, indeed, a centralized controller designed on the basis of an entire system may hardly be applicable for controlling MRRs. To avoid these problems, Liu et al. presented an online learning-based decentralized stabilization method [5,6] to deal with the decentralized optimal control problems of the classical nonlinear systems. However, the application of these methods are limited to address the optimal control problems of specific classes of robotic systems without implementing optimal dynamic compensation. Therefore, it is meaningful to investigate the decentralized optimal control approach by combining the model-based compensation control method and ADP-based optimal control policy for MRRs.

In this paper, a novel learning-based optimal control method is constructed to attain the decentralized controller design for MRRs with uncertain environment contact. The dynamic model of MRRs is described as a synthesis of interconnected subsystems, and the decentralized optimal control problem of the whole robotic system is reformulated as an optimal compensation issue of the model uncertainty. Moreover, a policy iteration-based learning algorithm is employed to solve the HJB equation with a modified cost function, and then a critic neural network is used to approximate the cost function, so that the approximate optimal control policy can be derived. Based on the Lyapunov theory, the asymptotic stability of the closed-loop robotic system are proved. Finally, simulations are conducted for 2-DOF MRRs with different configurations to investigate the effectiveness of the proposed decentralized optimal control approach.

2   Dynamic Model Formulation

By referencing the dynamic model of n-DOF MRR, which is proposed in our previous investigation [7], and the modeling approach for the robot manipulator with torque sensing [8], the dynamic model of the MRR system is described as a synthesis of interconnected subsystems, in which the subsystem dynamic model is formulated as:

$$I_{mi}\gamma_i\ddot{\theta}_i + f_i(\theta_i, \dot{\theta}_i) + Z_i(\theta, \dot{\theta}, \ddot{\theta}) + \frac{\tau_{fi}}{\gamma_i} = \tau_i, \tag{1}$$

where the subscript "i" represents the ith module, I_{mi} is the moment of inertia of the rotor about the axis of rotation, γ_i denotes the gear ratio, θ, $\dot{\theta}$ and $\ddot{\theta}$ represent the angular position, velocity and acceleration respectively, $f_i(\theta_i, \dot{\theta}_i)$ represents the frictional torque, $Z_i(\theta, \dot{\theta}, \ddot{\theta})$ indicates the interconnected joint coupling, τ_{fi} denotes the joint torque that including the dynamic information of the load torque and the external environment contact torque, and τ_i is the motor output torque. The friction term $f_i(\theta_i, \dot{\theta}_i)$ in (1), which is considered as a function of the joint position and velocity, is defined as:

$$f_i(\theta_i, \dot{\theta}_i) = \hat{b}_{fi}\dot{\theta}_i + \left(\hat{f}_{ci} + \hat{f}_{si}e^{(-\hat{f}_{\tau i}\dot{\theta}_i^2)}\right)\text{sgn}(\dot{\theta}_i) + f_{pi}(\theta_i, \dot{\theta}_i) + Y(\dot{\theta}_i)\tilde{F}_i, \quad (2)$$

where b_{fi}, f_{ci}, f_{si}, $f_{\tau i}$ and $f_{pi}(\theta_i, \dot{\theta}_i)$ are the nominal values of the friction model parameters, $\tilde{F}_i = \left[b_{fi} - \hat{b}_{fi}, f_{ci} - \hat{f}_{ci}, f_{si} - \hat{f}_{si}, f_{\tau i} - \hat{f}_{\tau i}\right]^T$ indicates the parametric uncertainty vector of the friction, $\hat{b}_{fi}$, $\hat{f}_{ci}$, $\hat{f}_{si}$ and $\hat{f}_{\tau i}$ represent the estimated values of the friction parameters, and the vector $Y(\dot{\theta}_i)$ is defined as

$$Y(\dot{\theta}_i) = \left[\dot{\theta}_i, \text{sgn}(\dot{\theta}_i), \quad e^{(-\hat{f}_{\tau i}\dot{\theta}_i^2)}\text{sgn}(\dot{\theta}_i), -\hat{f}_{si}\dot{\theta}_i^2 e^{(-\hat{f}_{\tau i}\dot{\theta}_i^2)}\text{sgn}(\dot{\theta}_i)\right]. \quad (3)$$

where $\left|\tilde{F}_i\right| \leq \rho_{Fil}$ $(l = 1, 2, 3, 4)$ and $\left|f_{pi}(\theta_i, \dot{\theta}_i)\right| \leq \rho_{fpi}$ are the known up-bounds. Moreover, according to the torque estimation method proposed in [9], one can estimate the joint torque τ_{fi} by substituting the position measurements into a control-oriented harmonic drive model, which is represented as

$$\tau_{fi} = \frac{1}{c_f}\tan\left(c_f k_{f0}\left(\Delta\theta_i - \frac{\text{sgn}(\tau_{wi})(1 - e^{-c_w|\tau_{wi}|})}{\gamma_i c_w k_{w0}}\right)\right), \quad (4)$$

where $\Delta\theta_i = \theta_{fOi} - \theta_{wIi}/\gamma_i$ is the harmonic drive torsional angle θ_{wIi} and θ_{fOi} denote the motor-side angular position and the link-side angular position, which are measured by using the motor-side and the link-side encoders respectively, τ_{wi} denotes the wave generator torque, which can be obtained by using the motor torque command, c_f, c_w, k_{f0} and k_{w0} are positive constants to be determined. Additionally, the interconnected joint coupling term $Z_i(\theta, \dot{\theta}, \ddot{\theta})$ in (1) is defined as follows:

$$Z_i(\theta, \dot{\theta}, \ddot{\theta}) = I_{mi}\sum_{j=1}^{i-1} z_{mi}^T z_{lj}\ddot{\theta}_j + I_{mi}\sum_{j=2}^{i-1}\sum_{k=1}^{j-1} z_{mi}^T (z_{lk} \times z_{lj})\dot{\theta}_k\dot{\theta}_j, \quad (5)$$

where z_{mi}, z_{lj} and z_{lk} are the unity vectors along the axis of rotation of the ith rotor, jth joint and kth joint respectively. In order to facilitate the analysis of the interconnected joint couplings, rewriting $I_{mi}\sum_{j=2}^{i-1}\sum_{k=1}^{j-1} z_{mi}^T (z_{lk} \times z_{lj})\dot{\theta}_k\dot{\theta}_j$ and $I_{mi}\sum_{j=1}^{i-1} z_{mi}^T z_{lj}\ddot{\theta}_j$ as

$$I_{mi}\sum_{j=1}^{i-1} z_{mi}^T z_{lj}\ddot{\theta}_j = \sum_{j=1}^{i-1} U_j^i, \quad (6)$$

$$I_{mi} \sum_{j=2}^{i-1} \sum_{k=1}^{j-1} z_{mi}^T \left(z_{lk} \times z_{lj} \right) \dot{\theta}_k \dot{\theta}_j = \sum_{j=2}^{i-1} \sum_{k=1}^{j-1} V_{kj}^i. \tag{7}$$

where $\left| \sum_{j=1}^{i-1} U_j^i \right| \leq \rho_{Uj}$ and $\left| \sum_{j=2}^{i-1} \sum_{k=1}^{j-1} V_{kj}^i \right| \leq \rho_{Vj}$ are the known up-bounds.

Define the system state vector $x_i = [x_{i1}, x_{i2}]^T = [\theta_i, \dot{\theta}_i]^T \in R^{2 \times 1}$, and the control input $u_i = \tau_i \in R^{1 \times 1}$, $i = 1, 2, \ldots n$. Then, the state space of ith subsystem is formulated as follows:

$$S_i \begin{cases} \dot{x}_{i1} = x_{i2} \\ \dot{x}_{i2} = -(\phi_i(x_i, \dot{x}_i) + h_i(x, \dot{x}, \ddot{x})) + B_i u_i . \\ y = x_{i1} \end{cases} \tag{8}$$

where $\phi_i(\theta_i, \dot{\theta}_i) = B_i \left(\hat{b}_{fi} \dot{\theta}_i + \left(\hat{f}_{ci} + \hat{f}_{si} e^{(-\hat{f}_{ri} \dot{\theta}_i^2)} \right) \mathrm{sgn}(\dot{\theta}_i) + \frac{\tau_{fi}}{\gamma_i} \right)$ represents the modeled and estimated part of the dynamic model, $B_i = (I_{mi} \gamma_i)^{-1} \in R^+$, and $h_i(\theta, \dot{\theta}, \ddot{\theta}) = B_i \left(Y(\dot{\theta}_i) \tilde{F}_i + f_{pi}(\theta_i, \dot{\theta}_i) + \sum_{j=1}^{i-1} U_j^i + \sum_{j=2}^{i-1} \sum_{k=1}^{j-1} V_{kj}^i \right)$ is the model uncertainty term.

3 Learning-Based Decentralized Optimal Control Method

3.1 Problem Transformation

Let the desired position, velocity and acceleration of the ith joint be x_{id}, $\dot{x}_{id}$ and $\ddot{x}_{id}$ respectively. Then, consider the MRR system (8) with an continuously differentiable infinite horizon cost function written as:

$$J_i(s_i(e_i)) = \int_0^\infty \left\{ U_i(s_i(e_i(\tau)), u_i(\tau)) + D_i^T D_i \right\} d\tau, \tag{9}$$

where $s_i(e_i)$ is defined as $s_i(e_i) = \alpha_{ei} e_i + \dot{e}_i$, in which $e_i = x_{i1} - x_{id}$ and $\dot{e}_i = \dot{x}_{i1} - \dot{x}_{id}$ denote the position and velocity tracking error of the ith joint respectively, α_{ei} is a determined constant, $U_i(s_i(e_i), u_i) = s_i^T Q_i s_i + u_i^T R_i u_i$ represents the utility function, in which $Q_i = Q_i^T$ and $R_i = R_i^T$ are determined positive constant matrixes, $D_i \in R^+$ denotes the up-bound function, then we can give a specifies form for the term D_i as:

$$D_i = B_i (|Y(\dot{x}_i)| \rho_{Fil} + \rho_{Ui} + \rho_{Vi} + \rho_{fpi}) \quad l = 1, 2, 3, 4, \tag{10}$$

Obviously, the model uncertainty term h_i and the up-bound function D_i satisfy the relation $h_i^T h_i \leq D_i^T D_i$. Then, for the MRR system (8) with the cost function (9), one can define the Hamiltonian function and the optimal cost function as

$$H_i(s_i, u_i, \nabla J_i) = U_i(s_i, u_i) + \nabla J_i(s_i)^T \left(-\phi_i - h_i + B_i u_i + \alpha_{ei} \dot{e}_i - \ddot{x}_{id} \right) + D_i^T D_i, \tag{11}$$

$$J_i^*(s_i) = \min_{u_i} \int_0^\infty \{U_i(s_i(e_i(\tau)), u_i(\tau)) + D_i^T D_i\} d\tau, \tag{12}$$

where $\nabla J_i(s_i) = \partial J_i(s_i)/\partial s_i$.

If the solution of J_i^* is existent and continuously differentiable, the optimal control law of the MRR system (8) can be computed as:

$$u_i^* = -\frac{1}{2} R_i^{-1} B_i^T \nabla J_i^*(s_i). \tag{13}$$

Rewriting the decentralized optimal control law u_i^* as the form of $u_i^* = u_{i1} + u_{i2}^*$ to deal with the terms of ϕ_i and h_i in (8) respectively, then one can modify the HJB equation as follows:

$$0 = U_i(s_i, u_i^*) + \nabla J_i^*(s_i)^T \left(-\phi_i - h_i + B_i u_{i1} + B_i u_{i2}^* + \alpha_{ei}\dot{e}_i - \ddot{x}_{id}\right) + D_i^T D_i. \tag{14}$$

Note that the terms $\alpha_{ei}\dot{e}_i$ and $\ddot{x}_{id}$ are measurable and known, as well as the term ϕ_i includes the certain part of the dynamic model, which is directly obtainable, so that the feedback control law u_{i1} can be designed as

$$u_{i1} = \hat{b}_{fi}\dot{x}_i + \left(\hat{f}_{ci} + \hat{f}_{si}e^{(-\hat{f}_{\tau i}\dot{x}_i^2)}\right) \mathrm{sgn}(\dot{x}_i) + \frac{\tau_{fi}}{\gamma_i} - B_i^{-1}(\alpha_{ei}\dot{e}_i) + B_i^{-1}\ddot{x}_{id}, \tag{15}$$

to compensate the modeled and estimated terms of the dynamic model.

3.2   Policy Iteration-Based Learning Algorithm

In this part, the online policy iteration-based learning algorithm is implemented to derive the solution of the HJB equation. The policy iteration algorithm consists of policy evaluation based on (13) and policy improvement based on (14). Specifically, the iterative procedure of the policy iteration algorithm with cost function (9) can be described in [10].

3.3   Neural Network Implementation

Neural network is a well-known tool for approximating nonlinear functions. Since the cost function is highly nonanalytic and nonlinear, in this part, the cost function $J_i(s_i)$ is approximated by using a single hidden layer neural network, which is defined as follows:

$$J_i(s_i) = W_{ci}^T \sigma_{ci}(s_i) + \varepsilon_{ci}, \tag{16}$$

where W_{ci} is the ideal weight vector, $\sigma_{ci}(s_i)$ denotes the activation function, and ε_{ci} is the approximation error of neural network. Then, the gradient of $\nabla J_i(s_i)$ is given as:

$$\nabla J_i(s_i) = (\nabla \sigma_{ci}(s_i))^T W_{ci} + \nabla \varepsilon_{ci}, \tag{17}$$

where $\nabla \sigma_{ci}(s_i) = \partial \sigma_{ci}(s_i)/\partial s_i$ and $\nabla \varepsilon_{ci}$ are the gradients of the activation function and the approximation error respectively. Since the ideal weight W_{ci} is always unknown, a critic neural network is built with approximated weight $\hat{W}_{ci}$ to estimate the cost function as:

$$\hat{J}_i(s_i) = \hat{W}_{ci}^T \sigma_{ci}(s_i). \tag{18}$$

According to the definition of Hamiltonian (11) and the HJB equation (14), the Hamiltonian is further expressed by

$$\begin{aligned} H_i(s_i, u_i, W_{ci}) = &U_i(s_i, u_i) + D_i^T D_i + \left(W_{ci}^T \sigma_{ci}(s_i)\right) \\ &\cdot (-\phi_i - h_i + B_i u_{i1} + B_i u_{i2} + \alpha_{ei}\dot{e}_i - \ddot{x}_{id}) - e_{cHi} \end{aligned}, \tag{19}$$

where e_{cHi} is the residual error that is brought from the neural network approximation error, and defined as follows:

$$e_{cHi} = -\nabla \varepsilon_{ci}^T (-\phi_i - h_i + B_i u_{i1} + B_i u_{i2} + \alpha_{ei}\dot{e}_i - \ddot{x}_{id}). \tag{20}$$

The approximate Hamiltonian function, in the same manner, is given as:

$$\begin{aligned} \hat{H}_i\left(s_i, u_i, \hat{W}_{ci}\right) = &U_i(s_i, u_i) + D_i^T D_i + \left(\hat{W}_{ci}^T \sigma_{ci}(s_i)\right) \\ &\cdot (-\phi_i - h_i + B_i u_{i1} + B_i u_{i2} + \alpha_{ei}\dot{e}_i - \ddot{x}_{id}) \end{aligned}. \tag{21}$$

Define the error function $e_{ci} = \hat{H}_i\left(s_i, u_i, \hat{W}_{ci}\right) - H_i(s_i, u_i, W_{ci})$, and the weight estimation error $\tilde{W}_{ci} = W_{ci} - \hat{W}_{ci}$, by combining (19) and (21), one obtain the expression of e_{ci} in terms of $\tilde{W}_{ci}$ as

$$e_{ci} = e_{cHi} - \tilde{W}_{ci}^T \nabla \sigma_{ci}(s_i) \cdot (-\phi_i - h_i + B_i u_{i1} + B_i u_{i2} + \alpha_{ei}\dot{e}_i - \ddot{x}_{id}). \tag{22}$$

For the purpose of training and adjusting the weight information of the critic neural network, we employ the objective function $E_{ci} = \frac{1}{2}e_{ci}^T e_{ci}$, which is minimized by $\hat{W}_{ci}$. Moreover, the neural network weight is updated by using

$$\dot{\hat{W}}_{ci} = -\alpha_{ci}\left(\frac{\partial E_{ci}}{\partial \hat{W}_{ci}}\right), \tag{23}$$

where $\alpha_{ci} > 0$ denotes the learning rate of the critic neural network.

When implementing the online policy iteration algorithm to accomplish the policy improvement, one obtain the approximate optimal control law $\hat{u}_{i2}^*$ as:

$$\hat{u}_{i2}^* = -\frac{1}{2}R_i^{-1}B_i^T (\nabla \sigma_{ci}(s_i))^T \hat{W}_{ci}. \tag{24}$$

From (24), one concludes that the optimal control law is derived depending on only critic neural network, unlike the conventional method that also relay on training of action neural network. Then, combining (15) and (24), the proposed decentralized optimal control law u_i^* is given as

$$\begin{aligned} u_i^* = &\hat{b}_{fi}\dot{x}_i + \left(\hat{f}_{ci} + \hat{f}_{si}e^{(-\hat{f}_{ri}\dot{x}_i^2)}\right)\text{sgn}(\dot{x}_i) + \frac{\tau_{fi}}{\gamma_i} - B_i^{-1}(\alpha_{ei}\dot{e}_i) + B_i^{-1}\ddot{x}_{id} \\ &-\frac{1}{2}R_i^{-1}B_i^T (\nabla \sigma_{ci}(s_i))^T \hat{W}_{ci} \end{aligned}. \tag{25}$$

Theorem. *Given an environmental contacted modular and reconfigurable robot comprised of n modules, with the joint dynamic model as formulated in (1), and the model uncertainties that exist in (2), (6) and (7) with the up-bound function (10). The closed-loop robotic system is asymptotically stable under the decentralized optimal control law designed by (25), with the weight update law given by (23).*

Proof. Select the Lyapunov function candidate as

$$V(t) = \sum_{i=1}^{n} V_i(t) = \sum_{i=1}^{n} \left(\frac{1}{2} s_i^T s_i + J_i^*(s_i) \right). \tag{26}$$

The time derivative of (26) is obtained as

$$\dot{V}(t) = \sum_{i=1}^{n} s_i^T \begin{pmatrix} -\phi_i - h_i + B_i u_{i1} - \ddot{x}_{id} \\ + B_i u_{i2}^* + \alpha_{ei}\dot{e}_i \end{pmatrix} + \sum_{i=1}^{n} \nabla J_i^*(s_i)^T \begin{pmatrix} -\phi_i - h_i + B_i u_{i1} \\ + B_i u_{i2}^* + \alpha_{ei}\dot{e}_i - \ddot{x}_{id} \end{pmatrix}. \tag{27}$$

It is noted that the control law u_{i1} is designed as (15) for the purpose of compensating the certain terms ϕ_i, $\alpha_{ei}\dot{e}_i$ and $\ddot{x}_{id}$ in the HJB equation (14), then, one can rewrite $\dot{V}(t)$ as

$$\dot{V}(t) = \sum_{i=1}^{n} \left(s_i^T \left(-h_i + B_i u_{i2}^* \right) - s_i^T Q_i s_i - u_i^{*T} R_i u_i^* - D_i^T D_i \right). \tag{28}$$

By Young's inequation, we know the (28) can be reformulated as:

$$\dot{V}(t) \leq \sum_{i=1}^{n} \left(\frac{1}{2}\|s_i\|^2 + \frac{1}{2}\|h_i\|^2 + \frac{1}{2}\|s_i\|^2 + \frac{1}{2}\|B_i\|^2\|u_{i2}^*\|^2 \right)$$
$$- \sum_{i=1}^{n} \left(\lambda_{\min}(Q_i)\|s_i\|^2 + \lambda_{\min}(R_i)\|u_{i1}\|^2 \right) - \sum_{i=1}^{n} \left(\lambda_{\min}(R_i)\|u_{i2}^*\|^2 + \|D_i\|^2 \right), \tag{29}$$

where $\lambda_{\min}(Q_i)$ and $\lambda_{\min}(R_i)$ denotes the minimum eigenvalue of Q_i and R_i respectively. Since h_i and D_i satisfy the relation $h_i^T h_i \leq D_i^T D_i$, then one obtains

$$\dot{V}(t) \leq -\sum_{i=1}^{n} \left(\lambda_{\min}(Q_i) - 1 \right) \|s_i\|^2 - \sum_{i=1}^{n} \frac{1}{2}\|D_i\|^2$$
$$- \sum_{i=1}^{n} \left(\lambda_{\min}(R_i) - \frac{1}{2}\|B_i\|^2 \right) \|u_{i2}^*\|^2 - \sum_{i=1}^{n} \lambda_{\min}(R_i)\|u_{i1}\|^2. \tag{30}$$

Therefore, one concludes that $\dot{V}(t) \leq 0$ if the following condition holds

$$\left\{ \lambda_{\min}(Q_i) \geq 1 \quad \lambda_{\min}(R_i) \geq \frac{1}{2I_{mi}^2 \gamma_i^2} \right. . \tag{31}$$

Besides, (30) also implies that $\dot{V}(t) < 0$ for any $s_i \neq 0$ when the condition (31) is hold, therefore, according to the Lyapunov theory, we conclude that the closed-loop MRR system is asymptotically stable under the proposed decentralized optimal control in (25). This concludes the proof of the Theorem.

4   Simulations

In order to verify the effectiveness of the proposed decentralized optimal control method, in this section, two 2-DOF MRRs with uncertain environment contact is used to conduct the simulations. The dynamic model, friction model parameters and desired trajectories are adopted by referring our previous investigation [11], and the parameters of the controller are given in Table 1. Let $Q_i = R_i = I$ (identity matrix), expressing the weigh vector $\hat{W}_{ci}$ $(i = 1, 2)$ as $\hat{W}_{c1} = \left[\hat{W}_{c11}, \hat{W}_{c12}, \hat{W}_{c13}\right]^T$ and $\hat{W}_{c2} = \left[\hat{W}_{c21}, \hat{W}_{c22}, \hat{W}_{c23}\right]^T$, and setting the activation function $\sigma_{ci}(s_i)$ $(i = 1, 2)$ as the form of $\sigma_{c1}(s_1) = \left[e_1^2, e_1 s_1, s_1^2\right]$ and $\sigma_{c2}(s_2) = \left[e_2^2, e_2 s_2, s_2^2\right]$. Two types of external environment contacts are considered in the simulations that including continuous time-varying environment constraint (configuration A) and collision at random time point (configuration B). The time-varying constraint force and the the constant collision force are still follow our previous study [12].

Table 1. Parameters of the controller

Name	Value	Name	Value	Name	Value	Name	Value	Name	Value	Name	Value
I_{mi}	120	$\hat{f}_{si}$	4.0	k_{w0}	1.33	ρ_{Ui}	2.37	c_w	83.5	$\hat{f}_{\tau i}$	80
k_{f0}	8.3e+3	ρ_{Vi}	2.2519	c_f	8.9e-2	$\hat{f}_{ci}$	3.0	$\hat{b}_{fi}$	1.2	ρ_{fpi}	0.32
ρ_{Fi1}	0.3	ρ_{Fi2}	1.0	α_{ei}	0.5	ρ_{Fi3}	0.7	ρ_{Fi4}	20	α_{ci}	0.8

Figure 1 illustrated the position tracking error curves. For configuration A, in the first 10 s, the tracking errors of both situations are relatively obvious due to the decentralized optimal controllers require a period of time for training the critic neural network, after that, the tracking errors may converge to a small range (less than $10e - 2rad$) since the model uncertainty has been compensated accurately. For configuration B, one observes that the instantaneous position deviations are occurred at the time points of 30 s and 45 s, which can be attributed to the influence of the environmental collision, after this, the tracking errors are converged rapidly under the action of the decentralized optimal control.

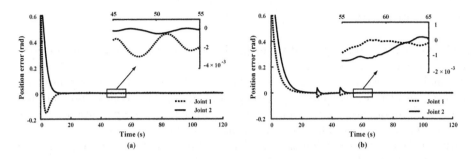

Fig. 1. Position tracking error curves. (a) Configuration A. (b) Configuration B

Figure 2 shows the control torque curves of the MRRs of configuration A and B. From this figure, one concludes that the control torques, which are continuous and smooth motor output torques, are available for implementing in the actual MRR systems. Besides, benefit from the proposed optimal control strategy, the torque consumptions are optimized in a suitable range for matching the output power of the motors in each joint module. Note that the decentralized optimal controller are suitable for different configurations of MRRs without the needs of readjusting the control parameters.

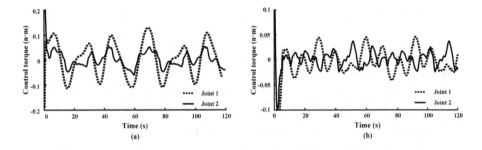

Fig. 2. Control torque curves. (a) Configuration A. (b) Configuration B.

During the implementation process of the online policy iteration algorithm and critic neural network training, for each isolated subsystem, we obtain that convergence results of the weights have occurred after two seconds for each situation. Actually, the weights of the critic neural networks converge to

$$\begin{cases} \hat{W}_{c1A} = [33.34\ 52.99\ 59.43] \\ \hat{W}_{c2A} = [45.66\ 50.16\ 46.78] \end{cases}, \begin{cases} \hat{W}_{c1B} = [23.20\ 4.70\ 43.96] \\ \hat{W}_{c2B} = [30.65\ 18.33\ 34.37] \end{cases}$$

for configuration A and configuration B respectively.

From the simulation results above, we conclude that the proposed decentralized optimal control method can provide accuracy and stability for MRRs to satisfy the requirements of various tasks with complex working environment.

5 Conclusions

This paper focus on investigating of MRRs with uncertain environment contact, and addresses the problem of decentralized control with a learning-based optimal compensation strategy. The dynamic model of MRRs are formulated as a synthesis of interconnected subsystems, and the optimal control problem for the whole robotic system is reformulated as an optimal compensation issue of the model uncertainty. The policy iteration algorithm is developed to solve the HJB equation by constructing a critic neural network, and then the approximate optimal control policy can be derived directly. The Lyapunov theory is used to prove the asymptotic stability of the closed-loop MRR systems. Finally, simulations are performed for two 2-DOF MRRs with uncertain environment contact to verify the effectiveness of the proposed decentralized optimal control method.

Acknowledgments. This work is supported by the National Natural Science Foundation of China (Grant no. 61374051), the State Key Laboratory of Management and Control for Complex Systems (Grant no. 20150102), the Scientific Technological Development Plan Project in Jilin Province of China (Grant nos. 20160520013JH, 20160414033GH and 20150520112JH) and the Science and Technology project of Jilin Provincial Education Department of China during the 13th Five-Year Plan Period (JJKH20170569KJ).

References

1. Patchaikani, P., Behera, L., Prasad, G.: A single network adaptive critic-based redundancy resolution scheme for robot manipulators. IEEE Trans. Ind. Electron. **59**, 3241–3253 (2012)
2. Tang, L., Liu, Y., Tong, S.: Adaptive neural control using reinforcement learning for a class of robot manipulator. Neural Comput. Appl. **25**, 135–141 (2014)
3. Li, Y., Chen, L., Tee, K., Li, Q.: Reinforcement learning control for coordinated manipulation of multi-robots. Neurocomputing **170**, 168–175 (2015)
4. Nageshrao, S., Lopes, G., Jeltsema, D., Babuska, R.: Passivity-based reinforcement learning control of a 2-DOF manipulator arm. Mechatronics **24**, 1001–1007 (2014)
5. Liu, D., Wang, D., Li, H.: Decentralized stabilization for a class of continuous-time nonlinear interconnected systems using online learning optimal control approach. IEEE Trans. Neural Netw. Learn. Syst. **25**, 418–428 (2014)
6. Wang, D., Liu, D., Mu, C., Ma, H.: Decentralized guaranteed cost control of interconnected systems with uncertainties: a learning-based optimal control strategy. Neurocomputing **214**, 297–306 (2016)
7. Dong, B., Li, Y.: Decentralized integral nested sliding mode control for time varying constrained modular and reconfigurable robot. Adv. Mech. Eng. **7**, 1–15 (2015)
8. Imura, J., Yokokohji, Y., Yoshikawa, T., Sugie, T.: Robust control of robot manipulators based on joint torque sensor information. Int. J. Robot. Res. **13**, 434–442 (1994)
9. Zhang, H., Ahmad, S., Liu, G.: Torque estimation for robotic joint with harmonic drive transmission based on position measurements. IEEE Trans. Robot. **31**, 322–330 (2015)

10. Zhao, B., Liu, D., Li, Y.: Online fault compensation control based on policy iteration algorithm for a class of affine non-linear systems with actuator failures. IET Control Theory Appl. **10**, 1816–1823 (2016)
11. Dong, B., Li, Y.: Decentralized reinforcement learning robust optimal tracking control for time varying constrained reconfigurable modular robot based on ACI and Q-function. Math. Probl. Eng. **2013**, 1–16 (2013)
12. Dong, B., Li, Y., Liu, K.: Decentralized control for harmonic drive–based modular and reconfigurable robots with uncertain environment contact. Adv. Mech. Eng. **9**, 1–14 (2017)

Decentralized Force/Position Fault-Tolerant Control for Constrained Reconfigurable Manipulators with Actuator Faults

Fan Zhou[1,2], Bo Dong[1], and Yuanchun Li[1(✉)]

[1] Changchun University of Technology, Changchun, China
{dongbo,liyc}@ccut.edu.cn
[2] Ryerson University, Toronto, ON M5B 2K3, Canada
zhoufandyouxiang@sina.com

Abstract. This paper addresses the problems of decentralized force/position fault-tolerant control for constrained reconfigurable manipulators. A novel decentralized force/position control method is proposed for constrained reconfigurable manipulators without torque sensing by estimating the joint torques with only position measurements. In addition, a modified sliding mode controller is designed to guarantee force/position tracking performance, and the actuator faults in independent subsystem can be compensated by using an adaptive algorithm. The stability of closed-loop system is analyzed using the Lyapunov method. Finally, simulations are performed to verify the advantages of the proposed method.

Keywords: Constrained reconfigurable manipulators · Force/position fault-tolerant control · Joint torque estimation · Sliding mode control

1 Introduction

Reconfigurable robot manipulators system can fulfill various tasks by changing its degree of freedom and task spaces. The main motive to design reconfigurable manipulators lie in its structural flexibility, low cost, easy maintenance, convenient modification, and portability. In many modern applications, especially for rehabilitative robot, military robots etc., the manipulators may make contact with environment, manipulating objects, or even working directly with people [1,2]. Once serious fault occurs to motor, physical injury and economic loss may be caused.

Passive fault-tolerant control (PFTC) and active fault-tolerant control (AFTC) are two basic strategies in fault-tolerant control. The PFTC is reliable only for the class of known faults and those faults are assumed to be known prior to the design of the controller [3–5]. In addition, it implements robustness to certain faults only possible at the expense of decreased nominal performance. The AFTC can deal with unknown faults based on a fault detection and diagnosis (FDD) unit [6]. When a fault occurs, the faulty system works under the normal

© Springer International Publishing AG 2017
D. Liu et al. (Eds.): ICONIP 2017, Part VI, LNCS 10639, pp. 22–31, 2017.
https://doi.org/10.1007/978-3-319-70136-3_3

controller until the fault is diagnosed and the controller is reconstructed [7–9]. The time delay may cause severe loss of stability and performance. It should be stressed that the contact force on the end-effector of manipulator may gradually increase in the period of time delay and cause more severe problems. Hence, how to guarantee transient and steady state performance and fast restoration of system stability after occurrence of faults are of substantial importance for constrained reconfigurable manipulators.

With the main advantages of integral sliding mode control (ISMC) such as fast response, ease of implementation and high robustness to model uncertainties [10,11], this paper selected ISMC for developing a novel torque sensorless robust decentralized force/position fault-tolerant control scheme for constrained reconfigurable manipulators system. The main features of the proposed approach are: (I) extend the results presented in [12] which only intended position decentralized fault-tolerant control for reconfigurable manipulators, this paper realizes position/force decentralized fault-tolerant control. Furthermore, the proposed scheme can reduce time delay as no FDD unit is required; and (II) unlike previous position/force control which are focused on position decentralized control [13], this paper takes into account the decentralized control of position and constraint force simultaneously, which has wider application potentials.

2   Dynamic Model Formulation

Considering the environment constraint, the dynamic model of constrained reconfigurable manipulators with n-DOF is described as follows:

$$M(q)\ddot{q} + C(q,\dot{q})\dot{q} + G(q) + F(q,\dot{q}) = u + \tau_c \tag{1}$$

where $q \in R^n$ is the vector of joint displacements, $M(q) \in R^{n \times n}$ is the symmetric and positive definite inertia matrix, $C(q,\dot{q}) \in R^n$ is the matrix of centripetal Coriolis matrix, $G(q) \in R^n$ is the gravity vector, $u \in R^n$ is the control torque of output side in harmonic drive transmission, $F(q,\dot{q}) \in R^n$ denotes the joint friction vector, τ_c is the joint constrained torque.

By separating the terms in Eq. (1), in which depending on only local variables $(q_i, \dot{q}_i, \ddot{q}_i)$ from those terms of other joint variables, the dynamical model of the ith subsystem is formulated in the joint space as:

$$M_i(q_i)\ddot{q}_i + C_i(q_i,\dot{q}_i)\dot{q}_i + G_i(q_i), + F_i(q_i,\dot{q}_i) + Z_i(q,\dot{q},\ddot{q}) = u_i + \tau_{ci}$$

$$Z_i(q,\dot{q},\ddot{q}) = \left\{ \sum_{j=1,j\neq i}^{n} M_{ij}(q)\ddot{q}_j + [M_{ii}(q) - M_i(q_i)]\ddot{q}_i \right\} + \left\{ \sum_{j=1,j\neq i}^{n} C_{ij}(q,\dot{q})\dot{q}_j \right.$$

$$\left. + [C_{ii}(q,\dot{q}) - C_i(q_i,\dot{q}_i)]\dot{q}_i \right\} + [\bar{G}_i(q) - G_i(q_i)]$$

$$\tag{2}$$

where the τ_{ci} can be obtained using the motor-side and link-side position measurements along with harmonic drive transmission (See Appendix A).

3   Design of Novel Adaptive Robust Fault-Tolerant Controller

According to Eq. (2) the constrained reconfigurable manipulators dynamic model of nonlinear interconnected subsystem S_i with actuator faults is presented by the following state equation:

$$S_i : \begin{cases} \dot{x}_i = A_i x_i + B_i \left[f_i(q_i, \dot{q}_i) + g_i(q_i)(u_i + \tau_{ci}) \right. \\ \qquad\qquad \left. + \varphi_i (q_i, \dot{q}_i, u_i) + h_i(q, \dot{q}, \ddot{q}) \right] \\ y_i = C_i x_i \end{cases} \tag{3}$$

where $x_i = [x_{i1}, x_{i2}]^T = [q_i, \dot{q}_i]^T$, $(i = 1, 2, ..., n)$ is the state vector of subsystem S_i, and y_i is the output of subsystem. $\varphi_i (q_i, \dot{q}_i, u_i) = g_i(q_i)\alpha(t-T_{if})\psi_i (q_i, \dot{q}_i, u_i)$, the term $\alpha(t - T_{if})$ is a step function defined by $\alpha(t - T_{if}) = \begin{cases} 0, \ t < T_{if} \\ 1, \ t \geq T_{if} \end{cases}$ and the $\psi_i (q_i, \dot{q}_i, u_i)$ denotes fault function. The matrices:

$$A_i = \begin{bmatrix} 0 & 1 \\ 0 & 0 \end{bmatrix}, B_i = \begin{bmatrix} 0 \\ 1 \end{bmatrix}, C_i = \begin{bmatrix} 1 & 0 \\ 0 & 1 \end{bmatrix}$$
$$f_i(q_i, \dot{q}_i) = M_i^{-1}(q_i) \left[-C_i(q_i, \dot{q}_i)\dot{q}_i - G_i(q_i) - F_i(q_i, \dot{q}_i) \right]$$
$$g_i(q_i) = M_i^{-1}(q_i)$$
$$h_i(q, \dot{q}, \ddot{q}) = -M_i^{-1}(q_i)Z_i(q, \dot{q}, \ddot{q})$$

Assumption 1. The kinematic restriction is given as a rigid surface and frictionless and refers to the fact that the end-effector involved has to track a certain prespecified desired position without losing contact with it.

Assumption 2. The reconfigurable manipulators stays away from singularities to ensure Jacobian matrix full rank.

Assumption 3. The error between joint constrained torque estimated value and its actual value is small enough so that it can be ignored.

Define the sliding surface of ISMC as:

$$s_i = \dot{q}_i - q_{ir} = \dot{e}_{qi} + k_{pi}e_{qi} + k_{\tau i} \int_0^t e_{\tau i}d\xi \tag{4}$$

$$e_{qi} = q_i - q_{id} \tag{5}$$

$$e_{\tau i} = \tau_{ci} - \tau_{di} \tag{6}$$

$$q_{ir} = \dot{q}_{id} - k_{pi}e_{qi} - k_{\tau i} \int_0^t e_{\tau i}d\xi \tag{7}$$

where e_{qi} is the position tracking error, $e_{\tau i}$ is the torque tracking error, τ_{di} is desired constrained torque, k_{pi} and $k_{\tau i}$ are positive constants.

The time derivative of sliding variable s_i along the trajectories of system (3) is:

$$\dot{s}_i = f_i(q_i, \dot{q}_i) + g_i(q_i)(u_i + \tau_{ci}) + \varphi_i(q_i, \dot{q}_i, u_i) + h_i(q, \dot{q}, \ddot{q}) + v_i \qquad (8)$$

where $v_i = \ddot{q}_{id} + k_{pi}\dot{e}_{qi} + k_{\tau i}e_{\tau i}$.

The terms of $f_i(q_i, \dot{q}_i)$, $g_i(q_i)$ and $h_i(q, \dot{q}, \ddot{q})$ are unknown continuous functions because of there are many possible configurations for reconfigurable modular manipulators. To overcome this difficulty, the Radial Basis Function (RBF) neural network is employed to approximate the unknown terms:

$$f_i(q_i, \dot{q}_i, W_{if}) = W_{if}^T \Phi_{if}(q_i, \dot{q}_i) + \varepsilon_{if} \quad \|\varepsilon_{if}\| \le \varepsilon_1 \qquad (9)$$

$$g_i(q_i, W_{ig}) = W_{ig}^T \Phi_{ig}(q_i) + \varepsilon_{ig} \qquad \|\varepsilon_{ig}\| \le \varepsilon_2 \qquad (10)$$

where W_{if} and W_{ig} are the ideal neural network weights, $\Phi(\cdot)$ is the neural network basis function, ε_{if} and ε_{ig} are the neural network approximation errors, ε_1, ε_2 are known constants.

Define $\hat{W}_{if}$ and $\hat{W}_{ig}$ as the estimations of W_{if} and W_{ig}, respectively. $\hat{f}_i\left(q_i, \dot{q}_i, \hat{W}_{if}\right)$ is the estimation value of $f_i(q_i, \dot{q}_i, W_{if})$ and $\hat{g}_i\left(q_i, \hat{W}_{ig}\right)$ is the estimation value of $g_i(q_i, W_{ig})$. $\hat{f}_i\left(q_i, \dot{q}_i, \hat{W}_{if}\right)$ and $\hat{g}_i\left(q_i, \hat{W}_{ig}\right)$ are expressed as:

$$\hat{f}_i\left(q_i, \dot{q}_i, \hat{W}_{if}\right) = \hat{W}_{if}^T \Phi_{if}(q_i, \dot{q}_i) \qquad (11)$$

$$\hat{g}_i\left(q_i, \hat{W}_{ig}\right) = \hat{W}_{ig}^T \Phi_{ig}(q_i) \qquad (12)$$

Define the estimation errors as $\tilde{W}_{if} = W_{if} - \hat{W}_{if}$ and $\tilde{W}_{ig} = W_{ig} - \hat{W}_{ig}$. Thus,

$$f_i(q_i, \dot{q}_i, W_{if}) - \hat{f}_i\left(q_i, \dot{q}_i, \hat{W}_{if}\right) = \tilde{W}_{if}^T \Phi_{if}(q_i, \dot{q}_i) + \varepsilon_{if} \qquad (13)$$

$$g_i(q_i, W_{ig}) - \hat{g}_i\left(q_i, \hat{W}_{ig}\right) = \tilde{W}_{ig}^T \Phi_{ig}(q_i) + \varepsilon_{ig} \qquad (14)$$

Assumption 4. [15]: The interconnection term $h_i(q, \dot{q}, \ddot{q})$ is bounded by:

$$|h_i(q, \dot{q}, \ddot{q})| \le \sum_{j=1}^{n} d_{ij} E_j \qquad (15)$$

where $d_{ij} \ge 0$, $S_j = 1 + |s_j| + |s_j|^2$ and define $p_i(|s_j|) = n \max_{i,j} \{d_{ij}\} S_j$.

Similarly, the RBF neural networks, which is used to approximate the interconnection term, are given as follows:

$$\hat{p}_i\left(|s_i|, \hat{W}_{ip}\right) = \hat{W}_{ip}^T \Phi_{ip}(|s_i|) \qquad (16)$$

where $\hat{W}_{ip}$ is the estimation value of W_{ip} and $\tilde{W}_{ip} = \hat{W}_{ip} - W_{ip}$ is the estimation error.

Define approximation error:

$$\omega_{i1} = W_{if}^T \tilde{\Phi}_{if}(q_i, \dot{q}_i) + W_{ig}^T \tilde{\Phi}_{ig}(q_i) u_i + \varepsilon_{if} + \varepsilon_{ig} u_i \tag{17}$$

$$\omega_{i2} = p_i(|s_i|) - \hat{W}_{ip}^T \hat{\Phi}_{ip}(|s_i|) \tag{18}$$

$$\omega_i = |\omega_{i1}| + |\omega_{i2}| \tag{19}$$

In order to enable fast restoration of the system's stability and performance after actuator fault occurrence, a continuous exponential reaching law is defined as follows:

$$\dot{s}'_i(t) = -\hat{\sigma}_i H(s_i) - k_i s_i \tag{20}$$

where $\hat{\sigma}_i$ represents a constant reaching rate with the adaptive $\dot{\hat{\sigma}}_i = \beta_i |s_i|$.

Note that, the discontinuous function $\text{sgn}(s_i)$ used in the traditional ISMC, which causes the chattering phenomenon that is undesired in practical applications, is replaced by a continuous nonlinear function expressed as follows:

$$H(s_i) = (\exp(4s_i) - 1) / (\exp(4s_i) + 1) \tag{21}$$

Assumption 5. During the worst scenario caused by a given disturbance φ_i $(q_i, \dot{q}_i, u_i)$ the sliding function s_i is assumed to become large enough so that we can assume $H(s_i) = |(\exp(4s_i) - 1) / (\exp(4s_i) + 1)| \approx (\exp(4s_i)) / (\exp(4s_i)) = 1$.

Theorem. Consider the fault nonlinear system (3) with Assumptions 1–5. If the following controller and adaptive laws are employed:

$$u_i = -\left[\hat{f}_i(q_i, \dot{q}_i, \hat{W}_{if}) + \text{sgn}(s_i)\hat{p}_i(|s_i|, \hat{W}_{ip}) + v_i + \hat{\omega}_i - \dot{s}' \right] / \hat{g}_i(q_i, \hat{W}_{ig}) - \tau_{ci} \tag{22}$$

$$\dot{\hat{W}}_{if} = \eta_{if} s_i \hat{\Phi}_{if}(q_i, \dot{q}_i) \tag{23}$$

$$\dot{\hat{W}}_{ig} = \eta_{ig} s_i \hat{\Phi}_{ig}(q_i)(u_i + \tau_{ci}) \tag{24}$$

$$\dot{\hat{W}}_{ip} = \eta_{ip} |s_i| \hat{\Phi}_{ip}(|s_i|) \tag{25}$$

$$\dot{\hat{\omega}}_i = \lambda_i |s_i| \tag{26}$$

where, η_{if}, η_{ig}, η_{ip} and λ_i are positive constants. Then the close-loop system is globally asymptotically bounded.

Proof. Let the Lyapunov function for the i th subsystem be given by:

$$V_i = \tfrac{1}{2} s_i^2 + \tfrac{1}{2} \tilde{W}_{if}^T \eta_{if}^{-1} \tilde{W}_{if} + \tfrac{1}{2} \tilde{W}_{ig}^T \eta_{ig}^{-1} \tilde{W}_{ig} + \tfrac{1}{2} \tilde{W}_{ip}^T \eta_{ip}^{-1} \tilde{W}_{ip} + \tfrac{1}{2} \lambda_i^{-1} \tilde{\omega}_i^2 + \tfrac{1}{2} \beta_i^{-1} \tilde{\sigma}_i^2 \tag{27}$$

Then, the derivative of V_i with respect to time generates:

$$
\begin{aligned}
\dot{V}_i &= s_i \dot{s}_i - \eta_{if}^{-1} \tilde{W}_{if}^T \dot{\hat{W}}_{if} - \eta_{ig}^{-1} \tilde{W}_{ig}^T \dot{\hat{W}}_{ig} - \eta_{ip}^{-1} \tilde{W}_{ip}^T \dot{\hat{W}}_{ip} - \lambda_i^{-1} \tilde{\omega}_i \dot{\hat{\omega}}_i - \beta_i^{-1} \tilde{\sigma}_i \dot{\hat{\sigma}}_i \\
&= s_i \left[f_i(q_i, \dot{q}_i) + g_i(q_i)(u_i + \tau_{ci}) + h_i(q, \dot{q}, \ddot{q}) + v_i + \varphi_i(q_i, \dot{q}_i, u_i) \right] \\
&\quad - \eta_{if}^{-1} \tilde{W}_{if}^T \dot{\hat{W}}_{if} - \eta_{ig}^{-1} \tilde{W}_{ig}^T \dot{\hat{W}}_{ig} - \eta_{ip}^{-1} \tilde{W}_{ip}^T \dot{\hat{W}}_{ip} - \lambda_i^{-1} \tilde{\omega}_i \dot{\hat{\omega}}_i - \beta_i^{-1} \tilde{\sigma}_i \dot{\hat{\sigma}}_i \\
&= s_i \left[f_i(q_i, \dot{q}_i) + \hat{g}_i(q_i)(u_i + \tau_{ci}) + (g_i(q_i) - \hat{g}_i(q_i)))(u_i + \tau_{ci}) \right. \\
&\quad \left. + h_i(q, \dot{q}, \ddot{q}) + v_i + \varphi_i(q_i, \dot{q}_i, u_i) \right] - \eta_{if}^{-1} \tilde{W}_{if}^T \dot{\hat{W}}_{if} - \eta_{ig}^{-1} \tilde{W}_{ig}^T \dot{\hat{W}}_{ig} \\
&\quad - \eta_{ip}^{-1} \tilde{W}_{ip}^T \dot{\hat{W}}_{ip} - \lambda_i^{-1} \tilde{\omega}_i \dot{\hat{\omega}}_i - \beta_i^{-1} \tilde{\sigma}_i \dot{\hat{\sigma}}_i \\
&= \tilde{W}_{if}^T \left(s_i \hat{\Phi}_{if}(q_i, \dot{q}_i) - \eta_{if}^{-1} \dot{\hat{W}}_{if} \right) + \tilde{W}_{ig}^T \left(s_i \hat{\Phi}_{ig}(q_i)(u_i + \tau_{ci}) - \eta_{ig}^{-1} \dot{\hat{W}}_{ig} \right) \\
&\quad + s_i \omega_{i1} - k_i s_i^2 - s_i \hat{\omega}_i - s_i \hat{\sigma}_i H(s_i) + s_i \left(h_i - \text{sgn}(s_i) \hat{W}_{ip}^T \hat{\Phi}_{ip}(|s_i|) \right) \\
&\quad + s_i \varphi_i(q_i, \dot{q}_i, u_i) - \eta_{ip}^{-1} \tilde{W}_{ip}^T \dot{\hat{W}}_{ip} - \lambda_i^{-1} \tilde{\omega}_i^T \dot{\hat{\omega}}_i - \beta_i^{-1} \tilde{\sigma}_i \dot{\hat{\sigma}}_i
\end{aligned}
\tag{28}
$$

Substituting (23) and (24) into (28) and considering (15), yields the expression:

$$
\begin{aligned}
\dot{V} \le \sum_{i=1}^{n} &\left(s_i w_{i1} - k_i s_i^2 + |s_i| \hat{\omega}_i - s_i \hat{\sigma}_i H(s_i) - |s_i| \hat{W}_{ip}^T \hat{\Phi}_{ip}(|s_i|) + s_i \varphi_i(q_i, \dot{q}_i, u_i) \right. \\
&\left. - \eta_{ip}^{-1} \tilde{W}_{ip}^T \dot{\hat{W}}_{ip} - \lambda_i^{-1} \tilde{\omega}_i^T \dot{\hat{\omega}}_i - \beta_i^{-1} \tilde{\sigma}_i \dot{\hat{\sigma}}_i \right) + \max_{ij}\{d_{ij}\} \sum_{i=1}^{n} |s_i| \sum_{j=1}^{n} E_j
\end{aligned}
\tag{29}
$$

Note that $|s_i| \le |s_j| \Leftrightarrow E_i \le E_j$, and by virtue of Chebyshev inequality:

$$
\sum_{i=1}^{n} |s_i| \sum_{j=1}^{n} E_j \le n \sum_{i=1}^{n} |s_i| E_i
\tag{30}
$$

By using Assumption 5 and (30), (29) can be rewritten as:

$$
\begin{aligned}
\dot{V} \le \sum_{i=1}^{n} &\left(|s_i| \omega_i - |s_i| \hat{\omega}_i - s_i \hat{\sigma}_i - k_i s_i^2 + \tilde{W}_{ip}^T \left(|s_i| \hat{\Phi}_{ip}(|s_i|) - \eta_{ip}^{-1} \dot{\hat{W}}_{ip} \right) \right. \\
&\left. + s_i \varphi_i(q_i, \dot{q}_i, u_i) - \lambda_i^{-1} \tilde{\omega}_i \dot{\hat{\omega}}_i - \beta_i^{-1} \tilde{\sigma}_i \dot{\hat{\sigma}}_i \right) \\
= \sum_{i=1}^{n} &\left(\tilde{\omega}_i \left(|s_i| - \lambda_i^{-1} \dot{\hat{\omega}}_i \right) - s_i \hat{\sigma}_i H + s_i \varphi_i(q_i, \dot{q}_i, u_i) - k_i s_i^2 \right. \\
&\left. + \tilde{W}_{ip}^T (|s_i| \hat{\Phi}_{ip}(|s_i|) - \eta_{ip}^{-1} \dot{\hat{W}}_{ip}) - \beta_i^{-1} \tilde{\sigma}_i \dot{\hat{\sigma}}_i \right)
\end{aligned}
\tag{31}
$$

Substituting (25) and (26) into (31), one has:

$$
\begin{aligned}
\dot{V} \le \sum_{i=1}^{n} &\left(-s_i \hat{\sigma}_i + s_i \varphi_i(q_i, \dot{q}_i, u_i) - k_i s_i^2 - \beta_i^{-1} \tilde{\sigma}_i \dot{\hat{\sigma}}_i \right) \\
= \sum_{i=1}^{n} &\left(-s_i \hat{\sigma}_i + s_i \varphi_i(q_i, \dot{q}_i, u_i) - k_i s_i^2 - \beta_i^{-1} \tilde{\sigma}_i \dot{\hat{\sigma}}_i + \sigma_i |s_i| - \sigma_i |s_i| \right) \\
\le \sum_{i=1}^{n} &\left(|s_i| (|\varphi_i(q_i, \dot{q}_i, u_i)|_{\max} - \sigma_i) + \tilde{\sigma}_i \left(|s_i| - \beta_i^{-1} \dot{\hat{\sigma}}_i \right) - k_i s_i^2 \right) \\
= \sum_{i=1}^{n} &\left(|s_i| (|\varphi_i(q_i, \dot{q}_i, u_i)|_{\max} - \sigma_i) - k_i s_i^2 \right)
\end{aligned}
\tag{32}
$$

Next, we assume that the parameters σ_i is large enough (i.e. $\sigma_i \gg \varphi_i(q_i, \dot{q}_i, u_i)$), which is considered only for the stability analysis purpose, the exact value of σ_i is not required in the fault-tolerant controller design. Therefore, the following conclusion can be obtained:

$$\dot{V} \leq 0 \tag{33}$$

This proves that applying the designed control law (24) with the update rules (25)–(28), the closed-loop system (3) is asymptotically stable and the control objective is met despite the actuator faults, i.e. $\lim_{t \to \infty} e(t) = 0$. This completes the proof.

4   Simulations and Analysis

To verify the effectiveness of the proposed novel adaptive robust fault-tolerant controller, two 2-DOF constrained reconfigurable manipulators with different configurations, whose configuration and dynamic model are same as those in Ref. [14], are employed for simulation.

The initial position and velocity are set as $q_1(0) = q_2(0) = 1$ and $\dot{q}_1(0) = \dot{q}_2(0) = 0$, respectively. We consider the following fault situation: for configuration a, $u_{a1} = 0.8u_1$ and $u_{a2} = 2\cos q_2 + u_2$ happen at $t = 5$ s for joint 1 and $t = 7$ s for joint 2, respectively; for configuration b, $u_{b2} = 10q_2^2 + \sin(u_2)u_2$ happened at $t = 4$ s for joint 2. Some related control parameters are listed in Table 1.

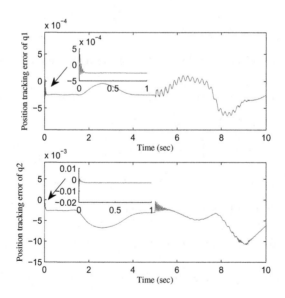

Fig. 1. Position tracking error of configuration a under actuator fault.

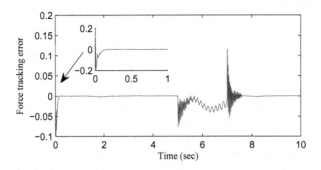

Fig. 2. Force tracking error of configuration a under actuator fault.

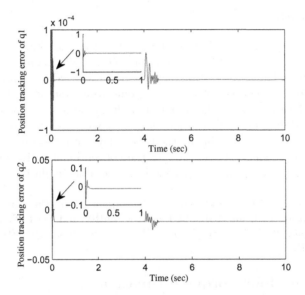

Fig. 3. Position tracking error of configuration b under actuator fault.

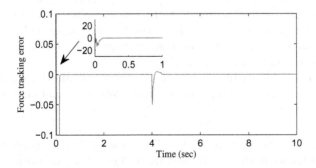

Fig. 4. Force tracking error of configuration b under actuator fault

Table 1. The parameters of the controller and adaptive laws

Parameters	k_{pi}	$k_{\tau i}$	k_i	η_{if}	η_{ig}	η_{ip}	λ_i	β_i
Values	500	500	0.5	0.002	0.002	500	0.5	0.5

Figures 1, 2, 3, and 4 show the position tracking error and force tracking error of configuration a and b under the fault condition. The tracking errors of position and force become greater at the fault occurrence time, but remain within the scope of the engineering allowable. From the Figures, one can conclude that the proposed control algorithms are capable of fault-tolerant control for two different configurations reconfigurable manipulators without any parameter modification.

5   Conclusion

A novel torque sensorless force/position robust decentralized fault-tolerant control scheme was proposed for constrained reconfigurable manipulators system. Torque estimation based on position measurements realized force/position decentralized control and reduced the cost of joint torque sensing. The proposed method aimed to deal with the actuator fault by adding compensation term to a modified sliding mode controller. It was shown that the proposed control algorithms were capable of reducing the time delay caused by online fault detection and diagnosis which is necessary in the conventional active fault tolerant control. The efficacy of proposed scheme was tested in simulation.

Acknowledgments. This work is financially supported by the National Natural Science Foundation of China (61374051 and 60974010) and Scientific and Technological Development Plan Project in Jilin Province of China (20160414033GH and 20160520013JH).

Appendix A. Joint torque estimation

Considering the constrained reconfigurable module manipulators consists of n-modules, each module provides an independently rotating joint with harmonic drive transmission. According the Ref. [16], we can obtain the joint torque τ_{fi} by using the torque estimation method based on the motor-side and link-side position measurements along with harmonic drive model for each joint module of constrained reconfigurable manipulators.

By the following formula, one can get the constrained torque, which is obtained by the constrained force on the end-effector of manipulator:

$$\tau_{ci} = \tau_{fie} - \tau_{fio},$$

where τ_{fio} denotes the joint torque which is obtained in free space, τ_{fie} denotes the total joint torque in the constrained space. The total joint torque τ_{fie} and/or joint torque in free space τ_{fio} is directly obtained by the method proposed in the Ref. [16] under the condition of constrained space and free space, respectively.

References

1. Gams, A., Nemec, B., Ijspeert, A.J., Ude, A.: Coupling movement primitives: inter-action with the environment and bimanual tasks. IEEE Trans. Rob. **30**(4), 816–830 (2014)
2. Li, Z., Cao, X., Tang, Y., Li, R., Ye, W.: Bilateral teleoperation of holonomic constrained robotic systems with time-varying delays. IEEE Trans. Instrum. Meas. **62**(4), 752–765 (2013)
3. Wang, W., Wen, C.: Adaptive compensation for infinite number of actuator failures or faults. Automatica **47**(10), 2197–2210 (2011)
4. Huang, S.T., Davison, E.J., Kwong, R.: Decentralized robust servomechanism problem for large flexible space structures under sensor and actuator failures. IEEE Trans. Autom. Control **57**(12), 3219–3224 (2012)
5. Yang, G.H., Ye, D.: Reliable control of linear systems with adaptive mechanism. IEEE Trans. Autom. Control **55**(1), 242–247 (2010)
6. Wang, H., Ye, D., Yang, G.H.: Actuator fault diagnosis for uncertain T-S fuzzy systems with local nonlinear models. Nonlinear Dyn. **76**(4), 1977–1988 (2014)
7. Shen, Q., Jiang, B., Shi, P., Lim, C.C.: Novel neural networks-based fault tolerant control scheme with fault alarm. IEEE Trans. Cybern. **44**(11), 2190–2201 (2014)
8. Tong, S.C., Huo, B.Y., Li, Y.M.: Observer-based adaptive decentralized fuzzy fault-tolerant control of nonlinear large-scale systems with actuator failures. IEEE Trans. Fuzzy Syst. **22**(1), 1–15 (2014)
9. Li, H., Liu, H., Gao, H., Shi, P.: Reliable fuzzy control for active suspension systems with actuator delay and fault. IEEE Trans. Fuzzy Syst. **20**(2), 342–357 (2012)
10. Balasubramaniam, P., Muthukumar, P., Ratnavelu, K.: Theoretical and practical applications of fuzzy fractional integral sliding mode control for fractional-order dynamical system. Nonlinear Dyn. **80**(1), 249–267 (2015)
11. Chen, C.C., Xu, S.S.D., Liang, Y.W.: Study of nonlinear integral sliding mode fault-tolerant control. IEEE/ASME Trans. Mechatron. **21**(2), 1160–1168 (2016)
12. Ahmad, S., Zhang, H.W., Liu, G.J.: Distributed fault detection for modular and reconfigurable robots with joint torque sensing: a prediction error based approach. Mechatronics **23**(6), 607–616 (2013)
13. Shen, Q., Jiang, B., Shi, P., Lim, C.: Novel neural networks-based fault tolerant control scheme with fault alarm. IEEE Trans. Cybern. **44**(11), 2190–2201 (2014)
14. Zhou, F., Li, Y., Liu, G.: Robust decentralized force/position fault-tolerant control for constrained reconfigurable manipulators without torque sensing. Nonlinear Dyn. **89**, 955–969 (2017). doi:10.1007/s11071-017-3494-1
15. Zhao, B., Li, Y.C.: Local joint information based active fault tolerant control for reconfigurable manipulator. Nonlinear Dyn. **77**(3), 859–876 (2014)
16. Zhang, H., Ahmad, S., Liu, G.: Modeling of torsional compliance and hysteresis behaviors in harmonic drives. IEEE/ASME Trans. Mechatron. **20**(1), 178–185 (2015)

Backward Path Tracking Control for Mobile Robot with Three Trailers

Jin Cheng$^{(\boxtimes)}$, Bin Wang, and Yuan Xu

School of Electrical Engineering, University of Jinan,
No. 336, West Road of Nan Xinzhuang, Jinan 250022, Shandong, China
{cse_chengj,cse_wangb,cse_xuy}@ujn.edu.cn

Abstract. The path tracking control problem of a mobile robot with three trailers in backward motion is addressed in this paper. Based on the proposed feedback control law, which can stabilize the orientations of the tractor and trailers on the desired reference angle, a fuzzy controller is designed to track given path. The controller is applicable to line segment path and is stable in backward motion. Numerical simulation experiments are implemented and the results show that the designed controller has excellent performance in backward tracking of line path.

1 Introduction

A mobile robot with trailers, also known as tractor-trailer mobile robot (TTMR), is a kind of modular robotic system that consists of a tractor and one or multiple trailers. The trailers are interconnected in a chain by the passive rotary joints of on-axle type or off-axle type. By exploiting passive trailers, a mobile robot can be conveniently realigned to take various service tasks. Compared to multiple individual mobile robots, TTMR has a remarkable lower operational cost. These advantages of TTMR have given rise to plenty research in industry transportation in recent years. It has acquired many successful application in large cargo transportation, baggage transferring in airport and railway station, and indoor service robot [1].

Due to the fact that there exit nonholonomic constraints in the kinematics, the system of mobile robot with trailers is considered as a nonlinear under-actuated system. Feedback stabilization and tracking control are challenging problems for such a complicated system. In addition, backward motion control of TTMR is difficult because the subsystem of trailers is open loop unstable, which results in the so-called jack-knife effects, that the trailers skid and end up colliding with the tractor or the front trailer [2].

A lot of research has been done on the control problems of mobile robot with one or more trailers, such as feedback stabilization on given configuration, tracking of reference trajectory, parallel parking, motion planning in complex environment, and formation control. Jack-knife effect during in backward motion has also been addressed and some anti-Jacknife feedback control laws are proposed in [3,4].

© Springer International Publishing AG 2017
D. Liu et al. (Eds.): ICONIP 2017, Part VI, LNCS 10639, pp. 32–41, 2017.
https://doi.org/10.1007/978-3-319-70136-3_4

Lamiraux presents a robust method to control a mobile robot towing a trailer that can solve both problems of trajectory tracking and steering to a given configuration in [5]. Altafini et al. proposes a control scheme for stabilization of backward driving along simple paths for a miniaturized vehicle composed of a truck and a two-axle trailer in [6]. A feedback stabilization control law via dynamic extension and linearization is proposed for a mobile robot with one trailer in [7]. Chang designed a fuzzy controller for the discrete LPV T-S fuzzy models constructed for truck-trailer mobile robot system and the stability conditions were derived via Lyapunov stability criteria based on the PDC concept [8].

Backing up a trailer system is important for parking control. Cuesta presents a backing up method in [9] which can realize autonomous parallel parking of a kind of mobile robot with trailer. In [10], Kwanghyun Yoo made a mechanical alteration which the passive trailers are connected to the front bumper of a car to improve the backward motion control performance and proposed a trailer-pushing control algorithm for the stable backing up motion.

Orientation tracking control for mobile robot with trailers is a new research hotspot that has few research work till now. Obviously, control of the orientation angle of the trailers is the critical part in backward motion. In this paper, the path tracking control problem of mobile robot with three trailers is addressed. First, an orientation angle tracking control law is presented. Then a fuzzy controller is designed to track the line segments path via setting the reference orientation angle according to the tracking errors.

The paper is organized as follows: In Sect. 2, the kinematic model of the mobile robot with three trailers is presented. In Sect. 3, the orientation tracking control law is proposed. The fuzzy path tracking controller is designed in Sect. 4. In Sect. 5, two numerical simulation examples are given to illustrate the effectiveness of the designed path tracking controller.

2   Vehicle Kinematics and Problem Statement

The structure of the TTMR system is illustrated in Fig. 1. Three passive trailers are hooked up with the previous axle of the tractor or trailer respectively via on-axle approach. The tractor is driven by rear-wheels with linear speed v and controlled by the steering angle φ, where φ is the the angle of the front wheels with respect to the longitudinal axis of the tractor. Define $\varphi > 0$ when the front wheels turn to the left along the forward motion and $\varphi < 0$ when to the right. $\theta_i (i = 1, 2, 3, 4)$ is the orientation angle of the tractor and three trailers with respect to x axis. $P_i(x_i, y_i)(i = 1, 2, 3, 4)$ are the Cartesian coordinates defined respectively at the center of the rear axle of the tractor and trailers. L_1 is the length of the wheelbase of the tractor and $L_i(i = 2, 3, 4)$ are the length parameters of the connecting link of the passive trailers.

The kinematic model of the mobile robot with three trailers can be deduced from the holonomic constraint caused by mechanical connection between bodies and the nonholonomic constraints arising from the assumption that there exits no slipping motion between the wheels and the ground. It can be given by

$$\dot{x}_1 = v \cos \theta_1$$
$$\dot{y}_1 = v \sin \theta_1$$
$$\dot{\theta}_1 = \frac{1}{L_1} v \tan \varphi$$
$$\dot{\theta}_2 = \frac{1}{L_2} v \sin \gamma_1 \tag{1}$$
$$\dot{\theta}_3 = \frac{1}{L_3} v \cos \gamma_1 \sin \gamma_2$$
$$\dot{\theta}_4 = \frac{1}{L_4} v \cos \gamma_1 \cos \gamma_2 \sin \gamma_3$$

where $\gamma_i = \theta_i - \theta_{i+1}$, $i = 1, 2, 3$.

Beside the constraints on kinematics, there are also mechanical limitations on the control input φ and the joint angles $|\gamma_i| < \pi/2(i = 1, 2, 3)$. It is can be seen that the system (1) is not controllable when $|\varphi| = \pi/2$ or $|\gamma_i| = \pi/2$, $(i = 1, 2, 3)$. Also, to avoid collision between bodies, the limitation $|\gamma_i| < \pi/2(i = 1, 2, 3)$ should be satisfied.

Also, the subsystem of trailers are open-loop unstable, for instance, define $s = \sin \theta_4$ and a Lypunove candidate function $V = \frac{1}{2} s^2$, it has

$$\dot{V} = \frac{v}{L_4} \sin \theta_4 \cos \theta_4 \cos \gamma_1 \cos \gamma_2 \sin(\theta_3 - \theta_4) \tag{2}$$

Assuming $\theta_3 = 0$ and $|\theta_4| < \pi/2$, for $v < 0$ in backward motion and $\cos \gamma_i > 0 (i = 1, 2)$ it has $\dot{V} \geq 0$. The joint angle γ_3 would rapidly increase beyond the limitation of $|\gamma_3| < \pi/2$.

For the practical application of TTMR, path tracking is one of the most required abilities. In this paper, a feedback control law that can stably reverse the trailers in backward motion to track the desired reference orientation angle is presented. Based on this stable feedback control law, a fuzzy controller is designed to track reference path composed of line segments. Also, the designed controller can successfully solve the backward docking problem of TTMR.

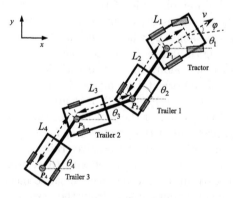

Fig. 1. Geometry of a mobile robot with three trailers

3   Orientation Tracking Control Law

In this section, a asymptotically stable feedback control law of φ for mobile robot with three trailers is proposed, which can stably reverse the robot to track the desired orientation in backward motion.

Considering the mechanical limitations of the robot, the control law is designed under assumptions that $\dot{\theta}_{4d} = 0$, $|\theta_4 - \theta_{4d}| < \pi/2$ and $|\gamma_i| < \pi/2 (i = 1, 2, 3)$.

Define the tracking error with

$$s_1 = \sin(\theta_4 - \theta_{4d}) - \sin\gamma_3 \tag{3}$$

and define a instrumental variable

$$s_2 = \frac{1}{L_4}\sin\gamma_3 - \frac{1}{L_3}\tan\gamma_2 + \frac{1}{L_4}\cos(\theta_4 - \theta_{4d})\tan\gamma_3 - k_1 s_1 \tag{4}$$

where $k_1 > 0$ is a design parameter.

Taking a Lyapunov candidate function

$$V_2 = \frac{1}{2}(s_1^2 + s_2^2) \tag{5}$$

it has

$$\dot{V}_2 = k_1 v \cos\gamma_1 \cos\gamma_2 \cos\gamma_3 s_1^2 + v \cos\gamma_1 \cos\gamma_2 \cos\gamma_3 s_1 s_2 + s_2 \dot{s}_2 \tag{6}$$

Define

$$\gamma_{1d} = \tan^{-1}(L_2 L_3 \cos^3\gamma_2(\cos\gamma_3 s_1 \\ + \frac{1}{L_3}\tan\gamma_2 \cdot g_1(\cdot) - \frac{1}{L_4}\sin\gamma_3 \cdot g_2(\cdot) - k_2 s_2)) \tag{7}$$

where $g_1(\cdot) = \frac{1}{L_4}\cos\gamma_3 + k_1 \cos\gamma_3 + \frac{1}{L_3}\sec^2\gamma_2 + \frac{1}{L_4}\cos(\theta_4 - \theta_{4d})\sec^2\gamma_3$, $g_2(\cdot) = \frac{1}{L_4}\cos\gamma_3 + k_1(\cos\gamma_3 + \cos(\theta_4 - \theta_{4d})) + \frac{1}{L_4}\sin(\theta_4 - \theta_{4d})\tan\gamma_3 + \frac{1}{L_4}\cos(\theta_4 - \theta_{4d})\sec^2\gamma_3$ and $k_2 > 0$ is a design parameter.

Let $\gamma_1 := \gamma_{1d}$ and substitute γ_1 with (7) into (6), it yields

$$\dot{V}_2 = k_1 v \cos\gamma_1 \cos\gamma_2 \cos\gamma_3 s_1^2 + k_2 v \cos\gamma_1 \cos\gamma_2 s_2^2 \tag{8}$$

For $k_1 > 0$, $k_2 > 0$, $v < 0$ and $|\gamma_i| < \pi/2 (i = 1, 2)$, it has $\dot{V}_2 \leq 0$. As a direct conclusion from Lyapunov technique, if $\gamma_1 := \gamma_{1d}$, it has $s_1 \to 0$ and $s_2 \to 0$ when $t \to \infty$.

The following is to design a stable control law with which γ_1 can asymptotically converge to γ_{1d}.

Define

$$s_3 = \sin\gamma_1 - \sin\gamma_{1d} \tag{9}$$

and the derivative of s_3 along system (1) is given by

$$\dot{s}_3 = v \cos \gamma_1 (\frac{1}{L_1} \tan \varphi - \frac{1}{L_2} \sin \gamma_1) - \cos \gamma_{1d} \dot{\gamma}_{1d} \qquad (10)$$

Design the control law for φ with

$$\varphi = \tan^{-1}(L_1(k_3 s_3 + \frac{1}{L_2} \sin \gamma_1 + \frac{1}{v} \sec \gamma_1 \cos \gamma_{1d} \dot{\gamma}_{1d})) \qquad (11)$$

where $k_3 > 0$ is a design parameter, it yields

$$\dot{s}_3 = k_3 v \cos \gamma_1 s_3 \qquad (12)$$

Define a Lyapunov candidate function $V_3 = \frac{1}{2} s_3^2$, for $k_3 > 0$, $v < 0$ and $|\gamma_1| < \pi/2$, it has

$$\dot{V}_3 = k_3 v \cos \gamma_1 s_3^2 \leq 0. \qquad (13)$$

So, with the control law (11), s_3 will asymptotically converge to the origin when $t \rightarrow \infty$, that is, γ_1 will converge to γ_{1d} asymptotically.

The stability of the closed-loop system (1) with the control law (11) can be proved with a Lemma on a cascade system. Rewrite the closed-loop system with the variables $s_i (i = 1, 2, 3)$, it has

$$\dot{\tilde{s}} = f_1(t, \tilde{s}, s_3) \qquad (14)$$
$$\dot{s}_3 = f_2(t, s_3) \qquad (15)$$

where $\tilde{s} = [s_1, s_2]^T$.

With s_3 as input, the unforced subsystem of (14) is

$$\dot{\tilde{s}} = f_1(t, \tilde{s}, 0) \qquad (16)$$

When $s_3 = 0$, it has $\gamma_1 = \gamma_{1d}$. From (8) it can easily be proven that the unforced system (16) has a exponentially stable equilibrium at the orgin $\tilde{s} = 0$. So the system (14) is input-to-state stable. From (13), it shows that the subsystem (15) is uniformly asymptotically stable at $s_3 = 0$. So, according to **Lemma 4.7** in [11], the cascade system (14) and (15) is uniformly asymptotically stable. As a conclusion, when $t \rightarrow \infty$, it has $s_i \rightarrow 0 (i = 1, 2, 3)$.

Define the orientation tracking error with

$$s_4 = \sin(\theta_4 - \theta_{4d}) \qquad (17)$$

The derivative of s_4 along the closed-loop system with the control input (11) is then given with

$$\dot{s}_4 = \frac{1}{L_4} v \cos(\theta_4 - \theta_{4d}) \cos \gamma_1 \cos \gamma_2 (s_4 - s_1) \qquad (18)$$

With s_1 as input of system (18), the stability of unforced system (18) can be proved with a Lyapunov candidate function $V_4 = \dfrac{1}{2}s_4^2$ and its derivative is given by

$$
\begin{aligned}
\dot{V}_4 &= \frac{1}{L_4}v\cos(\theta_4 - \theta_{4d})\cos\gamma_1\cos\gamma_2 s_4^2 \\
&\leq -\frac{1}{L_4}|v|\cos(\theta_4 - \theta_{4d})\cos\gamma_1\cos\gamma_2 s_4^2
\end{aligned}
\tag{19}
$$

So, the unforced system (18) is exponentially stable when the condition $|\gamma_i| < \pi/2(i = 1, 2)$ is satisfied. Apply **Lemma 4.7** in [11] here again, with the conclusion that s_1 is asymptotically stable at its origin, the system (18) is uniformly asymptotically stable at their origin $s_4 = 0$. When $s_i \to 0$, it has $\theta_4 \to \theta_{4d}$, $\gamma_i \to 0 (i = 1, 2, 3)$.

So, with the proposed control law (11), the robot can stably reverse the three trailers to track the desired orientation angle with asymptotic convergence.

4   Numerical Validation

The designed fuzzy controller and the orientation tracking control law are verified with two numerical simulations.

4.1   Backward Tracking of Line Segments Path

Backward tracking of line segments path is common in practical application of TTMR. A fuzzy controller is designed to track the line-segment reference path in this section.

Define the inputs of the fuzzy controller with E_Dist and E_Angle, which are the tracking errors of the third trailer to the line segment path as shown in Fig. 2.

$$
\begin{aligned}
E\_Dist &= |\overline{P_4 P_j}| \\
E\_Angle &= Path\_Angle - \theta_4
\end{aligned}
\tag{20}
$$

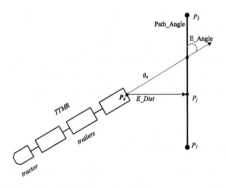

Fig. 2. Tracking of Line Path

Three linguistic variables, *Far*, *Near*, *Zero*, are defined to describe *E_Dist*, and five linguistic variables, *NegBig*, *NegSmall*, *Zero*, *PosSmall*, *PosBig*, for *E_Angle*. The output of the fuzzy controller is defined with $\Delta\Theta_d$. Five linguistic variables, *NegBig*, *NegSmall*, *Zero*, *PosBig* and *PosSmall*, are also defined to describe $\Delta\Theta_d$.

The fuzzy rules of the controller is showed in Table 1.

Table 1. Fuzzy rules

$\Delta\Theta$		E_Angle		
		Neg	Zero	Pos
E_Dist	NegFar	PosBig	PosBig	PosBig
	NegNear	PosSmall	PosSmall	PosBig
	NegSmall	Zero	PosSmall	PosBig
	PosNear	NegBig	NegSmall	NegSmall
	PosFar	NegBig	NegBig	NegBig

$$\theta_{4d} = Path\_Angle + \Delta\Theta_d \qquad (21)$$

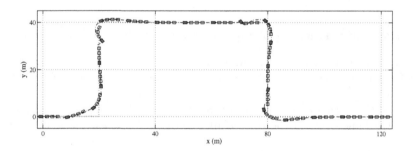

Fig. 3. Trace of TTMR

The reference angle for the third trailer is then designed based on the output of the fuzzy controller as in (21).

Results of numerical simulation are shown in Figs. 3 and 4. It can be seen that the controller successfully reversed the mobile robot with three trailers to track the reference line segments path. Form Fig. 4, it shows that the orientation angles both the tractor and trailer are stably controlled during the whole backward tracking process.

4.2 Backward Docking Task

Docking is defined as moving from the current configuration to a desired configuration while following a safe trajectory. Docking task is common for trucks, industrial fork-lifts, mobile manufacturing assembly robots, and rescue robots.

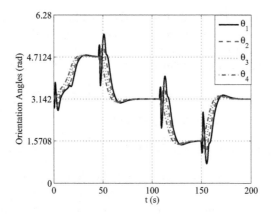

Fig. 4. Response of orientation angles of TTMR

In this section, the control law proposed above is applied to the docking task of the mobile robot with three trailers. As shown in Fig. 5, the tractor needs to reverse the the three trailers from the initial configuration to the docking config-uration. The docking strategy is designed with a *Line-of-Sight(LOS)* approach. The orientation angle θ_{4d} is defined as the direction pointed from the position P_4 of the third trailer to the reference point P_r on the virtual line generated by the docking configuration. Point P_j is defined as the projecting point of P_4 on the virtual line and the distance between P_j and P_r satisfies

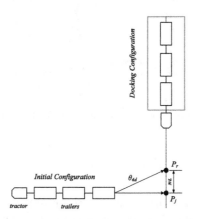

Fig. 5. Docking task of a mobile robot with three trailers

$$|P_r P_j| = nL$$

where $n > 0$ is a integer and L is often designed with the length of the trailers.

With this strategy, if the robot is reversed stably to track the desired θ_{4d}, the tractor and trailers would approach the virtual line and move along this line to the docking configuration.

The initial configuration is defined with

$$(x_1, y_1, \theta_1, \theta_2, \theta_3, \theta_4)|_{t=0} = (0, 0, \pi, \pi, \pi, \pi)$$

and the docking configuration is defined with

$$(x_1, y_1, \theta_1, \theta_2, \theta_3, \theta_4)|_{t=0} = (20, 44, 3\pi/2, 3\pi/2, 3\pi/2, 3\pi/2)$$

The speed of the robot is $v = -1\,\mathrm{m/s}$ and the design parameters are defined with $k = 1$ and $L = L_2 + L_3 + L_4 = 6\,\mathrm{m}$.

Simulation results are shown in Fig. 6, where the red filled rectangular represents the tractor and the other blank rectangulars represent the three trailers. It can be seen that with the proposed control law and LOS approach, the robot is successfully accomplish the docking task with adequate tolerances required by docking configuration.

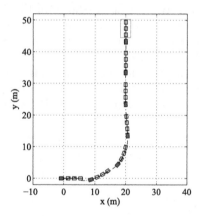

Fig. 6. Trace of robot in docking task (Color figure online)

5   Conclusion

Solution to the backward path tracking control problem for a mobile robot with three on-axle jointed trailers has been presented in this paper. The feedback control law can stabilize the orientations of the tractor and trailers on the desired reference angle with asymptotic stability in backward motion. With that, a fuzzy controller is designed to track given path. The controller is applicable to line segment path and is stable in backward motion. Also, a simple controller is designed for the backward docking task. The performance of the designed controllers have been verified with numerical simulation. Future work will be emphasized on the motion control problems of TTMR in off-axle form.

Acknowledgments. This work is supported by National Nature Science Foundation under Grant 61203335, and partly by National Natural Science Foundation of China (Nos. 61603150), and Doctoral Foundation of University of Jinan (No. XBS1605).

References

1. David, J., Manivannan, P.V.: Control of truck-trailer mobile robots: a survey. Intel. Serv. Robot. **7**, 245–258 (2014)
2. Martínez, J.L., Morales, J., Mandow, A., García-Cerezo, A.: Steering limitations for a vehicle pulling passive trailers. IEEE Trans. Control Syst. Technol. **16**(4), 809–818 (2008)
3. Stergiopoulos, J., Manesis, S.: Anti-jackknife state feedback control law for non-holonomic vehicles with trailer sliding mechanism. Int. J. Syst. Control Commun. **1**(3), 297–311 (2009)
4. Chen, L., Shieh, Y.: Jackknife prevention for articulated vehicles using model reference adaptive control. Proc. Inst. Mech. Eng. Part D: J. Automob. Eng. **225**(1), 28–42 (2011)
5. Lamiraux, F., Laumond, J.P.: A practical approach to feedback control for a mobile robot with trailer. In: ICRA, pp. 3291–3296 (1998)
6. Altafini, C., Speranzon, A., Wahlberg, B.: A feedback control scheme for reversing a truck and trailer vehicle. IEEE Trans. Robot. Autom. **17**(6), 915–922 (2001)
7. Cheng, J., Zhang, Y., Hou, S., Song, B.: Stabilization control of a backward tractor-trailer mobile robot. In: 2010 8th World Congress on Intelligent Control and Automation (WCICA), pp. 2136–2141. IEEE (2010)
8. Chang, W.J., Chen, P.H.: Stabilization for truck-trailer mobile robot system via discrete LPV T-S fuzzy models. In: Lee, S., Cho, H., Yoon, K.J., Lee, J. (eds.) Intelligent Autonomous Systems 12. AISC, vol. 193, pp. 209–217. Springer, Heidelberg (2013). doi:10.1007/978-3-642-33926-4_20
9. Cuesta, F., Gómez-Bravo, F., Ollero, A.: Parking maneuvers of industrial-like electrical vehicles with and without trailer. IEEE Trans. Industr. Electron. **51**(2), 257–269 (2004)
10. Yoo, K., Chung, W.: Pushing motion control of n passive off-hooked trailers by a car-like mobile robot. In: 2010 IEEE International Conference on Robotics and Automation (ICRA), pp. 4928–4933. IEEE (2010)
11. Khalil, H.K., Grizzle, J.: Nonlinear Systems, vol. 3. Prentice Hall, New Jersey (1996)

Adaptation-Oriented Near-Optimal Control and Robust Synthesis of an Overhead Crane System

Ding Wang$^{(\boxtimes)}$

The State Key Laboratory of Management and Control for Complex Systems,
Institute of Automation, Chinese Academy of Sciences, Beijing 100190, China
ding.wang@ia.ac.cn

Abstract. In this paper, we develop an adaptation-oriented approximate optimal control strategy and apply it to perform robust stabilization of an overhead crane system including complex nonlinearity. Via employing a novel updating rule to the adaptive critic structure, the near-optimal control law can be learnt based on the converged weight vector. By further considering the dynamical uncertainties, it is proven that the developed near-optimal control law can achieve uniform ultimate boundedness of the closed-loop state vector, thereby guaranteeing a certain extent of robustness for the uncertain nonlinear plant. An experimental simulation with respect to the overhead crane system is also conducted to verify the performance of the present control method.

Keywords: Adaptive and learning systems · Adaptive critic · Neural networks · Nonlinear control · Optimal control · Overhead crane · Robustness

1 Introduction

Optimal and robust feedback designs of complex dynamical plants are significant topics of automatic control community, in particular when the inclusion of system uncertainties occurs. Developing linear optimal regulators have been studied by control scientists and engineers for many years. However, it is not an easy task to acquire the analytic solution of the Hamilton-Jacobi-Bellman equation of nonlinear systems, like the nonlinear overhead crane plant. As a result, the optimal feedback of general nonlinear systems is difficult but considerable important. Fortunately, a series of iterative methods have been established to tackle the optimal control problems approximately. Among them, adaptive/approximate dynamic programming [1–5] is regarded as a typical strategy to design optimal control adaptively and forward-in-time, where the adaptive critic is taken as the basic structure and neural networks are often involved to serve as the function approximator. In general, employing the adaptive dynamic programming method always results in adaptive near-optimal feedback controllers [6–12].

© Springer International Publishing AG 2017
D. Liu et al. (Eds.): ICONIP 2017, Part VI, LNCS 10639, pp. 42–50, 2017.
https://doi.org/10.1007/978-3-319-70136-3_5

This paper focuses on developing an adaptation-oriented near-optimal control method with application to robust stabilization of an overhead crane system via an improved neural learning mechanism. The main contribution lies in that it brings a meaningfully reinforced component into the traditional critic learning algorithm, so that to achieve the adaptation-oriented nonlinear optimal regulation, but also guarantee a certain extent of robustness about the introduced dynamical uncertainties. This can be regarded as an improvement to the traditional adaptive-critic-based optimal control designs, like [6–8] and adaptive-critic-based robust feedback stabilization, such as [10–12]. Now, we list the main notations used in the paper as follows. $\mathbb{R}$ stands for the set of all real numbers. $\mathbb{R}^n$ is the Euclidean space of all n-dimensional real vectors. $\mathbb{R}^{n \times m}$ is the space of all $n \times m$ real matrices. $\| \cdot \|$ denotes the vector norm of a vector in $\mathbb{R}^n$ or the matrix norm of a matrix in $\mathbb{R}^{n \times m}$. I_n represents the $n \times n$ identity matrix. $\lambda_{\max}(\cdot)$ and $\lambda_{\min}(\cdot)$ calculate the maximal and minimal eigenvalues of a matrix, respectively. Let Ω be a compact subset of $\mathbb{R}^n$ and $\mathscr{A}(\Omega)$ be the set of admissible control laws on Ω. The superscript "T" represents the transpose operation and $\nabla(\cdot) \triangleq \partial(\cdot)/\partial\chi$ denotes the gradient operator.

2 General Control Design Description

2.1 Optimal Control Background

For performing a general description, we consider a class of continuous-time systems with control-affine inputs given by

$$\dot{\chi}(t) = f(\chi(t)) + g(\chi(t))\mu(t), \tag{1}$$

where $\chi(t) \in \Omega \subset \mathbb{R}^n$ is the state vector, $\mu(t) \in \Omega_\mu \subset \mathbb{R}^m$ is the control vector, and the system functions $f(\cdot)$ and $g(\cdot)$ are differentiable in the arguments satisfying $f(0) = 0$. We let the initial state at $t = 0$ be $\chi(0) = \chi_0$ and $\chi = 0$ be the equilibrium point of the controlled plant. The internal system function $f(\chi)$ is assumed to be Lipschitz continuous on a set Ω in $\mathbb{R}^n$ and containing the origin. Generally, the nonlinear plant (1) is assumed to be controllable.

For designing an infinite horizon optimal feedback control law $\mu(\chi)$, we let $Z(\chi(t), \mu(t)) = Q(\chi(t)) + \mu^{\mathsf{T}}(t)\mu(t)$ with $Q(\chi) \geq 0$ represent the utility function and define the cost function as

$$J(\chi(t), \mu) = \int_t^\infty Z(\chi(\tau), \mu(\tau))\mathrm{d}\tau. \tag{2}$$

For simplicity, the cost $J(\chi(t), \mu)$ is often written as $J(\chi(t))$ or $J(\chi)$ in the sequel. Particularly, we have $J(\chi(0)) = J(\chi_0)$. For an admissible control law $\mu(\chi) \in \mathscr{A}(\Omega)$, if the cost function (2) with respect to it is continuously differentiable, then the related infinitesimal version is the nonlinear Lyapunov equation

$$0 = Z(\chi, \mu(\chi)) + (\nabla J(\chi))^{\mathsf{T}}[f(\chi) + g(\chi)\mu(\chi)]$$

with $J(0) = 0$. Define the Hamiltonian of system (1) as

$$H(\chi, \mu(\chi), \nabla J(\chi)) = Z(\chi, \mu(\chi)) + (\nabla J(\chi))^\mathsf{T}[f(\chi) + g(\chi)\mu(\chi)].$$

In view of Bellman's optimality principle, the optimal cost function defined as

$$J^*(\chi) = \min_{\mu \in \mathscr{A}(\Omega)} \int_t^\infty Z(\chi(\tau), \mu(\tau))\mathrm{d}\tau,$$

satisfies the Hamilton-Jacobi-Bellman equation

$$\min_{\mu \in \mathscr{A}(\Omega)} H(\chi, \mu(\chi), \nabla J^*(\chi)) = 0.$$

Based on optimal control theory, the optimal control law is formulated as follows:

$$\mu^*(\chi) = \arg \min_{\mu \in \mathscr{A}(\Omega)} H(\chi, \mu(\chi), \nabla J^*(\chi)) = -\frac{1}{2}g^\mathsf{T}(\chi)\nabla J^*(\chi). \tag{3}$$

Using the control expression (3), the Hamilton-Jacobi-Bellman equation becomes

$$0 = Z(\chi, \mu^*(\chi)) + (\nabla J^*(\chi))^\mathsf{T}[f(\chi) + g(\chi)\mu^*(\chi)], \ J^*(0) = 0. \tag{4}$$

Note that (4) is actually $H(\chi, \mu^*(\chi), \nabla J^*(\chi)) = 0$, which is difficult to deal with in theory. Hence, it is not an easy task to obtain the optimal control law (3) for general nonlinear systems. This inspires us to devise an approximate control strategy to overcome the difficulty in what follows.

2.2   Adaptation-Oriented Near-Optimal Control

During the neural network implementation, we denote l_c as the number of neurons in the hidden layer. Taking the universal approximation property into consideration, the optimal cost function $J^*(\chi)$ can be expressed by a neural network with a single hidden layer on a compact set Ω as

$$J^*(\chi) = \omega_c^\mathsf{T}\sigma_c(\chi) + \varepsilon_c(\chi), \tag{5}$$

where $\omega_c \in \mathbb{R}^{l_c}$ is the ideal weight vector that is bounded by a positive constant such that $\|\omega_c\| \leq \lambda_\omega$, $\sigma_c(\chi) \in \mathbb{R}^{l_c}$ is the activation function, and $\varepsilon_c(\chi) \in \mathbb{R}$ is the reconstruction error. Then, the gradient vector is

$$\nabla J^*(\chi) = (\nabla \sigma_c(\chi))^\mathsf{T}\omega_c + \nabla\varepsilon_c(\chi).$$

Since the ideal weight is unknown, a critic neural network is developed to approximate the optimal cost function as

$$\hat{J}^*(\chi) = \hat{\omega}_c^\mathsf{T}\sigma_c(\chi), \tag{6}$$

where $\hat{\omega}_c \in \mathbb{R}^{l_c}$ denotes the estimated weight vector. Similarly, we derive the gradient vector as

$$\nabla\hat{J}^*(\chi) = (\nabla\sigma_c(\chi))^\mathsf{T}\hat{\omega}_c.$$

Considering the feedback formulation (3) and the neural network expression (5), the optimal control law function can be rewritten as

$$\mu^*(\chi) = -\frac{1}{2}g^{\mathsf{T}}(\chi)\big[(\nabla\sigma_c(\chi))^{\mathsf{T}}\omega_c + \nabla\varepsilon_c(\chi)\big]. \tag{7}$$

Using the critic network (6), the approximate optimal control function is

$$\hat{\mu}^*(\chi) = -\frac{1}{2}g^{\mathsf{T}}(\chi)(\nabla\sigma_c(\chi))^{\mathsf{T}}\hat{\omega}_c. \tag{8}$$

Based on the neural network formulation, the approximate Hamiltonian is

$$\hat{H}(\chi, \hat{\mu}^*(\chi), \nabla\hat{J}^*(\chi)) = Z(\chi, \hat{\mu}^*(\chi)) + \hat{\omega}_c^{\mathsf{T}}\nabla\sigma_c(\chi)[f(\chi) + g(\chi)\hat{\mu}^*(\chi)]. \tag{9}$$

By virtue of the fact $H(\chi, \mu^*(\chi), \nabla J^*(\chi)) = 0$, we acquire $e_c = \hat{H}(\chi, \hat{\mu}^*(\chi), \nabla\hat{J}^*(\chi))$. Clearly, we find that

$$\frac{\partial e_c}{\partial \hat{\omega}_c} = \nabla\sigma_c(\chi)[f(\chi) + g(\chi)\hat{\mu}^*(\chi)] \triangleq \eta, \tag{10}$$

where $\eta \in \mathbb{R}^{l_c}$. Based on [9], we choose $\mathcal{L}(\chi)$ as an additional Lyapunov function, so as to get the critic learning rule as follows:

$$\dot{\hat{\omega}}_c = -\beta_c\frac{\eta}{(1 + \eta^{\mathsf{T}}\eta)^2}e_c + \frac{1}{2}\beta_s\nabla\sigma_c(\chi)g(\chi)g^{\mathsf{T}}(\chi)\nabla\mathcal{L}(\chi), \tag{11}$$

where $\beta_c > 0$ and $\beta_s > 0$ are the learning rates.

We define the error vector between the ideal weight and the estimated value as $\tilde{\omega}_c = \omega_c - \hat{\omega}_c$ and then find that $\dot{\tilde{\omega}}_c = -\dot{\hat{\omega}}_c$. Here, let us introduce two new variables

$$\eta_1 = \frac{\eta}{1 + \eta^{\mathsf{T}}\eta}, \quad \eta_2 = 1 + \eta^{\mathsf{T}}\eta$$

with $\eta_1 \in \mathbb{R}^{l_c}$ and $\eta_2 \geq 1$. Then, by using the tuning rule (11), we derive that the critic error dynamics can be simply formulated as

$$\dot{\tilde{\omega}}_c = -\beta_c\eta_1\eta_1^{\mathsf{T}}\tilde{\omega}_c + \beta_c\frac{\eta_1}{\eta_2}e_{cH} - \frac{1}{2}\beta_s\nabla\sigma_c(\chi)g(\chi)g^{\mathsf{T}}(\chi)\nabla\mathcal{L}(\chi), \tag{12}$$

where the term $e_{cH} = -(\nabla\varepsilon_c(\chi))^{\mathsf{T}}[f(\chi) + g(\chi)\hat{\mu}^*(\chi)]$ denotes the residual error arisen in the neural network approximation process. The following assumption is provided, as often used in literature as [8, 9, 11].

Assumption 1. *The matrix $g(\chi)$ is upper bounded such that $\|g(\chi)\| \leq \lambda_g$, where λ_g is a positive constant. On the compact set Ω, the terms $\nabla\sigma_c(\chi)$, $\nabla\varepsilon_c(\chi)$, and e_{cH} are all upper bounded such that $\|\nabla\sigma_c(\chi)\| \leq \lambda_\sigma$, $\|\nabla\varepsilon_c(\chi)\| \leq \lambda_\varepsilon$, and $|e_{cH}| \leq \lambda_e$, where λ_σ, λ_ε, and λ_e are positive constants.*

Based on the results of [9], the critic weight error $\tilde{\omega}_c$ is upper bounded by a finite constant, i.e., $\|\tilde{\omega}_c\| \le \mathscr{B}_{\tilde{\omega}}$. Then, according to (7) and (8), we can find

$$\|\mu^*(\chi) - \hat{\mu}^*(\chi)\| = \frac{1}{2}\|g^{\mathsf{T}}(\chi)\left[(\nabla \sigma_c(\chi))^{\mathsf{T}}\tilde{\omega}_c + \nabla \varepsilon_c(\chi)\right]\|$$

$$\le \frac{1}{2}\lambda_g(\lambda_\sigma \mathscr{B}_{\tilde{\omega}} + \lambda_\varepsilon) \triangleq \mathscr{B}_\mu. \tag{13}$$

This implies that the near-optimal control $\hat{\mu}^*(\chi)$ can converge to a neighborhood of the optimal function $\mu^*(\chi)$ with a finite bound $\mathscr{B}_\mu$, where $\mathscr{B}_\mu$ is a positive constant. It is also worth mentioning that this bound can be set adequately small by adjusting the related parameters like the critic learning rate.

3   Application to Perform Robust Stabilization

If dynamical uncertainties are brought into system (1) by various changes during the operation process of the controlled plant, we have to pay attention to the robustness of the designed controller. We consider a class of nonlinear systems subjected to uncertainties and described by

$$\dot{\chi}(t) = f(\chi(t)) + g(\chi(t))[\mu(t) + d(\chi(t))], \tag{14}$$

where the term $g(\chi)d(\chi)$ reflects a kind of dynamical uncertainties matched with the control matrix. We assume $d(0) = 0$, so as to keep $\chi = 0$ as an equilibrium of the controlled plant. It is often assumed that the term $d(\chi)$ is bounded by a known function $d_M(\chi)$, i.e., $\|d(\chi)\| \le d_M(\chi)$ with $d_M(0) = 0$.

Considering the uncertain nonlinear system (14), for coping with the robust stabilization problem, we should design a control law $\mu(\chi)$, such that the closed-loop state vector is stable with respect to dynamical uncertainties. In this section, by adopting a positive constant ρ and specifying $Q(\chi) = \rho d_M^2(\chi)$, we will show that the robust control problem can be addressed by designing the optimal controller of the nominal plant (1), where the cost function is given as (2) and a modified utility is selected as

$$Z(\chi(t), \mu(t)) = \rho d_M^2(\chi(t)) + \mu^{\mathsf{T}}(t)\mu(t). \tag{15}$$

Note that in this situation, the optimal control function is kept unchanged even if the modified utility is employed. Observing the modified utility function (15) and substituting the optimal control law (3) into (4), the Hamilton-Jacobi-Bellman equation with respect to the modified optimal control problem becomes

$$0 = \rho d_M^2(\chi) + (\nabla J^*(\chi))^{\mathsf{T}} f(\chi)$$

$$- \frac{1}{4}(\nabla J^*(\chi))^{\mathsf{T}} g(\chi) g^{\mathsf{T}}(\chi) \nabla J^*(\chi), \quad J^*(0) = 0. \tag{16}$$

Theorem 1. *For the nominal system (1) and the cost function (2) with a modified utility function (15), the approximate optimal control obtained by (8) ensures that the closed-loop form of the uncertain nonlinear plant (14) possesses uniformly ultimately bounded stability if $\rho > 1$.*

Proof. The proof is performed via the Lyapunov stability theory. Denote the solution of the Hamilton-Jacobi-Bellman equation (16) as $J^*(\chi)$ and based on which, the optimal feedback control law is formulated as (3). According to the aforementioned definition, it is shown that $J^*(\chi)$ is a positive definite function. Combining the formula (3), i.e., $2\mu^{*\mathsf{T}}(\chi) = -(\nabla J^*(\chi))^\mathsf{T} g(\chi)$ with (16), we easily find that

$$(\nabla J^*(\chi))^\mathsf{T} f(\chi) = -\rho d_M^2(\chi) + \mu^{*\mathsf{T}}(\chi)\mu^*(\chi). \tag{17}$$

Applying the approximate optimal control law (8) and using (17), we obtain the time derivative $\dot{J}^*(\chi) = \mathrm{d}J^*(\chi)/\mathrm{d}t$ along the uncertain nonlinear plant (14) as follows:

$$\begin{aligned}
\dot{J}^*(\chi) &= (\nabla J^*(\chi))^\mathsf{T}[f(\chi) + g(\chi)\hat{\mu}^*(\chi) + g(\chi)d(\chi)] \\
&= -\rho d_M^2(\chi) + \mu^{*\mathsf{T}}(\chi)\mu^*(\chi) - 2\mu^{*\mathsf{T}}(\chi)[\hat{\mu}^*(\chi) + d(\chi)].
\end{aligned} \tag{18}$$

By bringing a quadratic term $d^\mathsf{T}(\chi)d(\chi)$ into (18), we have

$$\begin{aligned}
\dot{J}^*(\chi) = &- \rho d_M^2(\chi) + d^\mathsf{T}(\chi)d(\chi) + 2\mu^{*\mathsf{T}}(\chi)[\mu^*(\chi) - \hat{\mu}^*(\chi)] \\
&- (\mu^*(\chi) + d(\chi))^\mathsf{T}(\mu^*(\chi) + d(\chi)) \\
\leq &- [\rho d_M^2(\chi) - d^\mathsf{T}(\chi)d(\chi)] + 2\mu^{*\mathsf{T}}(\chi)[\mu^*(\chi) - \hat{\mu}^*(\chi)].
\end{aligned} \tag{19}$$

Performing the Young's inequality to second term of (19), we can derive that

$$2\mu^{*\mathsf{T}}(\chi)[\mu^*(\chi) - \hat{\mu}^*(\chi)] \leq \|\mu^*(\chi)\|^2 + \|\mu^*(\chi) - \hat{\mu}^*(\chi)\|^2. \tag{20}$$

Observing (7), the optimal control function $\mu^*(\chi)$ is upper bounded such that we have

$$\begin{aligned}
\|\mu^*(\chi)\| &\leq \frac{1}{2}\|g^\mathsf{T}(\chi)[(\nabla\sigma_c(\chi))^\mathsf{T}w_c + \nabla\varepsilon_c(\chi)]\| \\
&\leq \frac{1}{2}\lambda_g(\lambda_\sigma\lambda_w + \lambda_\varepsilon) \triangleq \lambda_{\mu^*},
\end{aligned} \tag{21}$$

where λ_{μ^*} is a positive constant. Considering (13) and (21), it follows from (20) that

$$2\mu^{*\mathsf{T}}(\chi)[\mu^*(\chi) - \hat{\mu}^*(\chi)] \leq \lambda_{\mu^*}^2 + \mathscr{B}_\mu^2. \tag{22}$$

Noticing $\|d(\chi)\|^2 = d^\mathsf{T}(\chi)d(\chi) \leq d_M^2(\chi)$ and (22), we further find that (19) becomes

$$\dot{J}^*(\chi) \leq -(\rho - 1)d_M^2(\chi) + \lambda_{\mu^*}^2 + \mathscr{B}_\mu^2.$$

In many circumstances, we can determine a quadratic bound of the uncertain component $d(\chi)$, such that $d_M(\chi) = \xi\|\chi\|$, where ξ is a positive constant. Hence, considering $\rho > 1$, we conclude that $\dot{J}^*(\chi) < 0$ if $\chi(t)$ lies outside

$$\Omega_\chi = \left\{\chi : \|\chi\| \leq \sqrt{\frac{\lambda_{\mu^*}^2 + \mathscr{B}_\mu^2}{\xi^2(\rho - 1)}} \triangleq \mathscr{B}_\chi\right\},$$

where $\mathscr{B}_\chi$ stands for a positive constant. In this sense, we say that with the approximate optimal control (8), the state trajectory of the closed-loop uncertain system is uniformly ultimately bounded as $\|\chi\| \leq \mathscr{B}_\chi$, which ends the proof. $\square$

4 Simulation Study of an Overhead Crane

In this section, an experimental simulation is carried out for the overhead crane given in [12], where the mass of trolley, the mass of load, the length of rope, and the gravitational acceleration are chosen as $1\,\text{kg}$, $0.8\,\text{kg}$, $0.305\,\text{m}$, and $9.81\,\text{m/s}^2$, respectively. We also make a modification to this plant by introducing an uncertain term $d(\chi) = 2\varpi\chi_1 \sin(\chi_2^2\chi_3)\cos(\chi_3\chi_4^2)$ with $\varpi \in [-0.5, 0.5]$, where $x = [\chi_1, \chi_2, \chi_3, \chi_4]^\mathsf{T}$. Then, we find that the bounded function can be selected as $d_M(\chi) = \|\chi\|$ and thus, the modified utility function can be written as $Z(\chi, \mu) = \rho\|\chi\|^2 + \mu^\mathsf{T}\mu$. For coping with the nonlinear near-optimal control problem including the modified utility with $\rho = 2$, we employ the improved adaptive critic control method, where the optimal cost function can be approximated by building a critic network

$$
\begin{aligned}
\hat{J}^*(\chi) = {}& \hat{\omega}_{c1}\chi_1^2 + \hat{\omega}_{c2}\chi_1\chi_2 + \hat{\omega}_{c3}\chi_1\chi_3 \\
& + \hat{\omega}_{c4}\chi_1\chi_4 + \hat{\omega}_{c5}\chi_2^2 + \hat{\omega}_{c6}\chi_2\chi_3 \\
& + \hat{\omega}_{c7}\chi_2\chi_4 + \hat{\omega}_{c8}\chi_3^2 + \hat{\omega}_{c9}\chi_3\chi_4 + \hat{\omega}_{c10}\chi_4^2.
\end{aligned}
$$

We set the learning rate parameters as $\beta_c = 2$ and $\beta_s = 0.01$ and then employ a probing noise for guaranteeing the persistence of excitation condition. Through a sufficient learning stage, the weight vector of the critic network converges to

$$
\begin{aligned}
[2.4188, 4.1442, 0.1583, 0.4370, 3.3129, \\
0.2046, 0.5664, -0.0631, -0.3990, 0.0751]^\mathsf{T}.
\end{aligned}
$$

In this simulation, we find that the convergence has occured in $t = 550\,\text{s}$ and after that we remove the probing signals. These results display a learning trend of approaching to the ideal weight and attaining the near-optimal controller.

Next, the performance of robust stabilization is checked by selecting $\varpi = 0.5$ and applying the derived control law to the uncertain system for $t = 20\,\text{s}$. Then, the system trajectory is depicted in Fig. 1(a) while the control curve is presented in Fig. 1(b). Hence, under the action of the developed controller, the state vector

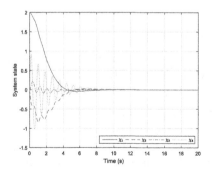
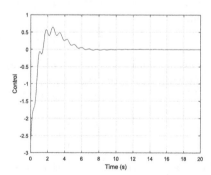

Fig. 1. (a) The state trajectory. (b) The control curve.

is nearly driven to zero as time goes on, which validates the good robustness with respect to the dynamical uncertainty.

5   Conclusions

In this paper, we aim at investigating the adaptation-oriented near-optimal control design and applying it to solve the robust control problem of an overhead crane system. The improved learning rule reduces the initial stabilizing control law and brings in a great convenience to the adaptive control implementation.

Acknowledgments. This work was supported in part by Beijing Natural Science Foundation under Grant 4162065, in part by the National Natural Science Foundation of China under Grants 61773373, U1501251, 61533017, and 61233001, and in part by the Early Career Development Award of SKLMCCS.

References

1. Werbos, P.J.: Approximate dynamic programming for real-time control and neural modeling. In: White, D.A., Sofge, D.A. (eds.) Handbook of Intelligent Control: Neural, Fuzzy, and Adaptive Approach. Van Nostrand Reinhold, New York (1992)
2. Wang, D., Mu, C., Liu, D.: Data-driven nonlinear near-optimal regulation based on iterative neural dynamic programming. Acta Automatica Sinica **43**, 366–375 (2017)
3. Liu, D., Wei, Q., Wang, D., Yang, X., Li, H.: Adaptive Dynamic Programming with Applications in Optimal Control. Springer, London (2017). doi:10.1007/978-3-319-50815-3
4. Vamvoudakis, K.G., Modares, H., Kiumarsi, B., Lewis, F.L.: Game theory-based control system algorithms with real-time reinforcement learning: how to solve multiplayer games online. IEEE Control Syst. Mag. **37**, 33–52 (2017)
5. Zhang, H., Zhang, X., Luo, Y., Yang, J.: An overview of research on adaptive dynamic programming. Acta Automatica Sinica **39**, 303–311 (2013)
6. Vamvoudakis, K.G., Lewis, F.L.: Online actor-critic algorithm to solve the continuous-time infinite horizon optimal control problem. Automatica **46**, 878–888 (2010)
7. Mu, C., Wang, D.: Neural-network-based adaptive guaranteed cost control of nonlinear dynamical systems with matched uncertainties. Neurocomputing **245**, 46–54 (2017)
8. Zhang, H., Cui, L., Luo, Y.: Near-optimal control for nonzero-sum differential games of continuous-time nonlinear systems using single-network ADP. IEEE Trans. Cybern. **43**, 206–216 (2013)
9. Wang, D., Mu, C.: A novel neural optimal control framework with nonlinear dynamics: closed-loop stability and simulation verification. Neurocomputing **266**, 353–360 (2017)
10. Jiang, Y., Jiang, Z.P.: Robust adaptive dynamic programming and feedback stabilization of nonlinear systems. IEEE Trans. Neural Netw. Learn. Syst. **25**, 882–893 (2014)

11. Zhang, Q., Zhao, D., Wang, D.: Event-based robust control for uncertain nonlinear systems using adaptive dynamic programming. In: IEEE Transactions on Neural Networks and Learning Systems (2017). in press
12. Wang, D., He, H., Liu, D.: Adaptive critic nonlinear robust control: a survey. IEEE Trans. Cybern. **47**(10), 3429–3451 (2017)

Deep CNN Identifier for Dynamic Modelling of Unmanned Helicopter

Shaofeng Chen, Yang Cao, Yu Kang$^{(\boxtimes)}$, Rongrong Zhu, and Pengfei Li

Department of Automation,
University of Science and Technology of China, Hefei, China
kangduyu@ustc.edu.cn

Abstract. Unmanned helicopter has broad application prospects, both in civil and military field. Helicopter is a strong coupled with many phenomena, inherently unstable, high-order, time-varying nonlinear complex system. It is a great challenge to investigate the system identification of helicopter, particularly when the non-stationary flight regimes are considered. In this paper, we address the system identification as dynamic regression. Inspired by the feature expression ability of deep learning, we use Deep convolutional neural networks (CNN) to represent dynamics model of helicopter. The parameters of the network are directly learned from the real flight data collected from helicopter. We provide model initialization method and optimization details for training. Since it captures the hidden states in aerobatic maneuvers without a-priori, the proposed identifier manifests strong robustness and high accuracy, even for untrained aerobatic maneuvers. The effectiveness of the proposed method is verified by various experiments on the real-world flight data from Stanford Autonomous Helicopter Project. Specifically, the Deep CNN identifier improves 71.60% overall in RMS acceleration prediction over the lasted Deep Rectified Linear Unit (ReLU) Network Model.

Keywords: Unmanned helicopter · Deep convolutional neural networks · System identification

1 Introduction

The unmanned helicopter has outstanding flight capabilities, such as fixed position hovering, sideward flight, collision avoidance maneuver and so on. These flight capabilities make helicopter has broad application prospect, both in civil and military field [1,2]. System identification (also referred to as modeling dynamic system) is one of the most basic and important part in control. The helicopter is a inherently unstable, high-order, time-varying nonlinear, strongly coupled with many phenomena system [3]. The complexity of helicopter system makes the system identification of helicopter become challenging.

The helicopter is coupled with many phenomena (aerodynamic forces, shaking, engine dynamics, internal control loops and so on) [4]. These phenomena

© Springer International Publishing AG 2017
D. Liu et al. (Eds.): ICONIP 2017, Part VI, LNCS 10639, pp. 51–60, 2017.
https://doi.org/10.1007/978-3-319-70136-3_6

are, substantially all, somewhat poorly comprehended and immeasurable up to date, and thus remain hidden. So we can not get the accurate dynamic model only by first-principles modelling [5], part of the dynamic of the helicopter need to be learned from data. Considering persons can fly helicopter effectively, even through complex maneuvers, this paper proposes a method to learn a dynamic model by utilizing captured state-action trajectories from expert demonstrations.

While the features extraction and features representation capabilities of deep learning methods in high dimensional space [6,7] make them have prominent performance in perception related tasks such as image and speech recognition, it has been more recently indicated that system identification problems also benefit from this method [8]. [8] leverages Deep Rectified Linear (ReLU) Network including 2500 hidden units to construct a global nonlinear model without prior or assumptions. Takens Theorem [9,10] provides theoretical basis of deep learning methods, which elucidates that the system state of a nonlinear dynamical systems with n-dimensional state space can be effectually reconstructed so long as there are 2n+1 former measurements of a single system output.

Although the Deep ReLU Network in [8] constructs a nonlinear dynamic model which contains the hidden states in the system dynamics by the features extraction and representation capabilities of deep learning methods, the Deep CNN has better performance in features extraction and representation compared with other deep neural network [11]. And Deep CNN has the prominent properties of sparse connectivity and parameter sharing [12]. These properties reduce the complexity of the network and avoid the complexity of data reconstruction in feature extraction and representation. Naturally, we consider using Deep CNN to construct a global nonlinear dynamic model of the helicopter that describing the hidden states and uncertainties from the collected flight data, without any assumptions or prior of flight regimes. The parameters of the Deep CNN network are learned from the real flight data of Stanford Autonomous Helicopter Project [13]. To demonstrate the effectiveness of the presented method, we compare the method with several baseline methods. The results reveal that the proposed method is more accurate in dynamic modeling and has good robustness on describing the dynamic behavior of hidden states and uncertainties in the dynamics model.

Our main contributions of this paper are:

(1) Compared with the former system identifiers, the proposed method in this paper identifies the dynamic behavior of hidden states (e.g. airflow) and uncertainties (e.g. shaking) from the aerobatic flight data, without any assumptions or prior of flight regimes. Therefore, the proposed identifier demonstrates a better performance at the complex flight environment. The Deep CNN Network Model improves 71.60% overall in RMS acceleration prediction over the latest Deep ReLU Network in [8].

(2) The presented Deep CNN network method indeed learns a set of submodels with their corresponding active regions in the state control space. Additionally, these sub-models express the features extracted from the state control space, and are integrated to construct a global nonlinear dynamic model of the

helicopter. Consequently, the presented Deep CNN network identifier manifests strong robustness and adaptivity across the untrained flight trajectories.

2   Problem Formulation and Baseline Models

Consider the unmanned helicopter with six degrees of freedom expressed in the inertial coordinate frame, which are the position $p = (x, y, z)^T \in \mathbb{R}^3$ and the attitude $\Theta = (\phi, \theta, \psi)^T \in \mathbb{R}^3$. And $v = (v_x, v_y, v_z) \in \mathbb{R}^3$ and $\omega = (\omega_x, \omega_y, \omega_z) \in \mathbb{R}^3$ represent the linear velocity and angular velocity, respectively. Subsequently, the dynamic model of the helicopter can be written as

$$\dot{v} = -S(w)v + G(R) + \frac{1}{m}\Gamma_1 + \frac{1}{m}\tau_1 + \Delta v \tag{1}$$

$$\dot{w} = J^{-1}S(Jw)\omega + J^{-1}\Gamma_2 + J^{-1}\tau_2 + \Delta\omega \tag{2}$$

where $S(\omega) \in \mathbb{R}^{3\times3}$ and $S(J\omega) \in \mathbb{R}^{3\times3}$ are skew symmetric matrix, $G(R) = [0, 0, g]^T \in \mathbb{R}^{3\times1}$ is gravity matrix with g the gravitational acceleration, $m \in \mathbb{R}$ represents the mass of the helicopter, $J \in \mathbb{R}^{3\times3}$ is the inertia matrix, $\Gamma_1 \in \mathbb{R}^{3\times1}$ and $\Gamma_2 \in \mathbb{R}^{3\times1}$ are the nonlinear aerodynamic forces, $\Delta v \in \mathbb{R}^{3\times1}$ and $\Delta\omega \in \mathbb{R}^{3\times1}$ represent other phenomena strong coupled with helicopter. $\tau_1 = [0, 0, u_4]^T \in \mathbb{R}^{3\times1}$ and $\tau_2 = [u_1, u_2, u_3]^T \in \mathbb{R}^{3\times1}$ are control inputs.

Γ_1, Γ_2, Δv and $\Delta\omega$ are somewhat poorly comprehended and immeasurable up to date, and thus remain hidden. The inertia matrix is time-varying during flight. In these tough and standard practice in helicopter modeling, we make an informed rewrite (1) and (2) into the following form:

$$\begin{bmatrix} \dot{v} \\ \dot{w} \end{bmatrix} = \begin{bmatrix} -S(\omega)v + G(R) + g_v(s, \tau, \lambda) \\ g_\omega(s, \tau, \lambda) \end{bmatrix} \tag{3}$$

g_v and g_ω represent the linear and angular uncertainties that contains hidden states, $s = [v, \omega]$ is the state vector, $\tau = [u_1, u_2, u_3, u_4]$ represents the control vector and λ is the model parameter. Making $g = [g_v^T, g_\omega^T]^T$.

Artificial neural networks (ANNs) have ability to approximate any nonlinear function and learn from data. ANNs have already been used to identify helicopter systems by their outstanding ability. So we choose typical back propagation (BP) Neural Networks [16] as a baseline model. The output of the BP Neural Networks is calculated by proceeding layer by layer, details as follows:

$$S_j^k(n) = \sum_{i=1}^{m} w_{ji}^k(n) s_j^{k-1}(n) \tag{4}$$

where S_j^k represents the output of neuron j in hidden layer k, n is the number of iterations, w_{ji}^k represents the weight which connects neuron j with neuron i in the layer k, s_j^k is the output of unit j in the layer k given by

$$s_j^k(n) = \frac{1}{1 + e^{-\alpha S_j^k(n)}} \tag{5}$$

where α is the hyper-parameter. The input of the BP Neural Network is $[x, y]$, $x = [v; \omega]^T$, $y = [\tau; \dot{\tau}]^T$. The reason why we consider the control derivatives $\dot{\tau}$ is that $\dot{u}_3$ is a better predictor of the yaw acceleration than u_3 by the presence of an internal gyroscope and control loop in the helicopter.

For better indicating the prominent performance of our model, we choose the up-to-date ReLU Network Model [8] as a baseline model. The model is proposed by Pieter Abbeel of the University of California, Berkeley. Algebraically, it can be written as follows:

$$g = P\beta(x_t) + \sum_{i=0}^{H} Q_i \beta(y_{t-i}) + \eta(p_t; \lambda) \tag{6}$$

$$\eta(p_t; \lambda) = w^T max\left(0, W^T p_t + B\right) + b \tag{7}$$

$$\beta(y_{t-i}) = \left[y_{t-i}, max\left(0, y_{t-i}\right)^2, min\left(0, y_{t-i}\right)^2\right]^T \tag{8}$$

where $P, Q_0...Q_H$ represent matrices of parameters to be learned, $\beta(z)$ is used to capture some simple nonlinearities, H is the length of the state-control trajectory segment $p_t = [x_{t-H}, y_{t-H}, x_{t-H+1}, y_{t-H+1}, ..., x_t, y_t]$ which corresponds to a small part of a helicopter maneuver, $\eta(p_t; \lambda)$ is a two-layer ReLU neural network of N hidden units with weights W, w and biases B, b.

3   Deep CNN Identifier

Takens Theorem points out that the system state of a nonlinear dynamical systems with n-dimensional state space can be effectually reconstructed so long as there are 2n+1 former measurements of a single system output. It means that if the H is large enough, the entire hidden state at the end of p_t can be reconstructed. Considering Deep CNN has better performance in features extraction and representation compared with another deep neural network. We propose a Deep CNN identifier for dynamic modelling of unmanned helicopter from the collected flight data without any assumptions or prior of flight regimes. It means using a Deep CNN model to identify g. The architecture of our Deep CNN model is shown as Fig. 1. It consists of eight layers (3 convolutional layers, 2 pooling layers and 3 inner product layers), not counting the input layer. The data type of the CNN is image, so we convert the vector p_t to a matrix $m_t = [x_{t-H}, y_{t-H}; x_{t-H+1}, y_{t-H+1}; ..., x_t, y_t]$ and view it as a $H \times 14$ pixel image with one channel. The values of the m_t need to be normalized so that the learning rate accelerates. Algebraically, the convolutional layers can be described as

$$o_j^l = f\left(\sum_{i \in M_j} o_j^{l-1} * k_{ij}^l + b_j^l\right) \tag{9}$$

where l is the layer index, k represents convolution kernel, M_j is the space consisted of m_t, b represents bias. The result of each convolution layer is the

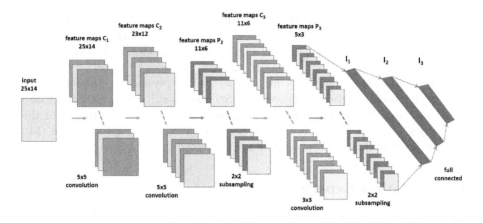

Fig. 1. Deep CNN architecture for a system identification task

input of the next pooling layer. The algebraic expression of the pooling layers can be written as follow:

$$o_j^l = f\left(\beta_j^{l-1} d\left(o_j^{l-1}\right) + b_j^l\right) \tag{10}$$

where $d\left(\cdot\right)$ represents pooling function, each feature graph has its β and b. For ease of description, convolutional layers are labeled C_x, pooling layers are labeled P_x, and inner product layers are labeled I_x, where x is the layer index.

Layer C_1 has 16 feature maps. Each neuron in the feature maps is connected to a 5×5 neighborhood in the input. The size of the feature maps is 25×14. C_1 contains 400 trainable parameters and 140000 connections. Layer C_2 has 32 feature maps of size 23×12. Each neuron in the feature maps is connected to a 5×5 neighborhood in the input. Layer C_2 has 800 trainable parameters and 220800 connections. Layer P_2 is a pooling layer with 32 feature maps. Each neuron in each feature map is connected to a 2×2 neighborhood in the corresponding feature map in C_2. The size of the feature maps is 11×6. Layer P_2 contains 128 trainable parameters and 8448 connections.

Layer C_3 has 64 feature maps of size 11×6. Each neuron in the feature maps is connected to a 3×3 neighborhood in the input. Layer C_3 has 576 trainable parameters and 39016 connections. Layer P_3 has 64 feature maps. Each neuron in each feature map is connected to a 2×2 neighborhood in the corresponding feature map in C_3. The size of the feature maps is 5×3. Layer P_3 contains 256 trainable parameters and 3840 connections. Layer I_1 contains 128 neurons and is fully connected to P_3. Layer I_2, I_3 contain 128, 1 neurons, respectively.

Our task is having minimize mean squared prediction error by adjusting λ,

$$\min_\lambda \sum_{i=1}^{N} \frac{1}{N} ||g_d - g\left(s, \tau, \lambda\right)||^2 \tag{11}$$

where g_d represents the observed values along a demonstration trajectory.

The optimization problem of constructing uncertainties in our work is splited into six subproblems, three for the linear uncertainties, three for the angular uncertainties. We work out these six subproblems individually. It means training six changed Deep CNN models. In our work, we adopt Stochastic Gradient Descent to train the Deep CNN models. It is also very easy to implement. In order to improve the training speed and precision, we divide our train set into many batches. The gradients of the objective over the batch in regard to the parameters of the Deep CNN models are figured using Backpropagation [14]. The details of optimization procedure are presented in Sect. 4.

4   Simulation Experiment

4.1   Modelling Dataset and Optimization

To examine the effectiveness of our proposed dynamic modelling method, we adopt data from the Stanford Autonomous Helicopter Project [13]. The project used a Synergy N9 model helicopter weighing 4.85 kg with the length of 138 cm and the height of 40 cm. The project invited the skilled pilot to flow the helicopter repetitively covering a range of aerobatic maneuvers.

Trajectories logged by the project included the estimated dataset from Kalman smoother in the 0.01 s sampling interval. These aerobatic maneuvers are divided into twenty categories. We serve ten seconds as interval to slice each trajectory, then muddle these trajectory parts. 75% of these parts are selected randomly as the training set, and the others are testing set. Among training set, 40% is selected randomly as validation set. The training set is used to optimize the parameters of dynamic model and validation set is used to pick hyperparameters. In the training process, the categories of aerobatic maneuvers are not used as labels. A global dynamic nonlinear model is trained across all maneuvers. Particularly, to verify the robustness, only 18 categories of aerobatic maneuvers are used for the training of modelling, while all categories are used for testing of modelling. The $turn - demos3$ and $orientation - sweeps - motions$ maneuvers are selected for testing.

The stochastic gradient descent method is chosen to optimize our Deep CNN model. To increase training speed, pretreatment (data type conversion and normalization) is needed to prepare the data. The value of momentum is 0.95. The learning rate is set to 0.001 and the stepsize is 100000. The value of weight decay is set to 0.005. The number of iterations is 200000, the batch size are both set to 256. To compute gradients of the objective, we choose an automatic differentiation library called Caffe [15].

4.2   Performance

In the experiments, the BP neural network model and the Deep RELU Network model are selected as baseline models. Compared with the BP neural network model only considered some simple nonlinear relatedness on the current

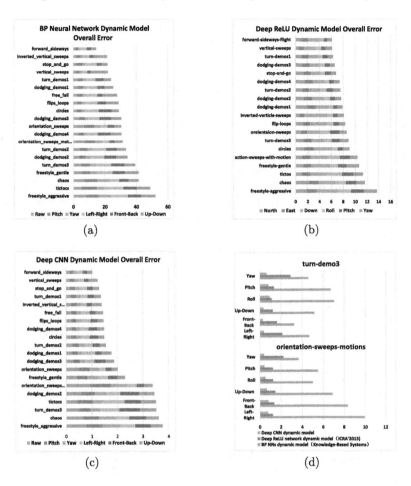

Fig. 2. RMS prediction error of: (a) BP neural network dynamic model; (b) Deep ReLU network dynamic model; (c) Deep CNN dynamic model; (d) Untrained maneuvers (m/s^2)

state and controls, the Deep ReLU Network model directly playes as the state-of-the-art performance baseline. The Deep ReLU Network model is the latest method so far and proposed by Pieter Abbeel of the University of California, Berkeley. Root Mean-Square (RMS) is chosen to the performance of the two models by its property of normalizing the length of trajectories. The contrastive test of our proposed model against the two baseline models were performed first. Figure 2(a)–(c) give the evaluation results on the overall test set. As seen, our novel Deep CNN model was far beyond the two baseline models in prediction accuracy. Our model improves 92.63% and 71.6% overall in RMS acceleration prediction over the two baseline models, respectively. Then the performances of our Deep CNN model and the two baseline models on the $turn - demos3$ and

the *orientationsweeps − motions* maneuvers are given in Fig. 2(d). Seeing the
Deep ReLU Network model and the BP neural network are fully trained on the
trajectory segmentations over the two maneuvers while our Deep CNN model
not. As shown, although our model is totally untrained across the two maneuvers, the best results were achieved. This well demonstrates the robustness of
our proposed Deep CNN model.

In addition, the observed and predicted accelerations in three directions of the
Deep ReLU Network model and our Deep CNN model are presented. The evaluation results across the *turn − demos*3 and *orientationsweepsmotions* maneuvers are given in Fig. 3. Noting all the trajectory segmentations over the two
maneuvers are not in the training of the Deep CNN model. As shown, our
Deep CNN model is far beyond the two baseline models in the accuracy of prediction, in particular when the acceleration is dramatically-shifted. We further
select the most dramatic trajectory segmentation (shown as the red line of the
trajectory in Fig. 4(a)(1) and (b)(1) to evaluate the identification accuracy of

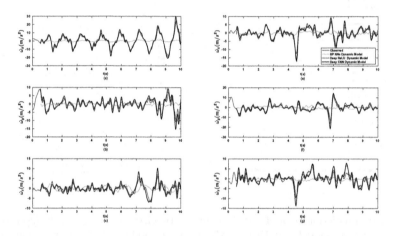

Fig. 3. Observed and predict angular accelerations in three direction over untrained
maneuvers: (a–c) orientation-sweeps-motions; (e–g) turn-demos3

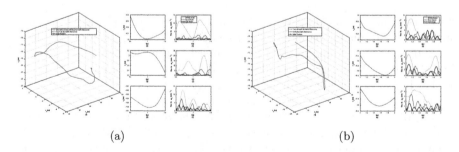

(a)   (b)

Fig. 4. Properties of untrained aerobatic maneuvers: (a) orientation-sweeps-motions;
(b) turn-demos3 (Color figure online)

the three models. The identification errors on angular acceleration are shown in Fig. 4(a)(5–7) and (b)(5–7). The evaluation results exhibit the capacity of our dynamic modeling method at the complex flight environment.

5 Conclusion and Future Work

This paper devotes the problem of dynamic modelling of unmanned helicopter. To identify the uncertainties and the hidden states in helicopter dynamics model, a Deep CNN model whose parameters are straightly learned from the real data of helicopter is proposed. The Deep CNN model significantly outperforms the latest Deep ReLU Network model in identification precision. And our model manifests strong robustness at complicated environment, even for untrained aerobatic maneuvers. Various experimental results on the real-world data from Stanford Autonomous Helicopter Project prove the effectiveness of the proposed dynamic model. However, the question of whether the Deep CNN model performs well enough to enable autonomous control through aerobatic maneuvers is not answered. We aim to solve this question in the future work.

Acknowledgments. This work was supported in part by the National Natural Science Foundation of China (61422307 and 61673361), the Scientific Research Staring Foundation for the Returned Overseas Chinese Scholars and Ministry of Education of China. Authors also gratefully acknowledge supports from the Youth Top-notch Talent Support Program and the Youth Yangtze River Scholar.

References

1. Starke, E.A., Staley, J.T.: Application of modern aluminum alloys to aircraft. Prog. Aerosp. Sci. **32**(2–3), 131–172 (1996)
2. Johnson, W.: Helicopter Theory. Courier Corporation, New York (2012)
3. Leishman, G.J.: Principles of Helicopter Aerodynamics with CD Extra. Cambridge University Press, Cambridge (2006)
4. Abbeel, P., Ganapathi, V., Ng, A.Y.: Learning vehicular dynamics, with application to modeling helicopters. In: Advances in Neural Information Processing Systems, pp. 1–8 (2006)
5. Padfield, G.D.: The Theory and Application of Flying Qualities and Simulation Modeling. Helicopter Flight Dynamics. AIAA: Education Series, Washington, DC (1996)
6. LeCun, Y., Bengio, Y., Hinton, G.: Deep learning. Nature **521**(7553), 436–444 (2015)
7. Schmidhuber, J.: Deep learning in neural networks: an overview. Neural Netw. **61**, 85–117 (2015)
8. Punjani, A., Abbeel, P.: Deep learning helicopter dynamics models. In: 2015 IEEE International Conference on Robotics and Automation (ICRA), pp. 3223–3230. IEEE (2015)
9. Takens, F.: Detecting strange attractors in turbulence. In: Rand, D., Young, L.-S. (eds.) Dynamical Systems and Turbulence, Warwick 1980. LNM, vol. 898, pp. 366–381. Springer, Heidelberg (1981). doi:10.1007/BFb0091924

10. Robinson, J.C.: A topological delay embedding theorem for infinite-dimensional dynamical systems. Nonlinearity **18**(5), 2135 (2005)
11. Krizhevsky, A., Sutskever, I., Hinton, G.E.: Imagenet classification with deep convolutional neural networks. In: Advances in Neural Information Processing Systems, pp. 1097–1105 (2012)
12. Bouvrie, J.: Notes on Convolutional Neural Networks (2006)
13. Abbeel, P., Coates, A., Ng, A.Y.: Autonomous helicopter aerobatics through apprenticeship learning. Int. J. Robot. Res. **29**(13), 1608–1639 (2010)
14. Riedmiller, M., Braun, H.: A direct adaptive method for faster backpropagation learning: the RPROP algorithm. In: 1993 IEEE International Conference on Neural Networks, pp. 586–591. IEEE (1993)
15. Jia, Y., Shelhamer, E., Donahue, J., Karayev, S., Long, J., Girshick, R., Darrell, T.: Caffe: convolutional architecture for fast feature embedding. In: Proceedings of the 22nd ACM International Conference on Multimedia, pp. 675–678. ACM (2014)
16. Guo, Z.H., Wu, J., Lu, H.Y., Wang, J.Z.: A case study on a hybrid wind speed forecasting method using BP neural network. Knowl.-Based Syst. **24**(7), 1048–1056 (2011)

Packet-Dropouts Compensation for Networked Control System via Deep ReLU Neural Network

Yi Cui, Yang Cao, Yu Kang$^{(\boxtimes)}$, Pengfei Li, and Xuefeng Wang

Department of Automation,
University of Science and Technology of China, Hefei, China
kangduyu@ustc.edu.cn

Abstract. This paper introduces a packet-dropouts compensation strategy for networked control systems. To achieve robustness with respect to packet-dropouts, the predictions of the feedback losses in network transmission are included in the data packets. To achieve high-precision predictions, a deep ReLU neural network is used to build the relationships between the system input and feedback losses. We show how to design the parameters of the deep neural network to ensure stability of the resulting feedback control systems when the number of packet-dropouts is bounded. Simulation results indicate that the proposed compensation strategy can achieve much better control performances than the widely used zero-input or hold-input strategies, especially when the system inputs include abundant noises.

Keywords: Networked control systems · Deep ReLU neural network · Packet-dropouts · Compensation

1 Introduction

Network control systems (NCSs) are used to communicate those which the controlled plant is located far away from the controller [1]. Many challenges arise since the feedback communication is made through unreliable and rate-limited communication channels such as wireless networks or the Internet [2]. Accordingly, effective NCS architecture need to consider both control and communication problems, such as network-induced delay, packet-dropouts, quantization and network constraint. However, it is well known that, for many applications, the full state vector is not accessible and only partial state information is available via the actually measured output [3]. In general, the zero-input and the hold-input strategy are used to compensate the packet-dropouts. But the predictive accuracy of the two methods is limited. Therefore, some compensation strategies were proposed to overcome the adverse effects of packet-dropouts on the system, such as spectral density analysis [4], and state observer or compensator [3]. However, these methods required rigorous and complex mathematical derivation, and ignored the effects of input noise.

Traditional artificial neural networks usually use sigmoid, tanh and other nonlinear functions as the activation function, thereby any function can be

© Springer International Publishing AG 2017
D. Liu et al. (Eds.): ICONIP 2017, Part VI, LNCS 10639, pp. 61–70, 2017.
https://doi.org/10.1007/978-3-319-70136-3_7

approximated by the nonlinear combination of neural network input. So that the neural network can be designed as a predictive controller, in which the prior data are used to predict the control value among a finite horizon of future time instants. The predictor can achieve real-time compensation of the packet-dropouts, and thus ensure the stability of the system. Moreover, the neural network is data-driven and only requires sufficient historical data to complete the training, so that the complex mathematical derivation can be avoided.

However traditional artificial neural networks still have the following problems: gradient disappeared, overfitting, and a huge amount of computation. Hinton et al. proposed the concept of deep learning in 2006 [5], and then many new methods were arose, such as the new activation function (ReLU), the new weight initialization method (layer initialization, XAVIER [9], etc.), the new loss function, the new anti-fitting method (Dropout [8], BN, etc.). Among them, ReLU activation function is similar to the brain neuron activation frequency function, which has the characteristic about unilateral inhibition, relatively broad excitatory boundary, sparse activation. Subsequently, many research work shows the new activation function ReLU was superior to the traditional activation function (sigmoid, tanh, etc.) in terms of computation and convergence speed [6, 10, 14].

Based on the above description, this paper proposes a packet-dropouts compensation strategy using deep ReLU neural network. The contributions of this paper are summarized as:

(1) A new packet-dropouts compensation strategy for network feedback control system is proposed. It can achieve good robustness when the number of packet-dropouts is bounded.
(2) The predictor via deep ReLU neural network can also suppress the noise of system input to a certain extent. It further improves the control performance of the proposed strategy.

2   Deep ReLU Neural Network Structure and Training Algorithm

2.1   Deep ReLU Neural Network Structure

The deep ReLU neural network consists an input layer, multiple hidden layers, and an output layer. The input layer unit only passes the input signal to the hidden layer, the hidden layer neurons are composed of ReLU activation function, and the output layer is a linear combination of the hidden units, plus a final bias, see Fig. 1(a). Algebraically, the model can be written

$$h_{ij} = \sum_{j=1}^{M} W_{ji} f\left(x_j\right) + B_i$$

$$O_{pq} = \sum_{q=1}^{Q} W_{qp} h_q + b_p$$

(1)

where x is the input vector, h_{ij} is the output of the jth neurons of the ith hidden layer, and M is the number of neurons in the ith hidden layer, W_{ij} is the weights, B_i is the biases. Similarly, o_{pq} is the output of a linear output layer with weights w_{qp} and biases b_p. The hidden unit activation function f is a soft threshold function, see Fig. 1(b), which can formulated as follows

$$f(x) = max(0, x) \tag{2}$$

In this work we minimize mean squared prediction error over a training set of demonstration data, solving

$$min \sum_{t=1}^{T} \frac{1}{T} \left\| \tilde{o_{pq}} - o_{pq} \right\|^2 \tag{3}$$

where $\tilde{o_{pq}}$ are the observed values of o_{pq} along a demonstration data.

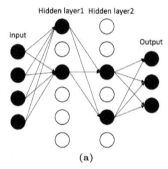
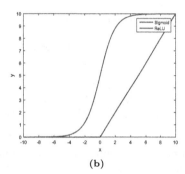

(a)   (b)

Fig. 1. The activation function and topology of deep ReLU neural network. **Note**: (a) is the curve of Sigmoid and ReLU activation function; (b) shows the deep neural network structure using ReLU as the activation function

2.2 Deep ReLU Neural Network Training Algorithm

In the training process, we optimize over the weights and biases of the neural network (W,B,w,b) using Stochastic Gradient Descent (SGD) [11]. SGD is the standard optimization method for training recent neural network models and is very simple to implement [7,12]. In each iteration, the objective in Eq. 3 is computed over a small subset of training data, called a minibatch. The gradient of the objective over the minibatch with respect to the parameters of the neural network is computed using Backpropagation [13]. An update step is computed as an average of the past update step and the current gradient, where the past step is weighted by a hyperparameter called momentum (typically set to 0.9). Parameters (weights and biases) are updated by the new update step, scaled by a learning rate. A new minibatch is randomly selected from training data and the next iteration proceeds. The learning rate is decreased during optimization.

3 Control Model and Compensation Strategy

3.1 Control Model

Figure 2 shows the networked control system which we are interested in this paper. The feedback signals in the NCS architecture are transmitted through an erasure channel. This channel introduces packet-dropouts, which we model via the discrete dropout process $\{d(k)\}_{k \in \mathbb{N}_0}$ in [2]:

$$d(k) \triangleq \begin{cases} 0, & \text{if packet-dropout occurs at instant } k \\ 1, & \text{if packet-dropout does not occur at time } k \end{cases} \tag{4}$$

Meanwhile, this system consists of a controlled plant, a digital controller, a buffer, and a deep neural network. The definitions of these systems are given as follows:

Plant: We consider discrete-time plant models:

$$\begin{aligned} \mathbf{x}(k+1) &= A\mathbf{x}(k) + Bu(k) + v(k), \quad k \in \mathbb{N}_0 \\ \mathbf{x}(0) &= \mathbf{x}_0 \end{aligned} \tag{5}$$

where $\mathbf{x}(k) \in \mathbb{R}^n$, $u(k) \in \mathbb{R}$, $v(k) \in \mathbb{R}^N$, $\mathbb{N}_0 = \{0, 1, 2, 3 \cdots \}$. Throughout this work, we assume that the pair (A, B) is reachable.

Buffer: In our proposal, at each time instant, a control error packet is sent to the buffer

$$\mathbf{e}(k) \triangleq [e_0(k), e_1(k), \cdots, e_N(k)]^T \in \mathbb{R}^N \tag{6}$$

Each data packet contains a sequence of control error predictive values for a finite horizon of future time instants. Packets which are successfully received at the controller side, are stored in a buffer to be used whenever later packets are dropped. When there are no packet-dropouts, the control system reduces to networked feedback control.

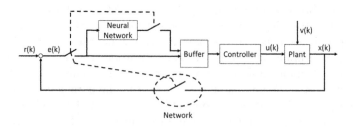

Fig. 2. NCS with deep ReLU neural network

Controller: The controller uses the control error $e(k)$ to produce the control vector $u(k)$. For example, because of the advantages of easy algorithm, high reliability and easy implementation, PID control is most widely used in the actual industrial production. The control algorithm is as follows:

$$u(k) = k_p e(k) + \frac{k_p}{T_I} \sum_{m=0}^{k} e(m) T + k_p T_D \frac{e(k) - e(k-1)}{T} \tag{7}$$

where k_p, T_I and T_D are respectively the proportional, integral, and differential constant. T is the sampling period, k is the sampling constant, $k = 1, 2, \cdots$, $e(k-1)$ and $e(k)$ are respectively the sampling error at the $k-1$ and the k constant.

Switching System Control Model: Based on the above description, we can model the network feedback control system as switching system. In order to facilitate system analysis and modeling, the system has the following assumptions:

Assumption 1: Packet-dropouts is a random process, and the maximum number of consecutive packet-dropouts is bounded.

Assumption 2: In Fig. 2, the three switches are linked. Namely, when the feedback signal is lost in some instant, no data is transferred to the buffer in the meantime.

Assumption 3: There is no delay in the network feedback control system.

The question can be modeled as switching system:

$$\begin{cases} \mathbf{x}(k+1) = A\mathbf{x}(k) + BK(r_k - x_k) \\ \mathbf{x}(k+1) = A\mathbf{x}(k) + BK\hat{e}_{k|k-1} \\ \cdots \\ \mathbf{x}(k+1) = A\mathbf{x}(k) + BK\hat{e}_{k|k-i} \\ \cdots \\ \mathbf{x}(k+1) = A\mathbf{x}(k) + BK\hat{e}_{k|k-N} \end{cases} \tag{8}$$

where $r(k)$ is the reference, K is the abbreviation of the controller, $\hat{e}_{k|k-i}$ is the control error we used when the number of consecutive packet-dropouts is i, N is the the maximum number of consecutive packet-dropouts.

3.2   Compensation Strategy

It is assumed that there is no packet loss in the network firstly, and then let the system run for a period of time, the control error data is collected, which is used to train the deep ReLU neural network. The training completed neural network can be used as a prediction model. The prediction model is SIMO structure:

◇ $x = e_0(k)$ is the neural network input which is the control error in the k instant;

◇ $\tilde{\mathbf{e}}(k) = [e_1(k), e_2(k), \cdots, e_N(k)]^T$ is the expected output sequence (ground truth) where N is the maximum number of consecutive packet-dropouts;

⋄ $w_n = \left[w_n^1, w_n^2, \cdots, w_n^m \right]^T$ is the weight matrix of the nth hidden layer, where m is the number of neurons in this hidden layer.

Suppose that at time instant k, we have $d(k) = 1$, i.e., the data $\mathbf{x}(k)$ is successfully feedback from the plant output side, that is, the data packet $\mathbf{e}(k) \triangleq \left[e_0(k), e_1(k), \cdots, e_N(k) \right]^T$ is successfully received. Then, this packet is stored in a buffer, overwriting its previous contents. If the next packet $\mathbf{e}(k+1)$ is dropped, then the controller input is set to $e_1(k)$, the second element of $\mathbf{e}(k)$. The elements of $\mathbf{e}(k)$ are then successfully used until some packet $\mathbf{e}(k+\ell)$, $\ell \geq 2$ is successfully received.

4   Simulation Experiment

In this section, we illustrate simulation results to show the effectiveness of the the proposed method in networked feedback control systems.

The matrices in the discrete-time state-space model (5) of the controlled plant P are taken as (the sampling time is 0.01 s)

$$A = \begin{bmatrix} -56 & 0 \\ 1 & 0 \end{bmatrix}, \quad B = \begin{bmatrix} 1 \\ 0 \end{bmatrix} \tag{9}$$

And the maximum number of consecutive packet-dropouts $N \leq 5$. The system noise is Gaussian noise, and the signal-to-noise ratio is set to 40 dB. We use the two reference: sinusoidal sequence and Wavelet basis function $Morlet$ sequence, see Fig. 3, and each set of data had 1000,000 training points. The motivation for using sinusoidal and $Morlet$ data to train is that any function can be approximated by a series of sinusoidal sequence (Fourier series) or Wavelet basis function (Wavelet transform).

In Figs. 4 and 5, the sinusoidal sequence and $Morlet$ sequence with system noise are used as the reference signal. Here, (I), (II) and (III) respectively

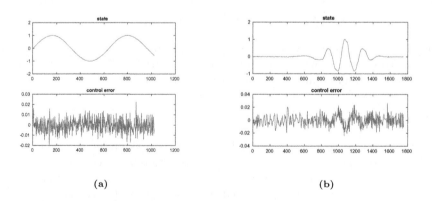

(a)   (b)

Fig. 3. The training data for deep ReLU neural network.
Note: (a) is the training data of sinusoidal sequence with system noise; (b) is the training data of $Morlet$ sequence with noise;

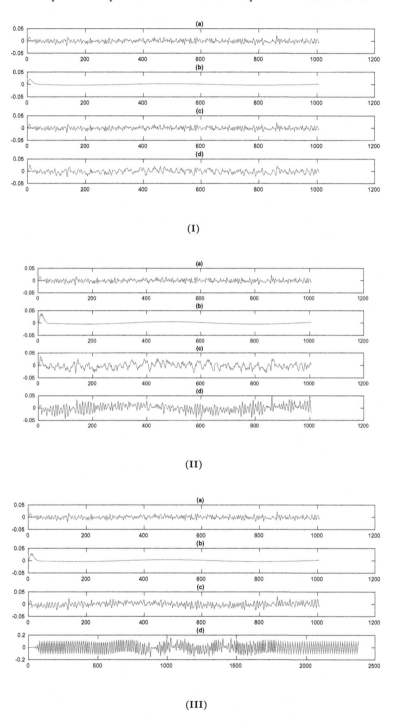

Fig. 4. The control error of the sinusoidal sequence with system noise.
Note: (a) is the control error reference value as training data; (b) is the control error using the compensation strategy proposed in this paper; (c) is the control error using zero-input compensation; (d) is the control error using hold-input compensation

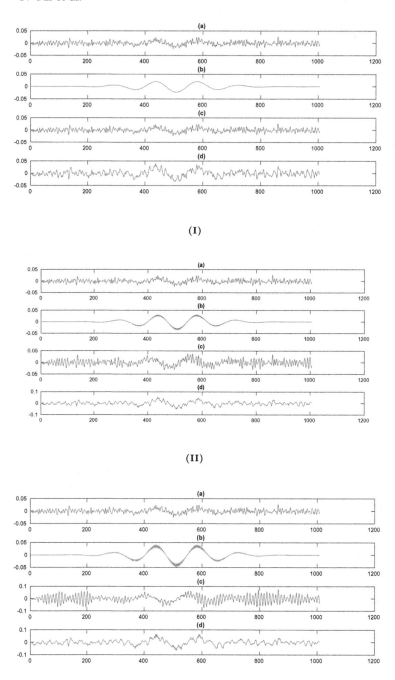

Fig. 5. The control error of the *Morlet* sequence with system noise.
Note: (a) is the control error reference value as training data; (b) is the control error using the compensation strategy proposed in this paper; (c) is the control error using zero-input compensation; (d) is the control error using hold-input compensation

show the simulation results which the maximum number of consecutive packet-dropouts is set as $N = 1$, $N = 3$ and $N = 5$. And (a) is the control error reference value as training data; (b), (c) and (d) are respectively the control error using the compensation strategy proposed, the zero-input compensation and the hold-input compensation. Simulation results prove that

(1) The networked feedback control system which use the deep ReLU neural network can filter out part of the system noise, resulting in strong robustness and stability;
(2) With the increase of the maximum number of consecutive packet-dropouts, ReLU network's performance advantage is more obvious. We can see that the system we proposed is still able to track the given signal and the tracking error is small.

5   Conclusion

In this project, we introduce the deep ReLU neural network for networked feedback control systems. The method proposed was used to compensate the packet-dropouts of feedback signal which are transmitted through rate-limited channels. The deep ReLU neural network is used as a predictive controller, which is data-driven and avoids complex mathematical derivation. Simulation results indicate that the proposed method have better performance than the use of zero-input compensation strategy or hold-input compensation strategy, and it can filter out the system noise to a certain extent. Future work may include further study of nonlinear system performance aspects and the effect of plant disturbances.

Acknowledgments. This work was supported in part by the National Natural Science Foundation of China (61422307 and 61673361), the Scientific Research Staring Foundation for the Returned Overseas Chinese Scholars and Ministry of Education of China. Authors also gratefully acknowledge supports from the Youth Top-notch Talent Support Program and the Youth Yangtze River Scholar.

References

1. Nagahara, M., Quevedo, D.E., Matsuda, T., Hayashi, K.: Compressive sampling for networked feedback control. In: 2012 IEEE International Conference on Acoustics, Speech and Signal Processing (ICASSP), pp. 2733–2736. IEEE (2012)
2. Nagahara, M., Quevedo, D.E., Ostergaard, J.: Packetized predictive control for rate-limited networks via sparse representation. In: 2012 IEEE 51st Annual Conference on Decision and Control (CDC), pp. 1362–1367. IEEE (2012)
3. Li, H., Sun, Z., Liu, H., Chow, M.Y.: Predictive observer-based control for networked control systems with network-induced delay and packet dropout. Asian J. Control **10**(6), 638–650 (2008)
4. Ling, Q., Lemmon, M.D.: Power spectral analysis of networked control systems with data dropouts. IEEE Trans. Autom. Control **49**(6), 955–959 (2004)
5. Hinton, G.E., Salakhutdinov, R.R.: Reducing the dimensionality of data with neural networks. Science **313**(5786), 504–507 (2006)

6. Jarrett, K., Kavukcuoglu, K., LeCun, Y.: What is the best multi-stage architecture for object recognition? In: 2009 IEEE 12th International Conference on Computer Vision, pp. 2146–2153. IEEE (2009)

7. Punjani, A., Abbeel, P.: Deep learning helicopter dynamics models. In: 2015 IEEE International Conference on Robotics and Automation (ICRA), pp. 3223–3230. IEEE (2015)

8. Hinton, G.E., Srivastava, N., Krizhevsky, A., Sutskever, I., Salakhutdinov, R.R.: Improving neural networks by preventing co-adaptation of feature detectors. arXiv preprint arXiv:1207.0580 (2012)

9. Glorot, X., Bengio, Y.: Understanding the difficulty of training deep feedforward neural networks. In: Proceedings of the Thirteenth International Conference on Artificial Intelligence and Statistics, pp. 249–256 (2010)

10. Krizhevsky, A., Sutskever, I., Hinton, G.E.: Imagenet classification with deep convolutional neural networks. In: Advances in Neural Information Processing Systems, pp. 1097–1105 (2012)

11. Bottou, L.: Online learning and stochastic approximations. On-line Learn. Neural Netw. **17**(9), 142 (1998)

12. Hinton, G., Deng, L., Yu, D., Dahl, G.E., Mohamed, A.R., Jaitly, N., Kingsbury, B.: Deep neural networks for acoustic modeling in speech recognition: the shared views of four research groups. IEEE Sig. Process. Mag. **29**(6), 82–97 (2012)

13. LeCun, Y., Bottou, L., Orr, G.B., Müller, K.-R.: Efficient backprop. In: Orr, G.B., Müller, K.-R. (eds.) Neural Networks: Tricks of the Trade. LNCS, vol. 1524, pp. 9–50. Springer, Heidelberg (1998). doi:10.1007/3-540-49430-8_2

14. Glorot, X., Bordes, A., Bengio, Y.: Deep sparse rectifier neural networks. In: Proceedings of the Fourteenth International Conference on Artificial Intelligence and Statistics, pp. 315–323 (2011)

Cloud-Based Knowledge Sharing in Cooperative Robot Tracking of Multiple Targets with Deep Neural Network

Hui Bao[✉], HuaiMin Wang, Bo Ding, and SuNing Shang

National Key Lab of Parallel and Distributed Processing,
National University of Defense Technology, Changsha 410073, China
{baohui15,hmwang,dingbo,shangsuning12}@nudt.edu.cn

Abstract. Cooperative robot tracking of multiple targets plays an important role in many realistic robot applications. In order to minimize the time during which any target is not tracked, target trading among robots at runtime is a common phenomenon. After a period of successful tracking, the robot can gain a lot of knowledge about the target details, for example, the appearance changes caused by motion and illumination. However, the accumulated knowledge is dropped simply in existing research while robots trading targets, which makes each robot has to learn the knowledge of target details from scratch. The absence of knowledge sharing heavily influences the tracking accuracy in practice. In this paper, we propose a novel approach named *Cloudroid Tracking* which enables knowledge sharing through the support of the back-end cloud infrastructure. Our approach adopts the deep neural network (DNN) and its online tuning mechanisms to enable the knowledge accumulation. The dynamic connection of multiple DNNs on the cloud infrastructure and multiple robots is enabled. No matter how the target changes, the robot can connect to the corresponding neural network which is responsible for a specific target. The experimental results on both open dataset and real robots show that our approach can promote the accuracy for robot tracking significantly.

Keywords: Cooperative robot tracking of multiple targets · Deep neural network · Cloud robotic architecture

1 Introduction

Target tracking has been a hot topic in robotics for decades. It concerns how to enable the robot to follow the specified moving target, allowing the robot to continuously observe it. A subversion of this problem in the multi-robot system is the Cooperative Multi-robot Observation of Multiple Moving Targets (CMOMMT), which is firstly formulated in [1] and can be stated in brief as follows: Assuming that a robot has the ability to track (i.e., observe and follow) a limited number of moving targets, how to control a group of mobile robots to simultaneously track a group of targets and minimize the time during which any target is not tracked. With the fast development and deployment of multi-robot systems, more and more CMOMMT applications have emerged in security, surveillance, and reconnaissance practices.

D. Liu et al. (Eds.): ICONIP 2017, Part VI, LNCS 10639, pp. 71–80, 2017.
https://doi.org/10.1007/978-3-319-70136-3_8

Traditional CMOMMT research mainly focuses on correctly assigning targets to robots and deciding when the robots should trade targets, such as the work presented in [9–14]. However, another major factor which can greatly contribute to the tracking accuracy, i.e., the sharing of accumulated knowledge in tracking process among robots, has not been discussed yet. In practice, when a target is assigned to a robot, the robot only has limited knowledge of this target, for example, only with a pre-trained tracker engine and one labeled example as the object to track specified in the first frame. However, after a period of successful tracking, it can gain a lot of knowledge about the target, for example, its appearance changes caused by motion, occlusion, illumination and other variations. In CMOMMT, if this accumulated knowledge cannot be successfully transferred while the robots switching tracking targets, each robot has to learn it from scratch. On these conditions, the tracking accuracy will be significantly influenced.

This paper proposes an approach named *Cloudroid Tracking* that addressing the above-mentioned challenge. In this approach, we adopt a deep neural network (DNN)-based tracking algorithm [2] which can accumulate the knowledge of the details of a specified target through dynamically fine-tuning the neural network. Unlike traditional solutions which running on the robot onboard computer, we introduce the cloud robotic architecture and a robotic cloud platform, Cloudroid [3], to enable the knowledge sharing. A group of such kind of neural networks is running on the back-end cloud and a different network is responsible for a different target. They can be accessed by all the robots and evolves (i.e. fine-tunes) while it gains more knowledge about the targets. The task-based adaptive switching mechanism, which is the kernel of our approach, enables the robot to select the appropriate neural network to track the newly-assigned targets, inheriting all knowledge learned by its predecessors. The experiments on both open datasets and real robot applications validate the advantage of introducing knowledge sharing in CMOMMT.

The rest of the paper is organized as follows. The background and related work are introduced in Sect. 2. Section 3 presents an overview of our proposed approach. Section 4 highlights the key mechanisms of our approach. Section 5 presents the experimental results both on open datasets and real robots.

2 Background and Related Work

This section first gives an introduction to related work in the field of robot tracking. And then we make an introduction on cloud robotics-based knowledge sharing.

2.1 Robot Tracking and CMOMMT

Robot tracking is the task that the mobile robot observes and follows the specific target. Traditional tracking algorithms adopt the combination of a group of features, which are usually predefined manually in advance, to make robotic movement decisions [4]. However, this approach cannot adapt well to the shape, angle and attitude changes of the moving target in complex tracking environments. Recent years, a newly emerging approach is based on the deep neural network and the "offline pre-training + online fine-tuning" paradigm, such as the work in [5–8]. It firstly trains a convolution neural network offline with the auxiliary dataset (e.g., video sequences). At runtime, the network is fine-tuned to meet the feature of the specific target by using samples collected online. With the "fine-tuning" stage, it can adapt itself to a specific target and promote tracking accuracy significantly.

As a sub-problem of robot target tracking, Cooperative Multi-Robot Observation of Multiple Moving Targets (CMOMMT) involves multiple robots and multiple targets. Robots cooperatively plan their motion in order to maximize the time during which each target lies within the sensing range of at least one robot [9]. The CMOMMT problem was first proposed by Parker and Emmons in 1997 [1]. In [10], Parker extends the initial work with a new approach called A-CMOMMT, which is based on the use of weighted local force vectors. Then, a method based on distributed architecture was proposed, called B-CMOMMT [11], which supports positive communication and cooperation between robots. A new tracking method P-CMOMMT based on altruism is given in [12], the effect of altruism on the tradeoff between the individual benefit and the collective benefit is studied. Formation-CMOMMT uses a flexible formation of robots instead of using local force vectors [13]. Model-predictive control strategies are introduced to solve CMOMMT problem for the first time in [14]. Although the effect is relatively good, the computational complexity is high. The expected motion patterns of the targets can be used to make the observation time of each target is equal for robots [9]. The above-mentioned work mainly focuses on cooperatively planning robot's motion. The sharing of target-related knowledge among robots, which is the focus of this paper, is not discussed yet.

2.2   Cloud Robotics-Based Knowledge Sharing

The concept of "cloud robotics" was put forward for the first time in 2010 [15], which refers to connect the robot with the cloud computing infrastructure. An important advantage of the cloud robotic architecture is enabling knowledge sharing. For example, RoboEarth [16] aims to construct a World Wide Web for robots, enabling robots to share data and experiences with each other. And RoboBrain [17], which is a cloud knowledge base, the database of knowledge comes from other robots, public data sets, and existing robot research projects, supports free learning and knowledge sharing among robots.

These efforts make knowledge sharing and collaborative learning between robots become more efficient. But as far as we know, there is no work focus on knowledge sharing in cooperative robot tracking of multiple targets problems.

3   Method Overview

The Cloudroid Tracking approach we proposed is based on the cloud robotic architecture (Fig. 1). A group of tracking engines is deployed on the cloud to enable robots to track specified targets. Each engine adopts a DNN-based tracking algorithm [2] which supports the "offline pre-training + online fine-tuning" paradigm. The knowledge of specific targets is able to be learned in the process of online fine-tuning. And then, we enable Knowledge sharing by introducing a switching mechanism between robots and the tracking engines on the cloud, which can support the robot switches the tracking engine from the previous one to an appropriate one when targets are redistributed. Another issue introduced by the cloud robotic architecture is the Cloud-robot collaborative following. Because the ROI (Region of Interest) of each frame is processed by the tracking engine on the cloud, while the relative distance of the target is calculated on the local robot. We introduce a frame identification mechanism to realize the collaboration. More details about the above-mentioned method and the online learning neural networks can be found in Sect. 4.

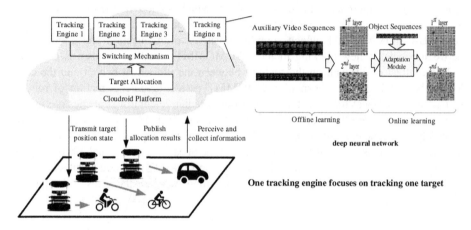

Fig. 1. The overview architecture of Cloudroid Tracking

4   Key Mechanisms

In this section, three key mechanisms of our approach are presented, including how to deploy the tracking engine on the cloud, how to realize the switching mechanism, and how to enable a robot to follow a target on the cloud robotic architecture.

4.1   Tracking Engine and Knowledge Sharing

The premise of knowledge sharing is the acquiring and representation of the accumulated knowledge. Some of the cloud robot projects, such as RoboBrain [17], represent knowledge in the form of cloud database. However, the knowledge learned by robots in tracking process is the feature of the moving target, which is hard to represente in a structured and explicit manner. Fortunately, the most important advantage of deep learning is that it can learn features automatically. Hence we deploy a DNN-based tracking algorithm [2] on the Cloudroid platform as the tracking engine to solve the problem. The hierarchical features robust to diverse motion patterns are learned via a two layer convolutional neural network from auxiliary video sequences, which is performed offline. Although the generic features are robust to complicated motion transformations in visual tracking, they do not include appearance information of specific targets, e.g. shape and texture. The domain adaptation module solved the problem by adapting the generic features online according to specific targets. Therefore, the target-related knowledge learned by each robot can be accumulated.

4.2 Knowledge Sharing of Robot Tracking

In the CMMOMT problem, robots often need to switch their targets dynamically according to the coordinated motion strategy. In order to achieve the goal of knowledge sharing among robots during the process of target switching, we propose a task-based adaptive switching mechanism. The overall procedure is presented in Table 1.

Table 1. Task-based adaptive switching algorithm

Input   : the previous tracking state y_{t-1}
Output: the predicted tracking state y_t
1: **repeat:**
2: Read the result of the assignment: {robot: r_1 -> object:o_1, ······, robot:r_i ->object:o_j,······}
3: Robots look for the corresponding tracking engines e
4:   **if match(o_j, e) = false, then**
5:      Initialize a tracking engine on the cloud
6:      Tag this tracking engine with the label of the object
7:      Input y_{t-1} to the tracking engine e_j to predict the tracking state y_t
8:   **else then**
9:      Input y_{t-1} to the tracking engine e_j to predict the tracking state y_t
10: Update the feature and the sample set every M frames.
11: **until** end of the tracking task

First, the results of the target assignment are obtained: {robot:r_1-> object:o_1, ..., robot:r_i ->object:o_j,......}. Then, when a robot r_i is assigned a new target, the robot looks for the corresponding tracking engine e according to the label of the target o_j. If it cannot find a corresponding one, which means the target is new for the robot group, the cloud does not have any accumulated knowledge of this target. In this case, initialize a new tracking engine e_j is initialized and it is tagged with the label of this new target. If the corresponding tracking engine e_j is found, the previous tracking state y_{t-1} is input to predict the tracking state y_t. Finally, the feature of the tracking engine and the sample set by using samples of y_t every M frames is update.

4.3 Cloud-Robot Collaborative Following

Typically, robot following is realized locally based on ROI and the corresponding distance information. The distance information refers to the depth values of the pixels corresponding to the target in the image, which is outputted by an RGB-D camera or laser scanner. However, in a cloud robotic architecture, the ROI is finally decided by the cloud tracking engine. And because of the delay of cloud service invocation, the result may be outdated in certain circumstances.

In order to synchronize the remote ROI and the local depth information on the robot, we introduce the *frame identification* mechanism. First, we cache the RGB image and depth image on the robot through the depth camera (Kinect) and mark them with the timestamp. Then we send the RGB image to the cloud tracking engine and obtain the ROI in sequence. The ROI of every frame y_t is predicted by the following equation in [2]:

$$y_t = \arg\max_{y_t^i} p(y_t^i | z_{1:t})$$ (1)

where y_t^i denotes the state of the ith ψ sample in the tth frame, $p(y_t^i | z_{1:t})$ indicates the posterior probability and $z_{1:t}$ denotes the feature representation. y_t is transmitted to the robot via publishing topics by ROS. Finally, we associate the ROI with the depth image pixels according to their timestamp. In addition, we set a threshold θ. When the time difference between the ROI returned from the cloud and the latest frame cached on the robot exceeds θ, that is, $|\text{timestamp}_{ROI} - timestamp_{latest}| > \theta$, the robot abandons the outdated ROI and obtains the latest one from the cloud. The corresponding depth value d_t is obtained by:

$$d_t = depthiamge.at(y_t)$$ (2)

The movement of the robot is based on the rotation speed and the linear speed, which can be directly calculated through y_t and d_t.

5   Experiments and Evaluation

In this section, we first evaluated our tracking method on public benchmark data sets. Then we used two robots to carry out the experiment in our laboratory environment in the real scene.

5.1   Evaluation on Open Dataset

Three comparative experiments on the open data sets OTB [18] and VOT2014 [19] are conducted. The tracking engine is deployed on a DELL PowerEdge R730 server with a 1.6 GHz Intel Xeon E5-2603 and NVIDIA Tesla K80 GPU through the Cloudroid platform [3]. The adaptation module to demonstrate the importance of accumulating knowledge is evaluated, and the comparison results between mean shift tracking algorithm [20] and the DNN-based algorithm we adopted are presented. We also evaluate our switching mechanism's capability of handling different targets in visual tracking.

In the last set of experiments, we change the input from one video sequence to two different video sequences. We divide the second video sequence into two segments and use the front one to fine tune a tracking engine. In the course of the experiment, input the first video sequence to a new tracking engine at first, after a period of time, change the input to the rest of the second video sequence. Under the switching mechanism, the previous tracking engine can be selected according to the label of the second video sequence. Figure 2 shows the comparison results on different video sequences. The red box indicates the tracking result by using our proposed method, and the white indicates the actual target position.

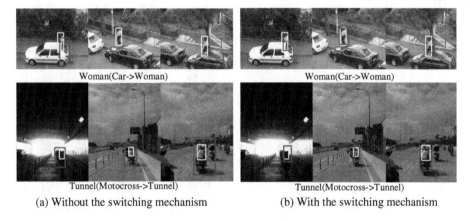

Tunnel(Motocross->Tunnel)

(a) Without the switching mechanism

(b) With the switching mechanism

Fig. 2. Comparison results on different video sequences (Color figure online)

Two measurements are used to quantitatively evaluate tracking performances. The first one is called center location error. This refers to the distance between the center of the rectangular box and the actual center position of the tracker output in pixels. The second one is called overlap rate. S_T denotes the tracking frame area of the tracker output, S_G denotes the actual target's area, the overlap rate is defined as the ratio of the intersection and union of the two, that is, area$(S_T \cap S_G)$/area$(S_T \cup S_G)$. The experimental results are illustrated in Fig. 3.

Figure 3(a) and (b) present the performance of the adapting feature algorithm we adopted with (with_adp) and without (no_adp) the adaptation module. From the quantitative comparison, we can observe that the adaptation module improves the tracking accuracy. It is due to the fact that the adaptation module is able to learn the appearance information of specific target and save the information as accumulate knowledge. Figure 3(c) and (d) present the comparison results between mean shift tracking algorithm (mean_shift) and the algorithm we adopted (adapted_feature). From the quantitative comparison, we can find that the adapting feature algorithm we adopted outperforms the mean shift tracking algorithm in the tracking accuracy. Figure 3(e) and (f) present the performance of the algorithm we adopted with (with_switch) and without (no_switch) the switching mechanism. From the quantitative comparison, we can observe that, without the switching mechanism, the tracking accuracy drops when

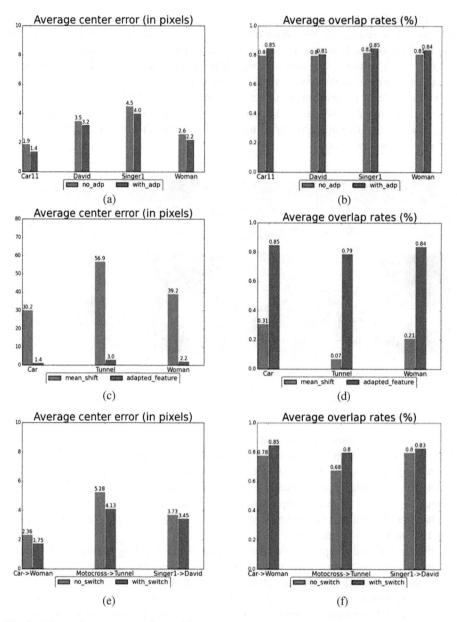

Fig. 3. The performances are denoted by average center error (in pixels) and average overlap rates (%), respectively

the video sequence changes from one to the other. It is due to the fact that different target and background in the two sequences have an impact on the adapting of features, while the switching mechanism makes one feature is adapted for one target, hence maintains the high accuracy.

5.2 Real World Environment

We used two suitable mobile robots (Turtlebot) R1 and R2 equipped with depth camera (Kinect) to track the students with large difference statures A and B in the laboratory environment. First, R1 and R2 execute the tracking task independently. Then the target of R1 is changed from A to B, and the target of R2 is also changed from B to A. The tracking results of R1 are shown below. In the process of R1 tracks A, R1 fine-tunes a tracking engine for A. Similarly, R2 fine-tunes a tracking engine for B. We can see that when the target changes from A to B for R1, R1 can still accurately distinguish them due to the fact that R1 can directly call the tracking engine for B by using the switching mechanism, even if A and B appear in the scene at the same time. The result proves the switching mechanism is effective (Fig. 4).

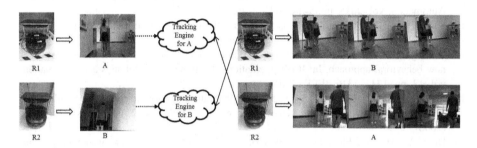

Fig. 4. The performances of switching mechanism in laboratory environment

6 Summary

In this paper, we propose a switching mechanism to realize the knowledge sharing among robots in the CMOMMT problem. We have carried out experiments to evaluate the proposed approach. The experimental results show that the Cloudroid Tracking is effective, with the support of the cloud.

Acknowledgment. This work is partially supported by the National Natural Science Foundation of China (nos. 91118008 and 61202117), the special program for the applied basic research of the National University of Defense Technology (no. ZDYYJCYJ20140601), and the Jiangsu Future Networks Innovation Institute Prospective Research Project on Future Networks (no. BY2013095-2-08).

References

1. Parker, L.E., Emmons, B.A.: Cooperative multi-robot observation of multiple moving targets. In: IEEE International Conference on Robotics and Automation, pp. 2082–2089 (1997)
2. Wang, L., Liu, T., Wang, G., Chan, K.L., Yang, Q.: Video tracking using learned hierarchical features. IEEE Trans. Image Process. Publ. IEEE Signal Process. Soc. **24**(4), 1424–1435 (2015)

3. Hu, B., Wang, H., Zhang, P., Ding, B., Che, H.: Cloudroid: A cloud framework for transparent and QoS-aware robotic computation outsourcing. arXiv preprint arXiv:1705.05691 (2017)
4. Dai, Y., Yu, G., Hirasawa, K.: New development on tracking algorithm with derivation measurement. IEEE Int. Conf. Syst. Man Cybernet. **5**, 3181–3186 (2001)
5. Wang, N., Yeung, D.Y.: Learning a deep compact image representation for visual tracking. In: Advances in Neural Information Processing Systems, pp. 809–817 (2013)
6. Nam, H., Han, B.: Learning multi-domain convolutional neural networks for visual tracking. In: Computer Science (2015)
7. Wang, N., Li, S., Gupta, A., Yeung, D.Y.: Transferring rich feature hierarchies for robust visual tracking. In: Computer Science (2015)
8. Nam, H., Baek, M., Han, B.: Modeling and propagating CNNs in a tree structure for visual tracking (2016)
9. Banfi, J., Guzzi, J., Giusti, A., Gambardella, L., Di Caro, G.A.D.: Fair multi-target tracking in cooperative multi-robot systems. In: IEEE International Conference on Robotics and Automation, vol. 2015, pp. 5411–5418. IEEE (2015)
10. Parker, L.E.: Distributed algorithms for multi-robot observation of multiple moving targets **12**(3), 231–255 (2002). Kluwer Academic Publishers
11. Kolling, A., Carpin, S.: Multirobot cooperation for surveillance of multiple moving targets-a new behavioral approach. In: IEEE International Conference on Robotics and Automation, vol. 12, pp. 1311–1316. IEEE (2006)
12. Ding, Y., Zhu, M., He, Y., Jiang, J.: P-CMOMMT algorithm for the cooperative multi-robot observation of multiple moving targets. In: WCICA 2006, vol. 2, pp. 9267–9271. IEEE (2006)
13. Ding, Y., He, Y.: Flexible formation of the multi-robot system and its application on CMOMMT problem. In: International Asia Conference on Informatics in Control, Automation and Robotics, vol. 1, pp. 377–382 (2010)
14. Kuhn, J., Reinl, C., Stryk, O.V.: Predictive control for multi-robot observation of multiple moving targets based on discrete-continuous linear models. IFAC Proc. Volumes **44**(1), 257–262 (2011)
15. Chen, Y., Du, Z., García-Acosta, M.: Robot as a service in cloud computing. In: Fifth IEEE International Symposium on Service Oriented System Engineering, pp. 151–158. IEEE (2010)
16. Waibel, M., Beetz, M., Civera, J., D'Andrea, R.: RoboEarth. Robot. Autom. Mag. IEEE **18**(2), 69–82 (2011)
17. Saxena, A., Jain, A., Sener, O., Jami, A., Misra, D.K., Koppula, H.S.: Robobrain: Large-scale knowledge engine for robots, arXiv preprint arXiv:1412.0691 (2014)
18. Wu, Y., Lim, J., Yang, M.H.: Object tracking benchmark. IEEE Trans. Pattern Anal. Mach. Intell. **37**(9), 1834–1848 (2015)
19. Kristan, M., et al.: The Visual object tracking VOT2014 challenge results. In: Agapito, L., Bronstein, Michael M., Rother, C. (eds.) ECCV 2014. LNCS, vol. 8926, pp. 191–217. Springer, Cham (2015). doi:10.1007/978-3-319-16181-5_14
20. Yang, C., Duraiswami, R., Davis, L.: Efficient mean-shift tracking via a new similarity measure. In: IEEE Computer Society Conference on Computer Vision & Pattern Recognition, vol. 1, pp. 176–183. IEEE (2005)

Backstepping and ADRC Techniques Applied to One-DOF Link Manipulator with External Disturbances and Input Saturation

Yang Yang$^{(\boxtimes)}$ and Jie Tan

College of Automation, Nanjing University of Posts and Telecommunications,
Nanjing 210023, People's Republic of China
yyang@njupt.edu.cn

Abstract. In this paper, via the active disturbance rejection control (ADRC), backstepping technique as well as the auxiliary system, we focus on the position control problem for one-DOF link manipulator with external disturbances and input saturation. The extended state observer (ESO) does not depend on the accurate model of systems, which is utilized to compensate external disturbances. The auxiliary system is employed to overcome the control input saturation. It is shown, from the input to state stability (ISS) and Lyapunov stability theorem, that the tracking error can be gradually converged into arbitrarily small neighborhood of the origin. The simulation results are given to illustrate the effectiveness of the proposed tracking control scheme.

Keywords: ADRC · Backstepping technique · Input saturation · Auxiliary system

1 Introduction

Manipulators have received increasing attention from industrial and academic communities because of its wide application in industrial automation, such as automobile manufacturing and aerospace field. Manipulators control methods were springing up like mushrooms [1–4], where [3] and [4] used an integral sliding mode control algorithm and two sliding-mode observers to deal with uncertainties and external disturbances of the manipulator. [5] and [6] were published a neural network sliding mode controller and an adaptive fuzzy sliding mode controller about the manipulator, respectively. As we know, the input saturation is inherent characteristics of the motor which might degrade the control performance of the closed-loop system, and even undermine stability in the case of severe saturation making the control task to fail [7]. [8] published an adaptive neural impedance controller and used the auxiliary system to deal with the problem of the input saturation. The tracking and stabilization control issue for a robot suffered from the input saturation was reported by Huang in [9].

The backstepping technique was proposed by Kanellakopoulos et al., which can effectively eliminate the constraints of the matching conditions [10]. As we

© Springer International Publishing AG 2017
D. Liu et al. (Eds.): ICONIP 2017, Part VI, LNCS 10639, pp. 81–89, 2017.
https://doi.org/10.1007/978-3-319-70136-3_9

known, manipulators can convert the general affine nonlinear system, which was researched by backstepping technique [11–13]. Both [11] and [12] were directed to a class of strictly feedback nonlinear systems and used backstepping to achieve trajectory control. The difference was that the former used the recursive fuzzy neural network method, and the latter used the robust control method in the case of external disturbances, both of them did not consider the system with the input saturation. Comparing with [11,12], [13] considered the spacecraft system with the input saturation and the unknown dead zone, and applied the adaptive neural network to the controller. However, it is difficult to derive the virtual control of the fuzzy and the neural basis function as the order of the system increases. Fortunately, the TD in ADRC can calculate the derivative of the signal for the signal without the mathematical expression. The ADRC was proposed by Han in 1998 to deal with uncertainty and disturbances [14,15]. Its core is to convert the system into a simple 'integral tandem' to control, the part of the system that is not 'integral tandem' is treated as 'total disturbance' [16–19]. The ESO in ADRC not only approximates the uncertainties of the system uniformly, but also calculates the unknown state of the system and restrains the disturbance of the system effectively [20]. The ADRC was adopted during every step of backstepping in [15]. Although both of them were based on the ADRC, they didn't consider the nonlinear system with the input saturation.

On the basis of the mentioned analysis, in order to overcome the impact of the uncertainties and disturbances on the control performance in the system and the inherent limiting characteristic of the torque in the case of one-DOF link manipulator control. The main contribution of this paper is three-fold. First, external disturbances of the manipulator is considered, which is compensated by ESO in this paper. The ESO not only approximates the uncertainties of the system uniformly, but also calculates the unknown state of the system and restrains the disturbance of the system effectively. Second, in order to solve the difficult problem that the differential of the virtual control is obtained in the controller. The TD in ADRC is employed to estimate the derivative of the virtual control, and avoid the complex mathematical operations. Third, the input saturation is taken into account in order to ensure that the motor can work safely. An auxiliary system constructed to compensate the characteristic of the input saturation, which can make the saturation time of the input control shorter and overcome the effect of the torque limitation.

2   Mathematical Model of One-DOF Link Manipulator

In general, the angle of manipulator arm is regarded as the output signal γ. $\dot{\gamma}$ is the manipulator's angular velocity. The moment of inertia is deemed as $B_0 = 4ml^2/3$, where m is the mass of the manipulator, l is distance from the centroid to the center of connecting rod rotation. The gravity of the manipulator is $H_0 = mglcos(\gamma)$. The viscous friction coefficient is E_0. The control torque is τ. d_e is regarded as a disturbance variable. Thus, the mathematical model of the one-DOF link manipulator system [21]

$$B_0\ddot{\gamma} + E_0\dot{\gamma} + H_0 = \tau + d_e, \tag{1}$$

where external disturbances d_e is about the system states. Further, we define $x_1 = \gamma$, $x_2 = \dot{\gamma}$, $\nu = \tau$, and (1) can be expressed as

$$\begin{cases} \dot{x}_1 = g_1(x_1, x_2), \\ \dot{x}_2 = g_2(\bar{x}_2, \nu), \\ y = x_1, \end{cases} \tag{2}$$

where $g_1(x_1, x_2) = x_2$, $\bar{x}_2 = [x_1, x_2]$, $g_2(\bar{x}_2, \nu) = -\frac{3E_0}{4ml^2}x_2 - \frac{3g}{4l}cosx_1 + \frac{3}{4ml^2}\nu + \frac{3d_e}{4ml^2}$, y is the output signal of the system, ν is the input control. Without loss of generality, the system states x_1 and x_2 is in a compact set, and is available for measurement [15]. The desired signal y_d and its derivative $\dot{y}_d$ are bounded over $\mathbb{R}$. Due to the one-DOF link manipulator has a limited characteristic about its own torquer, its saturation function is described as

$$\nu = \begin{cases} \nu_{max}, & if\ \nu_c > \nu_{max}, \\ \nu_c, & if\ \nu_{min} \leq \nu_c \leq \nu_{max}, \\ \nu_{min}, & if\ \nu_c < \nu_{min}, \end{cases} \tag{3}$$

where ν_c is the control signal to be specified later, $\nu_{max} \in (0, \infty)$ and $\nu_{min} \in (-\infty, 0)$ are known parameters.

3 One-DOF Link Manipulator Control System Based on ADRC and Backstepping Technique

We design the controller for a one-DOF link manipulator based on ADRC and backstepping technique. Firstly, the stability of the control system is analyzed after the controller was designed to achieve the expected performance index on the theoretical basis of ADRC and backstepping techniques. Then, the controller is analyzed and evaluated from the practical point of view.

Firstly, we define $G_1(x_1, x_2) = g_1(x_1, x_2) - P_2x_2$, $G_2(\bar{x}_2, \nu) = g_2(\bar{x}_2, \nu) - P_3\nu$, $p_1, p_2 \in (0, \infty)$ are designed constants, (2) can be expressed as

$$\begin{cases} \dot{x}_1 = G_1(x_1, x_2) + P_2x_2, \\ \dot{x}_2 = G_2(\bar{x}_2, \nu) + P_3\nu, \\ y = x_1, \end{cases} \tag{4}$$

where y is the output signal, ν is the input control. Using the backstepping technique to design the controller of system (4).

Step 1: We define the variable $\eta_1 = x_1 - y_d$ and obtain its differential coefficient

$$\dot{\eta}_1 = Q_1(x_1, x_2, \dot{y}_d) + P_2x_2, \tag{5}$$

where $Q_1(x_1, x_2, \dot{y}_d) = G_1(x_1, x_2) - \dot{y}_d$. The ESO can be constructed for the system (6) because $G_1(*)$ is an unknown part, and we get

$$\begin{cases} \delta_1 = \phi_{1,1} - \eta_1, \\ \dot{\phi}_{1,1} = \phi_{1,2} - \rho_1 \delta_1 + P_2 x_2, \\ \dot{\phi}_{1,2} = -\rho_2 |\delta_1|^{\sigma_1} \text{sign}(\delta_1), \end{cases} \tag{6}$$

where $\rho_1 > 0$ and $\rho_2 > 0$ are the gains of ESO, $\sigma_1 \in (0, 1)$ is an adjustable parameter. $\text{sign}(\bullet)$ is a symbolic function, and its form is as follows

$$\text{sign}(x) = \begin{cases} 1, & \text{if } x > 0, \\ 0, & \text{if } x = 0, \\ -1, & \text{if } x < 0. \end{cases} \tag{7}$$

The virtual control variable x_{2d} can be designed as

$$x_{2d} = -\frac{\phi_{1,2}}{P_2} - \frac{T_1 \eta_1}{P_2}, \tag{8}$$

where $T_1 > 0$ and $P_2 > 0$ are designed constants.

Subsequently, constructing the following Lyapunov function candidate

$$V_1 = \frac{1}{2} \eta_1^2. \tag{9}$$

The differential of (9) can be obtained by combining the virtual control of (8) with the defined variable $\eta_2 = x_2 - x_{2d}$,

$$\dot{V}_1 = -T_1 \eta_1^2 + \eta_1(Q_1 - \phi_{1,2}) + P_2 \eta_1 \eta_2. \tag{10}$$

If η_2 is equal to 0, and $(Q_1 - \phi_{1,2})$ is considered as the disturbance input of system. (10) can be written as

$$\dot{V}_1 \leq -(T_1 - \frac{1}{2})\eta_1^2 + \frac{(Q_1 - \phi_{1,2})^2}{2}. \tag{11}$$

According to the input to state stability (ISS) theory, when η_2 is equal to 0, the system (5) is the ISS. In other words, as long as $(Q_1 - \phi_{1,2})$ is bounded, η_1 is bounded. $P_2 \eta_1 \eta_2$ can be eliminated in the next step.

Step 2: The variable η_2 is differentiated

$$\dot{\eta}_2 = G_2 + P_3 \nu - \dot{x}_{2d}. \tag{12}$$

Due to x_{2d} contains the ESO state $\phi_{1,2}$, there will be the complex mathematical operations. So the TD is designed for estimating $\dot{x}_{1,2}$ to avoid this phenomenon [17], its form is as follows

$$\begin{cases} \dot{r}_{1,1} = r_{1,2}, \\ \dot{r}_{1,2} = -\pi^2 \text{sign}(r_{1,1} - x_{2d})|r_{1,1} - x_{2d}|^\sigma - \pi r_{1,2}, \end{cases} \tag{13}$$

where $r_{1,1}$ and $r_{1,2}$ are TD states. As long as the following inequality is satisfied: $0 < \sigma < 1$, $\pi > 0$, $r_{1,2}$ can be tracked $\dot{x}_{2d}$. The parameters of TD were given in Sect. 2.3 of Ref. [16].

Furthermore, due to $G_2(*)$ is unknown in (12) and treated as a compensation item for the model, the ESO can be constructed for the system (12)

$$
\begin{cases}
\delta_2 = \phi_{2,1} - \eta_2, \\
\dot{\phi}_{2,1} = \phi_{2,2} - \rho_{01}\delta_2 + P_3\nu - r_{1,2}, \\
\dot{\phi}_{2,2} = -\rho_{02}|\delta_2|^{\sigma_2}\text{sign}(\delta_2),
\end{cases}
\tag{14}
$$

where $\rho_{01} > 0$ and $\rho_{02} > 0$ are the gains of ESO, $\sigma_2 \in (0,1)$ is an adjustable parameter, $r_{1,2}$ is the TD state (13), the control scheme ν_c can be designed as

$$
\nu_c = -\frac{1}{p_3}\left(T_2\eta_2 + P_2\eta_1 + \phi_{1,2} - r_{1,2}\right) + T_s\lambda,
\tag{15}
$$

where T_2, T_s, P_2 and P_3 are designed constants, λ is the output of the auxiliary system which is designed for the system with the input saturation. The auxiliary system is expressed as

$$
\dot{\lambda} =
\begin{cases}
-T_a\lambda - \frac{|P_3\eta_2\Delta\nu|+0.5\Delta\nu^2}{\lambda} + \Delta\nu, & if\ |\lambda| \geq \mu, \\
0, & if\ |\lambda| < \mu,
\end{cases}
\tag{16}
$$

where $\Delta\nu = \nu - \nu_c$, T_a and μ are designed constants.

Theorem 1. *In the system (2), the tracking error can be bounded stabilized within a residue of the origin by the virtual control variable (8), the auxiliary system (16) and the control scheme (15) under the desired signal y_d.*

Proof. From (6), (13) and (14), $(Q_1 - \phi_{1,2})$ and $(G_2 - \phi_{1,2})$ are the estimated error of ESO. The total error of ESO and TD can be described as

$$
\psi = \sup\left[|Q_1 - \phi_{1,2}| + |G_2 - \phi_{2,2}| + |r_{1,2} - \dot{x}_{2d}|\right].
\tag{17}
$$

Subsequently, constructing the following Lyapunov function candidate

$$
V_2 = V_1 + \frac{1}{2}\eta_2^2 + \frac{1}{2}\lambda^2.
\tag{18}
$$

The differential of (18) can be obtained by combining the control scheme (15) with the auxiliary system (16)

$$
\dot{V}_2 = \eta_1(Q_1 + P_2x_{2d}) + P_2\eta_1\eta_2 + \lambda\dot{\lambda} + \eta_2(G_2 - P_2\eta_1 \\
- \phi_{1,2} - \dot{x}_{2d} + r_{1,2} - T_2\eta_2 + P_3T_s\lambda + P_3\Delta\nu).
\tag{19}
$$

Further, the auxiliary system is a piecewise function which can be divided into

① When $|\lambda| \geq \mu$, (19) can be expressed as

$$
\dot{V}_2 = \eta_1(Q_1 + P_2 x_{2d}) + P_2 \eta_1 \eta_2 + \eta_2(G_2 - P_2 \eta_1 - \phi_{1,2} - \dot{x}_{1,2} + r_{1,2} - T_2 \eta_2 \\
+ P_3 T_s \lambda + P_3 \Delta\nu) + \lambda \left(-T_a \lambda - \frac{|P_3 \eta_2 \Delta\nu| + 0.5\Delta\nu^2}{\lambda} + \Delta\nu \right). \tag{20}
$$

Utilizing (11), Young's inequality and $P_3 \eta_2 \Delta\nu - |P_3 \eta_2 \Delta\nu| \leq 0$, (20) can be written as

$$
\dot{V}_2 \leq -(T_1 - \frac{1}{2})\eta_1^2 - (T_2 - \frac{2 + P_3^2}{2})\eta_2^2 - \left(T_a - \frac{1}{2} - \frac{T_s^2}{2} \right) \lambda^2 \\
+ \frac{(Q_1 - \phi_{1,2})^2}{2} + \frac{(G_2 - \phi_{2,2})^2}{2} + \frac{(r_{1,2} - \dot{x}_{2d})^2}{2}. \tag{21}
$$

Further, utilizing (17) and (18), the inequality above can be further expressed as

$$
\dot{V}_2 \leq -2\min \left[(T_1 - \frac{1}{2}), (T_2 - \frac{2 + P_3^2}{2}), \left(T_a - \frac{1}{2} - \frac{T_s^2}{2} \right) \right] V_2 + \frac{\psi^2}{2}, \\
\leq -a_1 V_2 + b_1, \tag{22}
$$

where $a_1 = 2\min \left[(T_1 - \frac{1}{2}), (T_2 - \frac{2+P_3^2}{2}), \left(T_a - \frac{1}{2} - \frac{T_s^2}{2} \right) \right]$, $b_1 = \frac{\psi^2}{2}$.

② When $|\lambda| < \mu$, $\lambda\dot{\lambda} = 0$. (19) can be expressed as

$$
\dot{V}_2 = \eta_1(Q_1 + P_2 x_{2d}) + P_2 \eta_1 \eta_2 + \eta_2(G_2 - P_2 \eta_1 - \phi_{1,2} \\
- \dot{x}_{1,2} + r_{1,2} - T_2 \eta_2 + P_3 T_s \lambda + P_3 \Delta\nu). \tag{23}
$$

Utilizing (11), Young's inequality, $P_3 \eta_2 \Delta\nu \leq \frac{P_3^2 \eta_2^2}{2} + \frac{\Delta\nu^2}{2}$ and $\eta_2 P_3 T_s \lambda \leq \frac{P_3^2 \eta_2^2}{2} + \frac{T_s^2 \lambda^2}{2} \leq \frac{P_3^2 \eta_2^2}{2} - \frac{T_s^2 \lambda^2}{2} + T_s^2 \mu^2$, (23) can be written as

$$
\dot{V}_2 \leq -(T_1 - \frac{1}{2})\eta_1^2 - (T_2 - 1 - P_3^2)\eta_2^2 - \frac{T_s^2}{2}\lambda^2 + T_s^2 \mu^2 + \frac{\Delta\nu^2}{2} \\
+ \frac{(Q_1 - \phi_{1,2})^2}{2} + \frac{(G_2 - \phi_{2,2})^2}{2} + \frac{(r_{1,2} - \dot{x}_{2d})^2}{2}. \tag{24}
$$

Further, utilizing (17) and (18), the inequality above can be further expressed as

$$
\dot{V}_2 \leq -2\min \left[(T_1 - \frac{1}{2}), (T_2 - 1 - P_3^2), \frac{T_s^2}{2} \right] V_2 + T_s^2 \mu^2 + \frac{\psi^2}{2} + \frac{\Delta\nu^2}{2}, \\
\leq -a_2 V_2 + b_2, \tag{25}
$$

where $a_2 = 2\min \left[(T_1 - \frac{1}{2}), (T_2 - 1 - P_3^2), \frac{T_s^2}{2} \right]$, $b_2 = T_s^2 \mu^2 + \frac{\psi^2}{2} + \frac{\Delta\nu^2}{2}$. From (22) and (25), we obtain

$$
V_2 \leq V_2(0) \exp(-at) + \frac{b}{a}, \tag{26}
$$

where $a = \min(a_1, a_2)$ and $b = \max(b_1, b_2)$.

If the parameters of ESO and TD are chosen appropriately, and other parameters are met $T_1 > \frac{1}{2}, T_2 > 1 + P_3^2, T_a > \frac{1+T_s^2}{2}$ and $T_s > 0$, η_1, η_2 and λ are uniformly bounded by (26) and the definition of V_2. Furthermore, when $t \to \infty$, we have $|\eta_1| \leq \sqrt{\frac{2b}{a}}$ by (26). Therefore, the tracking error is bounded stable to a residue of the origin in the case where the desired input of the system (2) is y_d.

4 Simulation

The block diagram of the one-DOF link manipulator control system based on ADRC and backstepping technique is built in Simulation. Firstly, the desired signal is $y_d = \sin(t)$. Then, the parameters of one-DOF link manipulator are taken as follows: $E_0 = 2\,\mathrm{N \cdot m \cdot s/rad}$, $m = 1\,\mathrm{kg}$, $l = 0.25\,\mathrm{m}$, $g = 9.8\,\mathrm{m/s^2}$, and $d_e = x_2 \sin(x_1)$. The control input limits are $\nu_{\max} = 5\,\mathrm{N \cdot m}$, $\nu_{\min} = -5\,\mathrm{N \cdot m}$. The initial value of x_1 and x_2 are $[0.2\ 0]$. Finally, the parameters of the controller are obtained: $P_2 = 1$, $P_3 = 1$, $T_1 = 20$, $T_2 = 10$, $\lambda = 1$, $\sigma = 0.9$, $\sigma_1 = 0.9$, $\rho_1 = 100$, $\rho_2 = 1000$, $\sigma_{01} = 0.9$, $\rho_{01} = 10$, $\rho_{02} = 20$, $T_a = 10$, $T_s = 0.5$, $\mu = 0.01$, $\lambda(0) = 80$. The initial values for ESO and TD are zero.

As shown in Figs. 1, 2, 3 and 4, when the desired input is sinusoidal signal $\sin(t)$, the ESO can effectively estimate the unknown part of the system in this paper. By Fig. 5, when the desired input is the same, the auxiliary system is added to the controller so that the control law is shorter at a saturation time, and the tracking error becomes significantly smaller at the beginning. The stability time is obviously smaller and the tracking speed is obviously accelerated, thus improving the tracking performance of the system.

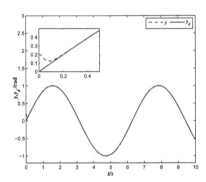

Fig. 1. The trajectory y and the desired one y_d.

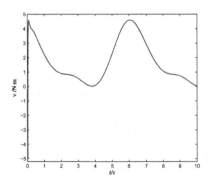

Fig. 2. The control input signal.

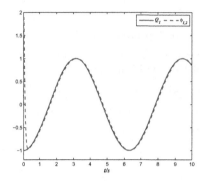
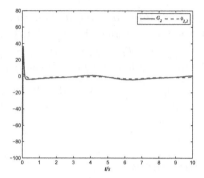

Fig. 3. The curves of Q_1 and $\phi_{1,2}$.   **Fig. 4.** The curves of G_2 and $\phi_{2,2}$.

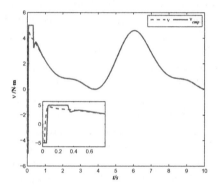

Fig. 5. The control input signal ν is a controller with auxiliary system, and ν_{cmp} is a controller without auxiliary system.

5   Conclusion

In this paper, the position control problem of one-DOF link manipulator with uncertainties and the input saturation is discussed by using ADRC and backstepping techniques. This paper is not directly to build the ideal controller, but the ADRC is adopted during every step of backstepping. The simulation results show that the proposed method in this paper is effective. The direction of this paper is the control of multi-degree-of-freedom manipulators.

Acknowledgments. This work is supported in part by National Natural Science Foundation of China under Grant 61503194 and 61533010, in part by the Research and Development Program of Jiangsu Province under Grant BE2016184, in part by Natural Science Foundation of Jiangsu Province under Grant BK20140877, in part by Key University Natural Science Research Project of Jiangsu Province under Grant 17KJA120003, in part by Jiangsu Government Scholarship for Overseas Studies under Grant 2017-037.

References

1. Li, S., He, J., Li, Y., et al.: Distributed recurrent neural networks for cooperative control of manipulators: a game-theoretic perspective. IEEE Trans. Neural Netw. Learn. Syst. **28**, 415–426 (2017)
2. Nikdel, N., Badamchizadeh, M., Azimirad, V., et al.: Fractional-order adaptive backstepping control of robotic manipulators in the presence of model uncertainties and external disturbances. IEEE Trans. Ind. Electron. **63**, 6249–6256 (2016)
3. Xiao, B., Yin, S., Kaynak, O.: Tracking control of robotic manipulators with uncertain kinematics and dynamics. IEEE Trans. Ind. Electron. **63**, 6439–6449 (2016)
4. Ho, H.F., Wong, Y.K., Rad, A.B.: Robust fuzzy tracking control for robotic manipulators. Simulat. Pract. Theor. **15**, 801–816 (2007)
5. Ertugrul, M., Kaynak, O.: Neuro sliding mode control of robotic manipulators. Mechatronics **10**, 239–263 (2000)
6. Guo, Y., Woo, P.Y.: An adaptive fuzzy sliding mode controller for robotic manipulators. IEEE Trans. Syst. Man Cybern. A. **33**, 149–159 (2003)
7. Wang, H., Chen, B., Liu, X., et al.: Adaptive neural tracking control for stochastic nonlinear strict-feedback systems with unknown input saturation. Inf. Sci. **269**, 300–315 (2014)
8. He, W., Dong, Y., Sun, C.: Adaptive neural impedance control of a robotic manipulator with input saturation. IEEE Trans. Syst. Man Cybern. **46**, 334–344 (2016)
9. Huang, J., Wen, C., Wang, W., et al.: Adaptive stabilization and tracking control of a nonholonomic mobile robot with input saturation and disturbance. Syst. Control Lett. **62**, 234–241 (2013)
10. Kanellakopoulos, I., Kokotovic, P.V., Morse, S.: Systematic design of adaptive controllers for feedback linearizable systems. IEEE Trans. Autom. Control. **36**, 1241–1253 (1991)
11. Han, S.I., Lee, J.M.: Recurrent fuzzy neural network backstepping control for the prescribed output tracking performance of nonlinear dynamic systems. ISA Trans. **53**, 33–43 (2014)
12. Chen, M., Zhang, S.Y.: Design of robust controller for predictive performance of nonlinear system based on backstepping. Control Decis. **30**, 877–881 (2015)
13. Yang, Q., Chen, M.: Adaptive neural prescribed performance tracking control for near space vehicles with input nonlinearity. Neurocomputing **174**, 780–789 (2016)
14. Zheng, Q., Gao, Z.Q.: Active disturbance rejection control: between the formulation in time and the understanding in frequency. Cont. Theor. Tech. **14**, 250–259 (2016)
15. Cheng, C.H., Hu, Y.A., Wu, J.H.: ADRC for non-affine pure feedback nonlinear systems. Acta Automatica Sinica **40**, 1528–1536 (2014)
16. Han, J.Q.: ADRC and application of ADRC. Control Decis. **13**, 19 (1998)
17. Gaom, Z.Q.: On the foundation of active disturbance rejection control. Cont. Theor. Appl. **30**, 1498–1510 (2013)
18. Guo, B.Z., Zhao, Z.L.: On the convergence of an extended state observer for nonlinear systems with uncertainty. Syst. Control Lett. **60**, 420–430 (2011)
19. Gao, Z.: Active disturbance rejection control: from an enduring idea to an emerging technology. In: International Workshop Robot Motion Control, pp. 269–282 (2015)
20. Han, J.Q.: Active Disturbance Rejection Control Technology: Uncertainty Estimation Compensation control Technology. National Defense Industry Press, Beijing (2008)
21. Shen, T.: Robot Robust Control Foundation. Tsinghua University Press, Beijing (2000)

A Causal Multi-armed Bandit Approach for Domestic Robots' Failure Avoidance

Nathan Ramoly[1]([✉]), Amel Bouzeghoub[1], and Beatrice Finance[2]

[1] SAMOVAR, Telecom SudParis, CNRS, Paris-Saclay University, Evry, France
{nathan.ramoly,amel.bouzeghoub}@telecom-sudparis.eu
[2] DAVID, University of Versailles Saint-Quentin-en-Yvelines, Versailles, France
beatrice.finance@uvsq.fr

Abstract. As there is a growing need for domestic healthcare, multiple projects are aiming to bring domestic robots in our homes. These robots aim to help users in their everyday life through various actions. However, they are subjected to task failure, making them less efficient and, possibly, bothering to the users. In this work, we aim to prevent task failures by understanding their causes through robot's experience. In order to guarantee high accuracy, our approach uses highly semantic data as well as user validation. Our approach can consolidate its knowledge or discover new possible causes, and uses a multi-armed bandit solution: R-UCB. In order to make it more efficient, R-UCB was improved using causal induction and causal graphs. Experiments show our proposition to achieve a very high rate of correct failure prevention.

Keywords: Domestic robotics · Task failure · Ontologies · Reasoning · Experience · Multi-armed bandit

1 Introduction

Nowadays, we observe the emergence of domestic robotics through multiple industrial and research projects. Indeed, there is a growing need for domestic healthcare, in particular for elderlies. We expect that robots will help to improve their quality of life. As stated in a recent report, if robots are very effective for precise, repetitive work in carefully designed settings, they cannot cope with an unfamiliar or uncertain situation.

This is typically encountered in home environments, that are various and unpredictable. Domestic robots are likely to encounter task failures in their plans, reducing their efficiency. For instance, a robot may be asked to remind the user to take his/her medicine, however, due to his/her audition problem, he/she is not able to hear the robot. There may be too much noise in the room, the TV is on and very loud, and/or the robot voice is not loud enough... If nothing is done, the patient may forget to take his/her treatment leading to a 'crisis' situation.

A robot can fail to reach its objective due to many reasons: it may have a breakdown, it may not understand the context correctly, it may miss some

© Springer International Publishing AG 2017
D. Liu et al. (Eds.): ICONIP 2017, Part VI, LNCS 10639, pp. 90–99, 2017.
https://doi.org/10.1007/978-3-319-70136-3_10

knowledge, etc. Indeed, it is very difficult for an expert to foresee all possible situations a robot might encounter in so many different homes, with users that might suffer from various disabilities, such as low vision or deafness.

The objective of this paper is to help the robot learning about repetitive failures and, by analyzing their causes from experience, avoid repeating them in the future by adapting its task-planner. A task-planner is an algorithm that computes a sequence of actions (or tasks) to do in order to reach a given objective according to a current context. There exist multiple ways for planning, however most solutions rely, at some point, on preconditions to generate the plan.

In the literature, there are two complementary ways to approach the problem. The first and most popular one, proposes solutions for overcoming the current failure [5, 7]. The second one, which has been less treated, addresses the problem of preventing failure by using previous experience [9, 14]. Our work corresponds to the second approach and extends the state-of-the-art by considering more complex failure causes and heterogeneous context data. Indeed, existing works only consider simple case of task failure and simple data, thus they are prone to error and bias, and may identify wrong failure causes.

In this paper, we propose a solution to identify causes that relies on semantic experience and user validation. Our approach relies on ontologies, multi-armed bandit solution and causal induction to achieve a high identification accuracy. It carries three contributions:

– Integration and adaption of an existing multi-armed bandit solution, R-UCB (Risk - Upper Confidence Bound), to efficiently balance discovery and consolidation before user validation.
– Improvement of the R-UCB algorithm by using a causal graph to guide the exploration.
– Generation of causal graph based on both causal induction and knowledge implicitly carried through rules.

The rest of the paper is constructed as follows. The first section presents our general approach and its overall principles. We then focus on the core of our contributions: the possible failure causes extraction. The literature is then quickly reviewed to point out the strength of our approach. Finally, we address our experiments before ending with concluding words and perspectives.

2   General Approach

In this section, we present our system from a general point of view. Figure 1 depicts the architecture of our approach. The key elements are labeled with numbers for referencing.

As it is very important to understand what is happening in the environment when a failure occurs, there is a need to gather and generate at all times **context data** about the environment. The **live situation** (box 1 in Fig. 1) is responsible for that and manages **context data** that are maintained in an ontology. An ontology is a set of triples that can be depicted as a graph. Thus, a context data

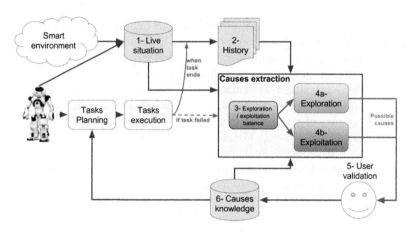

Fig. 1. System overview

is defined as a triple (subject, predicate, object), for example: *(Michel isDoing cooking)*. We rely on rules to infer further context data. Ontologies are known for their compatibility with reasoning through rules. In our work we rely on reasoning to generate further context data. Let us have a simple example, the following rule states that if a user is sitting in the kitchen, then he/she is eating (note that "?user" is a variable):

(?user isIn kitchen) ∧ *(?user hasStance sitting)* ∧ *(?user isA person)* → *(?user isDoing eating)*

In that case, if Michel is sitting in the kitchen, the context data *(Michel isDoing eating)* will be generated by the rule and added to the live situation. As the context acquisition is not the core of the paper, how the context data are acquired, formatted and modeled is not addressed there. You can find more in other works such as [8].

The robot maintains its experience through the **history** H (2 in Fig. 1). It is a set of situation snapshots acquired when the robot was executing tasks. Every time a task t starts, the live situation is stored in the history associated to t: H_t. It is then annotated with the outcome of this task: success or failure. H_t will be then used for identifying possible failure causes for task t as we will see later.

Whenever the robot fails a task, it launches the cause identification process. Be aware that it exclusively aims to identify the failure's causes, it doesn't find a reparation to the failed plan, see related work. The system will extract context data from the live situation and the history that are likely to be failure causes (3, 4a and 4b in Fig. 1). These aspects will be detailed in the next section.

These extracted causes are then submitted to the user for validation (5 in Fig. 1). Please note that the user only validates a given number of possible causes as he/she should not spend his/her time doing the robot's job: the robot shall only ask for the most accurate validation. We denote nV, the number of context data the user can validate in one session. According to this feedback, the checked causes are associated with a **causality belief** cb, representing their importance in the failure, and stored in the **cause knowledge** CK (6 in Fig. 1). A low cb means the context data has a little influence on the failure while a high cb points out a clear explanation of the task's outcome. In the end, the task planner can consult CK and can generate a plan that avoids tasks whose failure causes are observed, preventing further failure situations. Note that we used a lightly modified Hierarchical Task Network (HTN) as task planner.

The core and novelty of this work remains in the cause extraction process. The next sections present how it was modeled as a multi-armed bandit problem and how we adapted R-UCB to provide an efficient cause extraction process.

3   Cause Extraction

The cause extraction process aims to extract possible causes from the live situation that will then be checked by the user. As we will see, it can be modeled as a multi-armed bandits problem where exploring consists in checking new possible causes while exploiting allows to consolidate the knowledge. The cost is the validation by the user and the reward is the user feedback.

We based our approach on the R-UCB (Risk - Upper Confidence Bound) algorithm [4]. It aims to properly exploit according to the previous knowledge and context as well as balance exploration and exploitation according to the 'risk'. In our work, we represented the 'reliability' instead. The reliability represents the success rate of a task, it is computed as follows:

$$R = nbrSucc_N/N \tag{1}$$

$nbrSucc_N$ is the number of successful situations in the past N situations in H_t. With this variable, we compute ϵ, that is the ratio of exploitation over exploration:

$$\epsilon = \epsilon_{max} - (1 - R) * (\epsilon_{max} - \epsilon_{min}) \tag{2}$$

where R is the reliability of a task t over the past N situations. In other words, by applying these formulas, the more a task fails, meaning the knowledge we have is not accurate enough to prevent it correctly, the more our approach focuses on consolidating the knowledge. In this work we aim to use the strength of UCB for exploiting, but our main contribution remains in the exploration phase that we improved.

3.1   Exploitation

When exploiting, the system consolidates its knowledge. It selects a context data that was already checked by the user and is in the cause knowledge CK. When exploiting, the R-UCB algorithm selects the context data with the highest upper confidence bound d_{cd}. d_{cd} represents the confidence in the selection of cd according to its current weight cb_{cd}, its occurrence and the number F_t of feedback already provided by the user N_{cd}. Typically, a high d_{cd} means cd needs to be checked in priority. In this work, it is computed as follows:

$$d_{cd} = cb_{cd} * \sqrt{log(F_t)/N_{cd}} \tag{3}$$

3.2 Exploration

In R-UCB, the exploration relies on a random selection. In fact, we suppose we have no information until we try the bandits. This is however not the case in our context. In fact, based on previous experience, it is possible to have an idea on what context data is a cause of the failure. In other words, using the history H, we can assess which context data will have the best reward (positive user validation). To do so, we propose to generate and use a causal graph representing dependencies between context data, including the task outcome. It is the object of the next sections.

Causal Graph Generation

The causal graph [13] carries the causality relations between context data. A context data X causes another Y ($X \rightarrow Y$) if the value of Y is dependent, or partially dependent, of the value of X. For example, the context data "radio status on" causes "user doing listenToMusic". As the outcome of task is considered as a context data, the causal graph is then used to find direct or indirect context data that cause the task failure. The causal graph is built by applying causal induction on all pairs of context data using the history H. Bayesian causal induction is used to determine if a piece of context data X causes another Y, for example, if *"user doing listenToMusic"* causes *"taskWarnUser outcome failure"*. It relies on a probability tree that models two hypothesis: $\theta : X \rightarrow Y$ and $\neg\theta : Y \rightarrow X$, as depicted in Fig. 2. An intervention is then applied to the probability tree leading the tree to possibly be unbalanced: then, according to this unbalancing, we may assert that one hypothesis is true [12].

In our case, the tree is constructed based on the history H and the number of occurrence of each piece of context data according to the other. Let us consider two context data X = "radio status on" and Y = "user doing listenToMusic" whose causality relation is questioned. Let us say that X was observed two out of three times Y was observed in H, then $P(X|Y) = 2/3$ and $P(\neg X|Y) = 1/3$. The same process is applied for any proba-

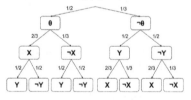

Fig. 2. Example of generated probability tree

bility needed in the tree to represent the two hypothesis θ and $\neg\theta$. An example of resulting tree is shown in Fig. 2. Note that $P(X|\theta) = P(X)$ (and similarly for other variables depending on variable θ) when building the tree.

Once constructed, an intervention is applied on the tree to determine the causality relation. The intervention consists in setting a probability of a currently observed piece of data to 1. Let us consider X = "radio status on" was observed, and let us consider the intervened variable $\hat{X}$. The tree is different with $\hat{X}$ as, for example: $P(\hat{X}|Y) = 1$. To see if the tree is now unbalanced, we compare $P(\theta|\hat{X}, Y)$ and $P(\theta|X, Y)$. If $P(\theta|\hat{X}, Y) > P(\theta|X, Y)$, the tree was unbalanced by the intervention, thus $Y \rightarrow X$. If $P(\theta|\hat{X}, Y) = P(\theta|X, Y)$, there is no causal relation. For more information and deeper information about causal induction please refer to [12] and to this link[1]. By repeating this operation on all pairs of context data, we get a set of pairwise causal relations. However it is not our only source for building these relations.

In fact, as we are relying on ontologies and rules, more context data can be derived in the live situation. Indeed, rules implicitly carry causal relation information. For example, let us consider the following rule:

(?rad status on) ∧ *(?rad isIn ?room)* ∧ *(?rad isA radio)* → *(?room noise Level medium)*

It this case, it implies that the data "noiseLevel" can be caused by a radio being turned on. In consequence, our approach also extracts the causal relation from the rules. It simply goes through all rules and associates all possible pairs from left and right parts of rules with causal relation.

The computed causal relations are then put in the causal graph. It carries context data as vertex and the causal relations as edges. Edges are labeled with a weight that represents how strong the causal relation is based on how much the tree was unbalanced. The weight matches the hypothesis's probability after intervention, in our example with X and Y, it would be $weight = P(\theta|\hat{X}, Y)$. In case of edges determined by a rule, the labeled weight is set to 1.0. If an edge is determined by both history analysis and rules, the rule method has priority and the weight is also set to 1.0. An example of generated causal graph can be found in Fig. 3, where the variable F represents the task failure. The causal graph is then used to select possible causes of failure.

Selecting Causes from the Causal Graph

As we aim to extract possible causes for a task failure, the causal graph is used by focusing on the context data related to the task outcome (F in Fig. 3). The principle is to select nodes, in other words context data, that have a path to the task failure's node. In fact, there might be multiple possible causes, yet, as the user only validates a certain number of causes, the aim of this step is to select the best candidates for validation. From a multi-armed bandit point of view, the aim is to select the candidates that are more likely to provide a high reward.

To do so, the possible causes of failure are ordered according-ing to the two following rules: (1) Priority is given to the vertex closer to the node 'task failure', (2) Priority is given to the vertex with the highest path weights. The path weight is computed by multiplying the weight of all edges composing the path. If multiple paths are possible for one vertex, the one with the highest path weight is used. For example, in Fig. 3 the resulting order would be: Y, W, X, V.

With the vertices, thus the possible failure's causes, ordered, a last filtering process is executed. In fact, this cause extraction is part of the exploration, thus only the non already

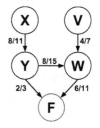

Fig. 3. Example of generated causal graph

[1] http://www.adaptiveagents.org/bayesian_causal_induction.

checked causes should be extracted. Indeed, the ones that were already validated (or invalidated) are selected through the method previously described for exploitation. In consequence, all causes that are registered in the cause knowledge are excluded from the list. For example, let say context data Y is already in the cause knowledge CK, it is removed from the list that now consists of: W, X, V. Once the ordered list is filtered, its nV first context data are selected for validation. The user validates or invalidates the causes, according to user's feedback, the causes are associated to 'causality belief' and stored in the causes knowledge. These newly discovered causes are then used in the planning and cause extraction process. How the user validates the data and how the causes are used by the planner is out of the scope of this paper.

4   Related Work

To the best of our knowledge, the proposition of Sariel and Kapotoglu [9,14] is the main work that uses the experience to prevent task failures. It is similar to our approach as they also aim to identify causes from previous failure situations in order for the task planner to avoid encountering them again. To do so, they use Inductive Logic Programming (ILP), an experiential learning framework that builds an experience by deriving hypothesis from failure situations. Their approach is based on associating and adjusting hypothesis (example: the object is a ball and red, task grab object fails) with probabilities, a low probability implying there is a lot of ambiguity. With these hypotheses and probabilities, the probabilist planner (POMDP) is adjusted to prevent failing situations. Although the problematic is similar, it differs from our approach on multiple aspects. First of all, they only consider a simple scenario (grabbing an object) with simple data, this is incompatible with real case scenarios for domestic applications. Indeed, in such cases, data are heterogeneous and various. By relying on ontologies, our approach can model any type of data and even use reasoning to infer new context data. Secondly, by using a causal graph, we are able to find indirect cause or the best candidates, while Sariel and Kapotoglu purely relies on statistic, making their approach more sensible to bias. Then, we efficiently include the user in the loop for validation, ensuring a low error rate in failures' causes identification. Lastly, as for the task planner, we rely on a Hierarchical Task Network that was lightly modified to take into consideration CK when planning.

The multi-armed bandit problem is a common problem of research, with tens of contributions. The Upper Confidence Bound (UCB) algorithm [1] is a solution that uses the context to select the best bandit. It has been improved various times, in particular with E-UCB [11] and R-UCB [3,4] that balance exploration and exploitation according to the context. However, in these approaches, the exploration is done randomly as we suppose there are no further information about the bandits. But in some context, including ours, we do have data that can help to determine the bandit with the best reward, allowing to converge faster to the optimal solution. That's why we used causal graph and causal induction for exploration. Using causality is not uncommon in the literature.

Lattimore et al. [10] address the idea of causal bandits, but they only focus on 'pure exploration', meaning they do not consider the exploitation phase. Some works [2,15] also use causal graph for contextual bandits, however they aim to tackle the issue of co-founders.

The experiments detailed in the next section illustrate how our approach allows to achieve better results.

5   Experiments

Our approach was implemented in Java and relies on Jena[2] to manage ontologies. It was integrated and tested on a Nao Robot [6] (via ROS Indigo[3]) operating in the Hadaptic[4] platform. Videos can be found online[5] and the core code is available on github[6].

We evaluated our approach on a randomly generated dataset. The dataset consists of multiple situations that include various possible task failures. The idea is to see how our approach learns and prevents the failures. Each run consists of a generation of 100 situations. For each run, we measure the correctness of the failure prevention according to the number of encountered situations. A prevention is correct if the robot selected the most efficient task without failing. The process was repeated 20 times, and we considered $nV = 3$. Note that nV influences the quickness of the learning of our approach, yet the tendency of the curve is similar. Results are depicted in Fig. 4. Each graph shows the evolution of the correctness of the simulated robot's risk evaluation as it gets more experience. Expectedly, the more experience the robot is, the less erroneous it is, yet the pattern of the learning curve varies according to the method used.

Based on this measure, we compared our approach to a state-of-the-art solution similar to Sariel and Kapotoglu one [9,14] in Fig. 4a. We observe that, with the state-of-the-art method, the curve rise quickly before stabilizing. As the approach of Sariel and Kapotoglu is not limited by validations, it can identify many causes at once and reach quickly (after 10 situations) its maximum correctness of 75%. However, their approach makes some errors, making it identify wrong causes that are not corrected by user validation. This explains why it can't go beyond 75% of correctness. As our approach relies on validation, the learning phase is longer as the robot has to ask the user multiple times. Indeed, after 10 situations, our approach only achieves 37% of correct task selection. However, thanks to the rich semantic representation and the user validation, our approach enables 95% when trained enough. This means that, once the robot has enough experience, it has only 5% chance to fail a task or select an inappropriate one, which is much lower than the 25% of the state-of-art solution. All in all, we can say our approach proves to identify and prevents accurately the failures, but at the expense of a longer learning time compared to the related works.

---

[2] https://jena.apache.org/.

[3] http://wiki.ros.org/indigo.

[4] http://hadaptic.telecom-sudparis.eu.

[5] http://nara.wp.tem-tsp.eu/what-is-my-work-about/leaf/.

[6] https://github.com/Nath-R/LEAF.

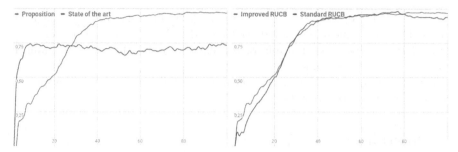

(a) Comparison between our proposition and a state of the art solution

(b) Comparison of our proposition with a standard and improved R-UCB

Fig. 4. Correctness of task risk evaluation according to the number of situations encountered

We also compared our approach with a standard R-UCB and with our improved version using causal graphs to assess its efficiency. Results are shown in Fig. 4b. Our improvement enables a quicker correctness increase at first, allowing to reach 30% of correctness after 8 situations, while the standard R-UCB reaches it after 12 situations. This proves the causal graph to be lightly more effective to find possible causes during exploration. The more experienced the robot is, the more it relies on knowledge consolidation, in consequence we expected the two versions to reach similar correctness as they should behave similarly. This is what we observe after 22 situations. Although it allows a better cause identification at first, the overall gain of the R-UCB improvement remains limited in this context. However, it may achieve a better profit in other less variable applications. This is out of the scope of this paper, but we are willing to tackle it in future works. Nevertheless, our improvement is pertinent as it allows the robot to be less faulty when it has little experience.

6   Conclusion and Future Works

In this paper, we presented an approach to identify causes of failure in domestic robots' plan by using experience. Our approach uses ontologies, reasoning and includes the user in the learning loop for validation. The problem was modeled as a multi-armed bandit one. Consequently, we adapted and improved the R-UCB algorithm by using causal graphs built by using causal induction on the experience of the robot. Experiments show our approach to enable a very accurate learning of failures by conceding on the learning time, allowing the robot's task planner to generate failure-free plan. Our improvement of R-UCB was shown to be more efficient at first, but it also sensible to bias. As for future works, we want to make our approach compliant to uncertain context data to ensure efficiency despite the inaccuracy of sensors. More complete experiments using a smart platform are also projected.

References

1. Auer, P., Cesa-Bianchi, N., Fischer, P.: Finite-time analysis of the multiarmed bandit problem. Mach. Learn. **47**(2–3), 235–256 (2002)
2. Bareinboim, E., Forney, A., Pearl, J.: Bandits with unobserved confounders: a causal approach. In: Advances in Neural Information Processing Systems, pp. 1342–1350 (2015)
3. Bouneffouf, D.: DRARS, a dynamic risk-aware recommender system. Ph.D. thesis, Institut National des Télécommunications (2013)
4. Bouneffouf, D., Bouzeghoub, A., Ganarski, A.L.: Risk-aware recommender systems. In: Lee, M., Hirose, A., Hou, Z.-G., Kil, R.M. (eds.) ICONIP 2013. LNCS, vol. 8226, pp. 57–65. Springer, Heidelberg (2013). doi:10.1007/978-3-642-42054-2_8
5. Ghezala, M.W.B., Bouzeghoub, A., Leroux, C.: RSAW: a situation awareness system for autonomous robots. In: 2014 13th International Conference on Control Automation Robotics and Vision (ICARCV), pp. 450–455. IEEE (2014)
6. Gouaillier, D., Hugel, V., Blazevic, P., Kilner, C., Monceaux, J., Lafourcade, P., Marnier, B., Serre, J., Maisonnier, B.: Mechatronic design of Nao humanoid. In: IEEE International Conference on Robotics and Automation, ICRA 2009, pp. 769–774. IEEE (2009)
7. Hanheide, M., Göbelbecker, M., Horn, G.S., Pronobis, A., Sjöö, K., Aydemir, A., Jensfelt, P., Gretton, C., Dearden, R., Janicek, M., et al.: Robot task planning and explanation in open and uncertain worlds. Artif. Intell. **247**, 119–150 (2015)
8. Jarraya, A., Ramoly, N., Bouzeghoub, A., Arour, K., Borgi, A., Finance, B.: FSCEP: a new model for context perception in smart homes. In: Debruyne, C., et al. (eds.) OTM 2016. LNCS, vol. 10033, pp. 465–484. Springer, Cham (2016). doi:10.1007/978-3-319-48472-3_28
9. Kapotoglu, M., Koc, C., Sariel, S.: Robots avoid potential failures through experience-based probabilistic planning. In: 2015 12th International Conference on Informatics in Control, Automation and Robotics (ICINCO), vol. 2, pp. 111–120. IEEE (2015)
10. Lattimore, F., Lattimore, T., Reid, M.D.: Causal bandits: learning good interventions via causal inference. In: Advances in Neural Information Processing Systems, pp. 1181–1189 (2016)
11. Li, W., Wang, X., Zhang, R., Cui, Y., Mao, J., Jin, R.: Exploitation and exploration in a performance based contextual advertising system. In: Proceedings of the 16th ACM SIGKDD International Conference on Knowledge Discovery and Data Mining, pp. 27–36. ACM (2010)
12. Ortega, P.A., Braun, D.A.: Generalized Thompson sampling for sequential decision-making and causal inference. Complex Adapt. Syst. Model. **2**(1), 2 (2014)
13. Pearl, J.: Causality. Cambridge University Press, New York (2009)
14. Sariel, S., Yildiz, P., Karapinar, S., Altan, D., Kapotoglu, M.: Robust task execution through experience-based guidance for cognitive robots. In: 2015 International Conference on Advanced Robotics (ICAR), pp. 663–668. IEEE (2015)
15. Sen, R., Shanmugam, K., Kocaoglu, M., Dimakis, A.G., Shakkottai, S.: Contextual bandits with latent confounders: an NMF approach. arXiv preprint arXiv:1606.00119 (2016)

Enabling Imagination: Generative Adversarial Network-Based Object Finding in Robotic Tasks

Huimin Che[✉], Ben Hu, Bo Ding, and Huaimin Wang

National Key Lab of Parallel and Distributed Processing, College of Computer,
National University of Defense Technology, Changsha, China
{chehuimin15,huben11,dingbo,hmwang}@nudt.edu.cn

Abstract. The skill to find objects in a real world situation is important for mobile robots. Existing works of robotic vision-based object finding is based on the traditional training and classification paradigm, which means that a robot can only detect objects with the fixed and pre-trained classification labels. It is of great challenge for robots to find an untrained object, even if a complex description of the object has been given. In this paper, we proposed a vision-based object detection approach for robotic finding names Generative Search. It is inspired by the object detection model that when an unfamiliar object needs to be found through a complex description, human would "imagine" the object in his or her brain and then find the object which is mostly like the imagined object profile. By adopting a Generative Adversarial Network (GAN), our approach enables the robot to generate the object virtually according to the given description. Then, we use pre-trained deep neural networks to match the generated image with images in the robotic vision. At the implementation level, we adopt the cloud robotic architecture to promote the algorithm efficiency. The experiments on both open datasets and real robotic scenarios have proved the significant promotion of object finding accuracy when a robot searching an unfamiliar object with a complex description.

Keywords: Robotic object finding · GAN · Image matching

1 Introduction

Finding objects is an essential task to many robotic tasks. For example, a patient may order a service robot to find (and fetch) an object through a natural language instruction such as "a cup", and a scientist may require a UAV (Unmanned Aerial Vehicle) to find a specific species such as "a bird" on a scientific expedition. In addition to moving and navigating in the environment, a core capability required in this process for the robot is to actively detect the object that matches the given instruction. In the former research, this goal is usually achieved by vision-based object detection algorithms (Fig. 1a). For example, DNNs (Deep Neural Networks) in [1] is used to detect and classify objects in the robotic vision into different categories according to pre-trained models and then output a label of it. The robot can judge whether the object is the search target by matching the label with the given instruction.

© Springer International Publishing AG 2017
D. Liu et al. (Eds.): ICONIP 2017, Part VI, LNCS 10639, pp. 100–110, 2017.
https://doi.org/10.1007/978-3-319-70136-3_11

Fig. 1. (a) is the traditional way of searching "a bird" for robots. (b) is the way of human thinking when searching objects with the description "a small yellow bird with black wings". (Color figure online)

However, the above-mentioned approach has limitations in many real cases. For example, the instruction given to the robot may be a complex description of the search target such as "a small yellow bird with black wings", which is not trained in advance. It is nearly impossible to train models to output labels which contain all possible combination of the additional features (such as "small", "yellow" and "with black wings" in our "bird" example), because of the lack of adequate training samples or the combination explosion problem.

In the human world, when a description "A small yellow bird with black wings" is given to a person, he or she can imagine the profile of the bird according to the existed knowledge, even if they have not seen such a specific bird before. And then he can find which object in his vision is mostly like the image he imagined. Inspired by this object detection process (Fig. 1b), we propose an imagination-based detection approach named *Generative Search* which can enable the robot to find objects that was not directly trained. The key challenge is to enable a robot to "imagine" an unfamiliar search target according to the given description. In our approach, we adopt a newly emerged neural network, Generative Adversarial Networks (GAN) [2] to achieve this goal. Then, we compare the "imagined" image with the object images captured by the robot while it roaming around the environment, by contrasting their features extracted from another deep neural network. We realized our approach based on the ROS (Robot Operating System) [3] platform[1] and the cloud robotic paradigm. The experiments on both open datasets and real robots have proved the significant promotion of object finding accuracy in our approach.

As far as we have known, Generative Search is the first successful application of GAN in the robotic search field, and it is also the first algorithm which enables the robots to find objects not being directly trained through imitating the human's "imagination-matching" process. The remain of this paper is organized as follows: The background and related work are discussed in Sect. 2. An overview of our approach and its key mechanisms are introduced in Sects. 3 and 4 respectively. The experiments and evaluation are presented in Sect. 5.

---

[1] https://github.com/SelinaChe/GAN-based-Object-Finding.

2   Background and Related Work

Object finding is the task of efficient searching for maximizing the probability of detecting a target within a given cost constraint [4]. This section first gives an introduction to related work in the field of object search, focusing on the difference from our research. And then, we introduce GAN, the core concept of Generative Search to enable the robot to "imagine" the search target according to a description.

2.1   Vision-Based Robotic Object Search

Finding and recognizing objects by vision is easy for humans, but remains an ongoing challenge for mobile robots. To search efficiently, robots must make use of various direct and indirect knowledge. A lot of former researches in this field focus on deciding where to search and how best to navigate to those locations [5]. For example, [6] proposed the idea of indirect target search, which is capable of finding objects in scenes by making use of semantic scene structure, e.g., searching "a bird" by searching assumptive obvious things such as "a tree"; [7] presents a context-based vision system for place and object detection. This system recognizes place first and recognizes objects at possible scenarios; [5] identifies inspection points that it considers likely to provide good views of the area it is searching, then creates efficient contingent plans.

The study of object detection, as the focus of this paper, is another core research issue in robotic object finding. As mentioned in Sect. 1, existing researches is based on robotic visual image processing and classification. For example, [4] uses machine learning algorithms to promote the speed of object detection, so that robots can maintain its detection accuracy when moving; [8] uses public cloud services when local SVM algorithm unable to ensure recognition accuracy; [1] uses DNNs to address this problem, which can not only classify but precisely locates objects of various classes. A sub-problem is how to control the robot's movements and promote object detection accuracy. For example, in [9], the training image is processed by RFCH and SIFT algorithms to provide a set of histograms and key points, and then robots move closer for more clear images of the object for successful searching. [10] studies the problem of determining camera viewpoints for successive views looking for distinguishing features of an object.

However, all of the previous object detection works in robotic research assume that the class of the robot search target is pre-trained. Our work in this paper concentrate on how to detect an object which is not directly trained but with a complex description. As we have mentioned, it is the first algorithm which enables the robots to find unfamiliar objects through imitating the human's "imagination-matching" process.

2.2   GAN and Its Application in Robotics

Generative adversarial networks (GANs) are a recently introduced class of generative models, designed to produce realistic samples. The main idea behind GAN is to train two networks: a generator network G tries to produce a sample, and a discriminator network D tries to distinguish between "real" samples and "fake" generated samples. One can train these networks against each other in a min-max game where the generator seeks to maximally fool the discriminator while simultaneously the discriminator seeks to detect which examples are fake.

Works using GAN on robotic applications have been applied in the field of self-driving cars [12] and robotic reinforcement learning [13]. Santana and Hotz [12] investigates variational autoencoders with classical and learned cost functions using GAN for embedding road frames. The model-free imitation learning algorithm in [13] obtains significant performance gains over existing model-free methods in imitating complex behaviors in large, high-dimensional environments. To our knowledge, Generative Search is the first successful application of GAN in the robotic finding field.

3   Method Overview

The problem this paper concerns is how to enable a robot to detect an untrained object with a complex description through "imagination" based on the knowledge it has possessed. For example, assuming a robot has been trained with a set of samples of "a bird with black wings" and "a bird with a shot pointed beak", we need to enable the robot to detect an object described by "a bird with black beak" in its finding process.

Imitating the human object detection model mentioned in Sect. 1, the proposed Generative Search method can be divided into three parts (Fig. 2): (1) *Image generation*, which generates an image with a probable appearance that matches a complex description in natural language. We use GANs based Generative Model to get the image. (2) *Region-to-image matching*, which segments all possible regions for objects in the robot's view, and calculates the similarity using the Euclidean distance between these regions and the generated image from the first process. (3) *Identifying interested region*, which identifies interested regions to determine whether the robot should be closer to objects. Besides, in order to support these compute-intensive DNNs running for robots, we adopt the *cloud robotic-based realization*.

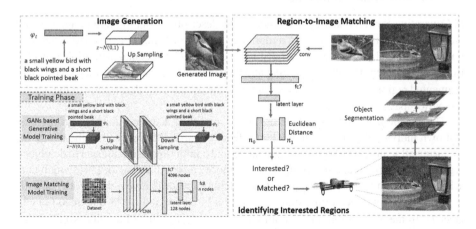

Fig. 2. Overview of Generative Search

In our approach, two neural networks are selected and designed as shown in Fig. 2. StackGAN [11] is selected to train generative model to generate images in the first process. The second process adopts fine-turn classic convolutional neural networks [14], to accomplish image matching. More details about the above-mentioned four mechanisms and these two neural networks can be found in Sect. 4.

4 Key Mechanisms

In this section, we introduce the key mechanisms of our approach, including how to enable a robot to imagine, how to realize region-to-image matching, how to identify interested regions, and how we realized our approach based on the cloud robotic architecture.

4.1 Enabling Imagination by GAN

The kernel of Generative Search is to generate a photo-realistic image according to the description. Since GAN has achieved excellent performances in the field of image generation, we apply it to achieve this goal. In details, we adopt StackGAN [10], which can not only imagine an unfamiliar object, but also generate a high quality image of this object from linearly interpolated sentence embedding. The performance of StackGAN is benefit from its two stages program. In Stage-I, the input variables are text description and a noise data z. StackGAN design mechanism of conditioning augmentation and adding a regularization term to draw rough shapes, correct colors for objects for generating more matched images. Stage-II takes Stage-I results and text descriptions as inputs, and following the steps similar to Stage-I to generate photo-realistic images.

4.2 Region-to-Image Matching

In Generative-Search system, after generating a description conditioning image g using StackGAN, robots need to roam in a room and search for similar images. However, the images captured by robots are generally a scene image C that contains multiple objects. Robots need to segment the image first, and then matches the generated image with each segmented region $\{c_1, c_2 \ldots c_n\}$. We summarize the pseudocode description of the whole region-to-image matching process in Table 1.

The function of object segmentation is to subdivide acquired images into regions that own individual objects. The method selective search [15], which has the nature of capturing all scales, supporting diversification and computing fast, is chosen to do object segmentation. The image matching network model refers to the work [14], which can achieve good matching results and has fast matching speed. This neural network consists of six convolution layers, full connection layers Fc7, Fc8 and a 128-dimension latent layer H. In the application phase, both g and $\{c_1, c_2 \ldots c_n\}$ should be processed by the first eight layers to produce 128-dimension feature. We extract the outputs of the latent layer as the image feature which is denoted by $latent\_layer(Image)$. For each bit $i = 1 \cdots l$ (where l is the number of nodes in the latent layer). The corresponding codes of each

Table 1. Region-to-image matching process.

Algorithm 1. Region-to-image Matching
Input: generated image g and scene images C captured by the robot
Output: the distance between the feature codes of g and the region of C

1	use StackGAN to generate photo-realistic images
2	use selective search to get proposal regions
3	$(c_1, c_2 \dots c_n) = Selective\_Search(C)$
4	$Vg = latent\_layer(x)$
5	**for** c_i **in** $(c_1, c_2 \dots c_l)$
6	$Vc_i = latent\_layer(c_i)$
7	$M_i^c = Euclidean\_distance(Vg, Vc_i)$
8	**endfor**
9	$\mathcal{M} = top\_n(sort(M_1^c, M_2^c, \dots, M_r^c))$

image are donated as $\Gamma_V = \{Vc_1, Vc_2, \dots, Vc_r\}$ (where r is the number of regions). After generating an image g and getting its feature codes Vg, we can get a pool of n candidates, $\mathcal{M} = \{M_1^c, M_2^c, \dots, M_n^c\}$, if the Euclidean distance between Vg and $Vc_i \in \Gamma_V$ is lower than a threshold.

4.3 Identifying Interested Regions in Robotic Vision

Often, the images that a robot captures are not immediately sufficient to perform accurate object detection, especially with low-resolution cameras. For successful detection, either moving closer or zooming in on the object is necessary. Most previous image matching works would retrieve all images I_i that need to be detected, and calculate the distance between features of given image and I_i. The image with the smallest distance would be selected to be the most similar one. However, robots need to match objects at runtime. They cannot wait for a result after retrieving all the objects in a room. In Generative Search, we implement a mechanism to allow a robot to find the interested regions as soon as the image is captured.

Because all the features are extracted by the same model. They are under the same probability distribution. Therefore, we use the normalized method to normalize results to $N(0, 1)$ in Eq. (1) to convert the Euclidean distances of the results into matching similarity scores. α is a coefficient controlling the degree of the sparseness of the score based on M_i^c mentioned in Sect. 4.2. S is a slack variable which represents the degree of tolerance for the difference of n_0 and n_i.

$$score_i = 2(1 + e^{\alpha(|M_i^c - S|)^{-1}})^{-1} - 1 \qquad 0 < i < r \qquad (1)$$

According to Eq. (1), the higher similarity score, the more likely the current region is that we are interested in. Users can define the distribution of similarity score by adjusting parameters α and S. We set two score threshold T_{match} and $T_{interest}$

($T_{interest} < T_{match}$) to do localization. While a robot roaming in a room, we design blew mechanism to decide the next action of the robot defined in Eq. 2:

Let $S = \{score_1, score_2, \ldots, score_r\}$ denote the calculated score of r regions of an image captured by the robot. In the searching process, robot actions are summarized as {A$_1$:*continue to roam*, A$_2$:*mark and report to human*, A$_3$:*closer to objects*}

$$action = \begin{cases} A_1 & score_i < T_{interest} \\ A_1 \ and \ A_2 & score_i \geq T_{match} \\ A_3 & T_{interest} \leq score_i < T_{match} \end{cases} \qquad (2)$$

4.4 Cloud Robotic-Based Realization

DNN-based processes in Generative Search are highly compute-intensive tasks which are hard to directly deploy on resources limited robots. "Cloud Robotics", which is a novel paradigm combining the robots with cloud computing to enhance robots' capabilities, can be used in our work. Because it is tedious to deploy and design the message transfer mechanism between robots and clouds, we adopt Cloudroid [16], a robotic cloud platform to support the ROS applications deployment directly, to outsource the complex computation of this method to cloud as shown in Fig. 3. With the help of this platform, robots only need to collect the images and send them to the cloud through wireless network, and wait for the detection result.

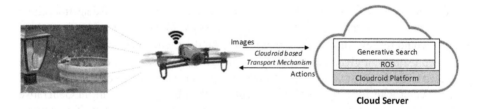

Fig. 3. Generative Search realization based on cloud robotic

5   Evaluation and Experiments

In this section, We first introduce the datasets and present our experimental results, which are the performance comparison between our method and classical detection algorithm on the public datasets, and then present our experimental results on robots in the real world.

5.1 Experiments on Public Dataset

In this section, we comprehensively train the generative model on the CUB [17] and the Oxford-102 dataset [18], and train image matching model on these datasets. CUB has

11,788 images of birds belonging to 200 different categories. The Oxford-102 contains 8,189 images of flowers from 102 different categories. As shown in Fig. 4, descriptions are inputted into Generative Search to generate photo-realistic images. Four matching results are shown in Fig. 4. For example in the first result, two strong positive correlation birds and a weak positive correlation bird are detected and matched exactly.

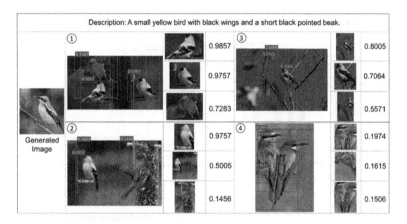

Fig. 4. Matching results on a description. (Color figure online)

As there is no relevant research on searching an object with a description, we compare Generative Search with Faster R-CNN [19], which is a classic DNN based object detection algorithm to illustrate our advantages. Since the output of Faster R-CNN is a signal label, the input sentence should be parsed first to get its subject, e.g., "bird" is parsed from the description "A small yellow bird with black wings". Let T_{match} values be 0.8, detection of searching task of Generative Search and Faster R-CNN can be regarded as binary classifications with results "detected" and "not detected". We randomly select 76 flower images and 89 bird images from the Internet as our test set.

To evaluate the performance of Faster R-CNN and our method, we select several criteria of binary classifications of the search field in Fig. 5(a–c). Figure 5(a) illustrates that accuracy, precision, F1-score of Generative Search are evenly increased by 78.7%, 49.64%, 23.1% than the results of Faster R-CNN in four descriptions. For the descriptions "A small yellow bird with a black crown and a short black pointed beak", we test it with 232 birds in which 36 birds match to the description, under different matching score thresholds T_{match}. The precision and accuracy curve in Fig. 5(b) presents that, as the accuracy increases, the precision of finding the specific bird by Faster R-CNN decreases, while our method shows a positive correlation. Figure 5(c) calculates the area under the curve of ROC (Receiver Operating Characteristic) to show the overall performance. The area of our method is larger than the Luck curve, but Faster R-CNN is smaller. It illustrates that our method performs better, while the Faster R-CNN performs even worse than randomly guessing in this task. Above results illustrate that the performance of our method is better than existing object detection algorithm in the task of searching an object though a complex description. For evaluating whether the region-to-image matching mechanism is good for Generative Search or not, we test it under the mechanism with or without region-to-Image matching by evaluating the number of TP (Ture Positive) on different thresholds. The result in Fig. 5(d) shows that, using region-to-image matching, more TP objects can be correctly figured out when fixing the value of T_{match}.

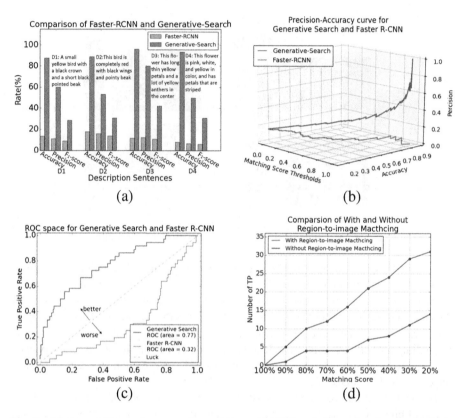

Fig. 5. (a) (b) and (c) are the comparison of Faster R-CNN and Generative Search. (d) is the comparison curve of with and without region-to-image matching mechanism of our method.

5.2   Experiment on a Real Robotic Scenario

In this experiment, neural networks related parts of Generative-Search engine are deployed on a DELL PowerEdge R730 server through Cloudroid. Parrot Robot, which is a kind of quadrotor, responsible for collecting vision information, receiving processed results from the cloud service, and then executing the corresponding actions. As shown in Fig. 6, a robot received an assignment to find an object with the description "This flower has long thin white petals and a lot of yellow anthers in the center". The robot sent the description to server first to generate a matched image. It stopped roaming until the matching score was higher than 60% and labeled the corresponding region as an interested one. Then the robot went closer to this region for a clear image. Finally, the object with the score larger than 90% was identified and reported to the human. Figure 6 contains some snapshot of this experiment, and it validates the effectivity of our approach on this real robotic object finding tasks.

Fig. 6. Results on Parrot Robot in a real environment (Color figure online)

6   Conclusion

In this paper, we proposed Generative Search for the robotic task of finding an unfamiliar object with a complex description. The proposed method generates an image that matches the description using StackGAN first, and then extracts the features of the generated image and intelligently divide regions of image captured by robots to calculate the similarity scores. The experiments on both open datasets and real quadrotor robots validate the effectivity and efficiency of our approach in comparison with existing works in this field. Our future work includes improving performance of Generative Search, and exploring other algorithms for completing the task of finding an object with a complex description more efficiently.

Acknowledgments.   This work is partially supported by the National Natural Science Foundation of China (nos. 91118008 and 61202117), the special program for the applied basic research of the National University of Defense Technology (no. ZDYYJCYJ20140601), and the Jiangsu Future Networks Innovation Institute Prospective Research Project on Future Networks (no. BY2013095-2-08).

References

1. Szegedy, C., Toshev, A., Erhan, D.: Deep neural networks for object detection. In: Advances in Neural Information Processing Systems, pp. 2553–2561 (2013)
2. Goodfellow, I., Pouget-Abadie, J., Mirza, M., Xu, B., Warde-Farley, D., Ozair, S., Courville, A., Bengio, Y.: Generative adversarial nets. In: Advances in Neural Information Processing Systems, pp. 2672–2680 (2014)

3. Quigley, M., Conley, K., Gerkey, B., Faust, J., Foote, T., Leibs, J., Wheeler, R., Ng, A.Y.: ROS: an open-source robot operating system. In: ICRA Workshop on Open Source Software (2009)
4. Aydemir, A., Sjöö, K., Jensfelt, P.: Object search on a mobile robot using relational spatial information. In: Proceedings of International Conference on Intelligent Autonomous Systems, pp. 111–120 (2010)
5. Saigol, Z., Ridder, B., Wang, M., Dearden, R., Fox, M., Hawes, N., Lane, D.M., Long, D.: Efficient search for known objects in unknown environments using autonomous indoor robots. In: IROS Workshop on Task Planning for Intelligent Robots in Service and Manufacturing (2015)
6. Garvey, T.D.: Perceptual strategies for purposive vision (1976)
7. Torralba, A., Murphy, K.P., Freeman, W.T., Rubin, M.A., et al.: Context-based vision system for place and object recognition. In: ICCV, vol. 3, pp. 273–280 (2003)
8. Li, Y., Wang, H., Ding, B., Shi, P., Liu, X.: Toward QoS-aware cloud robotic applications: a hybrid architecture and its implementation. In: 2016 International IEEE Conferences Ubiquitous Intelligence & Computing, pp. 33–40. IEEE (2016)
9. López, D.G., Sjo, K., Paul, C., Jensfelt, P.: Hybrid laser and vision based object search and localization. In: IEEE International Conference on Robotics and Automation, ICRA 2008, pp. 2636–2643. IEEE (2008)
10. Kim, H.S., Jain, R., Volz, R.: Object recognition using multiple views. In: Proceedings 1985 IEEE International Conference on Robotics and Automation, vol. 2, pp. 28–33. IEEE (1985)
11. Zhang, H., Xu, T., Li, H., Zhang, S., Huang, X., Wang, X., Metaxas, D.: Stackgan: text to photo-realistic image synthesis with stacked generative adversarial networks. arXiv preprint arXiv:1612.03242 (2016)
12. Santana, E., Hotz, G.: Learning a driving simulator. arXiv preprint arXiv:1608.01230 (2016)
13. Ho, J., Ermon, S.: Generative adversarial imitation learning. In: Advances in Neural Information Processing Systems, pp. 4565–4573 (2016)
14. Lin, K., Yang, H.F., Hsiao, J.H., Chen, C.S.: Deep learning of binary hash codes for fast image retrieval. In: Proceedings of the IEEE Conference on Computer Vision and Pattern Recognition Workshops, pp. 27–35 (2015)
15. Uijlings, J.R., Van De Sande, K.E., Gevers, T., Smeulders, A.W.: Selective search for object recognition. Int. J. Comput. Vision **104**(2), 154–171 (2013)
16. Hu, B., Wang, H., Zhang, P., Ding, B., Che, H.: Cloudroid: a cloud framework for transparent and QoS-aware robotic computation outsourcing. arXiv preprint arXiv:1705.05691 (2017)
17. Wah, C., Branson, S., Welinder, P., Perona, P., Belongie, S.: The caltech-ucsd birds-200-2011 dataset (2011)
18. Nilsback, M.E., Zisserman, A.: Automated flower classification over a large number of classes. In: Sixth Indian Conference on Computer Vision, Graphics & Image Processing, ICVGIP 2008, pp. 722–729. IEEE (2008)
19. Ren, S., He, K., Girshick, R., Sun, J.: Faster R-CNN: towards real-time object detection with region proposal networks. In: Advances in Neural Information Processing Systems, pp. 91–99 (2015)

Event-Based Target Tracking Control for a Snake Robot Using a Dynamic Vision Sensor

Zhuangyi Jiang[1][✉], Zhenshan Bing[1], Kai Huang[2], Guang Chen[1],
Long Cheng[1], and Alois Knoll[1]

[1] Department of Informatics, Technical University of Munich,
Boltzmannstr. 3, 85748 Munich, Germany
{jiangz,bing,guang,chengl,knoll}@in.tum.de
[2] School of Data and Computer Science, Sun Yat-Sen University,
Guangzhou, China
huangk36@mail.sysu.edu.cn

Abstract. Dynamic Vision Sensor (DVS) is a promising neuromorphic vision sensor for autonomous locomotion control of mobile robots, as the DVS acquires visual information by mimicking retina to sense and encode the world as neural signals. In this paper, we present an autonomous target detecting and tracking control approach for a snake-like robot with a monocular DVS. By using Hough transform based on the Spiking Neural Network (SNN), the target pole is detected as two parallel lines from the event-based visual input. Then a depth estimation method based on the pose and motion of the robot is proposed. Furthermore, by combining the periodic motion feature of the snake-like robot, an adaptive tracking method based on the estimated depth information is introduced. Experiments are conducted on a snake-like robot to demonstrate the practicality and accuracy of our proposed method to track a target pole dynamically with a monocular DVS.

Keywords: Target tracking · Spiking Neural Network · Dynamic Vision Sensor · Neuromorphic snake robot · Hough transform

1 Introduction

Autonomous locomotion capability, namely making decisions on how, when, and where to move, is important for mobile robots, especially for snake-like robots designed for disaster rescue [1]. A typical implementation of the autonomous locomotion is the target tracking. Sensing, deciding and acting are the three components of the target tracking procedure [2]. Most research has focused on the acting component. However, the sensors for snake-like robots and the corresponding method of decision-making have not been well explored.

Despite various vision sensors have been used, such as frame-based camera and stereo camera, there still exist many limitations and deficiencies. Conventional computer vision acquires information by examining a series of pictures

© Springer International Publishing AG 2017
D. Liu et al. (Eds.): ICONIP 2017, Part VI, LNCS 10639, pp. 111–121, 2017.
https://doi.org/10.1007/978-3-319-70136-3_12

at a fixed frame rate, regardless whether there is a change or not in the scene. It will lead to data redundancy, information loss, and dependency on lighting conditions. On the other hand, the cameras mounted on snake-like robots are not able to work in stable positions while the robots are moving, because of the periodic orientation of the body of the snake-like robot under 3D slithering gait.

Very few literature has explored the sensing and deciding approaches applied on snake-like robots. Ponte [2] proposed a pole tracking method by using a structured light sensor that can make 3D maps of the environment and IMU sensors to estimate the pose of the robot. Pfotzer [3] proposed an autonomous navigation method for the snake-like robots with wheels. However, these methods need to sense the environment in a static gait but not in real time, because of the blur caused by the moving of robots and the huge computation of processing image and making decisions.

As a promising solution, Dynamic Vision Sensor (DVS) [4] mimics the retina and generates spikes in response to the pixel-level changes in illumination caused by movement. Compared to a conventional frame-based camera, a DVS offers great advantages in terms of data rate, speed, and dynamic range [5], especially for mobile scenes. The DVS is suitable for working in critical scenarios with either bad light conditions or moving platforms. Moreover, events generated by a DVS can be directly fed into Spiking Neural Networks (SNNs) for fast target detecting and motion control.

Furthermore, it should be considered how to acquire depth information by DVS for target localizing and tracking. Everding [6] and Piatkowska [7] both extracted the depth information by streaming the events of stereo DVS. The stereo DVS camera is a good choice, however, it requires additional space than monocular DVS, which makes it difficult to be mounted on a snake-like robot with the small head module. Besides, there exists an extra blind area near the stereo DVS, so that the depth of objects in this area cannot be extracted.

In this paper, we present an autonomous pole detecting and tracking approach for a snake-like robot based on monocular DVS. First, we extract the line features of the target pole by streaming and processing event sequences from DVS with an SNN based on Hough Transform [5,8,9]. Two parallel lines are detected as pole boundaries when the membrane potential of the neurons in the SNN exceeds the pre-defined threshold. Then, a depth estimation method based on the pose and motion of the robot is proposed with the monocular DVS instead of the stereo DVS, which calculates the depth by the change of the width of the pole in pixels and the displacement of the snake-like robot in the forward direction. Furthermore, an adaptive tracking method based on the depth estimation is introduced. According to the pose of the robot and the offset of the target in the field of DVS, the relative depth and orientation between the target and the robot are estimated as the parameters for adaptive tracking control which uses a series of control signals of turning left or turning right. Finally, a set of target pole tracking experiments for the snake-like robots is conducted to demonstrate the accuracy and practicality of the proposed method.

The rest of the paper is organized as follows. Section 2 describes the relative background knowledge, including DVS camera and spiking neural network. Section 3 is the overview of the neural snake-like robot and the tracking system. Section 4 presents a spiking neural network designed for pole detection and pole detecting algorithm. The position estimation algorithm and tracking method are illustrated in Sect. 5. Section 6 shows the results of experiments conducted on a snake-like robot. Section 7 concludes this paper.

2 Background

The dynamic vision sensor (DVS) [10] is a silicon retina. Instead of wastefully sending entire images at fixed frame rates, only the local pixel-level changes caused by movement in a scene are transmitted. It records the change in illumination as events in real time. Once the intensity change exceeds a threshold, a positive or negative event will be generated to represent the change of dark-to-bright or bright-to-dark. An event is a 4-tuple (t,x,y,p), where t is the timestamp of the event, x and y are the position of the event in pixels, and p is the polarity which is binary $(+/-)$. The DVS used in this paper has a 128×128 spatial resolution and $1\,\mu s$ temporal accuracy.

Spiking neural network (SNN) is the third generation of neural network models, increasing the level of realism in a neural simulation [11]. Each Spiking Neuron [12] has some spike inputs and a spike output. A spiking input causes an increase or decrease of the neuron's Membrane Potential (MP). At the meantime, the MP is always decaying by a fixed rate. Whenever the MP exceeds the positive or negative threshold, a spike with the corresponding polarity is generated in the output. Then the MP is reset to zero and the neuron enters a refractory period, during which MP remains zero and input spikes are ignored.

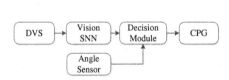

Fig. 1. The model of the neuromorphic snake robot for target tracking.

Fig. 2. The snake-like robot equipped with Dynamic Vision Sensor (DVS128)

3 Neuromorphic Snake Robot for Target Tracking

The method proposed in this paper for target detecting and tracking is tested on a neuromorphic snake-like robot we have developed. A neuromorphic snake-like robot model is designed in the robot simulator V-REP, consisting of 15 actuated modules and a head module mounting the DVS128 sensor as shown in Fig. 2. All the modules are connected alternately with the lateral and dorsal planes. Each module with angle sensor is allowed 180° rotation. The monocular DVS in the head module sends back the real-time event stream to the host server via remote API functions of V-REP. Our snake-like robot is developed with 3D locomotion capabilities by the Central Pattern Generator (CPG) [13] which generates parameter of the motion equation for locomotion control, so that the autonomous locomotion control can be implemented simply by sending a series of commands of turning left or right. The slithering gait [14] for target tracking has been implemented to make the snake-like robot move forward fast and have a head module with relatively stable direction, so that the DVS camera mounting in the head module could obtain the valid data.

The framework of our neuromorphic snake robot for target tracking is divided into 5 components as shown in Fig. 1, including the DVS camera for sensing the environment, the angel sensors for pose estimation, the vision SNN for event-based object detection, the decision module for motion decision and the CPG-based control module.

4   SNN-Based Pole Detection by DVS

The pole is one of the most common obstacles indoor. It usually has a textureless and smooth surface so that it is regarded as two lines in each address-event frame. In this paper, an SNN corresponding to the Hough transform parameter space is designed. The events in the stream are fed into the SNN to detect the pole.

4.1   Vision SNN for Line Detection

According to the Hough transform, assuming $n = (\sin\theta, \cos\theta)$ as the normal vector perpendicular to the line L and ρ as the normal distance from the line to the origin, for every point $p = (x, y)$ on the line:

$$\rho = n \cdot p = x\sin\theta + y\cos\theta. \tag{1}$$

Equation (1) maps every point (x, y) from Cartesian coordinate into parameter space (θ, ρ) as a sinusoidal curves as shown in Fig. 3(a).

A 2D SNN corresponding to the parameter space of Hough transform is built up as shown in Fig. 3(b) for line detection, which consists of 180×180 spiking neurons. One dimension of the SNN is for angle θ and the other is for distance ρ, the range of θ is from 0° to 179°, the range of ρ is from 1 to $128\sqrt{2} \approx 180$ pixels. Each neuron of the SNN represents a line, or a point (θ, ρ) in the parameter space. The leaky integrate-and-fire (LIF) neuron model is used in the SNN. We use Algorithm 1 to update a spiking neuron. For every time slot, the MP of the spiking neuron decreases at a constant rate λ as the decay. When an input spike arrives, the absolute value of MP increases s_i. Then if the MP exceeds the positive threshold or the negative one, an output spike δ is generated and the fired spiking neuron will be reset.

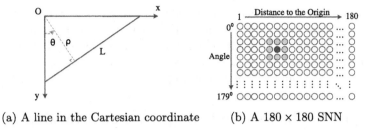

(a) A line in the Cartesian coordinate   (b) A 180 × 180 SNN

Fig. 3. θ is limited in $[0°, 180°)$ while ρ is limited in $[1, 180]$. The central neuron in (b) is corresponded to the line in (a), which is connected to all neurons in neighbor for local inhibition.

Algorithm 1. Updating of a spiking neuron ($\lambda = 0.3/\text{ms}$, $v_{th} = 40$)

---

for input spike s_i at t_i **do**
   $v_i \leftarrow sign(v_{i-1}) \cdot \max(|v_{i-1}| - \lambda(t_i - t_{i-1}), 0)$
   $v_i \leftarrow v_i + s_i$
   if $|v_i| \geq v_{th}$ **then**
      Generate output spike $\delta = sign(v_i)$ at t_i
      Reset all connected neurons
      $v_i \leftarrow 0$

Meanwhile, a local inhibition strategy is applied to suppress the noise. Every spiking neuron is connected to those in its neighborhood. Once a line is detected, a spiking neuron will fire and all the spiking neurons connected will be reset as 0. In this paper, the size of the neighborhood for local inhibition strategy is 7×7, which means the angle range is $\pm 3°$ and the distance range is ± 3.

4.2 SNN-Based Pole Detection

The vertical edge on both sides of the pole can be detected as two parallel lines. In the certain indoor environment, while the DVS camera is moving in the direction perpendicular to the pole, the change of lightness is opposite on both sides of the pole. The polarity of the events on the one side is positive, but negative on the other side. Once the DVS camera moves to the opposite direction, the polarity of the events on the two side would reverse. The two lines with opposite polarity can be considered as a pole. Furthermore, there should not be any other lines between the two sides of the pole which is textureless. Therefore, three conditions for line detection are found out as below:

- The polarities of two lines are different.
- The two lines are parallel or the difference of the angle is tiny.
- The distance between the two lines is the minimum in all pairs of line.

In this paper, all the lines are tested, which are detected by the SNN in each time slot. The pair of lines met the above conditions are found out. The target pole can be detected by Algorithm 2 and represented as a 4-tuple $P(t, \theta, w, l)$, where t is the timestamp, θ is the angle of the pole, the w is the width of the pole and the l is the offset to the left side of the view field. Moreover, the procedure in Algorithm 2 can be vectorized and accelerated by parallel methods, such as multi-thread, GPU and neuromorphic chip.

5   Depth Estimation and Adaptive Pole Tracking

When the pole is detected by the SNN, we can estimate the offset of the pole on the x-axis and the distance between the DVS camera and the pole on the z-axis. As shown in Fig. 4(a), In a period of time $\Delta t = t_2 - t_1$ the decrease of the distance $\Delta d = |d_2 - d_1|$ on the z-axis is relative to the increase of the width of the pole $\Delta w = |w_2 - w_1|$ in DVS. Assuming the robot moves at a constant speed, the Δd can be estimated by multiplying the time elapsed and the speed. Due to our snake-like robot moving slowly, the speed forwards is approximately constant. On the other hand, the distance d in meters is inversely proportional to the width of the pole w in pixels, the scale factor is the focus length f in pixels multiplying the width l in meters. According to Eqs. (2), (3) and (4), we

---

Algorithm 2. Event-based pole detecting in the SNN

---

    for event $e_i = (t_i, x_i, y_i, s_i)$ in each time slot **do**
      for every angle θ_j in SNN **do**
        Calculate distance $\rho_{\theta_j} = argmin \; |\rho - x_i \sin \theta_j - y_i \cos \theta_j|$
        Excite neuron $N(\theta_j, \rho_{\theta_j})$ at t_i with s_i (algorithm 1)
        Find out two output spikes met the pole conditions
        if a pole exits **then**
        Output the pole $P(t, \theta, w, l)$

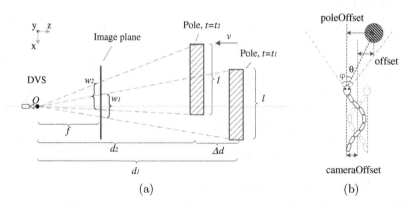

(a)   (b)

Fig. 4. (a) The geometric relationship between the DVS camera and the pole. When t = t1 the pole is on the right position. After the DVS camera moving at a certain velocity v, the pole is on the left position when $t = t_2$. (b) The periodic motion of the DVS camera while the snake-like robot moving forwards.

Algorithm 3. Position estimation and adaptive tracking for target ($v = 0.4\,\mathrm{m/s}$)

---

for pole $p_i(t_i, \theta_i, w_i, l_i)$ **do**

    if $i \geq 10$ **then**

        Calculate the distance, $d = v \cdot (t_i - t_{i-10}) \cdot \frac{w_{i-10}}{w_i - w_{i-10}}$

        Calculate the offset of the pole in DVS, $poleOffset = d \cdot \frac{|l_i - 64| \cdot \tan\frac{\phi}{2}}{64}$

        Calculate the offset of the camera $cameraOffset$

        $offset = poleOffset + robotOffset$

        Trun left when $offset < 0$

        Trun right when $offset > 0$

        Go straight when $offset == 0$

---

can calculate the distance d_2 depending on the displacement in a time period and the change of the pole's width in pixels.

$$\Delta d = |d_2 - d_1| = v \cdot \Delta t, \tag{2}$$

$$d = f \cdot l \cdot w^{-1}, \tag{3}$$

$$d_2 = \frac{f \cdot l}{w_2} = \frac{w_1 \cdot v \cdot \Delta t}{\Delta w}. \tag{4}$$

The snake-like robot moves slowly and the Δt and the Δw between two consecutive output spikes are tiny. Therefore, the error of distance calculated by the Eq. (4) is remarkable. To reduce the error, two discrete output spikes are selected for distance estimating and the interval is 10 spikes in this paper.

Actually, the pole cannot be detected in each time slot by our SNN, so that it is hard to track the target pole at a fixed frequency. Therefore, an adaptive method is proposed that the robot makes a decision to turn left or turn right immediately when the relative position of the target pole is estimated. The relative position, that is the offset to the symmetry axis while moving, consists of the offset of the pole in DVS and the offset of the camera mounted on the robot's head. Considering the mobile snake-like robot, as shown in Fig. 4(b), the offset of the pole is calculated by the ratio of $\tan\theta$ to $\tan\frac{\phi}{2}$ ($\phi = 65°$) and the ratio of l to half of the resolution of DVS. Then the offset of the camera is calculated just according to the periodic motion of the head module in the horizontal direction. The trajectory of the camera can be extracted so that the relationship between the angle of the head module and the amplitude can be calculated by FFT. Especially, the trajectory can be extracted directly in the simulator. Finally, the command of turning left, turning right or going straight is sent to the robot control module implemented by the Central Pattern Generator (CPG). Algorithm 3 is performed for each pole p_i. The distance is calculated by Eq. (4) and $Offset$ is calculated by $poleOffset$ and $cameraOffset$. Finally, the movement direction is decided according to $offset$.

6   Experiments

The proposed method was evaluated in the simulator V-REP, an indoor scene was built up with a pole in front of a snake-like robot mounted a DVS in the head module. Two cases were tested, the pole was on the left side as the case 1 and the pole was on the right side as the case 2. In case 1, the initial position of the left pole is $(-0.574, 1.550, 1.200)$, the initial position of the DVS is $(-0.021, -0.920, 0.046)$. In case 2, the initial position of the right pole is $(0.574, 1.550, 1.200)$, the initial position of the DVS is $(-0.021, -0.920, 0.046)$. The robot moves forwards at the speed of $0.04\,\mathrm{m/s}$, while the head module is rotating and swinging periodically. The event sequences that are obtained from the DVS in V-REP inspired the vision SNN which is implemented in Python. The trajectory of the head module of the snake-like robot, the angle of the servo and the relative distance are recorded while simulating.

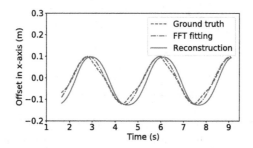

Fig. 5. The motion estimation of the head of snake-like robot while moving forwards.

The pole was detected in each time slot, the image and the position of the pole in case 2 were recorded and some of them were shown in Fig. 6. By using Algorithm 2, the pole was exactly detected at different distances. With the snake-like robot moving towards the pole, the width of the pole increased, as shown in Fig. 7. The offset of the pole to the left side of the image was obtained by calculating the center of two lines.

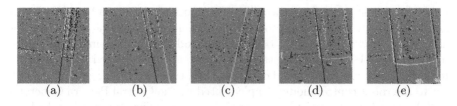

Fig. 6. The poles were detected in case 2. (a) A pole detected at 0.3 s. (b) A pole detected at 7.65 s. (c) A pole detected at 15.6 s when the robot turned right. (d) A pole detected at 36.45 s. (e) A pole detected at 42.65 s when the robot turned left.

Then the trajectory of the head module of the snake-like robot was analyzed by FFT while the robot moving straight. As shown in Fig. 5, the trajectory fitted by FFT was reconstructed, the peak amplitude was 0.112 m at the frequency 0.319. In the meantime, we reconstructed the trajectory of the head module by the angle θ extracted by V-REP. we obtained the offset of the DVS by the formula shown in Eq. (5). Further, the situation of turning was approximately treated as that moving straight.

$$y = -0.124 \cdot sin\theta - 0.010. \tag{5}$$

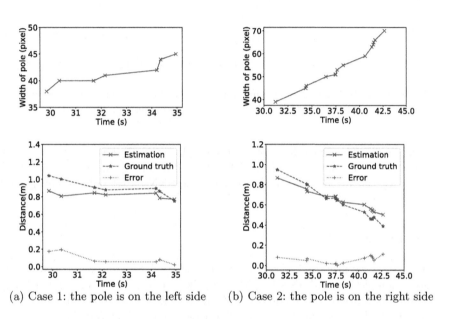

(a) Case 1: the pole is on the left side   (b) Case 2: the pole is on the right side

Fig. 7. The upper graphs show the increase of the width of the target pole in pixels. The lower graphs show the distance between the snake-like robot and the target pole.

For the pole offset to the snake-like robot, the offset of the pole in the address-event image is known after the pole is detected and the real offset of the pole is proportional to offset in DVS. So the ratio of offset in DVS to the real offset is decided by the ratio of the drift angle to the field angle as shown in Fig. 4(b) and Algorithm 3. The distance between the robot to the target pole was estimated first, as shown in Fig. 7, the depth was the estimated value from the tenth time when the pole was detected. Compared to the real distance extracted in V-REP, the error value is relatively small. Then the offset was calculated in every time when the pole was detected, and the control signals to the CPG of the snake-like robot were generated. As shown in Fig. 8, in the beginning the signal was 0 which means going straight. Then The robot turned left at 21.75 s and turned right at 34.95 s in case 1. The robot turned right at 15.6 s and turned left at 42.65 s in

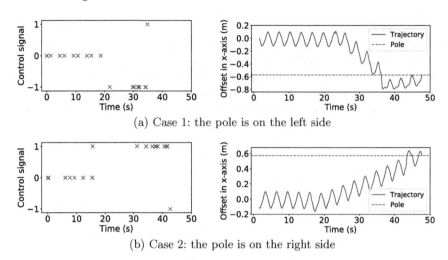

(a) Case 1: the pole is on the left side

(b) Case 2: the pole is on the right side

Fig. 8. Left: Control signals of turning left (-1), turning right (1) and going straight (0) for the snake-like robot. Right: The trajectory of the head module while tracking.

case 2. Finally The snake-like robot successfully arrived at the position of the target pole in the both two cases. The chart illuminates the practicality and accuracy of the method we proposed that the SNN-based pole detecting and tracking method.

7   Conclusion

In this paper, we proposed a pole detecting and tracking approach based on the combination of DVS and SNN for the snake-like robot. The combination is novel to be used in autonomous locomotion. A simulating scene is built up to test our approach on the neuromorphic snake-like robot. The target pole is detected in the address-event stream obtained from DVS. An adaptive tracking method is proposed, according to the change of relative position between the robot and the target pole. Experiments demonstrate the efficacy of the SNN for pole detecting and the practicality and accuracy of the adaptive tracking method.

References

1. Liljebäck, P., Pettersen, K.Y., Stavdahl, O., Gravdahl, J.T.: Snake Robots: Modelling, Mechatronics, and Control. Springer Science & Business Media, Heidelberg (2012)
2. Ponte, H., Queenan, M., Gong, C., Mertz, C., Travers, M., Enner, F.: Visual sensing for developing autonomous behavior in snake robots. In: 2014 IEEE International Conference on Robotics and Automation (ICRA), pp. 2779–2784. IEEE (2014)
3. Pfotzer, L., Klemm, S., Rönnau, A., Zöllner, J.M., Dillmann, R.: Autonomous navigation for reconfigurable snake-like robots in challenging, unknown environments. Robot. Auton. Syst. **89**, 123–135 (2017)

4. Weikersdorfer, D., Adrian, D.B., Cremers, D., Conradt, J.: Event-based 3D SLAM with a depth-augmented dynamic vision sensor. In: 2014 IEEE International Conference on Robotics and Automation (ICRA), pp. 359–364. IEEE (2014)
5. Seifozzakerini, S., Yau, W.Y., Zhao, B., Mao, K.: Event-based hough transform in a spiking neural network for multiple line detection and tracking using a dynamic vision sensor. In: BMVC (2016)
6. Everding, L., Walger, L., Ghaderi, V.S., Conradt, J.: A mobility device for the blind with improved vertical resolution using dynamic vision sensors. In: 2016 IEEE 18th International Conference on e-Health Networking, Applications and Services (Healthcom), pp. 1–5. IEEE (2016)
7. Piatkowska, E., Belbachir, A., Gelautz, M.: Asynchronous stereo vision for event-driven dynamic stereo sensor using an adaptive cooperative approach. In: Proceedings of the IEEE International Conference on Computer Vision Workshops, pp. 45–50 (2013)
8. Wiesmann, G., Schraml, S., Litzenberger, M., Belbachir, A.N., Hofstatter, M., Bartolozzi, C.: Event-driven embodied system for feature extraction and object recognition in robotic applications. In: Computer Vision and Pattern Recognition Workshops (CVPRW), pp. 76–82. IEEE (2012)
9. Auerbach, J.: Cross tracking on the DVS using an extended hough space method. In: Telluride Nueromorphic Cognition Engineering Workshop (2009)
10. Conradt, J., Galluppi, F., Stewart, T.C.: Trainable sensorimotor mapping in a neuromorphic robot. Robot. Auton. Syst. **71**, 60–68 (2015)
11. Maass, W.: Networks of spiking neurons: the third generation of neural network models. Neural Netw. **10**(9), 1659–1671 (1997)
12. Burkitt, A.N.: A review of the integrate-and-fire neuron model: I. Homogeneous synaptic input. Biol. Cybern. **95**(1), 1–19 (2006)
13. Bing, Z., Cheng, L., Huang, K., Zhou, M., Knoll, A.: CPG-based control of smooth transition for body shape and locomotion speed of a snake-like robot. In: 2017 IEEE International Conference on Robotics and Automation (ICRA), pp. 4146–4153. IEEE (2017)
14. Bing, Z., Cheng, L., Chen, G., Röhrbein, F., Huang, K., Knoll, A.: Towards autonomous locomotion: CPG-based control of smooth 3D slithering gait transition of a snake-like robot. Bioinspir. Biomim. **12**(3), 035001 (2017)

Data-Driven Nonlinear Adaptive Optimal Control of Connected Vehicles

Weinan Gao[1(✉)] and Zhong-Ping Jiang[2]

[1] Department of Electrical Engineering, Allen E. Paulson College of Engineering
and Information Technology, Georgia Southern University,
Statesboro, GA 30460, USA
wgao@georgiasouthern.edu
[2] Department of Electrical and Computer Engineering,
Tandon School of Engineering, New York University,
Brooklyn, NY 11201, USA
zjiang@nyu.edu

Abstract. This paper studies the cooperative adaptive cruise control
(CACC) problem of connected vehicles with unknown nonlinear dynamics. Different from the existing literature on CACC, a data-driven optimal control policy is developed by global adaptive dynamic programming
(GADP). Interestingly, the developed control policy achieves global stabilization of the nonlinear vehicular platoon system in the absence of the
a priori knowledge of system dynamics. Numerical simulation results are
presented to validate the effectiveness of the developed approach.

Keywords: Global adaptive dynamic programming · Cooperative adaptive cruise control · Nonlinear optimal control · Connected and
autonomous vehicles

1 Introduction

The construction of intelligent transportation systems (ITS) attracts considerable attention because of the increasing number of traffic accidents and conges-
tions all over the world. Adaptive/autonomous cruise control (ACC), an important design issue in the study of ITS, concerns how to automatically regulate
the dynamics of individual vehicles by measuring the headway and velocity via
on-board sensors [1,2]. Thanks to the dramatic development of wireless communication technologies, the cooperative adaptive cruise control (CACC) [3] is
believed realizable in the near future. Compared with ACC, the CACC has the
potential to further increase road safety and traffic throughput, reduce impact
of transportation on the environment, and refine passengers' comfort since it has
better predictive, communicative and collaborative abilities.

The issues of traffic throughput improvement and fuel usage reduction are
essential for both development and deployment of the CACC. An intuitive way to
tackle these issues is to design optimal feedback control laws by minimizing some

© Springer International Publishing AG 2017
D. Liu et al. (Eds.): ICONIP 2017, Part VI, LNCS 10639, pp. 122–129, 2017.
https://doi.org/10.1007/978-3-319-70136-3_13

predefined cost, that employs the idea from the optimal control theory. However, most of the existing optimal CACC approaches are model-based. Considering the presence of linear or nonlinear unmodeled dynamics and unknown human and mechanical parameters in the platoon system, classical adaptive control approaches have been applied to achieve the stabilization of connected vehicle systems [4,5]. Unfortunately, adaptive systems designed this way often do not address the optimality issue and are known to respond slowly to parameter variations from the plant. As a result, it is of both theoretical and practical importance to develop online adaptive and optimal approaches for connected vehicles.

Adaptive dynamic programming (ADP) is a non-model-based method to solve data-driven online optimal control problems. It is a new trend in control theory how to design model-free, online adaptive optimal controllers with assured stability for linear and nonlinear dynamic systems [6–9]. An extension to the adaptive optimal output regulation problem (or asymptotic tracking with disturbance rejection) can be found in [10]. In the recent paper [11], we have developed a new global adaptive dynamic programming (GADP) method, a tool for global optimal control of continuous-time nonlinear systems without using neural network approximation.

The main purpose of this paper is to solve the data-driven adaptive optimal control problem for a platoon of connected vehicles. As compared with the huge number of control solutions on the vehicular platoon, our paper offers the following novel contributions. First, because of the strongly nonlinear dynamics of the platooning vehicles, we are not aware of any global solutions to adaptive optimal control of connected vehicles with unknown dynamics. Second, different from existing adaptive control approaches of connected vehicles, the online GADP approach presented in this paper provides a systematic way to learn a near-optimal controller iteratively via real-time state/input data collected from system trajectories. Third, the neural network approximation is avoided for this kind of high-order connected vehicle systems which dramatically decreases the computational burden. As opposed to our previous work [12] considering a linearized model for a platoon of n human-operated vehicles with an automated vehicle in the tail, we study the case where all the vehicles are fully autonomous with unknown nonlinear polynomial dynamics.

The remainder of this paper is organized as follows. Section 2 provides the detailed formulation of optimal control problem of connected vehicles. The model-based policy iteration is presented in Sect. 3, whereby the online GADP approach for connected vehicle systems is developed in Sect. 4. Section 5 is dedicated to a numerical example demonstrating the benefit of the developed GADP methodology. Finally, conclusions are contained in Sect. 6.

Notations. Throughout this paper, $\mathcal{C}^1$ denotes the set of all continuously differentiable functions. $\mathcal{P}$ indicates the set of all functions in $\mathcal{C}^1$ that are positive definite and proper. Given a vector of polynomials $f(x)$, $\deg(f)$ represents the highest polynomial degree of all the entries in $f(x)$. For any integers $d_2 \geq d_1 > 0$,

$m_{d_1,d_2}(x)$ is the vector of all $\binom{n+d_2}{d_2} - \binom{n+d_1-1}{d_1-1}$ distinct monic monomials in $x \in \mathbb{R}^n$ with degree at least d_1 and at most d_2. $\mathbb{R}[x]_{d_1,d_2}$ denotes the set of all polynomials in $x \in \mathbb{R}^n$ with degree no less than d_1 and no greater than d_2. ∇V is the gradient of a function $V : \mathbb{R}^n \to \mathbb{R}$.

2   Problem Formulation and Preliminaries

In this paper, we consider the longitudinal control of a platoon of n automobile vehicles. For each vehicle $i = 1, 2, \cdots, n$ with $i = 1$ being the leader vehicle, s_i denotes the position of the vehicle. A nonlinear model of the dynamics of the ith vehicle is given by [4,5]

$$\ddot{s}_i = \frac{1}{M_i}(\mu_i - c_i \dot{s}_i^2 - F_i), \tag{1}$$

where c_i, M_i, F_i, μ_i are the effective aerodynamic drag coefficient, the effective inertia, the rolling resistance friction and the propulsive/braking effort on the ith vehicle. For $i = 2, 3, \cdots, n$, let $h_i := s_{i-1} - s_i$ be the headway. Our goal in this paper is to actuate each vehicle at desired headway $h^* > 0$ and velocity $v^* > 0$. Suppose the leader tracks a fictitious vehicle which operates in a constant velocity v^*. Then, the headway of the leader is $h_1 = s_1 - v^* t$. Defining $\tilde{h}_i = h_i - h^*$ and $\tilde{v}_i = v_i - v^*$, then we have the following equation

$$\begin{aligned}
\dot{\tilde{h}}_i &= \tilde{v}_{i-1} - \tilde{v}_i, \\
\dot{\tilde{v}}_i &= f_{i,2}(\tilde{v}_i) + w_i/M_i, \quad i = 1, 2, \cdots, n,
\end{aligned} \tag{2}$$

where $w_i = \mu_i - F_i - (v^*)^2 c_i$ is the control input of vehicle i, $f_{i,2}(\tilde{v}_i) = (-2c_i v^* \tilde{v}_i - c_i \tilde{v}_i^2)/M_i$ and $\tilde{v}_0 = 0$.

Letting $x = [\tilde{h}_1, \tilde{v}_1, \cdots, \tilde{h}_n, \tilde{v}_n]^T \in \mathbb{R}^{2n}$ and $u = [w_1, w_2, \cdots, w_n]^T \in \mathbb{R}^n$, we can write the mathematical model of the vehicular platoon in a compact form

$$\dot{x} = f(x) + Gu. \tag{3}$$

Consider the nonlinear polynomial system (3). The control objective in this paper is to design a control policy u^o that minimizes the following cost

$$J(x_0, u) = \int_0^\infty [Q(x) + u^T Ru]dt \tag{4}$$

where $Q(x)$ is a positive definite polynomial function and R is a symmetric positive definite matrix. The optimal control policy u^o can be achieved by

$$u^o(x) = -\frac{1}{2}R^{-1}G^T \nabla V^o(x) \tag{5}$$

where $V^o(x)$ is solved from the following Hamilton-Jacobi-Bellman (HJB) equation:

$$\nabla V^T(x)f(x) + Q(x) - \frac{1}{4}\nabla V^T(x)GR^{-1}G^T\nabla V(x) = 0 \qquad (6)$$

with the boundary condition $V(0) = 0$.

Generally, the analytical solution of the HJB equation is very difficult to be obtained. In the next section, we recall from [11] a sum of squares (SOS) based policy iteration method to find a suboptimal and globally stabilizing control policy.

3   SOS-Based Nonlinear Policy Iteration

The SOS-based policy iteration solves a relaxed semidefinite programming (SDP) in the policy evaluation step. Let us make the following assumption before expressing the details.

Assumption 1. *There exist smooth mappings* $V_0 : \mathbb{R}^{2n} \to \mathbb{R}, u_1 : \mathbb{R}^{2n} \to \mathbb{R}^n$, *such that* $V_0 \in \mathbb{R}[x]_{2,2r} \cap \mathcal{P}$ *and* $\mathcal{L}(V_0, u_1)$ *is SOS with*

$$\mathcal{L}(V, u) = -\nabla V^T(x)(f(x) + Gu) - Q(x) - u^T Ru, \forall V \in \mathcal{C}^1, \forall u \in \mathbb{R}^n. \qquad (7)$$

The SOS-based policy iteration algorithm is presented as follows.

Algorithm 1. SOS-based Policy Iteration Algorithm

1: Find V_0 and u_1 such that Assumption 1 is satisfied set. $j \leftarrow 1$.
2: **repeat**
3:     Solve an optimal solution p_j to the following optimization program:

$$\min_p \int_\Omega V(x)dx \qquad (8)$$

$$\text{s.t.} \quad \mathcal{L}(V, u_j) \quad \text{and} \quad V_{j-1} - V \quad \text{are} \quad \text{SOS} \qquad (9)$$

where $V = p^T m_{2,2r}(x)$. Denote $V_j = p_j^T m_{2,2r}(x)$
4:     Update the control policy by

$$u_{j+1}(x) = -\frac{1}{2}R^{-1}G^T\nabla V_j(x). \qquad (10)$$

5:     $j \leftarrow j+1$
6: **until** $|p_j - p_{j-1}| < \nu$

Remark 1. The cost function (8) can be described as $\int_\Omega V(x)dx = c^T p$, where $c = \int_\Omega m_{2,2r}dx$ and $p \in \mathbb{R}^{n_{2r}}$ with $n_{2r} = \begin{pmatrix} 2n + 2r \\ 2r \end{pmatrix} - \begin{pmatrix} 2n + 1 \\ 1 \end{pmatrix}$.

The following theorem demonstrates the convergence of Algorithm 1 when being applied to the nonlinear polynomial connected vehicles systems (3).

Theorem 1 ([11]). *Under Assumption 1, the following statements hold for all $j \geq 1$:*

1. *The SOS program (8)–(9) has a nonempty set.*
2. *The closed-loop system comprised of (3) and $u = u_j$ is globally asymptotically stable at the origin.*
3. *$V_j \in \mathcal{P}$ and $\forall x_0 \in \mathbb{R}^{2n}$, $V^o(x_0) \leq V_j(x_0) \leq V_{j-1}(x_0)$.*
4. *There exist $V^*(x)$ satisfying $V^*(x) \in \mathbb{R}[x]_{2,2r} \cap \mathcal{P}$, such that, for any $x_0 \in \mathbb{R}^{2n}$, $\lim\limits_{j \to \infty} V_j(x_0) = V^*(x_0)$.*
5. *Along the solutions of system (3) with $u^* = -\frac{1}{2}R^{-1}G^T \nabla V^*$, we have*

$$0 \leq V^*(x_0) - V^o(x_0) \leq -\int_0^\infty ((\nabla V^*)^T f + Q - \frac{1}{4}(\nabla V^*)^T GR^{-1}G^T \nabla V^*)dt$$

4   GADP for Connected Vehicle Systems

In this section, we develop a data-driven GADP method in this section which is not based on the knowledge of the system dynamics f and G.

To begin with, express the system input as $u = u_j + e$, where u_j is a globally stabilizing feedback control policy and e is a bounded exploration noise. Then, the system (3) is rewritten as

$$\dot{x} = f + G(u_j + e). \tag{11}$$

Remark 2. It has been shown in [11] that if there exists a $V_{j-1} \in \mathcal{P}$ such that $\mathcal{L}(V_{j-1}, u_j) \geq 0$, then the system (11) is forward complete [13]. In other words, for any initial condition $x_0 \in \mathbb{R}^{2n}$ and every bounded input signal e, the corresponding solution of system (11) is defined for all $t \geq 0$.

Under Assumption 1, we have $\mathcal{L}(V_j, u_j) \in \mathbb{R}[x]_{2,2d}, \forall j \geq 1$, if

$$d \geq \frac{1}{2}\max\{\deg(f) + 2r - 1, 2(2r - 1), \deg(Q)\}.$$

It is checkable that $u_i \in \mathbb{R}[x]_{1,d}$. More specifically, there is a matrix $K_i \in \mathbb{R}^{n \times n_d}$ such that $u_i = K_i \boldsymbol{m}_{1,d}(x)$, with $n_d = \binom{2n + d}{d} - \binom{2n + 0}{0}$. Then, along the solutions of the system (11), we have

$$\begin{aligned}
\dot{V} &= \nabla V^T(f + Gu_j) + \nabla V^T Ge \\
&= -Q(x) - u_j^T Ru_j - \mathcal{L}(V, u_j) + \nabla V^T Ge \\
&= -Q(x) - u_j^T Ru_j - l_p^T \boldsymbol{m}_{2,2d}(x) - 2\boldsymbol{m}_{1,d}(x)^T K_p^T Re
\end{aligned} \tag{12}$$

where the vector $l_p \in \mathbb{R}^{n_{2d}}$ and the matrix $K_p \in \mathbb{R}^{n \times n_d}$ with $n_{2d} = \binom{2n + 2d}{2d} -$
$\binom{2n + 1}{1}$ satisfy $\mathcal{L}(V, u_j) = l_p^T m_{2,2d}(x), -\frac{1}{2} R^{-1} G^T \nabla V = K_p m_{1,d}(x)$. Noticing
that $V = p^T m_{2,2r}(x)$, integrating both sides of (12) yields

$$V(x(t_0)) - V(x(t_1)) = \int_{t_0}^{t_1} [Q(x) + u_j^T R u_j + l_p^T m_{2,2d}(x) + 2 m_{1,d}(x)^T K_p^T Re] dt$$

Therefore, one can solve l_p and K_p for the given vector p, with enough collected input/state data. More specifically, define the following vector $\sigma_e \in \mathbb{R}^{n_{2d}+n_d n}$ and matrices $\Phi_j \in \mathbb{R}^{q_j \times (n_{2d}+n_d n)}, \Xi_j \in \mathbb{R}^{q_j}, \Theta_j \in \mathbb{R}^{q_j \times n_{2r}}$,

$$\sigma_e = -[m_{2,2d}^T, 2m_{1,d}^T \otimes (e^T R)]^T, \quad \Phi_j = [\int_{t_{0,j}}^{t_{1,j}} \sigma_e dt, \int_{t_{1,j}}^{t_{2,j}} \sigma_e dt, \cdots, \int_{t_{q_j-1,j}}^{t_{q_j,j}} \sigma_e dt]^T$$

$$\Xi_j = [\int_{t_{0,j}}^{t_{1,j}} (Q(x) + u_j^T R u_j) dt, \int_{t_{1,j}}^{t_{2,j}} (Q(x) + u_j^T R u_j) dt, \cdots, \int_{t_{q_j-1,j}}^{t_{q_j,j}} (Q(x) + u_j^T R u_j) dt]^T$$

$$\Theta_j = [m_{2,2r}|_{t_{0,j}}^{t_{1,j}}, m_{2,2r}|_{t_{1,j}}^{t_{2,j}}, \cdots, m_{2,2r}|_{t_{q_j-1,j}}^{t_{q_j,j}}]^T.$$

Then, we have

$$\Phi_j \begin{bmatrix} l_p \\ \text{vec}(K_p) \end{bmatrix} = \Xi_j + \Theta_j p. \tag{13}$$

Assumption 2. *For all $j = 1, 2, \cdots$, there exists a $q_j^* > 0$ such that for all $q_j > q_j^*$, the rank condition $\text{rank}(\Phi_j) = n_{2d} + n_d n$ holds.*

Now we are ready to give an online GADP Algorithm 2 for connected vehicles, using real-time input/state data along the solutions of connected vehicles. The following theorem discusses the convergence of the Algorithm 2 and the global stability of the closed-loop system.

Theorem 2. *Under Assumptions 1 and 2, the following properties hold.*

1. *The optimization problem (15)–(18) has a nonempty feasible set.*
2. *The sequences $\{V_j\}_{j=1}^{\infty}$ and $\{u_j\}_{j=1}^{\infty}$ satisfy properties 2–5 in Theorem 1.*

Proof. A pair (p_j', K_{pj}') is an optimal solution to the optimization problem (15)–(18) if p_j' is a feasible solution to (8)–(9) and K_{pj} satisfies

$$-\frac{1}{2} R^{-1} G^T \nabla((p_j')^T m_{2,2r}(x)) = K_{pj}' m_{1,d}(x). \tag{14}$$

On the other hand, if p_j' is a feasible solution to (8)–(9), then the pair (p_j', K_{pj}') must be a solution to (15)–(18). Moreover, the cost (8) is equivalent to (15). The optimal solutions solved by Algorithms 1 and 2 are the same at each iteration. Based on Theorem 1, the two properties in Theorem 2 thus hold.

Algorithm 2. Online GADP Algorithm

1: Find V_0 and u_1 such that Assumption 1 is satisfied. Let p_0 be the vector satisfying $V_0 = p_0^T m_{2,2r}(x)$. Set $j \leftarrow 1$ and select a small threshold $\nu > 0$.
2: **repeat**
3:     Apply $u = u_j + e$. Compute Φ_j, Ξ_j, Θ_j until Assumption 2 holds.
4:     Solve an optimal solution (p_j, K_{j+1}) to the following optimization program:

$$\min_{p, K_p} c^T p \tag{15}$$

$$\text{s.t.} \quad \Phi_j \begin{bmatrix} l_p \\ \mathrm{vec}(K_p) \end{bmatrix} = \Xi_j + \Theta_j p \tag{16}$$

$$l_p^T m_{2,2d}(x) \quad \text{is} \quad \text{SOS} \tag{17}$$

$$(p_{j-1} - p)^T m_{2,2r}(x) \quad \text{is} \quad \text{SOS} \tag{18}$$

5:     Update the control policy by $u_{j+1} = K_{j+1} m_{1,d}(x)$.
6:     $j \leftarrow j + 1$
7: **until** $|p_j - p_{j-1}| < \nu$

5 Numerical Examples

In this section, we validate the proposed Algorithm 2 on a platoon of three autonomous vehicles. By using the online GADP Algorithm 2, we update our control policy iteratively from $t = 0\,\mathrm{s}$ to $t = 60\,\mathrm{s}$. In order to show the performance of the learned control policy, we add $\Delta \tilde{h}_i = 8\,\mathrm{m}$ into the headway of each vehicle at $t = 60\,\mathrm{s}$. From Fig. 1, we observe that the updated control policy is able to stabilize the connected vehicle system.

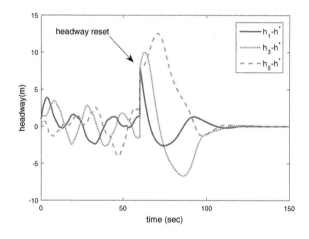

Fig. 1. Headway errors of autonomous vehicles #1-#3

6   Conclusions

This paper has studied the nonlinear and adaptive optimal control problem of connected vehicles, an emerging topic in intelligent transportation systems (ITS). The proposed design scheme avoids relying on the neural network approximation, which highly increases the computational efficiency. Instead of developing a local or semi-global stabilizing controller, this paper achieves global stabilization of nonlinear connected vehicle systems. More importantly, we present a non-model-based, data-driven methodology which is significant for practically connected vehicular platoons with strong model uncertainties. Simulation results show that the presented approach serves as an effective tool to provide online solutions to the data-driven optimal control problem for connected nonlinear vehicular systems.

Acknowledgments. This work has been supported in part by the U.S. National Science Foundation grant ECCS-1501044.

References

1. Ioannou, P.A., Stefanovic, M.: Evaluation of ACC vehicles in mixed traffic: lane change effects and sensitivity analysis. IEEE Trans. Intell. Transp. Syst. **6**(1), 79–89 (2005)
2. Rajamani, R.: Vehicles Dynamics and Control. Springer, New York (2011). doi:10.1007/978-1-4614-1433-9
3. Oncu, S., Ploeg, J., van de Wouw, N., Nijmeijer, H.: Cooperative adaptive cruise control: Network-aware analysis of string stability. IEEE Trans. Intell. Transp. Syst. **15**(4), 1527–1537 (2014)
4. Kwon, J.W., Chwa, D.: Adaptive bidirectional platoon control using a coupled sliding mode control method. IEEE Trans. Intell. Transp. Syst. **15**(5), 2040–2048 (2014)
5. Swaroop, D., Hedrick, J.K., Choi, S.B.: Direct adaptive longitudinal control of vehicle platoons. IEEE Trans. Veh. Technol. **50**(1), 150–161 (2001)
6. Jiang, Y., Jiang, Z.P.: Robust Adaptive Dynamic Programming. Wiley-IEEE Press, Hoboken (2017)
7. Lewis, F.L., Vrabie, D.: Reinforcement learning and adaptive dynamic programming for feedback control. IEEE Circuits Syst. Mag. **9**(3), 32–50 (2009)
8. Gao, W., Jiang, Y., Jiang, Z.P., Chai, T.: Output-feedback adaptive optimal control of interconnected systems based on robust adaptive dynamic programming. Automatica **72**, 37–45 (2016)
9. Gao, W., Huang, M., Jiang, Z.P., Chai, T.: Sampled-data-based adaptive optimal output-feedback control of a 2-degree-of-freedom helicopter. IET Control Theory Appl. **10**(12), 1440–1447 (2016)
10. Gao, W., Jiang, Z.P.: Adaptive dynamic programming and adaptive optimal output regulation of linear systems. IEEE Trans. Autom. Control **61**(12), 4164–4169 (2016)
11. Jiang, Y., Jiang, Z.P.: Global adaptive dynamic programming for continuous-time nonlinear systems. IEEE Trans. Autom. Control **60**(11), 2917–2929 (2015)
12. Gao, W., Jiang, Z.P., Ozbay, K.: Data-driven adaptive optimal control of connected vehicles. IEEE Trans. Intell. Transp. Syst. **18**(5), 1122–1133 (2017)
13. Angeli, D., Sontag, E.D.: Forward completeness, unboundedness observability, and their Lyapunov characterizations. Syst. Control Lett. **38**(4–5), 209–217 (1999)

Energy Management of Planetary Gear Hybrid Electric Vehicle Based on Improved Dynamic Programming

Xin Tang[1], Liang Chu[1], Nan Xu[1(✉)], Di Zhao[1], and Zhe Xu[2]

[1] State Key Laboratory of Automotive Simulation and Control,
Jilin University, Changchun 130022, China
nanxu@jlu.edu.cn
[2] R&D Center, China FAW Group Corporation,
Changchun 130011, China

Abstract. Dynamic Programming (DP) is often used in hybrid electric vehicle (HEV) energy management strategies to optimize fuel economy performance. When using the DP algorithm to find the optimal State of Charge (SOC) trajectory, we found that the optimal SOC trajectory is more than one. However, the traditional DP algorithm can just show one optimal path from masses of optimal SOC trajectories. In this paper, we proposed an improved DP algorithm to find a region which is made up of many optimal trajectories. Planetary gear hybrid electric vehicles as a research object in this paper and obtained the better fuel economy by the proposed algorithm with a lower computational complexity. At the same time, this method can offer the possibility for the further optimization of the vehicle ride comfort in the future.

Keywords: Energy management · Dynamic programming algorithm · Optimal trajectories · HEV

1 Introduction

In the process of vehicle development, hybrid electric vehicle (HEV) is a new type of vehicle which can effectively reduce emission, fuel consumption and it has many advantages of the traditional vehicle at the same time [1–3]. The control strategy for energy management of HEV is a research focus in recent years [4]. Many scholars have put forward a lot of control theories and ideas, including neural network [5, 6], fuzzy control [7], dynamic programming [8, 9] and so on. However, only dynamic programming (DP) can obtain the global optimal solution under the known driving cycle, and it can be used as a reference for other control strategies and real-time experiments [10, 11]. Its core idea is to find the optimal trajectory path that the control target is optimal under the given cycle conditions [12, 13]. The principle of dynamic programming allows finding the optimal State of Charge (SOC) trajectory of the battery to minimize the fuel consumption on a drive cycle known in advance.

© Springer International Publishing AG 2017
D. Liu et al. (Eds.): ICONIP 2017, Part VI, LNCS 10639, pp. 130–138, 2017.
https://doi.org/10.1007/978-3-319-70136-3_14

However, DP has the heavy computational burden because it would calculate every possible state. Therefore, the DP algorithm should be improved [14]. Some researchers considered the maximum charge and discharge current limit of the battery, thus greatly reducing the search area of DP [15]. Some researchers also improved the current limit of battery which is applied to discrete state variables, and this way can greatly reduce the search range of each step [16, 17]. Some scholars improved the algorithm by using three different structures of oil storage and compared their computation time [18]. Thus, in order to improve the efficiency of DP algorithm, this paper considers the battery charge and discharge current limiting to reduce the whole search scope and the range of state transition for each step.

Before using the DP algorithm, stage fuel consumption(the fuel consumption caused by each state transition) should be calculated. When calculating the stage fuel consumption, it is found that some fuel consumption values at each stage are equal. It enlightens the core of this study that the optimal trajectory may be more than one. By marking the SOC state points at these optimal trajectories, an optimal trajectory region can be formed. We can find a path in the premise of satisfying the lowest fuel consumption in this region. Moreover, other vehicle performance under this path is relatively better. For example, in the optimal trajectory region, we can find a better trajectory with lower fuel consumption, better shifting smoothness, or good handling stability at the same time. Selecting this trajectory as the control trajectory of vehicle will improve the performance of the whole vehicle. It is of great significance to the research of HEV energy management strategy in the future. The Sect. 2 of this paper introduces a planetary gear Hybrid Electric Vehicle model. The Sect. 3 focuses on the application of dynamic programming method in hybrid vehicle energy management. The Sect. 4 is about the solution for the optimal trajectory region problem.

2 Planetary Gear Hybrid Electric Vehicle Model

The structure of HEV with planetary gear is shown in Fig. 1. It is composed of an engine and two motors/generators, respectively called MG1 and MG2. The MG1 and the MG2 are connected with the battery through an inverter. The inverter is designed to achieve the transition between direct current and alternating current. The planetary gear enables the engine and the two motors to work in series, parallel and mixed states according to different driving conditions, so that the vehicle can optimize the fuel economy while satisfying the driving performance [19, 20]. The power separation device adopts a planetary gear mechanism, and the engine is connected with a planet carrier. The motor/generator MG1 is connected with the sun wheel, and the motor/generator MG2 is connected with the gear ring.

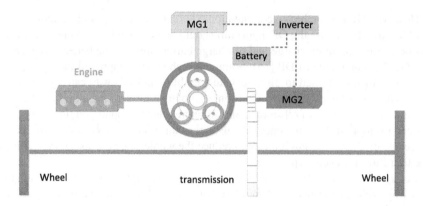

Fig. 1. Powertrain structure of hybrid vehicle

The power flow of the whole vehicle structure and the planetary gear are analyzed, and the power balance equation of the transmission system is obtained as follows:

$$
\begin{aligned}
P_{req} &= P_e + P_{MG1} + P_{MG2} \\
P_{req} &= T_{wh}\omega_{wh} \\
P_e &= T_e\omega_e \\
P_{MG1} &= T_{MG1}\omega_{MG1} \\
P_{MG2} &= T_{MG2}\omega_{MG2} \\
P_{bat} &= P_{MG1}/\eta_{MG1} + P_{MG2}/\eta_{MG2}
\end{aligned}
\tag{1}
$$

Where P_{req} is the demand power, P_e is engine power, P_{MG1} is MG1 power, P_{MG2} is MG2 power, P_{bat} is battery charging and discharging power, η_{MG1} is MG1 efficiency and η_{MG2} is MG2 efficiency. The motor efficiency is obtained from the motor's MAP by searching the speed and torque of motor.

2.1   Vehicle Demand Power Model

When the vehicle is running, the vehicle is subjected to traction, wind resistance, roll resistance, and slope resistance. Assuming that all forces act on a particle, force analysis is carried out to obtain the demand torque.

$$
\begin{cases}
\frac{T_{wh}}{R_{wh}} = \mu_r Mg \cos\theta + \frac{1}{2}\rho C_D A v^2 + \delta M \frac{dv}{dt} \\
v = 3.6\omega_{wh}T_{wh}
\end{cases}
\tag{2}
$$

Where T_{wh} is the wheel torque, R_{wh} is the wheel radius, μ_r is the rolling resistance coefficient, M is the total mass of vehicle, ρ is the air density, C_D is the air resistance coefficient, A is the windward area, v is the vehicle speed, δ is the rotational mass conversion factor and θ is the road slope.

2.2 Battery Power Model

The battery model is equivalent to a simple internal resistance model, and the formula for calculating the battery power is obtained:

$$V_{\text{ter}} = V_{oc} - \Delta SOC(2 \cdot 3600 \cdot R \cdot Q_{\text{bat}}) \tag{3}$$

$$P_{\text{bat}} = \frac{V_{oc}^2 - V_{\text{ter}}^2}{4R} \tag{4}$$

Where V_{oc} is the terminal voltage of the battery, V_{ter} is the terminal voltage of battery groups, ΔSOC is the change of SOC, Q_{bat} battery capacity.

2.3 Motor Power Model

Through the force analysis of the vehicle engine, MG1 and MG2, the relationship between the torque and the speed of planetary gear, the engine, MG1 and MG2 can be obtained:

$$\begin{cases} \omega_c(R_r + R_s) = \omega_r R_r + \omega_s R_s \\ T_r = \frac{R_r}{R_r + R_s} T_c, T_s = \frac{R_s}{R_r + R_s} T_c \\ J_{MG1}\dot{\omega}_{MG1} = T_s + T_{MG1} \\ J_e\dot{\omega}_e = T_e - T_c \\ J_{MG2}\dot{\omega}_{MG2} = T_r + T_{MG2} - T_{wh}/g_f \\ \omega_c = \omega_e, \omega_s = \omega_{MG1} \\ \omega_r = \omega_{MG2} = vg_f/R_{wh} \end{cases} \tag{5}$$

Where J_{MG1} is the MG1 rotary inertia, J_e is the engine rotary inertia, J_{MG2} is the MG2 rotary inertia and g_f is the transmission ratio. Where ω_s is the solar wheel speed, ω_r is the gear ring speed and ω_c is the planetary wheel speed. Where T_{MG1} is the MG1 output torque, T_{MG2} is the MG2 output torque, T_e is the engine output torque, T_s is solar wheel torque, T_r is gear ring torque and T_c is planetary wheel torque.

3 Energy Management Using Dynamic Programming for HEV

The core of HEV control is minimizing fuel consumption under the known driving cycle. The fuel consumption not only concern with engine but also with the battery and electric motor. Therefore, in this paper, we selected the SOC as the state variable. We can transform the control problem into the multi-stage decision problem. In every stage of SOC discrete points we would find the optimal decision until the end point to form the optimal decision sequence. Finally we would find an optimal SOC trajectory in SOC feasible region. This line represents the minimum fuel consumption of the vehicle. Using the principle of dynamic programming, the problem formulation is the following:

Firstly, the state variable SOC feasible region is determined, and the maximum charge and discharge current of the battery is taken into account. The upper and lower bound of the region (*SOC_max, SOC_min*) are determined by the battery characteristics. Common values are (40% and 80% [15]). The SOC feasible region of the boundary can be determined by SOC initial value (*SOC_start*), SOC termination value (*SOC_terminal*), *SOC_max* and *SOC_min* together. Thereafter, the search of the algorithm is carried out within this feasible region.

In addition, we would ensure the SOC maximum discrete interval and certain calculation accuracy. In this paper, the maximum charge and discharge current of the battery is taken into account when determining the maximum discrete interval. That provides convenience for future calculation. The feasible region after discretization is shown in the Fig. 2.

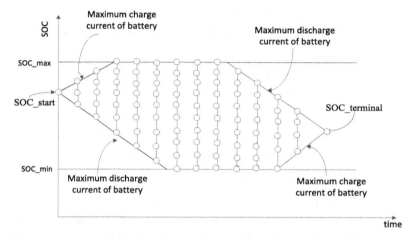

Fig. 2. The feasible region after discretization

To determine the final optimal path, it is necessary to know the fuel consumption generated by each state transition. Only between these discrete points is the fuel consumption in every stage calculated. The interval between the two sampling time points constitutes a stage. The fuel consumption at each stage corresponds to the change in the amount of two SOC state points (ΔSOC) at this stage and the speed at that moment. ΔSOC is defined as:

$$\Delta SOC = SOC(j, i) - SOC(k, i - 1) \qquad (6)$$

Where $SOC(j, i)$ is *jth* SOC state point from the top of the SOC feasible region to its bottom at the current *ith* moment, $SOC(k, i - 1)$ is *kth* point from the top of the SOC feasible region to its bottom at the $i - 1$ moment. The phase transition between the points also need to meet the maximum charge and discharge current limit, SOC state point can only be transferred from $SOC(k, i - 1)$ to $SOC(j, i)$ as the red line connection between the two state points in Fig. 3. The oil consumption in this transition can be obtained by ΔSOC combined with the formula in Sect. 2.

In order to increase the efficiency of the algorithm as much as possible, this paper chooses to record the fuel consumption at each stage in the form of three-dimensional fuel consumption matrix $fuel\_stage(k,j,i)$. When calculating the stage fuel consumption, we find that many stages have some equivalent stage fuel consumption. This question will be solved in detail in Sect. 4.

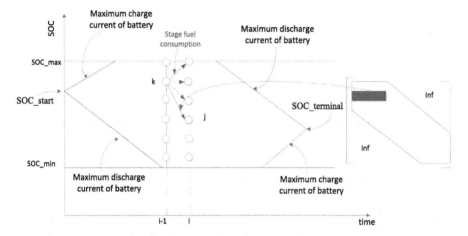

Fig. 3. Calculation of stage fuel consumption

Dynamic programming to find the optimal path is given by:
for i = from start to terminal moment

$$fuel\_total(j,i) = \min(fuel\_stage(k,j,i) + fuel\_total(k,i-1))$$

Where $fuel\_total(j,i)$ is the fuel consumption between $SOC(j,i)$ and SOC_start. Where $fuel\_total(k,i-1)$ is the fuel consumption between $SOC(k,i-1)$ and SOC_start.

4   Improved Dynamic Programming

The dynamic programming algorithm can find the global optimal solution, but the computing time is too long and neglected the existence of the other potential optimal paths. An improved dynamic programming is proposed in this section. The core idea of this theory is to find the optimal path region and all points which all shortest paths pass through. Based on the above ideas, this paper innovatively uses a matrix to record the points which the all optimal trajectories pass through.

Improved dynamic programming can be said: we would record the $SOC(k,i-1)$ when $fuel\_total(j,i) \leq (fuel\_stage(k,j,i) + fuel\_total(k,i-1))$. Within the SOC feasible region, we mark the SOC state points of all the best paths through as shown in the red dots below Fig. 4. These red SOC state points form a region in which the best SOC trajectories for all optimal fuel consumption trajectories can be found.

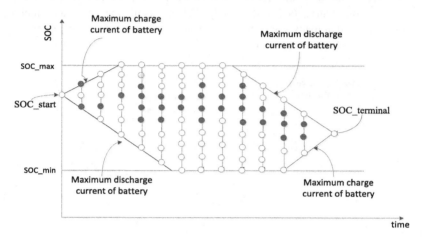

Fig. 4. SOC optimal trajectory area (Color figure online)

We verify the effectiveness of the DP algorithm using Matlab program in Urban Dynamometer Driving Schedule (UDDS), Extra Urban Driving Cycle (EUDC) and Japan-1015 driving cycle. We contrasted DP and instantaneous optimization method in Matlab. The instantaneous optimization method is performed by Advisor in Matlab. The DP program and Advisor have the same parameters. The simulation result of engine fuel consumption is shown in Fig. 5. We can see that DP can get better fuel consumption compared with instantaneous optimization method.

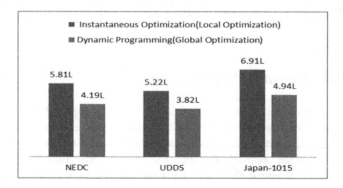

Fig. 5. Fuel consumption per 100 km(L)

5   Conclusion

For HEV energy management, traditional DP has long computation time and may neglect the existence of the other potential optimal paths when searching for the global optimum fuel consumption. In order to solve these problems, this paper has introduced the limitation of the charge/discharge current and use 3D matrix to storage stage fuel consumption. In this paper, we proposed an improved DP algorithm which can find every state point through all the optimal trajectories, and they form an optimal trajectory region instead of only one optimal trajectory. And the feasibility of the improved DP algorithm is verified. The determination of the optimal trajectory region will provide support for other performance optimizations and control parameters matching in the future. It is of great significance to the research of HEV energy management strategy in the future.

Acknowledgement. Supported by Jilin Province Science and Technology Development Fund (20150520115JH); Energy Administration of Jilin Province [2016]35.

References

1. Husain, I.: Electric and hybrid vehicles: design fundamentals. Circ. Dev. Magaz. IEEE **21**(5), 26–27 (2005)
2. Chan, C.C.: The state of the art of electric and hybrid vehicles. Proc. IEEE **90**(12), 247–275 (2002)
3. Miller, J.M.: Propulsion Systems for Hybrid Vehicles. Iet Digital Library (2004)
4. Barsali, S.: A control strategy to minimize fuel consumption of series hybrid electric vehicles. IEEE Trans. Energy Convers. **19**(1), 187–195 (2004)
5. Qi, Y., Wang, W.: Neural network and efficiency-based control for dual-mode hybrid electric vehicles. In: Control Conference, pp. 8103–8108, Hangzhou (2015)
6. Wang, D., et al.: Optimal control of unknown nonaffine nonlinear discrete-time systems based on adaptive dynamic programming. Automatica **48**(8), 1825–1832 (2012)
7. Pan, Y.: Study on Fuzzy Logic Based Energy Management Strategy of ISG-type Speed Coupling Hybrid Electric Vehicle Based on DP Algorithm. Chongqing University (2013)
8. Squartini, S., et al.: Computational energy management in smart grids. Neurocomputing **170**(11), 267–269 (2015)
9. Perez, L., et al.: Optimization of power management in a hybrid electric vehicle using dynamic programming. Math. Comput. Simul. **73**(1), 244–254 (2006)
10. Bellman, R.: Dynamic Programming. Princeton University Press (1957). 12(5), pp. 317–348
11. Kirk, D.E.: Optimal control theory. Am. Math. Monthly **83**(4), 261–288 (2012)
12. Perez, L.V., et al.: Optimization of power management in an hybrid electric vehicle using dynamic programming. Math. Comput. Simul. **73**(11), 244–254 (2006)
13. Vinot, E., et al.: Improvement of an EVT-based HEV using dynamic programming. IEEE Trans. Veh. Technol. **63**(11), 40–50 (2014)
14. Shen, C.Y., et al.: Control strategy of series hybrid electric vehicle based on improved dynamic programming. Control Theory Appl. **28**(3), 427–432 (2011)
15. Chau, K., et al.: Overview of power management in hybrid electric vehicles. Energy Convers. Manag. **43**(15), 1953–1968 (2002)

16. Sciarretta, A., et al.: Control of hybrid electric vehicles. IEEE Control Syst. **27**(12), 60–70 (2007)
17. Vinot, E.: Time reduction of the dynamic programming computation in the case of hybrid vehicle, pp. 1–15 (2014)
18. Scordia, J., et al.: Global optimization of energy management laws in hybrid vehicles using dynamic programming. Int. J. Veh. Des. **39**(14), 349–367 (2005)
19. Jeanneret, B., et al.: New Hybrid concept simulation tools, evaluation on the Toyota Prius car. In: 16th International electric vehicle symposium, Beijing (1999)
20. Trigui, R., et al.: Global Forward-Backward Approach for a Systematic Analysis and Implementation, Estoril, Portugal (2004)

Consensus Maneuvering of Uncertain Nonlinear Strict-Feedback Systems

Yibo Zhang[1], Dan Wang[1($\boxtimes$)], and Zhouhua Peng[1,2]

[1] School of Marine Engineering, Dalian Maritime University,
Dalian 116026, People's Republic of China
{zhangyibo1991,zhpeng}@dlmu.edu.cn, dwangdl@gmail.com
[2] Department of Computer Science, City University of Hong Kong,
Kowloon Tong, Hong Kong

Abstract. In this paper, a consensus maneuvering problem is investigated for uncertain nonlinear systems in strict-feedback form. Consensus maneuvering controllers are developed based on a modular design approach. Specifically, an estimation module is proposed, where a neural network is employed for approximating the unknown nonlinearities. Then, a controller module is designed based on a modified dynamic surface control method. Finally, the input-to-state stability of the close-loop system is analyzed via cascade theory, and the consensus maneuvering error is proved to converge to a residual set.

Keywords: Consensus maneuvering · Strict-Feedback system · Uncertain nonlinearity · Modular design approach

1 Introduction

In recent years, cooperative control has drawn tremendous attention due to its wide applications in military and civilian [1]. Cooperative control means that behaviors of all individuals among a group move towards a common goal. Cooperative control includes various topics such as consensus, flocking, and coverage. In particular, consensus is to force followers to track a desired trajectory [2–9]. The system models considered in previous contributions include first-order and second-order systems [2,3], higher-order systems [4,5], strict-feedback systems [6,7], Lagrangian systems [8,9]. It is notable that dynamic models [2–4,8,9] and time-related functions [5–7] are used to lead the group in the previous works. Generally, these contributions [2–9] are summed up as a consensus tracking problem. During the consensus tracking, the update of the leading trajectory is deterministic and time-related. However, in some cases, the leading trajectory can be a parameterized path. Furthermore, the information flow between the leader and followers is directed and short of a feedback from the followers to the leader.

Consensus maneuvering includes a geometric objective and a dynamic objective. The geometric objective is to force followers to steer along a parameterized path. The dynamic objective is to satisfy a desired dynamic behavior. The related

© Springer International Publishing AG 2017
D. Liu et al. (Eds.): ICONIP 2017, Part VI, LNCS 10639, pp. 139–146, 2017.
https://doi.org/10.1007/978-3-319-70136-3_15

study can be found in [10]. In [10], the maneuvering problem of strict-feedback system is studied. It is worth mentioning that the maneuvering controller in [10] is developed for a single system and is a centralized one in nature.

In this paper, we aim to address the consensus maneuvering problem of uncertain nonlinear systems in strict-feedback form. The path information is only available for a small number of followers and communication links among followers are directed. A modular design method is applied to develop consensus maneuvering controllers [11–14]. Specifically, an estimation module is proposed, where the neural network is utilized to approximate uncertain nonlinearities. Next, a controller module is developed based on a modified dynamic surface control (DSC) method [15]. A second-order linear tracking differentiator (TD) is used to extract the time derivative of virtual law accurately. The close-loop system is proved to be input-to-state stable (ISS).

The paper is organized as follows. Section 2 introduces some preliminaries and problem formulation. Main results of this paper are presented in Sect. 3. Section 4 concludes this paper.

2   Preliminaries and Problem Formulation

2.1   Graph Theory

Let $\mathcal{G} = (\mathcal{V}, \varepsilon, \Lambda)$ denote a directed graph. $\mathcal{V} = (n_1, ..., n_M)$ is a vertex set, where n_i is a node of the ith follower. $\varepsilon = \{(n_i, n_j) \in \mathcal{V} \times \mathcal{V}\}$ is an edge set, where $(n_i, n_j) \in \varepsilon$ represents a direct information access from agent i to agent j. $\Lambda = [a_{i,j}] \in \mathbb{R}^{M \times M}$ is an adjacency matrix, where if $(n_i, n_j) \in \varepsilon$, then $a_{i,j} > 0$, otherwise if $(n_i, n_j) \notin \varepsilon$ or $i = j$, then $a_{i,j} = 0$. There exists a spanning tree in the graph $\mathcal{G}$ if there exists a root node and a direct information flow from the root node to other nodes in the graph $\mathcal{G}$. The Laplacian matrix $L = [l_{i,j}] \in \mathbb{R}^{M \times M}$ is defined as $L = D - \Lambda$, and the degree matrix $D = \mathrm{diag}(d_1, ..., d_M)$ with $d_i = \sum_{j \in \mathcal{N}_i} a_{i,j}$, where $\mathcal{N}_i = \{j | (n_i, n_j) \in \varepsilon\}$ represents the neighbor set of node i. The leader adjacency matrix is defined as $B = \mathrm{diag}(b_1, ..., b_M)$, where $b_i > 0$ if and only if the ith agent has access to the leader, otherwise $b_i = 0$. There exists a directed spanning tree among followers, and the root node can receive the information from the leader.

2.2   Problem Formulation

Consider an uncertain nonlinear strict-feedback system consisting of M followers labeled as 1 to M and a virtual leader. The dynamics of the ith followers is:

$$\begin{cases} \dot{x}_{i,k} = x_{i,k+1} + f_k\left(\bar{x}_{i,k}\right) \\ \dot{x}_{i,n} = u_i + f_n\left(\bar{x}_{i,n}\right), \end{cases} \tag{1}$$

where $i = 1, 2, ..., M$, $k = 1, ..., n - 1$, $x_{i,k} \in \mathbb{R}$, $x_{i,n} \in \mathbb{R}$, $\bar{x}_{i,k} = [x_{i,1}, ..., x_{i,k}]^T \in \mathbb{R}^k$, $\bar{x}_{i,n} = [x_{i,1}, ..., x_{i,n}]^T \in \mathbb{R}^n$, $u_i \in \mathbb{R}$ is the control input, $y_i = x_{i,1} \in \mathbb{R}$ is the output, $f_k(\bar{x}_{i,k}) \in \mathbb{R}$ and $f_n(\bar{x}_{i,n}) \in \mathbb{R}$ denote the uncertain nonlinearities.

The virtual leader moves along a parameterized path $y_r(\theta)$ and θ signifies a path variable.

The objective of consensus maneuvering is to design adaptive control laws u_i for each follower. The output trajectory of each follower y_i nearly converges to the leader $y_r(\theta)$, and the derivative of path variable $\dot{\theta}$ nearly converges to a desired velocity signal v_s.

Assumption 1. *Assume that $y_r(\theta)$ and its derivative $y_r^\theta(\theta)$ are bounded.*

Lemma 1. *Assume that the nonlinear function $f_i(\xi_i)$ can be approximated by a neural network (NN) as follows:*

$$f_i(\xi_i) = W_i^T \varphi(\xi_i) + \varepsilon_i(\xi_i), \forall \xi_i \in \Omega, \tag{2}$$

where W_i is a weight matrix that satisfies $\|W_i\|_F \le W^*$ with W^* being a positive constant, ξ_i is the input of NN, Ω is a compact set, a vector form $\varphi(\xi)$ is $\varphi(\xi_i) = [\varphi_1(\xi_i), ..., \varphi_m(\xi_i), \varphi_0]$ that satisfies $\|\varphi(\xi_i)\| \le \varphi_i^*$ with φ_i^* being a positive constant and a positive bias φ_0, $\varphi(\cdot)$ is an activation function of NN, and $\varepsilon_i(\xi_i)$ is an approximation error, where satisfies $\|\varepsilon_i(\xi_i)\| \le \varepsilon^*$ with ε^* being a positive constant.

3   Consensus Maneuvering Controllers Design and Analysis

3.1   Estimation Module Design

Step 1. At first, a consensus maneuvering error $z_{i,1}$ is defined as

$$z_{i,1} = \sum_{j=1}^{M} a_{i,j}(y_i - y_j) + b_i(y_i - y_r(\theta)). \tag{3}$$

The time derivative of $z_{i,1}$ along (1) satisfies

$$\dot{z}_{i,1} = (d_i + b_i) x_{i,2} - \sum_{j=1}^{M} a_{i,j} x_{j,2} - b_i y_r^\theta(\theta)\dot{\theta} + g(x_{i,1}, x_{j,1}), \tag{4}$$

where $d_i = \sum_{j=1}^{M} a_{i,j}$, and $g(x_{i,1}, x_{j,1}) = (d_i + b_i)f_{i,1}(x_{i,1}) - b_i f_{j,1}(x_{j,1})$.

An NN is employed to approximate the uncertain nonlinearity $g(x_{i,1}, x_{j,1})$:

$$g(x_{i,1}, x_{j,1}) = W_{i,1}^T \varphi_{i,1}(\xi_{i,1}) + \varepsilon_{i,1}, \tag{5}$$

where $W_{i,1}$ is a weight matrix, $\varphi_{i,1}(\cdot)$ is an activation function, $\xi_{i,1} = [x_{i,1},\ x_{j,1}]^T$ is the input of NN with $j \in \mathcal{N}_i$, and $\varepsilon_{i,1}$ is an approximation error. An estimator for (4) is designed as:

$$\begin{aligned}
\dot{\hat{z}}_{i,1} = {} & (d_i + b_i) x_{i,2} - \sum_{j=1}^{M} a_{i,j} x_{j,2} - b_i y_r^\theta(\theta)\dot{\theta} + \hat{W}_{i,1}^T \varphi_{i,1}(\xi_{i,1}) \\
& - (\zeta_{i,1} + \rho_{i,1})(\hat{z}_{i,1} - z_{i,1}),
\end{aligned} \tag{6}$$

where $\zeta_{i,1} \in \mathbb{R}$ and $\rho_{i,1} \in \mathbb{R}$ are positive constants, and $\hat{W}_{i,1}$ is the estimate of $W_{i,1}$. An update law of $\hat{W}_{i,1}$ is designed as follows:

$$\dot{\hat{W}}_{i,1} = -\Gamma_{i,1}(\varphi_{i,1}(\xi_{i,1})\tilde{z}_{i,1} + \lambda_{i,1}\hat{W}_{i,1}), \tag{7}$$

where $\Gamma_{i,1} \in \mathbb{R}$ and $\lambda_{i,1} \in \mathbb{R}$ are positive constants, and $\tilde{z}_{i,1} = \hat{z}_{i,1} - z_{i,1}$.

Step k. Similar to *Step 1*, an error surface $z_{i,k}$ is defined as $z_{i,k} = x_{i,k} - v_{i,k-1}$, where $v_{i,k-1}$ comes from the virtual control law $\alpha_{i,k-1}$ passing through a second-order linear TD. Take the derivative of $z_{i,k}$ along (1) satisfying:

$$\dot{z}_{i,k} = x_{i,k+1} + f_k(\bar{x}_{i,k}) - v_{i,k-1}^d, \tag{8}$$

where $v_{i,k-1}^d$ is the derivative of $v_{i,k-1}$. The uncertain nonlinearity $f_k(\bar{x}_{i,k})$ is approximated by an NN:

$$f_k(\bar{x}_{i,k}) = W_{i,k}^T\varphi_{i,k}(\xi_{i,k}) + \varepsilon_{i,k}, \tag{9}$$

where $W_{i,k}$ is a weight matrix, $\varphi_{i,k}(\cdot)$ is an activation function, $\xi_{i,k} = \bar{x}_{i,k}$ is the input of NN, and $\varepsilon_{i,k}$ is an approximation error. An estimator for (8) is designed as:

$$\dot{\hat{z}}_{i,k} = x_{i,k+1} + \hat{W}_{i,k}^T\varphi_{i,k}(\xi_{i,k}) - (\zeta_{i,k} + \rho_{i,k})(\hat{z}_{i,k} - z_{i,k}) - v_{i,k-1}^d, \tag{10}$$

where $\zeta_{i,k} \in \mathbb{R}$ and $\rho_{i,k} \in \mathbb{R}$ are positive constants, and $\hat{W}_{i,k}$ is the estimate of $W_{i,1}$. An update law of $\hat{W}_{i,k}$ is designed as follows:

$$\dot{\hat{W}}_{i,k} = -\Gamma_{i,k}(\varphi_{i,k}(\xi_{i,k})\tilde{z}_{i,k} + \lambda_{i,k}\hat{W}_{i,k}), \tag{11}$$

where $\Gamma_{i,k} \in \mathbb{R}$ and $\lambda_{i,k} \in \mathbb{R}$ are positive constants, and $\tilde{z}_{i,k} = \hat{z}_{i,k} - z_{i,k}$.

Step n. Similar to *Step k*, an error surface $z_{i,n}$ is defined as $z_{i,n} = x_{i,n} - v_{i,n-1}$, where $v_{i,n-1}$ comes from the virtual control law $\alpha_{i,n-1}$ passing through a second-order linear TD. The derivative of $z_{i,n}$ along (1) satisfies:

$$\dot{z}_{i,n} = u_i + f_{i,n}(\bar{x}_{i,n}) - v_{i,n-1}^d; \tag{12}$$

where $v_{i,n-1}^d$ is the derivative of $v_{i,n-1}$. Similarly, let $f_n(\bar{x}_{i,n})$ approximated by an NN as follows:

$$f_n(\bar{x}_{i,n}) = W_{i,n}^T\varphi_{i,n}(\xi_{i,n}) + \varepsilon_{i,n}, \tag{13}$$

where $W_{i,n}$ is a weight matrix, $\varphi_{i,n}(\cdot)$ is an activation function, $\xi_{i,n} = \bar{x}_{i,n}$ is the input of NN, and $\varepsilon_{i,n}$ is an approximation error. An estimator for (12) is designed as:

$$\dot{\hat{z}}_{i,n} = u_i + \hat{W}_{i,n}^T\varphi_{i,n}(\xi_{i,n}) - (\zeta_{i,n} + \rho_{i,n})(\hat{z}_{i,n} - z_{i,n}) - v_{i,n-1}^d, \tag{14}$$

where $\zeta_{i,n} \in \mathbb{R}$ and $\rho_{i,n} \in \mathbb{R}$ are positive constants, and $\hat{W}_{i,n}$ is the estimate of $W_{i,n}$. An update law of $\hat{W}_{i,n}$ is designed as follows:

$$\dot{\hat{W}}_{i,n} = -\Gamma_{i,n}(\varphi_{i,n}(\xi_{i,n})\tilde{z}_{i,n} + \lambda_{i,n}\hat{W}_{i,n}), \tag{15}$$

where $\Gamma_{i,n} \in \mathbb{R}$ and $\lambda_{i,n} \in \mathbb{R}$ are positive constants, and $\tilde{z}_{i,n} = \hat{z}_{i,n} - z_{i,n}$.

Let $\tilde{W}_{i,1} = \hat{W}_{i,1} - W_{i,1}$, $\tilde{W}_{i,k} = \hat{W}_{i,k} - W_{i,k}$, and $\tilde{W}_{i,n} = \hat{W}_{i,n} - W_{i,n}$, and $\tilde{Z}_i = [\tilde{z}_{i,1}, ..., \tilde{z}_{i,n}]^T$, $\tilde{W}_i = [\tilde{W}_{i,1}, ..., \tilde{W}_{i,n}]^T$, $\varepsilon_i = [\epsilon_{i,1}, ..., \epsilon_{i,n}]^T$, $\varphi_i =$ diag$(\varphi_{i,1}(\xi_{i,1}), ..., \varphi_{i,n}(\xi_{i,n}))$, $\hat{W}_i = [\hat{W}_{i,1}, ..., \hat{W}_{i,n}]^T$, $\Gamma_i =$ diag$(\Gamma_{i,1}, ..., \Gamma_{i,n})$, $\rho_i =$ diag$(\rho_{i,1}, ..., \rho_{i,n})$, $\zeta_i =$ diag$(\zeta_{i,1}, ..., \zeta_{i,n})$, and $\lambda_i =$ diag$(\lambda_{i,1}, ..., \lambda_{i,n})$. The estimation subsystem is obtained as:

$$\begin{cases} \dot{\tilde{Z}}_i = -(\rho_i + \zeta_i)\tilde{Z}_i + \varphi_i^T \hat{W}_i - \epsilon_i \\ \dot{\tilde{W}}_i = -\Gamma_i(\varphi_i \tilde{Z}_i + \lambda_i \hat{W}_i). \end{cases} \tag{16}$$

The stability property of the subsystem (16) is presented as follows:

Lemma 2. *The subsystem (16) is ISS with state vectors being $\tilde{Z}_i$ and $\tilde{W}_i$, and input vectors being W_i and ϵ_i, where $W_i = [W_{i,1}, ..., W_{i,n}]^T$.*

Proof. Let a Lyapunov function for system (16) be $V_{i,p} = \frac{1}{2}(\tilde{Z}_i^T \tilde{Z}_i + \tilde{W}_i^T \Gamma_i^{-1} \tilde{W}_i)$. The time derivative of $V_{i,p}$ along (16) satisfies $\dot{V}_{i,p} = -\tilde{Z}_i^T(\rho_i + \zeta_i)\tilde{Z}_i - \tilde{Z}_i^T \varepsilon_i - \tilde{W}_i^T \lambda_i \tilde{W}_i - \tilde{W}_i^T \lambda_i W_i \leq -\lambda_{\min}(\rho_i + \zeta_i)\|\tilde{Z}_i\|^2 - \lambda_{\min}(\lambda_i)\|\tilde{W}_i\|^2 + \|\tilde{Z}_i\|\|\varepsilon_i\| + \lambda_{\max}(\lambda_i)\|\tilde{W}_i\|\|\varepsilon_i\| \leq -c_1\|E\|^2 + \|E\|\|h\|$, where $E = [\|\tilde{Z}_i\|, \|\tilde{W}_i\|]^T$, $h = [\|\varepsilon_i\|, \lambda_{\max}(\lambda_i)\|W_i\|]^T$, and $c_1 = \min\{\lambda_{\min}(\rho_i + \zeta_i), \lambda_{\min}(\lambda_i)\}$. Since $\|E\| \geq (\|\varepsilon_i\| + \lambda_{\max}(\lambda_i)\|W_i\|)/\eta_1 c_1 \geq \|h\|/\eta_1 c_1$ makes $\dot{V}_{i,p} \leq -(1 - \eta_1)c_1\|E\|^2$, where $0 < \eta_1 < 1$, it follows that the system (16) is ISS. Consider $\kappa_{ip1}(s) = \lambda_{\min}(P)s^2/2$ and $\kappa_{ip2}(s) = \lambda_{\max}(P)s^2/2$ with $P = $ diag$[1, \Gamma^{-1}]$, and there exists a $\mathcal{KL}$ function $\alpha_1(\cdot)$ and $\mathcal{K}_\infty$ functions $\kappa^{\epsilon_i}(\cdot)$ and $\kappa^{W_i}(\cdot)$ satisfying $\|E(t)\| \leq \alpha_1(\|E(t_0)\|, t - t_0) + \kappa^{\epsilon_i}(\|\epsilon_i\|) + \kappa^{W_i}(\|W_i\|)$, where $\kappa^{\epsilon_i}(s) = (s\sqrt{\lambda_{\max}(P)})/(\eta_1 c_1 \sqrt{\lambda_{\min}(P)})$ and $\kappa^{W_i}(s) = (s\lambda_{\max}(\lambda_i)\sqrt{\lambda_{\max}(P)})/(\eta_1 c_1 \sqrt{\lambda_{\min}(P)})$.

3.2   Controller Module Design

Step 1. In the previous subsection, we obtained the consensus maneuvering error $z_{i,1}$ and its estimate $\hat{z}_{i,1}$. Let the time derivative of path variable θ be $\dot{\theta} = v_s - \omega$. The derivative of estimated consensus maneuvering error $\hat{z}_{i,1}$ is rewritten as:

$$\dot{\hat{z}}_{i,1} = (d_i + b_i) x_{i,2} - \sum_{j=1}^{M} a_{i,j} x_{j,2} - b_i y_r^\theta(\theta)(v_s - \omega) + \hat{W}_{i,1}^T \varphi_{i,1}(\xi_{i,1}) - (\zeta_{i,1} + \rho_{i,1})\tilde{z}_{i,1}, \tag{17}$$

where v_s is a desired velocity, and ω is a speed assignment.

From (17), a virtual control law $\alpha_{i,1}$ is designed as follows:

$$\alpha_{i,1} = \frac{1}{d_i + b_i}\{-\rho_{i,1}z_{i,1} + \sum_{j=1}^{M} a_{i,j} x_{j,2} + b_i y_r^\theta(\theta)v_s - \hat{W}_{i,1}^T \varphi_{i,1}(\xi_{i,1})\}. \tag{18}$$

In DSC method [15], the first-order filter is used to take the derivative of $\alpha_{i,1}$. In this paper, the second-order linear TD is used to replace the first-order filter as follows:

$$\begin{cases} \dot{v}_{i,1} = v_{i,1}^d \\ \dot{v}_{i,1}^d = -\gamma_{i,1}^2[(v_{i,1} - a_{i,1}) + 2(v_{i,1}^d/\gamma_{i,1})], \end{cases} \tag{19}$$

where $\gamma_{i,1} \in \mathbb{R}$ is a positive constant. Substituting (18) and (17) into (6), one has:

$$\dot{\hat{z}}_{i,1} = -\rho_{i,1}\hat{z}_{i,1} - \zeta_{i,1}\tilde{z}_{i,1} + b_i y_r^\theta(\theta)\omega. \tag{20}$$

Step k. At first, an estimated error surface $\hat{z}_{i,k}$ is defined as:

$$\hat{z}_{i,k} = \hat{x}_{i,k} - v_{i,k-1}. \tag{21}$$

The derivative of $\hat{z}_{i,k}$ (10) has been obtained in the previous subsection. To stabilize (10), a virtual control law $\alpha_{i,k}$ is designed as follows:

$$\alpha_{i,k} = -\rho_{i,k}z_{i,k} + v_{i,k-1}^d - \hat{W}_{i,k}^T\varphi_{i,k}(\xi_{i,k}). \tag{22}$$

Let $\alpha_{i,k}$ pass through a second-order linear TD:

$$\begin{cases} \dot{v}_{i,k} = v_{i,k}^d \\ \dot{v}_{i,k}^d = -\gamma_{i,k}^2[(v_{i,k} - a_{i,k}) + 2(v_{i,k}^d/\gamma_{i,k})], \end{cases} \tag{23}$$

where $\gamma_{i,k} \in \mathbb{R}$ is a positive constant. Substituting (22) into (10), $\hat{z}_{i,k}$ is changed as:

$$\dot{\hat{z}}_{i,k} = -\rho_{i,k}\hat{z}_{i,k} - \zeta_{i,k}\tilde{z}_{i,k}. \tag{24}$$

Step n. Similar to the *Step k*, an estimated error surface $\hat{z}_{i,n}$ is defined $\hat{z}_{i,n} = \hat{x}_{i,n} - v_{i,n-1}$, The derivative of $\hat{z}_{i,n}$ has been obtained via the previous results (14), and a consensus maneuvering control law u_i is designed as follows:

$$u_i = -\rho_{i,n}z_{i,n} + v_{i,n-1}^d - \hat{W}_{i,n}^T\varphi_{i,n}(\xi_{i,n}). \tag{25}$$

Substituting (25) into (19), one has:

$$\dot{\hat{z}}_{i,n} = -\rho_{i,n}\hat{z}_{i,n} - \zeta_{i,n}\tilde{z}_{i,n}. \tag{26}$$

3.3   Path Update Law Design

In the consensus maneuvering problem, the update of parameterized path is affected by the leader and adjacent followers. Therefore, the speed assignment ω is designed as:

$$\omega = -\mu \sum_{i=1}^M b_i y_r^\theta(\theta)\hat{z}_{i,1}, \tag{27}$$

where $\mu \in \mathbb{R}$ is a positive constant. Let $\hat{Z}_i = [\hat{z}_{i,1}, ..., \hat{z}_{i,n}]^T$, and $Q = [b_i y_r^\theta(\theta)\omega, 0, ..., 0]^T$, and on the basis of (20), (24), (26) and (27), the error subsystem is expressed as:

$$\begin{cases} \dot{\hat{Z}}_i = -\rho_i\hat{Z}_i - \zeta_i\tilde{Z}_i + Q \\ \omega = -\mu \sum_{i=1}^M b_i y_r^\theta(\theta)\hat{z}_{i,1}. \end{cases} \tag{28}$$

The following lemma presents the stability of the subsystem (28):

Lemma 3. *The subsystem (28) with the state vector being $\hat{Z}_i$ and the input vector being $\tilde{Z}_i$ is ISS.*

Proof. Consider a Lyapunov function $V_d = \frac{1}{2}\hat{Z}_i^T \hat{Z}_i$, and its time derivative is put into: $\dot{V}_d \leq -\hat{Z}_i^T \rho_i \hat{Z}_i - \hat{Z}_i^T \zeta_i \tilde{Z}_i \leq -\lambda_{\min}(\rho_i)\|\hat{Z}_i\|^2 + \lambda_{\max}(\zeta_i)\|\hat{Z}_i\|\|\tilde{Z}_i\|$. Note that $\|\hat{Z}_i\| \geq \lambda_{\max}(\zeta_i)\|\tilde{Z}_i\|/\eta_2 \lambda_{\min}(\rho_i)$ makes $\dot{V}_d \leq -\lambda_{\min}(\rho_i)(1-\eta_2)\|\hat{Z}_i\|^2$, where $0 < \eta_2 < 1$. It follows that the system (28) is ISS, and there exists a $\mathcal{KL}$ function $\alpha_2(\cdot)$ and a $\mathcal{K}_\infty$ function $\kappa^{\tilde{Z}_i}(\cdot)$ such that $\|\hat{Z}_i(t)\| \leq \alpha_2(\|\hat{Z}_i(t_0)\|, t - t_0) + \kappa^{\tilde{Z}_i}(\|\tilde{Z}_i\|)$, where the gain function is given by $\kappa^{\tilde{Z}_i}(s) = (\lambda_{\max}(\zeta_i)s)/(\eta_2 \lambda_{\min}(\rho_i))$.

The stability of cascade system is presented in Theorem 1.

Theorem 1. *Under Assumptions 1–2, the system cascaded by (16) and (28) is ISS. Moreover, the consensus maneuvering error between the leader and followers converges to a residual set.*

Proof. By utilizing the conclusion of *Lemma* 1 in [14], the system cascaded by (16) and (28) is proved to be ISS. According to conclusions of *Lemmas* 2 and 3, $\|\tilde{Z}_i\|$ and $\|\hat{Z}_i\|$ are ultimately bounded.

Since $\|Z_i\| = \|\hat{Z}_i - \tilde{Z}_i\| \leq \|\hat{Z}_i\| + \|\tilde{Z}_i\|$, it follows that $\|Z_i\|_{t\to\infty} \leq \|\hat{Z}_i\|_{t\to\infty} + \|\tilde{Z}_i\|_{t\to\infty} \leq [\sqrt{\lambda_{\max}(P)}/(\eta_1 c_1 \sqrt{\lambda_{\min}(P)})][\varepsilon^* + \lambda_{\max}(\lambda_i)W^*][1 + \lambda_{\max}(\zeta_i)/(\eta_2 \lambda_{\min}(\rho_i))]$. Therefore, it is proved that the consensus maneuvering error between the leader and followers converges to a residual set.

4   Conclusion

In this paper, the consensus maneuvering problem of uncertain nonlinear strict-feedback systems guided by a virtual leader steering along a parameterized path is addressed. The information flow among followers is directed, and only a small number of followers can receive the leader information. The modular design method is employed to develop consensus maneuvering controllers, where the estimation module and the controller module are designed separately. The cascade system is to be proved ISS via cascade theory, and the consensus maneuvering error is proved to converge to a residual set.

Acknowledgments. The work of D. Wang was supported in part by the National Natural Science Foundation of China under Grants 61673081, and in part by the Fundamental Research Funds for the Central Universities under Grant 3132016313, and in part by the National Key Research and Development Program of China under Grant 2016YFC0301500. The work of Z. Peng was supported in part by the National Natural Science Foundation of China under Grants 51579023, and in part by the China Postdoctoral Science Foundation under Grant 2015M570247, and in part by High Level Talent Innovation and Entrepreneurship Program of Dalian under Grant 2016RQ036.

References

1. Ren, W., Bread, R.: Distributed Consensus in Multi-vehicle Cooperative Control. Springer, London (2008). doi:10.1007/978-1-84800-015-5
2. Jadbabaie, A., Jie, L., Morse, A.S.: Coordination of groups of mobile autonomous agents using nearest neighbor rules. IEEE Trans. Autom. Control **48**(6), 988–1001 (2003)
3. Olfati-Saber, R., Fax, J.A., Murray, R.M.: Consensus and cooperation in networked multi-agent systems. Proc. IEEE **95**(1), 215–233 (2007)
4. Ren, W., Moore, K.L., Chen, Y.Q.: High-order and model reference consensus algorithms in cooperative control of multivehicle systems. J Dyn. Syst-T. ASME. **129**(5), 678–688 (2007)
5. Wen, G., Hu, G., Yu, W., Cao, J., Chen, G.: Consensus tracking for higher-order multi-agent systems with switching directed topologies and occasionally missing control inputs. Syst. Control Lett. **62**(12), 1151–1158 (2013)
6. Yoo, S.J.: Distributed consensus tracking for multiple uncertain nonlinear strict-feedback systems under a directed graph. IEEE Trans. Neural Networks Learn. Syst. **24**(4), 666–672 (2013)
7. Wang, W., Wang, D., Peng, Z., Li, T.: Prescribed performance consensus of uncertain nonlinear strict-feedback systems with unknown control directions. IEEE Trans. Syst. Man Cybern. Syst. **46**(9), 1279–1286 (2016)
8. Ren, W.: Distributed leaderless consensus algorithms for networked Euler-Lagrange systems. Int. J. Control **82**(11), 2137–2149 (2009)
9. Mei, J., Ren, W., Ma, G.: Distributed containment control for Lagrangian networks with parameteric uncertaities under a directed graph. Automatica **48**(4), 653–659 (2012)
10. Skjetne, R., Fossen, T.I., Kokotovi, P.V.: Robust output maneuvering for a class of nonlinear systems. Automatica **40**(3), 373–383 (2004)
11. Peng, Z., Wang, J., Wang, D.: Distributed maneuvering of autonomous surface vehicles based on neurodynamic optimization and fuzzy approximation. IEEE Trans. Control Syst. Technol. (2017). doi:10.1109/TCST.2017.2699167
12. Peng, Z., Wang, J., Wang, D.: Distributed containment maneuvering of multiple marine vessels via neurodynamics-based output feedback. IEEE Trans. Ind. Electron. **64**(5), 3831–3839 (2017)
13. Peng, Z., Wang, J., Wang, D.: Containment maneuvering of marine surface vehicles with multiple parameterized paths via spatial-temporal decoupling. IEEE/ASME Trans. Mechatron. **22**(2), 1026–1036 (2017)
14. Peng, Z., Wang, D., Wang, J.: Cooperative dynamic positioning of multiple marine offshore vessels: a modular design. IEEE/ASME Trans. Mechatron. **21**(3), 1210–1221 (2016)
15. Wang, D., Huang, J.: Neural network-based adaptive dynamic surface control for a class of uncertain nonlinear systems in strictfeedback form. IEEE Trans. Neural Networks **6**(1), 195–202 (2005)

Partially-Directed-Topology-Based Consensus Control for Linear Multi-agent Systems

Chunping Shi[1], Qinglai Wei[2,3]([⊠]), and Derong Liu[4]

[1] School of Automation and Engineering, University of Science
and Technology Beijing, Beijing 100083, China
[2] The State Key Laboratory of Management and Control for Complex Systems,
Institute of Automation, Chinese Academy of Sciences, Beijing 100190, China
qinglai.wei@ia.ac.cn
[3] University of Chinese Academy of Sciences, Beijing 100049, China
[4] School of Automation, Guangdong University of Technology,
Guangzhou 510006, China

Abstract. This paper focuses on designing an adaptive controller for solving consensus control problem of continues-time linear multi-agent systems over partially directed topology. The main contribution of this paper is that the multi-agent system under partially directed topology is designed. Using the designed controller, the presented system is stable, which is proved in this paper. The convergence is also analysed. Finally, a simulation study is given to show its effectiveness.

Keywords: Multi-agent system · Consensus control · Partially directed topology · External disturbance

1 Introduction

In recent years, due to the applications of multi-agent systems, more and more researchers have begun their research in this field and have obtained many remarkable achievements [1–4]. The critical issue from the consensus control is to design a control protocol to enable the common states of the agents to reach an agreement [5]. Over the last decade, the consensus control problem has been extensively investigated by using many control methods, such as adaptive control [6–10], observer-based control, ADP [11–15] and so on.

Some preliminary results about the consensus control under fixed topology have been reported in [16–18]. In [17], the joint connectivity was a key condition to the leader-following consensus. Moreover, different static and dynamic consensus protocols were designed in [19], where the knowledge of the communication graph was required to determine the bound of the coupling weights. There are also many aspects for us to research though the consensus control has reached so many achievements. For example, in actual environment the external disturbance is unavoidable when designing a controller. Therefore, the controller is designed to solve the situation in this paper.

© Springer International Publishing AG 2017
D. Liu et al. (Eds.): ICONIP 2017, Part VI, LNCS 10639, pp. 147–156, 2017.
https://doi.org/10.1007/978-3-319-70136-3_16

Inspired by the existing work, based on the multi-agent system under undi-rected topology [20], we design a control protocol with partially directed topol-ogy. As shown in Fig. 1, the leader is globally reachable. The information between agents may not be able to pass each other completely in real environment. Hence, the theorem mentioned in this paper can be used to solve the actual problem.

The rest of this paper is organised as follows. In Sect. 2, graphs and prelim-inaries of multi-agent systems are presented. The consensus problem of multi-agent systems is introduced in Sect. 3. In Sect. 4, consensus control with partially directed topology is described. A simulation is shown in Sect. 5. In Sect. 6, a brief conclusion is given.

2   Graphs and Preliminaries of Multi-agent Systems

We can model the topology in a system by using graph theory which consists of N agents. Let $G = (V, E, \Delta)$ be an N-directed graph, where $V = \{v_1, v_2, \cdots, v_N\}$ is a nonempty finite set. $E \subseteq V \times V$ is a set of edges or arcs. The edges of G are denoted by e_{ij}. The weighted adjacency matrix $\Delta = [a_{ij}]$ is defined such that a_{ij} is positive, i.e., $a_{ij} > 0$ if and only if $e_{ij} \in E$. Moreover, we assume that $a_{ii} = 0$ for all i. If there is information flowing from vertex i to vertex j, $a_{ij} > 0$, otherwise, $a_{ij} = 0$. Laplacian matrix $L = \mathbb{D} - \Delta$, $\mathbb{D} = [\mathbb{D}_{ij}]$ is a diagonal matrix, $\mathbb{D}_{ii} = \sum\limits_{j=1}^{N} a_{ij}$. Therefore, the Laplacian matrix $L = [l_{ij}]$ can be written as

$$l_{ij} = \begin{cases} \sum\limits_{k=1, k \neq i}^{n} a_{ik}, & i = j, \\ -a_{ij}, & i \neq j. \end{cases}$$

According to the definition of L, the row sum of each row of the Laplacian matrix L is zero. A directed graph contains a directed spanning tree if there exists a directed path from the root to every other vertex in the graph.

For the multi-agent system with a leader and N followers, let 0 represent the leader and $1, 2, ..., N$ represent N followers, respectively. Define a diagonal matrix $D = \text{diag}[d_i], i = 1, 2, ..., N$. $d_i > 0$ if it is connected between the leader and the ith follower, otherwise, $d_i = 0$. G is defined on the vertices $0, 1, ..., N$.

3   The Consensus Problem of Multi-agent Systems

Consider the multi-agent system with an active leader indexed by 0 and N agents defined by $1, 2, ..., N$. In the graph G, the dynamics of the ith agent is represented as

$$\dot{z}_i(t) = A z_i(t) + B u_i(t) + \phi_i(t, z_i(t)) v(t), \quad i = 1, 2, ..., N, \tag{1}$$

where $z_i \in \mathbb{R}^n, i = 1, 2, ..., N$ is the state of the ith agent, and $u_i \in \mathbb{R}^m, i = 1, 2, ..., N$ is the control input of the ith agent, which can only use local infor-mation of its neighbours and itself. $A \in \mathbb{R}^{n \times n}$ and $B \in \mathbb{R}^{n \times m}$ are constant real matrices. $\phi_i(\cdot,\cdot) : \mathbb{R} \times \mathbb{R}^n \to \mathbb{R}^n$ is the external disturbance function vector and $v(t)$ is Gauss white noise generated by Brown motion $\omega(t)$. Therefore, the Eq. (1) can be written as

$$\mathrm{d}z_i(t) = \big[Az_i(t) + Bu_i(t)\big]\mathrm{d}t + \phi_i(t, z_i(t))\mathrm{d}\omega(t), \quad i = 1, 2, ..., N, \tag{2}$$

where $\omega(t)$ is a one-dimensional matrix and $E\{\omega(t)\} = 0$, where $E\{\cdot\}$ represents the expectation. The dynamic of the leader indexed by 0 is represented as

$$\mathrm{d}z_0(t) = Az_0(t)\mathrm{d}t + \phi_0(t, z_0(t))\mathrm{d}\omega(t), \tag{3}$$

where z_0 is the state of the leader. The leader is independent of others so that there is no control input. For further study, some assumptions are introduced.

Assumption 1. The pair (A, B) is stabilizable.

Assumption 2. The Lipschitz condition for the external disturbance function vector $\phi_i(\cdot,\cdot) : \mathbb{R}^n, i = 0, 1, ..., N$ is that there is a constant matrix θ satisfying the following inequality for all $x, y \in \mathbb{R}^n$

$$\|\phi_i(t, x) - \phi_0(t, y)\|^2 \le (x - y)^\mathsf{T}\theta(x - y). \tag{4}$$

Assumption 3. The leader represented by vertex 0 is globally reachable.

4   Consensus Control with Partially Directed Topology

In this section, the control protocol of the multi-agent system with partially directed topology shown in Fig. 1 is designed. The designed protocol satisfies the condition that the closed-loop system is stabilized.

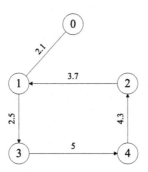

Fig. 1. The partially directed topology of multi-agent system

The distributed adaptive controller is represented as

$$u_i = K\Big[\sum_{j=1}^{N} \beta_{ij}a_{ij}(z_i - z_j) + \beta_i d_i(z_i - z_0)\Big],$$

$$\dot{\beta}_{ij} = \eta_{ij}a_{ij}(z_i - z_j)^\mathsf{T}\Gamma(z_i - z_j), \tag{5}$$

$$\dot{\beta}_i = \eta_i d_i(z_i - z_0)^\mathsf{T}\Gamma(z_i - z_0), \quad i = 1, 2, ..., N,$$

where u_i is the control input. K is the feedback gain of the multi-agent system. β_{ij} is the time-varying coupling weight between agent i and agent j and β_i is the time-varying coupling weight between agent i and agent 0. Because of $a_{ij} \neq a_{ji}$, the values of $\dot{\beta}_{ij}$ and $\dot{\beta}_{ji}$ are different, i.e., $\dot{\beta}_{ij} \neq \dot{\beta}_{ji}$. Besides, η_{ij} and η_i are both positive constants.

Let $e_i = z_i - z_0$ and $e = (e_1^\mathsf{T}, e_2^\mathsf{T}, \cdots, e_N^\mathsf{T})$. Thus, the state error e_i can be written as

$$de_i(t) = Ae_i dt + Bu_i(t)dt + \tilde{\phi}_i(t, e_i)d\omega(t), \qquad (6)$$

where $\tilde{\phi}_i(t, e_i) = \phi_i(t, z_i(t)) - \phi_0(t, z_0(t))$. Substituting (5) into (6), we obtain

$$de_i(t) = Ae_i dt + BK\left[\sum_{j=1}^{N} \beta_{ij} a_{ij}(e_i - e_j) + \beta_i d_i e_i\right]dt \qquad (7)$$
$$+ \tilde{\phi}_i(t, e_i)d\omega(t), i = 1, 2, ..., N.$$

Define a positive symmetric matrix S, which is the solution to the following inequality

$$\begin{aligned} S &< rI, \\ SA + A^\mathsf{T}S - 2SBB^\mathsf{T}S + r\theta &< 0, \end{aligned} \qquad (8)$$

where $r > 0$ is a tuning parameter. The feedback gain matrix is given as

$$K = -B^\mathsf{T}S. \qquad (9)$$

The constant gain matrix in (5) is represented as

$$\Gamma = SBB^\mathsf{T}S. \qquad (10)$$

The matrix H defined by $H = L + D$ is asymmetric because of the asymmetry of matrix L. We can obtain $\Gamma \geq 0$ from (10). Hence, the coupling weights β_{ij} and β_i are nondecreasing. In summary, the consensus problem can be solved by the adaptive controller (5) if the state error e converges to zero in the mean-square sense.

Theorem 1. *Assume that the Assumptions 1–3 hold and the multi-agent system is given by (2) and (3). Then, the consensus control problem can be solved by the controller protocol (5).*

Proof. Consider the following Lyapunov function candidate for states error system (7)

$$V(t) = \sum_{i=1}^{N} e_i^\mathsf{T} S e_i + \sum_{i=1}^{N} \sum_{j=1, j\neq i}^{N} \frac{(\beta_{ij} - \alpha)^2}{\eta_{ij}} + \sum_{i=1}^{N} \frac{(\beta_i - \alpha)^2}{\eta_i}, \qquad (11)$$

where α is a constant. By using (7), the derivative of $V(t)$ can be calculated as

$$dV(t) = \sum_{i=1}^{N} 2e_i{}^{\mathsf{T}}Sde_i(t) + \sum_{i=1}^{N} \tilde{\phi}_i^{\mathsf{T}}(t, e_i)S\tilde{\phi}_i(t, e_i)dt$$
$$+ 2\sum_{i=1}^{N}\sum_{j=1,j\neq i}^{N} \frac{(\beta_{ij} - \alpha)}{\eta_{ij}}d\beta_{ij}(t) + \sum_{i=1}^{N} \frac{2(\beta_i - \alpha)}{\eta_i}d\beta_i(t). \tag{12}$$

According to (7), (12) can be derived as

$$dV(t) = 2\sum_{i=1}^{N} e_i^{\mathsf{T}}SAe_idt + \sum_{i=1}^{N} \tilde{\phi}_i^{\mathsf{T}}(t, e_i)S\tilde{\phi}_i(t, e_i)dt + 2\sum_{i=1}^{N} e_i^{\mathsf{T}}S\tilde{\phi}_i(t, e_i)d\omega(t)$$
$$- 2\alpha\sum_{i=1}^{N}\sum_{j=1}^{N} a_{ij}e_i^{\mathsf{T}}SBB^{\mathsf{T}}S(e_i - e_j)dt - 2\alpha\sum_{i=1}^{N} d_ie_i^{\mathsf{T}}SBB^{\mathsf{T}}Se_idt$$
$$+ \sum_{i=1}^{N}\sum_{j=1}^{N} 2(\beta_{ji} - \alpha)a_{ji}e_i^{\mathsf{T}}SBB^{\mathsf{T}}S(e_i - e_j)dt. \tag{13}$$

Under the Assumption 2, we can get

$$\sum_{i=1}^{N} \tilde{\phi}_i^{\mathsf{T}}(t, e_i)S\tilde{\phi}_i(t, e_i)dt \leq r\sum_{i=1}^{N} \tilde{\phi}_i^{\mathsf{T}}(t, e_i)\tilde{\phi}_i(t, e_i)dt$$
$$\leq r\sum_{i=1}^{N} e_i^{\mathsf{T}}\theta e_idt, \tag{14}$$

where r is the maximum eigenvalue of the matrix S and $E\{\omega(t)\} = 0$. Then, substituting (14) into (13) and using the matrix L, we can get

$$dE\{V(t)\} \leq E\Big\{ \sum_{i=1}^{N} e_i^{\mathsf{T}}(2SA + r\theta)e_idt - 2\alpha\sum_{i=1}^{N}\sum_{j=1}^{N} H_{ij}e_i^{\mathsf{T}}SBB^{\mathsf{T}}Se_jdt$$
$$+ 2\sum_{i=1}^{N} M_ie_i^{\mathsf{T}}SBB^{\mathsf{T}}Se_idt - 2\sum_{i=1}^{N}\sum_{j=1}^{N} M_{ji}e_i^{\mathsf{T}}SBB^{\mathsf{T}}Se_jdt \Big\}, \tag{15}$$

where H_{ij} denotes the (i, j)th entry of the matrix $H = L + D \in \mathbb{R}^{N\times N}$. Let $M_{ji} = (\beta_{ji} - \alpha)a_{ji}$ and $M_i = \sum_{j=1}^{N} M_{ji}$. Denote $M^1 = \mathrm{diag}(M_1, M_2, \cdots, M_N) \in \mathbb{R}^{N\times N}$ and $M^2 = [M_{ji}] \in \mathbb{R}^{N\times N}$, $i, j = 1, 2, ..., N$. (15) can be rewritten as

$$dE\{V(t)\} \leq E\Big\{ e^{\mathsf{T}}\Big[I_N \otimes (SA + A^{\mathsf{T}}S + r\theta)$$
$$- 2(\alpha H - M^1 + M^2) \otimes SBB^{\mathsf{T}}S\Big]edt \Big\}. \tag{16}$$

Let $\alpha H - M^1 + M^2 = U^{\mathsf{T}} \Lambda U$, where U is an orthogonal matrix and we assume that Λ exists. Denoting $\delta = (U \otimes I_n)e$, the formula of (16) becomes

$$
\begin{aligned}
\mathrm{d}E\{V(t)\} &\leq E\left\{ \delta^{\mathsf{T}} \left[I_N \otimes (A^{\mathsf{T}}S + SA + r\theta) - 2\alpha\Lambda \otimes SBB^{\mathsf{T}}S \right] \delta \mathrm{d}t \right\} \\
&\leq E\left\{ \sum_{i=1}^{N} \delta_i^{\mathsf{T}} \left(A^{\mathsf{T}}S + SA - 2\alpha\lambda_i SBB^{\mathsf{T}}S + r\theta \right) \delta_i \mathrm{d}t \right\},
\end{aligned}
\tag{17}
$$

where $\lambda_i, i = 1, 2, ..., N$ are the eigenvalues of matrix $\alpha H - M^1 + M^2$. If $\alpha\lambda_i \geq 1, i = 1, 2, \cdots, N$ hold, according to (8), (17) becomes

$$
\frac{\mathrm{d}E\{V(t)\}}{\mathrm{d}t} < 0.
\tag{18}
$$

It is noted that $\mathrm{d}E\{V(t)\} < 0$ if $\delta \neq 0$ holds, which implies that $e \neq 0$ is also satisfied. Then, $V(t)$ is a decreasing function and bounded in the mean square. The matrix Γ is not a negative definite matrix so that β_{ij} and β_i can not decrease. In order to make $\alpha\lambda_i \geq 1$ hold for $i = 1, 2, ..., N$, the constant α can be large enough. Thus, the β_{ij} and β_i can converge to finite constants. It means that the system (7) can be globally stable so that all the following agents can follow the leader.

5   Simulation

In this paper, the partially directed topology of multi-agent system is strongly connected. A simulation study is given to explain the Theorem mentioned above (Figs. 2, 3, 4 and 5).

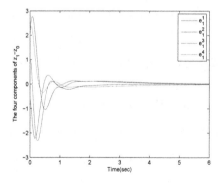

Fig. 2. The error trajectories of e_1 in Example 1

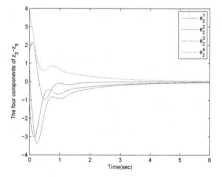

Fig. 3. The error trajectories of e_2 in Example 1

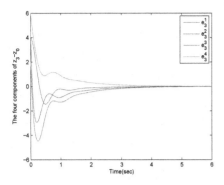
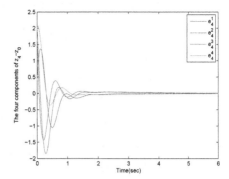

Fig. 4. The error trajectories of e_3 in Example 1

Fig. 5. The error trajectories of e_4 in Example 1

Example 1. Consider a multi-agent system with 4 followers represented by 1, 2, 3, 4 and a leader represented by 0. The dynamics of the ith agent is described as (2) and (3) with

$$A = \begin{bmatrix} -6 & -3 & 7 & 5 \\ -3 & -7 & 0 & -8 \\ -4 & 2 & -3 & -5 \\ -3 & 1 & 2 & 0 \end{bmatrix}, \quad B = \begin{bmatrix} 1 \\ 2 \\ 4 \\ 3 \end{bmatrix}.$$

We can get the Laplacian matrix of G and the adjacency matrix of the leader from the Fig. 1.

$$L = \begin{bmatrix} 2.5 & 0 & -2.5 & 0 \\ -3.7 & 3.7 & 0 & 0 \\ 0 & 0 & 5 & -5 \\ 0 & -4.3 & 0 & 4.3 \end{bmatrix}, \quad D = \begin{bmatrix} 2.1 & 0 & 0 & 0 \\ 0 & 0 & 0 & 0 \\ 0 & 0 & 0 & 0 \\ 0 & 0 & 0 & 0 \end{bmatrix}.$$

The state of multi-agent system is $z_i(t) = \begin{bmatrix} z_{i1}(t), z_{i2}(t), z_{i3}(t), z_{i4}(t) \end{bmatrix}^\mathsf{T}$. For simulation, the initial states are represented by $z_0 = \begin{bmatrix} 2, 3.5, 4, 6 \end{bmatrix}^\mathsf{T}$, $z_1 = [4.2, 2.9, 5, 8]^\mathsf{T}$, $z_2 = \begin{bmatrix} 3.6, 2.5, 5, 10 \end{bmatrix}^\mathsf{T}$, $z_3 = \begin{bmatrix} 6, 8, 6, 12 \end{bmatrix}^\mathsf{T}$, $z_4 = \begin{bmatrix} 2.4, 5.2, 6, 8 \end{bmatrix}^\mathsf{T}$. The external disturbance function is $\phi(t, z_i) = [1.3cos(z_{i1}(t)), 1.2cos(z_{i2}(t)), 1.4cos(z_{i3}(t)), 2cos(z_{i4}(t))]^\mathsf{T}$ (Figs. 6 and 7).

By Matlab, we get the solution of (8)–(10)

$$S = \begin{bmatrix} 0.1914, & -0.0216, & 0.0025, & -0.0150 \\ -0.0216, & 0.1970, & -0.0113, & -0.0471 \\ -0.0025, & -0.0113, & 0.1565, & -0.0776 \\ -0.0150, & -0.0471, & -0.0776, & 0.3241 \end{bmatrix},$$

$$K = \begin{bmatrix} -0.0932, & -0.1859, & -0.3681, & -0.5527 \end{bmatrix},$$

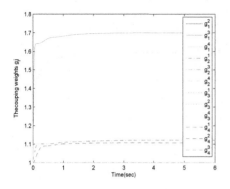

Fig. 6. The coupling weights trajectories of β_{ij} in Example 1

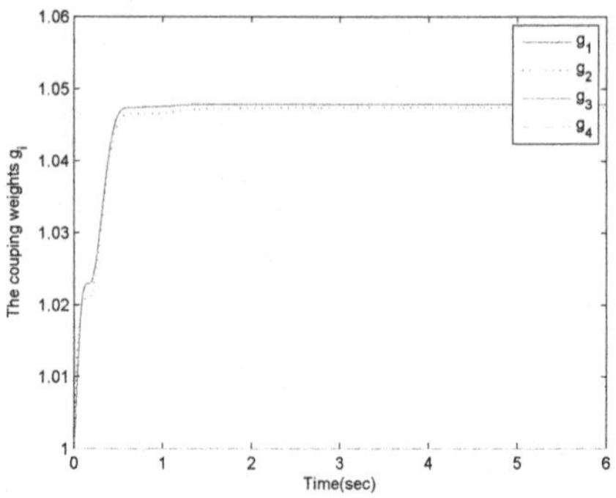

Fig. 7. The error trajectories of β_i in Example 1

and

$$\Gamma = \begin{bmatrix} 0.0087, \ 0.0173, \ 0.0343, \ 0.0515 \\ 0.0173, \ 0.0346, \ 0.0684, \ 0.1027 \\ 0.0343, \ 0.0684, \ 0.1355, \ 0.2034 \\ 0.0515, \ 0.1027, \ 0.2034, \ 0.3055 \end{bmatrix}.$$

The state error mentioned above is $e_i = z_i - z_0, i = 1, 2, 3, 4$. From the simulation results, the state errors converge to zero, which implies the leader achieving the consensus control of followers. The coupling weights trajectories of β_{ij} and β_i converge to some constants. Besides, the control signals of the multi-agent system converge to zero over time. It indicates that the controller does not give followers control inputs when the leader and followers are in the same moving trail.

6   Conclusion

In this paper, consensus control of multi-agent systems under external disturbance based on partially directed topology is proposed. The stability and convergence of the proposed method is analyzed as well. Finally, the simulation results illustrate the effectiveness of the designed algorithm. Future work will introduce the directed network with different constant matrix A_i and time-varying topology.

Acknowledgements. This work was supported in part by the National Natural Science Foundation of China under Grants 61233001, 61374105, 61722312, 61533017 and 61673054.

References

1. Porfiri, M., Roberson, D.G., Stilwell, D.J.: Tracking and formation control of multiple autonomous agents: a two-level consensus approach. Automatica **43**(8), 1318–1328 (2007)
2. Geng, H., Chen, Z.Q., Liu, Z.X., Zhang, Q.: Consensus of a heterogeneous multi-agent system with input saturation. Neurocomputing **166**, 382–388 (2015)
3. Chu, H., Cai, Y., Zhang, W.: Consensus tracking for multi-agent systems with directed graph via distributed adaptive protocol. Neurocomputing **166**, 8–13 (2015)
4. Cruz, D., McClintock, J., Perteet, B., Orqueda, O.A.A., Cao, Y., Fierro, R.: Decentralized cooperative control-a multivehicle platform for research in networked embedded systems. IEEE Control Syst. **27**(3), 58–78 (2007)
5. Yang, T., Zhang, P., Yu, S.: Consensus of linear multi-agent systems via reduced-order observer. Neurocomputing **240**, 200–208 (2017)
6. Wei, Q., Liu, D., Song, R.: Optimal self-learning cooperative control for continuous-time heterogeneous multi-agent systems. In: 34th Chinese Control Conference, pp. 3005–3010. IEEE Press, Hangzhou (2015)
7. Wei, Q., Liu, D.: Numerical adaptive learning control scheme for discrete-time non-linear systems. IET Control Theory Appl. **7**(11), 1472–1486 (2013)
8. Wei, Q., Lewis, F.L., Shi, G., Song, R.: Error-tolerant iterative adaptive dynamic programming for optimal renewable home energy scheduling and battery management. IEEE Trans. Industr. Electron. (2017). doi:10.1109/JAS.2016.7510262
9. Wei, Q., Lewis, F.L., Sun, Q., Yan, P., Song, R.: Discrete-time deterministic q-learning: a novel convergence analysis. IEEE Trans. Cybern. **47**(5), 1224–1237 (2017)
10. Wei, Q., Liu, D., Lewis, F.L., Liu, Y., Zhang, J.: Mixed iterative adaptive dynamic programming for optimal battery energy control in smart residential microgrids. IEEE Trans. Industr. Electron. **64**(5), 4110–4120 (2017)
11. Wei, Q., Liu, D., Lin, Q.: Discrete-time local value iteration adaptive dynamic programming: admissibility and termination analysis. IEEE Trans. Neural Netw. Learn. Syst. (2017). doi:10.1109/TCYB.2016.2542923
12. Wei, Q., Liu, D., Liu, Y., Song, R.: Optimal constrained self-learning battery sequential management in microgrid via adaptive dynamic programming. IEEE/CAA J. Autom. Sinica **4**(2), 168–176 (2017)
13. Wei, Q., Shi, G., Song, R., Liu, Y.: Adaptive dynamic programming-based optimal control scheme for energy storage systems with solar renewable energy. IEEE Trans. Industr. Electron. **64**(7), 5468–5478 (2017)
14. Wei, Q., Song, R., Yan, P.: Data-driven zero-sum neuro-optimal control for a class of continuous-time unknown nonlinear systems with disturbance using ADP. IEEE Trans. Neural Netw. Learn. Syst. **27**(2), 444–458 (2016)
15. Wei, Q., Liu, D., Lin, H.: Value iteration adaptive dynamic programming for optimal control of discrete-time nonlinear systems. IEEE Trans. Cybern. **46**(3), 840–853 (2016)
16. Su, Y., Huang, J.: Stability of a class of linear switching systems with applications to two consensus problems. IEEE Trans. Autom. Control **57**(6), 1420–1430 (2012)
17. Wen, G., Duan, Z., Chen, G., Yu, W.: Consensus tracking of multi-agent systems with lipschitz-type node dynamics and switching topologies. IEEE Trans. Circuits Syst. I Regul. Pap. **61**(2), 499–511 (2014)

18. Xiao, F., Wang, L.: Asynchronous consensus in continuous-time multi-agent systems with switching topology and time-varying delays. IEEE Trans. Autom. Control **53**(8), 1804–1816 (2008)
19. Seo, J.H., Shim, H., Back, J.: Consensus of high-order linear systems using dynamic output feedback compensator: low gain approach. Automatica **45**(11), 2659–2664 (2009)
20. Lin, H., Wei, Q., Liu, D., Ma, H.: Adaptive tracking control of leader-following linear multi-agent systems with external disturbances. Int. J. Syst. Sci. **47**(13), 3167–3179 (2016)

Synchronization in Networks of Nonidentical Discrete-Time Systems with Directed Graphs

Liang Hongjing[1], Zhou Yu[1], Zhou Qi[2], Li Hongyi[2], and Li Ping[1(✉)]

[1] College of Engineering, Bohai University, Jinzhou 121013, Liaoning, China
lianghongjing99@163.com, zhouyu6752@163.com, pinglime@gmail.com
[2] School of Automation, Guangdong University of Technology,
Guangzhou 510006, China
zhouqi2009@gmail.com, lihongyi2009@gmail.com

Abstract. This paper solves output synchronization problem for non-identical discrete-time multi-agent systems with directed graphs. All the agents suffer the disturbance form the leader. For the discrete-time case, we use the stabilization region regulator method and the variable restructured method to solve the output synchronization problem. At last, we give an example to show the effectiveness of the main result.

Keywords: Output synchronization · Multi-agent systems · Stabilization region

1 Introduction

Multi-agent systems have been received considerable attention [1–5] due to their distinctive advantages in many aries in recent years, such as non-minimum phase switch stabilization [6,7], containment control [8], near-optimal control [9], distributed optimal control [10], and network packet dropouts [11]. The consensus control is a popular problem of multi-agent systems which is to make the trajectory of all the agents run onto a common trajectory [12]. This techniques also have been widely applied to solve a lot of practical control problems.

The synchronization phenomenon is very common in the real world. Because of its widely applications in distributed sensor fusion, formation flying and so on, it has attracted many interest in the recent years. The synchronization control problem of multi-agent systems could be described as follows: the main attention is to keep synchronization by designing appropriate control laws on each agent by using the neighbor information of the agent. Reference [12] give a unified viewpoint between consensus of multi-agent systems and synchronization problem, in which the main unified viewpoint is the distributed control algorithm. Directed communication graphs was considered in [13] in handling the optimal synchronization phenomenon of discrete-time multi-agent systems based on riccati design method. Basical identical linear systems was studied in [14] under a directed interconnection and possibly time-varying structure.

© Springer International Publishing AG 2017
D. Liu et al. (Eds.): ICONIP 2017, Part VI, LNCS 10639, pp. 157–164, 2017.
https://doi.org/10.1007/978-3-319-70136-3_17

Further more, [15] considered the synchronization problem of multi-agent systems which contains the external disturbance, and an internal model method is used to handle the case that the system matrices are also uncertain. In addition, the exosystem is a general case and a transformation is add to the exosystem matrix to solve the problem. This problem also called the output regulation problem, in which the disturbance generated by an exosystem is rejected and the outputs of each node also asymptotic reach to same trajectory of the leader's output. A distributed leader-follower consensus control algorithms are presented in [16] to solve the output regulation problem for linear multi-agent systems, and this method is also used to obtain existing multi-agent coordination solutions to track an active leader with different dynamics and unmeasurable variables to allow the identical agents. Then [17] considered the discrete-time multi-agent systems and designed a stabilization region to keep the closed-loop systems without the external disturbance stable.

The purpose of this paper is to address distributed output synchronization problem for nonidentical discrete-time multi-agent systems with directed graphs. All the agents have different dynamics with others, and the disturbance generated by the leader node also influence the followers. For the discrete-time case, we should use the stabilization region regulator method which has been addressed in [17]. Then we use the variable restructured method to solve the output synchronization problem. At last, we give an example to improve the effectiveness of the result.

2   Preliminaries

Some basic concepts and notations in graph theory [18] should be introduced firstly. A weighted graph $\mathcal{G}_l = (\mathcal{N}_l, \mathcal{E}_l, \mathcal{A}_l)$, where $\mathcal{N} = \{v_1, v_2, \ldots, v_N\}$ is the set of nodes, $\mathcal{E}_l$ is the node set, and an edge of $\mathcal{G}_l$ denoted by $e_{ij} = (v_i, v_j) \in \mathcal{E}$ means that node v_i receives information from node v_j. $\mathcal{A} = [a_{ij}]$ is a weighted adjacency matrix, where $a_{ii} = 0$ and $a_{ij} \geq 0$ for all $i \neq j$. $a_{ij} > 0$ if and only if there is an edge from vertex j to vertex i. The set of neighbors of node v_i is denoted by $\mathcal{N}_i = \{v_j \in \mathcal{V} : (v_i, v_j) \in \mathcal{E}\}$. The communication topology between agents could be expressed by a diagonal matrix $\mathcal{D}_l =$ block diag$\{\Sigma_{j=1}^n a_{1j}, \Sigma_{j=1}^n a_{2j}, \ldots, \Sigma_{j=1}^n a_{Nj}\}$, where $\Sigma_{j=1}^n a_{ij}, i = 1, 2, \ldots, N$ is called a degree matrix of $\mathcal{G}_l$. The Laplacian with the directed graph $\mathcal{G}_l$ is defined as $\mathcal{L}_l = \mathcal{D}_l - \mathcal{A}_l$.

There is a sequence of edges with the form $(v_i, v_{k_1}), (v_{k_1}, v_{k_2}), \ldots, (v_{k_j}, v_j) \in \mathcal{E}$ composing a direct path beginning with v_i ending with v_j, then node v_j is reachable from node v_i. A directed graph contains a directed spanning tree if there exists at least one agent which is called root node that has a directed path to every other agents. A node is reachable from all the other nodes of graph, the node is called globally reachable.

3 Problem Formulation

In this paper, two types of the system dynamics of the multi-agent systems are given. The leaders of the agents are given as follows:

$$\begin{cases} x_i(k+1) = A_i x_i + B_i u_i + E_i \omega, \\ y_i = C_i x_i + D_i u_i, \end{cases} \qquad i = 1,\ldots,N. \tag{1}$$

where $x_i \in R^n$ and $y_i \in R^p$, are the state and output of the agents. $u_i \in R^m$ is the unknown consensus protocol to be designed later. ω is the exosystem state, and the exosystem is addressed as follows:

$$\begin{cases} \omega(k+1) = A_0 \omega, \\ y_r = Q\omega, \end{cases} \tag{2}$$

where $\omega \in R^q$ is the disturbance to be rejected and/or the reference input to be tracked, and $y_r \in R^p$ is the reference output.

The synchronization errors about the followers and the leader are given as follows:

$$e_i = y_i - y_r = C_i x_i + D_i u_i - Q\omega, \qquad i = 1,\ldots, N. \tag{3}$$

The output synchronization problem in networks of nonidentical discrete-time systems can be resolved if the following conditions are hold:

1. Under the appropriate distributed control law u_i, the nominal form of closed-loop system matrices are Hurwitz.
2. The output synchronization errors between the measured and reference outputs converge to zero, i.e.,

$$\lim_{k \to \infty} e_i(k) = 0. \tag{4}$$

4 Distributed Dynamic Feedback Design

The agents can only receive their neighbor's information. We have to use the distributed control method. Thus the distributed dynamic state feedback control law is designed as follows:

$$\begin{cases} \eta_i(k+1) = A_0 \eta_i + \theta L \sum_{j=0}^{N} a_{ij}(\eta_i - \eta_j), \\ z_i(k+1) = G_1 z_i + G_2(y_i - Q\eta_i(k)), \\ u_i = K_{1i} x_i + K_{2i} z_i, \end{cases} \tag{5}$$

in which $z_i \in R^s$ is the state of the compensator, $\eta_i \in R^p$ is the state of the distributed compensator. (G_1, G_2) incorporate the p-copy internal model of the matrix A_0, which is defined as follows:

$$\begin{aligned} G_1 &= \text{block diag}\{\varsigma_1, \varsigma_2, \ldots, \varsigma_p\}, \\ G_2 &= \text{block diag}\{\sigma_1, \sigma_2, \ldots, \sigma_p\}, \end{aligned} \tag{6}$$

in which σ_i is a constant column vector, ς_i is a constant square matrix, for any $i = 1, \ldots, p$ such that the minimal polynomial of A_0 divides the characteristic polynomial of ς_i and (ς_i, σ_i) is controllable.

Let

$$min \ det(\lambda I - A_0) = \lambda^{s_m} + a_1 \lambda^{s_m - 1} + \ldots + a_{s_m - 1} \lambda + a_{s_m}$$

be the minimal polynomial of A_0. Choose ς_i and σ_i in (6) as the following forms:

$$\varsigma_i = \varsigma = \begin{pmatrix} 0 & 1 & \ldots & 0 & 0 \\ 0 & 0 & \ldots & 0 & 0 \\ \vdots & \vdots & \vdots & \vdots & \vdots \\ 0 & 0 & \ldots & 0 & 1 \\ -a_{s_m} & -a_{s_m-1} & \ldots & -a_2 & -a_1 \end{pmatrix}, \ \sigma_i = \sigma = \begin{pmatrix} 0 \\ 0 \\ \vdots \\ 0 \\ 1 \end{pmatrix}, \quad (7)$$

with $s = ps_m, i = 1, 2, \ldots, p$ and $\varsigma_i \in R^{s_m \times s_m}, \sigma_i \in R^{s_m \times 1}$.

Consider the distributed compensator η_i, we have:

$$\eta_i(k+1) = A_0 \eta_i + \theta_i L \sum_{j=0}^{N} a_{ij} \eta_i - \theta_i L \sum_{j=0}^{N} a_{ij} \eta_j - \theta_i L a_{i0} \omega.$$

Let $\eta(k+1) = (\eta_1^T, \eta_2^T, \ldots, \eta_N^T)^T$, then one gets:

$$\eta(k+1) = (I_N \otimes A_0)\eta(k) + (\theta I_N \otimes I_q)((\mathcal{D} + \mathcal{A}_0) \otimes L)\eta \\ - (\theta I_N \otimes I_q)(\mathcal{A} \otimes L)\eta - (\theta I_N \otimes I_q)(\mathcal{A}_0 \otimes L)\bar{\omega}, \quad (8)$$

in which $\bar{\omega} = 1_N \otimes \omega$. Then submitting the distributed control law into the system dynamics, one gets:

$$x_i(k+1) = (A_i + B_i K_{1i})x_i + B_i K_{2i} z_i + E_i \omega$$
$$y(k) = (C_i + D_i K_{1i})x_i + D_i K_{2i} z_i$$
$$z(k+1) = G_2(C_i + D_i K_{1i})x_i + (G_1 + G_2 D_i K_{2i})z_i - Q_i \eta_i \quad (9)$$

Let $x(k) = (x_1(k), x_2(k), \ldots, x_N(k))^T$, and $z(k) = (z_1(k), z_2(k), \ldots, z_N(k))^T$, we have

$$x(k+1) = (A + BK_1)x + BK_2 z + E\bar{\omega}$$
$$z(k+1) = (I_N \otimes G_1 + (I_N \otimes G_2)DK_2)z + (I_N \otimes G_2)(C + DK_1)x, \quad (10)$$

in which

$$A = \text{block diag}\{A_1, A_2, \ldots, A_N\}$$
$$B = \text{block diag}\{B_1, B_2, \ldots, B_N\}$$
$$K_1 = \text{block diag}\{K_{11}, K_{12}, \ldots, K_{1N}\}$$
$$K_2 = \text{block diag}\{K_{21}, K_{22}, \ldots, K_{2N}\}$$
$$C = \text{block diag}\{C_1, C_2, \ldots, C_N\}$$
$$D = \text{block diag}\{D_1, D_2, \ldots, D_N\}$$
$$E = \text{block diag}\{E_1, E_2, \ldots, E_N\}.$$

Then the compacted closed-loop system could be obtained as follows:

$$\rho(k+1) = \Lambda\rho(k) + \Gamma\varrho(k), \tag{11}$$

in which $\rho(k) = (x(k)^T, z(k)^T)^T$, $\varrho(k) = (\bar{\omega}(k)^T, \eta(k)^T)^T$ and

$$\Lambda = \begin{pmatrix} A + BK_1 & BK_2 \\ (I_N \otimes G_2)(C + DK_1) & I_N \otimes G_1 + (I_N \otimes G_2)DK_2 \end{pmatrix}$$

$$\Gamma = \begin{pmatrix} E & 0 \\ 0 & -(I_N \otimes G_2)Q \end{pmatrix}.$$

To obtain the main result, we give the following assumptions and lemmas.

Assumption 1: The pairs $(A_i, B_i, C_i), i = 1, \ldots, N$ are stabilizable and detectable.

Assumption 2: Let $\lambda \in \sigma(A_0)$, where $\sigma(A_0)$ is the spectrum of A_0,

$$Rank \begin{pmatrix} A_i - \lambda I_n & B_i \\ C_i & D_i \end{pmatrix} = n + p. \tag{12}$$

Assumption 3: All the eigenvalues of A_0 span in the interior of the unit circle.

Lemma 1 [8]: If the Assumptions 1, 2 and 3 hold, and the matrix pair (G_1, G_2) incorporates a p-copy internal model of A_0, then the matrix pair

$$\left(\begin{pmatrix} A_i & \mathbf{0} \\ G_2C_i & G_1 \end{pmatrix} \begin{pmatrix} B_i \\ G_2D \end{pmatrix} \right)$$

is stabilizable.

Thus we obtain the following theorem.

Theorem 1: If the node 0 in the topology graph $\mathcal{G}_s$ is globally reachable, and the Assumption 1, 2 and 3 hold, the closed-loop system matrix Λ is stable under the distributed control law (5).

Proof: A transformation should be used as

$$\Lambda_t = (T \otimes I_n)\Lambda(T^{-1} \otimes I_n), \tag{13}$$

in which T is chosen as follows: the $(2k-1)$-th row is the k-th row of I_{2N} and the $(2k)$-th row of T is the $(k+N)$-th row of I_{2N} with $k = 1, \ldots, N$, and

$$\Lambda_t = \text{block diag}\{\Lambda_{1t}, \Lambda_{2t}, \ldots, \Lambda_{Nt}\},$$

with

$$\Lambda_{it} = \begin{pmatrix} A_i + B_iK_{1i} & B_iK_{2i} \\ G_2(C_i + DK_{1i}) & G_1 + G_2D_iK_{2i} \end{pmatrix}, i = 1, \ldots, N.$$

Then the matrix Λ_{it} can be rewritten as:

$$\begin{pmatrix} A_i & \mathbf{0} \\ G_2 C_i & G_1 \end{pmatrix} + \begin{pmatrix} B_i \\ G_2 D \end{pmatrix} \begin{pmatrix} K_{i1} & K_{i2} \end{pmatrix}$$

Therefore, according to Lemma 1, there exist appropriate K_{1i} and K_{2i} such that the matrix Λ is stable.

Theorem 2: Under the Assumption 1, 2 and 3, if the node 0 in the topology graph $\mathcal{G}_s$ is globally reachable, then the distributed dynamic control law (5) could solve synchronization for nonidentical discrete-time systems.

Proof: The Sylvester equation, which can be written as follows:

$$\Xi(I_{2N} \otimes A_0) = \Lambda\Xi + \Gamma, \tag{14}$$

with the unique solution Ξ. This theorem could be proved according to Theorem 1.

4.1   Example

To illustrate the validity of the proposed controller design strategy, we consider the system matrices of five agents as follows:

$$A_i = \begin{pmatrix} 0 & 1+0.1*i \\ 1 & 0 \end{pmatrix}, B_i = \begin{pmatrix} 0 \\ 1 \end{pmatrix}, C_i = \begin{pmatrix} 1 & 0 \end{pmatrix}, E_i = \begin{pmatrix} 0 & 0 & 0 \\ 0 & 0 & i \end{pmatrix},$$

and D_i are chosen as zero matrices. The leader's system matrix is

$$A_0 = \begin{pmatrix} 0 & 0 & 0 \\ 1 & 0 & -1 \\ 0 & 1 & 0 \end{pmatrix}.$$

Correspondingly, the internal model matrices are chosen as

$$G_1 = \begin{pmatrix} 0 & 1 & 0 \\ -1 & 0 & 1 \\ 0 & 0 & 0 \end{pmatrix}, G_2 = \begin{pmatrix} 0 \\ 0 \\ 1 \end{pmatrix}.$$

The agents communicate information with their neighbors. The information link can be shown in Fig. 1. At last, the tracking errors are shown in Fig. 2 by the appropriate distributed control law. It is shown that the outputs of the agents could reach on the same trajectories with the leader's output.

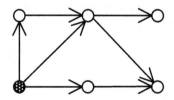

Fig. 1. The topology graph of five agents and leader

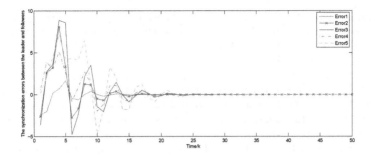

Fig. 2. Synchronization error of the outputs

5 Conclusion

Discrete-time multi-agent systems were studied in this paper, and distributed output synchronization problem has been solved by the appropriate distributed compensator and dynamic state feedback control law. Two main theorems were addressed and proved. At last, an example was shown to improve the main result.

Acknowledgments. This work was partially supported by the National Natural Science Foundation of China (61503037, 61703051, 61673071, 61673072, 61622302) and the Department of Education of Guangdong Province (2016KTSCX030).

References

1. Olfati-Saber, R., Murray, R.M.: Consensus problems in networks of agents with switching topology and time-delays. IEEE Trans. Autom. Control **49**(9), 1520–1533 (2004)
2. Fax, J.A., Murray, R.M.: Information flow and cooperative control of vehicle formations. IEEE Trans. Autom. Control **49**(9), 1465–1476 (2004)
3. Li, P., Lam, J.: Decentralized control of compartmental networks with H_∞ tracking performance. IEEE Trans. Industr. Electron. **60**(2), 546–553 (2013)
4. Zhou, X., Shi, P., Lim, C.C., Yang, C., Gui, W.: Event based guaranteed cost consensus for distributed multi-agent systems. J. Franklin Inst. **352**(9), 3546–3563 (2015)
5. Song, Q., Liu, F., Cao, J., Yu, W.: M-matrix strategies for pinning-controlled leader-following consensus in multiagent systems with nonlinear dynamics. IEEE Trans. Cybern. **43**(6), 1688–1697 (2013)
6. Yang, H., Jiang, B., Cocquempot, V., Zhang, H.: Stabilization of switched nonlinear systems with all unstable modes: application to multi-agent systems. IEEE Trans. Autom. Control **56**(9), 2230–2235 (2011)
7. Yang, H., Jiang, B., Zhang, H.: Stabilization of non-minimum phase switched nonlinear systems with application to multi-agent systems. Syst. Control Lett. **61**(10), 1023–1031 (2012)
8. Liang, H., Li, H., Yu, Z., Li, P., Wang, W.: Cooperative robust containment control for general discrete-time multi-agent systems with external disturbance. IET Control Theor. Appl. **11**(12), 1928–1937 (2017)

9. Zhang, J., Zhang, H., Feng, T.: Distributed optimal consensus control for nonlinear multiagent system with unknown dynamic. IEEE Trans. Neural Netw. Learn. Syst. doi:10.1109/TNNLS.2017.2728622
10. Zhang, H., Zhang, J., Yang, G., Luo, Y.: Leader-based optimal coordination control for the consensus problem of multiagent differential games via Fuzzy adaptive dynamic programming. IEEE Trans. Fuzzy Syst. **23**(1), 152–163 (2015)
11. Li, H., Wu, C., Shi, P., Gao, Y.: Control of nonlinear networked systems with packet dropouts: Interval type-2 fuzzy model-based approach. IEEE Trans. Cybern. **45**(11), 2378–2389 (2015)
12. Li, Z., Duan, Z., Chen, G., Huang, L.: Consensus of multiagent systems and synchronization of complex networks: a unified viewpoint. IEEE Trans. Circuits Syst. I: Regular Papers **57**(1), 213–224 (2010)
13. Hengster-Movric, K., You, K., Lewis, F.L., Xie, L.: Synchronization of discrete-time multi-agent systems on graphs using Riccati design. Automatica **49**(2), 414–423 (2013)
14. Luca, S., Rodolphe, S.: Synchronization in networks of identical linear systems. Automatica **45**(11), 2557–2562 (2009)
15. Xiang, J., Li, Y., Wei, W.: Brief paper - synchronisation of linear high-order multi-agent systems: an internal model approach. IET Control Theor. Appl. **7**(17), 2110–2116 (2013)
16. Hong, Y., Wang, X., Jiang, Z.: Distributed output regulation of leader-follower multi-agent systems. Int. J. Robust Nonlinear Control **23**(1), 48–66 (2013)
17. Liang, H., Zhang, H., Wang, Z., Wang, J.: Consensus robust output regulation of discrete-time linear multi-agent systems. IEEE/CAA J. Autom. Sinica **1**(2), 204–209 (2015)
18. Godsil, C.D., Royle, G.: Algebraic Graph Theory. Springer, New York (2001). doi:10.1007/978-1-4613-0163-9

Adaptive Neural Network Output-Feedback Control for a Class of Discrete-Time Nonlinear Systems in Presence of Input Saturation

Xin Wang[1(✉)], Tieshan Li[1], and C.L. Philip Chen[1,2]

[1] Navigation College, Dalian Maritime University,
Dalian 116026, People's Republic of China
18941190675@yeah.net
[2] Faculty of Science and Technology, University of Macau,
Macau, People's Republic of China

Abstract. In this paper, an adaptive neural network output-feedback control approach is presented for a class of discrete-time nonlinear strict-feedback systems in presence of input saturation. An auxiliary design system is employed to overcome the problem of input saturation constraint, and states of auxiliary design system are utilized to develop the tracking control. The high-order neural network (HONN) is employed to approximate unknown function. It is shown via Lyapunov theory that all the signals in closed-loop system are semi-globally uniformly ultimately bounded (SGUUB) and the tracking error converges to a small neighborhood of zero by choosing the control parameters appropriately. A simulation example is included to illustrate the effectiveness of the proposed approach.

Keywords: Discrete-time nonlinear systems · Output-feedback control · Neural network control · Input saturation constraint

1 Introduction

In general, NNs are often used as function approximator to approximate some suitable uncertainties appearing in controllers or systems. In recent years, a number of adaptive NN control schemes have been studied for uncertain nonlinear systems in state-feedback form [1–4] and output-feedback form [5–8]. But all of these methods can only be applied in continuous-time systems.

Comparing to the nonlinear continuous-time systems indicated in the above mentioned papers, adaptive control is less developed for nonlinear discrete-time systems. The reason is many adaptive control schemes for continuous-time systems may be not suitable for discrete-time systems. Recently, several significant developments have been achieved in adaptive NN control for discrete-time nonlinear systems, including strict-feedback form [9–13] and output-feedback form [14–18]. For example, the adaptive output-feedback control was proposed for a class of discrete-time multi-input-multi-output (MIMO) nonlinear systems with triangular form inputs in [16], and then the ideas was applied to MIMO systems with unknown control directions in [17].

© Springer International Publishing AG 2017
D. Liu et al. (Eds.): ICONIP 2017, Part VI, LNCS 10639, pp. 165–173, 2017.
https://doi.org/10.1007/978-3-319-70136-3_18

However, the discrete-time nonlinear systems studied in previous researches [9–18] did not consider the input saturation constraints problem. This problem is of great importance because almost all practical control systems have limitations on the amplitudes of control inputs, and such limitations can cause serious deterioration of control performances and even destroy the stability of the control systems [19]. Recently, the analysis and design of control systems with saturation nonlinearities have been studied in [20–23] and the references therein, such as in [20], robust adaptive NN tracking control was proposed for ocean surface vessels with input saturation by introducing the auxiliary design system. However, aforementioned elegant control approaches are studied for continuous-time systems, and due to difficulties in discrete-time systems, there is few research on the adaptive control for discrete-time nonlinear systems in presence of input saturation constraints.

Motivated by the aforementioned observations, in this paper, a robust adaptive neural network output-feedback control approach is presented for a class of discrete-time nonlinear strict-feedback systems in presence of input saturation.

2 Problem Formulation and Preliminaries

Consider the following single-input-single-output discrete-time nonlinear strict-feedback systems with input saturation:

$$\begin{cases} \xi_i(k+1) = f_i(\bar{\xi}_i(k)) + g_i(\bar{\xi}_i(k))\xi_{i+1}(k), & i = 1, 2, \ldots, n-1, \\ \xi_n(k+1) = f_n(\bar{\xi}_n(k)) + g_n(\bar{\xi}_n(k))u(k) \\ y_k = x_1(k) \end{cases} \tag{1}$$

where $\bar{\xi}_i(k) = [\xi_1(k), \xi_2(k), \ldots, \xi_i(k)]^T \in R^i$, $i = 1, 2, \ldots, n$ and $y_k \in R$ are the state variables and the output of the system; $f_i(\bar{\xi}_i(k))$ and $g_i(\bar{\xi}_i(k))$, $i = 1, 2, \ldots, n$ are unknown smooth functions; $u(k) \in R$ represents the control input with saturation constraint.

In this paper, considering the presence of input saturation constraints on $u(k)$ as

$$-u_{\min} \leq u(k) \leq u_{\max} \tag{2}$$

where $u_{\min}$ and $u_{\max}$ are the known lower limit and up limit of the input saturation constraints of $u(k)$, respectively. Thus,

$$u(k) = sat(u(k)) = \begin{cases} u_{\max} & \text{if } u(k) > u_{\max} \\ u(k) & \text{if } -u_{\min} \leq u(k) \leq u_{\max} \\ -u_{\min} & \text{if } u(k) < -u_{\min} \end{cases} \tag{3}$$

Assumption 1. The signal of $g_i(\bar{\xi}_i(k))$, $i = 1, 2, \ldots, n$ are known and there exist constants $\underline{g}_i > 0$ and $\bar{g}_i > 0$ such that $\underline{g}_i \leq |g_i(\bar{\xi}_i(k))| \leq \bar{g}_i, \forall \bar{\xi}_n(k) \in \Omega \subset R^n$.

Without losing generality, we shall assume that $g_i(\bar{\xi}_i(k))$ and $g_n(\bar{\xi}_n(k))$ are positive in this paper. The control objective is to design an adaptive NN controller for system

(1) such that: (i) all the signals in the closed-loop system are semi-globally uniformly ultimately bounded (SGUUB) and (ii) the system output y_k follows the desired reference signal $y_d(k)$.

Assumption 2. The desired reference signal $y_d(k) \in \Omega_y, \forall k > 0$ is smooth, known and bounded, where $\Omega_y := \{\chi | \chi = x_1\}$.

Definition 1. (see [15]) The solution of (1) is semi-globally uniformly ultimately bounded (SGUUB), if for any Ω, a compact subset of R^n and all $\bar{\xi}_n(k_0) \in \Omega$, there exist an $\varepsilon > 0$ and a number $N(\varepsilon, \bar{\xi}_n(k_0))$ such that $\left\| \bar{\xi}_n(k) \right\| < \varepsilon$ for all $k \geq k_0 + N$.

3 Output Feedback Adaptive NN Controller Design

This paper uses HONNs to approximate the unknown functions. Consider the discrete-time nonlinear strict-feedback system with input saturation described in (1). The original system is transformed to the following form [9]:

$$\begin{aligned}
&\xi_i(k+n-i+1) = F_i(\bar{\xi}_n(k)) + G_i(\bar{\xi}_n(k))\xi_{i+1}(k+n-i), \ i = 1, 2, \ldots, n-1, \\
&\xi_n(k+1) = f_n(\bar{\xi}_n(k)) + g_n(\bar{\xi}_n(k))u(k), \\
&y_k = \xi_1(k),
\end{aligned} \tag{4}$$

where $F_i(\bar{\xi}_n(k))$ and $G_i(\bar{\xi}_n(k))$, $i = 1, 2, \ldots, n-1$ are unknown highly nonlinear function which can approximated by using HONNs. For convenience of analysis and discussion, for $i = 1, 2, \ldots, n-1$, let

$$F_i(k) = F_i(\bar{\xi}_n(k)), \ G_i(k) = G_i(\bar{\xi}_n(k)), \ f_n(k) = f_n(\bar{\xi}_n(k)), \ g_n(k) = g_n(\bar{\xi}_n(k))$$

By a series of transformations, original system (4) is equivalent to the following form [9]:

$$y_{k+n} = x_n(k+1) = f_0(\underline{z}(k)) + g_0(\underline{z}(k))u_k \tag{5}$$

where
$$\begin{aligned}
f_0(\underline{z}(k)) &:= F_0(\underline{z}(k)) = f([x_1(k), \psi_2(\underline{z}(k)), \ldots, \psi_n(\underline{z}(k))]^T), \\
g_0(\underline{z}(k)) &:= G_0(\underline{z}(k)) = g([x_1(k), \psi_2(\underline{z}(k)), \ldots, \psi_n(\underline{z}(k))]^T).
\end{aligned}$$

Define tracking error as $e_y(k) = y_k - y_d(k)$. The tracking error dynamics are given by

$$e_y(k+n) = -y_d(k+n) + f_0(\underline{z}(k)) + g_0(\underline{z}(k))u_k. \tag{6}$$

Supposing that the nonlinear function $f_0(\underline{z}(k))$ and $g_0(\underline{z}(k))$ are known exactly, we present a desired control, $\bar{u}_k^*$, such that the output y_k follows the desired trajectory $y_d(k)$ in deadbeat step:

$$\bar{u}_k^* = -\frac{1}{g_0(\underline{z}(k))}(f_0(\underline{z}(k)) - y_d(k+n)). \tag{7}$$

Substituting the desired control $\bar{u}_k^*$ into error dynamics Eq. (6), it is obvious that $e_y(k+n) = 0$. This means that after n steps, we have $e_y(k) = 0$. Therefore, $\bar{u}_k^*$ is a n-step deadbeat control.

Accordingly, the desired control $\bar{u}_k^*$ can be expressed as

$$\bar{u}_k^* = \bar{u}^*(\bar{z}(k)), \quad \bar{z}(k) = [\underline{z}^T(k), y_d(k+n)]^T \in \Omega_{\bar{z}} \subset R^{2n}$$

where $\Omega_{\bar{z}} = \left\{(\underline{y}(k), \underline{u}_{k-1}, y_d) | \underline{u}_{k-1}(k) \in \Omega_u, \underline{y}(k) \in \Omega_y, y_d \in \Omega_y\right\}$.

Since $f_0(\underline{z}(k))$ and $g_0(\underline{z}(k))$ are unknown, they are not available for constructing control $\bar{u}_k^*$. However, $f_0(\underline{z}(k))$ and $g_0(\underline{z}(k))$ are function of $\underline{z}(k)$, therefore, we can use HONN to approximate $\bar{u}_k^*$ as follows:

$$\bar{u}^*(\bar{z}) = W^{*T}(k)S(\bar{z}(k)) + \varepsilon_{\bar{z}}, \quad \forall \bar{z} \in \Omega_{\bar{z}} \tag{8}$$

where $\varepsilon_{\bar{z}}$ is the NN estimation error satisfying $|\varepsilon_{\bar{z}}| < \varepsilon_0$.

For convenience of constraint effect analysis of the input saturation, the following auxiliary design system is given by

$$\varsigma(k+1) = \begin{cases} -k_1\varsigma(k) + \Delta u, & |\varsigma(k)| \geq \mu \\ 0, & |\varsigma(k)| < \mu \end{cases} \tag{9}$$

where $k_1 = k_2 + \frac{|e_y(k)\Delta u| + 0.5\Delta u^2}{\varsigma^2(k)} > 0$, $k_2 > 0$, Δu is the control input error, μ is a small positive design constant; $\varsigma(k)$ is a variable of the auxiliary design system introduced to ease the analysis of the effect of the input saturation.

Choose the control law:

$$u_k = \hat{W}(k)S(\bar{z}(k)) + \varsigma(k) \tag{10}$$

and the updating law is:

$$\hat{W}(k+1) = \hat{W}(k) - \Gamma[S(\bar{z}(k_1))e_y(k+1) + \sigma\hat{W}(k)], \tag{11}$$

where $k_1 = k - n + 1$.

Substituting controller (10) into (6), Eq. (6) can be re-written as

$$e_y(k+n) = f_0(\underline{z}(k)) + g_0(\underline{z}(k))[\tilde{W}^T(k)S(\bar{z}(k)) + \varsigma(k)] - y_d(k+n) \tag{12}$$

adding and subtracting $g_0(\underline{z}(k))\bar{u}^*(\bar{z}(k))$ on the right-hand side of (12) and noting (8), have

$$e_y(k+n) = f_0(\underline{z}(k)) - y_d(k+n) + g_0(\underline{z}(k))\bar{u}^*(\bar{z}(k)) + g_0(\underline{z}(k))$$
$$\times [\hat{W}^T(k)S(\bar{z}(k)) + \varsigma(k) - W^{*T}(k)S(\bar{z}(k)) - \varepsilon_{\bar{z}}] \tag{13}$$

substituting (7) into (13) leads to

$$e_y(k+n) = g_0(\underline{z}(k))[\tilde{W}^T(k)S(\bar{z}(k)) + \varsigma(k) - \varepsilon_{\bar{z}}] \tag{14}$$

The stability analysis of the closed-loop system is given as follows.

Theorem 1. (see [9]) Consider the closed-loop system consisting of system (1), controller (10), adaptive law (11). There exist compact sets $\Omega_{y0} \subset \Omega_y$, $\Omega_{w0} \subset \Omega_w$, $\Omega_{\delta 0} \subset \Omega_\delta$ and positive constants l^*, γ^*, and σ^* such that if (i) assumptions 1–3 being satisfied, the initial condition $y(0) \in \Omega_{y0}$, $\tilde{W}(0) \in \Omega_{w0}$, and (ii) the parameters are suitably chosen such that $l > l^*$, $\sigma > \sigma^*$ and $\bar{\gamma} > \gamma^*$ with $\bar{\gamma}$ being the largest eigenvalue of Γ, then the closed-loop system is SGUUB.

Proof: Choose the following lyapunov function candidate:

$$V(k) = \frac{1}{\bar{g}}e_y^2(k) + \tilde{W}^T(k)\Gamma^{-1}\tilde{W}(k) + \bar{g}\Gamma^{-2}\varsigma^2(k) \tag{15}$$

Based on the fact that $\tilde{W}^T(k)S(\bar{z}(k)) = \frac{1}{g_0(\underline{z}(k))}e_y(k+1) - \varsigma(k) + \varepsilon_{\bar{z}}$. The difference of (16) along (11) and (14) is given:

$$\Delta V = \frac{1}{\bar{g}}[e_y^2(k+1) - e_y^2(k)] + \tilde{W}^T(k+1)\Gamma^{-1}\tilde{W}(k+1) - \tilde{W}^T(k)\Gamma^{-1}\tilde{W}(k)$$
$$+ \bar{g}\Gamma^{-2}\varsigma^2(k+1) - \bar{g}\Gamma^{-2}\varsigma^2(k) \tag{16}$$

Using the fact and Young's inequality, we obtain:

$$\Delta V \le -\frac{\rho}{\bar{g}}e_y^2(k+1) - \frac{1}{\bar{g}}e_y^2(k) - \sigma(1 - \sigma\bar{\gamma} - \bar{g}\sigma\bar{\gamma})\|\hat{W}(k)\|^2$$
$$- \frac{\bar{g}(1 - \bar{\gamma} - 2k_1^2)}{\bar{\gamma}^2}\varsigma^2(k) + \beta \tag{17}$$

where $\rho = 1 - 2\bar{g}\bar{\gamma} - \bar{\gamma}l - \bar{g}\bar{\gamma}l$, $\beta = \varepsilon_{\bar{z}}^2/\bar{\gamma} + (1+\bar{\gamma})\Delta u^2 + \sigma\|W^*(k)\|^2$.

If we choose the design parameters as follows:

$$\gamma < \frac{1}{l + 2\bar{g} + \bar{g}l}, \quad \sigma < \frac{1}{(1+\bar{g})\bar{\gamma}}, \quad 0 < k_1 < \sqrt{\frac{1 - \bar{\gamma}}{2}} \tag{18}$$

then it is obvious that $\Delta V \le 0$ once $|e_y(k)| > \sqrt{\bar{g}\theta}$. This implies the boundedness of $V(k)$ for all $k \ge 0$, which leads to the boundedness of $e_y(k)$ and $\varsigma(k)$. Furthermore, the tracking error $e_y(k)$ will asymptotically converge to the compact set denoted by

$\varepsilon \le \sqrt{\bar{g}\beta}$. Due to negativity of ΔV, we can conclude that $y_{k+1} \in \Omega_y$ if all past outputs $y_{k-j} \in \Omega_y$, $j = 0, \ldots, n-1$, and compact set ε is small enough.

We can use the same techniques as in [9] to show that the NN weight error stays in a small compact set Ω_{we}, and $u_k \in L_\infty$. Finally, if we initialize state $y_0 \in \Omega_{y0}$, $\tilde{W}(0) \in \Omega_{w0}$, $\tilde{\delta}(0) \in \Omega_{\delta 0}$ and we choose suitable parameters γ, B, σ, β, k_1 according to (14) to make ε small enough, there exists a constant k^* such that all tracking errors asymptotically converges to Ω_{we} for all $k > k^*$. This implies that the closed-loop system is SGUUB. Then $y_k \in \Omega_y$, $\hat{W}(k) \in L_\infty$ and $\hat{\delta}(k) \in L_\infty$, will hold for all $k > 0$.

4 Simulation

To demonstrate the effectiveness of the proposed approach, consider the following discrete-time nonlinear strict-feedback systems with input saturation:

$$\begin{cases} \xi_1(k+1) = f_1(\xi_1(k)) + 0.3\xi_2(k) \\ \xi_2(k+1) = f_2(\bar{\xi}_2(k)) + u(k) \\ y_k = \xi_1(k) \end{cases} \tag{19}$$

where $f_1(\xi_1(k)) = \frac{1.4\xi_1^2(k)}{1+\xi_1^2(k)}$ and $f_2(\bar{\xi}_2(k)) = \frac{\xi_1(k)}{1+\xi_1^2(k)+\xi_2^2(k)}$. The tracking objective is to make the output y_k following a desired reference signal $y_d(k) = \sin(k\pi/20)/2 + \sin(k\pi/10)/2$.

The initial condition for system states is $x(0) = [0, 0]^T$, and the initial conditions of the adaptive law is $\hat{W}(0) = 0$. Other controller parameters are chosen as $l = 29$, $\Gamma = 0.01$, $\sigma = 0.2$, $k_2 = 0.01$. The input constraints are $u_{min} = u_{max} = 1.8$. The simulation results are presented in Figs. 1, 2, 3.

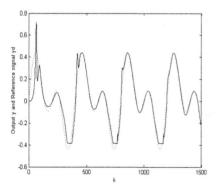
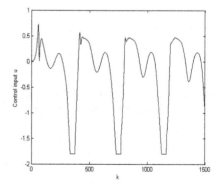

Fig. 1. y_d (dashed line) and y_k (solid line)   **Fig. 2.** Control input $u(k)$

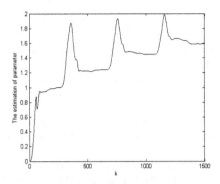

Fig. 3. $\|\hat{W}(k)\|$ (solid line)

Figure 1 shows the tracking performances of the output feedback. Figure 2 gives the control signal of the closed-loop system. Figure 3 illustrate the trajectory of parameter $\|\hat{W}(k)\|$.

5   Conclusion

By using the approximation property of the neural network, we have proposed a robust adaptive neural network output-feedback control scheme for a class of discrete-time nonlinear strict-feedback systems in presence of input saturation. An auxiliary design system is employed to address the problem of input saturation constraint. The high-order neural network (HONN) is employed to approximate unknown function, and the robustness of the closed-loop systems is improved obviously. The proposed approach can guarantees the boundedness of all the closed-loop signals and achieves asymptotic tracking performance. A simulation example is studied to demonstrate the effectiveness of the proposed approach. The future research will extend the proposed approach to control discrete-time nonlinear systems in presence of input saturation in pure-feedback form.

Acknowledgements. This work is supported in part by the National Natural Science Foundation of China under Grants 51309041, 51179019 and 61374114, the Fundamental Research Program for Key Laboratory of the Education Department of Liaoning Province under Grant LZ2015006, the Fundamental Research Funds for the Central Universities under Grants 3132016313 and 3132016311.

References

1. Ge, S.S., Wang, C.: Adaptive neural control of uncertain MIMO nonlinear systems. IEEE Trans. Neural Netw. **15**, 674–692 (2004)
2. Karimi, H.R., Babazadeh, A.: Modeling and output tracking of transverse flux permanent magnet machines using high gain observer and RBF neural network. ISA Trans. **44**, 445–456 (2005)
3. Wang, D., Huang, J.: Neural network-based adaptive dynamic surface control for a class of uncertain nonlinear systems in strict-feedback form. IEEE Trans. Neural Netw. **16**, 195–202 (2005)
4. Li, T.S., Wang, D., Feng, G.: A DSC approach to robust adaptive NN tracking control for strict-feedback nonlinear systems. IEEE Trans. Syst. Man Cybern. Part B Cybern. **40**, 915–927 (2010)
5. Choi, J.Y., Farrell, J.A.: Adaptive observer backstepping control using neural networks. IEEE Trans. Neural Netw. **12**, 1103–1112 (2001)
6. Stoev, J., Choi, J.Y., Farrell, J.: Adaptive control for output feedback nonlinear systems in the presence of modeling errors. Automatica **38**, 1761–1767 (2002)
7. Hua, C., Guan, X., Shi, P.: Robust output feedback tracking control for time-delay nonlinear systems using neural network. IEEE Trans. Neural Netw. **18**, 495–505 (2007)
8. Chen, W., Li, J.: Decentralized output-feedback neural control for systems with unknown interconnections. IEEE Trans. Syst. Man Cybern. Part B Cybern. **38**, 258–266 (2008)
9. Ge, S.S., Li, G.Y., Lee, T.H.: Adaptive NN control for a class of strict-feedback discrete-time nonlinear systems. Automatica **39**, 807–819 (2003)
10. Zhu, Q.M., Guo, L.Z.: Stable adaptive neuron control for nonlinear discrete-time systems. IEEE Trans. Neural Netw. **15**, 653–662 (2004)
11. Alanis, A.Y., Sanchez, E.N., Loukianov, A.G.: Discrete-time adaptive backstepping nonlinear control via high-order neural networks. IEEE Trans. Neural Netw. **18**, 1185–1195 (2007)
12. Chen, W.S.: Adaptive NN control for discrete-time pure-feedback systems with unknown control direction under amplitude and rate actuator constraints. ISA Trans. **48**, 304–311 (2009)
13. Wang, X., Li, T.S., Chen, C.L.P.: Adaptive robust control based on single neural network approximation for a class of uncertain strict-feedback discrete-time nonlinear systems. Neurocomputing **138**, 325–331 (2014)
14. Zhang, J., Ge, S.S., Lee, T.L.: Output feedback control of a class of discrete MIMO nonlinear systems with triangular form inputs. IEEE Trans. Neural Netw. **16**, 1491–1503 (2005)
15. Li, Y.N., Yang, C.G., Ge, S.S.: Adaptive output feedback NN control of a class of discrete-time MIMO nonlinear systems with unknown control directions. IEEE Trans. Syst. Man Cybern. Part B Cybern. **41**, 507–517 (2011)
16. Ge, S.S., Yang, C.G., Lee, T.H.: Adaptive predictive control using neural network for a class of pure-feedback systems in discrete time. IEEE Trans. Neural Netw. **19**, 1599–1614 (2008)
17. Liu, Y.J., Chen, C.L.P., Wen, G.X.: Adaptive neural output feedback tracking control for a class of uncertain discrete-time nonlinear systems. IEEE Trans. Neural Netw. **22**, 1162–1167 (2011)
18. Yang, C.G., Ge, S.S., Xiang, C.: Output feedback NN control for two classes of discrete-time systems with unknown control directions in a unified approach. IEEE Trans. Neural Netw. **19**, 1873–1886 (2008)

19. Gao, W.Z., Selmic, R.R.: Neural network control of a class of nonlinear systems with actuator saturation. IEEE Trans. Neural Netw. **17**, 147–156 (2006)
20. Chen, M., Ge, S.S., Choo, Y.: Neural network tracking control of ocean surface vessels with input saturation. In: Proceedings of the 2009 IEEE International Conference on Automation and Logistics, pp. 85–89. IEEE, Qingdao (2009)
21. Li, Y.M., Tong, S.C., Li, T.S.: Direct adaptive fuzzy backstepping control of uncertain nonlinear systems in the presence of input saturation. Neural Comput. Appl. **23**, 1207–1216 (2013)
22. Li, Y.M., Tong, S.C., Li, T.S.: Adaptive fuzzy output-feedback control for output constrained nonlinear systems in the presence of input saturation. Fuzzy Sets Syst. **248**, 138–155 (2014)
23. Li, T.S., Li, R.H., Li, J.F.: Decentralized adaptive neural control of nonlinear interconnected large-scale systems with unknown time delays and input saturation. Neurocomputing **74**, 2277–2283 (2011)

FPGA Implementation of the Projection Based Recurrent Neural Network Approach to Compute the Distance Between a Point and an Ellipsoid

Shenshen Gu$^{(\boxtimes)}$ and Xiaowen Wang

School of Mechatronic Engineering and Automation,
Shanghai University, Shanghai 200072, China
gushenshen@shu.edu.cn

Abstract. In this paper, an FPGA hardware implementation based on a recurrent neural network was proposed to compute the distance between a point and an ellipsoid. This implementation takes the 0–1 constraint box into consideration as well, it is also capable to solve the hyperellipsoid problem based on the methodology of an automatic generation of neural hardware tool. The hardware design is based on the Xilinx's System Generator development tool and experimental results show that the proposed hardware implementation method is very efficient with a high degree of parallelism.

Keywords: Recurrent neural network · FPGA · Hardware implementation · Optimization

1 Introduction

Computing the minimum distance between a point and an ellipsoid is a typical quadratic programming problem. There are plenty of mathematical methods to solve the problem, however the traditional method is very time consuming. The neural network is a kind of mathematical model with parallel structure with high efficiency to solve some mathematical problems. In the paper [1], a recurrent neural network model was presented for solving convex optimization problems with box constraint. Base on the model, a projection based recurrent neural network was proposed in paper [2] to compute the distance between a point and an ellipsoid with box constraint.

The field-programmable-gate-array (FPGA) is very suitable for parallel computing, it have been widely used to accelerate the neural network and machine learning algorithm [3,4]. In the paper [5], an FPGA implementation of a finite-time convergent recurrent neural network was proposed to solve the L smallest k-subsets sum problem. Integrated with Matlab, Xilinx's System Generator facilitates the process of building hardware implementation architecture. However it is very time consuming to manually construct large scale of network which

© Springer International Publishing AG 2017
D. Liu et al. (Eds.): ICONIP 2017, Part VI, LNCS 10639, pp. 174–181, 2017.
https://doi.org/10.1007/978-3-319-70136-3_19

contains hundreds of modules and connections. The paper [6] proposed an automatic generation of neural hardware tool called Automatic General Purpose Neural Hardware Generator (AGNE). Based on Matlab command programme, the AGNE can build the hardware implementation architecture efficiently.

In this paper the hardware implementation of the projection based recurrent neural network was proposed to compute the distance between a point and an ellipsoid. Based on the methodology of the AGNE, the hardware implementation network was automatically generated to solve the hyperellipsoid problem. After verification of the recurrent neural network model based on Xilinx Blockset in Simulink, the Verilog hardware description language (HDL) is used to describe the neural network in Xilinx's comprehensive FPGA development software Vivado.

The rest of this paper is organized as follows. Section 2 presents the problem formulation and illustrates the description of the problem with a projection based recurrent neural network. Section 3 introduces the design procedure of the hardware implementation and the methodology of automatic generation. And some issues during the design process is presented as well in this section. Next, in Sect. 4, experimental results are given to verify the efficiency of the FPGA implementation. Finally, a conclusion was drawn in the end to summarize this work.

2 Problem Formulation and Neural Network Model

The problem can be denoted as an equality constrained optimization problem, the objective function is the distance between a point and an ellipsoid (or hyperellipsoid). And the point on the ellipsoid is the constrained condition. To compute the minimum distance from a point A to the ellipsoid, the problem can be formulated as follows:

$$
\begin{aligned}
\min f(x) &= \sum_{i=1}^{n} (x_i - a_i)^2 \\
s.t.\, h(x) &= \tfrac{1}{2} x^T Q x + c^T x = v
\end{aligned}
\tag{1}
$$

where $A = (a_1, a_2, \ldots, a_n)$ is a random point, $f(x)$ denotes the distance and $h(x)$ is the ellipsoid equation. Q is an n-dimensional symmetry matrix and c is an n-dimensional vector.

For most practical applications of the problem, the box constraint should be taken into consideration. So a 0–1 box constrain is added to problem (1) and the problem is updated to a new problem as follows:

$$
\begin{aligned}
\min_{x \in \Omega} f(x) \\
s.t.\ h(x) = 0
\end{aligned}
\tag{2}
$$

where $\Omega \in [0,1]^n$.

In paper [2], based on the framework of the recurrent neural network, a projection based neural network was proposed to solve the problem. The dynamic equation for the proposed neural network is given as follows:

$$\dot{x}(t) = -\mu x(t) + \mu P_\Omega \{x(t) - \nabla f(x(t)) + \nabla h(x(t))$$
$$[-\mu \nabla h(x(t))^T \nabla f(x(t)) + \rho h(x(t))] \tag{3}$$
$$[\mu \nabla h(x(t))^T \nabla h(x(t))]^{-1}\}$$

where x is the state vector of the neural network, which corresponds to the decision vector in (1), ∇f is the gradient of f, ∇h is the gradient vector of h and P_Ω is a projection operator defined as

$$P_\Omega = \begin{cases} 0, & U_i < 0 \\ U_i, & 0 < U_i < 1 \\ 1, & U_i > 1 \end{cases} \tag{4}$$

The converge analysis of the neural network model is also presented in that paper.

3   FPGA Implementation

According to the dynamic equation shown above, a hardware implementation network was built to compute the distance between a point and the ellipsoid. Figure 1 shows the network model, it is a partial parallel network, the connection weights are consisted by the factors of the matrix Q and the vector c. As denoted in the dynamic equation, network contains four main calculation processes: ∇f, f, ∇h and h. After a series of calculation process, the state vector of the network x can be calculated as output signals, then the output signals will be propagated to the input ports to complete the feedback process. The data type of the output signal is fixed point with 15 bits and the binary point bits is 12.

The hardware implementation architecture is constructed with Xilinx Blockset in Simulink. The paper [7] introduced the use of the Xilinxs System Generator development tool for the hardware implementation on Xilinx FPGA in detail. Several issues which may create difficulties during the design process also have been mentioned in the paper. Two main issues should be noticed in the hardware implementation. The first one is the timing issue, during the calculation process, some nodes must receive signals from different branch circuits simultaneously to ensure the stability of the system and the mathematical results. So it's necessary to insert delay blocks in some brunch circuits. The second one is the data type issue, the definition of the data type within the hardware implementation flow is alternative of signed or unsigned, bits width and the position of binary point. Some logic blocks even support float point calculation. It is very significant to set the data type properly to guarantee the math preciseness and avoid overflow.

To build large scale of the hardware implementation architecture, hundreds blocks will be involved and the connections between them will be dramatically complex. It is very difficult to build the network and set up the parameter of blocks manually. In paper [6], an automatic generation of neural hardware tool called Automatic General Purpose Neural Hardware Generator (AGNE) was

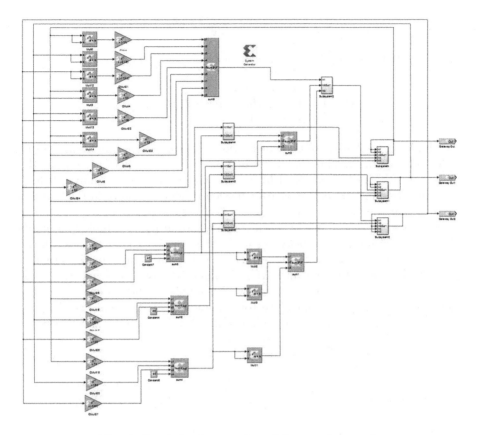

Fig. 1. Circuit implementation of the neural network

proposed. This tool is based on the Matlab programme and a GUI interface is also available to set the parameter of the hardware neural network. By compiling Matlab programme, user can add blocks and build connections in the Simulink project. A series of blocks can be integrated as subsystem which can be saved in a Simulink block library. By using Matlab command, the subsystems can be added into the project from the library, then the connections can be built between the subsystems and blocks automatically.

4 Simulation Results

To show the effectiveness and efficiency of the neural network hardware implementation, the following simulations are performed. To compute the distance between a point and an ellipsoid, the problem is presented as follows:

$$\min_{x \in \Omega} \quad f(x) = \sum_{i=1}^{3} (x_i - 0.5)^2$$

$$s.t. \quad h(x) = \frac{1}{2}x^T Q x + c^T x$$

where $\Omega \in [0,1]^3$, Q and C are given as follows:

$$Q = \begin{pmatrix} -26 & 43 & 79 \\ 43 & -63 & 158 \\ 79 & 158 & 345 \end{pmatrix}, c = (47, 65, 92)^T$$

After building the hardware implementation architecture, the simulation result of the network in Simulink is shown in Fig. 2. The Verilog HDL code of the neural network can be generated by System Generation, after running behavioral simulation in Vivado the wave simulation results are shown in Fig. 3 which indicates that the system converges at 2.430544 us.

To compute the distance between a point and an hyperellipsoid, the hardware implementation neural networks were generated automatically base on the methodology of ANGE. In the following cases the dimensions of the problem are set to be 5 and 10. The simulation results of the two cases and the hardware implementation are shown as follow. When Q is a 5-dimensional symmetry matrix and c is a 5-dimensional vector, function $f(x)$ represent the distance between point A and a hyperellipsoid. The problem is presented as follows:

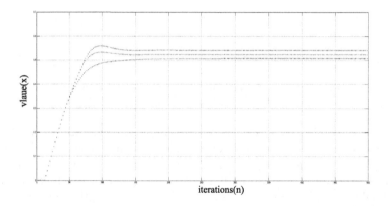

Fig. 2. The simulation result of the hardware implementation

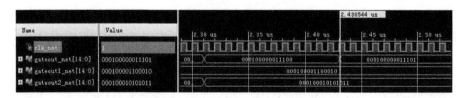

Fig. 3. The wave simulation result of The simulation result of the hardware implementation

$$\min_{x \in \Omega} \quad f(x) = \sum_{i=1}^{5} (x_i - 0.5)^2$$

$$s.t. \quad h(x) = \frac{1}{2}x^T Q x + c^T x$$

where $\Omega \in [0,1]^5$, Q and c are given as follows:

$$Q = \begin{pmatrix} -26 & 43 & 79 & 86 & 26 \\ 43 & -63 & 158 & 40 & 44 \\ 79 & 158 & -345 & 10 & 17 \\ 86 & 40 & 10 & -128 & 2 \\ 26 & 44 & 17 & 2 & -200 \end{pmatrix}, c = (43, 65, 92, 108, 128)^T$$

Figure 4 shows the simulation result of the 5-dimensional problem in Simulink and as Fig. 5 illustrates, the system converges at 4.970196 us.

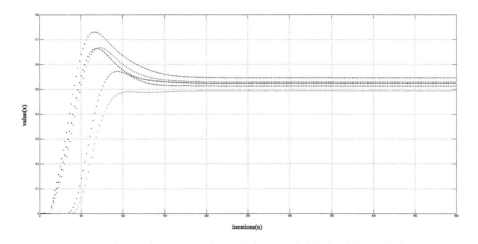

Fig. 4. The simulation result of the 5-dimensional problem

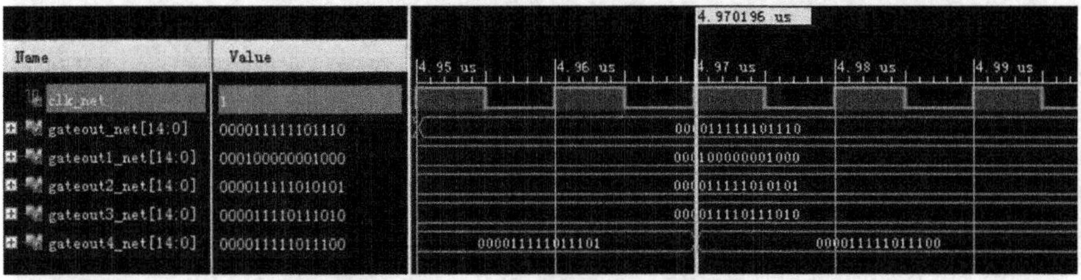

Fig. 5. The wave simulation result of the 5-dimensional problem

When Q is a 10-dimensional symmetry matrix and c is a 10-dimensional vector, Q and c are given as follows:

$$Q = \begin{pmatrix} -486 & 24 & -20 & 10 & -26 & 32 & -24 & 48 & -2 & -49 \\ 24 & -478 & -9 & 40 & -44 & 19 & -45 & -3 & 32 & -48 \\ -20 & -9 & -502 & 29 & 17 & 35 & -21 & -46 & 1 & 48 \\ 10 & 40 & 29 & -458 & -2 & 43 & 27 & -3 & -39 & -14 \\ -26 & -44 & 17 & -2 & -500 & 28 & -30 & -32 & 6 & -16 \\ 32 & 19 & 35 & 43 & 28 & -484 & -50 & -4 & -29 & 42 \\ -24 & -45 & -21 & 27 & -30 & -50 & -543 & 30 & -32 & 22 \\ 48 & -3 & -46 & -3 & -32 & -4 & 30 & -479 & -6 & -3 \\ -2 & 32 & 1 & -39 & 6 & -29 & -32 & -6 & 474 & -42 \\ -49 & -48 & 48 & -14 & -19 & 41 & 22 & -3 & -42 & -546 \end{pmatrix}$$

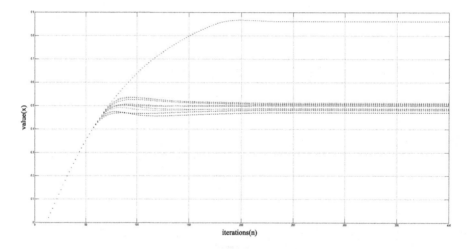

Fig. 6. The simulation result of the 10-dimensional problem

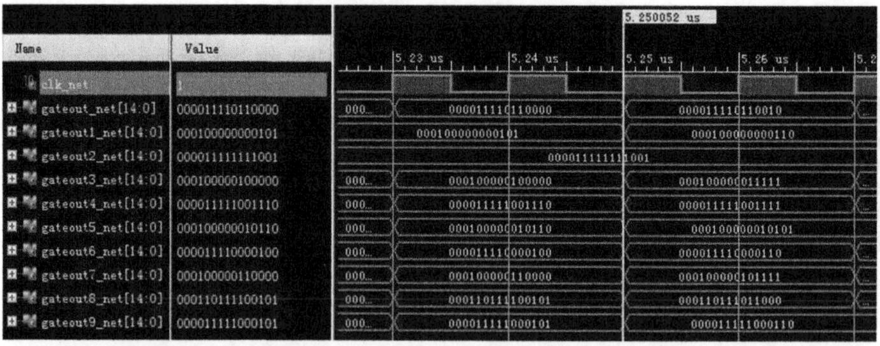

Fig. 7. The wave simulation result of the 10-dimensional problem

$$c = (\, 203,\, 245,\, 230,\, 215,\, 270,\, 206,\, 277,\, 278,\, 267,\, 288\,)^T$$

The simulation result of the 10-dimensional problem in Simulink is shown in Figs 6 and 7 illustrates the wave simulation result, the system converges at 5.25 us.

5   Conclusion

In this paper, based on a projection based recurrent neural network model combined with FPGA chips, a hardware implementation method was proposed by using System Generator to compute the distance between a point and an ellipsoid. By employing the methodology of ANGE the hardware implementation can be automatically generated to compute the distance between a point and a hyperellipsoid. The experimental results indicated that this hardware implementation demonstrated a high degree of parallelism and capable of pipelining of neural networks.

Acknowledgments. The work described in the paper was supported by the National Science Foundation of China under Grant 61503233.

References

1. Xia, Y., Leung, H., Wang, J.: A projection neural network and its application to constrained optimization problems. IEEE Trans. Circ. Syst. I Fundam. Theory Appl. **49**(4), 447–458 (2002)
2. Gu, S., Peng, J., Zhang, J.: A projection based recurrent neural network approach to compute the distance between a point and an ellipsoid with box constraint. In: Youth Academic Annual Conference of Chinese Association of Automation, pp. 459–462. IEEE Press, New York (2016)
3. Eriko, N., Jaewoong, S., David, S., Asit, M., Srivatsan, K., Debbie, M.: Accelerating recurrent neural networks in analytics servers: comparison of FPGA, CPU, GPU, and ASIC. In: IEEE 26th International Conference on Field Programmable Logic and Applications, pp. 1–4. IEEE Press, New York (2016)
4. Abdelrahman, T.S.: Accelerating k-means clustering on a tightly-coupled processor-FPGA heterogeneous system. In: IEEE 27th International Conference on Application-Specific Systems, Architectures and Processors, pp. 176–181. IEEE Press, New York (2016)
5. Gu, S., Wang, X.: FPGA implementation of the L smallest k-subsets sum problem based on the finite-time convergent recurrent neural network. In: Cong, F., Leung, A., Wei, Q. (eds.) ISNN 2017. LNCS, vol. 10261, pp. 337–345. Springer, Cham (2017). doi:10.1007/978-3-319-59072-1_40
6. Baptista, F.D., Morgado-Dias, F.: Automatic general purpose neural hardware generator. Neural Comput. Appl. **28**(1), 25–36 (2017)
7. Murthy, S.N., Alvis, W., Shirodkar, R., Valavanis, K., Moreno, W.: Methodology for implementation of unmanned vehicle control on FPGA using system generator. In: IEEE 7th International Caribbean Conference on Devices, Circuits and Systems, pp. 1–6. IEEE Press, New York (2008)

A Compliance Control Strategy for Minimizing Base Attitude Disturbance Using Variable Stiffness Joint Space Manipulator

Xingyu Wu[1(✉)], Ming Chu[1], and Zhenghong Dong[2]

[1] School of Automation, Beijing University of Posts and Telecommunications, Beijing, China
wuxingyu1012@163.com, buptchuming@163.com
[2] Department of Information Equipment, Academy of Equipment, Beijing 100876, People's Republic of China
dzh.bj@163.com

Abstract. The base attitude of a free-floating space robot is disturbed during capturing targets. Based on the variable stiffness technology, this paper presents a compliance control strategy for minimizing the base attitude disturbance. Firstly, the dynamic model of space manipulator system is established by using the Lagrange equation. Secondly, the differential evolution algorithm is utilized to design the control strategy of variable stiffness joint space manipulator. The simulation results reflect that the influence introduced by impact is obviously reduced, which verify the effectiveness of the control strategy.

Keywords: Minimize disturbance · Space manipulator · Variable stiffness · Differential evolution

1 Introduction

Space robotics is considered one of the most promising approaches for on-orbit servicing missions such as docking, berthing, repairing, upgrading, transporting, rescuing, and orbital debris removal [1]. When space robots accomplish above tasks, they need to capture the resting or moving targets. The main difference between the space robot and the ground robot is that the space robot base is not fixed and there exists the kinematics and dynamics coupling between the manipulator and the base. As a result, it is more difficult for space robots to capture targets. Apart from this, the impulse will influence the momentum of the system, bring the additional angular momentum to the base, which may lead to the whole system rolling over. At this moment, the disturbance may cause the reaction wheel saturation or seriously affect the quality of communication [2].

Therefore, many scholars have studied on how to reduce the disturbance of the base attitude. Among them, Yoshida's contribution is prominent. Generally, a capturing task consists of three specific phases: the pre-impact phase, the impact phase and the post-impact phase. The impulse brought by the impact

© Springer International Publishing AG 2017
D. Liu et al. (Eds.): ICONIP 2017, Part VI, LNCS 10639, pp. 182–191, 2017.
https://doi.org/10.1007/978-3-319-70136-3_20

phase makes the first phase and the third phase discontinuous. For this problem, Yoshida *et al.* [3] made a dynamic analysis on the impact phase and proposed a concept of the Extended Inverse Inertia Tensor (Ex-IIT) [4], realizing the impulse minimization. From the view of the angular momentum, Nenchev and Yoshida [5] decoupled manipulator dynamics from the base dynamics by utilizing the reaction null space approach, then the angular momentum was transferred from the base toward the manipulator after impact; simultaneously, the joint velocity was decreased through the joint damping control to ensure the stabilization of the base attitude in the post-impact phase. But the joint velocity got through the method would not affect the distribution of angular momentum. Then, Dimitrov and Yoshida [6] focused on the angular momentum distribution of the pre-impact phase and the post-impact phase, put forward the method of preloading angular momentum in manipulator and the base and applied distributed momentum control [7] and reaction null space control on the system after impact. The concept of zero disturbance direction based on bias momentum approach was raised in [8]. However, how to confirm the impact direction and the capture point remains to be solved. Zhang *et al.* [9] summarized the deficiencies of the above methods and put forward a scheme of pre-impact trajectory planning for minimizing the disturbance of base attitude caused by impact according to reaction null space method and particle swarm optimization algorithm. But, because of some additional constraints, the impact still introduces some disturbance to the base, and the stabilization control after impact needs to be considered. In recent years, Chen Li research team has done a lot of study on the capturing process and post-impact stabilization control. Results mainly concentrate in using different control methods to deal with the instability caused by impulse. There is neural network stabilization control, robust control, the real-time observation sliding-mode compensating control, etc. [10].

In this paper, a compliance control strategy to reduce the impulse is proposed. The variable stiffness joint [11] is used in the manipulator. When the end-effector contacts with the target, the impact force would be absorbed by the internal deformation of the elastic element in the variable stiffness joint. In addition, the internal deformation is related to the stiffness of the joint. Then we make use of the differential evolution algorithm to control the stiffness so that space robot can buffer the impact. Thereby, the disturbance of the base attitude will be minimized and the residual vibration can be suppressed.

2   Dynamic Modeling of Variable Stiffness Joint Free-Floating Space Manipulator

The free-floating space manipulator system is composed of a free-floating base and rigid links in series, which are connected with revolute and compliant joints. A planar two-DOF space manipulator is introduced in this paper, as shown in Fig. 1, where $O_j - x_j y_j$ $(j = 0, 1, 2)$ is the jth body frame and $O - XY$ the inertial frame. According to the geometry of the system, the vectors of the centroid of each body and the end-effector with respect to the inertial frame are

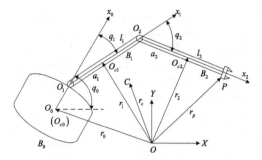

Fig. 1. Free-floating space manipulator model

$$r_1 = r_0 + l_0 + a_1,$$
$$r_2 = r_0 + l_0 + a_1 + b_1 + a_2, \qquad (1)$$
$$r_p = r_0 + l_0 + a_1 + b_1 + a_2 + b_2.$$

The symbols in the above equations are defined as follows:

r_j: inertial vector of the centroid of each body B_j

r_p: inertial vector of the end-effector

l_0: inertial vector from center of the base to the centroid of the first joint

a_i $(i = 1, 2)$: inertial vector from center of the joint to the centroid of B_i

b_i: inertial vector from the centroid of B_i to the $(i + 1)^{th}$ center of the joint

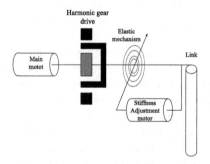

Fig. 2. Principle of variable stiffness

The space manipulator joint the paper studied is variable stiffness joint. Its principle of variable stiffness is shown in Fig. 2. The joint rotation is controlled by the main motor and the joint stiffness is regulated by the stiffness adjustment motor. As the space manipulator finishing positioning and trajectory tracking tasks, the joint stiffness is fixed. When interacting with the environment, the joint stiffness can be changed as the load changes. Due to the effect of the elastic mechanism, when the joint rotates an angle θ_{di}, the rotation of the link B_i is not consistent with θ_{di}. Therefore, the dynamic analysis of the free-floating space manipulator with variable stiffness joints should be separated into analysis of the space manipulator and the motor rotor. Thus, the kinetic energy of the system contains two parts: the kinetic energy of the rigid system composed of the base and rigid link and the total kinetic energy of each joint motor rotor. Because the motor rotor mass is negligible, the rotor kinetic energy is mainly rotational kinetic energy of its own.

Considering the kinetic energy of each part of the free-floating space manipulator system, there is

$$T_j = \frac{1}{2}m_j \dot{r}_j^2 + \frac{1}{2}J_j \omega_j^2, \tag{2}$$

where m_j is the mass of each part, J_j is the moment of inertia of each part, ω_j is the angular velocity vector of the jth part. The kinetic energy for each joint main motor rotor and stiffness adjustment motor rotor is

$$\begin{aligned} T_{Mdi} &= \tfrac{1}{2}J_{di}\dot{\theta}_{di}, \\ T_{Mri} &= \tfrac{1}{2}J_{ri}\dot{\theta}_{ri}, \end{aligned} \tag{3}$$

where J_{di} is the moment of inertia of the main motor rotor, J_{ri} is the moment of inertia of the stiffness adjustment motor rotor, θ_{di} is the angular vector of the main motor and θ_{ri} is the angular vector of the stiffness adjustment motor. So, the kinetic energy of the system can be presented by

$$T = \sum_{j=0}^{2} T_j + \sum_{i=1}^{2} T_{Mdi} + \sum_{i=1}^{2} T_{Mri}. \tag{4}$$

The total potential energy of the system is only elastic deformation potential energy generated by the stiffness adjustment mechanism, namely

$$V_i = \frac{1}{2}k_i \theta_{si}^2, \tag{5}$$

where k_i represents the stiffness of the elastic mechanism, $\theta_{si} = (q_i - \theta_{di})$ is the deformation owing to the elastic mechanism, then the total potential energy of the system is $V = \sum_{i=1}^{2} V_i$. The dynamic model of the free-floating flexible space manipulator derived from second Lagrange equation is expressed in the following form

$$M(q)\ddot{q} + H(q, \dot{q})\,\dot{q} + k_i(q_i - \theta_{di}) = \begin{bmatrix} \tau_b \\ 0 \\ 0 \end{bmatrix}, \tag{6}$$

$$\begin{aligned} J_{di}\ddot{\theta}_{di} - k_i(q_i - \theta_{di}) &= \tau_{di}, \\ J_{ri}\ddot{\theta}_{ri} &= \tau_{ri} - \tau_{Ri}, \end{aligned}$$

where $q = [q_0, q_1, q_2]^T$, τ_{di} and τ_{ri} are respectively the driving moment of the main motor and the stiffness adjustment motor, τ_{Ri} is the resistance torque on the stiffness adjustment motor.

In the process of contact with the target, the space manipulator is free floating. The reaction wheel and jet thruster are in closed state. At the same time, the base position and attitude are not controlled. So the base driving torque is zero. Assuming that the contact force between the end-effector and the target is F_e . With no regard for the torque acting on the end-effector, the contact force is expressed as

$$F_e = [F_x, F_y]^{\mathrm{T}}. \tag{7}$$

When the spacecraft contacts with the target, the main motor stops to work and the stiffness adjustment motor starts to work. At the moment of contact, the dynamic equation is changed into

$$M(\boldsymbol{q})\ddot{\boldsymbol{q}} + H\left(\boldsymbol{q}, \dot{\boldsymbol{q}}\right)\dot{\boldsymbol{q}} + k_i\left(\boldsymbol{q}_i - \boldsymbol{\theta}_{Di}\right) = J^{\mathrm{T}} F_e, \tag{8}$$

where J is the generalized kinematic Jacobian matrix of the end point velocity vectors $\dot{\boldsymbol{x}}_p$ and $\dot{\boldsymbol{y}}_p$ relative to the base attitude angular velocity $\dot{\boldsymbol{q}}_0$ and the joint angular velocity $\dot{\boldsymbol{q}}_1$ and $\dot{\boldsymbol{q}}_2$, $\boldsymbol{\theta}_{Di}$ is the terminate angle of the main motor.

3   Solving Optimal Joint Stiffness Based on Differential Evolution Algorithm

3.1   Differential Evolution Algorithm

Differential Evolution algorithm (DE) is a new evolutionary computation technique, which is mainly used for solving global optimization problems with continuous variables. In recent years, it has become a hot spot in domestic and foreign scholars. The process of solving DE is basically the same as genetic algorithm, including mutation, crossover and selection. An important symbol different from genetic algorithm is DE through the differential strategy to realize individual variation, reducing the complexity of genetic operations. In the standard DE algorithm, the binomial crossover strategy is usually used to form a new individual by sampling from the mutation and original individuals randomly [12]. The selection of DE is similar to the greedy algorithm, which adopts a one-by-one competitive strategy by individual adaptive value. Through an iterative calculation, retaining the excellent individuals, eliminating the inferior individuals, the DE algorithm guides the search process to the global optimum solution approximation. As with genetic algorithms, DE algorithm has a strong global convergence ability and robustness. Besides, on the one hand, DE algorithm has less parameter and only two main parameters need to be adjusted. On the other hand, the result is not affected by parameters and the DE algorithm is more convenient for use [13].

3.2   The Selection of the Objective Function

For the manipulator structure mentioned in the last section, after the collision, the impact force will make the system momentum alter. Meanwhile, the base attitude will occur large rotation due to disturbance. The control objective of the flexible arm is to achieve the minimum base attitude disturbance. So, we set up the objective function as follows

$$F = \eta_0 \left\| \dot{q}_0 \right\| + \eta_1 \left\| \dot{q}_1 \right\| + \eta_2 \left\| \dot{q}_2 \right\|. \tag{9}$$

where $\dot{q}_0$, $\dot{q}_1$, $\dot{q}_2$ are the velocities of the base, the first joint and the second joint. η_0, η_1 and η_2 are weighting coefficients which satisfy $\eta_0 + \eta_1 + \eta_2 = 1$. Owing to the coupling between the base and the manipulator, the angular velocity of them cant be reduced by zero at the same time. For the objective function 9, if the angular velocity is less than the set maximum, namely $F < 0.5$, the requirement of the control is met. The final weights are determined by the test.

3.3   The Algorithm Flow

In order to realize the minimum disturbance of space robot base attitude disturbance, we present the optimal stiffness value algorithm, the steps are as follows (which is also shown in Fig. 3.).

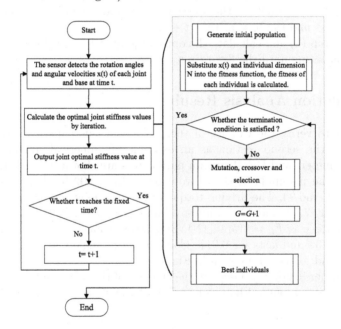

Fig. 3. The algorithm flow

(1) After the contact between the end of the space manipulator and the target, the motion sensor detects the rotation angles and angular velocities $x(t)$ of each joint and base at time t.

(2) According to the rotation angles, angular velocities, DE algorithm and Lagrange dynamics equation, by iteration, we calculate the optimal joint stiffness values at time t. The detailed process of solving consists of six steps.

2(a) Generate initial population N_p in the search space randomly. Define the individual dimension N according to number of joints. Set $G = 0$.

2(b) Substitute $x(t)$ and N into the fitness function, the fitness of each individual is calculated.

2(c) Determine whether the termination condition is satisfied or whether G reaches the maximum value generation. If true, the iteration is terminated and the optimal individual at this moment is the optimal output. Otherwise, continue to the next step.

2(d) Perform the mutation and crossover operations for each individual in the initial population. Deal with the boundary conditions and obtain the experimental populations.

2(e) Begin the selection operation. The individual fitness of the two populations is compared, and the individuals with small fitness are new individuals in the next generation.

2(f) Set $G = G + 1$. Go to step 2(c).

(3) Through adjusting stiffness of motor, output joint optimal stiffness value at time t. The sensor detects the rotation angles and angular velocities $x(t + 1)$ of the joint and the base at time $t + 1$.

(4) Repeat step (2) and calculate the optimal joint stiffness value at time $t + 1$. Keep repeating until the fixed time.

4   Simulation Analysis Results

In order to verify the validity of the method in this paper, use the model described in the second section as an example of numerical simulation. The system parameters and DE algorithm parameters are shown in Table 1.

Besides, the manipulator starts from $\boldsymbol{q} = [0.1, -0.02, 0.1]^T$ (rad) and $\dot{\boldsymbol{q}} = [0.5, 0.2, 0.3]^T$ (rad/s). The driving torque of the first joint and the second joint are respectively 7.5 N and 6 N. Stiffness adjustment range is $[50, 130]$ (N · m/rad) and impact force is $F_I = [15; 15]$ (N). Simulation time is 10 s and the impact occurs at $t = 3$ s and lasts for 0.01 s. Comparison of angle and angular velocity of the base and joints can be seen in Fig. 4.

On the other hand, Fig. 4 depicts the changes of the angle and angular velocity of the base and joints. Figure 5 proves that the changes of joint stiffness are

Table 1. Key simulation parameters

Parameter	Value	Parameter	Value	Parameter	Value
m_0	20 kg	m_1, m_2	1 kg	J_0	1.67 kg · m^2
J_1, J_2	0.33 kg · m^2	l_0	0.5 m	k_1, k_2	100 N · m/rad
a_1, a_2	0.5 m	b_1, b_2	0.5 m	Dimension	2
Variation rate	0.5	Crossover	0.9	Max iteration	100
J_{d1}, J_{d2}	0.106 kg · m^2	ph_1, ph_2	0.5 Nms/rad		

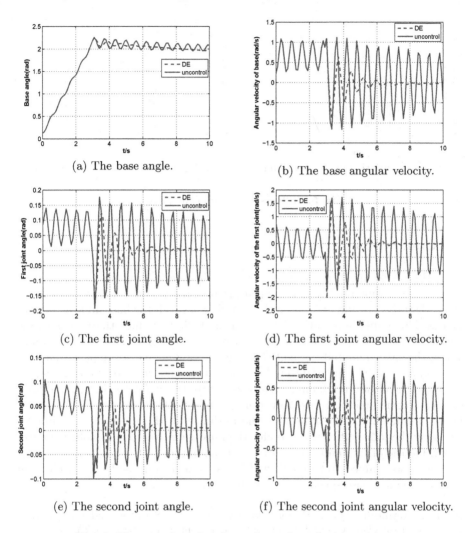

(a) The base angle.

(b) The base angular velocity.

(c) The first joint angle.

(d) The first joint angular velocity.

(e) The second joint angle.

(f) The second joint angular velocity.

Fig. 4. The variation of angles and angular velocities with t.

within the adjustment range. From the figures, it can be seen that the disturbance of the base and each joint is significantly weakened when using optimal control strategy. Though the amplitude of the angular velocity is not decreased immediately, it is also weakened in several seconds and the residual vibration is obviously suppressed. At about 7 s, base and joint velocities approach zero, and the sum value of them is less than the set maximum 0.5, which means the optimization is valid.

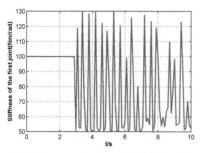
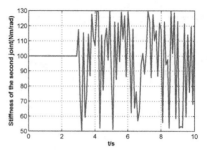

(a) Stiffness variation of the first joint.   (b) Stiffness variation of the second joint.

Fig. 5. Stiffness variation of the joints.

5   Conclusion

With the development of the space robotics, the free-floating space manipulator play an important role in space capturing operation. But the base attitude is easily disturbed by impact due to the coupling between the base and the manipulator. This paper summarizes the main methods to reduce the base attitude disturbance and proposes a new strategy on the basis of variable stiffness joint. When the space manipulator suffered from varying degrees of impact, the stiffness of joint can be regulated to reduce the impact and the impact energy can be stored in the elastic mechanism, which is clearly verified with the optimal joint stiffness control method based on differential evolution algorithm. The simulation results show that improving the flexibility of the space manipulator by changing the joint stiffness can buffer the impulse introduced by collision effectively. On the other hand, we find that the amplitude of the angular velocity is not decreased immediately. So we will focus on analyzing the factors which can improve the response speed in the future work.

Acknowledgment. This work was supported in part by Scientific and Technological Innovation Projects of General Armament Department under grant No. ZYX12010001 and National Key Basic Research Program of China under grant No. 2013CB733000.

References

1. Flores-Abad, A., Ma, O., Pham, K., et al.: A review of space robotics technologies for on-orbit servicing. Prog. Aerosp. Sci. **68**(8), 1–26 (2014)
2. Wu, J.W., Shi, S.C., Liu, H., Cai, H.G.: Spacecraft attitude disturbance optimization of space robot in target capturing process. Robot **33**, 16–22 (2011). China
3. Yoshida, K., Sashida, N., Kurazume, R., et al.: Modeling of collision dynamics for space free-floating links with extended generalized inertia tensor. In: Proceedings of the 1992 IEEE International Conference on Robotics and Automations, pp. 899–904, France (1992)

4. Yoshida, K., Sashida, N.: Modeling of impact dynamics and impulse minimization for space robots. In: Proceedings of the 1993 IEEE/RSJ International Conference on Intelligent Robots and Systems 1993, IROS 1993. pp. 2064–2069. Yokohama, Japan (1993)

5. Nenchev, D.N., Yoshida, K.: Impact analysis and post-impact motion control issues of a free-floating space robot subject to a force impulse. IEEE Trans. Robot. Automat. **15**(3), 548–557 (1999)

6. Nenchev, D.N., Yoshida, K.: Utilization of the bias momentum approach for capturing a tumbling satellite. In: Proceedings of 2004 IEEE/RSJ International Conference on Intelligent Robots and Systems, pp. 3333–3338. IEEE (2004)

7. Dimitrov, D.N., Yoshida, K.: Momentum distribution in a space manipulator for facilitating the post-impact control. In: Proceedings of 2004 IEEE/RSJ International Conference on Intelligent Robots and Systems, vol. 4, pp. 3345–3350. IEEE (2004)

8. Shui, H.T., Li, X., Peng, S.J., et al.: Zero disturbance planning for space robots during target capture. In: Proceedings of IEEE International Conference on Control and Automation, Xiamen, China, pp. 471–475 (2010)

9. Zhang, L., Jia, Q.X., Chen, G.: Pre-impact trajectory planning for minimizing base attitude disturbance in space manipulator systems for a capture task. Chin. J. Aeronaut. **28**(4), 1199–1208 (2015)

10. Dong, Q.H., Chen, L.: Neural network stabilization control of space mainipulator capturing operation. Huangzhong Univ. Sci. Tech. **43**(3), 22–27 (2015). China

11. Tsagarakis, N.G., Sardellitti, I., Caldwell, D.G.: A new variable stiffness actuator (CompAct-VSA): Design and modelling. In: IEEE/RSJ International Conference on Intelligent Robots and Systems, pp. 378–383. IEEE (2011)

12. Dorronsoro, B., Bouvry, P.: Cellular genetic algorithms without additional parameters. J. Supercomput. **63**(3), 156–162 (2013)

13. Qin, A.K., Huang, V.L., Suganthan, P.N.: Differential evolution algorithm with strategy adaptation for global numerical optimization. IEEE Trans. Evol. Comput. **13**(2), 656–665 (2009)

Path Following for Unmanned Surface Vessels Based on Adaptive LOS Guidance and ADRC

Hongyun Huang and Yunsheng Fan[✉]

Dalian Maritime University, Dalian 116026, China
yunsheng@dlmu.edu.cn

Abstract. This paper investigates the path following control problem for an unmanned surface vessel (USV). The method proposed is based on an identified model. The course keeping controller using active disturbance rejection control (ADRC) is employed to identify the environmental disturbance and model parameter perturbation. An improved adaptive line-of-sight (ALOS) guidance is proposed to follow reference path. The path can be either straight line or curve. The adaptive control law guarantees the uniformly globally asymptotically stable of the closed-loop USV system. Simulation results show the effectiveness of the proposed control approach.

Keywords: Unmanned surface vessel · Path following · Adaptive LOS guidance · ADRC

1 Introduction

The important technology of USV is path following. Commonly, path following is defined as USV with a certain speed to follow a desired path without temporal constraint.

One of the key components of motion controller is guidance. A popular and typical way to achieve convergence to the desired path is look-ahead line-of-sight (LOS) guidance mimicking an experienced sailor [1]. The method calculates the desired yaw angle by using geometry relationship of the problem, then fed to the attitude tracking subsystem [2]. However, the conventional LOS guidance law has several drawbacks: nonzero sideslip angle during path following for underactuation in the sway direction, and it is susceptible to the environmental disturbance such as ocean current and wind. Under the above-mentioned circumstances, problems of path deviation and convergence will occur [3]. Moreover, these problems can't be properly handled by simply adding an integral action to the heading controller.

An alternative method is to use the integral LOS (ILOS) guidance to alleviate the adverse effect of sideslip angle [4, 5]. In [6], the unknown sideslip angle is treat as a constant parameter, which is estimated by an adaptive law. Also, the adaptive LOS guidance in essence is ILOS. Based on [7], it has been proved that the LOS guidance law is uniformly globally asymptotically stable (UGAS) and uniformly locally exponentially stable (ULES).

In the paper, we present a novel adaptive LOS guidance law. The adaptive LOS guidance law calculates the desired yaw angle and estimates the currents for

© Springer International Publishing AG 2017
D. Liu et al. (Eds.): ICONIP 2017, Part VI, LNCS 10639, pp. 192–200, 2017.
https://doi.org/10.1007/978-3-319-70136-3_21

compensation. Then the ADRC deals with yaw tracking problem of USV. The paper is organized as follows. Models of USV and environmental disturbance such as ocean current and wind are established in Sect. 2. In Sects. 3 and 4, the course keeping controller and the adaptive LOS guidance law are proposed. In Sect. 5, simulations of the proposed control approaches are performed on MATLAB/Simulink platform. Finally, we conclude the paper and introduce future works in Sect. 6.

2 USV and Environmental Disturbance Model

2.1 Mathematic Model of USV Maneuvering

The object of the research is Dalian Maritime University "LANXIN" USV.

According to [8], the kinematics of a three degree-of-freedom USV in terms of surge speed u, sway speed v and yaw velocity r can be expressed as:

$$\begin{cases} \dot{x} = u\cos\psi - v\sin\psi \\ \dot{y} = u\sin\psi + v\cos\psi \\ \dot{\psi} = r \end{cases} \tag{1}$$

We adapt Norrbin model from the nonlinear mathematical of 3-DOF to formula:

$$T\ddot{\phi} + \dot{\phi} + \alpha\dot{\phi}^3 = K\delta \tag{2}$$

where T is the following coefficient and K is the turning coefficient, meanwhile, these coefficients are related to the speed of USV. By analyzing the data obtained from turning tests, it was revealed that the rudder response model could be described as a second order under-damped element:

$$\ddot{\delta} + 2\zeta\omega_n\dot{\delta} + \omega_n^2\delta = K\omega_n^2\delta_r \tag{3}$$

where δ, ω_n, ζ and δ_r represent rudder angle, natural oscillation frequency, damping ratio and desired rudder angle, respectively.

2.2 The Environmental Disturbance Model

According to [9], we can regard the disturbance as a combination of white noise and second order wave transfer function:

$$y(s) = h(s)\omega(s) \tag{4}$$

$$h(s) = \frac{K_\omega s}{s^2 + 2\xi\omega_0 s + \omega_0^2} \tag{5}$$

where $\omega(s)$, $h(s)$ are Gaussian white noise with zero mean and second order wave transfer function. K_ω, ω_0 are gain constant and dominated wave frequency.

3 Design of Course Keeping Controller Using ADRC

3.1 The Structure of ADRC

ADRC consists of three parts: tracking differentiator (TD), extended state observer (ESO) and nonlinear state error feedback (NLSEF).

Tracking Differentiator (TD). The main purpose of TD is to arrange a reasonable transient process and obtain the differential signal of input.

The discrete form of second order TD could be written as follows:

$$\begin{cases} v_1(k+1) = v_1(k) + hv_2(k) \\ v_2(k+1) = v_2(k) + hfhan(v_1(k) - v(k), v_2(k), r, h_0) \end{cases} \tag{6}$$

where $fhan(x_1, x_2, r, h)$ expression is:

$$\begin{cases} d = rh^2, \ a_0 = hx_2, \ y = x_1 + a_0, \ a_1 = \sqrt{d(d+8|y|)} \\ a_2 = a_0 + sign(y)(a_1 - d)/2 \\ a = (a_0 + y)fsg(y, d) + a_2(1 - fsg(y, d)) \\ fhan = -r(a/d)fsg(a, d) - rsign(a)(1 - fsg(a, d)) \\ fsg(x, d) = (sign(x+d) - sign(x-d))/2 \end{cases} \tag{7}$$

Extended State Observer (ESO). It can observe the real-time changes of the state variables in the control system. Extended state observer requires neither accurate system model nor accurate perturbation model, as long as isolating corresponding signal in the system's total disturbance by making compensation in the system of feedback channel.

The discrete form of extended state observer (ESO) is:

$$\begin{cases} e(k) = z_1(k) - y(k) \\ z_1(k+1) = z_1(k) + h((z_2(k) - \beta_{01}e(k)) \\ z_2(k+1) = z_2(k) + h(z_3(k) - \beta_{02}fal(e(k), 0.5, \delta) + b_0u(k)) \\ z_3(k+1) = z_3(k) - h\beta_{03}fal(e(k), 0.25, \delta) \end{cases} \tag{8}$$

where the nonlinear function $fal(e, \alpha, \delta)$ is defined as follows:

$$fal(\varepsilon, \ \alpha, \ \delta) = \begin{cases} |\varepsilon|^{\alpha} sign(\varepsilon), & |\varepsilon| > \delta \\ \varepsilon\delta^{\alpha-1}, & |\varepsilon| \le \delta \end{cases} \tag{9}$$

Nonlinear State Error Feedback (NLSEF). To obtain error signals, we subtract ESO outputs from TD outputs:

$$e_i = v_i - z_i, \quad i = 1, 2, \ldots, n \tag{10}$$

The discrete form of NLSEF is:

$$\begin{cases} e_1(k) = v_1(k) - z_1(k) \\ e_2(k) = v_2(k) - z_2(k) \\ u_0(k) = \beta_{01}fal(e_1(k), \alpha_1, \delta) + \beta_{02}fal(e_2(k), \alpha_2, \delta) \\ u(k) = u_0(k) - z_3(k)/b_0 \end{cases} \quad (11)$$

3.2 The Simulation of the Course Keeping Controller

PID controller's parameters are: $K_p = 0.41$, $K_i = 0.001$, $K_d = 0.22$.

The parameters of the ADRC controller are as follows: TD: $r_0 = 20$, $h_0 = 0.38$; ESO: $\alpha_1 = 0.5$, $\alpha_2 = 0.25$, $\beta_{01} = 40$, $\beta_{02} = 95$, $\beta_{03} = 200$, $\delta = 0.75$; NLSEF: $\beta_{01} = 0.044$, $\beta_{02} = 1.05$, $\alpha_1 = 0.75$, $\alpha_2 = 1.25$, $\delta = 1.71$.

Disturbance model parameters are: $K_\omega = 0.979$, $\omega_0 = 0.606$.

Case: course keeping with disturbance ($90°$ reference course angle).

Analysis: we conclude that USV always under the disturbance, from Figs. 1 and 2, ADRC performs well than PID. In the case of small disturbances, the course angle of the ADRC shows a relatively small oscillation amplitude, and the rudder angle output curve indicates that the steering servo is manipulated at a small angle, and the steady-state error is smaller than that of PID controller, achieving in the case of perturbation of the reference route more accurate tracking.

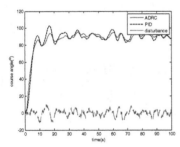

Fig. 1. Curve of course angle

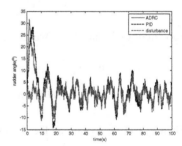

Fig. 2. Curve of rudder angle

4 Design of Adaptive LOS Guidance Controller

4.1 Problem Formulation

The geometry information of the LOS guidance is shown in Fig. 3.

For USV located at (x, y), we define the along-track and cross-track error (x_e, y_e). The errors are computed as:

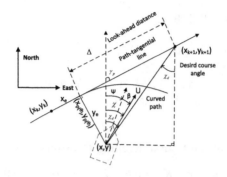

Fig. 3. Geometry information of the LOS guidance

$$\begin{bmatrix} x_e \\ y_e \end{bmatrix} = \underbrace{\begin{bmatrix} \cos(\gamma_p) & -\sin(\gamma_p) \\ \sin(\gamma_p) & \cos(\gamma_p) \end{bmatrix}}_{R(\gamma_p(\theta))} \begin{bmatrix} x - x_p(\theta) \\ y - y_p(\theta) \end{bmatrix} \tag{12}$$

In the paper, we don't consider the singularity when desired path consists of circular arc segment. Also, we just consider the along-track error ([5] points out when in a path- or target-tracking scenario needs to include the along-track error dynamics).

Taking the time derivative of y_e, we get

$$\begin{aligned} \dot{y}_e = & -(\dot{x} - \dot{x}_p(\theta))\sin(\gamma_p) - (x - x_p(\theta))\cos(\gamma_p)\dot{\gamma}_p \\ & + (\dot{y} - \dot{y}_p(\theta))\cos(\gamma_p) - (y - y_p(\theta))\sin(\gamma_p)\dot{\gamma}_p \end{aligned} \tag{13}$$

Substituting (1) into (13), we get

$$\begin{aligned} \dot{y}_e = & \; u\sin(\psi - \gamma_p) + v\cos(\psi - \gamma_p) - \dot{\gamma}_p(x - x_p(\theta))\cos(\gamma_p) \\ & + (y - y_p(\theta))\sin(\gamma_p) + \dot{\theta}\sqrt{x_p'(\theta)^2 + y_p'(\theta)^2}\sin(\gamma_p + \phi) \end{aligned} \tag{14}$$

Then y_e can be written as the amplitude-phase form:

$$\dot{y}_e = U\sin(\psi - \gamma_p + \beta) \tag{15}$$

where the amplitude $U = \sqrt{u^2 + v^2}$ and the phase sideslip angle $\beta = \arctan 2\,(v, u)$ are recognized as the speed and sideslip angle.

Assumption 1: The sideslip angle β is small and constant during path following.

Remark 1: When tracking the curve path, the sideslip angle is constant. It will largely affect the path following performance even if the sideslip is small.

4.2   Adaptive LOS Guidance Algorithm

Assumption 2: The heading autopilot can track the desired heading angle well, namely $\psi = \psi_d$.

Let $\hat{\beta}$ denote the estimate of the sideslip and $\tilde{\beta} = \beta - \hat{\beta}$ is the parameter estimation error. Then we propose the adaptive LOS guidance law:

$$\psi_d = \gamma_p + tan^{-1}(-\frac{1}{\Delta}y_e - \hat{\beta}) \tag{16}$$

$$\dot{\hat{\beta}} = k\frac{U\Delta y_e}{\sqrt{\Delta^2 + (y_e + \Delta\hat{\beta})^2}}, k > 0 \tag{17}$$

with $0 < \Delta_{min} < \Delta < \Delta_{max}$ and $0 < U_{min} < U \leq U_{max}$, the origin $(y_e, \tilde{\beta}) = (0,0)$ is UGAS.
Proof: Consider the Lyapunov function:

$$V(t, y_e, \tilde{\beta}) = \frac{1}{2}y_e^2 + \frac{1}{2k}\tilde{\beta}^2 > 0 \tag{18}$$

Then

$$\dot{V}(t, y_e, \tilde{\beta}) = y_e\dot{y}_e + \frac{1}{k}\tilde{\beta}\dot{\tilde{\beta}} \tag{19}$$

Concerning

$$\begin{aligned}\dot{y}_e &= -U\frac{y_e + \Delta\hat{\beta}}{\sqrt{\Delta^2 + (y_e + \Delta\hat{\beta})^2}} + U\frac{\Delta}{\sqrt{\Delta^2 + (y_e + \Delta\hat{\beta})^2}}\beta \\ &= -U\frac{y_e}{\sqrt{\Delta^2 + (y_e + \Delta\hat{\beta})^2}} + U\frac{\Delta}{\sqrt{\Delta^2 + (y_e + \Delta\hat{\beta})^2}}\tilde{\beta}\end{aligned} \tag{20}$$

Substituting (20) into (19), we get

$$\dot{V}(t, y_e, \tilde{\beta}) = -U\frac{y_e^2}{\sqrt{\Delta^2 + (y_e + \Delta\hat{\beta})^2}} + U\frac{\Delta y_e}{\sqrt{\Delta^2 + (y_e + \Delta\hat{\beta})^2}}\tilde{\beta} + \frac{1}{k}\tilde{\beta}\dot{\tilde{\beta}} \tag{21}$$

Based on Assumption 1, we have $\tilde{\beta} = \dot{\beta} - \dot{\hat{\beta}} \Rightarrow \dot{\tilde{\beta}} = -\dot{\hat{\beta}}$. Substituting (17) into (21), we get

$$\dot{V}(t, y_e, \tilde{\beta}) = -U\frac{y_e^2}{\sqrt{\Delta^2 + (y_e + \Delta\hat{\beta})^2}} \leq 0 \tag{22}$$

Hence, we can conclude the origin $(y_e, \tilde{\beta}) = (0,0)$ is UGAS.

5 Simulations

5.1 Straight-Line Path Following

The desired path is given as $(x_d, y_d) = (\theta, \theta)$ and USV's velocity is chosen as 5 m/s. Initial position is $(x, y) = (40$ m, -20 m$)$. Power spectrum density of $\omega(s)$ in (5) is 0.1. The results are shown in Figs. 4, 5, 6 and 7.

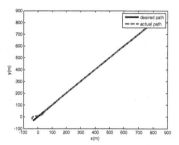

Fig. 4. Straight-line path following

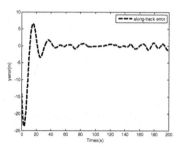

Fig. 5. Curve of the cross-track error

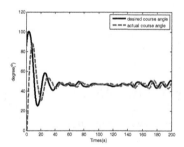

Fig. 6. Curve of course angle

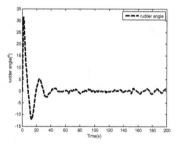

Fig. 7. Curve of rudder angle

Linear path tracking is quite accurate. If there is no sideslip compensation, the path may not be tracked so accurately and cross-track error may increase. As seen in Fig. 6, the actual course angle of the unmanned vessel has a mutation at the beginning, which ensures a good tracking effect in a short time. Figure 7 shows the change of rudder angle, and the rudder angle changes slightly within the acceptable range. As illustrated in the Fig. 5, the convergence to the desired path is guaranteed.

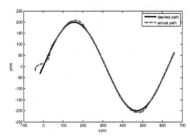

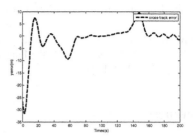

Fig. 8. Sinusoidal path following   **Fig. 9.** Curve of the cross-track error

5.2 Sinusoidal Path Following Simulation

The desired path is $.(x_d, y_d) = (200\sin(\theta/100), \theta)$. and USV's velocity is chosen as 5 m/s. Initial position is $(x, y) = (40 \text{ m}, -20 \text{ m})$. The results are shown in Figs. 8, 9, 10 and 11.

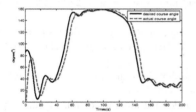

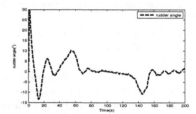

Fig. 10. Desired and actual course angle   **Fig. 11.** Curve of rudder angle

As illustrated in Figs. 8 and 9, the convergence to the desired path also be guaranteed, USV follows the sinusoidal path well. Maximum cross-track error is 10 m when USV move to the turn place of path. Figure 10 shows that ADRC can track the desired course angle. Figure 11 is the curve of rudder angle. In summary, curve path following is more difficult to achieve than straight line. In other words, the strategy of LOS guidance combining ADRC is feasible and the simulations verify the method is efficient.

6 Conclusion

In the paper, the adaptive LOS guidance is proposed using cross-track error and path-tangential angle to calculate the desired yaw angle and make the compensation of sideslip angle caused by ocean current. ADRC controller is used to track and keep the desired yaw angle. Based on MATLAB/Simulink, the feasibility of the proposed approach for straight-line and sinusoidal path following is verified. We will further study the LOS guidance algorithm and other control methods for USV in the future.

Acknowledgement. This work is partially supported by "the Nature Science Foundation of China" (grant NO. 51609033) and "the Fundamental Research Funds for the Central Universities" (grant NO. 3132016315).

References

1. Breivik, M., Fossen, T.I.: Guidance-based path following for autonomous underwater vehicles. In: Proceedings of MTS/IEEE, OCEANS, vol. 3, pp. 2807–2814 (2005)
2. Breivik, M., Fossen, T.I.: Path following for marine surface vessels. In: MTTS/IEEE TECHNO-OCEAN, OCEANS, vol. 4, pp. 2282–2289 (2005)
3. Borhaug, E., Pavlov, A., Pettersen, K.Y.: Integral LOS control for path following of underactuated marine surface vessels in the presence of constant ocean currents. In: IEEE Conference on Decision and Control, vol. 30, pp. 4984–4991 (2008)
4. Bibuli, M., Caharija, W., Pettersen, K.Y., et al.: ILOS guidance - experiments and tuning. In: IFAC Proceedings, vol. 47(3), pp. 4209–4214 (2014)
5. Lekkas, A.M., Fossen, T.I.: Integral los path following for curved paths based on a monotone cubic hermite spline parametrization. IEEE Trans. Control Syst. Technol. 22(6), 2287–2301 (2014)
6. Fossen, T.I., Pettersen, K.Y., Galeazzi, R.: Line-of-sight path following for dubins paths with adaptive sideslip compensation of drift forces. IEEE Trans. Control Syst. Technol. 23(2), 820–827 (2015)
7. Pettersen, K.Y., Lefeber, E.: Way-point tracking control of ships. In: Proceedings of the IEEE Conference on Decision and Control, vol. 1, pp. 940–945 (2001)
8. Fossen, T.I.: Handbook of Marine Craft Hydrodynamics and Motion Control, 1st edn. John Wiley & Sons Ltd., United Kingdom (2011)
9. Fossen, T.I.: Guidance and Control of Ocean Vehicles. 1st edn. John Wiley & Sons Ltd., chichester (1994)

Adaptive Neural Control for Pure Feedback Nonlinear Systems with Uncertain Actuator Nonlinearity

Maolong Lv[1(✉)], Ying Wang[1], Simone Baldi[2], Zongcheng Liu[3],
Chao Shi[3], Chaoqi Fu[1], Xiangfei Meng[1], and Yao Qi[1]

[1] College of Equipment Management and Safety Engineering,
Air Force Engineering University, Xi'an 710051, Shaanxi, China
18037707161@163.com
[2] Delft Center for Systems and Control, Delft University of Technology,
2628 CD Delft, Netherlands
[3] College of Aeronautics and Astronautics Engineering,
Air Force Engineering University, Xi'an 710038, Shaanxi, China

Abstract. For the pure feedback systems with uncertain actuator nonlinearity and non-differentiable non-affine function, a novel adaptive neural control scheme is proposed. Firstly, the assumption that the non-affine function must be differentiable everywhere with respect to control input has been canceled; in addition, the proposed approach can not only be applicable to actuator input dead zone nonlinearity, but also to backlash nonlinearity without changing the controller. Secondly, the neural network (NN) is used to approximate unknown nonlinear functions of system generated in the process of control design and a nonlinear robust term is introduced to eliminate the actuator nonlinearity modeling error, the NN approximation error and the external disturbances. Semi-globally uniformly ultimately boundedness of all signals in the closed loop system is analytically proved by utilizing Lyapunov theory. Finally, the effectiveness of the designed method is demonstrated via two examples.

Keywords: Adaptive neural control · Robust control · Actuator input nonlinearity · Non-affine function

1 Introduction

As we all know, pure feedback systems have a more general form than strict feedback systems, and many industrial applications such as biochemical process, mechanical systems and dynamic model in pendulum control have the form of pure feed feedback systems. Many approaches have been investigated for this class of systems [1–4]. However, it is worth mentioning that, for non-affine nonlinear pure feedback systems, the main difficulty of controller design is that there is no affine control appearance of control input in systems; therefore, the approaches developed for affine nonlinear systems cannot be directly applied to control design for pure feedback systems in non-affine form. To overcome this difficulty, some remarkable methods have been presented for pure feedback systems such as in [5, 6]. Nevertheless, it is worth noting

© Springer International Publishing AG 2017
D. Liu et al. (Eds.): ICONIP 2017, Part VI, LNCS 10639, pp. 201–211, 2017.
https://doi.org/10.1007/978-3-319-70136-3_22

that the commonly used assumption in the above schemes is that the non-affine function of the pure feedback system is always assumed to be differentiable with respect to the control input or state variable. This is a restrictive condition for non-affine function due to the fact that the non-affine functions in some practical systems are always continuous but not differentiable.

Evident examples of such functions are non-smooth nonlinear characteristics such as dead-zone, backlash, and hysteresis, which extensively appear in mechanical connection, hydraulic servo valves, piezoelectric translators, and electric servomotors, and which may lead to instability of the closed-loop system if their effect is not taken into account properly. Although some constructive methods have been designed to eliminate the adverse influence in closed-loop systems such as in [7], it should be noted that the approach in [7] is only applicable to strict feedback nonlinear systems but is not be suitable for pure feedback systems. What's more, to the best of the authors' knowledge, the research for control design of pure feedback systems with uncertain actuator nonlinearity is an open problem, which motivates us to explore new methods to solve this problem.

Motivated by above discussion, this work proposes a novel adaptive neural control scheme for pure feedback systems with uncertain actuator input nonlinearity. The main contributions of this paper are as follows:

(1) The restrictive differentiability condition for non-affine function of pure feedback systems is removed and only a semi-bounded condition is required.
(2) Different from all the previous researches, in this paper, actuator input dead zone nonlinearity and backlash nonlinearity of pure feedback systems are both considered by modeling actuator nonlinearity appropriately when designing controller, which is a completely new work for pure feedback systems. The proposed method is not only applicable to the actuator dead zone nonlinearity, but also is suitable for the backlash nonlinearity, which has a more relaxed application scope than existing works such as in [1, 2].

2   Problem Statement and Preliminaries

Consider a class of pure feedback systems with actuator input nonlinearity as follows:

$$\begin{cases} \dot{x}_i = x_{i+1}, \quad i = 1, 2 \ldots, n-1 \\ \dot{x}_n = f(x, v(u(t))) + d(x, t) \\ y = x_1 \end{cases} \tag{1}$$

where $x(t) = [x_1(t), x_2(t), \ldots, x_n(t)]^T \in R^n$ and $y \in R$ denote the system states and output, respectively; $d(x, t)$ represents systems external disturbance; $f(x, v(u(t)))$ is an unknown function such that $f(x, 0) = g(x)$; $u(t)$ and $v(u(t))$ are the actuator input and output, respectively. The actuator nonlinear model can be expressed as

$$v(u(t)) = k(u, t) \cdot u + \varepsilon_u \tag{2}$$

where $k(u, t)$ is an unknown positive constant and ε_u is a modeling error satisfying $|\varepsilon_u| \leq \varepsilon_u^*$ with ε_u^* being an unknown positive constant.

Assumption 1: There exist unknown constants m_1 and m_2 such that

$$0 < m_1 \leq k(u, t) \leq m_2 \tag{3}$$

Assumption 2: There exists an unknown positive constant d^* such that $|d(t)| \leq d^*$.

Assumption 3: Define $F(\mathbf{x}, v) = f(\mathbf{x}, v) - f(\mathbf{x}, 0)$, there always exists an unknown positive m_i $(i = 1, 2, 3, 4)$ making the following inequalities hold.

$$\begin{cases} m_1 v \leq F(\mathbf{x}, v) \leq m_2 v, & v \geq 0 \\ m_3 v \leq F(\mathbf{x}, v) \leq m_4 v, & v < 0 \end{cases} \tag{4}$$

Remark 1: It should be noted that the unknown function $f(\mathbf{x}, v(u(t)))$ is commonly assumed to satisfy $0 < g_1 \leq \partial f(\mathbf{x}, v(u(t))) / \partial v \leq g_2$ such as in [2, 8] with g_1 and g_2 being unknown positive constants, which is seen as the controllability condition of their systems. However, in this paper, Assumption 3 is utilized to guarantee the controllability of system (1), while the restrictive assumption that non-affine function must be differentiable has been removed. Moreover, we have also considered a class of uncertain actuator nonlinearity simultaneously when designing the control scheme.

According to Assumption 3, if $v < 0$, we have

$$F(\mathbf{x}, v) = [(1 - \theta_1(t))m_1 + m_2\theta_1(t)]v \tag{5}$$

where $\theta_1(t) \in [0, 1]$, if $v < 0$, we obtain

$$F(\mathbf{x}, v) = [(1 - \theta_2(t))m_3 + m_4\theta_2(t)]v \tag{6}$$

with $\theta_2(t) \in [0, 1]$.

Define

$$G(t) = \begin{cases} (1 - \theta_1(t))m_1 + m_2\theta_1(t), & v \geq 0 \\ (1 - \theta_2(t))m_3 + m_4\theta_2(t), & v < 0 \end{cases} \tag{7}$$

Then, one has $0 < \min_{i=1,2,3,4}\{m_i\} \leq G(t) \leq \max_{i=1,2,3,4}\{m_i\} = G_{\max}$ \tag{8}

Hence, the non-affine system (1) can be converted into the following affine system

$$
\begin{cases}
\dot{x}_i = x_{i+1}, \ i = 1, 2 \ldots, n-1 \\
\dot{x}_n = g(\boldsymbol{x}) + k(u, t)G(t)u(t) + G(t)\varepsilon_u + d(\boldsymbol{x}, t) \\
y = x_1
\end{cases} \tag{9}
$$

Radial basis function neural network can approximate any continuous nonlinear function $h(\boldsymbol{Z})$ with any precision. Namely

$$
h(\boldsymbol{Z}) = \boldsymbol{W}^{*T}\boldsymbol{\psi}(\boldsymbol{Z}) + \varepsilon \tag{10}
$$

where $\boldsymbol{Z} \in \boldsymbol{\Omega}_z \subset \boldsymbol{R}^n$ is a input vector; n is the input dimension of neural network; ε is the approximation error satisfying $|\varepsilon| \leq \varepsilon^*$ with ε^* being an unknown positive constant; $\boldsymbol{\psi}(\boldsymbol{Z}) \in \boldsymbol{R}^l$ is commonly selected as Gaussian function, and $\boldsymbol{W}^* \in \boldsymbol{R}^l$ is the optimal weight vector defined by

$$
\boldsymbol{W}^* = \arg \min_{\boldsymbol{W} \in \boldsymbol{R}^l} \left\{ \sup_{\boldsymbol{Z} \in \boldsymbol{\Omega}_Z} |h(\boldsymbol{Z}) - \boldsymbol{W}^T\boldsymbol{\psi}(\boldsymbol{Z})| \right\} \tag{11}
$$

where $\boldsymbol{W}$ is a weight vector.

The following definition and lemma are instrumental to stability analysis.

Definition 1: A function $N(\cdot)$ is called a Nussbaum-type function if it has the following properties

$$
\begin{aligned}
\limsup_{s \to \infty} \frac{1}{s} \int_0^s N(\zeta)d\zeta = +\infty, \\
\liminf_{s \to \infty} \frac{1}{s} \int_0^s N(\zeta)d\zeta = -\infty
\end{aligned} \tag{12}
$$

Lemma 1 [9]: $V(\cdot)$ and $\zeta(\cdot)$ are smooth functions defined on $[0, \ t_f)$ with $V(t) \geq 0$, and $N(\zeta)$ is a Nussbaum-type function. If the following inequality holds

$$
V(t) \leq c_1 + e^{-c_2 t} \int_0^t [g(x(\tau))N(\zeta(\tau)) + 1]\dot{\zeta}e^{-c_2\tau}d\tau \tag{13}
$$

where c_1 and c_2 are positive constants; $g(x(\tau))$ is a time-varying parameter which takes values in the intervals $I = [l^-, l^+]$ with $0 \notin I$, then, $V(t)$, $\zeta(t)$ and $\int_0^t N(\zeta(\tau))\dot{\zeta}d\tau$ are bounded in $[0, t_f)$.

We are now in the position to state the control objective.

Control objective: Design an adaptive neural network control law combined with the Nussbaum gain technology to make the system output y follow the desired trajectory y_d accurately. Assume that the desired reference trajectory y_d is bounded, namely, $y_d, y_d^{(1)}$, $y_d^{(2)}, \ldots, y_d^{(n)}$ are continuous and bounded, we define $\boldsymbol{x}_d = [y_d, \dot{y}_d, \ldots, y_d^{(n-1)}]^T$, $\boldsymbol{x}_d \in \boldsymbol{R}^n$, where $\boldsymbol{e} = \boldsymbol{x} - \boldsymbol{x}_d$ is the tracking error.

For compactness, in the following let $|\bullet|$ denote the Euclidean norm of vector $\bullet$, $\|\cdot\|$ represents the 2-norm, $\hat{\bullet}$ is the estimate of $\bullet^*$ with $\tilde{\bullet} = \bullet^* - \hat{\bullet}$, and the Nussbaum function is chosen as $N(\zeta) = e^{\zeta^2}\cos(\pi\zeta/2)$ in this paper.

3 Controller Design and Stability Analysis

To begin with the design, we firstly define a filtered tracking. Using the idea of sliding mode control, the filtered tracking error is designed as follows

$$r = [\Lambda^T \ 1]e \tag{14}$$

where $\Lambda = [\lambda_{n-1}, \lambda_{n-2}, \ldots, \lambda_1]^T$ is a design vector with $s^{n-1} + \lambda_1 s^{n-2} + \cdots + \lambda_{n-1}$ a Hurwitz polynomial. The time derivative of the filtered tracking error is

$$\begin{aligned}
\dot{r} &= g(x) + k(u,t)G(t)u(t) + G(t)\varepsilon_u \\
&+ d(x,t) - y_d^{(n)} + [0 \ \Lambda^T]e
\end{aligned} \tag{15}$$

To consider the stability of (15), define a quadratic function as follows

$$V_r = \frac{1}{2}r^2 \tag{16}$$

The time derivative of V_r along (15) is

$$\begin{aligned}
\dot{V}_r &= r[g(x) + k(u,t)G(t)u(t) + [0 \ \Lambda^T]e \\
&+ G(t)\varepsilon_u + d(x,t) - y_d^{(n)}]
\end{aligned} \tag{17}$$

From Assumption 2 and (8), we have

$$\begin{aligned}
\dot{V}_r &\leq rg(x) + rk(u,t)G(t)u(t) \\
&+ |r|(G_{max}\varepsilon_u^* + d^*) + rY_d
\end{aligned} \tag{18}$$

where $Y_d = -y_d^{(n)} + [0 \ \Lambda^T]e$. Since $g(x)$ is an unknown continuous function, we apply a RBF neural network to approximate it on a compact set, namely

$$g(x) = W^{*T}\psi(x) + \varepsilon \tag{19}$$

where ε is the approximation error. It follows from (10) that there exists an unknown positive ε^* such that $|\varepsilon| \leq \varepsilon^*$ with ε^* being an unknown positive constant. Since the optimal weight vector W^* is unknown, we will use its estimate $\hat{W}$ for the controller design. Substituting (19) into (18) yields

$$\dot{V}_r \leq r\boldsymbol{W}^{*T}\boldsymbol{\psi}(\boldsymbol{x}) + rk(u,t)G(t)u(t)$$
$$+ |r|(G_{\max}\varepsilon_u^* + d^* + \varepsilon^*) + rY_d \tag{20}$$
$$\leq r\boldsymbol{W}^{*T}\boldsymbol{\psi}(\boldsymbol{x}) + |r|\delta^* + rk(u,t)G(t)u(t) + rY_d$$

with $\delta^* = G_{\max}\varepsilon_u^* + d^* + \varepsilon^*$ being an unknown positive constant.

Consider the following Lyapunov function

$$V = V_r + \frac{1}{2}\tilde{\boldsymbol{W}}^T\boldsymbol{\Gamma}^{-1}\tilde{\boldsymbol{W}} + \frac{1}{2\gamma}\tilde{\delta}^2 \tag{21}$$

where $\boldsymbol{\Gamma} = \boldsymbol{\Gamma}^{-1}$ denotes adaptive gain matrix; and γ is an adaptive gain coefficient; $\tilde{\boldsymbol{W}} = \boldsymbol{W}^* - \hat{\boldsymbol{W}}$ and $\tilde{\delta} = \delta^* - \hat{\delta}$ are parameter estimation errors.

It follows from (20) that the time derivative of V is

$$\dot{V} \leq r\boldsymbol{W}^{*T}\boldsymbol{\psi}(\boldsymbol{x}) + |r|\delta^* + rk(u,t)G(t)u(t) + rY_d$$
$$- \tilde{\boldsymbol{W}}^T\boldsymbol{\Gamma}^{-1}\dot{\hat{\boldsymbol{W}}} - \frac{1}{\gamma}\tilde{\delta}\dot{\hat{\delta}} \tag{22}$$

Design the actual control law and adaptation laws as follows

$$u = N(\zeta)\left[\beta r + \hat{\boldsymbol{W}}^T\boldsymbol{\psi}(\boldsymbol{x}) + \hat{\delta} \cdot \tanh(\frac{r}{\tau}) + Y_d\right] \tag{23}$$

$$\dot{\zeta} = \beta r^2 + r\hat{\boldsymbol{W}}^T\boldsymbol{\psi}(\boldsymbol{x}) + \hat{\delta} \cdot r\tanh(\frac{r}{\tau}) + rY_d \tag{24}$$

$$\begin{cases} \dot{\hat{\boldsymbol{W}}} = \boldsymbol{\Gamma}(r\boldsymbol{\psi}(\boldsymbol{x}) - \sigma_1\hat{\boldsymbol{W}}) \\ \dot{\hat{\delta}} = \gamma(r\tanh(\frac{r}{\tau}) - \sigma_2\hat{\delta}) \end{cases} \tag{25}$$

where $\beta > 0$, $\tau > 0$, $\sigma_1 > 0$ and $\sigma_2 > 0$ are design parameters.

Then, the stability of the closed-loop system is analyzed as follows. Substituting (23) into (22), we obtain

$$\dot{V} \leq r\boldsymbol{W}^{*T}\boldsymbol{\psi}(\boldsymbol{x}) + |r|\delta^* + k(u,t)G(t)N(\zeta)\dot{\zeta}$$
$$+ rY_d - \tilde{\boldsymbol{W}}^T\boldsymbol{\Gamma}^{-1}\dot{\hat{\boldsymbol{W}}} - \frac{1}{\gamma}\tilde{\delta}\dot{\hat{\delta}} \tag{26}$$

From (26) we can further have

$$\dot{V} \leq k(u,t)G(t)N(\zeta)\dot{\zeta} + \delta^*\left[|r| - r\tanh(\frac{r}{\tau})\right]$$
$$- \tilde{\boldsymbol{W}}^T\boldsymbol{\Gamma}^{-1}\left[\dot{\hat{\boldsymbol{W}}} - r\boldsymbol{\Gamma}\boldsymbol{\psi}(\boldsymbol{x})\right] - \beta r^2 \tag{27}$$
$$- \frac{1}{\gamma}\tilde{\delta}\left[\dot{\hat{\delta}} - \gamma \cdot r\tanh(\frac{r}{\tau})\right] + \dot{\zeta}$$

and substituting (25) into (27), one has

$$\dot{V} \leq - \beta r^2 + k(u,t)G(t)N(\zeta)\dot{\zeta} + \sigma_1 \tilde{W}^{\mathrm{T}}\hat{W}$$
$$+ \sigma_2 \tilde{\delta}\hat{\delta} + \delta^* \left[|r| - r\tanh(\frac{r}{\tau}) \right] + \dot{\zeta} \tag{28}$$

Using the following inequality for any $\tau > 0$ and $r \in R$ [10].

$$|r| - r \cdot \tanh(r/\tau) \leq 0.2785\tau \tag{29}$$

Substituting (29) into (27), we obtain

$$\dot{V} \leq - \beta r^2 + k(u,t)G(t)N(\zeta)\dot{\zeta} + \dot{\zeta}$$
$$+ \sigma_1 \tilde{W}^{\mathrm{T}}\hat{W} + \sigma_2 \tilde{\delta}\hat{\delta} + 0.2785\tau\delta^* \tag{30}$$

Utilizing the following inequalities

$$\sigma_1 \tilde{W}^{\mathrm{T}}\hat{W} \leq - \frac{\sigma_1}{2} \left\| \tilde{W} \right\|^2 + \frac{\sigma_1}{2} \left\| W^* \right\|^2$$

$$\sigma_2 \tilde{\delta}\hat{\delta} \leq - \frac{\sigma_2}{2} \tilde{\delta}^2 + \frac{\sigma_2}{2} \delta^{*2}$$

Consequently, we can further have

$$\dot{V} \leq - \alpha_1 V + [k(u,t)G(t)N(\zeta) + 1]\dot{\zeta} + \alpha_0 \tag{31}$$

where $\alpha_1 = \min\left\{ 2\beta, \frac{\sigma_1}{\lambda_{\max}(\Gamma^{-1})}, \sigma_2\gamma \right\} \alpha_0 = 0.2785\tau\delta^* + \frac{\sigma_1}{2}\left\| W^* \right\|^2 + \frac{\sigma_2}{2}\delta^{*2}$.
Multiply (31) by $e^{\alpha_1 t}$ and integrate (31) over $[0,t]$, we have

$$V(t) \leq \frac{\alpha_0}{\alpha_1} + (V(0) - \frac{\alpha_0}{\alpha_1})e^{-\alpha_1 t} +$$
$$e^{-\alpha_1 t} \int_0^t [k(u,t)G(\tau)N(\zeta) + 1]\dot{\zeta}e^{\alpha_1 \tau}d\tau$$
$$\leq \frac{\alpha_0}{\alpha_1} + V(0)$$
$$+ \int_0^t [k(u,t)G(\tau)N(\zeta) + 1]\dot{\zeta}e^{-\alpha_1(t-\tau)}d\tau \tag{32}$$

In view of Lemma (1), we know that $V(t)$, $\zeta(t)$ and $\int_0^t k(u,t)G(\tau)N(\zeta)\dot{\zeta}d\tau$ are bounded on $[0, t_f)$. Therefore, let

$$\int_0^t |k(u,t)G(\tau)N(\zeta) + 1|\dot{\zeta}e^{-\alpha_1(t-\tau)}d\tau \leq Q \tag{33}$$

From (32) and (33), one has

$$\lim_{t \to \infty} V(t) \leq \frac{a_0}{a_1} + V(0) + Q \tag{34}$$

Since $V(t)$ is bounded, we derive that all signals of closed-loop system are SGUUB.

Then, define

$$C_0 = \sqrt{2(a_0/a_1 + V(0) + Q)} \tag{35}$$

According to (21) and (35), we obtain

$$r \leq \sqrt{2V(t)} \leq C_0 \tag{36}$$

Therefore, by invoking the definition of filter tracking error r, we know the tracking error e is bounded, moreover, when $r \to 0$, tracking error $e \to 0$. Consequently, the system output y can track the desired trajectory y_d accurately.

4 Simulation Results

Example 1: Consider a class of pure feedback nonlinear systems with actuator input dead zone nonlinearity as follows

$$\begin{cases} \dot{x}_1 = x_2 \\ \dot{x}_2 = -p_1 x_1 - p x_2 - x_1^3 + q \cos(wt) \\ \qquad + h(x, v(u(t))) + d(x, t) \\ y = x_1 \end{cases}$$

where $h(x, v(u(t))) = (1 + 0.1 \cos x_1)(1 + 0.2 \cos v(u(t))) \times v(u(t))$ is a non-affine term and $d(x, t) = 0.1(x_1^2 + x_2^2) \cdot \sin t$ denotes external disturbance; $p_1 = -0.2$; $q = 5 + 0.1 \cos(t)$; $p = 0.2 + 0.2 \cos(5x_1)$ and $w = 0.5 + 0.1 \sin(t)$ are uncertain parameters, initial conditions $x_1(0) = 0.5$, $x_2(0) = 0$ and we assume the desired trajectory $y_d = 0.5 \times (\sin t + \sin(0.5t))$.

The model of actuator dead zone nonlinearity is as follows

$$v(u(t)) = \begin{cases} (1 + 0.3 \sin(u))(u - 0.5) & 0.5 \leq u \\ 0 & -0.3 \leq u \leq 0.5 \\ (0.8 + 0.2 \cos(u))(u + 0.3) & u \leq -0.3 \end{cases}$$

In the simulation, the controller $u(t)$ is designed as (23), the parameter adaptation laws are chosen as (24) and (25), respectively. The Gaussian function is selected as the basis function of RBF neural network as follows

$$\psi(\mathbf{Z}) = e^{-(\mathbf{Z}-\mu_i)^T(\mathbf{Z}-\mu_i)/v_i^2}, i = 1, 2, \ldots, l$$

The parameters of RBF neural network are set as: $\hat{\mathbf{W}}^T\psi(\mathbf{x})$ contains $l = 27$ nodes, the center $\mu_i(i = 1, 2, \ldots, 27)$ is evenly distributed $[-10, 10] \times [-10, 10]$, width $v_i = 2(i = 1, 2, \ldots, 27)$. The initial values of neural networks weights $\hat{\mathbf{W}}(0)$ are set to zero and the initial conditions of parameters estimations are set as $\hat{\delta}(0) = 0$ and $\zeta(0) = 1$. The remaining parameters are selected as: $\boldsymbol{\Gamma} = diag[0.5]$, $\lambda_1 = 1.5$, $\sigma_1 = \sigma_2 = 0.5$, $\gamma = 1.5$, $\tau = 0.2$, $\beta = 2.5$. Simulation results are shown in Fig. 1. It is seen from Fig. 1 that the proposed approach is sufficient to make the systems output follow the desired reference trajectory and fairly good tracking performance has been achieved. In addition, the boundedness of variable x_2 and control input u can also be observed from Fig. 1.

Note that the non-affine function $h(\mathbf{x}, v(u(t)))$ contains dead zone nonlinearity and is therefore obviously non-differentiable, which implies that the existing methods cannot work, while our approach is adequate to control this system.

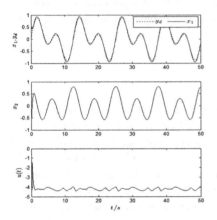

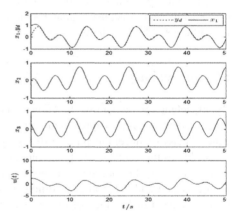

Fig. 1. The response curves of Example 1   **Fig. 2.** The responses of Genesio system

Moreover, when designing the controller, all the existing methods have not considered the influence of actuator input nonlinearity, while our scheme has taken it into account.

Example 2: Consider a Genesio system with parametric perturbations and actuator input backlash nonlinearity as follows

$$\begin{cases} \dot{x}_1 = x_2 \\ \dot{x}_2 = x_3 \\ \dot{x}_3 = -cx_1 - bx_2 - ax_3 + x_1^2 + h(\boldsymbol{x}, v(u(t))) + d(\boldsymbol{x}, t) \\ y = x_1 \end{cases}$$

where $h(\boldsymbol{x}, v(u(t))) = (2 + \cos x_1)(1 + 0.2 \sin^2 v(u(t))) \times v(u(t))$ is non-affine function; $d(\mathbf{x}, t) = \sin(0.1t)$ denotes external interference and $a = 1.6$; $b = 3$; $c = 6$; initial states are set as $x_1(0) = 1$, $x_2(0) = 0$, $x_3(0) = 0$. Set the desired output trajectory as $y_d = 0.5(\sin t + \sin(0.5t))$.

The model of actuator backlash nonlinearity is expressed as

$$v(u(t)) = \begin{cases} 1.2(u - 0.5), & \dot{u} > 0 \ \text{and} \ \varphi(u) = 1.2(u - 0.5) \\ 1.2(u + 0.6), & \dot{u} < 0 \ \text{and} \ \varphi(u) = 1.2(u + 0.6) \\ v(t_-) & \text{otherwises} \end{cases}$$

In the simulation, the design parameters are selected as: $\boldsymbol{\Gamma} = diag[0.5]$, $\lambda_1 = 2$, $\lambda_2 = 1$, $\sigma_1 = \sigma_2 = 0.3$, $\gamma = 1.2$, $\tau = 0.5$, $\beta = 5$ and the remaining parameters and the controller structure keep unchanged. The results are depicted in Fig. 2.

It can be easily seen from Fig. 2 that the proposed scheme can not only achieve good tracking performance even in the presence of actuator input dead zone nonlinearity while taking actuator input backlash nonlinearity, but also in the presence of non-differentiable non-affine functions.

5   Conclusions

By modeling the non-affine function and actuator dead zone and backlash model appropriately, a novel adaptive neural tracking control scheme is presented for a more general class of uncertain pure feedback systems. The proposed method is not only applicable to the actuator dead zone nonlinearity, but also is suitable for the backlash nonlinearity. In addition, the assumption that the actuator function must be known has been canceled and the restrictive differentiability condition of non-affine function has been relaxed. Finally, the performance of the proposed approach has been verified through two simulation examples.

References

1. Shi, C.: Robust adaptive neural control for a class of non-affine nonlinear systems. Neurocomputing **223**, 118–128 (2017)
2. Liu, Z., Dong, X., Xue, J., Li, H., Chen, Y.: Adaptive neural control for a class of pure-feedback nonlinear systems via dynamic surface technique. IEEE Trans. Neural Netw. Learn. Syst. **27**(9), 1969–1975 (2016)
3. Li, Y., Tong, S., Liu, L., Feng, G.: Adaptive output-feedback control design with prescribed performance for swithched nonlinear systems. Automatica **80**, 225–231 (2017)

4. Tong, S.C., Li, Y.M., Feng, G., Li, T.S.: Obeserver-based adaptive fuzzy backstepping dynamic surface control for a class of MIMO nonlinear systems. IEEE Trans. Syst. Man Cybern **41**(4), 1124–1135 (2011)
5. Yang, B.J., Calise, A.J.: Adaptive control of a class of non-affine systems using neural networks. IEEE Trans. Neural Netw. **18**(4), 1149–1159 (2007)
6. Hovakimyan, N., Yang, B.J., Calise, A.J.: Adaptive output feedback control methodology applicable to non-minimum phase nonlinear systems. Automatica **42**(4), 513–522 (2006)
7. Liu, Z.: Adaptive control for a class of nonlinear systems with uncertain actuator nonlinearity. Syst. Eng. Electron. Technol. **37**(1), 163–168 (2015)
8. Calise, A.J., Hovakimyan, N., Idan, M.: Adaptive output feedback control of nonlinear systems using neural networks. Automatica **37**(8), 1201–1211 (2001)
9. Lv, M.L., Sun, X.X., Liu, S.G., Wang, D.: Adaptive tracking control for non-affine nonlinear systems with non-affine function possibly being discontinuous. Int. J. Syst. Sci. **48**(5), 1115–1122 (2017)
10. Liu, Y.J., Li, J., Tong, S., Chen, C.P.: Neural network control-based adaptive learning design for nonlinear systems with full-state constraints. IEEE Trans. Neural Netw. Learn. Syst. **27**(7), 1562–1570 (2016)

Composite Learning Control of Hypersonic Flight Dynamics Without Back-Stepping

Yixin Cheng[1], Tianyi Shao[2], Rui Zhang[1], and Bin Xu[1,3(✉)]

[1] School of Automation, Northwestern Polytechnical University,
Xi'an 710072, China
yixin_cheng@mail.nwpu.edu.cn, ruidyx@sina.cn
[2] Shanghai Aerospace Control Technology Institute, Shanghai 201109, China
shao_tianyi@yeah.net
[3] Research Institute of Northwestern Polytechnical University in Shenzhen,
Shenzhen 518057, China
smileface.binxu@gmail.com

Abstract. In this paper, composite neural control is proposed for hypersonic flight control in presence of unknown dynamics. Using high gain observer (HGO), the controller of attitude subsystem is designed without back-stepping. This strategy simplifies the process of controller design and reduces the computation burden of parameter updating. To construct the composite neural controller, the filtered modeling error is further considered in the weight updating of RBF NN. Moreover, the composite neural controller can achieve the fast learning of system uncertainty. Simulation is presented to demonstrate the effectiveness of the design.

Keywords: Composite neural control · Output-feedback control · High gain observer · Hypersonic flight vehicle

1 Introduction

Owing to a more reliable way to access space and the more prominent capability of precise strike, hypersonic flight vehicles (HFVs) have attracted strong concern. HFVs is a highly nonlinear, time-varying and strong coupling system, thus, the controller design of hypersonic vehicles poses many challenges.

Back-stepping design [1,2] is widely applied on control of nonlinear system [3,4]. For back-stepping control of hypersonic flight dynamics, some papers can be referred to [5]. In [6,7] the control systems are transformed into the normal output-feedback form based on HGO which simplifies controller design since no virtual control signal is required for design.

The intelligent control has a great development in recent years. In [8], the back-stepping approach was proposed to achieve higher tracking accuracy of nonlinear system. Some adaptive back-stepping NN control methods in [3] are proposed to assure the stability of uncertain nonlinear system. The above-mentioned

© Springer International Publishing AG 2017
D. Liu et al. (Eds.): ICONIP 2017, Part VI, LNCS 10639, pp. 212–218, 2017.
https://doi.org/10.1007/978-3-319-70136-3_23

methods ignored the motivation of employing intelligent system to approximate nonlinear functions, which result in the learning accuracy of uncertainty is not high. To deal with this problem, some methods notice the accuracy of the desired identified models. In [9–11], the system modeling error is considered in the process of construct the composite updating law. Thus, More accurate tracking is achieved through composite learning.

In this paper, the attempt of composite neural learning is studied for hypersonic vehicles dynamics without back-stepping. In Sect. 2, the dynamics is given and Sect. 3 formulates the new dynamics. In Sect. 4, the composite neural controller is designed. Simulation results are given in Sect. 5. The conclusion is included in Sect. 6.

2   Problem Formulation

2.1   Hypersonic Flight Vehicle Model

A generic HFV is considered as follows

$$\dot{V} = \frac{T \cos \alpha - D}{m_g} - \frac{\mu \sin \gamma}{r^2} \tag{1}$$

$$\dot{h} = V \sin \gamma \tag{2}$$

$$\dot{\gamma} = \frac{L + T \sin \alpha}{m_g V} - \frac{\left(\mu - V^2 r\right) \cos \gamma}{V r^2} \tag{3}$$

$$\dot{\alpha} = q - \dot{\gamma} \tag{4}$$

$$\dot{q} = \frac{M_{yy}}{I_{yy}} \tag{5}$$

In system model, V is the velocity, h is the altitude, γ is the flight path angle, α is the attack angle, q is the pitch rate, δ_e is elevator deflection and β is the throttle setting. The detail of the dynamics can refer to literatures [6,7].

2.2   Strict-Feedback Formulation

Define the attitude of HFVs as $X = [x_1, x_2, x_3]^T$, $x_1 = \gamma$, $x_2 = \theta_p$, $x_3 = q$, where $\theta_p = \alpha + \gamma$. The attitude subsystem (3)–(5) can be written as the following strict-feedback form:

$$\begin{aligned}
\dot{x}_1 &= f_1(x_1) + g_1(x_1) x_2 \\
\dot{x}_2 &= f_2(x_1, x_2) + g_2(x_1, x_2) x_3 \\
\dot{x}_3 &= f_3(x_1, x_2, x_3) + g_3(x_1, x_2) u \\
y &= x_1 \\
u &= \delta_e
\end{aligned} \tag{6}$$

where the detailed expression of function f_i and g_i are given in [6,7].

2.3   Control Goal

This paper aim to design controller for attitude subsystem (6) to stabilize the system attitude and rapidly track the reference command h_d. However, it is complex to design controller for attitude subsystem due to the strict-feedback form and system uncertainties.

3   Output-Feedback Formulation and HGO Design

3.1   Output-Feedback Formulation

Define the new state variables $Z = [z_1, z_2, z_3]^T$, $z_1 \overset{\Delta}{=} y$, $z_2 \overset{\Delta}{=} \dot{z}_1 = f_1 + g_1 x_2$, $z_3 \overset{\Delta}{=} \dot{z}_2 = m_2 + n_2 x_3$. where $m_2 (x_1, x_2) = \left(\frac{\partial f_1}{\partial x_1} + \frac{\partial g_1}{\partial x_1} x_2 \right) (f_1 + g_1 x_2) + g_1 f_2$, $n_2 (x_1, x_2) = g_1 g_2 = g_1$.

Through this transformation, the attitude subsystem can be redescribed as

$$
\begin{aligned}
\dot{z}_1 &= z_2 \\
\dot{z}_2 &= z_3 \\
\dot{z}_3 &= m_3 + n_3 u \\
y &= z_1
\end{aligned}
\tag{7}
$$

where $m_3 (X) = \sum_{j=1}^{2} \left(\frac{\partial m_2}{\partial x_j} + \frac{\partial n_2}{\partial x_j} x_3 \right) (f_j + g_j x_{j+1}) + n_2 (f_3 + g_3 u)$, $n_3 (X) = g_1 g_3$. Because of system model exist uncertainties, we can obtain m_2 and m_3 are unknown.

3.2   HGO Design

Since the new states $Z = [z_1, z_2, z_3]^T$ are incomputable, the estimate value $\hat{Z} = [\hat{z}_1, \hat{z}_2, \hat{z}_3]^T$, $\hat{z}_1 = z_1, \hat{z}_2 = \frac{\xi_2}{\varepsilon}, \hat{z}_3 = \frac{\xi_3}{\varepsilon^2}$ as [6,7]

$$
\begin{aligned}
\dot{\xi}_1 &= \frac{\xi_2}{\varepsilon} \\
\dot{\xi}_2 &= \frac{\xi_3}{\varepsilon} \\
\dot{\xi}_3 &= \frac{-k_1 \xi_3 - k_2 \xi_2 - \xi_1 + y(t)}{\varepsilon}
\end{aligned}
\tag{8}
$$

where ε , k_1 and k_2 are positive design parameters.

To improve the learning accuracy and speed of system uncertainty, a filtered modeling error be used to construct composite neural control in subsequent controller design. This is the difference between the proposed strategy and other methods in [6,7].

4   Controller Design

Step 1: Define Y_d as

$$Y_d = [y_d, \dot{y}_d, \ddot{y}_d]^T \tag{9}$$

and

$$\hat{E} = \hat{Z} - Y_d \tag{10}$$

$$\hat{S} = \begin{bmatrix} H^T & 1 \end{bmatrix} \hat{E} \tag{11}$$

where $H = \begin{bmatrix} \eta^2, 2\eta \end{bmatrix}^T$ with $\eta > 0$.

Step 2: The unknown function $a_3(X)$ is approximated via RBF NN. Thus, the estimation of a_3 is obtained as

$$\hat{a}_3 = \hat{\omega}_a^T \theta_a(X) \tag{12}$$

The attitude controller is designed as

$$u = \frac{1}{b_3} \left(-k_A \hat{S} - \hat{\omega}_a^T \theta_a(X) + y_d^{(3)} \right) \tag{13}$$

where k_A is a positive design parameter.

The adaption law for $\hat{\omega}_a$ is designed as

$$\dot{\hat{\omega}}_a = \gamma_a \left[\left(\hat{S} + \gamma_{k_a} z_{NN} \right) \theta_a(X) - \delta_a \hat{\omega}_a \right] \tag{14}$$

where γ_a, γ_{k_a} and δ_a are positive design parameters. z_{NN} is the filtered modeling error and defined as

$$z_{NN} = \hat{z}_3 - \hat{z}_{3N} \tag{15}$$

The variable $\hat{z}_{3N}$ can be obtained from the following updating law

$$\dot{\hat{z}}_{3N} = \hat{a}_3 + b_3 u + \gamma_z (\hat{z}_3 - \hat{z}_{3N}) \tag{16}$$

where γ_z is a positive design parameter.

Remark 1. In [6,7], the HGO based neural control of hypersonic flight dynamics is studied. The design in this paper is different since the composite learning is included by using the important signal z_{NN}.

5   Simulation

In this section, some simulation tests are implemented with the winged-cone model to verify the effectiveness of the proposed algorithm. The altitude command can be generated by using the following filter:

$$\frac{\omega_{n1} \omega_{n2}^2}{(s + \omega_{n1})(s^2 + 2\varepsilon_c \omega_{n2} s + \omega_{n2}^2)} \tag{17}$$

where $\omega_{n1} = 0.5$, $\omega_{n2} = 0.2$, $\varepsilon_c = 0.7$.

For the altitude climbing, the reference altitude command can be followed in Fig. 1. In Fig. 2, it can be seen that the system states include flight path angle, attack angle and pitch rate are converging. The estimation of the HGO is presented in Fig. 3. The trajectory of composite learning weight updating law is shown in Fig. 4.

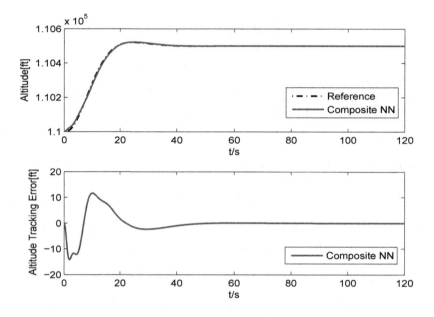

Fig. 1. Altitude tracking

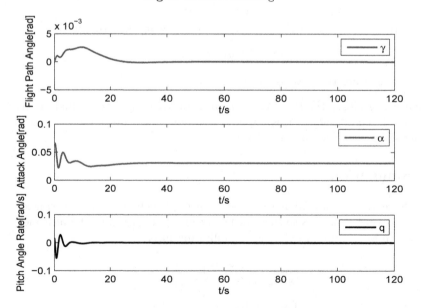

Fig. 2. System states

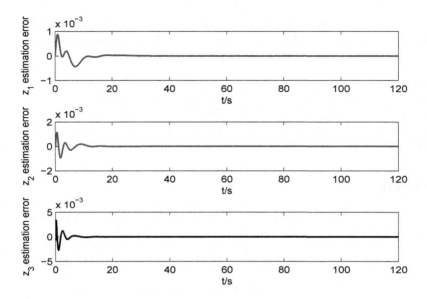

Fig. 3. HGO estimation error

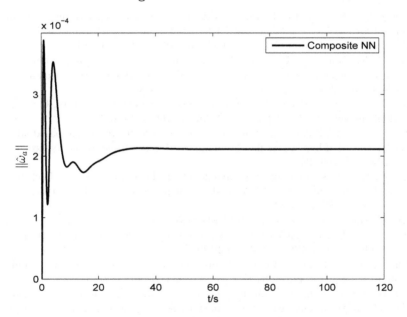

Fig. 4. Trajectory of $\|\hat{\omega}_a\|$

6   Conclusions

This paper studies the HGO based composite neural control of HFV without back-steeping. The lumped uncertain nonlinearity is approximated by using only one NN in the process of controller design. The composite neural updating law is constructed by using filtered tracking error and filtered modeling error. The simulation is presented to show the effectiveness of the controller design.

Acknowledgments. This work was supported by Fundamental Research Funds of Shenzhen Science and Technology Project (JCYJ20160229172341417), Natural Science Basic Research Plan in Shaanxi Province (2016KJXX-86), Aeronautical Science Foundation of China (2015ZA53003) and National Natural Science Foundation of China (61622308).

References

1. Farrell, J.A., Polycarpou, M., Sharma, M., Dong, W.: Command filtered backstepping. IEEE Trans. Autom. Control **54**(6), 1391–1395 (2009)
2. Dong, W., Farrell, J.A., Polycarpou, M.M., Djapic, V., Sharma, M.: Command filtered adaptive backstepping. IEEE Trans. Contr. Syst. Technol. **20**(3), 566–580 (2012)
3. Chen, W., Li, J.: Decentralized output-feedback neural control for systems with unknown interconnections. IEEE Trans. Syst. Man Cybern. Part B Cybern. **38**(1), 258–266 (2008)
4. Chen, W., Jiao, L., Li, J., Li, R.: Adaptive NN backstepping output-feedback control for stochastic nonlinear strict-feedback systems with time-varying delays. IEEE Trans. Syst. Man Cybern. B Cybern. **40**(3), 939–950 (2010)
5. Gao, D.X., Sun, Z.Q., Du, T.R.: Dynamic surface control for hypersonic aircraft using fuzzy logic system. In: IEEE International Conference on Automation and Logistics, pp. 2314–2319 (2007)
6. Xu, B., Gao, D.X., Wang, S.X.: Adaptive neural control based on HGO for hypersonic flight vehicles. Sci. China Ser. F **54**(3), 511–520 (2011)
7. Xu, B., Fan, Y., Zhang, S.: Minimal-learning-parameter technique based adaptive neural control of hypersonic flight dynamics without back-stepping. Neurocomputing **164**, 201–209 (2015)
8. Li, Y., Qiang, S., Zhuang, X., Kaynak, O.: Robust and adaptive backstepping control for nonlinear systems using RBF neural networks. IEEE Trans. Neural Netw. **15**(3), 693–701 (2004)
9. Xu, B., Sun, F., Pan, Y., Chen, B.: Disturbance observer based composite learning fuzzy control of nonlinear systems with unknown dead zone. IEEE Trans. Syst. Man Cybern. Syst. **47**(8), 1854–1862 (2017)
10. Xu, B., Shi, Z., Yang, C.: Composite fuzzy control of a class of uncertain nonlinear systems with disturbance observer. Nonlinear Dyn. **80**(1–2), 341–351 (2015)
11. Xu, B., Shi, Z., Yang, C., Sun, F.: Composite neural dynamic surface control of a class of uncertain nonlinear systems in strict-feedback form. IEEE Trans. Cybern. **44**(12), 2626–2634 (2014)

Disturbance Observer Based Optimal Attitude Control of NSV Using $\theta - D$ Method

Rongsheng Xia$^{(\boxtimes)}$, Qingxian Wu, and Xiaohui Yan

College of Automation Engineering, Nanjing University of Aeronautics
and Astronautics, Nanjing 211100, China
xrsh12ujs@126.com, wuqingxian@nuaa.edu.cn, xhyan_nuaa@163.com

Abstract. In this paper, a disturbance observer based optimal attitude control scheme using $\theta - D$ method is presented for the near space vehicle (NSV). Firstly, $\theta - D$ method is used to design the optimal controller for the nominal system without considering the disturbance. Secondly, nonlinear disturbance observer (NDO) technique is applied to estimate the disturbance and the estimation result can be used as the disturbance compensation term. Then, the composite controller consisting of optimal controller and disturbance compensation term is proposed. The closed-loop system signals are proved to be uniformly ultimately bounded (UUB) using Lyapunov method. Finally, simulation results show the effectiveness of proposed control scheme.

Keywords: Near space vehicle · Nonlinear disturbance observer · $\theta - D$ method · Optimal attitude control

1 Introduction

The near space vehicle (NSV) has attracted more and more research attentions since 21th century. The accurate and reliable control schemes of NSV, especially for flight attitude control, are more crucial in practical applications. However, some characteristics of NSV such as large flight envelope, high flight speed, strong nonlinearity and complex flight environments will further increase the difficulty of attitude controller design [1,2]. Furthermore, some external disturbances such as force disturbance, wind disturbance and moment disturbance should also be considered during the controller design. Therefore, how to design an effective attitude controller for NSV with external disturbance has a good research signification.

In recent years, many works have been done to develop the attitude controller for NSV [3–5]. But few researches attempt to control the attitude of NSV in an optimal way, meeting a suitable performance index requirements, especially when system existing external disturbance. In this paper, we focus on the optimal attitude controller design of NSV with unknown time-varying disturbance. Among existing numerous optimization methods, $\theta - D$ method is to find an approximation solution by using an intermediate variable θ and the optimal cost

© Springer International Publishing AG 2017
D. Liu et al. (Eds.): ICONIP 2017, Part VI, LNCS 10639, pp. 219–227, 2017.
https://doi.org/10.1007/978-3-319-70136-3_24

function can be written as a power series of θ [6]. The $\theta - D$ method has already been applied in many fields. In [7], an optimal attitude tracking controller was proposed using $\theta - D$ method for air-breathing air-to-air missile. In [8], $\theta - D$ method was used for trajectory control of miniature helicopter. In [9], a trajectory optimal scheme for powered-decent phase of Mars landing was proposed using $\theta - D$ method. When system exists external disturbance, NDO technique can be used to estimate the disturbance and its design process can be separated from the optimal feedback controller design [10]. In [11], a robust tracking controller was proposed for NSV attitude control problem with external time-varying disturbances using backstepping and disturbance observer methods. In [12], a sliding mode disturbance observer was proposed for attitude control of near space vehicle.

In this paper, a composed attitude controller consisting of $\theta-D$ based optimal feedback controller and NDO based disturbance compensation term is used for NSV attitude system with external disturbance. The closed-loop system signals are proved to be UUB using Lyapunov method. Simulations on NSV attitude control are given to show the effectiveness of proposed control scheme. The rest of this paper is organized as follows. The problem statement and preliminaries are shown in Sect. 2. Section 3 shows the process of compound controller design. Section 4 presents the attitude tracking controller design of NSV. Section 5 gives the simulation results and Sect. 6 concludes the whole paper.

2   Problem Statement and Preliminaries

The attitude model of NSV can be described as follows [6]:

$$
\begin{aligned}
\dot{\Omega} &= f_s(\Omega) + g_s(\Omega)\omega \\
\dot{\omega} &= f_f(\omega) + g_f(\omega)M_c + d_f
\end{aligned}
\tag{1}
$$

where $\Omega = [\alpha, \beta, \mu]^T$ and $\omega = [p, q, r]^T$ are attitude angle vector of slow-loop system and angle rate vector of fast-loop system, respectively. $M_c = [l_c, m_c, n_c]^T$ denotes the control moment input vector. $f_s(\Omega)$ and $f_f(\omega)$ are system state vector functions, $g_s(\Omega)$ and $g_f(\omega)$ are system control matrices. d_f is an external disturbance vector acting on fast-loop system. The specific form of each function can reference to [13]:

The control object of this paper is to design a disturbance observer based optimal attitude controller to ensure that the attitude angle Ω can track a desired signal Ω_d.

3   Disturbance Observer Based $\theta - D$ Optimal Control Design

The each loop of attitude dynamic system (1) can be written as

$$
\dot{x} = f(x) + g(x)u + d(t)
\tag{2}
$$

where $f(x)$ is continuously differentiable on a compact set $\hbar$ and $f(0) = 0$. $g(x)$ is the control matrix. u is the control input. For the purpose of controller design, we have following assumptions:

Assumption 1: The control matrices $g(x)$ is invertible and bounded such as $\|g(x)\| \leq \bar{g}_M$, where $\bar{g}_M$ is an unknown positive constant.

Assumption 2: For external disturbances $d(t)$, there exists an unknown positive constant $\bar{d}_M$, such that $\|d(t)\| \leq \bar{d}_M$.

Considering the system (2) without the disturbance yields

$$\dot{x} = f(x) + g(x)u. \tag{3}$$

For optimal controller design, the cost function to be minimized is given by

$$J = \frac{1}{2} \int_0^\infty (x^T Q x + u^T R u) dt \tag{4}$$

where Q is a semi-positive definite matrix and R is a positive definite matrix with suitable dimension.

The optimal controller can be obtained by solving the following HJB equation:

$$V_x(x) f(x) - \frac{1}{2} V_x(x) g(x) R^{-1} g^T(x) V_x(x) + \frac{1}{2} x^T Q \, x = 0 \tag{5}$$

where $V(x) > 0$ is the optimal cost with $V(0) = 0$ and $V_x(x) = \partial V(x)/\partial x$

Then the optimal controller is given by [7]

$$u^* = -R^{-1} g^T(x) V_x \tag{6}$$

Since nonlinear HJB Eq. (5) is intractable to solve by analytical approach, the $\theta - D$ suboptimal control method is used to obtain its approximate solution. Now, consider the perturbations added to the cost function (4)

$$J = \frac{1}{2} \int_0^\infty (x^T (Q + \sum_{i=1}^\infty D_i \theta^i) x + u^T R u) dt \tag{7}$$

where θ and D_i are chosen such $Q + \sum_{i=1}^\infty D_i \theta^i$ is semi-positive definite.

The original state equation can be written as

$$\dot{x} = f(x) + g(x)u = \left[A_0 + \theta(\frac{A(x)}{\theta}) \right] x + \left[B_0 + \theta(\frac{B(x)}{\theta}) \right] u \tag{8}$$

where A_0 and B_0 are constant matrixes such that (A_0, B_0) is a stable pair and $[A_0 + A(x), B_0 + B(x)]$ is point-wise controllable.

Defining $V_x = \sum\limits_{i=0}^{\infty} T_i \theta^i x$ and invoking (7) in (5), we have

$$(\sum_{i=0}^{\infty} T_i \theta^i x)^T f - \frac{1}{2}(\sum_{i=0}^{\infty} T_i \theta^i x)^T g R^{-1} g^T (\sum_{i=0}^{\infty} T_i \theta^i x) + \frac{1}{2} x^T \left[Q + \sum_{i=1}^{\infty} D_i \theta^i \right] x = 0 \tag{9}$$

where T_i is assume to be determined and to be symmetric.

Applying the $\theta - D$ method [6], the value of T_i can be obtained by solving perturbed HJB Eq. (9). Then the optimal controller can be written as

$$u = -R^{-1} g^T(x) \sum_{i=0}^{\infty} T_i \theta^i x \tag{10}$$

Remark 1: we denote $\hat{T}_0 = T_0$, $\hat{T}_i = \theta^i T_i$, $\epsilon_i = 1 - k_i e^{-l_i t}, i = 1, \cdots, n$. In the next section, we will discuss the propertied of $\sum\limits_{i=0}^{\infty} \hat{T}_i$ instead of $\sum\limits_{i=0}^{\infty} T_i \theta^i$. In practical applications, for the purpose of simplifying the calculating, only first several terms of T_i will be used.

For system (2), the following NDO is designed to estimate the disturbance $d(t)$.

$$\begin{cases} \dot{z} = -L\hat{d} - L(f(x) + g(x)u) \\ \hat{d} = z + P(x) \end{cases} \tag{11}$$

where z is the internal state of the disturbance observer, $\hat{d}$ is the estimation of d. $P(x) = [P_1(x), \ldots, P_n(x)]^T$ is the design function vector, $L = \partial P(x)/\partial x$ is a design matrix. Define $\tilde{d} = d - \hat{d}$, then we have $\dot{\tilde{d}} = \dot{d} - L\tilde{d}$.

Combining (10) and (11), the composite controller for system (2) is designed as

$$u_c = -R^{-1} g^T(x) \sum_{i=0}^{\infty} T_i \theta^i x - g^{-1}(x)\hat{d} \tag{12}$$

After design the composite controller, the stability of closed loop system is given. The main result is stated in Theorem 1. Before this, Lemma 1 is given, which will be applied in the proof of Theorem 1.

Lemma 1: If $\lambda_{min}[(A_0 - B_0 R^{-1} B_0^T \hat{T}_0) + (A_0 - B_0 R^{-1} B_0^T \hat{T}_0)^T] < 0$, where λ_{max} denotes the largest eigenvalue; Then the series $\sum_{i=0}^{\infty} \hat{T}_i(x)$ produced by the algorithm is convergent and positive definite [6,9].

Theorem 1: For the nonlinear system (2) with external disturbance. If the conditions in Lemma 1 is satisfied, the disturbance observer is shown in (11) and the composite controller is (12), then the disturbance estimation error $\tilde{d}$ and system states x are UUB. The details of proof process is in Appendix.

4   Attitude tracking controller design of NSV

It is well know that the condition $f(0) = 0$ needs to be satisfied during the $\theta - D$ optimal controller design so that $f(x)$ can be written as the linear-like structure $F(x)x$. The state-independent terms that make $f(0) \neq 0$ are the bias terms. In order to handle this problem, an augment state s satisfying $\dot{s} = -\lambda_s s$ is introduced, where λ_s is a positive number [6,7]. Then, the bias term denoted by $b(t)$ can be factorized as $b(t) = [\frac{b(t)}{s}]s$. Generally, $s(0)$ is set to 1.

4.1   Slow-Loop Controller Design

In order to deal with the optimal tracking control problem, the $\theta - D$ method is implemented as an integral servo-mechanism [7]. For the slow-loop of system (1), we define the augment states $\tilde{\Omega} = [\alpha_I \ \alpha \ \beta_I \ \beta \ \mu_I \ \mu \ s]$, where $\alpha_I = \int \alpha dt$, $\beta_I = \int \beta dt$, $\mu_I = \int \mu dt$. Define $\alpha_{cI} = \int \alpha_c dt$, $\beta_{cI} = \int \beta_c dt$, $\mu_{cI} = \int \mu_c dt$ are the integral of the reference attitude angle signals of α_c, β_c, μ_c, respectively. The control input vector $\omega = [p_c, q_c, r_c]$.

Then we choose the factorization of slow-loop system as the following form

$$\dot{\tilde{\Omega}} = [A_s(\tilde{\Omega}_0) + \theta(\frac{A_s(\tilde{\Omega}) - A_s(\tilde{\Omega}_0)}{\theta})]\tilde{\Omega} + [B_s(\tilde{\Omega}_0) + \theta(\frac{B_s(\tilde{\Omega}) - B_s(\tilde{\Omega}_0)}{\theta})]\omega \qquad (13)$$

where $\tilde{\Omega}_0$ is the initial value of $\tilde{\Omega}$. The design process of A_s and B_s can reference to [7] and their specific forms are omitted here for the limitation of article length.

Using $\theta - D$ method, the optimal controller for slow-loop system is given by

$$\omega = -R_s^{-1}B_s^T \sum_{i=0}^{\infty} T_i^s \cdot \theta^n[\alpha_I - \alpha_{cI}; \alpha - \alpha_c; \beta_I - \beta_{cI}; \beta - \beta_c; \mu_I - \mu_{cI}; \mu - \mu_c; s]$$
$$(14)$$

where R_s is the designed positive definite matrix.

4.2   Fast-Loop Controller Design

For the fast-loop system of (1) without disturbance, the augment state space is chosen to be $\tilde{\omega} = [p \ q \ r \ s]^T$, and the control input vector is $u_f = [l_c \ m_c \ n_c]^T$.

We choose the factorization of fast-loop system as following form

$$\dot{\tilde{\omega}} = [A_f(\tilde{\omega}_0) + \theta(\frac{A_f(\tilde{\omega}) - A_f(\tilde{\omega}_0)}{\theta})]\tilde{\omega} + B_f u_f \qquad (15)$$

where $\tilde{\omega}_0$ is the initial value of $\tilde{\omega}$. The design process of A_f and B_f can reference to [7] and their specific forms are omitted here for the limitation of article length.

Then, the $\theta - D$ based controller for fast-loop system is given by

$$u_f = -R_f^{-1}B_f^T \sum_{n=0}^{\infty} T_n^f \theta^n[p - p_c; q - q_c; r - r_c; s] \qquad (16)$$

Then the composite controller for fast-loop system is designed as

$$M_c = u_f - g_f^{-1}(\omega)\hat{d}_s \tag{17}$$

where $\hat{d}_s$ can be obtained by using nonlinear disturbance observer (11).

5   Simulation Results

The weight of NSV is 24500 kg and the engine thrust $T = 12500N$. The initial states for NSV system are chosen as $\alpha_0 = 4°, \beta_0 = 1°, \mu_0 = 4°, p_0 = q_0 = r_0 = 0, H_0 = 21000\,\mathrm{m}, V_0 = 2000\,\mathrm{m/s}$. The desired flight attitude angles are given by: $\alpha_c = 4(0.5sin(0.3t) + cos(0.4t) + 1), \beta_c = 0, \mu_c = 5(0.5sin(0.5t) + 0.5cos(0.4t))$. The external disturbance acting on fast-loop is $d_f = [0.388\sin(5t), 0.311\sin(6t), 0.311\sin(6t)]^T$. The correlation parameters and constants for simulations are given as $k_{s1} = k_{s2} = k_{f1} = k_{f2} = 0.99, l_{s1} = l_{s2} = l_{f1} = l_{f2} = 0.5, Q_s = diag\{10, 3 \times 10^8, 50, 6.3 \times 10^8, 50, 1 \times 10^8, 0\}, R_s = diag\{3 \times 10^7, 1 \times 10^6, 3 \times 10^6\}, Q_f = diag\{2 \times 10^5, 3 \times 10^5, 3.6 \times 10^4, 0\}, R_f = diag\{50, 10, 10\}, L_f = [100\ 0\ 0; 0\ 100\ 0; 0\ 0\ 100]$.

The simulation results are presented from Figs. 1, 2, 3 and 4. Firstly, the tracking performance of attitude angles are shown in Fig. 1 and the tracking errors are shown in Fig. 2. From the two figures, we observe that the actual attitude angles can quickly track the desired signals and the tracking errors can converge to a small bound. The estimation errors of disturbances are shown in Fig. 3, we can note that the NDO can effectively estimate the external disturbances. At the same time, the control input of control moments are shown in Fig. 4 which are roll, pitching and yaw control moments, respectively. Finally, it is concluded that the proposed disturbance based optimal attitude control scheme is feasible for the NSV system from the above simulation results.

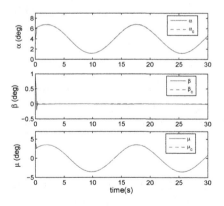

Fig. 1. Response curves of attitude angle

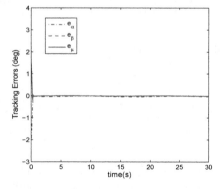

Fig. 2. The tracking errors of attitude angle

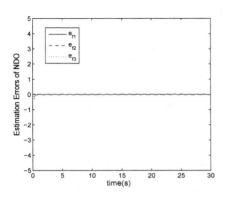

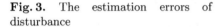

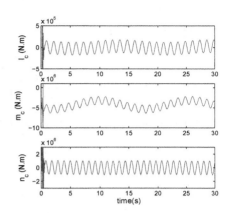

Fig. 3. The estimation errors of disturbance

Fig. 4. The control inputs of control moment

6 Conclusions

A disturbance observer based optimal attitude control scheme for NSV has been proposed in this paper. $\theta - D$ method is used to the optimal controller design and nonlinear disturbance observer method is introduced to estimate the unknown external disturbance to enhance the robustness of control system. Then the composite controller consisting of optimal controller and disturbance compensation term is proposed. Simulation results show the effectiveness of proposed control scheme.

Appendix

Proof: Choose a Lyapunov candidate function

$$L(t) = \frac{1}{2}x^T \sum_{i=0}^{\infty} \hat{T}_i x + \frac{1}{2}\tilde{d}^T \tilde{d} \tag{18}$$

Taking the time derivative of (13), we have

$$\dot{L}(t) = \left[x^T \sum_{i=0}^{\infty} \hat{T}_i + \frac{1}{2}x^T \sum_{i=0}^{\infty} \frac{\partial \hat{T}_i}{\partial x} x \right] [f(x) + g(x)u + d] + \tilde{d}^T(\dot{d} - L\tilde{d}) \tag{19}$$

Since $u = -R^{-1}g^T(x)\sum_{i=0}^{\infty}\hat{T}_i x - g^{-1}(x)\hat{d}$, then we have

$$\dot{L}(t) = -\frac{1}{2}u^T R u - \frac{1}{2}\left[Q + \sum_{i=0}^{\infty}D_i\theta^i\right]x + x^T\left[\frac{1}{2}\sum_{i=0}^{\infty}\frac{\partial\hat{T}_i}{\partial x}x\right]$$

$$\left[A_0 + A(x) - g(x)R^{-1}g^T(x)\sum_{i=0}^{\infty}\hat{T}_i\right]x + x^T\left[\frac{1}{2}\sum_{i=0}^{\infty}\frac{\partial\hat{T}_i}{\partial x}x\right]\tilde{d} + \tilde{d}^T(\dot{d} - L\tilde{d})$$

$$\leq -\frac{1}{2}\bar{\lambda}\|x\|^2 - \lambda_{min}(L)\|\tilde{d}\|^2 + \frac{1}{2}\|\tilde{d}\|^2 + \frac{1}{2}\dot{d}^2 + \|x\|^2\left\|\frac{1}{2}\sum_{i=0}^{\infty}\frac{\partial\hat{T}_i}{\partial x}x\right\|$$

$$\left\|A_0 + A(x) - g(x)R^{-1}g^T(x)\sum_{i=0}^{\infty}\hat{T}_i\right\| + \left\|\frac{1}{2}\sum_{i=0}^{\infty}\frac{\partial\hat{T}_i(x)}{\partial x}x\right\|\left(\frac{1}{2}\|x\|^2 + \frac{1}{2}\|\tilde{d}\|^2\right)$$

$$(20)$$

where $\bar{\lambda} = \lambda_{min}[Q + \sum_{i=0}^{\infty}D_i\theta^i]$.

Using the relationship $\frac{\partial\hat{T}_i}{\partial x} = \epsilon_i\frac{\partial\bar{T}_i}{\partial x}$, we have [6]

$$\dot{L}(t) \leq -\left[\frac{1}{2}\bar{\lambda} - \epsilon_i\left\|\frac{1}{2}\sum_{i=0}^{\infty}\frac{\partial\bar{T}_i}{\partial x}x\right\|\left(\left\|A_0 + A(x) - g(x)R^{-1}g^T(x)\sum_{i=0}^{\infty}\hat{T}_i\right\| + 1\right)\right]\|x\|^2$$

$$-\left[\lambda_{min}(L) - \frac{1}{2} - \epsilon_i\left\|\frac{1}{2}\sum_{i=0}^{\infty}\frac{\partial\bar{T}_i}{\partial x}x\right\|\right]\|\tilde{d}\|^2 + \frac{1}{2}\dot{d}_M^2$$

$$(21)$$

Note that as long as x lies in a compact set with $A(x)$ is bounded; $g(x)$ is bounded as shown in Assumption 1; $\sum_{i=0}^{\infty}\hat{T}_i(x)$ is converge and positive in Lemma 1, one can always choose a set of ϵ_i such that

$$M = \left[\frac{1}{2}\bar{\lambda} - \epsilon_i\left\|\frac{1}{2}\sum_{i=0}^{\infty}\frac{\partial\bar{T}_i}{\partial x}x\right\|\left(\left\|A_0 + A(x) - g(x)R^{-1}g^T(x)\sum_{i=0}^{\infty}\hat{T}_i\right\| + 1\right)\right] \geq 0$$

$$N = \left[\lambda_{min}(L) - \frac{1}{2} - \epsilon_i\left\|\frac{1}{2}\sum_{i=0}^{\infty}\frac{\partial\bar{T}_i}{\partial x}x\right\|\right] \geq 0; \quad B_d = \frac{1}{2}\dot{d}_M^2$$

$$(22)$$

then we have

$$\dot{L}(t) \leq -M\|x\|^2 - N\|\tilde{d}\|^2 + B_d \qquad (23)$$

If $\|x\| > \sqrt{\frac{B_d}{M}}$ or $\|\tilde{d}\| > \sqrt{\frac{B_d}{N}}$, we have $\dot{L}(t) < 0$, then the disturbance estimation error $\tilde{d}$ and system states x are proved to be UUB.

References

1. Liu, Z., Tan, X.M.: Adaptive trajectory tracking control system design for hyoersonic vehicles with parametric uncertainty. Proc. Inst. Mech. Eng. Part G J. Aerosp. Eng. **229**(1), 182–187 (2015)
2. Li, Y., Wu, Q.X., Jiang, C.S.: Robust predictive control for hypersonic vehicles using recurrent functional link artificial neural networks. Int. J. Innovation Comput. Inf. Control. **6**(12), 5351–5365 (2010)
3. Xu, B., Zhang, Q., Pan, Y.P.: Neural network based dynamic surface control of hypersonic flight dynamics using small-gain theorem. Neurocomputing **173**, 690–699 (2016)
4. Gao, Z.F., Jinag, B., Qi, R.Y.: Robust reliable control for a near space vehicle with parametric uncertainties and actuator faults. Int. J. Syst. Sci. **42**, 2113–2124 (2011)
5. Ge, S.S., Wang, C.: Adaptive neural control of uncertain MIMO nonlinear systems. IEEE Trans. Neural Netw. **15**, 674–692 (2004)
6. Xin, M., Balakrishnan, S.N., Stansbery, D.T.: A new method for suboptimal control of a class of nonlinear systems. Optim. Control Appl. Method **26**, 55–83 (2005)
7. Xin, M., Balakrishnan, S.N.: Nonlinear missile autopilot with theta-D technique. J. Guidance Control Dyn. **27**, 406–417 (2004)
8. Xin, M.: Trajectory control of miniature helicopters using a unified nonlinear optimal control technique. In: Aiaa Guidance, Navigation, and Control Conference, pp. 2417–2424 (2013)
9. Liu, R.J., Li, S.H., Chen, X.S.: Powered-decent trajectory optimization scheme for Mars landing. Ad. Space Res. **52**(11), 1888–1901 (2013)
10. Chen, W.H., Ballance, D.J., Cawthrop, P.J.: A nonlinear disturbance observer for robotic manipulators. IEEE Trans. Industr. Electron. **47**(4), 932–938 (2000)
11. Chen, M., Jiang, B.: Robust attitude control of near space vehicles with time-varying disturbances. Int. J. Control Autom. Syst. **11**(1), 182–187 (2013)
12. Chen, M., Yu, J.: Disturbance observer-based adaptive sliding mode control for near space vehicles. Nonlinear Dyn. **82**(4), 1671–1682 (2015)
13. Du, Y.L., Wu, Q.X., Wang, Y.H.: Adaptive robust predictive control for hypersonic vehicles using recurrent functionl link artificial neural networks. Int. J. Innovation Comp. Inf. Control **6**(12), 5351–5365 (2010)

Three-Dimensional Vibrations Control Design for a Single Point Mooring Line System with Input Saturation

Weijie Xiang[1], Wei He[1(✉)], Xiuyu He[1], Shuanfeng Xu[2], Guang Li[3], and Changyin Sun[4]

[1] School of Automation and Electrical Engineering,
University of Science and Technology Beijing, Beijing 100083, China
hewei.ac@gmail.com
[2] Science and Technology on Space Intelligent Control Laboratory,
Beijing Institute of Control Engineering, Beijing 100094, China
[3] School of Engineering and Materials Science,
Queen Mary University of London, London E1 4Ns, UK
[4] School of Automation, Southeast University,
Nanjing 210096, Jiangsu, China

Abstract. This paper presents a boundary control design for a single point mooring line system with input saturation in three-dimensional (3D) space. The system is described by some partial differential equations (PDEs) and ordinary differential equations (ODEs). The control strategy proposed in this paper at the tip payload of the mooring line and the control design uses Lyapunov's direct method (LDM) to ensure the stability of the system. In order to compensate the input saturation, we propose an auxiliary system. With the proposed boundary control, the mooring system's uniform boundedness under the effect of external environment is obtained. The presented boundary control is implementable with feasible equipment because all information in the system can be gained and calculated through various sensors or by applying a backward difference algorithm. Simulation results are provided to prove that the controller is effective in regulating the vibration of the system.

Keywords: Boundary control · Input saturation · Three-dimensional mooring line system · Distributed parameter system

1   Introduction

Nowadays, flexible mooring systems (FMSs) are widely used in the engineering fields, such as offshore gas and oil exploitation in deeper and harsher ocean environment. The marine environment is complex due to the influence of wind, wave, ocean current, tide, etc. Therefore, FMS will create large vibration problems in the 3D space. Unknown external disturbances will result in excessive vibration of the flexible structures, decrease the performance of the FMS, and further cause

© Springer International Publishing AG 2017
D. Liu et al. (Eds.): ICONIP 2017, Part VI, LNCS 10639, pp. 228–238, 2017.
https://doi.org/10.1007/978-3-319-70136-3_25

fatigue problem which has not been studied maturely. Therefore, suppressing and controlling the vibration of the FMS is a challenging research task.

Many engineering systems have flexible structures [1], such as flexible turbine tower, flexible marine risers [2], and flexible manipulators [3]. In [4], proposing a robust adaptive control with dynamic control allocation for the localization of marine vessels furnished with a thruster assisted mooring system. In [5], a robust adaptive control is used for solving the mooring system's vibration problem with thruster assisted positioning in one-dimensional space. In the process of dynamic analysis, we regard the flexible mooring system as a distributed parameter system (DPS) [6]. The DPS is mathematically described by PDEs [7] and a series of ODEs [8].

Many approaches have been used to suppress the vibration of the FMSs, for example, the Galerkin's method [9], the finite element method [10], and the transform of laplace [11]. Above methods are totally based on truncated finite-dimensional models [12,13]. The topic of using the FMSs for sea wave energy converters (WECs) is interesting. Now the researchers can model predictive control (MPC) of highly-coupled clusters of WECs [14]. Floating sea WECs must be anchored to the sea bed through mooring lines for safe operation of the devices [15].

In previous researches, many researchers discussed the situation of the system with input deadzone [16], input constraint [17], input backlash and input saturation. The system's vibration problem with input saturation is resolved by various control methods, for example, low-and-high gain control [18], neural network control [19], anti-windup compensation [20], and adaptive backstepping control [21]. In [22], a typical boundary control method is presented to regulate the flexible marine riser's vibration with input saturation. In [23], under the input saturation, a robust adaptive control is designed to solve the unknown parameters and the time-varying external disturbances from ocean environment for nonlinear systems. However, all the above researchers are confined to one dimensional space, namely, only the transverse vibration is discussed. Therefore we should discuss the system's dynamic in three-dimensional space. The flexible system will reduce performance subject to the disturbances between transverse deformation and axial displacement. Input saturation will affect the stability of the system. Therefore, the main contributions of this paper are summarized as follows:

(i) The single point mooring line system exists input saturations in the 3D space. In order to compensate the phenomenon, we propose an auxiliary method to achieve the stability of the system in three-dimensional space.

(ii) The mooring line system subjected to unknown external loads is derived by using the Hamilton's principle in three-dimensional space. We use a distributed parameter system (DPS) to model the mooring line system, which is described with a number of partial differential equations (PDEs) and ordinary differential equations (ODEs).

The rest of this paper are organized as follows. In Sect. 2, we present the dynamics of the three-dimensional mooring system. In Sect. 3, through the LDM, both model-based system and boundary control strategy are presented. The uniform boundedness and uniformly ultimate boundedness of the system are proven as well. Simulation numerations will be given in Sect. 4. Section 5 concludes this paper.

2   Problem Formulation and Dynamic Analysis

A typical single point mooring line system is provided in Fig. 1. We model the mooring line as a flexible string instead of an elastic beam. $u_1(t), u_2(t)$ and $u_3(t)$ represent control inputs in the X, Y, Z directions. $x(r,t)$ and $y(r,t)$ are the transverse displacements based on X and Y directions with respect to position r and time t. $z(r,t)$ is the longitudinal displacement of the mooring line based on Z direction with respect to position r and time t. The time-varying boundary disturbances $d_x(t), d_y(t)$ and $d_z(t)$ are on the top boundary in X, Y, Z directions. The time-varying disturbance loads $f_x(r,t), f_y(r,t)$ and $f_z(r,t)$ are along the mooring line in X, Y, Z directions. According to [21], considering the single point mooring line system with input saturation in X, Y, Z directions, we can obtain the input saturation functions as below

$$u(t) = \begin{cases} \text{sgn}(u_i(t))u_{\max}, & |u_i(t)| \geq u_{\max} \\ u_i(t), & |u_i(t)| < u_{\max} \end{cases}, (i = 1, 2, 3) \qquad (1)$$

where we define $u(t)$ as the FMS control input. $u_i(t)$ is the order of control design in X, Y, Z directions. $u_{\max}$ is the input saturation limitation. We have $-u_{\max} \leq u \leq u_{\max}$ in Fig. 1.

Remark 1: For clarity, we notate $(\dot{\cdot}) = \frac{\partial \cdot}{\partial t}, (\ddot{\cdot}) = \frac{\partial^2 \cdot}{\partial t^2}, (\cdot)' = \frac{\partial \cdot}{\partial r}, (\cdot)'' = \frac{\partial^2 \cdot}{\partial r^2}, (\cdot)''' = \frac{\partial^3 \cdot}{\partial r^3}, (\cdot)'''' = \frac{\partial^4 \cdot}{\partial r^4}, (\dot{\cdot})' = \frac{\partial \cdot}{\partial r \partial t}, (\cdot) = (\cdot)(r,t), (\cdot)_0 = (\cdot)(0,t)$ and $(\cdot)_L = (\cdot)(L,t)$ are adopted throughout the paper.

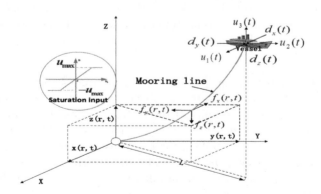

Fig. 1. A typical single point mooring line system with input saturation in 3D space

2.1   Dynamics of the Mooring Line in Three-Dimensional Space

The mooring line system's kinetic energy $E_k(t)$ can be written as

$$E_k(t) = \frac{1}{2}\rho \int_0^L \{\dot{x}^2 + \dot{y}^2 + \dot{z}^2\}dr + \frac{1}{2}M\{\dot{x}_L^2 + \dot{y}_L^2 + \dot{z}_L^2\} \tag{2}$$

where L is the length of the mooring line. r and t represent the displacement and time variables, respectively. M is the mass of the payload. ρ denotes the mass per unit length of the mooring line.

The potential energy $E_p(t)$ under the axial stiffness EA, and the constant tension T can be written as

$$E_p(t) = \frac{1}{2}EA \int_0^L \{\frac{1}{2}x'^2 + \frac{1}{2}y'^2 + z'\}^2 dr + \frac{1}{2}T \int_0^L \{x'^2 + y'^2\}dr \tag{3}$$

The virtual work due to the time-varying distributed disturbances (DD) $f_x(r,t), f_y(r,t), f_z(r,t)$ along the mooring line and the boundary disturbances $d_x(t), d_y(t), d_z(t)$ on the payload is given as

$$\delta W_f = \int_0^L [f_x(r,t)\delta x + f_y(r,t)\delta y + f_z(r,t)\delta z]dr + d_x(t)\delta x_L + d_y(t)\delta y_L + d_z(t)\delta z_L \tag{4}$$

The virtual work done by the control inputs can be written by

$$\delta W_m(t) = u_x(t)\delta x_L + u_y(t)\delta y_L + u_z(t)\delta z_L \tag{5}$$

Then all the virtual work appearing on the single point mooring system $\delta W(t)$ is obtained by

$$\delta W(t) = \delta W_f(t) + \delta W_m(t) \tag{6}$$

The Hamilton's principle is expressed by

$$\int_{t_1}^{t_2} \delta[E_k(t) - E_p(t) + W(t)]dt = 0 \tag{7}$$

where t_1 and t_2 are two time instants, $t_1 < t < t_2$ is the control time interval, δ represents the variational operator. $E_k(t)$ and $E_p(t)$ are the kinetic and potential energies of the FMS, respectively, and $W(t)$ represents the virtual work done by nonconservative force appeared in the FMS, incorporation control force and external disturbance.

Using the variation operator δ and integrating (2), (3) and (6) by parts, the governing equations of the FMS can be written as

$$\rho\ddot{x} = f_x + EA[z'x'' + z''x'] + Tx'' + \frac{3EA}{2}x'^2x'' + \frac{EA}{2}\{[x''[y']^2 + 2x'y'y'']\} \tag{8}$$

$$\rho\ddot{y} = f_y + EA[z'y'' + z''y'] + Ty'' + \frac{3EA}{2}y'^2y'' + \frac{EA}{2}\{[y''[x']^2 + 2y'x'x'']\} \tag{9}$$

$$\rho \ddot{z} = f_z + EAy''y' + EAz'' + EAx''x' \tag{10}$$

$\forall r \in (0, L)$ and $\forall t \in [0, \infty)$, also, boundary conditions can be obtained below

$$x_0 = y_0 = z_0 = 0, x_0'' = y_0'' = z_0'' = 0, x_L'' = y_L'' = z_L'' = 0 \tag{11}$$

$$M\ddot{x}_L + Tx_L' = \frac{EA}{2}x_L'^3 - u_x(t) + EAx_L'z_L' - d_x(t) + \frac{EA}{2}x_L'y_L'^2 \tag{12}$$

$$M\ddot{y}_L + Ty_L' = \frac{EA}{2}y_L'^3 - u_y(t) + EAy_L'z_L' - d_y(t) + \frac{EA}{2}y_L'x_L'^2 \tag{13}$$

$$M\ddot{z}_L + EAz_L' = \frac{EA}{2}x_L'^2 - u_z(t) + \frac{EA}{2}y_L'^2 - d_z(t) \tag{14}$$

2.2 Preliminaries

Assumption 1: In this section, we have the time-varying DD $f_x(r, t)$, $f_y(r, t)$, $f_z(r, t)$ and time-varying boundary disturbances $d_x(t)$, $d_y(t)$, $d_z(t)$. Therefore, we presume that constants $\bar{f}_x$, $\bar{f}_y$, $\bar{f}_z$, $\bar{d}_x$, $\bar{d}_y$, $\bar{d}_z \in \mathbb{R}^+$ exist, so that $|f_x(r, t)| \le \bar{f}_x$, $|f_y(r, t)| \le \bar{f}_y$, $|f_z(r, t)| \le \bar{f}_z$, $\forall r \in (0, L)$ and $\forall t \in [0, \infty)$, and $|d_x(t)| \le \bar{d}_x$, $|d_y(t)| \le \bar{d}_y$, $|d_z(t)| \le \bar{d}_z$, $\forall t \in [0, \infty)$. We conclude that the rational hypothesis as the DD $f_x(r, t)$, $f_y(r, t)$, $f_z(r, t)$ and boundary disturbances $d_x(t)$, $d_y(t)$, $d_z(t)$ have finite energy, and we can obtain $f_x(r, t)$, $f_y(r, t)$, $f_z(r, t)$, $d_x(t)$, $d_y(t)$, $d_z(t) \in L_\infty$.

3 Control Design

The boundary control target is to regulate the vibration of the FMS with input saturation in three-dimensional directions. In this section, we use LDM to design the control law $u_1(t)$, $u_2(t)$ and $u_3(t)$ at the tip payload of mooring line and to analyze the closed-loop stability of the system. Furthermore, in Fig. 2, the FMS's boundary control strategy is described by the block diagram.

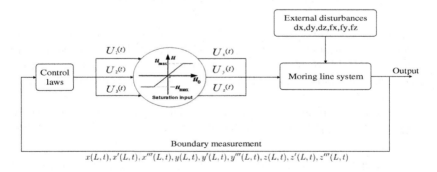

Fig. 2. Block diagram of the mooring system with input saturation

Because the mooring line system has an impact on input saturation, we design an auxiliary system to compensate for the input saturation and achieve better control performance. This auxiliary system are given below [19],

$$\dot{\zeta}_j(t) = \begin{cases} -k_j\zeta_j(t) - D_j + \Delta u_p(t), & |\zeta_j(t)| \geq \zeta_0 \\ 0, & |\zeta_j(t)| < \zeta_0 \end{cases} \tag{15}$$

where $D_j = \frac{u_j(t)\Delta u_p(t)+0.5[\Delta u_p(t)]^2}{\zeta_j(t)}(j = a,b,c; p = x,y,z)$, the auxiliary control gains are $k_a, k_b, k_c > 0$, $u_i(t)$ is the boundary control command which will be designed in the following parts, $u_p(t)$ is the control inputs with input saturations, $\Delta u_p(t) = u_p(t) - u_i(t)$, $\zeta_a(t)$, $\zeta_b(t)$, $\zeta_c(t)$ are the states of the auxiliary system, ζ_0 is a positive design parameter that can be chosen as an advisable value fits with the target of the system's performance.

Define $u_a(t)$, $u_b(t)$, $u_c(t)$ as $u_j(t) = \dot{p}_L + p'_L (j = a,b,c; p = x,y,z)$, in order to regulate the vibrations of the FMS in three directions, we present the following control laws as

$$u_1(t) = -M\dot{x}'_L - 2k_1\dot{x}_L - \text{sgn}[x'_L + \dot{x}_L]\bar{d}_x + k_4\zeta_a(t) \tag{16}$$

$$u_2(t) = -M\dot{y}'_L - 2k_2\dot{y}_L - \text{sgn}[y'_L + \dot{y}_L]\bar{d}_y + k_5\zeta_b(t) \tag{17}$$

$$u_3(t) = -M\dot{z}'_L - 2k_3\dot{z}_L - \text{sgn}[z'_L + \dot{z}_L]\bar{d}_z + k_6\zeta_c(t) \tag{18}$$

where k_1, k_2, k_3, k_4, k_5 and k_6 are the control gains.

Use the Lyapunov candidate function (LCF) as

$$V(t) = V_1(t) + V_2(t) + V_3(t) \tag{19}$$

where

$$V_1(t) = \frac{\alpha}{2}EA\int_0^L (\frac{x'^2}{2} + \frac{y'^2}{2} + z')^2 dr$$
$$+ \frac{\alpha}{2}\rho\int_0^L (\dot{x}^2 + \dot{y}^2 + \dot{z}^2)dr + \frac{\alpha}{2}T\int_0^L (x'^2 + y'^2)dr, \tag{20}$$

$$V_2(t) = \frac{\alpha}{2}M[z'_L + \dot{z}_L]^2 + \frac{\alpha}{2}\zeta_a^2(t) + \frac{\alpha}{2}M[x'_L + \dot{x}_L]^2 + \frac{\alpha}{2}\zeta_b^2(t)$$
$$+ \frac{\alpha}{2}M[y'_L + \dot{y}_L]^2 + \frac{\alpha}{2}\zeta_c^2(t) \tag{21}$$

$$V_3(t) = \beta\rho\int_0^L (r\dot{x}x' + r\dot{y}y' + r\dot{z}z')dr \tag{22}$$

where α and β in the equations represent two positive constants.

Then we can obtain the differentiation of LCF is upper bounded as

$$\dot{V}(t) \leq -\lambda V(t) + \varepsilon \tag{23}$$

where λ and ε in this equation represents two positive constants.

Theorem 1: For the dynamical systems of mooring line, which is described by (8)–(10) and boundary conditions (11)–(14), using Assumption 1 and the boundary control laws $u_i(t)$, with the initial conditions, the target states information $x_L, \dot{x}_L, y_L, \dot{y}_L, z_L$ and $\dot{z}_L$ can be derived. Therefore, we can obtain that:

(i) uniform boundedness (UB): the states of the closed-loop system $x(r,t)$, $y(r,t)$ and $z(r,t)$ will remain in the compact set Ω_1 defined by

$$\Omega_1 := \{x, y, z \in R | |x|, |y|, |z| \le D_1, \forall r \in (0,L) \text{ and } \forall t \in [0,\infty)\}, \tag{24}$$

where

$$D_1 = \sqrt{\frac{L}{\lambda_1}\left(V(0)e^{-\lambda t} + \frac{\varepsilon}{\lambda}\right)}, \forall r \in [0,L] \tag{25}$$

where λ and ε represent two positive constants.

(ii) uniform ultimate boundedness (UUB): the state fo the system $x(r,t)$, $y(r,t)$ and $z(r,t)$ will eventually converge to the compact Ω_2 defined by

$$\Omega_2 := \{x, y, z \in R | |\lim_{t\to\infty} |x|, \lim_{t\to\infty} |y|, \lim_{t\to\infty} |z| \le D_2\}, \forall r \in (0,L) \text{ and } \forall t \in [0,\infty) \tag{26}$$

where

$$D_2 = \sqrt{\frac{L\varepsilon}{\lambda_1 \lambda}} \tag{27}$$

Proof: Applying (16) through $e^{\lambda t}$, we have

$$\frac{\partial}{\partial t}(Ve^{\lambda t}) \le \varepsilon e^{\lambda t}, V(t) \le \left(V(0) - \frac{\varepsilon}{\lambda}\right)e^{-\lambda t} + \frac{\varepsilon}{\lambda} \le V(0)e^{-\lambda t} + \frac{\varepsilon}{\lambda} \in \mathcal{L}_\infty \tag{28}$$

which means $V(t)$ is bounded, then we can obtain

$$\frac{1}{L}x^2(r,t) \le \int_0^L [x'(r,t)]^2 dr \le \frac{1}{\lambda_1}V(t) \in \mathcal{L}_\infty \tag{29}$$

Furthermore, we have

$$|x(r,t)|, |y(r,t)|, |z(r,t)|| \le \sqrt{\frac{L}{\lambda_1}\left(V(0)e^{-\lambda t} + \frac{\varepsilon}{\lambda}\right)}, \forall r \in [0,L] \tag{30}$$

When there is no distributed disturbance, and the $\varepsilon = 0$, the Eq. (25) holds.

Remark 2: It should be emphasized that the above proof analyzes a situation when $|\zeta(t)| \ge \zeta_0$, that is, the input saturation is active. In order to decrease the influence from the nonlinear saturation function, an auxiliary system is designed. When $|\zeta(t)| < \zeta_0, \dot{\zeta}(t) = 0$, the input saturation is inactive, we can design control via the previous design methods.

4   Numerical Simulations

In this section, we use numerical simulations to verify the efficacy of the presented boundary controllers $u_1(t)$, $u_2(t)$ and $u_3(t)$ for the mooring line system. We choose the parameters of the flexible mooring line system as follows, $L = 150\,\text{m}$, $M = 5 \times 10^3\,\text{kg}$, $\rho = 100\,\text{kg/m}$, $T = 9 \times 10^4\,\text{N}$, $EA = 9 \times 10^3\,\text{Nm}^2$. According to the actual situation, we choose the length of the mooring line for a proper value is $150\,\text{m}$.

Choosing the initial conditions are $x(r,0) = y(r,0) = z(r,0) = \frac{12r}{L}$, $\dot{x}(r,0) = \dot{y}(r,0) = \dot{z}(r,0) = 0$. To solve the numerical simulation, we use the finite difference method. We discuss the different situations below:

(i) Without control: As shown in Figs. 3, 4 and 5, the system has no control inputs, i.e., $u_1(t) = u_2(t) = u_3(t) = 0$. Then the control gains $k_1 = k_2 = k_3 = k_4 = k_5 = k_6 = 0$. We can easily observe that the vibration of the mooring line is within the range of -20 m to +20 m in X, Y directions, and the vibration of the mooring line is within the range of -10 m to +10 m in Z directions. Therefore, it is necessary to devise the controller to regulate the vibration of the system.

(ii) Boundary control: In Figs. 6, 7 and 8, we use the proposed controllers $u_1(t)$, $u_2(t)$ and $u_3(t)$, where, giving the control gains $k_1 = k_2 = 500$, $k_3 = 400$, the input saturation control gains $k_4 = k_5 = 10$, $k_6 = 0.01$, and the auxiliary control gains $k_a = k_b = 100$, $k_c = 1$, it can be observed that the system is stable in X, Y, Z directions with the proposed control design. Figure 9 shows the system's control inputs. Figure 10 shows the input saturation signals in X, Y, Z directions.

According to the simulation results, we can observe that the vibration of the mooring line is suppressed well in X, Y and Z directions, and we can summarize that mooring line system can be stabilized at the small neighborhood of their equilibrium positions.

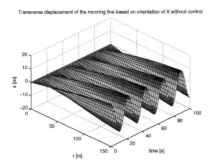

Fig. 3. Displacement in X direction without control

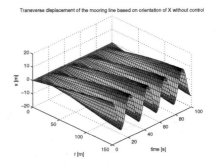

Fig. 4. Displacement in Y direction without control

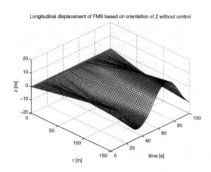

Fig. 5. Displacement in Z direction without control

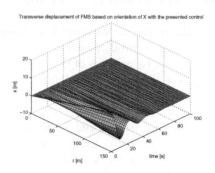

Fig. 6. Displacement in X direction with proposed control

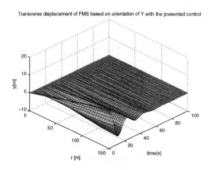

Fig. 7. Displacement in Y direction with proposed control

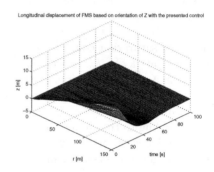

Fig. 8. Displacement in Z direction with proposed control

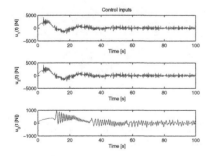

Fig. 9. Control inputs

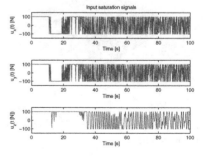

Fig. 10. Input saturation signals

5   Conclusion

This paper proposes the boundary control for suppressing the vibration of a mooring line with input saturation in 3D directions. A typical auxiliary system is proposed to compensate for the system's input saturation. we model the system as a DPS which is described by PDEs and ODEs. The proposed vibration control provides accurate and concise stability analysis for the single point mooring line system. With the proposed control design, all the signals of the closed-loop system have been verified to be uniformly bounded through applying the LDM. In addition, the ocean environment is complex and changeful, so a single point mooring line is not enough. Therefore, it is an interesting topic for mooring lines system's in future study. FMS with input saturation in three-dimensional space will have more significance as well. Finally, simulation results proved the efficacy of the controller.

Acknowledgments. This work was supported by the National Basic Research Program of China (973 Program) under Grant 2013CB733100, the National Natural Science Foundation of China under Grant 61522302, 61761130080, 61520106009, 61533008, the Newton Advanced Fellowship from The Royal Society, UK, under Grant NA160436, the Beijing Natural Science Foundation under Grant 4172041, and the Fundamental Research Funds for the China Central Universities of USTB under Grant FRF-BD-16-005A and FRF-TP-15-005C1.

References

1. Oueini, S.S., Nayfeh, A.H., Pratt, J.R.: A nonlinear vibration absorber for flexible structures. Nonlinear Dyn. **15**(3), 259–282 (1998)
2. Do, K.D.: Stochastic boundary control design for extensible marine risers in rhree dimensional space. Automatica **77**(3), 184–197 (2017)
3. Matsuno, F., Hatayama, M.: Robust cooperative control of two two-link flexible manipulators on the basis of quasi-static equations. Int. J. Robot. Res. **18**(4), 414–428 (1999)
4. Chen, M., Ge, S.S., How, B.V.E., Choo, Y.S.: Robust adaptive position mooring control for marine vessels. IEEE Trans. Control Syst. Technol. **21**(2), 395–409 (2013)
5. He, W., Zhang, S., Ge, S.S.: Robust adaptive control of a thruster ssisted psition mooring system. Automatica **50**(7), 1843–1851 (2014)
6. Luo, B., Huang, T., Wu, H.N., Yang, X.: Data-driven, H_∞, control for nonlinear distributed parameter systems. IEEE Trans. Neural Netw. Learn. Syst. **26**(11), 2949–2961 (2015)
7. Luo, B., Wu, H.N., Li, H.X.: Adaptive optimal control of highly dissipative nonlinear spatially distributed processes with neuro-dynamic programming. IEEE Trans. Neural Netw. Learn. Syst. **26**(4), 684–696 (2015)
8. Wang, J.M., Liu, J.J., Ren, B., Chen, J.: Sliding mode control to stabilization of cascaded heat PdeOde systems subject to boundary control matched disturbance. Automatica **52**, 23–34 (2015)
9. Do, K.D., Pan, J.: Boundary control of transverse motion of marine risers with actuator dynamics. J. Sound Vib. **318**(4), 768–791 (2008)

10. Mcnamara, J.F., O'Brien, P.J., Gilroy, S.G.: Nonlinear analysis of flexible risers using hybrid finite elements. J. Offshore Mech. Arct. Eng. **110**(3), 197–204 (1988)
11. Feliu, V., Rattan, K.S., Brown, H.B.J.: Adaptive control of a single-link flexible manipulator. IEEE Control Syst. Mag. **10**(2), 29–33 (1990)
12. Wang, N., Wu, H.N., Guo, L.: Coupling-observer-based nonlinear control for flexible air-breathing hypersonic vehicles. Nonlinear Dyn. **78**(3), 2141–2159 (2014)
13. Bhikkaji, B., Moheimani, S.O.R., Petersen, I.R.: A negative imaginary approach to modeling and control of a collocated structure. IEEE/ASME Trans. Mech. **17**(4), 717–727 (2012)
14. Li, G., Belmont, M.R.: Model predictive control of sea wave energy converters part i: a convex approach for the case of a single device. Renew. Energy. **69**(69), 453–463 (2014)
15. Johanning, L., Smith, G.H., Wolfram, J.: Measurements of static and dynamic mooring line damping and their importance for floating WEC devices. Ocean Eng. **34**(14–15), 1918–1934 (2007)
16. He, W., He, X., Sun, C.: Vibration control of an industrial moving strip in the presence of input deadzone. IEEE Trans. Ind. Electron. **64**(6), 4680–4689 (2017)
17. Wu, H.N., Wang, J.W., Li, H.X.: Design of distributed H_∞ fuzzy controllers with constraint for nonlinear hyperbolic PDE systems. Automatica **48**(10), 2535–2543 (2012)
18. Lin, Z., Saberi, A.: Low-and-high gain design technique for linear systems subject to input saturation-a direct method. In: Proceedings of the 35th IEEE Conference on Decision and Control. vol. 4, pp. 4788–4793. IEEE (1996)
19. Chen, M., Ge, S.S., Ren, B.: Adaptive tracking control of uncertain MIMO nonlinear systems with input constraints. Automatica **47**(3), 452–465 (2011)
20. Grimm, G., Hatfield, J., Postlethwaite, I., Teel, A.R., Turner, M.C., Zaccarian, L.: Antiwindup for stable linear systems with input saturation: an LMI-based synthesis. IEEE Trans. Autom. Control **48**(9), 1509–1525 (2003)
21. Zhou, J., Wen, C.Y.: Adaptive Backstepping Control of Uncertain Systems: Nonsmooth Nonlinearities, Interactions or Time-Variations. Springer, Berlin (2008)
22. He, W., He, X., Ge, S.S.: Vibration control of flexible marine riser systems with input saturation. IEEE/ASME Trans. Mech. **21**, 254–265 (2016)
23. Wen, C., Zhou, J., Liu, Z., Su, H.: Robust adaptive control of uncertain nonlinear systems in the presence of input saturation and external disturbance. J. IEEE Trans. Autom. Control **56**(7), 1672–1678 (2011)

Boundary Iterative Learning Control of an Euler-Bernoulli Beam System

Yu Liu[1(✉)], Xiao Deng[1], Fang Guo[1], and Wei He[2]

[1] School of Automation Science and Engineering,
South China University of Technology, Guangzhou 510640, China
auylau@scut.edu.cn, {auxdeng,maguo040201}@mail.scut.edu.cn
[2] School of Automation Engineering,
University of Science and Technology Beijing, Beijing 100083, China
hewei.ac@gmail.com

Abstract. In this article, through combining boundary control, adaptive technique with iterative learning control, a control strategy is developed for improving the tracing accurate and achieving the vibration suppression for the Euler-Bernoulli beam system. The dynamics of Euler-Bernoulli beam system can be written as partial-ordinary differential equations. With designed adaptive iterative learning control strategy, the unexpected spillover problem is suppressed and the learning convergence of iterative learning control is also mathematically achieved. Finally, the validity is illustrated by numerical simulation results.

Keywords: Euler-Bernoulli beam · Boundary control · Adaptive technique · Iterative learning control

1 Introduction

With the rapid development of modern industrial engineering, repetitive motion and task become more and more common, such as the robot arm manipulators and so on. Iterative learning control (ILC), as a prevalent solution to handle the controlled system with repetitive motion and same task, has gained more and more attention [1,2]. Considering that the reference trajectory is repeated over a given operational time, ILC needs the less prior knowledge, thus, it is widely adopted for achieving bounded error in tracking the expectations orbit in the tracking system and improving the tracing accurate of the controlled system.

Very often, the Euler-Bernoulli beam serves as a model to describe a number of mechanical flexible systems, including marine riser [3]. In the actual production process, under the influence of external disturbances, these flexible systems would occur the phenomenon of unwanted mechanical vibration, which will certainly cause negative effects upon the product performance, productivity and the service life of the flexible structures. Based on this consideration, the active vibration suppression of the flexible beam-like structure has aroused widespread concern and become a hot research topic [3–5].

© Springer International Publishing AG 2017
D. Liu et al. (Eds.): ICONIP 2017, Part VI, LNCS 10639, pp. 239–247, 2017.
https://doi.org/10.1007/978-3-319-70136-3_26

The design of controller aimed at realizing the vibration attenuation for Euler-Bernoulli beam system is a hard task. The Euler-Bernoulli beam system is modeled as a distributed parameter system and it is written as a PDE and several ODEs. The infinite-dimensional character of Euler-Bernoulli beam system makes it difficult to design the controller. The traditional methods for controlling PDE system are all based on truncation of system model [6,7], with these methods, some problems would arise, including spillover instability and so on. In addition, the dynamic model of the Euler-Bernoulli beam with unknown parameters and disturbance makes these traditional control methods unusable. For solving these problems, a group of scholars and researchers have tried to integrate boundary control with other present advanced control methods for controlling the infinite-dimensional system, including PID control, robust and adaptive control and so on [8–10]. In this article, we concentrate on the ILC for the Euler-Bernoulli beam system. And through combining iterative learning control, adaptive technique with boundary control, an appropriate control strategy is put forward for improving the tracing accurate and minimizing the vibration displacement for the Euler-Bernoulli beam system.

The arrangement of this article is given as follows. The system dynamic model and some preparations are given in Sect. 2. The adaptive iterative learning control strategy is put forward in Sect. 3. In Sect. 4, simulations are shown to verify its validity and the conclusion is presented in Sect. 5.

2   Dynamic Model

Figure 1 portrays a representative Euler-Bernoulli beam system subjected to unknown disturbance $d(t)$, $w(x,t)$ is vibration displacement of the beam and $u(t)$ is input force.

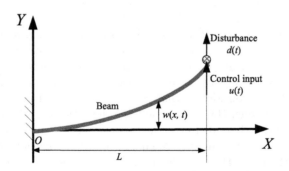

Fig. 1. A representative Euler-Bernoulli beam system.

In this article, the Euler-Bernoulli beam system given in [11] is reintroduced for further study, where the motion equations are

$$\rho \ddot{w} + EIw'''' - Tw'' = 0 \tag{1}$$

$\forall (x,t) \in (0,L) \times [0,+\infty)$, and

$$\begin{cases} w(0,t) = w'(0,t) = w''(L,t) = 0 \\ -EIw'''(L,t) + Tw'(L,t) = u(t) + d(t) - M_s\ddot{w}(L,t) \end{cases} \tag{2}$$

$\forall t \in [0,+\infty)$.

Remark 1. For designing and analysing the ILC strategy, the state variable $w(x,t)$ needs to be denoted as $w_k(x,t)$, where $k \in N$ is the iteration number.

Assumption 1. For $d(t)$, we can hypothesize that there exists a positive constant D, which satisfies $\mid d(t) \mid \le D$.

Assumption 2. The resetting condition can be meet, in other words, $w_k(x,0) = \dot{w}_k(x,0) = 0$ for all $k \in Z_+$.

Assumption 3. Considering that $\mid x \mid -x\tanh x \le \varepsilon = 0.2758$ stands for any $x \in R$, a positive constant $\bar{D}$ exists that makes the inequality $\mid \dot{w}_k(L,t)d_k(t) \mid \le \bar{D}\dot{w}_k(L,t)\tanh(\dot{w}_k(L,t))$ valid, where $\bar{D} > D$.

3   Boundary Iterative Learning Control Design

For the considered Euler-Bernoulli beam, through combining boundary control, adaptive technique with iterative learning control, an appropriate control strategy is designed for minimizing the vibration displacement and improving the tracing accurate.

Based on Assumptions 1–2, the boundary control strategy is introduced as

$$u_k(t) = -k_d\dot{w}_k(L,t) - \hat{\sigma}_k(t)\text{sgn}(\dot{w}_k(L,t)) \tag{3}$$

with

$$\hat{\sigma}_k(t) = \hat{\sigma}_{k-1}(t) + \gamma\dot{w}_k(L,t)\text{sgn}(\dot{w}_k(L,t)) \tag{4}$$

where $k_d, \gamma > 0$ and $\hat{\sigma}_{-1}(t) = 0$.

Theorem 1. Considering the Euler-Bernoulli beam system (1)–(2), under the proposed control strategy (3), Assumptions 1–2 and bounded initial conditions, the boundedness of $\dot{w}_k(L,t)$ and $u_k(t)$ can be concluded, for all $k \in Z_+$. Besides, it is also concluded that $\lim\limits_{k \to \infty} w_k(x,t) = \lim\limits_{k \to \infty} \dot{w}_k(x,t) = 0$, for all $t \in [0,T]$.

Proof. The following Lyapunov function is given

$$M_k(t) = V_k(t) + \frac{1}{2}\int_0^t \gamma^{-1}\tilde{\sigma}_k^2(\tau)d\tau \tag{5}$$

with $\tilde{\sigma}(t) = \sigma(t) - \hat{\sigma}(t)$, where $\sigma(t)$ is a unknown vector. $\hat{\sigma}(t)$ is the estimate of $\sigma(t)$, and the vector $\sigma(t)$ is defined as $\sigma(t) = D$.

The $V_k(t)$ in (5) is given as

$$V_k(t) = V_{1,k}(t) + V_{2,k}(t) \tag{6}$$

where

$$V_{1,k}(t) = \frac{1}{2}\rho \int_0^L \dot{w}_k^2 dx + \frac{1}{2}EI \int_0^L (w_k'')^2 dx + \frac{1}{2}T \int_0^L (w_k')^2 dx \tag{7}$$

and

$$V_{2,k}(t) = \frac{1}{2}M_s \dot{w}_k^2(L,t) \tag{8}$$

According to (5), the difference of $\Delta M_k(t)$ can be obtained as

$$\Delta M_k(t) = -\frac{1}{2}\int_0^t \gamma^{-1}(\bar{\sigma}_k^2(\tau) + 2\bar{\sigma}_k(\tau)\tilde{\sigma}_k(\tau))d\tau + V_k(t) - V_{k-1}(t) \tag{9}$$

where $\bar{\sigma}_k = \hat{\sigma}_k - \hat{\sigma}_{k-1}$.

In addition, $V_k(t)$ is rewritten as

$$V_k(t) = V_k(0) + \int_0^t \dot{V}_k(\tau)d\tau \tag{10}$$

where

$$\dot{V}_{1,k}(t) = [Tw_k'(L,t) - EIw_k'''(L,t)]\dot{w}_k(L,t) \tag{11}$$

and

$$\dot{V}_{2,k}(t) = [u_k(t) + d_k(t) + EIw_k'''(L,t) - Tw_k'(L,t)]\dot{w}_k(L,t) \tag{12}$$

Combining (6), (11) with (12) yields

$$\dot{V}_k(t) = [u_k(t) + d_k(t)]\dot{w}_k(L,t) \tag{13}$$

Substituting (13) into (10) results in

$$V_k(t) = V_k(0) + \int_0^t [u_k(\tau) + d_k(\tau)]\dot{w}_k(L,\tau)d\tau \tag{14}$$

Considering Assumption 1, we have

$$\dot{w}_k(L,t)d_k(t) \le D \mid \dot{w}_k(L,t) \mid D\dot{w}_k(L,t)\mathrm{sgn}(\dot{w}_k(L,t)) \tag{15}$$

Combining (14) with (15), we have

$$V_k(t) \le \int_0^t [u_k(\tau) + D\mathrm{sgn}(\dot{w}_k(L,\tau))]\dot{w}_k(L,\tau)d\tau + V_k(0) \tag{16}$$

Substituting (3) into (16) leads to

$$\begin{aligned} V_k(t) \le \int_0^t (D - \hat{\sigma}_k)\mathrm{sgn}(\dot{w}_k(L,\tau))\dot{w}_k(L,\tau)d\tau \\ -k_d \int_0^t \dot{w}_k^2(L,\tau)d\tau + V_k(0) \end{aligned} \tag{17}$$

Substituting (17) into (9) and combining (4), we can obtain

$$\Delta M_k(t) \le -V_{k-1}(t) - \tfrac{1}{2}\int_0^t \gamma^{-1}\tilde{\sigma}_k^2(\tau)d\tau - k_d\int_0^t \dot{w}_k^2(L,\tau)d\tau \le 0 \qquad (18)$$

Therefore, $M_k(t)$ is a non-increasing sequence. And for all $t \in [0,T]$, if the boundedness of initial value $M_0(t)$ is given, the boundedness of $M_k(t)$ can also be concluded.

Based on the above results, considering (5) with $k = 0$, we obtain

$$M_0(t) = V_0(t) + \frac{1}{2}\int_0^t \gamma^{-1}\tilde{\sigma}_0^2(\tau)d\tau \qquad (19)$$

Differentiating (19) yields

$$\dot{M}_0(t) \le -k_d\dot{w}_0^2(L,t) + \tfrac{1}{2}\gamma^{-1}\tilde{\sigma}_0^2(t) + \tilde{\sigma}_0(t)\dot{w}_0(L,t)\operatorname{sgn}(\dot{w}_0(L,t)) \qquad (20)$$

Considering that $\hat{\sigma}_{-1}(t) = 0$ and $\hat{\sigma}_0(t) = \hat{\sigma}_{-1}(t) + \gamma\dot{w}_0(L,t)\operatorname{sgn}(\dot{w}_0(L,t))$, we can obtain

$$\dot{M}_0(t) \le [\hat{\sigma}_0(t) + \frac{1}{2}\tilde{\sigma}_0(t)]\gamma^{-1}\tilde{\sigma}_0(t) - k_d\dot{w}_0^2(L,t) \qquad (21)$$

According to $\hat{\sigma}_0(t) = \sigma(t) - \tilde{\sigma}_0(t)$, (21) can be updated as

$$\dot{M}_0(t) \le -k_d\dot{w}_0^2(L,t) + \sigma(t)\gamma^{-1}\tilde{\sigma}_0(t) - \frac{1}{2}\gamma^{-1}\tilde{\sigma}_0^2(t) \qquad (22)$$

Using Young's inequality, we have

$$\sigma\gamma^{-1}\tilde{\sigma}_0 \le \lambda(\gamma^{-1}\tilde{\sigma}_0)^2 + \frac{1}{4\lambda}\sigma^2 \qquad (23)$$

for any $\lambda > 0$.

Substituting (23) into (22) leads to

$$\dot{M}_0(t) \le -k_d\dot{w}_0^2(L,t) - \frac{1}{2}\gamma^{-1}\tilde{\sigma}_0^2(t) + \lambda(\gamma^{-1}\tilde{\sigma}_0)^2 + \frac{1}{4\lambda}\sigma^2 \qquad (24)$$

Hence, we can obtain

$$\dot{M}_0(t) \le -k_d\dot{w}_0^2(L,t) - (\frac{1}{2\gamma} - \frac{\lambda}{\gamma^2})\tilde{\sigma}_0^2(t) + \frac{1}{4\lambda}\sigma^2 \qquad (25)$$

When λ and γ are selected to meet $\frac{1}{2\gamma} - \frac{\lambda}{\gamma^2} > 0$, i.e., $\lambda < \frac{1}{2}\gamma$, and considering that k_d is a positive constant, we can further obtain

$$\dot{M}_0(t) \le \frac{1}{4\lambda}\sigma^2 \le \frac{1}{4\lambda}\sigma_{\max}^2 \qquad (26)$$

which indicates that $M_0(t)$ is uniformly continuous and bounded for all $t \in [0,T]$. Therefore, combining (5), (6), (18) with the above analysis, the boundedness of

$V_{1,k}(t)$, $V_{2,k}(t)$ and $\int_0^t \gamma^{-1}\tilde{\sigma}_k^2(\tau)d\tau$ is obvious. Thus, for all $k \in Z_+$ and $t \in [0,T]$, the boundedness of $\dot{w}_k(L,t)$ and $u_k(t)$ can be concluded.

Considering that $M_k(t)$ given in (5) can be rewritten as

$$M_k(t) = M_0(t) + \sum_{j=1}^{k} \Delta M_j(t) \qquad (27)$$

Combining (27) with (18), we can further obtain the following inequality

$$M_k(t) \leq -\frac{1}{2}\sum_{j=1}^{k}(V_{1,j-1}(t) + V_{2,j-1}(t)) + M_0(t) \qquad (28)$$

Hence

$$\sum_{j=1}^{k}(V_{1,j-1} + V_{2,j-1}) \leq 2(M_0 - M_k) \leq 2M_0 \qquad (29)$$

Based on the above analysis, because of the boundedness of $M_k(t)$, we can conclude that $\lim_{k\to\infty} V_{1,k}(t) = \lim_{k\to\infty} V_{2,k}(t) = 0$, for all $t \in [0,T]$. Combining with (7), we can conclude that $\lim_{k\to\infty} w_k(x,t) = \lim_{k\to\infty} \dot{w}_k(x,t) = 0$, for all $t \in [0,T]$.

Considering that the proposed control strategy (3) and the adaptive law (4) contain the function sgn(t), which will inevitably cause the input chattering phenomenon. Thus, in this article, the function tanh(t) will be used to replace sgn(t) for avoiding the unwanted chattering phenomenon. Therefore, the designed boundary control strategy (3) can be updated as

$$u_k(t) = -k_d\dot{w}_k(L,t) - \hat{\sigma}_k(t)\tanh(\dot{w}_k(L,t)) \qquad (30)$$

with

$$\hat{\sigma}_k(t) = \hat{\sigma}_{k-1}(t) + \gamma\dot{w}_k(L,t)\tanh(\dot{w}_k(L,t)) \qquad (31)$$

Theorem 2. Considering the Euler-Bernoulli beam system (1)–(2), under the proposed control strategy (30), Assumptions 1–3 and bounded initial conditions, the boundedness of $\dot{w}_k(L,t)$ and $u_k(t)$ can be concluded, for all $k \in Z_+$. Besides, it is also concluded that $\lim_{k\to\infty} w_k(x,t) = \lim_{k\to\infty} \dot{w}_k(x,t) = 0$, for all $t \in [0,T]$.

Proof. In the proof process of Theorem 2, we use the same Lyapunov function candidate $M_k(t)$ (5), and the unknown vector $\sigma(t)$ is defined as $\sigma(t) = \bar{D}$.

According to the proof of Theorem 1 and Assumption 3, we have

$$V_k(t) \leq \int_0^t [u_k(\tau) + \bar{D}\tanh(\dot{w}_k(L,\tau))]\dot{w}_k(L,\tau)d\tau + V_k(0) \qquad (32)$$

Substituting (30) into (32) yields

$$V_k(t) \leq \int_0^t (\bar{D} - \hat{\sigma}_k)\tanh(\dot{w}_k(L,\tau))\dot{w}_k(L,\tau)d\tau - k_d\int_0^t \dot{w}_k^2(L,\tau)d\tau + V_k(0) \qquad (33)$$

Substituting (33) into (9) and combining (31), we can obtain

$$\Delta M_k(t) \leq -V_{k-1}(t) - \frac{1}{2}\int_0^t \gamma^{-1}\bar{\sigma}_k^2(\tau)d\tau - k_d \int_0^t \dot{w}_k^2(L,\tau)d\tau$$
$$\leq 0 \tag{34}$$

The remainder of the proof can refer to the above proof of Theorem 1.

4   Simulations

Numerical simulations by using FD method will be performed for validating the availability of designed control. The detailed parameters are $\rho = 1\,\text{kg/m}$, $M_s = 2\,\text{kg}$, $L = 10\,\text{m}$, $T = 10\,\text{N}$ and $EI = 50\,\text{Nm}^2$. The initial conditions are $w(x,0) = \dot{w}(x,0) = 0$, and $d(t) = 1 + 0.1\sin(0.1t) + 0.2\sin(0.2t) + 0.3\sin(0.3t)$.

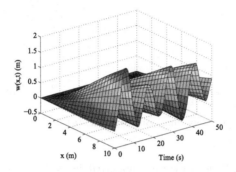

Fig. 2. Deflection of Euler-Bernoulli beam without control.

Figure 2 gives the deflection of considered Euler-Bernoulli beam system with no control. Figure 3 displays its deflection with the designed adaptive iterative learning control strategy by choosing the iteration numbers $k = 5$ and $k = 15$ respectively. The corresponding control inputs are shown in Fig. 4.

From Figs. 2–3, it can be concluded there is a violent vibration of the Euler-Bernoulli beam with no control. Besides, the designed adaptive iterative learning control strategy could suppress its vibration greatly, and the control performances are improved incrementally with the increase of the iteration number.

5   Conclusion

In this article, the active vibration suppression has been studied for the Euler-Bernoulli beam system. The adaptive iterative learning control strategy has been put forward for reducing the vibration displacement of the Euler-Bernoulli beam and achieving the learning convergence. Finally, simulation has been carried out for testifying the availability of formulated adaptive iterative learning control strategy.

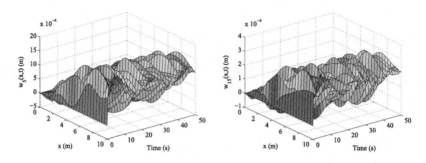

Fig. 3. Deflection of Euler-Bernoulli beam with control: (a) $k = 5$, (b) $k = 15$.

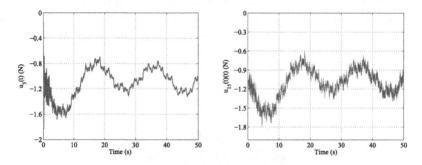

Fig. 4. Corresponding control input: (a) $k = 5$, (b) $k = 15$.

Acknowledgments. This work was supported in part by the Science and Technology Planning Project of Guangdong Province (2016B090912003, 2016A010106007, 2016B090927010, 2016B010126001, 2015B010101003, 2015B010919003), and by the Fundamental Research Funds for the Central Universities of SCUT (2017ZD058).

References

1. Li, X.F., Xu, J.X., Huang, D.Q.: An iterative learning control approach for linear time-invariant systems with randomly varying trial lengths. IEEE Trans. Autom. Control. **59**(7), 1954–1960 (2014)
2. Chen, Y.Q., Moore, K.L., Yu, J., Zhang, T.: Iterative learning control and repetitive control in hard disk drive industry-a tutorial. In: 45th IEEE Conference on Decision and Control, pp. 2338–2351. IEEE Press, San Diego (2006)
3. Liu, Y., Guo, F., Zhao, Z.J.: Boundary barrier-based control of a flexible riser system. IET Control Theory Appl. **11**(7), 923–930 (2017)
4. Liu, Z.J., Liu, J.K.: Boundary control of a flexible robotic manipulator with output constraints. Asian J. Control. **19**(1), 332–345 (2017)
5. Ge, S.S., Zhang, S., He, W.: Vibration control of an Euler-Bernoulli beam under unknown spatiotemporally varying disturbance. Int. J. Control. **84**(5), 947–960 (2011)
6. Balas, M.J.: Active control of flexible systems. J. Optimiz. Theory App. **25**(3), 415–436 (1978)

7. Sakawa, Y., Matsuno, F., Fukushima, S.: Modeling and feedback control of a flexible arm. J. Robot. Syst. **2**(4), 453–472 (1985)
8. Zhao, Z.J., Liu, Y., He, W., et al.: Adaptive boundary control of an axially moving belt system with high acceleration/deceleration. IET Control Theory Appl. **10**(11), 1299–1306 (2016)
9. Feng, Z.G., Lam, J., Shu, Z.: Dissipative control for linear systems by static output feedback. Int. J. Syst. Sci. **44**(8), 1566–1576 (2013)
10. Liu, Y., Zhao, Z.J., He, W.: Stabilization of an axially moving accelerated/decelerated system via an adaptive boundary control. ISA Trans. **64**, 394–404 (2016)
11. He, W., Ge, S.S.: Vibration control of a flexible beam with output constraint. IEEE Trans. Ind. Electron. **62**(8), 5023–5030 (2015)

Adaptive Control of an Output Constrainted Riser

Fang Guo and Yu Liu$^{(\boxtimes)}$

School of Automation Science and Engineering,
South China University of Technology, Guangzhou 510640, China
maguo040201@mail.scut.edu.cn, auylau@scut.edu.cn

Abstract. In this paper, the vibration control problem of an output constrainted riser is addressed. An adaptive Lyapunov-based barrier control is formulated for reducing the flexible riser's vibration by applying integral-barrier Lyapunov function, backstepping technique and adaptive technique. The unexpected spillover problem is suppressed under the designed control. The numerical simulation results illustrate the availability of formulated control.

Keywords: Output constrainted riser · Backstepping technique · Integral-barrier Lyapunov function · Disturbance observer

1 Introduction

Flexible marine riser, which possesses the advantages of high efficiency, low cost, convenient use and so on, is playing an increasingly important role in the process of oil and gas drilling and production [1–3]. It must be noted that vibration of these flexible structures would limit production efficiency and destroy equipment in offshore engineering. Thus, the vibration control of flexible riser is payed more and more attention by researchers and becomes a great interest over the recent years.

Mathematically, the flexible riser system regarded as an Euler-Bernoulli beam is actually a distributed parameter system (DPS) with the infinite-dimensional state space, which make the control design pose a challenging task. There are many studies and results in modelling and controlling for flexible riser system based on model truncation and spatial discretization. Compared with these traditional control methods, boundary control has been widely used in practical engineering [1–7], since it can avoid the spillover instability.

As is well known, a representative marine riser system consists of an production vessel, well head and flexible riser. In complex and harsh marine environment, the flexible riser's excessive vibration excited by external disturbances may produce much cracks on connection joint. Existing cracks and unwanted vibration will bring the oil and gas leakage from damaged areas or even environmental pollution. In order to solve the above hazards, regulating the riser's boundary vibration displacement in a proper range is a powerful strategy. In this paper,

© Springer International Publishing AG 2017
D. Liu et al. (Eds.): ICONIP 2017, Part VI, LNCS 10639, pp. 248–256, 2017.
https://doi.org/10.1007/978-3-319-70136-3_27

the riser's vibration abatement and the problem of output constraint satisfaction are considered simultaneously. For handling the effect of output constraint, the integral-barrier Lyapunov function (IBLF) is widely applied in control deign [8–11]. However, the studies of boundary control by integrating IBLF, finite-dimensional backstepping technology with adaptive technology are limited. The major contributions of this paper includes:

(1) An adaptive Lyapunov-based barrier control is developed to reduce riser's vibration and regulate the boundary vibration displacement by using Lyapunov direct method and IBLF.
(2) A disturbance observer is proposed including the barrier term of IBLF, which compensates for boundary disturbance and avoids chattering induced by using signum function.

The outline of this paper is proposed as follows. The dynamic equations of riser system with output constraint are given in Sect. 2. An adaptive Lyapunov-based barrier boundary control with disturbance observer is proposed in Sect. 3. In Sect. 4, numerical simulation is shown for demonstrating the availability of formulated control, and the conclusion is shown in Sect. 5.

2   Dynamic Model

Figure 1 portrays a representative riser system with output constraint $|w(L,t)| < Q$ $(Q > 0)$. And its dynamic model is given as

$$\rho\ddot{w} + EIw'''' - Tw'' - f + c\dot{w} = 0, \tag{1}$$

$\forall(s,t) \in (0,L) \times [0,+\infty)$, and

$$\begin{cases} w(0,t) = w'(0,t) = w''(L,t) = 0, \\ -EIw'''(L,t) + Tw'(L,t) = u(t) + d(t) - d_s\dot{w}(L,t) - M_s\ddot{w}(L,t), \end{cases} \tag{2}$$

$\forall t \in [0,+\infty)$.

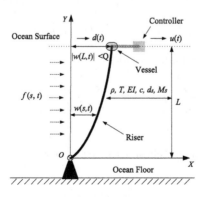

Fig. 1. Representative riser system with output constraint.

Assumption 1. For $f(s,t)$ and $d(t)$, assume that there exist constants $\bar{f}$, $\bar{d}$ and $D \in \mathbb{R}^+$, such that $\mid f(s,t) \mid \leq \bar{f}$, $\forall(s,t) \in [0,L] \times [0,+\infty)$, $\mid d(t) \mid \leq \bar{d}$ and $\mid \dot{d}(t) \mid \leq D$, $\forall t \in [0,+\infty)$.

3   Adaptive Lyapunov-Based Barrier Control

The closed-loop riser system (1)–(2) can be rewritten as

$$
\begin{cases}
\rho\ddot{w} = -EIw'''' + Tw'' + f - c\dot{w}, \\
w(0,t) = w'(0,t) = w''(L,t) = 0, \\
z_1(t) = w(L,t), \\
\dot{z}_1(t) = z_2(t), \\
\dot{z}_2(t) = \frac{1}{M_s}[u(t) + d(t) - d_s z_2(t) + EIw'''(L,t) - Tw'(L,t)].
\end{cases}
\tag{3}
$$

3.1   Step One

Define the observer error $e_0(t)$ as

$$
e_0(t) = z_2(t) - z_0(t),
\tag{4}
$$

where $z_0(t)$ is a virtual control of $z_2(t)$.

Select the Lyapunov function candidate as

$$
E_a(t) = E_x(t) + E_y(t),
\tag{5}
$$

where

$$
\begin{cases}
E_x(t) = \varpi\rho \int_0^L s\dot{w}w'ds, \\
E_y(t) = \frac{\kappa\rho}{2} \int_0^L \dot{w}^2 ds + \frac{\kappa EI}{2} \int_0^L (w'')^2 ds + \frac{\kappa T}{2} \int_0^L (w')^2 ds,
\end{cases}
\tag{6}
$$

where ϖ, $\kappa > 0$.

Lemma 1. Suppose that there exist $\iota_1 > 0$ and $\iota_2 > 0$ such that

$$
0 < \iota_1 E_y(t) \leq E_a(t) \leq \iota_2 E_y(t).
\tag{7}
$$

Proof. Using triangle inequality yields

$$
\mid E_x(t) \mid \leq \frac{\varpi\rho L}{2} \int_0^L \dot{w}^2 ds + \frac{\varpi\rho L}{2} \int_0^L (w')^2 ds \leq \iota E_y(t),
\tag{8}
$$

where $\iota = \frac{\varpi\rho L}{\min(\kappa\rho,\kappa T)}$.

The proper ϖ and κ are chosen to satisfy $0 < \iota < 1$, applying (9) results into

$$
\varpi < \frac{\min(\kappa\rho, \kappa T)}{\rho L}.
\tag{9}
$$

From Eq. (8), we can obtain

$$-\iota E_y(t) \le E_x(t) \le \iota E_y(t). \tag{10}$$

The following results can be given

$$\begin{cases} \iota_1 = 1 - \frac{\varpi\rho L}{\min(\kappa\rho,\kappa T)} = 1 - \iota > 0, \\ \iota_2 = 1 + \frac{\varpi\rho L}{\min(\kappa\rho,\kappa T)} = 1 + \iota > 1. \end{cases} \tag{11}$$

Utilizing (5), (10) and (11), we have

$$0 < \iota_1 E_y(t) \le E_a(t) \le \iota_2 E_y(t). \tag{12}$$

Taking differentiate for (5), we can obtain

$$\begin{aligned} \dot{E}_a(t) = {}& \kappa[Tw'(L,t) - EIw'''(L,t)][e_0(t) + z_0(t)] + \tfrac{\varpi TL}{2}[w'(L,t)]^2 \\ & - \varpi EILw'(L,t)w'''(L,t) - \tfrac{\varpi T}{2}\int_0^L (w')^2 ds + \tfrac{\varpi\rho L}{2}[e_0(t) \\ & + z_0(t)]^2 - \tfrac{3\varpi EI}{2}\int_0^L (w'')^2 ds + \varpi\int_0^L sw'(f - c\dot{w})ds \\ & + \kappa\int_0^L \dot{w}f ds - (c\kappa + \tfrac{\varpi\rho}{2})\int_0^L \dot{w}^2 ds. \end{aligned} \tag{13}$$

Applying the above results and analysis, give the following virtual control

$$z_0(t) = -k_1 w'(L,t) + k_2 w'''(L,t), \tag{14}$$

where $k_1,\ k_2 > 0$.

Thus, we obtain

$$\begin{aligned} \dot{E}_a(t) = {}& -(\varpi\rho Lk_1k_2 + \varpi EIL - \kappa Tk_2 - \kappa EIk_1)w'(L,t)w'''(L,t) \\ & - [(\varpi\rho Lk_1 - \kappa T)w'(L,t) + (\kappa EI - \varpi\rho Lk_2)w'''(L,t)]e_0(t) \\ & - (Tk_1\kappa - \tfrac{\varpi\rho L}{2}k_1^2 - \tfrac{\varpi TL}{2})[w'(L,t)]^2 - (c\kappa + \tfrac{\varpi\rho}{2})\int_0^L \dot{w}^2 ds \\ & - (EIk_2\kappa - \tfrac{\varpi\rho L}{2}k_2^2)[w'''(L,t)]^2 + \tfrac{\varpi\rho L}{2}e_0^2(t) - \tfrac{\varpi T}{2}\int_0^L (w')^2 ds \\ & - \tfrac{3\varpi EI}{2}\int_0^L (w'')^2 ds + \varpi\int_0^L sw'(f - c\dot{w})ds + \kappa\int_0^L \dot{w}f ds. \end{aligned} \tag{15}$$

3.2 Step Two

Substituting (3) and (14) into the time derivative of (4), we have

$$\begin{aligned} M_s\dot{e}_0(t) = {}& u(t) - d_s z_2(t) + EIw'''(L,t) - Tw'(L,t) + d(t) \\ & + M_s k_1\dot{w}'(L,t) - M_s k_2\dot{w}'''(L,t). \end{aligned} \tag{16}$$

Define the estimate of the system parameters as $\widehat{EI}(t)$, $\widehat{\rho}(t)$, $\widehat{M}_s(t)$, $\widehat{d}_s(t)$ and $\widehat{T}(t)$, and estimation errors as $\widetilde{EI}(t) = EI - \widehat{EI}(t)$, $\widetilde{\rho}(t) = \rho - \widehat{\rho}(t)$, $\widetilde{M}_s(t) = M_s - \widehat{M}_s(t)$, $\widetilde{d}_s(t) = d_s - \widehat{d}_s(t)$ and $\widetilde{T}(t) = T - \widehat{T}(t)$.

Select a new Lyapunov function candidate as

$$E_b(t) = E_a(t) + \frac{M_s}{2}e_0^2(t)\ln\frac{2Q^2}{Q^2 - z_1^2(t)}. \tag{17}$$

Substituting (15) and (16) into the time derivative of (17) leads to

$$
\begin{aligned}
\dot{E}_b(t) = & -[(\varpi \rho L k_1 - \kappa T)w'(L,t) + (\kappa EI - \varpi \rho L k_2)w'''(L,t)] \\
& \cdot e_0(t) + \tfrac{\varpi \rho L}{2}e_0^2(t) + [u(t) - d_s e_0(t) - d_s k_2 w'''(L,t) \\
& + d_s k_1 w'(L,t) + EIw'''(L,t) - Tw'(L,t) + M_s k_1 \dot{w}'(L,t) \\
& - M_s k_2 \dot{w}'''(L,t) + d(t)]e_0(t) \ln \tfrac{2Q^2}{Q^2 - z_1^2(t)} + M_s e_0^2(t) \tfrac{z_1(t)z_2(t)}{Q^2 - z_1^2(t)} \\
& - (Tk_1 \kappa - \tfrac{\varpi \rho L}{2}k_1^2 - \tfrac{\varpi TL}{2})[w'(L,t)]^2 - \tfrac{3\varpi EI}{2}\int_0^L (w'')^2 ds \\
& - (\varpi \rho L k_1 k_2 + \varpi EIL - \kappa T k_2 - \kappa EI k_1)w'(L,t)w'''(L,t) \\
& - (EI k_2 \kappa - \tfrac{\varpi \rho L}{2}k_2^2)[w'''(L,t)]^2 - (c\kappa + \tfrac{\varpi \rho}{2})\int_0^L \dot{w}^2 ds \\
& - \tfrac{\varpi T}{2}\int_0^L (w')^2 ds + \kappa \int_0^L \dot{w}f ds + \varpi \int_0^L sw'(f - c\dot{w})ds.
\end{aligned}
\tag{18}
$$

To make the flexible riser system (1)–(2) stable, we consider control input $u(t)$ as

$$
\begin{aligned}
u(t) = & \frac{[\varpi \widehat{\rho}(t)L k_1 - \kappa \widehat{T}(t)]w'(L,t) + [\kappa \widehat{EI}(t) - \varpi \widehat{\rho}(t)L k_2]w'''(L,t)}{\ln \tfrac{2Q^2}{Q^2 - z_1^2(t)}} - \widehat{M}_s(t)k_1 \dot{w}'(L,t) \\
& + \widehat{M}_s(t)k_2 \dot{w}'''(L,t) - k_3 e_0(t) - \widehat{d}(t) - \frac{\widehat{M}_s(t)e_0(t)\tfrac{z_1(t)z_2(t)}{Q^2 - z_1^2(t)} + k_4 e_0(t)}{\ln \tfrac{2Q^2}{Q^2 - z_1^2(t)}} \\
& - [\widehat{d}_s(t)k_1 - \widehat{T}(t)]w'(L,t) + [\widehat{d}_s(t)k_2 - \widehat{EI}(t)]w'''(L,t),
\end{aligned}
\tag{19}
$$

where $k_3, k_4 > 0$.

To estimate the boundary disturbance, we define a disturbance observer as

$$
\dot{\widehat{d}}(t) = e_0(t) \ln \frac{2Q^2}{Q^2 - z_1^2(t)} - k_5 \widehat{d}(t),
\tag{20}
$$

where $k_5 > 0$. Observer error is considered as $\widetilde{d}(t) = d(t) - \widehat{d}(t)$, thus

$$
\dot{\widetilde{d}}(t) = \dot{d}(t) - k_5 \widetilde{d}(t) - e_0(t) \ln \frac{2Q^2}{Q^2 - z_1^2(t)} + k_5 d(t).
\tag{21}
$$

To handle the effect that the system parameter are unknown, propose the following adaptive laws

$$
\begin{cases}
\dot{\widehat{EI}}(t) = -\zeta_1 \mu_1 \widehat{EI}(t) - [\kappa - \ln \tfrac{2Q^2}{Q^2 - z_1^2(t)}]w'''(L,t)\mu_1 e_0(t), \\
\dot{\widehat{\rho}}(t) = -\zeta_2 \mu_2 \widehat{\rho}(t) - \varpi L[k_1 w'(L,t) - k_2 w'''(L,t)]\mu_2 e_0(t), \\
\dot{\widehat{M}}_s(t) = -\zeta_3 \mu_3 \widehat{M}_s(t) + [k_1 \dot{w}'(L,t) - k_2 \dot{w}'''(L,t)]\mu_3 e_0(t) \ln \tfrac{2Q^2}{Q^2 - z_1^2(t)} \\
\qquad\quad + \tfrac{z_1(t)z_2(t)}{Q^2 - z_1^2(t)}\mu_3 e_0^2(t), \\
\dot{\widehat{d}}_s(t) = -\zeta_4 \mu_4 \widehat{d}_s(t) + [k_1 w'(L,t) - k_2 w'''(L,t)]\mu_4 e_0(t) \ln \tfrac{2Q^2}{Q^2 - z_1^2(t)}, \\
\dot{\widehat{T}}(t) = -\zeta_5 \mu_5 \widehat{T}(t) + [\kappa - \ln \tfrac{2Q^2}{Q^2 - z_1^2(t)}]w'(L,t)\mu_5 e_0(t).
\end{cases}
\tag{22}
$$

Consider the following Lyapunov function candidate

$$
E(t) = E_b(t) + E_o(t),
\tag{23}
$$

where $E_o(t) = \frac{\widetilde{EI}^2(t)}{2\mu_1} + \frac{\tilde{\rho}^2(t)}{2\mu_2} + \frac{\widetilde{M_s}^2(t)}{2\mu_3} + \frac{\tilde{d_s}^2(t)}{2\mu_4} + \frac{\widetilde{T}^2(t)}{2\mu_5} + \frac{\tilde{d}^2(t)}{2}$.

Combining (17), (23) with Lemma 1, we have

$$
\begin{aligned}
0 < \lambda_1[E_y(t) + \tfrac{M_s}{2}e_0^2(t)\ln\tfrac{2Q^2}{Q^2 - z_1^2(t)} + E_o(t)] &\leq E(t) \\
&\leq \lambda_2[E_y(t) + \tfrac{M_s}{2}e_0^2(t)\ln\tfrac{2Q^2}{Q^2 - z_1^2(t)} + E_o(t)],
\end{aligned}
\tag{24}
$$

where $\lambda_1 = \min(\iota_1, 1), \lambda_2 = \max(\iota_2, 1)$.

Lemma 2. For $\dot{E}(t)$, it is upper bounded as

$$
\dot{E}(t) \leq -\lambda E(t) + \varepsilon,
\tag{25}
$$

where $\lambda, \varepsilon > 0$.

Proof. Taking differentiate for (23) with respect to time t, and then substituting (18)–(19) and (21)–(22), we have

$$
\begin{aligned}
\dot{E}(t) \leq & - (d_s + k_3)e_0^2(t)\ln\tfrac{2Q^2}{Q^2 - z_1^2(t)} - (k_4 - \tfrac{\varpi\rho L}{2})e_0^2(t) - (Tk_1\kappa - \tfrac{\varpi TL}{2} \\
& - \tfrac{\varpi\rho Lk_1^2}{2} - \tfrac{|\varpi\rho Lk_1k_2 + \varpi EIL - \kappa Tk_2 - \kappa EIk_1|}{\delta_3})[w'(L,t)]^2 - (EIk_2\kappa \\
& - \tfrac{\varpi\rho Lk_2^2}{2} - |\varpi\rho Lk_1k_2 + \varpi EIL - \kappa Tk_2 - \kappa EIk_1|\delta_3) \\
& \cdot [w'''(L,t)]^2 - (c\kappa - \varpi cL\delta_6 - \kappa\delta_4 + \tfrac{\varpi\rho}{2})\int_0^L \dot{w}^2 ds + \delta_1 \dot{d}^2(t) \\
& - (k_5 - \tfrac{1}{\delta_1} - \tfrac{k_5}{\delta_2})\dot{d}^2(t) - (\tfrac{\varpi T}{2} - \varpi L\delta_5 - \tfrac{\varpi cL}{\delta_6})\int_0^L (w')^2 ds \\
& - \tfrac{\zeta_1}{2}\widetilde{EI}^2(t) - \tfrac{\zeta_2}{2}\tilde{\rho}^2(t) - \tfrac{\zeta_3}{2}\widetilde{M_s}^2(t) - \tfrac{\zeta_4}{2}\tilde{d_s}^2(t) - \tfrac{\zeta_5}{2}\widetilde{T}^2(t) \\
& + \tfrac{\zeta_1}{2}EI^2 + \tfrac{\zeta_2}{2}\rho^2 + \tfrac{\zeta_3}{2}M_s^2 + \tfrac{\zeta_4}{2}d_s^2 + \tfrac{\zeta_5}{2}T^2 + \delta_2 k_5 d^2(t) \\
& - \tfrac{3\varpi EI}{2}\int_0^L (w'')^2 ds + (\tfrac{\kappa}{\delta_4} + \tfrac{\varpi L}{\delta_5})\int_0^L f^2 ds,
\end{aligned}
\tag{26}
$$

where $\delta_1 \sim \delta_6 > 0$.

According to (9) and (26), $\varpi, \kappa, k_1 \sim k_5$ and $\delta_1 \sim \delta_6$ are chosen to satisfy conditions: $\varpi < \frac{\min(\kappa\rho, \kappa T)}{\rho L}, Tk_1\kappa - \frac{\varpi\rho Lk_1^2}{2} - \frac{\varpi TL}{2} - \frac{|\varpi\rho Lk_1k_2 + \varpi EIL - \kappa Tk_2 - \kappa EIk_1|}{\delta_3} \geq 0,$
$EIk_2\kappa - \frac{\varpi\rho Lk_2^2}{2} - |\varpi\rho Lk_1k_2 + \varpi EIL - \kappa Tk_2 - \kappa EIk_1|\delta_3 \geq 0, k_4 - \frac{\varpi\rho L}{2} \geq 0,$
$\tau_1 = c\kappa - \varpi cL\delta_6 - \kappa\delta_4 + \frac{\varpi\rho}{2} > 0, \tau_2 = \frac{3}{2}\varpi EI > 0, \tau_3 = \frac{\varpi T}{2} - \varpi L\delta_5 - \frac{\varpi cL}{\delta_6} > 0,$
$\tau_4 = d_s + k_3 > 0$ and $\tau_5 = k_5 - \frac{1}{\delta_1} - \frac{k_5}{\delta_2} > 0.$

Thus, combining (24) with (26), we obtain

$$
\begin{aligned}
\dot{E}(t) \leq & - \lambda_3 E_y(t) - \tau_4 e_0^2(t)\ln\tfrac{2Q^2}{Q^2 - z_1^2(t)} - \lambda_4 E_o(t) + \varepsilon \\
\leq & - \lambda_5[E_y(t) + \tfrac{M_s}{2}e_0^2(t)\ln\tfrac{2Q^2}{Q^2 - z_1^2(t)} + E_o(t)] + \varepsilon \\
\leq & - \lambda E(t) + \varepsilon,
\end{aligned}
\tag{27}
$$

where $\lambda_3 = \min(\frac{2\tau_1}{\kappa\rho}, \frac{2\tau_2}{\kappa EI}, \frac{2\tau_3}{\kappa T}), \lambda_4 = \min(2\tau_5, \zeta_1\mu_1, \zeta_2\mu_2, \zeta_3\mu_3, \zeta_4\mu_4, \zeta_5\mu_5)$ and $\varepsilon = \max\{\frac{\zeta_1}{2}EI^2 + \frac{\zeta_2}{2}\rho^2 + \frac{\zeta_3}{2}M_s^2 + \frac{\zeta_4}{2}d_s^2 + \frac{\zeta_5}{2}T^2 + \delta_1\dot{d}^2(t) + \delta_2 k_5 d^2(t) + (\frac{\kappa}{\delta_4} + \frac{\varpi L}{\delta_5})\int_0^L f^2 ds\}, \lambda_5 = \min(\lambda_3, \lambda_4, \frac{2\tau_4}{M_s}), \lambda = \frac{\lambda_5}{\lambda_2}.$

4   Simulation Analysis

Numerical simulations are performed for validating the availability of designed control (19). The system parameters are listed as $\rho = 500\,\text{kg/m}$, $M_s = 9.6 \times 10^6\,\text{kg}$, $L = 1000\,\text{m}$, $c = 5.0\,\text{Ns/m}^2$, $T = 8.11 \times 10^7\,\text{N}$, $EI = 1.5 \times 10^7\,\text{Nm}^2$, $d_s = 1000\,\text{Ns/m}$ and $Q = 0.02\,\text{m}$. Give the initial conditions as $w(s,0) = \dot{w}(s,0) = 0$, and $d(t) = [2 + 0.3\sin(0.5t) + 0.1\sin(0.3t) + 0.5\sin(0.9t)] \times 10^5$.

The deflections of the proposed riser under free vibration and the designed control (19) are depicted in Fig. 2. Figure 3 depicts riser's vibration displacement inspected at $s = 1000\,\text{m}$ and $s = 500\,\text{m}$. Figure 4 shows the disturbance observer error $\tilde{d}(t)$ and control input $u(t)$.

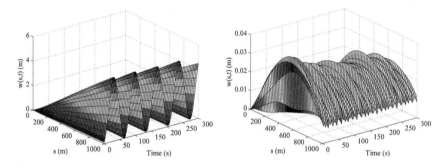

Fig. 2. Deflections of the riser system: (a) without control, (b) with designed control.

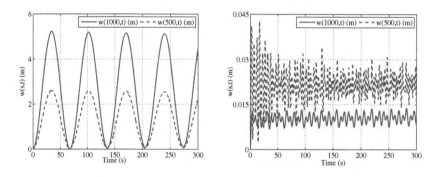

Fig. 3. Deflections of the riser at $s = 1000\,\text{m}$ and $s = 500\,\text{m}$: (a) without control, (b) with designed control.

It can be observed from Figs. 2, 3 and 4 that the formulated control (19) can efficaciously decrease riser's vibration and make boundary vibration displacement satisfy $|w(L,t)| < Q, Q = 0.02\,\text{m}$. Despite there exists the disturbance estimation error $\tilde{d}(t)$, the designed control (19) could still stabilize riser system. The control input $u(t)$ varies between $-0.5 \times 10^5\,\text{N}$ and $-3.5 \times 10^5\,\text{N}$, which is mainly used to counteract the external environmental disturbance.

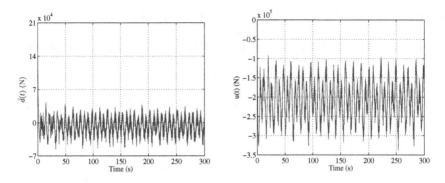

Fig. 4. (a) disturbance observer error $\widetilde{d}(t)$, (b) control input $u(t)$.

5 Conclusion

In this paper, vibration control of the riser system with output constraint has been addressed. An adaptive Lyapunov-based barrier control with disturbance observer has been designed based on integrating finite-dimensional backstepping technique and IBLF, where the adaptive laws have been developed to attenuate the parametric uncertainties and the IBLF has been considered to solve the effect of output constraint. The availability of formulated control has been testified by presented simulation results.

Acknowledgments. This work was supported in part by the Science and Technology Planning Project of Guangdong Province (2016A010106007), and by the Fundamental Research Funds for the Central Universities of SCUT (2017ZD058).

References

1. Do, K.D., Pan, J.: Boundary control of three-dimensional inextensible marine risers. J. Sound Vib. **327**(3–5), 299–321 (2009)
2. Nguyen, T.L., Do, K.D., Pan, J.: Boundary control of two-dimensional marine risers with bending couplings. J. Sound Vib. **332**(16), 3605–3622 (2013)
3. He, W., Ge, S.S., How, B.V., et al.: Robust adaptive boundary control of a flexible marine riser with vessel dynamics. Automatica **47**(4), 722–732 (2011)
4. Balas, M.J.: Active control of flexible systems. J. Optim. Theor. Appl. **25**(3), 415–436 (1978)
5. Liu, Y., Zhao, Z.J., He, W.: Stabilization of an axially moving accelerated/decelerated system via an adaptive boundary control. ISA Trans. **64**, 394–404 (2016)
6. Sakawa, Y., Matsuno, F., Fukushima, S.: Modeling and feedback control of a flexible arm. J. Robot. Syst. **2**(4), 453–472 (1985)
7. Zhao, Z.J., Liu, Y., He, W., et al.: Adaptive boundary control of an axially moving belt system with high acceleration/deceleration. IET Control Theor. Appl. **10**(11), 1299–1306 (2016)

8. He, W., Ge, S.S.: Vibration control of a flexible beam with output constraint. IEEE Trans. Ind. Electron. **62**(8), 5023–5030 (2015)
9. Liu, Z.J., Liu, J.K.: Boundary control of a flexible robotic manipulator with output constraints. Asian J. Control. **19**(1), 332–345 (2017)
10. He, W., Zhang, S., Ge, S.S.: Adaptive control of a flexible crane system with the boundary output constraint. IEEE Trans. Ind. Electron. **61**(8), 4126–4133 (2014)
11. He, W., Sun, C., Ge, S.S.: Top tension control of a flexible marine riser by using integral-barrier Lyapunov function. IEEE/ASME Trans. Mechatron. **20**(2), 497–505 (2015)

Vibration Suppression of an Axially Moving System with Restrained Boundary Tension

Zhijia Zhao[1], Yu Liu[2(✉)], and Kun Sun[2]

[1] School of Mechanical and Electrical Engineering,
Guangzhou University, Guangzhou 510006, China
zhao.zhijia@mail.scut.edu.cn
[2] School of Automation Science and Engineering,
South China University of Technology, Guangzhou 510640, China
auylau@scut.edu.cn, sunbaiwan9527@gmail.com

Abstract. In this paper, we concentrate on the vibration suppression of an axially moving string system subject to the restrained boundary tension. By introducing an appropriate barrier Lyapunov function, a boundary control is constructed to stabilize the vibration and insure that the boundary tension is maintained within limits. The derived control can guarantee the uniformly bounded stability of the closed-loop system and the satisfaction of the boundary tension constraint. Finally, the simulations validate the results.

Keywords: Axially moving system · Vibration suppression · Boundary control · Boundary tension constraint

1 Introduction

Axially moving systems such as cables, strings, belts, and others, can exhibit vibration in the course of the axial transport. However, the unwanted vibration of the system will cut down the associated manufacturing process productivity [1,2]. Hence, the vibration suppression of the axially moving system has aroused interest of many researchers in recent years.

In nature, the axially moving system is a typically infinite-dimensional distributed parameter system (DPS). There are two usual methods for controlling the DPS following modal approach and boundary control. Modal approach is the execution of the control design by neglecting the high frequency modes, which would bring about control spillover or even unstable problems [3,4]. Boundary control for the control design is on the basis of original infinite-dimensional model of the system and the modelling and control design for axially moving systems have made rapid progress in recent decades [5–9]. In [1], the adaptive and robust controls are presented to weaken the oscillation of a stretched string. In [2], the boundary control is constructed for damping the vibration of axially translating system under the effects of unknown disturbance derived from uncontrolled span using the energy approach. In [5,6], the adaptive robust boundary control

© Springer International Publishing AG 2017
D. Liu et al. (Eds.): ICONIP 2017, Part VI, LNCS 10639, pp. 257–265, 2017.
https://doi.org/10.1007/978-3-319-70136-3_28

is developed to globally stabilize a class of axially accelerated system by employing adaptive technique, Lyapunov theory and backstepping method. In [7], the vibration of an axially moving nonuniform system is attenuated through the developed output feedback control. In [8], adaptive isolation controllers are proposed to guarantee that the transverse vibration of the axially moving system is asymptotically convergent. In [9], the stabilization of an axially moving string is realized through the total energy dissipation. However, in all the research results on axially moving systems [1,2,5–9], despite boundary control for axially moving systems having made significant progress, there is little research on control design for copping with boundary tension constraint problem. The violation of the boundary tension constraint will give rise to serious hazards, such as degrading the control performance, causing damage to the equipment and even causing safety accident, which makes the control design more challenging. This motivates us for this research.

In this paper, we deal with the boundary control design problem for suppressing the vibration and preventing the constraint transgression for an axially moving string system. By constructing a novel barrier Lyapunov function (BLF), a boundary control is designed for stabilizing the string system and ensuring that the boundary tension constraint is never transgressed. The uniformly ultimately bounded stability of the closed-loop system is realized employing rigorous Lyapunov analysis without recourse to model reduction.

2   Problem Formulation

Figure 1 shows an axially moving string system. OXY denotes the reference frame, x and t denote the independent spatial and time variables, $z(x,t)$ denotes the vibration displacement, $v(t)$, ρ and c denote the axial speed, the mass per unit length and the viscous damping coefficient of the string, m and γ denote the mass and damping coefficient of the actuator, L denotes be the length of the controlled span, T_m denotes the boundary tension constraint, $d(t)$ and $f(x,t)$ denote unknown boundary and distributed disturbances, and $u(t)$ denotes the control input exerted at the right boundary of the string. We define notations $(\cdot)(t) = (\cdot), (\cdot)(x,t) = (\cdot), (\cdot)_x = \partial(\cdot)/\partial x$ and $(\cdot)_t = \partial(\cdot)/\partial t$ throughout the paper.

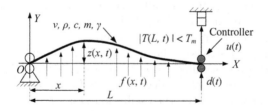

Fig. 1. Schematic of an axially moving system.

The kinetic energy $K_e(t)$ and potential energy $P_e(t)$ of the considered string system are respectively described by

$$\begin{cases} K_e(t) = \frac{1}{2}mz_t^2(L,t) + \frac{1}{2}\int_0^L \rho[z_t(x,t) + v(t)z_x(x,t)]^2 dx \\ P_e(t) = \frac{1}{2}\int_0^L T(x,t)z_x^2(x,t)dx \end{cases} \tag{1}$$

where the spatiotemporally-varying tension $T(x,t)$ is expressed as [1]

$$T(x,t) = T_0(x) + \kappa(x)z_x^2(x,t) \tag{2}$$

with $T_0(x) > 0$ being the initial tension and the scalar function $\kappa(x) \geq 0$ being the nonlinear elastic modulus.

The virtual work $\delta W_1(t)$ done by the nonconservative force and the virtual momentum transport $\delta W_2(t)$ across the boundaries are calculated as

$$\begin{cases} \delta W_1(t) = d(t)\delta z(L,t) - c\int_0^L [z_t(x,t) + v(t)z_x(x,t)]\delta z(x,t)dx \\ \qquad\qquad + [u(t) - \gamma z_t(L,t)]\delta z(L,t) + \int_0^L f(x,t)\delta z(x,t)dx \\ \delta W_2(t) = \rho v(t)[z_t(L,t) + v(t)z_x(L,t)]\delta z(L,t) \end{cases} \tag{3}$$

where δ denotes the variational operator.

Utilizing the Hamilton's principle to derive the dynamical model of the considered string system

$$\int_{t_1}^{t_2} [\delta K_e(t) - \delta P_e(t) + \delta W_1(t) - \delta W_2(t)]dt = 0 \tag{4}$$

where t_1 and t_2 $(t_1 < t < t_2)$ are two time instants.

Substituting (1) and (3) into (4), and then applying integration by parts, we derive the dynamical equation of the system as

$$\begin{aligned} \rho[z_{tt}(x,t) &+ v_t(t)z_x(x,t) + 2v(t)z_{xt}(x,t) + v^2(t)z_{xx}(x,t)] \\ &- T_0(x)z_{xx}(x,t) - T_{0x}(x)z_x(x,t) - 2\kappa_x(x)z_x^3(x,t) \\ &- 6\kappa(x)z_x^2(x,t)z_{xx}(x,t) + c[z_t(x,t) + v(t)z_x(x,t)] = f(x,t) \end{aligned} \tag{5}$$

$\forall(x,t) \in (0,L) \times [0,+\infty)$, and the boundary conditions as

$$\begin{cases} z(0,t) = 0 \\ mz_{tt}(L,t) + T_0(L)z_x(L,t) + 2\kappa(L)z_x^3(L,t) + \gamma z_t(L,t) - d(t) = u(t) \end{cases} \tag{6}$$

$\forall t \in [0,+\infty)$.

Assumption 1. We assume that $f(x,t)$, $v(t)$ and $d(t)$ are uniformly continuous and there exist constants b_1, b_2, $b_3 \in \mathbb{R}^+$, such that $| f(x,t) | \leq b_1$, $\forall(x,t) \in [0,L] \times [0,+\infty)$, and $0 < v(t) \leq b_2$, $| d(t) | \leq b_3$, $\forall t \in [0,+\infty)$.

Assumption 2. We assume the scalar function $T_0(x)$ and $\kappa(x)$ are uniformly bounded and there exist nonnegative constants b_4, b_5, b_6, b_7, b_8, b_9, such that $b_4 \leq T_0(x) \leq b_5$, $b_6 \leq \kappa(x) \leq b_7$, $|T_{0x}(x)| \leq b_8$, $|\kappa_x(x)| \leq b_9$, $\forall x \in [0,L]$.

3 Boundary Control Design

In this section, we develop a boundary control at the string's right boundary for restraining the vibration and simultaneously ensuring the boundary tension constraint satisfaction, i.e., $|T(L,t)| \leq T_m$. Afterwards, the BLF is constructed to analyze the stability of the controlled system.

To stabilize the considered system given by (5)–(6), we propose the following boundary control

$$u(t) = -[z_t(L,t) + k_2 z_x(L,t)][k_1 + \frac{mz_x(L,t)z_{xt}(L,t)}{\phi^2 - z_x^2(L,t)}]/\ln \frac{2\phi^2}{\phi^2 - z_x^2(L,t)} \quad (7)$$
$$- k_2 m z_{xt}(L,t) + T_0(L)z_x(L,t) + 2\kappa(L)z_x^3(L,t) + \gamma z_t(L,t)$$
$$- k_3[z_t(L,t) + k_2 z_x(L,t)] - 2\kappa(L)z_x^3(L,t)/\ln \frac{2\phi^2}{\phi^2 - z_x^2(L,t)}$$
$$- sgn\{[z_t(L,t) + k_2 z_x(L,t)]\ln \frac{2\phi^2}{\phi^2 - z_x^2(L,t)}\}b_3$$

with $k_1, k_2, k_3 > 0$ being the control gains, $sgn(\cdot)$ being the signum function, and $\psi > 0$ being related to the boundary tension constraint T_m such that $\psi = \sqrt{\frac{T_m - T_0(L)}{\kappa(L)}}$.

Consider the following Lyapunov function candidate (LFC)

$$V(t) = V_m(t) + V_n(t) + V_p(t) \quad (8)$$

with an energy term $V_a(t)$ with $\eta > 0$ being represented as

$$V_m(t) = \tfrac{1}{2}\mu \int_0^L \rho[z_t(x,t) + v(t)z_x(x,t)]^2 dx + \tfrac{1}{2}\mu \int_0^L T(x,t)z_x^2(x,t)dx \quad (9)$$

and a small crossing term $V_b(t)$ with $\mu > 0$ being defined as

$$V_n(t) = 2\epsilon\rho \int_0^L xz_x(x,t)[z_t(x,t) + v(t)z_x(x,t)]dx \quad (10)$$

and an auxiliary term $V_c(t)$ being expressed as

$$V_p(t) = \tfrac{1}{2}\mu m[z_t(L,t) + k_2 z_x(L,t)]^2 \ln \frac{2\psi^2}{\psi^2 - z_x^2(L,t)} \quad (11)$$

Lemma 1. The selected LFC (8) is with the following form

$$0 \leq \omega_1[V_m(t) + V_p(t)] \leq V(t) \leq \omega_2[V_m(t) + V_p(t)] \quad (12)$$

where $\omega_1, \omega_2 > 0$.

Proof. Applying $mn \leq \frac{m^2 + n^2}{2}$ to (10) gives

$$|V_n(t)| \leq \epsilon\rho L \int_0^L \{z_x^2(x,t) + [z_t(x,t) + v(t)z_x(x,t)]^2\}dx \leq \varpi V_m(t) \quad (13)$$

where ϖ is defined as

$$\varpi = \frac{2\epsilon\rho L}{\min(\mu\rho, \mu b_4)} \quad (14)$$

Choosing η and μ properly yields

$$\varpi_1 = 1 - \frac{2\epsilon\rho L}{\min(\mu\rho,\mu b_4)} > 0, \quad \varpi_2 = 1 + \frac{2\epsilon\rho L}{\min(\mu\rho,\mu b_4)} > 1 \tag{15}$$

(15) shows $0 < \varpi < 1$, and then the combination of (14) leads to

$$\epsilon < \frac{\min(\mu\rho,\mu b_4)}{2\rho L} \tag{16}$$

Rearranging (13) results in

$$-\varpi V_m(t) \le V_n(t) \le \varpi V_m(t) \tag{17}$$

Substituting (15) into (17), we get

$$0 < \varpi_1 V_m(t) \le V_m(t) + V_n(t) \le \varpi_2 V_m(t) \tag{18}$$

According to (8), we further derive

$$0 \le \omega_1[V_m(t) + V_p(t)] \le V(t) \le \omega_2[V_m(t) + V_p(t)] \tag{19}$$

where $\omega_1 = \min(\varpi_1, 1) > 0$ and $\omega_2 = \max(\omega_2, 1) > 0$.

Lemma 2. The time derivative of the LFC (8) can be upper bounded with

$$V_t(t) \le -\omega V(t) + \lambda \tag{20}$$

where $\omega, \lambda > 0$

Proof. Differentiating (8) to result in

$$V_t(t) = V_{mt}(t) + V_{nt}(t) + V_{pt}(t) \tag{21}$$

Differentiating (9) and (10), substituting (5), integrating by parts and applying $mn \le \frac{m^2}{\sigma} + \sigma n^2, \sigma > 0$, we have

$$
\begin{aligned}
V_{mt}(t) \le{}& -\frac{\mu v(t)[T_0(0) - \rho v^2(t)]}{2} z_x^2(0,t) - \frac{\mu\rho v(t)}{2}[z_t(L,t) + v(t)z_x(L,t)]^2 \\
&+ \frac{\mu T_0(L)}{2k_2}[z_t(L,t) + k_2 z_x(L,t)]^2 - \frac{\mu T_0(L)[k_2 - v(t)]}{2} z_x^2(L,t) \\
&+ \frac{3\mu v(t)}{2}[\kappa(L)z_x^4(L,t) - \kappa(0)z_x^4(0,t)] + 2\mu\kappa(L)z_t(L,t)z_x^3(L,t) \\
&- \frac{\mu T_0(L)}{2k_2} z_t^2(L,t) - (c\mu - \mu\chi_1)\int_0^L [z_t(x,t) + v(t)z_x(x,t)]^2 dx \\
&+ \frac{\mu}{2}\int_0^L v(t)\kappa_x(x)z_x^4(x,t)dx + \frac{\mu}{\chi_1}\int_0^L f^2(x,t)dx
\end{aligned}
\tag{22}
$$

$$V_{nt}(t) \leq \epsilon\rho L z_t^2(L,t) - \epsilon[\rho L v^2(t) - LT_0(L)]z_x^2(L,t) + \frac{2\epsilon L}{\chi_2}\int_0^L f^2(x,t)dx$$

$$- \epsilon[T_0(x) - xT_{0x}(x) - \rho v^2(t) - 2L\chi_2 - 2L\chi_3 c]\int_0^L z_x^2(x,t)dx$$

$$- \epsilon\rho\int_0^L z_t^2(x,t)dx + \frac{2\epsilon Lc}{\chi_3}\int_0^L [z_t(x,t) + v(t)z_x(x,t)]^2 dx$$

$$+ 3\epsilon L\kappa(L)z_x^4(L,t) - \epsilon\int_0^L [3\kappa(x) - x\kappa_x(x)]z_x^4(x,t)dx \qquad (23)$$

where $\chi_1, \chi_2, \chi_3 > 0$.

Differentiating (11) and substituting (6) and (7), we get

$$V_{pt}(t) = -\mu k_1[z_t(L,t) + k_2 z_x(L,t)]^2 - 2\mu\kappa(L)z_t(L,t)z_x^3(L,t) \qquad (24)$$

$$- 2\mu k_2\kappa(L)z_x^4(L,t) - \mu k_3[z_t(L,t) + k_2 z_x(L,t)]^2 \ln\frac{2\psi^2}{\psi^2 - z_x^2(L,t)}$$

Substituting (22)–(24) into (21), we derive

$$V_t(t) \leq -(\mu k_1 - \frac{\mu T_0(L)}{2k_2})[z_t(L,t) + k_2 z_x(L,t)]^2 - [\frac{\mu T_0(L)}{2k_2} - \epsilon\rho L]z_t^2(L,t)$$

$$- \frac{\mu v(t)[T_0(0) - \rho v^2(t)]}{2}z_x^2(0,t) - \mu k_3[z_t(L,t) + k_2 z_x(L,t)]^2 \ln\frac{2\psi^2}{\psi^2 - z_x^2(L,t)}$$

$$- \{\epsilon L\rho v^2(t) + \frac{\mu T_0(L)[k_2 - v(t)]}{2} - \epsilon LT_0(L)\}z_x^2(L,t)$$

$$- [2\mu k_2 - 3\epsilon L - \frac{3\mu v(t)}{2}]\kappa(L)z_x^4(L,t) - \frac{3\mu v(t)}{2}\kappa(0)z_x^4(0,t)$$

$$- (c\mu - \mu\chi_1 - \frac{2\epsilon Lc}{\chi_3})\int_0^L [z_t(x,t) + v(t)z_x(x,t)]^2 dx$$

$$- [\epsilon T_0(x) - \epsilon xT_{0x}(x) - \epsilon\rho v^2(t) - 2\epsilon L\chi_2 - 2\epsilon L\chi_3 c]\int_0^L z_x^2(x,t)dx$$

$$- \int_0^L [3\epsilon\kappa(x) - \epsilon x\kappa_x(x) - \frac{\mu}{2}v(t)\kappa_x(x)]z_x^4(x,t)dx$$

$$- \frac{\mu\rho v(t)}{2}[z_t(L,t) + v(t)z_x(L,t)]^2 + (\frac{\mu}{\chi_1} + \frac{2\epsilon L}{\chi_2})\int_0^L f^2(x,t)dx \qquad (25)$$

The choice of the parameters ϵ, μ, $k_1 \sim k_3$, $\chi_1 \sim \chi_3$ is to satisfy the following conditions

$$\begin{cases} \epsilon < \frac{\min(\mu\rho,\mu b_4)}{2\rho L}, \quad \frac{\mu v(t)[T_0(0)-\rho v^2(t)]}{2} \geq 0, \quad \mu k_1 - \frac{\mu T_0(L)}{2k_2} \geq 0 \\ \frac{\mu T_0(L)}{2k_2} - \epsilon\rho L \geq 0, \quad \epsilon L\rho v^2(t) + \frac{\mu T_0(L)[k_2-v(t)]}{2} - \epsilon LT_0(L) \geq 0 \\ \lambda = (\frac{\mu}{\chi_1} + \frac{2\epsilon L}{\chi_2})Lb_1^2, \quad \tau_1 = c\mu - \mu\chi_1 - \frac{2\epsilon Lc}{\chi_3} > 0 \\ \tau_2 = \min[\epsilon T_0(x) - \epsilon xT_{0x}(x) - \epsilon\rho v^2(t) - 2\epsilon L\chi_2 - 2\epsilon L\chi_3 c] > 0 \\ \tau_3 = \min[3\epsilon\kappa(x) - \epsilon x\kappa_x(x) - \frac{\mu}{2}v(t)\kappa_x(x)] > 0 \end{cases} \qquad (26)$$

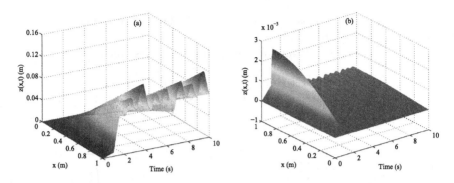

Fig. 2. Deflections of the string system: (a) without control, (b) with proposed control.

Substituting (26) into (25) gives

$$V_t(t) \leq - \tau_1 \int_0^L [z_t(x,t) + v(t)z_x(x,t)]^2 dx - \tau_2 \int_0^L z_x^2(x,t)dx \qquad (27)$$

$$- \tau_3 \int_0^L z_x^4(x,t)dx - \mu k_3 [z_t(L,t) + k_2 z_x(L,t)]^2 \ln \frac{2\psi^2}{\psi^2 - z_x^2(L,t)} + \lambda$$

$$\leq - \omega_3 [V_m(t) + V_p(t)] + \lambda$$

where $\omega_3 = \min(\frac{2\tau_1}{\mu\rho}, \frac{2\tau_2}{\mu b_6}, \frac{2\tau_3}{\mu b_7}, \frac{2k_3}{m})$. Then combining (12) and (28), we have

$$V_t(t) \leq -\omega V(t) + \lambda \qquad (28)$$

where $\omega = (\omega_3/\omega_2)$.

Multiplying (20) by $e^{\omega t}$ and integrating the consequence give

$$V(t) \leq [V(0) - \tfrac{\lambda}{\omega}]e^{-\omega t} + \tfrac{\lambda}{\omega} \leq V(0)e^{-\omega t} + \tfrac{\lambda}{\omega} \qquad (29)$$

Combining (9), (12) and Lemma 2 in [10], we get

$$\tfrac{\mu b_4}{2L} z^2(x,t) \leq \tfrac{\mu}{2} \int_0^L T_0(x)z_x^2 dx \leq V_m(t) \leq \tfrac{1}{\omega_1} V(t) \qquad (30)$$

Substituting (29) into (30), we derive

$$| z(x,t) | \leq \sqrt{\tfrac{2L}{\mu\omega_1 b_4}[V(0)e^{-\omega t} + \tfrac{\lambda}{\omega}]}, \quad \forall (x,t) \in [0, L] \times [0, +\infty] \qquad (31)$$

4   Numerical Simulations

In this section, we exploit the finite difference method to prove the effectiveness of the proposed control for the considered string system [11,12]. The detailed parameters are $\rho = 1\,\text{kg/m}$, $L = 1.0\,\text{m}$, $c = 1.0\,\text{Ns/m}^2$, $m = 5.0\,\text{kg}$, $\gamma = 1.0\,\text{Ns/m}$,

$v(t) = 2 + \sin t$, $T_0(x) = 100(1 + 0.1x)$ N, $\kappa(x) = 5000(1 + 0.1x)$. The corresponding initial conditions are $z(x, 0) = z_t(x, 0) = 0$.

The disturbances $f(x, t)$ and $d(t)$ are respectively described as

$$\begin{cases} f(x, t) = \frac{x}{10}[1 + \sin(\pi x t) + 2\sin(2\pi x t) + 3\sin(3\pi x t)] \\ d(t) = 10 + \sin(t) + 3\sin(3t) + 5\sin(5t) \end{cases} \tag{32}$$

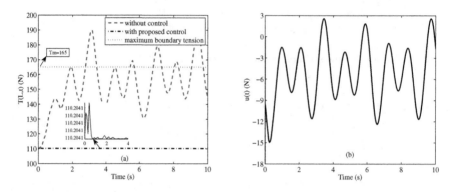

Fig. 3. (a) boundary tension $T(L, t)$ of the string, (b) proposed control input.

The string's deflection $z(x, t)$ under no control is displayed in Fig. 2(a) and the string's deflection $z(x, t)$ with proposed control is depicted in Fig. 2(b) by choosing control parameters as $k_1 = 5000$, $k_2 = 300$, $k_3 = 1000$ and $\phi = 0.1$. The boundary tension $T(L, t)$ of the string is shown in Fig. 3(a), and the time histories of the proposed control input is given in Fig. 3(b).

5   Conclusion

In this paper, the control design for an axially moving string system with restrained tension was addressed. Under the derived control law, the vibration of the string system was attenuated, and the boundary tension constraint was ensured. The stability of the controlled system was realized via Lyapunov analysis. In conclusion, the efficiency of the control proposed was verified conducting numerical simulation.

Acknowledgments. This work was supported in part by the National Natural Science Foundation of China (U1601204, 61603105), the Science and Technology Planning Project of Guangdong Province (2016B090912003, 2016B090927010, 2016B010126001, 2015B010101003, 2015B010919003), and by the Fundamental Research Funds for the Central Universities of SCUT (2017ZD058).

References

1. Qu, Z.H.: Robust and adaptive boundary control of a stretched string on a moving transporter. IEEE Trans. Autom. Contr. **46**(3), 470–476 (2001)
2. Yang, K.-J., Hong, K.-S., Matsuno, F.: Energy-based control of axially translating beams: varying tension, varying speed, and disturbance adaptation. IEEE Trans. Control Syst. Technol. **13**(6), 1045–1054 (2005)
3. Wu, H.-N., Wang, J.-W.: Observer design and output feedback stabilization for nonlinear multivariable systems with diffusion PDE-governed sensor dynamics. Nonlinear Dyn. **72**(3), 615–628 (2013)
4. Guo, B.Z., Yang, K.J.: Dynamic stabilisation of an Euler-Bernoulli Beam equation with time delay in boundary observation. Automatica **45**(6), 1468–1475 (2009)
5. Liu, Y., Zhao, Z.J., He, W.: Stabilization of an axially moving accelerated/decelerated system via an adaptive boundary control. ISA Trans. **64**, 394–404 (2016)
6. Liu, Y., Zhao, Z.J., He, W.: Boundary control of an axially moving accelerated/decelerated belt system. Int. J. Robust Nonlinear Control **26**(17), 3849–3866 (2016)
7. Zhao, Z.J., Liu, Y., Guo, F., Fu, Y.: Modelling and control for a class of axially moving nonuniform system. Int. J. Syst. Sci. **48**(4), 849–861 (2017)
8. Li, Y., Aron, D., Rahn, C.D.: Adaptive vibration isolation for axially moving strings: theory and experiment. Automatica **38**(3), 379–390 (2002)
9. Nguyen, Q.C., Hong, K.-S.: Asymptotic stabilization of a nonlinear axially moving string by adaptive boundary control. J. Sound Vib. **329**(22), 4588–4603 (2010)
10. Zhao, Z.J., Liu, Y., He, W., Luo, F.: Adaptive boundary control of an axially moving belt system with high acceleration/deceleration. IET Control Theory Appl. **10**(11), 1299–1306 (2016)
11. Zhao, Z.J., Liu, Y., Luo, F.: Output feedback boundary control of an axially moving system with input saturation constraint. ISA Trans. **68**, 22–32 (2017)
12. Zhao, Z.J., Liu, Y., Luo, F.: Boundary control for a vibrating string system with bounded input. Asian J. Control (2017, in press). doi:10.1002/asjc.1555

A High Accurate Vision Algorithm on Measuring Arbitrary Contour

Hongwei Xie[1], Kun Sun[2], Yu Liu[2(✉)], and Jiaxiang Luo[2]

[1] Guangzhou University, Guangzhou 510006, China
xhw_cn@foxmail.com
[2] South China University of Technology, Guangzhou 510640, China
sunbaiwan9527@gmail.com, {auylau,luojx}@scut.edu.cn

Abstract. In order to measure the error of arbitrary contours, a high accurate visual algorithm is proposed. Firstly, a subpixel edge extraction algorithm based on local grayscale fitting is used to extract subpixel contours. And then we use the coarse-to-fine matching strategy, which uses the shape context feature of contours to perform coarse matching, and then based on iterative closest points to complete fine matching step. Finally, the neighborhood algorithm is proposed to calculate the contour error. Experiments show that the accuracy of this algorithm can reach 0.5 pixel, and this algorithm can apply to error measurement of any shape of contours.

Keywords: Shape context descriptor · Iterative closest points · Sub-pixel contour extraction · Contour measurement

1 Introduction

The visual measurement technology of product defects is widely used in industrial applications. Compared with other measurement techniques, machine vision measurement technology has the advantages of high degree of intelligence, good real-time and high precision [1]. Contour measurement is just one of the important applications.

At present, the research on the contour detection and measurement algorithm is basically to divide the extracted contour into straight lines, ellipses, circles and other geometric primitives [2–4], and then fit them respectively [5, 6]. Based on the known number of breakpoints, [2] proposed an algorithm to determine the approximate function in the breakpoint interval to divide the contour curve into lines and circles. Based on the detection of arc and the dominant point, [3] divided the contours into straight lines and circles. And then the robustness of this algorithm is improved in [4], which using the adaptive tangential covering for the dominant point detection and the polygonal approximation of the contours on the tangent space. With the least squares method, [5] fitted circles, ellipses, hyperbolas, etc. A new method of nonparametric fitting and elliptic arc is proposed in [6], which improves the measurement accuracy of line segment and ellipse. Although these research works make the robustness and accuracy of contour segmentation and fit increased, these methods can only be used to detect and measure the contours of the regular shapes. Considering the fact that the actual workpiece shapes

© Springer International Publishing AG 2017
D. Liu et al. (Eds.): ICONIP 2017, Part VI, LNCS 10639, pp. 266–276, 2017.
https://doi.org/10.1007/978-3-319-70136-3_29

are varied and the contours may be made up of irregular curves, a new artifact detection algorithm for workpiece contour defects is proposed, which can accurately detect and measure the contour defects of any shape of the workpiece.

The algorithm proposed in this paper can be divided into three steps: extracting the contour, matching the contour and calculating the error. Firstly, the area of the workpiece is extracted on the image, and followed by denoising and closing contour. Then the sub-pixel edge is extracted based on the local area edge extraction algorithm [7]. Secondly, we will match contour by coarse-to-fine matching strategy. Select the sample points first, which are used to calculate the shape context descriptors for initial position registration of contours [8], and then fine matching using the iterative nearest point algorithm [9, 10]. Finally, the error of each position in the contour is calculated according to the matching result.

2 Extracting Contour

2.1 Image Preprocessing

In order to get a better contour of the workpiece, we use industrial camera with parallel backlight and telecentric lens to collect images. Firstly, the image is done binarization, erosion and dilation separately, followed by smoothing filter to extract region of interest (ROI). Then the first order gradient of ROI is obtained by the convolution of image with Prewitt operator and the pixels whose gradient value is greater than the threshold is noted as the contour edge. However, the contour obtained by the above method is likely not to be closed continuously, which will affect the accuracy of error calculation. So, the contours should be filled with appropriate erosion and dilation.

2.2 Contour Extracting

The existing sub-pixel edge extraction algorithm can be divided into three categories: based on the moment [10], based on the least squares [12] and based on interpolation [13]. The methods based on moments have high accuracy, but it is very sensitive to noise. The methods based on the minimum squared difference determines the edge parameters by minimizing the local energy function, and are robust to the noise, but the computation is time consuming. There are also some computationally efficient methods based on interpolation, but is susceptible to errors. Therefore, a new sub-pixel edge extraction algorithm which is different from the above three categories was proposed in 7. This method can obtain the sub-pixel information accurately, including the position, gray scale difference, normal vector and curvature of edges, based on the function on the neighborhood area. It is also computationally efficient, robust to noise near the edge, and accurate sub-pixel information. And particularly, accurate curvature will play an important role in removal of false matches and fine matching, which is not available in other edge extraction algorithms.

Assume that the edge is a quadratic curve

$$y = a + bx + cx^2 \tag{1}$$

This curve cut up the image into two parts, and the gray values are A and B. Take a 5×3 neighborhood centered on the given pixel, as shown in Fig. 1.

As shown in Fig. 2, the coordinate system is established with the center of the given pixel as the origin, and $F_{(i,j)}$ is the gray value of each pixel $p(i, j)$. The sum of gray values of each column is respectively marked as S_L, S_M, S_R. So

$$S_L = \sum_{n=j-2}^{j+2} F_{i-1,n} = 5B + \frac{A - B}{h^2}L \tag{2}$$

$$S_M = \sum_{n=j-2}^{j+2} F_{i,n} = 5B + \frac{A - B}{h^2}M \tag{3}$$

$$S_R = \sum_{n=j-2}^{j+2} F_{i+1,n} = 5B + \frac{A - B}{h^2}R \tag{4}$$

where L, M, and R denote the area of each column respectively, and the simultaneous equations are solved

$$a = \frac{2S_M - 5(A + B)}{2(A - B)} - \frac{1}{12}c, \ b = \frac{S_R - S_L}{2(A - B)}, \ c = \frac{S_L + S_R - 2S_M}{2(A - B)} \tag{5}$$

whereby the curvature of the pixel can be obtained

$$K = \frac{2c}{(1 + b^2)^{\frac{3}{2}}} \tag{6}$$

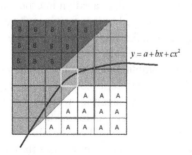
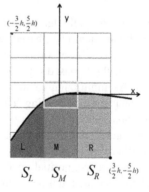

Fig. 1. The pixel in edge curve and its 5×3 neighborhood marked with a red box (Color figure online)

Fig. 2. The neighborhood of the quadratic curve

3   Contour Matching

3.1   Coarse Matching

Get Shape Context Descriptor

Since there are so many pixels of the target contour, it is very time consuming to compute the feature orderly, and the appropriate sampling will improve the matching speed. So firstly we will randomly sample the contours uniformly and get a sparse contour Q.

In 2002, Serge Belongie proposed the shape context descriptor (hereinafter referred to as SC), which had achieved a good effect in shape matching. Suppose the contour is $S = \{s_1, s_2, \ldots, s_n\}$, where any $s_i \in S$ is the origin of the log-polar coordinates, and SC of s_i is the distribution of the histogram of other n-1 point.

In the log-polar coordinate system, the coordinate plane is divided into $k = r \times l$ bins, where r is the equal segment number of the angle axis and l is the logarithm axis of the number of segments, to record the distribution of the remaining n-1 points. And this constructs the histogram $h_i(j)$, where i is the i-th point, j represents the j-th bins, where $1 \leq i \leq n, 1 \leq j \leq k$. This feature is invariant in translation. As the shape context descriptor using the logarithmic distance, which can accurate describe nearby points and approximate describe points faraway, we can take into account the local features and global features, as shown in Figs. 3 and 4.

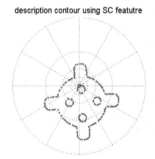

description contour using SC featutre

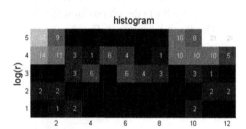

Fig. 3. The description of workpiece with SC descriptor

Fig. 4. Count the points in each bins of Fig. 4 and draw the histogram

Feature Matching

Assume $p_i \in P, q_i \in Q$, are the random points in contour P and Q respectively, the cost function between the two points can be described as

$$C_{i,j} = C(p_i, q_j) = \frac{1}{2} \sum_{k=1}^{K} \frac{[h_i(k) - h_j(k)]^2}{h_i(k) + h_j(k)} \tag{7}$$

where $h_i(k)$ and $h_j(k)$ is the histogram in pi and qi. Thus we can calculate the cost function of all corresponding points between P and Q

$$H(\pi) = \sum_i C(p_i, q_{\pi(i)}) \tag{8}$$

and expect to minimum the total cost function, which is a weighted bipartite graph matching problem. Here we use a more efficient algorithm proposed in [14] to calculate the best match.

Removing Mismatch

The mismatch between contour points often occurs, which will reduce the speed and accuracy of the contour matching. Therefore, a rejection function is designed with the curvature of sub-pixel,

$$r = \begin{cases} 1, & c_1 - c_2 \le c_0 \\ 0, & c_1 - c_2 > c_0 \end{cases} \tag{9}$$

where c_1 and c_2 are the curvatures of the corresponding points. When the curvature error of the corresponding point is greater than the threshold value c_0, it would be considered to be false match and the point pair will be discarded. Then, the rotation and translation matrices can be calculated based on matching result.

Calculating Rotation and Translation Matrix

According to the matching results of the corresponding points, the commonly used methods for calculating the rotation and translation matrices are: SVD decomposition [15], quaternion method [16], orthonormal matrix [17], dual quaternion method [18]. Here we use SVD decomposition to solve the problem.

The result is shown in Fig. 5.

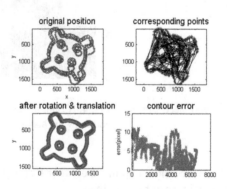

Fig. 5. Shape matching with SC descriptor

The first line of pictures are the sampled contours and correspondences with *SC* descriptor (connected with segments). The second line of pictures are the result after coarse matching and the error of each contour point. But it can be seen that the error range reaches 10 pixels, obviously cannot meet the measurement needs. So the more accurate measurement, at pixel or even sub-pixel level, is needed.

3.2   Fine Matching

The coarse matching result is used as the initial position for the *ICP* algorithm. This algorithm essentially is iteratively matching the corresponding points to calculate the optimal rigid transformation matrix, until the condition of stopping the convergence is satisfied. But the algorithm requires that the two contours have been approached to some extent or the initial position has been estimated, otherwise the process of searching for the nearest point will fall into the local optimum. So here we use the framework proposed in [15] to achieve fine matching of contours. The steps are as follows:

1. Select the data. Considering the results of the initial match has been more accurate, so all the points would be use directly. And it can be seen that it has reached the optimal in the first several iterations from Fig. 6.
2. Match contour points. Searching the nearest contour point is usually the most time-consuming step. There are three general approaches: The simplest but also most time-consuming method is traversing all $q_j \in Q$ to find the nearest point for all $p_i \in P$ In order to speed up the search process, generally use kD-tree or Delaunay algorithm. Here using kD-tree.
3. Determine the weight function. Considering error of the noise effects and error in the contour extraction process, a new weight function is designed based on the sub-pixel information.

$$w = e^{-(\alpha m_1 + \beta m_2 + \lambda m_3)} \tag{10}$$

Where

$$m_1 = \frac{|d_1 - d_2|}{mean(|d_P - d_Q|)}, \; m_2 = \frac{1}{\vec{n}_1 \cdot \vec{n}_2} \frac{1}{mean(|\vec{n}_P \cdot \vec{n}_Q|)}, \; m_3 = \frac{|c_1 - c_2|}{mean(|c_P - c_Q|)}. \tag{11}$$

where m1 is the normalized residual of the nearest points in P and Q, m2 is the normalized product of the normal vector of the nearest point, and m3 represents the normalized difference in the curvature of the nearest point. α, β, γ The corresponding scale factor, $\alpha + \beta + \gamma = 1$. Here $\alpha = 0.5$, $\beta = 0.3$, $\gamma = 0.2$.

4. Discard partial matching result. Discard the poor quality of the matching results, not incorporated into the error calculation. Here, the minimum weight of 10% of the corresponding points is discarded.
5. Determine the error metric function. After getting the matching result, the rest of the work is to measure the error and minimize the error function. There are two main error measurement methods:
One is calculating point-to-point distance proposed in [9]:

$$\sum_{i=1}^{n} \left\| w_i (Rp_i + t) - q_i \right\|^2 \tag{11}$$

Another is calculating point-to-tangent distance proposed in [10]:

$$\sum_{i=1}^{n} \left\| w_i \left(Rp_i + T - q_i \right) . n_i \right\|^2 \tag{12}$$

As the point-to-tangent distance is more accurate to describe the positional relationship of contours, it is better when the high precision is required. Here we adopt this method.

6. Minimum the contour error. Linearize the rotation matrix $\begin{pmatrix} \cos\theta & -\sin\theta \\ \sin\theta & \cos\theta \end{pmatrix}$ to $\begin{pmatrix} 1 & -\theta \\ \theta & 1 \end{pmatrix}$. Thus, the rotation angle θ and the translation distance t_x and t_y can be obtained by the least squares method. Although this approximation introduces errors, with the iteration the angle become smaller and smaller, and the linearized rotation matrix will be very close to true value.

In Fig. 6 below, first line on the left side of is the coarse matching result, and the right side is fine matching result. The second line on the left side is the contour error, the right is detailed iterations. It can be seen that the error has been completely less than one pixel.

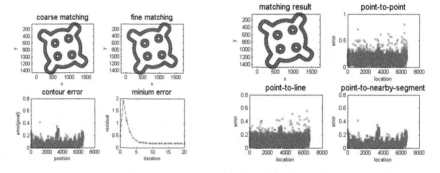

Fig. 6. The contour matching of workpiece   **Fig. 7.** Compare of three kind metric methods

4   Calculating Contour Error

The contour error will be calculated after the contour has been fine matched. As the contour is discrete and similar, so it is needed to try to make the results closer to the real value. There are three methods of error calculation:

1. Point to point. For any $p_i \in P$, whose nearest point in Q is denoted q_j, the error is

$$e_i = \left\| p_i - q_j \right\| \tag{13}$$

that is, the European distance of these two points. This approach depends on the quantity of points, when the contours are sparse, the results will be very inaccurate. Generally, this method is not used directly.

2. Point to tangent. For any $p_i \in P$, whose nearest point in Q is denoted q_i, the error is

$$e_i = \left\| (p_i - q_j).n_i \right\| \tag{14}$$

That is the distance of p_i to q_j where the tangent. It can be seen this method requires high precision of the normal vector.

3. Neighborhood method. Based on the advantages of the above two methods, we design the neighborhood method, that is, calculate the minimum distance from the point to the adjacent segment. For $p_i \in P$, find the n points nearest to p_i in Q, and clockwise connect them to n-1 line segments. Let $\{q'_1, q'_2, q'_3, \ldots q'_{n-1}\}$ be the minimum distance from pi to the n-1 segment, and it is just the error in contour point qi.

$$e_i = \min\{q'_1, q'_2, \ldots q'_{n-1}\} \tag{15}$$

Three error measurement methods are compared in Fig. 7. It can be seen that the neighborhood method proposed in this paper has the best effect. Because the distance of point-to- tangent is limited by the precision of the normal vector, and distance of point-to-point is limited by the quantity of the contour points, while the neighborhood method minimizes these negative factors, with better robustness.

5 Experiment and Analysis

5.1 Calibration Plate Experiment

The calibration plate with accuracy of 0.001 mm is used to verify the accuracy of the algorithm. As the measurement object, it would be randomly rotated and translated in the field of view, and then the circle, rectangle and triangle on the calibration plate would be extracted and compared to standard contours. The error distributions are as follow:

It can be seen from Figs. 8, 9 and 10 that the accuracy of our contour detection and measurement algorithm can up to 0.5 pixels, especially good result on the circle and rectangle. However, the error of triangle is large, this is because the edge of the intersection is very close, affecting the accuracy of contour extraction.

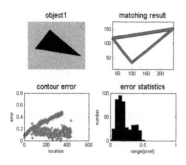
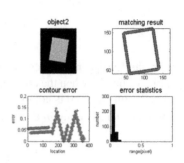

Fig. 8. Calibration plate experiment 1   **Fig. 9.** Calibration plate experiment 2

5.2 Workpiece Experiment

The workpiece with precision of 0.01 mm is placed in the field of view, and then compared extracted contour with the standard contour. The experimental results are as follows in Fig. 11.

It can be seen that for irregularly shaped workpiece, the accuracy of the contour measurement can also be within 0.5 pixels, but compared with the calibration plate experiment the error is significantly increased, which is caused by two reasons: First, the accuracy of workpiece is not high, with the fluctuation range of 0.2 pixels. Second, as the complexity of the contour increases, the extraction of corners and other edges of the contour would be less accurate.

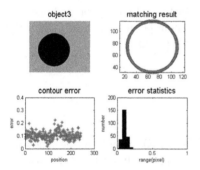
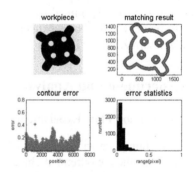

Fig. 10. Calibration plate experiment 3   **Fig. 11.** Workpiece Experiment

6   Summary and Outlook

In this paper, a contour error measurement algorithm is proposed to detect and measure the contour error of any shape, and the measurement accuracy can up to 0.5 pixels. The algorithm will greatly improve the application of error detection in industrial and improve the efficiency of production. In this paper, according to the requirements of contour error detection and the characteristics of sub-pixel contours, we design a rejection function to reduce the false matching in SC, propose a new weight function to increase the accuracy and robustness of *ICP*, and also design the neighborhood method to calculate the contour error. However, the robustness of the algorithm is not good enough to the affects from the noise point close to the edge. And as the increase of contour points, the extraction of sub-pixel edge and run time of *ICP* will increase accompanied, which is also an important factor restricting practical application of this algorithm. These are all needed to be improved in next steps.

Acknowledgements. This work was supported in part by the Science and Technology Planning Project of Guangdong Province (2015B090901049, 2014A090906010, 2014A090906009), and by the Fundamental Research Funds for the Central Universities of SCUT (2017ZD058).

References

1. Wang, Y., Chen, T., He, Z., Wu, C.: Review on the machine vision measurement and control technology for intelligent manufacturing equipment. Control Theor. Appl. **32**(3), 273–286 (2015)
2. Chen, J., Ventura, J.A., Wu, C.: Segmentation of planar curves into circular and line segments. Image Vis. Comput. **14**, 71–83 (1996)
3. Nguyen, T.P., Debled-Rennesson, I.: Decomposition of a curve into arcs and line segments based on dominant point detection. In: Heyden, A., Kahl, F. (eds.) SCIA 2011. LNCS, vol. 6688, pp. 794–805. Springer, Heidelberg (2011). doi:10.1007/978-3-642-21227-7_74
4. Ngo, P., Nasser, H., Debled-Rennesson, I.: A discrete approach for decomposing noisy digital contours into arcs and segments. In: Chen, C.-S., Lu, J., Ma, K.-K. (eds.) ACCV 2016. LNCS, vol. 10117, pp. 493–505. Springer, Cham (2017). doi:10.1007/978-3-319-54427-4_36
5. Sung, J., Wolfgang, R., Hans-JuKrgen, W.: Least-squares orthogonal distances fitting of circle, sphere, ellipse, hyperbola, and parabola. Pattern Recogn. **34**, 2283–2303 (2001)
6. Pătrăucean, V., Gurdjos, P., von Gioi, R.G.: A parameterless line segment and elliptical arc detector with enhanced ellipse fitting. In: Fitzgibbon, A., Lazebnik, S., Perona, P., Sato, Y., Schmid, Cordelia (eds.) ECCV 2012. LNCS, pp. 572–585. Springer, Heidelberg (2012). doi: 10.1007/978-3-642-33709-3_41
7. Agustín, T., Karl, K., Miguel, A., Daniel, S.: Accurate subpixel edge location based on partial area effect Accurate subpixel edge location based on partial area effect. Image Vis. Comput. **31**, 72–90 (2013)
8. Serge, B., Jitendra, M., Jan, P.: Shape matching and object recognition using shape contexts. IEEE Trans. Pattern Anal. Mach. Intell. **24**(4), 509–522 (2002). IEEE
9. Paul, J., Neil, D.: A method for registration of 3-D shapes. IEEE Trans. Pattern Anal. Mach. Intell. **14**(2), 239–256 (1992). IEEE
10. Yang, C., Gerard, M.: Object modeling by registration of multiple range image. Image Vis. Comput. **10**(3), 145–155 (1992)
11. Sugata, G., Rajiv, M.: Orthogonal moment operators for subpixel edge detection. Pattern Recogn. **26**(2), 295–306 (1993)
12. Kisworo, M., Venkatesh, S., West, G.: Modeling edges at subpixel accuracy using the local energy approach. IEEE Trans. Pattern Anal. Mach. Intell. **16**(4), 405–410 (1994)
13. Steger, C.: Subpixel-precise extraction of lines and edges. Int. Arch. Photogrammetry Remote Sens. **33**(3), 141–156 (2000)
14. Jonker, R., Volgenant, A.: A shortest augmenting path algorithm for dense and sparse linear assignment problems. Computing **38**(4), 325–340 (1987)

15. Arun, K., Huang, T., Blostein, S.: Least-squares fitting of two 3-D point sets. IEEE Trans. Pattern Anal. Mach. Intell. **9**(5), 698–700 (1987)
16. Horn, B.K.P.: Closed-form solution of absolute orientation using unit quaternions. Opt. Soc. Am. **4**(4), 629–642 (1987)
17. Horn, B.K.P., Hilden, H., Negahdaripour, S.: Closed form solution of absolute orientation using orthonormal matrices. Opt. Soc. Am. **5**(7), 1127–1135 (1988)
18. Walker, M., Shao, L., Volz, R.: Estimating 3-D location parameters using dual number quaternions. CVGIP Image Underst. **54**(3), 358–367 (1991)

Dynamic Phasor Modeling of a Hybrid AC/DC Microgrid

Jin Xu, Keyou Wang$^{(\boxtimes)}$, and Guojie Li

Shanghai Jiao Tong University, 800 Dongchuan RD. Minhang District, Shanghai, China
{xujin20506,wangkeyou}@sjtu.edu.cn

Abstract. The dynamic phasor (DP) model of a hybrid AC/DC microgird is proposed in this paper. This hybrid microgrid consists of an interlinking converter (ILC), wind turbine (WT) system, photovoltaic (PV) system and energy storage (ES) system, and can operate under either grid-connected mode or autonomous mode. A comprehensive definition of the dynamic phasor is given to make the developed model more compact and the physical meaning more clear. The developed microgrid model is validated by comparing with a detailed model considering switch operations in Matlab/Simulink. By comparison, the DP model turns out to consume much less time and have a satisfactory accuracy under various disturbances.

Keywords: Dynamic phasor · Energy storage · Hybrid microgrid · Interlinking converter · Multiple-Shifted-Frequency (MSF) method · Photovoltaic · Wind turbine

1 Introduction

Due to the increasing integration of distributed generations (DGs) into distribution network, microgrid has been proposed to manage these DGs and received more and more research attention [1, 2]. Among the various topologies, the hybrid AC/DC microgrid can effectively reduce the energy conversion processes of distribution generators and loads [3–6], thus needs fewer converters and has less energy loss. The hybrid microgrid has DGs or energy storage on both AC and DC subsystems, which requires more coordination for the voltage and power control [5]. A proper model on system level is necessary for the time-domain simulation, which provides useful information for control and protection design, harmonic and resonance analysis, stability evaluation, etc.

Detailed electromagnetic-transient (EMT) models [7], in which voltage and current variables are represented by instantaneous values, is widely used in electromagnetic transient simulation tools, such as Electromagnetic Transients Program (EMTP), EMTDC/PSCAD, and MATLAB/Simulink. In the microgrid simulation [8], the EMT model usually covers every detailed dynamic from the switching dynamics of power electronics to the mechanical or thermal dynamics of DGs, with a wide time frame from microseconds to seconds [9]. The simulation of microgrids may need to span over a long time due to the existence of slow responding sources [10]. Given the current computing power, the EMT simulation of a whole mcirogrid consisting of multiple DGs and

D. Liu et al. (Eds.): ICONIP 2017, Part VI, LNCS 10639, pp. 277–286, 2017.
https://doi.org/10.1007/978-3-319-70136-3_30

converters, which is extremely time-consuming, may be unacceptable [8]. Since the phenomena associated with the switching dynamics are not a major concern in microgrid simulation for system level study, the EMT model is excessively detailed and will cause unnecessary computation [11].

The average-value modeling (AVM) aims to develop efficient models which only represent the slow dynamics of power-electronic-based systems by neglecting the switching dynamics [12]. The dynamic phasor (DP) based modeling, an averaging technique, achieves this object by using the quasi-periodic nature of power-electronic switches, for which voltages and currents can be represented using time-varying Fourier coefficients. As the Fourier coefficients change much slower than the original variables, a lager time step is allowed in the DP-based simulation. Besides, the complexity of the dynamic phasor model can be changed as needed. Hence, the DP-based simulation can approach any required tradeoff between the accuracy and speed by adopting different orders of the DP model [13]. In addition, the DP model can be easily augmented to account for any harmonic components and negative-/zero- sequence components, if needed [12].

Some efforts have also been made to analyze and simulate the distribution [14, 15] system or microgrid [16] with AVM, whose dynamic phasor models only consist of the fundamental waveform. The modeling of DG dynamics and the complete microgrid control strategies are few involved in these researches [14–16].

This paper models a hybrid AC/DC microgrid with dynamic phasors and improves the modeling strategy in the following aspects.

- Microgrids under both grid-connected mode and autonomous mode are modeled under normal and unbalanced scenarios, and negative sequence compensation (NSC) control in unbalanced case is included.
- Slow dynamics of DGs behind the converters, e.g., the mechanic dynamics of the wind turbine, are taken into the consideration in the modeling. Thus, the more complete low-frequency dynamics of microgrids can be reflected in the DP model.
- Inspired by the Shifted-Frequency Analysis (SFA) proposed in [17, 18], a comprehensive definition of the dynamic phasor is given to make the developed model more compact and the physical meaning more clear.

The rest of this paper is organized as follows. In Sect. 2, the dynamic phasor theory with a more comprehensive definition is introduced. In the following Sect. 3, the complete DP model of a hybrid microgrid is presented. The simulation results of three cases and corresponding conclusions are given in the Sects. 4 and 5, respectively.

2 Dynamic Phasor Theory

From the perspective of communication technology, a voltage (or current) variable $u(t)$ containing harmonics can be seen as the superposition of the bandpass signals $u^k(t)$, $k = 0, 1, 2,..$, which are modulated by their corresponding carrier with the frequency of $k\omega_s$. Here ω_s is the fundamental frequency.

$$u(t) = \sum_{k=0}^{\infty} u^k(t) = \sum_{k=0}^{\infty} \left(u_I^k(t) \cos k\omega_s t - u_Q^k(t) \sin k\omega_s t \right) \tag{1}$$

where the low-pass signals $u_I^k(t)$ and $u_Q^k(t)$ are the in-phase and quadrature components of the bandpass signals $u^k(t)$, respectively. Then, the kth order dynamic phasor $<U(t)>_k$ can be defined as

$$\langle U(t) \rangle_k = u_I^k(t) + j u_Q^k(t) \tag{2}$$

The kth order dynamic phasor can be seen as the complex envelope of $u^k(t)$. From the definition, we can derive some properties of dynamic phasors which will be helpful for transforming an instantaneous value model into a dynamic phasor one.

1. Homogeneity

$$\langle a \cdot u(t) \rangle_k = a \cdot \langle U(t) \rangle_k. \tag{3}$$

   where a is a constant.
2. Differential Property

$$\left\langle \frac{du(t)}{dt} \right\rangle_k = \frac{d\langle U(t) \rangle_k}{dt} + jk\omega_s \langle U(t) \rangle_k \tag{4}$$

3. Convolutional Property

$$\langle u(t) \cdot i(t) \rangle_k = \frac{1}{2} \sum_{l=-\infty}^{\infty} \left[\langle U(t) \rangle_{k+l} \cdot \langle I(t) \rangle_{-l} \right] \tag{5}$$

These properties are very similar to those of the DPs defined by Fourier method. Actually, these two definitions are approximately equivalent in certain circumstance. However, the definition given in this paper eliminates the dynamic phasors of negative orders by Hilbert Transformation, thus there are two advantages over the traditional definition:

- The required number of the dynamic phasors is halved and the DP models can be expressed in a more compact form.
- The remaining positive- and zero-order dynamic phasors are corresponding to the harmonic components and DC component one to one, which makes the physical meaning more clear.

The instantaneous waveforms can be restored from the phasor results by the inverse transformation:

$$u(t) = \sum_{k=0}^{\infty} u^k(t) = \sum_{k=0}^{\infty} \text{Re}\left[\langle U(t) \rangle_k e^{jk\omega_s t} \right] \tag{6}$$

3 Hybrid Microgrid Configuration and Dynamic Phasor Modelling

The system diagram of the studied hybrid AC/DC microgrid is shown in Fig. 1.

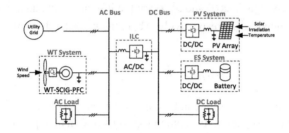

Fig. 1. A hybrid AC/DC microgrid system

3.1 Interlinking Converter (ILC)

The interlinking converter (ILC) is a four-quadrant operating voltage source converter (VSC). The typical topology is shown in Fig. 2 where u_{x0} ($x = a,b,c$) is the output voltage on the AC side, u_x is the AC bus voltage, u_{dc} is the DC bus voltage, i_x is the AC current, i_{dc0} is the output DC current and i_{dc} is the DC current after the capacitor.

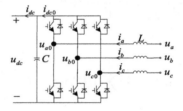

Fig. 2. Typical topology of VSC

According to the three properties in Sect. 2, the VSC model can be rewritten with dynamic phasors (taking "phase A" for example):

$$L\frac{d\langle I_a\rangle_k}{dt} = \langle U_a\rangle_k - \frac{1}{3}(\langle U_a\rangle_k + \langle U_b\rangle_k + \langle U_c\rangle_k) - (R + jk\omega_s L)\langle I_a\rangle_k - \langle U_{a0}\rangle_k \tag{7}$$

$$\langle U_{a0}\rangle_k = \frac{1}{2}\sum_{l=-\infty}^{\infty}\left[\langle U_{dc}\rangle_{k-l}\cdot\left(\frac{2}{3}\langle S_a\rangle_l - \frac{1}{3}\langle S_b\rangle_l - \frac{1}{3}\langle S_c\rangle_l\right)\right] \tag{8}$$

$$C\frac{d\langle U_{dc}\rangle_k}{dt} = \langle I_{dc0}\rangle_k - \langle I_{dc}\rangle_k - jk\omega_s C\langle U_{dc}\rangle_k \tag{9}$$

$$\langle I_{dc0}\rangle_k = \frac{1}{2}\sum_{l=-\infty}^{\infty}\left(\langle I_a\rangle_{k-l}\langle S_a\rangle_l + \langle I_b\rangle_{k-l}\langle S_b\rangle_l + \langle I_c\rangle_{k-l}\langle S_c\rangle_l\right) \tag{10}$$

where $<S_a>$, $<S_b>$, $<S_c>$ are the dynamic phasors of switch functions.

3.2 SCIG-WT System Model

The electrical part of the squirrel cage induction generator (SCIG) is represented by a fourth-order state-space model in the dq frame.

Since the mechanical part of SCIG and WT do not contain fast-fluctuating sinusoidal components, dynamic phasor form is not adopted. Assuming a rigid drive train, the equation of turbine rotor motion is given by

$$\frac{d\omega_m}{dt} = \frac{1}{2H}\left(T_e - T_m - F\omega_m\right) \tag{11}$$

$$T_e \approx \langle T_e \rangle_0 = \frac{3}{2}\left(\langle \varphi_{ds} \rangle_0 \langle I_{qs} \rangle_0 - \langle \varphi_{qs} \rangle_0 \langle I_{ds} \rangle_0\right) \tag{12}$$

$$T_m = \frac{1}{2}\pi\rho R_b^3 V_w^2 C_p(\lambda) \tag{13}$$

where T_e is the electrical torque. If the effect of electrical torque ripples on the shafting system is neglected, T_e is approximately given by (12). T_m is the aerodynamic torque of the wind turbine given by the wind power utilization formula [17] in (13). C_p is wind power utilization coefficient and λ is tip speed ratio, V_w is wind speed.

In order to compensate the reactive power consumed by the SCIG, a power factor correction (PFC) capacitor is connected to the AC bus. The PFC adopts the capacitor model similar to that in (9).

3.3 Photovoltaic (PV) System

The PV system is divided into two parts: a PV array and a boost circuit. The PV array can be seen as a current source.

Figure 3 shows the topology of the boost circuit. The DP model of the filters is written as

$$C_1 \frac{d\langle V_{pv} \rangle_k}{dt} = \langle I_{pv} \rangle_k - \langle I_1 \rangle_k - jk\omega_s C_1 \langle V_{pv} \rangle_k \tag{14}$$

$$C_2 \frac{d\langle V_{pv2} \rangle_k}{dt} = \langle I_2 \rangle_k - \langle I_{pv2} \rangle_k - jk\omega_s C_2 \langle V_{pv2} \rangle_k \tag{15}$$

$$L \frac{d\langle I_1 \rangle_k}{dt} = \langle V_{pv} \rangle_k - \langle V'_{pv} \rangle_k - (R + jk\omega_s L)\langle I_1 \rangle_k \tag{16}$$

where $<V'_{pv}>_k$ and $<I_2>_k$ can be approximately described by the 0th order DP of the switch function g, i.e., the duty cycle d.

$$\left\langle V'_{pv} \right\rangle_k \approx \left\langle V_{pv2} \right\rangle_k \left(1 - \langle g \rangle_0\right) = \left\langle V_{pv2} \right\rangle_k (1 - d) \tag{17}$$

$$\langle I_2 \rangle_k \approx \langle I_1 \rangle_k \left(1 - \langle g \rangle_0\right) = \left\langle I_{pv} \right\rangle_k (1 - d) \tag{18}$$

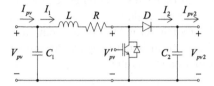

Fig. 3. Boost circuit

3.4 Energy Storage (ES) System

The ES system is also divided into two parts: a battery and a boost-buck circuit.

The battery can be seen as a voltage source whose terminal voltage V_b is related to discharge current I_b and state of charge (SOC) [19].

The topology of the boost-buck circuit is shown in Fig. 4. When the battery is discharging, gate signal g_1 is blocked. This bidirectional converter works as a boost circuit and has the same DP model with (17)–(18). When the battery is charging, gate signal g_2 is blocked. The bidirectional converter works as a buck circuit and the voltage and current on both sides have an approximate relationship as follows:

$$\langle I_1 \rangle_k \approx \langle I_2 \rangle_k d_1 \tag{19}$$

$$\langle V_2 \rangle_k \approx \langle V_1 \rangle_k d_1 \tag{20}$$

where d_1 is the duty circle of the upper gate.

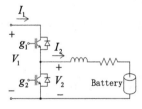

Fig. 4. Buck-boost circuit

4   Simulation Results

The DP model of the hybrid microgrid in Fig. 1 has been established in Matlab/Simulink, based on the DAEs described in Sect. 3. The instantaneous value (IV) model with identical topology and parameters is built with blocks in Simulink/SimPowerSystems, which is regarded as the benchmark in the case study. All the converters in IV model adopt switch function models.

4.1 Case 1: Environmental Disturbances

In this case, the hybrid microgrid is working at the autonomous mode. A series of environmental disturbances are imposed on the microgrid. First, a step change of irradiance on PV array (750 W/m^2–1000 W/m^2) occurs at 5.0 s, then a step change of wind speed (10 m/s–8 m/s) occurs at 10.0 s, finally a step change of DC load power (9.6 kW–14.6 kW) occurs at 15.0 s. Simulation results of both models are shown below.

The black curves in Fig. 5 represent the DP results of DC bus voltage, output current of PV and output current of ES; the gray ones represent the corresponding IV results. Likewise, the black curves in Fig. 6 represent the DP results of AC bus voltage, ILC current on the AC side and output current of WT; the gray ones represent the corresponding IV results with a fundamental frequency of 60 Hz.

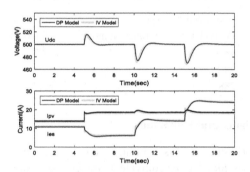

Fig. 5. DC bus voltage, output currents of PV and ES

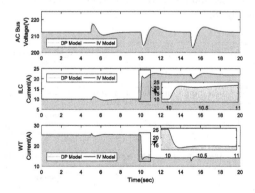

Fig. 6. Bus voltage and branch currents on the AC side

In Fig. 5, the 0th order DPs well fit the DC waveforms of the IV model, and in Fig. 6 the 1st order DPs well envelop the 60 Hz AC waveforms of the IV model. For clarity, the DC voltage error between the DP results and IV results are plotted in Fig. 7.

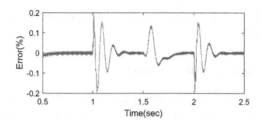

Fig. 7. Relative error of the DC bus voltage

All these figures indicate that the static and transient accuracy of the DP model is satisfactory.

Table 1 lists the consumed time of different models in this simulation. Obviously, the DP model consumes much less than the IV model.

Table 1. Comparison of consuming time

Simulated time (s)	Consumed time (s)	
	IV model (Switch function model)	DP model (Average model)
5	48.3	8.7
10	98.1	17.4
30	288	53.7

4.2 Case 2: Unbalance and Harmonics

In this case, the hybrid microgrid is working at the grid-connected mode. A negative sequence component is added to the equivalent voltage source of the utility grid. Simulations with and without the negative sequence compensation (NSC) control are performed. The DC voltage and AC currents (restored from the DP results using (5)) of the ILC are shown in Fig. 8.

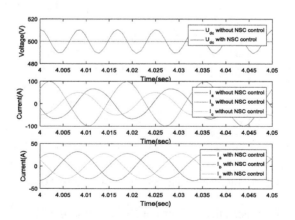

Fig. 8. DC voltage and AC currents of the ILC restored from the DP results

The unbalanced 1st order AC currents will lead to a 2nd order DC current, and the 2nd order DC voltage will lead to 3rd order AC voltages in return, which explains the existence of 120 Hz DC ripples and the 3rd AC harmonics. After the activation of the NSC controller, both the 120 Hz ripples and the 3rd harmonics die down and the 1st order AC currents return to the symmetry.

Table 2 shows the harmonic analysis results of the detailed-model-based and DP-based simulations. By comparing these two models, it indicates that the DP model accurately reflects the magnitudes of the fundamental component and the 3rd order harmonic under the unbalanced condition without NSC control and with NSC control. However, since the DP model in this paper only including the 0th order, 1st order, 2nd order and 3rd order, it cannot represent higher order harmonics. As a result, the total harmonic distortion (THD) ratio of the DP model is lower than that of the detailed model.

Table 2. Harmonic analysis results of the detailed model and DP model (phase A)

	Detailed model		DP model	
	Without NSC	With NSC	Without NSC	With NSC
Fundamental component (A)	68.35	32.17	67.17	32.4
3rd order harmonic (A)	2.42	0.08	2.22	0.03
THD (%)	4.26	0.70	3.31	0.10

5   Conclusion

In this paper, the dynamic phasor model of a complete hybrid AC/DC microgrid is developed, based on a more comprehensive definition of the dynamic phasor. The accuracy of this DP model is validated under various scenarios. The DP model shows a much faster simulation speed than the traditional one. Case study also demonstrates its ability to handle unbalance and harmonic issues. Both the fundamental control of power/voltage and the auxiliary control of NSC function correctly in the DP-based simulation. By neglecting the high frequency switch operations, the DP model can focus on slower dynamics, which makes its time frame more suitable for system level simulations of microgrids.

Acknowledgement.   This work was supported in part by National Key R&D Plan (2016YFB0900601) and State Grid Technology Program (study on principle, design and control technology of new operation mode of micro-grid based on electric spring).

References

1. Mariam, L., Basu, M., Conlon, M.F.: Microgrid: architecture, policy and future trends. Renew. Sustain. Energy Rev. **64**, 477–489 (2016)
2. Lasseter, R.H.: MicroGrids. In: IEEE Power Engineering Society Winter Meeting, New York, vol. 1, pp. 305–308 (2002)
3. Unamuno, E., Barrena, J.A.: Hybrid ac/dc microgrids—Part I: review and classification of topologies. Renew. Sustain. Energy Rev. **52**, 1251–1259 (2015)

4. Unamuno, E., Barrena, J.A.: Hybrid ac/dc microgrids—Part II: review and classification of control strategies. Renew. Sustain. Energy Rev. **52**, 1123–1134 (2015)
5. Nejabatkhah, F., Li, Y.W.: Overview of power management strategies of hybrid AC/DC microgrid. IEEE Trans. Power Electron. **30**(12), 7072–7089 (2015)
6. Eghtedarpour, N., Farjah, E.: Power control and management in a hybrid AC/DC microgrid. IEEE Trans. Smart Grid **5**(3), 1494–1505 (2014)
7. Watson, N., Arrillaga, J.: Power Systems Electromagnetic Transients Simulation, p. 448. Institution of Engineering & Technology (2003)
8. Xu, Y., Gao, H., Chen, Y., et al.: A fast EMT simulation method for control and protection studies of microgrids. In: IEEE Pes General Meeting | Conference & Exposition, National Harbor, pp. 1–5. (2014)
9. Shuai, Z., Sun, Y., Shen, Z.J., et al.: Microgrid stability: classification and a review. Renew. Sustain. Energy Rev. **58**, 167–179 (2016)
10. Soultanis, N.L., Papathanasiou, S.A., Hatziargyriou, N.D.: A stability algorithm for the dynamic analysis of inverter dominated unbalanced LV microgrids. IEEE Trans. Power Syst. **22**(1), 294–304 (2007)
11. Xu, Y., Chen, Y., Liu, C.C., et al.: Piecewise average-value model of PWM converters with applications to large-signal transient simulations. IEEE Trans. Power Electron. **31**(2), 1304–1321 (2015)
12. Daryabak, M., Filizadeh, S., Jatskevich, J., et al.: Modeling of LCC-HVDC systems using dynamic phasors. IEEE Trans. Power Delivery **29**(4), 1989–1998 (2014)
13. Liu, C., Bose, A., Tian, P.: Modeling and analysis of HVDC converter by three-phase dynamic phasor. IEEE Trans. Power Delivery **29**(1), 3–12 (2014)
14. Emadi, A.: Modelling of power electronic loads in AC distribution systems using the generalized state space averaging method. IEEE Trans. Industr. Electron. **51**(5), 992–1000 (2004)
15. Miao, Z., Piyasinghe, L., Khazaei, J., et al.: Dynamic phasor-based modeling of unbalanced radial distribution systems. IEEE Trans. Power Syst. **30**(6), 3102–3109 (2015)
16. Soultanis, N.L., Papathanasiou, S.A., Hatziargyriou, N.D.: A stability algorithm for the dynamic analysis of inverter dominated unbalanced LV microgrids. IEEE Trans. Power Syst. **22**(1), 294–304 (2007)
17. Shariatpanah, H., Fadaeinedjad, R., Rashidinejad, M.: A new model for PMSG-based wind turbine with yaw control. IEEE Trans. Energy Convers. **28**(4), 929–937 (2013)
18. Ropp, M.E., Gonzalez, S.: Development of a MATLAB/Simulink model of a single-phase grid-connected photovoltaic system. IEEE Trans. Energy Convers. **24**(1), 195–202 (2009)
19. Tremblay, O., Dessaint, L.A., Dekkiche, A.I.: A generic battery model for the dynamic simulation of hybrid electric vehicles. In: IEEE Vehicle Power and Propulsion Conference, VPPC, Arlington, pp. 284–289 (2007)

UAV Path Planning Based on Adaptive Weighted

Pigeon-Inspired Optimization Algorithm

Na Lin, Siming Huang[✉], Changqing Gong, Liang Zhao, and Jiacheng Tang

College of Computer Science, Shenyang Aerospace University,
Shenyang 110136, Liaoning, China
13654950820@163.com

Abstract. In the complex environment, using traditional pigeon-inspired optimization algorithm for the UAV route planning leads local optimum and slow convergence speed and unstable problem. In order to solve this problem, this paper introduces an adaptive weighted pigeon-inspired optimization algorithm. The adaptive weight coefficient is applied to calculate the speed and position of the individuals in the population which enhances the quality and efficiency of route planning. In addition, this paper done many simulation experiment from different aspect for providing enough evident in path planning. This paper also have these simulation experiment by designing different environment model including the simple and complex environment. The simulation results show that the adaptive weighted pigeon-inspired optimization algorithm provides a shorter route distance, a lower threat cost consumption and the algorithm running time while comparing with pigeon-inspired optimization algorithm and particle swarm optimization than basic pigeon-inspired optimization algorithm and Particle swarm intelligence algorithm. After the spline smoothing, the UAV route is flyable.

Keywords: Unmanned aerial vehicle (UAV) · Adaptive weighted pigeon optimization (PIO) · Spline smoothing method

1 Introduction

Unmanned aerial vehicle (UAV) path-planning is to point to under some certain constraint conditions, according to the characters of the task goal to reach an optimal UAV flight path. Superiority of UAV path planning performance directly identifies the task execution efficiency. If the global information about the environment at hand, the problem is called offline planning [1–5]. If the circumstance is partially known or completely unknown in advance, the path will be planned online [1, 2, 6–8]. In the complex environment, the existed algorithm have some disadvantage when it is used in the practical application. In addition, these algorithm haven't enough performance during UAV flight.

In recent years, there are a lot of population-based swarm intelligence algorithms. All the bio-inspired optimization algorithms are trying to simulate the natural ecosystem mechanisms, which have greatly improved the feasibility of the modern optimization

© Springer International Publishing AG 2017
D. Liu et al. (Eds.): ICONIP 2017, Part VI, LNCS 10639, pp. 287–297, 2017.
https://doi.org/10.1007/978-3-319-70136-3_31

techniques, and offered practical solutions for those complicated combinatorial optimization problems.

In addition, Evolutionary Algorithms including Genetic Algorithm ect. have become very popular in the optimization community and successfully applied to a wide range of problems. In 2014, foreign experts Goel, S. et al. published the paper that Pigeon optimization algorithm: A novel approach for solving optimization problems is proposed the concept of pigeon optimization algorithm [9]. But did not apply to the pigeon optimization algorithm to practical problems. The domestic professor Huabin Duan inspired by this, in the UAV path planning application of a novelty intelligent bionic algorithm, pigeon-inspired optimization algorithm [10]. In 2016 Bo Zhang and Duan Haibin proposed a path planning method based on Predator-Prey Pigeon-Inspired Optimization for Uninhabited Combat Aerial Vehicle [11]. Using the communication function between the pigeons to realize the information sharing of the multi-UAV. Zhang Shujian, Duan Haibin et al. published Gaussian pigeon-inspired optimization approach to orbital spacecraft formation which path planning based on the Gaussian distribution algorithm [12].

Pigeon-inspired Optimization algorithm motivated by the homing characteristics of pigeons, two operators including a map and compass operator and landmark operator have been designed. PIO algorithm has previously proven itself as a worthy competitor to its better known rivals. However, the PIO runs into local optima easily because of its fast convergence. In this study, the adaptive inertia weight is exploited for the generation of the new individual to avoid the local optima. Finally, a novel variant of PIO algorithm, named Adaptive Weighted Pigeon-inspired Optimization Algorithm (AWPIO) is proposed here.

In summary, in order to enhance the performance of UAV route planning and efficiency issues, this paper presents an adaptive weights pigeon optimization algorithm. First, the increase in the initial stage of the initialization process route, based on the difference between the size of UAV missions and terrain, using different ways to route initialization. Second, increasing the adaptive-weighted coefficients of the basic pigeon-optimization algorithm during geomagnetic operational phase. Through reasonable regulation of this factor, thereby controlling the flight direction and speed of the particle populations. Third, after the spline smoothing, the UAV route is pliable that it is based on the different demands of different kind of UAVs.

2   The Cost of Threat Evaluation Model

UAV route planning performance indicators include the completion of specified tasks of the safety performance and fuel performance indicators, that is the minimum cost of the threat of cost performance and fuel cost minimum performance indicators.

$$\min J_t = \int_0^L w_t dl \tag{1}$$

The minimum threat cost is calculated as follow Eqs. (1) and (2). Among them, the letter L is the route length.

$$\min J_f = \int_0^L w_f dl \tag{2}$$

The total cost of the threat assessment model is as follow Eq. (3).

$$\min J = kJ_t + (1-k)J_f \tag{3}$$

When UAVs fly along the route, the total threat cost to each threat source is calculated as follow Eq. (4).

$$w_{t,L_{ij}} = \int_0^{L_{ij}} \sum_{k=1}^{N_t} \frac{t_k}{\left[(x-x_k)^2 + (y-y_k)^2\right]^2} dl \tag{4}$$

To simplify the calculation of the cost of the threat, taking five points to calculate the cost of this edge threat suffered, if the threat from the point of the edge to within a radius of a threat, according to the following Eq. (5) to calculate the cost of a threat.

In Eq. (5), Lij is connected to node i, j edge length, $d_{(0,1,k)}$ represents the k-th distance between the edge of the center of the source of the threat 1/10 pitch, is a threat factor k, T represents a threat to the current threat of UAVs.

$$w_{t,L_{ij}} = \frac{L_{ij}^5}{5} \sum_{k=1}^{N_t} t_k \left(\frac{1}{d_{0.1,k}^4} + \frac{1}{d_{0.3,k}^4} + \frac{1}{d_{0.5,k}^4} + \frac{1}{d_{0.7,k}^4} + \frac{1}{d_{0.9,k}^4} \right) \tag{5}$$

3   Adaptive Weighted Pigeon-Inspired Optimization Algorithm

According to a pigeon excellent navigation ability, the pigeons-inspired optimization algorithm is proposed. A mathematical model of the optimization algorithm mainly divides into two parts: the geomagnetic operator and a landmark operator. According to the two operators operating updates the optimal particle's speed and position. The *pigeonnum* is the number of pigeon population. That also is to say population size.

First of all, introduced the geomagnetic operator, one of magnetic induction in the brain map out briefly, then according to the direction of the sun to identify the direction of the destination. In D dimension of search space, each round of iteration individuals in a population according to the following Eqs. (6) and (7) to calculate

$$v_i(t) = v_i(t-1) \cdot e^{-Rt} + rand \cdot (x_g - x_i(t-1)) \tag{6}$$

and update the particle's speed and position [10]. Among them, R is geomagnetic operator.

$$x_i(t) = x_i(t-1) + v_i(t) \tag{7}$$

Then, a landmark operator is introduced, and a pigeon on the basis of whether the current position and destination, if similar to determine the position and a pigeon fly directly to the destination. Otherwise, using a pigeon for the most close to the center of the particles destination location. Each iteration processes the population size in half. The t-th iteration, updates the position of the population and population scale by the following Eqs. (8), (9) and (10):

$$N_p = \frac{N_p(t-1)}{2} \tag{8}$$

$$x_c(t) = \frac{\sum x_i(t) \cdot fitness(x_i(t))}{N_p \sum fitness(x_i(t))} \tag{9}$$

$$x_i(t) = x_i(t-1) + rand \cdot (x_c(t) - x_i(t-1)) \tag{10}$$

Among them, the function *fitness()* as a threat modeling after it is concluded that the threat of cost minimum. Through the calculation of the landmark operation can be faster to find the location of the destination, thus pigeons was faster to fly to the destination, improve the efficiency of the flight.

After it was found that the basic pigeons algorithm, in the process of realization of UAV route planning, has a slow convergence speed, the threat of consumption price higher defect. In this paper, the existing pigeon algorithm was improved. PIO for UAV route planning, these are directly using a pigeon algorithm for the calculation of the optimal solution, and no initial path for initialization of unmanned Aerial vehicle navigation, this article increases the initialization part of the route, for after a pigeon algorithm provides a better initial optimal value. After initialized to sail, it can reduce the computation time algorithms, and improve the pigeon execution efficiency of the algorithm.

The basic pigeon algorithm in solving the global optimal solutions and a local optimal solution, it is easy to fall into local extremum problems. Therefore, in order to balance a pigeon local search ability and global search ability of the algorithm, in a pigeon geomagnetic operation part of the algorithm is introduced into nonlinear dynamic inertia weight coefficient (That is the adaptive weight coefficient), so as to improve the efficiency of the algorithm in the route planning. Adaptive weight coefficient calculated according to the following Eq. (11).

$$\omega = \begin{cases} \omega_{min} - \dfrac{(\omega_{max} - \omega_{min}) * (f - f_{min})}{f_{avg} - f_{min}}, & f \leq f_{avg} \\ 0, & f > f_{avg} \end{cases} \tag{11}$$

In Eq. (11), w_{min} and w_{max} respectively inertia weight coefficient of minimum and maximum, the threat of cost function, said a pigeon in the current threat generation value on average, according to the current pigeon value in minimum threat generation.

Application with inertia weight in a pigeon-inspired optimization algorithm to solve UAV route planning problem, in each round of iteration. There must be a part of the particle movement to better fitness value, other particles movement to the fitness value worse position. By the above analysis, this paper proposes using adaptive weight inertia to improve basic pigeon-inspired optimization algorithm. In each iteration, the fitness value of variation of the particle, particle inertia weight adverse to the convergence of algorithm, make its inertia weight, thereby eliminating the negative influence of inertial component; For fitness values become the optimal particle, particle inertia weight convergence of algorithm, make its inertia weight according to the rules of updating.

To sum up, in a pigeon-inspired optimization proposed adaptive weighting algorithm can improve the efficiency of the algorithm, in the actual application can also reduce the threat to the cost of consumption.

4   Path Smoothing

Directly using a pigeon algorithm calculation of routing exists around the corner, as showed in left of Fig. 1. But in the process of the actual UAV mission, according to the needs of the task must often change the sailing directions, which require to meet the minimum turning radius constraint UAV itself. Therefore, a pigeon algorithm of course cannot be directly applied to the actual UAV voyage, need to smooth the planning of the route.

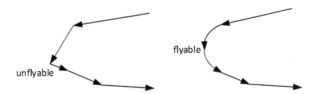

Fig. 1. Smooth contrast figure before and after processing

To solve above problems, this paper puts forward using spline smoothing algorithm for planning the path smoothly after treatment, so as to achieve the purpose of the airway can fly. Spline smoothing algorithm is mainly based on the parameters of the control after the smooth effect, can accord to demand a custom parameter values [13]. The basic principle of spline smoothing is shown in the following equation.

$$p \sum_i w_i(y_i - s(x_i))^2 + (1-p) \int (\frac{d^2s}{dx^2})^2 dx \qquad (12)$$

The parameter p for smoothing parameter, and the value range is from 0 to 1. w_i is weight coefficient, and the value range is from 0 to 1. By default, $w_i = 1$. After airway smooth out the results as showed in right of Fig. 1.

5   Simulation Experiment and Comparative Analysis

Adaptive weight pigeon algorithm through the adjustment of parameters in the algorithm can solve the problem of different situations of unmanned aerial vehicle route planning, it can freely according to the application field of unmanned aerial vehicle and the change of factors such as constraints to change parameters, so as to achieve better planning

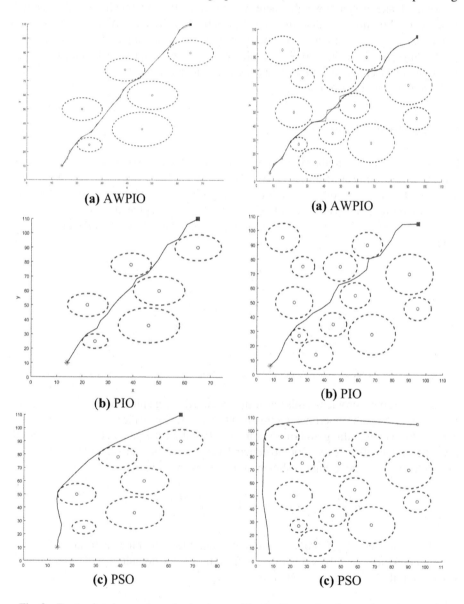

(a) AWPIO

(a) AWPIO

(b) PIO

(b) PIO

(c) PSO

(c) PSO

Fig. 2. Route planning roadmap in simple environment

Fig. 3. Route planning roadmap in complex environment

effect. In addition, through a series of experiments show that the improved adaptive pigeon algorithm feasibility and effectiveness, and the improved adaptive weighting pigeon algorithm with the original pigeon algorithms and particle swarm optimization algorithm was analyzed.

The whole simulation part of the unmanned aerial vehicle route planning in the Windows 7 operating system using Matlab R2016 threat modeling and route simulation platform. Hardware configuration is: Intel I5-2400@3.10 GHz processor, 4 GB of memory. Including the geographical scope for 80 * 110 km, 1 km distance per unit length in the coordinate system. Set the threat source and threat source of the threat factor and other data are shown in Figs. 2 and 3, respectively. Starting point in the area of the set of threats to the environment coordinates (14, 10), target coordinates of (65, 110) in a simple environment. Starting point in the area of the set of threats to the environment coordinates (8, 6), target coordinates of (95, 105) in a complex environment. Simulation experiments using the related parameters are shown in Table 1.

Table 1. Parameters setting

AWPIO	PIO	PSO
	k = 0.3	
	D = 20	
T1 = 100, T2 = 40, pigeonnum = 120, R = 0.2		c1 = 2, c2 = 2, w = 0.7298,
w_{max} = 0.7, w_{min} = 0.4		MaxDT = 200, N = 150

The performance of the improved algorithm is verified from multiple angles by simulating experiments in different complexity. According to the actual situation, the simulation terrain is divided into simple and complex two, so as to fully explain the reliability of the algorithm. To the threat's constraint conditions, respectively, using improved adaptive pigeon optimization algorithms, the common pigeon optimization algorithms and particle swarm optimization algorithm for UAV route planning simulation experiment. In order to guarantee the feasibility and the accuracy of contrast experiment, each algorithm under the same constraint conditions. According to the set parameters calculated simulation results as showed in Figs. 2 and 3.

In the same environment, the threat of using AWPIO, PIO and PSO for UAV route planning. Through three algorithms on route distance, threat of cost analysis and calculation time of the three parameters, can effectively analyze the performance of the algorithm. Three algorithms are respectively the performance parameters are shown in Tables 2 and 3.

Table 2. The data of three algorithm's performance in simple environment

Algorithm	Path distance (km)	Threat cost
AWPIO	113.6354	82.2668
PIO	115.8751	83.0129
PSO	121.2275	84.8867

Table 3. The data of three algorithm's performance in complex environment

Algorithm	Path distance (km)	Threat cost
AWPIO	139.3299	106.4090
PIO	146.3601	109.259
PSO	185.5639	129.9060

According to the above data can be concluded that the improved pigeon optimization algorithm is relative to the improvement in front of a pigeon algorithm and particle swarm optimization algorithm in route distance, threats, cost and execution time has significant improvement. To ensure an unmanned aerial vehicle mission can ensure more low resource consumption, also can minimize the task execution speed.

In addition, the convergence rate of the algorithm is executed, it is also an important factor to distinguish algorithm faster and more stable can ensure the execution efficiency of algorithm convergence speed and stability of the algorithm. Through the simulation experiment of three kinds of algorithm convergence curve calculated as showed in Figs. 4 and 5 in two kinds of different environment. In figure, horizontal iterations of the algorithm and ordinate said the threat of it in the process of route planning generation value.

In Fig. 4, it can be seen from Fig. 4(a), AWPIO algorithm convergence faster, in the route planning can be faster to calculate the minimum threat cost, and the convergence trend is relatively stable, indicating that the stability of the algorithm better Calculate the threat cost with higher stability. As can be seen from the trend of the curve in Fig. 4(b), although the threat value has been decreasing, the improved algorithm has some shortcomings and stability. It can be seen from Fig. 4(c), PSO compared with the other two algorithms, there are obvious defects, the convergence rate is slow, the cost of the threat of higher consumption, the number of iterations is also more than two other algorithms.

In Fig. 5, we can see that in the complex environment, the improved AWPIO algorithm can still be solved accurately, the cost of the threat is low, the algorithm also has a certain stability, and maintain the convergence speed and convergence time may be small. From Fig. 5(b), we can conclude that the convergence trend and algorithm stability of PIO algorithm in complex environment are obviously lower than AWPIO. In Fig. 5(c), it can be concluded that the PSO algorithm has the ability to reduce the path planning ability in the complex environment, the threat of consumption is higher and the convergence speed is not.

The convergence trend curves of the three algorithms are compared and analyzed, AWPIO algorithm can realize the path planning function in the environment with different complexity and ensure the stability and threat cost of the algorithm as low as possible; PIO algorithm in a simple environment, better stability; PSO algorithm in a complex environment, the convergence rate faster, but the threat cost is too high.

According to the above trend of the convergence curve diagram can clear it is concluded that improved algorithms in the process of unmanned aerial vehicle route planning have a better pigeon effect of convergence. Compared with other two kinds of algorithms has faster convergence speed, more stable, and minimum cost algorithm consumption threats. Through the above analysis can be possible to conclude that the

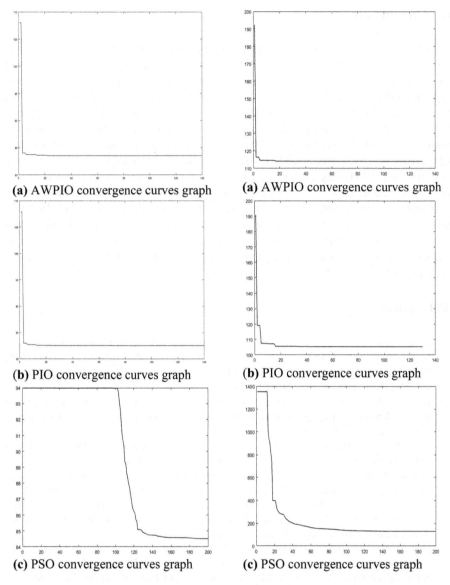

(a) AWPIO convergence curves graph

(a) AWPIO convergence curves graph

(b) PIO convergence curves graph

(b) PIO convergence curves graph

(c) PSO convergence curves graph

(c) PSO convergence curves graph

Fig. 4. The convergence curves graph of simple environment algorithm

Fig. 5. The convergence curves graph of complex environment algorithm

improved algorithm of adaptive weighted pigeon in unmanned aerial vehicle route planning has a better planning effectiveness and efficiency.

6   Conclusion

In order to solve this problem, the basic pigeon algorithm is improved to solve the problem of route planning for UAVs. The algorithm is applied to calculate and solve route planning with adaptive weighting. Problem optimal way point and uses mathematical models to ask approach points smooth the path calculation operation. Finally, the algorithm simulation analysis, the flock algorithm simulation results show improved results in better UAV route planning, adaptive weight flock algorithm derived from the route compared to PIO algorithm reduces the 2.2397 km compared with the PSO algorithm reduces 7.5921 km; and PSO algorithm reduces the time-consuming compared with the PIO 0.154 s algorithm; the threat of depletion expense compared with PIO algorithm reduces the 0.7461, compared with the PSO algorithm reduces the 2.6199 a decrease of 1.514 s. Able to overcome the existing flock algorithm of Path Planning deficiencies. The algorithm can compare with the particle swarm optimization algorithm. The results of the path planning show that the improved pigeon algorithm can show the advantage of the improved pigeon algorithm, which can fully show the availability of adaptive weight pigeon algorithm in the UAV route planning.

References

1. Besada-Portas, E., de la Torre, L., de la Cruz, J.M., Andres-Toro, B.: Evolutionary trajectory planner for multiple UAVs in realistic scenarios. IEEE Trans. Robot. **26**(4), 619–634 (2010)
2. Zheng, C., Li, L., Xu, F., Sun, F., Ding, M.: Evolutionary route planner for unmanned air vehicles. IEEE Trans. Robot. **21**(4), 609–620 (2005)
3. Nikolos, I.K., Valavanis, K.P., Tsourveloudis, N.C., Kostaras, A.N.: Evolutionary algorithm based offline/online path planner for UAV navigation. IEEE Trans. Syst. Man Cybern. B Cybern. **33**(6), 898–912 (2003)
4. Szczerba, R.J., Galkowski, P., Glicktein, I.S., Ternullo, N.: Robust algorithm for real-time route planning. IEEE Trans. Aerosp. Electron. Syst. **36**(3), 869–878 (2000)
5. Obermeyer, K.J., Oberlin, P., Darbha, S.: Sampling-based path planning for a visual reconnaissance unmanned air vehicle. J. Guidance, Control, Dynamics **35**(2), 619–631 (2012)
6. Nikolos, I.K., Tsourveloudis, N.C., Valavanis, K.P.: Evolutionary algorithm based path planning for multiple UAV cooperation. In: Valavanis, K.P. (ed.) Advances in Unmanned Aerial Vehicles, vol. 33, pp. 309–340. Springer, Dordrecht (2007)
7. De La Cruz, J.M., Besada-Portas, E., de la Torre, L., Andres-Toro, B., Lopez-Orozco, J.A.: Evolutionary path planner for UAVs realistic environments. In: Proceedings of the 10th Annual Conference on Genetic and Evolutionary Computation, pp. 1477–1484 (2008)
8. Sujit, P.B., Beard, R.: Multiple UAV path planning using anytime algorithms. In: Proceeding of the American Control Conference, pp. 2978–2983 (2009)
9. Goel, S.: Pigeon optimization algorithm: a novel approach for solving optimization problems. In: International Conference on Data Mining and Intelligent Computing (2014)
10. Duan, H., Qiao, P.: Pigeon-inspired optimization: a new swarm intelligence optimizer for air robot path planning. Int. J. Intell. Comput. Cybern. **7**(1), 24–37 (2015)
11. Zhang, B., Duan, H.: Three-dimensional path planning for uninhabited combat aerial vehicle based on predator-prey pigeon-inspired optimization in dynamic environment. IEEE/ACM Trans. Comput. Biol. Bioinform. **14**, 97–107 (2016)

12. Zhang, S., Duan, H.: Gaussian pigeon-inspired optimization approach to orbital spacecraft formation reconfiguration. Chin. J. Aeronaut. **28**(1), 200–205 (2015)
13. Nagahara, M., Martin, C.F.: L1 Control theoretic smoothing splines. IEEE Signal Process. Lett. **21**(11), 1394–1397 (2014)

Multi-Agent Q(λ) Learning for Optimal Operation Management of Energy Internet

Lingxiao Yang[1(✉)] ⓘ, Qiuye Sun[1] ⓘ, and Yue Han[2] ⓘ

[1] Northeastern University, Shenyang 110819, Liaoning, China
ylxiao66@163.com
[2] State Grid Liaoning Electric Power Research Institute, Shenyang 110819, Liaoning, China

Abstract. This paper proposes an optimal operation management methodology based on the multi-agent reinforcement learning (MARL) in energy internet (EI). An integrated approach to minimize the total cost of operation of such an electrical, natural gas and district heating network simultaneously is studied. A novel multi-agent Q(λ) learning method is presented to form a coordinated optimal management strategy of energy internet with multiple We-Energy(WE), and an equal interval sampling method is proposed to find the optimal discrete action sets so as to enhance the performance of the control areas. Furthermore, a global Q operator is designed to produce a global Q function considering the local reward from each agent which optimizes simultaneously. The proposed method verified by case studies applied to the modified energy network. Compared with the centralized approach, the test results show that the proposed method can provide a fast solution for the optimal operation management which can be applied to multiple We-Energy internet with sufficient accuracy.

Keywords: Multi-Agent reinforcement learning · Optimal operation management · Q(λ) learning · Energy internet · We-Energy

1 Introduction

The optimal operation management of energy has become an important socioeconomic problem in which exploring renewable energy and improving the supply efficiency are among important issues for realizing the EI of economic and security operation to reduce the network loss [1]. Under the development of renewable energy systems, the energy source will no longer be provided only in the form of the traditional energy supplier, and there will be several types of energy producers which means that users can choose the energy suppliers according to their own needs. In this supply mode, a novel energy accessing mode for energy Internet called We-Energy is proposed that it will be not only energy producer but also energy consumer [2]. In this regard, the cooperation among multiple energy forms and economic opportunities for enhancing the supply efficiency in EI was overlooked.

In [3–6], the optimal power flow of electricity and natural gas combined system is discussed. Paper [7] proposed the generalized heuristic algorithm to study the optimal

© Springer International Publishing AG 2017
D. Liu et al. (Eds.): ICONIP 2017, Part VI, LNCS 10639, pp. 298–306, 2017.
https://doi.org/10.1007/978-3-319-70136-3_32

power flow of multiple energy system. While with the increasing utilization of co-generation plants, there is a challenge to find the optimal strategy in such a way for this class of complex nonlinear multi objective optimization problems. The domestic and foreign scholars made in-depth study in this question for more efficient algorithm. In addition to improve the basic heuristic algorithm for optimal energy flow [8], distributed algorithm has become a research focus [9].

Recently, reinforcement learning (RL) algorithm as a kind of machine learning algorithms attracts people's attention. Some learning strategies on the basis of RL to solve deterministic optimal control problems in continuous state spaces can be found in some studies such as [10–15]. The MARL which is a new branch of reinforcement learning algorithm has been developed rapidly in various areas including distributed control, robotic teams, collaborative decision support systems, and economics [16]. MARL is defined to be composed of multiple agents, the whole system will achieve the learning goals through each agent executing part of reinforcement mission independently. All performance of MARL exhibits its advantage on the collaborative multi-task problems, and the features that aim at strategic decision make MARL widely used [17].

In this paper, the optimal operation management in EI is investigated at the transmission level. We propose an optimal model to improve the performance of environment for EI. The proposed formulation for multi-agent systems can be solved by machine learning algorithms which could find the optimization strategy intelligently. We present a MARL for distributed multicarrier energy network, which computes a global optimal policy in cooperative subsystems on the basis of the implementation of independent optimization for subsystems. A policy is defined as a set of actions deriving from the reward function connecting the environment. With the preprocessing method of action sets, the performance of the system will be improved.

This paper is organized as follows. In Sect. 2, the mathematical model of optimal management problem in EI is represented to improve the energy economy while Sect. 3 discussed about the multi-agent reinforcement learning methodology to solve this problem. Section 4 presents the case studies with a typical EI consists of several types of WEs. Finally, Sect. 5 concludes the discussion.

2   Optimal Operation Management Model of EI

In EI, different structure of prosumers will lead to a variety of supply and demand situations. WE, as a novel energy sub-region in EI, can exchange electricity, gas and heat from modern communications, power electronic conversion and automation technology with other WEs. As shown in Fig. 1, the main body of WE will be the individual, company or community that consists of energy production, user load or storage devices such as distributed generation, energy storage, CCHP and so on. WEs coordinate with each other to guarantee multi energy to reliable transport. Each WE is connected to be considered as the generalized node of EI.

In order to achieve the optimal energy flow of EI with multiple WEs, an operation management model is to find the optimal solution in a sense that required objective function is minimized while several equality and inequality constraints are satisfied.

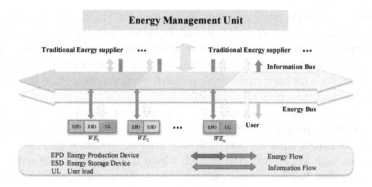

Fig. 1. Energy flow model of WEs in energy internet.

Through the coordinated optimization of WEs, the network will achieve the overall optimization.

The objective function in this paper is to optimize the operation cost which can be expressed by:

$$
\begin{cases}
\min T = \sum_{i=1}^{n} F_i(\boldsymbol{P}_i, \boldsymbol{F}_\alpha) \\
s.t. \begin{cases}
L = CP \\
\boldsymbol{G}_\alpha(\boldsymbol{P}_i) = 0 \\
\boldsymbol{F}_\alpha \min \leq \boldsymbol{F}_\alpha \leq \boldsymbol{F}_\alpha \max \\
\boldsymbol{P}_i \min \leq \boldsymbol{P}_i \leq \boldsymbol{P}_i \max
\end{cases}
\end{cases}
\tag{1}
$$

Where $i = 1, 2, \ldots, n$, n is the number of WEs. $\boldsymbol{P}_i$ is the state variables of WE_i. $\boldsymbol{F}_\alpha$ is the energy flow of multi-energy network including electric power network, natural gas network and centralized heating network. The first constraint stands for the input and output balance of an energy hub in WE which can be identified as a unit to achieve conversion and storage of multi-energy carriers. The second constraint and the third constrain respectively express the power balance equation of energy flow in EI and the variable limits to obtain a feasible operating point. And the last constrain is the limits of the network input. All the equality and inequality constraints which can refer to [18] will not be described in detail here.

For each WE, the total cost of operation in 24 h will be defined as the sum of the fuel consumed by WE which can be formulated as follows:

$$
F_i = \sum_{t=1}^{24} \sum_{\beta=1}^{N} (a_\beta P_\beta(t) + b_\beta P_\beta^2(t))
\tag{2}
$$

Where t is the operation time. Generally, the cost of operation is formulated in a quadratic function on the basis of energy input power with several kinds of fuel such as natural gas, coal and so on. In addition, a_β, b_β are the unique coefficients for each fuel.

3   Proposed Methodology

Considering the energy network structure as well as the operation management model, the multi-agent reinforcement learning algorithm was applied to solve the problem innovatively.

3.1   Multi-Agent Q(λ) Learning Algorithm

MARL is a method which expands the single-agent RL. Each agent can obtain the rewards from adjacent agent with a few information. The global system use iteration to influence non-adjacent agent so as to optimize the performance of the whole system based on reinforcement learning.

According to the distributed structure of EI, each WE coordinates and interacts with each other to solve the complex problems. A optimal operation management of EI is a tuple $\langle n, \{S_i\}_{i=1,\ldots,n}, \{A_i\}_{i=1,\ldots,n}, \{R_i\}_{i=1,\ldots,n}, T \rangle$ where n is the number of WEs, S_i is the state space of WE_i, A_i is the action set of WE_i and $\{A_i\}_{i=1,\ldots,n}$ are the sets of actions available to the WEs, yielding the joint action set $A = A_1 + A_2 + \cdots + A_n$ that every WEs parallel compute for reinforcement learning. $T{:}S \times A \times S \to [0, 1]$ means the state transition probability. $R_i{:}\, S \times A \to R$ is the direct reward functions of each WE.

Given the MARL iteration rule for WE, the eligibility traces for the state-action will be updated as follows which can realize the delay control of signal during the optimization:

$$e_t(s, a) = \begin{cases} \gamma \lambda e_{t-1}(s, a) + 1 & if\ s = s_t\ and\ a = a_t \\ \gamma \lambda e_{t-1}(s, a) & otherwise \end{cases} \tag{3}$$

Where γ is the discount factor and λ is the recession coefficient. By adding the eligibility traces in the iteration, the problem of time reliability assignment in the optimization process will be solved.

The Q(λ) learning operation is defined as:

$$\delta_t = r_t(s, s', a_t) + \gamma \max Q_t(s', a_{t+1}) - Q_t(s, a_t) \tag{4}$$

$$Q_{t+1}(s, a) = Q_{t-1}(s, a) + \alpha \delta_t e_t(s, a) \tag{5}$$

Where α is the learning factor with $0 < \alpha < 1$, α indicates the proportion of update part in Q value.

3.2   Equal Interval Sampling for Action Sets

As a matter of fact, by considering the character of Markov Decision Processes for RL, the operational state of EI should be transformed into a discrete form. To do so, an equal interval sampling approach is given to each action set in such way that individuals with better fitness value improve the accuracy and generalization of computing.

In the MARL optimal operation management model, the energy hub is the key link of multiple energy coupling in each WE. Thus, for each control area, control variables studied in this paper is the power exchanged between the WEs and the hybrid energy network which contains electrical power P_e, natural gas power P_g and so on. Equal interval sampling approach for action sets is expressed as follows.

For P_e and P_g, the continuous attribute $a \in C$ and the range of P_a is $\min(P_a)$, $\max(P_a)$, the interval value can be designed as:

$$d = \frac{\max(P_a) - \min(P_a)}{k_a + 1} \tag{6}$$

Where the integer parameter k_a is the number of pre-set split points. And the split point set can be described as:

$$C_a^{k_a} = \begin{cases} \varnothing, & k_a = 0 \\ \{\min(V_a) + id, i = 1, \dots, k_a\}, & k_a \geq 1 \end{cases} \tag{7}$$

If the integer parameter K_a is the maximum split points, split point set space can be expresses as:

$$\Omega_a = \{C_a^{k_a} : 0 \leq k_a \leq K_a\} \tag{8}$$

Therefore, the discrete action sets will be obtained by adjusting the parameters to find the optimal set of points. By preprocessing the action set, the learning speed will be accelerated and the accuracy of optimization could be improved.

3.3 Design of Reward Function for MARL

For MARL, in order to achieve the goal of optimal operation management, rewards in reinforcement learning should be combined with the objective function and constraint conditions.

The local immediate reward value R of each WE need satisfy the constraint conditions of power flow calculation to ensure the validity of the calculation results for each subsystem. Each WE will obtain the optimal strategy by maximizing reward function values. The local reward for WE is defined as formula (9).

Every WE will check control variables through connected transmission lines to see whether they meet the corresponding boundary conditions. If all of constraints are satisfied, the local reward signal will be set to the negative objective function. Otherwise, it will be zero. The local rewards are applied to each WE to guide action strategy.

$$R_{i,0}^K = \begin{cases} 0, & \text{if constraint s are violated} \\ \dfrac{1}{F_i^K(X)}, & \text{otherwise} \end{cases} \tag{9}$$

The aim of optimal operation management is to seek a best strategy from the action space, so that the global reward is presented as an average value of summation of local rewards from each WE. According to the global information discovery algorithm, the global reward signal can be discovered by using signals of node agents.

$$R^K = \frac{1}{n} \sum_{i=1}^{n} R_{i,0}^K \tag{10}$$

3.4 Implementation of the Algorithm for the Optimization of EI

The structure of MARL is shown below as Fig. 2. Through the multi-energy flow calculation for EI, the running status of each WE will be acquired. The following steps should be accomplished to solve the optimal energy flow problem in an EI using MARL algorithm.

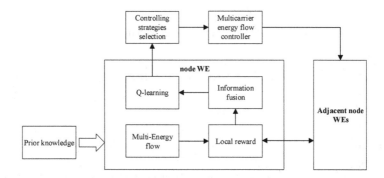

Fig. 2. MARL optimization structure.

Each WE uses multi-energy flow calculation module to obtain the operation state. The local reward of WE will be obtained from the information interaction with environment according to the formula (9). Then, the global reward will be updated with the local reward if all the information is available in information fusion unit. The Q-learning unit will operate based on RL iteration rule to find the optimal strategy. Meanwhile, combined with the prior knowledge for initial action set, the learning state and learning efficiency could be improved. Each optimization iteration process contains four operation phases which includes detection of local signals, calculation of local reward function, exploration of the global signals, update the local Q matrix.

4 Simulations and Results

4.1 Test System

In this section, we apply the proposed multi-agent Q(λ) learning algorithm to the optimal energy flow problem for EI with the structure of 9-node internet with three WEs which is shown in Fig. 3. Percentages of the electric and heat demand in a 24 period compared to their basic values are illustrated in Fig. 4.

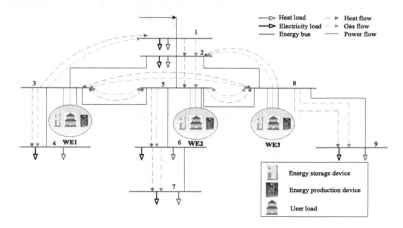

Fig. 3. 9-Node energy internet with three WEs.

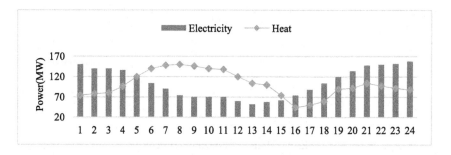

Fig. 4. Electric and heat demand of EI during 24 h.

The interconnection between WEs includes information communication and energy transmission according to the demand. The energy coupling part is also achieved through the energy hub and its energy equipment from WEs includes energy storage device, energy production device and user load. The number of actions for MARL optimal power flow algorithm in this modified network is $120 + 136 + 114 = 370$ which is the sum of the action number from each WE according to the limits of input.

4.2 Simulation Results

As seen in Fig. 5, in order to achieve the overall energy costs and satisfy the needs of users, the optimal strategy is to obtain more energy from the power system, while reducing the natural gas from the natural gas system. And Fig. 6 shows the MARL convergence results at 1358.

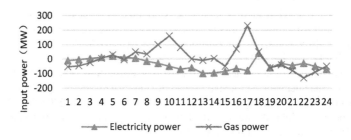

Fig. 5. Input power of WE2 during 24 h.

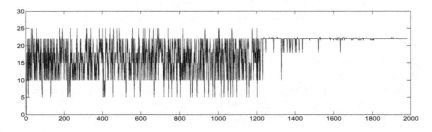

Fig. 6. MARL process at $\alpha = 0.99, \gamma = 0.2$

Through the reinforcement learning of each WE, it can be concluded that the energy consumption of the EI is reduced by 27% under the constraints of the system.

5 Conclusion

This paper proposes an optimal operation management model and presents the multi-agent Q(λ) learning algorithm that can drive these agents to parallel learn behaviors. Compared with the centralized approach, they tend to reduce the calculation difficulty and require consideration of multiple aspects. Multi-Agent Reinforcement Learning is an effective way to improve the learning efficiency and solve the problem of "dimension disaster". The method of utilizing each WE to undertake the task independently to reach the coordinated system is suitable for hierarchical control mode of energy internet. Above all, experimental results revealed that distributed algorithm has a faster convergence speed for the optimal energy flow model.

References

1. Shabanpour-Haghighi, A., Seifi, A.: Energy flow optimization in multicarrier systems. IEEE Trans. Ind. Inf. **11**(5), 1067–1077 (2016)
2. Hu, J., Sun, Q., Teng, F.: A game-theoretic pricing model for energy internet in day-ahead trading market considering distributed generations uncertainty. In: International Conference on Computational Intelligence (SSCI), pp. 1–7. (2016)
3. Correa-Posada, C.M., Sánchez-Martín, P.: Integrated power and natural gas model for energy adequacy in short-term operation. IEEE Trans. Power Syst. **30**(6), 3347–3355 (2015)

4. Alabdulwahab, A., Abusorrah, A., Zhang, X.: Coordination of interdependent natural gas and electricity infrastructures for firming the variability of wind energy in stochastic day-ahead scheduling. IEEE Trans. Sustain. Energy **6**(2), 606–615 (2015)
5. Xu, X., Jia, H., Chiang, H.D.: Dynamic modeling and interaction of hybrid natural gas and electricity supply system in microgrid. IEEE Trans. Power Syst. **30**(3), 1212–1221 (2015)
6. Zhang, X., Shahidehpour, M., Alabdulwahab, A.: Optimal expansion planning of energy hub with multiple energy infrastructures. IEEE Trans. Smart Grid **6**(5), 2302–2311 (2015)
7. Shabanpour-Haghighi, A., Seifi, A.R.: Energy flow optimization in multicarrier systems. IEEE Trans. Industrial Inf. **11**(5), 1067–1077 (2015)
8. Ríos-Mercado, R.Z., Borraz-Sánchez, C.: Optimization problems in natural gas transportation systems: a state-of-the-art review. Appl. Energy **147**, 536–555 (2015)
9. Sun, Q., Han, R., Zhang, H.: A Multiagent-based consensus algorithm for distributed coordinated control of distributed generators in the energy internet. IEEE Trans. Smart Grid **6**(6), 3006–3019 (2015)
10. Liu, D., Wei, Q.: Policy iteration adaptive dynamic programming algorithm for discrete-time nonlinear systems. IEEE Trans. Neural Netw. Learn. Syst. **25**(3), 621–634 (2014)
11. Modares, H., Lewis, F.L., Naghibi-Sistani, M.B.: Integral reinforcement learning and experience replay for adaptive optimal control of partially-unknown constrained-input continuous-time systems. Automatica **50**(1), 193–202 (2014)
12. Zhang, H., Cui, L., Zhang, X.: Data-driven robust approximate optimal tracking control for unknown general nonlinear systems using adaptive dynamic programming method. IEEE Trans. Neural Netw. **22**(12), 2226–2236 (2011)
13. Kamalapurkar, R., Dinh, H., Bhasin, S.: Approximate optimal trajectory tracking for continuous-time nonlinear systems. Automatica **51**, 40–48 (2015)
14. Wei, Q., Liu, D.: Adaptive dynamic programming for optimal tracking control of unknown nonlinear systems with application to coal gasification. IEEE Trans. Autom. Sci. Eng. **11**(4), 1020–1036 (2014)
15. Kamalapurkar, R., Andrews, L., Walters, P.: Model-based reinforcement learning for infinite-horizon approximate optimal tracking. IEEE Trans. Neural Netw. Learn. Syst. **28**(3), 753–758 (2017)
16. Yu, C., Zhang, M., Ren, F.: Emotional multiagent reinforcement learning in spatial social dilemmas. IEEE Trans. Neural Netw. Learn. Syst. **26**(12), 3083–3096 (2015)
17. Plamondon, P., Chaib-draa, B., Benaskeur, A.R.: A Q-decomposition and bounded RTDP approach to resource allocation. In: Proceedings of the 6th International Joint Conference on Autonomous Agents and Multiagent Systems, p. 200. (2007)
18. Shabanpour-Haghighi, A., Seifi, A.R.: Simultaneous integrated optimal energy flow of electricity, gas, and heat. Energy Convers. Manage. **101**, 579–591 (2015)

Mixed Installation to Optimize the Position and Type Selection of Turbines for Wind Farms

Xiaoyu Tang[1], Yun Shen[2], Siliang Li[2], Qinmin Yang[1(✉)], and Youxian Sun[1]

[1] State Key Laboratory of Industrial Control Technology,
College of Control Science and Engineering, Zhejiang University,
Hangzhou 310027, China
qmyang@zju.edu.cn
[2] WindMagics (Wuhan) Energy Corporation, Wuhan 430206, China

Abstract. The optimal deployment of turbines in a wind farm, namely micro-sitting, is crucial to improve the economical returns of a wind power plant. Traditionally, a wind farm layout is designed with identical turbines. In this work, installation of multiple types of turbines is introduced in the first time to further increase the efficiency of the farm, namely mixed installation. Firstly, The optimization problem of micro-siting with mixed installation is established, which is then approached via a GA-based method, obtaining the type selection and positioning of turbines simultaneously. Finally, a complex scenario with practical wind conditions is utilized to demonstrate the feasibility of the proposed scheme.

Keywords: Wind farm micro-siting · Mixed installation · Turbine positioning and type selection

1 Introduction

Nowadays, renewable energies are investigated as substitutes of traditional energy resources. Wind energy is of great quantity on earth, and is also one of the fastest developing renewable energies. The wind energy industry has great prospect, as well as difficulties in utilizing, due to the spatial non-uniformity and temporal instability of wind energy, as well as the complicated mutual effects between turbines.

Over a certain wind farm the wind energy distribution is explicit after statistical analysis based on long-term records. Micro-siting [5] is carried out to improve the utilization efficiency of the wind energy. Therefore the position of each wind turbine must be chosen appropriately, in order to reduce the interactions, the wake effects, between turbines. Meanwhile, the positions of all wind turbines should be arranged to gain the maximum power generation.

However, the optimization problem of micro-siting is quite complicated. Commonly, the fitness function is chosen to maximize the power output or to minimize the power generating cost, while the constraints are various, including

© Springer International Publishing AG 2017
D. Liu et al. (Eds.): ICONIP 2017, Part VI, LNCS 10639, pp. 307–315, 2017.
https://doi.org/10.1007/978-3-319-70136-3_33

keeping turbines away no shorter than a certain distance mutually because of safety. Both the fitness and the constraints are coupled, nonlinear and multi-disciplinary. It is difficult to solve it via calculus-based optimization algorithms. Therefore, the heuristic optimization algorithms are usually adopted. Since 1994 [11], a lot of optimization approaches on wind farm optimizations have been proposed [3,4,12–15].

Recently, some researchers have made some accomplishments on further improvements of turbine positioning, such as installing turbines with different hub-heights to make full use of the wind energy in three dimensional spaces [1,2]. Thus, it is believed that multiple types of turbines installed within a farm (named mixed installation), rather than just placing only one type of turbines, will improve the farm efficiency significantly. It is a novel idea and worth further investigation. In previous researches, the other characteristics of the wind turbines, such as sizes of diameters and power generation characteristics are not considered, which would further increase the efficiency of the whole wind farms. This paper is presented to bring out the idea of mixed installation, and validate that multiple turbines of different types can avoid wake effects when arranged properly. Additionally, we are motivated to study the micro-siting for wind farms with mixed installation, and present a method based on heuristic algorithms to accomplish the micro-siting optimization with mixed installation.

2   Problem Formulation

In this section, the optimization problem of micro-sitting is described and formulated. The simplified models in this paper are all able to be adopted in practical engineering, also can be modified or removed according to actual requirements.

2.1   Wind Modeling

The wind directions and velocities are changing over time, and are analyzed and summarized into a wind rose. The historical data are measured, recorded and processed by method of bins [7], which can be written in matrix as

$$\mathbf{F} = (F_{wk}) \quad with \quad w = 1, 2, \ldots, N_{ws}$$
$$k = 1, 2, \ldots, N_{wd} \quad (1)$$

where $F_{wk} = f(v_w, \theta_k)$ denotes the frequency of wind occurrence with speed v_w in direction θ_k, N_{ws} and N_{wd} are the number of bins for wind speed and the number of bins for wind direction, respectively. For long-term horizons, and with the data observed in many sites, F_{wk} at a given location, height follows a Weibull distribution [8].

To estimate the energy distribution, the wind resource at each position in the wind farm is considered. The linear model is often adopted for offshore farms or farms in planes. In this paper, the thermal effects of the atmosphere are negligible in the surface layer. H_{ref} is the reference height. The wind velocities at different heights are described by [10]

$$\frac{v}{v_m} = \frac{\ln(H/z_0)}{\ln(H_{ref}/z_0)} \tag{2}$$

where v_m donates the wind speed measured at a height of H_{ref}, v denotes the wind speed predicted at a height H, and z_0 is the roughness length.

2.2 Wake Modeling

The wakes are the reactions between turbines, which have a significant impact on the power generation. The wake decay model developed by Jensen [6] is adopted to calculate the velocity deficit for a turbine in the wake of another:

$$V_{def} = 1 - v_a/v_0 = \frac{\sqrt{1-C_T}}{(1+\alpha d/R)^2} \tag{3}$$

where V_{def} denotes the normalized velocity deficit, C_T denotes the trust coefficient of turbines, α is the wake spread coefficient, R is the radius of turbine blade scanning rotor, d denotes the distance between the two turbines in the wind flow direction, v_a denotes the effective velocity arriving at turbine in the wake, and v_0 denotes the velocity of wind flow without any wakes.

When there are multi-types of turbines installed, Partial shelter will occur, calculated in the following equation:

$$V_{def\_ji} = \frac{\sqrt{1-C_{Tj}}}{\left(1+\alpha_j d_{ji}/R_j\right)^2} \cdot \frac{A_{overlap\_ji}}{A_i} \tag{4}$$

where $A_{overlap\_ji}$ is the area of turbine i that is in the wake of turbine j, A_i is the blade scanning area of turbine i; d_{ji} denotes the distance between the two turbines in current wind direction.

Since a turbine is affected by multiple turbines in the wind farm, the total deficit in velocity when the wind direction is θ_k, can be computed as

$$V_{def\_i\_k} = \sqrt{\sum_{j=1}^{N} V_{def\_j,i}^2 \cdot W_{k\_i}(i,j)} \tag{5}$$

where $W_{k\_i}(i,j)$ denotes the wake filter, expressed as

$$W_{k\_i}(i,j) = \begin{cases} 1 & j \in F_{k\_i} \\ 0 & \text{otherwise} \end{cases} \tag{6}$$

where F_{k_i} donates the set of turbines which have a wake effect on turbine i when the wind direction is θ_k.

2.3   Mixed Installation and Turbines Modeling

Mixed installation is considered here, as one of the main contributions in this paper. Turbines with different characteristics are arranged within one wind farm. Since too many types of wind turbines means more kinds of spare parts and more O&M cost, 2 to 4 types of turbines are usually selected in one wind power site according to the practical conditions. Before optimization, the optional types of turbines are selected based on the wind resource analysis of extreme cases and turbulence intensity conditions. Supposing M kind of turbines are installed, $N_1, N_2, \ldots, N_M$ represent the number of each type of turbines, which are to be computed by the optimization algorithm. Then the total number of wind turbines in a wind farm N can be calculated as $N_1 + N_2 + \ldots + N_M = N$.

According to [3,9], the power generation model is given as follows

$$P_i = \begin{cases} 0 & \text{if} \quad v_i < u_{\text{in}\_i}, \quad \text{or} \quad v_i > u_{\text{out}\_i} \\ \frac{1}{2}\rho C_{p\_i} A_i v_i^3 & \text{if} \quad u_{\text{in}\_i} \leq v_i < u_{\text{rate}\_i} \\ P_{\text{rate}\_i} & \text{if} \quad u_{\text{rate}\_i} \leq v_i \leq u_{\text{out}\_i} \end{cases} \tag{7}$$

where ρ denotes the air density, C_{p_i} denotes the power generation coefficient of wind turbine i, P_{rate_i} denotes the rated power, u_{in_i}, u_{out_i} and u_{rate_i} denote the cut-in velocity, cut-out velocity, and rated velocity of turbine i, respectively.

Moreover, the annual power generation of the whole farm (AEP) is

$$\text{AEP} = \sum_t \sum_{k=1}^{N_{wd}} \sum_{w=1}^{N_{ws}} \sum_{i=1}^{N} P_{ikw} \cdot p(\theta_k, v_w) \tag{8}$$

where t denotes the average power generating time in hour in one year, $p(\theta_k, v_w)$ denotes the probability of wind flow with velocity v_w in direction θ_k.

2.4   Cost Modeling

The cost of a wind farm consists of many factors including O&M cost, investment cost, land rent capital and etc. To simplify the fitness function, only the investment cost on buying turbines is considered [11], and modified for mixed installation:

$$\text{cost} = \sum_{s=1}^{M} C_s \cdot N_s \left(\frac{2}{3} + \frac{1}{3} e^{-0.00174 N_s^2} \right) \tag{9}$$

where C_s is the cost of buying a single turbine of kind s, $s = 1, 2, \ldots, M$.

2.5   Objective Function and Constrains

In micro-siting discussed here, the cost of energy (CoE = cost/AEP) is considered as the fitness function.

In practice, the wind turbine positioning and selection is an optimization problem with constraints, since the safe distance between two wind turbines must be satisfied. The safe distance (D_s) between turbines usually is $3D$ to $8D$, with D being the diameter of turbines. Then, the optimization problem and constraints can be formulated as follows

$$\min CoE$$
$$\text{s.t.} \quad \begin{cases} dis_{ij} \geq D_s & i,j = 1,2,...,N, i \neq j \\ x_i \in [\underline{x}, \bar{x}] & i = 1,2,...,N \\ y_i \in [\underline{y}, \bar{y}] & i = 1,2,...,N \end{cases} \quad (10)$$

where $dis_{ij} = \sqrt{(x_i - x_j)^2 + (y_i - y_j)^2}$ is the distance between the turbines; $[\underline{x}, \bar{x}]$ and $[\underline{y}, \bar{y}]$ are the ranges of the wind farm in x-direction and y-direction, respectively.

3   Methodology

Wind farm is a very complicated MIMO nonlinear system with state-varying, strong-coupling and faulty characteristics [16]. To simplify the micro-sitting problem, we only investigate the wind farms built in planes. However, the optimization of micro-siting is beyond the traditional calculus-based optimization algorithms. GA has been proven to be one of the optimal tools to solve positioning problems in wind farms. In this paper, GA is also adopted for the position search for turbines as well as the turbine type selection.

As shown in Mosetti's paper [11], to keep safe distance between turbines, a wind farm can be divided into grids with the side-length of D_s. It is only needed to consider whether to place a turbine inside a grid or not in the optimization algorithm, which makes the optimization problem much more easy to be solved. In this work, we also use the "grids" to meet the safe distance criterion.

The target of the evolution of GA is to find the best turbine positions and types as the configuration for a wind farm on a given terrain. CoE is set as the fitness for GA in this paper. When the grids is adopted, each individual in GA represents a turbine arranging scheme to with N vectors representing turbines to be installed in the farm. Each vector represents information of a turbine as $[x, y, s]$, with (x, y) denoting the grid position of the turbines, and s denoting the type of turbine selected in this grids. For example, if $[x, y, s] = [1, 4, 1]$, it means the wind turbine of type A (A is represented by $s = 1$ in the algorithm) is set in the first row and fourth column grid. Individuals are encoded and the population of GA is set to be $20N$. After calculating the fitness value of each individual, the relative superior ones are transferred to the next generation after steps of selection, crossover and mutation. Here the rates of selection, crossover are 0.9, 0.8 and 0.01 respectively. When iterations are carried on till convergence criteria are satisfied, the global optimal individual is exported as the solution to the position and type selection scheme for micro-siting adopting mixed installation. 10000 generations are set to as GA to finish the evolution, except that the iterations reach the minimum residuals set to 10^{-6}.

4   Case Study

Nowadays, 1.5 MW or 2 MW turbines, unlike the 750 kW turbines in Mosetti's paper, are widely installed with fast developments in turbine manufacture industry. Therefore, the identical 750 kW turbine given in [11] is replaced by 4 different types of turbines with different diameters, different hub heights and different power generation curves, parameters given in Table 1. It should be noticed that the different characteristics between turbine types are not limited to the items listed in Table 1. In this case study, characteristics in the table are just to illustrate mixed installation and the effectiveness of the optimization method provided in Sect. 3. In Mosetti's work, the wind field with 10×10 grids is considered. In our study, to simplify the calculation, a wind farm with 5×5 grids is considered. The safe distance is selected as 4 times the maximum diameter of the turbines as listed in Table 1. The width of each grid is 440 m. A 2.2 km $\times$ 2.2 km wind farm is to be optimized with 8 wind turbines to be set. Therefore, 25 grids are the possible wind turbine locations in the farm. Additionally, the surface roughness length z_0 is set to 0.003 m. The air density is set to 1.225 kg/m^3, and the reference height H_{ref} is 80 m.

Table 1. Parameters of the turbines

Type no.	A	B	C	D
Turbine diameter R (m)	77	77	110	110
Hub height H (m)	65	80	80	90
Rated power P_{rated} (MW)	1.5	1.5	2	2
Price C (CNY $\times 10^6$)	6.00	6.02	10.00	10.03

This case considers eight different wind directions and three wind speeds with unequal probability of occurrence as shown in Fig. 1(a). It is much more similar to the actual conditions over a wind farm. Wind from a certain direction which occurs most frequently in a certain wind farm, is called the dominant direction. The results with identical type of turbines are also shown for comparison, adopting method provided in [3].

Results of the case are shown in Table 2 and Fig. 1(b). Along the dominant wind direction, 225°, the turbines are laid away from each other as far as possible, in order to reduce the wake effect as illustrated in Fig. 1(b). Right behind the highest and largest turbines towards the wind from northeast, the lowest and smallest turbines are installed to take full use of the energy in the wakes. Downstream the wind, several higher and larger turbines are set behind the lower and smaller ones. Meanwhile, the turbines are arranged to scatter along the NW-SE direction, perpendicular to the dominant wind direction, to reduce the partial shelter effects of the wakes. The vertical arrangements with different sizes turbines at different heights are able to make used of the wind energy spatially, by reducing the sheltered rotor scanning areas and turbine overlaps.

The result analysis is presented in Fig. 2(a). In Fig. 2(b), the power generation per direction is in accordance with the wind rose. Directions with more wind power distributed have more power generation, for example, in the dominant direction, 225°, the most wind energy is produced. The power generation deficit caused by wake effects are also shown in Fig. 2(b). The turbine positioning and type selections scheme has provided a minimum wake deficit in the dominant wind direction, compared with that of any other directions.

Additionally, B is not chosen in layout of this case for the following reasons. When a turbine B is placed near another turbine, the partial shelter effect and the wake effect is much larger, for example, compared with an A near a D. Besides, v_{rate} of A and B is smaller than that of C and D, which means that the wakes have more effects on A and B than they do on C and D.

From the results of the optimization of the turbine positioning and type selection as shown in Table 2, the CoE is reduced substantially with mixed installation, compared with identical turbine installations. Correspondingly, the wake deficit of mixed installation is the lowest among the five results, which means it can improve the utilization efficiency of wind energy distributed over the wind farm.

Table 2. Results of mixed installation

Case A	Mixed installation	A	B	C	D
AEP (10^6 kWh)	35.033	23.648	26.976	37.575	37.808
CoE (CNY/kWh)	0.1575	0.4896	0.3786	0.5136	0.4512
Wake deficit (%)	0.26	3.27	3.29	0.82	0.45

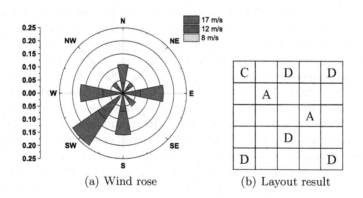

(a) Wind rose   (b) Layout result

Fig. 1. Micro-siting result analysis

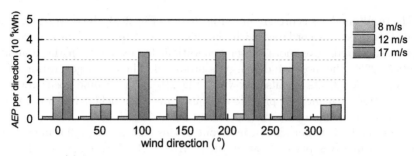

(a) Power generation for wind from different directions

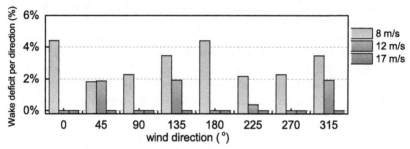

(b) Wake deficit for wind from different directions

Fig. 2. Results of turbine positioning and type selection with mixed installation

5   Conclusion

In this paper, a novel attempt is presented for wind farm micro-siting adopting multi-types turbines. The optimization problem in micro-citing is modelled, and minimizing CoE is chosen as the object function. Then a method based on GA is presented to solve the optimization problem with multiple turbines, which includes positioning and turbine type selection. Case study is presented to illustrate the significance of mixed installation as well as the effectiveness of the optimization method. With the wind condition of variable speeds and variable directions, the mixed installation makes full use of the wind energy distributed in the 3 dimensional spatial ranges over the farm, and reduces the wake effects. The algorithm presented solves the equilibrium and optimal point between cost and power generation, leading to an remarkable improvement of the farm efficiency and a lower CoE. In future work, efforts can be made to extend this methodology to practical wind farms over complex terrains, or to integrate with wind turbine controls [9].

Acknowledgements. This work is supported by the National Natural Science Foundation of China (61673347).

References

1. Abudulrahman, M.: Wood: investigation the power-COE trade-off for wind farm layout optimization considering commercial turbine selection and hub height variation. Renew. Energy **102**, 267–278 (2017)
2. Chen, Y., Li, H., Jin, K., Song, Q.: Wind farm layout optimization using genetic algorithm with different hub height wind turbines. Energy Convers. Manag. **70**, 56–65 (2013)
3. Grady, S.A., Hussaini, M.Y., Abdullah, M.M.: Placement of wind turbines using genetic algorithms. Renew. Energy **30**(2), 259–270 (2005)
4. Gu, H., Wang, J.: Irregular-shape wind farm micro-siting optimization. Energy **57**(8), 535–544 (2013)
5. Herbert-Acero, J.F., Probst, O., Réthoré, P.E., Larsen, G.C., Castillo-Villar, K.K.: A review of methodological approaches for the design and optimization of wind farms. Energies **7**(11), 6930–7016 (2014)
6. Katic, I., Højstrup, J., Jensen, N.O.: A simple model for cluster efficiency. In: European Wind Energy Association Conference and Exhibition, pp. 407–410 (1986)
7. Kusiak, A., Song, Z.: Design of wind farm layout for maximum wind energy capture. Renew. Energy **35**(3), 685–694 (2010)
8. Manwell, J.F., Mcgowan, J.G., Rogers, A.L.: Wind Energy Explained: Theory, Design and Application. Wiley, West Sussex (2006)
9. Meng, W., Yang, Q., Ying, Y., Sun, Y., Yang, Z., Sun, Y.: Adaptive power capture control of variable-speed wind energy conversion systems with guaranteed transient and steady-state performance. IEEE Trans. Energy Convers. **28**(3), 716–725 (2013)
10. Mortensen, N.G., Landberg, L., Troen, I., Petersen, E.L.: WAsP utility programs (2004)
11. Mosetti, G., Poloni, C., Diviacco, B.: Optimization of wind turbine positioning in large windfarms by means of a genetic algorithm. J. Wind Eng. Ind. Aerodyn. **51**(1), 105–116 (1994)
12. Ozturk, U.A., Norman, B.A.: Heuristic methods for wind energy conversion system positioning. Electr. Power Syst. Res. **70**(3), 179–185 (2004)
13. Rivas, R.A., Clausen, J., Hansen, K.S., Jensen, L.E.: Solving the turbine positioning problem for large offshore wind farms by simulated annealing. Wind Eng. **33**(3), 287–297 (2009)
14. Wan, C., Wang, J., Yang, G., Zhang, X.: Optimal micro-siting of wind farms by particle swarm optimization. In: Proceedings of the First International Conference on Advances in Swarm Intelligence, ICSI 2010, Beijing, China, 12–15 June 2010, pp. 198–205 (2010)
15. Yang, J., Feng, J., Shen, W.: Optimization of wind farm layout: a refinement method by random search, pp. 624–633. Technical University of Denmark (2013)
16. Yang, Q., Ge, S.S., Sun, Y.: Adaptive actuator fault tolerant control for uncertain nonlinear systems with multiple actuators. Automatica **60**, 92–99 (2015)

Kinematic, Static and Dynamic Analyses of Flapping Wing Mechanism Based on ANSYS Workbench

Youpeng Li[1], Chen Qian[1], Bingqi Zhu[2], and Yongchun Fang[1(✉)]

[1] Nankai University, Tianjin, China
fangyc@nankai.edu.cn
[2] Hohai University Changzhou Campus, Changzhou, China

Abstract. A method for kinematic, static and dynamic analyses of single degree of freedom flapping wing aircraft is shown in this paper. All the analyses are realized completely by using *ANSYS Workbench*. A 3D model built in *SolidWorks* is imported into *ANSYS Workbench*. Firstly, a rigid body dynamic analysis is implemented to judge the connections among joints and get the maximum joint forces to find potentially dangerous positions of the movement. Then, a static analysis is carried out to check deformation and stress of the mechanism. On the basis of above analyses, modal analysis and transient dynamic analysis are respectively achieved to determine the stress under dynamic loads, with the obtained results clearly demonstrating the rationality of the designed flapping wing mechanism.

Keywords: Flapping wing aircraft · ANSYS Workbench · Rigid body dynamic analysis · Static analysis · Transient dynamic analysis

1 Introduction

Flapping wing aircraft has been becoming a hotspot in science field in recent years [1–5]. Prototypes of flapping wing aircraft can be divided into multi-degree flapping mechanism by imitating insects [6–9] and single degree of freedom flapping wing mechanism by imitating birds [10–12]. A designed single degree of freedom flapping wing structure is used in this paper. For most researches of single degree of freedom flapping wing mechanism, kinematic analysis is implemented by using *Adams* [12] firstly and then static and dynamic analyses are achieved by three-dimensional modeling software such as *SolidWorks*, *UG* [13] and *Pro/E* afterwards. *ANSYS Workbench* can be used to complete all above analyses for the flapping wing mechanism to check its strength and stiffness.

ANSYS Workbench is used to analyze kinematic, static and dynamic properties of the single degree of freedom flapping wing aircraft in this paper. Due to its high accuracy, more accurate results are obtained. And it provides a simpler and easier way to analyze kinematic, static and dynamic properties of a mechanism as there is just one software being used.

© Springer International Publishing AG 2017
D. Liu et al. (Eds.): ICONIP 2017, Part VI, LNCS 10639, pp. 316–323, 2017.
https://doi.org/10.1007/978-3-319-70136-3_34

What we have done is shown below. Before analyses, a 3D assembly model (the model built in *SolidWorks* is three dimensional) of flapping wing mechanism built in *SolidWorks* is imported into *ANSYS Workbench*. Firstly, connections are judged to be correct, and maximum joint forces are obtained from rigid body dynamic analysis. And then total deformations and stresses of all components are checked by static analysis, all results are satisfied for the check condition. On the basis of above analyses, modal analysis and transient dynamic analysis are carried out. First 6-order mode natural frequencies and mode shapes of vibration are acquired through modal analysis, which are supposed to be avoided when motors are chosen. Through the transient dynamic analysis, stresses of the flapping wing mechanism are checked at all six potentially dangerous positions under dynamic loads, and results at all positions are satisfied for the stress check condition.

2   Modeling of Flapping Wing Mechanism

Double-stage wing structure, composed by two parts and connected by joint in the middle, is basically used in the body of medium and large birds. To simulate the movement of birds in this paper, a double-stage wing structure is chosen. For the designs of the mechanism, Negrello and Silvestri's paper [10] has been taken as a reference. A crank rocker mechanism ($l_1 \sim l_4$) is used to simulate the movement of the internal semi-wing (the part of a wing near wing root), and a parallelogram mechanism is connected to the internal semi-wing to simulate the movement of external semi-wing (the part of a wing near wing tip). Flapping wing mechanism schematic diagram is shown in Fig. 1. In the parallelogram mechanism, input rod (l_5) is a part of connecting rod (l_3) of the crank rocker mechanism, and output rod (l_7) is on the opposite side of the input rod. The size of internal semi-wing (l_6) is close to the size of pull rod (l_8), those are not same because a design like this can improve movement flexibility of external semi-wing and make the whole mechanism behave more like birds.

All 3D solid models of corresponding components are designed according to Fig. 1 and all those components are assembled in *SolidWorks*. Final overall assembly diagram of flapping wing mechanism model, is shown in Fig. 2.

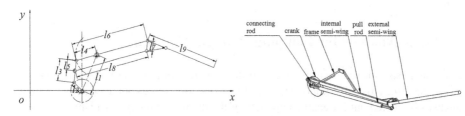

Fig. 1. Flapping wing mechanism schematic diagram

Fig. 2. Overall assembly diagram of flapping wing mechanism model

3 Rigid Body Dynamic Analysis of Flapping Wing Mechanism

The process of rigid body dynamic analysis on the Rigid Dynamics platform involves defining engineering materials, importing geometric data, preprocessing, model solving, results, and post-processing. Choose aluminum alloy material, set solution time as 3 s, and apply 50 r/min rotational velocity to the crank, then solve the model. At last, results can be obtained as followed: internal semi-wing velocity, acceleration of time and external semi-wing velocity, acceleration of time (see Fig. 3).

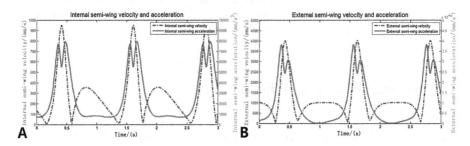

Fig. 3. Internal semi-wing velocity and acceleration (A) and external semi-wing velocity and acceleration (B). Maximum internal and external semi-wing velocity are 0.96 m/s and 4.10 m/s respectively; And maximum internal and external semi-wing acceleration are $0.8\,\text{m/s}^2$ and $38.0\,\text{m/s}^2$ respectively.

Maximum joint forces are shown in Table 1. It can be seen from it that their values for all joints are less than 600 N, which are not large for components. In the first flapping cycle, extreme values of joint forces occur at the time of 0.36 s and 0.47 s respectively, when the mechanism may suffer danger of break for dynamic analysis. Based on all these above joint forces, a static analysis is carried out.

Table 1. Maximum joint forces for joint 1–7

Joint	1	2	3	4	5	6	7
Maximum joint force/N	580.95	580.95	229.26	361.01	579.35	359.22	357.95

4 Static Analysis for Flapping Wing Mechanism

Static analysis can be used to determine the displacement and stress of components. Applying forces to each component according to the joint forces obtained above, a static analysis is carried out for each component of the flapping wing mechanism.

The flapping wing mechanism is a test prototype, so its total deformation requirement is not strict. For each component, total deformation can be considered to meet the deformation check condition as long as its value is no more than 1% of its total length. Total deformation results of all components are shown in Table 2, where total deformation ratio of a component is ratio of total deformation and total length of it. As can be seen from Table 2, total deformation ratios of all components are less than 1%, which means that all components satisfy the deformation check condition.

Table 2. Flapping wing mechanism static analysis deformation check

Name of component	Total length of component/mm	Total deformation of component/mm	Total deformation ratio of component/%
Crank	80	0.034	0.042
Connecting rod	61.08	0.11	0.18
Internal semi-wing	472	0.45	0.096
Pull rod	473	0.031	0.0066
External semi-wing	480	0.63	0.13

All components of the mechanism are plastic, so the third strength theory is used to check. Select Equivalent Stress of solution in *ANSYS Workbench* to solve, and results indicate that the maximum stress, 119 MPa, occurs at the internal semi-wing, and is less than tensile strength of aluminum alloy material, so the flapping wing mechanism is satisfied for the stress check condition in statics.

5 Dynamic Analysis for Flapping Wing Mechanism

5.1 Modal Analysis for Flapping Wing Mechanism

Modal analysis is a common type of dynamic analyses, and is also the basis for harmonic response analysis, response spectrum analysis and transient dynamic analysis. Natural frequencies and mode shapes of vibration of the flapping wing mechanism can be determined according to it.

The model in the situation that considered as dangerous position during the rigid body dynamic analysis is imported into *ANSYS Workbench* to carry out a static analysis. Based on above static analysis for the flapping wing mechanism, a pre-stressing modal analysis is achieved. And the first 6 order natural frequencies of the flapping wing mechanism can be obtained and shown in Table 3. Mode shapes of vibration at above natural frequencies can also be easily obtained in *ANSYS Workbench*, shown in Fig. 4.

Table 3. First 6 order natural frequencies of the flapping wing mechanism

Mode	1	2	3	4	5	6
Frequency/Hz	23.454	46.361	59.027	144.52	217.39	297.68

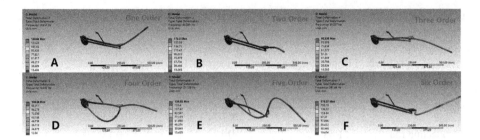

Fig. 4. 1–6 order mode shapes of vibration (A–F)

The natural frequencies given above should be avoided in this design and movement of the flapping wing mechanism so as to avoid resonance with the mechanism and affect its motion stability during the movement. When resonance happens, the mechanism is easily unsteady, shortening all components' life.

5.2   Transient Dynamic Analysis of Flapping Wing Mechanism

Time-varying air resistance load is introduced into the process of movement for the flapping wing mechanism. Therefore, transient dynamic analysis is necessary.

There are six positions (A–F) for the flapping wing mechanism in transient dynamic analysis: two potentially dangerous positions (maximum points of acceleration) in one movement period, flapping motion initial position, lowest extreme position, horizontal position and highest extreme position (see Fig. 5). The first position is taken as an example for following analysis.

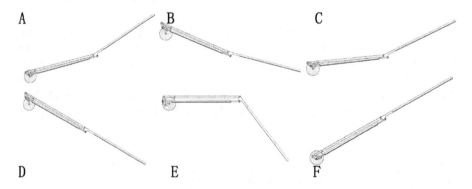

Fig. 5. Main positions for transient dynamic analysis (A–F)

As can be seen from Figs. 3 and 4, flapping motion period is about 1.2 s. Solution time is set to 1.5 s to shorten solving time as much as possible. In one cycle, direction of air resistance load of the flapping wing mechanism changes twice, so set step numbers to 3. Proper transient response time step can be calculated as followed: $t = 1/20f = 1/(20 \times 23.454) = 0.0021s$. In order to make solution results more accurate, maximum time step is set as 0.001 s, as shown in Table 4.

Table 4. Initial parameters setting in transient dynamic analysis for the mechanism

Step Controls			
Number of steps	3	3	3
Current step number	1	2	3
Step end time	0.2817	1.111	1.500
Initial time step	0.001	0.001	0.001
Minimum time step	0.0005	0.0005	0.0005
Maximum time step	0.001	0.001	0.001

Take the air resistance formula for fixed-wing aircraft design as reference:

$$F_d = -\frac{1}{2}\rho v^2 C_d A \tag{1}$$

where F_d is air resistance of aircraft, ρ is density of air fluid, whose value is 1.293 kg/m³, v is relative velocity of the aircraft to the fluid, C_d is coefficient of drag, taken as 0.6, A is windward area, taken as 0.2 m² for internal semi-wing and 0.3 m² for external semi-wing.

Velocities of internal semi-wing, pull rod and external semi-wing in three directions of x, y and z can be obtained by rigid body dynamic analysis. Bring these velocities into formula (1), and corresponding air resistances are obtained. Results indicate that it is less than 0.5 N for internal semi-wing and pull rod, while less than 1.5 N for external semi-wing. For the sake of convenience, consider their values as constants, 1.0 N for internal semi-wing and pull rod and 2.0 N for externa semi-wing.

Table 5. Direction reversal time for internal semi-wing, pull rod and external semi-wing

Direction reversal time for internal semi-wing/s	Direction reversal time for pull rod/s	Direction reversal time for external semi-wing/s
0 ↑	0 ↑	0 ↑
0.2184 ↓	0.2298 ↓	0.2817 ↓
1.014 ↑	1.045 ↑	1.111 ↑
1.423 ↓	1.435 ↓	1.474 ↓
2.218 ↑	2.252 ↑	2.321 ↑
2.618 ↓	2.630 ↓	2.682 ↓
3.416 ↑	3.447 ↑	3.500 ↑

Direction reversal time of internal semi-wing, pull rod and external semi-wing can be found by velocity curve of them. Time points and directions of speed change of each component within 3.5 s are shown in Table 5, where "↑" means that component moves upwardly from that moment, and "↓" indicates that component moves downwardly from that moment.

Loads on each component are set according to direction reversal time. Since air resistance is mainly applied to the surface of the whole mechanism, [Remote Force] is set for internal semi-wing, pull rod and external semi-wing to simulate actual forces.

Final loads condition is shown in Fig. 6. After solving, results of stress change can be obtained, shown in Fig. 7. Generally, stress for the whole mechanism fluctuates up and down around 120 MPa and is relatively stable. At the time of 0.9557 s, maximum stress occurs in front section of external semi-wing, whose value is 233 MPa and within elastic deformation range of aluminum alloy material, and can be accepted. It can be considered to satisfy the transient dynamic stress check condition.

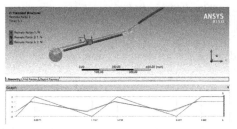   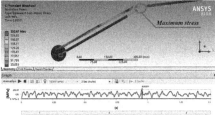

Fig. 6. Loads condition in transient dynamic analysis   **Fig. 7.** Equivalent stress for transient dynamic analysis

Results of maximum stress at each position in transient dynamic analysis are shown in Table 6. As can be seen, the maximum stress of all components occurs at the third position (flapping motion initial position), is 328 MPa (taking data before 1.25 s to analyze, a steady state having not reached yet between 1.25 s and 1.5 s), which is satisfied for the transient dynamic stress check condition. In summary, the stress check condition is satisfied in all six potentially dangerous positions for the flapping wing mechanism, and it is appropriate to use aluminum alloy material to make the flapping wing mechanism.

Table 6. Maximum stress at each position in transient dynamic analysis

Positions	1	2	3	4	5	6
Maximum stress/MPa	233	321	328	193	114	82

6   Conclusion and Perspectives

A rigid body dynamic analysis, a static analysis, a modal analysis and a transient dynamic analysis are implemented for the single degree of freedom flapping wing aircraft in *ANSYS Workbench* in the paper. Connections are judged to be correct, and maximum joint forces are obtained from the rigid body dynamic analysis. And total deformations and stresses of all components are checked by the static analysis, all of which are satisfied for the check condition. First 6-order mode natural frequencies and mode shapes of vibration are acquired through the modal analysis, which are supposed to be avoided when motors are chosen. According to the transient dynamic analysis, stresses of the flapping wing mechanism at all six potentially dangerous positions under dynamic loads are checked, and results show that stress at all positions are satisfied for the stress check condition. In summary, the model performs well through all analyses, the design of the flapping wing mechanism is reasonable.

Based on the results presented, the authors believe that it is feasible to build a real operational prototype of the biomimetic flapping MAV (Micro Aerial Vehicle) for test. This represents the next step of our work.

References

1. Mahjoubi, H., Byl, K.: Efficient flight control via mechanical impedance manipulation: energy analyses for hummingbird-inspired MAVs. J. Intell. Robot. Syst. **73**(1), 487–512 (2014)
2. Colmenares, D., Kania, R., Zhang, W., Sitti, M.: Compliant wing design for a flapping wing micro air vehicle. In: 2015 IEEE Conference on IROS, Hamburg, Germany, pp. 32–39 (2015)
3. Ryu, S., Kwon, U., Kim, H.J.: Autonomous flight and vision-based target tracking for a flapping-wing MAV. In: 2016 IEEE Conference on IROS, Daejeon, South Korea, pp. 5645–5650 (2016)
4. Hassanalian, M., Abdelkefi, A., Wei, M., Ziaei-Rad, S.: A novel methodology for wing sizing of bio-inspired flapping wing micro air vehicles: theory and prototype. J. Acta Mech. **228**(3), 1097–1113 (2017)
5. Ramezani, A., Chung, S.J., Hutchinson, S.: A biomimetic robotic platform to study flight specializations of bats. J. Sci. Robot. **2**(3), 1–12 (2017)
6. Phan, H.V., Park, H.C.: Remotely controlled flight of an insect-like tailless flapping-wing micro air vehicle. In: 2015 IEEE Conference on URAI, Goyang, South Korea, pp. 315–317 (2015)
7. Sreetharan, P.S., Wood, R.J.: Passive torque regulation in an underactuated flapping wing robotic insect. Auton. Robots **31**, 225 (2011)
8. İşbitirici, A., Altuğ, E.: Design of a flapping-wing aerial vehicle based on four-bar mechanism. In: 2016 IEEE Conference on ICUAS, Arlington, USA, pp. 1240–1245 (2016)
9. İşbitirici, A., Altuğ, E.: Design and control of a mini aerial vehicle that has four flapping-wings: Theory and prototype. J. Intell. Robot. Syst. pp. 1–19 (2017)
10. Negrello, F., Silvestri, P., Lucifredi, A., Guerrero, J.E., Bottaro, A.: Preliminary design of a small-sized flapping UAV: II Kinematic and structural aspects. J. Meccanica **51**(6), 1369–1385 (2016)
11. Jitsukawa, T., Adachi, H., Abe, T., Yamakawa, H., Umezu, S.: Bio-inspired wing-folding mechanism of micro air vehicle (MAV). Artif. Life Robot. **22**, 203–208 (2016)
12. Jiang, H., Zhou, C., Xie, P.: Design and kinematic analysis of seagull inspired flapping wing robot. In: 2016 IEEE Conference on ICIA, pp. 1382–1386, Ningbo, China (2016)
13. Ma, N., He, G.P., Di, J.J.: Study of velocity fluctuation of bat-like flapping wing air vehicle. J. Mech. Trans. **38**, 131–137 (2014)

Homography-Based Visual Servo Tracking Control of Wheeled Mobile Robots with Simultaneous Depth Identification

Yu Qiu, Baoquan Li$^{(\boxtimes)}$, Wuxi Shi, and Yimei Chen

Tianjin Key Laboratory of Advanced Technology of Electrical Engineering
and Energy, School of Electrical Engineering and Automation,
Tianjin Polytechnic University, Tianjin 300387, China
qiuyuqiuyu000@163.com, {libq,chenyimei}@tjpu.edu.cn, shiwuxi@163.com

Abstract. In this paper, a visual servo tracking control method is developed for the wheeled mobile robot subject to nonholonomic motion constraints, while the unknown feature depth information is simultaneously identified in the visual servoing process. Firstly, a video feature points are prerecorded as the desire trajectory for the mobile robot. Secondly, Euclidean homographies are constructed by utilizing projective geometric relationships of feature points. Subsequently, trajectory tracking errors are obtained after Euclidean homographies decomposition. Then, the kinematic controller is designed for the mobile robot to achieve the visual servo trajectory tracking task. Moreover, by utilizing the concurrent learning framework, the historical and current system data is used to construct an adaptive updating mechanism for recovering the unknown feature depth. Simulation results are collected to prove the efficiency and utility of the proposed strategy.

Keywords: Wheeled mobile robot · Visual servo control · Adaptive control · Depth identification

1 Introduction

Nowadays, wheeled mobile robots always have to deal with system uncertainties when they are operated in unstructured environment. It is quite feasible and effective when we use some kinds of sensors for robots navigation, such as the works in [1–3]. The issue of controlling underactuated systems, has been a important direction for both theoretical and practical research purposes [4]. The missing of available control inputs causes much difficulty for both controller design and stability analysis [5,6]. Visual servoing has three main schemes, they are position-based visual servoing (PBVS), image-based visual servoing (IBVS), and hybrid visual serving (2.5DVS) [7]. However, general visual servo control methods have one main drawback due to the perspective projection model of visual camera, which is the missing of the scene depth information. Then, how

© Springer International Publishing AG 2017
D. Liu et al. (Eds.): ICONIP 2017, Part VI, LNCS 10639, pp. 324–333, 2017.
https://doi.org/10.1007/978-3-319-70136-3_35

to accomplish the function of identifying the depth information while completing the visual servoing tasks is quite a difficult problem.

With the rapid development of the image recognition, some researchers have achieved trajectory tracking tasks. Li *et al.* design a time-varying continuous controller to implement both tracking and regulation tasks [8]. MacKunis *et al.*, also using the way of decomposing the Euclidean homographies, address the unified tracking and regulation visual servo control problem [9]. A Broyden population partition method is used in state-space, which can track fast and complicated target [10]. In [11], Li *et al.* propose a visual servoing strategy for wheeled mobile robot to complete both unified tracking and regulation tasks. In [12], the mobile robot tracks a moving target using a novel image-based visual approach. In [13], Mahony *et al.* develop an image-based visual servoing controller for unmanned aerial vehicles to track parallel linear visual features. Tan *et al.* adopted PID control for mobile robot to track the desired trajectory [14]. In [15], Chen *et al.* make the wheeled mobile robot track the desired trajectory, which is defined by a prerecorded image sequence, and they also employ the method of decomposing the Euclidean homography.

Recently, there are some results about identifying the unknown range information for robots, such as position of manipulator end-effector [16], position of moving object [17], and robot manipulator velocities [18]. In [19], an adaptive algorithm is designed, which can estimate the position of the mobile robot through target features while performing the task of visual trajectory tracking. Moreover, Parikh *et al.* have completed the task of identifying the scene depth while tracking the trajectory for an robot manipulator [20].

Inspired by the visual servo tracking control method in [15] and depth identification method in [20], this paper investigates a strategy to simultaneously achieve mobile robot tracking control and depth identification. Firstly, the kinematic model of the problem is introduced. Secondly, from the current image and desired trajectory image, the Euclidean homography matrixes are decomposed to get the unmeasurable signals. Then, an augmented adaptive updating law for the unknown feature depth and the tracking controller is designed. The main contribution of this paper is that, compared with [15], it solves the problem of unknown depth identification.

2   Problem Formulation

2.1   System Description

As shown in Fig. 1, we define the origin of the orthogonal coordinate system of the camera $\mathcal{F}^c$ above the center of the wheel axis of the wheeled mobile robot. The plane of motion is defined by the x and z axis of the $\mathcal{F}^c$, z axis is vertical to the wheel axis while x axis is parallel to it. The y axis is defined perpendicular to the wheel axis. $v_c(t)$ is the linear velocity along the z axis and $w_c(t)$ is the angular velocity along y axis. A time-varying trajectory of $\mathcal{F}^d$ is recorded previously by image sequence. $\mathcal{F}^*$ is defined as the fixed reference frame.

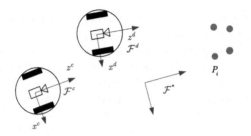

Fig. 1. Wheeled mobile robot coordinate systems

The plane decided by four non-liner feature points $\boldsymbol{P}_i$ is the reference plane π. The normal vector of the plane π is denoted as n^*. The 3-d Euclidean coordinates of $\boldsymbol{P}_i$ in $\mathcal{F}^c$, $\mathcal{F}^d$ and $\mathcal{F}^*$ are $\boldsymbol{P}_i(t)$, $\boldsymbol{P}_i^d(t)$ and $\boldsymbol{P}_i^* \in \mathbb{R}^3$, respectively, which are defined as follows:

$$\begin{cases} \boldsymbol{P}_i(t) = [X_i(t), Y_i(t), Z_i(t)]^T, \\ \boldsymbol{P}_i^d(t) = \left[X_i^d(t), Y_i^d(t), Z_i^d(t)\right]^T, \\ \boldsymbol{P}_i^* = [X_i^*, Y_i^*, Z_i^*]^T. \end{cases} \tag{1}$$

It is known that the distance from the originals of the coordinates to the feature plane along the optical axis is positive. The rotation from $\mathcal{F}^*$ to $\mathcal{F}^c$ is $_*^c R(t) \in SO(3)$, and the translation from $\mathcal{F}^*$ to $\mathcal{F}^c$ is $^c T_*(t) \in \mathbb{R}^3$, wherein the $^c T_*(t)$ is expressed under $\mathcal{F}^c$. In the same way, the desired time-varying rotation from $\mathcal{F}^*$ to $\mathcal{F}^d$ is $_*^d R(t) \in SO(3)$, and the desired translation from $\mathcal{F}^*$ to $\mathcal{F}^d$ is $^d T_*(t) \in \mathbb{R}^3$, wherein the $^d T_*(t)$ is expressed under $\mathcal{F}^d$.

The $_*^c R(t)$ and $_*^d R(t)$ are defined as follows:

$$_*^c R = \begin{bmatrix} \cos\theta & 0 & \sin\theta \\ 0 & 1 & 0 \\ -\sin\theta & 0 & \cos\theta \end{bmatrix}, _*^d R = \begin{bmatrix} \cos\theta_d & 0 & \sin\theta_d \\ 0 & 1 & 0 \\ -\sin\theta_d & 0 & \cos\theta_d. \end{bmatrix} \tag{2}$$

where $\theta(t)$ is the right-handed rotation angle about $Y_i(t)$ that aligns the rotation of $\mathcal{F}^c$ with $\mathcal{F}^*$, and $\theta_d(t)$ is the right-handed rotation angle about $Y_i^d(t)$ that aligns the rotation of $\mathcal{F}^d$ with $\mathcal{F}^*$. From (2), it is clear that

$$\dot{\theta} = -w_c, \dot{\theta}_d = -w_{cd} \tag{3}$$

where $w_{cd}(t) \in \mathbb{R}$ is the desired angular velocity of the wheeled mobile robot expressed in $\mathcal{F}^d$.

The distance from $\mathcal{F}^*$ to π along the unit normal vector of π is defined as $d^* \in \mathbb{R}$:

$$d^* = \boldsymbol{n}^{*T} \boldsymbol{P}_i^*. \tag{4}$$

where $\boldsymbol{n}^* \in \mathbb{R}^3$ is the unit normal vector of π.

2.2   Euclidean Reconstruction

Symbols $\bar{\boldsymbol{p}}_i(t)$, $\bar{\boldsymbol{p}}_i^d(t)$ and $\bar{\boldsymbol{p}}_i^*$ are denoted as the normalized Euclidean coordinates of $\boldsymbol{P}_i$ in $\mathcal{F}^c$, $\mathcal{F}^d$, and $\mathcal{F}^*$, respectively.

The relationship of the rotations and translations between the coordinate systems and the normalized Euclidean coordinates is shown as follows:

$$\begin{cases} \bar{\boldsymbol{p}}_i = \frac{Z_i^*}{Z_i} \underbrace{\left({}_*^cR + {}^c\boldsymbol{T}_{*h}\boldsymbol{n}^{*T}\right)}_{H} \bar{\boldsymbol{p}}_i^*, \\ \bar{\boldsymbol{p}}_i^d = \frac{Z_i^*}{Z_i^d} \underbrace{\left({}_*^dR + {}^d\boldsymbol{T}_{*h}\boldsymbol{n}^{*T}\right)}_{H_d} \bar{\boldsymbol{p}}_i^*. \end{cases} \tag{5}$$

where $H(t)$ and $H_d(t)$ are Euclidean homographies.

${}^c\boldsymbol{T}_{*h}(t), {}^d\boldsymbol{T}_{*h}(t) \in \mathbb{R}^3$ are defined as the scaled translation vectors:

$$\begin{cases} {}^c\boldsymbol{T}_{*h} = \left[{}^cT_{*h2}, 1, {}^cT_{*h1}\right]^T = \frac{{}^c\boldsymbol{T}_*}{d^*}, \\ {}^d\boldsymbol{T}_{*h} = \left[{}^dT_{*h2}, 1, {}^dT_{*h1}\right]^T = \frac{{}^d\boldsymbol{T}_*}{d^*}. \end{cases} \tag{6}$$

Then, the Euclidean reconstruction technologies in [15, 22–24] can be used to obtain ${}_*^cR(t), {}_*^dR(t), {}^c\boldsymbol{T}_{*h}(t), {}^d\boldsymbol{T}_{*h}(t), \theta(t), \theta_d(t)$.

3   Design of Control Theory

3.1   Open Loop Error System

One goal of the control progress is to force the coordinate $\mathcal{F}^c$ track the time-varying trajectory under $\mathcal{F}^d$.

We define $\boldsymbol{e}(t) = [e_1, e_2, e_3]^T$ as the rotation and translation errors, that is

$$\begin{cases} e_1 = {}^cT_{*h1} - {}^dT_{*h1}, \\ e_2 = {}^cT_{*h2} - {}^dT_{*h2}, \\ e_3 = \theta - \theta_d \end{cases} \tag{7}$$

where ${}^cT_{*h1}(t), {}^cT_{*h2}(t), {}^dT_{*h1}(t)$ and ${}^dT_{*h2}(t)$ are defined in (6), and $\theta(t), \theta_d(t)$ are defined in (2).

Moreover, the auxiliary variable $\bar{e}_2(t) \in \mathbb{R}$ is defined as

$$\bar{e}_2 = e_2 - {}^dT_{*h1}e_3. \tag{8}$$

Inspired by [15], the open-loop error dynamics are presented as follows:

$$\begin{cases} d^*(\dot{e}_1 - {}^cT_{*h2}w_c + {}^d\dot{T}_{*h1}) = -v_c, \\ \dot{\bar{e}}_2 = -(e_1w_c + {}^d\dot{T}_{*h1}e_3), \\ \dot{e}_3 = -(w_c + \theta_d). \end{cases} \tag{9}$$

3.2   Adaptive Controller Development

The depth estimation error $\tilde{d}^*$ is defined as follows:

$$\tilde{d}^* = d^* - \hat{d}^* \tag{10}$$

where $\hat{d}^*(t)$ is the depth estimate. The unknown depth information is effectually identified when $\tilde{d}^*(t)$ converge to zero.

We design the linear and angular velocity control inputs for the wheeled mobile robot as follows:

$$v_c = k_v e_1 - \bar{e}_2 w_c + \hat{d}^*({}^cT_{*h2}w_c - {}^d\dot{T}_{*h1}), \tag{11}$$

$$w_c = k_w e_3 - \dot{\theta}_d - {}^d\dot{T}_{*h1}(t)\bar{e}_2(t). \tag{12}$$

According to the concurrent learning method in [20,21], we design the adaptive updating law for the depth estimate $\hat{d}^*(t)$ as follows:

$$
\dot{\hat{d}}^* = \text{Proj}\{-\Gamma_1 e_1({}^cT_{*h2}w_c - \dot{T}_{hd1}) + \Gamma_1\Gamma_2 \sum_{k=1}^{N}
$$
$$
\left[\dot{e}_1(t_k) - {}^cT_{*h2}(t_k)w_c(t_k) + {}^d\dot{T}_{*h1}(t_k)\right][-v_c(t_k)]
$$
$$
-\Gamma_1\Gamma_2 \sum_{k=1}^{N}\left[\dot{e}_1(t_k) - {}^cT_{*h2}(t_k)w_c(t_k) + {}^d\dot{T}_{*h1}(t_k)\right]
$$
$$
\left\{\left[\dot{e}_1(t_k) - {}^cT_{*h2}(t_k)w_c(t_k) + {}^d\dot{T}_{*h1}(t_k)\right]\hat{d}^*\right\}\} \tag{13}
$$

wherein $\Gamma_1, \Gamma_2 \in \mathbb{R}^+$ are updating gains. The $N \in \mathbb{Z}^+$ in (13) denotes a positive constant which presents the number of sampling periods from the beginning. $t_k \in [0, t]$ in (13) are the sampling time points.

It can be seen that, the concurrent learning items in the adaptive updating law (13) use data recorded in N sampling periods, thus optimal smoothers can be utilized to accurately estimate values of $\dot{e}_1(t_k)$, ${}^d\dot{T}_{*h1}(t_k)$, $w_c(t_k)$, ${}^cT_{*h2}(t_k)$, $v_c(t_k)$. In this way, we could see an prominent improvement of the parameter estimation [20].

Symbol $\text{Proj}\{\chi\}$ is used to present the projection function as follows:

$$\text{Proj}\{\chi\} = \begin{cases} 0, & \text{for } \hat{d}^* = d^*_{\min} \text{ and } \chi < 0 \\ \chi, & \text{else} \end{cases} \tag{14}$$

wherein $d^*_{\min} \in \mathbb{R}^+$ represents the positive lower bound of $d^*(t)$. It can be seen from (14) that $d^*(t) \geq d^*_{min} > 0$.

As parameters amount is quite small (k_v, k_w, Γ_1, Γ_2), which makes it easy to be tuned to the right performance, the scheme in this paper is suitable for practical application.

From the former deduction in the paper, the closed-loop error dynamics are obtained as follows:

$$\begin{cases} d^*\dot{e}_1 = -k_v e_1 + \bar{e}_2 w_c + \tilde{d}^*(^c T_{*h2} w_c - {}^d \dot{T}_{*h1}), \\ \dot{\bar{e}}_2 = -(e_1 w_c + {}^d \dot{T}_{*h1} e_3), \\ \dot{e}_3 = -k_w e_3 + {}^d \dot{T}_{*h1} \bar{e}_2. \end{cases} \tag{15}$$

4   Stability Analyses

Theorem 1. *Control inputs designed in (11), (12) and the parameter updating law (13) drive the wheeled mobile robot track the trajectory and simultaneously identify the scene depth in the sense that*

$$\lim_{t \to \infty} e_1, e_2, e_3, \tilde{d}^* = 0. \tag{16}$$

Assuming that the time derivative of the desired trajectory satisfies the condition below:

$$\lim_{t \to \infty} {}^d \dot{T}_{*h1} \neq 0. \tag{17}$$

Proof: details are available upon request.

5   Simulation Results

In this part, simulation results are offered to validate the feasibility of the proposed strategy. Four coplanar feature points are randomly arranged to get the homographies.

The controller and depth identification robustness against disturbances is tested by adding image noise with standard deviation $\sigma = 0.1$ pixels. Control parameters are tuned as $k_v = 0.605, k_w = 0.100, \Gamma_1 = \Gamma_2 = 0.900$. N is selected as 100, which means that the simulation progress records data in the first 100 sampling periods.

In the process of writing the program for the adaptive updating law, firstly, arrays that each has 103 array elements are defined for each parameter $e_1(t_k)$ $^d T_{*h1}(t_k)$ $^c T_{*h2}(t_k)$ $w_c(t_k)$ $v_c(t_k)$ and a variate named *counter* is used to denote the array index. After assigning the value of each parameter in each time period to the array, we use a loop statement to sum up the value of each period to get the sum needed. Thus, the whole adaptive updating law be written into the program.

From the motion path of wheeled mobile robot shown in Fig. 2, it can be seen that the mobile robot successfully tracks the desired trajectory. It can be known that in Fig. 3 the current feature points image trajectory tracks the desired feature points image trajectory efficiently. From Fig. 4, it can be seen that the system errors converge to zero. Figure 5 shows $v_c(t)$ and $w_c(t)$ of the wheeled mobile robot. Figure 6 shows that the depth estimate converges to its true value quickly and efficiently, which means the unknown depth information is successfully identified.

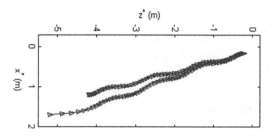

Fig. 2. The desired and current motion pathes of the wheeled mobile robot

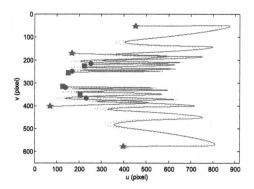

Fig. 3. The image trajectory of feature points [dash lines: desired trajectory; solid lines: current trajectory]

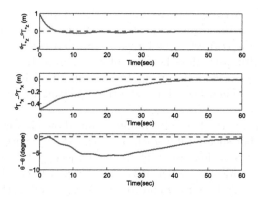

Fig. 4. The evolution of system errors [dash lines: desired value; solid lines: true value]

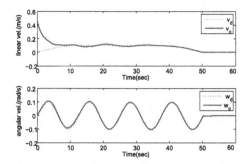

Fig. 5. The velocities of the wheeled mobile robot

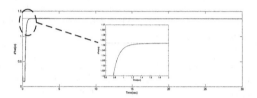

Fig. 6. The evolution of $\hat{d}^*$ by the parameter updating law [dash line: the true value of d^*; solid lines: the estimate value of d^*]

6 Conclusion

In this paper, a scheme for the wheeled mobile robot is developed. The position/orientation of the robot are forced to track a desired time-varying trajectory defined by a prerecorded sequence of images, and meanwhile the unknown depth information is identified simultaneously. By using multiple views of four targets, the homographies are constructed. Then, Euclidean homographies are decomposed into separate translations and rotations, thus the reconstructed Euclidean information can be used to develop controller and adaptive updating law. Then, we design the augmented adaptive updating law to identify the unknown depth from the origin of reference coordinate system to the feature plane. Simulation results are provided to illustrate the performance of the controller.

Acknowledgments. This work is supported in part by National Natural Science Foundation of China under Grant 61603271, and in part by the Natural Science Foundation of Tianjin under Grant 15JCYBJC47800 and Grant 16JCQNJC03800.

References

1. Sun, N., Wu, Y., Fang, Y., Chen, H.: Nonlinear antiswing control for crane systems with double-pendulum swing effects and uncertain parameters: design and experiments. J. IEEE Trans. Autom. Sci. Eng. **PP**, 1–10 (2017)
2. Kriegman, D.J., Triendl, E., Binford, T.O.: Stereo vision navigation in buildings for mobile robots. J. IEEE Trans. Robot. Autom. **5**(6), 792–803 (1989)

3. Thorpe, C.E., Hebert, M., Kanade, T., Shafer, S.: Vision and navigation for the Carnegie-Mellon Navlab. J. IEEE Trans. Pattern Anal. Mach. Intell. **10**(3), 362–373 (1988)
4. Sun, N., Fang, Y., Chen, H., Lu, B.: Amplitude-saturated nonlinear output feedback antiswing control for underactuated cranes with double-pendulum cargo dynamics. J. IEEE Trans. Ind. Electron. **64**(3), 2135–2146 (2017)
5. Hebert, M., Kanade, T.: 3-D vision for outdoor navigation by an autonomous vehicle. In: Proceedings of Image Understanding Workshop, pp. 593–601. MIT Press, San Mateo (1988)
6. Sun, N., Fang, Y., Chen, H., Fu, Y., Lu, B.: Nonlinear stabilizing control for ship-mounted cranes with ship roll and heave movements: design, analysis, and experiments. J. IEEE Trans. Syst. Man Cybern. Syst. **PP**, 1–13 (2017)
7. Assa, A., Janabi-Sharifi, F.: Virtual visual servoing for multicamera pose estimation. J. IEEE/ASME Trans. Mechatron. **20**(2), 789–798 (2015)
8. Li, B., Fang, Y., Hu, G., Zhang, X.: Model-free unified tracking and regulation visual servoing of wheeled mobile robots. J. IEEE Trans. Control Syst. Technol. **24**(4), 328–1339 (2016)
9. MacKunis, W., Gans, N., Kaiser, K., Dixon, W.E.: Unified tracking and regulation visual servo control for wheeled mobile. In: IEEE International Conference on Control Applications, pp. 88–93, Singapore (2007)
10. Hao, M., Sun, Z.: A universal state-space approach to uncalibrated model-free visual servoing. J. IEEE/ASME Trans. Mechatron. **17**(5), 833–846 (2012)
11. Li, B., Fang, Y., Zhang, X.: Visual servo regulation of wheeled mobile robots with an uncalibrated onboard camera. J. IEEE/ASME Trans. Mechatron. **21**(4), 2230–2342 (2016)
12. Wang, H.Y., Itani, S., Fukao, T., Adachi, N.: Image-based visual adaptive tracking control of nonholonomic mobile robots. In: Proceedings IEEE/RSJ International Conference on Intelligent Robots and Systems. IEEE Press, Maui (2001)
13. Mahony, R., Hamel, T., Visual servoing using linear features for under-actuated rigid body dynamics. In: Proceedings IEEE/RSJ International Conference on Intelligent Robots and Systems, pp. 1153–1158. IEEE Press, Maui, Hawaii (2001)
14. Tan, F.X., Guan, X.P., Chen, Y., Sun, D.D.: Tracking control of nonholonomic mobile robot based on unfalsified adaptive PID theory. In: 8th World Congress on Intelligent Control and Automation. IEEE Press, Jinan (2010)
15. Chen, J., Dixon, W., Dawson, M., McIntyre, M.: Homography-based visual servo tracking control of a wheeled mobile robot. J. IEEE Trans. Robot. **22**(2), 406–415 (2006)
16. Liang, X., Wang, H., Liu, Y.H., Chen, W., Hu, G., Zhao, J.: Adaptive task-space cooperative tracking control of networked robotic manipulators without task-space velocity measurements. J. IEEE Trans. Cybern. **46**(10), 2386–2398 (2016)
17. Wang, H., Liu, Y.H., Chen, W., Wang, Z.: A new approach to dynamic eye-in-hand visual tracking using nonlinear observers. J. IEEE/ASME Trans. Mechatron. **16**(2), 387–394 (2011)
18. Wang, H., Liu, Y.H., Chen, W.: Uncalibrated visual tracking control without visual velocity. J. IEEE Trans. Control Syst. Technol. **18**(6), 1359–1370 (2010)
19. Wang, K., Liu, Y., Li, L.: Visual servoing trajectory tracking of nonholonomic mobile robots without direct position measurement. J. IEEE Trans. Robot. **30**(4), 1026–1035 (2014)
20. Parikh, A., Kamalapurkar, R., Chen, H.Y., Dixon, W.E.: Homography based visual servo control with scene reconstruction. In: 54th IEEE Conference on Decision and Control, pp. 6972–6977. IEEE Press, Osaka, Japan (2015)

21. Li, B., Fang, Y., Zhang, X., Shi, W.: Visual servo regulation of wheeled mobile robots with simultaneous depth identification. J. IEEE Trans. Ind. Electron. **PP**, 1 (2017)
22. Faugeras, O.: Three-Dimensional Computer Vision. MIT Press, Cambridge (2001)
23. Zhang, Z., Hanson, A.R.: Scaled Euclidean 3D reconstruction based on externally uncalibrated cameras. In: Proceedings of International Symposium on Computer Vision, pp. 37–42. IEEE Press, Coral Gables (1995)
24. Zhang, X., Fang, Y., Li, B., Wang, J.: Visual servoing of nonholonomic mobile robots with uncalibrated camera-to-robot parameters. J. IEEE Trans. Ind. Electron. **64**(1), 390–400 (2017)

Amended Disturbance Observer Compensation-Based Vibration Control for an All-Clamped Stiffened Plate

Shengquan Li[1(✉)], Juan Li[1,2], Jiawei Zhou[1], Yanqiu Shi[1],
and Shenghua Yuan[1]

[1] School of Hydraulic, Energy and Power Engineering,
Yangzhou University, Yangzhou 225127, China
sqli@yzu.edu.cn
[2] Key Laboratory of Measurement and Control of Complex Systems
of Engineering, Ministry of Education, Southeast University,
Nanjing 210096, China

Abstract. The design of an acceleration sensor based active vibration control for an all-clamped stiffened panel with boned piezoelectric patches is studied. The unmodeled error, harmonic effect and acceleration sensor noise, which degrade the performance of the system or even induce instability in real vibration control system, are considered. An amended disturbance observer plus linear feedback control strategy is developed to suppress these defects. First, the unmodeled error of the current controlled mode, harmonic effects, uncontrolled mode effects and high-frequency measurement noise, etc., are regarded as the lumped disturbances which can be estimated by the disturbance observe (DO), and the estimated value is used for the feed-forward compensation design. Then, a PID controller combing the acceleration sensor feedback is employed for the feedback design. A rigorous analysis is also given to show why the DO can effectively suppress the lumped disturbances. In order to verify the proposed algorithm, the dSPACE real-time simulation platform is used and an experimental platform for the all-clamped stiffened panel smart piezoelectric structure active vibration control is set up. The experimental results demonstrate the effectiveness, practicality and strong anti-disturbance ability of the proposed control strategy.

Keywords: Active vibration control · Disturbance observer · Stiffened plate · Piezoelectric actuator

1 Introduction

Stiffened panel structure, consisting of deep frame, long truss and rivets, is one of the most typical aircraft skin. Substantial value vibration of the aircraft skin structure is easily caused, because the aircraft is suffered from various external disturbances in the process of flight. This kind of long-term vibration of stiffened panel may lead to fatigue crack and structure damage, even hidden trouble of heavy accidents. Piezoelectric materials structure is one of the most attractive smart structures for structural vibration

© Springer International Publishing AG 2017
D. Liu et al. (Eds.): ICONIP 2017, Part VI, LNCS 10639, pp. 334–344, 2017.
https://doi.org/10.1007/978-3-319-70136-3_36

suppression because of good mechanical-electrical coupling characteristics, frequency response and reliability [1].

In order to meet the need for high vibration performance and overcome the complexity of piezoelectric stiffened panel, the issue on active vibration control for this kind of structure is more important than ever. It is well known that linear control schemes, e.g., the optimal linear quadratic regulator (LQR) strategy and velocity negative feedback controller, which should know the precise model a priori, are already widely applied in the vibration control of stiffened panel due to their relative simple implementation [2, 3]. However, the error inevitably exists between the model of actual stiffened structure and theoretical model with unavoidable and unmeasured disturbances, such as harmonic effects, uncontrolled mode effects, etc., as well as external disturbance excitations. This makes it very difficult for this kind of linear vibration controllers to obtain sufficient high performance of these stiffened structures. So, we should rationally design the active control algorithm for vibration suppression of these structures, aiming to possess the robustness of the whole closed-loop system. Recently, with the rapid process in microprocessors, especially microcontroller and modern control theories, many researches have aimed to develop many kinds of active control methods for the smart structures, not merely stiffened panels. And, various active vibration suppression algorithms have been proposed, e.g., intelligent control [4], PID control [5], sliding-mode control [6], and robust control [7]. These algorithms have improved the vibration suppression performance of piezoelectric structures from the different aspects.

To copy with the existing internal dynamic and external disturbances, one efficient way is to introduce a feed-forward compensation part into the controller besides conventional feedback part. Thus a composite control method is obtained. Since, in real stiffened panel applications, it is usually impossible to measure the disturbances directly. So, disturbance estimation techniques have to be developed. The disturbances observer (DO)-based control method was originally presented by Ohnishi in 1987 for servo system [8]. Following this direction, many DO-based control methods have been reported in different applications because of their simplicity and powerful ability to compensate various disturbances, e.g., mechatronics system [8], robotic systems [9], motion control [10], vibration control of hard disk drive systems [11]. Among these results, different kinds of DOs have been developed, including linear DOs, Fuzzy DOs, neural network-based DOs, nonlinear-DOs, etc.

To measure and control vibrations, an accelerometer which unavoidably imports measurement noise, easier to measure than displacement or velocity, is often used as sensor in structure vibration system in stiffened panel vibration systems [12]. The conventional disturbance observer-based (DOB) controller cannot do anything about the measurement noise. In this paper, a composite control approach combining a feed-forward compensation part based on an amended DOB and a feedback regulation part based on PID (amended DOB+PID) is developed to improving the vibration suppression performance of the all-clamped piezoelectric stiffened panel. One novelty of this work lies in that the terms of model mismatches in the closed-loop structure are merged into the disturbance term; meanwhile the amended DOB has the capacity of eliminating the influence of high-frequency measurement noise on the system output. The other novelty lies in that an active vibration composite control algorithm based on

PID and DOB is proposed, thus the PID+DOB approach inherits many advantages of both PID and DOB, moreover the PID feedback control part is optimization by chaotic technique with a transient performance function, which can satisfy the anticipated response of the closed-loop system.

The organization of the paper is as follows. In Sect. 2, the electromechanical model of the all-clamped piezoelectric stiffened panel with acceleration sensor is derived. The design of an amended DOB composite controller is presented in detail in Sect. 3. A rigorous analysis of the general disturbances and high-frequency accelerator measurement noisy observed and compensated for the whole stiffened panel is deduced. In Sect. 4, an experimental apparatus of piezoelectric smart stiffened panel for active vibration control is designed and built up. Experiment is carried out and the performance of the proposed DOB composite approach is given. Finally, conclusions are given in Sect. 5.

2 Mathematical Model

In this section, a mathematical model is derived for stiffened panel structure equipped with an acceleration sensor and piezoelectric (PZT) actuator. Here, an accelerometer and one PZT patch are used as sensor and actuator, respectively. The surface mounted PZT actuator patch is collocated in the middle of panel, and accelerometer is mounted near the PZT patch, shown in Fig. 1.

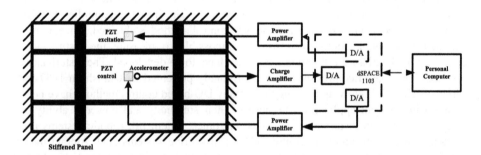

Fig. 1. Schematic diagram of the experimental set-up

Almost all engineering structures, including beams, panels and shell, are a continuum, but their vibration can be expressed as the superposition of modal vibrations using modal coordinator. For active vibration control, the independent modal space control method is adopted, so we should obtain the modal state equation. When using classical assumptions on analytical structural modeling, and finite element modeling, the dynamical behavior equations of a piezoelectric structure can be written as [13]:

$$m\ddot{z} + c\dot{z} + k^e z = f_p + f_e \tag{1}$$

where z is the displacement vector, m, c and k^e are the mass, damping and stiffness matrices, respectively. f_p is the electrically dependent part of the force applied by piezoelectric elements on the structure, f_e represents the external force applied to the structure.

The piezoelectric elements bonded on the host structure ensure the electromechanical coupling described by Eqs. (2) and (3)

$$f_p = -\alpha V \tag{2}$$

$$I = \alpha \dot{z} - C_o \dot{V} \tag{3}$$

where α is the electromechanical coupling coefficient and V is the piezoelectric element voltage vector. I is the outgoing current from piezoelectric elements, C_o is the blocked capacitance of the piezoelectric elements. After modal analysis, the natural frequency and modal function can be obtained. The natural frequency of the first mode is 163.6 Hz.

The physical model Eq. (1) can be described by modal equation after the following change of variables:

$$z = \phi \eta$$

where ϕ and η are the modal function and modal coordinator of the structure mode, respectively. Ignoring the effect of the force for excitation (f_e), the model function of the piezoelectric structure is shown as following,

$$M\ddot{\eta} + C\dot{\eta} + K^E \eta = -\alpha_s V_s - \alpha_a V_a \tag{4}$$

$$I = \theta_s^T \dot{\eta} - C_o \dot{V} \tag{5}$$

where M, C and K^E are the mass, damping and stiffness in modal coordinator, respectively. $\theta = \phi^T \alpha$ is the modal electromechanical coupling coefficient. In order to further simply the Eq. 4, the structural modal mass M is defined by:

$$M = \phi^T m \phi = I \tag{6}$$

So, the Eq. (4) can be rewritten as:

$$\ddot{\eta} + C_\prime \dot{\eta} + K_r^E \eta = -\theta_s V_s - \theta_a V_a \tag{7}$$

So the modal damping and the modal stiffened of Eq. (7) can be written as:

$$C_\prime = diag(2\pi\xi f_{sc}) \tag{8}$$

$$K_r^E = diag((2\pi f_{sc})^2) \tag{9}$$

where f_{sc} is the eigen frequency when all the piezoelectric elements are in short circuit. In an open circuit or when the sensor voltage is monitored with a voltage amplifier, sensor intensity is null, therefore, the Eq. (5) can be rewritten as following:

$$\theta_s^T \eta - C_o V_s = 0 \tag{10}$$

and by reintroducing the Eq. (10) in Eq. (7):

$$\ddot{\eta} + C_i \dot{\eta} + (K_r^E + \theta_s (C_o)^{-1} \theta_s^T) \eta = -\theta_a V_a \tag{11}$$

there

$$K_r^E + \theta_s (C_o)^{-1} \theta_s^T = diag(2\pi f_{oc}) \tag{12}$$

with f_{oc} is the eigen frequency when all the piezoelectric elements are in open circuit. The first natural frequency is considered in this paper, so the electromechanical coupling coefficient of first mode can be calculated, whether it is an actuator or a sensor:

$$\theta = 2\pi \sqrt{C_o (f_{oc}^2 - f_{sc}^2)} \tag{13}$$

Linear system (11) and current Eq. (5) can be rewritten in modal state equation:

$$\begin{cases} \dot{x} = Ax + Bu \\ y_p = C_p x \end{cases} \quad x = \begin{bmatrix} \eta \\ \dot{\eta} \end{bmatrix} \tag{14}$$

where x being the state vector, and $u = V_a$ is the control signal, $y_p = V_s$ is the output of piezoelectric patches. A, B, and C_p are the state matrices shown as following:

$$A = \begin{bmatrix} 0 & 1 \\ -K_r^E + \theta_s (C_o)^{-1} \theta_s^T & -C_i \end{bmatrix}, B = \begin{bmatrix} 0 \\ \theta_a \end{bmatrix}, C_p = \begin{bmatrix} C_o^{-1} \theta_s^t & 0 \end{bmatrix}$$

And the measured acceleration signal by the fixed accelerometer is:

$$y_a = C_a \dot{x} \tag{15}$$

with $C_a = \begin{bmatrix} 0 & \phi_{(x_s,y_s)} \end{bmatrix}$, where x_s, y_s are the distances between the fixed points of the accelerometer and the middle of the stiffened panel.

3   Control Strategy

3.1   Amended DOB Based Control System

The block diagram of the amended DOB+PID scheme for piezoelectric stiffened panel is shown in Fig. 2. In Fig. 2, $G(s)$ and $G_o(s)$ are the transfer functions of the actual stiffened and the normal plant of the structure, respectively. And r u_o, u, d, $\hat{d}$, ξ

represent reference signal, feedback controller signal, composite controller signal, general disturbances, estimation of the disturbance and measurement noise, respectively. Compared with the classical DOB-based control system, another compensator $f_2(s)$ is added to compensate the feedback signal of system output aiming to high-frequency measurement noise. The transfer function between the system output and the reference, the disturbances, and measurement noise are given, respectively, as following:

$$G_{yr}(s) = \frac{G(s)C_c(s)}{G(s)C_c(s) + 1 + (f_1(s)G_o^{-1}(s) - C_c(s)f_2(s))(G(s) - G_o(s))} \tag{16}$$

$$G_{yd}(s) = \frac{1 - (f_1(s)G_o^{-1}(s) - C_c(s)f_2(s))G_o(s)}{G(s)C_c(s) + 1 + (f_1(s)G_o^{-1}(s) - C_c(s)f_2(s))(G(s) - G_o(s))} \tag{17}$$

$$G_{y\xi}(s) = \frac{G(s)\left[(f_1(s)G_o^{-1}(s) - C_c(s)f_2(s)) + C_c(s)\right]}{G(s)C_c(s) + 1 + (f_1(s)G_o^{-1}(s) - C_c(s)f_2(s))(G(s) - G_o(s))} \tag{18}$$

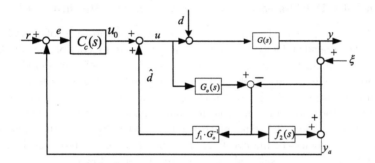

Fig. 2. The schematic diagram of the amended DOB-based controller

In general, to eliminate the influence of disturbances and measurement noise on the output, the conditions should be considered as $G_{yd}(s) = 0$ and $G_{y\xi}(s) = 0$.

That is to say,

$$\begin{cases} 1 - (f_1(s)G_o^{-1}(s) - C_c(s)f_2(s))G_o(s) = 0 \\ G_o(s)\left[(f_1(s)G_o^{-1}(s) - C_c(s)f_2(s)) + C_c(s)\right] = 0 \end{cases} \tag{19}$$

Then, we have

$$\begin{cases} f_1(s)G_o^{-1}(s) - C_c(s)f_2(s) = G_o^{-1}(s) \\ f_1(s)G_o^{-1}(s) - C_c(s)f_2(s) = -C_c(s) \end{cases} \tag{20}$$

It is necessary at different frequency ranges to simultaneously eliminate the disturbance and measurement noise, because the disturbance and measurement noise respectively belong to the low and the high frequency ranges. So the Eq. (20) can be written as:

$$
\begin{cases}
f_1(s)G_o^{-1}(s) - C_c(s)f_2(s) = G_o^{-1}(s), & \omega \in (0, \omega_d) \\
f_1(s)G_o^{-1}(s) - C_c(s)f_2(s) = -C_c(s) & \omega \in (\omega_\xi, \infty)
\end{cases}
\tag{21}
$$

where $\omega_d < \omega_\xi$. And we should rationally choose the solutions $f_1(s)$ and $f_2(s)$ to satisfy the Eq. (21). The stiffened panel is a stable system, so we choose the nominal plant $G_o(s)$ is also stable minimum-phase plant. That is to say the inverse of $G_o(s)$ exists as well as stable. Thus, there are $f_1(s)G_o^{-1}(s) = G_o^{-1}(s)$ and $f_2(s) = 0$ in the low frequency range $\omega \in (0, \omega_d)$; while there are $f_1(s) = 0$ and $f_2(s) = 1$ in the high frequency range $\omega \in (\omega_d, \infty)$. Consequently, the amended DOB-based control system not only guarantees perfect anti-disturbances capability in the low frequency, but also eliminates the influence of the high-frequency measurement noise, because the structure of DOB-based controller have been improved.

3.2   Amended DOB-Based Controller for Piezoelectric Stiffened Panel

The method of this work focuses on obtaining well performance of vibration suppression. An amended DOB+PID scheme is proposed to control the all-clamped piezoelectric stiffened panel. Note that the stiffened panel considered her is a second-order system because of the first natural frequency of the piezoelectric structure being studied. From the Separation Principle, we can respectively deign the feedback part and feed-forward part. The feed-forward channel consists of amended DOB approach shown in Sect. 3.1. Fine effects can be achieved by tuning the parameters of PID and the parameters of the two filters $f_1(s)$ and $f_2(s)$ in the proposed DOB. Here $f_1(s)$ and $f_2(s)$ are selected as a second-order-low-pass filter and a second-order-high-pass filter with the stead-state gain of 1 in them relative frequency range, respectively. The structure of the filters are expressed as

$$
f_1(s) = \frac{1}{(\tau_1 s + 1)^2}
\tag{22}
$$

$$
f_2(s) = \frac{k_o s^2}{s^2 + \varphi \omega_0 s + \omega_o^2}
\tag{23}
$$

It should be pointed out that the implementation of this proposed DOB is rather simple, thus the introduction of feed-forward compensation part does not increase much computational complexity.

4   Experimental Results

To valuate the performance of the proposed amended DOB+PID composite method, experimental research was conducted on a piezoelectric stiffened panel. To implement the proposed collocated acceleration sensor based composite controller, an experiment setup was constructed, as shown in Fig. 3. The whole vibration control algorithms, including the amended DOB technique, are implemented by the dSPACE1103 board with a sample frequency of 10 kHz. The control algorithm is simulated on Matlab2009a. The accelerometer is bonded at the middle of the panel. There are two PZT patches: one is used for the external excitation, the other is for the control.

Fig. 3. Experimental test setup

The resulting response of whole control system is measured by a collocated accelerometer. The control input, calculated on the basis of the sensor signals, is amplified and then applied to the actuator. The whole closed-loop sampling period is 100 μs. The control parameters of PID controller are chosen by chaotic algorithms.

The time-domain closed-loop vibration response of the first mode suppressed by the amended DOB-based composite control algorithm is shown in Fig. 4. And its control voltage applied to the PZT actuator for the first mode is in Fig. 5. From the time–domain experiment results, it can be seen that the amended DOB+PID control algorithm can decrease to nearly one sixth of without control. In order to further explain the capability of the proposed method, the frequency-domain response of the first mode is shown in Fig. 6. And the spectrum of the normalized sensor signal is expressed in decibel as follows:

$$\text{The decibel value} = 20\log_{10}(f(y/y_R))$$

where f is the symbol of Fourier Transformation and y_R is the reference output of acceleration sensor for normalization. The value of y_R is set to 1 v in the following sections so that 0 dB is equivalent to 1 mm and-20 dB is equivalent to 0.1 v.

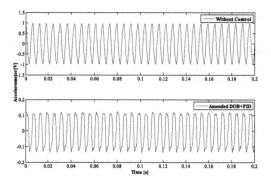

Fig. 4. Time-domain response of the first mode with proposed amended DOB+PID

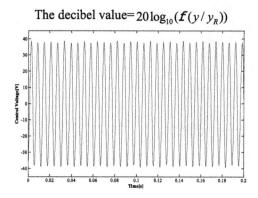

Fig. 5. Control voltage of the proposed amended DOB+PID

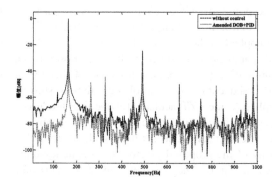

Fig. 6. Frequency-domain response with proposed amended DOB+PID

Figure 6 shows the corresponding frequency for the case in which the plate is excited at the first resonant frequency (163.6 Hz). The results shown in Fig. 6 illustrate that many other modes, the harmonic frequencies and measurement noise come out when the stiffened panel is excited at the frequency 163.6 Hz, because of the complexity of the panel. Figure 6 indicates that the response amplitude values of first natural frequency of 163.6 Hz are very small after proposed control method. The vibration amplitude is reduced by 17.35 dB at the frequency of 163.6 Hz. Figure 6 also shows that the response amplitude values of frequencies of 327.3 Hz, 491 Hz and 654.6 Hz, i.e., the double-frequency, triple-frequency and quadruple-frequency of the nature frequency, are reduced by 2.9 dB, 7.2 dB and 6.7 dB, respectively. The frequencies of 449.4 Hz and 654.6 Hz maybe easy to provoked when the all-clamped piezoelectric stiffened panel is excited by the piezoelectric actuator at 163.6 Hz, i.e., the first resonance frequency. Obviously,their response values have been suppressed very well. And, the high frequencies of 749.9 Hz, 818.3 Hz, 850 Hz, 950.2 Hz and 981.9 Hz maybe injected from accelerometer. Figure 6 shows these high frequencies effects also have been attenuated to the relatively small values. Obviously, the various harmonic interferences caused by the first nature frequencies and effects of high-frequency of accelerometer noise can be compensated well by the amended DOB. It's the reason that the amended DOB+PID have very well performance with robust stability.

However, there is an exceptional frequency of 263.8 Hz which is the second natural mode of the stiffened panel. Figure 6 and Table 1 show that the second mode has provoked after first nature vibration mode suppression. And the spillover phenomenon more or less exists in active vibration system, because the truncated modes are ignored for easy vibration suppression. Moreover, the design of proposed active vibration algorithm in Sect. 3, shows that the proposed amended DOB-based vibration controller aims to improve the performance of vibration suppression. The proposed active vibration controller simultaneously deals with the relative low-frequency disturbances and high-frequency accelerometer noise by improved the architecture of the DOB-based controller. The control spillover of other modes can be regard as one kind of the disturbances. For actual vibration control, we should rationally choose the frequency ranges of filters to obtain a compromise between the disturbances and the accelerometer noise. So, this is the reason that the decibel value of second mode of the all-clamped stiffened panel appeared to bigger after control. However, combining the time-domain response curve, Figs. 4 and 6 show that the stability of the whole closed-loop system is maintained very well with good performance. So, the new control system structure has raised a way to overcome the conflict between performance and stability in the traditional active vibration controller.

5 Conclusion

In this study, a new active vibration suppression method based on an amended DOB-based composite controller is proposed for the kinds of disturbances, i.e., effects of harmonic frequencies, error between the actual mode and nominal mode, and high-frequency accelerometer noise. This strategy combines a PID and a DOB for the all-clamped piezoelectric stiffened. Two kinds of techniques have been introduced to enhance the vibration suppressing property of the active control system. Firstly, an amended DOB, whose structure is different from the conventional DOB, has been introduced to observer the general disturbances and eliminate the high-frequency accelerometer noise on the system output, simultaneously. Second, in order to auto-acquire the appropriate parameters of PID feedback control for suppressing the smart piezoelectric stiffened panel, the chaotic algorithm is introduced to achieve a good vibration suppression performance. The experimental result of the stiffened panel vibration damping shows that proposed DOB-based strategy can achieve a very well performance with whole closed-loop stabling. Meanwhile, the amended DOB-based control system structure has the potential to overcome the conflict between stability and performance in the traditional active vibration control.

Acknowledgments. This work was supported in part by the National Natural Science Foundation of China (Grant nos. 51405428, 61773335), Natural Science Foundation of Jiangsu Province (Grant nos. BK20140490, BK20171289), the Open Project Program of Ministry of Education Key Laboratory of Measurement and Control of CSE, (Grant nos. MCCSE2015A01 and MCCSE2016A01)

References

1. Qiu, J., Ji, H.: The application of piezoelectric materials in smart structures in China. Int. J. Aeronaut. Space Sci. **11**(4), 266–284 (2010)
2. Mukherjee, A., Joshi, S., Ganguli, A.: Active vibration control of piezolaminated stiffened plates. Compos. Struct. **55**(4), 435–443 (2002)
3. Balamurugan, V., Narayanan, S.: Finite element modeling of stiffened piezolaminated plates and shells with piezoelectric layers for active vibration control. Smart Mater. Struct. **19**(3), 1–21 (2010)
4. Lin, J.: An active vibration absorber of smart panel by using a decomposed parallel fuzzy control structure. Eng. Appl. Artif. Intell. **18**(8), 985–998 (2005)
5. Suhariyono, A., Goo, N.S., Park, H.C.: Use of lightweight piezo-composite actuators to suppress the free vibration of an aluminum beam. J. Intell. Mater. Syst. Struct. **19**(1), 101–112 (2008)
6. Qiu, Z., Han, J., Zhang, X., et al.: Active vibration control of a flexible beam using a non-collocated acceleration sensor and piezoelectric patch actuator. J. Sound Vib. **326**(3–5), 438–455 (2009)
7. Kar, I., Miyakura, T., Seto, K.: Bending and torsional vibration control of a flexible plate structure using HN-based robust control law. IEEE Trans. Control Syst. Technol. **8**(3), 545–553 (2000)
8. Ohnishi, K.: A new servo method in mechatronics. Trans. Jpn. Soc. Electr. Eng. **107**(D), 83–86 (1987)
9. Chen, W., Balance, D.: Nonlinear disturbance observer for two-link robotic manipulators. IEEE Trans. Ind. Electron. **47**(4), 932–938 (2000)
10. Sun, N., Fang, Y., Chen, H., et al.: Amplitude-saturated nonlinear output feedback antiswing control for underactuated cranes with double-pendulum cargo dynamics. IEEE Trans. Ind. Electron. **64**(3), 2135–2146 (2017)
11. Sun, N., Fang, Y., Chen, H., et al.: Nonlinear stabilizing control for ship-mounted cranes with disturbances induced by ship roll and heave movements: design, analysis, and experiments. IEEE Trans. Syst. Man Cybern. Syst. (in press). doi:10.1109/TSMC.2017. 2700393
12. Ye, J., Ding, Y.: Vibration test and analysis of an aircraft maintenance hangar under multi-support excitations. Adv. Struct. Eng. **13**(4), 695–706 (2010)
13. Ji, H., Qiu, J., Zhu, K., et al.: Multi-modal vibration control using a synchronized switch based on a displacement switching threshold. Smart Mater. Struct. **18**(1), 1–8 (2009)

Dynamics Analysis of Underactuated Cherrypicker Systems with Friction

Yiming Wu[1,2], Yifa Liu[1,2], Ning Sun[1,2(✉)], and Yongchun Fang[1,2]

[1] Institute of Robotics and Automatic Information System (IRAIS),
College of Computer and Control Engineering, Nankai University, Tianjin, China
{ymwu,yifaliu}@mail.nankai.edu.cn, {sunn,fangyc}@nankai.edu.cn
[2] Tianjin Key Laboratory of Intelligent Robotics (tjKLIR),
Nankai University, Tianjin, China

Abstract. The cherrypicker system has long mechanical arms and an unactuated bucket, which helps raise up workers to implement difficult aerial works on high up towers, power lines, and buildings. However, due to the gravity and inertia, the bucket has residual vibration which brings safety concerns. In order to design controllers to suppress the oscillation, this paper first provides a dynamic model of a two-armed cherrypicker system with friction by using Lagrange's modeling method and also derives the matrix form dynamic equation. Numerical simulation results verify the feasibility of the model.

Keywords: Underactuated system · Cherrypicker · Lagrange's dynamics · System modeling

1 Introduction

Currently, advanced control of nonlinear systems has been a hot research direction [1–13]. Among them, an important branch is named as underactuated systems, which are widely used in practical applications. Specifically, as shown in Fig. 1, as a typical representative, a cherrypicker system usually has more than two long arms and one bucket, which exhibits underactuated characteristics. The underactuated characteristics bring many merits, such as low costs and high flexibility. The cherrypicker system is a special underactuated system. While the arms raising up, the unactuated bucket oscillates back and forth due to the gravity and inertia. Considering that the oscillation of the bucket is likely to bring safety concerns, for the cherrypicker system, we also have some important control problems to solve: (1) The system should be able to realize accurate orientation when raising up people. (2) It is also necessary to make sure that the residual vibration is eliminated effectively.

In the past few years, studies on underactuated cherrypicker systems are still few and open. References [14–16] design the mechanical construction of different cherrypicker-like aerial lifts. Reference [17] derives the system model by

---

Yiming Wu and Yifa Liu contribute equally to this paper.

© Springer International Publishing AG 2017
D. Liu et al. (Eds.): ICONIP 2017, Part VI, LNCS 10639, pp. 345–354, 2017.
https://doi.org/10.1007/978-3-319-70136-3_37

Fig. 1. Different kinds of cherrypickers.

using rotation matrices and uses a common proportional-derivative (PD) controller to reach the expected joint angles. Additionally, in order to eliminate the residual vibration, besides the conventional way of improving the transmission-mechanism structure, few control strategies are proposed. Reference [18] presents a motion control architecture to realize trajectory tracking and vibration suppression. Moreover, some input shaping methods are proposed in [19–21], which eliminate the residual vibration by shaped trajectories. However, for the cherrypicker system in the presence of friction, there is still no general dynamic model. In this paper, the dynamic model with friction terms and its matrix form of a two-armed cherrypicker system are first obtained based on Lagrange's modeling method, which is fundamental for subsequent high performance controller design and analysis. Then, in order to verify the feasibility of the proposed model, numerical simulation results are provided.

2   System Modeling

A schematic illustration of the cherrypicker is shown in Fig. 2, where $\{x_g O z_g\}$ denotes the truck-fixed coordinate and the system parameters are defined in Table 1.

Based on Lagrange's modeling method, we first calculate the entire energy of the cherrypicker system. Since the bucket is usually designed without lateral deviations, the slewing angle θ_1 is not considered for simplicity. Then the total kinetic energy K can be divided into three parts in the sense that $K = K_1 + K_2 + K_M$, where K_1, K_2, K_M denote the kinetic energies of the lower arm, the upper arm, and the bucket, respectively. After some physical analysis and mathematical arrangements, K_1, K_2, K_M can be obtained as follows:

$$K_1 = \frac{1}{6} m_1 L_1^2 \dot{\theta}_2^2, \tag{1}$$

$$K_2 = \frac{1}{2} m_2 \left(L_1^2 + \frac{1}{3} L_2^2 + L_1 L_2 \cos \theta_3 \right) \dot{\theta}_2^2 + \frac{1}{6} m_2 L_2^2 \dot{\theta}_3^2$$
$$+ \frac{1}{2} m_2 \left(\frac{2}{3} L_2^2 + L_1 L_2 \cos \theta_3 \right) \dot{\theta}_2 \dot{\theta}_3, \tag{2}$$

$$K_M = \frac{1}{2} M \left(L_1^2 + L_2^2 + 2 L_1 L_2 \cos \theta_3 \right) \dot{\theta}_2^2 + \frac{1}{2} M L_2^2 \dot{\theta}_3^2$$
$$+ \frac{1}{2} M \left(2 L_1 L_2 \cos \theta_3 + 2 L_2^2 \right) \dot{\theta}_2 \dot{\theta}_3$$
$$+ M L_1 L \dot{\phi} \sin \left(\phi - \theta_2 \right) \dot{\theta}_2 + M L_2 L \dot{\phi} \sin \left(\phi - \theta_2 - \theta_3 \right) \dot{\theta}_2$$
$$+ M L_2 L \dot{\phi} \sin \left(\phi - \theta_2 - \theta_3 \right) \dot{\theta}_3 + \frac{1}{2} M L^2 \dot{\phi}^2. \tag{3}$$

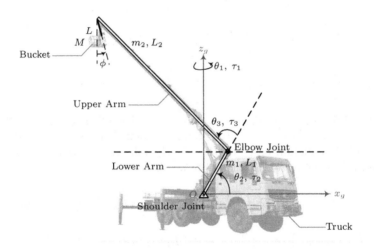

Fig. 2. A schematic illustration of a kind of cherrypicker system.

Similarly, the total potential energies of the system can also be divided into three parts as $P = P_1 + P_2 + P_M$, where P_1, P_2, and P_M are the potential energy of the lower arm, the upper arm and the bucket. By setting the truck platform as the zero potential energy surface, the total potential energy P can be easily obtained such that:

$$P = \frac{1}{2} m_1 g L_1 \sin \theta_2 + m_2 g \left[L_1 \sin \theta_2 + \frac{L_2}{2} \sin \left(\theta_2 + \theta_3 \right) \right]$$
$$+ M g \left[L_1 \sin \theta_2 + L_2 \sin \left(\theta_2 + \theta_3 \right) - L \cos \phi \right]. \tag{4}$$

Table 1. The physical significance of the system parameters.

Parameters	Physical significance	Units
M, m_1, m_2	Bucket, lower arm and upper arm masses	kg
L_1, L_2, L	Lower arm, upper arm, and bucket rope lengths	m
$\theta_1, \theta_2, \theta_3$	Slewing, shoulder joint, and elbow joint angles	rad
ϕ	Bucket rotational angle	rad
g	Gravity constant	N/kg
τ_1, τ_2, τ_3	Input torques	N·m

Then, based on (3) and (4), by considering the friction of each joint, we can derive Lagrange's function $\mathcal{L} = K - P$ and establish the system dynamic model by using the following Lagrange's equations:

$$\frac{d}{dt}\frac{\partial \mathcal{L}}{\partial \dot{\theta}_2} - \frac{\partial \mathcal{L}}{\partial \theta_2} = \tau_2 + d_1, \tag{5}$$

$$\frac{d}{dt}\frac{\partial \mathcal{L}}{\partial \dot{\theta}_3} - \frac{\partial \mathcal{L}}{\partial \theta_3} = \tau_3 + d_2, \tag{6}$$

$$\frac{d}{dt}\frac{\partial \mathcal{L}}{\partial \dot{\phi}} - \frac{\partial \mathcal{L}}{\partial \phi} = d_3, \tag{7}$$

where the friction terms $d_1(t), d_2(t), d_3(t)$ are defined as $d_1 = -\lambda_1 \dot{\theta}_2, d_2 = -\lambda_2 \dot{\theta}_3, d_3 = -\lambda_3 \dot{\phi}$ with the positive damping coefficients $\lambda_1, \lambda_2, \lambda_3$. After some mathematical deduction based on (5)–(7), the following system dynamic model of the cherrypicker system is finally obtained:

$$\left[\left(\frac{1}{3}m_1 + m_2 + M\right)L_1^2 + \left(\frac{1}{3}m_2 + M\right)L_2^2 + (m_2 + 2M)L_1L_2\cos\theta_3\right]\ddot{\theta}_2$$

$$+ \left[\left(\frac{1}{3}m_2 + M\right)L_2^2 + \left(\frac{1}{2}m_2 + M\right)L_1L_2\cos\theta_3\right]\ddot{\theta}_3$$

$$+ \left[ML_1L\sin(\phi - \theta_2) + ML_2L\sin(\phi - \theta_2 - \theta_3)\right]\ddot{\phi}$$

$$- 2L_1L_2\left(\frac{1}{2}m_2 + M\right)\sin\theta_3 \cdot \dot{\theta}_2\dot{\theta}_3 - L_1L_2\left(\frac{1}{2}m_2 + M\right)\sin\theta_3 \cdot \dot{\theta}_3^2$$

$$+ \left[ML_1L\cos(\phi - \theta_2) + ML_2L\cos(\phi - \theta_2 - \theta_3)\right]\dot{\phi}^2$$

$$+ \left(\frac{1}{2}m_1 + m_2 + M\right)gL_1\cos\theta_2$$

$$+ \left(\frac{1}{2}m_2 + M\right)gL_2\cos(\theta_2 + \theta_3) = \tau_2 + d_1, \tag{8}$$

$$\left(\frac{1}{3}m_2 + M\right) L_2^2 \ddot{\theta}_3 + \left[\left(\frac{1}{3}m_2 + M\right) L_2^2 + \left(\frac{1}{2}m_2 + M\right) L_1 L_2 \cos\theta_3\right] \ddot{\theta}_2$$

$$+ M L_2 L \sin\left(\phi - \theta_2 - \theta_3\right) \ddot{\phi} + \left(\frac{1}{2}m_2 + M\right) L_1 L_2 \sin\theta_3 \cdot \dot{\theta}_2^2$$

$$+ M L_2 L \cos\left(\phi - \theta_2 - \theta_3\right) \dot{\phi}^2 + \left(\frac{1}{2}m_2 + M\right) g L_2 \cos\left(\theta_2 + \theta_3\right) = \tau_3 + d_2, \quad (9)$$

$$[M L_1 L \sin\left(\phi - \theta_2\right) + M L_2 L \sin\left(\phi - \theta_2 - \theta_3\right)] \ddot{\theta}_2$$
$$+ M L_2 L \sin\left(\phi - \theta_2 - \theta_3\right) \cdot \ddot{\theta}_3 + M L^2 \ddot{\phi}$$
$$- [M L_1 L \cos\left(\phi - \theta_2\right) + M L_2 L \cos\left(\phi - \theta_2 - \theta_3\right)] \dot{\theta}_2^2$$
$$- M L_2 L \cos\left(\phi - \theta_2 - \theta_3\right) \cdot \dot{\theta}_3^2$$
$$- 2 M L_2 L \cos\left(\phi - \theta_2 - \theta_3\right) \cdot \dot{\theta}_2 \dot{\theta}_3 + M g L \sin\phi = d_3, \quad (10)$$

The dynamic model shown in (8)–(10) can usually represented by the following matrix form dynamic equation:

$$M(q)\ddot{q} + C(q,\dot{q})\dot{q} + G(q) = U + d, \quad (11)$$

where $q \in \mathbb{R}^3$ is the system state vector defined as $q = [\,\theta_2,\,\theta_3,\,\phi\,]^\mathsf{T}$. The matrices $M(q) \in \mathbb{R}^{3\times3}$, $C(q,\dot{q}) \in \mathbb{R}^{3\times3}$, $G(q) \in \mathbb{R}^3$, $U \in \mathbb{R}^3$, and $d \in \mathbb{R}^3$ denote the inertial matrix, the centripetal-Coriolis matrix, the gravity vector, the control input vector, and the friction vector. Specifically, the expression of $M(q)$ is given as:

$$M(q) = \begin{bmatrix} m_{11}, m_{12}, m_{13} \\ m_{21}, m_{22}, m_{23} \\ m_{31}, m_{32}, m_{33} \end{bmatrix},$$

where

$$m_{11} = \left(\frac{1}{3}m_1 + m_2 + M\right) L_1^2 + \left(\frac{1}{3}m_2 + M\right) L_2^2 + (m_2 + 2M) L_1 L_2 \cos\theta_3,$$

$$m_{12} = m_{21} = \left(\frac{1}{3}m_2 + M\right) L_2^2 + \left(\frac{1}{2}m_2 + M\right) L_1 L_2 \cos\theta_3,$$

$$m_{13} = m_{31} = M L_1 L \sin\left(\phi - \theta_2\right) + M L_2 L \sin\left(\phi - \theta_2 - \theta_3\right),$$

$$m_{22} = \left(\frac{1}{3}m_2 + M\right) L_2^2,$$

$$m_{23} = m_{32} = M L_2 L \sin\left(\phi - \theta_2 - \theta_3\right),$$

$$m_{33} = M L^2.$$

The matrix $C(q,\dot{q})$ is expressed as

$$C(q,\dot{q}) = \begin{bmatrix} c_{11}, c_{12}, c_{13} \\ c_{21}, 0, c_{23} \\ c_{31}, c_{32}, 0 \end{bmatrix} \quad (12)$$

where

$$c_{11} = -L_1 L_2 \left(\frac{1}{2}m_2 + M\right) \sin\theta_3 \cdot \dot\theta_3,$$

$$c_{12} = -L_1 L_2 \left(\frac{1}{2}m_2 + M\right) \sin\theta_3 \cdot \left(\dot\theta_2 + \dot\theta_3\right),$$

$$c_{13} = \left[ML_1 L \cos\left(\phi - \theta_2\right) + ML_2 L \cos\left(\phi - \theta_2 - \theta_3\right)\right] \dot\phi,$$

$$c_{21} = \left(\frac{1}{2}m_2 + M\right) L_1 L_2 \sin\theta_3 \dot\theta_2,$$

$$c_{23} = ML_2 L \cos\left(\phi - \theta_2 - \theta_3\right) \dot\phi,$$

$$c_{31} = -ML_1 L \cos\left(\phi - \theta_2\right) \cdot \dot\theta_2 - ML_2 L \cos\left(\phi - \theta_2 - \theta_3\right) \cdot \left(\dot\theta_2 + \dot\theta_3\right),$$

$$c_{32} = -ML_2 L \cos\left(\phi - \theta_2 - \theta_3\right) \cdot \left(\dot\theta_2 + \dot\theta_3\right),$$

and the vectors $G(q), U, d$ are expressed as follows:

$$G(q) = \begin{bmatrix} \left(\frac{1}{2}m_1 + m_2 + M\right) gL_1 \cos\theta_2 + \left(\frac{1}{2}m_2 + M\right) gL_2 \cos\left(\theta_2 + \theta_3\right) \\ \left(\frac{1}{2}m_2 + M\right) gL_2 \cos\left(\theta_2 + \theta_3\right) \\ MgL \sin\phi \end{bmatrix},$$

$$U = \left[\tau_1, \tau_2, 0\right]^\top,$$

$$d = \left[-\lambda_1 \dot\theta_2, -\lambda_2 \dot\theta_3, -\lambda_3 \dot\phi\right]^\top.$$

Obviously, $M(q)$ is a positive definite symmetric matrix and $\dot M(q) - 2C(q, \dot q)$ is a skew symmetric matrix which satisfies that

$$\xi^\top \left(\dot M(q) - 2C(q, \dot q)\right) \xi = 0, \ \forall \xi \in \mathbb{R}^3. \tag{13}$$

The property shown in (13) will be utilized in the ensuing analysis.

3   Controller Design

We consider the following storage energy of the cherrypicker system:

$$E = \frac{1}{2}\dot q^\top M(q)\dot q + MgL(1 - \cos\phi). \tag{14}$$

Then, by taking the time derivative of E, we have

$$\dot E = \dot q^\top M(q)\ddot q + \frac{1}{2}\dot q^\top \dot M(q)\dot q + MgL\dot\phi \sin\phi$$

$$= \dot q^\top \left(U - G(q) + d\right) + MgL\dot\phi \sin\phi$$

$$= \dot\theta_2 \left[\tau_2 - \left(\frac{1}{2}m_1 + m_2 + M\right) gL_1 \cos\theta_2 - \left(\frac{1}{2}m_2 + M\right) gL_2 \cos\left(\theta_2 + \theta_3\right)\right]$$

$$+ \dot\theta_3 \left[\tau_3 - \left(\frac{1}{2}m_2 + M\right) gL_2 \cos\left(\theta_2 + \theta_3\right)\right] - \lambda_1 \dot\theta_2^2 - \lambda_2 \dot\theta_3^2 - \lambda_3 \dot\phi^2, \tag{15}$$

where (11) and (13) are used. Because all the system parameters are exactly known, for $\tau_2(t)$ and $\tau_3(t)$, we can naturally design the following controller:

$$\tau_2 = k_{p1}\left(\theta_{2r} - \theta_2\right) + k_{d1}(\dot{\theta}_{2r} - \dot{\theta}_2)$$
$$+ \left(\frac{1}{2}m_1 + m_2 + M\right)gL_1\cos\theta_2 + \left(\frac{1}{2}m_2 + M\right)gL_2\cos\left(\theta_2 + \theta_3\right), \quad (16)$$

$$\tau_3 = k_{p2}\left(\theta_{3r} - \theta_3\right) + k_{d2}(\dot{\theta}_{3r} - \dot{\theta}_3) + \left(\frac{1}{2}m_2 + M\right)gL_2\cos\left(\theta_2 + \theta_3\right), \quad (17)$$

where θ_{2r}, θ_{3r} denote the expected angular values and $k_{p1}, k_{d1}, k_{p2}, k_{d2}$ are positive control gains. The designed controller is a PD-based controller which cancels out the gravity-induced terms.

4   Simulation Results

In this paper, the dynamic model of the cherrypicker system is simulated by applying the MATLAB/Simulink software. In order to testify the feasibility of the model and the controller (16) and (17), we have implemented numerical simulations under the following two cases:

- **Case 1.** Considering the natural status of the system without any control, the system parameters are set as $m_1 = 2\,\text{kg}$, $m_2 = 2\,\text{kg}$, $m = 2\,\text{kg}$, $L_1 = 1\,\text{m}$, $L_2 = 1\,\text{m}$, $L = 0.05\,\text{m}$, $g = 9.8\,\text{m/s}^2$, the damping coefficients are given as $\lambda_1 = \lambda_2 = \lambda_3 = 0.01$, and the initial angular values are chosen as $\theta_2(0) = -\pi/2$, $\theta_3(0) = \pi/6$, $\phi(0) = 0$.[1]
- **Case 2.** Considering applying the designed controller shown in (16) and (17) to the system model with the same system parameters and damping coefficients as **Case 1**. Specifically, the initial angular values are chosen as $\theta_2(0) = 0$, $\theta_3(0) = \pi$, $\phi(0) = 0$ (which are the same as the initial conditions of a real cherrypicker), the expected joint angles are such that $\theta_{2r} = \pi/6$, $\theta_{3r} = 5\pi/6$, and the control gains are given as $k_{p1} = 3000$, $k_{d1} = 40$, $k_{p2} = 2500$, $k_{d2} = 100$.

The simulation results are shown in Figs. 3 and 4. In Fig. 3, the system states oscillate persistently, which is accordance with the behavior of the real system without control. In Fig. 4, the designed PD-based controller with gravity compensation is applied to the system. The joint angles converge to their expected values $\theta_{2r} = \pi/6$, $\theta_{3r} = 5\pi/6$ correctly within $1\,\text{s}$, while the bucket keeps oscillating until $4\,\text{s}$ due to the inertia. The residual vibration brings safety concerns to workers and also makes the control problem difficult to solve. The simulation results of the two cases indicate that the proposed dynamic model shown in

---

[1] In **Case 1**, the simulation results are only used to testify the correctness of the model without considering the angular constraints. Actually, the joint angle constraints of a practical cherrypicker (usually $-\pi/2 \le \theta_1 \le \pi/2, 0 \le \theta_2 \le \pi/2, -\pi \le \theta_3 \le \pi$) can be easily realized by mechanical design.

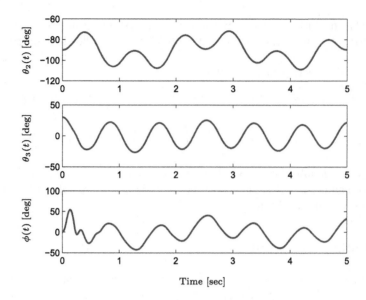

Fig. 3. The simulation results without any controller.

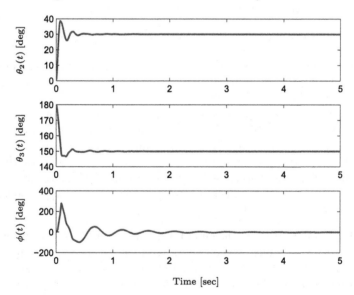

Fig. 4. The simulation results of the PD controller with gravity compensation.

(8)–(10) is able to reflect the real characteristics of the cherrypicker system with friction and is feasible to be used directly for designing more advance controllers in future works. In addition, the results in Fig. 4 reflect the effectiveness of the designed controller in (16) and (17).

5   Conclusions

This paper first provides a general dynamic model of a kind of two-armed cherrypicker system with friction by using Lagrange's modeling method and also obtains the matrix form dynamic equation. A PD-based controller with gravity compensation is utilized and numerical simulation results verify the feasibility of the presented model. In future works, based on the proposed dynamic model of the cherrypicker system, numerous advanced control methods can be designed directly for tackling different control problems.

Acknowledgments. This work is supported by the National Natural Science Foundation of China under Grant 61503200, the Natural Science Foundation of Tianjin under Grant 15JCQNJC03800, and the China Postdoctoral Science Foundation under Grant 2016M600186 and under Grant 2017T100153.

References

1. Yang, C., Li, Z., Li, J.: Trajectory planning and optimized adaptive control for a class of wheeled inverted pendulum vehicle models. IEEE Trans. Cybern. **43**, 24–36 (2013)
2. Sun, N., Fang, Y., Chen, H., Lu, B.: Amplitude-saturated nonlinear output feedback antiswing control for underactuated cranes with double-pendulum cargo dynamics. IEEE Trans. Industr. Electron. **64**, 2135–2146 (2017)
3. Li, B., Fang, Y., Hu, G., Zhang, X.: Model-free unified tracking and regulation visual servoing of wheeled mobile robots. IEEE Trans. Control Syst. Technol. **24**, 1328–1339 (2016)
4. Zhang, M., Ma, X., Chai, H., Rong, X., Tian, X., Li, Y.: A novel online motion planning method for double-pendulum overhead cranes. Nonlinear Dyn. **85**, 1079–1090 (2016)
5. Sun, N., Wu, Y., Fang, Y., Chen, H.: Nonlinear antiswing control for crane systems with double pendulum swing effects and uncertain parameters: design and experiments. IEEE Trans. Autom. Sci. Eng. (2017, in press). doi:10.1109/TASE.2017.2723539
6. Cheng, L., Wang, Y., Ren, W., Hou, Z.-G., Tan, M.: Containment control of multiagent systems with dynamic leaders based on a PI^n-type approach. IEEE Trans. Cybern. **46**, 3004–3017 (2016)
7. Sun, N., Yang, T., Fang, Y., Lu, B., Qian, Y.: Nonlinear motion control of underactuated 3-dimensional boom crane systems with hardware experiments. IEEE Trans. Industr. Inform. (2017, in press). doi:10.1109/TII.2017.2754540
8. Bai, L., Zhou, Q., Wang, L., Yu, Z.: Observer-based adaptive control for stochastic nonstrict-feedback systems with unknown backlash-like hysteresis. Int. J. Adapt. Control Signal Process. (2017, in press). doi:10.1002/acs.2780
9. Sun, N., Wu, Y., Fang, Y., Chen, H., Lu, B.: Nonlinear continuous global stabilization control for underactuated RTAC systems: design, analysis, and experimentation. IEEE/ASME Trans. Mechatron. **22**, 1104–1115 (2017)
10. Li, S., Li, J.: Output predictor-based active disturbance rejection control for a wind energy conversion system with PMSG. IEEE Access **5**, 5205–5214 (2017)

11. Li, S., Li, J., Mo, Y.: Piezoelectric multimode vibration control for stiffened plate using ADRC-based acceleration compensation. IEEE Trans. Industr. Electron. **61**, 6892–6902 (2014)
12. Sun, N., Fang, Y., Chen, H., Fu, Y., Lu, B.: Nonlinear stabilizing control for ship-mounted cranes with disturbances induced by ship roll and heave movements: design, analysis, and experiments. IEEE Trans. Syst. Man Cybern. Syst. (2017, in press). doi:10.1109/TSMC.2017.2700393
13. He, W., Chen, Y., Yin, Z.: Adaptive neural network control of an uncertain robot with full-state constraints. IEEE Trans. Cybern. **46**, 620–629 (2016)
14. Lee, S., Gil, M., Lee, K., Lee, S., Han, C.: Design of a ceiling glass installation robot. In: 24th International Symposium on Automation and Robotic in Construction, pp. 247–252. Construction Automation Group, I.I.T. Madras (2007)
15. Hong, Y., Han, S.-H., Lee, J.-J., Hong, D.-P., Kim, Y.-M.: Structural analysis of boom system in 42 m aerial platform truck. Key Eng. Mater. **353–358**, 2817–2821 (2007)
16. Ge, M., Li, E., Liang, Z., Tan, M.: Design of a hydraulic-cylinder-pressure-based anti-overturning module for aerial work platforms. In: Fourth International Conference on Intelligent Computation Technology and Automation, Shenzhen, Guangdong, China, pp. 974–977 (2011)
17. Hernandez, E.C.: Dynamic characterization and analysis of aerial lifts. Georgia Institute of Technology (2012)
18. Yuan, Q.H., Lew, J., Piyabongkarn, D.: Motion control of an aerial work platform. In: American Control Conference, pp. 2873–2878. Hyatt Regency Riverfront, St. Louis (2009)
19. Maleki, E., Pridgen, B., Xiong, J.Q., Singhose, W.: Dynamic analysis and control of a portable cherrypicker. Am. Soc. Mech. Eng. **2**, 477–482 (2010)
20. Pridgen, B., Maleki, E., Singhose, W., Seering, W., Glauser, U., Kaufmann, L.: A small-scale cherrypicker for experimental and educational use. In: American Control Conference, O'Farrell Street, San Francisco, CA, USA, pp. 681–686 (2011)
21. Hongxia, J., Wanli, L., Singhose, W.: Using two-mode input shaping to suppress the residual vibration of cherrypickers. In: Third International Conference on Measuring Technology and Mechatronics Automation, Shanghai, China, pp. 1091–1094 (2011)

A PD Controller of Flexible Joint Manipulator Based on Neuro-Adaptive Observer

Xin Liu[1], Chenguang Yang[1(✉)], Min Wang[1], and Wei He[2]

[1] Key Laboratory of Autonomous Systems and Networked Control,
College of Automation Science and Engineering,
South China University of Technology, Guangzhou 510640, China
x.liu_scut@qq.com, cyang@ieee.org, auwangmin@scut.edu.cn
[2] School of Automation and Electrical Engineering,
University of Science and Technology Beijing, Beijing 100083, China
hewei.ac@gmail.com

Abstract. Due to inevitable uncertainties associated with the dynamics and kinematics of flexible joint manipulators, accurate models would not be available for control design. Furthermore, practically we may face the problem that state variables required by the controller are not measurable. In this paper, we focus on the control system design using a neural network observer to solve the aforementioned unmeasurable problem. A state observer of a general multivariable nonlinear systems based on neural network is proposed. It can be applied to systems with unknown dynamic model. To test the effectiveness of the state observer we design a PD controller combining with the observer proposed for the flexible joint manipulator whose model is unknown. The stability of the controlled system is shown by Lyapunov method. To test and verify the effectiveness of the state controller simulation studies are performed.

Keywords: State observer · RBF Neural network · Flexible joint manipulator system

1 Introduction

In recent years, robotic technology has achieved a great development. Increasing new technologies and new methods are applied to robots. Along with the progress of technology and towards new applications, Customers no longer satisfy with the safety of rigid manipulators. Then researchers put forward a new type of manipulator system, flexible joint manipulator system. Flexible joints provide the manipulator with a compliant behaviour so if the flexible joint manipulators encounter obstacles during operation, the contact force between manipulators and obstacles may be relatively slight and manipulators may stop immediately. Thus, in contrast to rigid manipulator the safety of flexible joint manipulator is relatively high. Recent years flexible joint manipulators have been widely applied in the field of teaching and engineering. In [1], They build a variable stiffness

© Springer International Publishing AG 2017
D. Liu et al. (Eds.): ICONIP 2017, Part VI, LNCS 10639, pp. 355–364, 2017.
https://doi.org/10.1007/978-3-319-70136-3_38

joint for a manipulator, the leaf springs are used to generate the compliance and two actuators are used to control the position and stiffness of the joint. In [2] a servo-controller which can estimate unknown parameters online is proposed to regulate the driving torque of flexible joint manipulators. However, considering the complexity and uncertainty of the joint flexible manipulator model, the exact mathematical model of the system is difficult to obtain. Neural network is an applicable method to approximate unknown models. In [3–5], the neural networks are used to compensate for uncertainties of dynamic models for the robot arms.

Due to constraints of sensor deployment, we may not be able to measure all the state variables, then the controller based on state feedback is unavailable. Thus, observers which can estimate the state variables unmeasurable are necessary. Conventional nonlinear observers are generally applicable to systems whose models are precisely known [6], while we consider systems with unknown models. Thanks to the adaptive behavior, neural network has been a powerful tool for state observation with unknown models. In [7] an observer for a general nonlinear system is built, a feedforward neural network is adopted to deduce the gain of the observer. In [8], a scheme based on neural networks is presented to estimate the states of a nonlinear system with a single-input-single-output model. In [9], a recurrent neural network for a nonlinear system with a multiple-input-multiple-output model is presented. The update rate of the weights is based on the back propagation (BP) algorithm. [10]. An RBF network is adopted to approximate the nonlinearities of the dynamic model.

In this paper we build the observer based on RBF network, then we combined the observer with a PD controller to control the flexible joint manipulator which the angular position and angular velocity of motor shaft is unknown. First we propose an observer based on RBF network for a general nonlinear system with unknown model in Sect. 2. Then we propose a PD controller with gravity compensation for the flexible joint manipulator whose parts of model is unknown in Sect. 3. Finally, in Sect. 4 we perform simulation studies to test the effectiveness of the proposed controller.

2   Neuro-Adaptive Observer

2.1   The Proposed Neuro-Adaptive Observer

First we propose a state observer based on RBF neural network. The model of a general nonlinear system is

$$\dot{x}(t) = Ax + h(x, u)$$
$$y(t) = Cx(t) \tag{1}$$

where $u \in R^{M_u}$ is the input, $y \in R^{M_y}$ is the output, $x \in R^{M_x}$ are the states of the system, $h(x, u)$ is unknown, A is a Hurwitz matrix and C is the output matrix of the system. We propose the model of observer as:

$$\dot{\hat{x}}(t) = A\hat{x} + \hat{h}(\hat{x}, u) + G(y - C\hat{x})$$
$$\hat{y}(t) = C\hat{x}(t) \tag{2}$$

where $\hat{x}$ is the state variables of the observer, and $G \in R^{n \times m_y}$ is the observer gain. We select G such that $A - CG$ is a Hurwitz matrix. We model the unknown parts of the system through RBF neural network. Thus, $h(x, u)$ can be represented as:

$$h(x, u) = W^T S(\overline{x}) + \epsilon(x) \tag{3}$$

where W is the weight matrix of the output layer, $\overline{x} = [x^T, u^T]^T$, $\epsilon(x)$ is the approximation error of the neural network. $S(\cdot)$ is the transfer function of the hidden neurons which is a Gaussian function: $S_j(\overline{x}) = exp(-\frac{\|\overline{x} - c_j\|^2}{b_j^2})$. We assume there is the upper bound on weight matrices W such that $\|W\| \leq W_{max}$. And as we all know there is a bound of Gaussian function $\|S(\overline{x})\| \leq S_{max}$. We assume $h(x, u)$ can be approximated by RBF neural network. Then we can rewrite (2)

$$\dot{\hat{x}}(t) = A\hat{x} + \hat{W}^T S(\hat{\overline{x}}) + G(y - C\hat{x})$$
$$\hat{y}(t) = C\hat{x}(t). \tag{4}$$

We define the weight error $\tilde{W} = \hat{W} - W$ and state variable error $\tilde{x} = \hat{x} - x$. Then according to (4) we can obtain

$$\dot{\tilde{x}}(t) = AG\tilde{x} + \tilde{W}^T S(\hat{\overline{x}}) + w(t)$$
$$\tilde{y}(t) = C\tilde{x}(t) \tag{5}$$

where $AG = A - GC$, $w(t) = W^T[S(\hat{\overline{x}}) - S(\overline{x})] + \epsilon(x)$, $w_{max} > 0$ satisfy $\|w(t)\| \leq w_{max}$ due to the boundedness of W and $S(\overline{x})$.

2.2   Stability Analysis

First we define the adaptive update rate of weights as follow

$$\dot{\hat{W}} = \Gamma[S(\hat{\overline{x}})\tilde{y}^T C - \gamma\|C\tilde{x}\|\hat{W}] \tag{6}$$

where $\Gamma = \Gamma^T$ is a positive definite matrix. Since the optimal weight W is a constant matrix thus we obtain $\dot{W} = 0$. In terms of the weight errors $\tilde{W} = \hat{W} - W$ we obtain

$$\dot{\tilde{W}} = \dot{\hat{W}} = \Gamma[S(\hat{\overline{x}})\tilde{y}^T C - \gamma\|C\tilde{x}\|(\tilde{W} + W)] = \Gamma[S(\hat{\overline{x}})\tilde{x}^T C^T C - \gamma\|C\tilde{x}\|(\tilde{W} + W)]. \tag{7}$$

The Lyapunov function is selected as follow

$$V_1 = \frac{1}{2}\tilde{x}^T P\tilde{x} + \frac{1}{2}tr(\tilde{W}^T \Gamma^{-1}\tilde{W}) \tag{8}$$

where P is a positive definite matrix. Then, we define a variable $Q = -(AG^T P + PAG)$ where AG is a Hurwitz matrix, Q is positive definite matrix. According to the inequality $tr[\tilde{W}^T(-W - \tilde{W})] \leq W_{max}\|\tilde{W}\| - \|\tilde{W}\|^2$ and

$tr(\tilde{W}^T S(\hat{\tilde{x}})\tilde{x}^T C^T C) \leq S_{max}\|C\|^2\|\tilde{x}\|\|\tilde{W}\|$. We can obtain

$$
\begin{aligned}
\dot{V}_1 =& -\frac{1}{2}\tilde{x}^T Q\tilde{x} + \tilde{x}^T P\tilde{W}^T S(\hat{\tilde{x}}) + \tilde{x}^T Pw + tr[\tilde{W}^T S(\hat{\tilde{x}})\tilde{x}^T C^T C - \tilde{W}^T \gamma\|C\tilde{x}\| \\
& (\tilde{W} + W)] \\
\leq& -\frac{1}{2}\lambda_{min}(Q)\|\tilde{x}\|^2 + S_{max}\|P\|\|\tilde{x}\|\|\tilde{W}\| + w_{max}\|P\|\|\tilde{x}\| + S_{max}\|C\|^2\|\tilde{x}\|\|\tilde{W}\| \\
& + \gamma W_{max}\|C\|\|\tilde{x}\|\|\tilde{W}\| - \gamma\|C\|\|\tilde{x}\|\|\tilde{W}\|^2 \\
\leq& -\frac{1}{2}\lambda_{min}(Q)\|\tilde{x}\|^2 + [-\gamma\|C\|(\|\tilde{W}\| - \frac{S_{max}\|P\| + S_{max}\|C\|^2 + \gamma\|C\|W_{max}}{2\gamma\|C\|})^2 \\
& + \frac{(S_{max}\|P\| + S_{max}\|C\|^2 + \gamma\|C\|W_{max})^2}{4\gamma\|C\|}]\|\tilde{x}\| + w_{max}\|P\|\|\tilde{x}\|
\end{aligned}
\tag{9}
$$

where $\lambda_{min}(Q) > 0$ is the smallest eigenvalue of Q.
Since $-\gamma\|C\|(\|\tilde{W}\| - \frac{S_{max}\|P\| + S_{max}\|C\|^2 + \gamma\|C\|W_{max}}{2\gamma\|C\|})^2 < 0$, we can obtain

$$
\begin{aligned}
\dot{V}_1 <& -\frac{1}{2}\lambda_{min}(Q)\|\tilde{x}\|^2 + \frac{(S_{max}\|P\| + S_{max}\|C\|^2 + \gamma\|C\|W_{max})^2}{4\gamma\|C\|}\|\tilde{x}\| \\
& + w_{max}\|P\|\|\tilde{x}\| \\
=& L.
\end{aligned}
\tag{10}
$$

Let us define $M = \frac{(S_{max}\|P\| + S_{max}\|C\|^2 + \gamma\|C\|W_{max})^2}{4\gamma\|C\|} > 0$. We can obtain

$$
L = -\frac{1}{2}\lambda_{min}(Q)\|\tilde{x}\|^2 + w_{max}\|P\|\|\tilde{x}\| + M\|\tilde{x}\|.
\tag{11}
$$

And if $\|\tilde{x}\| > \frac{2Pw_{max} + 2M}{\lambda_{min}(Q)} = v$ then $\dot{V}_1 < L < 0$. When $\tilde{x} > v$, $\dot{V}_1 < 0$ is negative, then $\tilde{x}$ is bounded. By the rational choice of parameters γ and AG we can keep v get any small value. Then, we notice that $\tilde{x}$, W, C and $S(\hat{\tilde{x}})$ are all bounded, and $\gamma > 0$. According to (7) we obtain a system whose input $\Gamma[S(\hat{\tilde{x}})\tilde{x}^T C^T C - \gamma\|C\tilde{x}\|W]$ is bounded and state matrix of the system $-\gamma\|C\tilde{x}\|$ is a Hurwitz matrix. Thus, this system is stable, $\tilde{W}$ is also bounded.

3   Controller of the Flexible Joint Manipulator Based on Neuro-Adaptive Observer

3.1   Problem Formulation

First, we establish precise mathematical model of flexible joint manipulator as follows [11].

$$
M(q)\ddot{q} + C(q,\dot{q})\dot{q} + g(q) = \tau + DK^{-1}\dot{\tau} + \tau_e
\tag{12}
$$

$$
B\ddot{\theta} + \tau + DK^{-1}\dot{\tau} = u_m
\tag{13}
$$

$$
\tau = K(\theta - q)
\tag{14}
$$

The angular position of motor shaft is $\theta \in \mathbb{R}^n$, the angular position of manipulator shaft is $q \in \mathbb{R}^n$. $M(q) \in \mathbb{R}^{n \times n}$ is the inertia matrix of the manipulator, $C(q, \dot{q}) \in \mathbb{R}^{n \times n}$ is the Coriolis and centripetal vector of the manipulator, and $g(q) \in \mathbb{R}^n$ is the gravity vector of the manipulator. The torque provided by spring-damper is denoted by $\tau_a = \tau + DK^{-1}\dot{\tau} = K(\theta - q) + D(\dot{\theta} - \dot{q})$. The spring torque denoted by $\tau \in \mathbb{R}^n$ is defined by (14) where $K = diag(k_i) \in \mathbb{R}^{n \times n}$ is the joint stiffness matrix which is diagonal and positive definite, and $D = diag(d_i) \in \mathbb{R}^{n \times n}$ is the joint damping matrix which is diagonal and positive semi-definite. The external torques acting on the robot are denoted by $\tau_e \in \mathbb{R}^n$. The relationship between the spring-damper torque τ and the motor torque $u_m \in \mathbb{R}^n$ is shown in (13) where $B = diag(b_i) \in \mathbb{R}^{n \times n}$ is the motor inertia matrix which is diagonal and positive definite.

3.2   Torque and Position Controller Design

There are many control methods of robots have been proposed in recent years such as adaptive neural network control [12,13], robust control [14] and cooperative control [15]. For systems with unknown models, PD control is a simple and effective method. In this section we propose a PD controller for flexible joint manipulator, through the controller combining with the observer we can control the flexible joint manipulator system without the accurate mathematical expression of the model parameters. First we assume we can not measure the angular position θ and angular velocity $\dot{\theta}$ of motor shaft. We use the observer proposed in the previous section estimate θ and $\dot{\theta}$. We put u_m and $y = (q, \dot{q})^T$ which is considered as the input and the output of the manipulator respectively into the observer (4). Thus, we define $\hat{\theta} - \theta = \tilde{\theta}$, $\dot{\hat{\theta}} - \dot{\theta} = \tilde{\dot{\theta}}$. According to the previous section we can obtain $\|\tilde{\theta}\|$ is bounded and by the rational choice of parameters we can keep convergence radius get any small value. Thus, we assume $\hat{\theta}$ and $\dot{\hat{\theta}}$ can substitute for θ and $\dot{\theta}$. In order to simplify the analysis we divide the designing process of the joint state feedback controller into two steps, torque feedback and position feedback. First we consider the torque feedback, we propose a controller of the form

$$u_m = BB_\theta^{-1}u + \tau + DK^{-1}\dot{\tau} - BB_\theta^{-1}(\tau + D_s K^{-1}\dot{\tau}) \qquad (15)$$

where $u \in \mathbb{R}$ is an intermediate variable of the controller, D_s is a diagonal matrix and B_θ is a positive definite diagonal matrix which satisfies $b_{\theta i} < b_i$. Then we consider the position feedback, we obtain a controller of the form

$$u = -K_\theta \hat{\tilde{\theta}} - D_\theta \dot{\hat{\theta}} + g(q_d) \qquad (16)$$

where $g(q_d)$ is the gravity compensation based on the desired position q_d. The desired value of θ is given by $\theta_d = q_d + K^{-1}g(q_d)$ then the error is defined as $\hat{\tilde{\theta}} = \hat{\theta} - \theta_d$. Then if we substitute (16) into (15) we can obtain

$$u_m = -K_P \hat{\tilde{\theta}} - K_D \dot{\hat{\theta}} + K_T(g(q_d) - \tau) - K_S \dot{\tau} + g(q_d) \qquad (17)$$

where $K_P = BB_\theta^{-1}K_\theta$, $K_D = BB_\theta^{-1}D_\theta$, $K_T = BB_\theta^{-1} - I$ and $K_S = (BB_\theta^{-1}D_s - D)K^{-1}$. From (17) we can see the controller can control the manipulator system without the priori models $M(q)$ and $C(q, \dot{q})$.

3.3   Stability Analysis

Theorem: Considering the flexible joint manipulator described by (12)–(14), the controller described by (17), the observer described by (4) and the adaptive update rates of weights described by (6). For any bounded initial conditions, there exists suitable parameters G, K_θ, D_θ, Γ and γ such that the proposed control scheme guarantees:

(1) all the variables in the controlled system are bounded;
(2) the tracking errors converges to a arbitrarily small neighborhood of zero.

Proof: First we bulid the Lyapunov function for the whole system consists of controller and observer as follow

$$V(v) = \frac{1}{2}\tilde{v}^T P\tilde{v} + \frac{1}{2}tr(\tilde{W}^T \Gamma^{-1}\tilde{W}) + V_2(v, \dot{v}) \tag{18}$$

where $v = (\hat{\theta}, q)^T$, $\tilde{v} = (\hat{\theta} - \theta, 0)^T$ and

$$V_2(v) = \frac{1}{2}(\dot{q}M(q)\dot{q} + \hat{\dot{\theta}}B_\theta\hat{\dot{\theta}}) + U_p(v) - U_p(v_d) - \frac{\partial U_p(v_d)}{\partial v}(v - v_d). \tag{19}$$

$U_P(v)$ is defined as $U_P(v) = \frac{1}{2}(\hat{\theta} - q)^T K(\hat{\theta} - q) + \frac{1}{2}\hat{\dot{\theta}}K_\theta\hat{\dot{\theta}} + V_g(q)$ where $V_g(q)$ which is the potential function of gravity torques $g(q)$ satisfies $g(q) = (\frac{\partial V_g(q)}{\partial q})^T$. Then we can obtain the time derivative of V_2

$$\dot{V}_2(\dot{v}) = -\hat{\dot{\theta}}^T D_\theta\hat{\dot{\theta}} - (\hat{\dot{\theta}} - \dot{q})^T D(\hat{\dot{\theta}} - \dot{q}) + \hat{\dot{\theta}}^T(D - D_s)(\hat{\dot{\theta}} - \dot{q}) \tag{20}$$

If $D > \frac{1}{4}(D - D_s)^T D_\theta(D - D_s)$, $\dot{V}_2(\dot{v})$ is negative definite. According to the stability analysis of observer, we can see if $\|\tilde{v}\| > \frac{2Pv_m}{\lambda_{min}(Q)} = d$ then $\frac{1}{2}\tilde{v}^T P\tilde{v} + \frac{1}{2}tr(\tilde{W}^T \Gamma^{-1}\tilde{W}) < 0$. Then we can obtain the Lyapunov function $V(v)$ is negative definite. Then we can obtain all the signal of system is bounded.

4   Simulation

In order to prove the effectiveness of the observer and controller, We perform simulation studies with MATLAB software.

First of all we build the model of double joint manipulator as follows

$$\begin{bmatrix} m_{11} & m_{12} \\ m_{12} & m_{22} \end{bmatrix}\ddot{q} + \begin{bmatrix} -c\dot{q}_2 & -c(\dot{q}_1 + \dot{q}_2) \\ c\dot{q}_1 & 0 \end{bmatrix}\dot{q} + \begin{bmatrix} g_1 \\ g_2 \end{bmatrix} = \tau + DK^{-1}\dot{\tau} \tag{21}$$

$$B\ddot{\theta} + \tau + DK^{-1}\dot{\tau} = u_m \qquad (22)$$

$$\tau = K(\theta - q) \qquad (23)$$

where

$$m_{11} = (m_1 + m_2)r_1^2 + m_2 r_2^2 + 2m_2 r_1 r_2 cosq_2 \qquad (24)$$

$$m_{12} = m_2 r_2^2 + m_2 r_1 r_2 cosq_2 \qquad (25)$$

$$m_{22} = m_2 r_2^2 \qquad (26)$$

$$c = m_2 r_1 r_2 sinq_2 \qquad (27)$$

$$g_1 = (m_1 + m_2)r_1 cosq_2 + m_2 r_2 cos(q_1 + q_2) \qquad (28)$$

$$g_2 = m_2 r_2 cos(q_1 + q_2) \qquad (29)$$

We choose $m_1 = 1$, $m_2 = 1$, $r_1 = 0.5$, $r_2 = 0.5$, $B = \begin{bmatrix} 1 & 0 \\ 0 & 1 \end{bmatrix}$, $D = \begin{bmatrix} 1 & 0 \\ 0 & 1 \end{bmatrix}$ and $K = \begin{bmatrix} 1 & 0 \\ 0 & 1 \end{bmatrix}$.

The reference trajectory is

$$q_{d1} = q_{d2} = sin(t) \qquad (30)$$

Then, we select the initial values of each variable as $q_1 = 0$, $q_2 = 0$, $\theta_1 = 0$, $\theta_2 = 0$, parameters of controller as $B_\theta = 0.1B = \begin{bmatrix} 0.1 & 0 \\ 0 & 0.1 \end{bmatrix}$, $D_s = \begin{bmatrix} 1 & 0 \\ 0 & 1 \end{bmatrix}$, $K_\theta = \begin{bmatrix} 1000 & 0 \\ 0 & 1000 \end{bmatrix}$ and $D_\theta = \begin{bmatrix} 10 & 0 \\ 0 & 10 \end{bmatrix}$, parameters of observer as

$$A = \begin{bmatrix} -20 & 1 & 1 & 1 \\ 0 & -20 & 1 & 1 \\ 0 & 0 & -20 & 1 \\ 0 & 0 & 0 & -20 \end{bmatrix} \quad G = \begin{bmatrix} 1200 \\ 1200 \\ 1200 \\ 1200 \end{bmatrix}$$

Results of simulation are shown as follows:

Figures 1 and 2 show the relationship between the actual output q and the reference trajectory q_d. From Figs. 1 and 2 we can see that the actual output q can accurately track reference trajectory q_d within $5s$. Figures 3, 4, 5 and 6 show the relationship between the estimated value $\hat{\theta}$ and $\dot{\hat{\theta}}$ from observer and the actual state variable θ and $\dot{\theta}$. It is clear that the states of the observer can follow the actual state variable accurately and quickly. To sum up, we can obtain the PD controller based on RBF network observer is able to achieve good tracking performance in the presence of unknown model.

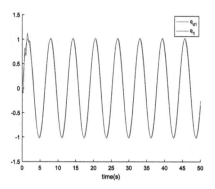

Fig. 1. q_1 and q_{d1}

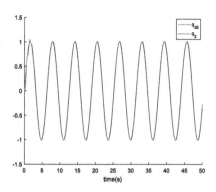

Fig. 2. q_2 and q_{d2}

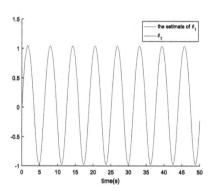

Fig. 3. θ_1 and $\hat{\theta}_1$

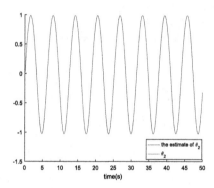

Fig. 4. θ_2 and $\hat{\theta}_2$

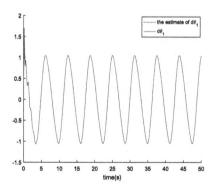

Fig. 5. $\dot{\theta}_1$ and $\dot{\hat{\theta}}_2$

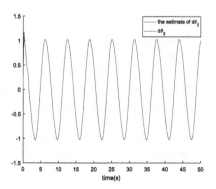

Fig. 6. $\dot{\theta}_2$ and $\dot{\hat{\theta}}_2$

5 Conclusion

In this paper we propose a PD controller with gravity compensation based on neuro-adaptive observer for the flexible joint manipulator with unknown model. The effect of observer is estimating the state variables unmeasurable from the manipulator. RBF network is used to construct the unknown dynamic model. Stability of the controller combining with observer is rigorously proved by the Lapunov method. To test the effectiveness of the proposed controller Simulation studies is performed. From the results of simulation we can confirm the reliable performance of the proposed controller.

Acknowledgments. This work was partially supported by National Nature Science Foundation (NSFC) under Grant 61473120, Guangdong Provincial Natural Science Foundation 2014A030313266 and International Science and Technology Collaboration Grant 2015A050502017, Science and Technology Planning Project of Guangzhou 201607010006, State Key Laboratory of Robotics and System (HIT) Grant SKLRS-2017-KF-13, and the Fundamental Research Funds for the Central Universities.

References

1. Choi, J., Hong, S., Lee, W., Kang, S., Kim, M.: A robot joint with variable stiffness using leaf springs. IEEE Trans. Rob. **27**(2), 229–238 (2011)
2. Navarro-Alarcon, D., Wang, Z., Yip, H.M., Liu, Y.H.: A method to regulate the torque of flexible-joint manipulators with velocity control inputs. In: IEEE International Conference on Robotics and Biomimetics, pp. 2437–2442 (2014)
3. Yang, C., Jiang, Y., Li, Z., He, W., Su, C.Y.: Neural control of bimanual robots with guaranteed global stability and motion precision. IEEE Trans. Ind. Inf. **PP**(99), 1 (2016)
4. Yang, C., Wang, X., Cheng, L., Ma, H.: Neural-learning-based telerobot control with guaranteed performance. IEEE Trans. Cybern. **PP**(99), 1–12 (2016)
5. Yang, C., Li, Z., Cui, R., Xu, B.: Neural network-based motion control of an under-actuated wheeled inverted pendulum model. IEEE Trans. Neural Netw. Learn. Syst. **25**(11), 2004 (2014)
6. Nicosia, S., Tomei, P., Tornamb, A.: An Approximate Observer for a Class of Nonlinear Systems. Elsevier Science Publishers B.V., Amsterdam (1989)
7. Ahmed, M.S., Riyaz, S.H.: Dynamic observers—a neural net approach. J. Intell. Fuzzy Syst. **9**(1–2), 113–127 (2000). IOS Press
8. Kim, Y.H., Lewis, F.L., Abdallah, C.T.: Nonlinear observer design using dynamic recurrent neural networks. In: Proceedings of the IEEE Conference on Decision and Control, vol. 1, pp. 949–954 (1996)
9. Abdollahi, F., Talebi, H.A., Patel, R.V.: A stable neural network observer with application to flexible-joint manipulators. In: International Conference on Neural Information Processing, vol. 4, pp. 1910–1914 (2006)
10. Wu, Q., Saif, M.: Neural adaptive observer based fault detection and identification for satellite attitude control systems. In: Proceedings of the American Control Conference, vol. 2, pp. 1054–1059 (2005)
11. Spong, M.W.: Modeling and control of elastic joint robots. ASME J. Dyn. Sys. Meas. Contr. **109**(4), 310–319 (1987)

12. He, W., Chen, Y., Yin, Z.: Adaptive neural network control of an uncertain robot with full-state constraints. IEEE Trans. Cybern. **46**(3), 620 (2016)
13. Chen, M., Tao, G.: Adaptive fault-tolerant control of uncertain nonlinear large-scale systems with unknown dead zone. IEEE Trans. Cybern. **46**(8), 1851–1862 (2015)
14. Chen, M., Shi, P., Lim, C.C.: Robust constrained control for mimo nonlinear systems based on disturbance observer. IEEE Trans. Autom. Control **60**(12), 3281–3286 (2015)
15. He, W., Ge, S.S.: Cooperative Control of a Nonuniform Gantry Crane with Constrained Tension. Pergamon Press Inc., Tarrytown (2016)

Transient Tracking Performance Guaranteed Neural Control of Robotic Manipulators with Finite-Time Learning Convergence

Tao Teng[1], Chenguang Yang[1(✉)], Wei He[2], Jing Na[3], and Zhijun Li[1]

[1] Key Laboratory of Autonomous Systems and Networked Control,
College of Automation Science and Engineering,
South China University of Technology, Guangzhou 510640, China
`tao.teng@foxmail.com`, `cyang@ieee.org`, `auzli@scut.edu.cn`
[2] School of Automation and Electrical Engineering,
University of Science and Technology Beijing, Beijing 100083, China
`hewei.ac@gmail.com`
[3] Kunming University of Science and Technology,
Kunming 650093, China
`najing25@163.com`

Abstract. An adaptive finite-time (FT) neural control scheme is proposed for robotic manipulators, which could guarantee transient tracking performances in the presence of model uncertainties. With the introduction of an error transformation mechanism, the original constrained manipulator system can be transformed into an unrestricted system. Moreover, the FT neural learning algorithm motivated by the estimated weights error, under persistent excitation (PE) condition, can guarantee the estimated neural weights converge to a small neighborhoods around the optimal values in finite time. Subsequently, the adaptive FT neural controller could ensure uniformly ultimate boundedness of all the signals in the closed-loop system and guarantee prescribed tracking and neural learning performances. The simulation results are given to illustrate the feasibility of the algorithm and correctness of theoretical analysis.

Keywords: Robotic manipulator · Neural network · Finite-time convergence · Predefined performances

1 Introduction

Along with the rapid development of automation science and technology, robotic manipulators are widely used in industrial production, aerospace and military application fields [1–4]. Controlling manipulators is a challenging task since the unique characteristics of the manipulators.

There are especial aims required to take the characteristics of manipulators into consideration. Although, there are a large number of valuable literature [5] on the issue of dynamics modeling of robotic manipulators, the exact knowledge of manipulators dynamics is still limited. Over the last few decades, neural

© Springer International Publishing AG 2017
D. Liu et al. (Eds.): ICONIP 2017, Part VI, LNCS 10639, pp. 365–375, 2017.
https://doi.org/10.1007/978-3-319-70136-3_39

network (NN) [6] has seen successful development that has wide applications due to the effort of industrial and academic communities. With the powerful approximation ability of NN, it has been evolved into many promising fields [7,8], such as modeling and identification of complex and nonlinear systems and optimization and automatic control.

In adaptive control systems, an unsatisfied transient performance might appear in the initial stage of parameter adaptation, especially when initial parameter estimation errors is too large. The problem of adaptive control systems with guaranteed transient performances has not been fully studied in the literature. Recently, adaptive NN learning control with prescribed performance was presented in [9] for nonlinear systems. The adaptive control with prescribed performance was applied in robot-tracking control systems [10]. And a global adaptive NN control with prescribed performance was applied in Hypersonic Flight Vehicle systems [11].

Furthermore, the conventional adaptive NN controls only focus on steady performance of the system rather than transient and neural learning performance. For the sake of polishing up conventional NN learning performance, the FT adaptive learning method is utilized. In [12], the parameter estimation error was obtained by a novel method. Therefore, the estimation error acts as an original prime mover was presented to achieve the FT learning process. To achieve the convergence of the estimated parameters, persistent excitation (PE) condition is usually necessary [13].

Inspired by the aforementioned works, in this paper an adaptive FT neural control is designed for robotic manipulators with guaranteed transient tracking performances in the presence of model uncertainties. To expedite the learning speed of neural networks, the FT adaptive learning mechanism is presented to boost the performance of neural learning. Moreover, a prescribed performance function is utilized to restrict the robotic manipulators system transients performance.

The remainder of this paper is outlined as follows: Preliminaries is first introduced in Sect. 2. Section 3 shows the detailed steps of adaptive FT neural controller design. In Sect. 4, the simulation results indicate the feasibility of the algorithm. Finally, Sect. 5 summarizes the main work and conclusions of this paper.

2   Preliminaries

2.1   Robotic Manipulator System

The dynamic equation of n-degrees of freedom (n-DOFs) robotic manipulator can be described as follows:

$$M(\Theta)\ddot{\Theta} + C(\Theta, \dot{\Theta})\dot{\Theta} + G(\Theta) = \tau, \tag{1}$$

where $\Theta = [\Theta_1, ..., \Theta_n]^T \in R^n$, $\dot{\Theta} = [\dot{\Theta}_1, ..., \dot{\Theta}_n]^T \in R^n$ and $\ddot{\Theta} = [\ddot{\Theta}_1, ..., \ddot{\Theta}_n]^T \in R^n$ represent the robot manipulator position vector, joint velocity vector and joint acceleration vector, respectively. $M(\Theta) \in R^{n \times n}$, $L(\Theta, \dot{\Theta}) \in R^{n \times n}$, and $G(\Theta) \in R^n$ are the inertia matrix, Coriolis/centripetal torque matrix and gravity vector, respectively. According to [14], the following properties hold for the robotic system (1):

Property 1. The matrix $M(\Theta) \in R^{n \times n}$ is symmetric positive-definite.

Property 2. The matrix $\dot{M}(\Theta) - 2C(\Theta, \dot{\Theta})$ is skew-symmetric, i.e., $z^T(\dot{M}(\Theta) - 2C(\Theta))z = 0$, $\forall z \in R^n$.

Property 3. The matrices $M(\Theta)$, $C(\Theta, \dot{\Theta})$ and $G(\Theta)$ are all bounded.

2.2   RBF NN and Localized Approximation

The RBF NN [11] is employed to emulate function:

$$\hat{f}\left(X_{in}, \hat{W}\right) = \sum_{i=1}^{N} \hat{\omega}_i h_i \left(X_{in}\right) = \hat{W}^T H \left(X_{in}\right) \tag{2}$$

where $\hat{f}(X_{in}, \hat{W}) \in R$ is the estimation of $f(X_{in})$, the input vector $X_{in} \in \Omega_{X_{in}} \subset R^M$, and $\hat{W} = [\hat{\omega}_1, ..., \hat{\omega}_N]^T \in R^N$ is the weights parameter vector, and N is the number of neurons in hidden layer. $H(X_{in}) = [h_1(X_{in}), ..., h_N(X_{in})]^T$ is kernel function, whose composition is

$$h_i \left(X_{in}\right) = \exp\left[-\frac{(X_{in} - \xi_1)^T (X_{in} - \xi_1)}{\vartheta^2}\right], \ i = 1, ..., N, \tag{3}$$

where $\xi_1 = [\xi_{i1}, \xi_{i2}, ..., \xi_{iM}]^T \in R^M$ is the center of the ith kernel function, ϑ is variance. The optimal NN weights W^* is defined as:

$$W^* = \arg\min_{(W)} \left[\sup_{X_{in} \in \Omega_{X_{in}}} |f(X_{in}) - \hat{f}(X_{in}, \hat{W})|\right]. \tag{4}$$

2.3   Partial PE Condition

Definition 1 [12]: A vector or matrix $\Upsilon(t)$ is called persistently excited if there exist $T_0 > 0$, $\varsigma > 0$, such that

$$\int_t^{t+T_0} \Upsilon^T(\tau)\Upsilon(\tau)d\tau \geq \varsigma I, \forall t \geq 0. \tag{5}$$

The motivation of using RBF NN in the paper mainly stems from the satisfaction of PE condition [9].

2.4   Predefined Transient Tracking Performance

The predefined performance is achieved by bounding the tracking error to a predefined region. The expression of predefined tracking performance is as follows:

$$- \underline{\vartheta}_i \eta_i(t) < \tilde{x}_{1,i}(t) < \overline{\vartheta}_i \eta_i(t), \ i = 1, ..., n \tag{6}$$

where $\underline{\vartheta}_i$, $\overline{\vartheta}_i$ are positive design constants, and $\eta_i(t)$ is an exponential decay function with $\lim_{t \to \infty} \eta_i(t) = \eta_{i,\infty}$, regarded as a performance function [9]. In this design, $\eta(t)$ is selected as:

$$\eta_i(t) = (\eta_{i,0} - \eta_{i,\infty}) exp(-\alpha_i t) + \eta_{i,\infty}, \ i = 1, ..., n \tag{7}$$

where $\eta_{i,0}$, $\eta_{i,\infty}$ and α_i are positive constants.

3   Adaptive FT Neural Control

3.1   Error Transformation Mechanism

To achieve the tracking control system satisfying the constrained performance, a suitable output error transform function [9] is employed to solve the constrained problem. For this purpose, define a smooth and strictly increasing function $T(z_{1,i})$ with $z_{1,i} \in R, i = 1, ..., n$ satisfying

$$\begin{cases} -\underline{\vartheta}_i < T(z_{1,i}) < \overline{\vartheta}_i, \forall z_{1,i} \in R_\infty \\ \lim_{z_{1,i} \to -\infty} T(z_{1,i}) = -\underline{\vartheta}_i \\ \lim_{z_{1,i} \to +\infty} T(z_{1,i}) = \overline{\vartheta}_i \end{cases} \tag{8}$$

Using the properties of $T(z_{1,i})$, the constrained tracking performance (6) can be rewritten by

$$\tilde{x}_{1,i}(t) = T(z_{1,i})\eta_i(t), \quad i = 1, ..., n \tag{9}$$

where $z_{1,i} \in R$ is defined as a transformed error.

In this paper, we choose the smooth and strictly increasing transformed function $T(z_{1,i})$ as follows [10]:

$$T(z_{1,i}) = \frac{\overline{\vartheta}_i e^{z_{1,i}} - \underline{\vartheta}_i e^{-z_{1,i}}}{e^{z_{1,i}} + e^{-z_{1,i}}} \tag{10}$$

Then, we have

$$z_{1,i} = \frac{1}{2} \ln \left(\frac{\gamma_i(t) + \underline{\vartheta}_i e^{-z_{1,i}}}{\overline{\vartheta}_i - \gamma_i(t)} \right), \quad i = 1, 2, 3 \tag{11}$$

where $\gamma_i(t) = \dfrac{\tilde{x}_{1,i}(t)}{\eta_i(t)}$.

Differentiating (11) with respect to time yields

$$\dot{z}_{1,i} = \phi_i \left(\dot{\tilde{x}}_{1,i} - \psi_i \tilde{x}_{1,i} \right), \quad i = 1, ..., n \tag{12}$$

where $\phi_i = \dfrac{1}{2\eta_i(t)} \left[\dfrac{1}{\gamma_i(t) + \underline{\vartheta}_i} - \dfrac{1}{\gamma_i(t) - \overline{\vartheta}_i} \right]$, $\psi_i = \dfrac{\dot{\eta}_i(t)}{\eta_i(t)}$.

Define $z_1 = [z_{1,1}, ..., z_{1,n}]^T \in R^n$, $\Phi = diag\,[\phi_1, \phi_2, ..., \phi_n]$, $i = 1, ...n$, and $\Psi = diag\,[\psi_1, \psi_2, ..., \psi_n]$, $i = 1, ...n$.

$$\dot{z}_1 = \Phi \left(\dot{\tilde{x}}_1 - \Psi \tilde{x}_1 \right) \tag{13}$$

3.2   Controller Design

The robotic manipulators joint position error is defined as $\tilde{x}_1 = \theta - \theta_d = x_1 - x_{1d}$, where $x_1 = \theta$, $x_{1d} = \theta_d$. So that

$$\dot{z}_1 = \Phi \left(\dot{\tilde{x}}_1 - \Psi \tilde{x}_1 \right) = \Phi \left(x_2 - \dot{x}_{1d} - \Psi \tilde{x}_1 \right) \tag{14}$$

Take x_{2d} as the virtual control of (14) and design the signal x_{2d} as:

$$x_{2d} = -K_{11}\tilde{z}_1 - K_{12}\mathrm{sign}\,(\tilde{z}_1) + \dot{x}_{1d} + \Psi \tilde{x}_1, \tag{15}$$

where K_{11} and K_{12} are control gains. Define $\tilde{x}_2 = x_2 - x_{2d}$ and (14) is calculated as:

$$\dot{z}_1 = \Phi \left(\dot{\tilde{x}}_1 - \Psi \tilde{x}_1 \right) = \Phi \left(\tilde{x}_2 - K_{11}\tilde{z}_1 - K_{12}\mathrm{sign}\,(\tilde{z}_1) \right) \tag{16}$$

The robotic manipulators joint velocity error can be written as $\tilde{x}_2 = x_2 - x_{2d}$, where $x_2 = \dot{\theta}$. Rewrite the Eq. (1), we have:

$$M\dot{\tilde{x}}_2 + C\tilde{x}_2 = \tau - M\dot{x}_{2d} - Cx_{2d} - G. \tag{17}$$

where $M\dot{\tilde{x}}_2$ is a function of the robotic manipulators joint acceleration $\ddot{\theta}$, which is noise-sensitive. To get around this problem, inspired by [12], the Eq. (17) is transformed as:

$$\dot{F}_1 \left(\bar{x} \right) + F_2 \left(\bar{x} \right) = \tau + F_3 \left(\bar{x} \right), \tag{18}$$

where $\bar{x} = [\theta, \dot{\theta}, x_{2d}, \dot{x}_{2d}]$, $F_1 = M\tilde{x}_2$, $F_2 = -\dot{M}\tilde{x}_2 + C\tilde{x}_2$ and $F_3 = -M\dot{x}_{2d} - Cx_{2d} - G$. Using RBF NN to approximate the unknown functions F_1, F_2 and F_3, respectively.

Then, the Eq. (18) is further formulated as:

$$F_{1,i} = H_1^T W_{1,i}^* + \varepsilon_{1,i}^*, F_{2,i} = H_2^T W_{2,i}^* + \varepsilon_{2,i}^*, F_{3,i} = H_3^T W_{3,i}^* + \varepsilon_{3,i}^*. \tag{19}$$

where $W_{1,i}^*$, $W_{2,i}^*$ and $W_{3,i}^*$ are ith column of the matrices W_1^*, W_2^* and W_3^*, $i = 1, ..., n$.

Then, the Eq. (19) is divided into n subsystems as:

$$\dot{H}_1^T W_{1,i}^* + \dot{\varepsilon}_{1,i}^* + H_2^T W_{2,i}^* + \varepsilon_{2,i}^* - H_3^T W_{3,i}^* - \varepsilon_{3,i}^* = \bar{H}^T W_i^* + \bar{\varepsilon}_i^* = \tau_i. \tag{20}$$

where $W_i^* = \left[W_{1,i}^{*T} W_{2,i}^{*T} W_{3,i}^{*T}\right]^T$, $\bar{H}^T = \dot{\bar{H}}_1^T + \bar{H}_2^T - \bar{H}_3^T$ and $\dot{\bar{H}}_1 = [\dot{H}_1^T, \mathbf{0}_N^T, \mathbf{0}_N^T]^T$, $\bar{H}_2 = [\mathbf{0}_N^T, H_2^T, \mathbf{0}_N^T]^T$, $\bar{H}_3 = [\mathbf{0}_N^T, \mathbf{0}_N^T, H_3^T]^T$, $N_{\bar{H}} = 3 \times N$, $\bar{\varepsilon}_i = \dot{\varepsilon}_{1,i}^* + \varepsilon_{2,i}^* - \varepsilon_{3,i}^*$.

The adaptive FT neural controller can be designed as:

$$\tau_i = -z_{1,i} - k_{21,i}\tilde{x}_{2,i} - k_{22,i}\text{sign}\,(\tilde{x}_{2,i}) - u_i^N \tag{21}$$

where $u_i^N = \hat{W}_i^T \bar{H}_3(z)$, and $K_{21} = \text{diag}(k_{21,1}, ..., k_{21,n})$, and $k_{21,i} > 0, i = 1, ..., n$, $K_{22} = \text{diag}(k_{22,1}, ..., k_{22,n})$, and $k_{22,i} > 0, i = 1, ..., n$.

Design the following filters to accelerate weights estimation:

$$\begin{cases} \beta\dot{\tau}_{if} + \tau_{if} = \tau_i, & \tau_{if}\,|_{t=0} = 0_n, \\ \beta\dot{\bar{H}}_{1f} + \bar{H}_{1f} = \bar{H}_1, \, \bar{H}_{1f}\,|_{t=0} = \mathbf{0}_{N_{\bar{H}}}, \\ \beta\dot{\bar{H}}_{2f} + \bar{H}_{2f} = \bar{H}_2, \, \bar{H}_{2f}\,|_{t=0} = \mathbf{0}_{N_{\bar{H}}}, \\ \beta\dot{\bar{H}}_{3f} + \bar{H}_{3f} = \bar{H}_3, \, \bar{H}_{3f}\,|_{t=0} = \mathbf{0}_{N_{\bar{H}}}, \end{cases} \tag{22}$$

where $\bar{H}_{1f}$, $\bar{H}_{2f}$, $\bar{H}_{3f}$ and τ_{if} are the filtered version of $\bar{H}_1$, $\bar{H}_2$, $\bar{H}_3$ and τ_i, respectively. And $\beta > 0$ is design parameter. According to (18) and (22), one can obtain:

$$W_i^{*T}\left(\frac{\bar{H}_1 - \bar{H}_{1f}}{\beta} + \bar{H}_{2f} - \bar{H}_{3f}\right) = W_i^{*T}\bar{H}_f = \tau_{if} - \bar{\varepsilon}_{if}. \tag{23}$$

Let us define matrices $B_i \in R^{N_{\bar{H}}}$, $P \in R^{N_{\bar{H}} \times N_{\bar{H}}}$:

$$\begin{cases} \dot{B}_i = -\ell B_i + \bar{H}_f \tau_{if}, \\ \dot{P} = -\ell P + \bar{H}_f \bar{H}_f^T, \end{cases} \tag{24}$$

where $\ell > 0$ is design parameter. The solution of (24) is derived as:

$$\begin{cases} B_i(t) = \int_0^t e^{-\ell_i(t-r)}\bar{H}_f \tau_{if} dr, \\ P(t) = \int_0^t e^{-\ell_i(t-r)}\bar{H}_f \bar{H}_f^T dr, \end{cases} \tag{25}$$

Define auxiliary vector $E_i \in R^{N_{\bar{H}}}$, which can be calculated from B_i, P:

$$E_i = P\hat{W}_i - B_i = P\hat{W}_i - PW_i^* - \varphi_i = -P\tilde{W}_i - \varphi_i, \tag{26}$$

where $B_i = PW_i^* + \psi_i$ with $\varphi_i = \int_0^t e^{-\ell_i(t-r)}\bar{H}_f \bar{\varepsilon}_{if} dr$.

We can obtain the closed-loop error equation:

$$M\dot{\tilde{x}}_2 + C\tilde{x}_2 = -z_1 - K_{21}\tilde{x}_2 - K_{22}\text{sign}\,(\tilde{x}_2) + \tilde{F}_3 + \varepsilon_3 \tag{27}$$

where $\tilde{F}_{3,i} = \tilde{W}_{3,i}^T H_3(z) = \tilde{W}_i^T \bar{H}_3(z)$, $\tilde{W}_{3,i} = W_{3,i}^* - \hat{W}_{3,i}$, $\tilde{W}_i = W_i^* - \hat{W}_i$.

The adaptive neural learning law of the weights are designed as:

$$\dot{\hat{W}}_i = \Gamma_i\left(\bar{H}_3\tilde{x}_{2,i} - \delta_i\frac{P^T E_i}{\|E_i\|}\right), \quad i = 1, \cdots, n, \tag{28}$$

where δ_i is designed positive parameter, and Γ_i is symmetric positive definitive matrix.

3.3   Stablity Analysis

According to the closed-loop error system (27), and adaptive laws (28). Select the following Lyapunov function:

$$L = L_1 + L_2, \tag{29}$$

with $L_1 = \frac{1}{2}\tilde{z}_1^T \Phi^{-1} \tilde{z}_1$, $L_2 = \frac{1}{2}\tilde{x}_2^T M \tilde{x}_2 + \frac{1}{2}\sum_{i=1}^{n}\left(E_i^T P^{-1}\Gamma^{-1}P^{-1}E_i\right)$, where Γ^{-1} is a positive-definite matrix. L_1 yields:

$$
\begin{aligned}
\dot{L}_1 &= \tilde{z}_1^T \Phi^{-1}\dot{\tilde{z}}_1 + \frac{1}{2}\tilde{z}_1^2 \dot{\Phi}^{-1} = \tilde{z}_1^T\left(\tilde{x}_2 - K_{11}\tilde{z}_1 - K_{12}\mathrm{sign}\left(\tilde{z}_1\right)\right) + \frac{1}{2}\tilde{z}_1^2 \dot{\Phi}^{-1} \\
&\leq -\sum_{i=1}^{n}\left(k_{12,i}|\tilde{z}_{1,i}|\right) + \tilde{z}_1^T\tilde{x}_2 \leq -K_1^*\sqrt{L_1} + \tilde{z}_1^T\tilde{x}_2,
\end{aligned} \tag{30}
$$

where $K_{11} = K_{11}^* + K_{11}' > 0$, with $K_{11}^* = \mathrm{diag}[k_{11,1}^*, k_{11,2}^*, \cdots, k_{11,n}^*]$, $k_{11,i}^* > 0, i = 1, \cdots, n$, $K_{11}' = \frac{1}{2}\dot{\Phi}^{-1}$, $\dot{\Phi}^{-1} = diag[-\phi_1/\dot{\phi}_1^2, -\phi_2/\dot{\phi}_2^2, ..., -\phi_n/\dot{\phi}_n^2]$, and $K_{12} = \mathrm{diag}[k_{12,1}, k_{12,2}, \cdots, k_{12,n}]$, $k_{12,i} > 0, i = 1, \cdots, n$, $K_1^* = \sqrt{2}\lambda_{min}\left(K_{12}\right)$.

According to (26), we have:

$$\frac{\partial(P^{-1}E_i)}{\partial t} = -\dot{\hat{W}}_i + P^{-1}\dot{P}P^{-1}\psi_i - P^{-1}\dot{\psi}_i = \dot{\hat{W}}_i + \psi_i', \tag{31}$$

where $\psi_i' = P^{-1}\dot{P}P^{-1}\psi_i - P^{-1}\dot{\psi}_i$.

Taking the derivative of L_2 yields:

$$
\begin{aligned}
\dot{L}_2 =& \tilde{x}_2^T M \dot{\tilde{x}}_2 + \frac{1}{2}\tilde{x}_2^T \dot{M}\tilde{x}_2 + \sum_{i=1}^{n}\left(E_i^T P^{-1}\Gamma^{-1}\left(\dot{\hat{W}}_i + \psi_i'\right)\right) \\
=& -\tilde{z}_1^T\tilde{x}_2 - \tilde{x}_2^T K_{21}\tilde{x}_2 - \sum_{i=1}^{n}\left(k_{22,i}|\tilde{x}_{2,i}|\right) + \tilde{x}_2^T\left(\tilde{F}_3 + \varepsilon_3\right) \\
&+ \sum_{i=1}^{n}\left(E_i^T P^{-1}\Gamma^{-1}\dot{\hat{W}}_i\right) + \sum_{i=1}^{n}\left(E_i^T P^{-1}\Gamma^{-1}\psi_i'\right) \\
=& -\tilde{z}_1^T\tilde{x}_2 - \tilde{x}_2^T K_{21}\tilde{x}_2 - \sum_{i=1}^{n}\left(k_{22,i}|\tilde{x}_{2,i}|\right) + \tilde{x}_2^T\varepsilon_3 \\
&+ \sum_{i=1}^{n}\left(-\psi_i^T P^{-1}\bar{H}_3\tilde{x}_{2,i}\right) + \sum_{i=1}^{n}\left(E_i^T P^{-1}\Gamma^{-1}\psi_i' - \delta_i\frac{E_i^T P^{-1}P^T E_i}{\|E_i\|}\right).
\end{aligned} \tag{32}
$$

And then, we have:

$$\dot{L}_2 \leq - \tilde{z}_1^T \tilde{x}_2 - \tilde{x}_2^T K_{21} \tilde{x}_2 - \sum_{i=1}^n \left(k_{22,i} |\tilde{x}_{2,i}|\right) + \sum_{i=1}^n \left(\varepsilon_{3,i}^* |\tilde{x}_{2,i}|\right)$$

$$- \sum_{i=1}^n \left(|\tilde{x}_{2,i}| \|\psi_i^T P^{-1} \bar{H}_3\|\right) - \sum_{i=1}^n \left(\|E_i^T\| \left(\delta_i - \|P^{-1} \Gamma^{-1} \psi_i'\|\right)\right)$$

$$\leq - \sum_{i=1}^n \left(|\tilde{x}_{2,i}| \left(k_{22,i} - \varepsilon_{3,i}^* + \|\psi_i^T P^{-1} \bar{H}_3\|\right)\right) \tag{33}$$

$$- \sum_{i=1}^n \left(\|E_i^T\| \left(\delta_i - \|P^{-1} \Gamma^{-1} \psi_i'\|\right)\right) - \tilde{z}_1^T \tilde{x}_2$$

$$\leq - K_2^* \sqrt{L_2} - \tilde{z}_1^T \tilde{x}_2,$$

where $K_2^* = \min[\sqrt{2/\lambda_{max}(M)} \times (k_{22,i} - \varepsilon_{3,i}^* + \|\psi_i^T P^{-1} \bar{H}_3\|), (\delta_i - \|P^{-1} \Gamma^{-1} \psi_i'\|) \delta_p \sqrt{\lambda_{max}(\Gamma^{-1})}]$.

$$\dot{L} = \dot{L}_1 + \dot{L}_2 \leq -K\sqrt{L}, \tag{34}$$

where $K = \min[K_1^*, K_2^*]$.

The output position error $\tilde{x}_1$ converges to zero in a finite time $t_c = 2K\sqrt{L(0)}$ with appropriately chosen design parameters. For any recurrent orbit $\dot{\theta}_d(t)|_{t \geq 0}$, and initial conditions $[x_1^T(0), x_2^T(0)]^T \in \Omega_0$ where Ω_0 is an appropriately chosen compact set). The NN weights estimation $\hat{W}_i$ converge to small neighborhoods of the optimal value W_i^*, and the parameter error $\tilde{W}_i$ satisfies $\lim_{t \to \infty} \tilde{W}_i = -P^{-1} \psi_i$.

4 Simulation Study

To illustrate the feasibility of the proposed scheme, simulation experiments are carried out based on the 7 DOF Baxter robot arm model as shown in Fig. 1.

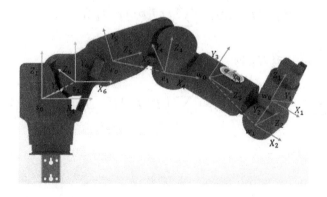

Fig. 1. An overlook of Baxter robot.

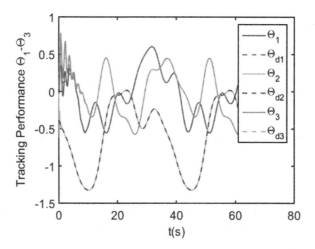

Fig. 2. Trajectory tracking performances of $\theta 1 - \theta 3$.

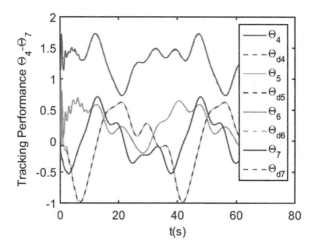

Fig. 3. Trajectory tracking performances of $\theta 4 - \theta 7$.

It has seven rotational joints which are named S_0, S_1, e_0, e_1, w_0, w_1, w_2, respectively [1]. The physical DH parameters of Baxter robot are shown in [1]. To ensure the $H_i, i = 1, 2, 3$ to satisfy the PE condition, periodic and bandlimited excitation joint reference trajectories, θ_d, $\dot{\theta}_d$, $\ddot{\theta}_d$ are generated by using the Fourier expansion and optimization in [5]. The control gains are chosen $K_{11}^* = \text{diag}[200, 1000, 180, 200, 60, 80, 60]$, $K_{12} = \text{diag}[0.0001, 0.0001, 0.0001, 0.0001, 0.0001, 0.0001, 0.0001]$, while $K_{21} = \text{diag}[20, 17.5, 8, 5, 4, 1.5, 0.5]$, $K_{22} = \text{diag}[0.0001, 0.0001, 0.0001, 0.0001, 0.0001, 0.0001, 0.0001]$. The gains of the adaptation law are selected to be $\Gamma_i = 15I(i = 1, \cdots, 7)$, $\delta_i = 0.005(i = 1, \cdots, 7)$. The NN weight matrix are initialized as $\hat{W}_1(0) = \hat{W}_2(0) =$

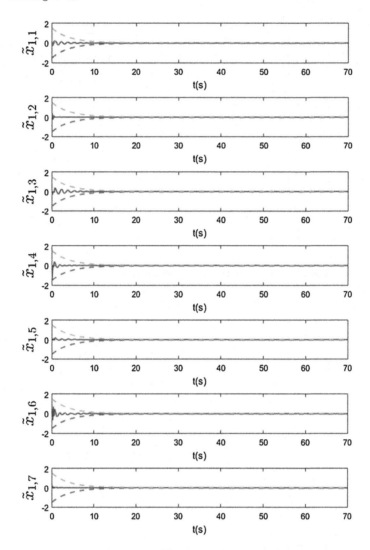

Fig. 4. Tracking errors $\tilde{x}_1$.

$\hat{W}_3(0) = \hat{W}_4(0) = \hat{W}_5(0) = \hat{W}_6(0) = \hat{W}_7(0) = \mathbf{0} \in R^{128}$. The simulation results are presented in Figs. 2, 3 and 4.

5   Conclusion

In this work, an adaptive FT neural control is designed for robotic manipulators with guaranteed transient tracking performances in the presence of model uncertainties. A prescribed performance function is utilized to restrict the robotic manipulators system transients performance. Moreover, to expedite the learning speed of neural networks, the FT adaptive learning mechanism is presented to boost the performance of neural learning. Simulation experiments illustrate the feasibility of the algorithm.

Acknowledgments. This work was partially supported by National Nature Science Foundation (NSFC) under Grant 61473120, Guangdong Provincial Natural Science Foundation 2014A030313266 and International Science and Technology Collaboration Grant 2015A050502017, Science and Technology Planning Project of Guangzhou 201607010006, State Key Laboratory of Robotics and System (HIT) Grant SKLRS-2017-KF-13, and the Fundamental Research Funds for the Central Universities 2017Z-D057.

References

1. Yang, C., Wang, X., Cheng, L., Ma, H.: Neural-learning-based telerobot control with guaranteed performance. IEEE Trans. Cybern. **47**(10), 3148–3159 (2016)
2. Newton, R.T., Xu, Y.: Neural network control of a space manipulator. IEEE Control Syst. **13**(6), 14–22 (1994)
3. Sun, F., Sun, Z., Woo, P.: Neural network-based adaptive controller design of robotic manipulators with an observer. IEEE Trans. Neural Netw. **2**(1), 54–67 (2001)
4. Sun, F., Sun, Z., Zhang, R., Chen, Y.: Neural adaptive tracking controller for robot manipulators with unknown dynamics. IEE Proc. Control Theor. Appl. **147**(3), 366–370 (2000)
5. He, W., Ge, W., Li, Y., et al.: Model identification and control design for a humanoid robot. IEEE Trans. Syst. Man Cybern. Syst. **47**(1), 1–13 (2016)
6. Fierro, R., Lewis, F.L.: Control of a nonholonomic mobile robot using neural networks. IEEE Trans. Neural Netw. **9**(4), 589–600 (1998)
7. Lewis, F.L., Jagannathan, S., Yesildirek, A.: Neural Network Control of Robot Manipulators and Nonlinear Systems. Taylor & Francis, London (1999)
8. Yang, C., Li, Z., Cui, R., Xu, B.: Neural network-based motion control of an underactuated wheeled inverted pendulum model. IEEE Trans. Neural Netw. Learn. Syst. **25**(11), 2004–2016 (2014)
9. Dai, S., Wang, M., Wang, C.: Neural learning control of marine surface vessels with guaranteed transient tracking performance. IEEE Trans. Ind. Electron. **63**(3), 1717–1727 (2016)
10. Na, J., Chen, Q., Ren, X., Guo, Y.: Adaptive prescribed performance motion control of servo mechanisms with friction compensation. IEEE Trans. Ind. Electron. **61**(1), 486–494 (2014)
11. Teng, T., Yang, C., Dai, S., Wang, M.: Tracking performance and global stability guaranteed neural control of uncertain hypersonic flight vehicle. Int. J. Adv. Robot. Syst. 1–11 (2017). doi:10.1177/1729881416678140
12. Na, J., Mahyuddin, M.N., Herrmann, G., et al.: Robust adaptive finite-time parameter estimation and control for robotic systems. Int. J. Robust Nonlinear Control **25**(16), 3045–3071 (2015)
13. Anderson, B.: Exponential stability of linear equations arising in adaptive identification. IEEE Trans. Autom. Control **22**(1), 83–88 (1977)
14. Slotine, J., Li, W.: Adaptive manipulator control a case study. In: IEEE International Conference on Robotics and Automation, pp. 1392–1400 (1987)

Guaranteeing Predefined Full State Constraints for Non-Affine Nonlinear Systems Using Neural Networks

Min Wang$^{(\boxtimes)}$ and Yanwen Zhang

School of Automation Science and Engineering,
Guangzhou Key Laboratory of Brain Computer Interaction and Applications,
South China University of Technology, Guangzhou 510641, China
auwangmin@scut.edu.cn

Abstract. This paper presents adaptive neural control (ANC) design for a class of nonaffine nonlinear systems with full state constraints. A novel transformed function is presented to convert the origin system into an equivalent nonaffine systems with new unconstrained states. By combining dynamic surface control, the explosion of complexity is avoided in the backstepping design. Subsequently, a novel ANC control scheme is proposed by Lyapunov synthesis. The proposed adaptive control guarantees that all closed-loop signals are uniformly ultimately bounded and all system states do not violate the predefined constraints. Simulation studies are performed to show the effectiveness of the proposed control scheme.

Keywords: Neural control · Full state constraints · State transformation · Dynamic surface control

1 Introduction

With the development of control theory, the constraints of the system variables in control design stage have become one of the most important subjects in recent years. Constraints problems often exist in many practical systems, which makes the study of constraints meaningful. For the control of constraints problem, there are many notable methods include model predictive control [1], extremum seeking control [2], nonovershooting control [3], adaptive variable structure control and error transformation [4]. Some studies [5] and [6] have investigated on the restricted tracking control problem which is one of the common forms in constraints problem. However these methods ignore the constraints for the output or states of the nonlinear systems which are more common in practical systems.

The barrier Lyapunov function (BLF) [7] is one of the effective methods for the control of nonlinear systems with output or state constraints. BLF involves the construction of a control Lyapunov function that grows to infinity whenever its arguments approaches some limits [8]. Then, it guarantees the limits are satisfied by keeping the BLF bound in the closed-loop system. The BLF method

© Springer International Publishing AG 2017
D. Liu et al. (Eds.): ICONIP 2017, Part VI, LNCS 10639, pp. 376–383, 2017.
https://doi.org/10.1007/978-3-319-70136-3_40

can achieve its control object well, but it has deficiencies because it has to transform the constraints of the states into the constraints of the corresponding errors. Therefore, the BLF method often causes the conservative of the controller design. In this paper, a new transformed function is used to directly transform the constrained states into the corresponding unconstrained states. And then, the controller is designed for the transformed systems with the unconstrained states, which effectively reduces the conservative of the controller design. Moreover, backstepping has been a popular design method for many nonlinear systems since adaptive backstepping design was presented for a class of nonlinear systems in parametric strict-feedback form in [9]. However, traditional backstepping method has to calculate the derivation of the virtual controller which may be cause the explosion of complexity. To avoid the problem, dynamic surface control [10,11] is proposed by introducing a first-order filter at each step of the traditional backstepping approach.

In this paper, we aim to achieve full state constraints for nonaffine nonlinear systems. A transformation function is constructed to transform the original constrained systems into an equivalent unconstrained nonaffine system. Dynamic surface control method is utilised to avoid the explosion of complexity in the backstepping design. Then we use the implicit function theorem and the mean value theorem [12] to obtain the implicit desired control input in an affine form. Radial basis function (RBF) neural networks (NNs) are employed to approximate the desired control input. Using the Lyapunov synthesis, a novel adaptive neural control scheme is proposed to guarantee the tracking performance of system output and the non-violation of the predefined full state constraints.

2   Problem Formulation

Consider a second-order non-affine nonlinear system in the following form

$$\begin{cases} \dot{x}_1 = x_2 \\ \dot{x}_2 = f\left(\overline{x}_2, u\right) \end{cases} \tag{1}$$

where $x_1, x_2 \in \mathbb{R}$ denote the system states; $f\left(\overline{x}_2, u\right)$ is an unknown smooth function; $\overline{x}_2 = [x_1, x_2]^T$; u is the system input; and $y = x_1$ is the system output.

Define the smooth function

$$g\left(\overline{x}_2, u\right) = \frac{\partial f\left(\overline{x}_2, u\right)}{\partial u} \tag{2}$$

Assumption 1. *[12] The sign of nonlinear function $g\left(\overline{x}_2, u\right)$ is known and $g\left(\overline{x}_2, u\right) \neq 0$, and there exists unknown positive constants g_0 and g_1 such that $0 < g_0 < g\left(\overline{x}_x, u\right) < g_1$.*

Assumption 2. *The desired trajectory $y_d\left(t\right)$ is continuous and known, and $y_d\left(t\right) \in \Omega_d$ where Ω_d is the known compact set within the output constraint boundness. Moreover, $\dot{y}_d\left(t\right)$ and $\ddot{y}_d\left(t\right)$ are continuous, bounded, and available.*

The control objective is to design a novel adaptive NN controller u, such that y is driven to track a desired trajectory $y_d(t)$ and all the signals in the closed-loop system are bounded and the full state constraints are not violated.

3   Adaptive Neural Control with Prescribed Constraints

In this paper, the states of the system must satisfy their upper bound and lower bound constraints:

$$- \underline{k}_i \le x_i \le \overline{k}_i \qquad i = 1, 2 \tag{3}$$

A transformed function $T_i(x_i) = k_{ai} \arctan \left(s_i - \tan \left(\frac{k_{bi}}{k_{ai}} \right) \right) + k_{bi}$ is used in this paper, which can transform the constrained states into the equivalent unconstrained ones according to its monotonic increasing and boundness properties.

Then the transformed state s_i can be expressed as

$$s_i = T_i^{-1}(x_i) = \tan \left(\frac{x_i}{k_{ai}} - \frac{k_{bi}}{k_{ai}} \right) + \tan \left(\frac{k_{bi}}{k_{ai}} \right) \tag{4}$$

where $k_{ai} = \frac{\overline{k}_i + \underline{k}_i}{\pi}, k_{bi} = \frac{\overline{k}_i - \underline{k}_i}{2}$.

The derivative of the transformed state is calculated:

$$\dot{s}_1 = \left[1 + \left(s_1 - \tan \frac{k_{b1}}{k_{a1}} \right)^2 \right] \frac{1}{k_{a1}} T_2(s_2) = F_1 + s_2 \tag{5}$$

$$\dot{s}_2 = \left[1 + \left(s_2 - \tan \frac{k_{b2}}{k_{a2}} \right)^2 \right] \frac{1}{k_{a2}} f(\overline{x}_2, u) \tag{6}$$

where $F_1 = \left[1 + \left(s_1 - \tan \frac{k_{b1}}{k_{a1}} \right)^2 \right] \frac{1}{k_{a1}} T_2(s_2) - s_2$

Step 1: We choose the error as follows

$$z_1 = s_1 - s_d \tag{7}$$

where s_d is the transformed desired trajectory. It can be proved that the tracking error $e_1 = x_1 - y_d \to 0$ as $z_1 \to 0$.

Then, we obtain

$$\dot{z}_1 = F_1 + s_2 - \dot{s}_d \tag{8}$$

We construct the virtual control α_1 as:

$$\alpha_1 = -k_1 z_1 - F_1 + \dot{s}_d \tag{9}$$

where k_1 is a positive design constant.

Next, we define a first-order filter as follows

$$\tau_2 \dot{\alpha}_{2f} + \alpha_{2f} = \alpha_1, \qquad \alpha_{2f}(0) = \alpha_1(0) \tag{10}$$

where α_{2f} is the output of the filter and τ_2 is a designed constant.

Then, defining $z_2 = s_2 - \alpha_{2f}$, it can be obtained that

$$\dot{z}_1 = -k_1 z_1 + z_2 \tag{11}$$

Step 2: Then the derivative of z_2 is given by

$$\dot{z}_2 = \left[1 + \left(s_2 - \tan \frac{k_{b2}}{k_{a2}}\right)^2\right] \frac{1}{k_{a2}} f(\overline{x}_2, u) - \dot{\alpha}_{2f} + z_1 - z_1 \tag{12}$$

$$= F_2(\overline{x}_2, u) + A - z_1$$

where $A = -\dot{\alpha}_{2f} + z_1$ and $F_2(\overline{x}_2, u) = \left[1 + \left(s_2 - \tan \frac{k_{b2}}{k_{a2}}\right)^2\right] \frac{1}{k_{a2}} f(\overline{x}_2, u)$.

According to the implicit function theorem and the mean value theorem, the derivative of z_2 can be rewritten as

$$\dot{z}_2 = F_2(\overline{x}_2, u^*) + A + Q_2(s_2) g_\mu (u - u^*) - z_1 \tag{13}$$

$$= Q_2(s_2) g_\mu (u - u^*) - z_1$$

where $Q_2(s_2) = \left[1 + \left(s_2 - \tan \frac{k_{b2}}{k_{a2}}\right)^2\right] \frac{1}{k_{a2}} \geq \frac{1}{k_{a2}} > 0$ and u^* is the unknown dynamics. We employ the RBF NNs $W^{*T} S(Z)$ to approximate $Q_2(s_2) u^*$ as follows

$$Q_2(s_2) u^* = W^{*T} S(Z) + \epsilon(Z) \tag{14}$$

where $Z = [x_1, x_2, \dot{\alpha}_{2f}, z_1]^T$ is the NN input vector, $\epsilon(Z)$ is the approximation error and satisfies $|\epsilon(Z)| \leq \epsilon^*$ with the constant $\epsilon^* > 0$.

Let $\hat{W}$ be the estimation of ideal weights W^*, and $\tilde{W} = \hat{W} - W^*$ be the estimate error. The control law u is taken as

$$u = -k_{20} z_2 + \frac{1}{Q_2(s_2)} \hat{W}^T S(Z) \tag{15}$$

Next, we construct the following neural weight updated law

$$\dot{\hat{W}} = \dot{\tilde{W}} = -\Gamma \left[S(Z) z_2 + \sigma \hat{W}\right] \tag{16}$$

where Γ is a positive-definite symmetric matrix and σ is a positive design parameter.

According to (11) and (13), the error system can be expressed as:

$$\begin{cases} \dot{z}_1 = -k_1 z_1 + z_2 \\ \dot{z}_2 = -Q_2(s_2) g_\mu k_{20} z_2 + g_\mu \tilde{W}^T S(Z) - g_\mu \epsilon(Z) - z_1 \end{cases} \tag{17}$$

Then we design the layer error as:

$$y_2 = \alpha_{2f} - \alpha_1 \tag{18}$$

whose derivative can be calculated by

$$\dot{y}_2 = \dot{\alpha}_{2f} - \dot{\alpha}_1$$
$$= -\frac{y_2}{\tau_2} - \dot{\alpha}_1 \qquad (19)$$

and $\dot{\alpha}_1 = -k_1\dot{z}_1 - \dot{F}_1 + \ddot{s}_d$ is a continuous function.

Theorem 1. *Consider the closed-loop system consisting of the plant (1), the state transformation with transformed state (4), the proposed ANC law (15) and the NN updated law (16). Then, we have:*

1) all the signals in the closed-loop system are uniformly ultimately bounded;
2) the error z_1, z_2, y_2 converges to a small residual set of zero;
3) states x_1, x_2 of the origin system (1) remain in their predefined constraints;
4) the error e_1 converges to the adjustably small neighborhood of zero.

Proof : We construct the following Lyapunov function candidate:

$$V = \frac{1}{2}z_1^2 + \frac{1}{2}z_2^2 + \frac{1}{2}\tilde{W}^T \Gamma^{-1} \tilde{W} + \frac{1}{2}y_2^2 \qquad (20)$$

Then, its derivative along (11), (13), (15), (16) and (19) is

$$\dot{V} = -k_1 z_1^2 - Q_2(s_2)g_\mu k_{20} z_2^2 + g_\mu \tilde{W}^T S(Z) z_2$$
$$- g_\mu z_2 \epsilon(Z) + \tilde{W}^T S(Z) z_2 - \sigma \tilde{W}^T \hat{W} - \frac{y_2^2}{\tau_2} - \dot{\alpha}_1 y_2 \qquad (21)$$

Using appropriate inequalities and combining the Assumption 1 and $Q_n(s_n) \geq \frac{1}{k_{an}}$, we obtain

$$\dot{V} \leq -k_1 z_1^2 - \frac{g_0}{k_{a2}} k_{20} z_2^2 + (1+g_1) r S^{*2} z_2^2 + \frac{1+g_1}{4r}\|\tilde{W}\|^2 + \frac{g_1 \epsilon^{*2}}{4k_\epsilon}$$
$$+ g_1 k_\epsilon z_2^2 - \frac{\sigma}{2}\|\tilde{W}\|^2 + \frac{\sigma}{2}\|W^*\|^2 - \frac{y_2^2}{\tau_2} + \frac{N_2^2 y_2^2}{4\gamma} + \gamma \qquad (22)$$
$$\leq -k_1 z_1^2 - k_2 z_2^2 - k_w\|\tilde{W}\|^2 - k_y y_2^2 + \frac{g_1 \epsilon^{*2}}{4k_\epsilon} + \frac{\sigma}{2}\|W^*\|^2 + \gamma$$
$$\leq -aV + b$$

where $k_2 = \frac{k_{20}g_0}{k_{a2}} - (1+g_1)rS^{*2} - g_1 k_\epsilon$, $k_w = \frac{\sigma}{2} - \frac{1+g_1}{4r}$, $k_y = \frac{1}{\tau_2} - \frac{N_2^2}{4\gamma}$, $a = \min\{2k_i, \frac{2k_w}{\lambda(\Gamma^{-1})}, 2k_y\}$ and $b = \frac{g_1 \epsilon^{*2}}{4k_\epsilon} + \frac{\sigma}{2}\|W^*\|^2 + \gamma$.
Let $\zeta = b/a$, we have

$$V \leq (V(0) - \zeta)\exp(-at) + \zeta \qquad (23)$$

which means that as $t \to \infty$, we have

$$z_i \leq \sqrt{2\zeta} \qquad (24)$$

According to (23) and (24), the errors z_1, z_2, the neural weight error $\tilde{W}$ and the layer error y_2 are bounded and converge to a small residual set of zero. Hence, $\hat{W}$ is bounded according to the boundedness of $\tilde{W}$ and the desired weight W^*. According to the state transformation, the tracking error e_1 converges to a small neighborhood of zero. Since the boundedness of $z_1, z_2, e_1 = x_1 - y_d, y_d$, it follows that s_1, s_2 are bounded and all states x_1, x_2 of the origin system (1) remain in their predefined constraints. Hence, all the signals in the closed-loop system remain uniformly ultimately bounded. ∎

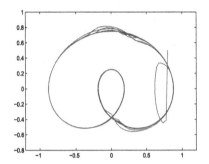
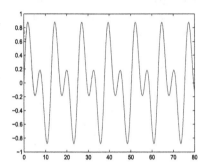

Fig. 1. System state x_i with ANC method based on transformation ("–")

Fig. 2. System output y ("–") and desired trajectory y_d ("-.-")

4   Simulation Results

In this section, a second-order van der Pol example is simulated to illustrate the proposed adaptive NN control scheme. Consider the following second-order van der Pol oscillator described by:

$$\begin{cases} \dot{x}_1 = x_2 \\ \dot{x}_2 = -x_1 + \beta(1 - x_1^2)x_2 + (2 + \sin(x_1 x_2))(u + (u^3/3) + \sin(u)) \\ y = x_1 \end{cases} \quad (25)$$

where $x_1, x_2 \in \mathbb{R}$ denote the states of the system, $\beta = 0.7$ is a system parameter, and y is the output of the system. Obviously, the model is not in affine form, because the control input u appears nonlinearly in (25). In this example, we suppose that there is no a priori knowledge of system nonlinearities except for some of its properties.

The reference trajectory is chosen as the following form:

$$y_d = 0.5(\sin(t) + \sin(0.5t))) \quad (26)$$

The objective of the section is to apply the proposed stable adaptive NN control law u (15) with the weight adaptation law (16) for system (25) such that the system states x_1 and x_2 satisfy their predefined constraints, the output y of system tracks the reference trajectory x_d in a finite time, and the implicit desired control input u^* is accurately approximated by localized RBF NNs along trajectories of NN inputs.

The predefined constraints of the states are chosen as

$$-1.2 \leq x_1 \leq 1.2, -0.8 \leq x_2 \leq 1 \tag{27}$$

In the simulation studies, we construct the Gaussian RBF network $\hat{W}^T S(Z))$ using 3200 nodes, with the center evenly spaced on $[-0.9, 0.9] \times [-0.6, 0.8] \times [-0.1, 0.3] \times [-3, 4]$ and the width are $0.22, 0.22, 0.11, 1.1$. The design parameters are $k_1 = 2, k_{20} = 1, \Gamma = 7, \sigma = 0, \tau = 0.005$. The initial conditions are $\hat{W} = 0, x(0) = [0.8, 0.5]^T$. Simulation results for adaptive NN control are shown in Figs. 1, 2, 3 and 4.

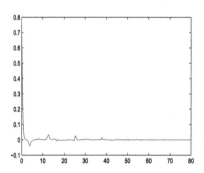

Fig. 3. Tracking error $e_1(\text{"-"})$

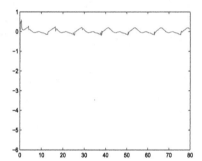

Fig. 4. Control signal $u(\text{"-"})$ with ANC method based on transformation

Figure 1 shows the tracking results in the phase space which indicates the system states x_1 and x_2 are in the predefined constraints. It can be seen from Fig. 2 that the system output y tracks the desired trajectory y_d quickly. Figure 3 shows the tracking error e_1. The boundedness of the control signal is shown in Fig. 4.

5   Conclusion

In this paper, we addressed the tracking control problem for a class of non-affine nonlinear system in the presence of full-state constraints. The constrained states were transformed into the equivalent unconstrained ones via a state transformation function. The system unknown dynamic was approximated by RBF NNs. A novel adaptive neural control was proposed to guarantee that the tracking error converges to a small residual set of zero and the prescribed state constraints are not violated. In our future work, the learning capacity of adaptive neural controller will be studied to improve the performance of the control scheme.

Acknowledgments. This work was partially supported by the National Natural Science Foundation of China under Grants 61773169, 61374119, 61473121, and 61611130214, by the Guangdong Natural Science Foundation under Grant 2014A030312005, and by the Fundamental Research Funds for the Central Universities.

References

1. Mayne, D.Q., Rawlings, J.B., Rao, C.V., Scokaert, P.O.: Constrained model predictive control: stability and optimality. Automatica **36**(6), 789–814 (2000)
2. DeHaan, D., Guay, M.: Extremum-seeking control of state-constrained nonlinear systems. Automatica **41**(9), 1567–1574 (2005)
3. Krstic, M., Bement, M.: Non-overshooting control of strict-feedback nonlinear systems. In: American Control Conference, pp. 4494–4499. IEEE Press (2007)
4. Do, K.D.: Control of nonlinear systems with output tracking error constraints and its application to magnetic bearings. Int. J. Control **83**(6), 1199–1216 (2010)
5. Wang, M., Wang, C., Shi, P., Liu, X.: Dynamic learning from neural control for strict-feedback systems with guaranteed predefined performance. IEEE Trans. Neural Netw. Learn. Syst. **27**(12), 2564–2576 (2016)
6. Dai, S.-L., Wang, M., Wang, C.: Neural learning control of marine surface vessels with guaranteed transient tracking performance. IEEE Trans. Industr. Electron. **63**(3), 1717–1727 (2016)
7. Tee, K.P., Ge, S.S., Tay, E.H.: Barrier Lyapunov functions for the control of output-constrained nonlinear systems. Automatica **45**(4), 918–927 (2009)
8. Li, J., Liu, Y.J.: Control of nonlinear systems with full state constraints using integral Barrier Lyapunov Functionals. In: International Conference on IEEE Informative and Cybernetics for Computational Social Systems, pp. 66–71 (2015)
9. Kanellakopoulos, I., Kokotovic, P.V., Morse, A.S.: Systematic design of adaptive controllers for feedback linearizable systems. In: American Control Conference, pp. 649–654. IEEE (1991)
10. Yip, P.P., Hedrick, J.K.: Adaptive dynamic surface control: a simplified algorithm for adaptive backstepping control of nonlinear systems. Int. J. Control **71**(5), 959–979 (1998)
11. Swaroop, D., Hedrick, J.K., Yip, P.P., Gerdes, J.C.: Dynamic surface control for a class of nonlinear systems. IEEE Trans. Autom. Control **45**(10), 1893–1899 (2000)
12. Ge, S.S., Wang, C.: Adaptive NN control of uncertain nonlinear pure-feedback systems. Automatica **38**(4), 671–682 (2002)

Self-repairing Learning Rule for Spiking Astrocyte-Neuron Networks

Junxiu Liu[1]([⊠]), Liam J. McDaid[1], Jim Harkin[1], John J. Wade[1],
Shvan Karim[1], Anju P. Johnson[2], Alan G. Millard[2], David M. Halliday[2],
Andy M. Tyrrell[2], and Jon Timmis[2]

[1] School of Computing, Engineering and Intelligent Systems,
Ulster University, Derry BT48 7JL, UK
{j.liu1,lj.mcdaid,jg.harkin,jj.wade,haji_karim-s}@ulster.ac.uk
[2] Department of Electronic Engineering, University of York, York YO10 5DD, UK
{anju.johnson,alan.millard,david.halliday,andy.tyrrell,
jon.timmis}@york.ac.uk

Abstract. In this paper a novel self-repairing learning rule is proposed which is a combination of the spike-timing-dependent plasticity (STDP) and Bienenstock, Cooper, and Munro (BCM) learning rules: in the derivation of this rule account is taken of the coupling of GABA interneurons to the tripartite synapse. The rule modulates the plasticity level by shifting the plasticity window, associated with STDP, up and down the vertical axis as a function of postsynaptic neural activity. Specifically when neurons are inactive, the window is shifted up the vertical axis (open) and as the postsynaptic neuron activity increases and, as learning progresses, the plasticity window moves down the vertical axis until learning ceases. Simulation results are presented which show that the proposed approach can still maintain the network performance even with a fault density approaching 80% and because the rule is implemented using a minimal computational overhead it has potential for large scale spiking neural networks in hardware.

Keywords: Astrocyte-neuron network · Learning window · Self-repair · Fault tolerance

1 Introduction

Spiking neural networks (SNNs) use models derived from the spike timing of neurons to encode and process information. Recent research has demonstrated the advantages of these computing paradigms in modelling memory [1], pattern recognition [2], fault tolerance [3] and also in many other applications [4,5]. Astrocytes have been shown to co-exist with neurons [6] where these cells communicate with synapses and neurons, and in doing so, regulate synaptic morphology and formation [6]. Artificial astrocyte cells together with spiking neurons form an astrocyte-neuron network (S-ANN) which facilitates a distributed and fine-grained self-repair capability. The authors have proposed this self-repairing

D. Liu et al. (Eds.): ICONIP 2017, Part VI, LNCS 10639, pp. 384–392, 2017.
https://doi.org/10.1007/978-3-319-70136-3_41

mechanism in an earlier paper [7] and also applied it to hardware systems with the aim of enhancing the fault-tolerant capability of the system [8,9]. In these papers, the pre-synaptic terminal receives the feedback signals from the post-synaptic neuron and astrocyte cell, respectively, which modulate the probability of release (PR) of all synapses associated with the postsynaptic neuron. For example, if synapses are damaged to such an extent that postsynaptic neural activity ceases, then other undamaged synapses will be potentiated by the astrocyte cell until the neural activity is restored (repair) [7].

In this paper, we go further and propose a novel self-repairing learning rule that uses recent evidence [7] to explain how the spike-timing-dependent plasticity (STDP) and Bienenstock, Cooper, and Munro (BCM) learning rules co-exist to give a learning function that is under the control of postsynaptic neuron activity. The key novelty in this work is that we now couple a GABA interneuron with tripartite synapses and show that this interaction can implement a presynaptic frequency selectivity capability through modulation of PR at synaptic sites, and that the PR parameter is also under the control of the postsynaptic firing activity: modulation of PR by postsynaptic activity underpins self-repair. The rest of paper is organized by follows. Section 2 presents the self-repairing learning rule in detail. Section 3 gives the simulation results and Sect. 4 concludes the paper.

2   Self-repairing Learning Rule

This section discusses the biophysical interactions that occur at the tripartite synapse in the presence of GABA interneurons and subsequently shows how such interactions can be interpreted to give rise to a self-repairing capability.

2.1   Activity-Dependent Mechanism in the S-ANNs

Figure 1 represents the signalling pathways between a GABA interneuron and the tripartite synapse [10] at a low presynaptic frequency (A) and at a high presynaptic frequency (B). The conventional tripartite synapse consists of a presynaptic terminal, a postsynaptic terminal, and an astrocyte terminal. However, we now consider the new additional signalling pathways between these terminals and a GABA interneuron terminal. Note also that we are taking the presynaptic spiking frequency (f_{pre}) to be the same as that of the GABA neuron [10].

At low f_{pre} GABA binds to GABA-A receptors on the presynaptic terminal and to GABA-B receptors on the astrocyte (Fig. 1A). However, because of inosotil 1, 4, 5-trisphosphate (IP_3) degradation within the astrocyte an insufficient amount of GABA is released to open calcium stores in the astrocyte at low f_{pre} and therefore there is no gliotransmitter release from the astrocyte. Consequently because GABA is binding to GABA-A receptors at the presynaptic terminal under low f_{pre}, then this has an inhibitory effect represented as a low PR value (Fig. 1A). However, if f_{pre} is increased (Fig. 1B), a point is reached whereby a sufficient amount of IP_3 exists within the astrocyte to trigger the opening of the calcium store and in this case gliotransmitter is released and

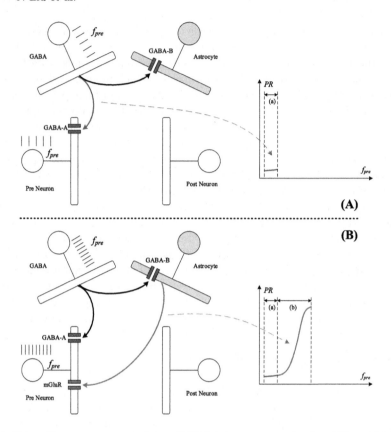

Fig. 1. Tripartite synapse coupled to a GABA interneuron under low (A) and high (B) presynaptic firing.

binds to group I metabotropic Glutamate Receptors (mGluR) on the presynaptic receptors. This overrides the inhibitory effect and causes a rapid increase in PR at the presynaptic terminal, as shown in Fig. 1B. However, if f_{pre} continuous to increase the IP_3 within the astrocyte increase and an upper threshold level is reached whereby the calcium oscillations stops and the release of gliotransmitter by the astrocyte ceases. This causes a fall-off in PR as shown in Fig. 2. Therefore, inhibitory GABA interneurons coupled to tripartite synapses appears to give rise to a frequency filtering effect where the effective passband is a function of cell morphology, receptor density and other factors.

To minimise the computational overhead we describe the relationship between the spike frequency (f_{pre}) and synaptic PR using a Gaussian function, as per Fig. 2, with the three stages of (a)–(c) as described above.

The Gaussian curve is described by

$$PR = e^{-\frac{(f_{pre} - f_s)^2}{2\sigma^2}}, \tag{1}$$

where f_s is the centre frequency and σ is the width of the Gaussian passband.

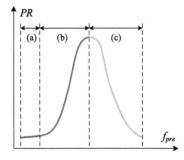

Fig. 2. PR vs f_{pre} for a tripartite synapse and GABA interneuron.

2.2   Self-repairing Learning Rule

In this paper, the Leaky Integrate-and-Fire (LIF) neuron model [11] is employed due to its relatively low computing and minimal parameter tuning requirements. It is given by

$$\tau_m \frac{dv}{dt} = -v(t) + R_m \sum_{i=1}^{n} I_{syn}^i(t), \qquad (2)$$

where τ_m is the neuron membrane time constant, v is the neuron membrane potential, R_m is the membrane resistance, I_{syn}^i is the current injected to the neuron membrane by i^{th} synapse, and n is the total number of synapses associated with the neuron. When the neuron membrane potential v is greater than the firing threshold value v_{th}, the neuron fires and outputs a spike. Subsequently, it goes to the reset state and remains for the duration of the refractory period ($\sim 2\,\text{ms}$).

To implement a self-repairing mechanism for the S-ANN, a learning algorithm needs to be designed. In this approach, the STDP [12,13], together with BCM learning rule [14,15], are combined to develop the BCM-STDP rule. STDP uses the time difference between presynaptic and postsynaptic spikes to adjust the synaptic weights, where the equations in (3) cause long-term potentiation (LTP) for $\Delta t \leq 0$ and long-term depression (LTD) for $\Delta t > 0$. In this approach, potentiation/depression is described by

$$\delta w(\Delta t) = \begin{cases} A_0 exp(\dfrac{\Delta t}{\tau_+}), & \Delta t \leq 0 \\ -A_0 exp(\dfrac{\Delta t}{\tau_-}), & \Delta t > 0 \end{cases} \qquad (3)$$

where $\delta w(\Delta t)$ is the weight update, Δt is the time difference between presynaptic and postsynaptic spike events, A_0 is the height of STDP learning window controlling the maximum levels of weight potentiation and depression, τ_+ and τ_- control the decay rate of weight updating for potentiation and depression, respectively. A symmetrical plasticity window is assumed and $\tau_+ = \tau_- = 40\,ms$.

In addition, the BCM learning rule modulates the height of the STDP plasticity window as a function of the actual firing rate of neuron according to

$$A_0 = \frac{A}{1 + e^{a(f-f_o)}} - A_- \tag{4}$$

where f and f_o are the actual and target firing rates of the postsynaptic neuron, respectively. A is the maximum height of plasticity window and A_- is the maximum height of the plasticity window for depression. The parameter a is constant which controls the opening/closing speed of the plasticity window and is found experimentally to be 0.1.

While the model in (4) does not capture the detailed biophysical processes underpinning the functional relationship between postsynaptic neural activity and the level of plasticity, we offer up here a plausible explanation for this. In a recent paper [7] it was shown that the endocannabinoid retrograde signaling pathways cause the level of IP_3 within astrocytes to increase (the indirect pathway) due to postsynaptic activity. Therefore, if f_{pre} is such that the PR value is maximum (see Fig. 2) then the IP_3 level within the astrocyte is between a lower and upper threshold limit and a calcium wave results. Under this condition and with little or no postsynaptic neural activity, the level of IP_3 will remain unchanged and PR will be at its maximum level (high level of plasticity). However, as learning progresses and the postsynaptic activity increases the indirect retrograde pathway strengthens causing the level of IP_3 within the astrocyte to increase and with sufficiently high postsynaptic activity (after a period of learning) the level of IP_3 moves above the upper threshold and the calcium wave ceases resulting in a falloff in PR (low level of plasticity). Hence it is proposed in this work that the retrograde signaling pathway may be the link between neural activity and the level of plasticity as proposed in the BCM rule. However, the authors are currently exploring this retrograde signaling pathway further to distill out a more detailed and biophysical based model, which will be the subject of a subsequent publication.

3   Results

This section presents simulation results where, in Fig. 3, the S-ANN includes two presynaptic neurons (N1 and N2), a postsynaptic neuron (N3) and two astrocyte cells connecting to the synapses. Each pre-post neural coupling has multiple synaptic pathways (8 in total) where each pathway is assumed to be of morphology modelled by a different delay: each synaptic pathway is delayed from its neighbour by 2 ms and therefore with a minimum delay of zero, the maximum delay of a pathway is 14 ms. As presented in Sect. 2.1, astrocyte cell modulates the synaptic transmission and determines the activities of postsynaptic neurons. In this experiment, we are using an input Poisson spike train for both presynaptic neurons and the centre frequency for all "filter" synapses is 25 Hz, i.e. when $f_{pre} = 25$ Hz, PR is maximum. The target frequency of N3 is also set to 25 Hz. The performance of this S-ANN is analysed under two different conditions.

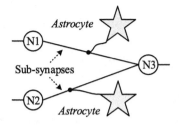

Fig. 3. An S-ANN with three neurons and two astrocyte cells.

The first condition is a healthy S-ANN with different input patterns, through which the pattern recognition capability of the network can be evaluated. The second condition is a faulty S-ANN where several synapses are damaged and the self-repairing mechanism of the S-ANN will be evaluated.

3.1 No Faults

Two input spike trains (25 Hz) are used to test the network performance under the no fault condition. As a 25 Hz spike train is compatible with the center frequency of the filter synapses we anticipate that a normal learning phase will occur with the postsynaptic target frequency also set to 25 Hz. Figure 4 shows the results of output spike frequency of N3 under the above conditions and, as can be seen, the spike frequency of N3 increases gradually during the training phase and eventually stabilizes at 25 Hz after ~60 s. Figure 5 shows the results of synaptic weights which as expected, show a slow potentiation over the learning period and stabilizes at ~80 s. Additional simulations (not shown) were carried out with presynaptic spike train frequencies outside the filter window and showed that no learning occurred, which verified that our network was selective to the input spike train patterns centered at or close to 25 Hz.

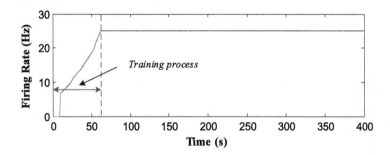

Fig. 4. Firing rate of N3 under the condition of no faults.

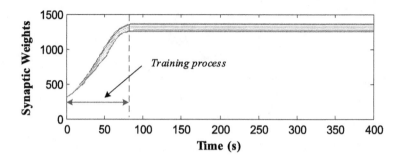

Fig. 5. Synaptic weights under the condition of no faults.

3.2   Partial Faults

To evaluate the self-repairing capability of the proposed S-ANN, the spike train frequency of both N1 and N2 were again set to the center frequency of the Gaussian curve (=25 Hz) and the S-ANN was trained as before (see Fig. 6) with a target frequency of 25 Hz for N3. However, after a normal training period had finished (200 s) 6 of the 8 synapses connecting N2 to N3 were broken (PR was forced low) which represents a fault density of 75%. Figure 6 shows the activity of N3 diminishes at 200 s where its activity drops to ˜17 Hz due to the impact of the faults. From time 200 s the learning window re-opens and the training process then restarts and the healthy synapses have their PR increased. Figure 7 shows the synapse re-training or adjustment. This process of retraining the network to recover the firing rate of N3 defines the self-repairing process. It can be seen that the synaptic weights of the remaining healthy synapses potentiate further within a time frame of ˜75 s and the firing rate of N3 recovers in a little under 60 s (see Fig. 6) to the pre-fault value. Based on this self-repairing mechanism, even when the faults occur and the synaptic connections are damaged, the network still retains the capability to reorganize itself by re-training and consequently recover to the pre-fault mapping. This is a very important capability for the fault-tolerant hardware systems due to the distributed, fine-grained repair capability which will yield a significantly enhanced reliable performance over conventional approaches [8].

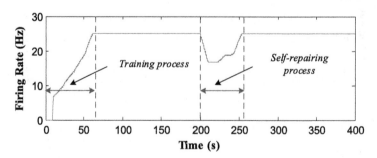

Fig. 6. Firing rate of N3 under the condition of partial faults.

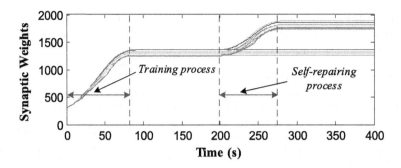

Fig. 7. Synaptic weights under the condition of partial faults.

4   Conclusion

A self-repairing astrocyte-neuron network is proposed where a GABA interneuron is coupled with a tripartite synapse. This coupling facilitates a presynaptic frequency selectivity capability which can route input data, coded in spike trains, to different neuron within the S-ANN. Furthermore, the probability of release at tripartite synapses is modulated by both the pre and post synaptic frequency which provides a novel self-repairing learning rule which can learn new data patterns, assign them to neurons in the output layer and maintain this mapping in the presence of faulty connections between neurons. This self-repairing learning rule combines both the STDP and BCM rule and a plausible biophysical explanation for this was presented. Results presented demonstrate that when faults occur, the firing rate of post-synaptic neuron drops which re-opens the learning window and the S-ANN then re-trains to maintain the original input/output mapping. It was also shown that this mapping can be recovered for fault densities as high as 75% and future work will explore the biophysical under-pinning for this self-repairing capability and developed S-ANNs that can be applied to real world fault-tolerant application domains, e.g. robotics, automotive or aerospace.

Acknowledgments. This work is part of the EPSRC funded SPANNER project (EP/N007141X/1) (EP/N007050/1).

References

1. Hu, J., Tang, H., Tan, K.C.: A hierarchical organized memory model using spiking neurons. In: International Joint Conference on Neural Networks, pp. 1–6 (2013)
2. McCarroll, N., Belatreche, A., Harkin, J., Li, Y.: Bio-inspired hybrid framework for multi-view face detection. In: Arik, S., Huang, T., Lai, W.K., Liu, Q. (eds.) ICONIP 2015. LNCS, vol. 9492, pp. 232–239. Springer, Cham (2015). doi:10.1007/978-3-319-26561-2_28
3. Liu, J., Harkin, J., McElholm, M., McDaid, L., Jimenez-Fernandez, A., Linares-Barranco, A.: Case study: Bio-inspired self-adaptive strategy for spike-based PID controller. In: IEEE International Symposium on Circuits and Systems (ISCAS), pp. 2700–2703 (2015)

4. Service, R.F.: The brain chip. Science **345**(6197), 614–616 (2014)
5. Furber, S.B.: Brain-inspired computing. IET Comput. Digital Tech. **10**(6), 299–305 (2015)
6. Stevens, B.: Neuron-astrocyte signaling in the development and plasticity of neural circuits. Neurosignals **16**(4), 278–288 (2008)
7. Wade, J., McDaid, L., Harkin, J., Crunelli, V., Kelso, S.: Self-repair in a bidirectionally coupled astrocyte-neuron (AN) system based on retrograde signaling. Front. Comput. Neurosci. **6**(76), 1–12 (2012)
8. Liu, J., Harkin, J., Maguire, L.P., Mcdaid, L.J., Wade, J.J.: SPANNER: A self-repairing spiking neural network hardware architecture. IEEE Trans. Neural Netw. Learn. Syst. 1–14 (2017)
9. Johnson, A.P., Halliday, D.M., Millard, A.G., Tyrrell, A.M., Timmis, J., Liu, J., Harkin, J., Mcdaid, L., Karim, S.: An FPGA-based hardware-efficient fault-tolerant astrocyte-neuron network. In: IEEE Symposium Series on Computational Intelligence, pp. 1–8 (2016)
10. Perea, G., Gómez, R., Mederos, S., Covelo, A., Ballesteros, J.J., Schlosser, L., Hernández-Vivanco, A., Martín-Fernández, M., Quintana, R., Rayan, A., Díez, A., Fuenzalida, M., Agarwal, A., Bergles, D.E., Bettler, B., Manahan-Vaughan, D., Martín, E.D., Kirchhoff, F., Araque, A.: Activity-dependent switch of GABAergic inhibition into glutamatergic excitation in astrocyte-neuron networks. eLife **5**, 1–26 (2016)
11. Gerstner, W., Kistler, W.M.: Spiking Neuron Models: Single Neurons, Populations, Plasticity. Cambridge University Press, Cambridge (2002)
12. Abbott, L.F., Nelson, S.B.: Synaptic plasticity: taming the beast. Nat. Neurosci. **3**, 1178–1183 (2000)
13. Song, S., Miller, K.D., Abbott, L.F.: Competitive Hebbian learning through spike-timing-dependent synaptic plasticity. Nat. Neurosci. **3**, 919–926 (2000)
14. Bienenstock, E.L., Cooper, L.N., Munro, P.W.: Theory for the development of neuron selectivity: orientation specificity and binocular interaction in visual cortex. J. Neurosci. **2**(1), 32–48 (1982)
15. Bear, M.F., Cooper, L.N., Ebner, F.F.: A physiological basis for a theory of synapse modification. Science **237**(4810), 42–48 (1986)

Finite-Time Adaptive Attitude Stabilization for Spacecraft Based on Modified Power Reaching Law

Meiling Tao, Qiang Chen, Xiongxiong He[✉], and Hualiang Zhuang

Data-Driven Intelligent Systems Laboratory, College of Information Engineering,
Zhejiang University of Technology, Hangzhou 310023, China
hxx@zjut.edu.cn

Abstract. In this paper, a finite-time adaptive sliding mode control scheme is proposed for the attitude stabilization of spacecrafts with lumped uncertainties. By introducing an exponential function in the reaching law design, an improved reaching law is developed such that the faster convergence of sliding mainfold can be achieved. Then, an adaptive controller is proposed based on the modified reaching law to guarantee the finite time attitude stabilization of spacecrafts by adaptive estimating the bounds of uncertainties. Besides, the chattering problem is reduced by using a power rate term in the controller design. Simulations are given to illustrate the effectiveness and superior performance of the proposed method.

Keywords: Finite-time adaptive stabilization · Spacecraft system · Sliding mode control · Power reaching law

1 Introduction

Attitude stabilization for spacecrafts has gained extensive interest in recent years, however, it is still a challenge to achieve the attitude stabilization with rapid convergence and high accuracy. Recently, there have been numerous researches in the literature on spacecraft attitute control (see, for instance, [1–4]).

Due to the excellent properties such as robustness to uncertainties and faster convergence, sliding mode control has been widely used in spacecraft attitude control. In [2], two sliding mode controllers are proposed to drive system states to the origin with the finite-time convergence for spacecraft attitude stabilization. In [3], an adaptive sliding mode control (SMC) is proposed for spacecrafts to ensure that the attitude control can be achieved with actuator saturation. In [4], an adaptive finite-time fault-tolerant controller has been proposed for rigid spacecrafts with external disturbances subject to four types of actuator faults. In [5], a power rate reaching strategy based on the conventional reaching law is applied to reduce chattering, but it increased the reaching time. Recently, an exponential reaching law (ERL) was proposed in [6]. By introducing an exponential function in the reaching law design, the faster convergence of sliding

© Springer International Publishing AG 2017
D. Liu et al. (Eds.): ICONIP 2017, Part VI, LNCS 10639, pp. 393–402, 2017.
https://doi.org/10.1007/978-3-319-70136-3_42

mode variable can be achieved. Considering the convergence rate and the chattering problem, the choice of coefficient of sign function becomes sensitive. Based on ideas in [6], this paper proposes an adaptive controller based on the modified reaching law, and the finite time attitude stabilization is guaranteed for spacecrafts with system uncertainties and disturbances. Besides, the chattering problem is reduced by using a power rate term in the controller design.

The rest of this paper is organized as follows. In Sect. 2, a spacecraft attitude model is constructed based on unit quaternion and the transformed attitude dynamics is developed in a more convenient way. In Sect. 3, an adaptive controller with modified power reaching law (MPRL) is designed to ensure that the sliding states can converge in finite time rapidly, then the system states can converge into a small region through Lyapunov stability analysis. Simulation results are presented in Sect. 4. Finally, this paper is concluded in Sect. 5.

2 Preliminaries

2.1 Spacecraft Dynamics and Kinematics Equations

Consider the following attitude kinematics and dynamics equations of the spacecraft in terms of quaternion [7]:

$$J\dot{\omega} = -\omega^{\times} J\omega + u + d(t) \tag{1}$$

$$\dot{q}_v = \frac{1}{2} \left(q_v^{\times} + q_0 I_3 \right) \omega \tag{2}$$

$$\dot{q}_0 = -\frac{1}{2} q_v^T \omega \tag{3}$$

where $\omega \in \mathbb{R}^3$ is the angular velocity of the spacecraft; $I \in \mathbb{R}^{3\times3}$ is the identity matrix; $J \in \mathbb{R}^{3\times3}$ is the innertia matrix of the spacecraft, $u \in \mathbb{R}^3$ and $d(t) \in \mathbb{R}^3$ are the control torque and the external unknow disturbances including environmental disturbances, respectively. The unit quaternion $Q = [q_0, q_1, q_2, q_3]^T = [q_0, q_v^T]^T \in \mathbb{R} \times \mathbb{R}^3$ describes the attitude orientation and satisfies the constraint $q_0^2 + q_v^T q_v = 1$. The notation $a^{\times}$ for a vector $a = [a_1, a_2, a_3]^T$ is used to denote the skew-symmetric matrix $a^{\times} = [0, -a_3, a_2; a_3, 0, -a_1; -a_2, a_1, 0]$.

Assume that the inertia matrix J is a form of $J = J_0 + \Delta J$, where J_0 and ΔJ denote the nominal part and the uncertain part of J, respectively. Then, (1) can be rewritten as

$$J_0\dot{\omega} = -\omega^{\times} J_0\omega + u + d(t) - \Delta J\dot{\omega} - \omega^{\times} \Delta J\omega \tag{4}$$

Property 1. The nominal part J_0 is a symmetric and positive definite matrix and satisfies:

$$J_1\|x\|^2 \leq x^T J_0 x \leq J_2\|x\|^2, \forall x \in \mathbb{R}^3, \tag{5}$$

where J_1 and J_2 are positive constants, denoting the lower and upper bounds of J_0, respectively.

2.2 Transformed Spacecraft Attitude Dynamics

For a more convenient way to express the attitude dynamics controller design, the Lagrange-like equation in [4] is utilized to describe the spacecraft attitude dynamic (1). Let $T = \frac{1}{2}\left(q_v^\times + q_0 I_3\right) \in \mathbb{R}^{3\times3}$, and (2) can be rewritten as

$$\omega = P\dot{q}_v \tag{6}$$

with

$$P = T^{-1} = \left[\frac{1}{2}\left(q_v^\times + q_0 I_3\right)\right]^{-1} \tag{7}$$

Then, differentiating (6) yields:

$$\dot{\omega} = \dot{P}\dot{q}_v + P\ddot{q}_v \tag{8}$$

Substituting (6) and (8) into (4) and premultiplying both sides of the resulting expression by P^T leads to

$$J^*\ddot{q}_v = -\Xi\dot{q}_v + P^T u + T_d \tag{9}$$

where $J^* = P^T J_0 P$, $\Xi = P^T J_0 \dot{P} - P^T \left(J_0 P\dot{q}_v\right)^\times P$, and $T_d = P^T d\left(t\right) - P^T \Delta J\dot{\omega} - P^T \omega^\times \Delta J\omega$. Here, T_d is considered as the lumped disturbances and uncertainties. Regarding the dynamic model given in (9) and Property 1, some more properties and assumptions are given as follows.

Property 2. [8] The inertia matrix J^* is symmetric and positively definite, and the matrix $\dot{J}^* - 2\Xi$ satisfies the following skew-symmetric relationship:

$$x^T\left(\dot{J}^* - 2\Xi\right)x = 0, \quad \forall x \in \mathbb{R}^3, \tag{10}$$

Property 3. [8] The inertia matrix J^* satisfies the following bounded condition:

$$J_{\min}\|x\|^2 \le x^T J^* x \le J_{\max}\|x\|^2, \forall x \in \mathbb{R}^3, \tag{11}$$

where J_{min} and J_{max} are positive constants, denoting the lower and upper bounds of J^*, respectively.

Assumption 1. [8] *To guarantee the existence of P defined in (7), the following condition should be satisfied:*

$$\det\left(T\right) = \frac{1}{2}q_0 \ne 0 \quad \forall t \in [0, \infty) \tag{12}$$

Assumption 2. [9] *The lumped term T_d of the disturbances and uncertainties satisfies the following relationship:*

$$\|T_d\| \le \gamma_0 \Phi \tag{13}$$

where $\Phi = 1 + \|\omega\| + \|\omega\|^2$ and γ_0 is a positive constant.

3   Finite Time Adaptive Control

3.1   Modified Power Reaching Law

In this subsection, the sliding mainfold $s \in \mathbb{R}^3$ is selected as

$$s = \dot{q}_v + \alpha q_v + \beta sig(q_v)^r \tag{14}$$

where α and β are positive constants; $r = \frac{r_1}{r_2}$, r_1 and r_2 are positive odd integers and $0 < r_1 < r_2$; the function $sig(q_v)^r$ is defined as

$$sig(q_v)^r = \left[|q_{v1}|^r sign(q_{v1}), |q_{v2}|^r sign(q_{v2}), |q_{v3}|^r sign(q_{v3})\right]^T$$

Differentiating (14) with respect to time yields

$$\dot{s} = \ddot{q}_v + \alpha \dot{q}_v + \beta \cdot r \cdot diag\left(|q_v|^{r-1}\right) \dot{q}_v \tag{15}$$

where $diag\left(|q_v|^{r-1}\right) = diag\left(\left[|q_{v1}|^{r-1}, |q_{v2}|^{r-1}, |q_{v3}|^{r-1}\right]\right) \in \mathbb{R}^{3\times3}$.

Remark 1. If $q_{vj} = 0$ and $\dot{q}_{vj} \neq 0$, the singularity occurs because of a negative fractional power $r - 1$. To avoid singularity, the first-order derivative of s is modified as [10]

$$\dot{s} = \ddot{q}_v + \alpha \dot{q}_v + \beta q_{vr} \tag{16}$$

with $q_{vr} \in \mathbb{R}^3$ defined as

$$q_{vr,j} = \begin{cases} r|q_{vj}|^{r-1}\dot{q}_{vj} & ,\text{if } |q_{vj}| \geq \epsilon \text{ and } \dot{q}_{vj} \neq 0 \\ r|\epsilon|^{r-1}\dot{q}_{vj} & ,\text{ if } |q_{vj}| < \epsilon \text{ and } \dot{q}_{vj} \neq 0 \\ 0, & \dot{q}_{vj} = 0 \end{cases} \tag{17}$$

where ϵ is a small constant. Then, considering (9), (14), and (16), it can be shown that

$$J^*\dot{s} = -\Xi s + P^T u + F + T_d \tag{18}$$

where $F = \Xi \alpha q_v + \Xi \beta sig(q_v)^r + J^*\alpha \dot{q}_v + J^*\beta q_{vr}$.

In this paper, a modified reaching law is proposed and expressed as

$$\dot{s} = -\frac{K}{D(s)}|s_j|^\theta sign(s) \tag{19}$$

$$D(s) = \mu + (\varphi - \mu)e^{-\vartheta\|s\|} \tag{20}$$

where $0 < \theta < 1$, $K > 0$, $0 < \mu < 1$, $\varphi = 1$ and $\vartheta > 0$.

In the proposed approach, as pointed out in [6], the $D(s)$ is strictly positive, so it does not affect the stability of SMC. If $\|s\|$ grows, $D(s)$ goes towards μ and $K|s_j|^\theta/D(s)$ would be $K|s_j|^\theta/\mu$, which is greater than K. In contrast, when $\|s\|$ decreases, it tends to $K|s_j|^\theta/\varphi$. This phenomenon makes the controller gain to be modified between $K|s_j|^\theta/\mu$ and $K|s_j|^\theta/\varphi$. Therefore, the MPRL specifies faster reaching speed compared with the conventional reaching law in [5] considering similar gain K. In addition, a term $|s_j|^\theta$ is employed to reduce the chattering problem which compares with the ERL in [6].

3.2   Controller Design and Stability Analysis

The finite-time adaptive control law is designed as

$$u = -P \left[u_{nom} + \frac{K}{D(s) \|P\|^2} |s_j|^\theta sign(s) \right] \tag{21}$$

with

$$u_{nom} = \frac{(\|F\| + \hat{\gamma}_0 \Phi) \|s\| s}{\|Ps\|^2} \tag{22}$$

where $\hat{\gamma}_0$ is the estimated values of γ_0, and the adaptive law is chosen as

$$\dot{\hat{\gamma}}_0 = c_0 (\Phi \|s\| - \varepsilon_0 \hat{\gamma}_0) \tag{23}$$

where c_0 and $\varepsilon_0 > 0$ are the designed parameters then the selection of c_0 is according to (29) and the initial estimated values satisfy $\hat{\gamma}_0(0) > 0$.

Lemma 1. [4] *Suppose $a_1, a_2, \ldots, a_n$ are positive numbers and $0 < p < 2$. Then, the following relationship exists:*

$$(a_1^2 + a_2^2 + \cdots + a_n^2)^p \le (a_1^p + a_2^p + \cdots + a_n^p)^2 \tag{24}$$

Lemma 2. [2] *Consider the nolinear system $\dot{x} = f(x, u)$. Suppose that there exist continuous function $V(x)$, scalars $\lambda > 0$, $0 < \alpha < 1$ and $0 < \eta < \infty$ such that*

$$\dot{V}(x) \le -\lambda V^\alpha(x) + \eta \tag{25}$$

Then, the trajectory of system $\dot{x} = f(x, u)$ is pratical finite-time stable (PFS).

Lemma 3. [4] *Consider the sliding mode mainfold s defined by (14). If the sliding mode mainfold satisfies $s = 0$, then the system states q_v and $\dot{q}_v$ can converge to $q_v = 0$ and $\dot{q}_v = 0$ in finite time, respectively.*

Theorem 1. *Considering the attitude control systems (1)–(3), the adaptive controllers in (21)–(22), and the update law in (23) under Assumptions 1-2, the sliding mode mainfold s, spacecraft attitude q_{vj} and angular velocity ω_j $(j = 1, 2, 3)$ are locally finite-time uniformly ultimately bounded.*

Proof. Consider the following Lyaounov function candidate V_1

$$V_1 = \frac{1}{2} s^T J^* s + \frac{1}{2c_0} \tilde{\gamma}_0^2$$

$$\begin{aligned}
\dot{V}_1 &= \tfrac{1}{2} s^T \dot{J}^* s + s^T J^* \dot{s} - \tfrac{1}{c_0} \tilde{\gamma}_0 \dot{\hat{\gamma}}_0 \\
&= \tfrac{1}{2} s^T \dot{J}^* s + s^T \left(-\Xi s + P^T u + F + T_d \right) - \tfrac{1}{c_0} \tilde{\gamma}_0 \dot{\hat{\gamma}}_0 \\
&\le -\|F\| \|s\| - \tfrac{K}{D(s)} \sum_{j=1}^3 |s|^{\theta+1} + \|F\| \|s\| + (\|T_d\| - \gamma_0 \Phi) \|s\| + \varepsilon_0 \tilde{\gamma}_0 \hat{\gamma}_0 \quad (26) \\
&\le -\tfrac{K}{D(s)} \sum_{j=1}^3 |s|^{\theta+1} + \varepsilon_0 \tilde{\gamma}_0 \hat{\gamma}_0
\end{aligned}$$

Note that for any positive scalar $\delta_0 > \frac{1}{2}$, the following inequlity exists:

$$\varepsilon_0 \tilde{\gamma}_0 \hat{\gamma}_0 = \varepsilon_0 \tilde{\gamma}_0 \left(-\tilde{\gamma}_0 + \gamma_0 \right) \leq \frac{-\varepsilon_0 (2\delta_0 - 1)}{2\delta_0} \tilde{\gamma}_0^2 + \frac{\varepsilon_0 \delta_0}{2} \gamma_0^2 \tag{27}$$

Thus inequality (26) can be expressed as

$$
\begin{aligned}
\dot{V}_1 &\leq -\frac{K}{D(s)} \sum_{j=1}^{3} |s|^{\theta+1} - \left(\frac{\varepsilon_0 (2\delta_0 - 1)}{2\delta_0} \tilde{\gamma}_0^2 \right)^{\frac{\theta+1}{2}} + \left(\frac{\varepsilon_0 (2\delta_0 - 1)}{2\delta_0} \tilde{\gamma}_0^2 \right)^{\frac{\theta+1}{2}} + \varepsilon_0 \tilde{\gamma}_0 \hat{\gamma}_0 \\
&\leq -\varsigma \left[\left(\tfrac{1}{2} s^T J^* s \right)^{\frac{\theta+1}{2}} + \left(\frac{1}{2c_0} \tilde{\gamma}_0^2 \right)^{\frac{\theta+1}{2}} \right] + \left(\frac{\varepsilon_0 (2\delta_0 - 1)}{2\delta_0} \tilde{\gamma}_0^2 \right)^{\frac{\theta+1}{2}} + \varepsilon_0 \tilde{\gamma}_0 \hat{\gamma}_0
\end{aligned}
\tag{28}
$$

where

$$\varsigma = \frac{K}{D(s) \left(\tfrac{1}{2} J_{\max} \right)^{(\theta+1)/2}}, \quad c_0 = \frac{\delta_0 \varsigma^{2/(\theta+1)}}{\varepsilon_0 (2\delta_0 - 1)} \tag{29}$$

Note that Lemma 1, $\delta_0 > \frac{1}{2}$ and $\frac{1}{2} < \frac{\theta+1}{2} < 1$

$$\dot{V}_1 \leq -\varsigma V_1^{\frac{\theta+1}{2}} + \left(\frac{\varepsilon_0 (2\delta_0 - 1)}{2\delta_0} \tilde{\gamma}_0^2 \right)^{\frac{\theta+1}{2}} + \varepsilon_0 \tilde{\gamma}_0 \hat{\gamma}_0 \tag{30}$$

According to [2], the following inequality can be obtained:

$$\left(\frac{\varepsilon_0 (2\delta_0 - 1)}{2\delta_0} \tilde{\gamma}_0^2 \right)^{\frac{\theta+1}{2}} + \varepsilon_0 \tilde{\gamma}_0 \hat{\gamma}_0 \leq \frac{\varepsilon_0 \delta_0}{2} \gamma_0^2 \tag{31}$$

Thus, from (30) and (31), we can obtain

$$\dot{V}_1 \leq -\varsigma V_1^{\frac{\theta+1}{2}} + \phi \tag{32}$$

where $\phi = \frac{\varepsilon_0 \delta_0}{2} \gamma_0^2$.

From (32), the sliding mainfold is finite-time uniformly ultimately bounded by using Lemma 2. Hence, the bounded convergence region Δs is obtained as

$$|s_j| \leq \Delta s = \sqrt{\frac{2}{J_{\max}}} \left(\frac{\phi}{\varsigma} \right)^{\frac{1}{\theta+1}}, j = 1, 2, 3 \tag{33}$$

Then, the sliding mode mainfold defined in (14) can be expressed as follows:

$$\dot{q}_{vj} + \alpha q_{vj} + \beta sig(q_{vj})^r = \eta_j , \ |\eta_j| \leq \Delta s \tag{34}$$

Then, (34) can be written in the following two forms:

$$\dot{q}_{vj} + \left(\alpha - \frac{\eta_j}{q_{vj}} \right) q_{vj} + \beta sig(q_{vj})^r = 0, \tag{35}$$

$$\dot{q}_{vj} + \alpha q_{vj} + \left(\beta - \frac{\eta_j}{sig(q_{vj})^r} \right) sig(q_{vj})^r = 0, \tag{36}$$

From (35) and (36), if $\alpha - \frac{\eta_j}{q_{vj}} > 0$ and $\beta - \frac{\eta_j}{sig(q_{vj})^r} > 0$, they have similar structures to the proposed sliding mode mainfold. Therefore, by using Lemma 3, the attitude q_{vj} converges to the regions

$$|q_{vj}| \le \frac{|\eta_j|}{\alpha} \le \frac{\Delta s}{\alpha} \tag{37}$$

$$|q_{vj}| \le \left(\frac{|\eta_j|}{\beta}\right)^{\frac{1}{r}} \le \left(\frac{\Delta s}{\beta}\right)^{\frac{1}{r}} \tag{38}$$

in finite time. Finally, the attitude q_{vj} converges to the region

$$|q_{vj}| \le \min\left\{\frac{\Delta s}{\alpha}, \left(\frac{\Delta s}{\beta}\right)^{\frac{1}{r}}\right\} \tag{39}$$

in finite time. Moreover, from (34), $\dot{q}_{vj}$ converges to the region

$$|\dot{q}_{vj}| \le |\eta_j| + \alpha |q_{vj}| + \beta |q_{vj}|^r \le 3\Delta s \tag{40}$$

in finite time.

It should be noticed that $\|q_v^\times + q_0 I_3\| = 1$. From (2), $\|\omega\|_\infty \le 2\sqrt{3}\|\dot{q}_v\|_\infty$ is obtained. However, because $|\dot{q}_{vj}| \le 3\Delta s$ $(j = 1, 2, 3)$ in finite time, $\|\dot{q}_v\|_\infty \le 3\Delta s$ can be satisfied in finite time. Therefore, considering (6) and Assumption 1, $|\omega_j| \le 6\sqrt{3}\Delta s$ can be concluded. Based on the above analysis, the sliding mode mainfold s, spacecraft attitude q_{vj} and angular velocity ω_j are locally finite-time uniformly ultimately bounded. This completes the proof.

Remark 2. From (33), it can be seen that the larger parameter ς or the smaller parameter ϕ will lead to the smaller Δs. Besides, as seen from (39), larger parameters α and β or smaller parameter r can result in the smaller accuracy of the attitude stabilization.

Remark 3. In order to avoid the chattering problems caused by the discontinous term $\frac{s}{\|Ps\|^2}$ in (22), we employ the continuous function $\frac{s}{\|Ps\|^2+\xi}$ to replace it in the following simulation section, where $\xi > 0$.

4   Simulation Results

In this section, some simulation results are provided to illustrate the effectiveness of the proposed controller. For comparison, the ERL in [5] and conventional reaching law in [6] are also simulated. The expressions can be writen as follows respectively

$$\dot{s} = -\frac{K}{D(s)} sign(s) \tag{41}$$

$$\dot{s} = -K \cdot sign(s) \tag{42}$$

where K and $D(s)$ is similar chosen as (19) and (20), respectively.

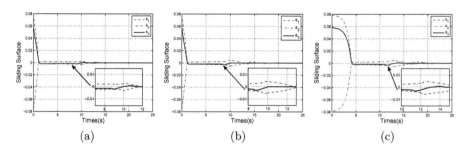

Fig. 1. Sliding surface with different reaching laws. (a)MPRL. (b)ERL. (c)Conventional reaching law.

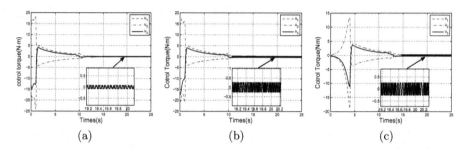

Fig. 2. Control torque with different reaching laws. (a)MPRL. (b)ERL. (c)Conventional reaching law.

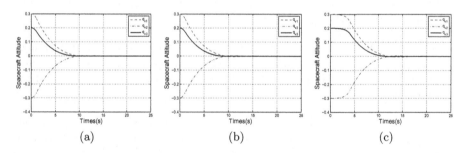

Fig. 3. Spacecraft attitude with different reaching laws. (a)MPRL. (b)ERL. (c)Conventional reaching law.

Considering the spacecraft model given in (1)–(3), the nominal inertia matrix of the spacecraft is $J_0 = diag\left([140, 120, 130]\right)$ kg $\cdot$ m^2 and the uncertainty in the inertia matrix $\Delta J = diag[sin(0.1t), 2sin(0.2t), 3sin(0.3t)]$ kg $\cdot$ m^2. The initial attitude orientation is chosen as $q_v(0) = [0.3, -0.3, 0.2]^T$ rad/s and $q_0(0) = 0.8832$. The initial angualar velocity is $\omega(0) = [0, 0, 0]^T$ rad/s. The external disturbance model is $d(t) = 0.005 \times [sin(0.8t), cos(0.5t), cos(0.3t)]^T$ N $\cdot$ m. For the sake of fairness, the parameters given in (19)–(20), the ERL in (41) and conventional reaching law in (42) are identical. Those parameters are chosen as $K = 0.5$, $\mu = 0.01$, $\theta = 0.1$, $\vartheta = 50$ and $\varphi = 1$. The parameters defined in (14) are chosen

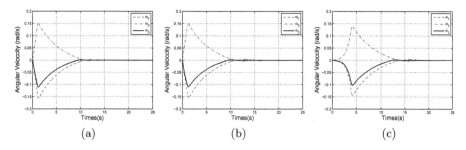

Fig. 4. Angular velocity response with different reaching laws. (a)MPRL. (b)ERL. (c)Conventional reaching law.

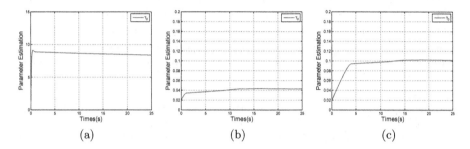

Fig. 5. Parameter estimation with different reaching laws. (a)MPRL. (b)ERL. (c)Conventional reaching law.

as $\alpha = 0.1$, $\beta = 0.1$, $r_1 = 3$, $r_2 = 5$. The parameters of adaptive law defined in (23) is chosen $\varepsilon_0 = 0.01$. The parameters in (29) is set as $J_{max} = 560$, $\delta_0 = 1$. The initial value of $\hat{\gamma}_0(0) = 0.02$. The parameter ξ is 0.0002.

Figures 1 and 2 show the sliding surface and control torque response, respectively. If $\|s\|$ grows, $D(s)$ goes towards 0.01 and $K/D(s)$ in (19) and ERL would be 50, which is greater than $K = 0.5$ in the conventional reaching law. In contrast, when $\|s\|$ decreases, it tends to 0.5. This phenomenon makes the controller gain to be modified between 50 and 0.5. As shown in Figs. 1 and 2, the convergence time of sliding surface using the MPRL and ERL are approximately 1.2 s, then the convergence time of sliding surface using the conventional reaching law is approximately 4.2 s. The MPRL and ERL outperforms the conventional reaching law, with higher steady performance and shorter reaching time. In addition, a term $|s_j|^\theta$ in (19) of MPRL reduces the chattering problem which compares with the ERL and conventional reaching law obviously.

The spacecraft attitude quaternion and angular velocity are shown in Figs. 3 and 4, respectively. The results show that both approaches can realize finite-time uniformly ultimately bounded. The convergence time of attitude quaternion using the MPRL and ERL are approximately 10 s, which are almost faster 2 s than the conventional reaching law. Moreover, the convergence time of angular velocity using the MPRL and ERL are approximately 11 s, which are nearly faster 3 s than the conventional reaching law. Based on similar analysis, the convergence speed of attitude quaternion and angular velocity using the MPRL and ERL are faster than that using the conventional reaching law. The corresponding estimated parameter is shown in Fig. 5. From Figs. 1, 2, 3, 4 and 5, it is clear that the proposed MPRL method can achieve superior control performance than the other two methods.

5   Conclusion

In this paper, the problem of attitude stabilization for spacecrafts with external disturbance and internal uncertainty has been considered. The main contribution of this paper is to propose an adaptive controller based on the modified reaching law, and the finite time attitude stabilization is guaranteed for spacecrafts with system uncertainties and disturbances. Besides, the chattering problem has been reduced by using a power rate term in the controller design. Simulation studies have been presented to verify that the proposed controller has stronger robustness and better control performance.

Acknowledgments. This work is supported by the National Natural Science Foundation of China under Grant No.61473262, No.6157332 and No.61403343, Zhejiang Provincial Natural Science Foundation under Grant No. Y17F030063.

References

1. Lu, K., Xia, Y., Zhu, Z., Basin, M.V.: Sliding mode attitude tracking of rigid spacecraft with disturbances. J. Franklin Inst. **349**(2), 413–440 (2012)
2. Zhu, Z., Xia, Y.Q., Fu, M.Y.: Attitude stabilization of rigid spacecraft with finite-time convergence. Int. J. Robust Nonlinear Control **21**(6), 686–702 (2011)
3. Zhu, Z., Xia, Y.Q., Fu, M.Y.: Adaptive sliding mode control for attitude stabilization with actuator saturation. IEEE Trans. Ind. Electron. **58**(10), 4898–4907 (2011)
4. Shen, Q., Wang, D., Zhu, S., Poh, E.K., Liu, T.: Finite-time fault-tolerant attitude stabilization for spacecraft with actuator saturation. IEEE Trans. Aerosp. Electron. Syst. **51**(3), 2390–2405 (2013)
5. Gao, W., Hung, J.C.: Variable structure control of nonlinear systems: a new approach. IEEE Trans. Ind. Electron **40**(1), 45–55 (1993)
6. Fallaha, C.J., Saad, M., Kanaan, H.Y., Al-Haddad, K.: Sliding-mode robot control with exponential reaching law. IEEE Trans. Ind. Electron. **58**(2), 600–610 (2011)
7. Sidi, M.J.: Spacecraft Dynamics and Control. Cambridge University Press, Cambridge (1997)
8. Costic, B.T., Dawson, D.M., De Queiroz, M.S., Kapila, V.: Quaternion-based adaptive attitude tracking controller without velocity measurements. J. Guidance Control Dyn. **24**(6), 1214–1222 (2001)
9. Wu, B.L., Wang, D.W., Poh, E.K.: Decentralized robust adaptive control for attitude synchronization under directed communication topology. J. Guidance Control Dyn. **34**(4), 1276–1282 (2011)
10. Zhao, D.Y., Li, S.Y., Zhu, Q.M.: A new TSMC prototype robust nonlinear task space control of a 6 DOF parallel robotic manipulator. Int. J. Control Autom. Syst. **8**(6), 1189–1197 (2010)

Neural Network Based Finite-Time Adaptive Backstepping Control of Flexible Joint Manipulators

Qiang Chen, Huihui Shi, and Mingxuan Sun[✉]

Data Driven Intelligent Systems Laboratory, College of Information Engineering,
Zhejiang University of Technology, Hangzhou, China
mxsun@zjut.edu.cn

Abstract. This paper proposes a finite-time adaptive backstepping control for an n-link flexible joint manipulator based on neural network approximation. In each recursive step, an adaptive virtual controller or practical controller is designed to guarantee that all the state errors can converge into a small region within a finite time. Besides, two simple neural networks are employed to approximate and compensate for the lumped uncertainties, and the finite time stability analysis is provided based on Lyapunov synthesis. Finally, simulation results show the effectiveness of the proposed method.

Keywords: Neural network · Finite-time adaptive control · Backstepping technique · Flexible joint manipulators

1 Introduction

Robotic manipulators are widely used in high performance areas, such as the industrial design, spacecraft, medical industry and so on. Lots of efforts have been done for the tracking control of robotic manipulators, such as fuzzy control [1], adaptive control [2–4], finite-time control [5], dynamic learning control [6], [7], sliding mode control [8], backstepping control [9] and so on.

However, most research works aforementioned mainly focus on rigid manipulators without considering joint flexibilities, which may reduce the effectiveness of the system. For the requirement of a high precision and performance, the joint flexibility of manipulators should be taken into account in both the modeling and control design. An adaptive control is first proposed in [10], and based on the idea of [10,11] presented a distributed adaptive containment control scheme. In [12], an adaptive fuzzy output feedback control is developed for a single-link flexible robot manipulator based on backstepping technique. In [13], a new robust output feedback control approach is proposed for flexible joint robots via the observer dynamic surface design approach by introducing a first-order low-pass filter at each recursive step of the backstepping design procedure, which can avoid the explosion of complexity.

© Springer International Publishing AG 2017
D. Liu et al. (Eds.): ICONIP 2017, Part VI, LNCS 10639, pp. 403–412, 2017.
https://doi.org/10.1007/978-3-319-70136-3_43

Although all the control schemes mentioned above are effective for the tracking control of flexible joint manipulators, most of them can only guarantee that the state errors are uniformly ultimately bounded as the time goes to infinity. Finite-time control is carried out in [14], which can guarantee the stability of system in finite time. According to the properties of the finite-time control, it is widely applied in various fields, such as servo systems, manipulators, spacecrafts and so on. An adaptive backstepping-based TSM control is proposed for uncertain nonlinear systems in [15], which can only guarantee the state error in final step converge in finite time. In [16], a non-singular terminal sliding mode (NTSM) backstepping control is developed, such that the errors reach the sliding manifold in finite time, but the system model should be known exactly.

In this paper, a finite-time adaptive backstepping control is proposed for an n-link flexible joint manipulator based on neural network approximation. Finite-time virtual controllers are designed in each recursive steps, which can guarantee all the state errors converge to a small neighbourhood around zero in finite time. What's more, neural networks are employed to approximate the unknown nonlinear function, and simulations are given to validate the effectiveness and satisfactory performance of the proposed method.

2 Dynamic Model of Flexible Joint Manipulator

The dynamic model of an n-link flexible joint manipulator is given as follows [10]:

$$\begin{cases} M(q)\ddot{q} + h(q,\theta) + K(q-\theta) = 0 \\ J\ddot{\theta} - K(q-\theta) = u \end{cases} \tag{1}$$

where $q \in R^n$ and $\theta \in R^n$ are the vectors of link positions and motor positions, respectively; $M(q) \in R^{n \times n}$ is the link inertia matrix; $J \in R^{n \times n}$ is the motor inertia matrix; $M(q)$ and J are symmetric nonsingular positive define; $K \in R^{n \times n}$ is a diagonal and positive define matrix representing the joint spring stiffness; $h(q,\theta)$ is a geometric term caused by the flexibility of the joint. $u \in R^n$ is the control torque.

Define $x_1 = q, x_2 = \dot{q}, x_3 = \theta, x_4 = \dot{\theta}$ and the system (1) can be rewritten in the following state space form

$$\begin{cases} \dot{x}_1 = x_2 \\ \dot{x}_2 = M^{-1}(x_1)\left(-h(x_1,x_2) - K(x_1 - x_3)\right) \\ \dot{x}_3 = x_4 \\ \dot{x}_4 = J^{-1}\left(u + K(x_1 - x_3)\right) \end{cases} \tag{2}$$

where $x_i, i = 1,2,3,4$ are measurable. $M(x_1), h(x_1,x_2), K$ and J are unknown terms.

The control objective is to design the controller u for the uncertain manipulator (2), such that the system output x_1 tracks a given smooth and bounded reference trajectory x_d within a finite time.

3   Controller Design

In this section, the proposed finite-time adaptive controller is designed according to the following recursive procedures.

Step1: Define the tracking error variable z_1 as

$$z_1 = x_1 - x_d \tag{3}$$

and its derivative can be written as

$$\begin{aligned} \dot{z}_1 &= \dot{x}_1 - \dot{x}_d \\ &= z_2 - \dot{x}_d + a_1 \end{aligned} \tag{4}$$

where $z_2 = x_2 - a_1$, and a_1 is a virtual controller given by

$$a_1 = -h_1 z_1 - k_1 z_1^{2\alpha - 1} + \dot{x}_d \tag{5}$$

where h_1 and k_1 are positive constants; $\alpha = \alpha_1/\alpha_2$, with α_1 and α_2 being positive odd integers, satisfying $\alpha_2 > \alpha_1$.

Then (4) can be rewritten as

$$\dot{z}_1 = z_2 - h_1 z_1 - k_1 z_1^{2\alpha - 1} \tag{6}$$

Step2: From (2), the derivative of z_2 is

$$\begin{aligned} \dot{z}_2 &= \dot{x}_2 - \dot{a}_1 \\ &= M^{-1}(x_1) K \left(-f_1(\overline{x}_1) - (x_1 - x_3) \right). \end{aligned} \tag{7}$$

where $f_1(\overline{x}_1) = K^{-1} h(x_1, x_2) + M(x_1) K^{-1} \dot{a}_1$ is an unknown function; $\overline{x}_1 = [x_1^T, x_2^T, \dot{a}_1^T]^T \in R^{3n}$.

In order to estimate $f_1(\overline{x}_1)$, we employ a simple sigmoid neural network (NN1) [17], and then $f_1(\overline{x}_1)$ can be expressed as

$$f_1(\overline{x}_1) = w_1^{*T} \Phi_1(\overline{x}_1) + \varepsilon_1 \tag{8}$$

where $w_1^* \in R^{i \times n}$ is a constant ideal weight matrix, and i is the number of neurons; ε_1 is the approximation error, satisfying $\|\varepsilon_1\| \leq \varepsilon_{1N}$, ε_{1N} is a positive constant; $\Phi_1(x)$ is the basis function represented as

$$\Phi_1(\overline{x}_1) = \frac{a_1}{b_1 + e^{-\frac{\overline{x}_1}{c_1}}} + d_1 \tag{9}$$

where a_1, b_1, c_1 and d_1 are all constant parameters.

Define $z_3 = x_3 - a_2$, and the derivative of z_2 is

$$\dot{z}_2 = M^{-1}(x_1) K \left(z_3 + a_2 - x_1 - w_1^{*T} \Phi_1(\overline{x}_1) - \varepsilon_1 \right) \tag{10}$$

where

$$a_2 = -z_1 - h_2 z_2 - k_2 z_2^{2\alpha - 1} + x_1 + \hat{w}_1^T \Phi_1(\overline{x}_1) - \hat{\varepsilon}_{1N} \frac{z_2}{\|z_2\|} \tag{11}$$

with h_2 and k_2 being positive constants; $\hat{w}_1$, $\hat{\varepsilon}_{1N}$ are the estimates of w_1^*, ε_{1N}. The update laws of $\hat{w}_1$ and $\hat{\varepsilon}_{1N}$ are given by

$$\dot{\hat{w}}_1 = -\Gamma_1(\Phi_1(\overline{x}_1)z_2^T + \sigma_1 \hat{w}_1) \qquad \dot{\hat{\varepsilon}}_{1N} = \gamma_1(\|z_2\| - \rho_1 \hat{\varepsilon}_{1N}) \qquad (12)$$

where $\Gamma_1 = \Gamma_1^T$, $\gamma_1 = \gamma_1^T$ are positive definite diagonal matrices; $\sigma_1 \hat{w}_1$ and $\rho_1 \hat{\varepsilon}_{1N}$ are introduced to enhance the robustness.

Substituting (11) into (10), we have

$$\dot{z}_2 = M^{-1}(x_1)K\left(z_3 - z_1 - h_2 z_2 - k_2 z_2^{2\alpha-1} - \tilde{w}_1^T \Phi_1(\overline{x}_1) - \hat{\varepsilon}_{1N}\frac{z_2}{\|z_2\|} - \varepsilon_1\right) \qquad (13)$$

Step3: Take the derivative of z_3 as

$$\begin{aligned}\dot{z}_3 &= \dot{x}_3 - \dot{a}_2 = x_4 - \dot{a}_2 \\ &= z_4 - \dot{a}_2 + a_3\end{aligned} \qquad (14)$$

where $z_4 = x_4 - a_3$, and a_3 is a virtual controller given by

$$a_3 = -z_2 - h_3 z_3 - k_3 z_3^{2\alpha-1} + \dot{a}_2 \qquad (15)$$

with h_3 and k_3 being positive constants.

Combining (14) with (15), $\dot{z}_3$ becomes

$$\dot{z}_3 = z_4 - z_2 - h_3 z_3 - k_3 z_3^{2\alpha-1} \qquad (16)$$

Step4: From (2), the derivative of z_2 is

$$\begin{aligned}\dot{z}_4 &= \dot{x}_4 - \dot{a}_3 \\ &= J^{-1}(u + f_2(\overline{x}_2))\end{aligned} \qquad (17)$$

where $f_2(\overline{x}_2) = K(x_1 - x_3) - J\dot{a}_3$, and $\overline{x}_2 = [x_1^T, x_3^T, \dot{a}_3^T]^T \in R^{3n}$.

Similar with step 2, $f_2(\overline{x}_2)$ can be approximated by using the second neural network (NN2), and written as

$$f_2(\overline{x}_2) = w_2^{*T} \Phi_2(\overline{x}_2) + \varepsilon_2 \qquad (18)$$

where $w_2^* \in R^{i \times n}$ is a constant ideal weight matrix; ε_2 is the approximation error, satisfying $\|\varepsilon_2\| \leq \varepsilon_{2N}$, ε_{2N} is a positive constant. $\Phi_2(\overline{x}_2)$ is the basis function represented as

$$\Phi_2(\overline{x}_2) = \frac{a_2}{b_2 + e^{-\frac{\overline{x}_2}{c_2}}} + d_2 \qquad (19)$$

where a_2, b_2, c_2 and d_2 are all constant parameters.

Differentiating z_4 yields

$$\dot{z}_4 = J^{-1}\left(u + w_2^{*T} \Phi_2(\overline{x}_2) + \varepsilon_2\right) \qquad (20)$$

and the practical controller is designed as

$$u = -z_3 - h_4 z_4 - k_4 z_4^{2\alpha-1} - \hat{w}_2^T \Phi_2(\overline{x}_2) - \hat{\varepsilon}_{2N} \frac{z_4}{\|z_4\|} \tag{21}$$

where h_4 and k_4 are positive constants; $\hat{w}_2$, $\hat{\varepsilon}$ are the estimates of w_2^*, ε_{2N}.
   The update laws of $\hat{w}_2$ and $\hat{\varepsilon}_{2N}$ are given by

$$\dot{\hat{w}}_2 = \Gamma_2(\Phi_2(\overline{x}_2)z_4^T - \sigma_2 \hat{w}_2) \qquad \dot{\hat{\varepsilon}}_{2N} = \gamma_2(\|z_4\| - \rho_2 \hat{\varepsilon}_{2N}) \tag{22}$$

where $\Gamma_2 = \Gamma_2^T$, $\gamma_2 = \gamma_2^T$ are positive definite diagonal matrices; $\sigma_2 \hat{w}_2$ and $\rho_2 \hat{\varepsilon}_{2N}$ are introduced to enhance the robustness.
   Then substituting (21) into (20), we can obtain

$$\dot{z}_4 = J^{-1}\left(-z_3 - h_4 z_4 - k_4 z_4^{2\alpha-1} + \widetilde{w}_2^T \Phi_2(\overline{x}_2) + \varepsilon_2 - \hat{\varepsilon}_{2N} \frac{z_4}{\|z_4\|}\right) \tag{23}$$

4   Stability Analysis

Lemma 1 [18]. Considering the system $\dot{x} = f(x, u)$, suppose there exists a Lyapunov function $V(x)$; scalars a, b are positive constants, satisfying $0 < a < 1, b > 1$; $\alpha > 0$, $\beta > 0$ and $0 < \eta < \infty$ such that $\dot{V}(x) \leq -\alpha V(x)^a - \beta V(x)^b + \eta$. Then, the trajectory of this system is finite-time stable. Therefore, the state errors of the closed-loop system is uniformly ultimately bounded into $\varrho_0 = \{\lim_{t \to T} x \mid V(x) \leq min\{(\frac{\eta}{(1-\theta)\alpha})^{\frac{1}{a}}, (\frac{\eta}{(1-\theta)\beta})^{\frac{1}{b}}\}\}$ in finite-time, where θ is a scalar, satisfying $0 < \theta \leq 1$.

Lemma 2 [19]. Suppose $a_1, a_2, \cdots, a_n$ and $0 \leq p_1 \leq 1$ are all positive numbers, then the following inequality holds:

$$(a_1^2 + a_2^2 + \cdots + a_n^2)^{2p_1} \leq \left(a_1^{2p_1} + a_2^{2p_1} + \cdots + a_n^{2p_1}\right)^2 \tag{24}$$

Theorem 1. Considering the flexible joint manipulator dynamic model (1) with the controller (21), the virtual controllers (5), (11) and (15), the update laws are (12) and (22), then

(1) All the signals of the closed-loop system are uniformly ultimately bounded.
(2) The tracking error z_1 can converge to a small neighborhood around zero in finite time.

Proof. (1) Choose the Lyapunov function

$$V = \frac{1}{2}z_1^T z_1 + \frac{1}{2}z_2^T M(x_1)K^{-1}z_2 + \frac{1}{2}z_3^T z_3 + \frac{1}{2}z_4^T J z_4 + \frac{1}{2}\widetilde{w}_1^T \Gamma_1^{-1}\widetilde{w}_1$$

$$+ \frac{1}{2}\widetilde{w}_2^T \Gamma_2^{-1}\widetilde{w}_2 + \frac{1}{2}\widetilde{\varepsilon}_{1N}^T \gamma_1^{-1}\widetilde{\varepsilon}_{1N} + \frac{1}{2}\widetilde{\varepsilon}_{2N}^T \gamma_2^{-1}\widetilde{\varepsilon}_{2N} \tag{25}$$

where $\widetilde{w}_1 = w_1^* - \hat{w}_1, \widetilde{w}_2 = w_2^* - \hat{w}_2, \widetilde{\varepsilon}_{1N} = \varepsilon_{1N} - \hat{\varepsilon}_{1N}, \widetilde{\varepsilon}_{2N} = \varepsilon_{2N} - \hat{\varepsilon}_{2N}$.

Differentiating (25) with respect to time and substituting (6), (13), (16) and (23) yield

$$
\begin{aligned}
\dot{V} &= z_1^T \dot{z}_1 + z_2^T M(x_1) K^{-1} \dot{z}_2 + z_3^T \dot{z}_3 + z_4^T J \dot{z}_4 - \sum_{k=1}^{2} \widetilde{w}_k^T \Gamma_k^{-1} \dot{\hat{w}}_k - \sum_{l=1}^{2} \widetilde{\varepsilon}_{lN}^T \gamma_l^{-1} \dot{\hat{\varepsilon}}_{lN} \\
&= - \sum_{i=1}^{4} h_i z_i^T z_i - \sum_{j=1}^{4} k_j z_j^T z_j^{2\alpha-1} - z_2^T \varepsilon_1 + z_4^T \varepsilon_2 - z_2^T \hat{\varepsilon}_{1N} \frac{z_2}{\|z_2\|} - z_4^T \hat{\varepsilon}_{2N} \frac{z_4}{\|z_4\|} \\
&\quad - z_2^T \widetilde{w}_1^T \Phi_1(\overline{x}_1) + z_4^T \widetilde{w}_2^T \Phi_2(\overline{x}_2) - \sum_{k=1}^{2} \widetilde{w}_k^T \Gamma_k^{-1} \dot{\hat{w}}_k - \sum_{l=1}^{2} \widetilde{\varepsilon}_{lN}^T \gamma_l^{-1} \dot{\hat{\varepsilon}}_{lN}
\end{aligned}
\tag{26}
$$

Using the update laws (12) and (22), we can obtain

$$
\begin{aligned}
\dot{V} &= - \sum_{i=1}^{4} h_i z_i^T z_i - \sum_{j=1}^{4} k_j z_j^T z_j^{2\alpha-1} - z_2^T \varepsilon_1 + z_4^T \varepsilon_2 - z_2^T \hat{\varepsilon}_{1N} \frac{z_2}{\|z_2\|} - z_4^T \hat{\varepsilon}_{2N} \frac{z_4}{\|z_4\|} \\
&\quad + \sigma_1 \widetilde{w}_1^T \hat{w}_1 + \sigma_2 \widetilde{w}_2^T \hat{w}_2 - z_2^T \widetilde{\varepsilon}_{1N} + \rho_1 \widetilde{\varepsilon}_{1N}^T \hat{\varepsilon}_{1N} - z_4^T \widetilde{\varepsilon}_{2N} + \rho_2 \widetilde{\varepsilon}_{2N}^T \hat{\varepsilon}_{2N} \\
&\leq - \sum_{i=1}^{4} h_i z_i^T z_i + \sigma_1 \widetilde{w}_1^T \hat{w}_1 + \sigma_2 \widetilde{w}_2^T \hat{w}_2 + \rho_1 \widetilde{\varepsilon}_{1N}^T \hat{\varepsilon}_{1N} + \rho_2 \widetilde{\varepsilon}_{2N}^T \hat{\varepsilon}_{2N}
\end{aligned}
\tag{27}
$$

By the triangle inequality, we have

$$
\begin{aligned}
\sigma_i \widetilde{w}_i^T \hat{w}_i &= \sigma_i \widetilde{w}_i^T (w_i^* - \widetilde{w}_i) & \rho_i \widetilde{\varepsilon}_{iN}^T \hat{\varepsilon}_{iN} &= \rho_i \widetilde{\varepsilon}_{iN}^T (\varepsilon_{iN} - \widetilde{\varepsilon}_{iN}) \\
&\leq -\sigma_i \|\widetilde{w}_i\|^2 + \sigma_i \|\widetilde{w}_i\| \|w_i^*\| & &\leq -\rho_i \|\widetilde{\varepsilon}_{iN}\|^2 + \rho_i \|\widetilde{\varepsilon}_{iN}\| \|\varepsilon_{iN}\| \\
&\leq -\tfrac{1}{2} \sigma_i \|\widetilde{w}_i\|^2 + \tfrac{1}{2} \sigma_i \|w_i^*\|^2 & &\leq -\tfrac{1}{2} \rho_i \|\widetilde{\varepsilon}_{iN}\|^2 + \tfrac{1}{2} \rho_i \|\varepsilon_{iN}\|^2
\end{aligned}
$$

where $i = 1, 2$.

We can obtain that

$$
\begin{aligned}
\dot{V} &\leq - \sum_{i=1}^{4} h_i z_i^T z_i - \tfrac{1}{2} \sigma_1 \|\widetilde{w}_1\|^2 - \tfrac{1}{2} \sigma_2 \|\widetilde{w}_2\|^2 - \tfrac{1}{2} \rho_1 \|\widetilde{\varepsilon}_{1N}\|^2 - \tfrac{1}{2} \rho_2 \|\widetilde{\varepsilon}_{2N}\|^2 \\
&\quad + \tfrac{1}{2} \sigma_1 w_1^{*2} + \tfrac{1}{2} \sigma_2 w_2^{*2} + \tfrac{1}{2} \rho_1 \varepsilon_{1N}^2 + \tfrac{1}{2} \rho_2 \varepsilon_{2N}^2
\end{aligned}
\tag{28}
$$

Then $\dot{V}$ can be rewritten to be

$$
\begin{aligned}
\dot{V} &\leq -\eta_1 V + \tfrac{1}{2} \sigma_1 w_1^{*2} + \tfrac{1}{2} \sigma_2 w_2^{*2} + \tfrac{1}{2} \rho_1 \varepsilon_{1N}^2 + \tfrac{1}{2} \rho_2 \varepsilon_{2N}^2 \\
&\leq -\eta_1 V + \delta_1
\end{aligned}
\tag{29}
$$

where $\eta_1 = Min\{2h_1, 2h_2 \lambda_{min}\{M^{-1}(x_1)K\}, 2h_3, 2h_4 \lambda_{min}\{J^{-1}\}, \sigma_1 \lambda_{min}\{\Gamma_1\}, \sigma_2 \lambda_{min}\{\Gamma_2\}, \rho_1 \lambda_{min}\{\gamma_1\}, \rho_2 \lambda_{min}\{\gamma_2\}\}$; $\delta_1 = \tfrac{1}{2} \sigma_1 w_1^{*2} + \tfrac{1}{2} \sigma_2 w_2^{*2} + \tfrac{1}{2} \rho_1 \varepsilon_{1N}^2 + \tfrac{1}{2} \rho_2 \varepsilon_{2N}^2$ which is bounded.

Therefore, we can obtain that z_i is bounded, $\|z_i\| \leq Z_{iN}$, $i = 1, 2, 3, 4$. It can be seen from the formula (29), $\widetilde{w}_1$ and $\widetilde{w}_2$ are bounded, $\|\widetilde{w}_1\| \leq W_{1N}, \|\widetilde{w}_2\| \leq W_{2N}$. Considering the definition of $\widetilde{\varepsilon}_{1N}, \widetilde{\varepsilon}_{2N}$, they are bounded, satisfying $\|\widetilde{\varepsilon}_{1N}\| \leq E_{1\mu}, \|\widetilde{\varepsilon}_{2N}\| \leq E_{2\mu}$. What's more, the given reference trajectory x_d and $\dot{x}_d$ are bounded too. Combining (3) and (4), it can be obtained that x_i and $\dot{x}_i$, $i = 1, 2, 3, 4$ are both bounded. Thus, all the signals in the closed-loop system are uniformly ultimately bounded.

Proof. (2) According to the expression of (9) and (19), $\Phi_i(\overline{x}_i)$ is bounded by $-d_i \leq \Phi_i(\overline{x}_i) \leq \frac{a_i}{b_i} + d_i, \|\Phi_i(\overline{x}_i)\| \leq \Phi_{iN}, i = 1, 2$. Meanwhile, according to the property of Frobenius norm, we can obtain that

$$\|\widetilde{w}_i^T \Phi_i(\overline{x}_i)\|_F \leq W_{iN} \Phi_{iN} \quad i = 1, 2 \tag{30}$$

Select the Lyapunov function as

$$V = \frac{1}{2} z_1^T z_1 + \frac{1}{2} z_2^T M(x_1) K^{-1} z_2 + \frac{1}{2} z_3^T z_3 + \frac{1}{2} z_4^T J z_4 \tag{31}$$

Differentiating V, we have

$$\begin{aligned}
\dot{V} &= z_1^T \dot{z}_1 + z_2^T M(x_1) K^{-1} \dot{z}_2 + z_3^T \dot{z}_3 + z_4^T J \dot{z}_4 \\
&= -\sum_{i=1}^{4} h_i z_i^T z_i - \sum_{j=1}^{4} k_j z_j^T z_j^{2\alpha-1} - z_2^T \varepsilon_1 + z_4^T \varepsilon_2 - z_2^T \widetilde{w}_1^T \Phi_1(\overline{x}_1) \\
&\quad + z_4^T \widetilde{w}_2^T \Phi_2(\overline{x}_2) - z_2^T \hat{\varepsilon}_{1N} \frac{z_2}{\|z_2\|} - z_4^T \hat{\varepsilon}_{2N} \frac{z_4}{\|z_4\|}
\end{aligned} \tag{32}$$

With the similar proof process of (1), we can directly obtain

$$\begin{aligned}
\dot{V} &\leq -\eta_2 V - \eta_3 V^\alpha + \|z_2\| \|\widetilde{w}_1\| \|\Phi_1(\overline{x}_1)\| + \|z_2\| \|\widetilde{\varepsilon}_{1N}\| + \|z_4\| \|\widetilde{w}_2\| \|\Phi_2(\overline{x}_2)\| + \|z_4\| \|\widetilde{\varepsilon}_{4N}\| \\
&\leq -\eta_2 V - \eta_3 V^\alpha + Z_{2N} W_{1N} \Phi_{1N} + Z_{4N} W_{2N} \Phi_{2N} + Z_{2N} E_{1\mu} + Z_{4N} E_{2\mu} \\
&\leq -\eta_2 V - \eta_3 V^\alpha + \delta_2
\end{aligned} \tag{33}$$

where $\eta_2 = Min\{2h_1, 2h_2 \lambda_{min}\{M^{-1}(x_1)K\}, 2h_3, 2h_4 \lambda_{min}\{J^{-1}\}\}$, $\eta_3 = Min\{2^\alpha k_1, (2M^{-1}(x_1)K)^\alpha k_2, 2^\alpha k_3, (2J^{-1})^\alpha k_4\}$, $\delta_2 = Z_{2N} W_{1N} \Phi_{1N} + Z_{4N} W_{2N} \Phi_{2N} + Z_{2N} E_{1\mu} + Z_{4N} E_{2\mu}$.

According to Lemma 1, the closed-loop system is finite-time stabe, and the system state errors $z_i, i = 1, 2, 3, 4$ converge to the region $\varrho = \{\lim_{t \to T} x \mid V(x) \leq min\{(\frac{\delta_2}{2(1-\theta)\eta_2}), (\frac{\delta_2}{2(1-\theta)\eta_3})^{\frac{1}{\alpha}}\}\}$ in finite time.

Remark. For avoiding the singularity problem due to the power term $(2\alpha - 1) < 1$, the $z_i^{2\alpha-1}$ is replaced by

$$\lambda(z_i) = \begin{cases} |z_i|^{2\alpha-1} \triangle z_i & if |z_i| \geq \epsilon \\ l_1 z_i + l_2 z_i^2 \triangle z_i & if |z_i| < \epsilon \end{cases} \quad i = 1, 2, 3, 4 \tag{34}$$

where $l_1 = (3 - 2\alpha)\epsilon^{2\alpha-2}$, $l_2 = (2\alpha - 2)\epsilon^{2\alpha-3}$. The expression of $\triangle z_i$ is

$$\triangle z_i = \begin{cases} sgn(z_i) & if \|\frac{z_i}{\varphi}\| \geq 1 \\ \frac{\|z_i\|}{\|z_i\|+\varphi} & if \|\frac{z_i}{\varphi}\| < 1 \end{cases} \quad i = 1, 2, 3, 4 \tag{35}$$

where φ is a positive constant.

5   Simulation Results

In this section, a single-link flexible joint manipulator system is expressed as follows

$$\begin{cases} M\ddot{q} + K(q - \theta) + mgLsin(q) = 0 \\ J\ddot{\theta} - K(q - \theta) = u \end{cases} \tag{36}$$

where m is the mass, g is the gravitational acceleration and L is the length of link. The parameters of the system is given as $m = 2.3, L = 1, g = 9.8, M = mL^2, J = 0.5$ and $K = 15$.

The parameters of the sigmoid functions (9) and (19) and the parameters in the update rules (12) and (22) are chosen as $a_1 = 10, b_1 = 2, c_1 = 1$ and $d_1 = -1.8; a_2 = 5, b_2 = 0.2, c_2 = 1$ and $d_2 = -4$. $\Gamma_1 = 0.05, \Gamma_2 = 0.1; \sigma_1 = 0.1, \sigma_2 = 0.1, \gamma_1 = 1, \gamma_2 = 0.5; \rho_1 = 5; \rho_2 = 5$. The virtual controllers (5), (11) and (15), the coefficients are given as $h_1 = 4, h_2 = 0.8, h_3 = 2, h_4 = 5; k_1 = 2.2, k_2 = 0.3, k_3 = 3, k_4 = 5; \alpha = 13/15$. The reference trajectory is defined as $x_d = sin(t)$. The initial state variable is selected as $x_d(0) = x_1(0) = x_2(0) = x_3(0) = x_4(0) = 0$; the initial weights $\hat{w}_1(0), \hat{w}_2(0), \hat{\varepsilon}_{1N}(0)$ and $\hat{\varepsilon}_{2N}(0)$ are chosen as random vectors, evenly spaced on $[-1, 1]$.

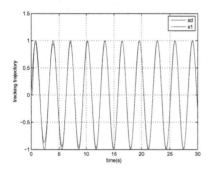

Fig. 1. Tracking trajectory

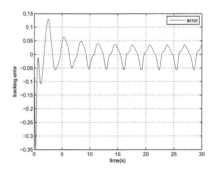

Fig. 2. Tracking error

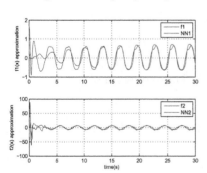

Fig. 3. Function approximation

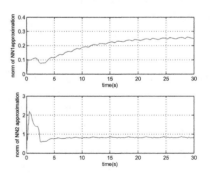

Fig. 4. The norm of NN weights

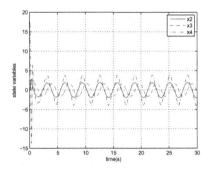

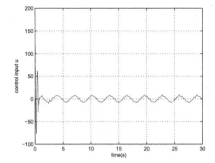

Fig. 5. Other state variables   **Fig. 6.** Control input

In Figs. 1 and 2, the tracking performance and corresponding tracking errors are provided, respectively. As shown in Figs. 1 and 2, we can see that the output x_1 can track the desired trajectory x_d rapidly, and the tracking error is guaranteed within a small region around zero. The performance of neural network approximation is shown in Figs. 3 and 4. From Figs. 3 and 4, it is clear that the neural networks (11) and (21) are able to approximate the unknown functions well with bounded weight norms. In Figs. 5 and 6, the other state variables and control input torque are given respectively. As shown in Figs. 1, 2, 3, 4, 5 and 6, the proposed controller (21) can achieve a satisfactory tracking performance and guarantee the tracking error converge to a small region.

6   Conclusion

This paper focus on a neural network based finite-time adaptive backstepping control for an n-link flexible joint manipulator. Within the finite-time virtual controllers, state errors are uniformly ultimately bounded in finite time, and neural network is employed to approximate the uncertainties of the system. Satisfactory tracking performance is achieved and finite-time stability is guaranteed with the designed practical controller. The effectiveness of the proposed method is proved the simulation results.

Acknowledgments. The authors would thank the support from the National Natural Science Foundation (NNSF) of China under Grant No. 61573320, No. 61473262 and No. 61403343, and Zhejiang Provincial Natural Science Foundation under Grant No. Y17F030063.

References

1. Li, Z., Yang, C., Tang, Y.: Decentralised adaptive fuzzy control of coordinated multiple mobile manipulators interacting with non-rigid environments. IET Control Theory Appl. **7**(3), 397–410 (2013)
2. He, W., David, A.O., Yin, Z., et al.: Neural network control of a robotic manipulator with input deadzone and output constraint. IEEE Trans. Syst. Man Cybern. Syst. **46**(6), 759–770 (2016)

3. He, W., Amoateng, D.O., Yang, C., et al.: Adaptive neural network control of a robotic manipulator with unknown backlash-like hysteresis. IET Control Theory Appl. **11**(4), 567–575 (2017)
4. Na, J., Chen, Q., Ren, X., et al.: Adaptive prescribed performance motion control of servo mechanisms with friction compensation. IEEE Trans. Industr. Electron. **61**(1), 486–494 (2013)
5. Liu, H., Tian, X., Wang, G., et al.: Finite-Time H_∞ control for high-precision tracking in robotic manipulators using backstepping control. IEEE Trans. Industr. Electron. **63**(9), 5501–5513 (2016)
6. Wang, M., Yang, A.: Dynamic learning from adaptive neural control of robot manipulators with prescribed performance. IEEE Trans. Syst. Man Cybern. Syst. **PP**(99), 1–12 (2017)
7. Dai, S.L., Wang, M., et al.: Learning from adaptive neural output feedback control of robot manipulators. IFAC Proc. Vols. **46**(20), 737–742 (2013)
8. Wang, L., Chai, T., Zhai, L.: Neural-network-based terminal sliding-mode control of robotic manipulators including actuator dynamics. IEEE Trans. Industr. Electron. **56**(9), 3296–3304 (2009)
9. Hu, Q., Xu, L., Zhang, A.: Adaptive backstepping trajectory tracking control of robot manipulator. J. Franklin Inst. **349**(3), 1087–1105 (2012)
10. Ghorbel, F., Hung, J.Y., Spong, M.W.: Adaptive control of flexible joint manipulators. IEEE J. Mag. **9**(7), 9–13 (1989)
11. Yoo, S.J.: Distributed adaptive containment control of networked flexible-joint robots using neural networks. Expert Syst. Appl. **41**(2), 470–477 (2014)
12. Li, Y., Tong, S., Li, T.: Adaptive fuzzy output feedback control for a single-link flexible robot manipulator driven DC motor via backstepping. Nonl. Anal. Real World Appl. **14**(1), 483–494 (2013)
13. Yoo, S.J., Park, J.B., Choi, Y.H.: Adaptive output feedback control of flexible-joint robots using neural networks: dynamic surface design approach. IEEE Trans. Neural Networks **19**(10), 1712–1726 (2008)
14. Haimo, V.T.: Finite time controllers. Soc. Industr. Appl. Math. **24**(4), 760–770 (1986)
15. Zheng, J.F., Feng, Y., Zheng, X.M., et al.: Adaptive backstepping-based terminal-sliding-mode control for uncertain nonlinear systems. Control Theory Appl. Chin. **26**(4), 410–414 (2009)
16. Zheng, X., Li, L., Zheng, J., et al.: Non-singular terminal sliding mode backstepping control for the uncertain chaotic systems. In: 2nd International Symposium on Systems and Control in Aerospace and Astronautics, pp. 1–5. IEEE Press, Shenzhen (2008)
17. Tang, X., Chen, Q., Nan, Y., et al.: Backstepping funnel control for prescribed performance of robotic manipulators with unknown dead zone. In: The 27th Chinese Control and Decision Conference, pp. 1508–1513. IEEE Press, Qingdao (2015)
18. Lu, K., Xia, Y., Yu, C., et al.: Finite-time tracking control of rigid spacecraft under actuator saturations and faults. IEEE Trans. Autom. Sci. Eng. **13**(1), 368–381 (2016)
19. Yu, S., Yu, X., Shirinzadeh, B., Man, Z.: Continuous finite-time control for robotic manipulators with terminal sliding mode. Automatica **41**, 1957–1964 (2005)
20. Modares, H., Ranatunga, I., Lewis, F.L., et al.: Optimized assistive human-robot interaction using reinforcement learning. IEEE Trans. Cybern. **46**(3), 655–667 (2016)

Pattern Recognition

An Approach to Pulse Coupled Neural Network Based Vein Recognition

Ting Yu and Xiaodong Gu[(✉)]

Department of Electronic Engineering, Fudan University,
Shanghai 200433, China
xdgu@fudan.edu.cn

Abstract. Hand vein recognition has received increasing attention in biometric identification for the uniqueness, stability, and easiness of collection of the vein image. Local Binary Pattern (LBP) has been a widely used texture descriptor, being well developed in vein recognition. However, the use of histogram in LBP as the feature of the vein image leads to the loss of global spatial information. That loss results in final accuracy reduction for absence of geometry structure, being essential to vein representation. In this paper we use Pulse Coupled Neural Network (PCNN) to process original LBP feature map as a solution to spatial information loss, because in PCNN pulse emitting and spreading reflects the intensity distribution pattern related to the vein geometry. The image time signature (image icon) produced by pulse emitting and spreading in PCNN is used as the vein feature. Using PCNN to extract time signature, we adopt a multi-valued linking channel in each neuron of the network to control the neighboring influence more precisely, and we introduce an adaptive linking strength (β) to address the less information on vein pattern of the dark region in the vein image. As for the vein binary representation, Unit-linking PCNN is employed. It uses pulse spreading to perform eroding operation on the K-clustering binarization result of the vein image. After computing the time signature and the binary representation, Support Vector Machine (SVM) fusion strategy is used to fuse them. The EER (Equal Error Rate) of our approach is 0.03% on the CASIA Multi-spectral Palmprint Image Database, which is better than four other approaches, including the multi-sampling method, mutual foreground LBP (MF_LBP) method, and so on.

Keywords: Palm vein recognition · Pulse Coupled Neural Network (PCNN) · Unit-linking PCNN · Local Binary Pattern

1 Introduction

Hand vein recognition has drawn increasing attention from both academia and industrial community. Similar to other biometrics like iris, face, and fingerprint, hand vein are individually different, even between twins. Besides, hand vein pattern has advantages over other biometrical features in the difficulty to forge, stability and contactless recognition environment.

In most literatures, hand vein recognition is divided as preprocessing, feature extraction, and matching. Among the procedures, extracting discriminative features from

© Springer International Publishing AG 2017
D. Liu et al. (Eds.): ICONIP 2017, Part VI, LNCS 10639, pp. 415–422, 2017.
https://doi.org/10.1007/978-3-319-70136-3_44

vein network is the key to the good performance of the whole system. The prevalent features extracted by literatures can be classified as local invariant-based features like SIFT [1], geometry-based features like line-like feature [2], and statistical-based features like local binary pattern (LBP) [3] and local derivative pattern (LDP).

As a local texture descriptor, LBP extracts the local pattern of each pixel from intensity comparisons between center and neighboring pixels. The approach uses the histogram, that is, the proportion of each feature value as the feature for matching. The local pattern can be well represented by the comparisons. However, the method ignores the holistic spatial information, or the global geometry of a vein image which is of great importance to the individual distinctiveness of vein network. In this paper Pulse Coupled Neural Network is used as a solution to the global geometry loss. The pulses burst and spread over the network relating to the intensity variation in the processed sample, therefore recording the global geometry in it. In this way, the geometry information is fused in the intensity distribution automatically. In the iteration process number of pulses generated in each iteration, called time signature, is used as the feature. The experiment is conducted on CASIA Multi-spectral palmprint database [4] and obvious improvement is obtained, compared to the original LBP method. Besides, we use Unit-linking PCNN which is a simplified version of PCNN to erode binary image, getting a truthful binary vein feature. The fusion of the time signature and binary feature produces an EER of 0.03% by SVM fusion. The overview and some intermediate results are shown in Fig. 1.

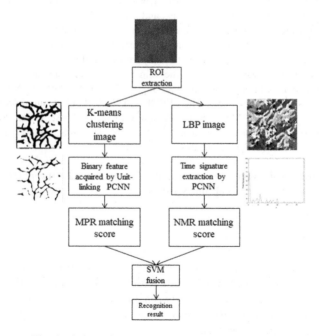

Fig. 1. Schematic overview of the proposed approach

2 Proposed Recognition System

2.1 Preprocessing

To reduce the effect caused by posture variations in CASIA database, Region of Interest (ROI) is first extracted using segmentation method proposed in [5]. All the segmented image are scaled to a size of 200×200.

2.2 PCNN Based Time Signature Extraction

LBP is a typical texture descriptor in pattern recognition, which extracting the pattern of a small local neighborhood by intensity comparisons between center and neighboring pixels. The algorithm has been successfully applied to hand vein to describe local vein patterns [6]. In most of the applications, the use of histogram as the feature, computing the proportion of each LBP pattern value in all the possible ones, ignores the geometric structure, or the spatial information contained in the neighboring pixels. Such geometric structure contains information on the trend and shape of the vein line, the intensity transition detail from vein to background, and so on. Obviously, the information is of great importance for identifying the vein sample.

Inspired from the practice of using the Unit-linking PCNN to process gray image to obtain the time signature which reflects the image intensity distribution pattern related to the geometry of the original image [7], we use PCNN to process the original LBP feature map, aiming at fusing global geometry information with the statistical feature. For a simple procedure of processing, the work is conducted based on the simplified structure of PCNN—Unit-linking PCNN [7] with some adjustments. LBP feature map of vein is used as the feeding input F of a PCNN consisting of the same Pulse Coupled Neurons (PCNs) in [7] of the same size as the map with one-to-one correspondence. Besides, each neuron is also connected with neurons in its 8-neighbor field, which can be represented by a kernel matrix $K = \begin{bmatrix} 1 & 1 & 1 \\ 1 & 1 & 1 \\ 1 & 1 & 1 \end{bmatrix}$ with 1 suggesting connections and 0 on the contrary.

According to the structure of PCN, the internal activity of each neuron, which determines whether the neuron fires by comparison with current inspiring threshold, consists of both its connected LBP feature value and the linking input decided by its neighbors. In this way, the neurons inspired each time can be divided as two parts; one part is the ones with enough feeding input from LBP feature map, firing at the beginning of each iteration (no previous emitted pulses exit); the other is neurons inspired by the combined influence of the feeding input, which singly is not enough to surpass the current inspiring threshold, and the linking input from the pulses emitted by the first part. In the situation of the second, the pulses generated at the beginning of current iteration are spread around because of the gradual intensity change in the LBP feature map, thus recording the geometry structure contained in it. By expanding the right side of modulation expression mathematically (Eq. (1), '.$*$' stands for array multiplication.), the resulted two expressions can represent the above mentioned two situations separately. If U stands for the internal activities of all fired neurons in one iteration, then U_b represents for the ones inspired at the beginning of each iteration with no emitted neighboring pulses $(L = 0)$, while U_s represents the ones fired following the former with the neighboring influence from the former.

$$U = F. * (1 + \beta L) \tag{1}$$

$$U_b = F \tag{2}$$

$$U_s = F + F. * \beta L \tag{3}$$

The numbers of pulses generated, that is, the inspired neurons in PCNN, in all iterations are arranged in time order and is called the time signature of vein. Obviously, the precise representation of neighboring firing states by the linking channel, is the key to an effective global geometry preservation. Observing Eq. (3) we can conclude that the influence of the linking channel on the center neuron's internal activity is represented in $F. * \beta L$, indicating a relationship between neighboring influence and both the linking strength β and linking input L. Note that the neighboring influence is not exactly the linking input (the linking channel L).

Multi-valued Linking Channel

Linking channel determines the linking input from neighboring field. Different firing states of the neighborhood indicates different geometry structures: the firing of one neuron, half of the neurons, and all the neurons may indicates the random noise, transition from vein to background, and the vein region respectively. Therefore, it is necessary to represent them differently to give a more precise reflection of the neighboring inspiring state.

In this paper the number of inspired neighboring neurons is used as the linking input, instead of the binary designation in Unit-linking PCN which only indicates whether there are inspired neurons. The linking channel L_k (of a neuron) is expressed as Eq. (4).

$$L_k = \sum_{j \in N_{(k)}} Y(j) \tag{4}$$

In Eq. (4), $N_{(k)}$ are 8-neighbor field of the center neuron and $Y(j)$ is the neighboring output.

Adaptive Linking Strength

Obviously, the neighboring influence $F. * \beta L$ in Eq. (3) is influenced by the feeding input F, that is, the connected LBP feature value, beside the L and β. In other words, the neurons connected with larger LBP feature value receive larger neighboring influence under the same neighboring inspiring states or linking input. In this condition, the pulses generated are more likely to spread in brighter area. As the result, the designation produces a time signature with more information of bright area while less information of dark area. However, areas of different brightness contribute equally to the distinctiveness of the sample. To increase the less information of dark region, an adaptive linking strength is used in this paper, which is expressed in Eq. (5).

$$\beta^n = \frac{\beta}{N-n} \tag{5}$$

With the new β, the U_s is expressed in Eq. (6). In $\boldsymbol{F}. * \frac{\beta}{N-n}\boldsymbol{L}$ of Eq. (6), the synchronous decreases of both $\boldsymbol{F}$ (of inspired neurons) with the decreasing inspiring threshold, and $N - n$ with the increase of iteration index n, addresses the less influence of neighborhood and the resulted less information of dark region in Eq. (3).

$$\boldsymbol{U}_s = \boldsymbol{F} + \boldsymbol{F}. * \frac{\beta}{N-n}\boldsymbol{L} \tag{6}$$

2.3 Unit-Linking PCNN Based Binary Representation

Beside the time signature extraction, the Unit-linking PCNN-based binary image thinning method proposed by [8] is adopted to erode or correct the inflated vein lines and get truthful binary vein lines, after K-means clustering on the Maximal Principal Curvature enhanced image [3]. The binary image got from K-clustering is connected as the feeding input with a Unit-linking PCNN of the same size as it with one-to-one correspondence. With 4-neighbor field connection mode which indicates a neuron fires as long as there are fired neurons in its top, bottom, left and right neighbor, the pulses generated by bright background region spread to the dark vein region, thinning it gradually. The 4-neighbor field Unit-linking PCNN-based binary image processing retain both the position information and the size information of the object [8].

A little adjustment is that our work use a fixed iteration number as the end of processing. The fixed iteration number is selected to produce an as truthful reflection to the original image as possible.

2.4 Matching Approach

For the vein time signature, we use simple Normalized Manhattan Distance (NMD) shown in Eq. (7) to do matching. In the expression, $\boldsymbol{TI}_1$ and $\boldsymbol{TI}_2$ are two time signatures for matching, L is the length of the obtained time signature vectors.

$$NMD(\boldsymbol{TI}_1, \boldsymbol{TI}_2) = \sum_{i=1}^{L} \frac{|\boldsymbol{TI}_1(i) - \boldsymbol{TI}_2(i)|}{\boldsymbol{TI}_1(i) + \boldsymbol{TI}_2(i)} \tag{7}$$

For the binary representation, the common used Matched Pixel Ratio (MPR) is used.

$$MPR(\boldsymbol{I}_1, \boldsymbol{I}_2) = \frac{\sum_j \sum_i [\boldsymbol{I}_1(i,j) \cdot \boldsymbol{I}_2(i,j)]}{\sum_j \sum_i \boldsymbol{I}_1(i,j) + \sum_j \sum_i \boldsymbol{I}_1(i,j)} \tag{8}$$

Kang *et al.* points out in [3] that SVM fusion is superior to other common fusing strategies, through comparing their performances in the same experimental setting. We also adopt the SVM fusion to do the score-level fusion on NMD and MPR.

3   Empirical Results

In this work, 1500 intra-class matches and 3000 inter-class matches are constructed from all the 600 left hand under 940 nm NIR light of CASIA Multi-Spectral Palmprint Image Database to evaluate the performance of proposed method.

For the simpleness of recognition process, uniform LBP is used. Figure 2 shows the score distribution of time signature matching and the ROC Curve. In (a), the green part represents the intra-class matching scores and the red part the inter-class ones, which demonstrates a separate score distribution of the two classes. The score on the crossing point of two classes is figured out as the threshold of classification, which give an EER of 1.62% in Fig. 2(b).

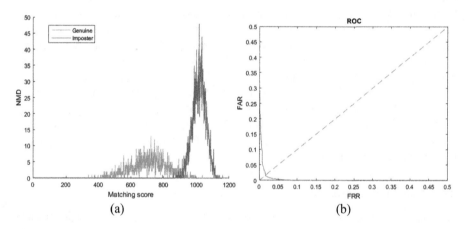

Fig. 2. Classification results of the time signature: (a) Scores distribution; (b) ROC curve (Color figure online)

Table 1 gives the comparison of the performances of the time signature and that of traditional LBP feature (histogram vector). Considering most of the LBP applications on vein recognition divides the LBP feature map into subblocks and concatenates histograms of each subblock together, we also do the division for a fair comparison. In Table 1, traditional histogram gives the best EER of 2.53% when the original feature map is divided into 5 × 5 subblocks. However, the time signature obtained from PCNN performs best at the 6 × 6 division, with an EER of 1.62%, 0.91% less than the histogram method. In each size of the subblock, the time signature representation gives an obviously lower EER than of the traditional method with a difference of 0.17%–4.07%. The table illustrates the effectiveness of the proposed PCNN algorithm on the combination of the intensity distribution and geometry structure of the sample.

Table 1. EER comparisons between the histogram and the time signature with different subblock numbers

Subblock number	Histogram	Time signature
3 × 3	8.35%	4.28%
4 × 4	3.23%	3.06%
5 × 5	2.53%	2.16%
6 × 6	2.96%	**1.62%**
7 × 7	3.83%	1.71%

The influence of linking strength β and iteration number N of PCNN on the performance is discussed in Table 2. Obviously, the larger is the β, the more likely that a center neuron fires by the influence from the neighborhood, and the emitted pulses in the beginning of the present iteration are more likely to spread around. However, if β is too large, the LBP feature distribution information will be little. On the other hand, a larger N produce more precise distribution information and better performance, while the improvement will reach the ceiling when N is too large. When β and N is set to 0.1 and 59, the best EER is obtained as 1.62%.

Table 2. EERs of the time signature with different linking strengths and iteration times

β	N = 49	N = 54	N = 59	N = 64	N = 69
0	2.69%	2.66%	2.53%	2.53%	2.53%
0.05	1.93%	1.89%	1.71%	1.84%	1.73%
0.1	1.87%	1.72%	**1.62%**	1.89%	1.83%
0.15	1.70%	1.91%	1.84%	2.12%	1.99%
0.2	2.02%	2.44%	2.32%	2.05%	2.12%
0.25	2.19%	2.86%	2.43%	2.26%	2.37%

On the other hand, the MPR matching reaches an EER of 3.08%, 2.55%. 2.31%, and 2.76% when Unit-linking PCNN iterates 1, 2, 3, 4 times, using the same classification protocol as NMD. We choose the best situation (iterates 3 times) to fuse the MPR score with time signature matching score and an EER of 0.03% is obtained. Table 3 illustrates the performance comparisons with other algorithms. Among the literatures, all the other algorithms design the experiment in the same way as ours, in which all the possible intra-class and inter-class matches are classified as a whole. The table illustrates the superior performance of our algorithm over those of others.

Table 3. Summary of performances of work on the CASIA database

Reference	Methodology	EER
[1]	Rootsift feature	0.996%
[2]	Contour Code representation	0.778%
[3]	Mutual foreground LBP	0.267%
[9]	Fuse features from multi-sample	0.16%
Proposed method	Feature fusion based on PCNN	**0.03%**

4 Conclusion

Compared to the conventional LBP histogram feature, the time signature produced by PCNN achieves better performance, for the time signature reflects not only the intensity but also the geometry structure of the vein image. Adopting an adaptive linking strength (β) instead of a constant one, the model extracts the geometry structure in a more precise way from the linking channel. The linking channel is multi-valued, which reflects more neighboring firing states. The EER of the proposed approach combining the PCNN time signature and the Unit-linking PCNN binary representation is 0.03% on the CASIA Multi-Spectral Palmprint Image Database, which is 0.15% lower than multi-sampling method, 0.237% lower than mutual foreground LBP method, and so on.

Acknowledgments. This work was supported in part by National Natural Science Foundation of China under grants 61371148 and 61771145.

References

1. Kang, W., Liu, Y., Wu, Q., Yue, X.: Contact-free palm-vein recognition based on local invariant features. PLoS ONE **9**, 97548 (2014)
2. Khan, Z., Mian, A., Yiqun, H.: Contour Code: robust and efficient multispectral palmprint encoding for human recognition. In: 2011 IEEE International Conference on Computer Vision (ICCV), pp. 1935–1942 (2011)
3. Kang, W., Wu, Q.: Contactless palm vein recognition using a mutual foreground-based local binary pattern. IEEE Trans. Inf. Forensics Secur. **9**, 1974–1985 (2014)
4. CASIA-MS-PalmprintV1. http://biometrics.idealtest.org/
5. Zhou, Y., Kumar, A.: Human identification using palm-vein images. IEEE Trans. Inf. Forensics Secur. **6**, 1259–1274 (2011)
6. Mirmohamadsadeghi, L., Drygajlo, A.: Palm vein recognition with local binary patterns and local derivative patterns. In: 2011 International Joint Conference on Biometrics (IJCB), pp. 1–6 (2011)
7. Gu, X.: Feature extraction using unit-linking pulse coupled neural network and its applications. Neural Process. Lett. **27**, 25–41 (2008)
8. Gu, X., Yu, D., Zhang, L.: Image thinning using pulse coupled neural network. Pattern Recogn. Lett. **25**, 1075–1084 (2004)
9. Yan, X., Kang, W., Deng, F., Wu, Q.: Palm vein recognition based on multi-sampling and feature-level fusion. Neurocomputing **151**(Part 2), 798–807 (2015)

A Regularized Margin Fisher Analysis Method for Face Recognition

Xiaoyu Xue[1,2], Xiaohu Ma[1,2(✉)], Yuxin Gu[1,2], Xiao Sun[1,2], and Zhiwen Ni[1,2]

[1] School of Computer Science and Technology,
Soochow University, Suzhou 215006, China
xhma@suda.edu.cn
[2] Collaborative Innovation Center of Novel Software Technology
and Industrialization, Nanjing 210023, China

Abstract. Margin Fisher Analysis is a typical graph-based dimensionality reduction technique and has been successfully applied to face recognition. However, it always suffers from the over-fitting, noise, and singular matrix problems. Common preprocessing methods such as PCA lose certain discriminant information in data, which leads the poor classification rate. We propose a novel method called Regularized Margin Fisher Analysis, which decomposes the inter-class similarity matrix into three subspace: principal space, noise space and null space. Then, we regularize the three subspaces in different ways to deal with the noise and over-fitting problems. Moreover, we use twice standard eigendecompositions instead of single generalized eigendecomposition which avoids the singular matrix problem. The experiments on Extended YaleB, CMU PIE and FERET face databases demonstrates that the proposed method is effective and can improve the classification ability.

Keywords: Face recognition · Graph embedding · Dimensionality reduction · Regularization · Margin fisher analysis

1 Introduction

Face recognition has attracted lots of researchers in area of pattern recognition, machine learning and computer vision. However, how to design a reliable dimensionality reduction method remains an open problem. There are some issues in pattern recognition point of views. One of the critical issue is how to extract discriminative and stable feature for classification. Linear subspace analysis has been extensively studied and has become a popular feature extraction method, such as principal component analysis (PCA) [14], linear discriminant analysis (LDA) [2]. Some theoretical analysis showed that low-dimensional linear subspace could capture the set of image of an object produced by variety of lighting condition [1]. Moreover, some nonlinear methods were proposed to capture the nonlinear structure of high-dimensional image data. The kernel methods [9,16] have achieved success in face recognition. And manifold learning [3,6] has also been applied in face recognition.

© Springer International Publishing AG 2017
D. Liu et al. (Eds.): ICONIP 2017, Part VI, LNCS 10639, pp. 423–433, 2017.
https://doi.org/10.1007/978-3-319-70136-3_45

Graph embedding framework was proposed as a method to unify several well-known dimensionality reduction techniques and provides an insight to design new method for dimensionality reduction [15]. The instances are Neighborhood Preserving Embedding (NPE) [5], Locality Preserving Projections (LPP) [10] and Margin Fisher Analysis [15] etc. In general, Graph embedding framework seeks an embedded low-dimensional manifold based on data similarities on an affinity graph [11].

Graph embedding framework tries to maximally preserve data locality after embedding. It could get the ultimate goal under the perfect information environment which is unrealistic. In the real world, data locality is estimated based on finite noisy training samples. [7] performed a thorough analysis on how to reliably restore the population statistics based on regularization technique. The classic MFA suffer the over-fitting and noise problems under the limited training sample, which leads to unsatisfactory classification accuracy. Inspired by [7], we proposed a novel graph embedding dimensionality reduction method called Regularized Margin Fisher Analysis (RMFA) to deal with these problems. The proposed method was examined on three public face database: Yale Face Database B (YaleB) [4,8], CMU Pose, Illumination and Expression (PIE) [13] and Facial Recognition Technology (FERET) [12].

In Sect. 2 the related work is briefly reviewed. Our method is proposed in Sect. 3. Section 4 shows the experimental results and analysis. Finally Sect. 5 draws the conclusion.

2   Related Work

LDA [2] is a global method and MFA is a local method based on graph embedding framework. Both of them try to find an optimal projection matrix, which is the best for classification task. Moreover, both of them suffer the problem of over-fitting due to the limitation of training samples.

2.1   The Linear Dimensionality Reduction Problem

The generic problem of linear dimensionality reduction is the following. Given a set of points $[\mathbf{x}_1, \ldots, \mathbf{x}_m] \in \mathbb{R}^{n \times m}$ and their labels $[l_1, \ldots, l_m], l_i \in \{1, 2, \ldots, c\}$, find a transformation matrix P which maps these m points to a set of points $[\mathbf{y}_1, \ldots, \mathbf{y}_m] \in \mathbb{R}^{d \times m}$ $(d < n)$, and $\mathbf{y}_i = P^T \mathbf{x}_i$.

2.2   Margin Fisher Analysis

The linear discriminant analysis is proposed with the assumption that the data of each class is of a Gaussian distribution, a property that often does not exist in real-world problems. The Margin Fisher Analysis (MFA) algorithm overcomes the limitation of LDA by developing new criteria which characterizes intraclass compactness and interclass separability. In MFA, there are two graphs, intrinsic graph and penalty graph.

In the intrinsic graph, intraclass compactness is characterized by the term

$$\Phi(\mathbf{p}) = \mathbf{p}^T X (D^w - W^w) X^T \mathbf{p} \tag{1}$$

$$W_{ij}^w = \begin{cases} 1, \text{ if } i \in N_{k_1}^+(j) \text{ or } j \in N_{k_1}^+(i) \\ 0, \text{ otherwise} \end{cases} \tag{2}$$

where, W^w is the intraclass adjacency matrix, D^w is a diagonal matrix and $D_{ii}^w = \sum_j W_{ij}^w$, $N_{k_1}^+(i)$ indicates the index set of the k_1-nearest neighbors of the sample $\mathbf{x}_i$ in the same class.

In the penalty graph, interclass separability is characterized by the term

$$\Psi(\mathbf{p}) = \mathbf{p}^T X (D^b - W^b) X^T \mathbf{p} \tag{3}$$

$$W_{ij}^b = \begin{cases} 1, \text{ if } i \in N_{k_2}^-(j) \text{ or } j \in N_{k_2}^-(i) \\ 0, \text{ otherwise} \end{cases} \tag{4}$$

where, W^b is the interclass adjacency matrix, D^b is a diagonal matrix and $D_{ii}^b = \sum_j W_{ij}^b$, $N_{k_2}^-(i)$ indicates the index set of the k_2-nearest neighbors of the sample $\mathbf{x}_i$ in the different classes.

MFA finds the optimal projection directions via the following Marginal Fisher Criterion:

$$\mathbf{p}^* = \arg \max_{\mathbf{p}} \frac{\Phi(\mathbf{p})}{\Psi(\mathbf{p})} = \arg \max_{\mathbf{p}} \frac{\mathbf{p}^T X (D^b - W^b) X^T \mathbf{p}}{\mathbf{p}^T X (D^w - W^w) X^T \mathbf{p}} \tag{5}$$

3   Regularized Margin Fisher Analysis

In this section, we develop a novel supervised subspace learning method called Regularized Margin Fisher Analysis (RMFA). Our method tries to deal with the over-fitting and noise problems in MFA and do not need the data distribution assumption compared with ERE [7]. In RMFA, we decompose the intraclass adjacency matrix to three subspaces: principal space, noise space and null space. And we regularize the three subspaces in different ways, then data are projected into regularized eigenspace. When data is regularized, we can find the optimal solution by decomposing the interclass similarity matrix.

Similar to MFA, we first construct the intraclass similarity matrix:

$$XLX^T = X(D^w - W^w)X^T \tag{6}$$

Then we can get an objective function to characterize the intraclass locality with the projection direction $\mathbf{a}$:

$$\begin{cases} \arg \min_{\mathbf{a}} \mathbf{a} X L X^T \mathbf{a} \\ \\ \text{s.t. } \mathbf{a}^T \mathbf{a} = 1 \end{cases} \tag{7}$$

this problem can be solved by the following eigendecompostion problem:

$$XLX^T \mathbf{a} = \hat{\lambda} \mathbf{a} \tag{8}$$

The projection matrix is constructed by $A = [\mathbf{a}_1, \ldots, \mathbf{a}_n]$, where $\mathbf{a}_i$ is the eigenvector corresponding to the ith smallest eigenvalue.

3.1   Regularization on Eigenspace

From Eqs. (7) and (8), the smaller $\hat{\lambda}$ represents the stronger locality. If we sort $\hat{\lambda}_i$ by the non-increasing order $\hat{\lambda}_1 \geq \hat{\lambda}_2 \geq, \ldots, \geq \hat{\lambda}_n$ we can get an eigenspectrum of the intraclass similarity matrix showed in Fig. 1. Here, we assume that noise is distributed in $[-\lambda_1/1000, \lambda_1/1000]$. And the whole space of the intraclass similarity matrix ($A = [\mathbf{a}_1, \ldots, \mathbf{a}_n]$) is decomposed into three subspace, the principal space ($A^P = [\mathbf{a}_1, \ldots, \mathbf{a}_u]$), the noise space ($A^N = [\mathbf{a}_{u+1}, \ldots, \mathbf{a}_r]$) and the null space ($A^\Phi = [\mathbf{a}_{r+1}, \ldots, \mathbf{a}_n]$).

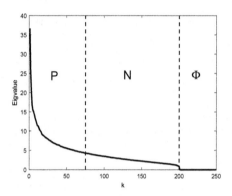

Fig. 1. The eigenspectrum of the intraclass similarity matrix

The next step of our work is to model the true eigenspectrum line. Firstly, we assume that the eigenspectrum is distributed as the function of the form $1/f$ [7]. Given the range of the number of eigenvalues $1 \leq k \leq r$, the v_k is the intrinsic eigenvalue, the ϵ_k is the noise component.

$$\hat{\lambda}_k = v_k + \epsilon_k = \frac{\alpha}{(k+\beta)^t} + \epsilon_k, \qquad 1 \leq k \leq r \tag{9}$$

where, λ_k is the eigenvalue calculated from the finite number of training samples, α, β and t are parameters.

The Principal Space and Noise Space. The key step of the next work is to determine the start point of the noise space. It is truth that median operation works well in separating outliers from a data set. We first find a point near the center of the noise region by

$$\lambda_{med} = \text{median}\{\forall \lambda_k | k \leq r\} \tag{10}$$

where r is the index of the smallest non-zero eigenvalue. Then the start point of the noise region is

$$\lambda_{u+1} = \max\{\forall \lambda_k | \lambda_k < (\lambda_{med} + \mu(\lambda_{med} - \lambda_r))\} \tag{11}$$

where μ is a constant.

As the eigenspectrum in the principal space is dominated by the principal structural component, the parameters of α and β are determined by fitting the principal portion of the model $\hat{\lambda}_k = \alpha/(k+\beta)^t$ to the real eigenspectrum in the principal space. In our experiment, we simply determine α and β using $v_1 = \hat{\lambda}_1$ and $\hat{\lambda}_u = v_u$:

$$\alpha = \lambda_1 \left(1 + \frac{u\lambda_1^{\frac{1}{t}} - \lambda_u^{\frac{1}{t}}}{\lambda_u^{\frac{1}{t}} - \lambda_1^{\frac{1}{t}}} \right)^t \tag{12}$$

$$\beta = \frac{u\lambda_1^{\frac{1}{t}} - \lambda_u^{\frac{1}{t}}}{\lambda_u^{\frac{1}{t}} - \lambda_1^{\frac{1}{t}}} \tag{13}$$

The Null Space. For the null space, we simply let the first point which is smaller than 10^{-10} be the start point of null space.

The Whole Eigenspace Regularization. In different subspaces, we model the eigenvalues as follows:

$$\tilde{\lambda}_k^w = \begin{cases} \lambda_k & k \leq u \\ \frac{\alpha}{(k+\beta)^t} & u+1 \leq k \leq r \\ \frac{\alpha}{(k+1+\beta)^t} & r < k \leq n \end{cases} \tag{14}$$

The feature weighting function can be calculated as follows:

$$\tilde{w}_k = \frac{1}{\sqrt{\tilde{\lambda}_k^w}}, \qquad k = 1, 2, \ldots, n \tag{15}$$

Using this weight function, we can regularize the training data by project data into the regularized space.

$$\tilde{Y} = \tilde{A}^T X \tag{16}$$

where

$$\tilde{A} = [\tilde{w}_1 \mathbf{a}_1, \ldots, \tilde{w}_n \mathbf{a}_n] \tag{17}$$

In this step $\tilde{A}$ is a full rank matrix which transforms the image vector to a regularized feature vector. So there is no dimension reduction in the transformation.

After the feature regularization, we construct the interclass similarity matrix of the regularized image vectors like MFA.

$$\tilde{Y}\tilde{L}\tilde{Y}^T = \tilde{Y}(\tilde{D} - W^b)\tilde{Y}^T \tag{18}$$

where $\tilde{D}_{ii} = \sum_j W_{ij}^b$.

In order to find the optimal projection matrix P, we first find the projection matrix U defined in the regularized space. By the Margin Fisher Analysis criterion, we have

$$\begin{cases} \arg \max_{\mathbf{u}} \mathbf{u}^T \tilde{Y}\tilde{L}\tilde{Y}^T \mathbf{u} \\ \\ \text{s.t. } \mathbf{u}^T \mathbf{u} = 1 \end{cases} \tag{19}$$

Then we get the following eigen equation

$$\widetilde{Y}\widetilde{L}\widetilde{Y}^{T}\mathbf{u} = \lambda\mathbf{u} \tag{20}$$

The projection matrix U is consisted of the eigenvectors corresponding to the first d largest eigenvalues.

$$U = [\mathbf{u}_1, \dots, \mathbf{u}_d] \tag{21}$$

The projection matrix from the original space to the optimal space is

$$P = \widetilde{A}U \tag{22}$$

Once the projection matrix P has been learned from the training data by RMFA, the image of any new point $\mathbf{x}_i \in \mathbb{R}^n$ could be represented by $\mathbf{y}_i = P^T\mathbf{x}_i$, where $\mathbf{y}_i \in \mathbb{R}^d$. The detail about RMFA is given in Algorithm 1.

Algorithm 1. Regularized Margin Fisher Analysis

Input: Training set $X = [\mathbf{x}_1, \dots, \mathbf{x}_m] \in \mathbb{R}^{n \times m}$, output dimension d
Output: Projection matrix P
1: Construct intraclass similarity matrix XLX^T using (6) and (7)
2: Sort eigenvalues by descending order, according to (8)
3: Determine the start point of noise space by (11) and decompose the eigenspace to three subspaces.
4: Determine parameters α and β using (12), (13), and get $\tilde{w}_k$ by (15)
5: Use (17), (16) to get regularized projection matrix $\widetilde{A}$, and regularized feature vectors $\widetilde{Y}$
6: Construct interclass similarity matrix $\widetilde{Y}\widetilde{L}\widetilde{Y}^T$ using (18)
7: Solve equation (20) and get matrix U consisting of the eigenvectors according to the d largest eigenvalues.
8: Compute optimal projection matrix $P = \widetilde{A}U$
9: **return** P

---

4   Experiment

In all experiments presented in this work, three databases YaleB, PIE and FERET are used to test. The proposed RMFA method is compared with the unsupervised method PCA, and supervised methods LDA, LPP, NPE, MFA and ERE. Moreover, two experimental results of each dataset are numerically recorded in two tables which includes more results for comparison. In our experiment, the parameter t is fixed to be 1 and we apply PCA to data in LDA, NPE, LPP and MFA to void the singular matrix problem which keeps the 99% energy.

4.1 Results on YaleB Database

The extended YaleB database contains 2414 frontal face images of 38 people. There about 64 images for each person. The original images were cropped to 32×32 pixels. We randomly select 10 images per person as training set and other for testing.

The testing set against the number of features and the testing results are numerically recorded in Table 1. We can find that the RMFA get the best recognition rate compared with other algorithms.

Table 1. The result on YaleB Database

Method	K1	K2	Dimension	Recognition (%)
PCA	-	-	110	43.33 ± 0.21
NPE	3	-	60	79.32 ± 1.16
LPP	3	-	75	79.04 ± 1.12
LDA	-	-	43	77.40 ± 0.63
ERE	-	-	50	79.97 ± 0.75
MFA	5	65	35	79.89 ± 1.03
RMFA	5	110	45	$\mathbf{81.27 \pm 0.56}$

Moreover, Table 2 records the recognition rate under different numbers of training samples per person on YaleB database. In this comparison, the proposed RMFA method also consistently outperforms other methods.

Table 2. The recognition rate (%) under different numbers of training samples on YaleB database, r indicates the number of training samples per category

Method	r = 5	r = 10	r = 15	r = 20
PCA	30.93 ± 0.12	43.33 ± 0.21	51.70 ± 0.37	57.73 ± 0.36
NPE	66.57 ± 0.97	79.11 ± 1.16	84.85 ± 0.93	88.56 ± 1.36
LPP	66.39 ± 1.20	79.04 ± 1.12	85.31 ± 1.17	88.77 ± 1.35
LDA	63.91 ± 0.68	77.40 ± 0.63	84.62 ± 0.35	88.78 ± 0.38
ERE	66.93 ± 1.03	79.97 ± 0.75	86.29 ± 0.77	90.07 ± 1.06
MFA	65.25 ± 0.77	79.89 ± 1.03	86.37 ± 1.31	89.98 ± 1.30
RMFA	$\mathbf{67.92 \pm 0.63}$	$\mathbf{81.27 \pm 0.56}$	$\mathbf{87.23 \pm 0.83}$	$\mathbf{91.97 \pm 0.56}$

4.2   Results on CMU PIE Database

CMU PIE database was acquired by using 13 synchronized cameras and an array of flashes as light sources. These camera flashes were placed in specific positions relative to the subject. The database includes 41368 images of 68 people. The original images were cropped to 32×32 pixels. We randomly select 20 images per person as the training set and other for testing.

The testing results are also numerically recorded in Table 3. We can find that the RMFA get the best recognition rate compared with other algorithms.

Table 3. The results on CMU PIE database.

Method	K1	K2	Dimension	Recognition (%)
PCA	-	-	200	49.60 ± 0.26
NPE	3	-	95	81.84 ± 1.06
LPP	3	-	65	85.39 ± 1.25
LDA	-	-	70	83.67 ± 0.33
ERE	-	-	30	89.02 ± 1.16
MFA	5	50	35	90.51 ± 1.26
RMFA	5	70	50	$\mathbf{92.10 \pm 0.56}$

Table 4 records the recognition rate under different numbers of training samples per person on CMU PIE database. In this comparison, the proposed RMFA method also consistently outperforms other methods.

Table 4. The recognition rate (%) under different numbers of training samples on PIE database, r indicates the number of training samples per category

Method	r = 5	r = 10	r = 15	r = 20
PCA	22.43 ± 0.17	34.32 ± 0.28	42.76 ± 0.37	49.60 ± 0.26
NPE	55.98 ± 0.97	67.06 ± 1.21	75.32 ± 0.93	81.84 ± 1.06
LPP	56.91 ± 1.13	71.11 ± 1.07	79.16 ± 1.17	85.39 ± 1.25
LDA	58.46 ± 1.08	70.48 ± 0.53	78.44 ± 0.35	83.67 ± 0.33
ERE	63.30 ± 1.03	78.85 ± 0.75	85.64 ± 0.77	89.02 ± 1.16
MFA	62.57 ± 0.97	80.65 ± 1.23	87.49 ± 1.31	90.51 ± 1.26
RMFA	$\mathbf{65.53 \pm 1.03}$	$\mathbf{82.37 \pm 0.77}$	$\mathbf{89.16 \pm 0.83}$	$\mathbf{92.10 \pm 0.56}$

4.3   Results on FERET Database

The key goal in assembling FERET database is to support the United State government in enhancing face recognition technology. It contains 200 images, and each person has 7 images with different illuminations and expressions. We randomly select 4 samples per person as training set and others for testing.

The testing results are also numerically recorded in Table 5. We can find that the RMFA get the best recognition rate compared with other algorithms.

Table 5. The results on FERET database.

Method	K1	K2	Dimension	Recognition (%)
PCA	-	-	170	39.50 ± 0.23
NPE	3	-	150	27.87 ± 1.76
LPP	3	-	175	28.27 ± 1.25
LDA	-	-	200	28.73 ± 0.33
ERE	-	-	15	83.33 ± 1.36
MFA	3	40	25	86.87 ± 1.22
RMFA	3	100	20	$\mathbf{88.73 \pm 1.06}$

Table 6 records the recognition rate under different numbers of training samples per person on FERET database. In this comparison, the proposed RMFA method also consistently outperforms other methods.

Table 6. The recognition rate (%) under different numbers of training samples on FERET database, r indicates the number of training samples per category

Method	$r = 3$	$r = 4$	$r = 5$
PCA	35.03 ± 0.25	39.50 ± 0.23	45.30 ± 0.21
NPE	27.35 ± 0.77	27.87 ± 1.76	32.35 ± 1.15
LPP	26.13 ± 1.26	28.27 ± 1.25	32.30 ± 1.07
LDA	2.67 ± 0.56	28.73 ± 0.33	32.25 ± 0.58
ERE	77.28 ± 1.17	83.33 ± 1.36	86.70 ± 0.85
MFA	78.13 ± 0.87	86.87 ± 1.22	89.65 ± 1.17
RMFA	$\mathbf{82.62 \pm 0.93}$	$\mathbf{88.73 \pm 1.06}$	$\mathbf{91.10 \pm 0.76}$

5   Conclusion

Graph embedding method tries to find the optimal projection which projects high-dimensional data to low-dimensional space for better recognition performance. However, limited training samples may cause the overfitting and noise problem. The estimation of true data locality could be biased. In order to solve the problem, we proposed a novel graph embedding method called Regularized Margin Fisher Analysis (RMFA). The eigenspace of intra-class similarity matrix is decomposed into three subspace, and is regularized in different ways. Moreover, the proposed method uses two standard eigen decomposition instead a generalized Rayleigh quotient that avoids the singular matrix problem. The experiment result on three public face database shows that the proposed RMFA outperforms other graph embedding techniques.

Acknowledgments. This work is partially supported by the National Natural Science Foundation of China (61402310). Natural Science Foundation of Jiangsu Province of China (BK20141195).

References

1. Basri, R., Jacobs, D.W.: Lambertian reflectance and linear subspaces. In: Proceedings of the Eighth IEEE International Conference on Computer Vision, ICCV 2001, vol. 2, pp. 383–390 (2003)
2. Belhumeur, P.N., Hespanha, J.P., Kriegman, D.J.: Eigenfaces vs. fisherfaces: recognition using class specific linear projection. IEEE Trans. Pattern Anal. Mach. Intell. **19**(7), 711–720 (1997)
3. Belkin, M., Niyogi, P.: Laplacian eigenmaps and spectral techniques for embedding and clustering. In: NIPS, vol. 14, pp. 585–591 (2001)
4. Georghiades, A.S., Belhumeur, P.N., Kriegman, D.J.: From few to many: illumination cone models for face recognition under variable lighting and pose. IEEE Trans. Pattern Anal. Mach. Intell. **23**(6), 643–660 (2001)
5. He, X., Cai, D., Yan, S., Zhang, H.J.: Neighborhood preserving embedding. In: Tenth IEEE International Conference on Computer Vision, ICCV 2005, vol. 2, pp. 1208–1213. IEEE (2005)
6. He, X., Yan, S., Hu, Y., Niyogi, P., Zhang, H.J.: Face recognition using Laplacianfaces. IEEE Trans. Pattern Anal. Mach. Intell. **27**(3), 328–340 (2005)
7. Jiang, X., Mandal, B., Kot, A.: Eigenfeature regularization and extraction in face recognition. IEEE Trans. Pattern Anal. Mach. Intell. **30**(3), 383–394 (2008)
8. Lee, K.C., Ho, J., Kriegman, D.J.: Acquiring linear subspaces for face recognition under variable lighting. IEEE Trans. Pattern Anal. Mach. Intell. **27**(5), 684–698 (2005)
9. Liu, Q., Lu, H., Ma, S.: Improving kernel fisher discriminant analysis for face recognition. IEEE Trans. Circ. Syst. Video Technol. **14**(1), 42–49 (2004)
10. Niyogi, X.: Locality preserving projections. In: Neural Information Processing Systems, vol. 16, p. 153. MIT (2004)
11. Pang, Y.H., Teoh, A.B.J., San Hiew, F.: Locality regularization embedding for face verification. Pattern Recogn. **48**(1), 86–102 (2015)
12. Phillips, P.J., Moon, H., Rizvi, S.A., Rauss, P.J.: The feret evaluation methodology for face-recognition algorithms. IEEE Trans. Pattern Anal. Mach. Intell. **22**(10), 1090–1104 (2002)
13. Sim, T., Baker, S., Bsat, M.: The CMU pose, illumination, and expression (PIE) database. In: Proceedings of the IEEE International Conference on Automatic Face and Gesture Recognition, pp. 46–51 (2002)

14. Turk, M., Pentland, A.: Eigenfaces for recognition. J. Cogn. Neurosci. **3**(1), 71–86 (1991)
15. Yan, S., Xu, D., Zhang, B., Zhang, H.J., Yang, Q., Lin, S.: Graph embedding and extensions: a general framework for dimensionality reduction. IEEE Trans. Pattern Anal. Mach. Intell. **29**(1), 40–51 (2007)
16. Yang, J., Frangi, A.F., Yang, J.Y., Zhang, D., Jin, Z.: KPCA plus LDA: a complete kernel fisher discriminant framework for feature extraction and recognition. IEEE Trans. Pattern Anal. Mach. Intell. **27**(2), 230–44 (2005)

The Abstraction for Trajectories with Different Numbers of Sampling Points

Peng Li, Qing Xu$^{(\boxtimes)}$, Hao Wei, Yuejun Guo, Xiaoxiao Luo, and Mateu Sbert

School of Computer Science and Technology, Tianjin University, Tianjin, China
qingxu@tju.edu.cn
http://cs.tju.edu.cn/faculty/qingxu/pages/index.html

Abstract. Trajectory abstraction is an efficient way to handle the large amount of information included in complex trajectory data. Based on the previous work, this paper proposes an improved framework for abstracting trajectories, which consists of three major stages. First, the original trajectories in different lengths are matched into groups according to their similarities, and then a non-local denoising approach, based on the wavelet thresholding technique, is performed on these groups to summarize trajectories. Last, a combined version of the compacted trajectories is obtained as the final trajectory abstraction. To avoid loss of trajectory features introduced by the resampling technique, we provide a novel method to convert trajectories in different lengths into suppositional equal, which serves for the similarity measurement and the wavelet thresholding. Extensive experiments on real and synthetic trajectory datasets demonstrate that the proposed trajectory abstraction achieves very potential results dealing with complex trajectory data.

Keywords: Trajectory abstraction · Outliers detection · Different sampling points · Similarity measurement · Wavelet thresholding

1 Introduction

With rapid development of location-aware sensors in a variety of new applications, massive spatial temporal data, i.e., trajectory data, will soon be accumulated [1]. Trajectory data has a brand range of practical applications in many fields such as intelligent transportation, location-based social networks [2] and so on [3]. The analysis of trajectory data is traditionally based on clustering to exact the patterns and underlying knowledge of these data. Unfortunately, clustering performance degrades when handling trajectory data with complex appearance [4].

To better understand the trajectory data, the framework [4] has been proposed for abstracting trajectories from the perspective of signal processing. In that framework, a resampling technique is firstly exploited to make trajectories have the same number of sampling points for trajectory abstracting framework. Extensive experiments show that the framework for trajectory abstraction gives

© Springer International Publishing AG 2017
D. Liu et al. (Eds.): ICONIP 2017, Part VI, LNCS 10639, pp. 434–442, 2017.
https://doi.org/10.1007/978-3-319-70136-3_46

very pleasant results for most trajectory data. Unfortunately, the performance degrades in special cases in which there are very tortuous trajectories, as shown in Figs. 4 and 5. The important shape or direction attributes of trajectories have inevitable distortion, leading to information loss of original trajectories. This is mainly because the resampling procedure discards original sampling points, meanwhile new points maybe introduced in the resampled trajectories, thus detailed information of original trajectories are changed to some extent.

This paper is a great leap of the work [4], and the main contribution is that we develop a new method for combating the situation that trajectories have different numbers of sampling points. In concrete, the reinforced framework starts without resampling, and matches original trajectories to form similarity groups. Here, the distance between trajectories is computed in a new way. That is, given any two trajectories in a dataset, for every sampling point of each trajectory, we obtain its corresponding point of the other trajectory by determining a position, where has the same length percentage with the sampling point under consideration. The distance between two trajectories is an average of all distances between sampling points and their corresponding points. We reuse all the virtual points in the following denoising approach. And the final combining is consistent with the previous framework.

The rest of this paper is organized as follows. The next section covers the related work. The improved trajectory abstracting framework is described in Sect. 3. Experimental results are presented and discussed in Sect. 4. The final section concludes the paper.

2   Related Work

Data mining is an interdisciplinary field of computer science [5–7]. It is the computational process of discovering patterns in large datasets involving methods at the intersection of artificial intelligence, machine learning, statistics, and database systems [5]. Among many data mining algorithms, clustering maybe the most popular way to present patterns of data. Many clustering algorithms have been proposed and developed, such as Density Based Spatial Clustering of Applications with Noise (DBSCAN) [8], Ordering Points to Identify the Clustering Structure (OPTICS) [9], k-means [10], Statistical Information Grid (STING) [11] and so on [12]. Due to simplifying and easily understanding, k-means is widely used, however, it is hard to obtain the number of clusters k adaptively, which influences the clustering performance directly. DBSCAN is a density-based clustering algorithm, which is less effective when handling high-dimensional data. Moreover, border points that are reachable from more than one cluster can be classified into either cluster, depending on the order in which the data is processed.

These clustering algorithms are often used to mine information and find outliers from the data, but for complex trajectory data, the performance may not be so satisfactory. To process and analyze trajectories effectively, a trajectory abstraction framework is proposed in [4], which summarizes trajectories from perspective of signals. The experiments show that it is suitable to deal with most of the general trajectory data, meanwhile some distortions maybe introduced. Therefore, this paper provides a novel framework based on the previous framework in order to handle more intractable trajectory abstracting application and distinguish outliers in a more appropriate way.

3   The Framework for Trajectory Abstraction

3.1   Distance Measurement

In practical applications, different trajectories always have different numbers of sampling points, which brings difficulty to measure the distance between trajectory data. In the work [4], all the trajectories are firstly resampled to have the same numbers of sampling points, making the distance measurement much easier. While in fact, the sampling technique may somehow destroy original shapes of trajectories, especially when dealing with very tortuous trajectory data. For instance, the sampling procedure may smooth out several turning points of a complex trajectory. As a result, the accuracy of distance measurement can be largely degraded. In order to improve the performance, we propose a new distance measurement to overcome the distortion generated by sampling.

In concrete, given the i-th trajectory in a dataset with m sampling points defined as

$$S_i = \{S_{i,1}, S_{i,2}, S_{i,3}, ..., S_{i,m}\}, \tag{1}$$

where $S_{i,j}$ is the j-th sampling point of trajectory S_i. The key to compute the distance between S_i and another trajectory S_j is to find out the "corresponding" sampling points in S_j for each point in S_i. We define the points with the equal *percentage* values have the "corresponding" relation. The *percentage* of the sampling point $S_{i,j}$ is calculated by the ratio of the trajectory length between $S_{i,1}$ and $S_{i,j}$ to the total length. Here, by length we mean the sum of Euclidean distances between adjacent sampling points. For example, as shown in Fig. 1. The length between $S_{i,1}$ and $S_{i,4}$ is actually the length of the red line, and similarly, the total length of the trajectory is the sum length of red and blue segments. Notice that, the corresponding point in S_j may a the new one, the position of which is computed by *percentage*. With all the corresponding points in S_j being located for sampling points in S_i, we can obtain the distance between $S_{i,1}$ and $S_{i,4}$ by the average of all distances between the pairwise points with corresponding relations. Figure 2 illustrates such an example of calculating the distance between trajectories S_i and S_j. The corresponding sampling point of $S_{i,k}$ is noted as $S'_{i,k}$, and for $S_{j,p}$ it is $S'_{j,p}$. Obviously, the final distance is the average length of all dashed lines.

Hausdorff and Euclidean distances may be the most widely used distance measures. While in fact, Euclidean distance is simple but requires the trajectories under consideration to have equal numbers of sampling points. Hausdorff distance does not have such requirement, but it is difficult to distinguish the directions of the trajectories, and it fails to deal with complex trajectories with

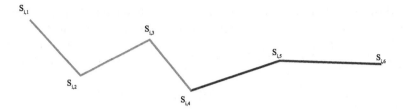

Fig. 1. An example of a trajectory with 6 sampling points.

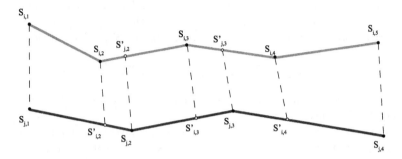

Fig. 2. Computation the trajectory distance between S_i and S_j

circular paths. By contrast, our proposed distance measurement possesses the simplicity of Euclidean distance and the general applicability of Hausdorff distance, and simultaneously overcomes the shortcomings of them.

3.2 Trajectory Abstraction

The improved trajectory abstraction framework is based on the work [4]. Different from the prior work, resampling is ignored in this paper, remaining the non-local denoising phase, including matching, thresholding and combining. Due to different numbers of sampling points, we also make a variant in thresholding. The reinforced framework can also iteratively output trajectory abstractions with multi-granularities and outliers.

Matching. In this step, each trajectory is regarded as a reference, for the purpose of matching its similar trajectories to establish groups. During the matching procedure, two trajectories S_i and S_j is matched into the same group when their distance is less than a threshold τ, which can be selected adaptively [4]. We adopt the new distance metric to measure the similarity between trajectories. Thus resampling can be avoided and shape feature of trajectories can be reserved. Note that a trajectory can be matched into more than one groups. That means a trajectory may have several duplicates in different groups, and they are independent of each other.

Thresholding. After matching, the wavelet thresholding technique is operated on every group. Notice that the similarity groups consist of similar trajectories but with different numbers of actual sampling points. Assume that the reference trajectory is S_r, and its similarity group TG_r with m trajectories is defined as

$$TG_r = \{S_j | Diff(S_r, S_j) < \tau\} \tag{2}$$

where $Diff(.)$ is the new distance metric mentioned in Sect. 3.1. We perform the wavelet thresholding on each sampling points of every trajectories in the group. That is, given a trajectory S_j from the group, we find all the virtual points in the whole group corresponding to each actual point of this trajectory. The collection of all virtual points together with the sampling point $S_{j,k}$ is now denoted as

$$s_{j,k} = \left[S'_{j,1}, S'_{j,2}, \ldots, S_{j,k}, \ldots, S'_{j,m} \right]^{\mathbf{T}}. \tag{3}$$

Thus, we transform trajectories into signals, which are then filtered by the wavelet thresholding technique.

Figure 3 presents a simple example. Suppose we have already formed a group of three trajectories. The red trajectory consists of two sampling points. The green is of three sampling points and the blue is four.

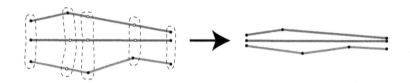

Fig. 3. Construction of points for filtering in a group (Color figure online)

We do the thresholding for every sampling point, i.e., each solid point in Fig. 3 will be filtered. In the figure, each dotted circle contains three points, which are either all solid points or a solid point with two hollow points. And the three points in a dotted circle have the same percentage value in their respective trajectories, and they will be filtered by wavelet thresholding. After filtering, only solid points will update their respective trajectories in the group, and hollow points will be discarded due to their fictionality. In case that there is a real sampling point corresponding to the sampling point to be filtered, we always use the original version of the real point, instead of the one being filtered.

Combining. With all groups filtered by thresholding, we obtain the filtered and condensed trajectories in each group. Notice that a trajectory can have different duplicates after filtering, since it is reasonable to exploit a same trajectory in several groups. Therefore, we perform the combining, by averaging its duplicates in all groups, to get the final form for each trajectory.

4   Experimental Results

In this section, to evaluate the performance of the improved framework, we have studied 7 trajectory datasets, including real and synthetic data, as listed in Table 1. In addition, comparison with the previous method [4] has been made. For reasons of space, only two real datasets, $video^1$ and GPS^2 [13–15], are illustrated in the following.

Table 1. Evaluation on outlier detection [4]

Database	Recall			Precision		
	Improved	Previous	DBSCAN	Improved	Previous	DBSCAN
Video[d]	**1.0**	0.67	0.67	1.0	1.0	1.0
GPS[b][13–15]	**1.0**	0.67	0.67	1.0	1.0	1.0
Highway [16]	0.93	0.89	**0.94**	**0.89**	**0.89**	0.84
Simulation [17]	**1.0**	**1.0**	**1.0**	**1.0**	**1.0**	0.95
Edinburgh[a]	**0.95**	**0.95**	0.76	**0.94**	0.81	0.86
Aircraft[c]	**0.95**	0.88	0.89	**1.0**	0.95	0.81
CROSS [18]	0.93	**0.98**	0.93	0.91	**0.92**	0.81

[a] http://homepages.inf.ed.ac.uk/rbf/forumtracking/
[b] http://research.microsoft.com/en-us/downloads/b16d359d-d164-469e-9fd4-daa38f2b2e13/default.aspx
[c] https://c3.nasa.gov/dashlink/resources/132/,2011
[d] http://www-users.cs.umn.edu/~aleks/inclof/

As shown in Fig. 4(a), the *video* is a really complex dataset, which includes 189 trajectories with the number of sampling points ranging from 174 to 645. The abstraction results by the improved and the previous methods are presented in Figs. 4(b) and (c), respectively. Note that, the previous method requires the resample process, which firstly smooths the trajectories and makes them in equal numbers of sampling points. Obviously, it is very difficult to summarize the trajectories due to their intricate shapes. By contrast, the performance of the improved method is more satisfying. For instance, in Fig. 4(a), 24 blue and 1 red trajectories seem to be similar with respect to the small waves of the lower half parts, while obviously the red one has relatively gradual shape changes of the upper half parts. Our improved method successfully smooths the blue trajectories, without largely losing the shape information from the overall perspective, and clearly detects the red one as an outlier. Unfortunately, the previous method mixes the blue trajectories with the outlier and gives the final abstraction result.

---

[1] http://www-users.cs.umn.edu/~aleks/inclof/.
[2] http://research.microsoft.com/en-us/downloads/b16d359d-d164-469e-9fd4-daa38f2b2e13/default.aspx.

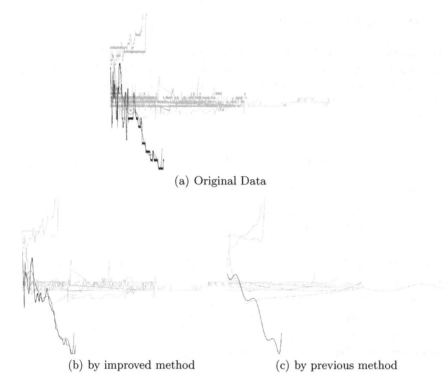

(a) Original Data

(b) by improved method   (c) by previous method

Fig. 4. Comparison of abstraction results on *Video* (Color figure online)

Figure 5(a) is the original 77 trajectories of *GPS*, where the red one is an outlier. These trajectories are of different numbers of sampling points, up to 370. The abstracted trajectories of original data are in Fig. 5(b). The resampled abstracted trajectories are in Fig. 5(c). In Fig. 5(b), three normal trajectories in blue overlap with each other, the same situation happens in Fig. 5(c). The difference is that the red anomaly trajectory is identified by our improved method due to the appropriate distance metric, as shown in Fig. 5(b), while the previous method treated the blue normal trajectories and the outlier as similar items due to the smoothing by resampling, as shown in Fig. 5(c).

Additionally, we make use of recall and precision metrics [16] to quantitatively measure the effect of our improvements in terms of anomaly detection. Table 1 shows the comparison results of our improved method, the previous method and DBSCAN. In all, our improved method and the previous method outperform the typical DBSCAN, and the improved version indeed enhances the ability of handling complex trajectory data.

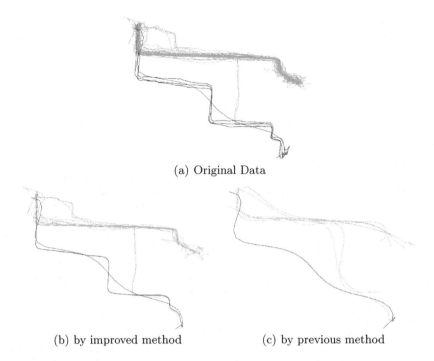

(a) Original Data

(b) by improved method   (c) by previous method

Fig. 5. Comparison of abstraction results on *GPS* (Color figure online)

5 Conclusion

The framework of doing trajectory abstracting [4] is able to process trajectory data more effectively than the common clustering algorithms. In order to preserve the advantages of the trajectory abstraction framework and meanwhile, to avoid the problem introduced by resampling, this paper has enhanced the previous trajectory abstracting framework to better deal with complex trajectories with massive details. We have made progresses in trajectory thresholding, that is, the wavelet thresholding can be handled on trajectories of various numbers of sampling points. And we have designed a new distance metric for tortuous and littery trajectories. The experimental results show that the improved framework has a stronger ability to abstract trajectory data with varied lengths and distinguish outliers.

Several improvements for the framework of trajectory abstraction will be tried in our future research. The time consumption of the trajectory abstraction should be reduced in order to handle a greater mount of trajectories efficiently. Furthermore, the abstraction method should be reinforced to handle trajectories of 3-Dimension or higher dimension data.

Acknowledgments. This work has been funded by Natural Science Foundation of China (61471261, 61179067, U1333110), and by grants TIN2013-47276-C6-1-R from Spanish Government and 2014-SGR-1232 from Catalan Government (Spain).

References

1. Chakka, V.P., Everspaugh, A.C., Patel, J.M.: Indexing large trajectory data sets with seti. Ann Arbor **1001**(48109–2122), 12 (2003)
2. Zheng, Y.: Tutorial on location-based social networks. In: Proceedings of the 21st International Conference on World Wide Web, WWW, vol. 12 (2012)
3. Morris, B.T., Trivedi, M.M.: Understanding vehicular traffic behavior from video: a survey of unsupervised approaches. J. Electron. Imaging **22**(4), 041113 (2013)
4. Luo, X., Xu, Q., Guo, Y., Wei, H., Lv, Y.: Trajectory abstracting with group-based signal denoising. In: Arik, S., Huang, T., Lai, W.K., Liu, Q. (eds.) ICONIP 2015. LNCS, vol. 9491, pp. 452–461. Springer, Cham (2015). doi:10.1007/978-3-319-26555-1_51
5. Chakrabarti, S., Ester, M., Fayyad, U., Gehrke, J., Han, J., Morishita, S., Piatetsky-Shapiro, G., Wang, W.: Data mining curriculum: a proposal (version 1.0). Intensive Working Group of ACM SIGKDD Curriculum Committee (2006)
6. Christopher, C.: Encyclopaedia britannica: definition of data mining. Technical report (2010). Accessed 09 Dec 2010
7. Hastie, T., Tibshirani, R., Friedman, J., Franklin, J.: The elements of statistical learning: data mining, inference and prediction. Math. Intell. **27**(2), 83–85 (2005)
8. Ester, M., Kriegel, H.-P., Sander, J., Xu, X.: A density-based algorithm for discovering clusters in large spatial databases with noise. In: KDD 1996, pp. 226–231 (1996)
9. Ankerst, M., Breunig, M.M., Kriegel, H.-P., Sander, J.: Optics: ordering points to identify the clustering structure. In: ACM SIGMOD Record, vol. 28, pp. 49–60. ACM (1999)
10. Lloyd, S.: Least squares quantization in PCM. IEEE Trans. Inf. Theory **28**(2), 129–137 (1982)
11. Wang, W., Yang, J., Muntz, R., et al.: Sting: a statistical information grid approach to spatial data mining. In: VLDB 1997, pp. 186–195 (1997)
12. Rui, X., Wunsch, D., et al.: Survey of clustering algorithms. IEEE Trans. Neural Netw. **16**(3), 645–678 (2005)
13. Zheng, Y., Li, Q., Chen, Y., Xie, X., Ma, W.-Y.: Understanding mobility based on GPS data. In: Proceedings of the 10th International Conference on Ubiquitous Computing, pp. 312–321. ACM (2008)
14. Zheng, Y., Xie, X., Ma, W.-Y.: Geolife: a collaborative social networking service among user, location and trajectory. IEEE Data Eng. Bull. **33**(2), 32–39 (2010)
15. Zheng, Y., Zhang, L., Xie, X., Ma, W.-Y.: Mining interesting locations and travel sequences from GPS trajectories. In: Proceedings of the 18th International Conference on World Wide Web, pp. 791–800. ACM (2009)
16. Anjum, N., Cavallaro, A.: Multifeature object trajectory clustering for video analysis. IEEE Trans. Circ. Syst. Video Technol. **18**(11), 1555–1564 (2008)
17. Piciarelli, C., Micheloni, C., Foresti, G.L.: Trajectory-based anomalous event detection. IEEE Trans. Circ. Syst. Video Technol. **18**(11), 1544–1554 (2008)
18. Morris, B.T., Trivedi, M.M.: Trajectory learning for activity understanding: unsupervised, multilevel, and long-term adaptive approach. IEEE Trans. Pattern Anal. Mach. Intell. **33**(11), 2287–2301 (2011)

A Deep Orthogonal Non-negative Matrix Factorization Method for Learning Attribute Representations

Bensheng Lyu$^{(\boxtimes)}$, Kan Xie, and Weijun Sun

School of Automation, Guangdong University of Technology,
Guangzhou 510006, China
lbshehe@163.com

Abstract. Orthogonal non-negative matrix factorization (ONMF) is a powerful unsupervised learning method because it is equivalent to the K-means method and can be more robust and flexible for clustering analysis. Arguing that ONMF with a single layer implementation often fails to capture the potential hierarchical features of complex objects, a deep orthogonal NMF (deep ONMF) model with cascaded multiple ONMF layers was proposed in this paper. We demonstrated how deep ONMF is able to reveal the hierarchy information of data and hence lead to improved clustering performance by both theoretical analysis and experiments on real-world data.

Keywords: Nonnegative matrix factorization · Orthogonal nonnegative matrix factorization · Clustering analysis

1 Introduction

Non-negative Matrix Factorization (NMF) is a widely-used method in data analysis. It aims to decompose a given non-negative matrix X into two low-rank nonnegative matrices Z and H, such that $X \approx ZH$. NMF was *discovered* several times by different scientists; however, it regained its popularity recently largely due to the word by Lee and Seung [1,2]. Due to the nonnegativity constraints, the factors are expected to be sparse, and particularly, the objects in data matrix are represented as purely additive-without subtractive-combinations of components. This feature of NMF is referred to as the learning-parts ability, which is one major advantage of NMF against other relative dimensionality reduction approaches. For this reason, NMF has been successfully applied in many fields, include pattern recognition and machine learning [3], data mining [4], signal processing [5], spectral data analysis [6], face recognition [7], speech recognition [8], hyperspectral image applications [9,10], and more. In recent years, orthogonal NMF (ONMF) that additionally imposes orthogonal constraints has attracted great attention as it proved to be equivalent to the K-means method [11,12,16]. In fact, the nonnegativity and the orthogonality constraints make the

© Springer International Publishing AG 2017
D. Liu et al. (Eds.): ICONIP 2017, Part VI, LNCS 10639, pp. 443–452, 2017.
https://doi.org/10.1007/978-3-319-70136-3_47

factor naturally almost strictly sparse, hence this factor can be used to indicate which category/cluster the associated object belongs to.

In order to impose the orthogonal constraints, two different multiplicative update (MU) algorithms were proposed in [11,12], respectively. An EM-like algorithm for ONMF using the augmented Lagrange multipliers method was presented in [16] and obtained satisfactory results in clustering analysis. All these methods have focused on strict orthogonal constraints, which make them like a hard K-means method. In practice, a sample can often have a degree of membership in each cluster, an approximate ONMF (AONMF) model together two efficiently algorithms was recently proposed [17]. This approach can control the strength of orthogonality and can be viewed as an analogy of the fuzzy K-means method.

Both ONMF and AONMF take a single layer structure and hence can only capture one level of features. In practice, it is common that complex data objects have hierarchical features, each of which denotes a different level of abstract understanding of the objects. It is therefore meaningful to develop ONMF models with a deep architecture, which allows ONMF to discover the hierarchy of data. To this end, a multi-layer ONMF was developed in this paper, allowing better high-level feature presentation, as show in Fig. 1.

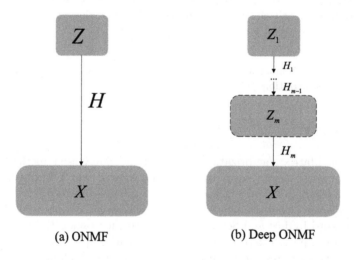

(a) ONMF   (b) Deep ONMF

Fig. 1. (a) A ONMF is presented in a linear transformation space. (b) Deep ONMF learn hidden representations that lie in revealing the low dimensional data.

The paper was organized as follows. In Sect. 2, a brief review of ONMF and AONMF was presented. In Sect. 3, a deep ONMF model was proposed, together with an efficient algorithm to optimize the cost function. Experimental results were presented in Sect. 4, justifying the superiority of the proposed deep ONMF. Finally, conclusion was made in Sect. 2.

2   A Brief Review on ONMF and AONMF

In recent years, there has been a significant amount of research on orthogonal NMF (ONMF) that imposes orthogonal constraints on a factor matrix. Given an nonnegative data matrix $X \in \mathbb{R}_+^{M \times N}$ (or simply $X \geq 0$), where $\mathbb{R}_+^{M \times N}$ denotes the set of M-by-N nonnegative matrices, by ONMF we obtain nonnegative matrices $Z \in \mathbb{R}_+^{M \times R}$ and $H \in \mathbb{R}_+^{N \times R}$, $R \ll \min(M, N)$, and H is column-wisely orthogonal, such that $X \approx ZH^T$. ONMF is typically achieved by solving the following constrained optimization problem:

$$\min_{Z \geq 0, H \geq 0} \|X - ZH^T\|_F^2, \quad s.t. \quad H^T H = I. \tag{1}$$

The orthogonality constraints $H^T H = I$ in NMF actually consist of two parts: the unit-norm constraints, i.e. $h_r^T h_r = 1$, and the orthogonal constraints $h_r^T h_j = 0$ for any $r \neq j$. Due to the nonnegativity, each row of Z contains only one nonzero entry, indicating which category the corresponding object belongs to. This builds direction connection between ONMF and the K-means method. Arguing that each object in practice may have a degree of membership, but not completely belongs to a category, the following approximate ONMF method has been proposed by Li and Zhou, et al.:

$$f(Z, H) = \frac{1}{2}\|X - ZH^T\|_F^2 + \frac{\lambda}{2}\sum_{r=1}^{R}\sum_{j \neq r} h_r^T h_j. \tag{2}$$

Apparently, when $\lambda \to +\infty$, $H^T H \to I$; otherwise, a trade-off between orthogonality against fitting error will be achieved, which is why we called (2) approximately orthogonal NMF (AONMF).

Several efficient algorithms have been proposed to solve (1) and (2) [11,12]. All these methods adopt the block coordinate descent method, where partial parameters (one factor matrix or even only one column of a factor matrix) will be optimized first while keeping the others fixed; all parameters must be updated at least once in each iteration. Among them, the hierarchical alternating least squares (HALS) method is quite effective as it is able to give the closed-form solution for each sub-problem. In details, if we hope to optimize H_r, the rth column of H, minimizing (2) is equivalent to minimizing

$$f_r = \frac{1}{2}\|X_r - z_r h_r^T\|_F^2 + \lambda \sum_{i \neq r} h_i^T h_r, \tag{3}$$

where $X_r = X - ZH^T + z_r h_r^T$. We use the Lagrange multiplier method and define the following Lagrange function:

$$L_r = f_r + \sum_{n=1}^{N} \mu_{nr} h_{nr}, \tag{4}$$

where μ_{nr} are the Lagrange multipliers. Suppose $z_r^T z_r \neq 0$ and consider the Karush-Kuhn-Tucker (KKT) conditions: (1) $\frac{\partial L_r}{\partial h_r} = 0$; (2) $b_{nr} \geq 0$; (3) $\mu_{nr} \geq 0$;

and $(4)\mu_{nr}h_{nr} = 0$; then there holds that

$$h_r \leftarrow \mathcal{P}_+ \left(h_r + \frac{X^T z_r - H(Z^T z_r)}{z_r^T z_r} - \frac{\lambda \breve{H}_r 1_{R-1}}{z_r^T z_r} \right),$$ (5)

where $\breve{H}_r$ is a sub-matrix of H by removing its rth column, 1_R is an all-one R-by-1 column vector. Note that (5) gives the unique global minimum of f_r with respect to h_r, which explains the high efficiency of this approach. The hierarchical alternating lease square (HALS) update rule for z_r can be similarly obtained:

$$z_r \leftarrow \mathcal{P}_+ \left(z_r + \frac{X h_r - Z(H^T h_r)}{h_r^T h_r} \right).$$ (6)

The factor matrix H given by AONMF is not only orthogonal but also approximately orthogonal. From the perspective of clustering, we regard $Z = [z_1, z_2, \ldots, z_k]$ as the cluster centroids, and $H = [h_1, h_2, \ldots, h_n]$ can be regarded as the cluster indicators for each data point. Hence, ONMF is equivalent to the K-means whereas AONMF corresponds to the fuzzy K-means method.

3   Deep Orthogonal Non-negative Matrix Factorization

In many cases, the data are complex, which have a collection of differences and unknown characteristics. In this article, we deal with face databases, which are not only from the representation of subjects, but also from head pose or facial expression in relation to camera. In addition, each face contains hierarchical features denoting different level of abstract conceptions. Clustering analysis of such type of data can be very challenging. In order to deal with such cases, one is polyadic decomposition [13–15], and the other is deep model decomposition. Here we use the latter method.

Our aim is to further decompose Z to equip ONMF with a deep architecture, which enables ONMF to: (1) Automatically learn latent hierarchy of attributes; (2) Find representations of data that are more suitable for clustering analysis based on high-level of abstraction. To this end, the data matrix $X \in \mathbb{R}_+^{M \times N}$ is decomposed as $X \approx Z_1 H_1^T$, where $Z_1 \in \mathbb{R}^{M \times k_1}$ and $H_1 \in \mathbb{R}^{N \times k_1}$ with $k_1 < \min(M, N)$, and $H_1^T H_1 = I$. Then, Z_1 will be treated as the new data matrix and ONMF will be applied such that $Z_1 = Z_2 H_2^T$, where $Z_2 \in \mathbb{R}^{M \times k_2}$ and $H_2 \in \mathbb{R}^{k_1 \times k_2}$ with $k_2 < k_1$, and $H_2^T H_2 = I$. Following this procedure, each matrix $Z_{i-1} \in \mathbb{R}_+^{M \times k_{i-1}}$ will be factorized by applying ONMF as $Z_{i-1} \approx Z_i H_i^T$, till sufficient depth is reached:

$$Z_{i-1} \approx Z_i H_i^T$$
$$Z_{i-2} \approx Z_{i-1} H_{i-1}^T$$
$$\vdots$$
$$Z_1 \approx Z_2 H_2^T$$
$$X \approx Z_1 H_1^T.$$

In such a way, we obtain an extended ONMF with a deep architecture, where the given data matrix X is decomposed the product of $i + 1$ factor matrices:

$$X \approx Z_1 H_1^T H_2^T \cdots H_i^T, \; H_l^T H_l = I, l = 1, 2, \ldots, i. \tag{7}$$

Note that for notation convenience, we invert the order of subscript indices of H and Z.

We use two steps to find the factors $Z_1, H_1, \ldots, H_i$:

Pre-training Step: The matrices $H_i, \; H_{i-1}, \ldots, H_1, Z_1$ will be initialized by applying standard ONMF or AONMF algorithms sequentially to obtain (3). The purpose of this step is to provide *good* initial values for all factor matrices. This step is quite critical and has been tactic widely used in deep autoencoder networks [18]. In this paper, the HALS-AONMF algorithm is adopted due to its very high efficiency and flexibility.

Fine-tuning Step: In order to fine tune each layer, we minimize the following cost function:

$$C_{deep} = \frac{1}{2} \| X - Z H_1^T \cdots H_i^T \|_F^2, \tag{8}$$

where $H_l^T H_l = I, l = 1, 2, \ldots, i$. Clearly, the matrices Z and H_i can be updated as done in [17]. The major difficulty is how to update the hidden layers. Because $H_l, l = 1, 2, \ldots, i$ are approximately orthogonal, we can transform the cost function as follows:

$$C_{deep} = \frac{1}{2} \| X H_i \cdots H_{l+1} - Z H_1^T \cdots H_l^T \|_F^2. \tag{9}$$

Then, we can view $X H_i H_{i-1} \cdots H_{l+1}$ and $Z H_1 H_2 \cdots H_{l-1}$ as X and Z in (1) and (2), respectively, suggesting that H_l can be updated using (5). See Algorithm 1 for the pseudo-code of the proposed algorithm.

4   Experiments and Clustering Results

Our main purpose is to show that a Deep ONMF is able to learn better high-level representations of data than a single one-layer ONMF. In order to evaluate this purpose, we have compared the performance of the proposed Deep ONMF with state-of-the-art on the task of clustering analysis of face images in 3 datasets. These datasets are:

- **CMU PIE:** This dataset comprises of 2,856 grayscale 32×32 face images of 68 subjects. Each person has 42 facial images under different light and illumination conditions. In this experiment images taken from pose27 were tested [19].
- **JAFFE:** The Japanese Female Facial Expression [20] Database contains 213 images of 7 facial expressions taken from 10 Japanese female models. Each image has been rated on 6 emotion adjectives by 60 Japanese subjects.

Algorithm 1. Suggested algorithm for training a Deep ONMF model. Initially we approximate the factors greedily using the HALS-AONMF algorithm and we fine tune the factors until we reach the convergence criterion.

Input: $X \in \mathbb{R}^{M \times N}$, list of layer sizes
Output: weight matrices Z_i and feature matrices H_i for each of the layers
Initialize layers
for all layers **do**
    $Z_i, H_i \leftarrow ONMF(Z_{i-1})$
end for
repeat
    for $l = 1, 2, \ldots, i$ **do**
    Update H_l by minimizing (9) using, e.g., the HALS algorithm
    end for
    $\Psi = \Pi_{l=1}^{i} H_l^T$
    $Z_1 \leftarrow Z_1 \odot \dfrac{X\Psi^T}{Z_1 \Psi \Psi^T}.$
    end for
until Stopping criterion is reached

- **YALE:** The Yale Face Database [21] contains 165 grayscale images in GIF format of 15 individuals. There are 11 images per subject, one per different facial expression or configuration: center-light, w/glasses, happy, left-light, w/no glasses, normal, right-light, sad, sleepy, surprised, and wink.

In order to evaluate the performance of our model, we also compare it with other NMF methods that could be used in learning this representations. Especially, we performed the clustering experiment of a Deep Semi-NMF algorithm [23], which could learn such hidden representations that allow themselves to an interpretation of clustering according to different, unknown attributes of a given dataset. Finally, we compared each algorithm with the best clustering results according to the different layers on the same dataset.

4.1 Implementation Details

In order to impose stronger orthogonal constraints, it is crucial to select proper parameter λ to achieve satisfactory performance. For the proposed algorithm, the regularization parameter λ was empirically set as $\lambda = 0.001$. For the Deep Semi-NMF experimental setup, Semi-NMF [22] is used to initialize, we choose a suitable number of components so that we can have good clustering performance.

It is important for the experimental setup to select suitable number of components. After preliminary careful experiments, we focused on experiments that involve five hidden layer architectures for the Deep ONMF and Deep Semi-NMF. When the number of layers increase, we use the top layer of H for clustering to get best clustering results according to adjust number of components.

4.2 Clustering Results

To evaluate the clustering performance of each algorithm, we used K-means clustering, following the experimental plan in [24]. These datasets were already labelled. The accuracy (AC) and the normalized mutual information metric (NMI) were used as two metrics [25] we compared.

Table 1. The best clustering performance on three datasets

Dataset	AC					
	NMF	GNMG	Semi-NMF	Deep Semi-NMF	ONMF	Deep ONMF
PIE	0.6488	0.5447	0.4322	0.8140	0.6761	0.8449
JAFFE	0.8667	0.9343	0.4399	0.9530	0.9445	0.9765
YALE	0.3660	0.3921	0.4521	0.4648	0.4321	0.5296

AC is the highest values of average that 10 test runs are conducted on the top layer against different NMF variants.

Table 2. The best clustering performance on three datasets

Dataset	NMI					
	NMF	GNMG	Semi-NMF	Deep Semi-NMF	ONMF	Deep ONMF
PIE	0.7735	0.7544	0.5858	0.9417	0.7954	0.9682
JAFFE	0.8920	0.9188	0.4383	0.9475	0.9319	0.9657
YALE	0.4286	0.4615	0.5112	0.5247	0.4879	0.5310

NMI is the highest values of average that 10 test runs are conducted on the top layer against different NMF variants.

Tables 1 and 2 show the highest clustering results on the three different datasets, the clustering results were conducted with layer ranging from one to five. Using K-means on the feature representations produced by six different NMF algorithms generated accuracy and normalized mutual information. For each clustering results, 10 test runs were conducted on the top layer. The average performance is reported on the table and figures. On the three datasets, only Deep ONMF and Deep Semi-NMF can change the layer, which have the most clustering results in different layer, other algorithms only have one layer for clustering. When the layer increases from one to five, we can compare the best clustering results with previous layer. The difference is obvious in Fig. 2, which can be a sign that after the initialization of Deep ONMF and Deep Semi-NMF, We continue to fine tune Z and H to get better clustering results.

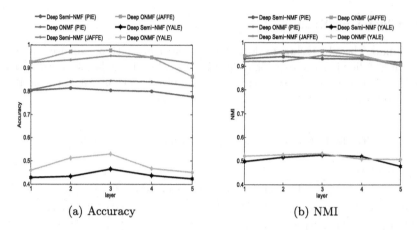

(a) Accuracy   (b) NMI

Fig. 2. Accuracy and NMI for clustering based on the representations learned by the two deep models on different datasets. The layer of each model is from one to five, the representations used are from the top layer. In parenthesis we show these different datasets.

5   Conclusion

We introduced a novel deep model for orthogonal non-negative matrix factorization, the Deep ONMF, which can automatically learn hierarchical features of given datasets for clustering. Experimental results show that the deep model of NMF has better clustering performance than single-layered NMF variants, and the clustering performance of Deep ONMF is better than that of Deep Semi-NMF on these datasets. We compare the previous layer and the latter layer of clustering performance in the deep model of NMF. The clustering performance of the first three layers is increased, and then decreased, which means that the number of layers increases to a certain extent, the clustering performance will decline.

Our next step is that we will use more datasets to test the new model and compare it with other NMF algorithms. Another line of work will focus on clustering performance of deep non-negative matrix factorization with different decomposed dimension.

Acknowledgements. This work was supported by the National Natural Science Foundation of China (No. 61673124), Guangdong Natural Science Foundation (No. 2014A030308009) and Guangdong Science and Technology Planning Project (Nos. 2016B030308001 and 2013B091300009).

References

1. Lee, D., Seung, H.: Learning the parts of objects by non-negative matrix factorization. Nature **401**(6755), 788–791 (1999)
2. Lee, D., Seung, H.: Algorithms for non-negative matrix factorization. In: Proceedings of the Advances in Neural Information Processing Systems, pp. 556–562 (2001)
3. Cichocki, A., Zdunek, R., Phan, A.H., Amari, S.: Non-negative Matrix and Tensor Factorization: Applications to Exploratory Multi-way Data Analysis and Blind Source Separation. Wiley-Blackwell, Oxford (2009)
4. Berry, M., Browne, M., Langville, A., Pauca, V., Plemmons, R.: Algorithms and applications for approximate nonnegative matrix factorization. Comput. Stat. Data Anal. **52**(1), 155–173 (2007)
5. Buciu, I.: Non-negative matrix factorization, a new tool for feature extraction: theory and applications. Int. J. Comput. Commun. Control **3**, 67–74 (2008)
6. Chu, M., Plemmons, R.: Nonnegative matrix factorization and applications. Bull. Int. Linear Algebra Soc. **34**, 2–7 (2005)
7. Zafeiriou, S., Tefas, A., Buciu, I., Pitas, I.: Exploiting discriminant information in nonnegative matrix factorization with application to frontal face verification. IEEE Trans. Neural Network **17**(3), 683–695 (2006)
8. Zdunek, R., Cichocki, A.: Non-negative matrix factorization with quasi-Newton optimization. In: Proceedings of the Eighth International Conference Artificial Intelligence and Soft Computing, pp. 870–879 (2006)
9. Wang, W., Li, S., Qi, H., Ayhan, B., Kwan, C., Vance, S.: Identify anomaly component by sparsity and low rank. In: IEEE Workshop on Hyperspectral Image and Signal Processing: Evolution in Remote Sensor (WHISPERS), Tokyo, Japan, 2–5 June 2015
10. Qu, Y., Guo, R., Wang, W., Qi, H., Ayhan, B., Kwan, C., Vance, S.: Anomaly detection in hyperspectral images through spectral unmixing and low rank decomposition. In: IEEE International Geoscience and Remote Sensing Symposium (IGARSS), Beijing, pp. 1855–1858, July 2016
11. Ding, C., Li, T., Peng, W., Park, H.: Orthogonal nonnegative matrix trifactorizations for clustering. In: Proceedings of the 12th ACM SIGKDD International Conference on Knowledge Discovery and Data Mining, KDD 2006, New York, NY, USA, pp. 126–135 (2006)
12. Choi, S.: Algorithms for orthogonal nonnegative matrix factorization. In: Proceedings of the IEEE International Joint Conference on Neural Networks (IJCNN), pp. 1828–1832 (2008)
13. Zhou, G., Cichocki, A., Zhao, Q., Xie, S.: Efficient nonnegative tucker decompositions: algorithms and uniqueness. IEEE Trans. Image Process. **24**(12), 4990–5003 (2015)
14. Zhou, G., Cichocki, A., Zhao, Q., Xie, S.: Nonnegative matrix and tensor factorizations: an algorithmic perspective. IEEE Signal Process. Mag. **31**(3), 54–65 (2014)
15. Zhou, G., Cichocki, A., Xie, S.: Accelerated canonical polyadic decomposition by using mode reduction. IEEE Trans. Neural Netw. Learn. Syst. **24**(12), 2051–2062 (2013)
16. Pompili, F., Gillis, N., Absil, P.-A., Glineur, F.: Two algorithms for orthogonal nonnegative matrix factorization with application to clustering. Neurocomputing **141**, 15–25 (2014)

17. Li, B., Zhou, G., Cichocki, A.: Two efficient algorithms for approximately orthogonal nonnegative matrix factorization. IEEE Signal Process. Lett. **22**(7), 843–846 (2015)
18. Hinton, G.E., Salakhutdinov, R.R.: Reducing the dimensionality of data with neural networks. Science **313**(5786), 504–507 (2006)
19. Sim, T., Baker, S., Bsat, M.: The CMU pose, illumination, and expression (PIE) database. TPAMI **25**(12), 1615–1618 (2003)
20. Lyons, M.J., Akamatsu, S., Kamachi, M., Gyoba, J.: Coding facial expressions with gabor wavelets. In: Third IEEE International Conference on Automatic Face and Gesture Recognition, pp. 200–205, 14–16 April 1998
21. Bellhumer, P.N., Hespanha, J., Kriegman, D.: Eigenfaces vs. Fisherfaces: recognition using class specific linear projection. IEEE Trans. Pattern Anal. Mach. Intell. **17**(7), 711–720 (1997). Special Issue on Face Recognition
22. Ding, C., Li, T., Jordan, M.I.: Convex and semi-nonnegative matrix factorizations. TPAMI **32**, 45–55 (2010)
23. Trigeorgis, G., Bousmalis, K., Zafeiriou, S., Schuller, W.B.: A deep semi-NMF model for learning hidden representations. In: ICML, vol. 32 (2014)
24. Cai, D., He, X., Han, J., Huang, T.S.: Graph regularized nonnegative matrix factorization for data representation. TPAMI **33**(8), 1548–1560 (2011)
25. Xu, W., Liu, X., Gong, Y.: Document clustering based on nonnegative matrix factorization. In: SIGIR, pp. 267–273. ACM (2003)

An Event-Driven Computational System with Spiking Neurons for Object Recognition

Yuhao Ma, Rong Xiao, and Huajin Tang$^{(\boxtimes)}$

Neuromorphic Computing Research Center, College of Computer Science,
Sichuan University, Chengdu, China
{yhma,rxiao}@stu.scu.edu.cn, htang@scu.edu.cn

Abstract. We propose a biologically plausible computational system
using spiking neural networks for object recognition, which processes the
data from a temporal contrast address event representation (AER) sensor. The spike-based features are obtained through event-driven Gabor
function and LIF neurons. And a time-to-first spike operation (also as
a temporal Winner-Take-All (WTA) operation) with lateral reset in the
same pooling area is implemented for reducing memory and computational costs. An address lookup table (LUT) is also applied to adjust the
feature maps via address mapping and reordering. Then, the extracted
spike feature patterns are classified by tempotron neurons. Our system
can not only capture temporal visual information, but also learn features
entirely based on the timing spikes information. Experiments conducted
on two AER datasets have proved its efficiency for object recognition.

Keywords: Neuromorphic computing · Address event representation
(AER) · Event driven · Spiking neural network (SNN) · Object recognition

1 Introduction

Last decade has witnessed the researchers exploring different event-driven neuromorphic systems inspired by biological studies of the visual ventral pathway
[1]. Notable examples of such biomimetic vision sensors include the Asynchronous
Time-based Image Sensor (ATIS) [2], event-driven Dynamic Vision Sensor (DVS)
[3], and the DAVIS sensor [4]. Unlike the traditional camera, AER vision sensors
enable pixel-parallel image processing at the focal plane. Each pixel in the sensor
can individually monitor the relative change of light intensity, and it will request
to output an event (x, y, t, p) once the change is greater than a user-defined threshold, where t denotes the timestamp, (x, y) corresponds to a local receptive field
and independently senses the light change, where x and y denote the positions of
the pixel. The polarity $p = 1$ denotes the increasing light (i.e., dark-to-light) and
$p = -1$ denotes exactly the opposite (i.e., light-to-dark). However, the majority
of existing methods are based on frame-driven image sensors, the one that cannot be directly used to handle the event information. To solve this problem, some
impressive works have been proposed. Inspired by the huge success of deep learning, Chen et al. adopt the frame-based CNN for training SNNs implementing them

© Springer International Publishing AG 2017
D. Liu et al. (Eds.): ICONIP 2017, Part VI, LNCS 10639, pp. 453–461, 2017.
https://doi.org/10.1007/978-3-319-70136-3_48

in FPGA [5]. Meanwhile, the convolutional neural network with an event-driven multi-kernel convolution processor module was extended for high-speed recognition examples [6]. In recent years, SNN has gained a lot of attention, which simulates the fundamental mechanism of our brain and provides greater computational power and more biological realism [7], in which the neuronal communication is predominantly carried out by the propagation of action potentials or spikes [8]. SNN has achieved promising performance in various pattern recognition problems. A recent study has further demonstrated the computational power of spiking neurons for processing spatiotemporal patterns, and illustrated their computational benefits to process visual information [9]. As a result, it is optimally suited for processing signals from event-based sensors such as DVS. The spiking neuron model was introduced, which captured temporal visual information and learned features in an unsupervised manner (Spike-Timing Dependent Plasticity (STDP)) [10]. [11] performed fast and accurately in tests for objects in multiple orientations. Moreover, Zhao et al. [12] proposed another AER feedforward categorization system, where a HMAX model and tempotron classifier are adopted. Orchard et al. also proposed a new hierarchical spiking neural network structure - HFirst [13], which extracts orientations using oriented Gabor filters. The one that relies on the strongly activated neurons tend to fire first. Besides, Tsitiridis et al. presented a biologically-inspired Gabor feature approach and have been trained via the Remote Supervision Method [14].

Similar to these biological networks, we exploit spike timing to our advantage in computation for object recognition in this paper. This work introduce an event-driven recognition system of Leaky-Integrate and Fire (LIF) spiking neurons [15] that can fully exploit retina sensor data in real-time. In this system, it trains SNNs directly on spatio-temporal event streams from a temporal contrast

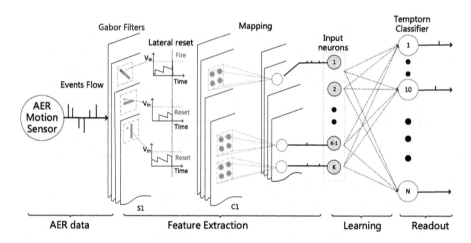

Fig. 1. A schematic of the event-driven feedforward categorization system for object recognition. It can be divided into three parts, namely, feature extraction layer, learning layer and readout layer.

AER vision sensor. The spike-based features are obtained through event-driven Gabor function and LIF neurons, which perform orientation selective edge detection spatiotemporally. In order to reduce memory and computational costs, a time-to-first spike operation with lateral reset in the same pooling area is implemented. Unlike the frame-based MAX operation, which outputs a number representing the strength of the strongest input, the temporal WTA can only output a spike, but by responding with low latency to its inputs. There is a lateral inhibition mechanism after firing the first spike. When a neuron fires, in a specific location, it inhibits other neurons (belonging to other orientations) and forces them to reset as well as enter a refractory period [13]. These together provide a sparse but highly informative coding. An addresses LUT is also applied to adjust the feature maps by addresses mapping and reordering [12]. Then, the extracted spike feature patterns are classified by a network of tempotron neurons [16] (see Fig. 1). The main contributions of this paper are summarized as following: (1) We use time encoding of signal strength and ensure that non-maximal responses are not propagated; (2) Our system can capture temporal visual information and learn features based on the timing spikes information entirely. Experiments conducted on two AER datasets have proved its efficiency for object recognition.

2 Methodology

2.1 Feature Extraction

Inspired by feedforward models of cortical information processing [12], we utilize a two-layer (S1 and C1 layers) hierarchical network to extract bio-inspired feature information from the input event data for simplifying the calculation and ensuring the precision. The detailed operation is described as follows.

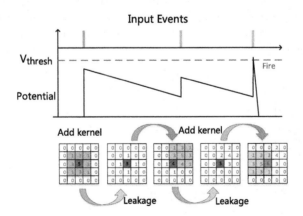

Fig. 2. The dynamics of S1 LIF neuron are illustrated. Adapted from [18].

Input to S1 Layer. For the incoming AER data, the Gabor filters are believed to match the response of simple cells in receptive fields [17], which is a linear filter defined as the product of a complex sinusoid with a two dimensional Gaussian envelope and for values in pixel coordinates (x, y). Each filter has a certain size of receptive field and responds best to a basic feature of a certain orientation. The function of Gabor filter can be described as:

$$G(x, y) = \exp(-\frac{(X^2 + \gamma^2 Y^2)}{2\sigma^2})cos(\frac{2\pi}{\lambda}X) \tag{1}$$

$$X = xcos\theta + ysin\theta, Y = -xsin\theta + ycos\theta \tag{2}$$

The filter parameter γ is the aspect ratio. Parameter λ is known as the wavelength of the cosine factor and together with parameter σ, the effective width, specify the spatial tuning accuracy of the Gabor filter. After these S1 cells perform edge detection operations on all incoming AER information by using Gabor filters, the LIF neurons [15] are used for integrating the related event-driven convolution. In this paper, the dynamics of an S1 LIF neuron are illustrated in Fig. 2. Here we show the change of the membrane voltage at the center point with the different incoming events. When a new event comes in, the Gabor filter is covered to the location specified by the input event's address, which will update the membrane voltage at the center point (equal to 5). However, the leakage needs to be updated first before the next event arriving. Once the membrane potential crosses the firing threshold after several calculations (equal to 6), it can generate a spike.

S1 to C1 Layer. After all the events flow into S1 layer, we observe which neuron responds first rather than perform MAX operation across all different RF sizes and orientations. When the response of a neuron to the stimulus crosses its spiking threshold before other neurons first, it will generate a spike transmitted to the next layer for computation. Lateral inhibition is also implemented, which is a mechanism that promotes the activity of maximally firing spikes by reducing the activity of their neighbours. In our work, the first spike from a pooling

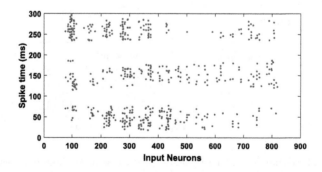

Fig. 3. The input spatiotemporal spike pattern where each dots denotes a spike time.

region can be used to reset other orientations through lateral reset connections. Only a minority neurons can generate spikes through these methods. Meanwhile, S1 neurons are divided into adjacent non-overlapping $n \times n$ pixel regions. For example, each S1 unit (4×4 pixel) feeds into C1 map (9×9 size) with 12 different orientations. In C1 layer, a low threshold voltage and refractory period are also used for reducing the number of spikes [13]. Then, the input spikes are organized into a column vector as the input of SNN for learning. There are $9 \times 9 \times 12$ input neurons since each pixel is connected to a neuron. And each neuron can fire single spike or multiple spikes (see Fig. 3).

2.2   Learning Layer

Tempotron [16] has only two output results: firing or not firing. The firing state is used to respond to a class (P^+), while no firing state is presented with a pattern corresponding to another class (P^-). It will modify the synaptic weights (w_i) whenever an error is present, which applies the gradient descent method to minimize the cost. We update the weights using the following:

$$\Delta w_i = \begin{cases} \lambda \sum_{t_i < t_{max}} K(t_{max} - t_i), & \text{if } P^+ \text{ error;} \\ -\lambda \sum_{t_i < t_{max}} K(t_{max} - t_i), & \text{if } P^- \text{ error;} \\ 0, & \text{otherwise.} \end{cases} \tag{3}$$

where t_{max} denotes the time at which the neuron reaches its maximum potential value in the time domain. λ is a constant representing the learning rate. It denotes the maximum change on the synaptic efficacy. In this learning rule, if one output spike is not elicited on a P^+ pattern, each synaptic efficacy is increased ($\lambda > 0$), and vice verse.

2.3   Readout Layer

The purpose of the readout layer is to classify stimuli from the responses of spiking neural network. We select the simple one hot coding scheme to label the tempotron neurons. If a class belongs to the first class, then the first tempotron neuron should fire, and all the other neurons' outputs are not fire. To further improve the performance, we can use group coding for each class. The number of tempotron neurons for each category is set as 10. We then use the majority of voting scheme to make the final decision: to check which category has the most firing neurons.

3   Experimental Setup

Experiments are conducted to analyse the performance of the proposed system by using two different event-based databases (see Fig. 4).

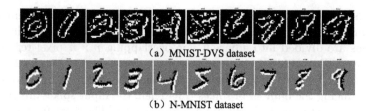
(a) MNIST-DVS dataset

(b) N-MNIST dataset

Fig. 4. Some reconstructed images from the used databases. (a) and (b) show the MNIST-DVS and N-MNIST databases including ten classes which correspond to digit 0 to 9.

3.1 On N-MNIST Dataset

N-MNIST dataset [19] was a spiking version of the original frame-based MNIST dataset and consisted of the same 60 000 training and 10 000 testing samples. It was generated by moving an asynchronous time-based image sensor (ATIS) in front of projected images of digits at the same visual scale. A 3-phase saccadic movement of the sensor was responsible for generating events, and shifted the position of the digit in pixel space.

In this section, we examine the scalability performance of our system, Hfirst method, and SKIM network. This experiment is run on the N-MNIST dataset. For the Hfirst method as described in Orchard et al. [13], two different classifiers were used. In SKIM network, a learning method based on principles of dendritic computation is used. In our work, we adopt the spiking neural network with tempotron learning rule for classification. The membrane time constant tau_m was set as 20 ms, and the ratio between the membrane and the synaptic constants is fixed at $\tau_m/\tau_s = 4$. The threshold V_{thr} is set to 30, and learning rate is set as $\lambda = 0.1$. The number of tempotron neurons for each category was set as 10. In addition, there are several parameters in our algorithm that is tuned according to specific applications, since the Hfirst model has not been tuned or optimized for the N-MNIST dataset. The parameters used in the feature extraction layer (S1 and C1 layers) are summarized in Table 1 for our system and optimal Hfirst method. Figure 5 reports the classification accuracy which shows that our method optimized is superior to the other investigated methods in classification accuracy. Compared with Hfirst method, the accuracy achieved is 22.87% and 35.62% higher achieved by Orchard's two different classifiers. In the SKIM network, the accuracy of the network is increasing with markedly

Table 1. Optimized neuron parameters

Layer	V_{thresh}	I_l/C_m	t_refr	Kernel Size	Layer size
S1	100	15	5	$7 \times 7 \times 1$	$34 \times 34 \times 12$
C1	1	0	5	$4 \times 4 \times 1$	$9 \times 9 \times 12$
Unit	mV	mV/ms	ms	Synapses	Neurons

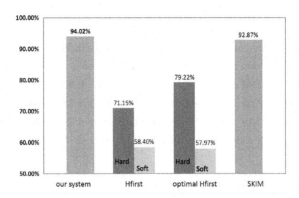

Fig. 5. The classification performance of our work, Hfirst, optimized Hfirst and SKIM on the AER N-MNIST dataset.

accelerating large number of hidden layer neurons. It can achieve an overall accuracy of 92.87% with 10,000 hidden neurons at a very high computational cost. However, the accuracy still is 1.15% lower than our method.

3.2 On MNIST-DVS Dataset

MNIST-DVS dataset [3] consists of a set of dynamic vision sensor (DVS) recordings of different handwritten digits. 10, 000 original 28 × 28 pixel digits were chosen from the standard 70,000-picture dataset and displayed on an LCD monitor with slow movements and a 128 × 128 pixel AER DVS at three different scales (scale-4, scale-8, and scale-16) for about 2–3 s. In this section, two feature extraction methods with the same tempotron classifier are compared for further estimating the performance of the proposed system. In Zhao's method, MAX operation and motion symbol detector module are used to model S1 and C1 cells in the visual cortex. At that moment, C1 feature maps are fed to a set of TFS neurons, where C1 responses are converted into spikes (only one spike as input). We use a simple temporal Winner-Take-All (WTA) rather than performing a synchronous MAX operation, which simplifies computation of the max. This is an important property ensuring that no computation is performed when there is insufficient activity in the scene. Meanwhile, the lateral reset connections between orientations is introduced by reducing the activity of their neighbours. Since the spike is emitted in WTA mechanism when the membrane potential exceeds the threshold, the same position can generate multiple spikes as input.

In our experiments, 90% of MNIST-DVS dataset are randomly selected for training and the others are used for testing. This evaluation process is repeated ten times to obtain the average performance. And all the tested methods employ the same parameters of Gabor filters as in [12]. We evaluated 100, 200, 500 ms and full length (about 2 s). Compared with Zhao's method, Table 2 shows the propose method gives a lower performance with the train set but a higher performance with the test set for different time lengths. The reason is that the tempotron

Table 2. The classification performance

Length	Zhao's method		Our method	
	Train set	Test set	Train set	Test set
100	98.86 ± 0.09	76.86 ± 1.27	88.09 ± 0.90	77.09 ± 1.09
200	99.08 ± 0.04	82.61 ± 1.17	93.84 ± 0.58	86.01 ± 0.73
500	99.19 ± 0.02	85.89 ± 0.84	96.97 ± 0.34	90.83 ± 0.88
Full	99.13 ± 0.02	88.14 ± 0.70	97.56 ± 0.25	93.09 ± 0.96

network can better fit the training data with single spike. Nevertheless, if we only consider the single spike as input, a large amount of information is missing. As a result, it causes the classification accuracy of Zhao's method with test set is lower than our method with multiple spikes as input. Through the comparison of two methods, it proves that our method has better adaptability and indicate that with proper feature extracting method to represent the AER datasets, spiking neural network could perform as well as, or even better than the state-of-art learning method.

4   Conclusion

We present a computational model which is a preliminary attempt to process data collected by using asynchronous AER image sensors. The external stimuli are sparsely represented after using hierarchical maps of leaky integration neurons. Then, the simple temporal-winner-take-all and lateral inhibition are also explored, which can ensure that maximal response (it spiked first) is propagated to subsequent layers. Through the network, the tempotron learning rule is applied to process various event-based datasets. The performance of the system applied to object recognition is comparable to the Zhao's method and Orchard's method under the same condition. The experimental results have shown that the proposed event-driven system maintains competitive accuracy for two different datasets.

In addition, temporal encoding and learning as a consistent model has also been successful in emulating the memory formulation mechanisms [20]. Our proposed computational model provides an efficient method for object recognition. In the future, we could extend the method to more complex cognitive and memory tasks.

Acknowledgments. This work was supported by the National Natural Science Foundation of China under grant number 61673283.

References

1. Indiveri, G., Linaresbarranco, B., Hamilton, T.J., Van, S.A., Etiennecummings, R., Delbruck, T., Liu, S.C., Dudek, P., Häfliger, P., Renaud, S.: Neuromorphic silicon neuron circuits. Front. Neurosci. 5(5), 73 (2011)

2. Posch, C., Matolin, D., Wohlgenannt, R.: A QVGA 143 dB dynamic range frame-free PWM image sensor with lossless pixel-level video compression and time-domain CDS. IEEE J. Solid State Circ. **46**(1), 259–275 (2010)
3. Lichtsteiner, P., Posch, C., Delbruck, T.: A 128 ×128 120 dB 15μs latency asynchronous temporal contrast vision sensor. IEEE J. Solid State Circ. **43**(2), 566–576 (2008)
4. Brandli, C., Berner, R., Yang, M., Liu, S.C., Delbruck, T.: A 240 × 180 130 dB 3μ s latency global shutter spatiotemporal vision sensor. IEEE J. Solid State Circ. **49**(10), 2333–2341 (2014)
5. Chen, S., Martini, B., Culurciello, E.: A bio-inspired event-based size and position invariant human posture recognition algorithm. In: IEEE International Symposium on Circuits and Systems, vol. 9, no. 4, pp. 775–778 (2009)
6. Camunas-Mesa, L., Zamarreno-Ramos, C., Linares-Barranco, A., Acosta-Jimenez, A.J., Serrano-Gotarredona, T., Linares-Barranco, B.: An event-driven multi-kernel convolution processor module for event-driven vision sensors. IEEE J. Solid State Circ. **47**(2), 504–517 (2012)
7. Indiveri, G., Liu, S.C.: Memory and information processing in neuromorphic systems. Proc. IEEE **103**(8), 1379–1397 (2015)
8. Memmesheimer, R.M., Rubin, R., Ölveczky, B.P., Sompolinsky, H.: Learning precisely timed spikes. Neuron **82**(4), 925–938 (2014)
9. Yu, Q., Tang, H., Tan, K.C., Li, H.: Rapid feedforward computation by temporal encoding and learning with spiking neurons. IEEE Trans. Neural Netw. Learn. Syst. **24**(10), 1539–1552 (2013)
10. Bichler, O., Querlioz, D., Thorpe, S.J., Bourgoin, J.P., Gamrat, C.: Extraction of temporally correlated features from dynamic vision sensors with spike-timing-dependent plasticity. Neural Netw. **32**(2), 339–348 (2012)
11. Wang, H., Xu, J., Gao, Z., Lu, C., Yao, S., Ma, J.: An event-based neurobiological recognition system with orientation detector for objects in multiple orientations. Front. Neurosci. **10**, 498 (2016)
12. Zhao, B., Ding, R., Chen, S., Linaresbarranco, B., Tang, H.: Feedforward categorization on aer motion events using cortex-like features in a spiking neural network. IEEE Trans. Neural Netw. Learn. Syst. **26**(9), 1963–1978 (2015)
13. Orchard, G., Meyer, C., Etienne-Cummings, R., Posch, C., Thakor, N., Benosman, R.: HFirst: a temporal approach to object recognition. IEEE Trans. Pattern Anal. Mach. Intell. **37**(10), 2028–2040 (2015)
14. Tsitiridis, A., Conde, C., Diego, I.M.D., Saez, J., Gomez, J.R., Cabello, E.: Gabor feature processing in spiking neural networks from retina-inspired data. In: International Joint Conference in Neural Networks, pp. 1–8 (2015)
15. Gerstner, W., Kistler, W.M.: Spiking Neuron Models: Single Neurons, Populations, Plasticity. Cambridge University Press, New York (2002)
16. Gütig, R., Sompolinsky, H.: The Tempotron: a neuron that learns spike timing-based decisions. Nat. Neurosci. **9**(3), 420–428 (2006)
17. Dayan, P., Abbott, L.F.: Theoretical neuroscience: computational and mathematical modeling of neural systems. Q. Rev. Biol. **15**, 154–155 (2005)
18. Zhao, B., Chen, S., Tang, H.: Bio-inspired categorization using event-driven feature extraction and spike-based learning. In: International Joint Conference on Neural Networks, pp. 3845–3852 (2014)
19. Orchard, G., Jayawant, A., Cohen, G.K., Thakor, N.: Converting static image datasets to spiking neuromorphic datasets using saccades. Front. Neurosci. **9**, 178 (2015)
20. Hu, J., Tang, H., Tan, K.C., Li, H.: How the brain formulates memory: a spatio-temporal model. IEEE Comput. Intell. Mag. **11**(2), 56–68 (2016)

Subspace Clustering via Adaptive Low-Rank Model

Mingbo Zhao[1]($\boxtimes$), Wenlong Cheng[1], Zhao Zhang[2], and Choujun Zhan[3]

[1] Donghua University, Shanghai, People's Republic of China
mzhao4@dhu.edu.cn
[2] Soochow University, Suzhou, People's Republic of China
[3] Nanfang College of Sun Yat-Sen University,
Guangzhou, People's Republic of China

Abstract. Subspace Clustering has been a major issue in many real-world task and sparse and low-rank representation based methods have received considerable attention during the past decades. However, both above methods need huge computation in order to solve sparse or trace-norm minimization problem, which may not be scalable to large-scale data. In this paper, we develop an efficient and effective sparse and low-rank model for subspace clustering. Starting from the basic idea of Robust Principal Component Analysis (RPCA), we observe that the optimal solution of RPCA can be equivalently solved by an iterative procedure, where the low-rank matrix is reformulated by two factorizations. We thereby further impose the group sparse constraint on such factorizations and additionally non-negative constraint on all variable matrix. As a result, the coefficient matrix S can both achieve sparcity and capture the global structure of whole data, which can be utilized to construct the graph for subspace clustering. Extensive simulations have verified the effectiveness of the proposed methods.

Keywords: Subspace clustering · Low-rank model · $l_{2,1}$-norm regularization

1 Introduction

Subspace Clustering has been a major issue in many real-world task, such as machine learning, pattern recognition, image analysis and data compression [1,6,14,17]. During the past decades, sparse representation [2,5,7] and low-rank approximation [8,9,16] based methods for subspace clustering have received considerable attention because they are able to handle images with occlusion [7], and do not require any priori knowledge of dimensions and the number of subspaces. The segmentation of data is then obtained by applying spectral clustering on the similarity graph based on sparse or low-rank representation.

It should be noted that a good affinity graph should simultaneously preserve the local geometrical structure and the global information of the data points. As mentioned by work in [2], the SR based methods have three advantages of high

© Springer International Publishing AG 2017
D. Liu et al. (Eds.): ICONIP 2017, Part VI, LNCS 10639, pp. 462–470, 2017.
https://doi.org/10.1007/978-3-319-70136-3_49

discriminating power, low sparsity and data-adaptive. But SR based methods usually do not characterize the global structure of data. To handle this problem, low-rank representation (LRR) has been utilized to compute the weights that represent the affinities among all the data samples [8]. But LRR will need huge computation in order to solve trace-norm minimization problem and the negative values in LRR lack of physically meanings for graph construction.

In this paper, we develop an efficient and effective sparse and low-rank model for subspace clustering. Starting from the basic idea of one popular low-rank model, i.e. Robust Principal Component Analysis (RPCA) [4], we observe that the optimal solution of RPCA can be equivalently solved by an iterative procedure, where the low-rank matrix is reformulated by two factorizations. Such factorizations can be viewed as a under-complete dictionary B multiplied by a matrix S representing the corresponding coefficients for data matrix X. We thereby further impose the group sparse constraint [19,20] on such factorizations and additionally non-negative constraint on all variable matrix. As a result, the coefficient matrix S can both achieve sparcity and capture the global structure of whole data, which can be utilized to construct the graph for subspace clustering. Extensive simulations have verified the effectiveness of the proposed methods.

2   Subspace Clustering via Adaptive Low-Rank Model

2.1   Adaptive Low-Rank Model

We starting from basic idea of one popular low-rank model, i.e. Robust Principle Component Analysis (RPCA) [4]. Let $X = [X_l, X_u] \in R^{d \times (l+u)}$ be the data matrix, where d is the number of data features, the first l and the remaining u samples in X represent the labeled set X_l and unlabeled set X_u, respectively. Assuming X is generated by corrupting some of entries of a clean and low-rank matrix L, where the corruption can be represented by an additive noise matrix O so that $X = L + O$. Since the corruptions only affects parts of entries of X, the noise matrix O is assumed to be sparsely supported. Then, in order to recover such clean and low-rank matrix L from the highly corrupted data matrix X, RPCA aim to minimize the following problem:

$$\min_{L,E} \|L\|_* + \gamma \|O\|_{2,1} \quad s.t. \ X = L + O. \tag{1}$$

where $\|L\|_*$ denotes the nuclear norm (the sum of singular values of L), which is to approximate the rank of L, $\|M\|_{2,1} = \sum_{i=1}^{n} \sqrt{\sum_{j=1}^{d} M_{ji}^2}$ is the $\ell_{2,1}$-norm of M encouraging the columns in M to be zero, which assumes the error is "sample-specific", i.e. some samples are corrupted and the others are clean [12]. In one of its formulations, RPCA can be pursued by solving the following convex problem:

$$\min_{L,O} \frac{1}{2} \|X - L - O\|_F^2 + \lambda \|L\|_* + \gamma \|O\|_{2,1}. \tag{2}$$

In addition, [15] has shown that the nuclear norm of a matrix of L can be reformulated as penalty over all possible factorizations:

$$\|L\|_* = \min_{B,S} \frac{1}{2}\|B\|_F^2 + \frac{1}{2}\|S\|_F^2 \quad s.t. \ B^T S = L. \tag{3}$$

where the optimal solution to Eq. (3) is obtained via the SVD of $L = U\Sigma V^T$, i.e. $B = \Sigma^{1/2}U^T \in R^{q\times d}$ and $S = \Sigma^{1/2}V^T \in R^{q\times n}$, and q the low-rank value. Here, denote $P = [B;S] \in R^{q\times(d+n)}$ as a joint matrix, we then have:

$$\|P\|_F^2 = \|[B;S]\|_F^2 = \|B\|_F^2 + \|S\|_F^2. \tag{4}$$

Combined Eqs. (2) and (3) with Eq. (4), Eq. (2) is roughly equivalent to the following convex problem:

$$\min_{B,S,O} \frac{1}{2}\left\|X - B^T S - O\right\|_F^2 + \lambda\|P\|_F^2 + \gamma\|O\|_{2,1}. \tag{5}$$

It can be easily noted that Eq. (5) shares similar formulation to the problem of sparse representation [13,18] if we let B as the dictionary matrix and S as the coefficient matrix. Here, following Eq. (4), one needs to initially fix the low-rank value q before solving the optimization problem. In general, a large value of q can make the objective function in Eq. (4) smaller. But this can greatly increase the computational complexity. Therefore, the low-rank value q is a key parameter and how to set a proper q is an important issue in order to achieve both small objective function and low computation complexity. To this end, we in this paper add a new $l_{2,1}$-norm term $\|P\|_{2,1}$ to the objective function of Eq. (5) as follows:

$$\min_{B,S,O} \frac{1}{2}\left\|X - B^T S - O\right\|_F^2 + \lambda\|P\|_{2,1} + \gamma\|O\|_{2,1} \quad s.t. \ B \geq 0, S \geq 0, O \geq 0 \tag{6}$$

where λ and γ are the parameters balancing the tradeoff between three terms, and $B \geq 0$, $S \geq 0$, $O \geq 0$ are three non-negative constraint in order to guarantee the non-negativity of $X = B^T S + O$. Here, since optimizing the $l_{2,1}$-norm $\|P\|_{2,1}$ in Eq. (6) is to encourage the columns of P sparse, i.e. some columns are close to zero while some are non-zero, the best value of q can naturally be determined and optimized in the iterative procedure. Finally, by solving the optimization problem of Eq. (6), the optimal matrix S can both achieve sparse property and the global structure of data, which is good to construct graph. We will discuss this point in the following subsections.

2.2   Iterative Solution

In this subsection, we will present an iterative algorithm to solve the optimization problem of Eq. (6). Note that there are two non-smooth terms involved in Eq. (6), i.e. $\|P\|_{2,1}$ and $\|O\|_{2,1}$, making the problem non-convex in P and O simultaneously. To solve the problem of Eq. (6), we propose an iterative method for optimization, in which we update one of variables (O, B or S) alternately with other variables fixed in each iterative procedure. Following [13], we introduce multiplicative updating rules and give the Lagrange function to the problem of Eq. (6) by considering non-negative constraints as follows:

$$\min_{B,S,O} \left\| X - B^T S - O \right\|_F^2 + \gamma \|O\|_{2,1} + \lambda \|P\|_{2,1} + Tr(\phi O) + Tr(\varphi B) + Tr(\psi S) \tag{7}$$

where ϕ, φ and ψ are the Lagrange multiplier for constraint $O_{ij} \geq 0$, $B_{ij} \geq 0$ and $S_{ij} \geq 0$. By setting the derivative w.r.t. O_{ij} to zero and using the Karush-Kuhn-Tuckre (KKT) condition $\gamma_{ij} O_{ij} = 0$, the updating rules of O_{ij} can be given as follows:

$$O_{ij} \leftarrow O_{ij} \frac{\left(X - B^T S\right)_{ij}}{\left(O + \gamma O H\right)_{ij}} \tag{8}$$

Similarly, we can also get the updating rules of B and O as follows:

$$S_{ij} \leftarrow S_{ij} \frac{(B(X-O))_{ij}}{(BB^T S + \lambda GS)_{ij}}, B_{ij} \leftarrow B_{ij} \frac{\left(S(X-O)^T\right)_{ij}}{(SS^T B + \lambda GB)_{ij}} \tag{9}$$

where $G \in R^{q \times q}$ and $H \in R^{n \times n}$ is a diagonal matrix satisfying:

$$G \leftarrow \begin{bmatrix} \frac{1}{2\|p_1\|_2} & & \\ & \ddots & \\ & & \frac{1}{2\|p_q\|_2} \end{bmatrix} \quad H \leftarrow \begin{bmatrix} \frac{1}{2\|o_1\|_2} & & \\ & \ddots & \\ & & \frac{1}{2\|o_n\|_2} \end{bmatrix} \tag{10}$$

This iterative procedure will continue until convergence. The basic steps for calculating the sparse coefficients can be seen in Algorithm 1.

Algorithm 1. Iterative solution for calculating low-rank representation

---

1 **Input**: Data matrix $X \in R^{d \times n}$, low-rank value q.
2 Initialize the dictionary $B \in R^{q \times d}$ as k-means clustering center, S via sparse coding algorithm[7, 5], and noise matrix as $O = \max\left(0, X - B^T S\right) \in R^{d \times n}$.
3 **repeat**
4 | Iteratively update S, B and O following Eqs. (8), (9) and (10).
5 **until** $J(B, S, O) = \min_{B,S,O} \left\| X - B^T S - O \right\|_F^2 + \gamma \|O\|_{2,1} + \lambda \|P\|_{2,1}$ *does not change*;
6 **Output**: Low-rank representation $S \in R^{q \times n}$.

It should be noted that following Algorithm 1, we needs to (1) initialize the B by k-means clustering and low-rank representation S; (2) alternatively update the dictionaries and sparse coding. In the first stage, the computational complexity for k-means clustering in each iteration is $O(qn)$; in the second stage, the computational complexity for updating S and B is $O(q^2 n)$ and $O(dq^2)$, respectively, hence the total complexity for this stage is $O\left(q^2 n + dq^2\right)$. Considering a large-scale dataset, i.e. $q \ll n$ and $d < n$, the above complexity can be approximately $O\left(\left(q^2 + d\right) n\right)$, which is linear with the number of dataset. Hence the sparse coding is suitable for handle large-scale dataset.

2.3   Subspace Clustering

So far, we have obtained q dictionaries and the sparse coefficient s_j to represent each data point x_j. To design the adjacency matrix by the sparse representation S, an natural method is to define it by using the formulation of inner product of S [10,11], which can be shown as follows:

$$W^s = S^T \Delta^{-1} S = Q^T Q. \tag{11}$$

where $\Delta \in R^{q \times q}$ is a diagonal matrix with each element Δ_{jj} being the sum of the jth row in S, i.e., $\Delta_{jj} = \sum_{i=1}^{l+u} S_{ij}$, $Q = \Delta^{-1/2} S$. One can easily check that the affinity matrix W^s is symmetric, normalized and doubly-stochastic. We can then perform subspace clustering by optimizing the following problems:

$$\min_F Tr\left(FL^s F^T\right) \quad s.t.\ FF^T = I \tag{12}$$

or

$$\max_F Tr\left(FW^s F^T\right) \quad s.t.\ FF^T = I \tag{13}$$

where $L^s = I - W^s$ is the Laplacian matrix of W^s. The optimal solution of F is to perform the eigen-decomposition of W^s, where the computational complexity is $O\left(n^3\right)$. Fortunately, with the form of $W^s = Q^T Q$, we only need to perform the eigen-decomposition of Q, where the computational complexity is $O\left(ndk\right)$ and k the average number of non-zeros elements in Q. Finally, we give the basic steps of the proposed methods as Algorithm 2.

Algorithm 2. The proposed method for subspace clustering

---

1 **Input**: Data matrix $X \in R^{d \times n}$, the number of low-rank value q and other relative parameters.
2 Calculate the sparse coding S as Table 1.
3 Form the weight matrix $W^s = S^T \Delta^{-1} S = QQ^T$ following Eq. (11).
4 Performing the eigen-decomposition of Q and form F as the first k eigenvectors of Q.
5 Each row of F is a data point and apply k-means to get the clusters.
6 **Output**: The clustering result of dataset.

---

3   Application to Image Clustering

In this section, we carry out extensive experiments on real datasets to illustrate the effectiveness and efficiency of the proposed algorithms. We also compare the proposed method with several state-of-the-art subspace clustering algorithms such as, Spectral Curvature Clustering (SCC) [3], Sparse Subspace Clustering (SSC) [5], Low-Rank Representation (LRR) [8,9] and Low-Rank Subspace Clustering (LRSC).

3.1   Data Sets and Evaluation Metric

We choose four datasets for our experimental studies: Coil-20, USPS and YaleB. Coil-20 is toy images, USPS is digit images, YaleB are face images. **Coil-20 dataset** contains 32×32 gray-scale images of 20 objects. **USPS dataset** contains ten classes (09 digit characters) and 11000 handwritten digit samples in total. All of these images are normalized to the size of 16×16 pixels. **Extended Yale B dataset** contains of 32×32 pixels cropped face images of 38 individuals, each class (individual) contains 64 frontal face images acquired under different illumination conditions. We then use two criterions to evaluate the performance of clustering for the proposed method:

Clustering Accuracy shows the one-to-one relationship between clusters and classes and measures the extent to which each cluster contained data points from the corresponding class.

Normalized Mutual Information (NMI) is used for determining the quality of clusters. Given a clustering result, the NMI is estimated by

$$NMI = \frac{\sum_{i=1}^{C} \sum_{j=1}^{C} n_{i,j} \log(\frac{n \cdot n_{i,j}}{n_i \hat{n}_j})}{\sqrt{\left(\sum_{i=1}^{C} n_i \log(\frac{n_i}{n})\right) \left(\sum_{j=1}^{C} \hat{n}_j \log(\frac{\hat{n}_j}{n})\right)}} \qquad (14)$$

where n_i denotes the number of data contained in the cluster $C_i (1 < i < c)$, is the number of data belonging to the $L_j (1 < j < c)$, and n_{ij} denotes the number of data that are in the intersection between cluster C_i and the class L_j.

3.2   Image Clustering

The average Accuracy and Mutual Information are listed in Tables 1, 2 and 3. We use k-means as the baseline clustering algorithm, k-means can be performed on the original feature space (baseline) or the "concept" space (matrix factorization methods). In order to randomize the experiments, we evaluate the clustering performance with different cluster number k. For each given cluster number, 20 tests were conducted on different randomly chosen classes over these 20 tests.

Tables 1, 2 and 3 shows the clustering results of the six compared methods on different datasets. We can see that our proposed method significantly outperforms other methods, which can achieve the best clustering results with 2% gain

Table 1. Clustering performance based on k-means, SCC, SSC, LLR, LRSC and the proposed method on the Coil-20 Dataset

k	Accuracy (%)						Normalized Mutual Information (%)					
	k-means	SCC	SSC	LRR	LRSC	Proposed	k-means	SCC	SSC	LRR	LRSC	Proposed
2	92.2	93.1	96.2	96.7	97.3	97.5	80.4	85.4	88.7	90.8	92.2	91.5
4	82.6	82	81.5	83.8	89.1	86.2	77.5	80.7	84.6	87.3	87.7	89.8
6	73.3	77.4	80.6	81.9	81.6	82.3	72.3	85.8	85.9	86.2	89.1	89.3
8	70.1	69.1	78.2	77	82.9	82.3	75.3	79.8	86.4	86.8	90.1	88.3
10	66.2	68.4	77.1	74.9	77.2	80.2	74.1	79.8	85.7	85.9	89.5	91.5
12	63.8	66.5	75.1	74.3	76.8	76.7	75.4	80.6	84.7	86.8	90	88.8
14	61.1	62.3	69.9	71.5	73.9	74.4	74.1	79	85.3	85.6	88.6	91.0
16	61.4	63.3	68.1	71	73.5	74.3	74.8	79.6	84.9	84.1	88.9	90.1
18	59.5	62.8	67.1	69.8	72.1	73.0	74.9	79.7	84.4	84.6	88.8	89.7
20	59.8	60.2	66.7	61	70.8	73.6	75.8	79.1	85.5	86.4	90.1	91.0
Average	69	70.5	76.1	76.2	79.5	80.0	75.5	81	85.6	86.5	89.5	90.1

Table 2. Clustering performance based on k-means, SCC, SSC, LLR, LRSC and the proposed method on the YaleB Dataset

k	Accuracy (%)						Normalized Mutual Information (%)					
	k-means	SCC	SSC	LRR	LRSC	Proposed	k-means	SCC	SSC	LRR	LRSC	Proposed
10	30.2	58.1	67	67.8	70.8	71.5	25.5	68	72.8	73.8	76.6	76.5
15	22.6	52.4	58	58.2	62.5	63.9	20.5	64.4	69.9	70.9	72.2	73.2
20	23.8	49.8	56.8	57.3	60.3	62.5	24.3	62.2	66.6	68.6	68.7	69.1
30	16.9	49.5	58	58.1	60.1	60.3	19.4	55.7	59.3	60.3	63.8	64.0
38	13.8	48.3	55.8	56.5	56.5	57.8	16.5	49.7	55.6	56.6	58.3	59.0
Average	21.5	51.6	59.1	59.6	62	63.2	21.2	60	64.8	66	67.9	68.3

Table 3. Clustering performance based on k-means, SCC, SSC, LLR, LRSC and the proposed method on the USPS Dataset

k	Accuracy (%)						Normalized Mutual Information (%)					
	k-means	SCC	SSC	LRR	LRSC	Proposed	k-means	SCC	SSC	LRR	LRSC	Proposed
2	94.1	94.3	94.2	94.6	95.4	96.3	75.9	76.2	81.4	82.8	91.3	91.0
3	88.1	88.8	89.3	89.3	91.7	91.2	72.1	73.4	79.8	80.9	85.3	85.9
4	78.2	79.2	83.3	84	85.1	86.0	67.1	72.2	79.4	80.3	83.3	85.2
5	75.1	78.2	79.1	80.8	82.3	82.6	67	71.7	77.9	78.6	82.2	83.0
6	70.4	74.3	75.2	75.1	78.3	80.0	65.1	69.7	76.3	77.6	82.2	83.5
7	71.8	73.3	74.2	75.6	77.7	79.1	64.7	76.2	81.4	82.8	81.1	82.7
8	70.5	71.8	74.3	76.3	76.6	78.1	64.3	73.4	79.8	80.9	80.2	81.6
9	68.7	69.2	75.3	75	74.3	75.6	63.4	72.2	79.4	80.3	80.7	81.1
10	64.4	63.3	74.2	74.3	75.1	76.0	62.9	69.7	77.3	77.6	79.6	79.8
Average	75.7	76.9	79.9	80.6	82	82.7	66.9	72.7	79.2	80.2	82.9	83.7

in Accuracy and 1% gain in NMI over the second best algorithm LRSC. By incorporating a low-rank representation, LRSC gains significant improvement over the traditional sparse coding approach (SCC). Compared with l_1-norm minimization based Sparse subspace Clustering (SSC), our method obviously performs better with 4% gain in Accuracy and 4% gain in NMI.

4   Conclusions

This paper presents an effective subspace clustering methods via a adaptive low-rank model. Based on the theoretical analysis and extensive results, we can draw the conclusion as follows: (1) the proposed methods can achieve an adaptive low-rank coding via an iterative procedure; (2) the proposed methods can achieve better clustering results compared with state-of-the-art methods. Both theoretical analysis and extensive experimental studies demonstrate the effectiveness and efficiency of the proposed methods.

Aknowledgements. This work was supported by the National Natural Science Foundation of China under Grant no. 61601112, the Fundamental Research Funds for the Central Universities and DHU Distinguished Young Professor Program.

References

1. Allen, Y.: Unsupervised segmentation of natural images via lossy data compression. Comput. Vis. Image Underst. **110**(2), 212–225 (2008)
2. Bin, C.: Learning with l1-graph for image analysis. IEEE Trans. Image Process. **19**(4), 858–866 (2010)
3. Cai, D., Hujun, B., Xiaofei, H.: Sparse concept coding for visual analysis. In: 2011 IEEE Conference on Computer Vision and Pattern Recognition (CVPR), pp. 2905–2910 (2011)
4. Candès, E.J., Li, X., Ma, Y., Wright, J.: Robust principal component analysis? J. ACM (JACM) **58**(3), 11 (2011)
5. Elhamifar, E., Vidal, R.: Sparse subspace clustering: algorithm, theory, and applications. IEEE Trans. Pattern Anal. Mach. Intell. **35**(11), 2765–2781 (2013)
6. Ho, J.: Clustering appearances of objects under varying illumination conditions. In: ICCV (2003)
7. John, W.: Robust face recognition via sparse representation. IEEE Trans. Pattern Anal. Mach. Intell. **31**(2), 210–227 (2009)
8. Liu, G., Lin, Z., Yan, S., Sun, J., Yu, Y., Ma, Y.: Robust recovery of subspace structures by low-rank representation. IEEE Trans. Pattern Anal. Mach. Intell. **35**(1), 171–184 (2013)
9. Liu, G., Zhouchen, L., Yong, Y.: Robust subspace segmentation by low-rank representation. In: Proceedings of the 27th International Conference on Machine Learning (ICML 2010), pp. 663–670 (2010)
10. Liu, W., He, J., Chang, S.F.: Large graph construction for scalable semi-supervised learning. In: Proceedings of the 27th International Conference on Machine Learning (ICML 2010), pp. 679–686 (2010)
11. Liu, W., Wang, J., Chang, S.F.: Robust and scalable graph-based semisupervised learning. Proc. IEEE **100**(9), 2624–2638 (2012)
12. Nie, F., Huang, H., Cai, X., Ding, C.: Efficient and robust feature selection via joint l21-norms minimization. In: NIPS (2010)
13. Pan, Q., Kong, D., Ding, C.H., Luo, B.: Robust non-negative dictionary learning. In: AAAI, pp. 2027–2033 (2014)
14. Parsons, L., Ehtesham, H., Huan, L.: Clustering appearances of objects under varying illumination conditions. In: ACM SIGKDD, pp. 90–105 (2004)

15. Srebro, N., Shraibman, A.: Rank, trace-norm and max-norm. In: Auer, P., Meir, R. (eds.) COLT 2005. LNCS, vol. 3559, pp. 545–560. Springer, Heidelberg (2005). doi:10.1007/11503415_37

16. Vidal, R., Paolo, F.: Low rank subspace clustering (LRSC). Pattern Recogn. Lett. **43**, 47–61 (2014)

17. Wenyi, Z.: Face recognition: a literature survey. ACM Comput. Surv. **35**(4), 399–458 (2003)

18. Wright, J., Yang, A.Y., Ganesh, A., Sastry, S.S., Ma, Y.: Robust face recognition via sparse representation. IEEE Trans. Pattern Anal. Mach. Intell. **31**(2), 210–227 (2009)

19. Xu, H., Caramanis, C., Sanghavi, S.: Robust PCA via outlier pursuit. IEEE Trans. Inf. Theory **58**(5), 3047–3064 (2012)

20. Yang, J., Yin, W., Zhang, Y., Wang, Y.: A fast algorithm for edge-preserving variational multichannel image restoration. SIAM J. Imaging Sci. **2**(2), 569–592 (2009)

Affine-Constrained Group Sparse Coding Based on Mixed Norm

Jianshu Zhang[1], Zhongyu Chen[1], Changbing Tan[1], Feilong Lin[1], Jie Yang[2], and Zhonglong Zheng[1(✉)]

[1] Department of Computer Science, Zhejiang Normal University, Jinhua, China
zhonglong@zjnu.edu.cn
[2] Institute of Pattern Recognition and Image Analysis,
Shanghai Jiaotong University, Shanghai, China

Abstract. Recently, sparse coding has received an increasing amount of interests. In this paper, a new algorithm named affine-constrained group sparse coding based on mixed norm (MNACGSC) is presented, which further extends the framework of sparse representation-based classification (SRC). From the perspective of geometry, affine-constrained group sparse coding based on mixed norm (MNACGSC) not only finds out the vector that can be best edcoded according to the given dictionary in the convex hull spanned by input samples, but also establishes on multiple regularization terms which can leverage the collaborative effects of those regularization terms to strength the robustness. This paper mainly discusses L_1-norm and L_2-norm. The experimental results have demonstrated that the proposed model is effective, robust to noise and outperforms some representative methods.

Keywords: Affine-constrained · Group sparse coding · Mixed norm

1 Introduction

With the explosive growth of data, how to find the useful information in large amount of data is particularly vital in many areas. In the field of pattern classification, people have been committed to improving classification accuracy for actual tasks such as face recognition and zip code classification. The easiest way is to compare the test image with the existing image directly. The highest score of existing image means the same class with the test sample. However, this method is too naive and crude which makes it very difficult to achieve the expectation of folks. Further, changing an image which could be seemed as a matrix into a numerical vector makes its dimension increase exponentially. The high dimensionality, which usually leads to the curse of dimensionality [1], is one of a main reasons for the decrease of recognition rate. Therefore, PCA [2] and LPP [3] are explored as very magic ways of reducing the dimension, respectively. There are also some other types of methods for dimensionality reduction. For example, 2DPCA [4] is based on two-dimensional images directly to make classification.

© Springer International Publishing AG 2017
D. Liu et al. (Eds.): ICONIP 2017, Part VI, LNCS 10639, pp. 471–480, 2017.
https://doi.org/10.1007/978-3-319-70136-3_50

CLEAR [5] uses the local neighorhood and reconstruction criterion to find data group or clusters while reducing dimensions. SLPP [6] aims to reformulate the tradition locality preserving projection method in a sparse regression framework. FDLR [7] combines fisher criterion with low rank constraints in order to extract more discriminant information from the data.

However, these methods for the application of data are still inefficient and relatively simple. Until sparse representation-based classification (SRC) [8] model was introduced into the fields of image classification and face recognition, for the application of large-scale data, SRC in terms of improving the classification accuracy had played a qualitative leap, because it utilized content characteristic of data—sparsity. Also, Feature extraction is one of the advantage in SRC. These crucial matters guaranteed the effectiveness and robustness in face recognition. From then on, a series of superior methods based on sparse representation had been proposed and implemented [9–11]. Among them, KSVD [9] wanted to learn a redundant dictionary using singular value decomposition (SVD) technique and a sparse coefficient at the same time. Traditional SRC was an unsupervised classification algorithm while FDDL [10] employed Fisher discriminative term which could utilize the between and within class information. GraphSC [11] harnessed the theory of local manifold structure of the datum and added a laplacian operator to sparse representation. These proposed algorithm greatly extended the framework of SRC.

Above methods are just based on a single input sample. The algorithm model can be enhanced through multiple inputs in the case of sufficient test sources. The group sparse coding (GSC) [12] and affine-constrained group sparse coding [13] (ACGSC) have been implemented based on such theory. Given a set of test samples, GSC reconstructed the dictionary and learnt corresponding coefficient of the sample in the group using L_1 or L_2 regular term, iteratively. ACGSC proposed a novel technique which needed to learn a affine-constrained coefficient to make full use of samples information in a group meanwhile the coefficient was still needed to be learned. Recently, the idea of group has been extended to some other scenario, like deep learning [14–16].

In this paper, a new algorithm named affine-constrained group sparse coding based on mixed norm (MNACGSC) which further extends the framework of sparse representation-based classification (SRC) is presented, referring to affine-constrained group sparse coding (ACGSC) and block and group regularized sparse modeling for dictionary learning [17] (BGSC). In contract to ACGSC, our algorithm is established on multiple regularization terms. Here, we mainly discuss L_1-norm and L_2-norm, and we conclude the introduction by summarizing the main contributions of this paper:

- We propose a larger sparse representation-based classification framework: affine-constrained group sparse coding based on mixed norm, and it provides a principled extension of the current ACGSC framework with multiple input samples and norms.

– We extend feature-sign search algorithm to solve the mixed L_1-norm and L_2-norm sparse issue, give detailed explanation of the optimization scheme and conduct some experimental evaluations on image classification.

2 Algorithm

In this section, we firstly give an overview of the sparse coding framework and affine-constrained group sparse coding, then discuss our proposed affine-constrained group sparse coding based on mixed norm model.

2.1 Sparse Coding Model

Denoted by $D = [D_1, \cdots, D_i, \cdots, D_k] \in \Re^{n \times m}$ a set of n dimensional, m training samples from k classes, where D_i is the training set of i-th class. Given a test sample $x \in \Re^{n \times 1}$, sparse representation coding (SRC) hopes to find coefficient vector such that:

$$x = \sum_{i=1}^{c} D_i c_i \tag{1}$$

If the test sample belongs to class i, only the coefficient c of class i is non-zero, the others are all zeros, and SRC framework is cropped as follows:

$$min\|x - Dc\|^2 + \lambda f(c) \tag{2}$$

where $\lambda \geq 0$ is the scalar constant, function $f(c)$ is a sparse-including regularizer. In the training model (2), the data fidelity term $\|x - Dc\|^2$ ensures the representation ability of dictionary$D$. Function $f(c)$ ensures the sparse of representation coefficient. A straightforward choice of $f(c)$ is the L_0-norm which counts the nonzero entries of c. However, the training model (2) when function $f(c)$ represents the L_0-norm of c, is a NP-hard problem and is difficult even to approximate [18–20]. Recently, compressive sensing [18] proves that if the solution of L_0-norm minimization problem of (2) is sparse enough, its solution is equal to the solution of L_1-norm. So, in practice, L_0-norm can be replaced by L_1-norm.

2.2 Affine-Constrained Group Sparse Coding

Affine-constrained group sparse coding [13] (ACGSC) further utilizes the sufficient data sources. Given a set of test samples and training samples, it uses the following objective function to perform sparse coding:

$$min\|Xa - Dc\|^2 + \lambda f(c) \tag{3}$$

where $a(\sum_{i=1}^{k} a_i = 1,\ and\ a_1, a_2, \cdots, a_k \geq 0)$ is affine-constrained coefficient, λ is scalar constant, which ensure the balance of model. $f(c)$ is sparse-including regularizer which ensures the sparse of representation coefficient. In (3), the data fidelity term $\|Xa - Dc\|^2$ ensures the representation ability of D. Different with group sparse coding [12] (GSC), there is no group coefficient a, and sparse coefficients c is a matrix in GSC. The geometry explanation of affine-constrained group sparse coding is shown in Fig. 1.

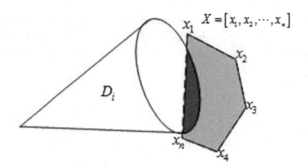

Fig. 1. Illustration of the principle of affine constraint coefficient and a group of test samples. The light shadow represents the product of test samples X and affine constraint coefficient a, and the dark shadow is the union set or solution according to Xa and the i-th class of training samples D. The idea of affine constraint is to obtain the points in the convex cone as many as possible.

2.3   Affine-Constrained Group Sparse Coding Based on Mixed Norm

This paper further extends the framework of ACGSC while ACGSC extends the framework of SRC. Let $X = [x_1, x_2, \cdots, x_k]$ denotes a group of input test data, and D is the given dictionary. Our proposed affine-constrained group sparse coding based on mixed norm aims to minimize the following objective function:

$$min\|Xa - Dc\|^2 + \lambda f(c) + \beta g(c) \qquad (4)$$

where $a(\sum_{i=1}^{k} a_i = 1, \ and \ a_1, a_2, \cdots, a_k \geq 0)$ is affine-constrained coefficient which aims to select the excellent vector for sparse coding as shown in Fig. 1. λ, β are scalar constants which ensure the balance of every terms. The loss function $\|Xa - Dc\|^2$ ensures the representation ability of D. $f(c)$ is sparse-including regularizer which shoulders the responsibility of algorithms sparse. $g(c)$ are other regularizers, such as L_2-norm, fisher discriminative term. Here, we use the L_2-norm as explanation. Embodying the above formula, we get:

$$min\|Xa - Dc\|^2 + \lambda\|c\|_1 + \beta\|c\|^2$$
$$s.t. \sum_{i=1}^{k} a_i = 1, \ and \ a_1, a_2, \cdots, a_k \geq 0 \qquad (5)$$

where $\lambda, \beta \geq 0$ are scalar constants. Note that in affine-constrained group sparse coding there is no regularizer $\|c\|^2$. A schematic illustration of the difference between the affine-constrained group sparse coding and our proposed version is shown in Fig. 2.

Next, we will demonstrate the process of affine-constrained group sparse coding based on L_1-norm and L_2-norm. MNACGSC needs to learn sparse coding coefficient c and affine-constrained coefficient a. We follow the method of ACGSC

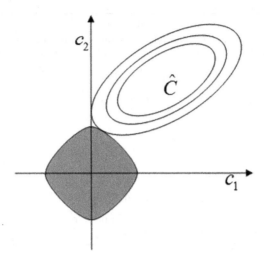

Fig. 2. Illustration of the difference between affine-constrained group sparse coding (ACGSC) and affine-constrained group sparse coding based on mixed norm (MNACGSC), and the effects of mixed norm on classification. Shown are contours of the error and constraint function. The gray area is mixed L_1-norm and L_2-norm constraint region, and those ellipses represent the contours of least square error function.

[13], which iteratively optimizes the objective function. Thus, (5) is resolved into a L_2-regularized least square problem and a least square problem with restrictions. MNACGSC is divided into two parts: fixing affine-constrained coefficient a, learning sparse coding coefficient c, and fixing sparse coding coefficient c, learning affine-constrained coefficient a. The standard MNACGSC algorithm is shown in Algorithm 1.

2.4   Optimization

Firstly, we discuss how to solve problem (5) by fixing the affine-constraint coefficient D. The problem (5) can be rewritten as:

$$min\|Xa - Dc\|^2 + \lambda\|c\|_1 + \beta\|c\|^2 \tag{6}$$

where λ, β are scalar constants.

The optimization problem (6) with L_1-norm and L_2-norm regularizer is convex about coefficient c, but it is non-differentiable when c contains value of zeros. Some commonly unconstrained optimization methods cannot be directly applied such as basis pursuit [21] (BP), orthogonal matching pursuit [22] (OMP). There are several indirect approaches to solving this problem, such as generalized lasso [23], Elastic net [24] as well as novel locally linear KNN [25] (LLKNN) model. In this paper, we follow feature-sign search algorithm [26] and get a general feature-sign search algorithm which is shown in Algorithm 2. The general feature-sign

---

Algorithm 1. Affine-constrained group sparse coding based on mixed norm.

Input: Train samples D, test samples X, group number n, parameters k, λ, β.
1: Preprocess samples, and for each subject, randomly select test samples as a group.
2: Initialize

$$a = \left[\frac{1}{n}, \frac{1}{n}, \cdots, \frac{1}{n}\right]^T, c = 0.$$

3: For $i = 1 : k$ do
      Update a by (6)
      Update c by (7)
   End for
4: Determine the class label by

$$L(X) = \arg\min \|Xa - D_i c_i\|^2$$

   Where D_i and c_i are the $i - th$ block of D and c, respectively.
Output: Class label L.

---

algorithm also maintains an active set of potentially nonzero coefficients and their corresponding signs. The algorithm systematically searches for the optimal active set and coefficient signs.

Secondly, we will fix sparse regularization, and learn affine-constrained coefficient a. When we fix sparse regularization coefficient c, the problem becomes the least squares problem with constraints.

$$min\|Xa - Dc\|^2$$
$$s.t. \sum_{i=1}^{k} a_i = 1, \ and \ a_i, a_2, \cdots, a_k \geq 0 \tag{7}$$

The constrained least square problem is a kind of constrained optimization algorithm, which can be solved by primal projection [13] or using conjugate gradient method after eliminating the limit by augmented Lagrangian method [27].

3   Experimental Results

In this section, in order to demonstrate the applicability of the proposed MNACGSC model, we select two moderate scale databases AR face database [28] and Extended YaleB database [29], and conduct some experiments for image classification problem to evaluate the performance. These databases are widely used in a variety of previous works to assess the quality of their algorithms [8,13,25].

AR database has 126 individuals frontal view images and all of the images is over 4000. We follow the experimental settings defined in [8] to make fair comparisons that training images includes 100 folks and each of them has 7 images, which only have illumination and expression changes and test samples includes 100 folks and each of them has the other 7 images, which also only have

Algorithm 2. General feature-sign search algorithm.

Input: Data D, x, parameters λ, β.

1: Initialize $c = \vec{0}, \theta = \vec{0}$, and active set $\Lambda = \{\}$, where $\theta \in \{-1, 0, 1\}$ denotes sign(c_i).

2: From zero coefficients of c, select

$$i = max_i \frac{\partial \|x - Dc\|^2 + \beta \|c\|^2}{\partial c_i}$$

Activate c_i (add i to the active set) only if it locally improves the objective, this is:

If $\frac{\partial \|x - Dc\|^2 + \beta \|c\|^2}{\partial c_i} > \lambda$, then set $\theta_i = 1, \Lambda = \{i\} \bigcup \Lambda$.

If $\frac{\partial \|x - Dc\|^2 + \beta \|c\|^2}{\partial c_i} < \lambda$, then set $\theta_i = -1, \Lambda = \{i\} \bigcup \Lambda$.

3: Feature-sign step:

Let $\hat{D}$ be a submatrix of D that contains only the columns corresponding to the active set. Let $\hat{c}$ and $\hat{\theta}$ be subvectors of c and θ corresponding to the active set. Compute the analytical solution to the resulting unconstrained QP : $min_{\hat{c}}\|x - \hat{D}\hat{c}\|^2 + \beta \|\hat{c}\|^2 + \lambda \hat{\theta}^T \hat{c}$, get:

$$\hat{c}_{new} = \left(\hat{C}^T C + \beta I\right)^{-1} \left(\hat{C}^T x - \lambda \hat{\theta}/2\right)$$

Perform an discrete line search on the closed line segment from $\hat{c}$ to $\hat{c}_{new}$:

Check the objective value at $\hat{c}_{new}$ and all points where any coefficient changes sign. Update $\hat{c}$ (and the corresponding entries in c) to the point with the lowest objective value.

Remove zero coefficients of $\hat{c}$ from the λ and update $\theta = $ sign (x).

4: Check the optimality conditions:

(a) Optimality condition for nonzero coefficients:

$\frac{\partial \|x - Dc\|^2 + \beta \|c\|^2}{\partial c_i} + \lambda$ sign $(c_j) = 0, \forall c_j \neq 0$. If condition (a) is not satisfied, go to Step 3 (without any new activation); else check condition (b).

(b) Optimality condition for zero coefficients:

$\frac{\partial \|x - Dc\|^2 + \beta \|c\|^2}{\partial c_i} \leq \lambda, \forall c_j \neq 0$. If condition (b) is not satisfied, go to Step 2; otherwise return as the solution.

Output: Sparse coefficient c.

illumination and expression changes. Extended YaleB database is a set of 2414 face images of 38 individuals. We randomly select 29 images as training samples, and 29 images as test samples. Some images of AR and Extended YaleB database are shown in Fig. 3(a) and (b).

Before applying these algorithms, the dimension of the face vector is reduced to 100 by PCA for AR database and EYaleB database. We use the training samples directly as atoms of dictionary D, and perform SRC when set the parameter $\theta = 0, k = 10, and \lambda = 0.01$. Then, we process elastic net (EN) when the experimental settings are essentially the same as SRC except $\theta = 0.01$. For affine-constraint group sparse coding, the group number is 3 or 5 and the test samples are randomly selected in the same class. We also randomly select the test samples at the next time and repeat 3 times in AR database and 10 times in

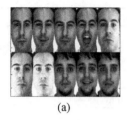

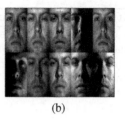

(a)   (b)

Fig. 3. Samples of AR (a) and EYaleB (b) database.

EYaleB database for every person. Notice that the parameters and the selected test samples are similar as before when conduct ourselves algorithm. The comparison methods include PCA [2], LPP [3], SRC [8], EN [10], FDDL [11], and ACGCS [13]. Tables 1 and 2 present the simulation results on AR and EYaleB database, respectively.

Table 1. Results on AR database

Methods	3 group	5 group
PCA	52.34%	58.76%
LPP	72.81%	78.69%
SRC	84.67%	84.67%
EN	85.33%	85.33%
FDDL	87.58%	88.15%
ACGSC	89.33%	89.33%
MNACGSC	90.17%	90.30%

Table 2. Results on EYaleB database

Methods	3 group	5 group
PCA	63.12%	66.87%
LPP	84.22%	86.37%
SRC	98.95%	98.95%
EN	97.89%	97.89%
FDDL	97.87%	98.92%
ACGSC	100.00%	100.00%
MNACGSC	100.00%	100.00%

4 Conclusion

In this paper, a new algorithm named affine-constrained group sparse coding based on mixed norm (MNACGSC) is presented, which further extends the framework of sparse representation-based classification (SRC) and the group strategy. The proposed model is effective, robust to noise and outperforms some other representative methods.

Acknowledgements. This work was supported in part by National Natural Science Foundation of China (Grant no. 61672467) and National Science Foundation of Zhejiang Province (Grant no. 2015C31095).

References

1. Hastie, T., Tibshirani, R., Friedman, J.: The Elements of Statistical Learning, 2nd edn. Springer, New York (2009)
2. Turk, M., Pentland, A.: Eigenfaces for recognition. J. Cogn. Neurosci. **3**(1), 71–86 (1991)
3. Belkin, M., Niyogi, P.: Laplacian eigenmaps for dimensionality reduction and data representation. Neural Comput. **15**, 1373–1396 (2003)
4. Yang, J., Zhang, D., Frangi, A.F., Yang, J.: Two-dimensional PCA: a new approach to appearance-based face representation and recognition. IEEE Trans. Pattern Anal. Mach. Intell. **26**(1), 131–137 (2004)
5. Zheng, Z., Mao, M., Ma, S.: CLEAR: clustering based on locality embedding and reconstruction. In: ICDE, pp. 791–798 (2016)
6. Zheng, Z., Huang, X., Chen, Z., He, X., Liu, H., Yang, J.: Regression analysis of locality preserving projections via sparse penalty. Inf. Sci. **303**, 1–14 (2015)
7. Zheng, Z., Mudan, Y., Jia, J., Liu, H., Xiang, D., Huang, X., Yang, J.: Fisher discrimination based low rank matrix recovery for face recognition. Pattern Recogn. **47**(11), 3502–3511 (2014)
8. Wright, J., Yang, A.Y., Ganesh, A., Sastry, S.S., Ma, Y.: Sparse representation for computer vision and pattern recognition. Proc. IEEE **96**(6), 1031–1044 (2010)
9. Aharom, M., Elad, M., Bruscktein, M.: K-SVD: an algorithm for designing over complete dictionaries for sparse representation. IEEE Trans. Sig. Process. **54**(11), 4311–4322 (2006)
10. Yang, M., Zhang, L., Feng, X., Zhang, D.: Fisher discriminative dictionary learning for sparse representation. In: ICCV (2011)
11. Zheng, M., Bu, J., Chen, C., Wang, C., Zhang, L., Qiu, G., Cai, D.: Graph regularized sparse coding for image representation. IEEE Trans. Image Process. **20**(5), 1327–1335 (2011)
12. Bengio, S., Pereria, F., Singer, Y., Strelow, D.: Group sparse coding. Adv. NIPS **22**, 82–89 (2009)
13. Chi, Y.T., Ali, M., Rajwade, A., Ho, J.: Affine-constrained group sparse coding and its application to image-based classifications. In: CVPR (2013)
14. Zhuang, B., Liu, L., Li, Y., Shen, C., Reid, I.: Attend in groups: a weakly-supervised deep learning framework for learning from web data. In: CVPR (2017)
15. Shu, T., Todorovic, S., Zhu, S.-C.: CERN: confidence-energy recurrent network for group activity recognition. In: CVPR (2017)
16. Ioannou, Y., Robertson, D., Cipolla, R., Criminisi, A.: Deep roots: improving CNN efficiency with hierarchical filter groups. In: CVPR (2017)
17. Chi, Y.T., Ali, M., Rajwade, A., Ho, J.: Block and group regularized sparse modeling for dictionary learning. In: IEEE Conference on CVPR, pp. 377–382 (2013)

18. Donoho, D.L.: For most large underdetermined systems of linear equations the minimal norm solution is also the sparsest solution. Comm. Pure Appl. Math. **59**(6), 797–829 (2006)
19. Amaldi, E., Kann, V.: On the approximability of minimizing nonzero variables or unsatisfied relations in linear systems. Theoret. Comput. Sci. **209**, 237–260 (1998)
20. Natarajan, B.: Sparse approximate solutions to linear systems. SIAM J. Comput. **24**(2), 227–234 (1995)
21. Chen, S.S., Donoho, D.L., Saunders, M.A.: Atomic decomposition by basis pursuit. SIAM J. Sci. Comput. **20**(1), 33–61 (1999)
22. Pat, Y.C., Rezaiif, R., Krishnapraa, P.S.: Orthogonal matching pursuit. IEEE Trans. Sig. Process. (1993)
23. Roth, V.: The generalized LASSO. IEEE Trans. Neural Netw. **15**(1), 16–28 (2004)
24. Zou, H., Hastie, T.: Regression Shrinkage and Selection Via the Elastic Net, with Applications to Microarrays. Stanford University (2003)
25. Liu, Q., liu, C.: A novel locally linear KNN model for visual recognition. In: CVPR, pp. 1329–1335 (2015)
26. Lee, H., Battle, A., Raina, R., Ng, A.Y.: Efficient sparse coding algorithms. Adv. Neural Inf. Process. Syst. **20**, 801–808 (2007)
27. Boyd, S., Vandenberghe, L.: Convex Optimization. Cambridge University, New York (2004)
28. Martinez, A., Benavente, R.: The AR Face Database. CVC Technical Report (1998)
29. Georghiades, A., Belhumeur, P., Kriegman, D.: Form few to many: ilumination cone models for face recognition under variable lighting and pose. IEEE Trans. Pattern Anal. Mach. Intell. **23**(6), 643–660 (2001)

Elastic Net Based Weighted Iterative Method for Image Classification

Bingrong Xu and Qingshan Liu$^{(\boxtimes)}$

School of Automation, Huazhong University of Science and Technology,
Wuhan 430074, China
{bingrongxu,qsliu}@hust.edu.cn

Abstract. This paper presents a weighted elastic net constrained sparse coding method for solving the sparse representation (SR) based image classification problem. First, the original model is transformed into the unconstrained basis pursuit denoising (BPDN) problem under the assumption that the residual error of the SR follows Gaussian distribution. The probability density function (PDF) of the residual error is approximated by the first order Taylor expansion and a weighted diagonal matrix is calculated according to the Taylor expansion formulation, which aims to eliminate the sparse representation error. Second, the weighted BPDN problem is solved by dual augmented Lagrangian method (DALM). The consistency and convergence of the proposed method are analysed. Finally, experiments conducted on three well-known face data sets present the effectiveness of the proposed method compared with some other algorithms for face recognition, especially with noisy and disguise situations.

Keywords: Elastic net based weighted iterative method · Sparse representation · Consistency

1 Introduction

Since sparse representation has become a useful tool in statistic machine learning, it has been widely used in signal processing and pattern recognition [10,12]. The main idea of sparse representation is to use a sparse linear combination of the atoms from a known dictionary to represent a test sample with the minimum error.

In general, the sparse coding problem with constrained condition can be formulated as L_0-norm, which counts the number of nonzero entries in a vector. However, the optimization problem in L_0-norm for underdetermined system of linear equations is NP-hard. According to the Restricted Isometry Property (R.I.P) condition, if the solution to L_0-norm problem is sparse enough, it can be calculated in L_1-norm, formulated as

$$
\begin{aligned}
&\text{minimize } \|x\|_1, \\
&\text{subject to } Ax = b,
\end{aligned}
\tag{1}
$$

© Springer International Publishing AG 2017
D. Liu et al. (Eds.): ICONIP 2017, Part VI, LNCS 10639, pp. 481–489, 2017.
https://doi.org/10.1007/978-3-319-70136-3_51

where $\| \cdot \|_1$ is the L_1-norm, $x \in \mathbb{R}^n$ is an unknown signal, $b \in \mathbb{R}^m$ is the given vector to be measured, and $A \in \mathbb{R}^{m \times n}$ is a matrix which is generally considered as a dictionary.

Another form of problem (1) is described as the unconstrained basis pursuit denoising (BPDN) problem which takes the residual $e = Ax - b$ into consideration, formulated as

$$\text{minimize } \frac{1}{2} \|Ax - b\|_2^2 + \lambda \|x\|_1, \tag{2}$$

where λ is a positive scalar weight.

In [17], Zou and Hastie proposed an elastic net model, which added another L_2-norm constraint term, formulated as follows

$$L(\lambda_1, \lambda_2, x) = \|Ax - b\|_2^2 + \lambda_1 \|x\|_1 + \lambda_2 \|x\|_2^2, \tag{3}$$

where λ_1 and λ_2 are non-negative regularization parameters. If λ_2 sets as 0, the elastic-net formulation is equivalent to BPDN or lasso problem.

The L_1-min problems can be converted into a linear program (LP), which can be solved by some traditional algorithms. For example, the interior-point method [1] whose main idea is to solve the constrained problem by Newton method, but the computational complexity is relatively high. There are many improved algorithms to be proposed to solve the problems mentioned above for various real applications. Malioutov et al. [6] proposed the Homotopy method which exploits the fact that the function to be optimized undergoes a homotopy from the L_2 constraint to the L_1 objective as the regularization parameter decreased. Also augmented Lagrangian method (ALM) and dual augmented Lagrangian method (DALM) have been put up for both L_1-min and cross-and-bouquet (CAB) problem [11,13]. More recently, some novel methods have proposed to solve the optimization problems based on neurodynamic approach, such as continuous-time recurrent neural networks [4] and projection neural networks [5]. The dynamical behaviors of neural networks have been analyzed and been applied to applications [3].

In this paper, we choose the elastic net model for optimization. There are two terms in the BPDN model. The first one is the L_2-norm error term which ensure that the recovery signal can approximate the original signals, especially with the noisy situation. The second one is L_1-norm which can characterize the signal sparsity. As for the elastic net, the newly added L_2-norm constraint term increases the possibility of obtaining optimum solution. The elastic net model is transformed into BPDN problem, and focused on improving the new residual term $\|b^* - A^* x^*\|_2$ which has high impact on finding the sparse coding result. Inspired by the former work, we assume that the residual term follows Gaussian or Laplacian distribution, which probability density function (PDF) is organized and expand to first-order Taylor expansion. Then the weighted diagonal matrix of residual term is obtained. In the experiments, the efficiency of the proposed method is proved.

2 Proposed Algorithm

2.1 Algorithm Description

First, with the known test image b and dictionary A, we define the artificial data as

$$b^* = \begin{pmatrix} b \\ 0 \end{pmatrix}, A^* = (1 + \lambda_2)^{-1/2} \begin{pmatrix} A \\ \sqrt{\lambda_2}I \end{pmatrix}. \tag{4}$$

Let $\lambda^* = \lambda_1/\sqrt{1 + \lambda_2}$, $x^* = \sqrt{(1 + \lambda_2)}x$. Then the elastic net model can be written as

$$L(\lambda^*, x^*) = \|b^* - A^*x^*\|_2^2 + \lambda^*\|x^*\|_1. \tag{5}$$

Let

$$\widetilde{x}^* = \arg\min_{x^*} L(\lambda^*, x^*),$$

and then we can get the optimal solution of (3) as

$$\widetilde{x} = \frac{1}{\sqrt{1 + \lambda_2}}\widetilde{x}^*.$$

Now, taking the problem (5) into consideration, with the dictionary $A^* = [a_1^*, a_2^*, \cdots, a_n^*]$, the residual is calculated as

$$e = b^* - A^*x^* = [e_1, e_2, \cdots, e_{m+n}]^T.$$

Suppose the residuals are independently and identically distributed (i.i.d) with some probability density function (PDF) $f_\theta(e_i)$, where θ is the parameter represents the distribution and $i = 1, 2, \cdots, m + n$. In order to get the maximum likelihood estimation (MLE) solution, the likelihood of the estimator is formulated as

$$L_\theta(e_1, e_2, \cdots, e_{m+n}) = \prod_{i=1}^{m+n} f_\theta(e_i).$$

Let $\rho_\theta = -\ln f_\theta(e_i)$, the estimator will be converted into $-\ln L_\theta = \sum \rho_\theta(e_i)$. And we define $F_\theta(e) = \sum \rho_\theta(e_i)$, the first-order Taylor expansion of $F_\theta(e)$ is

$$\widetilde{F}_\theta(e) = F_\theta(e_0) + (e - e_0)^T F_\theta'(e_0) + o(e), \tag{6}$$

where $F_\theta'(e)$ is the first order partial derivative of $F_\theta(e)$ which can be written as $F_\theta'(e) = [\rho_\theta'(e_{0,1}), \rho_\theta'(e_{0,2}), \cdots, \rho_\theta'(e_{0,m+n})]^T$, and $o(e)$ is the high order residual approximated by $o(e) = (e - e_0)^T W(e - e_0)/2$, in which W is the weighted diagonal matrix for e.

At $e = e_0$ (generally $e_0 = 0$), $F(e)$ gets the minimum value, and $\widetilde{F}_\theta(e)$ also requires to reach the minimum value. Let $F_\theta'(e_0) = 0$ and $e_0 = 0$, the weighted diagonal matrix W formulated as $W_{i,i} = \omega_\theta(e_{0,i}) = \rho_\theta'(e_{0,i})/e_{0,i}$, then the Eq. (6) can be formulated as $\widetilde{F}_\theta(e) = \|W^{1/2}e\|_2^2/2 + b$.

Since the elements of diagonal matrix W are the weight assigned to each pixel of the query image y. And in face recognition problem, the outlier noises should have low weight values. Thus, we choose the logistic function as weighted function

$$\omega_\theta(e_{0,i}) = \exp(\mu\omega - \mu e_{0,i}^2)/(1 + \exp(\mu\omega - \mu e_{0,i}^2)), \tag{7}$$

where μ and ω are positive parameters.

The diagonal elements $\omega_\theta(e_{0,i})$ of the weighted diagonal matrix W are obtained from (7). When the residual error is getting close to 0, the corresponding weighted diagonal element is to become 1, conversely, the bigger the residual error is, the smaller the diagonal element's value is. To some extent, the weighted matrix W could eliminate the sparse representation error in the following iterative process.

Then the problem can be rewritten as

$$\text{minimize } \|W^{1/2}(A^*x^* - b^*)\|_2^2 + \lambda^*\|x^*\|_1. \tag{8}$$

As for problem (8), it can be solved by some well-known algorithms. In this paper, the DALM is selected.

The sparse reconstruction algorithm is written as:

Algorithm 1. Weighted Iterative Method (WIM)

Initialization:
1: Normalize test image b and each column of dictionary A with unit L_2-norm, and set the maximum iterative step K, regularization parameters λ_1 and λ_2;
2: Set $k = 0$;
3: Compute the λ^*, A^*, b^* by (4), and the problem is formulated as
   $\min \|A^*x^k - b^*\|_2^2 + \lambda^*\|x^k\|_1$.
Iteration:
4: **while** $k \neq K$ **do**
5:    Calculate the residual
      $e^k = b^* - A^*x^k$;
6:    Calculate the weights
      $\omega_\theta(e_{0,i}) = \exp(\mu\delta - \mu e_i^2)/(1 + \exp(\mu\delta - \mu e_i^2))$;
7:    Compute the weighted BPDN problem using DALM method
      $x^k \leftarrow \min \|W^{1/2}(A^*x^* - b^*)\|_2^2 + \lambda^*\|x^*\|_1$;
8:    $k = k + 1$;
9: **end while**
10: **return** $x^* \leftarrow x^k$.

As for the classification problem, the residual of each class is calculated as $e_i = \|b - A_ix^*\|_2$, and the object will be assigned to the class i which leads to the minimum error.

Remark 1. Considering the extreme condition that all elements of b are so huge which may lead all the elements of weighted diagonal matrix W to be 0, and the solution of x could be zero vector. However, in this case, before calculating the matrix elements $\omega_\theta(e_{0,i})$, all the vectors' dimension will be deduced by PCA which can ensure the vector to be represented is in the proper dimension, and then the weighted diagonal matrix is composed, which can prevent most elements of W to be 0.

2.2 Validity Analysis of the Proposed Algorithm

According to the analysis in [15], a calculated sparse coding x^* is equal to the true value of sparse coding $\hat{x}$, if and only if

$$\text{sgn}(x^*) = \text{sgn}(\hat{x}), \tag{9}$$

where $\text{sgn}(\cdot)$ is a signal function which maps the positive entries and negative entries to 1 and -1 respectively, zero entries stay 0.

Assume the support set $S = \text{supp}(\hat{x}) = \{j : \hat{x}_j \neq 0\}$, where $\hat{x}$ is the true value of sparse coding, $\text{supp}(\cdot)$ is the sign of the support set. Denote S^n is the non-support set that $\hat{x}_j = 0$. The corresponding vectors (x_S, x_{S^n}) and matrices (A_S, A_{S^n}) are defined on S and S^n subspace respectively. For Lasso problem, assume that

$$\frac{1}{m}A^T A \to C, \tag{10}$$

where C is a positive definite matrix, $A = WA^*$ in the proposed model.

According to the analysis in [16], we can have C expressed in a block-wise form which block element $C_{11} = A_S^T A_S$ is the matrix related to the active set S, and is invertible.

There exists a positive constant $\omega > 0$ such that

$$\|C_{21}C_{11}^{-1}\text{sgn}(x_S)\|_\infty \leq 1 - \omega, \tag{11}$$

where the inequality holds for element-wise. This is the irrepresentable condition (IC) which describe a constraint on regression coefficients between the relevant elements x_S and the irrelevant elements x_{S^n}. And (9) holds true if and only if the IC is satisfied which proves that the x^* obtained equals to the true sparse coding $\hat{x}$.

Then we compare the elastic net models with and without the L_1-norm or L_2-norm terms. The sparsity level and the residual error are both taken into consideration in the proposed algorithm. Here we choose one image randomly from the ORL data set, and the dictionary is composed of three images of each class and the image's dimension is reduced by Principal Component Analysis (PCA) method. Then the situations (a. original elastic net; b. elastic net without L_1-norm term; c. elastic net without L_2-norm term) are compared by classifying the same test image which parameter (λ_1 or λ_2) in the situation (b) and (c) is set as the same value as situation (a).

The comparison results of sparse coefficient are shown in Fig. 1. It is obviously that elastic net performs better in that it keeps the coefficient of the correct classes larger, while that of incorrect classes smaller. From Fig. 1(a) and (b), it is

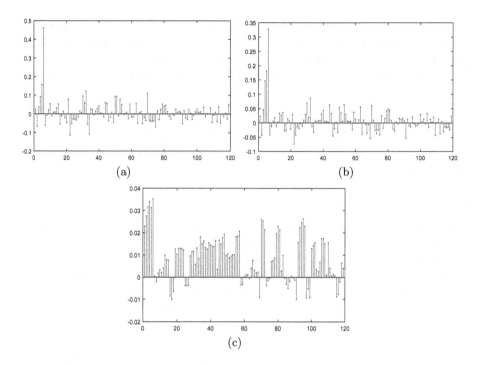

Fig. 1. The reconstruction coefficients of the same image with: (a) original elastic net (error term, L_1-norm term, L_2-norm term); (b) original model without L_2-norm term; (c) original model without L_1-norm term.

clear that the L_2-norm constraint term increase the discrimination of solution, and from Fig. 1(a) and (c), it can be figured out that the L_1-norm plays an important role in sparse representation.

3   Experimental Results

Before the experiments start, the values of the four parameters λ_1 and λ_2 in (5), ω and μ in (7) should be determined. Parameter ω is the demarcation parameter, and parameter μ controls the decreasing rate of weight value from 1 to 0. Let $\mu = c/\omega$, where c is a given constant. In the experiments, the value of ω is set in the range of $[0.5, 1]$ it can be changed under different data sets. And set c at 8, then we can obtain the value of μ. As for the parameters λ_1 and λ_2, λ_2 is usually dozens of time λ_1, the actual value of the two parameters depends on the real statistics. Normally we set $\lambda_2 = 0.05$, and λ_1 varies through the experiments.

The first experiment is conducted on ORL data set [8]. Figure 2 shows some samples faces of this data set. The proposed algorithm WIM is compared with primal-dual interior-point algorithm (PDIPA), prime augmented Lagrangian method (PALM), truncated Newton interior-point method (TNIPM/L1LS) and fast iterative soft-thresholding algorithm (FISTA) algorithms.

Fig. 2. Some image samples of ORL face data set.

The dimensions of both training and testing images are reduced to 200 by using PCA method. The N (N = 3, 4, 5) training images of each class are randomly selected, and the rests are for testing. λ_1 is set as 0.01 and λ_2 is set as 0.05. From Table 1, it is obvious that the recognition rate of the WIM performs better slightly than the other algorithms.

Table 1. Recognition rate on ORL data set (%)

Algorithms	PDIPA	PALM	L1LS	FISTA	WIM
$N = 3$	**74.17**	**74.17**	74.00	73.68	**74.17**
$N = 4$	80.62	84.14	84.00	84.25	**84.30**
$N = 5$	84.50	84.50	89.00	86.50	**89.35**

In the second experiment, the Extend Yale B data set [2] is chosen to demonstrate the ability of PIM dealing with noise pixel images. The parameters in the algorithms are set as λ_1 = 0.0001 and λ_2 = 0.05. For each class, 20 images are selected to compose the learning dictionary, and the rest testing images are cropped with different percentage (20, 40 and 60) of random Gaussian noise. Table 2 proves that the WIM has the highest recognition rate in all corruption degrees. The higher corrosion rate is, the more prominent the WIM performances (Fig. 3).

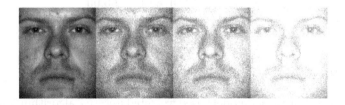

Fig. 3. EYB image samples under different levels random noise.

The third experiment is conduct on AR data set [7] to demonstrate the ability of the proposed WEN dealing with the disguise faces. Images in each class are with various facial expressions, illumination circumstances and occlusions. Some images are masked with sunglasses or scarf. First, all the images are converted

Table 2. Recognition rate under different noise levels of EYB data set (%)

Corruption rate	PDIPA	PALM	L1LS	FISTA	WIM
0	94.04	78.54	72.80	74.72	**94.56**
20	92.62	80.35	72.07	77.37	**93.11**
40	89.60	79.32	71.77	74.61	**90.68**
60	79.50	75,51	69.35	70.98	**85.73**

into gray version, then the images' dimension are reduced to 100 using PCA. For each class, the 14 face images without disguise are used for training, and other images with sunglasses or scarf are used for testing separately. The parameters are set the same as previous ones.

In this experiment, the proposed WIM is compared with original DALM [9] and CRC [14] which proved efficient and fast in face recognition. The face disguise recognition rates are presented in Table 3, which shows the effectiveness and superiority of the WIM, and it proves the weighted diagonal matrix makes a great contribution to dealing with outliers and disguise (Fig 4).

Fig. 4. Some AR image samples with sunglasses and scraf.

Table 3. Recognition rates with face disguise (%)

Algorithms	CRC	DALM	WIM
Sunglasses	53.50	60.30	**90.00**
Scarf	30.70	51.33	**71.67**

4   Conclusion

In this paper, an elastic net model based weighted iterative algorithm is proposed. First, the elastic net model is converted to BPDN form, and the representation residuals are calculated. Then, the weighted diagonal matrix is composed according to the first order Taylor expansion of the residuals and the logistic function. Finally, the DALM method are used to solve the problem with weighted matrix. The consistency and convergency of the proposed method is analysed. In the experiments, the proposed WIM is proved effectiveness especially with noise and disguise situations.

Acknowledgments. This work was supported in part by the National Natural Science Foundation of China under Grant 61473333.

References

1. Byrd, R.H., Hribar, M.E., Nocedal, J.: An interior point algorithm for large-scale nonlinear programming. SIAM J. Optim. **9**(4), 877–900 (1999)
2. Georghiades, A.S., Belhumeur, P.N., Kriegman, D.J.: From few to many: illumination cone models for face recognition under variable lighting and pose. IEEE Trans. Pattern Anal. Mach. Intell. **23**(6), 643–660 (2001)
3. Liu, Q., Huang, T., Wang, J.: One-layer continuous- and discrete-time projection neural networks for solving variational inequalities and related optimization problems. IEEE Trans. Neural Netw. Learn. Syst. **25**(7), 1308–1318 (2014)
4. Liu, Q., Wang, J.: A one-layer recurrent neural network with a discontinuous hard-limiting activation function for quadratic programming. IEEE Trans. Neural Netw. **19**(4), 558–570 (2008)
5. Liu, Q., Wang, J.: A one-layer projection neural network for nonsmooth optimization subject to linear equalities and bound constraints. IEEE Trans. Neural Netw. Learn. Syst. **24**(5), 812–824 (2013)
6. Malioutov, D.M., Cetin, M., Willsky, A.S.: Homotopy continuation for sparse signal representation. In: Proceedings of IEEE International Conference on Acoustics, Speech, and Signal Processing, vol. 5, p. v–733 (2005)
7. Martínez, A.M., Kak, A.C.: PCA versus LDA. IEEE Trans. Pattern Anal. Mach. Intell. **23**(2), 228–233 (2001)
8. Samaria, F.S., Harter, A.C.: Parameterisation of a stochastic model for human face identification. In: Proceedings of the Second IEEE Workshop on Applications of Computer Vision, pp. 138–142 (1994)
9. Tomioka, R., Sugiyama, M.: Dual-augmented lagrangian method for efficient sparse reconstruction. IEEE Sig. Process. Lett. **16**(12), 1067–1070 (2009)
10. Wright, J., Yang, A.Y., Ganesh, A., Sastry, S.S., Ma, Y.: Robust face recognition via sparse representation. IEEE Trans. Pattern Anal. Mach. Intell. **31**(2), 210–227 (2009)
11. Wright, S.J., Nowak, R.D., Figueiredo, M.A.: Sparse reconstruction by separable approximation. IEEE Trans. Sig. Process. **57**(7), 2479–2493 (2009)
12. Xu, Y., Zhong, Z., Yang, J., You, J., Zhang, D.: A new discriminative sparse representation method for robust face recognition via l_2 regularization. IEEE Trans. Neural Netw. Learn. Syst. (2016). doi:10.1109/TNNLS.2016.2580572
13. Yang, A.Y., Zhou, Z., Balasubramanian, A.G., Sastry, S.S., Ma, Y.: Fast l_1-minimization algorithms for robust face recognition. IEEE Trans. Image Process. **22**(8), 3234–3246 (2013)
14. Zhang, L., Yang, M., Feng, X.: Sparse representation or collaborative representation: which helps face recognition? In: Proceedings of IEEE International Conference on Computer Vision, pp. 471–478 (2011)
15. Zhao, P., Yu, B.: On model selection consistency of lasso. J. Mach. Learn. Res. **7**, 2541–2563 (2006)
16. Zhou, S., van de Geer, S., Bühlmann, P.: Adaptive lasso for high dimensional regression and Gaussian graphical modeling. arXiv preprint arXiv:0903.2515 (2009)
17. Zou, H., Hastie, T.: Regularization and variable selection via the elastic net. J. Roy. Stat. Soc. Ser. B (Stat. Methodol.) **67**(2), 301–320 (2005)

Cognitive Load Recognition Using Multi-threshold United Complex Network

Jian Shang and Qingshan Liu$^{(\boxtimes)}$

School of Automation, Huazhong University of Science and Technology,
Wuhan 430074, China
{shangjian,qsliu}@hust.edu.cn

Abstract. Finding effective representations from electroencephalogram (EEG) data is challenging. Complex network (CN) analysis has been proved to be one of the efficient way in the EEG time series analysis, such as modeling the cognitive events of human beings. But most of the network analysis is just using the time domain statistical features and often has a fixed threshold for the network's connectivity. Herein, based on our previous work with an adaptive threshold, we propose a novel approach using a set of thresholds which fit to the data distribution to construct connections between different EEG channels to generate a multi-channel network. Inspired by the multi-frame method of video processing, we also divide the EEG data of one trial into several frames without overlap. The final classification is based on the multi-threshold and multi-frame network structural features. The results on the cognitive load classification dataset demonstrate that the proposed approach is more efficient than the deep learning method, and reduce the mean classification error to 8.1%.

Keywords: Cognitive events · Electroencephalogram (EEG) · Frequency domain features · Multi-threshold · United complex network

1 Introduction

Human activity analysis is a hot topic, and there has been a lot of researches in traditional physical activity, such as human gait recognition [15]. However, the brain activity also plays a crucial role in human activity analysis, which is more challenging and difficult and can only be analysed by some potentiating method, such as Magnetic Resonance Imaging(MRI) [8] and Brain-Computer Interfaces(BCI).

Modeling cognitive events and recognizing cognitive load are in Brain-Computer Interfaces(BCI). Cognitive processing capacity is important for everyone, for it determines the mental function capacity, such as working memory. But the capacity is varying between different person, and excessive cognitive pressure could lead to overload state which may cause confusion and lower the learning ability [14]. Because of its high temporal resolution, non-invasion and

© Springer International Publishing AG 2017
D. Liu et al. (Eds.): ICONIP 2017, Part VI, LNCS 10639, pp. 490–498, 2017.
https://doi.org/10.1007/978-3-319-70136-3_52

low cost, EEG has been widely used in measuring changes of electrical voltage on the scalp. Here, we use EEG to explore the cognitive activities. In fact, there has been numerous researches using EEG data and applying machine learning method in EEG recognition [2,10]. Deep learning has achieved great success in many recognition tasks such as computer vision, whose signal is more robust than the EEG data [6,9]. Convolutional neural networks (CNN) and recurrent neural networks (RNN) have shown their potential applications in processing and extracting features from EEG signals [4,11]. Concetto et al. [13] propose to read the mind and explore to use human visual capabilities for automated visual classification using RNN and CNN. But using deep learning method directly for the EEG time series may not get better results than the classical machine learning approach. On the one hand, the EEG dataset is not large enough for the training of deep learning modules in the most time. On the other hand, there are often lots of channels in the EEG dataset of which not all of them are related to the specific cognitive task. So learning robust representations of EEG is significant. Bashivan et al. [2] propose a novel method to transform the EEG time series into 2-D images, by which they find representations which are invariant to inter- and intra-subject differences, and gets state-of-the-art classification accuracy.

We have demonstrated the effectiveness of the complex network approach in our precious work [12]. In fact, there has been many successful applications in learning representation of EEG time series using complex network, such as motor imagery, sleep stage classification and Alzheimer's disease recognition [3, 5,16]. Several methods have been proposed to transform EEG time series into complex networks. He and Liu [5] propose to use probabilistic graphical models in motor imagery analysis [7], constructing Bayesian network with Gaussian distribution. Zhang and Small [17] use a single node to represent each cycle of pseudo-periodic time series to construct complex networks. Wang and Yang [16] propose a limited penetrable visibility graph (LPVG) and phase space method to map single EEG series into networks. Diykh and Li [3] use different statistical features of divided EEG sub-segments to construct networks. The networks' topologies can help better understand the relationships between nodes which represent different channel or different time series. However, the threshold to determine the connection of networks has to be set manually according to the classification performance and is often a fixed value. But one single threshold could not demonstrate the relationship of different channels clearly, and the network constructed from the single threshold is just one representation of the signal, which is seriously influenced by the threshold. In [1], Backes et al. use degree measurements to compose a set of texture descriptors. In other words, they set many thresholds to construct many networks of one trial. But the set of thresholds are uniform distribution and can be only determined by experiment.

In this paper, we present a new approach to determine a set of thresholds according to the distribution of the frequency domain features which we use to construct multi-channel network. And inspired by the multi-frame method of video processing, we also divide the EEG data of one trial into several continuous frames without overlap. Every frame of one trial can use the set of thresholds to construct several networks which are comprehensive representations of relationship of different channels. These networks can represent the EEG time series of one trial from not only the spatial but also the temporal perspective. Our approach is different from the previous one which attempts to use fixed threshold or the mean distance between different channels. Then the set of networks' structural features such as degree distribution will be extracted and fed to a classifier. The results on the cognitive load classification dataset demonstrate that the proposed approach is more efficient than the deep learning method, and reduce the mean classification error to 8.1%.

2   Main Method

This paper proposes an efficient multi-threshold united complex network method to classify different cognitive load levels. Figure 1 illustrates the whole procedure of the proposed method. First, the EEG data's three frequency bands features are extracted to represent the nodes of the networks. Then, we compute the space distance of every two nodes and determine the multi-threshold to construct networks. To evaluate the effectiveness of the method, the extracted features of multi-threshold united complex network are forwarded to the SVM classifiers. We also compare the classification error with our previous adaptive threshold method [12] and the deep learning method in [2]. The details are explained in the following sections.

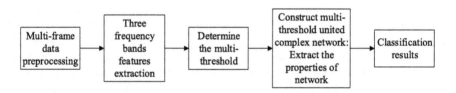

Fig. 1. Block diagram of the proposed multi-threshold united complex network method.

2.1   Multi-frame Data Preprocessing

The dataset [2] used in this paper is collected during a working memory experiment. There are 2670 samples from 13 subjects' data which are not damaged by the excessive noise and artifacts in the recording process, and every sample has the length of 3.5 s. Four classes mean the different cognitive load levels. Multi-frame data is divided from the 3.5 s data, and each has 7 frames with the length of 0.5 s. Our purposed method is to map the multi-frame EEG time series to a network representation. The three frequency bands, theta (4–7 Hz), alpha (8–12 Hz) and beta (13–30 Hz), which are related to the memory operations, are extracted to represent every channel. So every channel of each frame EEG data has a representation of three frequency band features.

2.2   Generate a Multi-threshold United Complex Network from the Frequency Domain Representations

A network can describe the relationship between different channels, and a union of several networks can reveal the distribution of the relationship. The connection between each pair of nodes which represent different channels refers to the relationship. In this work, we employ the frequency domain features to generate the network for the four different load levels. Each channel can be considered as a data point or a basic node in the network. Then the connections between every two nodes have to be determined. Finally the structural properties of the generated networks can be forwarded to a classifier. As for the connections, we employ the space distance as the measurement according to [17]. Let $d(x_i, x_j)$ represents the space distance between two nodes x_i, x_j, if the distance is less or equal to the predetermined threshold D_m, there is a connection; i.e., $d(x_i, x_j) \leq D_m$, where D_m is the m-th predetermined threshold. Here, we choose multi-threshold to generate several complex networks. The set of thresholds are determined according to the distribution of the space distance of the three frequency domain features. The details of the thresholds and the comparison with other methods will discussed in the following section.

After the network is constructed, we get one of the adjacent matrix A_m corresponding to D_m using

$$A_m(x_i, x_j) = \begin{cases} 1, & \text{if} \quad d(x_i, x_j) \leq D_m \\ 0, & \text{otherwise} \end{cases} \tag{1}$$

Figure 2 shows an example of constructed complex networks consisting of 64 nodes with two different thresholds. The lines represent the connections between two nodes.

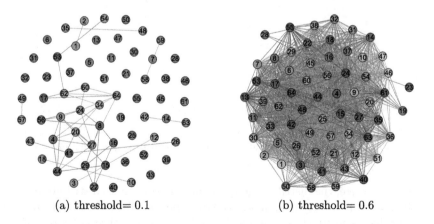

(a) threshold= 0.1   (b) threshold= 0.6

Fig. 2. The constructed complex networks with different thresholds. The number of each node refer to the different electrode in the scalp. Different color means different degree for each node, which is the main feature we use for classification.

2.3   Classification Methods

In this work, in order to demonstrate our approach's efficiency, we employ SVM to classify the network's structural features. The k-fold cross validation's test error are used to evaluate the performances. Let y_k represents the k-th fold classification accuracy, then the performance can be evaluated using $\frac{1}{k}\sum y_k$, where k is the number of folds, and the performance is the average accuracy of k folds.

3   Experimental Results

In this section, we compare our threshold determined approach with other methods. Then, we use 10-fold cross validation's test error to evaluate the efficiency of our approach. We also compare the test error of the proposed approach with the popular deep learning method in [2].

3.1   Determine the Set of Thresholds

Threshold influences the structure of the network. We propose to set several thresholds instead of previous single one. And the set of thresholds are determined according to the distribution of the three spectral features' space distance. The distribution of these distance is extraordinarily unequal, so we should set the thresholds according to our needs. Figure 3 shows the whole distribution of all the samples, or you can just use the training data to compute the distribution.

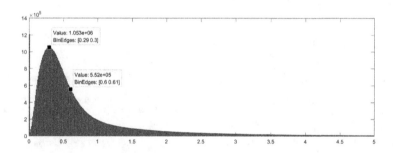

Fig. 3. The whole distribution of spectral features' space distance.

As you can see, the distribution is unequal: most samples distribute in $(0, 1)$, and the data's distribution results in the distribution of the threshold, so we set more thresholds in $(0, 1)$. A simplified way is to put the thresholds of different interval to be uniform distribution according to density. For example, in Fig. 3, the data is denser in $(0, 1)$, to be more precisely, the peak is at 0.3, and we set 0.3 to be one of the boundary points. So we set the thresholds as follows: 0.05, 0.1, 0.15, 0.2, 0.25, 0.3, 0.4, 0.5, 0.6, 0.7, 0.8, 0.9, 1, 1.5, 2, 3, 5, 8, 12. The interval

Table 1. Comparisons of test error (%) among different threshold determine methods

Method	Threshold	Threshold numbers	Test error
Adaptive threshold	Threshold=mean(distance)	1	10.36
Uniform thresholds	(0,2], interval=0.1	20	8.52
Uniform thresholds	(0,4], interval=0.2	20	10.58
Our method	(0,12], different interval	19	8.16

of threshold in $(0.05, 0.3)$ is 0.05, and $(0.3, 1)$ is 0.1, which are smaller than the other interval.

We also compare our approach with the previous adaptive threshold method [12], which use the mean distance of every sample, and the uniform thresholds method. The results are shown in Table 1.

3.2   Construct Multi-threshold United Complex Network

The method is based on the concept that the structures of different cognitive load level's network topologies are different. In the above section, we have determined the set of thresholds from the distribution. So, for every frame of the sample EEG time series, we'll have a specific network, that is to say, there'll be a union of networks for each sample, which is called multi-threshold united complex network. Figure 4 illustrates an example of the networks' adjacency matrixes of different frames and different thresholds. For visualization, we transform the adjacency matrixes into grayscale images, in which the horizontal axis and vertical axis represent the 64 nodes of the network. And every white point means the connection between the corresponding two nodes, while the black point means no connection. As you can see, the number of connection grows as the threshold become larger, from which we can see how the connections distribute.

3.3   Performance Comparison

In the experiment, we use the degree distribution as the classification feature. Every sample has 7 frames' degree features, and the SVM is adopted to be the classifier, and the multi-class classification is achieved by one-by-one classification. The average accuracy of 10-fold cross validation is 91.84%. The 10-fold test error's details are showed in Table 2. As you can see, the test errors vary from different folds, and the best is 5.24%, indicating that partitioning of training data is important for the final classification.

As mentioned above, for the classification experiment, we extract the degree distribution as features of the multi-threshold united complex networks using SVM classifier. We compare our results with the popular deep learning method in [2]. We also compare the multi-frame and single-frame method in the same threshold condition.

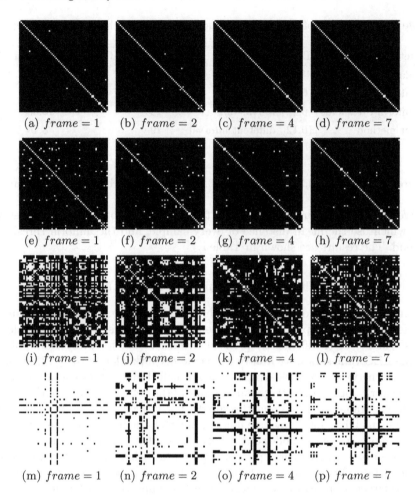

Fig. 4. Differences of adjacency matrixes of typical networks of different frames and different thresholds. Fig(a)-(d), Fig(e)-(h), Fig(i)-(l) and Fig(m)-(p) corresponding to threshold=0.05, 0.1, 0.3, 1 respectively.

The results are shown in Table 3, we can find that the performance of our proposed method is better than the deep learning method. And the deep learning method have a tremendous numbers of parameters and needs a long time to train the deep learning model and to generate the images from EEG time series. By comparing the results of multi-frame and single-frame method, we can see the

Table 2. Test error (%) of 10-fold cross validation

Fold	1	2	3	4	5	6	7	8	9	10
Test error	11.61	7.12	8.61	5.99	5.24	6.37	7.87	7.87	9.74	11.24

Table 3. Comparisons of test error (%) among different models

Models	Test error	Number of parameters
Multi-threshold united networks (multi-frame) + SVM	8.16	–
Multi-threshold networks (single-frame) + SVM	9.88	–
ConvNet + 1D−Conv [2]	11.32	441 k
ConvNet + LSTM [2]	10.54	1.34 mil
ConvNet + LSTM/1D−Conv [2]	8.89	1.62 mil

necessity of the multi-frame data processing, it has reduced the classification error from 9.88% to 8.16%. The reason may be the full use of the temporal and spatial information, which is important in EEG classification.

4   Conclusions

This paper proposes a novel approach using the distribution of space distance to set multi- thresholds to construct connections between different EEG channels. The idea is to express the EEG features based on the united complex network. And the classification is based on the network structural features. The results indicate that the proposed method is more efficient than others in the cognitive load recognition task, and reduce the classification error. However, the proposed method uses all of the channels in the EEG time series, but in some tasks, the brain activities are only related to several critical channels, such as emotion recognition and motor imagery [5, 18]. So the proposed approach has its limitation in the degree of generalization. But investigating critical frequency bands and channels of EEG in different tasks is still challenging, which will be included in our next work.

Acknowledgments. This work was supported in part by the National Natural Science Foundation of China under Grant 61473333.

References

1. Backes, A.R., Casanova, D., Bruno, O.M.: Texture analysis and classification: a complex network-based approach. Inf. Sci. **219**(1), 168–180 (2013)
2. Bashivan, P., Rish, I., Yeasin, M., Codella, N.: Learning representations from EEG with deep recurrent-convolutional neural networks. arXiv preprint arxiv:1511.06448 (2015)
3. Diykh, M., Li, Y.: Complex networks approach for EEG signal sleep stages classification. Expert Syst. Appl. **63**, 241–248 (2016)
4. Güler, N.F., Übeyli, E.D., Güler, I.: Recurrent neural networks employing Lyapunov exponents for EEG signals classification. Expert Syst. Appl. **29**(3), 506–514 (2005)

5. He, L., Liu, B., Hu, D., Wen, Y., Wan, M., Long, J.: Motor imagery EEG signals analysis based on Bayesian network with Gaussian distribution. Neurocomputing **188**, 217–224 (2016)
6. Karpathy, A., Toderici, G., Shetty, S., Leung, T., Sukthankar, R., Fei-Fei, L.: Large-scale video classification with convolutional neural networks. In: Proceedings of the IEEE conference on Computer Vision and Pattern Recognition, pp. 1725–1732 (2014)
7. Koller, D., Friedman, N.: Probabilistic Graphical Models: Principles and Techniques. MIT press, Cambridge (2009)
8. Kovalev, V.A., Kruggel, F., Gertz, H.J., von Cramon, D.Y.: Three-dimensional texture analysis of MRI brain datasets. IEEE Trans. Med. Imaging **20**(5), 424–433 (2001)
9. Krizhevsky, A., Sutskever, I., Hinton, G.E.: Imagenet classification with deep convolutional neural networks. In: Advances In Neural Information Processing Systems, pp. 1097–1105 (2012)
10. Lotte, F., Congedo, M., Lécuyer, A., Lamarche, F., Arnaldi, B.: A review of classification algorithms for EEG-based brain-computer interfaces. J. Neural Eng. **4**(2), 1–24 (2007). R1
11. Mirowski, P., Madhavan, D., LeCun, Y., Kuzniecky, R.: Classification of patterns of EEG synchronization for seizure prediction. Clin. Neurophysiol. **120**(11), 1927–1940 (2009)
12. Shang, J., Zhang, W., Xiong, J., Liu, Q.: Cognitive load recognition using multi-channel complex network method. In: Cong, F., Leung, A., Wei, Q. (eds.) ISNN 2017. LNCS, vol. 10261, pp. 466–474. Springer, Cham (2017). doi:10.1007/978-3-319-59072-1_55
13. Spampinato, C., Palazzo, S., Kavasidis, I., Giordano, D., Shah, M., Souly, N.: Deep learning human mind for automated visual classification. arXiv preprint arxiv:1609.00344 (2016)
14. Sweller, J., Van Merrienboer, J.J., Paas, F.G.: Cognitive architecture and instructional design. Educ. Psychol. Rev. **10**(3), 251–296 (1998)
15. Tao, D., Li, X., Wu, X., Maybank, S.J.: General tensor discriminant analysis and gabor features for gait recognition. IEEE Trans. Pattern Anal. Mach. Intell. **29**(10), 1700–1715 (2007)
16. Wang, J., Yang, C., Wang, R., Yu, H., Cao, Y., Liu, J.: Functional brain networks in Alzheimers disease: EEG analysis based on limited penetrable visibility graph and phase space method. Physica A **460**, 174–187 (2016)
17. Zhang, J., Small, M.: Complex network from pseudoperiodic time series: topology versus dynamics. Phys. Rev. Lett. **96**(23), 238701 (2006)
18. Zheng, W.L., Lu, B.L.: Investigating critical frequency bands and channels for eeg-based emotion recognition with deep neural networks. IEEE Trans. Auton. Ment. Dev. **7**(3), 162–175 (2015)

ELM-Based Signal Detection Scheme of MIMO System Using Auto Encoder

Fei Long[1] and Xin Yan[1,2(✉)]

[1] School of Electrical and Information Engineering, Guizhou Institute of Technology,
Guiyang 550001, China
946566983@qq.com
[2] College of Big Data and Information Engineering, Guizhou University, Guiyang 550025, China

Abstract. Signal detection scheme is the key technology to the implementation of multiple-input multiple-output (MIMO) wireless communication system, while the spatial-multiplexing coded MIMO systems cause a severe design challenge for signal detection algorithms. Although many researches focus on searching the solution space for optimal solution based on more efficient searching algorithm, the signal detection of MIMO system does not regarded as a classification problem. In this paper, the detection problem is considered as a feature classification, and a novel signal detection scheme of MIMO system based on extreme learning machine auto encoder (ELM-AE) is proposed. The proposed algorithm can efficiently extract the features of input data by ELM-AE and classify these representations to corresponding groups rapidly by using extreme learning machine (ELM). This paper has constructed a theoretical model of the proposed signal detector for MIMO system and carried out simulations to evaluating its performance. Simulation results indicate that the proposed detector outperforms many traditional schemes and state-of-the-art algorithms.

Keywords: MIMO · Signal detection · Extreme learning machine · Auto encoder · Feature classification

1 Introduction

Multiple-input multiple-output (MIMO) technology has been one of the most significant techniques of wireless communication system. The attractions of MIMO are the high performance gain and channel capacity which linear increase with the number of transmitter and receiver antennas due to the multipath parallel data transmission in the same frequency band [1]. The key to the implementation of MIMO system is the signal detection algorithm. Although many reliable signal detection methods for MIMO system have been proposed, it is still urgent for researchers to seek more efficient signal detection schemes to improve the current systems' performances and adapt to the applications of massive MIMO and super massive MIMO systems in the future. Therefore, it is a hot topic of MIMO system that how to search the better signal detection algorithms balancing the relationship of complexity and performance of detection scheme.

© Springer International Publishing AG 2017
D. Liu et al. (Eds.): ICONIP 2017, Part VI, LNCS 10639, pp. 499–509, 2017.
https://doi.org/10.1007/978-3-319-70136-3_53

There are many signal detection algorithms for MIMO system available, and maximum likelihood (ML) detector is the optimal detector which can minimize the bit-error-rate (BER) of detection but it has the highest computational complexity at the same time [2]. Zero-forcing (ZF) and minimum-mean-square-error (MMSE) algorithms are typical linear detection schemes with much lower complexities but less BER perform-ances than ML [3]. Zero-forcing successive-interference-cancellation (ZF-SIC) [4] and minimum-mean-squared-error successive-interference-cancellation (MMSE-SIC) [5] are improved algorithms of ZF and MMSE respectively based on SIC method, they utilize the cancellation of the former detected symbol's information to decrease BER. Radial basis function network optimized by quantum genetic algorithm (QGA-RBF) [6] and quantum ant colony algorithm (QACA) [7] are intelligent optimization algorithm that can shrink the searching region where the optimal solution exists, but the compu-tational complexity will increase concurrently with respect to the population size of QGA. Though there are many signal detection algorithms, but few of them have applied machine learning methods to signal detection of MIMO system, and none of them regards the problem as pattern recognition or feature classification problem, while this kind of issue transformation might be necessary in the process of high dimensional received data of massive MIMO systems in the future.

Deep learning and machine learning algorithms have been successfully applied in feature extraction and classification tasks in decades, and extreme learning machine algorithm stands out from others in virtue of its fast training speed, good generalization and universal approximation capability [8, 9]. In this paper, a novel signal detection algorithm based on extreme learning machine auto encoder (ELM-AE) [10] has been proposed. The proposed algorithm consists of two parts; the feature extractor based on ELM-AE can obtain useful feature representations of input samples by separating the channel state information via the projection of the learnt connection weights parameters from the unsupervised learning of the ELM-AE, the trained ELM classifier is used to recognize the corresponding original symbols of the features. Due to the fast learning speed and high classification accuracy of ELM, simulation results indicate that the proposed algorithm is more efficient than ML, QGA-RBF and the performance outper-forms ZF, MMSE, and ZF-SIC, MMSE-SIC algorithms.

The rest of this paper is organized as follows. Section 2 introduces the MIMO system model, and ELM, ELM-AE algorithms. The proposed signal detection algorithm is described in Sect. 3. Section 4 presents the simulation results. Finally, conclusions are drawn in Sect. 5.

2   MIMO System, ELM and ELM Auto-Encoder

2.1   MIMO System

This paper investigates a point-to-point MIMO system with N transmitter antennas and M receiver antennas, where $N \leq M$. The structure of MIMO wireless system is presented as in Fig. 1.

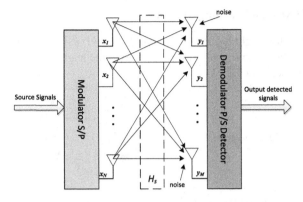

Fig. 1. The block diagram of MIMO system. This system includes three parts: transmitter, channel and receiver. x are the transmitting signals, y are receiving symbols and H_s represents channel state.

As shown in Fig. 1, the input-output relationship of MIMO system can be expressed in vector form as follows:

$$y = H_s \cdot x + n. \tag{1}$$

where $y = [y_1, y_2, \dots, y_M]^T$ is received signal vector, the corresponding transmitted vector $x = [x_1, x_2, \dots, x_N]^T$, H_s denotes a $M \times N$ channel state matrix and n is the additive white Gaussian noise with zero mean and variance of σ^2 [11].

In MIMO system the received symbol on every receiving antenna contains all information from transmitted symbols [12], as presented in Eq. (2).

$$y_k = \sum_{i=1}^{N} \left(h_{k,i} \cdot x_i \right) + n_k \tag{2}$$

where $h_{k,i}$ denotes the channel gain from the ith transmitting antenna to the kth receiving antenna, n_k represents the white Gaussian additive noise on k^{th} receiving antenna.

Signal detection of MIMO system is to obtain the optimal solution $\ddot{x}$ which has the minimum difference compares to the source signal x from the received symbols y.

The maximum likelihood (ML) detection is an optimal detection algorithm; it searches the entire solution space Φ to find the optimal solution $\ddot{x}$ which can minimize the cost function

$$\ddot{x} = \arg \min_{x \in \Phi} \left\{ \|y - H \cdot x\|^2 \right\}. \tag{3}$$

On account of the high complexity, suboptimal detection scheme is required. Thus linear detection methods (ZF and MMSE) and nonlinear detection methods (QGA-RBF, QACA etc.) are designed based on optimal detection theory [7].

2.2   Original Extreme Learning Machine

In order to solve the single hidden layer neural network (SLFNs), Huang [8, 13] has proposed a novel fast learning algorithm called extreme learning machine (ELM). The original ELM is shown in Fig. 2.

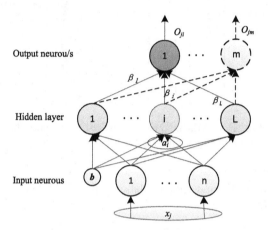

Fig. 2. Structure of ELM with additive hidden nodes: a_i is the total input of i_{th} hidden neuron, dotted lines denote multi-classification case. x_j is the j_{th} input data, O_{ji} represents the i_{th} output.

The first layer's parameters of ELM are randomly generated and does not need to be fine turned and the output weights are obtained by Eq. (8). Huang has proved that ELM has the same solution formula in binary classification case, multi-classification case and regression case [14], thus ELM has the generic form in the application of classification and regression as presents in Fig. 2. Original ELM model is described as follows:

(1) **Define parameters of ELM.** Suppose $\{x_k, t_k | x_k \in R^d, t_k \in R^m, k = 1, \ldots, N\}$ is the training set, where x_k is the k_{th} training vector, t_k represents the k_{th} target output (label) of corresponding training sample, and d, m denote the dimension of training samples and labels respectively, N is the number of training samples. w_{ij} is defined as the random connection weight between i_{th} input neuron and j_{th} hidden neuron, b_j is the bias of j_{th} hidden neuron, they are randomly generated based on Gaussian distribution, and g is a activation function of hidden layer, typically is given by users.

(2) **Calculate the output feature representation matrix H of hidden layer**

$$H = \begin{bmatrix} h_1(x) \\ \vdots \\ h_L(x) \end{bmatrix}^T = \begin{bmatrix} h_1(x_1) & \cdots & h_1(x_N) \\ \vdots & \ddots & \vdots \\ h_L(x_1) & \cdots & h_L(x_N) \end{bmatrix}. \tag{4}$$

$$\text{Where } h_j(x_n) = g\left(\sum_i x_n(i) \cdot w_{i,j} + b_j\right). \tag{5}$$

and $(i = 1, ..., d, j = 1, ..., L, L$ is the number of hidden neurons) [15].

(3) **Calculate the output weights**. The target of our training is to obtain a weight matrix β which satisfies the equation:

$$T = \beta \cdot H \tag{6}$$

where

$$T = \begin{bmatrix} t_1 \\ \vdots \\ t_N \end{bmatrix}^T = \begin{bmatrix} t_{11} & \cdots & t_{1N} \\ \vdots & \ddots & \vdots \\ t_{m1} & \cdots & t_{mN} \end{bmatrix} \tag{7}$$

is the target matrix (labels). Then we can obtain the output weight matrix

$$\beta = T \cdot H^\dagger. \tag{8}$$

where $T = [t_1, ..., t_N]$, $\mathbf{H}^\dagger$ is the Moore-Penrose generalized inverse of matrix $\mathbf{H}$. Typically we can calculate the MP inverse efficiently with the orthogonal projection method [15]: $\mathbf{H}^\dagger = (\mathbf{H}^T\mathbf{H})^{-1}\mathbf{H}^T$, for nonsingular case of $\mathbf{H}^T\mathbf{H}$; if $\mathbf{H}^T\mathbf{H}$ is singular, $\mathbf{H}^\dagger = \mathbf{H}^T(\mathbf{H}\mathbf{H}^T)^{-1}$. According to [14], if a positive value C is added to the diagonal of $\mathbf{H}^T\mathbf{H}$ or $\mathbf{H}\mathbf{H}^T$, the solution could be more stable and has better generalization performance based on the ridge regression theory [16]. Thus the modified β is

$$\beta = T \cdot H^T \left(\frac{I}{C} + HH^T\right)^{-1}. \tag{9}$$

$$\text{or } \beta = T \cdot \left(\frac{I}{C} + H^TH\right)^{-1} H^T. \tag{10}$$

(4) **Trained ELM for classification and regression etc.** The trained output weights β and random connection weights w and biases b is our target parameters for application. If testing data set is $\{S_i \mid S_i \in R^d, i = 1, ..., N_s\}$, then the corresponding output of ELM is as follows while $\mathbf{H}^T\mathbf{H}$ is nonsingular.

$$f(S) = h(S) \cdot \beta = g(w \cdot S + b) \cdot TH^T \left(\frac{I}{C} + HH^T\right)^{-1}. \tag{11}$$

2.3   ELM Auto-Encoder

Auto encoder (AE) is a representative unsupervised deep learning method, typically AE is used for feature extraction from unlabeled input data [17], and it can reduce the redundancies of input data. In addition a multilayer or a deep hierarchy's structure can be built by stacking AEs on top of each other [18].

The ELM auto-encoder (ELM-AE) is a kind of auto encoder which is established based on the random projection and fast learning speed of ELM, it could be seen as a special case of ELM where the input is the target output meanwhile [10], the ELM-AE is consist of three layers as shown in Fig. 3.

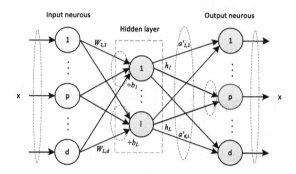

Fig. 3. ELM based auto encoder consists of input, hidden and output layers, w and b are random connection weights and biases, a is the trained output connection weights.

The working process of ELM-AE is as the same as ELM as show in Fig. 2. There are connection weights w, a' between adjacent layers and bias b in hidden layer.

The input weights w and bias b of ELM-AE are randomly generated as the same as ELM in this paper, thus as show in Fig. 3 the input data x is mapped to L-dimensional ELM random feature space first, then transformed to a more stable and generalized feature space by activation function g. The output weights a' form a more stable and generalized projection of the input data than w via the unsupervised learning of ELM, therefore $(a')^\mathrm{T}$ is used as the input weights instead of $(w)^\mathrm{T}$ in ELM-AE as show in Fig. 4.

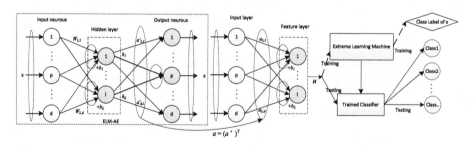

Fig. 4. The schematic diagram of the proposed detector based on ELM-AE for MIMO system

3   ELM Auto-Encoder for MIMO Signal Detection

The signal detection problem of MIMO system is regarded as a classification or pattern recognition problem in this paper, thus it is reasonable to resolve the problem with machine learning algorithms. In this paper, a novel detector for MIMO system based on unsupervised feature learning and classification via ELM based auto-encoder and ELM classifier is proposed, the schematic diagram is presented in Fig. 4. The detection algorithms is designed as follows:

(1) **Train ELM based auto encoder.** ELM based auto-encoder is a special case of ELM, thus the training processing of ELM-AE is the same to ELM: First the input weights and biases of hidden layer $[W, b]$ are randomly initialized based on Gaussian distribution, then the codes and the weights which are utilized to reconstruct input data can be obtained:

$$\text{Random projection code:} h = g(W \cdot x + b). \tag{12}$$

$$\text{The output weights: } a' = x \cdot h^T \left(I/C + h \cdot h^T \right)^{-1}. \tag{13}$$

(2) **Feature projection.** The output weight matrix a' of ELM-AE is served as the output of ELM-AE, and its transposed matrix a is set as the input weight of feature projection layer of the proposed detector:

$$a = \left(a' \right)^T. \tag{14}$$

The output H of feature layer are the feature representations of input data, they are more stable and generalized than the random projection code of ELM-AE:

$$H = g(a \cdot x + b). \tag{15}$$

(3) **Train ELM classifier.** The next step as the dotted arrow shown in Fig. 4 is to train the original ELM classifier after the representations of input data x are obtained. The training sample of the ELM is H. The training label of H is the same to x, it's the target output of our detector. The class label of x could be the corresponding transmitted signal of the received signals x of MIMO system or the class number (corresponds to the transmitted signal) of x, in this paper the class label of x is the later one.

(4) **Testing the detector.** Feature extractor and classifier are obtained from the training above. Then the proposed detector is ready to extract the features of input samples and classify the features to corresponding classes which can reconstruct the information of the transmitted symbols.

4   Simulation and Performance Evaluation

Computer simulations are conducted to investigate the performance of the proposed ELM-AE detector. Simulations are based on a simplified 4×4 point to point BPSK modulated MIMO system. Suppose the channel state H is known.

4.1 Parameter Selection

In this section, some simulations have been conducted to search for the best parameters of the proposed detector.

Figure 5(a) shows the testing result of positive value C and the number of hidden neurons L. In this simulation C and L are set as $\{10^{-9}, 10^{-8}, ..., 10^0, ..., 10^7, 10^8, 10^9\}$, $\{10, 20, ..., 440, 450\}$ respectively. The '*TestingRate*' represents the difference value of bit error rate (BER) of ML detector and the proposed detector. The results indicate that the BER performance could be better when C ranges form 10^{-3} to 10^1 and L is more than 100, in the next simulations L is set as 120, and C is set as $1/snr$ in this paper where *snr* represents signal to noise ratio.

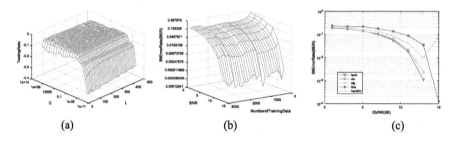

(a)   (b)   (c)

Fig. 5. (a) The error rate performance of the proposed detector compare to ML detection at different point of (C, L) when Eb/N0 = 7; (b) The BER performance of different number of training data; (c) Activation function testing.

Figure 5(b) shows the BER performance of different number of training data. Based on the results the training samples is set as 2400 × 4 in the next experiments under the premise that the performance is guaranteed.

This paper selects and uses *tanh* as the activation function of ELM and ELM-AE, as show in Fig. 5(c), arc-tan function *tanh* outperforms sine function *sin*, hard limit function *hardlim*, and sigmoid function *sig*, while the hidden layer number is 1, hidden neurons L = 120, the positive value C = 1/snr.

4.2 Comparisons Between ELM-AE Detector and Other Detection Methods

In order to verify the good performance of the proposed ELM-AE detector, this section carried out the traditional detection algorithms ML, ZF, MMSE in Fig. 6(a), and several state-of-the-art detection algorithms such as ZF-SIC, MMSE-SIC, QGA-RBF for comparison in Fig. 6(b).

Figure 6 and Table 1 illustrate the bit error rate, the mean detection time and the mean error rates compares to ML detector of these algorithms. It is event that the proposed detector outperforms the detector based on ZF, MMSE, and reaches a similar performance to the optimal detector ML from Fig. 6(a). Figure 6(b) indicates that the performance of the proposed detector outperforms ZF-SIC, MMSE-SIC, and exceeds QGA-RBF detection when SNR is more than 9 dB. The detection time of the proposed algorithm is 0.9402 s which is 20-times the detection speed of ML while detecting the

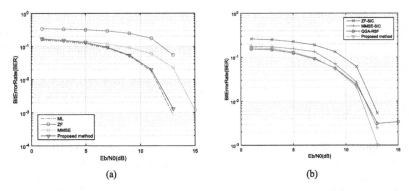

Fig. 6. (a) The performance curve of traditional algorithms (ML, ZF, MMSE) and the proposed method for MIMO signal detection; (b) The performance curve of several different state-of-the-art algorithms (ZF-SIC, MMSE-SIC, QGA-RBF) and the proposed method for MIMO signal detection.

symbols one by one, but the proposed algorithm supports the way of block detection and detection efficiency increase 4.4 times.

Table 1. The mean detection time and error rates to ML detector.

Methods	Detection time (s)	Mean error rate $\sum(BER_x - BER_{ML})/n$
Traditional detection algorithms		
ML	20.2356	0
ZF	0.7630	0.1525
MMSE	0.7594	0.0217
State-of-the-art detection algorithms		
ZF-SIC	4.7704	0.0695
MMSE-SIC	4.7386	0.0206
QGA-RBF	19.3495	0.0013
Proposed method	0.9402/0.2119	0.0042

In addition, channel estimation is not required in the proposed algorithm while the channel sate is contained in the output connection weights learnt from the unsupervised learning of ELM-AE.

5   Conclusion

In this paper, the Extreme Learning Machine based auto encoder is applied to MIMO system for signal detection. The signal detection scheme for MIMO system based on ELM-AE is proposed, channel estimation is embedded in learnt connection weights of ELM-AE, and the simulations of detection performance are made and analyzed, the simulation results show that the proposed scheme not only has better performance than many linear and nonlinear detection schemes, but also reaches much lower complexity than these methods, and its performance is very close to optimal detection algorithm. Massive MIMO system is a wide concerned MIMO system, its channel capacity is much higher than normal MIMO system, while the detection complexity is much higher at the same time, which is a big obstacle for its application. In the future works we will going to apply this detection scheme to massive MIMO system, and searching the possibility of reducing the detection complexity.

Acknowledgments.   The authors would like to thank the anonymous reviewers for their constructive and insightful comments for further improving the quality of this work. The research work was partially supported by the National Natural Science Foundation of China under Grant (61263005, 61563009), New Century Talents Project of the Ministry of Education under Grant No. NCET-12-0657.

References

1. Telatar, E.: Capacity of multi-antenna Gaussian channels. Trans. Emerg. Telecommun. Technol. **10**(6), 585–595 (1999)
2. Zhu, X., Murch, R.D.: Performance analysis of maximum likelihood detection in a MIMO antenna system. IEEE Trans. Commun. **50**(2), 187–191 (2002)
3. Liu, D.N., Fitz, M.P.: Low complexity affine MMSE detector for iterative detection-decoding MIMO OFDM systems. IEEE Trans. Commun. **56**(1), 150–158 (2008)
4. Xu, J., Tao, X., Zhang, P.: Analytical SER performance bound of M-QAM MIMO system with ZF-SIC receiver. In: IEEE International Conference on Communications, pp. 5103–5107 (2008)
5. Sarkar, S.: An advanced detection technique in MIMO-PSK wireless communication systems using MMSE-SIC detection over a Rayleigh fading channel. CSI Trans. ICT **3**(10), 1–7 (2016)
6. Li, F., Zhou, M., Li, H.: A novel neural network optimized by quantum genetic algorithm for signal detection in MIMO-OFDM systems. In: IEEE Symposium on Computational Intelligence in Control & Automation, CICA, pp. 170–177. IEEE (2011)
7. Yang, Y., Hu, F., Jiang, Z.: Signal detection of MIMO system based on quantum ant colony algorithm. In: IEEE International Conference on Signal Processing, Communications and Computing, ICSPCC, pp. 1–5. IEEE (2016)
8. Huang, G.B., Li, M.B., Chen, L., Siew, C.K.: Incremental extreme learning machine with fully complex hidden nodes. Neurocomputing **71**(4–6), 576–583 (2008)
9. Huang, G.B.: An insight into extreme learning machines: random neurons, random features and kernels. Cogn. Comput. **6**(3), 376–390 (2014)
10. Kasun, L.L.C., Zhou, H., Huang, G.B., Chi, M.V.: Representation learning with ELMs for Big Data. IEEE Intell. Syst. **28**(6), 31–34 (2013)
11. Liu, L., Lofgren, J., Nilsson, P.: Low-complexity likelihood information generation for spatial-multiplexing MIMO signal detection. IEEE Trans. Veh. Technol. **61**(2), 607–617 (2012)
12. Rusek, F., Persson, D., Lau, B.K., Larsson, E.G., Marzetta, T.L., Edfors, O., Tufvesson, F.: Scaling up MIMO: opportunities and challenges with very large arrays. IEEE Signal Process. Mag. **30**(1), 40–60 (2012)

13. Huang, G.B., Chen, L., Siew, C.K.: Universal approximation using incremental constructive feedforward networks with random hidden nodes. IEEE Trans. Neural Networks **17**(4), 879–892 (2006)
14. Huang, G.B., Zhou, H., Ding, X., Zhang, R.: Extreme learning machine for regression and multiclass classification. IEEE Trans. Syst. Man Cybern. Part B **42**(2), 513–529 (2012)
15. Tang, J., Deng, C., Huang, G.B.: Extreme learning machine for multilayer perceptron. IEEE Trans. Neural Netw. Learn. Syst. **27**(4), 809 (2016)
16. Hoerl, A.E., Kennard, R.W.: Ridge regression: biased estimation for nonorthogonal problems. Technometrics **12**(1), 55–67 (1970)
17. Fei, W., Ye, X., Sun, Z., Huang, Y., Zhang, X., Shang, S.: Research on speech emotion recognition based on deep auto-encoder. In: IEEE International Conference on Cyber Technology in Automation, Control, and Intelligent Systems, CYBER (2016)
18. Masci, J., Meier, U., Cireşan, D., Schmidhuber, J.: Stacked convolutional auto-encoders for hierarchical feature extraction. In: Honkela, T., Duch, W., Girolami, M., Kaski, S. (eds.) ICANN 2011. LNCS, vol. 6791, pp. 52–59. Springer, Heidelberg (2011). doi: 10.1007/978-3-642-21735-7_7

Low-Frequency Representation for Face Recognition

Bangjun Wang[1,2], Li Zhang[2(✉)], and Fanzhang Li[1,2]

[1] Machine Learning and Cognitive Computing Lab., School of Computer and Information Technology, Beijing Jiaotong University, Beijing 100044, China
[2] School of Computer Science and Technology & Joint International Research Laboratory of Machine Learning and Neuromorphic Computing, Soochow University, Suzhou 215006, China
{wangbangjun,zhangliml}@suda.edu.cn

Abstract. This paper proposes a low-frequency representation (LFR) method for face images based on support value transform. LFR works directly on 2D image matrices rather than 1D vectors, thus the image matrix does not need to be transformed into a vector prior to feature extraction. In LFR, the simple and slowly variational features for face images are remained. To demonstrate the effectiveness of LFR, a series of experiments are performed on two face image databases: ORL and UMIST face databases. Experimental results indicate that LFR provides a better representation for face images with multi-view and slightly various illumination.

Keywords: Face recognition · Support value transform · Low-frequency representation · Feature extraction · Image representation

1 Introduction

In machine learning, the study of face recognition has been underway for quite a long time [1]. Face recognition is usually divided into four processes [2]: face segmentation (detection), face alignment, feature extraction, and face matching. This paper deals with feature extraction for face recognition. The main purpose of feature extraction is to reduce the distance between similar images, and enlarge the distance between dissimilar images at the same time. Feature extraction can improve the robustness of face recognition and ease the problem of small scale samples.

Face feature extraction normally adopts one of the following two types of extractions, or geometric feature based or appearance based extraction. Geometric feature based methods focus on the facial features, such as the relationships between the jaw, nose, mouth and eyes [3,4]. Appearance based methods view an image as a point in an $m \times n$ dimensional space. Particularly, there are two widely used linear methods, principal component analysis (PCA) and linear discriminant analysis (LDA). Eigenfaces was used to represent face images based

© Springer International Publishing AG 2017
D. Liu et al. (Eds.): ICONIP 2017, Part VI, LNCS 10639, pp. 510–519, 2017.
https://doi.org/10.1007/978-3-319-70136-3_54

on PCA [5]. Belhumeur et al. proposed Fisherfaces based on LDA and PCA [6]. The nonlinear versions of PCA and LDA methods have also been proposed [7–9]. Another popular face features are Laplacianfaces which are generated by locality preserving projections (LPP) and PCA [10]. In [11,12], a random projection (RP) method was used for face feature extraction, and experimental results suggested that RP is an effective dimension reduction method in face recognition when applying sparse representation-based classifier.

Appearance based methods do not consider the spacial information in an image. To extract sufficient discriminant information and reduce the computational complexity, two-dimensional (2D) appearance-based feature extraction methods have been proposed [13–15]. Two-dimensional principal component analysis (2DPCA) was presented in [13]. In 2DPCA, an image covariance matrix is constructed by using the original image matrices. Since it directly works on 2D images, 2DPCA is more computationally efficient than PCA. Li et al. proposed two-dimensional linear discriminant analysis (2DLDA) [14,15].

This paper proposes a novel 2D feature extraction method by using a filtering method. In this method, a set of filters are first designed based on multiscale mapped least squared support vector machine (LS-SVM) [16]. Then the low-frequency representation (LFR) for a given face image is extracted by using support value transform and the designed filters. Similar to 2DPCA and 2DLDA, LFR is also based on 2D image matrices rather than 1D vectors, thus the image matrix does not need to be transformed into a vector prior to feature extraction.

The rest of this paper is organized as follows. In Sect. 2, we propose a novel feature extraction method for face recognition. We show experimental results on two face datasets in Sect. 3 and conclude this paper in Sect. 4.

2 Face Recognition Using Support Value Transform

In this section, we introduce support value transform (SVT) to extract face features for face recognition.

2.1 Multiscale Mapped LS-SVM

The multiscale mapped LS-SVM [16] is an extension of the mapped LS-SVM [18] which was proposed for estimating the underlying intensity surface of an image. Both the multiscale mapped LS-SVM and the mapped LS-SVM are variants of LS-SVM [19]. In fact, all three LS-SVMs have the same optimization formulation. Below we only introduce the multiscale mapped LS-SVM.

Given a set of training samples $\{\mathbf{x}_i, y_i\}_{i=1}^{\ell}$, where $\mathbf{x}_i \in \mathbb{R}^2$ denotes a pixel coordinate in a given image, $y_i \in \mathbb{R}$ is the intensity value of this image, and ℓ is the number of training samples, the multiscale mapped LS-SVM tries to find a function $f(\mathbf{x})$ to approximate the relationship between $\mathbf{x}_i$ and y_i. For a $(2m + 1) \times (2n + 1)$ image block, the training sample $\mathbf{x}_i$ takes value from the interval $\{-m, -m+1, \cdots, m\} \times \{-n, -n+1, \cdots, n\}$ when subtracting the center coordinate of image block, and $\ell = (2m + 1) \times (2n + 1)$. Usually, $m = n$.

In the multiscale mapped LS-SVM, the estimated regression function $f(\mathbf{x})$ has the form:

$$f(\mathbf{x}) = \sum_{i=1}^{\ell} \sum_{j=1}^{r} \left(\alpha_i^j k_j(\mathbf{x}_i, \mathbf{x}) + b_j \right) \tag{1}$$

where r is the number of decomposition level, $k_j(\mathbf{x}_i, \mathbf{x}_j)$ is the jth Mercer kernel function, α_i^j is the jth coefficient corresponding to the training sample $\mathbf{x}_i$ and b_j is the jth threshold. α_i^j and b_j are deduced from the jth kernel function, which could be the multiscale Gaussian kernels, or

$$k_j(\mathbf{x}_i, \mathbf{x}_p) = \exp\left(-\frac{\|\mathbf{x}_i - \mathbf{x}_p\|^2}{2^j \sigma^2} \right), \quad j = 1, 2, \cdots, r \tag{2}$$

where $\sigma > 0$ is the kernel parameter. Let $\mathbf{K}$ be the Gram kernel matrix, in which the element on the ith row and pth column is $k(\mathbf{x}_i, \mathbf{x}_p)$. Thus, we can obtain a series Gram matrix $\{\mathbf{K}_1, \mathbf{K}_2, \cdots, \mathbf{K}_r\}$ according to (2).

To solve the multiscale mapped LS-SVM, a sequential strategy is used [16]. At each level j, we need to find the solution to the set of linear equations as follows:

$$\begin{bmatrix} 0 & \mathbf{e}^T \\ \mathbf{e} & \boldsymbol{\Omega}_j \end{bmatrix} \begin{bmatrix} b_j \\ \boldsymbol{\alpha}^j \end{bmatrix} = \begin{bmatrix} 0 \\ \mathbf{Y}_j \end{bmatrix} \tag{3}$$

where $\mathbf{e}$ is the column vector of ones, $\boldsymbol{\alpha}^j = [\alpha_1^j, \cdots, \alpha_\ell^j]$, $\boldsymbol{\Omega}_j = \mathbf{K}_j + C_j \mathbf{I}$, $\mathbf{I}$ is the identify matrix, $C_j \geq 0$ is the jth regularization factor, $\mathbf{K}_j$ is constructed from $k_j(\cdot, \cdot)$, and

$$\mathbf{Y}_j = \begin{cases} \mathbf{Y}_{j-1} - \sum_{i=1}^{\ell} \left(\alpha_i^{j-1} \mathbf{k}_{j-1}(\cdot, \mathbf{x}_i) + b_{j-1} \right), & if \ \ j > 1 \\ \mathbf{Y}_1, & if \ \ j = 1 \end{cases} \tag{4}$$

where $\mathbf{k}_{j-1}(\cdot, \mathbf{x}_i) = [k_{j-1}(\mathbf{x}_1, \mathbf{x}_i), \cdots, k_{j-1}(\mathbf{x}_\ell, \mathbf{x}_i)]^T$ and $\mathbf{Y}_1 = [y_1, \cdots, y_\ell]^T$.

The solution to (3) can be expressed as

$$\boldsymbol{\alpha}^j = \boldsymbol{\Omega}_j^{-1}(\mathbf{Y}_j - b_j \mathbf{e}) \tag{5}$$

and

$$b_j = \frac{\mathbf{e}^T \boldsymbol{\Omega}_j^{-1} \mathbf{Y}_j}{\mathbf{e}^T \boldsymbol{\Omega}_j^{-1} \mathbf{e}}. \tag{6}$$

where $\boldsymbol{\Omega}_j^{-1}$ is the inverse matrix of $\boldsymbol{\Omega}_j$.

2.2   Multiscale Support Value Filters

The multiscale support value filters (MSVFs) are constructed by using the multiscale mapped LS-SVM. Let

$$\mathbf{A}_j = \boldsymbol{\Omega}_j^{-1} \tag{7}$$

and

$$\mathbf{B}_j = \frac{\mathbf{e}^T \boldsymbol{\Omega}_j^{-1}}{\mathbf{e}^T \boldsymbol{\Omega}_j^{-1} \mathbf{e}}. \tag{8}$$

Then, we can respectively rewritten (5) and (6) as

$$\boldsymbol{\alpha}^j = \mathbf{A}_j(\mathbf{Y} - b_j\mathbf{e}) \tag{9}$$

and

$$b_j = \mathbf{B}_j^T\mathbf{Y}. \tag{10}$$

Substituting (10) into (9), we have

$$\boldsymbol{\alpha}^j = \mathbf{A}_j(\mathbf{I} - \mathbf{e}\mathbf{B}_j^T)\mathbf{Y} = \mathbf{Q}_j\mathbf{Y}, \tag{11}$$

where $\mathbf{Q}_j \in \mathbb{R}^{\ell \times \ell}, j = 1, 2, \cdots, r$. The jth support value filter $\mathbf{SV}_j$ is deduced from the central row vector of the matrix $\mathbf{Q}_j$ by reshaping this row vector into a $(2m + 1) \times (2m + 1)$ matrix.

2.3 Extracting Face Features Based on Support Value Transform

By using MSVFs, we can perform support value transform (SVT), which is a multiresolution transform with frame elements indexed by scale and location parameters [16,17]. Given a face image $\mathbf{P}$ and a series of scaled-related support value filters $\{\mathbf{SV}_1, \cdots, \mathbf{SV}_r\}$, the support value images can be generated by

$$\mathbf{S}_j = \mathbf{LP}_j * \mathbf{SV}_j, j = 1, \cdots, r, \tag{12}$$

where $*$ denotes the convolution operation, $\mathbf{S}_j$ is the jth support value image, $\mathbf{LP}_1 = \mathbf{P}$ and $\mathbf{LP}_{j+1} = \mathbf{LP}_j - \mathbf{S}_j, j = 1, \cdots, r$. $\mathbf{LP}_{r+1}$ is the resulted low-frequency image.

Therefore, we can obtain the low-frequency component image $\mathbf{LP}_{r+1}$ and the series of support value images $\{\mathbf{S}_1, \cdots, \mathbf{S}_r\}$ when applying SVT on a face image. In [16–18], these support value images $\{\mathbf{S}_1, \cdots, \mathbf{S}_r\}$ are considered as the salient features of the original image. However, we found that these images are useless to classify face images. The only useful image is the low-frequency one, which contains the main information of face images. Figure 1 gives an example of SVT, which explains why the low-frequency is taken as the feature image. The original face image is one sample coming from the ORL dataset. Let the decomposition level $r = 2$. We get two SVIs $\mathbf{S}_i, i = 1, 2$ and one low-frequency image $\mathbf{LP}_3$. We can see that $\mathbf{S}_1$ and $\mathbf{S}_2$ are contours of the original face. The low-frequency image $\mathbf{LP}_3$ is very similar to the original face image, which contains the main information of the face image.

2.4 Face Recognition Using LRF

As mentioned above, we know that SVT is a transform that can extract the low-frequency representation of a given face image. The low-frequency representations of all original face images are obtained by using the same SVT. Note that SVT is definitely independent of the given face images. The nearest neighbor (NN) classifier is used for classify the low-frequency representations of test

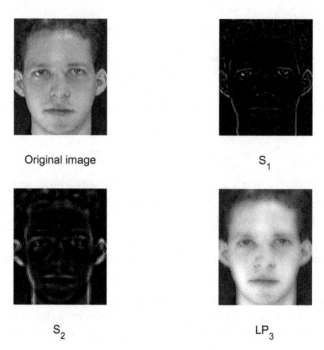

Original image

S_1

S_2

LP_3

Fig. 1. An example of SVT on face image, (a) Original image, (b) SVI: S_1, (c) SVI: S_2 and (d) Low-frequency image: LP_3. The decomposition level $r = 2$.

face images. The reason we use NN is that it is one of the simplest methods for performing general, non-parametric classification. The Euclidean metric is used as our distance measure. However, there might be some more sophisticated and better distance metric, e.g., variance normalized distance, which may be used to improve the recognition performance. In addition, other classifiers could also be adopted, such as support vector machines. In this paper, we focus on the feature representation of the original images instead of their classifiers.

Given a set of training images $\{\mathbf{P}_i, v_i\}_{i=1}^{L}$, we use the series of scaled-related support value filters $\{\mathbf{SV}_1, \cdots, \mathbf{SV}_r\}$ to obtain the set of corresponding LFRs $\{\mathbf{Z}_i, v_i\}_{i=1}^{L}$ where $\mathbf{Z}_i = (\mathbf{LP}_{r+1})_i$ are the LFR images. Given a test sample $\mathbf{P}$, we also compute its LFR $\mathbf{Z}$. The distance between $\mathbf{Z}$ and the training LFR images is defined by

$$d(\mathbf{Z}, \mathbf{Z}_i) = \|\mathbf{Z} - \mathbf{Z}_i\|_F, \tag{13}$$

where $\|\cdot\|_F$ is the Frobenius norm. If $d(\mathbf{Z}, \mathbf{Z}_j) = \min_i d(\mathbf{Z}, \mathbf{Z}_i)$, then $\mathbf{Z}$ or $\mathbf{P}$ will be assigned a class label v_j.

3   Experimental Results

To validate the efficiency of feature extraction using SVT, we perform experiments on two face datasets, the ORL and UMIST datasets. All numerical experiments are performed on a personal computer with a 2.93 GHz Intel(R) Core(T)2 Duo CPU and 2 G bytes of memory. This computer runs on Windows 7, with Matlab 7.01 and VC++ 6.0 compiler installed.

3.1   Compared Methods and Their Parameters

We compare LRF with other feature extraction methods for face images, including Eigenface, Fisherface, Laplacianface, random projection, 2DPCA and 2DLDA. For 2DPCA and 2DLDA, we keep the number of non-zero eigenvalues as the features of subspace. The parameters of other algorithms are described as follows:

Eigenface: It is the PCA method. To keep all useful information, the number of selected features is set to be the number of non-zero eigenvalues.

Fisherface: It is the PCA+LDA method. Generally, the dimensionality of the reduced space is $(c - 1)$, where c is the number of face classes.

Laplacianfaces: It is the PCA+LPP method. Similar to Eigenface, the dimensionality of the reduced space is the number of non-zero eigenvalues.

Random projection (RP): In this method, a Gaussian random matrix is taken as the projection matrix.

Low-frequency representation: In SVT, let the kernel parameter $\sigma = 1/\sqrt{2}$, and the regularization factors $C_j = 2^{1-j}, j = 1, \cdots, r - 1$ and $C_r = 0$, where r is the defined decomposition level. When $r = 1$, the support value filter can be described as:

$$
\begin{pmatrix}
-0.0405 & -0.0402 & -0.0401 & -0.0402 & -0.0405 \\
-0.0402 & -0.0398 & -0.0493 & -0.0398 & -0.0402 \\
-0.0401 & -0.0493 & 1.0000 & -0.0493 & -0.0401 \\
-0.0402 & -0.0398 & -0.0493 & -0.0398 & -0.0402 \\
-0.0405 & -0.0402 & -0.0401 & -0.0402 & -0.0405
\end{pmatrix}
\tag{14}
$$

3.2   Experiments on ORL Dataset

We perform experiments on the ORL face database [20] and take into account the effect of decomposition level r on face recognition. The ORL face data set has 10 different images for each subject and consists of 40 distinct subjects. All subjects are in up-right, frontal position (with tolerance for some side movement). The size of each face image is 112×92. In addition, the features for NN take values from the interval $[0, 1]$. The number of images for both training and test is 200. We randomly sample the dataset 100 trials and report the average results. Since SVT can not implement dimension reduction, we first use the down-sampling method to reduce the size of face images. Three sizes are adopted, 112×92, 64×64 and 32×32. Small size is for some method, say LDA, which can not be directly applied to high-dimensional data due to the memory limitation of a personal computer.

In the size of 112×92, the decomposition size r varies from 1 to 5. The low-frequency representations of a person under different levels are shown in Fig. 2.

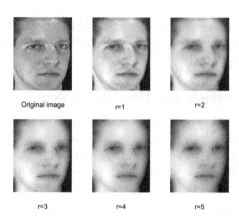

Fig. 2. Low-frequency representations of a person under different levels.

On the ORL dataset, the smaller the level is, the closer the low-frequency representation is to the original image. The larger the level is, the smoother the low-frequency representation. In order words, the simple and slowly variational features are remained. For the sizes of 64 × 64 and 32 × 32, r respectively changes from 1 to 4 and from 1 to 3. A similar phenomenon as in Fig. 2 can be observed. Thus, the low-frequency images in the two sizes are not shown. Table 1 lists the running time for obtaining low-frequency representations of all 400 face images and the average error rates on 100 test sets. We can see that the higher the level is, the better the performance and the higher the running time on the ORL dataset. All things considered, the three-level decomposition works quite well on this dataset. In addition, the adoption of down-sampling does not damage the feature information when combining with SVT. In the case of 32 × 32, a better performance is achieved.

The average test errors obtained by all methods are shown in Table 2. For our method, only the results of $r = 3$ are given. Note that we try to extract all useful features instead of dimension reduction. Thus, we keep the maximum

Table 1. Performance of the ORL dataset using LFR

112 × 92	Decomposition level	1	2	3	4	5
	Time(sec.)	0.0624	0.1092	0.4424	4.9140	112.2895
	Error rate (%)	5.45 ± 1.72	5.18 ± 1.73	4.99 ± 1.68	4.82 ± 1.83	4.69 ± 1.81
64 × 64	Decomposition level	1	2	3	4	-
	Time(sec.)	0.06404	0.1028	0.4524	4.8048	-
	Error rate (%)	5.42 ± 1.76	5.02 ± 1.74	4.71 ± 1.75	4.54 ± 1.71	
32 × 32	Decomposition level	1	2	3	-	-
	Time(sec.)	0.0736	0.098	0.4356	-	-
	Error rate (%)	4.90 ± 1.76	4.55 ± 1.63	3.99 ± 1.55	-	-

Table 2. Average test error rates (%) on the ORL dataset

Size	Eigenface	Fisherface	Laplacianface	RP	2DPCA	2DLDA	LFR
112 × 92	-	-	-	5.87 ± 1.74	5.79 ± 1.66	**4.33** ± 1.60	4.99 ± 1.68
64 × 64	5.63 ± 1.72	7.73 ± 1.95	20.29 ± 2.98	5.75 ± 1.67	5.63 ± 1.72	**4.39** ± 1.61	4.71 ± 1.75
32 × 32	5.38 ± 1.70	7.46 ± 2.04	15.23 ± 2.61	5.52 ± 1.61	5.38 ± 1.70	4.76 ± 1.63	**3.99** ± 1.55

feature number for each method. The symbol "-" in Table 2 denotes that there is no result for the corresponding method due to out of memory. 2DLDA has the best performance for the size of 112 × 92 and 64 × 64, and is followed by our method. In addition, LRF obtains the best result 3.99% in the case of 32 × 32.

3.3   Experiments on UMIST Face Dataset

We also test our method on the UMIST face database [21]. The UMIST face database is a multi-view database which consists of 574 cropped gray-scale images of 20 subjects, each covering a wide range of poses from profile to frontal views as well as race, gender and appearance. Each original image in the database is 112 × 92. We resize them to 32 × 32 using the down-sampling method.

We consider how the training number affects recognition accuracy. The number of the training samples in each subject varies from 1 to 11, and the rest samples are test ones. We randomly select the training samples from the dataset and repeat 100 trials. Let $r = 3$ for LFR. The average results are reported in Fig. 3. Observation on this figure indicates that the classification performance of

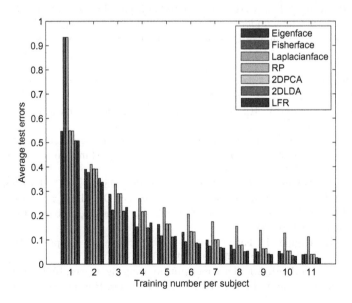

Fig. 3. Average test errors vs. training number.

all methods improves as the training number increases. When there is only one training number in each subject, all methods have bad performance. The test errors are larger than 50%. 2DLDA and LFR are better than other methods on the UMIST dataset. LFR outperforms 2DLDA except for the case of when the training number in each subject is 3, 4 or 8.

4 Conclusion

This paper introduces support value transform to extract the low-frequency representation of given face images. LFR is based on 2D image matrices rather than 1D vectors so the image matrix does not need to be transformed into a vector prior to feature extraction. SVT can extract a LFR for the original face image. In LFR, the simple and slowly variational features are remained. However, LFR can not directly implement dimension reduction. In experiments, we combine LFR with the down-sampling method to reduce the dimensionality of the original face images. Experimental results show the efficiency of our scheme. The experiments are performed on two public face datasets available, ORL and UMIST datasets. Average test errors on both ORL and UMIST indicate that the performance of LFR and 2DLDA are comparable, and are better than other methods.

LFR can achieve satisfactory performance on face images with multi-view and slightly various illumination, such as the ORL and UMIST face databases. In the future, we try to deal with face images greatly various lighting conditions using LFR.

Acknowledgments. This work was supported in part by the National Natural Science Foundation of China under Grant Nos. 61373093 and 61672364, and by the Natural Science Foundation of Jiangsu Province of China under Grant No. BK20140008.

References

1. Bruner, I.S., Tagiuri, R.: The Perception of People. American Psychologist. Addison-Wesley, Boston (1954)
2. Introna, L.D., Nissenbaum, H.: Facial recognition technology: a survey of policy and implementation issues. Social Science Electronic Publishing, New York University (2009)
3. Wiskott, L., Fellous, J.-M., Krüger, N., von der Malsburg, C.: Face recognition by elastic bunch graph matching. In: Sommer, G., Daniilidis, K., Pauli, J. (eds.) CAIP 1997. LNCS, vol. 1296, pp. 456–463. Springer, Heidelberg (1997). doi:10.1007/3-540-63460-6_150
4. Brunelli, R., Poggio, T.: Face recognition: features versus templates. IEEE Trans. Pattern Anal. Mach. Intell. **15**(10), 1042–1052 (1993)
5. Turk, M.A., Pentland, A.P.: Face recognition using eigenfaces. In: IEEE Conference on Computer Vision and Pattern Recognition, Maui, Hawaii, vol. 84, pp. 586–591 (2002)

6. Belhumeur, P.N., Hespanha, J.P., Kriegman, D.J.: Eigenfaces vs. Fisherfaces: recognition using class specific linear projection. In: Buxton, B., Cipolla, R. (eds.) ECCV 1996. LNCS, vol. 1064, pp. 43–58. Springer, Heidelberg (1996). doi:10.1007/BFb0015522

7. Baudat, G., Anouar, F.: Generalized Discriminant Analysis Using a Kernel Approach. MIT Press, Cambridge (2000)

8. Kim, K.I., Jung, K., Hang, J.K.: Face recognition using kernel principal component analysis. IEEE Signal Process. Lett. 9(2), 40–42 (2002)

9. Zhang, L., Zhou, W.D., Zhang, H., Jiao, L.C.: Generalized nonlinear discriminant analysis. In: International Conference on Pattern Recognition, vol. 74, pp. 1–4. IEEE (2008)

10. He, X., Yan, S., Hu, Y., Niyogi, P., Zhang, H.J.: Face recognition using Laplacianfaces. IEEE Trans. Pattern Anal. Mach. Intell. 27(3), 328–340 (2005)

11. Wright, J., Yang, A.Y., Ganesh, A., Sastry, S.S., Ma, Y.: Robust face recognition via sparse representation. IEEE Trans. Pattern Anal. Mach. Intell. 31(2), 210–227 (2009)

12. Zhang, L., Zhou, W.D., Chang, P.C., Liu, J., Yan, Z., Wang, T., Li, F.Z.: Kernel sparse representation-based classifier. IEEE Trans. Signal Process. 60(4), 1684–1695 (2012)

13. Yang, J., Zhang, D., Frangi, A.F., Yang, J.Y.: Two-dimensional PCA: a new approach to appearance-based face representation and recognition. IEEE Trans. Pattern Anal. Mach. Intell. 26(1), 131–137 (2004)

14. Li, M., Yuan, B.: 2D-LDA: a statistical linear discriminant analysis for image matrix. Pattern Recogn. Lett. 26(5), 527–532 (2005)

15. Liang, Z., Shi, P., Zhang, D.: Two-dimensional fisher discriminant analysis and its application to face recognition. In: Narayanan, P.J., Nayar, S.K., Shum, H.-Y. (eds.) ACCV 2006. LNCS, vol. 3851, pp. 130–139. Springer, Heidelberg (2006). doi:10.1007/11612032_14

16. Zheng, S., Shi, W.Z., Liu, J., Tian, J.W.: Remote sensing image fusion using multiscale mapped LS-SVM. IEEE Trans. Geosci. Remote Sens. 46(5), 1313–1322 (2008)

17. Zheng, S., Shi, W.A., Liu, J., Zhu, G.X., Tian, J.W.: Multisource image fusion method using support value transform. IEEE Trans. Image Process. 16(7), 1831–1893 (2007)

18. Zheng, S., Sun, Y.Q., Tian, J., Liu, J.: Mapped least squares support vector machine regression. Int. J. Pattern Recogn. Artif. Intell. 19(3), 459–475 (2005)

19. Suykens, J.A.K., Vandewalle, J.: Least squares support vector machine classifiers. Neural Process. Lett. 9(3), 293–300 (1999)

20. Samaria, F.S., Harter, A.C.: Parameterisation of a stochastic model for human face identification. In: Proceedings of the 2nd IEEE International Workshop on Applications of Computer Vision, Sarasota, Florida, pp. 138–142 (1994)

21. Graham, D.B., Allinson, N.M.: Characterising virtual eigensignatures for general purpose face recognition. In: Wechsler, H., Phillips, P.J., Bruce, V., Soulié, F.F., Huang, T.S. (eds.) Face Recognition: From Theory to Applications. NATO ASI Series F, Computer and Systems Sciences, vol. 163, pp. 446–456. Springer, Heidelberg (1998). doi:10.1007/978-3-642-72201-1_25

Robustness of Selective Desensitization Perceptron Against Irrelevant and Partially Relevant Features in Pattern Classification

Tomohiro Tanno[✉], Kazumasa Horie, Jun Izawa, and Masahiko Morita

University of Tsukuba, 1-1-1 Tennodai, Tsukuba, Ibaraki, Japan
{tanno,mor}@bcl.esys.tsukuba.ac.jp, horie@bipl-sdnn.org,
izawa@emp.tsukuba.ac.jp

Abstract. Recent practical studies have shown that a selective desensitization neural network (SDNN) is a high-performance function approximator that is robust against redundant input dimensions. This paper examined the classification performance of a single-output-SDNN, which we refer to as a selective desensitization perceptron (SDP), through a numerical experiment on binary classification problems that include some irrelevant features and partially relevant features and compared these results with multilayer perceptron (MLP) and support vector machine (SVM) classification methods. The results show that SDP was highly effective not only in dealing with irrelevant features but also in a dataset including a partially relevant feature, which is irrelevant in most of the domain but affects the output in a specific domain. These results indicate that the previously observed SDNN's high-performance in the practical problems might be originated from the fact that SDP does not require a precise feature selection with taking account of the various degrees of feature relevance.

Keywords: Binary classification · Selective desensitization perceptron · Irrelevant feature · Partially relevant feature

1 Introduction

When one uses a classifier for solving a practical problem with a multidimensional dataset, it is typically unknown whether the dataset includes redundant dimensions and which dimensions are actually redundant for this classification problem. Therefore, the user of a classifier often uses all features available even though many irrelevant features may be included. However, irrelevant features are known to have harmful effects on learning processes, such as increases in learning time and degradation of classification accuracy. For example, although support vector machines (SVMs) with radial basis function (RBF) kernel are known to exhibit excellent performance with binary classification problems, their accuracy severely decreases when the dataset includes irrelevant features [1,2]. To deal with this, multiple methods of feature selection have been proposed in

© Springer International Publishing AG 2017
D. Liu et al. (Eds.): ICONIP 2017, Part VI, LNCS 10639, pp. 520–529, 2017.
https://doi.org/10.1007/978-3-319-70136-3_55

order to improve the performance via removal of irrelevant features [2,3]. However, these methods often require prior and technical knowledge, time, and effort. Besides, the accuracy may not be improved by feature selection when some features seem to be irrelevant but are actually relevant in a specific condition. For example, the features may be irrelevant in most of the domain but relevant in a certain range of their (or other feature's) respective domains. We refer to these features as "partially relevant features" here. These features may degrade the classification accuracy like irrelevant features, but they should not be completely removed because they may be critical to solve the pattern in a certain domain.

For example, a multilayer perceptron (MLP) is a layered neural network known to be relatively robust to irrelevant features, i.e., the degradation of the classification accuracy is small. This is because its structure enables it to ignore their effects by decaying the synaptic weight of the input [4]. However, because it completely ignores the feature, it is predicted that the MLP cannot consider the partial relevance of the feature.

In contrast, a selective desensitization neural network (SDNN) is another layered neural network that exhibits some superiority as a function approximator. A study on continuous-state reinforcement learning showed that SDNN performed well when approximating a value function that included some redundant dimensions [5]. Furthermore, Nonaka et al. showed that SDNN could accurately approximate a complicated function that outputs a constant value in a specific domain; this can be considered as the case that the features are partially irrelevant to the output [6]. Although the SDNN is a function approximator, the output layer of SDNN is comprised of a set of simple perceptrons, each of which can be regarded as a binary classifier. Considering these properties of SDNN combined with its previously reported robustness, we hypothesized that a single-output-SDNN, which we refer to as a selective desensitization perceptron (SDP), is advantageous in binary classification for dealing with data that includes irrelevant and partially relevant features.

To test this idea, we systematically examined the robustness of SDP against irrelevant and partially relevant features. We conducted a numerical experiment on binary classification problems that included some irrelevant features or partially relevant features, and then compared the performances of SDP, MLP, and RBF kernel SVM.

2   Selective Desensitization Perceptron

SDP is a single-output-SDNN that can be applied as a binary classifier. It is constructed by applying manipulations of pattern coding and selective desensitization to a simple perceptron. The structure of an SDP is shown in Fig. 1. Pattern coding and selective desensitization are performed from the first to the second layer and the second to the third layer, respectively. The third to the fourth layer comprises a simple perceptron for binary classification, which is the only part that SDP trains.

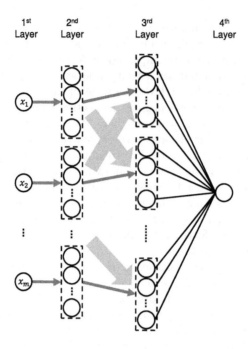

Fig. 1. Structure of an SDP with m dimensional input.

2.1 Pattern Coding

Pattern coding converts each analog input value into high-dimensional binary vectors known as code patterns. We specifically adopt the following procedures for all the input variables using different random sequences.

(1) After we quantized the analog input value x into q bins, we assigned an n-dimensional vector whose elements take only $+1$ or -1 to each bin. (2) We set P_1, the pattern vector of the first bin, by selecting $+1$ and -1 randomly for each element so that half of the elements take positive values and the rest take negative values. (3) For P_2, the pattern after the first bin (that is, P_1), we randomly selected r elements from those with positive value and the other r elements from those with negative value and then flipped the signs of these $2r$ elements. (4) Subsequently, we repeated this process for P_k based on the pattern of $P_{(k-1)}$ until we completed the same for the last bin.

This method results in a coded pattern that gradually changes from the first bin to the last bin, while ensuring that the correlation between two consecutive patterns is high and that the correlation between two patterns that are apart is near zero. If the code patterns fulfill these conditions, the values of the parameters, n, q, and r, do not affect the performance of SDNN (and SDP) significantly. A large n and q are always preferable if we disregard computational costs [6].

2.2   Selective Desensitization

Selective desensitization integrates two binary code patterns into one ternary $(-1, 0, +1)$ pattern by modifying one with the other. When there are two code patterns, $X = (x_1, x_2, ..., x_n)$ and $Y = (y_1, y_2, ..., y_n)$, x_i is desensitized if $y_i = -1$; that is, X is modified with Y into

$$X(Y) = (\frac{1+y_1}{2}x_1, ..., \frac{1+y_n}{2}x_n). \tag{1}$$

This makes $X(Y)$ a ternary pattern whose half of the elements are zero and the other half are the same as X. Note that different code patterns should be used for respective input variables to avoid undesirable bias in the modification (for example, $X(Y)$ never contains an element -1 if $X = Y$). Likewise, $Y(X)$, or Y modified with X, can be considered, and we use both $X(Y)$ and $Y(X)$ as the input pattern to the perceptron (Fig. 1).

In general, if the input dimension m is greater than two, selective desensitization is conducted for all combinations of modified and modifier variables, so that $m(m-1)$ ternary patterns are created in the third layer (Fig. 1).

2.3   Simple Perceptron

The output unit is a threshold element receiving signals from the third layer and emits 0 or 1, which works as a simple perceptron. In mathematical terms,

$$z = f(\sum_{i=1}^{s} w_i p_i + h), \tag{2}$$

where s is the input size (number of elements in the third layer); p_i and w_i are the i-th input signal (output of the third layer) and its weight, respectively; h is the threshold input; and $f(u)$ denotes the Heaviside step function taking 1 for $u > 0$ and 0 otherwise. Only this part is trained, with an error-correcting rule generally used for simple perceptrons. Specifically, the input weights and the threshold are updated as

$$w_i(t+1) = w_i(t) + (d-z)p_i, \tag{3}$$

$$h(t+1) = h(t) + (d-z), \tag{4}$$

where d is the target signal (0 or 1).

3   Numerical Experiment

We conducted an experiment on binary classification problems that included one or more irrelevant features and/or partially relevant features and compared the performance of SDP, MLP, and SVM. Here, an irrelevant feature is an element in the input vector that does not affect the output at all. A partially relevant feature, on the other hand, does not affect the output in most of its domain, but affects the output in a specific domain.

A dataset was generated using a binary (black and white) image of size 101×101 (10201 pixels in total) which represents the correct classification boundary (Fig. 2). For each pixel, the horizontal-vertical coordinates (normalized to $[0, 1]$) were used as the first and second components of the feature vector, and the luminance (white is 1 and black is 0) was used as the class number. Those two features were the relevant features that determined the output class. One or more random values of range $[0, 1]$ were included in each feature vector as the third or later components, which were the irrelevant features.

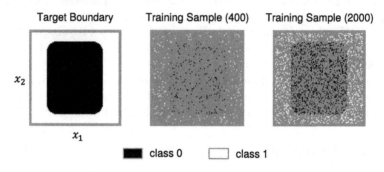

Fig. 2. The target class boundary and examples of the training sample set. The (x_1, x_2) coordinates were the two feature values that determined the output class value shown by the luminance.

The experiment was conducted as per the following procedures:

1. A certain number (k) of pixels on a binary image was pseudo-randomly selected with no overlap. The training sample set was created using these pixel points.
2. Each classifier learned the training samples.
3. Each classifier made predictions of the output class of 50000 unlearned points. Here, the rate of misclassified points was evaluated as the generalization error.
4. The above steps were repeated for 10 trials with different pseudo-random sequences.

The training parameters of classifiers are described below:

SDP: The pattern coding parameters were $n = 5000$, $q = 101$, and $r = 100$. The model was trained until every training sample was correctly classified.

MLP: One hidden layer of 100 units was applied between the input and the output layer. For hidden and output layers, hyperbolic tangent ($tanh$) was used as the activation function. Training was done with a standard backpropagation algorithm until the mean squared error of training reached below 0.005.

SVM: The RBF kernel was used. Kernel parameters were searched for the values of $C = 2^{-5}, 2^{-3}, ..., 2^{15}$ and $\gamma = 2^{-15}, 2^{-13}, ..., 2^{3}$ for every learning trial by five-fold cross-validation and grid search. LIBSVM was used [1].

3.1   Results

First, we examined the influence of irrelevant features. Figure 3 shows the mean generalization error of each classifier against the number of irrelevant features included in the input. The number of training samples was 400 for (a) and 2000 for (b). The error of SVM increased considerably as the number of irrelevant features increased, while the error of SDP and MLP did not.

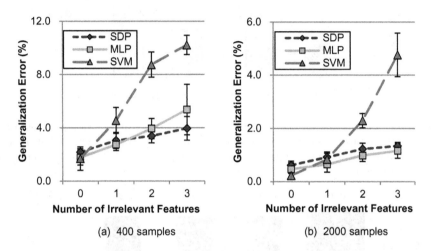

Fig. 3. Mean generalization error against the number of irrelevant features. The number of samples was 400 in (a) and 2000 in (b). Error bars indicate standard deviation.

Then, we introduced a partially relevant feature. Here, the third feature x_3 was the partially relevant feature; specifically, the output class was always 0 when x_3 was less than 0.1, and always 1 when x_3 was greater than 0.9. Otherwise the output was determined by the first two relevant features. In other words, x_3 is relevant to the output near the domain of $x_3 = 0.1$ and $x_3 = 0.9$, and irrelevant otherwise.

Figures 4 and 5 show the results of learning data with one partially relevant feature and one irrelevant feature. The number of training samples was 2000. In Fig. 4, the mean generalization error was compared with the case of two irrelevant features. The error of MLP and SVM increased substantially as one of the irrelevant features became partially relevant, while the increase was much smaller for SDP. Figure 5 shows some examples of the boundaries that each classifier constructed according to its predictions. It shows that MLP and SVM could not make accurate predictions, especially, when the output should be always 0 or 1 (where $x_3 < 0.1$ or $x_3 > 0.9$). In contrast, SDP showed more accurate predictions for the entire domain of x_3.

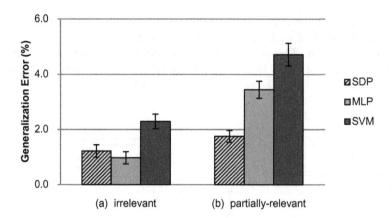

Fig. 4. (a) Mean generalization error for the problem with two irrelevant features. (b) Mean generalization error for the problem with one partially relevant feature and one irrelevant feature. The number of training samples was 2000. Error bars indicate standard deviation.

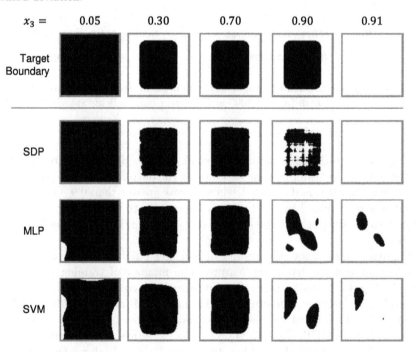

Fig. 5. Cross-sectional views of the class boundary constructed by each classifier, each of which is plotted in the (x_1, x_2) coordinate. The value for x_4 was fixed at 0.50.

4   Discussion

These results show that SDP is a more robust classifier than MLP and SVM for irrelevancy and partial-relevancy in classification problems. Here, we discuss how these three are influenced by irrelevant features, and why SDP is more robust.

SVM with an RBF kernel is known to be susceptible to irrelevant features [2], and this was confirmed in our experiment (Fig. 3). This is considered to be because its structure does not allow it to ignore a specific input variable. Because the input space became larger with the addition of irrelevant features, training samples became sparse and the training of SVM was directly affected.

MLP is known to be relatively robust to irrelevant features [4], a trend which was also shown in our experiment (Fig. 3). Because MLP determines the output according to the combination of the weighted sum of the input variables, it can ignore a specific variable by setting the synaptic weight for that variable to zero. However, Fig. 3 indicates that MLP cannot be trained to ignore the irrelevant features with fewer training samples. Furthermore, because MLP can only ignore the feature completely, the error increased when the feature was partially relevant to the output (Fig. 4). Figure 5 shows how the output of MLP was affected by the value of x_3 (partially relevant feature) in the domain where x_3 is irrelevant to the output.

In contrast to SVM and MLP, the influences of irrelevant features and partially relevant features were very small for SDP (Figs. 3 and 4). Figure 5 shows that the predictions of SDP were highly accurate in the entire domain of x_3, which indicates that SDP can remove the influence of a specific input variable without completely ignoring it. One possible reason for this is the mapping to the high-dimensional space by manipulations of pattern coding and selective desensitization. Because the weights in SDP are connected from each element of the high-dimensional vectors to the output, SDP can delete the influence of a certain variable by making the weighted sum of the elements zero, which can be achieved without setting the weight itself to zero. For example, consider the case that $P(x_3 = 0.30) = [+1, -1, ...]$ and $P(x_3 = 0.70) = [-1, +1, ...]$, which are the vectors (code patterns) that the values of 0.30 and 0.70 are converted into, and suppose that the third and later elements are all desensitized and that the weights for the first and second elements are equal. Then the weighted sum becomes zero for both $x_3 = 0.30$ and $x_3 = 0.70$, but if $P(x_3 = 0.05) = [+1, +1, ...]$, the weighted sum will not be zero for $x_3 = 0.05$, meaning that the output is affected by x_3 around 0.05 but not around 0.30 and 0.70. This enables SDP to remove the influence of the variable only in a specific domain.

Although SDP converts the inputs to higher dimensional code patterns, the computational cost does not increase much because it does not train hidden layer(s) and also because the input pattern for the simple perceptron is simple containing only $+1$, -1, and 0. Furthermore, the time for training (including parameter setting) of SDP was much smaller than that of MLP and SVM. However, because the computational cost of SDP increases in proportion to the square of the input dimension, SDP is especially suitable for problems with relatively low dimension (less than several dozens).

For these reasons, SDP is a useful and a practical classifier that can be applied when there is not much prior knowledge about a problem, or how each feature is related to the output. This characteristic of SDP is potentially one of the factors that contributed to achieving high performance and practicability in several previous studies using SDNN, such as discriminating multiple hand motions from surface electromyogram signals at high accuracy in real-time without precise adjustment of the number and position of sensors [7,8].

5   Conclusion

We compared the performance of SDP, MLP, and an RBF kernel SVM on binary classification problems that include some irrelevant features and partially relevant features (features that are irrelevant in most of the domain but affect the output in a specific domain).

The experimental results showed that SVM performed worse as more irrelevant features were included in the input, whereas MLP and SDP showed only a slight degradation in performance. The performance of MLP degraded when a partially relevant feature was included in the input. In contrast, SDP showed a much smaller increase in classification error. Thus, we conclude that SDP is highly robust to both the entire and the partial irrelevance of features.

According to this result, we suggest that using SDP allows us to keep relevant, irrelevant, and partially relevant dimensions in the given dataset with less worry of losing important information by unintentionally removing relevant or partially relevant features. In other words, SDP is a very practical binary classifier that can be easily used without prior knowledge of the problem, or highly technical feature selection methods. These advantages of SDP might be a reason for the previously reported high practicability of SDNN as a function approximator since it is composed of a set of multiple SDPs.

In future research, we plan to carry out experiments on higher dimensional problems with various types of features, such as those with different redundancies and distributions, to further clarify the robustness of SDP in detail.

References

1. Chang, C.C., Lin, C.J.: LIBSVM: a library for support vector machines. ACM Trans. Intell. Syst. Technol. **2**(3), 27:1–27:27 (2011)
2. Weston, J., Mukherjee, S., Chapelle, O., Pontil, M., Poggio, T., Vapnik, V.: Feature selection for SVMs. In: Leen, T.K., Dietterich, T.G., Tresp, V. (eds.) NIPS 2000. Advances in Neural Information Processing Systems, vol. 13, pp. 647–653. MIT Press, Cambridge (2001)
3. Guyon, I., Elisseeff, A.: An introduction to variable and feature selection. J. Mach. Learn. Res. **3**(May), 1157–1182 (2003)
4. Gasca, E., Sanchez, J.S., Alonso, R.: Eliminating redundancy and irrelevance using a new MLP-based feature selection method. Pattern Recogn. **39**(2), 313–315 (2006)

5. Kobayashi, T., Shibuya, T., Morita, M.: Q-learning in continuous state-action space with noisy and redundant inputs by using a selective desensitization neural network. J. Adv. Comput. Intell. Intell. Inform. **19**(6), 825–832 (2015)
6. Nonaka, K., Tanaka, F., Morita, M.: Empirical comparison of feedforward neural network on two-variable function approximation. IEICE Trans. Inf. Syst. J. **94**(12), 2114–2125 (2011). (in Japanese)
7. Kawata, H., Tanaka, F., Suemitsu, A., Morita, M.: Practical surface EMG pattern classification by using a selective desensitization neural network. In: Wong, K.W., Mendis, B.S.U., Bouzerdoum, A. (eds.) ICONIP 2010. LNCS, vol. 6444, pp. 42–49. Springer, Heidelberg (2010). doi:10.1007/978-3-642-17534-3_6
8. Horie, K., Suemitsu, A., Morita, M.: Direct estimation of hand motion speed from surface electromyograms using a selective desensitization neural network. J. Sig. Process. **18**(4), 225–228 (2014)

Single Sample Face Recognition
Based on Global Local Binary Pattern
Feature Extraction

Meng Zhang, Li Zhang$^{(\boxtimes)}$, and Chengxiang Hu

School of Computer Science and Technology & Joint International Research
Laboratory of Machine Learning and Neuromorphic Computing,
Soochow University, Suzhou 215006, China
zhangliml@suda.edu.cn

Abstract. To improve the recognition rate of single sample per person (SSPP), in this paper we propose a novel single sample face recognition method based on global LBP feature extraction. We first calculate the LBP value of each pixel based on the whole image and obtain the corresponding LBP image. Then, we segment the LBP image into non-overlapping image blocks. For each image block, we take its statistical histograms as its global LBP feature. Finally, we use the nearest neighbor (NN) classifier for face classification. Experimental results on three widely used face databases, including AR, FERET and ORL databases, demonstrate the effectiveness and robustness of the proposed method.

Keywords: Face recognition · Single sample · Feature extraction · Local binary pattern (LBP)

1 Introduction

With the development of computer science, face recognition has attracted more and more attention from the world. Feature-based recognition methods have been widely used in face recognition, and can be divided into two categories [1]: recognition methods based on global features and recognition methods based on local features. Methods of the first category extract features from whole images to obtain global information. Representative and popular methods include principal component analysis (PCA) [2], linear discriminant analysis (LDA) [3], independent component analysis (ICA) [4] and discrete cosine transform (DCT) [5]. Methods of the second category extract local features to reflect detailed information. Typical and widely used methods include local binary pattern (LBP) [6], local ternary patterns (LTP) [7], local directional pattern (LDP) [8] and histogram of oriented gradient (HOG) [9].

Traditional face recognition methods always believe that there are multiple training samples per person to use in the process of feature extraction. However, in many real-world face recognition applications, such as ID card identification, e-passport and law enhancement, it is hard to meet the requirement because it is inconvenient to collect multiple photos and usually there is a single sample per person (SSPP) recorded in these systems. Under these circumstances, many face recognition methods often

D. Liu et al. (Eds.): ICONIP 2017, Part VI, LNCS 10639, pp. 530–539, 2017.
https://doi.org/10.1007/978-3-319-70136-3_56

suffer from the lack of training samples and cannot obtain satisfactory results [10]. Therefore, many novel face recognition methods dealing with SSPP problems have been proposed.

Both global feature and local feature play a significant role in addressing SSPP problems. The LBP feature of an image is interrelated only with the image itself and can describe local information well, so it is widely applied to solving SSPP problems [6, 11]. However when it is performed on the blocks after segmentation, a part of edge information may be lost. In another word, the smaller blocks are, the more information will be lost which would result in bad recognition performance. But blocks with a large scale may decrease their ability to describe local information. Thus, we propose a novel single sample face recognition method based on global LBP feature extraction.

First, we calculate the LBP value of each pixel based on the whole image to retain global information, which can reduce information loss. Then we partition a LBP image into multiple non-overlapping blocks to obtain local feature of images. Afterwards, we use statistical histograms of blocks to represent the feature of images. Finally, we employ the nearest neighbor (NN) classifier for face recognition. Experimental results indicate that the proposed method retains both global feature and local feature and improves the accuracy of recognition.

2 Proposed Method

Figure 1 shows the framework of the proposed method. First, to avoid information loss after segmentation, we extract LBP features from training samples and test samples (unknown), and partition feature images into multiple non-overlapping blocks evenly. Then we cascade the statistical histograms obtained from blocks. Finally, we calculate the distances between blocks in the testing sample and those in the training samples and employ NN to classify the unknown sample.

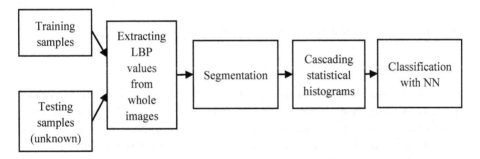

Fig. 1. Framework of the proposed method

2.1 Global LBP

Let $X = \{x_1, x_2, \ldots, x_c\}$ be the training set, where c is the number of individuals in the training set and x_i is the training sample for the i-th person, $1 \leq i \leq c$, $x_i \in R^{m \times n}$. In the original image partitioning methods based on LBP, x_i is directly divided into multiple non-overlapping blocks whose features are separately extracted by the LBP operator [6, 11]. The calculation of the LBP value requires a 3×3 neighborhood. But it is difficult for edge pixels to meet this requirement, so blocks would lose some useful information. Therefore, we propose a novel global LBP extracting scheme.

To reduce feature information loss, we first extract the LBP features from the whole image. Generally, the LBP operator adopts a neighborhood with 3×3 pixels to extract features [6, 11]. The 3×3 neighborhood takes the center pixel value as a threshold. In the neighborhood, the pixels would be marked as 1 if their values are greater than or equal to the threshold; the other pixels are marked as 0. Then we can get an eight-bit unsigned binary digit corresponding to pixels in the neighborhood, and covert it to a decimal number. The decimal number is the LBP value of the center pixel. The specific formula is defined as follows:

$$LBP_{(x_c, y_c)} = \sum_{p=0}^{7} 2^p s(I_p - I_C) \tag{1}$$

where $LBP_{(x_c, y_c)}$ is the LBP value of the pixel locating in x_c-th row and y_c-th column; I_C is the pixel value located at (x_c, y_c); I_p and 2^p are the p-th pixel in the neighborhood and its weight, respectively; and $s(x)$ is defined as follows:

$$s(x) = \begin{cases} 1, & \text{if } x > 0 \\ 0, & \text{if } x \leq 0 \end{cases} \tag{2}$$

To obtain local and global feature at the same time, the proposed method partitions the LBP value image into t non-overlapping blocks and uses the statistical histogram to describe the features of each block. Then the feature matrix of x_i can be described as follows:

$$H_{x_i} = [h_{x_i}^1, h_{x_i}^2, \ldots, h_{x_i}^t] \tag{3}$$

where $h_{x_i}^r$ is the statistical histogram of the r-th block in x_i.

2.2   NN Classifier

Let H_{x_i} be the feature matrix of the i-th image in the training set, H_{y_j} be the feature matrix of the j-th image (unknown) in the test set, and $d(H_{x_i}, H_{y_j})$ be the distance between them. Popular distance formulas include the Euclidean distance, the Manhattan distance, the cosine distance and the χ^2 distance, as defined in Table 1.

Since there is a single sample per person in the training set, we can obtain the classification result of each image in the test set through calculating the distances between the test sample and the training images and finding out the shortest distance.

Table 1. Distance formulas

Distance	Formula
Euclidean distance	$d(H_{x_i}, H_{y_j}) = \sum_{r=1}^{t} \left\| h_{x_i}^r - h_{y_j}^r \right\|$
Manhattan distance	$d(H_{x_i}, H_{y_j}) = \sum_{r=1}^{t} \left| h_{x_i}^r - h_{y_j}^r \right|$
Cosine distance	$d(H_{x_i}, H_{y_j}) = 1 - \dfrac{\sum_{r=1}^{t} (h_{x_i}^r h_{y_j}^r)}{\left\| H_{x_i} \right\| \cdot \left\| H_{y_j} \right\|}$
χ^2 distance	$d(H_{x_i}, H_{y_j}) = \sum_{r=1}^{t} \dfrac{(h_{x_i}^r - h_{y_j}^r)^2}{h_{x_i}^r - h_{y_j}^r}$

3 Experimental Results and Analysis

To illustrate the effectiveness and robustness of the proposed method, we conduct several SSPP recognition experiments on three widely used databases: ORL [12], AR [13] and FERET [14]. Since the proposed method is an improvement on feature-extraction-after-segmentation (FEAS) method [11], we compare the proposed method with FEAS in the experiments.

3.1 Experiments on ORL Database

The ORL database [12] consists of 400 images of 40 people with different illumination, facial expressions (open/closed eyes, smiling/not smiling) and facial details (glasses/not glasses). Figure 2 indicates the statistical histograms of the feature blocks obtained from the proposed method and the FEAS method. We can observe from Fig. 2 that the proposed method obtains more comprehensive information than the FEAS method when extracting features from blocks of the same image. The main reason is that the proposed method uses the global LBP in feature extraction, which can extract local feature and preserve the border information of blocks at the same time.

We can also see from Fig. 2 that the dimension number of histograms obtained by the proposed method is the same as the proposed method. Thus, the complexity of the proposed method and FEAS is identical and decided by the number of blocks.

Each image is cropped to the size of 60×60, which is further partitioned into 100 blocks with the size of 6×6. We select the i-th image of an individual as the training sample and the rest as the testing samples, where $i = 1, 2, \ldots, 10$. In other words, we take each image of one person as the training sample. The NN classifier uses the Manhattan distance. Results are shown in Fig. 3. We can see from Fig. 3 that the proposed method is overall better than FEAS while using different training samples. It indicates that the proposed method is more robust than FEAS under various facial expressions, lighting conditions and poses.

3.2 Experiments on AR Database

The AR database [13] consists of over 4000 color images of 126 people (70 men and 56 women) with different facial expressions, lighting conditions and occlusions

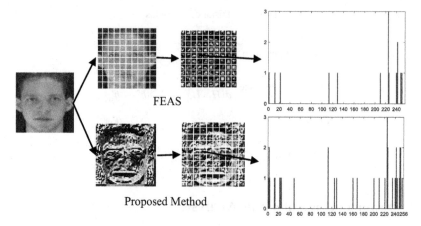

Fig. 2. Statistical histograms of feature blocks obtained from two methods

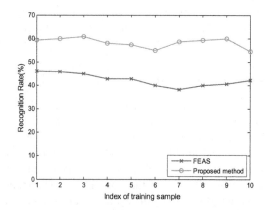

Fig. 3. Recognition rates of two methods on the ORL database

(sunglasses and scarves). In our experiments, 2600 images of 100 individuals are selected, and the 26 images of each individual were taken in two sessions. In the following, we validate our method from four aspects: different distances in the NN classifier, LBP feature extracting methods, light conditions and occlusions.

Different Distances. To evaluate the performance of the proposed method with different distances in the NN classifier, we conduct experiments with four popularly used distances: the Euclidean distance, the Manhattan distance, the cosine distance and the χ^2 distance, as shown in Table 1. In the experiment, we choose the first image of each individual as the training sample and the rest 25 images as test samples. All images are resized to the size of 60×60. Further, each resized image is partitioned into blocks with the size of 20×20, 15×15, 12×12, 10×10, 6×6, 5×5, 4×4 and 3×3, respectively. In doing so, we can observe the effect of the number of blocks on the classification accuracy.

The highest accuracy of two methods is shown in Table 2, and the corresponding size of the blocks is also shown in parentheses. We can learn from Table 2 that NN with the Manhattan distance has best classification performance in four kinds of distances. The proposed method obtains significantly higher recognition rate than FEAS using any of the four distances. And from the size of blocks in parentheses, we can know that compared to FEAS, the proposed method achieves the highest accuracy with smaller blocks, which also proves that FEAS may suffer from too much information loss with small blocks. Thus, the proposed method can extract global LBP features and minimize the impact of information loss.

Table 2. The highest recognition rates (%) of two methods

	FEAS method	Proposed method
Euclidean distance	81.52 (4 × 4)	83.32 (3 × 3)
Manhattan distance	88.96 (6 × 6)	91.28 (4 × 4)
Cosine distance	81.56 (4 × 4)	90.04 (4 × 4)
χ^2 distance	87.68 (6 × 6)	90.24 (4 × 4)

Different LBP Feature Extracting Methods. To demonstrate that the idea of the proposed method is suitable for different LBP feature extracting methods, we add a control group using the uniform LBP feature [15] in our experiment. Because the idea of global LBP and that of the global uniform LBP are similar, we do not regard the global uniform LBP as a novel feature. The results of two groups are shown in Fig. 4. According to the results in Fig. 4, we can know that the recognition rates of FEAS with LBP or uniform LBP both decrease after reaching a maximum value due to feature information loss. However, the proposed method applies global idea to feature extraction and can reduce the impact of blocks. In other words, the smaller the size of sub-image is, the higher the classification accuracy is. Moreover, Fig. 4 proves that the

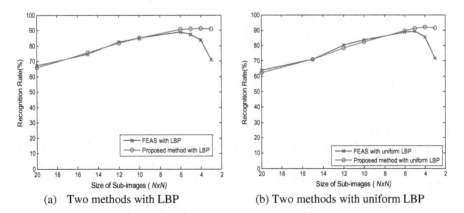

(a)   Two methods with LBP   (b) Two methods with uniform LBP

Fig. 4. Recognition rates of two groups on the AR database

proposed method is an improvement based on original methods and is suitable for different LBP feature extracting schemes.

Different Light Conditions. In the AR database, the main change of the first and fifth to seventh images in two sessions is light condition. To validate the robustness to illumination of the proposed method, we set the first image of each individual in the first session as the training sample, and the rest seven images as the test samples. We divide the testing samples into four subsets according to different light conditions, as shown in Table 3.

The best performances of FEAS and the proposed method are presented in Fig. 5. It is obvious that the proposed method obtains more global and local information under different light condition and is more robust to illumination than FEAS.

Table 3. Illumination subsets of AR database

Number of subset	Illumination direction	Number of samples
1	Left light on	200
2	Right light on	200
3	All side lights on	200
4	Soft light	100

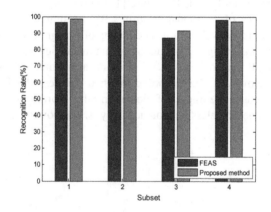

Fig. 5. The best performances of two methods under different light conditions

Different Occlusions. To evaluate the recognition effectiveness of the proposed method with partially occluded face images, we choose the first images of each individual for training and the eighth to thirteenth images in each session to test. The specific classification of subsets is shown in Table 4.

The recognition rates of two methods with varied sizes of blocks on different subsets are illustrated in Table 5, and the highest rates of two methods on six subsets are shown in Fig. 6. We can see from Table 5 and Fig. 6 that two methods perform better without the interference of light, because illumination may influence the relative

Table 4. Occlusion subsets of AR database

Number of subset	Outside conditions	Number of samples
1	Wearing sunglasses	200
2	Wearing sunglasses and left light on	200
3	Wearing sunglasses and right light on	200
4	Wearing scarf	200
5	Wearing scarf and left light on	200
6	Wearing scarf and right light on	200

Table 5. Recognition rates (%) of two methods with different occlusions

Subset	Method	3 × 3	4 × 4	5 × 5	6 × 6	10 × 10	12 × 12	15 × 15	20 × 20
1	FEAS	73.00	89.00	89.50	90.00	87.00	86.50	75.00	65.50
	Proposed method	90.50	93.00	93.00	92.50	89.00	89.00	78.00	63.00
2	FEAS	61.00	74.50	79.50	81.00	76.00	65.50	47.50	33.60
	Proposed method	86.00	86.50	84.50	83.00	69.50	61.50	53.00	30.00
3	FEAS	51.00	70.00	77.50	77.50	63.50	57.50	39.50	33.50
	Proposed method	80.50	82.50	79.00	77.50	63.00	55.50	43.50	30.00
4	FEAS	77.00	91.50	92.50	94.00	92.00	92.00	87.00	84.50
	Proposed method	95.50	95.00	94.50	95.50	93.00	91.00	88.00	85.00
5	FEAS	75.00	84.50	89.00	88.00	81.00	76.00	67.50	55.50
	Proposed method	91.50	91.50	91.50	90.50	81.00	71.00	65.00	52.50
6	FEAS	64.50	80.50	80.50	87.00	81.50	76.50	67.00	51.00
	Proposed method	90.50	88.50	89.50	89.50	81.00	75.00	65.00	51.50

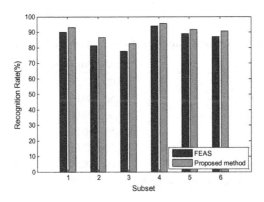

Fig. 6. The highest recognition rates of two methods on six occlusion subsets

values between the center pixel and those in the 3 × 3 neighborhood, resulting in deviations from original LBP values. Overall, the recognition rates of the proposed method are much better than FEAS no matter under variable illumination or occlusion conditions.

3.3   Experiments on FERET Database

The FERET database [14] is a comprehensive database containing over 10000 images. We choose a subset of 1400 images corresponding to 200 people in the FERET database in the experiment. The specific information of subsets is tabulated in Table 6.

We choose the Ba subset as the training sample. All images are resized to 60 × 60 and the NN classifier calculates with the Manhattan distance. Table 7 shows the recognition rates of two methods.

Table 6. Specific information of subsets on FERET database

Subset string	Pose angle (degree)	Description	Number of samples
Ba	0	Regular facial expression	200
Bg	−25	Subject faces to his left which is the photographer's right	200
Bf	−15		200
Be	+15	Subject faces to his right which is the photographer's left	200
Bd	+25		200
Bj	0	Alternative expression to ba	200
Bk	0	Different illumination to ba	200

As we can see from Table 7, when the pose angle varies from −25° to +25°, the recognition rates of the proposed method are 6.5%, 3.5%, 3.5% and 5% higher than those of FEAS in four subsets. And the proposed method performs better than FEAS under illumination variations. Therefore, the proposed method using global LBP feature can preserve both global and local information of images and is robust to complex conditions.

Table 7. Recognition rates (%) of two methods on FERET database

	FEAS	Proposed method
Bg	45.00	51.50
Bf	85.50	89.00
Be	89.50	93.00
Bd	51.50	56.50
Bj	93.50	93.00
Bk	83.00	88.50
Average recognition rate	74.67	78.58

4   Conclusion

In this paper, we propose a single face recognition method based the on global LBP extracting scheme. First, we perform LBP feature extraction on the whole original images and partition the obtained feature images into blocks. Then we use cascaded statistical histograms obtained from blocks to represent the feature of images. Finally, we apply the NN classifier for classification. Experimental results on three databases confirm the effectiveness and robustness of the proposed method.

Acknowledgments. This work was supported in part by the National Natural Science Foundation of China under Grant 61373093, by the Natural Science Foundation of Jiangsu Province of China under Grant BK20140008, and by the Soochow Scholar Project.

References

1. Wan, Y., Li, H., Wu, K., Tong, H.: Fusion with layered features of LBP and HOG for face recognition. J. Comput. Aided Design Comput. Graph. **27**, 640–650 (2015)
2. Zhou, C., Wang, L., Zhang, Q., et al.: Face recognition based on PCA and logistic regression analysis. Optik Int. J. Light Electron Optics **125**, 5916–5919 (2014)
3. Zhou, C., Wang, L., Zhang, Q., et al.: Face recognition based on PCA image reconstruction and LDA. Optik Int. J. Light Electron Optics **124**, 5599–5603 (2013)
4. Bartlett, M.S., Movellan, J.R., Sejnowski, T.J.: Face recognition by independent component analysis. IEEE Trans. Neural Netw. **13**, 1450–1464 (2002)
5. Li, Z., Yang, N., Xie, B., et al.: A two-phase face recognition method in frequency domain. Optik Int. J. Light Electron Optics **124**, 6333–6337 (2013)
6. Liu, L., Fieguth, P., Zhao, G., et al.: Extended local binary patterns for face recognition. Inf. Sci. **358–359**, 56–72 (2016)
7. Tan, X., Triggs, B.: Enhanced local texture feature sets for face recognition under difficult lighting conditions. IEEE Trans. Image Process. **19**, 1635 (2010)
8. Luo, Y., Zhang, T., Zhang, Y.: A novel fusion method of PCA and LDP for facial expression feature extraction. Optik Int. J. Light Electron Optics **127**, 718–721 (2016)
9. Dalal, N., Triggs, B.: Histograms of oriented gradients for human detection. In: CVPR, vol. 1, pp. 886–893 (2005)
10. Tan, X., Chen, S., Zhou, Z.H., et al.: Face recognition from a single image per person: a survey. Pattern Recogn. **39**, 1725–1745 (2006)
11. Ahonen, T., Hadid, A., Pietikäinen, M.: Face description with local binary patterns: application to face recognition. IEEE Trans. Pattern Anal. Mach. Intell. **28**, 2037–2041 (2006)
12. The database of faces. http://www.cl.cam.ac.uk/research/dtg/attarchive/facedatabase.html
13. AR face database. http://www2.ece.ohio-state.edu/ ~ aleix/ARdatabase.html
14. Pllillips, E.J., Moon, H., Rizvi, S.A., Rauss, E.J.: The feret evaluation methodology for face recognition algorithms. IEEE Trans. Pattern Anal. Mach. Intell. **22**, 1090–1104 (2000)
15. Ojala, T., Pietikinen, M., et al.: Multiresolution gray-scale and rotation invariant texture classification with local binary patterns. IEEE Trans. Pattern Anal. Mach. Intell. **24**, 971–987 (2002)

Multi-Features Fusion Based Face Recognition

Xianzhong Long[1,2,3]($\boxtimes$) and Songcan Chen[1]

[1] College of Computer Science and Technology, Nanjing University of Aeronautics
and Astronautics, Nanjing 211106, China
lxz@njupt.edu.cn, s.chen@nuaa.edu.cn
[2] School of Computer Science and Technology,
Nanjing University of Posts and Telecommunications, Nanjing 210023, China
[3] Jiangsu Key Laboratory of Big Data Security and Intelligent Processing,
Nanjing 210023, China

Abstract. In order to accelerate data processing and improve classification accuracy, some classic dimension reduction techniques have been proposed in the past few decades, such as Principal Component Analysis (PCA), Linear Discriminant Analysis (LDA), Non-negative Matrix Factorization (NMF), etc. However, these methods only use single feature and do not consider multi-features. In this paper, for the sake of exploiting the complementarity between multiple features, we put forward an efficient data dimensionality reduction scheme based on multi-features fusion. Specifically, gray value and local binary pattern features of all images are first extracted, and then some representative dimension reduction methods are applied. A series of experimental results are carried out on two benchmark face data sets to demonstrate the effectiveness of our proposed scheme.

Keywords: Multi-features fusion · Dimensionality reduction · Support vector machine · Face recognition

1 Introduction

As one of the most challenging tasks in computer vision and pattern recognition fields, face recognition have recently attracted many researchers' attention. Some face recognition techniques have been proposed in the past few decades. We usually represent a face image of size $m \times n$ pixels by an $m \times n$ dimensional vector. However, these $m \times n$ dimensional vectors are too large to allow fast processing. In order to resolve this problem, many dimensionality reduction techniques have been proposed, such as Principal Component Analysis (PCA) [1], Linear Discriminant Analysis (LDA) [2], Non-negative Matrix Factorization (NMF)[3], etc. Some corresponding projection matrices are generated after using these methods mentioned above. Each column of these projection matrices is a basis image, so the dimensionality reduction techniques are used to learn the representation of a face as linear combination of basis images. The basis images of PCA are orthogonal and have a statistical interpretation as the directions of

D. Liu et al. (Eds.): ICONIP 2017, Part VI, LNCS 10639, pp. 540–549, 2017.
https://doi.org/10.1007/978-3-319-70136-3_57

the largest variance of data. LDA tries to find a linear transformation that can maximize the between-class scatter matrix and meanwhile minimize the within-class scatter matrix. NMF aims to find two non-negative matrices whose product provides a good approximation to the original matrix. The nonnegativity properties lead to a parts-based representation because they allow only additive, not subtractive, combinations.

In the face recognition field, an image of 300×260 size can be transformed into a 32×32 matrix by using down-sampling technique. Then the image can be represented by a 1024×1 column vector. In order to eliminate redundant information in the image representation, PCA, LDA and NMF algorithms are used to learn a projected matrix which can be employed to reduce the dimensionality of data.

However, existing dimensionality reduction algorithms only extract single features of the image, inspired by the multi-features learning [4–6], we use two different features to describe the image, i.e., gray value and local binary patterns. Local Binary Patterns (LBP) is a type of visual descriptor used for classification, which was first described in [7]. It has since been found to be a powerful feature for texture classification. In this paper, we reduce the dimensionality of data based on the multi-features fusion and use SVM [8] to classify. Experiments show that our scheme achieves better recognition accuracy than those classical dimensionality reduction techniques based on single feature.

The remainder of the paper is organized as follows: Sect. 2 introduces the basic idea of existing dimensionality reduction techniques. Our method is proposed in Sect. 3. In Sect. 4, the comparison results of face recognition on two widely used data sets are reported. Finally, conclusions are made in Sect. 5.

2   Related Work

Let $\mathbf{X}$ be a data matrix of n m-dimensional samples $\mathbf{x}_1, \mathbf{x}_2, \cdots, \mathbf{x}_n$, i.e., $\mathbf{X} = [\mathbf{x}_1, \mathbf{x}_2, \cdots, \mathbf{x}_n] \in \mathbb{R}^{m \times n}$. Each column of $\mathbf{X}$ represents a face image with m dimensions. Usually, the image representation contains redundant information and this may lead to low recognition accuracy. Thus, dimensionality reduction is necessary before recognition, this section briefly reviews four classical dimensionality reduction techniques.

2.1   Principal Component Analysis

Principal Component Analysis (PCA) [1] tries to find a subspace whose basis vectors correspond to the maximum-variance direction in the original image space. Without loss of generality, let $\mathbf{W} \in \mathbb{R}^{m \times k}$ represent the linear transformation that maps the original m-dimensional space onto a k dimensional feature subspace where $k \ll m$, the new feature vectors $\mathbf{y}_i \in \mathbb{R}^k (i = 1, 2, \cdots, n)$ are obtained via the linear transformation:

$$\mathbf{y}_i = \mathbf{W}^T \mathbf{x}_i \tag{1}$$

The columns of $\mathbf{W}$ are the first k eigenvectors $\mathbf{w}_j \in \mathbb{R}^m (j = 1, 2, \cdots, k)$, which can be achieved by solving the following problem:

$$\mathbf{C}\mathbf{w}_j = \lambda_j \mathbf{w}_j \tag{2}$$

where $\mathbf{C} = \mathbf{X}\mathbf{X}^T$, $\mathbf{C} \in \mathbb{R}^{m \times m}$ is the covariance matrix and λ_j is the eigenvalue associated with the eigenvector $\mathbf{w}_j$. It is noteworthy that we should accomplish two things before obtaining the eigenvectors of $\mathbf{C}$: (1) the column vectors in $\mathbf{X}$ are normalized such that $\|\mathbf{x}_i\|_2 = 1$ and (2) the average vector of all images is subtracted from all column vectors of $\mathbf{X}$.

2.2   Linear Discriminant Analysis

Linear Discriminant Analysis (LDA) [2] seeks those vectors in the low-dimensional space that best discriminate among classes. From all samples, two matrices are defined. The first is called between-class scatter matrix, given by

$$\mathbf{S}_b = \sum_{t=1}^{c} N_t (\mu^t - \mu)(\mu^t - \mu)^T \tag{3}$$

where $\mathbf{S}_b \in \mathbb{R}^{m \times m}$, c is the number of classes, N_t is the number of training samples in class t, $\mu^t \in \mathbb{R}^m$ is the mean vector of samples belonging to class t, and $\mu \in \mathbb{R}^m$ represents the mean vector of all samples. The second matrix is called within-class scatter matrix:

$$\mathbf{S}_w = \sum_{t=1}^{c} \sum_{i=1}^{N_t} (\mathbf{x}_i^t - \mu^t)(\mathbf{x}_i^t - \mu^t)^T \tag{4}$$

where $\mathbf{S}_w \in \mathbb{R}^{m \times m}$, and $\mathbf{x}_i^t \in \mathbb{R}^m$ is the i-th sample of class t. The goal of LDA is to maximize the between-class scatter matrix while minimizing the within-class scatter matrix.

2.3   Non-negative Matrix Factorization

Non-negative matrix factorization (NMF) [3] decomposes a matrix $\mathbf{X} \in \mathbb{R}^{m \times n}$ into a product of two matrices $\mathbf{W} \in \mathbb{R}^{m \times k}$ and $\mathbf{H} \in \mathbb{R}^{k \times n}$ ($k \ll \min(m, n)$), i.e., $\mathbf{X} \approx \mathbf{W}\mathbf{H}$. Some algorithms for NMF have been proposed in [3,9], such as multiplicative update algorithms, gradient descent algorithms and alternating least squares algorithms.

Multiplicative update rules were firstly considered in [3]. The most commonly used criterion function of NMF is based on minimizing the Euclidean distance between $\mathbf{X}$ and $\mathbf{W}\mathbf{H}$. The corresponding optimization problem is as follows:

$$\begin{aligned} \min_{\mathbf{W}, \mathbf{H}} & \quad \|\mathbf{X} - \mathbf{W}\mathbf{H}\|_F^2 \\ \text{s.t.} & \quad \mathbf{W} \geq 0, \mathbf{H} \geq 0 \end{aligned} \tag{5}$$

where $\| \cdot \|_F$ denotes the matrix Frobenius norm, $\mathbf{X} \in \mathbb{R}^{m \times n}$ is a sample matrix, $\mathbf{W} \in \mathbb{R}^{m \times k}$ is called the basis matrix and $\mathbf{H} \in \mathbb{R}^{k \times n}$ is the coefficient matrix. In the machine learning, $\mathbf{W}$ can be used as a projected matrix to reduce the dimension of data, and $\mathbf{H}$ is employed to cluster. All the entries of $\mathbf{X}$, $\mathbf{W}$ and $\mathbf{H}$ are non-negative. The well-known multiplicative update rules are as follows [3]:

$$
\begin{aligned}
W_{iq} &\longleftarrow W_{iq} \frac{(XH^T)_{iq}}{(WHH^T)_{iq}} \\
H_{qj} &\longleftarrow H_{qj} \frac{(W^T X)_{qj}}{(W^T W H)_{qj}}
\end{aligned}
\tag{6}
$$

2.4 Graph Regularized Non-negative Matrix Factorization

Recently, the graph regularized non-negative matrix factorization (GNMF) was proposed in [10] to encode the data geometric structure in an nearest neighbor graph. GNMF solved the following optimization problem:

$$
\begin{aligned}
\min_{\mathbf{W}, \mathbf{H}} & \ \|\mathbf{X} - \mathbf{WH}\|_F^2 + \lambda \mathrm{Tr}(\mathbf{HLH}^T) \\
\text{s.t.} & \ \mathbf{W} \geq 0, \mathbf{H} \geq 0
\end{aligned}
\tag{7}
$$

where $\mathbf{L}$ is the graph Lpalacian matrix and $\mathbf{L} = \mathbf{B} - \mathbf{C}$ [11]. $\mathbf{C}$ is a weight matrix, $\mathbf{B}$ is a diagonal matrix whose entries are column or row sum of $\mathbf{C}$. Regularization parameter $\lambda \geq 0$ controls the smoothness of the new representation. The Tr is the trace of matrix, i.e., the sum of matrix diagonal entries.

The corresponding multiplicative update rules for solving (7) are as follows:

$$
\begin{aligned}
W_{iq} &\longleftarrow W_{iq} \frac{(XH^T)_{iq}}{(WHH^T)_{iq}} \\
H_{qj} &\longleftarrow H_{qj} \frac{(W^T X + \lambda HC)_{qj}}{(W^T W H + \lambda HB)_{qj}}
\end{aligned}
\tag{8}
$$

3 Multi-Features Fusion Based Face Recognition

Existing research applied the above algorithms to classify images, however, they only used gray value to denote image. Experimental results show that multi-features can complement each other, for example, for different kinds of flowers, we should simultaneously extract color information and shape feature. In our paper, we employ gray value and LBP features at the same time. Specifically, we employ $\mathbf{X}^1 \in \mathbb{R}^{m_1 \times n}$ and $\mathbf{X}^2 \in \mathbb{R}^{m_2 \times n}$ to indicate gray value and LBP feature extracted from images respectively. m_1 and m_2 represent the dimension of gray value and LBP feature. n denotes the total number of images in training set. Combining the above two kinds of features, we can get $\mathbf{X} = [\mathbf{X}^1; \mathbf{X}^2] \in \mathbb{R}^{m \times n}$, $m = m_1 + m_2$. After obtaining the feature combination $\mathbf{X}$, we put it into object function of PCA, LDA, NMF and GNMF respectively, and obtain the corresponding projected matrix. The dimensionality of samples in training set and testing set are reduced according to using projected matrix. Finally, SVM is used to predict the label of the testing sample.

4   Experimental Results

In this section, we first introduce relevant face data sets, and then illustrate our experiment settings, finally compare our scheme based on multi-features fusion with algorithms using single feature on two face data sets, i.e., ORL and UMIST.

4.1   Data Sets

Two face data sets are used in the experiment. The important statistics of these data sets are summarized in Table 1.

Table 1. Statistics of the two face data sets

Data set	Number of samples/classes	Dimensionality of gray value/LBP
ORL	400/40	256/256
UMIST	575/20	256/256

The ORL face data set[1] consists 400 images of 40 different classes in PGM format. Each class has 10 images. Classes were asked to face the camera and no restrictions were imposed on expression; only limited side movement and limited tilt were tolerated. For most classes, the images were shot at different times and with different lighting conditions, but all the images were taken against a dark homogeneous background. Some classes were captured with and without glass.

The UMIST face data set[2] consists 575 image of 20 different classes in PGM format. Each class has $19 \sim 48$ images and is shown in a range of poses from profile to frontal views.

4.2   Experiment Settings

First, we extract gray value of images. Specifically speaking, the image is transformed into gray image if original image is color, and down sampling technology is carried to extract 256 dimensional gray value vector for each image. Then, 256 dimensional LBP feature vector is computed for each image. Extracting the LBP feature consists of the following six steps. (1) Divide the examined window into cells, e.g. 16×16 pixels for each cell. (2) For each pixel in a cell, compare the pixel to each of its 8 neighbors and follow the pixels along a circle, i.e. clockwise or counter-clockwise. (3) Where the center pixel's value is greater than the neighbor's value, write "0", otherwise, write "1". This gives an 8-digit binary number which is usually converted to decimal for convenience. (4) Compute the histogram over the cell of the frequency of each "number" occurring, i.e., each combination of which pixels are smaller and which are greater than the center. This histogram can be seen as a 256-dimensional feature vector. (5) Optionally

---

[1] http://www.cl.cam.ac.uk/research/dtg/attarchive/facedatabase.html.

[2] https://www.sheffield.ac.uk/eee/research/iel/research/face.

normalize the histogram. (6) Concatenate the histograms of all cells. This gives a feature vector for the entire window. According to the above method, we can get gray values and LBP features respectively. After combining the gray value matrix and LBP feature matrix, we can obtain multi-features matrix $\mathbf{X}$. Each image in $\mathbf{X}$ is represented as a 512-dimensional column vector. The $\mathbf{X}$ is then scaled to [0,1] divided by L_2 norm of column vector. The parameter k in the PCA, NMF and GNMF is set to 30 respectively, which denotes that the dimensionality of face data is reduced to 30. In the LDA, the reduced dimensionality is one less than the total number of classes. In the GNMF, we use the $0-1$ weighting scheme for constructing the p nearest neighbor graph. The number of nearest neighbor p is set to 5 and the parameter λ is set to 0.5 empirically. We randomly select some samples from each class to construct training set, and the remaining samples of each class are constructed into testing set. For getting a more stable estimation of recognition accuracy, the random selection for each group of training data and testing data are repeated 50 times. The linear SVM will be used in all methods for the final classification. The average accuracy and the standard deviation are reported. All experiments are conducted in MATLAB 2011, which is executed on a PC with an Intel Core i7-4790 CPU (3.60 GHz) and 8 GB RAM.

4.3 Comparative Analysis

The classification result is evaluated by comparing the obtained label of each testing sample with the label provided by the data set.

Tables 2 and 5 show the recognition accuracy on the ORL and UMIST face data sets respectively using multi-features fusion. Tables 3 and 6 show the recognition accuracy only using gray value feature. Tables 4 and 7 show the recognition

Table 2. The result on the ORL using multi-features fusion (mean acc ± std dev %)

Method	3 Train	5 Train	7 Train
PCA	90.3 ± 1.7	94.6 ± 1.9	96.1 ± 1.6
LDA	93.0 ± 1.8	96.0 ± 1.4	97.2 ± 1.4
NMF	84.4 ± 2.6	90.9 ± 2.2	93.4 ± 2.8
GNMF	86.7 ± 2.5	92.7 ± 2.2	95.0 ± 2.0

Table 3. The result on the ORL only using gray value (mean acc ± std dev %)

Method	3 Train	5 Train	7 Train
PCA	86.9 ± 2.0	92.4 ± 1.7	94.4 ± 1.9
LDA	89.6 ± 2.0	91.6 ± 2.1	75.7 ± 4.1
NMF	81.5 ± 3.1	87.4 ± 2.7	90.6 ± 2.9
GNMF	82.5 ± 2.3	88.9 ± 2.3	91.5 ± 2.8

Table 4. The result on the ORL only using LBP feature (mean acc ± std dev %)

Method	3 Train	5 Train	7 Train
PCA	71.1 ± 2.7	77.3 ± 2.7	82.0 ± 3.0
LDA	67.8 ± 2.3	59.0 ± 3.4	18.6 ± 2.9
NMF	56.8 ± 3.0	63.5 ± 2.6	68.2 ± 4.3
GNMF	66.7 ± 2.3	71.8 ± 2.8	76.2 ± 3.6

Table 5. The result on the UMIST using multi-features fusion (mean acc ± std dev %)

Method	4 Train	10 Train	16 Train
PCA	83.8 ± 3.5	95.3 ± 1.5	97.3 ± 1.3
LDA	91.4 ± 2.1	97.8 ± 1.3	98.7 ± 0.9
NMF	78.7 ± 3.4	92.3 ± 2.2	94.9 ± 2.0
GNMF	82.7 ± 3.6	93.6 ± 1.9	96.1 ± 1.7

Table 6. The result on the UMIST only using gray value (mean acc ± std dev %)

Method	4 Train	10 Train	16 Train
PCA	76.7 ± 3.3	90.8 ± 2.5	95.5 ± 2.0
LDA	82.3 ± 2.8	92.4 ± 2.3	93.6 ± 1.7
NMF	72.8 ± 3.7	88.8 ± 2.3	93.6 ± 2.0
GNMF	73.9 ± 3.3	90.3 ± 2.2	94.4 ± 1.7

Table 7. The result on the UMIST only using LBP feature (mean acc ± std dev %)

Method	4 Train	10 Train	16 Train
PCA	74.4 ± 3.3	86.8 ± 2.5	90.4 ± 2.4
LDA	79.1 ± 2.6	72.6 ± 3.1	65.5 ± 3.6
NMF	68.5 ± 3.9	81.8 ± 2.5	85.3 ± 2.5
GNMF	73.9 ± 3.5	86.3 ± 2.5	89.3 ± 2.5

accuracy only using LBP feature. From the Tables, we can see that classification performance can be improved obviously by using multi-features fusion. The reason is that the complementarity between multiple features is fully exploited. The gray value denotes the intensity of light at each pixel and LBP indicates the statistical histogram of local intensity information. Two kinds of features are used to describe images from different perspectives and get better representation ability.

Besides, from the Tables, we observe that the recognition accuracy obtained by using only LBP is lower than using only gray values, this phenomenon shows

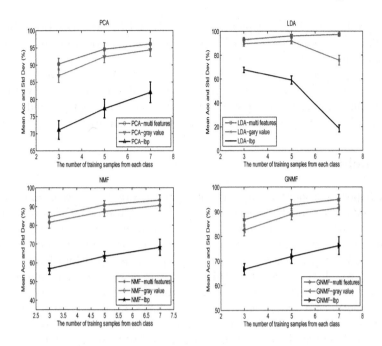

Fig. 1. Various reduced dimensionality algorithms on ORL face data set.

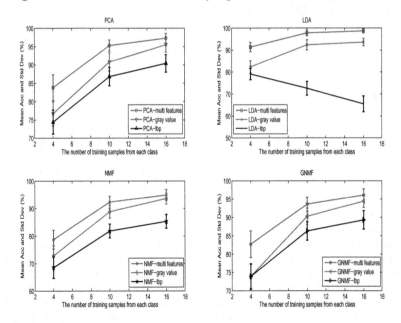

Fig. 2. Various reduced dimensionality algorithms on UMIST face data set.

that gray values can better depict face images than LBP features. However, when gray values are combined with LBP features, better recognition results can be obtained than using only one of them.

In the Figs. 1 and 2, the recognition results of PCA, LDA, NMF and GNMF are presented. Each subgraph corresponds to one kind of algorithms with multi-features and single feature. From the figures, we can see that multi-features fusion method is able to improve the recognition accuracy.

5   Conclusions

In this paper, in order to make use of complementarity between multiple features, an efficient multi-features fusion algorithm is proposed. We have compared our scheme for face recognition with four algorithms only using single feature. Experimental results on two face data sets demonstrate that recognition result of our method are much better than the several previous algorithms based on single feature. Through the research in this paper, we again show that multi-features fusion can improve performance results. From the experiment, the inspiration is that sometimes a simple feature combination can be used to achieve better results than a complex objective function. In our future research, we will explore other different kinds of feature combinations and test on more data sets.

Acknowledgments. This work is supported in part by the Postdoctoral Research Plan of Jiangsu Province (Grant No. 1501054B), the Postdoctoral Science Foundation of China (Grant No. 2016M591840), the Natural Science Foundation of Jiangsu Province (Grant No. BK20150856), the NUPTSF (Grant No. NY214168).

References

1. Turk, M.A., Pentland, A.P.: Face recognition using eigenfaces. In: IEEE Computer Society Conference on Computer Vision and Pattern Recognition, pp. 586–591 (1991)
2. Belhumeur, P.N., Hespanha, J.P., Kriegman, D.J.: Eigenfaces vs. fisherfaces: recognition using class specific linear projection. IEEE Trans. Pattern Anal. Mach. Intell. **19**(7), 711–720 (1997)
3. Lee, D.D., Seung, H.S.: Learning the parts of objects by non-negative matrix factorization. Nature **401**(6755), 788–791 (1999)
4. Yan, H.B., Lu, J.W., Zhou, X.Z., Shang, Y.Y.: Multi feature multi manifold learning for single sample face recognition. Neurocomputing **143**(16), 134–143 (2014)
5. Wu, X., Li, Q., Xu, L.L., Chen, K.W., Yao, L.: Multi-feature kernel discriminant dictionary learning for face recognition. Pattern Recogn. **66**, 404–411 (2017)
6. Huang, L.H., Li, W., Chen, C., Zhang, F., Lang, H.T.: Multiple features learning for ship classification in optical imagery. Multimedia Tools Appl. **2**, 1–27 (2017)
7. Ojala, T., Harwood, I.: A comparative study of texture measures with classification based on feature distributions. Pattern Recogn. **29**(1), 51–59 (1996)
8. Cortes, C., Vapnik, V.: Support-vector networks. Mach. Learn. **20**(3), 273–297 (1995)

9. Berry, M.W., Browne, M., Langville, A.N., Pauca, V.P., Plemmons, R.J.: Algorithms and applications for approximate nonnegative matrix factorization. Comput. Stat. Data Anal. **52**(1), 155–173 (2007)
10. Cai, D., He, X., Han, J., Huang, T.S.: Graph regularized nonnegative matrix factorization for data representation. IEEE Trans. Pattern Anal. Mach. Intell. **33**(8), 1548–1560 (2011)
11. Belkin, M., Niyogi, P.: Laplacian eigenmaps for dimensionality reduction and data representation. Neural Comput. **15**(6), 1373–1396 (2003)

Visual Saliency Based Blind Image Quality Assessment via Convolutional Neural Network

Jie Li and Yue Zhou[(⊠)]

Institute of Image Processing and Pattern Recognition,
Shanghai Jiao Tong University, Shanghai, China
{jaylee,zhouyue}@sjtu.edu.cn

Abstract. Image quality assessment (IQA), as one of the fundamental techniques in image processing, is widely used in many computer vision and image processing applications. In this paper, we propose a novel visual saliency based blind IQA model, which combines the property of human visual system (HVS) with features extracted by a deep convolutional neural network (CNN). The proposed model is totally data-driven thus using no hand-crafted features. Instead of feeding the model with patches selected randomly from images, we introduce a salient object detection algorithm to calculate regions of interest which are acted as training data. Experimental results on the LIVE and CSIQ database demonstrate that our approach outperforms the state-of-art methods compared.

Keywords: Blind image quality assessment · Visual saliency · Human visual system · Convolutional neural network

1 Introduction

Recently, digital images or videos have become the most intuitive medium for us to touch and understand this world and these digital information exists in almost every corner of our life. However, these images mediated by smartphones or televisions are distorted more or less for various reasons such as compression, storage and transmission. Since that, it is of great importance to evaluate the distortion level by image quality assessment (IQA).

Existing IQA methods can be classified into three categories according to the amount of additional information about the reference image: full-reference IQA (FR-IQA) e.g. [12,14,15], reduced-reference IQA (RR-IQA), and no-reference/blind IQA (BIQA) e.g. [3,4,8–10,13]. The first and the second method require full or partial information of the reference image, while the third method does not. Thus, BIQA is more applicable and significant in practice. The DIIVINE [9], based on natural scene statistic (NSS) model, uses a two-stage framework to identify the distortion type of an image first and then uses a distortion-specific regression model to predict the quality. BLIINDS-II [10] proposes a simple Bayesian inference model to obtain the quality with features

© Springer International Publishing AG 2017
D. Liu et al. (Eds.): ICONIP 2017, Part VI, LNCS 10639, pp. 550–557, 2017.
https://doi.org/10.1007/978-3-319-70136-3_58

extracted in DCT domain. BRISQUE [8] extracts features in spatial domain and is also based on a NSS model. CORNIA [13] introduces k-means clustering to extract features from raw-image-patches.

However, in recent years, many deep learning IQA methods have been proposed. These algorithms, without any NSS features extraction or special model construction, simply learns a certain map function from raw image pixels to perceived numerical quality scores. For example, Kang et al. [4] propose a CNN model to extract features from image patches automatically and then estimate the quality score. This method, known as the pioneer, bridges the gap between BIQA and CNN at the first time. Bosse et al. [1] treat the deep CNN as a feature extraction backbone in their BIQA algorithm and also give a choice to combine two of these architecture for further FR-IQA model. Nevertheless, those deep learning based approaches mentioned above only randomly select patches to feed CNN and acquire the image quality by averaging all the patches' scores simply. Thus they do not consider human visual system properties such as visual saliency.

In this paper, we utilize the idea of visual saliency to calculate the weight of each patch in an image and select top weighting patches as training data at first. Then we propose a CNN model to extract features and estimate the quality of every single patch. Finally, by weighting scores of all the patches, we obtain the predicted quality respectively. The most similar work with ours is [7], however, Li et al. [7] does not consider the importance of salient regions thus may use insignificant patches during training and testing. Furthermore, Experimental result on LIVE [11] and CSIQ [6] shows that our method achieves better performance.

2   Proposed Method

In this section, we introduce our implementation in details. Firstly, an efficient salient object detection algorithm as well as Prewitt operator is adopted for choosing significant patches from a complete image. Secondly, we illustrate the pipeline of our method from the view of data stream. Finally, training details are explained.

2.1   Salient Patches Selection

Inspired by the hypothesis that HVS only focus on part of an image in details, while ignoring rest insignificant regions, we crop the most important and informative patches from images and then feed these patches to our CNN model. Those patches should be representative thus need to contain as many salient regions as possible. Therefore, a simple but powerful salient region detection algorithm, proposed by Cheng et al. [2], is used here to generate salient map (Fig. 1(b)). Named as HC, this algorithm calculate pixel-wise salient value based on color statistics of an image. Defined by color contrast of one pixel with all other pixels in an image, the salient value of a pixel I_k in image I can be calculated as

$$S(I_k) = \sum_{i=1}^{N} D(I_k, I_i), \tag{1}$$

where $D(I_k, I_i)$ represents the color distance between pixel I_k and I_i in the *Lab* color space and N denotes the total number of pixels in image I. Since pixels with the same color share the same salient value, the terms with the same color value c_j can be grouped together. Thus for each color, saliency value is defined as

$$S(I_k) = S(c_l) = \sum_{j=1}^{n} f_j D(c_l, c_j), \tag{2}$$

where c_l represents the color value of pixel I_k, n is the number of distinct pixel colors, and f_j denotes the probability of color c_j in image I. Cheng et al. [2] also accelerate the algorithm by smartly reducing the number of colors with color histogram, and then color space smoothing is adopted to filter noise. Anyway, the simple but effective idea is to use salient value of each pixel to distinguish the salient regions from the background.

Considering the fact that HVS is also sensitive to the contour and edge information in an image, we introduce the Prewitt operator to generate gradient map from the original image and then calculate the corresponding weight of each patch. Suppose $S(i, j)$ to be the saliency value at the location (i, j) and $P(i, j)$ is the gradient value respectively. The weight of the patch is defined as follow:

$$W = \lambda \sum_{i=1}^{N} \sum_{j=1}^{M} S(i, j) + (1 - \lambda) \sum_{i=1}^{N} \sum_{j=1}^{M} P(i, j), \tag{3}$$

where λ is a balancing parameter which ranges in $[0, 1]$. N and M represent patch's width and height respectively and $N = M = 32$. Patches are selected in terms of their weights. Note that W is also used to weight local quality, which will be discussed later. Figure 1 shows the results where patches are illustrated in a heat map.

2.2   Architecture of the Method

As shown in Fig. 2, the architecture of our method can be divided into three parts: patches selection, CNN model and quality weighting.

For each image, we subdivide it into 32×32 sized patches without overlap at first, and then every each path is weighted based on Eq. 3. Finally, we sort all the patches according to their scores from high to low and choose the top N patches as training data. In experiment, we use $N = 256$, which means the quality of one image is decided by its most representative 66% patches. Under this assumption, we achieve the best performance.

We design a new 6 layers CNN model to extract features followed by 2 fully connected (FC) layers for regression while a simple linear regression layer with

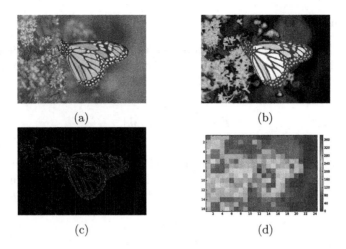

(a) (b)

(c) (d)

Fig. 1. (a) original image, (b) saliency map, (c) gradient map, (d) heat map.

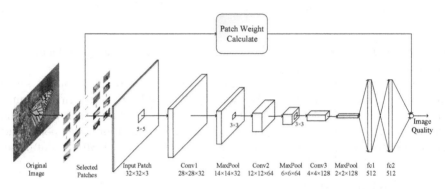

Fig. 2. The architecture of our method

one node is used to give the quality score at the end. Thus the structure is $32 \times 32 \times 3 - 28 \times 28 \times 32 - 14 \times 14 \times 32 - 12 \times 12 \times 64 - 6 \times 6 \times 64 - 4 \times 4 \times 128 - 2 \times 2 \times 128 - 512 - 512 - 1$ in detail. The first convolutional layer apply 5×5 pixel-sized convolutional kernels and the remaining two use 3×3 pixel-sized convolutional kernels. All max-pooling layers apply 2×2 pixel-sized kernels. This CNN model is totally data-driven and can be trained end-to-end.

Since we get all the patches' scores which represent the corresponding quality respectively, we do not acquire the image quality by averaging all patches' scores like in [4]. Instead, the weight defined in Eq. 3 is used here for weighted average pooling. Suppose q to be the estimated score of a patch, we compute the quality of the image as follow:

$$Q = \frac{\sum_{i=1}^{N} W_i q_i}{\sum_{i=1}^{N} W_i}, \tag{4}$$

where N is the number of selected patches.

2.3 Training

Inspired by [4], the score of each patch is set to be the same as its source image's ground truth score because of the homogeneity in all distortion images. The loss function is defined by mean absolute error (MAE):

$$L = \frac{1}{N} \sum_{i=1}^{N} |q_i - y_i|, \tag{5}$$

where q_i represents the estimated quality and y_i denotes the ground truth quality. Backpropagation is used to optimize the loss function and the learning rate is updated adaptively by using the ADAM method [5]. The Parameter θ is updated as follow:

$$m_t = \beta_1 m_{t-1} + (1 - \beta_1)g_t, \tag{6}$$

$$v_t = \beta_2 v_{t-1} + (1 - \beta_2)g_t^2, \tag{7}$$

$$\theta = \theta_{t-1} - \alpha \frac{m_t}{\sqrt{v_t} + \epsilon}, \tag{8}$$

where $\beta_1 = 0.9$, $\beta_2 = 0.999$, $\epsilon = 10^{-8}$, and $\alpha = 10^{-4}$. $g_t = \nabla_\theta f_t(\theta)$ denotes the gradient w.r.t θ at a time step t.

When training, the parametwr λ in Eq. 3 is set to 0.6. The training set is divided into several mini-batches randomly. We apply 4 images in one mini-batch and each image is represented by its top 256 patches, which means the effective batch size is 1024. The proposed model is trained for 8000 epochs and outperforms other methods compared on the LIVE [11] and CSIQ [6] database.

3 Experimental Results

In this section, two experiments are performed based on the LIVE [11] and CSIQ [6] database to evaluate the performance and the robustness of the proposed method. The LIVE [11] database contains 808 color images, which include 29 reference images and 779 distorted images. All the distorted images are generate from the source images at different distortion levels under five distortion types: JPEG2000 compression (JP2K), JPEG compression (JPEG), Gaussian blur (BLUR), fast fading (FF) and white noise (WN). Differential Mean Opinion Scores (DMOS) which range in [0, 100] are provided for each image. Lower DMOS indicts higher quality. The CSIQ [6] database include 30 reference images which are distorted under 6 different types and the Mean Opinion Score (MOS) of each image lies in a range [0, 1]. On the contrary, Lower MOS denotes lower quality. The Pearson linear correlation coefficient (LCC) and Spearman rank-order correlation coefficient (SROCC) are used as evaluation benchmark.

3.1 Performance Evalution

For single database evaluation, we randomly select 80% of reference images and their corresponding distortion images from each distortion types as training set and remaining 20% as test set. Tables 1 and 2 show the experimental results on the LIVE database. The best result is shown in red.

Table 1. LCC of different methods on LIVE.

Method	JP2K	JPEG	WN	GBLUR	FF	ALL
PSNR	0.873	0.876	0.926	0.779	0.870	0.856
SSIM [12]	0.921	0.955	0.893	0.893	0.939	0.906
FSIM [15]	0.910	0.985	0.978	0.978	0.912	0.960
BLIINDS-II [10]	0.950	0.978	0.981	0.939	0.912	0.936
DIVINE [9]	0.922	0.921	0.981	0.939	0.912	0.917
BRISQUE [8]	0.934	0.969	0.988	0.923	0.888	0.944
CORNIA [13]	0.917	0.912	0.984	0.935	0.901	0.936
CNN [4]	0.953	0.981	0.984	0.953	0.933	0.953
Li's method [7]	0.978	0.977	0.993	0.945	0.960	0.966
Ours	0.970	0.953	0.993	0.986	0.985	0.981

Table 2. SROCC of different methods on LIVE.

Method	JP2K	JPEG	WN	GBLUR	FF	ALL
PSNR	0.870	0.885	0.942	0.763	0.874	0.866
SSIM [12]	0.939	0.946	0.964	0.907	0.941	0.913
FSIM [15]	0.970	0.981	0.967	0.972	0.949	0.964
BLIINDS-II [10]	0.942	0.956	0.978	0.934	0.917	0.920
DIVINE [9]	0.913	0.910	0.984	0.921	0.863	0.916
BRISQUE [8]	0.942	0.944	0.967	0.903	0.871	0.940
CORNIA [13]	0.903	0.895	0.937	0.924	0.917	0.906
CNN [4]	0.952	0.977	0.978	0.962	0.908	0.956
Li's method [7]	0.964	0.935	0.988	0.941	0.945	0.958
Ours	0.950	0.944	0.990	0.976	0.963	0.970

Tables 1 and 2 show that our method has a superior performance to state-of-the-art FR and blind IQA methods. Furthermore, our method outperforms on WN, GBLUR and FF distortion types and all of distortion types together on the LIVE database. Figure 3 illustrates the scatter plots of DMOS versus predict

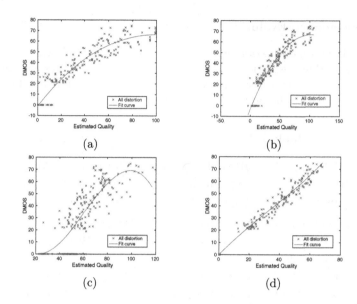

Fig. 3. Scatter plots of DMOS versus prediction of the test methods. (a) BLIINDS-II, (b) BRISQUE, (c) CORNIA, (d) Proposed Method.

quality scores. It can be shown that points with our method are closer to the fitting curve compared to other methods, which means the proposed method is in line with HVS.

3.2   Cross-Database Experiment

Table 3 shows the cross-database experimental result. We train our CNN model on the full LIVE database and test on the subset of CSIQ. Note that the subset contains only the 4 distortions that are shared with LIVE. The results shows that our method has a certain robustness.

Table 3. LCC and SROCC results of the cross-database experiment.

	JP2K	JPEG	WN	GBLUR	ALL
LCC	0.931	0.965	0.878	0.941	0.916
SROCC	0.924	0.935	0.841	0.907	0.874

4   Conclusion

In this paper, we propose a novel CNN based blind image quality assessment (BIQA) method. Firstly, we adopt a color contrast based salient region detection algorithm and the Prewitt gradient to select representative patches. Then, a new CNN model is applied to extract features from each patch and evaluate its quality score. Finally we weight all scores of patches and obtain the quality of the image. Experiments have been performed on the LIVE and CSIQ and the results demonstrate that our method is competitive with state-of-the-art methods.

Acknowledgments. This research is supported by the National High-Tech R&D Program of China (863 Program) under Grant 2015AA016402 and Shanghai Natural Science Foundation under Grant 14Z111050022.

References

1. Bosse, S., Maniry, D., Müller, K.R., Wiegand, T., Samek, W.: Deep neural networks for no-reference and full-reference image quality assessment. arXiv preprint arxiv:1612.01697 (2016)
2. Cheng, M.M., Mitra, N.J., Huang, X., Torr, P.H., Hu, S.M.: Global contrast based salient region detection. IEEE Trans. Pattern Anal. Mach. Intell. **37**(3), 569–582 (2015)
3. Hou, W., Gao, X., Tao, D., Li, X.: Blind image quality assessment via deep learning. IEEE Trans. Neural Netw. Learn. Syst. **26**(6), 1275–1286 (2015)
4. Kang, L., Ye, P., Li, Y., Doermann, D.: Convolutional neural networks for no-reference image quality assessment. In: Proceedings of the IEEE Conference on Computer Vision and Pattern Recognition, pp. 1733–1740 (2014)
5. Kingma, D., Ba, J.: Adam: A method for stochastic optimization. arXiv preprint arxiv:1412.6980 (2014)
6. Larson, E.C., Chandler, D.M.: Most apparent distortion: full-reference image quality assessment and the role of strategy. J. Electron. Imaging **19**(1), 011006 (2010)
7. Li, J., Zou, L., Yan, J., Deng, D., Qu, T., Xie, G.: No-reference image quality assessment using prewitt magnitude based on convolutional neural networks. SIViP **10**(4), 609–616 (2016)
8. Mittal, A., Moorthy, A.K., Bovik, A.C.: No-reference image quality assessment in the spatial domain. IEEE Trans. Image Process. **21**(12), 4695–4708 (2012)
9. Moorthy, A.K., Bovik, A.C.: Blind image quality assessment: from natural scene statistics to perceptual quality. IEEE Trans. Image Process. **20**(12), 3350–3364 (2011)
10. Saad, M.A., Bovik, A.C., Charrier, C.: Blind image quality assessment: a natural scene statistics approach in the dct domain. IEEE Trans. Image Process. **21**(8), 3339–3352 (2012)
11. Sheikh, H.R., Sabir, M.F., Bovik, A.C.: A statistical evaluation of recent full reference image quality assessment algorithms. IEEE Trans. Image Process. **15**(11), 3440–3451 (2006)
12. Wang, Z., Bovik, A.C., Sheikh, H.R., Simoncelli, E.P.: Image quality assessment: from error visibility to structural similarity. IEEE Trans. Image Process. **13**(4), 600–612 (2004)
13. Ye, P., Kumar, J., Kang, L., Doermann, D.: Unsupervised feature learning framework for no-reference image quality assessment. In: 2012 IEEE Conference on Computer Vision and Pattern Recognition (CVPR), pp. 1098–1105. IEEE (2012)
14. Zhang, L., Shen, Y., Li, H.: VSI: a visual saliency-induced index for perceptual image quality assessment. IEEE Trans. Image Process. **23**(10), 4270–4281 (2014)
15. Zhang, L., Zhang, L., Mou, X., Zhang, D.: FSIM: a feature similarity index for image quality assessment. IEEE Trans. Image Process. **20**(8), 2378–2386 (2011)

Multi-task Modular Backpropagation for Feature-Based Pattern Classification

Rohitash Chandra[(✉)]

Centre for Translational Data Science, The University of Sydney,
Sydney, NSW 2006, Australia
rohitash.chandra@sydney.edu.au

Abstract. Modular knowledge development in neural networks have the potential to feature robust decision given sudden changes in the environment or the data during real-time implementation. It can also provide a means to address robustness in decision making given certain features of the data are missing post training stage. In this paper, we present a multi-task modular backpropagation algorithm that features developmental learning where the training takes into account several groups of features that constitute the overall task. The proposed algorithm employs multi-task learning where knowledge from previously trained neural network modules are used to guide knowledge developmental in future modules. The results show that it is possible to implement a modular network without losing training or generalization performance.

Keywords: Backpropagation · Modular network design · Multi-task learning · Modular pattern classification

1 Introduction

Embedded control systems guided with machine learning can encounter states that have disruptions in stream of data from sensors [8]. This can as a result provide poor decision making for actuators. Modular knowledge development in neural networks can provide features of robustness and scalability given the changes in the environment or the data [2]. Examples include block-based neural networks that have been implemented and reconfigured in digital hardware such as field programmable gate arrays [12]. Modular neural networks have been popular for hardware implementations [11]. Due to knowledge representation as modules, the system should be able to make decisions with some degree of uncertainty even if some of the modules are damaged or missing. Such motivations come from biological neural systems, i.e. due to modular knowledge representation, one is able to see even if one eye is damaged [9].

Multi-task learning considers a shared knowledge representation that exploits knowledge learned from different but related tasks that can be helpful for each other during learning [4]. An example multi-task learning is a system that learns to recognise the face and facial expression recognition at the same time [17].

© Springer International Publishing AG 2017
D. Liu et al. (Eds.): ICONIP 2017, Part VI, LNCS 10639, pp. 558–566, 2017.
https://doi.org/10.1007/978-3-319-70136-3_59

Transfer learning, on the other hand, considers a one-way transfer of knowledge from source tasks into target task [13] and recently have been popular for deep learning [16]. The main goal of transfer learning is to improve the training or generalization performance of the target task. In some problems, more than one source data would exist and hence the area is known as multi-source transfer learning [15]. In cases where the source task data has features that are not alighted directly or inconsistent with target task, the problem is knowledge as heterogeneous and multi-view transfer learning [14]. The notion of multi-task learning has been incorporated in the field of time series to address dynamic time series problems [5] and multi-step ahead prediction [6]. These methods incorporate elements of transfer and multi-task learning.

The motivations from related learning techniques is incorporated, in particular, multi-task learning for modular knowledge representation in neural networks. In this paper, a multi-task modular back-propagation algorithm is presented that takes into account feature groups that are partitioned from the data. The method produces a modular network that provides decision making for the partitioned feature groups.

The rest of the paper is organised as follows. Section 2 presents the proposed method and Sect. 3 presents experiments and results. Section 4 concludes the paper with a discussion of future work.

2   Multi-task Modular Backpropagation

As mentioned earlier, the proposed algorithm feature properties of transfer and multi-task learning. The training takes into account several groups of overlapping features partitioned from the original dataset. The proposed multi-task modular backpropagation (MTMB) algorithm considers knowledge from smaller network modules to guide knowledge development for larger cascaded network modules. Although multi-task learning typically employs a set of datasets for the tasks, a single dataset is decomposed into overlapping feature groups which are referred as subtasks. Essentially, the network can be viewed as a cascaded network architecture that increases in size with the subtasks.

A feature group, X_m, is a subset of features. The overlapping subtasks $\Omega_1, \ldots, \Omega_m$ are defined as the union of selected feature groups $X_1, \ldots X_m$, for $m = 1, \ldots, M$, where M is the total number of feature groups, so that;

$$\Omega_1 = [X_1] \tag{1}$$
$$\Omega_2 = [X_1, X_2]$$
$$\Omega_3 = [X_1, X_2, X_3]$$
$$\Omega_M = [X_1, X_2, ..., X_M]$$

In the example in Fig. 1, the first feature group is defined to be $X_1 = \{S1, S2\}$ and the second to be $X_2 = \{S3\}$. The overlapping subtasks are then $\Omega_1 = X_1$ and $\Omega_2 = \{X_1, X_2\}$. The input-hidden layer ω_m weights and the hidden-output layer υ_m weights are combined for the respective network module Φ_m. Hence, the cascaded network module θ_m of subtask m is constructed by combining with current Φ_m and previous network module Φ_{m-1} as follows.

$$\Phi_1 = [\omega_1, \upsilon_1]; \quad \theta_1 = (\Phi_1)$$
$$\Phi_2 = [\omega_2, \upsilon_2]; \quad \theta_2 = [\theta_1, \Phi_2]$$
$$\vdots$$
$$\Phi_M = [\omega_M, \upsilon_M]; \quad \theta_M = [\theta_{M-1}, \Phi_M] \tag{2}$$

The list of network modules considered for training or optimisation is therefore $\Phi = (\Phi_1, \ldots, \Phi_M)$.

The size of the feature group and feature space needs to be defined experimentally or can be dependent on the problem given the contribution of the features. It is important to have the most contributing features in the first feature space in order to make use of the full potential of the algorithm. There is a need for appropriate feature selection algorithms as a pre-processing stage in finding the value of the features. Since feature selection is beyond the scope, the decomposition for feature groups would be arbitrary done as the goal is to develop an algorithm that provides robust decision making given some of the feature groups are missing.

The number of input i, hidden h and output o neurons in a cascaded network architecture defines a knowledge module $\theta_n = f(i_n, h_n, o)$. The number of output neurons o is same for all the respective modules and $f(.)$ represents the modules of the cascaded network. Hence, n modules are defined by concatenation of knowledge modules which can also be viewed as network ensembles. Note that the input size for a given module is given by the size of the corresponding subtask, $i_n = s(\Omega_n)$ where s represents the size. The number of hidden neurons for different modules can vary. In the proposed modular network architecture, we consider that the hidden neurons used in a given module is computed simply by considering the number of hidden neurons used in the previous module, $h_n = h_{n-1} + \bar{h}$ where $\bar{h}$ refers to the number of hidden neurons in the base knowledge module θ_1.

Algorithm 1 gives an overview of the multi-task modular backpropagation algorithm that employs gradient descent. The training of the network modules are implemented in a incremental mode where each module is trained for a short period of time given by a fixed or adaptive depth d which is predetermined experimentally. The procedure repeats in a round-robin fashion until the termination condition is met which could be given by the number of epochs or the minimal training performance. This incremental training strategy can be viewed as developmental learning [7,10] while the transfer of knowledge from the smaller modules to larger ones could be seen as heterogeneous transfer learning [15]. Figure 1 shows the stage of the network with module 1 and module 2 after knowledge has been incorporated. The incorporation of knowledge considers weights and bias in the respective layers as shown in the figure. The implementation of Algorithm 1 in Python is given online[1].

---

[1] https://github.com/rohitash-chandra/modular-backpropagation-classification.

Algorithm 1. Multi-task modular backpropagation

Step 1: Partition n subtasks Ω_n from data.
Step 2: Define cascaded neural network of modules: $\theta_n = f(i_n, h_n, o)$
while until termination **do**
  for each Module θ_n **do**
    for Depth d **do**
      i. Forwardpropagate(θ_n, Ω_n)
      ii. Backpropagate using Gradient-descent(θ_n, Ω_n)
      iii. a) Calculate gradients
        b) Weight updates
    end for
    transfer-knowledge(θ_n, θ_{n+1})
  end for
end while

---

3 Simulation and Analysis

This section presents performance evaluation of the proposed multi-task modular backpropgation method for feature-based and modular pattern classification. We compare the results with canonical backpropagation that features gradient descent for pattern benchmark classification tasks.

3.1 Experimental Design

Twelve problems from the University of California, Irvine machine learning data repository [1] were selected and the data was partitioned into 4 groups that contained overlapping features given the respective subtasks. The size δ of each subtask (Ω_m) is given by the proportion β considering the total number of features for the given problem p.

$$\beta = [0.25, 0.5, 0.75, 1] \tag{3}$$

$$\delta_n = \beta_n * p \tag{4}$$

Table 1 gives details of the respective problems used with details about the number of features, number of classes, and number of instances. The termination condition is also given. The number of hidden neurons for foundation module that corresponds to Ω_1 is given by $\hat{h}$ in Table 1. The rest of the hidden neurons in the respective network modules are incremented by $h_n = \hat{h} + h_{n-1} + \epsilon$, given that $h_1 = \hat{h}$. $\epsilon = 2$ is used in all the experiments.

Note that the two major strategies in multi-task modular back-propagation algorithm deal with number of iterations used for each module while they are evolved or trained in a round-robin fashion. The performance is evaluated where adaptive and fixed depth of search strategies are used. The fixed depth of $f = 5$ is used. The adaptive depth α considers a set of values where $\alpha = [10, 7, 4, 1]$. The motivation behind the adaptive depth is to use more training time for the subtasks that represent the building blocks of knowledge. The termination

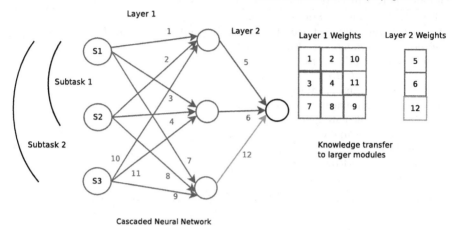

Fig. 1. Knowledge transfer through multi-task modular backpropagation. Note that the modules are represented by different colours. The neural network is implemented as a cascaded network architecture defined by the subtasks. (Color figure online)

condition is defined by maximum epochs or when minimum training performance (97%) has been reached.

Table 2 show the classification performance results that mean (Train and Test) and standard deviation (std) for 30 independent experimental runs. The results for MTMB for the instances of fixed and adaptive depth are further compared with canonical backpropagation that employs gradient descent (BP-GD). Note that the results of the different feature space for the respective problem has been shown (Ω_n) in Table 2. The results compare the fixed and adaptive depth in terms of training and generalisation performance. The two strategies have similar performance for most of the problems. The major difference is shown for the Balloon problem where the fixed depth gives a much better training and test performance when compared to adaptive depth strategy. In the Heart problem, the fixed depth Ω_4 gives a much better training performance, howsoever, both methods give a similar test performance. The Tic-Tac-Toe problem also gets better training and test performance by fixed depth strategy. The Lenses problem gets better training performance by fixed depth strategy, howsoever, both methods have the same test performance. In general, the results show that the fixed depth strategy provides better performance when compared to the adaptive depth. Next, the results of the proposed algorithm are compared with BP-GD. Ω_4 is selected specifically for comparison since it uses all the features. The fixed depth strategy (Ω_4) gives similar or better training performance when compared to BP-GD in most of the problems except for the Tic-Tac-Toe problem. In the test performance, it is observed that fixed depth strategy gives better performance for most of the problems, except for the Tic-Tac-Toe problem. Similarly,

Table 1. Configuration

Dataset	Features	Classes	Instances	$\hat{h}$	Max. Time
Iris	4	3	150	6	500
Wine	13	3	178	6	500
Cancer	9	2	699	6	1000
Heart	13	2	270	16	2000
Credit	15	2	690	20	3000
Baloon	4	2	20	5	500
Tic-Tac-Toe	9	2	269	30	2000
Ionosphere	34	2	351	8	500
Zoo	17	7	101	6	300
Lenses	4	3	24	5	500
Balance	4	3	625	8	200
Robot (Four)	4	4	5456	14	2000
Robot (TwentyFour)	24	4	5456	14	2000

the adaptive depth strategy (Ω_4) also gives better test performance than BP-GD in general.

3.2 Discussion

The results suggest that modularity enforced through backpropagation helped to retain the knowledge of the smaller network modules that are used as building blocks of knowledge for multi-task learning. Heterogeneous form of transfer learning is employed to transfer knowledge from small network modules to larger network modules which link with the respective subtasks. Hence, through transfer learning, the knowledge in foundational modules are projected through the learning of the entire network. This network architecture can be very useful in hardware implementations [11] given that real-time embedded systems may not have full information from sensors in some cases, the network will be able to provide a decision from knowledge in the foundational building blocks or modules. Multi-task modular back-propagation implements an ensemble of cascaded network modules that employ heterogeneous transfer learning for utilizing knowledge in smaller modules. This can also be viewed as a form of dynamic programming [3] as the problem is decomposed into modules and knowledge from the base network modules are used in larger modules through transfer learning. The proposed algorithm implements a neural network that would be operational with a degree of error even when some of the neurons or links in the larger modules are damaged. Moreover, it would be operational with a degree of error in decision making when selected subtasks are unavailable during an event.

Table 2. Results

Problem	Domain	Adapt Depth MTMB				Fixed Depth MTMB				BP-GD
		Ω_1	Ω_2	Ω_3	Ω_4	Ω_1	Ω_2	Ω_3	Ω_4	
Iris	Train	55.73	60.52	74.79	80.18	52.70	59.27	89.76	95.09	93.30
	(std)	4.89	3.72	4.96	4.39	4.95	5.04	3.16	1.38	0.89
	Test	85.25	88.67	89.42	93.08	88.75	90.00	91.08	94.42	83.50
	(std)	5.38	5.07	3.14	4.46	5.31	4.38	4.36	2.56	2.47
Wine	Train	98.26	99.81	99.83	99.95	98.09	99.86	100.00	100.00	98.45
	(std)	0.91	0.42	0.55	0.26	1.25	0.34	0.00	0.00	0.87
	Test	99.75	100.00	100.00	100.00	99.75	99.83	100.00	100.00	83.25
	(std)	0.75	0.00	0.00	0.00	0.75	0.62	0.00	0.00	9.90
Cancer	Train	86.32	90.03	93.59	93.84	86.03	89.56	94.00	94.56	94.07
	(std)	0.75	0.90	0.65	0.81	0.53	0.85	0.48	0.73	0.54
	Test	97.73	97.49	98.37	98.44	97.46	97.67	98.22	98.41	96.24
	(std)	0.47	0.87	0.27	0.39	0.55	0.91	0.27	0.41	0.57
Heart	Train	49.61	56.76	68.39	77.03	47.89	55.21	71.99	88.20	90.92
	(std)	3.72	4.36	2.11	2.45	4.21	5.15	2.96	2.69	1.44
	Test	74.78	75.67	72.56	79.11	75.22	76.22	73.41	77.56	70.63
	(std)	1.84	1.63	2.65	2.19	1.70	1.74	1.88	2.42	3.14
Credit	Train	19.79	42.53	82.34	84.35	18.94	40.62	83.24	87.44	89.64
	(std)	2.91	4.46	1.86	2.26	4.15	5.18	1.97	1.39	1.07
	Test	56.97	61.82	82.22	82.64	55.23	62.40	82.71	82.06	78.79
	(std)	3.32	2.96	1.73	1.43	4.59	2.76	1.67	1.48	1.56
Balloon	Train	7.14	15.00	34.76	44.29	8.57	12.14	45.24	99.52	100.00
	(std)	10.10	9.82	12.61	6.23	10.50	11.97	10.49	1.78	0.00
	Test	50.00	50.00	58.33	81.67	50.00	50.00	62.78	100.00	91.11
	(std)	0.00	0.00	14.75	21.24	0.00	0.00	15.33	0.00	14.74
Tic-Tac	Train	33.05	42.18	61.81	71.14	36.07	40.06	62.10	79.65	97.40
	(std)	9.04	6.68	3.83	2.85	9.33	7.18	4.52	3.54	0.24
	Test	0.00	8.29	12.08	24.97	0.00	8.39	13.22	38.96	61.24
	(std)	0.00	3.40	2.33	6.65	0.00	3.39	3.38	12.18	6.90
Ionosph.	Train	85.03	91.07	94.39	94.80	80.98	88.98	93.58	95.97	94.88
	(std)	1.92	1.54	1.55	2.58	2.32	2.01	1.53	0.86	1.32
	Test	89.54	92.48	94.19	93.94	90.00	92.26	94.40	94.74	84.62
	(std)	4.42	2.12	1.43	2.07	4.70	1.47	2.34	1.72	1.99
Zoo	Train	100.00	100.00	100.00	100.00	100.00	100.00	100.00	100.00	99.81
	(std)	0.00	0.00	0.00	0.00	0.00	0.00	0.00	0.00	0.60
	Test	100.00	100.00	100.00	100.00	100.00	100.00	100.00	100.00	98.44
	(std)	0.00	0.00	0.00	0.00	0.00	0.00	0.00	0.00	3.93
Lenses	Train	83.12	75.42	83.96	61.67	79.17	77.92	94.17	95.21	99.81
	(std)	15.15	17.60	21.51	24.72	14.99	15.46	9.12	5.97	0.60
	Test	100.00	100.00	100.00	100.00	100.00	100.00	100.00	100.00	98.44
	(std)	0.00	0.00	0.00	0.00	0.00	0.00	0.00	0.00	3.93
Balance	Train	94.09	95.62	95.98	93.35	93.94	95.36	96.11	94.65	92.29
	(std)	0.00	0.72	0.63	1.05	0.57	0.97	0.53	1.60	7.85
	Test	100.00	100.00	99.98	100.00	100.00	100.00	100.00	100.00	88.33
	(std)	0.00	0.00	0.10	0.00	0.00	0.00	0.00	0.00	8.50
Robot (Four)	Train	99.95	100.00	100.00	100.00	99.93	100.00	100.00	100.00	95.95
	(std)	0.15	0.00	0.00	0.00	0.17	0.00	0.00	0.00	1.69
	Test	100.00	100.00	100.00	100.00	100.00	100.00	100.00	100.00	98.81
	(std)	0.00	0.00	0.00	0.00	0.00	0.00	0.00	0.00	2.39
Robot (Twenty Four)	Train	100.00	100.00	100.00	100.00	100.00	100.00	100.00	100.00	98.69
	(std)	0.00	0.00	0.00	0.00	0.00	0.00	0.00	0.00	0.75
	Test	100.00	100.00	100.00	100.00	1.17	100.00	100.00	100.00	94.35
	(std)	0.00	0.00	0.00	0.00	2.17	0.00	0.00	0.00	6.21

4   Conclusions and Future Work

The paper presented a cascaded network architecture that employs multi-task modular backpropgation algorithm for feature-based pattern classification. The method incorporates heterogeneous transfer learning in order to utilize knowledge from smaller modules into larges ones. The goal of the method was to provide modularity in knowledge representation and decision making so that it can be applied to problems where real-time implementations may have cases where full feature space or all the features are available. The results shows that the proposed algorithm can deliver similar or better performance to that of canonical (non-modular) backpropagation network. Hence, the proposed algorithm can train neural networks that do not lose performance although their knowledge representation featured modularity. Moreover, although unexpected, the algorithm outperformed canonical backpropagation in several cases.

In future work, the method can be adapted for other types of problems that include image classification. Moreover, the modular method needs to be adapted further so that the trained network is operational even when the foundation or base subtask is unavailable during test phase. Uncertainty quantification through Bayesian inference methods for modular networks can also be explored. Furthermore, the method can be extended to the application of deep learning.

References

1. Asuncion, A., Newman, D.: UCI machine learning repository (2007). http://archive.ics.uci.edu/ml/datasets.html
2. Auda, G., Kamel, M.: Modular neural networks: a survey. Int. J. Neural Syst. **9**(02), 129–151 (1999)
3. Boutilier, C., Dearden, R., Goldszmidt, M.: Stochastic dynamic programming with factored representations. Artif. Intell. **121**(1), 49–107 (2000)
4. Caruana, R.: Multitask learning. In: Thrun, S., Pratt, L. (eds.) Learning to Learn, pp. 95–133. Springer, Boston (1998). doi:10.1007/978-1-4615-5529-2_5
5. Chandra, R., Ong, Y.S., Goh, C.K.: Co-evolutionary multi-task learning for dynamic time series prediction. CoRR abs/1703.01887 (2017). http://arxiv.org/abs/1703.01887
6. Chandra, R., Ong, Y.S., Goh, C.K.: Co-evolutionary multi-task learning with predictive recurrence for multi-step chaotic time series prediction. Neurocomputing **243**, 21–34 (2017)
7. Geschwind, N., Behan, P.: Left-handedness: association with immune disease, migraine, and developmental learning disorder. Proc. Natl. Acad. Sci. **79**(16), 5097–5100 (1982)
8. Hunt, K.J., Sbarbaro, D., Żbikowski, R., Gawthrop, P.J.: Neural networks for control systems-a survey. Automatica **28**(6), 1083–1112 (1992)
9. Johnson, M.K.: A multiple-entry, modular memory system. Psychol. Learn. Motiv. **17**, 81–123 (1983). Academic Press
10. Lee, M.H., Meng, Q., Chao, F.: Developmental learning for autonomous robots. Robot. Auton. Syst. **55**(9), 750–759 (2007)
11. Misra, J., Saha, I.: Artificial neural networks in hardware: a survey of two decades of progress. Neurocomputing **74**(1–3), 239–255 (2010)

12. Moon, S.W., Kong, S.G.: Block-based neural networks. IEEE Trans. Neural Netw. **12**(2), 307–317 (2001)

13. Pan, S.J., Yang, Q.: A survey on transfer learning. IEEE Trans. Knowl. Data Eng. **22**(10), 1345–1359 (2010)

14. Sun, S.: A survey of multi-view machine learning. Neural Comput. Appl. **23**(7–8), 2031–2038 (2013)

15. Xu, Z., Sun, S.: Multi-source transfer learning with multi-view adaboost. In: Huang, T., Zeng, Z., Li, C., Leung, C.S. (eds.) ICONIP 2012. LNCS, vol. 7665, pp. 332–339. Springer, Heidelberg (2012). doi:10.1007/978-3-642-34487-9_41

16. Zeng, T., Ji, S.: Deep convolutional neural networks for multi-instance multi-task learning. In: 2015 IEEE International Conference on Data Mining (ICDM), pp. 579–588, November 2015

17. Zheng, H., Geng, X., Tao, D., Jin, Z.: A multi-task model for simultaneous face identification and facial expression recognition. Neurocomputing **171**, 515–523 (2016)

On-Road Object Detection Based on Deep Residual Networks

Kang Chen, Qi Zhao, Yaorong Lin[✉], and Jun Zhang

School of Electronic and Information Engineering, South China University of Technology,
Guangzhou, China
eeyrlin@scut.edu.cn

Abstract. In this paper, we explore the performance of deep residual networks in on-road object detection based on Faster R-CNN algorithm. We first optimize the setting of anchors through cluster analysis of training data. To achieve higher accuracy, we introduce a network design to combine multi-layers features. We also use a ROI spatial pyramid pooling layer to improve system performance on small objects. Experiment results show that the proposed method achieves better performance compared with baseline method.

Keywords: Object detection · CNN · Deep learning · ResNet

1 Introduction

On-road object detection is one of the key challenges in fields such as autonomous vehicles and advanced driver assistant systems. In recent years, convolutional neural networks have been widely used in areas such as object detection and image classification due to the powerful capability in both representation and learning. The region based CNN (R-CNN) algorithms [1] outperforms the traditional object detection systems such as DPM [2] in generic object detection.

The Faster R-CNN algorithm [1] achieves high accuracy on the PASCAL dataset [3]. However, the performance degrades in on-road object detection. On-road objects exhibit significant scale variation, occlusion or truncation. There are a lot of small objects including pedestrians, cars, cyclists and so on. And only a limited amount of annotated data are available for such scenarios.

Many methods have been proposed to overcome the problems mentioned above. MS-CNN [5] uses multiple scale-specific detectors on multiple output layers to match objects of different scales. Sub-CNN [6] utilizes subcategory information to guide the proposal generating process, and a new network is designed for joint object detection and subcategory classification. Feature Pyramid Network [7] in a basic Faster R-CNN system shows significant improvement.

In this work, we propose a new approach to get better performance in on-road object detection. Generally we use the framework of Faster R-CNN algorithm. We improve the algorithm as follows:

© Springer International Publishing AG 2017
D. Liu et al. (Eds.): ICONIP 2017, Part VI, LNCS 10639, pp. 567–574, 2017.
https://doi.org/10.1007/978-3-319-70136-3_60

1. We optimize the anchors setting by cluster analysis of training data. Using the optimized anchors we can achieve comparable accuracy compared to the hand-crafted anchors with less computation.
2. We introduce a network design to combine multi-layers features and construct a ROI spatial pyramid pooling layer for small object detection.
3. We use online hard example mining (OHEM) [8] in the training process, and adopt the bounding box voting method [9] to improve the algorithm further.

The rest of the paper is organized as follows: Sect. 2 describes our proposed methods, Sect. 3 describes the experimental result and Sect. 4 closes with a conclusion.

2   Proposed Method

2.1   Baseline Model

The R-CNN algorithm consists of a proposal generation step and a detection step. In Faster R-CNN, Region Proposal Network (RPN) is used to generate proposals instead of region proposal methods. Faster R-CNN is much more effective because RPN shares convolutional layers with the object detection network.

He et al. [11] introduces a detection method based on the Faster R-CNN system with ResNet-101. ResNet-101 has no hidden fully-connected layers. The full-image shared convolutional feature maps are computed using those layers whose strides are not greater than 16 pixels (i.e., conv1, conv2_x, conv3_x, and conv4_x, totally 91 conv layers in ResNet101). These layers are shared by a region proposal network (RPN) and a Fast R-CNN detection network [1]. RoI pooling [1] is performed before conv5_1. All layers of conv5_x and up are adopted as region detection network on the RoI-pooled feature. In our experiments, we use Faster R-CNN with ResNet-101 as baseline model. And the architecture of our backbone network is similar to ResNet-101.

2.2   Anchors Optimization

As mentioned above in Sect. 1, there are various objects, especially many small objects in on-road scenarios. To achieve higher accuracy with Faster R-CNN algorithm, we need to select more anchors manually. Experiments show that we can get better result with 70 anchors instead of the original 9 anchors. However, more anchors need more computation. To refine anchors, we adopt K-means algorithm to cluster bounding boxes on training data. The centroid of clusters are used as anchors. The distance metric is defined as

$$dist(gt, centroid) = 1 - IOU(gt, centroid) \tag{1}$$

Here, IOU is intersection over union, gt denotes the ground truth bounding box, and centroid is the centroid of cluster. The goal of IOU is to compute the intersection of union between two bounding boxes. IOU is defined as follows

$$IOU(gt, centroid) = \frac{gt \cap centroid}{gt \cup centroid} \tag{2}$$

2.3 Proposed Model

Multi-layer features combination. Multi-scale detection performs better especially for small objects. The feature hierarchy of a deep ConvNet has an inherent multi-scale pyramid hierarchy [7]. The output of conv4_x is up-sampled by a factor of 2. The output of conv3_x undergoes a 1 x 1 convolutional layer to increase channel dimensions to 1024. They are merged by element-wise addition. Finally, a 3×3 convolution is appended on the merged map to generate the 1024-d multi-scale feature map. The multi-scale feature map are shared by RPN and R-CNN.

ROI spatial pyramid pooling. Faster R-CNN with ResNet takes the 1024-d feature as input of ROIPooling layer. For each ROI, $14 \times 14 \times 1024$-d feature is generated by the ROIPooling layer. To improve the performance of small object classification, the ROIPooling layer is replaced with a ROI spatial pyramid pooling layer [10]. The ROI spatial pyramid pooling layer consists of three ROI pooling layers of different scales, which output $12 \times 12 \times 1024$-d, $6 \times 6 \times 1024$-d, $4 \times 4 \times 1024$-d features respectively. The features are concatenated together as final ROI-pooled feature. The ROI SPP architecture is shown in Fig. 1.

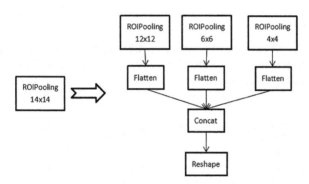

Fig. 1. ROI spatial pyramid pooling layer.

OHEM and Bounding box voting. Online Hard Example Mining [8] has been verified to be effective for optimizing the training process of Faster R-CNN like algorithms. It can improve these algorithms by constructing minibatches using high-loss examples. Bounding box voting [9] is an effective way to refine the output bounding boxes.

3   Experimental Results

3.1 Dataset

The KITTI dataset [4] consists of video frames of driving scenes. Object classes of car, pedestrian and cyclist are evaluated for object detection. Images are RGB images and mostly have a resolution of 1242×375. Each object in training set is labeled with a bounding box. The dataset is divided into 3 categories: Easy, Moderate and Hard, based on the minimum bounding box height, maximum occlusion and truncation level. The benchmark provides an evaluation toolkit. We split the KITTI training images into a training set and a validation set for analysis (5236 images for training and 2245 images for testing).

3.2 Implementation Details

We fine tune our networks on top of ResNet101 which is pre-trained on ImageNet. We randomly initialize all new layers by drawing weights from a zero-mean Gaussian distribution with standard deviation 0.01. During both training and testing stage, we re-scale all the images so that the shorter side of the images is fixed. In addition, if the longer side of the rescaled images is still too large, it is limited to a given size while maintaining the image's aspect ratio. We scale the shorter side to 560 pixels and make sure the longer side is no more than 2200 pixels. In all the experiments, we use an initial learning rate of 0.001, a step size of 10000 and a momentum of 0.9. A total of 40 K iterations are run for training.

We evaluate object detection performance by average precision (AP). AP is calculated by the toolkit provided in KITTI. All evaluations are run on an Intel i7-6700 CPU and a NVIDIA Titan X GPU (Maxwell architecture).

3.3 Comparison

Improvement by Multi-layer Feature and ROI SPP. We evaluate our method on KITTI object detection dataset with the network we discussed in Sect. 2.3. We use 15 anchors generated by K–means clustering. Table 1 shows the average precision for each object categories.

Table 1. AP improvement by multi-layer feature and ROI SPP.

Object	Car		
Level	Easy	Medium	Hard
Faster RCNN+ResNet-101	0.909	0.854	0.758
Proposed method	**0.970**	**0.896**	**0.803**
Object	Cyclist		
Level	Easy	Medium	Hard
Faster RCNN+ResNet-101	0.848	0.771	0.695
Proposed method	**0.893**	**0.806**	**0.804**
Object	Pedestrian		
Level	Easy	Medium	Hard
Faster RCNN+ResNet-101	0.790	0.687	0.609
Proposed method	**0.810**	**0.715**	**0.627**

Improvement by Anchors Optimization. Through clustering on training data with K-means algorithm, we can get better anchors setting even with less anchors. To balance between accuracy and time efficiency, we set 15 clusters when running K-means algorithm on training data. This results in 15 anchors. The anchors' scales and ratios are shown in Table 2. The network is the same as previous section. We use 70 hand-crafted anchors for comparison. Table 3 shows the AP of using two anchors settings. Table 4 shows the average testing time per image. It is shown that comparable accuracy is maintained even with less anchors by anchors optimization.

Table 2. Anchors generated by K-means. Scales mean width *length, ratios mean width / length.

Anchor	1	2	3	4	5	6	7
Scale	370*185	223*116	125*51	182*76	83*34	21*56	43*29
Ratio	2:1	1.9:1	2.5:1	2.4:1	2.4:1	0.4:1	1.5:1
Anchor	8	9	10	11	12	13	14	15
Scale	70*163	126*88	24*22	56*44	83*62	39*97	136*185	260*175
Ratio	0.4:1	1.4:1	1.1:1	1.3:1	1.3:1	0.4:1	0.7:1	1.5:1

Table 3. AP of different settings of Anchors.

Object	Car		
Level	Easy	Medium	Hard
70anchors	0.963	0.892	0.802
15anchors	0.952	0.883	0.793
Object	Cyclist		
Level	Easy	Medium	Hard
70anchors	0.897	0.808	0.719
15anchors	0.896	0.806	0.719
Object	Pedestrian		
Level	Easy	Medium	Hard
70anchors	0.809	0.718	0.629
15anchors	0.812	0.717	0.629

Table 4. Detection time of different settings of Anchors.

Anchors	Time (s)
15	0.578
70	0.669

Discussion. Table 1 shows that our model can achieve better AP than the baseline model, especially for car detection. But for cyclist and pedestrian, the improvement is less obvious. It may be due to the smaller size of pedestrian and cyclist training data. Tables 3 and 4 show that optimized anchors are helpful to improve detection efficiency while maintaining the accuracy meanwhile. The precision-recall curves in Fig. 2 shows that our method has higher precision when recall increases. Selected examples of object detection results are shown in Fig. 3.

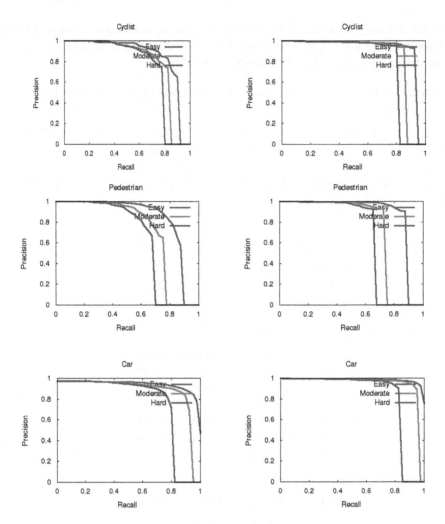

Fig. 2. PR curve. The left column is for comparison, the right one is that of proposed model.

Fig. 3. Selected examples of object detection results.

4   Conclusion

We propose a new network design to improve Faster R-CNN's detection performance in driving scenarios. We optimize anchors by clustering on training data with K-means. We merge multi-layers' features and construct ROI spatial pyramid pooling layer to improve detection accuracy for smaller objects in driving scenes. For further improvement, we use OHEM and bounding box voting to boost our method. Experiments show that our method can achieve better results than the baseline one.

Acknowledgements.   The work was supported in part by the National Natural Science Foundation of China under Grant numbers 61372083.

References

1. Ren, S., He, K., Girshick, R., et al.: Faster R-CNN: Towards real-time object detection with region proposal networks. IEEE Trans. Pattern Anal. Mach. Intell. **39**(6), 1137–1649 (2017)
2. Felzenszwalb, P.F., Girshick, R.B., Mcallester, D., et al.: Object detection with discriminatively trained part-based models. IEEE Trans. Pattern Anal. Mach. Intell. **32**(9), 1627–1645 (2010)
3. Everingham, M., Gool, L., Williams, C.K., et al.: The pascal visual object classes (VOC) challenge. Int. J. Comput. Vis. **88**(2), 303–338 (2010)
4. Urtasun, R., Lenz, P., Geiger, A.: Are we ready for autonomous driving? The KITTI vision benchmark suite. In: IEEE Conference on Computer Vision and Pattern Recognition, pp. 3354–3361. IEEE (2012)
5. Cai, Z., Fan, Q., Feris, R.S., Vasconcelos, N.: A unified multi-scale deep convolutional neural network for fast object detection. In: Leibe, B., Matas, J., Sebe, N., Welling, M. (eds.) ECCV 2016. LNCS, vol. 9908, pp. 354–370. Springer, Cham (2016). doi: 10.1007/978-3-319-46493-0_22
6. Xiang, Y., Choi, W., Lin, Y., et al.: Subcategory-aware convolutional neural networks for object proposals and detection (2016). arXiv:1604.04693
7. Lin, T., Dollár, P., Girshick, R., He, K., et al.: Feature pyramid networks for object detection. In: IEEE Conference on Computer Vision and Pattern Recognition. IEEE (2017)
8. Shrivastava, A., Gupta, A., Girshick, R.: Training region-based object detectors with online hard example mining. In: IEEE Conference on Computer Vision and Pattern Recognition, pp. 761–769. IEEE (2016)
9. Spyros, G., Nikos, K.: Object detection via a multi-region & semantic segmentation aware CNN model. In: 2015 IEEE International Conference on Computer Vision, pp. 1134–1142. IEEE (2015)
10. He, K., Zhang, X., Ren, S., Sun, J.: Spatial pyramid pooling in deep convolutional networks for visual recognition. In: Fleet, D., Pajdla, T., Schiele, B., Tuytelaars, T. (eds.) ECCV 2014. LNCS, vol. 8691, pp. 346–361. Springer, Cham (2014). doi:10.1007/978-3-319-10578-9_23
11. He, K., Zhang, X., Ren, S., et al.: Deep residual learning for image recognition. In: Proceedings of the IEEE Conference on Computer Vision and Pattern Recognition, pp. 770–778. IEEE (2016)

Supervised Deep Canonical Correlation Analysis for Multiview Feature Learning

Yan Liu, Yun Li[✉], Yun-Hao Yuan[✉], Ji-Peng Qiang, Min Ruan, and Zhao Zhang

School of Information Engineering,
Yangzhou University, Yangzhou 225137, China
{liyun,yhyuan}@yzu.edu.cn

Abstract. Recently, a new feature representation method called deep canonical correlation analysis (DCCA) has been proposed with high learning performance for multiview feature extraction of high dimensional data. DCCA is an effective approach to learn the nonlinear mappings of two sets of random variables that make the resulting DNN representations highly correlated. However, the DCCA learning process is unsupervised and thus lacks the class label information of training samples on the two views. In order to take full advantage of the class information of training samples, we propose a discriminative version of DCCA referred to as supervised DCCA (SDCCA) for feature learning, which explicitly considers the class information of samples. Compared with DCCA, the SDCCA method can not only guarantee the nonlinear maximal correlation between two views, but also minimize within-class scatter of the samples. With supervision, SDCCA can extract more discriminative features for pattern classification tasks. We test SDCCA on the handwriting recognition and speech recognition using two popular MNIST and XRMB datasets. Experimental results show that SDCCA gets higher performance than several related algorithms.

Keywords: Deep learning · Canonical correlations · Multiview learning

1 Introduction

In practical applications, an object can usually be described from different viewpoints in numerous scientific fields such as pattern recognition and multimedia retrieval. A simple example is that an image on internet can be depicted by original pixel feature and text feature. Since such data often called multi-view data contain more useful information than those only with one feature representation, learning from multi-view high-dimensional data, which is referred to as multi-view learning, has attracted more and more attention and become a hot research direction.

At present, there have been a number of multi-view learning methods. Canonical correlation analysis (CCA) [1] is one of the most widely used approaches in computer vision and pattern recognition. CCA linearly projects two sets of random variables into a lower-dimensional space where they are maximally correlated. However, CCA is an unsupervised method, thus difficult to generate discriminative low-dimensional projections for classification tasks. To deal with this issue, Sun et al. [2] proposed a

© Springer International Publishing AG 2017
D. Liu et al. (Eds.): ICONIP 2017, Part VI, LNCS 10639, pp. 575–582, 2017.
https://doi.org/10.1007/978-3-319-70136-3_61

generalized CCA (GCCA), which can not only guarantee the maximal correlation between two sets of the projected data, but also minimize the within-class scatter of training samples. On the other hand, CCA is essentially a linear subspace learning method. It is not capable of revealing the nonlinear correlations effectively between two-set data. To this end, kernel CCA [3] has been proposed where two-view original data are, respectively, projected into higher-dimensional Hilbert spaces by the implicit nonlinear mappings determined by kernels.

Different from the idea from kernels, deep variants of CCA have been developed for learning multi-view nonlinear low-dimensional features. Deep CCA (DCCA) [4] integrates deep neural network and CCA together, which can effectively uncover the nonlinear correlation structure hidden in multi-view high dimensional data. Due to the advantage, Yan et al. [5] used DCCA to propose a caption-image matching algorithm which produces the state-of-the-art results on three benchmark image-text datasets. In addition, deep variational CCA [6] and deep canonical correlation autoencoder [7] have also been presented.

Motivated by recent progress in deep learning and canonical correlations, in this paper we propose a supervised deep CCA (SDCCA) approach for multi-view feature learning, which explicitly considers the class label information of the training samples and can thus find *good* feature representations in classification. Experimental results show that SDCCA is encouraging.

2 Related Work

2.1 CCA

Given n pairs of centered samples $\{(x_i, y_i) \in \mathbb{R}^p \times \mathbb{R}^q\}_{i=1}^n$ with p and q as the sample dimensions, let $X = (x_1, x_2, \cdots, x_n) \in \mathbb{R}^{p \times n}$ and $Y = (y_1, y_2, \cdots, y_n) \in \mathbb{R}^{q \times n}$. CCA aims to seek pairs of projection directions $\alpha \in \mathbb{R}^p$ and $\beta \in \mathbb{R}^q$ such that the correlation coefficient of canonical projections $\alpha^T X$ and $\beta^T Y$ is maximized:

$$\rho(\alpha, \beta) = \frac{\alpha^T XY\beta}{\sqrt{\alpha^T XX^T \alpha}\sqrt{\beta^T YY^T \beta}} = \frac{\alpha^T S_{xy}\beta}{\sqrt{\alpha^T S_{xx}\alpha}\sqrt{\beta^T S_{yy}\beta}}, \tag{1}$$

where S_{xx} and S_{yy} are the within-set covariance matrices of samples X and Y, and S_{xy} is the between-set covariance matrix of X and Y.

Obviously, the canonical correlation coefficient ρ is affine-invariant to arbitrary scaling of α and β. Therefore, CCA needs to normalize the directions by

$$\alpha^T S_{xx}\alpha = 1 \text{ and } \beta^T S_{yy}\beta = 1. \tag{2}$$

With (2), CCA can be formulated as a constrained optimization problem:

$$(\alpha^*, \beta^*) = \arg\max_{\alpha,\beta} \alpha^T S_{xy}\beta$$
$$s.t. \quad \alpha^T S_{xx}\alpha = 1 \text{ , } \beta^T S_{yy}\beta = 1. \tag{3}$$

There are several ways to calculate pairs of solutions to CCA. Following the approach in [8], let us define

$$H = S_{xx}^{-1/2} S_{xy} S_{yy}^{-1/2}, \tag{4}$$

The singular value decomposition (SVD) of the matrix H is the following

$$H = U\Sigma V^T, \tag{5}$$

where U and V are the left and right singular vector matrices of H and Σ is a diagonal matrix with diagonal entries as the descending singular values of H. Then, the kth direction pair is the kth column vectors of matrices $S_{xx}^{-1/2}U$ and $S_{yy}^{-1/2}V$, respectively, where $k \leq rank(H)$. More details about CCA solution can be found in [8].

2.2   Deep CCA (DCCA)

The purpose of deep CCA [4] is to simultaneously learn two deep nonlinear mappings of two-view data that are highly correlated. Compared with KCCA where nonlinear representation is limited by fixed kernel, DCCA is able to learn flexible nonlinear representations by passing two-view data through multiple stacked layers of nonlinear transformation.

In DCCA, assume f and g denote two deep neural networks (DNNs) which are used to extract nonlinear features of two views. Let the learned features of X and Y by DNNs be[1] $f(X)$ and $g(X)$, respectively, where X and Y are defined in (1). Then, the DCCA model is the following:

$$\max \ \text{tr}\left(U^T f(X) g(Y)^T V\right)$$
$$s.t. \ \begin{cases} U^T f(X) f(X)^T U = I, \\ V^T g(Y) g(Y)^T V = I, \end{cases} \tag{6}$$

where tr(A) denotes the trace of matrix A, U and V are pairs of projection directions that project the final outputs of f and g into a space where the projections are highly correlated, and I is the identity matrix. In addition, denoising autoencoder [9] is adopted to initialize the values of weights in the two DNNs f and g.

3   Proposed SDCCA

The proposed SDCCA aims to find the nonlinear representations with the class label information of training samples. Thus, from the viewpoint of pattern classification, it would improve the classification ability of deep CCA. Specifically, consider n pairs of

---

[1] Here DNNs f and g are regarded as two nonlinear mappings. Thus, $f(X)$ and $g(Y)$ denote the DNN outputs (top-level representations) on the two views.

samples $x_{ij} \in \mathbb{R}^p$ and $y_{ij} \in \mathbb{R}^q$ with c classes, $i = 1, 2, \cdots, c, j = 1, 2, \cdots n_i$, and n_i is the number of samples in class i, satisfying $\sum_{i=1}^{c} n_i = n$. Let us denote

$$X = (X_1, X_2, \cdots, X_c) \in \mathbb{R}^{p \times n},$$

$$Y = (Y_1, Y_2, \cdots, Y_c) \in \mathbb{R}^{q \times n},$$

and let

$$f(X) = (f(X_1), f(X_2), \cdots, f(X_c)),$$

$$g(Y) = (g(Y_1), g(Y_2), \cdots, g(Y_c)),$$

be the top-level representations of data matrices X and Y obtained by DNNs f and g, where X_i and Y_i are the sample matrices of ith class on the two views. Our proposed SDCCA method solves the following optimization problem:

$$\max_{W_f, W_g, U, V} \operatorname{tr}(U^T S_{fg} V) \tag{7}$$
$$s.t. \quad U^T S_{wf} U = I, \ V^T S_{wg} V = I,$$

where W_f and W_g separately denote all the weight parameters of DNNs f and g, U and V are the projection matrices that make $f(X)$ maximally correlated with $g(Y)$, and

$$S_{fg} = \frac{1}{n-1} \sum_{i=1}^{c} \sum_{j=1}^{n_i} (f(x_{ij}) - m^x)(g(y_{ij}) - m^y)^T, \tag{8}$$

$$S_{wf} = \sum_{i=1}^{c} p(i) \sum_{j=1}^{n_i} \frac{1}{n_i} (f(x_{ij}) - m_i^x)(f(x_{ij}) - m_i^x)^T, \tag{9}$$

$$S_{wg} = \sum_{i=1}^{c} p(i) \sum_{j=1}^{n_i} \frac{1}{n_i} (g(y_{ij}) - m_i^y)(g(y_{ij}) - m_i^y)^T, \tag{10}$$

m^x and m^y are separately the mean of the DNN outputs $f(X)$ and $g(Y)$, m_i^x and m_i^y are respectively the mean of the DNN outputs in class i, $p(i)$ is the prior probability of class i which is set to $n_i/(n-1)$ in this paper. Here we refer to (9) and (10) as *deep within-class covariance matrices*.

Fixing the DNNs f and g in problem (7), i.e., W_f and W_g, we are easily able to obtain projection matrices U and V by the SVD of the matrix $S = S_{wf}^{-1/2} S_{fg} S_{wg}^{-1/2}$. Analogously to the CCA's solution, let the SVD of the matrix S be $S = \tilde{U} \Sigma \tilde{V}^T$, where $\tilde{U} \tilde{U}^T = \tilde{U}^T \tilde{U} = I$ and $\tilde{V} \tilde{V}^T = \tilde{V}^T \tilde{V} = I$, Σ is the diagonal matrix with diagonal entries as sorted singular values in descending order. Then, the optimal U and V are obtained by $U = S_{wf}^{-1/2} \tilde{U}$ and $V = S_{wg}^{-1/2} \tilde{V}$, and the optimal objective value of problem (7) is the sum of singular values, i.e., $\operatorname{tr}(\Sigma)$.

On the other hand, since the objective function in (7) is different from traditional DNN objectives (e.g., regression and classification training objectives), it is difficult to precisely optimize the weights W_f and W_g of two DNNs. To find W_f and W_g under the supervised case, we directly replace Andrew et al.'s gradient [4] of the correlation objective (i.e., $\text{tr}(\Sigma)$) w.r.t. $f(X)$ with the following

$$\frac{\partial \text{tr}(\Sigma)}{\partial f(X)} \leftarrow \frac{1}{n-1} \left[2\nabla_{ff} \cdot \bar{f}(X) + \nabla_{fg} \cdot \bar{g}(Y) \right], \tag{11}$$

where $\bar{f}(X) = (\bar{f}(X_1), \bar{f}(X_2), \cdots, \bar{f}(X_c))$ with $\bar{f}(X_i) = f(X_i) - (1/n_i)f(X_i)\mathbf{1}$, $\bar{g}(Y)$ has the similar definition to $\bar{f}(X)$, and

$$\nabla_{fg} = S_{wf}^{-1/2} \tilde{U} \tilde{V}^T S_{wg}^{-1/2}, \tag{12}$$

$$\nabla_{ff} = -\frac{1}{2} S_{wf}^{-1/2} \tilde{U} \Sigma \tilde{U}^T S_{wf}^{-1/2}. \tag{13}$$

For $g(Y)$, $\partial \text{tr}(\Sigma)/\partial g(Y)$ has a similar replacement. After that, we are able to compute the gradients w.r.t. W_f and W_g using a backpropagation procedure.

4   Experiment

To test the effectiveness of our proposed SDCCA, we perform several recognition experiments and compare it with existing methods: CCA, GCCA, DCCA, Partially Linear CCA (PLCCA) [10] and Nonparametric CCA (NCCA) [10]. To train SDCCA, we follow Andrew et al.'s method [4]. The initialization of the parameters on each layer of DNNs is obtained by a denoising autoencoder [9].

4.1   MNIST Dataset

In the first experiment, we learn correlated representations of the left and right halves of handwritten digit images and test the classification accuracy. We use the MNIST handwritten image dataset[2], which consists of 60,000 training images and 10,000 testing images. We randomly select 10,000 images from the training set to tune the hyperparameters. Each image is a 28×28 matrix of pixels, each representing one of 256 grayscale values. The left and right 14 columns are separated to form the view 1 and view 2, making 392 features in each view. For DCCA and SDCCA, the number of hidden layers is chosen as three, with 800 nodes in each layer. For the output layer, the number of nodes is 100. Linear SVM [11] is used as a classifier. Table 1 shows the recognition results of CCA, GCCA, DCCA, PLCCA, NCCA, and SDCCA. Also, Table 2 lists the total correlations from the different methods above.

---

[2] http://yann.lecun.com/exdb/mnist/.

Table 1. Recognition accuracy of CCA, GCCA, DCCA, PLCCA, NCCA, and our SDCCA on the MNIST dataset.

Method	CCA	GCCA	DCCA	PLCCA	NCCA	SDCCA
Accuracy	88.62%	92.35%	96.41%	95.32%	97.00%	97.25%

From Table 1, we can see that our SDCCA attains the higher recognition accuracy than CCA, GCCA, DCCA, PLCCA, and NCCA. In order to know why our proposed method can get the higher recognition rates, we calculate the total correlations of the projected features for all the methods, as shown in Table 2. From Table 2, we can find that the method that has higher recognition rate can achieve a higher total correlation. This may be the reason that the method with higher total correlation can get higher recognition accuracy.

Table 2. Total correlations of CCA, GCCA, DCCA, PLCCA, NCCA, and our SDCCA on the MNIST dataset.

Method	CCA	GCCA	DCCA	PLCCA	NCCA	SDCCA
Total correlation	24.13	32.54	53.96	50.68	61.50	70.33

4.2   XRMB Dataset

We further test our SDCCA method using the data from the University of Wisconsin X-ray Microbeam Database (XRMB)[3], which records the speech and articulatory measurements of 47 American English speakers (22 male, 25 female). Each speaker has about 20 min of read speech: multi-sentence recordings, individual sentences, isolated word sequences, and number sequences, as well as non-speech oral motor tasks. We remove isolated words and motor tasks and thus each speaker has 53 utterances. The articulatory measurements are horizontal and vertical displacements of 8 pellets on the tongue, lips, and jaw.

In this experiment, we follow Wang et al.'s experimental settings [12]. That is, 273-dimensional acoustic inputs and 112-dimensional articulatory inputs are taken as two views, and 35 speakers are fixed for SDCCA training, while the remaining 12 are used in a 6-fold experiment (recognizer training on 4 2-speaker folds, tuning on 1 fold, and testing on the last fold). More details can be found in [12]. In addition, we select hyperparamenters based on recognition accuracy on the tuning set. For DCCA and SDCCA, the number of hidden layers is chosen to be three layers with 1024 nodes per layer. For the output layers, we extract 112-dimensional projections for each method. Table 3 shows the recognition results of CCA, GCCA, DCCA, PLCCA, NCCA, and SDCCA and Table 4 shows the total correlations of each method.

From Table 3, we can see that our proposed SDCCA gets better recognition accuracy than other methods. Also, from Table 4, we can also see that CCA, GCCA,

---

[3] http://ttic.uchicago.edu/~klivescu/XRMB_data/full/README.

Table 3. Recognition accuracy of CCA, GCCA, DCCA, PLCCA, NCCA, and our SDCCA on the XRMB dataset.

Method	CCA	GCCA	DCCA	PLCCA	NCCA	SDCCA
Accuracy	73.3%	73.2%	75.2%	74.7%	75.2%	75.4%

Table 4. Total correlations of CCA, GCCA, DCCA, PLCCA, NCCA, and our SDCCA on the XRMB dataset.

Method	CCA	GCCA	DCCA	PLCCA	NCCA	SDCCA
Total correlation	21.7	29.6	107.6	79.4	107.9	131.3

and PLCCA have lower total correlations than other models. DCCA and NCCA get the comparable results with our SDCCA. The SDCCA method obtains the highest total correlation.

5 Conclusion

We propose a new method called SDCCA to extract deep features, which outperforms many existing related methods including state of the art DCCA, PLCCA, and NCCA methods. Similarly to DCCA, our SDCCA also benefits from the DNN model, which implies that SDCCA does not suffer from the shortcomings (such as limited kernel representation as mentioned in Sect. 2.2) of KCCA. In addition, SDCCA can not only guarantee the nonlinear maximal correlation, but also minimize the within-class scatter of the training samples in two views. Compared with DCCA, it can make the intraclass samples more close, which leads to improvements of recognition accuracy. A future direction is to study a fast stochastic optimization procedure for SDCCA.

Acknowledgements. This work is supported by National Natural Science Foundation of China under Grant No. 61402203. In addition, it is also supported in part by the National Natural Science Foundation of China under Grant Nos. 61472344, 61611540347, the Natural Science Foundation of Jiangsu Province of China under Grant Nos. BK20161338, BK20170513, and sponsored by Excellent Young Backbone Teacher Project.

References

1. Hotelling, H.: Relations between two sets of variates. Biometrika **28**(3/4), 321–377 (1936)
2. Sun, Q.S., Liu, Z.-D., Heng, P.-A., Xia, D.-S.: A theorem on the generalized canonical projective vectors. Pattern Recogn. **38**(3), 449–452 (2005)
3. Lai, P.L., Fyfe, C.: Kernel and nonlinear canonical correlation analysis. Int. J. Neural Syst. **10**(5), 365 (2000)
4. Andrew, G., Arora, R., Bilmes, J., Livescu, K.: Deep canonical correlation analysis. In: ICML, pp. III-1247–III-1255. JMLR: W&CP, Atlanta (2013)

5. Yan, F., Mikolajczyk, K.: Deep correlation for matching images and text. In: CVPR, pp. 3441–3451. IEEE, Boston (2015)
6. Wang, W., Yan, X., Lee, H., Livescu, K.: Deep variational canonical correlation analysis arXiv preprint arXiv:1610.03454v3 (2017)
7. Wang, W., Arora, R., Livescu, K., Bilmes, J.: On deep multi-view representation learning. In: ICML, pp. 1083–1092. JMLR: W&CP, Lille (2015)
8. Melzer, T., Reiter, M., Bischof, H.: Appearance models based on kernel canonical correlation analysis. Pattern Recogn. **36**(9), 1961–1971 (2003)
9. Vincent, P., Larochelle, H., Lajoie, I., Bengio, Y., Manzagol, P.-A.: Stacked denoising autoencoders: learning useful representations in a deep network with a local denoising criterion. J. Mach. Learn. Res. **11**, 3371–3408 (2010)
10. Michaeli, T., Wang, W., Livescu, K.: Nonparametric canonical correlation analysis. In: ICML, pp. 1967–1976. JMLR: W&CP, New York (2016)
11. Chang, C.-C., Lin, C.-J.: LIBSVM: a library for support vector machines. ACM TIST **2**(3) (2011). Article No. 27
12. Wang, W., Arora, R., Livescu, K., Bilmes, J.: Unsupervised learning of acoustic features via deep canonical correlation analysis. In: ICASSP, pp. 4590–4594. IEEE, Brisbane (2015)

Handwritten Digit String Recognition by Combination of Residual Network and RNN-CTC

Hongjian Zhan, Qingqing Wang, and Yue Lu[✉]

Shanghai Key Laboratory of Multidimensional Information Processing,
Department of Computer Science and Technology, East China Normal University,
Shanghai 200062, China
ylu@cs.ecnu.edu.cn

Abstract. Recurrent neural network (RNN) and connectionist temporal classification (CTC) have showed successes in many sequence labeling tasks with the strong ability of dealing with the problems where the alignment between the inputs and the target labels is unknown. Residual network is a new structure of convolutional neural network and works well in various computer vision tasks. In this paper, we take advantage of the architectures mentioned above to create a new network for handwritten digit string recognition. First we design a residual network to extract features from input images, then we employ a RNN to model the contextual information within feature sequences and predict recognition results. At the top of this network, a standard CTC is applied to calculate the loss and yield the final results. These three parts compose an end-to-end trainable network. The proposed new architecture achieves the highest performances on ORAND-CAR-A and ORAND-CAR-B with recognition rates 89.75% and 91.14%, respectively. In addition, the experiments on a generated captcha dataset which has much longer string length show the potential of the proposed network to handle long strings.

Keywords: Digit string recognition · End to end · Convolutional neural network · Recurrent neural network · Connectionist temporal classification

1 Introduction

Recent years, with the advancement of deep learning, handwritten digit string recognition (HDSR) has archived great improvements [1–3]. An intuitive approach to recognize these handwriting strings is to segment string images into pieces which correspond to single characters or part of them, then combine the recognition results of these pieces with path-search algorithms to get global optimal results. These methods are known as over-segmentation strategy. Wu et al. [1] transformed the string image into a sequence of primitive image segments after

© Springer International Publishing AG 2017
D. Liu et al. (Eds.): ICONIP 2017, Part VI, LNCS 10639, pp. 583–591, 2017.
https://doi.org/10.1007/978-3-319-70136-3_62

binarization, then combined these segments to generate candidate character patterns, forming a segmentation candidate lattice. After that a beam search algorithm was used to find an optimal path over the candidate lattice. This method won the first place on the ICFHR2014 HDSR competition [1]. Saabni [3] used sliding window and deep neural network to attain high recognition rates. Gattal et al. [2] applied three segmentation methods to handle handwritten digit strings by combining these segmentation methods depending on the configuration link between digits. But this kind of methods faced many problems in practice, such as various handwritten styles, connected characters or background noises.

An alternative to handle such sequence recognition task is segmentation-free methods. Benefitting from the ability of modelling the alignment between inputs and labels directly, connectionist temporal classification (CTC) [4] is specifically suitable for temporal classification tasks, such as speech and string recognition. CTC is often used as an output layer for recurrent neural network (RNN). In practice such RNN-CTC framework usually combines with a deep neural network, which generates the feature representation of inputs. Messina [5] firstly applied a LSTM-RNN model to off-line Chinese handwritten text recognition. Without well-designed architecture it achieved competitive performance with the state-of-the-art of tradition method [6]. Shi et al. [7] proposed a network with CNN and RNN named CRNN and applied it to scene text recognition. The CRNN is built with Torch. We rebuild the experimental environment in our machine and apply it to HDSR for comparison.

In this paper, we propose a new network based on RNN-CTC framework. First we use the more efficient Residual network [8], which was the champion of ILSVRC 2015 classification task, to extract more discriminative feature sequences. Then we modify the standard bi-direction LSTM by adding fully connected layer before combining the two directions for convergence. At the top of our model, a standard CTC is used to calculate the loss and yield the recognition result. By taking the advantages of these models, this new model works well in HDSR task. Compared with the submitted methods in ICFHR 2014 HDSR competition, as well as CRNN, our approach makes significant improvements and achieves the state-of-the-art performance. We conduct our experiments[1] with Caffe [9] toolkit.

The rest of this paper is organized as follows. In Sect. 2 we describe the methods. Then, the details of our experiments are presented in Sect. 3. Section 4 concludes this paper and discusses the future work.

2   The Proposed Architecture

The main idea of our model is using a recurrent neural network to model contextual information, namely, the features extracted by a powerful convolutional neural network from raw images and yield elementary results, then get the final recognition results with the output layer connectionist temporary classification.

---

[1] https://github.com/LPAIS/HDSR-with-RNN.

2.1   Feature Extractor: Convolutional Neural Networks

Convolutional neural networks are successful in most computer vision tasks. It remains the space structure of image then fully connected network and generates highly-efficient features that defeats traditional methods. CNN has great improvements since it was put forward. Many fantastic CNN architectures were proposed such as AlexNet [10], GoogleNet [11] and network in network (NIN) [12].

When the networks going deeper, a degradation problem has been exposed. In order to address this issue, He et al. [8] introduced a deep residual learning framework, i.e. the ResNet. The essential structure of ResNet is shortcut connection. Shortcut connections are those that skip one or more layers. With this kind of connections, we can handle the vanishing gradient problem and build deeper networks, which means that we can get more excellent feature representations. In practice the way of shortcut connection is flexible according to specific tasks.

In our model, we design a 10 layers residual network without global pooling layers. With the reason of connecting a deep RNN following, we don't employee much deep CNN to avoid divergence. We take the advantages of the residual learning to enhance gradient propagation.

2.2   Sequence Labelling: Recurrent Neural Network

A recurrent neural network is a class of neural network models where many connections among its neurons form a directed cycle. With self-connections, it has an important benefit to use contextual information when mapping between input and output sequences. But for traditional RNN, the range of context that can be in practice accessed is quite limited due to vanishing gradient problem. One solution is to impose a memory structure into the RNN, resulting in the so-called long-short time memory (LSTM) [13] cell. Such LSTM version of RNN is shown to overcome some fundamental problems of traditional RNN and can be able to efficiently learn to solve long time dependency problems. Nowadays, LSTM becomes one of the most widely used RNN.

For sequence labelling task it is beneficial to have access to future as well as past context. However, the standard LSTM only consider the past information and ignore future context. An alternative solution is to add another LSTM to handle data reversely, which is so-called bi-direction LSTM [14], short for BiL-STM. BiLSTM presents each training sequence forwards and backwards to two separate LSTM layers, both of which are connected to the same output layer. This structure provides the output layer with complete past and future context for every point in the input sequence.

2.3   Connectionist Temporal Classification

Connectionist temporal classification [4] is a kind of output layer. It has two main functions. One is to calculate the loss, the other is to decode the output of RNN.

For a sequence labelling task, the labels are drawn from a set A (in HDSR task, A is the ten digits). With an extra label named *blank*, we get a new set $A' = A \cup \{blank\}$, which is used in reality. The input of CTC is a sequence $y = y_1, ..., y_T$, where T is the sequence length. The corresponding label donates as I over A. Each y_i is a probability distribution on the set A'. We define a many-to-one function $\mathscr{F} : A'^T \mapsto A^{\leq T}$ to resume the repeated labels and blanks. For example $\mathscr{F}(1 - 22 - -333 - -) = 123$. Then, a conditional probability is defined as the sum of probabilities of all π which are mapped by $\mathscr{F}$ onto I:

$$p(I|y) = \sum_{\pi \in \mathscr{F}^{-1}(I)} p(\pi|y) \tag{1}$$

where the conditional probability of π is defined as:

$$p(\pi|y) = \prod_{t=1}^{T} y_{\pi_t}^t \tag{2}$$

$y_{\pi_t}^t$ is the probability of having label π_t at timestep t. Directly computing Eq. 1 is not feasible. In practice, Eq. 1 is usually calculated using the forward-backward algorithm.

Donate the training dataset by $S = (\boldsymbol{X}, \boldsymbol{I})$, where X is the training image and I is the ground truth label sequence. The CTC object function $\mathscr{O}(S)$ is defined as the negative log probability of ground truth all the training examples in training set S,

$$\mathscr{O}(S) = - \sum_{(x,i) \in S} \log p(I|y) \tag{3}$$

where y is the sequence produced by the recurrent layers from x. Therefore, the network can be end-to-end trained on pairs of images and sequences, without the procedure of manually labelling all individual components in training images.

3   Experiments

To evaluate the effectiveness of proposed model, we designed two experiments. One is to show the recognition performance on public datasets, the other is to verify the potential of our model for long digit strings recognition.

The network configuration used in our experiments is described in Table 1. The input images are resized to fixed size. The CNN part is derived from the residual network with necessary modifies. We reduce the kernel size to better suit for CTC decoding and remove the global pooling layer in ordinary ResNet. After deep convolutional layers, there is a bidirectional LSTM, each direction has two layers of LSTM.

For implementation, by using the fundamental LSTM layer in Caffe and a custom reverse layer, we build the Bi-LSTM layer in C++ without combining them into a single Bi-LSTM layer. This proposed architecture contains deep convolutional layers and deep recurrent layers which are known to be hard to

Table 1. Network configuration summary. The first row is the top layer. k, s, p stand for kernel, stride and padding sizes respectively. The 'reverse' layer reverses the input. For example, a input of 'reverse' layer is $x_1, ..., x_n$, the corresponding output is $x_n, ..., x_1$.

Type	Configuration	
CTC	Calculate the loss and decode	
Elewise	Sum	
Reverse	Reverse features	-
InnerProduct	#units:11	#units:11
InnerProduct	#units:100	#hunits:100
LSTM	#hidden units:100	#hidden units:100
LSTM	#hidden units:100	#hidden units:100
Reverse	Reverse features	-
permuted	Permute the blob to fit lstm	
Eltwise	Sum	
Convolution	#maps:512, k3x3, s1x1, p1x1	#maps:512, k1x1, s2x2
Convolution	#maps:512, k3x3, s2x2, p1x1	-
Eltwise	Sum	
Convolution	#maps:256, k3x3, s1x1, p1x1	#maps:256, k1x1, s2x2
Convolution	#maps:256, k3x3, s2x2, p1x1	-
Eltwise	Sum	
Convolution	#maps:128, k3x3, s1x1, p1x1	#maps:128, k1x1, s2x2
Convolution	#maps:128, k3x3, s2x2, p1x1	-
Eltwise	Sum	
Convolution	#maps:64, k3x3, s1x1, p1x1	-
Convolution	#maps:64, k3x3, s1x1, p1x1	-
MaxPooling	k3x3, s1x1	
Convolution	#maps:64, k5x5, s1x1, p1x1	
Input	Input raw image	

train. In practice the network is trained with ADADELTA, setting the essential parameter delta to 10^{-6}.

Our experiments are performed on a DELL workstation. The CPU is Intel Xeon E5-1650 with 3.5 GHz and the GPU is NVIDIA TITAN X. The software is the latest version of Caffe [9] with cuDNN V5 accelerated on Ubuntu 14.04 LTS system. The average testing time is 3.5 ms per image.

We use a hard metric to evaluate our methods. We calculate the recognition rate, which is defined as the number of correctly recognized digit strings divided by the total number of strings. Because there are more than one digit label in a string, we consider one string being recognized correctly only if when all labels are recognized correctly.

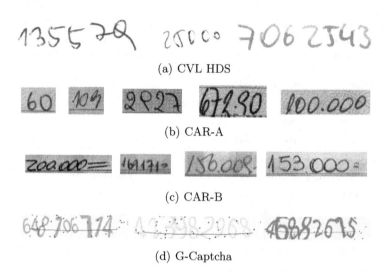

(a) CVL HDS

(b) CAR-A

(c) CAR-B

(d) G-Captcha

Fig. 1. Samples of the datasets used in our experiments.

3.1 Datasets

There are two public datasets used in our experiments. The first dataset, named as Computer Vision Lab Handwritten Digit String (CVL HDS), is collected from about 300 writers. The variability of writers brings high variability with respect to handwritten styles. The CVL HDS dataset has 7960 images, from which 1262 images for training and the other 6698 images for testing. Some examples are shown in Fig. 1(a) with different written styles.

The other dataset is ORAND-CAR, consisting of 11719 images obtained from the Courtesy Amount Recognition (CAR) field of real bank checks. The ORAND-CAR images come from two different sources with different characteristics. Considering the two different sources, ORAND-CAR is divided into two subsets, ORAND-CAR-A and ORAND-CAR-B, which are abbreviated to CAR-A and CAR-B.

Table 2. Distribution of the databases with respect to string length.

Length	Training set				Testing set			
	CVL	CAR-A	CAR-B	G-Captcha	CVL	CAR-A	CAR-B	G-Captcha
Below 7	883	1978	2862	0	4933	3686	2767	0
7	379	29	137	0	1765	87	157	0
8	0	2	1	1500	0	11	2	2000
9	0	0	0	1500	0	0	0	2000
10	0	0	0	1500	0	0	0	2000
11	0	0	0	1500	0	0	0	2000

The CAR-A database consists of 2009 images for training and 3784 images for testing. The CAR-B database consists of 3000 training images and 2926 testing images. Some samples are shown in Fig. 1(b)–(c).

String lengths of samples in these two datasets are mostly not larger than 7. For string recognition, the longer strings are the harder task is. So we create two captcha datasets by using a Python package named 'captcha'[2]. This package can generate arbitrary length captcha images with dirty background, and the styles of digits are varieties, which are similar to human handwriting.

The generated captcha dataset is named G-Captcha, in which string length is extended to 11. The distribution of the four different datasets with respect to string length are show in Table 2. With the Python package 'captcha', we can create arbitrary lengths of captcha images. This dataset contains 14,000 images, in which 6,000 for training and 8,000 for testing. The examples of G-Captcha are shown in Fig. 1(d).

3.2 Results and Analysis

The experimental results are shown in Table 3. We can see that the proposed network achieves the state-of-the-art on both ORAND-CAR-A and ORAND-CAR-B with a huge advance. But it performs very bad on CVL HDS dataset. On the other side, traditional methods performed outstandingly. There are 300 writers that contribute to CVL HDS. For each writer, 26 different digit strings were collected. Only 10 kinds of strings occur in training set. For segmentation methods, this is not a problem because the total categories of numbers are ten. But for methods based on RNN-CTC, it gets into trouble due to the lack of sample diversity. The CRNN architecture [7] which is also derived from

Table 3. Recognition rates of different models on the datasets described above. (The top five methods are proposed on the HDSRC 2014 [1], the following two are proposed in newest papers. Especially, last but one method uses the ORAND-CAR dataset as a whole.)

Methods	CAR-A	CAR-B	CVL HDS	G-Captcha
Tebessa I [1]	0.3705	0.2662	0.5930	-
Tebessa II [1]	0.3972	0.2772	0.6123	-
Singapore [1]	0.5230	0.5930	0.5040	-
Pernambuco [1]	0.7830	0.7543	0.5860	-
BeiJing [1]	0.8073	0.7013	**0.8529**	-
CRNN [7]	0.8801	0.8979	0.2601	0.9312
Saabni [3]	0.8580		-	-
Proposed	**0.8975**	**0.9114**	0.2707	**0.9515**

---

[2] https://pypi.python.org/pypi/captcha/0.1.1.

RNN-CTC faces the same problem. The result on G-Captcha shows the strong ability of handling very long strings.

The above experiments demonstrate that the proposed method can work well on handwritten digit string recognition. Apart from the shorter length strings in public datasets, it can recognize much longer strings. Although this method fails to handle CVL HDS, it is also an efficient approach to deal with digit string recognition, even if the string is long.

4 Conclusion and Future Work

In this paper, we have presented a new model based on RNN-CTC architecture. Combined with ResNet, we archive the new arts on the handwritten digit string recognition benchmarks ORAND-CAR with a great improvement. The experiments on G-Capthca dataset, which consists of much longer string images, indicate our model is very competitive of handling long sequence labelling. But it gets into trouble when handling data like CVL HDS. It seems a common failing for such kind of method. In future, we will refine our model based on elaborate analysis the results in this paper, and exploit the potential on relative areas.

References

1. Diem, M., Fiel, S., Kleber, F., Sablatnig, R., Saavedra, J.M., Contreras, D., Barrios, J.M., Oliveira, L.S.: ICFHR 2014 competition on handwritten digit string recognition in challenging datasets (HDSRC 2014). In: 14th International Conference on Frontiers in Handwriting Recognition, pp. 779–784. IEEE Press, Crete (2014)
2. Gattal, A., Chibani, Y., Hadjadji, B.: Segmentation and recognition system for unknown-length handwritten digit strings. Pattern Anal. Appl. **20**, 307–323 (2017)
3. Saabni, R.: Recognizing handwritten single digits and digit strings using deep architecture of neural networks. In: 3th International Conference on Artificial Intelligence and Pattern Recognition, pp. 1–6 (2016)
4. Graves, A., Fernández, S., Gomez, F., Schmidhuber, J.: Connectionist temporal classification: labelling unsegmented sequence data with recurrent neural networks. In: 23th International Conference on Machine Learning, pp. 369–376 (2006)
5. Messina, R., Louradour, J.: Segmentation-free handwritten Chinese text recognition with LSTM-RNN. In 13th IAPR International Conference on Document Analysis and Recognition, pp. 171–175 (2015)
6. Wang, Q.-F., Yin, F., Liu, C.-L.: Handwritten chinese text recognition by integrating multiple contexts. IEEE Trans. Pattern Anal. Mach. Intell. **34**, 1469–1481 (2012)
7. Shi, B., Bai, X., Yao, C.: An end-to-end trainable neural network for image-based sequence recognition and its application to scene text recognition (2016). doi:10.1109/TPAMI.2016.2646371
8. He, K., Zhang, X., Ren, S., Sun, J.: Deep residual learning for image recognition. In: 29th IEEE Conference on Computer Vision and Pattern Recognition, pp. 770–778 (2016)

9. Jia, Y., Shelhamer, E., Donahue, J., Karayev, S., Long, J., Girshick, R., Guadarrama, S., Darrell, T.: Caffe: convolutional architecture for fast feature embedding. arXiv preprint arXiv:1408.5093 (2014)
10. Krizhevsky, A., Sutskever, I., Hinton, G.E.: Imagenet classification with deep convolutional neural networks. In: Advances in Neural Information Processing Systems, pp. 1097–1105 (2012)
11. Szegedy, C., Liu, W., Jia, Y., Sermanet, P., Reed, S., Anguelov, D., Erhan, D., Vanhoucke, V., Rabinovich, A.: Going deeper with convolutions. In: 28th IEEE Conference on Computer Vision and Pattern Recognition, pp. 1–9 (2015)
12. Lin, M., Chen, Q., Yan, S.: Network in network. arXiv preprint arXiv:1312.4400 (2014)
13. Hochreiter, S., Schmidhuber, J.: Long short-term memory. Neural Comput. **9**, 1735–1780 (1997)
14. Graves, A., Schmidhuber, J.: Framewise phoneme classification with bidirectional lstm and other neural network architectures. Neural Netw. **18**, 602–610 (2005)

Highly Occluded Face Detection: An Improved R-FCN Approach

Lin Liu, Fei Jiang, and Ruimin Shen[✉]

Department of Computer Science and Engineering, Shanghai Jiao Tong University,
No. 800 Dongchuan Road, Minhang District, Shanghai, China
{l_liulin,jiangf,rmshen}@sjtu.edu.cn

Abstract. For highly occluded faces, only few features exist, which makes such face detection more challenging. In this paper, we propose a novel algorithm to make full use of the facial features. The proposed algorithm is based on Region-based Fully Convolutional Network (R-FCN) with two improved parts for robust face detection, including the multi-scale training and a new feature-fusion scheme. Firstly, instead of utilizing fixed scales for all faces, we adopt multi-scale inputs to strengthen the features of the partial faces and increase the training set diversity. Up-sampling the training images can efficiently enlarge the features of the occluded faces. Secondly, we make a feature fusion by combining layers with different sizes of receptive fields, which can preserve the details of the faces with only partial faces available. Our method achieves superior accuracy over the stat-of-the-art techniques on massively-benchmarked face dataset (WIDER FACE), and shows great improvements for highly occluded face detection.

Keywords: Face detection · Fully convolutional neural network · Occlusions

1 Introduction

Face detection is one of the fundamental computer vision tasks. It is essential to many face applications, such as facial expression analysis and face recognition. Recently, tremendous progress has been made in face detection [1]. However, in many real scenarios, faces recorded by cameras are often highly occluded, which imposes great challenges for detecting such faces.

Early researches on face detection tend to train effective classifiers with features which are manually designed and extracted. Most researches focus on designing more representative features or more distinctive classifiers. While, hand-crafted features are hard to handle the highly occluded faces. Recently, the convolution neural network (CNN) has achieved significant success in computer vision, and has been widely used for object detection, image segmentation and image classification. One of the most outstanding frameworks for general object detection is the region-based convolutional neural network (RCNN) [2],

© Springer International Publishing AG 2017
D. Liu et al. (Eds.): ICONIP 2017, Part VI, LNCS 10639, pp. 592–601, 2017.
https://doi.org/10.1007/978-3-319-70136-3_63

which can be seen as an extension of CNN based on region proposals generalized by different algorithms. Though tremendous progress has been made in face detection by deep learning, highly occluded face detection is still a challenging, due to lacking of clues for such faces.

In this paper, we look deep into this challenge, and propose a novel algorithm to make full use of the facial features. The proposed algorithm is based on Region-based Fully Convolutional Network (R-FCN) [3] with two improved parts for robust face detection, including the multi-scale training and a new feature-fusion scheme. To deal with the problem that features of highly occluded faces are too tiny to be detected, we utilize a multi-scale training scheme to enlarge the size of the features, making it more possible to be detected. Moreover, we make a feature fusion by combining layers with different sizes of receptive fields, which can preserve the details of the faces with only partial parts available. To make the feature maps from different layers have the same size, we introduce a deconvolution operator [4]. The efficiency and effectiveness of the proposed algorithm have been demonstrated on the widely used benchmark, WIDER FACE [5].

2 Related Work

In the literature of computer vision, face detection has been a prevalent research area all the time and has been extensively studied. Since 2001,Viola and Jones [6] first made face detection apply to the real-world scenario, tremendous progress has been achieved in face detection research.

Viola and Jones face detector can be regarded as an instance of boosting algorithms. It utilizes the integral image to compute the Haar-like features rapidly and takes the AdaBoost classifier in a cascaded manner. The most important keys in this kind of method are feature extraction and learning algorithms. Various features have been designed to represent faces in the follow-up works. Mita et al. [7] proposed a kind of joint Haar-like features which used the co-occurrence of multiple Haar-like features to capture more powerful characteristics of faces. In [8,9], local binary pattern (LBP) is applied for facial feature extraction for its robustness to illumination variations. Further more, linear features are introduced for face representation in [10–12]. Another well-known feature for face detection is based on histograms. In [13], local edge orientation histograms was proposed, which compute the histogram of edge orientations in subregions of the test windows and later Dalal et al. [14] proposed a similar feature called histogram of oriented gradients (HoG), which has been popular among pedestrian detection till now. At the same time, massive advanced classifiers are explored for face detection. In [15], a method for frontal face detection using bayesian discriminating features was proposed. The famous support vector machines are also applied to face detection in [16,17].

Convolutional neural networks have recently been another widely used approach in the face detection literature and show great advantages in performance. In [18], a cascade architecture built on convolutional neural networks was proposed which operates at multiple resolutions, rejects the background regions in the fast low resolution stages and evaluates a small number of challenging candidates in the last high resolution stage. Li et al. [19] presented a method for detecting faces in the wild, which integrates a ConvNet and a 3D mean face model in an end-to-end multi-task discriminative learning framework. Zhang et al. [20] introduced a framework using multi-task cascaded convolutional networks which exploits the inherent correlation between face detection and alignment to boost up their performance. In [21], an improved faster RCNN approach was proposed using hard negative mining and feature concatenation. More recently, Hu et al. [22] provided an in-depth analysis of image resolution, object scale, and spatial context for the purpose of finding small faces.

In this work, we introduced an improved scheme based on R-FCN to enlarge the size of the feature maps and make full use of the limited facial features to achieve better result under the scenario of heavy occlusions.

3   Our Approach

In this section, we will describe our approach for the highly occluded face detection in detail. We firstly introduce the main architecture for the face detection. Then we present the training process of the proposed model. After that, we give more details for two schemes we proposed, including the multi-scale training and the feature fusion scheme.

3.1   CNN Architecture

The overall pipeline of our approach is shown in Fig. 1. Given an image, we initially resize it to different scales to build an image pyramid as the input. We call the training process for different scaling inputs as multi-scale training, and for more details please see Sect. 3.3. Then, we follow the main architecture of

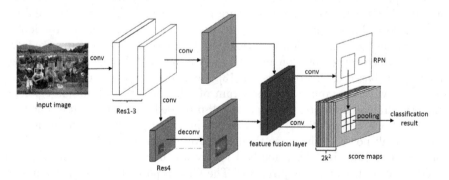

Fig. 1. Overall architecture of our network. The crucial part is the deconvolutional layer (deconv) and the fusion layer after Res4. The deconvolutional layer outputs the feature map with the same scale as Res3 and the feature fusion layer combines these two feature maps with different receptive fields. Both region proposal networks and the position-sensitive RoI pooling layer can share the syncretic feature maps.

R-FCN [3] with some improvements to form our face detection architecture. Similar to R-FCN, the proposed deep architecture consists of two modules: (i) a Region Proposal Network (RPN); and (ii) a Fully Convolutional Network (FCN). RPN is used for generating region proposals and FCN is used for the classification of the proposals from RPN and refining the bounding boxes of them. Our loss function is the same as Faster-RCNN [21], using softmax loss for classification and smooth L1 loss for bounding box regression. The total loss defined on each RoI is as follows:

$$L(p_i, t_i) = \frac{1}{N_{cls}} \sum_i L_{cls}(p_i, p_i^*) + \lambda \frac{1}{N_{reg}} \sum_i p_i^* L_{reg}(t_i, t_i^*). \tag{1}$$

$$L_{reg}(t_i, t_i^*) = \begin{cases} 0.5(t_i - t_i^*)^2 & \text{if } |t_i - t_i^*| \le 1 \\ |t_i - t_i^*| - 0.5 & \text{otherwise,} \end{cases} \tag{2}$$

Here i is the index of RoI generated from one image. p_i is the predicted probability of proposal i and t_i is a vector of 4 coordinates representing the result of bounding box regression. p_i^* and t_i^* are ground truth of them respectively. p_i^* has two values 1 and 0 which means face and non-face respectively. $L_{cls}(p_i, p_i^*)$ is the classification loss for predicted probability p_i and the ground truth p_i^* and we use softmax loss for this term. $L_{reg}(t_i, t_i^*)$ represents the bounding box regression loss using smooth L1 loss [23] formulated as Eq. 2. Moreover, only RoIs regarded as faces have the second bounding box loss term. Other details about the architecture, please refer to [3].

The main different part between our architecture and R-FCN is the feature fusion layer. In our architecture, the feature fusion layer combines the feature maps from Res3 and Res4 ahead of RPN by a deconvolution operator, where Res3 and Res4 represent the stack of layers named by res3_x and res4_x in the backbone Resnet [24] respectively. The feature fusion layer combines the features learned from different receptive fields. We will discuss the details of feature fusion in Sect. 3.4.

3.2   Training

We train our face detection model following the procedure in Fig. 2. First, our architecture takes the initial values from ResNet pre-trained on ImageNet classification dataset [25]. Then we train the proposed model on WIDER FACE with the size of original images. After that, we get a preliminary model. During the training procedure, we adopt the online hard example mining [26] to speed up. The last step is scaling original images to the double size and using the scaled images to train the final model. The whole process is end-to-end similar to R-FCN.

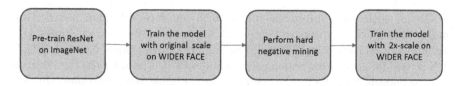

Fig. 2. The training procedure of our face detection model.

3.3 Multi-scale Training

The R-FCN model typically utilizes only one fixed scale for all the training images. Under the situation of faces with merely few parts available, the feature maps are too small to detect as in position-sensitive pooling these small areas are easy to be evaluated as non-faces. By scaling the original images to double size, score maps are also effectively scaled to the double size that the occluded faces are more prone to be considered as positive examples in the position-sensitive pooling. The multi-scale training procedure is shown in Fig. 3. Our empirical results show that the use of multi-scale training makes our model more robust towards occluded faces, and improve the detection performance on benchmark results.

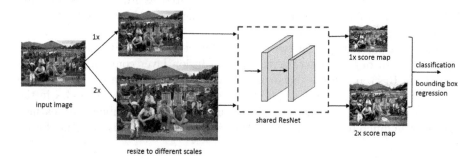

Fig. 3. The multi-scale training details. We scale the input image to 2× size and feed both the original image and the scaled image to the network. After the final layer of ResNet, we have two scales of score maps which offer more information for the next pooling operations that contributes to more precise classification and bounding box regression results.

3.4 Feature Fusion

According to [22], feature maps corresponding to the smaller receptive fields are more suitable for small faces. Motivated by this concept, we adopt a feature fusion scheme for the feature maps generated by Res3 and Res4 as they are reported in [22] to have better performance for tiny faces. As the fact that convolutional features at higher layers tend to have wider receptive fields, it is

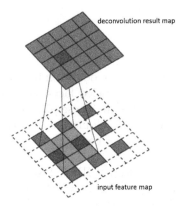

Fig. 4. Intuitive display of the deconvolution operator. Here kernel size is 3, padding is 1 and stride is 2.

prone for feature maps of higher layers to miss details, especially when the key information have limited area. In this work, we maintain the size of feature map from Res3 layer and perform a deconvolution operator to the result of Res4 layer. We set the stride of the deconvolution layer as 2 to double the size of feature map generated by Res4 layer so that the element-wise fusion can be conducted. Equation 3 defines the deconvolution formulation and Fig. 4 displays the operator in a more intuitive manner. As shown in Fig. 5, through the combination of these two feature maps, we preserve the low layer details and obtain more complicated features which are then fed to the position-sensitive pooling layer at the same time.

$$\hat{y}^c = \sum_{k=1}^{K} z_k * f^c. \tag{3}$$

Here f^c represents the input feature map with c channels to perform deconvolution, $\hat{y}^c$ is the deconvolution result map and K is the number of the deconvolution filters. z_k is the k-th learnable filter. $*$ represents the 2D convolution operator between z_k and f^c.

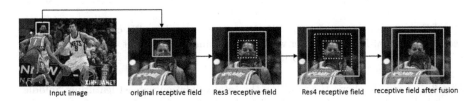

Fig. 5. Sizes of receptive fields in different layers. The highest layer Res4 owns the largest receptive field while for occluded faces, the context around them is more fundamental as a large area of features are overlaid by the surroundings. With the feature fusion layer, we obtain the global information from Res4 and preserve the detail context from Res3 at the same time which results in a better performance for occlusions.

4   Experiments

4.1   Dataset

WIDER FACE [5] is a widely used face detection benchmark dataset, it contains totally 32,203 images and 393,703 labeled faces which have a high diversity in scale, pose, illumination and occlusion. These pictures are divided into 61 event classes with different scenarios. For each picture, the faces are divided into three partitions: easy, medium and hard according to the detection rate associated with scale, pose and occlusion.

We train our improved model on WIDER FACE training set using 159424 faces in 10307 images and evaluate our model on the whole WIDER FACE validation set. Besides, to test the impact on occluded faces, we take all images in validation set whose occlusion labels equal to 2 as an additional set. In WIDER FACE, a face with occlusion label 1 is defined as 'partially occluded' that 1%–30% of the total face area is occluded and a face with occluded area over 30% has occlusion label 2 which means 'heavily occluded'.

4.2   Setup

We utilize Caffe framework [27] to implement deep networks. We adopt ResNet with 101 layers as our backbone network which has been pre-trained on ImageNet.

We randomly sample one image per batch for training. Our momentum is set to be 0.9 and the weight decay is 0.0005. We generate 2000 proposals during the

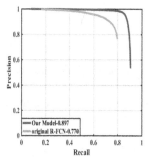 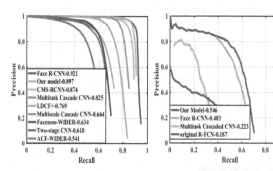

(a) PR curve on the total set with original R-FCN.

(b) PR curve on the total set with other advanced algorithms.

(c) PR curve on the occlusion set

Fig. 6. (a) and (b) shows the result on the total validation dataset featuring "middle" set. (a) shows the comparision with original R-FCN that our algorithms improves the accuracy by 12%. (b) is the comparision with other advanced algorithms where our model achieves quite comparable results. (c) shows results on additional dataset with occlusion label 2 which means heavy occlusions. For the reason that highly occluded faces are defined as over 30% occlusions, we only select those faces larger than $20 * 20$ pixels. Our model performs 6% better than other state-of-the-art models.

RPN layer and use 0.3 as the IoU threshold which means positive samples have IoU overlap over 70% and negative samples have IoU overlap below 30%. We first run the stochastic gradient descent solver 70k iterations with a base learning rate of 0.001 and then run another 30k iterations with the reduced learning rate 0.0001.

4.3   Result

The precision-recall curve is used as our evaluation criterion. Figure 6 shows the comparison results on 'total' dataset and additional 'occlusion' dataset. In Fig. 6, part (a) shows that our model improves the accuracy by *12%* percent compared with original R-FCN model and part (b) shows that our improved model achieves quite comparable performance compared to all advanced face detection algorithms. Moreover, for the evaluation of heavy occlusions, we implement several state-of-the-art models and perform the experiments on the 'occlusion' dataset. We can see from part (c) of Fig. 6 that our model achieves over *6%* accuracy than these state-of-the-art algorithms. More qualitative results are shown in Fig. 7.

| Easy | Middle | Hard |

Fig. 7. Qualitative results on different subsets.

5   Conclusions

We propose an improved framework based on R-FCN for finding highly occluded faces. To strengthen the features available of the occluded faces, we adopt multiscale training. The features of the occluded faces will be easy and efficient enlarged by up-sampling the original input images. Moreover, a new feature fusion scheme is proposed, which combines the feature maps with different sizes of receptive fields that the details of occluded faces can be preserved. The experimental results on WEDER FACE dataset demonstrate the efficiency and effectiveness of our method.

Acknowledgments. The authors would like to thank the editor and all the anonymous reviewers of this paper for their constructive suggestions and comments. This work is supported by NSFC (No. 61671290) in China, the Key Program for International S&T Cooperation Project of China (No. 2016YFE0129500), and the Shanghai Committee of Science and Technology, China (No. 17511101903).

References

1. Zafeiriou, S., Zhang, C., Zhang, Z.: A survey on face detection in the wild: past, present and future. Comput. Vis. Image. Underst. **138**, 1–24 (2015)
2. Girshick, R., Donahue, J., Darrell, T., Malik, J.: Rich feature hierarchies for accurate object detection and semantic segmentation. In: 27th IEEE Conference on Computer Vision and Pattern Recognition, pp. 580–587. IEEE Press, Columbus (2014)
3. Dai, J., Li, Y., He, K., Sun, J.: R-FCN: object detection via region-based fully convolutional networks. In: 30th Conference on Neural Information Processing Systems, Barcelona, pp. 379–387 (2016)
4. Zeiler, M.D., Krishnan, D., Taylor, G.W., Fergus, R.: Deconvolutional networks. In: 23th IEEE Conference on Computer Vision and Pattern Recognition, pp. 2528–2535. IEEE Press, San Francisco (2010)
5. Yang, S., Luo, P., Loy, C.C., Tang, X.: Wider face: a face detection benchmark. In: 27th IEEE Conference on Computer Vision and Pattern Recognition, pp. 5525–5533. IEEE Press, Las Vegas (2016)
6. Viola, P., Jones, M.: Rapid object detection using a boosted cascade of simple features. In: 14th IEEE Conference on Computer Vision and Pattern Recognition, pp. 511–518. IEEE Press, Hawaii (2001)
7. Mita, T., Kaneko, T., Hori, O.: Joint Haar-like features for face detection. In: 10th IEEE International Conference on Computer Vision, pp. 1619–1626. IEEE Press, Beijing (2005)
8. Ahonen, T., Hadid, A., Pietikäinen, M.: Face recognition with local binary patterns. In: Pajdla, T., Matas, J. (eds.) ECCV 2004. LNCS, vol. 3021, pp. 469–481. Springer, Heidelberg (2004). doi:10.1007/978-3-540-24670-1_36
9. Zhang, G., Huang, X., Li, S.Z., Wang, Y., Wu, X.: Boosting local binary pattern (LBP)-Based face recognition. In: 5th Chinese Conference on Advances in Biometric Person Authentication, Guangzhou, pp. 179–186 (2004)
10. Liu, C., Shum, H.Y.: Kullback-leibler boosting. In: 16th IEEE Conference on Computer Vision and Pattern Recognition, pp. 587–594. IEEE Press, Madison (2003)
11. Meynet, J., Popovici, V., Thiran, J.P.: Face detection with boosted Gaussian features. Pattern Recognit. **40**, 2283–2291 (2007)
12. Chen, X., Gu, L., Li, S.Z., Zhang, H.J.: Learning representative local features for face detection. In: 14th IEEE Conference on Computer Vision and Pattern Recognition, pp. 1126–1131. IEEE Press, Hawaii (2001)
13. Levi, K., Weiss, Y.: Learning object detection from a small number of examples: the importance of good features. In: 17th IEEE Conference on Computer Vision and Pattern Recognition, pp. 53–60. IEEE Press, Washington (2004)
14. Dalal, N., Triggs, B.: Histogram of oriented gradients for human detection. In: 18th IEEE Conference on Computer Vision and Pattern Recognition, pp. 886–893. IEEE Press, San Diego (2005)
15. Liu, C.: A Bayesian discriminating features method for face detection. IEEE Trans. Pattern Anal. Mach. Intell. **25**, 725–740 (2003)

16. Li, Y., Gong, S., Liddell, H.: Support vector regression and classification based multi-view face detection and recognition. In: 4th IEEE International Conference on Automatic Face and Gesture Recognition, p. 300. IEEE Press, Grenoble (2000)
17. Wang, P., Ji, Q.: Multi-view face detection under complex scene based on combined SVMs. In: 17th International Conference on Pattern Recognition, Cambridge, pp. 179–182 (2004)
18. Li, H., Lin, Z., Shen, X., Brandt, J., Hua, G.: A convolutional neural network cascade for face detection. In: 28th IEEE Conference on Computer Vision and Pattern Recognition, pp. 5325–5334. IEEE Press, Boston (2015)
19. Li, Y., Sun, B., Wu, T., Wang, Y.: Face detection with endto-end integration of a convnet and a 3d model. arXiv preprint arxiv: 1606.00850 (2016)
20. Zhang, K., Zhang, Z., Li, Z., Qiao, Y.: Joint face detection and alignment using multi-task cascaded convolutional networks. arXiv preprint arxiv: 1604.02878 (2016)
21. Sun, X., Wu, P., Hoi, S.C.H.: Face detection using deep learning: an improved faster rcnn approach. arXiv preprint arxiv: 1701.08289 (2017)
22. Hu, P., Ramanan, D.: Finding Tiny Faces. arXiv preprint arxiv: 1612.04402 (2017)
23. Girshick, R.: Fast R-CNN. In: 20th IEEE International Conference on Computer Vision, pp. 1440–1448. IEEE Press, Santiago (2015)
24. He, K., Zhang, X., Ren, S., Sun, J.: Deep residual learning for image recognition. In: 27th IEEE Conference on Computer Vision and Pattern Recognition, pp. 770–778. IEEE Press, Las Vegas (2016)
25. Russakovsky, O., Deng, J., Su, H.: Imagenet large scale visual recognition challenge. Int. J. Comput. Vis. **115**, 211–252 (2015)
26. Shrivastava, A., Gupta, A., Girshick, R.: Training region-based object detectors with online hard example mining. In: 27th IEEE Conference on Computer Vision and Pattern Recognition, pp. 761–769. IEEE Press, Las Vegas (2016)
27. Jia, Y.Q., Shelhamer, E., Donahue, J.: Caffe: Convolutional architecture for fast feature embedding. arXiv preprint arxiv: 1408.5093 (2014)

Partial Fingerprint Matching via Phase-Only Correlation and Deep Convolutional Neural Network

Jin Qin[1], Siqi Tang[1], Congying Han[1,2,3(✉)], and Tiande Guo[1,2,3]

[1] University of Chinese Academy of Sciences, Beijing, China
{qinjin13,tangsiqi14}@mails.ucas.ac.cn, hancy@ucas.ac.cn
[2] School of Mathematical Science, UCAS, Beijing, China
[3] Key Laboratory of Big Data Mining and Knowledge Management,
UCAS, Beijing, China

Abstract. A major approach for fingerprint matching today is based on minutiae. However, due to the lack of minutiae, their accuracy degrades significantly for partial-to-partial matching. We propose a novel matching algorithm that makes full use of the distinguishing information in partial fingerprint images. Our model employs the Phase-Only Correlation (POC) function to coarsely assign two fingerprints. Then we use a deep convolutional neural network (CNN) with spatial pyramid pooling to measure the similarity of the overlap areas. Experiments indicate that our algorithm has an excellent performance.

Keywords: Partial fingerprint matching · Phase-only correlation · Polar Fourier transform · Deep convolutional neural networks

1 Introduction

Nowadays fingerprint has become more popular on commercial and residential such as authentication in mobile devices. The sensors embedded in these devices are generally small and the resulting fingerprints are, therefore, limited in size. Although the minutiae pattern of each finger is quite unique, there are often insufficient minutiae in partial fingerprints. And, it is difficult to efficiently extract the minutia points from a poor quality fingerprint image. As a result, the existing minutia-based method [1] performs not well. The image-based methods (SIFT, KAZE [2]) utilized texture descriptors, which can increase the number of key points. But it is not designed to make full use of fingerprint structures. And the performance of image-based techniques is also easily influenced by non-linear distortions and noise in the image. Our method takes care of the difficulties in partial fingerprint matching. To keep the robustness and adaptability of the algorithm, we make it independent from any particular feature of the fingerprint to adapt to the arbitrary size of partial fingerprint image.

Recently, deep models such as CNN have been proved effective for object detection and face recognition [3–5]. In face recognition, two face image should

© Springer International Publishing AG 2017
D. Liu et al. (Eds.): ICONIP 2017, Part VI, LNCS 10639, pp. 602–611, 2017.
https://doi.org/10.1007/978-3-319-70136-3_64

be aligned firstly via facial landmarks such as the two eye centers, the nose tip, and the two mouth corners. Unlike with face recognition, fingerprint has no reference points that are similar to facial landmarks. The singular points of fingerprint are not stable enough. There is always an error detection rate when extracting singular points. Especially in partial fingerprint, the singular points are often unavailable. Hence, we can hardly use any artificial landmarks to align two fingerprints.

In this paper, we propose a novel matching algorithm that makes the most of distinguishing information in fingerprint images. First, we coarsely align two fingerprints by algorithm based on phase-only correlation. Then, the overlap region will be extracted. Finally, we employ a deep convolutional neural network (CNN) with spatial pyramid pooling to verify whether these two fingerprint regions come from the same finger. We have two contributions. First, compared with the existing method, our method is independent from any particular handcrafted features and fingerprint quality. Second, Our overall framework is a novel matching algorithm framework. We utilize a deep CNN with spatial pyramid pooling to learn features from the overlapping areas of any size. It makes full use of fingerprint structures. Moreover, the automatic training samples selected strategy saves a lot of manual labour.

The rest of this paper is organized as follows. In Sect. 2, the proposed alignment method based on POC is presented. In Sect. 3, we employ a deep CNN to extract a vector on common regions and get the similarity by these vectors. In Sect. 4, the experimental results of the proposed method are presented.

2　Partial Fingerprint Alignment

Our partial fingerprint alignment method uses modified phase-only correlation and Polar Fourier transform. The advantages of the proposed alignment method are high discriminating power, numerical efficiency, robustness against noise, and strong adaptability (it does not rely on any particular feature).

In this section, Fig. 1 shows the flow diagram of the proposed partial fingerprint alignment algorithm. Our alignment algorithm consists of the three steps: the rotation angle estimation; the displacement estimation; common region extraction.

POC is a digital image processing technique which derives correlation of two images based on the value of two phases. We use $\mathcal{F}$ to represent the 2-D Discrete Fourier Transform. Let $f(x, y)$ and $g(x, y)$ be $M \times N$ images and let $F(u, v)$ and $G(u, v)$ be the 2-D Discrete Fourier Transform of these two images. $F(u, v)$ and $G(u, v)$ are given by

$$F(u, v) = \mathcal{F}(f(x, y)) = \frac{1}{MN} \sum_{x=0}^{M-1} \sum_{y=0}^{N-1} f(x, y) e^{-i2\pi(\frac{ux}{M} + \frac{vy}{N})}, \tag{1}$$

$$G(u, v) = \mathcal{F}(g(x, y)) = \frac{1}{MN} \sum_{x=0}^{M-1} \sum_{y=0}^{N-1} f(x, y) e^{-i2\pi(\frac{ux}{M} + \frac{vy}{N})}, \tag{2}$$

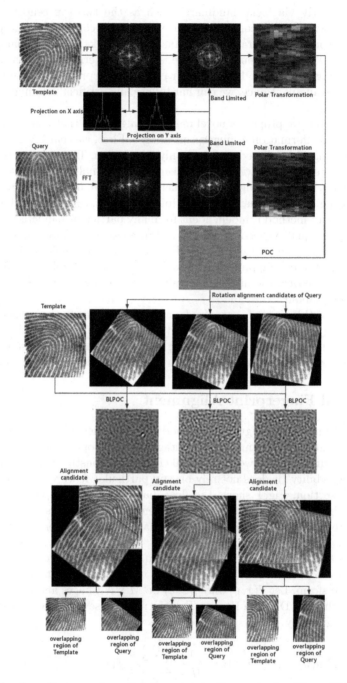

Fig. 1. The flow diagram of partial fingerprint alignment algorithm. (Color figure online)

where $\mathbf{i} = \sqrt{-1}$.

The normalized cross-spectrum $K(u, v)$ is defined as

$$K(u, v) = \frac{F(u, v) \cdot G^*(u, v)}{|F(u, v) \cdot G^*(u, v)|},\tag{3}$$

where $\cdot$ denotes Hadamard product and $*$ denotes complex conjugate operation.

The POC function will be given by

$$POC_{f,g}(x, y) = \mathcal{F}^{-1}\left(\frac{F(u, v) \cdot G^*(u, v)}{|F(u, v) \cdot G^*(u, v)|}\right) = \sum_{u=0}^{M-1}\sum_{v=0}^{N-1} K(u, v)e^{\mathbf{i}2\pi(\frac{ux}{M} + \frac{vy}{N})}.\tag{4}$$

If $g(x, y)$ is the displaced version of $f(x, y)$ that is $g(x, y) = f(x + \Delta x, y + \Delta y)$, where $(\Delta x, \Delta y)$ are the displacements. $POC_{f,g}(x, y)$ between $f(x, y)$ and $g(x, y)$ will show the maximum value at $(\Delta x, \Delta y)$. So, we can estimate the image displacement by detecting the peaks of the function.

The width of the fingerprint ridges vary from 100 um to 300 um. Generally, the period of a ridge/valley cycle is about 500 um. Due to this property, we can use the bandpass filtering to remove the noise and significantly improve the performance. In our algorithm, we use a ring bandpass filter to filter the high frequency part and low frequency part, and reserve the middle part. The high frequency threshold is chosen by the method described in [6]. The low frequency threshold is selected by experiment.

$$g(x, y) = f(x\cos(\theta) + y\sin(\theta), -x\sin(\theta) + y\cos(\theta)).$$
$$\Updownarrow\tag{5}$$
$$G(u, v) = F(u\cos(\theta) + v\sin(\theta), -u\sin(\theta) + v\cos(\theta)).$$

Due to the rotation invariance of frequency domain and space domain (Eq. (5)), we execute the polar coordinate transform on frequency domain, namely Polar Fourier transform. Then the estimate of rotation angles converts to the displacement estimation problem. In order to improve the performance of the algorithm, we select the highest N peaks of POC function as candidates. The same strategy can be use in the displacement estimation part. If N is larger, the performance will be better, but the running time will also increase accordingly. It's a trade-off problem between performance and efficiency. We set N_A (the number of rotation candidates) $= 6$ and N_D (the number of displacement candidates) $= 3$ in our experiment (Fig. 1 shows the situation that $N_A = 3, N_D = 1$). Each candidate will get a similarity score by the verification procedure (See Sect. 3). The final similarity score is the maximum of all alignment candidates' similarity score.

3 Fingerprint Verification

3.1 Motivation

The traditional POC method use the correlation value obtained in POC function, or the value obtained by calculate Normalized Cross Correlation (NCC) on

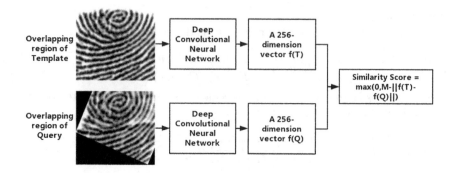

Fig. 2. The verification procedure.

common region, to determine the final similarity. The above evaluation methods are powerless, because the impressions of different fingers may appear very similar to each other (high inter-class similarity) and likewise, different acquisition of the same finger may be dissimilar from each other (high intra-class variation). An example is shown in Fig. 3. So the final similarity evaluation on common region must consider the nonlinear deformation problem. Moreover, it's hard to obtain a precisely alignment (need complex methods and huge computation cost). Inspired by [4], in this paper, we employ a deep convolution neural network to deal with this problem. A clearly flowchart of the verification procedure is shown in Fig. 2, the deep network converts the common regions (various size) to a fixed-length vector, And the final similarity is evaluated by using the the squared Euclidean distance between these vectors. This method not only takes into account the deformation, but also reduces the dependence on the alignment accuracy.

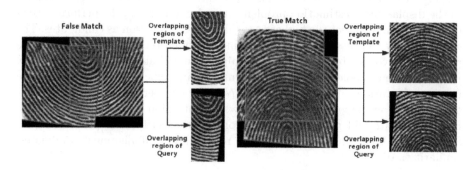

Fig. 3. Examples of false match and true match. These situations are difficult to distinguish. (Color figure online)

3.2   Network Configurations

Our deep network is described in Fig. 4. Let $f(x)$ denote the feature vector that is extracted by the deep network on overlapping region x (can be regard as an image). Because most overlapping regions are irregular, we extract the bounding box of the overlapping region as the boundary (Yellow box in Figs. 1 and 3), and fill zero to all invalid area (invalid area are black, see overlapping regions in Figs. 1 and 3). Moreover, the overlapping regions on different match pairs are different size. To adapt various size inputs, we equip the deep network with a spatial pyramid pooling layer [7], that makes our network can generate a fixed-length representation regardless of image size. Meanwhile, pyramid pooling is robust to object deformations. The spatial pyramid pooling layer used in our model is 3-level, and have 3×3, 2×2 and 1×1 bins respectively. The residual learning module [5] is also used in our network.

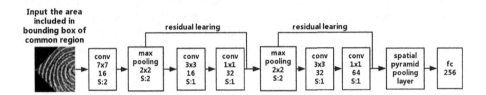

Fig. 4. The deep network configuration.

3.3   Loss-Function

We adopt the loss function Eq. (8), which combine the L2 loss Eq. (6) and the generalized logistic loss Eq. (7).

$$L_{L_2}(T_i, Q_i, y_i) = \begin{cases} \frac{1}{2}\|f(T_i) - f(Q_i)\|_2^2 & \text{if } y_i = 1 \\ \frac{1}{2}(max(0, m - \|f(T_i) - f(Q_i)\|_2))^2 & \text{if } y_i = -1 \end{cases}, \quad (6)$$

where y_i is the label of i-th training sample. $y_i = 1$ means that (T_i, Q_i) is a positive sample. $y_i = -1$ means that (T_i, Q_i) is a negative sample. m is a given constant representing the margin enforced between positive and negative samples.

$$L_{logistic}(T_i, Q_i, y_i) = \frac{1}{2}g(1 - y_i(m - \|f(T_i) - f(Q_i)\|_2)^2), \quad (7)$$

where $g(x) = \frac{1}{\beta}\log(1 + e^{\beta x})$ is the generalized logistic loss function [4].

$$Loss = \frac{1}{N}\sum_{i}^{N}(L_{L_2}(T_i, Q_i, y_i) + \lambda L_{logistic}(T_i, Q_i, y_i)). \quad (8)$$

3.4   Training Samples

A pair of overlapping regions, created by template and query respectively, is a training sample. If two overlapping regions come from the same region of the same finger, this overlapping region pair is a positive sample. Otherwise, this overlapping region pair is a negative sample. It's easy to create negative samples (the match pair come from different fingers), but most negative samples are quite different that can hardly give contributions to the network distinguish ability. On the other hand, it's hard to create positive samples. Because it's difficult to automatically determine whether an overlapping region pair come from the same region of the same finger (equivalent to verification problem). And if the positive samples are created by manual confirmation (in other papers about deep learning, this is the primary source of current deep learning samples), the workload will be enormous. So it's quite important for automatically sample production. In this paper, we use the following strategy to create samples: (1) For each match pair of overlapping regions, we use the similarity computing method, which is derived from [6], to rough evaluate the similarity score; (2) If the coarsely similarity score is higher than a threshold, this pair is selected as a sample. (3) If this pair comes from the same finger, this pair is labeled as a positive sample. Otherwise, this pair is labeled as a negative sample.

4   Experimental Results

One of our model advantage is that we can use different size fingerprints to train the verification network while the method [8] can not. And the well trained model can support different size fingerprint recognition without retraining (the method [8] need revise model and retrain). Hence, we can make full use of the existing fingerprint database. The database used in experiment is as follows: (1) FVC2000 [9], (2) FVC2002 [10], (3) FVC2004 [11], (4) FingerPass DB7 [12], (5) in-house partial fingerprints database.

The FingerPass DB7 dataset [12] comprises 8640 fingerprints of size 144×144 pixels and 500 dpi resolution from 720 fingers, each finger has 12 impression. In-house database consists of 1690 fingerprint impressions of 169 fingers, and each finger has 10 impressions, and the 10 impressions from one finger were manually confirmed that contain a common fingerprint region. The fingerprint image size of in-house database is 160×160 pixels at 508 dots-per-inch. In order to obtain as much partial fingerprint data as possible, we use traditional publicly available fingerprint database FVC [9–11] to simulate partial fingerprints. The simulate method is derived from [13]. Size of the simulated partial fingerprints is 150×150. The simulate method can not ensure the partial fingerprints which come from the same finger contain a common fingerprint region, hence we do not use simulated partial fingerprints to test in experiment. We use all simulated partial fingerprints, half FingerPass DB7 and half in-house partial fingerprints to train the verification network. For one match pair of fingerprints, our alignment algorithm could output N alignment candidates (See Sect. 2, $N = 6 \times 3 = 18$ in

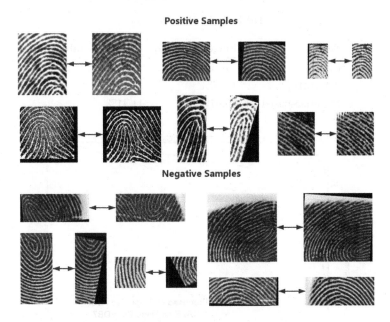

Fig. 5. Some training samples.

our experiment), hence one match pair of fingerprints could create N samples at most. Some of our training samples are shown in Fig. 5.

The proposed partial fingerprint matching algorithm was implemented by C++, and the tools used include OpenCV 2.4.10, FFTW and Caffe [14]. The kernel of A-KAZE algorithm is the publicly available code in [15].

Table 1 shows the comparison of proposed method with existing methods [1,2] in terms of EER metric on FingerPass DB7 dataset and in-house database. And the Fig. 6 shows ROC (Receiver Operating Characteristic) curves. Our model outperforms minutiae-based algorithm and A-KAZE. We analysed the failure cases of the above method. The average number of minutiae is around 5 and 12 on FingerPass DB7 dataset and in-house database respectively (the average foreground region size of all fingerprints in FingerPass DB7 dataset is around 120 × 120 pixels), which is not enough for minutiae-based algorithms. A-KAZE often fails among different collection environment, especially in dirty fingers and wet fingers case. Moreover, A-KAZE needs more overlap area to distinguish true-false match. Our model shows great power of deep convolutional network. Almost all failure cases are caused by incorrect alignment. Although, we have enough alignment candidates, it's very difficult to obtain the correct alignment in some situations, such as severe non-linear deformation, severe noise interference and insufficient overlap area. In these cases, other methods are equally powerless.

Table 1. EER on test set.

Method	FingerPass DB7	In-house database
Proposed	4.01%	1.32%
A-KAZE [2]	15.55%	4.60%
Minutiae-based [1]	30.67%	11.41%

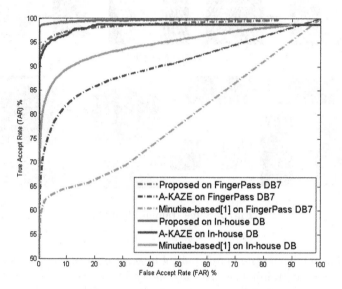

Fig. 6. Receiver Operating Characteristic curves.

5   Conclusion

In this paper, a novel frame for partial fingerprint matching problem was proposed. Partial fingerprint alignment and similarity evaluation were solved by POC-based method and deep CNN respectively. Experimental results show that proposed method performs better than some existing state-of-art methods. In future, we will design new deep network frame that could contain alignment and verification.

Acknowledgments. This work was funded by the Chinese National Natural Science Foundation (11331012, 11571014, 11731013).

References

1. Jea, T.Y., Govindaraju, V.: A minutia-based partial fingerprint recognition system. Pattern Recogn. **38**(10), 1672–1684 (2005)
2. Mathur, S., Vjay, A., Shah, J.: Methodology for partial fingerprint enrollment and authentication on mobile devices. In: International Conference on Biometrics, pp. 1–8. IEEE (2016)

3. Sun, Y., Chen, Y., Wang, X.: Deep learning face representation by joint identi-fication verification. In: Advances in Neural Information Processing Systems, pp. 1988–1996 (2014)
4. Hu, J., Lu, J., Tan, Y.P.: Discriminative deep metric learning for face verification in the wild. In: Computer Vision and Pattern Recognition, pp. 1875–1882. IEEE (2014)
5. He, K., Zhang, X., Ren, S.: Deep residual learning for image recognition. In: Pro-ceedings of the IEEE Conference on Computer Vision and Pattern Recognition, pp. 770–778 (2016)
6. Koichi, I.T.O., Nakajima, H., Kobayashi, K.: A fingerprint matching algorithm using phase-only correlation. IEICE Trans. Fundam. Electron. Commun. Comput. Sci. **87**(3), 682–691 (2004)
7. He, K., Zhang, X., Ren, S.: Spatial pyramid pooling in deep convolutional networks for visual recognition. IEEE Trans. Pattern Anal. Mach. Intell. **37**(9), 1904–1916 (2015)
8. Zhang, F., Feng, J.: High-resolution mobile fingerprint matching via deep joint KNN-triplet embedding. In: AAAI, pp. 5019–5020 (2017)
9. Maio, D., Maltoni, D., Cappelli, R.: FVC2000: fingerprint verification competition. IEEE Trans. Pattern Anal. Mach. Intell. **24**(3), 402–412 (2002)
10. Maio, D., Maltoni, D., Cappelli, R.: FVC2002: second fingerprint verification com-petition. In: Proceedings of the 16th International Conference on Pattern recogni-tion, vol. 3, pp. 811–814. IEEE (2002)
11. Maio, D., Maltoni, D., Cappelli, R.: FVC2004: third fingerprint verification com-petition. In: Biometric Authentication, pp. 31–35 (2004)
12. Jia, X., Yang, X., Zang, Y.: A cross-device matching fingerprint database from multi-type sensors. In: 2012 21st International Conference on Pattern Recognition (ICPR), pp. 3001–3004. IEEE (2012)
13. Roy, A., Memon, N., Ross, A.: MasterPrint: exploring the vulnerability of partial fingerprint-based authentication systems. IEEE Trans. Inf. Forensics Secur. **12**(9), 2013–2025 (2017)
14. Jia, Y., Shelhamer, E., Donahue, J.: Caffe: convolutional architecture for fast fea-ture embedding. In: Proceedings of the 22nd ACM International Conference on Multimedia, pp. 675–678. ACM (2014)
15. Alcantarilla, P.F., Solutions, T.: Fast explicit diffusion for accelerated features in nonlinear scale spaces. IEEE Trans. Pattern Anal. Mach. Intell. **34**(7), 1281–1298 (2011)

Adaptively Weighted Facial Expression Recognition by Feature Fusion Under Intense Illumination Condition

Yuechuan Sun and Jun Yu[(✉)]

Department of Automation,
University of Science and Technology of China, Hefei 230027, China
ycsun@mail.ustc.edu.cn, harryjun@ustc.edu.cn

Abstract. Accurate and robust facial expression recognition under complex environment is a challenging task. In this paper, we propose an adaptively weighted facial expression recognition approach to overcome the intense illumination difficulty by fusing diverse illumination invariant appearance features. First, a novel neural-network-based adaptive weight assignment strategy is designed to eliminate the adverse illumination variations efficiently and effectively. Then, a feature fusion strategy is developed to combine two of the most successful illumination invariant appearance descriptors, namely Gabor and Local Binary Patterns (LBP), for giving comprehensive and robust description of facial expressions. Extensive experiments demonstrate the superiority of the proposed approach on the common used CK+ dataset, especially the adaptive weight assignment for the significant improvement of recognition accuracy under extreme and intense illumination conditions.

Keywords: Facial expression recognition · Illumination · Feature fusion · Adaptive weight

1 Introduction

Facial expression plays a vital role in our daily communication and facial expression recognition (FER) has attracted significant research interest in the past few decades due to its potential applications in human-computer interaction (HCI). However, there still remains many challenges posed by uncontrolled environments that must be overcome to develop a robust and accurate FER system. Some of these challenges are posed by the uncontrolled environments under difficult lighting conditions and large head poses.

This paper mainly focuses on the issue of robust FER under significant illumination changes. The variation of the illumination condition causes dramatic changes in the face appearance. Intense illumination, in particular, can lead to major differences in the shading and shadows on the face. For example, face images captured under strong sunshine contain uneven textual distributions and less discriminative information for FER.

D. Liu et al. (Eds.): ICONIP 2017, Part VI, LNCS 10639, pp. 612–621, 2017.
https://doi.org/10.1007/978-3-319-70136-3_65

Existing approaches addressing the illumination problem can be classified mainly into passive approaches and active approaches [1]. The former attempt to overcome this problem by studying the visible spectrum images in which face appearance has been changed by illumination variations. Passive approaches usually seek for normalization techniques (e.g., Multiscale Retinex [2] and Self Quotient Image [3]) and illumination invariant features (e.g., Gabor [4] and LBP [5]). Active approaches employ active imaging techniques to obtain different modalities of face images that are invariant or insensitive to illumination changes. These modalities incorporate 3D face model [6], thermal infrared image [7], and hyperspectral image [8]. However, additional photo devices are required for modality collection.

Contrary to the difficulty of applying normalization techniques and modality collection, this paper presents a block-based adaptively weighted FER system using neural network by features fusion. Specifically, we first preprocess the raw face images for normalization. Then, a three-layer Back Propagation (BP) neural network is trained for adaptive weight assignment to achieve illumination invariance based on *local image entropy* and *illumination intensity*. Gabor and LBP features with illumination invariance are extracted and Principal Component Analysis (PCA) is implemented before feature fusion for dimensionality reduction. The obtained feature vector is then fed to Linear Discriminant Analysis (LDA) for feature optimization and support vector machine (SVM) is used for expression classification. Figure 1 shows the framework of the proposed method.

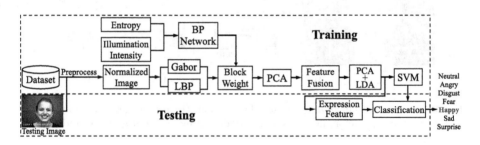

Fig. 1. The framework of the proposed method.

In summary, our main contributions are: (1) We present an effective feature fusion scheme that promotes the performance of FER. (2) To the best of our knowledge, this is the first time for quantitatively addressing the intense illumination problem using a given FER dataset under different illumination levels. We select target images by defining *illumination intensity*, which can be extended for any other dataset. (3) We propose using a neural network to adaptively assign weights for face image sub-blocks in order to tackle illumination changing problem. Compared with previous methods in which constant weights are assigned manually [5,9,10], ours is more robust as the network is trained using the real dataset under various illumination distributions. The proposed method is also applicable to other face analysis tasks.

The rest of this paper is organized as follows: in Sect. 2 we describe the proposed method in detail in terms of preprocessing, feature extraction, adaptive weight assignment and feature fusion. We evaluate the performance of the proposed method on the CK+ dataset and give a detailed discussion in Sect. 3. Section 4 concludes the paper.

2   The Proposed Approach

2.1   Preprocessing

Preprocessing is a fundamental step in FER. An ideal preprocessing is supposed to eliminate the irrelevant information (e.g., background and rotation) for pure expression images with uniform size and normalized intensity. For a given face image, we first localize the centers of eyes with OpenCV's implementation of Adaboost learning algorithm [11] for reference points. Images are then rotated, scaled, and cropped into 108×120 size to remove the background using the face model shown in Fig. 2(a). Histogram equalization is finally adopted for preliminary illumination compensation.

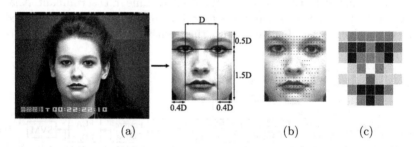

(a)   (b)   (c)

Fig. 2. (a) Original image and cropped face region. (b) Inhomogeneous sampling. (c) The weight mask, black indicates weight 2.0, dark grey 1.5, light grey 1.0, and white 0.

2.2   Feature Extraction

Gabor Representation. A Gabor wavelet filter is widely used for extracting local features and presents the best simultaneous localization of spatial and frequency information. The Gabor function can be defined as:

$$\psi_{u,v}(z) = \frac{\|k_{u,v}\|}{\sigma^2} e^{(-\|k_{u,v}\|^2 \|z\|^2 / 2\sigma^2)} \left[e^{ik_{u,v}z} - e^{-\sigma^2/2} \right]. \tag{1}$$

$z = (x, y)$ gives the pixel position in the spatial domain, and frequency vector $k_{u,v} = k_{\max} e^{i\phi_u} / f_v$ stands for the frequency vector, where $\phi_u = u\pi/u_{\max}, \phi_u \in [0, \pi)$, and u and v denote the orientation and scale factors of Gabor filters respectively. In our system, we adopt the Gabor filters of five scales ($v = 0, 1, \cdots, 4$)

and eight orientations ($u = 0, 1, \cdots, 7$), with $\sigma = 2\pi$, $k_{max} = \pi/2$ and $f = \sqrt{2}$. The same parameters were also chosen in [4].

The Gabor representation is obtained by convolving an input face image with a set of Gabor filters, and the magnitude of the convolution output is used for FER for its invariance to displacement. For dimensionality reduction, 279 fiducial points are selected to refine distinct expression information mainly located at eyes, mouth and nose (see Fig. 2(b)).

Local Binary Patterns. LBP was originally introduced by Ojala et al. [12] for texture description and later applied to FER [5]. The LBP operator labels the pixels of an image by thresholding P sampling points evenly distributed on a circle (of radius R) centered at the pixel with the center pixel value and considering the result as a binary number, and bilinear interpolation is used for these points that do not fall within the pixels.

A classic extension to the original LBP is the definition of so-called *uniform patterns*. A local binary pattern is called uniform if it contains at most two bitwise transitions from 0 to 1 or vice versa when the binary string is considered circular. A preliminary experiment is conducted to find the optimal parameters for this application, resulting in $P = 8$ and $R = 1$.

A histogram of the labeled image $f(x, y)$ can be defined as:

$$H_i = \sum_{x,y} I\{f(x, y) = i\}, i = 0, \cdots, n - 1, \tag{2}$$

where n is the number of different labels produced by LBP operator and

$$I\{A\} = \begin{cases} 1, & if\ A\ is\ true \\ 0, & otherwise \end{cases}. \tag{3}$$

The obtained histogram contains information about the distribution of the local micropatterns over the whole image. However, spatial information should also be considered to represent the shape information of faces for efficient face representation. For this purpose, face images are first divided into small sub-blocks and the LBP features extracted from each block are subsequently concatenated into a single, spatially-enhanced feature histogram. In our system, the face images are divided into 49 (7×7) sub-blocks, giving a good trade-off between recognition performance and feature vector length.

2.3   Adaptive Weight Assignment

Although Gabor and LBP descriptors are insensitive to illumination to some extent, the generated feature vectors are not suitable for FER without further processing, as the overexposure areas hardly carry texture information or contribute to FER. Considering the spatial texture difference of a face image, we design a block-based adaptively weighted strategy to reduce the adverse effect of overexposure parts of image by assigning lower weights to them and emphasize on the partitions with more discriminative information.

Previous work generates weights for image blocks by designing weight mask [5,9] or defining functions [10] by hand, which are not robust and sensitive to illumination changes. In this work, we propose training a BP neural network for automatically assigning weights. The network takes image entropy E and illumination intensity η as input and outputs weight $w \in [0,1]$. Gabor and LBP features extracted from a certain block are then multiplied by the corresponding w. Since the network is trained on real dataset and has only three layers, it can model the actual illumination information and make fast prediction. In practice, we first manually assign weights to each block of approximately one third of the dataset and they are used for training the neural network for generating weights for unseen images. A handcrafted weight mask is then designed to further enhance distinct face areas based on [10] (see Fig. 2(c)).

Local Image Entropy. According to Shannon theory, entropy depicts the quantity of information for a series of random variables. Being motivated by this, we compute the local entropy of each image block to investigate the contribution of the block to feature extraction:

$$E = - \sum_{i=1}^{N_t} P(i) \log P(i), \tag{4}$$

where N_t is the overall number of gray levels in the image sub-block and $P(i)$ is the gray value's probability in that block.

Illumination Intensity. In order to quantify the illumination level, we originally propose the definition of illumination intensity. For a two dimension $W \times H$ digital image, the illumination intensity η is defined as:

$$\eta = \frac{\sum_{x,y} I\left\{ f\left(x,y\right) > \tau \right\}}{W \times H}, \tag{5}$$

where τ is the threshold intensity.

2.4   Feature Fusion

Most of the existing approaches to FER use features of just one type. However, research indicates that the fusion of multiple features can enhance the performance of pattern recognition problems [13]. Of all the feature fusion strategies, a simple but effective one is to combine several sources of raw features to produce a new feature vector, which is expected to be more synthetic and informative.

Suppose that the feature vectors of Gabor and LBP descriptors are α_0 and β_0, PCA is first adopted to obtain α and β. In order to eliminate the numerical unbalance between these two features and gain satisfactory fusion performance, we first adopt feature normalization to turn α and β into unit vectors:

$$\begin{cases} \bar{\alpha} = \alpha/\|\alpha\| \\ \bar{\beta} = \beta/\|\beta\| \end{cases}. \tag{6}$$

Considering that the dimensions of $\bar{\alpha}$ and $\bar{\beta}$ are usually unequal, the higher-dimensional one is more powerful than the lower-dimensional one as it plays a more important role in the scatter matrices in terms of the linear feature extraction after combination. Therefore, we adopt the weighted combination strategy introduced in [13] to remove the adverse effect resulting from unequal dimensions. Suppose that the dimensions of $\bar{\alpha}$ and $\bar{\beta}$ are m and n respectively, the combined feature vector can be defined as $\gamma = [\bar{\alpha}, \theta\bar{\beta}]$, where θ be m^2/n^2. LDA is eventually employed for feature optimization.

3 Experiments

3.1 Dataset

Most FER systems recognize six basic expressions (i.e., Anger = AN, Disgust = DI, Fear = FE, Happiness = HA, Sadness = SA and Surprise = SU) proposed by Ekman [14]. In this work, 6-class as well as 7-class (including Neutral = NE) expression classification experiments are conducted on the Cohn-Kanade (CK+) Facial Expression Dataset [15]. This well-known dataset consists of 593 image sequences from 123 subjects. The image sequences vary in duration from neutral faces to peak expressions. Ambient room lighting augmented by a high-intensity lamp was used for approximately one third of subjects, resulting in partially overexposure under intense illumination. In our study, 309 sequences from 106 subjects are selected which were annotated with six basic expressions. Only the first and last frames were used. Since we are concerned with the illumination problem in this paper, image subsets under five levels of illumination are selected according to the definition of *illumination intensity* ($\eta \geq 0.1, 0.15, 0.2, 0.25, 0.3$). As there is no consent for publication for the intense illumination images, they cannot be depicted here.

3.2 Experiments on the Intense Illumination Subsets

We first evaluate the effectiveness of our proposed feature fusion and adaptive weight assignment strategies on intense illumination subsets and the results are presented in Fig. 3. Considering the limited amount of images in the dataset, we propose the use of leave-one-out scheme for performance evaluation. SVM is used to classify different facial expressions.

From Fig. 3, it can be seen that fusing Gabor and LBP features (blue line) obtains higher recognition rates than using any descriptor alone, since the fused feature takes the advantage of both and contains more discriminative information. It also shows that the performance of our FER system can be further promoted using the adaptive weight assignment framework (red line). This is achieved as the trained network emphasizes on the reliable blocks and removes the adverse impact from intense illumination areas. The overall performance deteriorates with the increase of illumination intensity, this is reasonable as the face images contain less information and the dataset gets smaller under

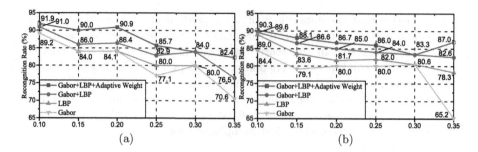

Fig. 3. Recognition rates under different illumination intensities. (a) 6-class experiment. (b) 7-class experiment. (Color figure online)

more intense illumination condition. However, there is a sharp increase in 7-class experiment when $\eta \geq 0.35$ (red line), this results from the occasionality caused by the lack of training data.

3.3 Experiments on the Whole CK+ Dataset

In order to verify the generalizability of our approach under random illumination condition, we also performed 10-fold cross validation experiments on the whole CK+ dataset, which covers images under all kinds of illumination intensities. Comparative results which adopted similar experimental protocols are reported in Tables 1 and 2.

Table 1. Recognition rates on CK+ dataset (6-class)

Method	AN	DI	FE	HA	SA	SU	Ave.
Baseline [15]	75.0	94.7	65.2	**100**	68.0	96.0	83.2
Hybrid feature [16]	**100**	96.6	84.0	**100**	78.6	**98.8**	93.0
SFP [17]	87.8	93.3	94.3	94.2	**96.4**	98.5	94.1
CNN based [18]	–	–	–	–	–	–	93.2
3D CNN [19]	**100**	**100**	84.0	**100**	89.3	**98.8**	95.4
3DCNN-DAP [20]	91.1	96.6	80.0	98.6	85.7	96.4	91.4
Proposed	93.3	**100**	**96.0**	**100**	92.9	**98.8**	**96.8**

As for the 6-class experiment, Lucey et al. [15] extracted geometric features based on Active Appearance Model when they proposed the dataset. Similar to us, [16,17] proposed block or patch based descriptors for feature extraction. Nevertheless, they did not consider the spatial texture disparity caused by illumination. Although deep convolutional neural networks (CNN) are effective for extracting high-level visual features, CNN based methods [18–20] still fall behind ours as the networks did not learn features related to illumination.

Table 2. Recognition rates on CK+ dataset (7-class)

Method	AN	DI	FE	HA	SA	SU	NE	Ave.
Gabor+LBP [21]	53.6	75.4	79.7	96.6	**79.1**	96.9	**96.2**	82.5
LDCRF [22]	76.7	81.5	**94.4**	98.6	77.2	**99.1**	73.5	85.9
AUDN [23]	81.8	95.5	82.7	99.6	71.4	97.6	95.4	89.1
Proposed	**88.9**	**98.3**	88.0	**100**	75.0	97.6	**96.2**	**92.0**

The 7-class experiment turns out to be more challenging as Neutral expression causes considerable amount of confusion with subtle expressions including Anger and Sadness. However, our method shows equal superiority to the state-of-the-art ones.

The result shows that Happiness and Surprise are easiest to recognize. This is an intuitive result as these expressions cause many more facial movements mainly located around mouth. Other expressions, such as Anger and Sadness, attain lower classification accuracies due to the lack of facial deformation and training samples.

4   Conclusion

In this paper, we propose a framework of recognizing facial expressions with 2D images under intense illumination condition. We show that the FER performance can be improved by using the proposed feature fusion method. In addition, we present an effective adaptive weight assignment strategy based on BP neural network. Extensive experiments on the CK+ dataset clearly demonstrate the effectiveness and generalizability of our new approach. It is noticeable that the proposed approach is applicable to other datasets and face analysis tasks (e.g., face recognition).

Acknowledgments. This work is supported by the National Natural Science Foundation of China (61572450, 61303150), Anhui Provincial Natural Science Foundation (1708085QF138), the Fundamental Research Funds for the Central Universities (WK2350000002), the Open Funding Project of State Key Lab of Virtual Reality Technology and Systems, Beihang University (BUAA-VR-16KF-12), the Open Funding Project of State Key Lab of Novel Software Technology, Nanjing University (KFKT2016B08).

References

1. Zou, X., Kittler, J., Messer, K.: Illumination invariant face recognition: a survey. In: IEEE International Conference on Biometrics: Theory, Applications, and Systems, pp. 1–8 (2007)
2. Jobson, D.J., Rahman, Z., Woodell, G.A.: A multiscale retinex for bridging the gap between color images and the human observation of scenes. IEEE Trans. Image Process. **6**(7), 965–976 (1997)

3. Wang, H., Li, S.Z., Wang, Y.: Face recognition under varying lighting conditions using self quotient image. In: IEEE International Conference on Automatic Face and Gesture Recognition, pp. 819–824 (2004)

4. Ou, J., Bai, X.B., Pei, Y., Ma, L., Liu, W.: Automatic facial expression recognition using gabor filter and expression analysis. In: International Conference on Computer Modeling and Simulation, vol. 2, pp. 215–218 (2010)

5. Shan, C., Gong, S., McOwan, P.W.: Facial expression recognition based on local binary patterns: a comprehensive study. Image Vis. Comput. **27**(6), 803–816 (2009)

6. Paysan, P., Knothe, R., Amberg, B., Romdhani, S., Vetter, T.: A 3D face model for pose and illumination invariant face recognition. In: IEEE International Conference on Advanced Video and Signal Based Surveillance, pp. 296–301 (2009)

7. Wang, S., Liu, Z., Lv, S., Lv, Y., Wu, G., Peng, P., Chen, F., Wang, X.: A natural visible and infrared facial expression database for expression recognition and emotion inference. IEEE Trans. Multimedia **12**(7), 682–691 (2010)

8. Di, W., Zhang, L., Zhang, D., Pan, Q.: Studies on hyperspectral face recognition in visible spectrum with feature band selection. IEEE Trans. Syst. Man Cybern. Part A Syst. Hum. **40**(6), 1354–1361 (2010)

9. Ahonen, T., Hadid, A., Pietikäinen, M.: Face description with local binary patterns: application to face recognition. IEEE Trans. Pattern Anal. Mach. Intell. **28**(12), 2037–2041 (2006)

10. Mohamed, A.A., Gavrilova, M.L., Yampolskiy, R.V.: Artificial face recognition using wavelet adaptive LBP with directional statistical features. In: International Conference on Cyberworlds, pp. 23–28 (2012)

11. Viola, P., Jones, M.: Rapid object detection using a boosted cascade of simple features. In: IEEE Computer Society Conference on Computer Vision and Pattern Recognition, vol. 1, pp. 511–518 (2001)

12. Ojala, T., Pietikäinen, M., Mäenpää, T.: Multiresolution gray-scale and rotation invariant texture classification with local binary patterns. IEEE Trans. Pattern Anal. Mach. Intell. **24**(7), 971–987 (2002)

13. Yang, J., Yang, J., Zhang, D., Lu, J.: Feature fusion: parallel strategy vs. serial strategy. Pattern Recogn. **36**(6), 1369–1381 (2003)

14. Ekman, P., Friesen, W.: Facial Action Coding System: A Technique for the Measurement of Facial Movement. Consulting Psychologists, San Francisco (1978)

15. Lucey, P., Cohn, J.F., Kanade, T., Saragih, J., Ambadar, Z., Matthews, I.: The extended Cohn-Kanade dataset (CK+): a complete dataset for action unit and emotion-specified expression. In: IEEE Computer Society Conference on Computer Vision and Pattern Recognition Workshops, pp. 94C–101 (2010)

16. Chen, J., Chen, Z., Chi, Z., Fu, H.: Facial expression recognition in video with multiple feature fusion. IEEE Trans. Affect. Comput. **PP**, 1 (2016)

17. Happy, S., Routray, A.: Automatic facial expression recognition using features of salient facial patches. IEEE Trans. Affect. Comput. **6**(1), 1–12 (2015)

18. Mollahosseini, A., Chan, D., Mahoor, M.H.: Going deeper in facial expression recognition using deep neural networks. In: IEEE Winter Conference on Applications of Computer Vision, pp. 1–10 (2016)

19. Jung, H., Lee, S., Yim, J., Park, S., Kim, J.: Joint fine-tuning in deep neural networks for facial expression recognition. In: International Conference on Computer Vision, pp. 2983–2991 (2015)

20. Liu, M., Li, S., Shan, S., Wang, R., Chen, X.: Deeply learning deformable facial action parts model for dynamic expression analysis. In: Asian Conference on Computer Vision, pp. 143–157 (2014)

21. Zavaschi, T.H., Britto, A.S., Oliveira, L.E., Koerich, A.L.: Fusion of feature sets and classifiers for facial expression recognition. Expert Syst. Appl. **40**(2), 646–655 (2013)
22. Jain, S., Hu, C., Aggarwal, J.K.: Facial expression recognition with temporal modeling of shapes. In: International Conference on Computer Vision Workshops, pp. 1642–1649 (2011)
23. Liu, M., Li, S., Shan, S., Chen, X.: AU-aware deep networks for facial expression recognition. In: IEEE International Conference and Workshops on Automatic Face and Gesture Recognition, pp. 1–6 (2013)

A Deep Model Combining Structural Features and Context Cues for Action Recognition in Static Images

Xinxin Wang, Kan Li$^{(\boxtimes)}$, and Yang Li

Beijing Institute of Technology, Beijing, China
{2120161059,likan,yanglee}@bit.edu.cn

Abstract. In this paper, we present a deep model for the task of action recognition in static images, which combines body structural information and context cues to build a more accurate classifier. Moreover, to construct more semantic and robust body structural features, we propose a new body descriptor, named *limb angle discriptor(LAD)*, which uses the relative angles between the limbs in 2D skeleton. We evaluate our method on the PASCAL VOC 2012 Action dataset and compare it with the published results. The result shows that our method achieves 90.6% mean AP, outperforming the previous state-of-art approaches in the field.

Keywords: Action recognition · Deep model · Body descriptor · Context cue

1 Introduction

Human action recognition in static images is an important task in computer vision. It has many important applications and practical values in different areas, such as intelligent surveillance, action or behavior based image retrieval and human-computer interaction (HCI). Unlike traditional methods for action recognition in image sequences or videos that can provide spatial-temporal information, there is no temporal information in static images. However, only spatial features in static images may be not enough to characterize and judge one's action. Therefore, recognizing actions in static images is more challenging.

To accurately recognize actions in static images, one effective way is to extract discriminative appearance features (including *statistical features* and *structural features*) of the human body from static images. Recently, CNN features are widely applied to action recognition because of their state-of-the-art performance on various computer vision tasks. Another effective way is to extract informative context cues from static images. Context cues are helpful when we address the problem of intra-class variability, since people may perform the same action in different ways, or even one person may perform a specific action differently in different situations [22]. However, recognizing actions using these two ways

D. Liu et al. (Eds.): ICONIP 2017, Part VI, LNCS 10639, pp. 622–632, 2017.
https://doi.org/10.1007/978-3-319-70136-3_66

in static images still faces some challenges. On one hand, CNN features have been demonstrated to have a powerful representation capability to learn high-level features, but they do not use the semantic information of body structures. It leads to misclassification of fine-grained actions with subtle appearance difference. On the other hand, the context cues will have some negative effects if the image scene is too noisy and crowded. Because they may provide disturbing information to distinguish actions. As shown in Fig. 1, there are two persons in the scene, skiing and walking respectively. The snowboards and ski poles in the scene are context cues that interfere with the recognition of walking.

Fig. 1. An example that context cues provide disturbing information to distinguish actions.

In order to solve the challenges mentioned above in action recognition, we proposed an approach that combines body structural features and the context cues into a unified CNN model. We fuse the classification score made through CNN features with the score predicted through body structure features to enhance the discriminability of body appearance. Furthermore, the model learns different weights on different score terms to jointly determine the final results. To address the problem caused by complex context in images, inspired by [9], we select the most informative cue from all available context cues to reduce the interference caused by unrelated cues. To construct more semantic body structural features, we propose a new body descriptor, named *limb*[1] *angle descriptor (LAD)*, which uses the relative angles between the limbs in 2D skeleton to represent one's action. LAD has more semantics in representing human actions and works in more similar way with human brain. And we can set up the motion constraints according to the LAD, for example, the knee cannot bend back, the head can only rotate in a certain range around. Moreover, the LAD is robust in image rotation and scaling.

We quantify the performance of our model for action recognition using the PASCAL VOC 2012 Action dataset [5]. The results demonstrate that our method outperforms all of the recent approaches, especially for the actions in which the context cues are not discriminative enough to distinguish them. In summary, the contribution of this paper are list as follows:

---

[1] We refer to part pairs as limbs for clarity, despite the fact that some pairs are not human limbs (e.g., the torso).

1. We proposed a deep model to address the task of action recognition in static images. It simultaneously fuse the informative context and the discriminative appearance features to make more accurate predictions.
2. We proposed a new body descriptor (LAD) which is more semantic and robust to represent body structural information by using the relative angles between the limbs in 2D skeleton.
3. The proposed method is evaluated on the Pascal VOC 2012 Action dataset. Our approach achieves 90.6% mean AP outperforming all other approaches in the field.

2   Related Work

Action Recognition. There is a variety of work in the field of action recognition in static images. The conventional approaches are based on hand-engineered features such as HOG [3] and SIFT [15]. Most leading methods use part detectors to learn specific action classifier. In detail, Maji et al. [16] constructed poselet activation vector based on poselets [1] as a distributed representation for each person and used SVMs to classify the actions. Hoai et al. [10] used body-part based detectors to get their part based features and then aligned them to their corresponding body part with a similar distance. Recently, CNNs have achieved state-of-the-art performance in computer vision. For the task of action recognition, Oquab et al. [17] used a CNN on ground-truth boxes for the task of action classification. Hoai [11] extracted fc7 features of an 8-layer network from image regions at multiple locations and got the final prediction by fusing the scores of these regions. Gkioxari et al. [8] used deep version of poselets to train part detectors for head, torso, legs region and trained holistic CNN to classify actions. However, those methods do not use the semantic information of body structures. It is easy to lead to misclassification in actions with subtle appearance difference.

Context Cues. Context cues and their roles in image-based action recognition have been studied for a long time. Maji et al. [16] obtained contextual cues in two ways: they explicitly detected related objects using pre-trained models and explored action knowledge from other people in the image. Prest et al. [18] located the action objects by finding recurring action patterns in images, and then captured their relative spatial relationships. Hoai et al. [10] integrated part-based features into object detection scores and trained non-linear SVMs to classify actions. Gkioxari et al. [9] adapted R-CNN to use more than one region to explore all available cues. Gkioxari et al. [7] relied on action and pose appearance cues to predict the interactions with objects in the scene. Inspired by [9], we use more than one context region for classification and select the most informative context region from all available context regions.

Structural Features. In recent research work, several structured descriptor features have been proposed to describe human action. Most of them are based on the human skeleton under 3D space with 20 joints [14] or 15 joints [4]. Some descriptors used the distances or variant distances [4,12,13,21] between joints to describe actions. For example, Ellis et al. [4] proposed a descriptor using the distances between every two joints to represent actions. The descriptors proposed by Yang et al. [21] use the position difference between joints. Kerola et al. [13] represented human pose using graph model, and let the nodes and edges correspond to the human joints and the joint distances respectively. However, it is difficult to reconstruct 3D skeletons in 2D images. Besides, it is also difficult for distance-based descriptors to set up the motion constraints.

3   Method

We proposed a CNN model that combines body structural features and the context cues to recognize actions in static images. The overview of the architecture is shown in Fig. 2. Given an image with the person bounding box, our network sequentially processes the input image with several convolutional and max pooling layers to obtain the feature map of the image. Then we branch out three scoring branches (followed by *the whole person branch*, *the context branch* and *the body structure branch*). On the first two branches, we use the features of different bounding box regions on the *conv*5 feature maps through ROI Pooling operation. Specifically, on *the whole person branch*, the feature vector is obtained from the bounding box of the target person and then passed through two fully connected layers $fc6$ and $fc7$ to predict the action score. On *the context branch* we predict the score for each candidate box, and then use a global max pooling operation to select the most informative box c for each action α. The third branch is *the body structure branch* where we incorporate the body structure features. On this branch we estimate the joint positions of the target person and use them to construct the LAD. After that, the descriptor vector is passed through

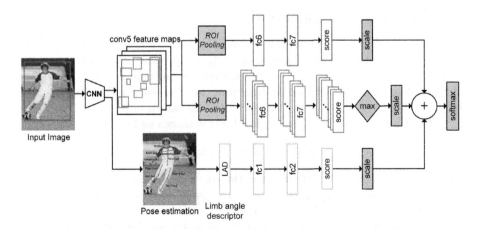

Fig. 2. The overview of our model architecture.

two fully connected layers to predict the score. Finally, the scores of these three branches are weightedly summed to generate the final score for action prediction.

3.1 The Model

Our goal is to recognize human action in a static image. To recognize actions accurately, we extract the CNN features and the structural features of the human bounding box, as well as pick the most informative contextual cue. Suppose for a target person bounding box h in image I, we have estimated all the positions of the joints J_i and applied them to construct the LAD as $\varphi(h)$. Then we define the score of action α as the weighted sum of three terms:

$$score(\alpha; h, I) = \underbrace{\lambda_1 \cdot w_h^\alpha \cdot \phi(h; I)}_{person\ CNN\ features} + \underbrace{\lambda_2 \cdot w_j^\alpha \cdot \varphi(h; I)}_{person\ structural\ features}$$

$$+ \underbrace{\lambda_3 \cdot \max_{c \in R(c)} w_c^\alpha \cdot \phi(c; I)}_{context\ cues} . \quad (1)$$

where $R(c)$ defines a set of candidate context regions for the target person. $\phi(h)$, $\phi(c)$ are the vectors of $fc7$ features extracted from the person region and the context region in I, and $\varphi(h)$ is the vector of the LAD. While w_h^α, w_j^α and w_c^α are the corresponding scoring weights for action α respectively. λ_1, λ_2 and λ_3 define the weights corresponding to the three scoring terms. Given the score for each action $\alpha \in A$, the probability that the person is performing action α is obtained by a softmax function:

$$P(\alpha|h, I) = \frac{exp(score(\alpha|h, I))}{\sum\limits_{\alpha' \in A} exp(score(\alpha'|h, I))} . \quad (2)$$

3.2 Limb Angle Descriptor(LAD)

Human body structure information is essential for action recognition. In order to express the human action more accurately, we present *limb angle descriptor* (LAD), and use it to extract structure information of human body. Unlike the distance descriptor, the limb angle descriptor uses the relative angle between the limbs in 2D skeleton to represent one's action, as shown in Fig. 3.

The vector we used to represent the LAD is shown as follows:

$$\varphi(h; I) = (a_0, a_1, \cdots, a_9, a_{10})^T . \quad (3)$$

where a_0 represents the angle between the torso and y-axis, as well as $a_1 - a_{10}$ respectively indicate the angles between the torso and each of the other limbs (including the head, the shoulder, the left arm, the right arm, the left forearm, the right forearm, the left thigh, the right thigh, the left leg and the right leg).

To construct the descriptor, we suppose that the positions of the joints $\{J_i, J_j\}$, which are belong to a specific limb, are (x_i, y_i) and (x_j, y_j). Here, we

Fig. 3. The example of the limb angle descriptor.

estimate the positions of the joints using the method proposed by Cao et al. [2], which has relatively high speed and good accuracy. Then we construct the limb vector $\overrightarrow{J_iJ_j}$ through the coordinates of these two joints. After obtaining the vector of each limb, we can calculate the relative angle of any two limbs. Let (x_i, y_i), (x_j, y_j) and (x_k, y_k), (x_t, y_t) denote the positions of limbs $\overrightarrow{J_iJ_j}$ and $\overrightarrow{J_kJ_t}$. The relative angle of these two limbs is calculated as:

$$a(i, j, k, t) = \frac{\overrightarrow{J_iJ_j} \cdot \overrightarrow{J_kJ_t}}{|\overrightarrow{J_iJ_j}| \cdot |\overrightarrow{J_kJ_t}|} . \tag{4}$$

In this way, we construct the limb angle descriptor, which is robust in rotation and scaling, as well as contains rich semantic information about actions.

3.3 Context Cues

In the context branch of our network, our aim is to get the most informative context region. Inspire by [9], we extend Fast R-CNN [6] to use more than one region for classification. We generate candidate context regions using Selective Search method [20] and pass them into the network. To obtain the most informative context region, we select the region that generates the highest score.

$$c_\alpha{}^* = \underset{c \in R(c)}{\mathrm{argmax}}\, w_c^\alpha \cdot \phi(c; I) . \tag{5}$$

The reason why we obtain the most informative context region is that there are multiple cues in an image. Irrelevant cues will prevent the classifier to accurately reveal what action a person is doing. So we need to select the most relevant and informative context cue for the target person from all available cues. The global max pooling operation can ensure that the training error back-propagates only to the network weights corresponding to the most informative candidate region in the image. Thus, we are able to capture the most informative region from large number of candidates.

3.4 Learning

We train the model with stochastic gradient descent (SGD) using backpropagation. The loss over a batch of training images is defined as:

$$loss(B) = -\frac{1}{N} \sum_{i=1}^{N} log p_a \ . \tag{6}$$

where $B = \{I_i\}_{i=1}^{N}$ represents a batch of training images and N is the number of the images in a batch. We fine-tune our network starting with VGG-16 [19], which has been pre-trained on the ImageNet-1K for the image classification task. In particular, we only tune the fully connected layers of all three branches and fix all the convolutional layers. We set the learning rate to 0.0001 and consider 2 images per batch, and train them for 40 K iterations. In order to fully exploit the design of our network, we augment the training data by randomly cropping patches from each ground-truth person bounding box. And each patch is more than 1/2 size of the original box. All the patches are used to train our model.

4 Experiments

We evaluate the performance of our model using the PASCAL VOC 2012 Action dataset. In this section, we introduce the details of the dataset used for our experiments firstly. Then we evaluate our method and compare it with the variants of our method as well as the published results. And we demonstrate the effectiveness of our method for action recognition in static images. At last, we present some experiment results of our method.

4.1 Dataset

We use the PASCAL VOC 2012 Action dataset in our experiments. The PASCAL VOC 2012 Action dataset consists of 10 different behaviors, including *Jumping, Phoning, Playing Instrument, Reading, Riding Bike, Riding Horse, Running, Taking Photo, Using Computer, and walking*. In addition, there also have some examples of people who do not perform the above action, which are marked as *Other*. In the experiments, we use our model to recognize the above 10 actions. To train our CNN model we use the train set, which consists of 2296 images and 3134 instances (with their bounding box and action labels). And we use the test set to evaluate our approach during testing stage. The evaluation criterion defined by the PASCAL VOC action task, which computes the AP on the ground truth test boxes. For every example we provide probabilities for all actions and compute AP.

4.2 Performance

We experiment with the variants of our method to illustrate the validity of our method in the PASCAL VOC 2012 Action val set. In detail, we compared with the model without consideration of context cues and LAD (R-CNN), the model without consideration of LAD (R-CNN + Context) and the model without consideration of context cues (R-CNN + LAD).

1. **R-CNN.**
   This is the baseline approach that we train Fast R-CNN for action classification task. This network only exploits the information provided from the integral human body region.
2. **R-CNN + Context.**
   In this method, we jointly train the first two branches in order to take advantage of the information from both the integral human body region and context regions.
3. **R-CNN + LAD.**
   We validate the effectiveness of LAD in our experiment. We first estimate the human pose in the image, and then jointly train the whole person branch and the body structure branch for this task.

Table 1. AP of the variants of our model on the PASCAL VOC 2012 Action val set.

AP(%)	Jumping	Phoning	Playing Instrument	Reading	Riding Bike	Riding Horse	Running	Taking Photo	Using Computer	Walking	mAP
R-CNN	86.9	68.0	91.9	72.4	91.9	92.8	85.2	80.2	81.4	68.8	81.9
R-CNN+Context	88.6	80.0	95.3	81.5	93.9	96.9	87.9	84.4	92.6	71.4	87.3
R-CNN+LAD	87.7	68.5	92.2	72.5	92.0	93.2	86.4	80.8	81.4	70.3	82.5
Ours	**88.9**	**80.8**	**95.4**	**81.8**	**94.2**	**97.0**	**89.4**	**84.9**	**92.9**	**72.8**	**87.8**

Table 1 shows the performance of all the variants on the PASCAL VOC 2012 Action val set. The results present that our method outperforms across all categories. In particular, our method performs significantly better than the baseline approach. And we can observe that taking both body structure features and context cues into account is a promising way to improve the performance of action recognition in static images.

4.3 Comparison with the Published Results

In this section, we compare the performance of our model with the published results of recent approaches on the PASCAL VOC 2012 Action test set.

We compare our model with recent methods shown in Table 2. Gkioxari et al. [8] trained holistic CNN to classify actions and use deep version of poselets to train part detectors. Hoai [11] extracted feature vectors at multiple sub-windows at multiple locations and scales, then they fused their scores to get the final prediction. Simonyan et al. [19] used multi-scale convolutional features that are computed using two very deep convolutional networks and obtained the result by a SVM classifier. Gkioxari et al. [9] used R*CNN to make use of all available cues to perform action recognition. As shown in Table 2, the results of our approach are explicitly better than the recent methods that just consider the context cues and the CNN features of the image. Our method achieves significant improvement in walking and running, in which the context cues are not discriminative enough to distinguish them, by fusing the body structural information in the model. Our method also obtains high scores for *Using Computer*, *Riding Bike*, *Playing Instrument* and *Phoning* by considering the most informative context cue.

We present some experiment results of our method on the test set in Fig. 4. We highlight the person in question with red box and the body structure with red sticks, while the most informative context region with green box. Our method can obtain an accurate prediction for each action on this data set.

Table 2. AP of published approaches on the PASCAL VOC 2012 Action test set.

AP(%)	Jumping	Phoning	Playing Instrument	Reading	Riding Bike	Riding Horse	Running	Taking Photo	Using Computer	Walking	mAP
Gkioxari et al. [8]	77.9	54.5	79.8	48.9	95.3	95.0	86.9	61.0	68.9	67.3	73.6
Hoai et al. [11]	82.3	52.9	84.3	53.6	95.6	96.1	89.7	60.4	76.0	72.9	76.3
Simonyan et al. [19]	89.3	71.3	94.7	71.3	97.1	98.2	90.2	73.3	88.5	66.4	84.0
Gkioxari et al. [9]	91.5	84.4	93.6	83.2	96.9	98.4	93.8	85.9	92.6	81.8	90.2
Ours	91.9	84.7	93.9	83.6	97.3	98.5	94.5	86.9	92.6	82.4	90.6

Fig. 4. Top predictions on the PASCAL VOC Action test set. (Color figure online)

5 Conclusions

We propose a new model for the task of action recognition in static images. The body structural features and the most informative context cue are both considered in our model. And we propose a new body descriptor (LAD), which uses the relative angles between the limbs in 2D skeleton, to construct more semantic and robust body structural features. Finally, we propose a end-to-end CNN network architecture to achieve the task. Our method achieves state-of-art results on PASCAL VOC 2012 Action dataset. The result shows that exploiting body structural information is a promising way to improve the accuracy of action recognition in static images.

Acknowlwdgements. The work is partly supported by Beijing Natual Science Foundation (4172054).

References

1. Bourdev, L., Malik, J.: Poselets: Body part detectors trained using 3d human pose annotations, pp. 1365–1372 (2010)
2. Cao, Z., Simon, T., Wei, S.E., Sheikh, Y.: Realtime multi-person 2d pose estimation using part affinity fields. arXiv preprint arXiv:1611.08050 (2016)
3. Dalal, N., Triggs, B.: Histograms of oriented gradients for human detection. In: IEEE Computer Society Conference on Computer Vision and Pattern Recognition, CVPR 2005, vol. 1, pp. 886–893. IEEE (2005)
4. Ellis, C., Masood, S.Z., Tappen, M.F., Laviola, J.J., Sukthankar, R.: Exploring the trade-off between accuracy and observational latency in action recognition. Int. J. Comput. Vis. **101**(3), 420–436 (2013)
5. Everingham, M., Van Gool, L., Williams, C.K.I., Winn, J., Zisserman, A.: The pascal visual object classes (voc) challenge. Int. J. Comput. Vis. **88**(2), 303–338 (2010)
6. Girshick, R.: Fast r-cnn. In: Proceedings of the IEEE International Conference on Computer Vision, pp. 1440–1448 (2015)
7. Gkioxari, G., Girshick, R., Dollár, P., He, K.: Detecting and recognizing human-object interactions. arXiv preprint arXiv:1704.07333 (2017)
8. Gkioxari, G., Girshick, R., Malik, J.: Actions and attributes from wholes and parts, pp. 2470–2478 (2015)
9. Gkioxari, G., Girshick, R., Malik, J.: Contextual action recognition with r*cnn, pp. 1080–1088 (2015)
10. Hoai, M., Ladicky, L., Zisserman, A.: Action recognition from weak alignment of body parts (2014)
11. Hoai12, M.: Regularized max pooling for image categorization (2014)
12. Hussein, M.E., Torki, M., Gowayyed, M.A., Elsaban, M.: Human action recognition using a temporal hierarchy of covariance descriptors on 3D joint locations, pp. 2466–2472 (2013)
13. Kerola, T., Inoue, N., Shinoda, K.: Spectral graph skeletons for 3D action recognition, pp. 417–432 (2014)
14. Li, W., Zhang, Z., Liu, Z.: Action recognition based on a bag of 3D points, pp. 9–14 (2010)
15. Lowe, D.G.: Distinctive image features from scale-invariant keypoints. Int. J. Comput. Vis. **60**(2), 91–110 (2004)
16. Maji, S., Bourdev, L., Malik, J.: Action recognition from a distributed representation of pose and appearance, pp. 3177–3184 (2011)

17. Oquab, M., Bottou, L., Laptev, I., Sivic, J.: Learning and transferring mid-level image representations using convolutional neural networks. In: Proceedings of the IEEE conference on computer vision and pattern recognition, pp. 1717–1724 (2014)
18. Prest, A., Schmid, C., Ferrari, V.: Weakly supervised learning of interactions between humans and objects. IEEE Trans. Pattern Anal. Mach. Intell. **34**(3), 601–614 (2012)
19. Simonyan, K., Zisserman, A.: Very deep convolutional networks for large-scale image recognition. arXiv preprint arXiv:1409.1556 (2014)
20. Uijlings, J.R., Van De Sande, K.E., Gevers, T., Smeulders, A.W.: Selective search for object recognition. Int. J. Comput. Vis. **104**(2), 154–171 (2013)
21. Yang, X., Tian, Y.L.: Eigenjoints-based action recognition using nave-bayes-nearest-neighbor, pp. 14–19 (2012)
22. Ziaeefard, M., Bergevin, R.: Semantic human activity recognition: A literature review. Pattern Recogn. **48**(8), 2329–2345 (2015)

Face Hallucination and Recognition Using Kernel Canonical Correlation Analysis

Zhao Zhang, Yun-Hao Yuan$^{(\boxtimes)}$, Yun Li$^{(\boxtimes)}$, Bin Li,
and Ji-Peng Qiang

School of Information Engineering, Yangzhou University,
Yangzhou 225127, China
{yhyuan,liyun}@yzu.edu.cn

Abstract. Canonical correlation analysis (CCA) is a classical but powerful tool for image super-resolution tasks. Since CCA in essence is a linear projection learning method, it usually fails to uncover the nonlinear relationships between high-resolution (HR) and low-resolution (LR) facial image features. In order to solve this issue, we propose a new face hallucination and recognition algorithm based on kernel CCA, where the nonlinear correlation between HR and LR face features can be well depicted by implicit high-dimensional nonlinear mappings determined by specific kernels. First, our proposed method respectively extracts the principal component features from high-resolution and low-resolution facial images for computational efficiency and noise removal. Then, it makes use of kernel CCA to learn the nonlinear consistency of HR and LR facial features. The proposed approach is compared with existing face hallucination algorithms. A number of experimental results on LR face recognition have demonstrated the effectiveness and robustness of our proposed method.

Keywords: Face hallucination · Kernel CCA · Face recognition

1 Introduction

Face hallucination [1] aims at inferring high-resolution (HR) facial images from low-resolution (LR) ones. Since there are large volumes of low-quality face images in many practical applications, face hallucination is a fundamental issue in numerous computer vision tasks. From the perspective of face recognition, face hallucination is an effective approach for finding discriminative facial image features and improving the recognition performance of LR face images.

Over the decades, various face hallucination techniques have been proposed, which can be roughly divided into manifold-based, dictionary-based and regression-based methods. Manifold-based methods assume that face images in the HR space share the same local neighborhood structures as those in the LR space. Under this assumption, HR face images corresponding to LR ones can be generated by sample reconstruction. Typical methods include locally linear embedding [2–4], sparse neighbor embedding [5]. Dictionary-based methods generate HR face images by seeking sparse coding coefficients regarding dictionaries learned from LR and HR feature spaces, whose two representative directions are based on orthogonal dictionary [6, 7] and over-complete

© Springer International Publishing AG 2017
D. Liu et al. (Eds.): ICONIP 2017, Part VI, LNCS 10639, pp. 633–641, 2017.
https://doi.org/10.1007/978-3-319-70136-3_67

dictionary [8, 9]. Regression-based methods first learn a mapping function from LR feature space to HR one, and then reconstruct HR face images for LR inputs using the learnt mapping. Typical methods include Markov random fields [10], kernel regression [11], neural network [12–14], and support vector regression [15].

Apart from above-mentioned methods, Huang and He [16] proposed a canonical correlation analysis (CCA) based image super-resolution method for face recognition, which maximizes the linear correlations between HR and LR facial images and then projects LR and HR image features into a coherent space. Since canonical correlations can enhance the topological consistency of HR and LR facial images, CCA-based super-resolution method obtains better recognition results than conventional methods. However, CCA is a linear learning approach in essence. This means that it is difficult to measure the nonlinear relationships between HR and LR facial images.

To solve this issue, we propose a new face hallucination and recognition approach based on kernel CCA, where the nonlinear correlation between the HR and LR facial features can be well described by two implicit high-dimensional nonlinear mappings determined by kernels. It first extracts the global principal component features of HR and LR facial images for improving the computational efficiency and reducing noise. It then employs kernel CCA to learn the nonlinear consistency between HR and LR facial features. The proposed method is compared with the existing face hallucination methods. Many experimental results show that our proposed approach is superior to the existing methods.

2   A Brief of CCA

Assume n pairs of sample vectors are given as $\{(x_i, y_i) \in \Re^p \times \Re^q\}_{i=1}^n$, where p and q denote the dimensions of vectors. Let $X = [x_1, x_2, \cdots, x_n]$ and $Y = [y_1, y_2, \cdots, y_n]$ be two data matrices. Assume both $\{x_i\}_{i=1}^n$ and $\{y_i\}_{i=1}^n$ are centered, i.e., $\sum_{i=1}^n x_i = 0$ and $\sum_{i=1}^n y_i = 0$. CCA aims to find two projection vectors, $w_x \in \Re^p$ and $w_y \in \Re^q$, such that the following correlation coefficient

$$\rho(w_x, w_y) = \frac{w_x^T XY^T w_y}{\sqrt{w_x^T XX^T w_x} \cdot \sqrt{w_y^T YY^T w_y}} \tag{1}$$

is maximized. As ρ is invariant with respect to the scaling of w_x and w_y, we can reformulate (1) as

$$\begin{aligned} \max_{w_x, w_y} \quad & w_x^T XY^T w_y \\ s.t. \quad & w_x^T XX^T w_x = 1, \ w_y^T YY^T w_y = 1. \end{aligned} \tag{2}$$

With Lagrange multipliers technique, the maximization problem in (2) can be solved by the generalized eigenvalue problem.

3 Proposed Approach

3.1 Formulation

Assume n pairs of LR and HR facial training image vectors are given as $\{(I_i^l, I_i^h)\}_{i=1}^n$, where $I_i^l \in \Re^p$ is an LR facial image vector with p dimensions and $I_i^h \in \Re^q$ is the corresponding HR image vector with q dimensions. First, we center LR and HR face training images by $\hat{I}_i^l = I_i^l - m^l$ and $\hat{I}_i^h = I_i^h - m^h$, where m^l and m^h denote the mean faces of LR and HR face images, respectively. Then, to improve the computational efficiency and reduce the noise, we use principal component analysis (PCA) to extract the global facial features of LR and HR face training images by the following:

$$x_i^l = W_l^T \hat{I}_i^l \text{ and } x_i^h = W_h^T \hat{I}_i^h, \tag{3}$$

where x_i^l and x_i^h are the facial feature vectors of $\hat{I}_i^l$ and $\hat{I}_i^h$, and W_l and W_h are the PCA's projection matrices where each column denotes a basis vector.

Since PCA-transformed face features are derived from the same faces, it is natural that they have the intrinsic consistency. Now, let us employ nonlinear CCA to exploit the consistent features of LR and HR facial image data. Let $\phi(x_i^l)$ and $\varphi(x_i^h)$ be two implicit nonlinear mapping functions which project facial image features x_i^l and x_i^h into higher-dimensional Hilbert spaces, respectively. Let us denote

$$X_\phi^l = [\phi(x_1^l), \phi(x_2^l), \cdots, \phi(x_n^l)] \text{ and } X_\varphi^h = [\varphi(x_1^h), \varphi(x_2^h), \cdots, \varphi(x_n^h)]. \tag{4}$$

Then, our goal is to find projection vectors, v_l and v_h, such that nonlinear correlation between the projections $v_l^T X_\phi^l$ and $v_h^T X_\varphi^h$ is maximized. The optimization model is the following:

$$(v_l^*, v_h^*) = \arg\max_{v_l, v_h} \frac{v_l^T X_\phi^l (X_\varphi^h)^T v_h}{\sqrt{v_l^T X_\phi^l (X_\phi^l)^T v_l} \cdot \sqrt{v_h^T X_\varphi^h (X_\varphi^h)^T v_h}}. \tag{5}$$

Since the objective criterion is scale-invariant to v_l and v_h, the optimization problem in (5) can be reformulated equivalently as

$$\max_{v_l, v_h} v_l^T X_\phi^l (X_\varphi^h)^T v_h$$
$$s.t. \begin{cases} v_l^T X_\phi^l (X_\phi^l)^T v_l = 1, \\ v_h^T X_\varphi^h (X_\varphi^h)^T v_h = 1. \end{cases} \tag{6}$$

Solving the optimization problem in (6), we are able to obtain the projection vectors v_l and v_h for LR and HR facial image features in the Hilbert spaces. To understand our proposed method visually, Fig. 1 shows the flowchart of our face hallucination and recognition method.

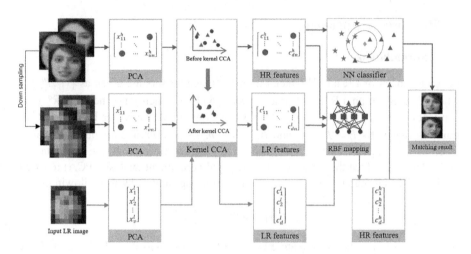

Fig. 1. The flowchart of our face hallucination and recognition method based on kernel CCA.

3.2   Solution

Using the dual representation theory, i.e.,

$$v_l = \sum_{i=1}^{n} a_i \phi(x_i^l) = X_\phi^l \alpha \text{ and } v_h = \sum_{i=1}^{n} b_i \varphi(x_i^h) = X_\varphi^h \beta, \tag{7}$$

where $\alpha^T = (a_1, a_2, \cdots, a_n) \in \Re^n$ and $\beta^T = (b_1, b_2, \cdots, b_n) \in \Re^n$, we are able to obtain the following

$$\max_{\alpha, \beta} \quad \alpha^T (X_\phi^l)^T X_\phi^l (X_\varphi^h)^T X_\varphi^h \beta$$
$$s.t. \quad \begin{cases} \alpha^T (X_\phi^l)^T X_\phi^l (X_\phi^l)^T X_\phi^l \alpha = 1, \\ \beta^T (X_\varphi^h)^T X_\varphi^h (X_\varphi^h)^T X_\varphi^h \beta = 1. \end{cases} \tag{8}$$

Let $K_l = (X_\phi^l)^T X_\phi^l = [k(x_i^l, x_j^l)] \in \Re^{n \times n}$ and $K_h = (X_\varphi^h)^T X_\varphi^h = [\tilde{k}(x_i^h, x_j^h)] \in \Re^{n \times n}$ be two kernel matrices computed by radial basis functions (RBFs) in this paper. It follows from (8) that

$$\max_{\alpha, \beta} \quad \alpha^T K_l K_h \beta$$
$$s.t. \quad \alpha^T K_l K_l \alpha = 1, \beta^T K_h K_h \beta = 1. \tag{9}$$

By the Lagrange multiplier technique, we are able to obtain the dual vectors α and β by the following generalized eigenvalue problem:

$$\begin{bmatrix} & K_l K_h \\ K_h K_l & \end{bmatrix} \begin{bmatrix} \alpha \\ \beta \end{bmatrix} = \lambda \begin{bmatrix} K_l K_l & \\ & K_h K_h \end{bmatrix} \begin{bmatrix} \alpha \\ \beta \end{bmatrix}. \tag{10}$$

Note that, to prevent the overfitting, we regularize (10) using the following strategy:

$$\begin{bmatrix} & K_l K_h \\ K_h K_l & \end{bmatrix} \begin{bmatrix} \alpha \\ \beta \end{bmatrix} = \lambda \begin{bmatrix} (K_l + \mu I)^2 & \\ & (K_h + \kappa I)^2 \end{bmatrix} \begin{bmatrix} \alpha \\ \beta \end{bmatrix}, \tag{11}$$

where μ and κ are two small positive numbers such as 0.001, and I is the identity matrix.

Like CCA, we select the eigenvectors corresponding to the top d eigenvalues of (11) to form dual vector matrices $D_l = [\alpha_1, \alpha_2, \cdots, \alpha_d]$ and $D_h = [\beta_1, \beta_2, \cdots, \beta_d]$ with d as user-specified parameter. After that, we can get the low-dimensional correlational features C^l and C^h of LR and HR facial features in the form of

$$C^l = [v_{l,1}, v_{l,2}, \cdots, v_{l,d}]^T X_\phi^l = D_l^T (X_\phi^l)^T X_\phi^l = D_l^T K_l, \tag{12}$$

$$C^h = [v_{h,1}, v_{h,2}, \cdots, v_{h,d}]^T X_\varphi^h = D_h^T (X_\varphi^h)^T X_\varphi^h = D_h^T K_h. \tag{13}$$

3.3   Mapping LR Correlational Features to HR Ones

Following Huang and He's strategy [16], we establish the relationship between the correlational features of LR and HR facial images using the following mapping:

$$C^h = W\Phi^l, \tag{14}$$

where $\Phi^l \in \Re^{n \times n}$ is a matrix and its (i, j)th entry $(\Phi^l)_{ij}$ is

$$(\Phi^l)_{ij} = \exp(-\|c_i^l - c_j^l\| / 2\sigma^2) \tag{15}$$

with c_i^l as the ith column in C^l and σ as the parameter of RBF chosen empirically in this paper. It follows from (14) that

$$W = C^h (\Phi^l)^{-1}. \tag{16}$$

In practice, once W is obtained, we can get the corresponding HR correlational face features of given LR facial images for recognition purpose.

4   Experiment

To verify the effectiveness of our proposed method, we have done several recognition experiments on the benchmark Yale and ORL face databases and compared it with Bicubic-PCA [17], PCA-RBF [18], and state-of-the-art Huang and He's method [16] (denoted as Huang's method for short). The nearest neighbor (NN) classifier is used in all the experiments. In our method, we retain the 96% of spectral energy for HR face images and 97% for LR ones in the PCA transformation.

4.1   Experiment on Yale Face Database

The Yale face database contains 15 individuals with a total of 165 grayscale images. Each subject has 11 images that have different facial expressions and environmental parameters. In this experiment, we use the first five images per individual for training, and the rest for testing. The size of HR facial images is set to 32 × 32. The size of LR face images varies from 4 × 4 to 10 × 10. Both Gaussian kernel parameters in kernel CCA are set to 1.06 empirically for avoiding exhaustive search. In addition, the RBF parameter σ in (15) is set to 2. The experimental results are shown in Table 1 and Fig. 2. As can be seen, our method outperforms Bicubic-PCA, PCA-RBF, and Huang's method.

Table 1. Recognition rates with different resolutions on the Yale face database.

Resolution	Our method	Huang's method	PCA-RBF	Bicubic-PCA
4 × 4	**0.678**	0.644	0.578	0.289
6 × 6	**0.778**	0.744	0.733	0.456
8 × 8	**0.811**	0.800	0.778	0.611
10 × 10	**0.811**	0.789	0.778	0.756

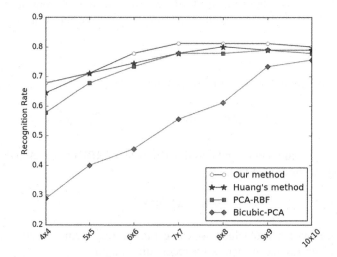

Fig. 2. Recognition rates versus different resolutions on the Yale face database.

To further test the recognition performance of our method with different training sample sizes, we choose the first m images per class as training set and the remaining $11 - m$ images as testing set. The HR face image size is still set to 32 × 32, and the LR image size is 8 × 8. Table 2 shows the results of each method. Note that the RBF parameter σ in (15) is still 2 and both Gaussian parameters in kernel CCA are set to the same and chosen empirically, whose values are recorded in parentheses in Table 2. As seen, our method achieves better results than other methods on the whole, and worse result than PCA-RBF only on the one-training-sample case.

Table 2. Recognition rates with different training samples per class on the Yale face database.

#/class	Our method	Huang's method	PCA-RBF	Bicubic-PCA
1	0.320 (1.4)	0.300	**0.340**	0.300
2	**0.548** (1.0)	0.519	0.511	0.407
3	**0.625** (2.0)	**0.625**	0.611	0.483
4	**0.676** (2.3)	0.667	0.642	0.533
5	**0.811** (1.1)	0.800	0.778	0.611

4.2   Experiment on ORL Face Database

There are 40 different individuals in the ORL face database, each of which has 10 images. For some subjects, images were taken at different times, varying the lighting, facial expressions.

In this experiment, the first five images per class are used for training and the rest for testing. We set the size of HR training face images as 32×32 and let LR image size change from 5×5 to 11×11. We set the two Gaussian parameters in kernel CCA to 0.9, respectively, and the parameter σ in (15) to 2. The experimental results are recorded in Table 3 and Fig. 3. From Table 3 and Fig. 3, we are able to see that our approach is superior to PCA-RBF, Bicubic-PCA, and Huang's method.

Table 3. Recognition rates with different resolutions on the ORL face database.

Resolution	Our method	Huang's method	PCA-RBF	Bicubic-PCA
5×5	**0.865**	0.845	0.780	0.495
7×7	**0.935**	0.915	0.870	0.790
9×9	**0.945**	0.910	0.875	0.840
11×11	**0.930**	0.905	0.890	0.756

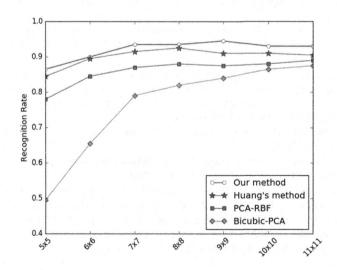

Fig. 3. Recognition rates versus different resolutions on the ORL face database.

5 Conclusion

In this paper, we have presented a kernel CCA-based face hallucination approach for recognition. It first extracts the global principal component features of HR and LR facial images. It then employs kernel CCA to learn the nonlinear consistency between HR and LR facial features. Many experimental results have shown that our proposed method is promising.

Acknowledgements. This work is supported by National Natural Science Foundation of China under Grant No. 61402203. In addition, it is also supported in part by the National Natural Science Foundation of China under Grant Nos. 61472344, 61611540347, the Natural Science Foundation of Jiangsu Province of China under Grant Nos. BK20161338, BK20170513, and sponsored by Excellent Young Backbone Teacher Project.

References

1. Baker, S., Kanade, T.: Hallucinating faces. In: 4th IEEE International Conference on Automatic Face and Gesture Recognition, pp. 83–88. IEEE, Grenoble (2000)
2. Chang, H., Yeung, D.Y., Xiong Y.: Super-resolution through neighbor embedding. In: CVPR, pp. 275–282. IEEE, Washington (2004)
3. Glasner, D., Bagon, S., Irani, M.: Super-resolution from a single image. In: ICCV, pp. 349–356. IEEE, Kyoto (2009)
4. Lu, X., Yuan, Y., Yan, P.: Image super-resolution via double sparsity regularized manifold learning. IEEE T-CSVT **23**(12), 2022–2033 (2013)
5. Gao, X., Zhang, K., Tao, D., Li, X.: Image super-resolution with sparse neighbor embedding. IEEE T-IP **21**(7), 3194–3205 (2012)
6. Dong, W., Zhang, L., Lukac, R., Shi, G.: Sparse representation based image interpolation with nonlocal autoregressive modeling. IEEE T-IP **22**(4), 1382–1394 (2013)
7. Mallat, S., Yu, G.: Super-resolution with sparse mixing estimators. IEEE T-IP **19**(11), 2889–2900 (2010)
8. He, L., Qi, H., Zaretzki, R.: Beta process joint dictionary learning for coupled feature spaces with application to single image super-resolution. In: CVPR, pp. 345–352. IEEE, Portland (2013)
9. Zeyde, R., Elad, M., Protter, M.: On single image scale-up using sparse-representations. In: Boissonnat, J.-D., Chenin, P., Cohen, A., Gout, C., Lyche, T., Mazure, L., Schumaker, L. (eds.) Curves and Surfaces 2010. LNCS, vol. 6920, pp. 711–730. Springer, Heidelberg (2012). doi:10.1007/978-3-642-27413-8_47
10. Freeman, W.T., Pasztor, E.C., Carmichael, O.T.: Learning low-level vision. Int. J. Comput. Vis. **40**(1), 25–47 (2000)
11. Kim, K.I., Kwon, Y.: Single-image super-resolution using sparse regression and natural image prior. IEEE T-PAMI **32**(6), 1127–1133 (2010)
12. Dong, C., Loy, C.C., He, K., Tang, X.: Learning a deep convolutional network for image super-resolution. In: Fleet, D., Pajdla, T., Schiele, B., Tuytelaars, T. (eds.) ECCV 2014. LNCS, vol. 8692, pp. 184–199. Springer, Cham (2014). doi:10.1007/978-3-319-10593-2_13
13. Kim, J., Lee, J.K., Lee K.M.: Accurate image super-resolution using very deep convolutional networks. In: CVPR, pp. 1646–1654. IEEE, Las Vegas (2016)

14. Shi, W., Caballero, J., Huszar, F., Totz, J., Aitken, A.P., Bishop, R., Rueckert, D., Wang, Z.: Real-time single image and video super-resolution using an efficient sub-pixel convolutional neural network. In: CVPR, pp. 1874–1883. IEEE, Las Vegas (2016)
15. Ni, K.S., Nguyen, T.Q.: Image super resolution using support vector regression. IEEE T-IP **16**(6), 1596–1610 (2007)
16. Huang, H., He, H.: Super-resolution method for face recognition using nonlinear mappings on coherent features. IEEE Trans. Neural Netw. **22**(1), 121–130 (2011)
17. Li, Y., Cai, C., Qiu, G., Lam, K.M.: Face hallucination based on sparse local-pixel structure. Pattern Recogn. **47**(3), 1261–1270 (2014)
18. Wang, X., Tang, X.: Hallucinating face by eigentransformation. IEEE Trans. Syst. Man, Cybern. Part C **35**(3), 425–434 (2005)

RGB-D Object Recognition
Using the Knowledge Transferred from Relevant
RGB Images

Depeng Gao, Rui Wu[✉], Jiafeng Liu, Qingcheng Huang, Xianglong Tang,
and Peng Liu

Research Center for Pattern Recognition and Intelligent Systems,
Harbin Institute of Technology, Harbin, China
gaodepeng@stu.hit.edu.cn

Abstract. The availability of depth images provides a new possibility to
solve the challenging object recognition problem. However, when there is
not enough labeled data, we cannot learn a discriminative classifier even
using depth information. To solve this problem, we extend LCCRRD
method by kernel trick. First, we construct two RGB classifiers with all
labeled RGB images from source and target domain. The significant samples for both classifier are boosted and the non-significant ones are inhib-
ited by exploiting the relationship between two domains. In this process,
the knowledge of source RGB classifier can be transferred to target RGB
classifier effectively. Then to improve the performance of RGB-D classifier by applying the knowledge from source domain, the predicted results
of RGB-D classifier are made consistent to target RGB classifier. Furthermore all the parameters are optimized in a unified objective function.
Experiments on four cross-domain dataset pairs shows that our approach
is indeed effective and promising.

Keywords: RGB-D object recognition · Transfer learning · Depth
images

1 Introduction

Object recognition has been widely researched in last two decades [1–3], it is an
important step to get the semantic information from original images. Recently,
with the availability of depth information captured by the low-cost RGB-D sensors such as Kinect, more and more people concern RGB-D object recognition
[4–6]. The depth image is robust to the change of illumination, background and
color etc. and can be used to solve some classical problems in computer vision.
But it is hard to get enough labeled RGB-D images to learn a discriminative
classifier because the labeling process is expensive and time-consuming. However
there are many relevant, labeled RGB images, an immediately idea is that we
can transfer some useful information from these RGB images to help create a
high-performance classifier for RGB-D object recognition [7,8].

© Springer International Publishing AG 2017
D. Liu et al. (Eds.): ICONIP 2017, Part VI, LNCS 10639, pp. 642–651, 2017.
https://doi.org/10.1007/978-3-319-70136-3_68

There are many differences in feature space and data distribution between RGB and RGB-D images, it does not satisfy the assumption of the traditional machine learning approaches that the testing data and training data come from the same domain. Methods coping with this domain difference problem is called transfer learning, which can apply previously learned knowledge to solve new problems faster or with better solutions [9,10]. Generally most methods take RGB images as the source and target domain, but in this work there are additional depth images in target domain to learn a discriminatory RGB-D classifier.

Li [8] proposed a method, Learning Coupled Classifiers with RGB images for RGB-D object recognition (LCCRRD). This method learns the coupled classifiers using RGB images from source domain, the combined RGB and depth images from target domain and RGB images from target domain. The predicted results of the two target classifiers are made to be similar to make them more accurate. It also utilize the correlation between source and target RGB images to boost the relevant features and eliminate the irrelevant features. Furthermore, a unified objective function is presented to learn the classifier parameters. Although it achieve competitive performance against the state-of-art methods, the learned classifiers are linear least square classifier, which is unable to represent the non-linear map from feature space to label space. Thus we use kernel trick on LCCRRD and learn three kernel least-squares (KLS) classifiers to solve this problem.

2 Background Knowledge

2.1 Notations

We refer the source domain as $D_s = \{\mathbf{X}_{sv}, \mathbf{Y}_s\}$ and the labeled RGB-D images in the target domain as $D_t = \{\mathbf{X}_{tv}, \mathbf{X}_{td}, \mathbf{Y}_t\}$ in which $\mathbf{X}_{sv} \in R^{d_{sv} \times n_s}$, $\mathbf{X}_{tv} \in R^{d_{tv} \times n_t}$ and $\mathbf{X}_{td} \in R^{d_{td} \times n_t}$. The variable $\mathbf{X}$ denote the feature matrixes, the subscript s and t represent source domain and target domain, v and d represent visual features and depth features, superscript d represents the dimension of features and the n represents the number of samples. In this paper, we assume that all the features have the same dimension means that $d_{sv} = d_{tv} = d_{td} = d$. $\mathbf{Y}_s \in R^{n_s \times c}$ and $\mathbf{Y}_t \in R^{n_t \times c}$ are the labels of source and target domain, c is the number of categories. Each sample corresponds to a row vector $\mathbf{y}_i = [0, ..., 1, ..., 0] \in R^{1 \times c}$, the column where 1 locates represents its category. We use superscript $'$ represent the transpose of matrix in this paper.

2.2 The LCCRRD Method

To learn a discriminative classifier using limited labeled RGB-D images with abundant related labeled RGB images, the LCCRRD method [8] learns three coupled classifiers in a uniform objective function:

$$\min_{\mathbf{W}_{sv}, \mathbf{W}_{tv}, \mathbf{W}_{tvd}} \|\mathbf{Y}_s - \mathbf{X}'_{sv}\mathbf{W}_{sv}\|_F^2 + \|\mathbf{Y}_t - \mathbf{X}'_{tv}\mathbf{W}_{tv}\|_F^2 + \|\mathbf{Y}_t - \mathbf{X}'_{tvd}\mathbf{W}_{tvd}\|_F^2$$
$$+ \alpha(\|\mathbf{W}_{sv}\|_F^2 + \|\mathbf{W}_{tv}\|_F^2 + \|\mathbf{W}_{tvd}\|_F^2) + \beta \|\mathbf{X}'_{tv}\mathbf{W}_{tv} - \mathbf{X}'_{tvd}\mathbf{W}_{tvd}\|_F^2 \qquad (1)$$
$$+ \gamma\|\mathbf{W}\|_{2,1} + \lambda(tr(\mathbf{W}'_{sv}\mathbf{X}_{sv}\mathbf{L}_s\mathbf{X}'_{sv}\mathbf{W}_{sv}) + tr(\mathbf{W}'_{tvd}\mathbf{X}_{tvd}\mathbf{L}_t\mathbf{X}'_{tvd}\mathbf{W}_{tvd})).$$

in which $\mathbf{X}_{tvd}$ denotes the combination of the target RGB and depth features. This function can be divided into four parts: the first part is the structural risks containing the first six terms, which minimizes the expected error. The second part of the objective function contain the seventh term of Eq. (1), it builds relationship between the two target classifiers by making the estimated results of the two target classifiers consistent. The third part of the objective function contain the eighth term of Eq. (1), it select relevant features and discard the irrelevant features by minimizing $L_{2,1}$ norm on $\mathbf{W} = [\mathbf{W}_{sv}, \mathbf{W}_{tv}]$, so the target RGB classifier is connected to the source classifier. The fourth part of the objective function is the graph laplace regularization, it contains the last two terms of Eq. (1) and is used to protect the geometric structure of both domain. $\mathbf{L}_s$ and $\mathbf{L}_t$ are the graph Laplace matrices of source and target domain, the detailed construct process can be seen in [8]. The $\alpha, \beta, \gamma, \lambda$ are the balance parameters.

2.3   Kernel Trick

Kernel trick is a common method to realize the nonlinear classification. The discrimination function of least squares classifier for c categories and n samples can be regarded as the combination of c original least squares classifiers for the two class problem presented in Eq. (2), where $\mathbf{X} = [\mathbf{x}_1, ..., \mathbf{x}_n] \in R^{d \times n}$ denotes the feature matrix, $\mathbf{Y} \in R^{n \times c}$ is label matrix and $y_{ij} \in \{0, 1\}$ when the value is 1 means the ith sample belongs to jth category.

$$f(\mathbf{X}) = \mathbf{X}'\mathbf{W} = [\mathbf{X}'\mathbf{w}_1, \mathbf{X}'\mathbf{w}_2, ..., \mathbf{X}'\mathbf{w}_c] = \mathbf{Y}. \tag{2}$$

For a linear inseparable problem, suppose there is a nonlinear mapping function ϕ transforming the feature space to a higher dimension space in which a linear least squares classifier $\mathbf{W}^\phi = [\mathbf{w}_1{}^\phi, \mathbf{w}_2{}^\phi, ..., \mathbf{w}_c{}^\phi]$ is build. According to the theory of reproducing kernels the $\mathbf{w}_i{}^\phi$ can be expressed by the linear combination of all feature vectors belongs to $\phi(\mathbf{X})$ [11], therefor $\mathbf{W}^\phi$ can be constructed in the form of

$$\begin{aligned}
\mathbf{W}^\phi &= [\mathbf{w}_1{}^\phi, \mathbf{w}_2{}^\phi, ..., \mathbf{w}_c{}^\phi] \\
&= \left[\sum\nolimits_{i=1}^{n} \phi(\mathbf{x}_i)\alpha_{i1}, \sum\nolimits_{i=1}^{n} \phi(\mathbf{x}_i)\alpha_{i2}, ..., \sum\nolimits_{i=1}^{n} \phi(\mathbf{x}_i)\alpha_{ic}\right] \\
&= [\phi(\mathbf{X})\boldsymbol{\alpha}_1, \phi(\mathbf{X})\boldsymbol{\alpha}_2, ..., \phi(\mathbf{X})\boldsymbol{\alpha}_c] = \phi(\mathbf{X})[\boldsymbol{\alpha}_1, \boldsymbol{\alpha}_2, ..., \boldsymbol{\alpha}_c] = \phi(\mathbf{X})\mathbf{A}.
\end{aligned} \tag{3}$$

where $\phi(\mathbf{X}) = [\phi(\mathbf{x}_1), ..., \phi(\mathbf{x}_n)]$, $\mathbf{A} = [\alpha_{ij}] \in R^{n \times c}$ is the coefficient matrix, the element α_{ij} describes the significance of each sample in the classifier $\mathbf{W}^\phi$. By using Eq. (3) and the kernel function

$$k(\mathbf{x}_i, \mathbf{x}_j) = <\phi(\mathbf{x}_i), \phi(\mathbf{x}_j)>. \tag{4}$$

the discrimination function $f(\mathbf{X})$ can translate to the form of

$$f^\phi(\mathbf{X}) = \phi(\mathbf{X})'\mathbf{W}^\phi = \phi(\mathbf{X})'\phi(\mathbf{X})\mathbf{A} = \mathbf{K}\mathbf{A}. \tag{5}$$

in which $\mathbf{K} = \{k_{ij} | k_{ij} = k(\mathbf{x}_i, \mathbf{x}_j)\}, i, j = 1, ..., n$ is the positive semi-definite kernel matrix meets the Mercer condition.

3   The Proposed Method

The LCCRRD method [8] aims to learn a linear classifier for recognizing RGB-D images, it is not suitable for the non-linear problem. We combine the kernel trick with LCCRRD to build a non-linear classifier.

3.1   Minimize Structural Risk

From the theory of reproducing kernels [11] and Eq. (3), we know that any solution of source RGB classifier $\mathbf{W}_{sv}^{\phi}$ lies in the space of all training samples from source domain, so in the wider space of all training samples from source and target domain must has solutions. Therefor we can construct the $\mathbf{W}_{sv}^{\phi}$ in the form of

$$
\begin{aligned}
\mathbf{W}_{sv}^{\phi} &= [\sum_{i=1}^{n_s} \phi(\mathbf{X}_{sv})_i \alpha_{i1} + \sum_{i=n_s+1}^{n_s+n_t} \phi(\mathbf{X}_{tv})_{i-n_s} \alpha_{i1}, ..., \\
&\quad \sum_{i=1}^{n_s} \phi(\mathbf{X}_{sv})_i \alpha_{ic} + \sum_{i=n_s+1}^{n_s+n_t} \phi(\mathbf{X}_{tv})_{i-n_s} \alpha_{ic}] \\
&= [\phi(\mathbf{X}_{sv})_1, ..., \phi(\mathbf{X}_{sv})_{n_s}, \phi(\mathbf{X}_{tv})_1, ..., \phi(\mathbf{X}_{tv})_{n_t}][\boldsymbol{\alpha}_1, ..., \boldsymbol{\alpha}_c] \\
&= [\phi(\mathbf{X}_{sv}), \phi(\mathbf{X}_{tv})]\mathbf{A}_{sv} = \phi(\mathbf{X}_v)\mathbf{A}_{sv}.
\end{aligned}
\tag{6}
$$

in a similar way the target RGB classifier $\mathbf{W}_{tv}^{\phi}$ is in the form of

$$
\mathbf{W}_{tv}^{\phi} = \phi(\mathbf{X}_v)\mathbf{A}_{tv}.
\tag{7}
$$

the $\mathbf{X}_v = [\mathbf{X}_{sv}, \mathbf{X}_{tv}] \in R^{d\times(n_s+n_t)}$ is the jointly feature matrix of source and target RGB features. Then learning the objective classifier $\mathbf{W}_{tvd}^{\phi}$ with the combined target RGB and depth features $\mathbf{X}_{tvd} = [\mathbf{X}_{tv}; \mathbf{X}_{td}] \in R^{2d\times n_t}$

$$
\begin{aligned}
\mathbf{W}_{tvd}^{\phi} &= [\sum_{i=1}^{n_t} \phi(\mathbf{X}_{tvd})_i \alpha_{i1}, ..., \sum_{i=1}^{n_t} \phi(\mathbf{X}_{tvd})_i \alpha_{ic}] \\
&= [\phi(\mathbf{X}_{tvd})_1, ..., \phi(\mathbf{X}_{tvd})_{n_t}][\boldsymbol{\alpha}_1, ..., \boldsymbol{\alpha}_c] = \phi(\mathbf{X}_{tvd})\mathbf{A}_{tvd}.
\end{aligned}
\tag{8}
$$

$\mathbf{A}_{sv}, \mathbf{A}_{tv} \in R^{(n_s+n_t)\times c}$ and $\mathbf{A}_{tvd} \in R^{n_t\times c}$ are the coefficients matrixes describing the significance of each sample. According to Eqs. (3) and (5) the regularization $\left\|\mathbf{W}^{\phi}\right\|_F^2$ can be written as

$$
\left\|\mathbf{W}^{\phi}\right\|_F^2 = tr(\mathbf{W}^{\phi\prime}\mathbf{W}^{\phi}) = tr(\mathbf{A}'\phi(\mathbf{X})'\phi(\mathbf{X})\mathbf{A}) = tr(\mathbf{A}'\mathbf{K}\mathbf{A}).
\tag{9}
$$

According Eqs. (5) to (9) the optimizing function to minimize the structural risk is

$$
\begin{aligned}
\min_{\mathbf{A}_{sv},\mathbf{A}_{tv},\mathbf{A}_{tvd}} &\left\|\mathbf{Y}_s - \mathbf{K}_{sv}\mathbf{A}_{sv}\right\|_F^2 + \left\|\mathbf{Y}_t - \mathbf{K}_{tv}\mathbf{A}_{tv}\right\|_F^2 + \left\|\mathbf{Y}_t - \mathbf{K}_{tvd}\mathbf{A}_{tvd}\right\|_F^2 \\
&+ \alpha(tr(\mathbf{A}'_{sv}\mathbf{K}_v\mathbf{A}_{sv}) + tr(\mathbf{A}'_{tv}\mathbf{K}_v\mathbf{A}_{tv}) + tr(\mathbf{A}'_{tvd}\mathbf{K}_{tvd}\mathbf{A}_{tvd}))
\end{aligned}
\tag{10}
$$

in which $\mathbf{K}_{sv} = k(\mathbf{X}_{sv}, \mathbf{X}_v) \in R^{n_s\times(n_s+n_t)}$, $\mathbf{K}_{tv} = k(\mathbf{X}_{tv}, \mathbf{X}_v) \in R^{n_t\times(n_s+n_t)}$, $\mathbf{K}_v = k(\mathbf{X}_v, \mathbf{X}_v) \in R^{(n_s+n_t)\times(n_s+n_t)}$ and $\mathbf{K}_{tvd} = k(\mathbf{X}_{tvd}, \mathbf{X}_{tvd}) \in R^{n_t\times n_t}$ are the kernel matrixes constructed by different feature matrixes.

3.2   Build Relationship Between Two Domains

To utilize the knowledge from source domain, the target domain must be connected to source domain. We have learned the source and target RGB classifier constructed by all RGB images. To establish a correlation between the two classifiers, we combine the coefficient matrix as $\mathbf{A} = [\mathbf{A}_{sv}, \mathbf{A}_{tv}] \in R^{(n_s+n_t)\times 2c}$. Each row of $\mathbf{A}$ reflects the significance of each sample in both source and target RGB classifier. We use $L_{2,1}$ regularization to restrict $\mathbf{A}$. Through minimizing the $L_{2,1}$ norm can make each row of $\mathbf{A}$ to be all zeros or non-zeros simultaneously. It means that if the sample is important for source RGB classifier, it is also important for target RGB classifier. Thus, source RGB images can be utilized to learn a more discriminative target RGB classifier. The objective function can be written as

$$\min_{\mathbf{A}_{sv},\mathbf{A}_{tv}} \|\mathbf{A}\|_{2,1} \tag{11}$$

Furthermore, the parts of correlation between two target classifiers and the graph laplace regularization are consistent to the LCCRRD method [8], so the overall objective function can be rewrite as

$$\min_{\mathbf{A}_{sv},\mathbf{A}_{tv},\mathbf{A}_{tvd}} \|\mathbf{Y}_s - \mathbf{K}_{sv}\mathbf{A}_{sv}\|_F^2 + \|\mathbf{Y}_t - \mathbf{K}_{tv}\mathbf{A}_{tv}\|_F^2 + \|\mathbf{Y}_t - \mathbf{K}_{tvd}\mathbf{A}_{tvd}\|_F^2$$
$$+ \alpha(tr(\mathbf{A}'_{sv}\mathbf{K}_v\mathbf{A}_{sv}) + tr(\mathbf{A}'_{tv}\mathbf{K}_v\mathbf{A}_{tv}) + tr(\mathbf{A}'_{tvd}\mathbf{K}_{tvd}\mathbf{A}_{tvd}))$$
$$+ \beta\|\mathbf{K}_{tv}\mathbf{A}_{tv} - \mathbf{K}_{tvd}\mathbf{A}_{tvd}\|_F^2 + \gamma\|\mathbf{A}\|_{2,1}$$
$$+ \lambda(tr(\mathbf{A}'_{sv}\mathbf{K}'_{sv}\mathbf{L}_s\mathbf{K}_{sv}\mathbf{A}_{sv}) + tr(\mathbf{A}'_{tvd}\mathbf{K}'_{tvd}\mathbf{L}_t\mathbf{K}_{tvd}\mathbf{A}_{tvd})) \tag{12}$$

3.3   The Optimization

In this part, we will introduce the optimized results of Eq. (12). The main idea is alternating and iterating, each time two independent variables are fixed and the partial derivative of Eq. (12) w.r.t. another variable equal to zero. The process is repeated until convergence.

In addition, the objective function involves a $L_{2,1}$ form which is not contained in the former looping. To solve it, we suppose $R = diag(r_1, \ldots\ldots, r_{n_s+n_t})$ is a diagonal matrix, and each

$$r_i = \frac{1}{2\|\mathbf{A}_i\|}, i = 1, 2, \ldots\ldots, n_s + n_t \tag{13}$$

Therefor the $\|\mathbf{A}\|_{2,1}$ can be written as [8]

$$\|\mathbf{A}\|_{2,1} = tr(\mathbf{A}'\mathbf{R}\mathbf{A}) \tag{14}$$

Computing Every Coefficient Matrix. For example, $\mathbf{A}_{tv}$ and $\mathbf{A}_{tvd}$ are fixed to compute the $\mathbf{A}_{sv}$, this is equal to solve the following optimization problem

$$\min_{\mathbf{A}_{sv}} \|\mathbf{Y}_s - \mathbf{K}_{sv}\mathbf{A}_{sv}\|_F^2 + \alpha(tr(\mathbf{A}'_{sv}\mathbf{K}_v\mathbf{A}_{sv}))$$
$$+ \gamma\|\mathbf{A}\|_{2,1} + \lambda(tr(\mathbf{A}'_{sv}\mathbf{K}'_{sv}\mathbf{L}_s\mathbf{K}_{sv}\mathbf{A}_{sv}) \tag{15}$$

then setting the partial derivative of Eq. (15) w.r.t. $\mathbf{A}_{sv}$ equals to zero, so

$$\mathbf{A}_{sv} = (\mathbf{K}'_{sv}\mathbf{K}_{sv} + \alpha\mathbf{K}_v + \gamma\mathbf{R} + \lambda\mathbf{K}'_{sv}\mathbf{L}_s\mathbf{K}_{sv})^{-1}\mathbf{K}'_{sv}\mathbf{Y}_s \qquad (16)$$

with the same way, we can get $\mathbf{A}_{tv}$ and $\mathbf{A}_{tvd}$ as

$$\mathbf{A}_{tv} = ((1 + \beta)\mathbf{K}'_{tv}\mathbf{K}_{tv} + \alpha\mathbf{K}_v + \gamma\mathbf{R})^{-1}(\mathbf{K}'_{tv}\mathbf{Y}_t + \beta\mathbf{K}'_{tv}\mathbf{K}_t\mathbf{A}_{tvd}) \qquad (17)$$

$$\mathbf{A}_{tvd} = ((1 + \beta)\mathbf{K}'_t\mathbf{K}_t + \alpha\mathbf{K}_t + \gamma\mathbf{R} + \lambda\mathbf{K}'_t\mathbf{L}_t\mathbf{K}_t)^{-1}(\mathbf{K}'_t\mathbf{Y}_t + \beta\mathbf{K}'_t\mathbf{K}_{tv}\mathbf{A}_{tv}) \qquad (18)$$

Based on the above formulation, the corresponding algorithms to the presented method is summarized in Algorithm 1. The convergence criterion in our experiment is that $|obj_{t+1} - obj_t|/|obj_t| < 10^{-4}$ in which obj represents the value of objective function.

Algorithm 1. The corresponding algorithms to our works

Input: Labeled source RGB features $\mathbf{X}_{sv}$, target RGB features $\mathbf{X}_{tv}$ and depth features $\mathbf{X}_{td}$, parameters $\alpha, \beta, \gamma, \lambda$.
1: Initialize the $\mathbf{A}_{sv}, \mathbf{A}_{tv}, \mathbf{A}_{tvd}$ randomly and calculate graph laplacian matrixes $\mathbf{L}_s$ and $\mathbf{L}_t$.
2: Update $\mathbf{A} = [\mathbf{A}_{sv}, \mathbf{A}_{tv}]$ and calculate $\mathbf{R}$ via Eq. (13).
3: **repeat**
4:    Calculate $\mathbf{A}_{sv}$ via Eq. (16).
5:    Calculate $\mathbf{A}_{tv}$ via Eq. (17).
6:    Update $\mathbf{A} = [\mathbf{A}_{sv} \ \mathbf{A}_{tv}]$ and calculate $\mathbf{R}$ via Eq. (13).
7:    Calculate $\mathbf{A}_{tvd}$ via Eq. (18).
8: **until** convergence
Output: All classifiers $\mathbf{A}_{sv}, \mathbf{A}_{tv}, \mathbf{A}_{tvd}$.

---

4   Experiments and Analysis

4.1   Dataset Description

The dataset Caltech-256 [12], ImageNet [13] and dataset RGB-D [14], B3DO [15] are respectively used as the source and target domain. The RGB-D dataset is cropped from video sequences, so the adjacent images are very similar. In order to increase the difficulty, we subsample every 4th images as the used dataset. The RGB images and depth images of B3DO are cropped by using the provided bounding boxes of objects. We choose some common classes between different cross-domain dataset pairs for the experiments[1].

---

[1] Caltech-256/RGB-D: ball, calculator, box, mug, Flashlight, keyboard, light-bulb, mushroom, can, tomato, total 1132/1824 images. Caltech-256/B3DO: bottle, can, cup, keyboard, monitor, mouse, phone, spoon, total 776/1129 images. ImageNet/RGB-D: apple, banana, mug, keyboard, soda-can, water-bottle, plate, calculator, cereal-box, light-bulb, total 968/1823 images. ImageNet/B3DO: bottle, cup, keyboard, monitor, mouse, phone, plate, spoon, total 789/1135 images [8].

We use $m\%$ target samples as training data and the others as test data. The Multipath Hierarchical Matching Pursuit(M-HMP) method [16] is used to extract a highly discriminative feature for both RGB and depth images. Then the features are deduced to 500-dimensional by Principal Component Analysis (PCA) method.

4.2   Experimental Results

The multiclass classification accuracy is used as the evaluation criteria. We conducted our experiments ten times and report the average precision of the classification w.r.t. the different percentage of target labeled data. We use the same balance parameters with LCCRRD as $\alpha = 0.01$, $\beta = 1$, $\gamma = 0.1$ and $\lambda = 0.1$ [8]. The nearest neighbor to construct the graph Laplace matrix is set as $k = 10$. Specially, the kernel function and parameter used in our method for Caltech-256/B3DO are (G1.2, L1.9, L1.7, G1.9, G1.7), for Caltech-256/RGB-D are (L1.3, G1.5, G1.8, L1.2, G1.3), for ImageNet/B3DO are (G1.0, G1.7, L1.9, L1.5, L1.5), for ImageNet/RGB-D are (G2.0, G2.0, L1.2, L1.9, G1.5), in which G represents Gauss kernel and L represents Laplace kernel. In this paper, we use 10 fold cross-validation scheme to select the kernel parameter, the best parameter found is used to classify the complete testing set.

The comparison results are shown in Fig. 1 and Table 1. We can see that our method obviously perform better than LCCRRD approach with different percentage of labeled target data on all dataset pairs. To illustrate the advantage of our method, some actual examples are given in Fig. 2. For the target objects in Fig. 2, they are misclassified to other class using LCCRRD method while classified correct using the proposed method. This is because the classifier learned in LCCRRD is just a linear classifier, for the linear inseparable samples it will be failure. Our method can map the original feature space of samples to a higher dimensional, linear separable space by kernel method, in this space the samples can be classified correct.

Table 1. Comparison of multiclass classification accuracy (%) w.r.t. the percentage of labeled data on different cross domain dataset pairs.

Dataset pairs	Method	2%	3%	5%	8%	10%
Caltech-256/B3DO	LCCRRD	38.43	44.59	48.76	53.72	54.33
Caltech-256/B3DO	Ours	43.76	50.55	55.63	60.80	62.89
Caltech-256/RGB-D	LCCRRD	57.39	62.07	70.46	77.86	81.04
Caltech-256/RGB-D	Ours	63.19	69.08	79.49	86.46	88.09
ImageNet/B3DO	LCCRRD	38.11	44.08	48.38	52.88	56.27
ImageNet/B3DO	Ours	44.65	50.04	54.92	59.67	62.72
ImageNet/RGB-D	LCCRRD	61.14	69.14	77.73	81.75	86.28
ImageNet/RGB-D	Ours	69.14	76.04	85.47	90.22	92.54

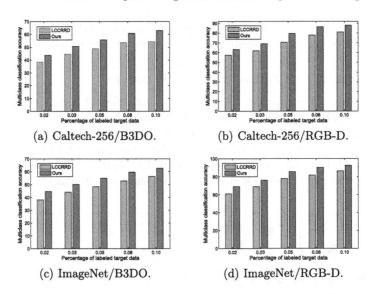

Fig. 1. Performance comparison w.r.t. the percentage of labeled data on different cross domain dataset pairs.

	method result	LCCRRD	Ours
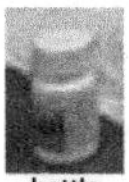 object bottle		cup	bottle
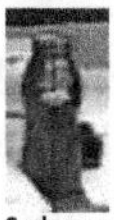 Soda-can		bottle	Soda-can

Fig. 2. The results of some samples classified by LCCRRD and the proposed method on Caltech-256/B3DO dataset

4.3 Influence of Depth Information and Transfer Learning

To investigate the influence of depth information and transfer learning on the object recognition problem, we learn a KLS classifier with only labeled target RGB images and another KLS classifier with labeled target RGB and depth images. The comparison result is show in Fig. 3, we can see that the performance of the classifier with depth information is just a little better than only with RGB images because there is not enough labeled data to train a discriminative classifier. Our method achieved the best performance because it use not only the depth information but also the knowledge learned from source domain.

The experiment result shows that applying the knowledge transferred from source RGB images can promote the performance of target RGB-D classifier.

4.4 Comparison of Different Kernel Functions

In this section, we compared the performance of different commonly used kernel function [17] in Fig. 4. The gauss and laplace kernel belongs to radial basis function (RBF) kernel, their performance are better than others in most case, because they are more suitable to classify the non-linear problem. The linear kernel is slightly worse than the RBF kernel, but as it does not need to select parameter and calculate the kernel matrix, its time is more efficient.

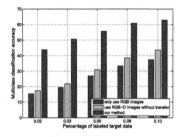

Fig. 3. Demonstrate the validity of depth information and transfer learning

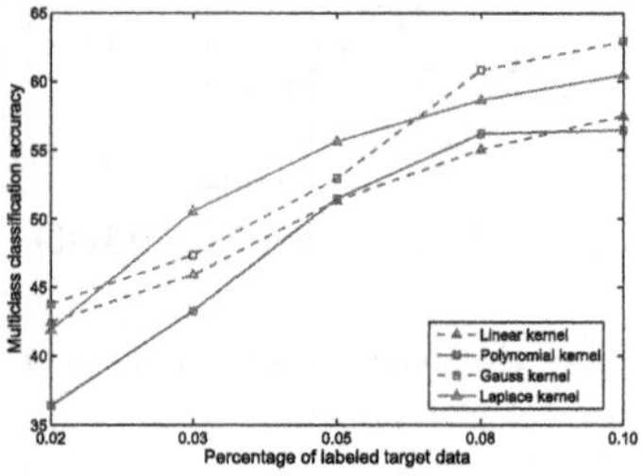

Fig. 4. Comparison of different kernel function.

5 Conclusion

We investigate the problem of how to utilize labeled RGB data to learn a more discriminative classifier for RGB-D images of limited labels by introducing kernel trick to the LCCRRD method. Moreover, in this work we use all samples from source and target domain to construct source and target RGB classifier. In this process, the knowledge can be transferred between two domain effectively. All the classifiers learned in the proposed method are non-linear, their representation ability are more powerful and one can choose different kernel function and parameter in different situations, so that the proposed method is more flexible and promising. In fact, the LCCRRD is only a special case when the propose method use the linear kernel function. The proposed method can allow us to learn a accurate classifier using only a tiny amount of labeled RGB-D data and a large amount of relevant RGB data, even when RGB-D data are not sufficient to train a classifier alone. Experimental results on different cross-domain dataset pairs demonstrate that our approach leads a significant performance gain over the state-of-the-art methods.

Acknowledgments. This research is supported by Natural Science Foundation of Heilongjiang Province, China (No. F201012) and National Science Foundation of China (No. 61370162, No. 61672190, No. 61671175).

References

1. Lowe, D.G.: Object recognition from local scale-invariant features. In: IEEE International Conference on Computer Vision, pp. 1150–1157 (1999)
2. Belongie, S., Malik, J., Puzicha, J.: Shape matching and object recognition using shape contexts. IEEE Trans. Pattern Anal. Mach. Intell. **24**(4), 509–522 (2002)
3. Donahue, J., Jia, Y., Vinyals, O., et al.: DeCAF: a deep convolutional activation feature for generic visual recognition. In: International Conference on Machine Learning, vol. 32, pp. 647–655 (2014)
4. Bo, L., Ren, X., Fox, D.: Unsupervised feature learning for RGB-D based object recognition. In: Desai, J., Dudek, G., Khatib, O., Kumar, V. (eds.) Experimental Robotics. STAR, vol. 88, pp. 387–402. Springer, Heidelberg (2013). doi:10.1007/978-3-319-00065-7_27
5. Lai, K., Bo, L., Ren, X., Fox, D.: RGB-D object recognition: features, algorithms, and a large scale benchmark. In: Fossati, A., Gall, J., Grabner, H., Ren, X., Konolige, K. (eds.) Consumer Depth Cameras for Computer Vision. ACVPR, pp. 167–192. Springer, London (2013). doi:10.1007/978-1-4471-4640-7_9
6. Eitel, A., Springenberg, J.T., Spinello, L., et al.: Multimodal deep learning for robust RGB-D object recognition. In: IEEE/RSJ International Conference on Intelligent Robots and Systems, pp. 681–687 (2015)
7. Okamoto, M., Nakayama, H.: Unsupervised visual domain adaptation using auxiliary information in target domain. In: IEEE International Symposium on Multimedia, pp. 203–206 (2014)
8. Li, X., Fang, M., Zhang, J.J., et al.: Learning coupled classifiers with RGB images for RGB-D object recognition. Pattern Recogn. **61**, 433–446 (2017)
9. Pan, S.J., Yang, Q.: A survey on transfer learning. IEEE Trans. Knowl. Data Eng. **22**(10), 1345–1359 (2010)
10. Weiss, K., Khoshgoftaar, T.M., Wang, D.D.: A survey of transfer learning. J. Big Data **3**(1), 1–40 (2016)
11. Mika, S., Ratsch, G., Weston, J., et al.: Fisher discriminant analysis with kernels. In: IEEE Signal Processing Society Workshop, pp. 41–48 (1999)
12. Griffin, G., Holub, A., Perona, P.: Caltech-256 object category dataset (2007)
13. Deng, J., Dong, W., Socher, R., et al.: Imagenet: a large-scale hierarchical image database. In: IEEE Conference on Computer Vision and Pattern Recognition, pp. 248–255 (2009)
14. Lai, K., Bo, L., Ren, X., et al.: A large-scale hierarchical multi-view RGB-D object dataset. In: International Conference on Robotics and Automation, pp. 1817–1824 (2011)
15. Janoch, A., et al.: A category-level 3D object dataset: putting the kinect to work. In: Fossati, A., Gall, J., Grabner, H., Ren, X., Konolige, K. (eds.) Consumer Depth Cameras for Computer Vision. ACVPR, pp. 141–165. Springer, London (2013). doi:10.1007/978-1-4471-4640-7_8
16. Bo, L., Ren, X., Fox, D.: Multipath sparse coding using hierarchical matching pursuit. In: IEEE Conference on Computer Vision and Pattern Recognition, pp. 660–667 (2013)
17. Shawe, T.J., Cristianini, N.: Kernel Methods for Pattern Analysis. Cambridge University Press, Cambridge (2004)

Image Inpainting by Recursive Estimation Using Neural Network and Wavelet Transformation

Hiromu Fujishige, Junichi Miyao, and Takio Kurita$^{(\boxtimes)}$

The Department of Information Engineering, Graduate School of Engineering,
Hiroshima University, Higashi-Hiroshima, Japan
tkurita@hiroshima-u.ac.jp

Abstract. This paper proposes image inpainting algorithms in which the pixel values of the regions to be inpainting are recursively estimated by using multi-layered Perceptron from the original input image and its wavelet transformation. Instead of forward estimation by using the deep neural network such as convolutional neural network (CNN), we use shallow neural network and the pixel values are recursively estimated. To improve the estimation quality, wavelet transformation is also used as the input of the neural network. The effectiveness of the proposed approach was experimentally confirmed by using the face databases.

Keywords: Image inpainting · Multi-layered perceptron · Recursive estimation

1 Introduction

The technique to compensate small damaged regions of an image has received considerable attention in recent years [1]. This technique is called image inpainting. There are several applications such as removing unwanted people, text, logos from photographs or videos.

One of the most simple method for image inpainting is to select the image regions to be inpainting and propagate color information inward from the regions boundaries. Bertalmio et al. proposed a method propagating pixel values along isophote directions interleaved with some anisotropic diffusion steps [2]. Telea proposed a fast algorithm that uses the fast marching method from level sets [3].

Takahashi et al. [4] proposed an approach for constructing a classifier which has ability to compensate occluded regions in a given image.

Recently the deep neural networks become very popular for image recognition and image processing. Xie et al. proposed an approach for image denoising and inpainting in which sparse coding and deep networks pre-trained with denoising auto-encoder were combined [5]. Cai et al. proposed a blind inpainting method based on fully convolutional neural network [6]. Iizuka et al. proposed an approach for image completion using both locally and globally consistent in images with fully convolutional neural network [7]. Compared with approach proposed by Takahashi et al., their methods are one pass algorithm and not iterative.

© Springer International Publishing AG 2017
D. Liu et al. (Eds.): ICONIP 2017, Part VI, LNCS 10639, pp. 652–661, 2017.
https://doi.org/10.1007/978-3-319-70136-3_69

In this paper, we use the approach by Takahashi et al. and extend for image inpainting by using both the original image and its wavelet transformation. Since the regions to be inpainting are usually known beforehand, it is not necessary to detect them. This means that the image inpainting is easier than the occlusion compensation. However, the requirement to the quality of the compensation in image inpainting is much higher than the classification for the partly occluded images.

A shallow neural network is used to estimate the regions to be inpainting instead of the deep neural network. By iterative recall the pixel values of the regions to be inpainting, we can gradually improve the quality of the inpainting. To improve the quality of the inpainting further, the wavelet transformations of the original image are also used as the input of the neural network.

The paper is structured as follows. In Sect. 2, the related works are briefly reviewed. The proposed approach is explained in Sect. 3 and experimental results are shown in Sect. 4. Section 5 is for conclusion and future works.

2 Related Works

2.1 Image Inpainting

In the most simple inpainting method, the image regions to be inpainting are selected and color information is propagated inward from the regions boundaries. Bertalmio et al. proposed a method propagating pixel values along isophote directions interleaved with some anisotropic diffusion steps [2]. Telea developed an image inpainting method based on propagating an image smoothness estimator along the image gradient [3]. In his method, the image smoothness is estimated as a weighted average over a known image neighborhood of the pixel to inpaint. The missing regions are treated as level sets and the fast marching method (FMM) [8] is used to propagate the image information.

The example-based texture generation techniques are also used by filling the holes from the outside. Criminisi et al. used example-based texture synthesis by ordering depending on the strength of the gradient along the region boundary [9]. When a large database of source images is available, for example, when images are taken from a photo sharing site, it is possible to copy a single contiguous image region to fill the hole.

2.2 Occlusion Compensation by Auto-associative Network

To improve the image classification accuracy for the partly occluded image, Takahashi et al. [4] proposed an approach in which the auto-associative network is used to recall the pixel values in the occluded regions. As the auto-associative network can recall the original image from a partly occluded input image, it is used to detect occluded regions and compensate the input image by replacing those regions with recalled pixel values. By repeating this reconstruction process, the target objects with occlusions can be robustly reconstructed by this network. This auto-associative network for occlusion compensation is integrated with the feed-forward classifier to improve the classification accuracy for the partly occluded images.

To implement the auto-associative network, the authors use a three-layer Perceptron. The Perceptron consists of linear units and performs linear dimensionality reduction and reconstruction. This network is equivalent to the principal component analysis (PCA).

Takahashi et al. [4] proposed a method composed of two steps: (1) detecting occluded pixels in each input image and (2) replacing each pixels in the occluded regions with the estimated values. In the first step, pixel-wise errors between the input image and the reconstructed image are computed. If the pixel values are included in the occluded regions, the error might be large. So in the second step, the detected pixels are replaced with the corresponding pixels in the reconstructed image and the modified input image is used as the input image of the next iteration. These steps are repeatedly applied to get the clear image.

In this paper, we implemented the auto-associative memory which is the same as Takahashi's method to estimate the pixel values of the local regions to be inpainting and used to compare the performance with the proposed algorithms. We call this algorithm as AAM-G-G(Takahashi).

2.3   Image Inpainting by Deep Neural Network

Recently the deep neural networks becomes very popular for image recognition and image processing. Several approaches for image inpainting have been already proposed in the literature [5,6,10].

Xie et al. proposed an approach for image denoising and inpainting in which sparse coding and deep networks pre-trained with Denoising Auto-encoder (DA) [11,12] were combined [5]. The authors employed DA to perform pre-training to train a two-layer neural network which reconstructs the original input from a noisy version of it.

Cai et al. proposed a blind inpainting method based on fully convolutional neural network. Three convolutional layers are cascaded to directly learn an end-to-end mapping between a corrupted and ground truth sub-images [6].

Iizuka et al. proposed an approach for image completion using both locally and globally consistent in images with fully convolutional neural network [7]. The authors used locally and globally context network to discriminate real image and restored ones. The image completion network is trained to fool the both discriminator networks, which requires it to generate images that are indistinguishable from real ones with regard to overall consistency as well as in details. Since natural images, despite their diversity, are highly structured, we can understand this structure and make visual predictions even when seeing only parts of the scene. Pathak et al. showed that it is possible to learn and predict this structure using convolutional neural networks (CNNs). A CNN is trained to regress to the missing pixel values for an given image with missing region [10]. In their architecture, encoder features and decoder features are fully connected channel wise manner and adversarial loss based on Generative Adversarial Networks (GAN) [13] is introduced to produce a plausible hypothesis for the missing parts.

These methods for inpainting using deep architectures are one pass algorithm and not iterative. In this paper, we use iterative reconstruction algorithm similar with the method proposed by Takahashi et al. [4].

2.4 Multi-resolution Analysis of Image by Using Wavelet Transformation

The theory of wavelet transformation offers a methodology to generate continuous-time compact support orthogonal filter banks through the design of discrete-time finite length filter banks with multiple time and frequency resolutions. By wavelet transformation, the signal can be decomposed into the sparse representation with multiple time and frequency resolutions.

One of the many active application areas of wavelet transformation has been of denoising [14]. For applications of denoising, the noise is rarely entirely Gaussian nor signal independent. Therefore wavelet transformation that can be applied to realistic scenarios are of continuing interest.

It is known that the signals obtained by wavelet transformation are sparse. The notion of sparseness is a source of the effectiveness of wavelet transformations for compression or denoising. Recently L_1-norm minimization have been introduced to reconstruct the original signal. This method is know as Compressed Sensing [15].

3 Proposed Approach

In this paper, we propose three algorithms for image inpainting based on the method proposed by Takahashi et al. [4]. To estimate the pixel values of a local region to be inpainting, we use a multi-layered Perceptron. As the input of the Perceptron, we use the input image itself, the 2 dimensional wavelet transformation of the input image, or the concatenation of these two.

The multi-layered Perceptron is trained to estimate the original image by using some training samples. The mean squared errors between the original input vector and the reconstructed vector.

Here we assume that the pixels to be inpainting is know beforehand. Thus we can define the $M \times M$ diagonal matrix $D = \mathrm{diag}(\alpha_1, \alpha_2, \ldots, \alpha_{M \times M})$ where α is 0 if the corresponding pixel is included in the region to be inpainting and α is 1 otherwise.

3.1 Auto-associative Memory Using the Wavelet Transformation

The first algorithm uses auto-associative memory. In this algorithm, the gray image is transformed by 2-dimensional wavelet transformation and the wavelet coefficients are used as the input of the auto-associative memory. So, we call the first algorithm as AAM-W-W. To train the auto-associative memory, the mean

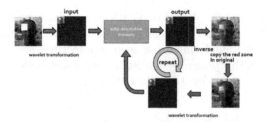

Fig. 1. Estimation scheme by auto-associative memory using the wavelet transformation.

squared errors between the original wavelet coefficients and the reconstructed wavelet coefficients are used as the objective function of the optimization.

Figure 1 shows that the recursive estimation scheme for this algorithm. For each iteration, the wavelet coefficients are estimated by the trained Perceptron as $q_t = B_1^T A_1^T \tilde{p}_t$ where A_1 and B_1 are the weights of the trained auto-associative memory. Then the pixel values of the original image z_t are reconstructed by the inverse wavelet transformation from the estimated wavelet coefficients q_t and the pixel values in the regions to be inpainting are replaced with the estimated values as $\tilde{x}_{t+1} = Dx + (I - D)z_t$.

The details of the recursive estimation algorithm is shown in Algorithm 1.

Algorithm 1. Estimation of pixel values in the local regions to be inpainting by using the wavelet transformation.

Require: The coefficient matrix A_1 and B_1 of the trained Perceptron are given. The regions to be inpainting are specified in the matrix D. The number of iterations T is specified. The input image is stored in the vector x.

$t \Leftarrow 0, \tilde{x}_0 = x$
while $t < T$ **do**
    Wavelet transformation from $\tilde{x}_t$ to $\tilde{p}_t$
    $q_t = B_1^T A_1^T \tilde{p}_t$
    Inverse Wavelet transformation q_t to z_t
    $\tilde{x}_{t+1} = Dx + (I - D)z_t$
    $t \leftarrow t + 1$
end while

3.2 Multi-layered Perceptron Estimating the Gray Image with the Gray Image and the Wavelet Transformation

The second algorithm uses multi-layered Perceptron. In this algorithm, the gray image is concatenated with the wavelet coefficients and they are used as the input image of the multi-layered Perceptron. The output of the muliti-layered Perceptron is the estimation of the original image. So, we call the second algorithm as MLP-GW-G. Similar with the first algorithm, for each iteration the wavelet coefficients $\tilde{p}_t$ is obtained from the estimated image $\tilde{x}_t$. The concatenated vector $\tilde{r}_t = \begin{bmatrix} \tilde{x}_t \\ \tilde{p}_t \end{bmatrix}$ is used as the input of the trained Perceptron. Then the pixel values of the original image are estimated by using the trained Perceptron as $z_t = B_2^T A_2^T \tilde{r}_t$ where A_2 and B_2 are the weights of the trained Perceptron. Finally the pixel values of the region to be inpainting are replaced with the estimated pixel values as $\tilde{x}_{t+1} = Dx + (I - D)z_t$.

3.3   Multi-layered Perceptron Estimating the Wavelet Coefficients with the Gray Image and the Wavelet Transformation

The third algorithm also uses multi-layered Perceptron. In this algorithm, the gray image is concatenated with the wavelet coefficients and they are used as the input image of the multi-layered Perceptron. The output of the multi-layered Perceptron is the estimation of the wavelet coefficients. So, we call the third algorithm as MLP-GW-W. Similar with the second algorithm, for each iteration the wavelet coefficients $\tilde{p}_t$ is obtained from the estimated image $\tilde{x}_t$. The concatenated vector $\tilde{r}_t = \begin{bmatrix} \tilde{x}_t \\ \tilde{p}_t \end{bmatrix}$ is used as the input of the trained Perceptron. For each iteration, the wavelet coefficients are estimated by the trained Perceptron as $q_t = B_3^T A_3^T \tilde{r}_t$ where A_3 and B_3 are the weights of the trained Perceptron. Then the pixel values of the original image z_t are reconstructed by the inverse wavelet transformation from the estimated wavelet coefficients q_t. Finally the pixel values of the region to be inpainting are replaced with the estimated pixel values as $\tilde{x}_{t+1} = Dx + (I - D)z_t$.

4   Experiments

4.1   Conditions of the Experiments

Face images were taken from Caltech 101 datasets. The training data set consists of 300 images. All the images are converted to the same size (64×64 pixels). Also all images are converted to gray scale and the pixel values are normalized in the range from 0 to 1.

For fair comparison, the number of neurons in hidden layer are determined so that three approaches show the same mean squared errors. They are 280 for AAM-W-W, 200 for MLP-GW-G and 200 for MLP-GW-W. The initial value of the pixels in the region to be inpainting is set to 0.5.

We have also implemented the auto-associative memory using CNN for comparison. We call this algorithm as AAM(CNN)-G-G.

4.2   Comparisons of the Methods

Figure 2 shows the results of the inpainting by proposed three algorithms, AAM-G-G(Takahashi) and AAM(CNN)-G-G. The upper image in the left part is the original image. This image is included in the training samples. The lower image in the left part is the image with missing regions. The missing region are shown in gray square. The center and right parts show the reconstructed images by the proposed three algorithms and two algorithms to compare with the proposed ones. The iterations are increased from left to right as 1st, 2nd, 10th, and 30th. The upper row in the center part is a result of AAM-W-W. The middle row and lower row are results of MLP-GW-G and MLP-GW-W. The results of AAM-G-G(Takahashi) and AAM(CNN)-G-G are shown in the upper row and lower row of the right part. It is noticed that the estimation quality of the pixel values in the missing regions are gradually improved as the number of iterations increase except for the results of AMM(CNN)-G-G. Especially MLP-GW-W and AAM-G-G(Takahashi) give good results in the five algorithms.

Figure 3 shows the graph of the mean squared errors of each iteration in the missing region of Fig. 2 by five algorithms. Algorithms through 1 to 3, AAM-G-G(Takahashi) and AAM(CNN)-G-G are shown in red, yellow, green, blue and purple, respectively. The numerical values of the mean squared errors at each iterations are shown in Table 1. From Fig. 3 and Table 1, we can notice that MLP-GW-W is the best in terms of the mean squared error and the convergence speed becomes faster when we use the wavelet transformation. The reason for this is probably that the sparseness of the wavelet coefficients can contribute to improve the generalization ability. We can find this phenomena in other images of training samples. Also we can find the phenomena that there is a minimum around 3 iterations and the mean squared errors in the missing region increase until around 15 iterations for the case only the gray image is used. However these phenomena is not observed for the algorithms in which the wavelet transformation is used. This means that the wavelet transformation can contribute for the stability of the recursive estimation.

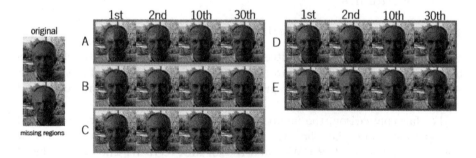

Fig. 2. Examples of the inpainting by using five algorithms for the image in the training samples. The upper image in the left part is the original and the lower is the image with missing regions (gray square region). The center and right parts show the reconstructed images by five algorithms (A (red row): AAM-W-W, B (yellow row): MLP-GW-G, C (green row): MLP-GW-W, D (blue row): AAM-G-G(Takahashi), E (purple row): AAM(CNN)-G-G). (Color figure online)

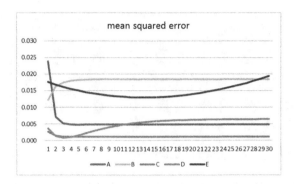

Fig. 3. Graph of the mean squared errors of each iteration in missing region of Fig. 2 applying five inpainting algorithms. A (red line) is AAM-W-W, B (yellow line) is MLP-GW-G, C (green line) is MLP-GW-W, D (blue line) is AAM-G-G(Takahashi), E (purple line) is AAM(CNN)-G-G. (Color figure online)

Table 1. The mean squared errors of each iteration in the missing region

	Iterations	AAM-W-W	MLP-GW-G	MLP-GW-W	AAM-G-G(Takahashi)	AAM(CNN)-G-G
Figure 2	$t = 1$	0.02381	0.01220	0.00263	0.00367	0.01760
	$t = 10$	0.00488	0.01841	**0.00113**	0.00445	0.01331
	$t = 30$	0.00488	0.01842	**0.00113**	0.00643	0.01938
Figure 4	$t = 1$	0.01450	0.05150	0.00833	0.00305	0.05966
	$t = 10$	**0.00141**	0.05436	0.00633	0.00187	0.06571
	$t = 30$	**0.00141**	0.05436	0.00633	0.00187	0.09564

Similarly Fig. 4 shows the results of the inpainting by five algorithms. But in this case, the image is not included in the training samples. It is noticed that the pixel values in the missing region are correctly estimated by four algorithms except for AAM(CNN)-G-G.

Figure 5 shows the results of the inpainting by two algorithms using color image which is not included in training samples. The upper row are the results of the auto-associative memory based on wavelet transformation of the color image which is based on the first proposed method. The lower row are the results of the auto-associative memory based on the color image which is based on the method proposed by Takahashi et al. [4]. The color image is divided in RGB channels. Each channels are transformed by 2-dimensional wavelet transformation and the wavelet coefficients are used as the input the auto-associative memory. It is noticed that the auto-associative memory based on wavelet transformation of the color image gives good results.

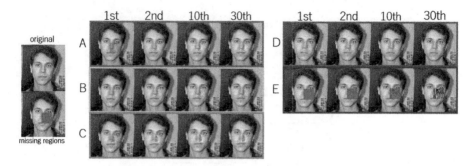

Fig. 4. Examples of the inpainting by five algorithms using test image which is not included in the training samples.

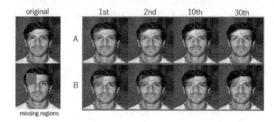

Fig. 5. Examples of the inpainting by the proposed two algorithms using test image which is not included in the training samples. The upper image in the left part is the original and the lower is the image with missing regions (gray square region). The right part shows the reconstructed images by the two algorithms (A (upper row): the auto-associative memory based on the wavelet transformation of the color image, B (lower row): the auto-associative memory based on the color image.

5   Conclusion and Future Works

In this paper, we proposed three algorithms for image inpainting in which the trained multi-layered Perceptron was used in the recursive estimation of the pixel values of the original image. Instead of forward estimation by using the deep neural network such as convolutional neural network (CNN), we used the shallow neural network and the pixel values were recursively estimated. To improve the estimation quality, wavelet coefficients were also used as the input of the neural network. From the experiments using the face images, the effectiveness of the proposed approaches was confirmed.

Mallat pointed out the relation between the wavelet transformation and the deep convolutional neural networks [16]. This means that there is a possibility to use the deep covolutional neural networks instead of the standard wavelet transformation. We think these extensions of our algorithms are our future works.

Acknowledgment. This work was partly supported by JSPS KAKENHI Grant Number 16K00239.

References

1. Szeliski, R.: Computer Vision: Algorithms and Applications. Springer, London (2011). doi:10.1007/978-1-84882-935-0
2. Bertalmio, M., Sapiro, G., Caselles, V., Ballester, C.: Image inpainting. In: Proceedings of ACM SIGGRAPH 2000 Conference, pp. 417–424 (2000)
3. Telea, A.: An image inpainting technique based on the fast marching method. J. Graph. Tools **9**, 23–34 (2012)
4. Takahashi, T., Kurita, T.: A robust classifier combined with an auto-associative network for completing partly occluded images. Neural Netw. **18**(7), 958–966 (2005)
5. Xie, J., Xu, L., Chen, E.: Image denoising and inpainting with deep neural networks. In: Advances in Neural Information Processing Systems, vol. 25, pp. 341–349 (2012)
6. Cai, N., Su, Z., Lin, Z., Wang, H., Yang, Z., Wing-Kuen Ling, B.: Blind inpainting using the fully convolutional neural network. Visual Comput. **33**(2), 249–261 (2017)
7. Iizuka, S., Simo-Serra, E., Ishikawa, H.: Globally and locally consistent image completion. ACM Trans. Graph. **36**(4), 107 (2017)
8. Sethian, J.A.: A fast marching level set method for monotonically advancing fronts. Proc. Natl. Acad. Sci. **93**(4), 1591–1595 (1996)
9. Criminisi, A., Pérez, P., Toyama, K.: Region filling and object removal by exampler-based inpainting. IEEE Trans. Image Process. **13**(9), 1200–1212 (2004)
10. Pathak, D., Donahue, J., Efros, A.A.: Context encoders: feature learning by inpainting. In: Proceedings of the IEEE Conference on Computer Vision and Pattern Recognition (2016)
11. Salakhutdinov, R., Hinton, G.E.: Deep Boltzmann machines. In: Proceedings of the International Conference on Artificial Intelligence and Statistics, vol. 5, no. 2, pp. 448–455 (2009)
12. Vincent, P., Larochelle, H., Lajoie, I., Bengio, Y., Manzagol, P.A.: Stacked denoising autoencoders: learning useful representations in a deep network with a local denoising criterion. J. Mach. Learn. Res. **11**, 3371–3408 (2010)
13. Goodfellow, I., Pouget-Abadie, J., Mirza, M., Xu, B., Warde-Farley, D., Ozair, S., Courville, A., Bengio, Y.: Generative adversarial nets. In: Advances in Neural Information Processing Systems (2014)
14. Akansu, A.N., Serdijn, W.A., Selesnick, I.W.: Emerging applications of wavelets: a review. Phys. Commun. **3**, 1–18 (2010)
15. Eland, M.: Sparse and Redundant Representations: From Theory to Applications in Signal and Image Processing. Springer, New York (2010). doi:10.1007/978-1-4419-7011-4
16. Mallat, S.: Understanding deep convolutional networks. Philos. Trans. R. Soc. A **374**, 1–16 (2015)

Experimental Study on the Effects of Watermarking Techniques on EEG-Based Application System Performance

Trung Duy Pham, Dat Tran[(✉)], and Wanli Ma

University of Canberra, Bruce, ACT 2162, Australia
{duy.pham,dat.tran,wanli.ma}@canberra.edu.au

Abstract. Watermarking has been suggested as a means to improve security of e-Health systems or to add additional functionalities to such system. All watermarking methods alter the host signal to some extent, though the acceptability of this modification varies with the watermarking scheme and depends on a particular application. However, the effect of watermarking methods on Electroencephalogram (EEG)-based applications has not been investigated. In this paper, we propose a robust EEG watermarking scheme and experimentally investigate the impact of applying the proposed method on the recognition performance of some EEG-based application systems such as emotion recognition and user authentication. We have found that the proposed EEG watermarking scheme results in a small degradation of performance.

Keywords: EEG · User authentication · Watermarking · Discrete Wavelet Transform (DWT) · SVD (Sigular Value Decomposition) · Quantization Index Module (QIM)

1 Introduction

Electroencephalogram (EEG) has contributed in various fields of research including in medical, neuron-ergonomics and smart environment, neuron-marketing and advertisement, education and self-regulation, games and entertainment, and security and authentication fields [1]. The widespread emergence of computer networks has made such EEG data to be shared across the world [3]. This sometimes results in crucial critical issues of misuse of digital content leading to severe consequences. To overcome this problem, digital watermarking has been introduced as a safeguard for the copyright protection [10,19]. Digital watermarking [8] is defined as embedding imperceptible information (named as watermark) of multimedia data in the host signal. Watermarking techniques have been thoroughly studied as a means to achieve proof of ownership and transaction tracking [9]. However, several issues have not been resolved or investigated thoroughly in this context. One of these issues is the possible impact of applied watermarking

© Springer International Publishing AG 2017
D. Liu et al. (Eds.): ICONIP 2017, Part VI, LNCS 10639, pp. 662–671, 2017.
https://doi.org/10.1007/978-3-319-70136-3_70

method on the recognition accuracy of the e-Health systems that should be augmented with this technology (this question of course only applies to watermarking scenarios, where the host data actually are biometric sample data which are used in biometric recognition and have been modified by watermarking process).

Mostly, the development of digital watermarking is connected to their evolution. In the literature, different strategies are introduced to provide a wide and comparable evaluation of watermarking algorithms. These existing evaluation techniques differ in their strategies and procedure. For example, a simple evaluation procedure for robustness can be provided by using single attacks with following detection or retrieval of the embedded information. If the watermarking schemes should be evaluated in the context of application scenarios, profiles are more realistic and can be better used for the evaluation. With profiles, the evaluation is easier, abstracted and useable for the developers as well as for end users with no or only few inside knowledge. Hereby, application profiles provide a typical used application scenario. Furthermore, the comparability of given watermarking schemes can be analyzed for a specific application scenario or a subset of application fields.

The impact of watermarking on recognition system performance has been investigated in some previous studies. The effect of watermarking methods on biometrics, in particular iris detection, has been investigated for robust techniques [11,12] and fragile techniques [20]. While Dong et al. [11] do not report on performance degradation when investigating a single watermark embedding algorithm and one iris recognition technique only, Hämmerle et al. [12] find partially significant reduction in recognition accuracy when assessing two iris recognition schemes and a couple of robust watermarking algorithms. This study in [20] showed that fragile watermarking significantly affects iris recognition performance in many cases. Hong et al. [13] discuss the application of robust watermark and symmetric encryption techniques for the exchange of compressed biometric sample data, where they also investigate the impact on accuracy of a fingerprint recognition scheme. Based on first evaluation [25,33], the authors [15] present a new application profile and exemplary test results for audio watermarking evaluations. However, the impact of watermarking scheme on EEG-based application performance has not been studied. Our main purpose is to study the effects of watermarking application on EEG-based application performance in general means rather than to compare which watermarking algorithm is better for EEG watermarking scheme. Hence, robust EEG watermarking scheme will be investigated.

In this paper, we propose a robust watermarking scheme to protect rightful ownership of outsourced EEG data, and investigate thoroughly its effects on performance of EEG-based application systems such as Emotion Recognition System and User Authentication System. Experimental results show that our proposed not only strengthen the security of overall system, but also do not affect significantly on system performance.

The rest of paper is organized as follows. We first present the proposed watermarking scheme for EEG data in Sect. 2. Section 3 presents EEG-based application test scenarios including emotion recognition system and user authentication system. Experiments and results are presented in Sect. 4. We conclude the paper with a conclusion and future works in Sect. 5.

2   Watermarking Scheme for EEG Data

Transform domains are proven to be more robust toward different attacks [24] and SVD-based watermarking is one of the most powerful watermarking schemes in this domain. The robust performance of existing SVD-based watermarking methods is not always better than that of frequency-based methods such as Gaussian filtering and noising [32] for most of attacks [4] developed in the spatial domain. A better approach to enhance the robustness of SVD-based methods is to employ this transform along with the frequency transform for biomedical data. It has been reported that among the transform domain methods, Discrete Wavelet Transform (DWT) is more suitable for achieving robust watermarking and imperceptible [22]. In addition, DWT is widely used for the time-frequency analysis of EEG data due to its non-stationary characteristics [26,31]. In our watermarking scheme, we choose the popular QIM [5] method in the embedding process because of its good robustness and blind nature [17]. The present work uses DWT-SVD hybrid transform integrated with QIM to carry out watermarking scheme for EEG data, shown in Fig. 1. The proposed approach includes two main phases: watermarking embedding and watermarking extraction.

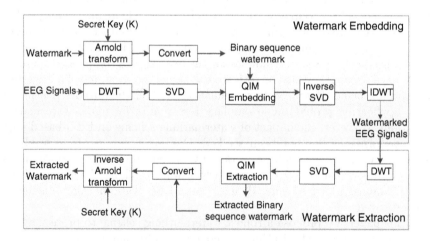

Fig. 1. Diagram of the watermark scheme.

Firstly, watermark after transformed by Arnold with secret K to improve security, is converted to binary sequence watermark. Next, EEG signals are decomposed by two-level DWT using Haar wavelet filter and then performed by SVD.

Binary sequence watermark is embedding to SVD matrix by QIM method. Watermarked EEG signals are reconstructed by inverse SVD and inverse DWT.

In the extraction phase, watermarked EEG signals are transformed by DWT and SVD, then binary sequence watermark is extracted by QIM extraction method. Extracted watermark is obtained by converting and transformed by Arnold with secret K from extracted binary sequence watermark.

It is obvious that the quantization step in QIM method is significant in terms of both robustness and imperceptibility. The larger the quantization step is, the more robust, but less imperceptibility, the watermarking scheme is and vice versa.

3   EEG-Based Application Test Scenarios

In this research, we make a first attempt to investigate applications about EEG watermarking and make some analysis on the influences which are caused by watermarking scheme to EEG-based application performance. There are two popular application scenarios about EEG watermarking: emotion recognition system and user authentication system.

3.1   EEG-Based Emotion Recognition System

Emotions play an extremely important role in how we make a decision, planning, reasoning and other human states. The recognition of these emotions is becoming a vital task for e-healthcare systems [2]. Through many studies, EEG signals have been proven to provide informative characteristics in response to the emotional states [6,18,27]. Automatic emotion recognition system has been one of the most popular research topics in the fields of computer vision, speech recognition, brain machine interface, and computational neuron-science [7].

EEG-based emotion recognition model in [30] has two phases: training phase and recognition phase, using autoregressive (AR) model, Saviztky-Golay smoother and support vector data description (SVDD) method for feature extraction, feature smoothing and emotion model building, respectively. Figure 2 shows the emotion recognition system based on EEG signals with proposed

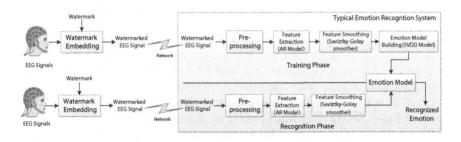

Fig. 2. EEG-based emotion recognition system scenario

robust watermarking scheme. We study the impact of the watermark embedding on the overall emotion recognition performance, by studying the recognition rate changes with and without watermarking.

3.2   EEG-Based User Authentication System

In recent year, researchers start to establish the fact that brain wave patterns are unique to every individual, thus EEG signals can be used in biometrics [21]. They explore the potential of EEG in biometric authentication because of its advantages. A critical problem related with biometrics such as EEG based authentication for remote application is how to protect the biometric information securely from unauthorized accesses [23].

EEG signal is watermarked as authentication purpose, which provides an extra authenticity level before transmission. At receiver, features are extracted and used to train the model which is kept securely in a database for this person.

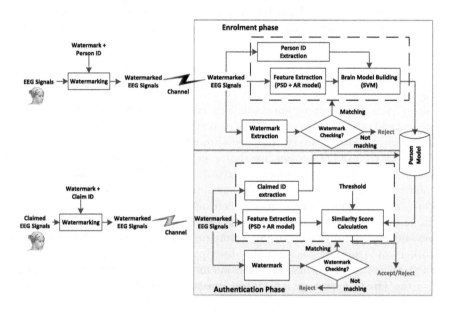

Fig. 3. EEG-based user authentication system scenario

Based on EEG-based User Authentication System in [28,29], Fig. 3 shows the general process of authentication based on enrollment data and test data including watermarking embedding and retrieving. In this scenario, performance of a system is evaluated by Detection Error Trade-off curves (DET) which is a plot of False Acceptance Rate (FAR) on y-axis versus False Rejection Rate (FRR) on x-axis. To compare the accuracy of the system with different DET curves, we use Equal Error Rate (EER) that is a point on a DET curve where FAR and FRR are equal. The lower DET curves, as well as smaller EER is considered as the better authentication system. We investigate the effects of the proposed watermarking on authentication system performance based on DET curves and EER measure.

4   Experiments and Results

4.1   Experiments

Experiments were performed using DEAP dataset [14] for EEG-based Emotion Recognition System and Graz 2008 B [16] for EEG-based User Authentication System. A binary logo image with size 32×32 will be used as watermark image and we consider how the proposed watermarking scheme with different quantization steps ($\Delta = 5, 10$, and 20) affects to the performance of the two systems.

4.2   Results

To evaluate the effects on emotion recognition accuracy with and without watermarking, we embedded watermark with various quantization step that was explained in Sect. 2. The accuracy is degraded slightly (on average, from about 2% to 3% in accuracy reduction, depending on quantization step), but for some subjects, the watermarking decreases significantly the accuracies of classifiers for the reason that quantization step is not suitable, leading to major distortion of EEG signals. This problem could be solved by adjusting the quantization step of watermarking scheme to find the best one. Finding the best quantization step needs to be investigated in the further studies.

Figure 4 shows the classification performance of two-level class. In general, the accuracy of emotion recognition system decreases, however for some subjects, the

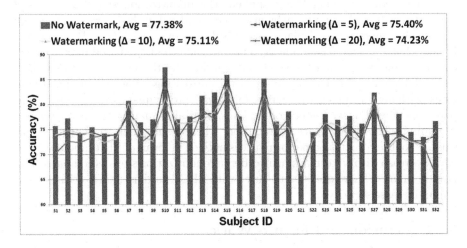

Fig. 4. The accuracy of emotion recognition system of two level-class affected by watermarking with different quantization steps

smoothed feature sequence decreases the accuracies of classifiers for the reason that the smoothing causes information lost in some degree. This problem could be solved by adjusting the parameters of smoothers to find the best parameters. Finding the best parameters needs to be investigated in the further studies.

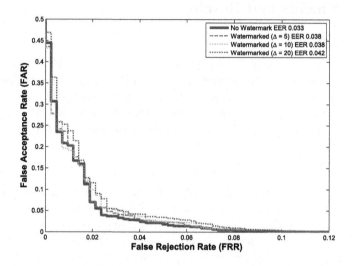

Fig. 5. DET curves for system performance by watermarking with different quantization steps

In EEG-based user authentication system, the blue solid DET curve in Fig. 5 is the baseline, which is the original DET curves generated from the un-watermarked datasets.

In case watermarking being applied, the quantization step ($\Delta = 5, 10$ and 20) curves depicted with magenta, green, and red dashed curve, respectively are the average results, calculated over 9 subjects of 2 tasks (Graz B dataset). It is clear that EEG watermarking does not degrade the EEG based user authentication system performance, severely in experiments. However, we notice a slight reduction of recognition accuracy across the entire range of investigated matching rates, with higher impact when embedding with larger quantization step as compared to embedding with smaller one. Thus, a suitable quantization step is critical to minimize the performance degradation. These results indicate that no significant loss of the recognition performance is noticed in terms of EER (about 0.5% to 0.9% decrease with watermarking in different quantization steps as compared with no watermark). Therefore, it can be used with EEG-based user authentication system to increase security.

5   Conclusion and Future Works

As to be expected, watermarking affects the EEG-based application performance including emotion recognition and user authentication in this study, we have found that the proposed watermarking results in minor impact on recognition performance for both EEG-based applications, however, embedding with different quantization steps causes significant recognition degradations for some subjects. This implies that when designing a watermarking scheme for employment in an EEG context, it is important to consider those issues to find the best quantization step for each subject.

In near future, we will experiment our proposed EEG watermarking with other EEG-based application context. In addition, finding the best parameters of watermarking scheme will be investigated to enhance the performance of EEG watermarking scheme.

References

1. Abdulkader, S.N., Atia, A., Mostafa, M.S.M.: Brain computer interfacing: applications and challenges. Egypt. Inf. J. **16**(2), 213–230 (2015)
2. Ali, M., Mosa, A.H., Al Machot, F., Kyamakya, K.: EEG-based emotion recognition approach for e-healthcare applications. In: 2016 Eighth International Conference on Ubiquitous and Future Networks (ICUFN), pp. 946–950. IEEE (2016)
3. Bhatnagar, G., Wu, Q.J.: Biometrics inspired watermarking based on a fractional dual tree complex wavelet transform. Future Gener. Comput. Syst. **29**(1), 182–195 (2013)
4. Chang, C.C., Tsai, P., Lin, C.C.: SVD-based digital image watermarking scheme. Pattern Recogn. Lett. **26**(10), 1577–1586 (2005)
5. Chen, B., Wornell, G.W.: Quantization index modulation methods for digital watermarking and information embedding of multimedia. J. VLSI Signal Process. Syst. **27**(1–2), 7–33 (2001)
6. Coan, J.A., Allen, J.J.: Frontal EEG asymmetry as a moderator and mediator of emotion. Biol. Psychol. **67**(1), 7–50 (2004)
7. Cowie, R., Douglas-Cowie, E., Tsapatsoulis, N., Votsis, G., Kollias, S., Fellenz, W., Taylor, J.G.: Emotion recognition in human-computer interaction. IEEE Signal Process. Mag. **18**(1), 32–80 (2001)
8. Cox, I., Miller, M.: A review of watermarking and the importance of perceptual watermarking. In: Proceedings of Electronic Imaging (1997)
9. Cox, I., Miller, M., Bloom, J., Fridrich, J., Kalker, T.: Digital Watermarking and Steganography. Morgan Kaufmann, San Francisco (2007)
10. Cox, I.J., Kilian, J., Leighton, F.T., Shamoon, T.: Secure spread spectrum watermarking for multimedia. IEEE Trans. Image Process. **6**(12), 1673–1687 (1997)
11. Dong, J., Tan, T.: Effects of watermarking on iris recognition performance. In: 2008 10th International Conference on Control, Automation, Robotics and Vision, ICARCV 2008, pp. 1156–1161. IEEE (2008)
12. Hämmerle-Uhl, J., Raab, K., Uhl, A.: Experimental study on the impact of robust watermarking on iris recognition accuracy. In: Proceedings of the 2010 ACM Symposium on Applied Computing, pp. 1479–1484. ACM (2010)
13. Hong, S., Kim, H., Lee, S., Chung, Y.: Analyzing the secure and energy efficient transmissions of compressed fingerprint images using encryption and watermarking. In: 2008 International Conference on Information Security and Assurance, ISA 2008, pp. 316–320. IEEE (2008)

14. Koelstra, S., Muhl, C., Soleymani, M., Lee, J.S., Yazdani, A., Ebrahimi, T., Pun, T., Nijholt, A., Patras, I.: Deap: a database for emotion analysis; using physiological signals. IEEE Trans. Affect. Comput. **3**(1), 18–31 (2012)
15. Lang, A., Dittmann, J.: Digital watermarking of biometric speech references: impact to the EER system performance. In: Security, Steganography, and Watermarking of Multimedia Contents 9 (2007)
16. Leeb, R., Brunner, C., Müller-Putz, G., Schlögl, A., Pfurtscheller, G.: BCI Competition 2008-Graz Data set B. Graz University of Technology, Austria (2008)
17. Lei, B., Soon, Y., Zhou, F., Li, Z., Lei, H.: A robust audio watermarking scheme based on lifting wavelet transform and singular value decomposition. Sig. Process. **92**(9), 1985–2001 (2012)
18. Li, X., Hu, B., Zhu, T., Yan, J., Zheng, F.: Towards affective learning with an EEG feedback approach. In: Proceedings of the First ACM International Workshop on Multimedia Technologies for Distance Learning, pp. 33–38. ACM (2009)
19. Liu, R., Tan, T.: An SVD-based watermarking scheme for protecting rightful ownership. IEEE Trans. Multimedia **4**(1), 121–128 (2002)
20. Lock, A., Allen, A.: Effects of reversible watermarking on iris recognition performance. Int. J. Comput. Electr. Autom. Control Inf. Eng. **8**(4), 574–579 (2014)
21. Marcel, S., Millán, J.d.R.: Person authentication using brainwaves (EEG) and maximum a posteriori model adaptation. IEEE Trans. Pattern Anal. Mach. Intell. **29**(4) (2007)
22. Mishra, A., Agarwal, C., Sharma, A., Bedi, P.: Optimized gray-scale image watermarking using DWT-SVD and firefly algorithm. Expert Syst. Appl. **41**(17), 7858–7867 (2014)
23. Moon, D., Kim, T., Jung, S.H., Chung, Y., Moon, K., Ahn, D., Kim, S.-K.: Performance evaluation of watermarking techniques for secure multimodal biometric systems. In: Hao, Y., Liu, J., Wang, Y.-P., Cheung, Y., Yin, H., Jiao, L., Ma, J., Jiao, Y.-C. (eds.) CIS 2005. LNCS, vol. 3802, pp. 635–642. Springer, Heidelberg (2005). doi:10.1007/11596981_94
24. Mousavi, S.M., Naghsh, A., Abu-Bakar, S.: Watermarking techniques used in medical images: a survey. J. Digit. Imaging **27**(6), 714–729 (2014)
25. Oermann, A., Lang, A., Vielhauer, C.: Digital speech watermarking and its impact to biometric speech authentication. In: New Advances in Multimedia Security, Biometrics, Watermarking and Cultural Aspects (2006)
26. Orhan, U., Hekim, M., Ozer, M.: Eeg signals classification using the k-means clustering and a multilayer perceptron neural network model. Expert Syst. Appl. **38**(10), 13475–13481 (2011)
27. Petrantonakis, P.C., Hadjileontiadis, L.J.: A novel emotion elicitation index using frontal brain asymmetry for enhanced EEG-based emotion recognition. IEEE Trans. Inf Technol. Biomed. **15**(5), 737–746 (2011)
28. Pham, T., Ma, W., Tran, D., Nguyen, P., Phung, D.: EEG-based user authentication in multilevel security systems. In: Motoda, H., Wu, Z., Cao, L., Zaiane, O., Yao, M., Wang, W. (eds.) ADMA 2013. LNCS, vol. 8347, pp. 513–523. Springer, Heidelberg (2013). doi:10.1007/978-3-642-53917-6_46
29. Pham, T., Ma, W., Tran, D., Nguyen, P., Phung, D.: A study on the feasibility of using EEG signals for authentication purpose. In: Lee, M., Hirose, A., Hou, Z.-G., Kil, R.M. (eds.) ICONIP 2013. LNCS, vol. 8227, pp. 562–569. Springer, Heidelberg (2013). doi:10.1007/978-3-642-42042-9_70

30. Pham, T.D., Tran, D., Ma, W., Tran, N.T.: Enhancing performance of EEG-based emotion recognition systems using feature smoothing. In: Arik, S., Huang, T., Lai, W.K., Liu, Q. (eds.) ICONIP 2015. LNCS, vol. 9492, pp. 95–102. Springer, Cham (2015). doi:10.1007/978-3-319-26561-2_12

31. Subasi, A.: EEG signal classification using wavelet feature extraction and a mixture of expert model. Expert Syst. Appl. **32**(4), 1084–1093 (2007)

32. Tsai, H.H., Jhuang, Y.J., Lai, Y.S.: An SVD-based image watermarking in wavelet domain using SVR and PSO. Appl. Soft Comput. **12**(8), 2442–2453 (2012)

33. Vielhauer, C., Scheidat, T., Lang, A., Schott, M., Dittmann, J., Basu, T., Dutta, P.: Multimodal speaker authentication-evaluation of recognition performance of watermarked references. In: Proceedings of the 2nd Workshop on Multimodal User Authentication (MMUA), Toulouse, France (2006)

A Self Organizing Map Based Multi-objective Framework for Automatic Evolution of Clusters

Naveen Saini[1(✉)], Shubham Chourasia[2], Sriparna Saha[1],
and Pushpak Bhattacharyya[1]

[1] Indian Institute of Technology, Patna, India
naveen.pcs16@iitp.ac.in, nsaini1988@gmail.com
[2] Sikkim Manipal Institute of Technology, East Sikkim, India

Abstract. The current paper reports about the development of an automatic clustering technique which builds upon the search capability of a self-organizing multi-objective differential evolutionary approach. The algorithm utilizes new search operators which are developed after considering the neighbor-hood relationships of solutions of a population extracted using a self organizing map (SOM). Variable number of cluster centers are encoded in different solutions of the population which are evolved using the new search operators of differential evolution to automatically determine the number of clusters. Two cluster validity indices capturing different goodness measures of partitioning are used as objective functions. The effectiveness of the proposed framework namely, self organizing map based multi-objective (MO) clustering technique (SMEA_clust) is shown for automatically partitioning four artificial and four real-life data sets in comparison with a multi-objective differential evolution based clustering technique (similar to our proposed approach but without using SOM concept), two recent multi-objective clustering based techniques, VAMOSA and MOCK. Results are further validated using statistical significance tests.

Keywords: Self organizing map · Unsupervised classification · Clustering · Evolutionary algorithm · Cluster validity measures

1 Introduction

Clustering [1], an unsupervised approach of patten classification, aims to partition the given data set into various K-groups where members belonging to a particular group should have similar properties. Here the value of K may or may not be known *a priori*. Traditional approaches [2] of determining the appropriate number of clusters mainly apply different clustering algorithms like K-means [1], hierarchical [1] approaches for different values of K and then select the optimal partitioning based on the value of a cluster validity index, measuring the goodness of a partitioning. Most of the existing clustering algorithms implicitly optimize a single cluster quality measure capturing different cluster properties

© Springer International Publishing AG 2017
D. Liu et al. (Eds.): ICONIP 2017, Part VI, LNCS 10639, pp. 672–682, 2017.
https://doi.org/10.1007/978-3-319-70136-3_71

like compactness, separation, connectivity, density or symmetricity. But in real-life, clusters of a given data set possess different structures which can not be detected with the use of a single cluster quality measure. Thus the optimization of multiple cluster quality measures simultaneously using the search capacity of a multiobjective optimization algorithm [3, 4] became popular in recent years. This leads to the development of some multi-objective based clustering algorithms [5]. Moreover automatic optimization of cluster validity indices also guides the algorithm to automatically determine the number of clusters. Most of the existing multi-objective clustering approaches utilize different evolutionary techniques (EAs) like genetic algorithm (GA) [6], differential evolution (DE) [7] or particle swarm optimization (PSO) [8] as the underlying optimization strategy.

In [9], Handl et al. developed a multi-objective automatic clustering algorithm, MOCK. But the application of MOCK is limited in determining only some well-separated or hyper-spherical shaped clusters. It does not perform well in detecting overlapping clusters. Moreover the complexity of MOCK increases linearly with the increase in the number of data points. In recent years some symmetry based multiobjective clustering techniques are proposed in [10,11] utilizing AMOSA [3] as the underlying optimization technique. Suresh et al. [7] have proposed some multi-objective differential evolution based clustering techniques and have shown that differential evolution can serve as a promising backbone for devising multi-objective clustering techniques. In general it was shown in the literature that DE based approaches converge faster compared to other EA based techniques [7]. Motivated by this, current paper also exploits the search capability of DE in proposing an automatic clustering technique in collaboration with self organizing map (SOM) [12].

Self organizing map (SOM) is an unsupervised learning method of artificial neural network to map high dimensional input space to low dimensional output space preserving the topological structure of the input data. In recent years researchers are working towards integrating SOM with evolutionary algorithms to develop some new optimization techniques like SMOEA/D [13], SMEA [14]. Motivated by this in the current paper we have developed a self organizing evolutionary algorithm based clustering technique where at each generation, a new solution is generated using the neighborhood relationship identified by SOM trained on solutions present in the current population as done in SMEA [14]. For a given solution, only the neighboring solutions in the topographical map identified by SOM are participated in the genetic operations of DE to generate high quality solutions. The proposed clustering approach simultaneously optimizes two cluster validity indices, PBM index [15] and Silhouette score [11] for the purpose of automatic determination of the number of clusters.

Similar to any other MOO based approach our proposed clustering approach, SMEA_clust, also produces a set of solutions at the end on the final Pareto optimal front. A single best solution is selected using an external cluster validity index namely Adjusted Rand Index (ARI) [7]. The supremacy of the proposed approach is shown on automatically partitioning four artificial and four real-life data sets of varying complexities. The obtained partitioning results are compared with some existing MOO based clustering techniques like MOCK [9] and VAMOSA [10]. In a part of the paper, in order to show the adequacy of SOM based genetic operators, experiments are also performed with normal genetic operators in association with MOO based clustering approach developed in the paper, namely MEA_clust. Results clearly show the strength of using SOM in mating pool generation process of the proposed MOO based clustering approach. This clearly illustrates that participation of nearest neighbors of a solution in generating the mating pool helps in exploring the search space in an efficient way. Furthermore in order to validate the obtained results, some statistical tests guided by [16] are also conducted to show the superiority of our algorithm.

2   Methodology

In the current work we have proposed a self organizing evolutionary algorithm based clustering technique. The key attributes of the current work are the following: (i) a recently developed self organizing multi-objective evolutionary algorithm [14] is utilized as the underlying optimization technique. Here neighborhood information extracted by a SOM for a given solution is used during genetic operations. This helps in exploring the search-space steadily. (ii) optimization of two cluster validity indices, PBM index [15] and Silhouette score [11], simultaneously enables the proposed clustering approach to automatically determine the appropriate partitioning from a given data set. A flow-chart of the proposed approach is shown in Fig. 2 and the basic operations are described below.

2.1   Self Organizing Map

Self Organizing Map or SOM developed by Kohonen [12] is a special type of artificial neural network which makes use of unsupervised learning to produce a low-dimensional mapping of input space of the training samples. Low-dimensional space (output space) consists of regular, usually 2-D grid of neurons (or map units or prototype vectors). Neurons in low dimensional space have *position vectors* and *weight vectors* associated with them.

Fig. 1. Traditional approach for SOM training. Here η_0: initial learning rate, σ_0: initial neighborhood size, η and σ are continuously decreasing functions at each iteration, i_{max} is the maximum number of iterations for SOM training

Main objective of SOM is to create a topographic preserving map in the output space such that different regions of the output space respond similarly

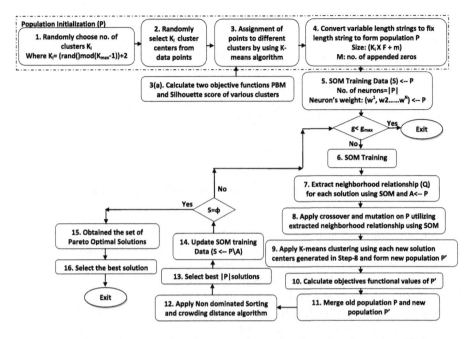

Fig. 2. SMEA based proposed architecture for multi-objective clustering. Here, g_{max} is the maximum number of generation, F is no. of features in data

to certain input patterns. Learning of SOM starts by assigning each neuron a weight vector, a randomly chosen data point from the available training samples. At each iteration, the weight vectors of the neurons are updated by using the training samples closer to them. In this work, we have utilized the traditional learning algorithm [17] as shown in Fig. 1 for training of SOM using neighborhood relationships among neurons which returns the weight vectors of different neurons.

2.2   String Representation and Population Initialization

In SMEA based clustering, the strings (solutions or chromosomes) are made up of real numbers which represent the coordinates of cluster centers. Our algorithm attempts to find the appropriate number of cluster centers that represent the partitioning of the data. Thus the number of cluster centers present in different chromosomes varies over a range, 2 to $\sqrt{N}$, where N is the total number of data points. For ith chromosome a random number (K_i) in the range $[2, \sqrt{N}]$ is generated and then K_i number of data points are randomly selected from the data set which are considered as the initial cluster centers. But as these chromosomes further take part in training of SOM to generate the neighborhood information, we have converted the variable length chromosomes to some fixed length vectors. Reason for keeping the fix length for all solutions is that weight vector corresponding to a neuron of SOM must be of same length as input vector (here solutions are the input vectors). Maximum length of the string can be $(K * d + m)$, where K is the number of clusters present in a solution, d is the number of features in the data, m is the number of appended zeros which can vary between '0' to $(K * d - 2 * d)$ because of the constraint of having minimum two clusters. This means string length should be $\sqrt{N}$*d. For an example, if a particular string encodes the centers of 3 clusters in 2-d space and N = 16, then string will be represented as $< 2.31.47.612.92.13.40.00.0 >$ which encodes three cluster centers (2.3, 1.4), (7.6, 12.9) and (2.1, 3.4), where m is 2. This set of strings with varying number of clusters will form the initial population.

2.3   Euclidean Distance Calculation and Weight Updation

The vectors (strings) present in the population further take part in SOM training to find the neighborhood of all these solutions. As string length is fixed in the population, during Euclidean distance calculation between training vector and weight vector of neuron, only that much length of the vector is considered which has the maximum number of appended zeros. For example, let one vector be (a, b, c, d, 0, 0) and second vector be (a, b, 0, 0, 0, 0) then during distance calculation or weight updation, consider the length of vector (or number of features) as 2 and consider the remaining features as zero because second vector has maximum number of appended zeros.

2.4   Objective Functions

In this paper, two well known internal cluster validity measures, PBM (Pakhira-Bandyopadhyay-Maulik) index [15] and Silhouette score [11] are used as objective functions which need to be simultaneously optimized. These two objective functions measure the compactness and the separation of the partitionings in term of the Euclidean distance in two different ways and should be maximized.

Algorithm 1. MatingPool_Construction(M, P, H, β, $\overline{x_{current}}$)

1: Find out winning neuron 'h' mapped by solution $\overline{x_{current}}$ based on minimum Euclidean distance.
2: Sort hth row of M in ascending order and keep the sorted indices in I.

$$Q = \begin{cases} \cup_{k=1}^{H}\{\overline{x^k}\} & \text{if rand}() < \beta, \text{and k} < H \\ P & \text{otherwise} \end{cases}$$

Where rand() is a random number generated between 0 and 1. $\overline{x^k}$ is the kth neuron present in list I.
3: **return** Q for solution $\overline{x_{current}}$

Algorithm 2. $y = \text{Generate}(Q,CR,MP,\overline{x_{current}})$

1: Randomly select two parents $\overline{x^1}$ and $\overline{x^2}$ from mating pool Q of solution $\overline{x_{current}}$
   such that $\overline{x^1} \neq \overline{x^2} \neq \overline{x_{current}}$
2: Generate a trial solution $\overline{y}'$ using the following

$$\text{if rand}() \leq CR, \text{then } y_i' = x_{current_i} + F \times (x_i^1 - x_i^2), \text{ Otherwise } y_i' = x_{current_i}$$

$i = 1\ldots,k$
3: Here only the non-zero values (say k) of $\overline{x_{current}}$ are updated with the help of
   corresponding k values of x_1 and x_2 keeping remaining values from (k+1) to n
   unchanged.
4: Repair the trial solution to generate $\overline{y}''$

$$\text{if } y_i' < a_i, \text{then } y_i'' = a_i, \text{elseif } y_i' > b_i, \text{then } y_i'' = b_i, \text{Otherwise }, y_i'' = y_i'$$

Where, $i = 1, 2, \ldots, k$ and a_i, b_i are the lower and upper boundaries of variable
$x_{current_i}$.
5: Mutate the trial solution by using the following Equation to generate $\overline{y}$
   (i) if $0 \leq MP < 0.6$:   ▷ Perform normal mutation

$$\text{if rand}() \leq p_m, \text{then } y_i = y_i'' + \delta_i \times (b_i - a_i), \text{ otherwise } y_i = y_i''$$

where $i = (1, 2, \ldots, k)$, $r = rand()$ is a random number between 0 and 1, and

$$
\delta_i = \begin{cases}
\left[2r + (1 - 2r)(\frac{b_i - y_i''}{b_i - a_i})^{\eta_m + 1} \right]^{\frac{1}{\eta_m + 1}} - 1, & \text{if } r < 0.5 \\[4mm]
1 - \left[2 - 2r + (1 - 2r)(\frac{y_i'' - a_i}{b_i - a_i})^{\eta_m + 1} \right]^{\frac{1}{\eta_m + 1}} & \text{Otherwise}
\end{cases}
$$

   (ii) if $0.6 \leq MP < 0.8$:   ▷ Perform insert mutation
        Pick a random sample from the data set and add that starting from (k+1) th
        position of the string.
   (iii) if $0.8 \leq MP \leq 1.0$:   ▷ Perform delete mutation
         Randomly select a cluster center and delete that from the given string.
6: **return** the new solution $\overline{y}$

2.5   Extracting Neighborhood Relationship

The neighborhood relationship of current solution is established with the use of
SOM which identifies the solutions closer to the current solution. This phenomenon is known as mating pool construction. Mating pool constructed is denoted
as Q shown in Fig. 2. These neighboring (closer) solutions can mate to generate a new solution. Steps of constructing mating pool Q for current solution
$\overline{x_{current}} \in P$ are shown in Algorithm 1 [14]. In the algorithm we have used the
following parameters, M: distance matrix created using position vectors of neu-
rons, P: the population containing solutions $(\overline{x^1}, \overline{x^2}, \ldots..\overline{x^n})$, H: mating pool size,
β : threshold probability of selecting the closer solution and $\overline{x_{current}}$: current
solution for which we want to generate mating pool.

2.6   Crossover and Mutation Operations

Mating pool generated in the previous step is participated in crossover and mutation operation. Two more changes over traditional DE are incorporated to generate the trial solution $\overline{y'}$ and new solution y. Firstly only non-zeros values (say k) of the current solution (excluding appended zeros) are used to generate the trial solution. Second change was made in the mutation operation. A new solution is generated from the current solution $\overline{x_{current}}$ by using any of the three types of mutation operations - normal mutation, insert mutation and delete mutation to explore the search space of solutions efficiently. Any of these three types of mutation operations is selected based on some random probability lying within a range as similar to [10]. The detailed algorithm [14] on genetic operations with changes incorporated is discussed in Algorithm 2. In the algorithm, F and CR are the two control parameters of the DE operator; p_m is the threshold mutation probability for mutation of each component of y'' in case of normal mutation; CR is the crossover probability to generate the trial solution; MP is the mutation probability of current solution deciding which type of mutation should be performed and η_m denotes the distribution index of mutation.

2.7   Selection of Best Solution

Any MOO algorithm produces a large number of non-dominated solutions [4] on the final Pareto optimal set and all these solutions are equally important from optimization perspective. But sometimes, user may want to select only a single solution. Therefore, in this paper to select a single solution, we have used an external cluster validity index, *Adjusted Rand Index (ARI)* [7]. ARI utilizes the true partitioning information in its computation. The similarity between the obtained partitioning and the true partitioning is measured in ARI. Definition of ARI suggests that higher value corresponds to most perfect partitioning. Thus we have computed the ARI values for all the partitioning solutions present in the final Pareto front and the solution corresponding to the higher value of ARI is reported here.

3   Experiments and Results

The parameters of the proposed clustering approach, SMEA_clust, are as follows: H (mating pool size) = 5, $\eta_0 = 0.1$, $\sigma_0 = 2$, $g_{max} = 50$, F = 0.8, CR = 0.8, the probability ranges for normal, insertion and deletion mutation operators are 0 to 0.6, 0.6 to 0.8 and 0.8 to 1, respectively. As seen from Fig. 2, in Step-14, we are updating SOM's training data by excluding those solutions which are already covered in SOM training i.e., at the end of each generation, S will contain only new solutions and if no new solutions are left for training then we will exit the loop. Otherwise, the loop will continue till the maximum number of generations, g_{max}, is reached. As MOO gives a set of non-dominated Pareto optimal solutions, therefore best solution is identified by the method discussed in Sect. 2.7. For the purpose of comparison, some other MOO clustering techniques, MEA_clust (similar to our proposed clustering approach except the use of SOM), MOCK [9] and VAMOSA [10], are also executed on the above mentioned data sets with default parameter settings.

3.1 Data Sets Used for Experiments

The proposed clustering based approach is tested on several data sets. Due to space constriant, here results are provided only for eight datasets, four of them are artificial data sets namely, AD_5_2 [10], AD_10_2 [10], Spherical_6_2 [18], Spherical_4_3 [18] and four are real-life data sets namely, Iris, Newthyroid, Wine and LiverDisorder. These real life data sets are taken from Ref. [19]. Detailed descriptions of these data sets are provided in Table 1. Note that for all the data sets used here, actual class label information is available.

3.2 Discussion of Results

In order to quantify the goodness of the obtained partitionings by different MOO based approaches, an external cluster validity index, namely *Adjusted Rand Index* [7] is utilized. But, for the purpose of comparison of results attained by different clustering approaches, corresponding values of Minkowski Score (MS) [10] for different partitionings and the corresponding number of clusters identified by different MOO based techniques are reported in Table 1. MS is an external cluster validity index to measure the quality of predicted clustering solution with respect to the given true clustering solution. Lower MS value yields better partitioning.

Table 1. Experiment results showing comparison between our proposed approach, SMEA_clust, and two existing MOO based clustering techniques, MOCK and VAMOSA, and another variant of our proposed approach, MEA_clust. Here, AC = actual number of clusters, OC = obtained number of clusters, MS = Minkowski Score, #F = No. of features, #N = No. of data points.

Data set	#F	#N	AC	MOCK		VAMOSA		MEA_clust		SMEA_clust	
				OC	MS	OC	MS	OC	MS	OC	MS
AD_5_2	2	250	5	6	0.39	**5**	**0.25**	5	0.35	**5**	**0.25**
AD_10_2	2	500	10	6	1.01	10	0.43	**10**	**0**	**10**	**0**
Spherical_6_2	2	300	6	**6**	**0**	6	0	6	0	6	0
Spherical_4_3	3	400	4	**4**	**0**	4	0	4	0	4	0
Iris	4	150	3	2	0.82	2	0.80	2	0.72	**3**	**0.67**
Newthyroid	5	215	3	2	0.82	5	0.57	3	0.59	**3**	**0.56**
Wine	13	178	3	3	0.90	3	0.97	2	0.36	**3**	**0.33**
LiveDisorder	6	345	2	3	0.98	**2**	**0.98**	**2**	**0.98**	2	0.98

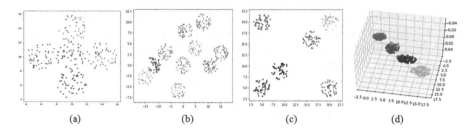

Fig. 3. Automatically clustered *(a) AD_5_2, (b) AD_10_2, (c) Spherical_6_2, (d) Spherical_4_3* by SMEA_clust approach

Results on Artificial Data Sets: As can be seen from Table 1, (i) for AD_5_2 data set, SMEA_clust and VAMOSA both are able to determine the appropriate number of clusters and provide the lowest MS values compared to other techniques, (ii) for AD_10_2, SMEA_clust and MEA_clust perform similarly and are better than other two MOO based techniques, MOCK and VAMOSA, (iii) for Spherical_6_2, because of the well-separated structure of the partitioning, all the clustering approaches are capable of determining the same optimal partitioning, (iv) for Spherical_4_3 again all the clustering approaches are capable of determining the optimal partitioning. Final partitionings obtained by SMEA_clust for AD_5_2, AD_10_2, Spherical_6_2 and Spherical_4_3 data sets are shown in Fig. 3(a), (b), (c) and (d) respectively.

Table 2. p-values returned by t-test comparing the performance of SMEA_clust with other MOO based clustering techniques over different data sets with respect to MS values

Data set	MOCK	VAMOSA	MEA_clust
AD_5_2	1.60815E-237	0.788494	5.34939E-153
AD_10_2	0	0	0.788494
Spherical_6_2	0.788494	0.788494	0.788494
Spherical_4_3	0.788494	0.788494	0.788494
Iris	1.12289E-255	8.12717E-215	2.53903E-51
Newthyroid	6.77E-04	0	2.73576E-21
Wine	0	0	2.73576E-21
LiverDisorder	0.788494	0.788494	0.788494

Results on Real-life Data Sets: As can be seen from Table 1, for LiveDisorder data set, VAMOSA, MEA_clust and SMEA_clust are able to determine the exact number of clusters as well as attain the same MS values. But, for other data sets, Iris, Newthyroid and Wine, our proposed algorithm performs better than other clustering techniques.

Statistical Test: To further establish the superiority of our proposed clustering algorithm, here we have conducted some statistical tests guided by [16]. Statistical t-test which provides some p-value is conducted to check whether the improvements obtained by the proposed SMEA_clust are significant or not. Minimum p-value implies that the proposed clustering algorithm is better than others. The obtained p-values (reported in Table 2) evidently support the results of Table 1.

4   Conclusions and Future Works

In the current study we have developed a new automatic multi-objective clustering approach utilizing the search capability of differential evolution. The current algorithm is a hybridization of DE and SOM where the neighborhood information identified by SOM trained on the current population of solutions is utilized for generating the mating pool which can further take part in genetic operations. The use of SOM at new solution generation helps the proposed clustering algorithm to better explore the search space of optimal partitioning. The potency of the proposed clustering technique is shown in automatically partitioning several artificial and real-life data sets of varying complexities. Results are compared with those obtained by a simple multi-objective DE based clustering technique as well as by several popular MOO based clustering techniques and it was found that the proposed approach converges faster compared to other MOO based clustering techniques.

As a future work, we would like to test the proposed approach for solving some real-life problems like text-summarization, search result clustering etc.

References

1. Jain, A.K., Dubes, R.C.: Algorithms for Clustering Data. Prentice-Hall Inc., Upper Saddle River (1988)
2. Maulik, U., Bandyopadhyay, S.: Performance evaluation of some clustering algorithms and validity indices. IEEE Trans. Pattern Anal. Mach. Intell. **24**(12), 1650–1654 (2002)
3. Bandyopadhyay, S., Saha, S., Maulik, U., Deb, K.: A simulated annealing-based multiobjective optimization algorithm: AMOSA. IEEE Trans. Evol. Comput. **12**(3), 269–283 (2008)
4. Deb, K.: Multi-objective Optimization Using Evolutionary Algorithms. Wiley, New York (2005)
5. Bandyopadhyay, S., Maulik, U.: Nonparametric genetic clustering: comparison of validity indices. IEEE Trans. Syst. Man Cybern. Part C (Applications and Reviews) **31**(1), 120–125 (2001)
6. Konak, A., Coit, D.W., Smith, A.E.: Multi-objective optimization using genetic algorithms: a tutorial. Reliab. Eng. Syst. Saf. **91**(9), 992–1007 (2006)
7. Suresh, K., Kundu, D., Ghosh, S., Das, S., Abraham, A.: Data clustering using multi-objective differential evolution algorithms. Fund. Inform. **97**(4), 381–403 (2009)

8. Kennedy, J.: Encyclopedia of machine learning. In: Saul, L., Fu, M.C. (eds.) Particle Swarm Optimization, pp. 760–766. Springer, New York (2011). doi:10.1007/978-1-4419-1153-7_200581

9. Handl, J., Knowles, J.: An evolutionary approach to multiobjective clustering. IEEE Trans. Evol. Comput. **11**(1), 56–76 (2007)

10. Saha, S., Bandyopadhyay, S.: A symmetry based multiobjective clustering technique for automatic evolution of clusters. Pattern Recogn. **43**(3), 738–751 (2010)

11. Saha, S., Bandyopadhyay, S.: A generalized automatic clustering algorithm in a multiobjective framework. Appl. Soft Comput. **13**(1), 89–108 (2013)

12. Kohonen, T.: The self-organizing map. Neurocomputing **21**(1), 1–6 (1998)

13. Zhang, H., Zhang, X., Gao, X.Z., Song, S.: Self-organizing multiobjective optimization based on decomposition with neighborhood ensemble. Neurocomputing **173**, 1868–1884 (2016)

14. Zhang, H., Zhou, A., Song, S., Zhang, Q., Gao, X.Z., Zhang, J.: A self-organizing multiobjective evolutionary algorithm. IEEE Trans. Evol. Comput. **20**(5), 792–806 (2016)

15. Pakhira, M.K., Bandyopadhyay, S., Maulik, U.: Validity index for crisp and fuzzy clusters. Pattern Recogn. **37**(3), 487–501 (2004)

16. Demšar, J.: Statistical comparisons of classifiers over multiple data sets. J. Mach. Learn. Res. **7**(Jan), 1–30 (2006)

17. Haykin, S.S.: Neural Networks and Learning Machines, vol. 3. Pearson, Upper Saddle River, NJ, USA (2009)

18. Bandyopadhyay, S., Maulik, U.: Genetic clustering for automatic evolution of clusters and application to image classification. Pattern Recogn. **35**(6), 1197–1208 (2002)

19. Lichman, M.: UCI machine learning repository (2013)

A Genetic Programming Based ECOC Algorithm for Microarray Data Classification

HanRui Wang, KeSen Li, and KunHong Liu[✉]

Software School of Xiamen University, Xiamen 361005, China
{hrwang,kslee}@stu.xmu.edu.cn, lkhqz@xmu.edu.cn

Abstract. Microarray technology aims to discover the relationship between genes and cancers. But the analysis of multiclass microarray datasets is a difficult problem in considering the small sample size along with the class imbalance problem. In this paper, we propose a Genetic Programing (GP) based Error Correcting Output Codes (ECOC) algorithm to tackle this problem. In our GP framework, each individual represents a codematrix, and a legality checking mechanism is applied to avoid the production of illegal codematrices. So the algorithm evolves towards optimum ECOC codematrices. In experiments, our algorithm is compared with other methods based on four famous microarray datasets. Experimental results prove that our algorithm can achieve better results in most cases.

Keywords: Error Correcting Output Codes · Genetic programing · Codematrix

1 Introduction

Cancers pose great threats to human's life, but the development of microarray techniques makes it possible to diagnose cancers in the early stage based on gene expression levels, bringing the hope of saving millions of people's lives. Many researchers have been devoted to the discovery of relationship between genes and cancers [1]. However, as the number of tumor samples tends to be much smaller than the number of genes, microarray data is a typical "large p, small n" problem [2], resulting difficulties in finding effective approaches to further analysis. It is a harder problem for the case of multiclass classification because of the class imbalance problem and the data distribution overlapping among classes.

An effective solution for the multiclass classification problem is to break it down into several simpler binary classification problems. And the combination of all these problems produces a final solution for the original problem. Based on this strategy, many feasible frameworks had been put forward, and Error Correcting Output Codes (ECOC) [3, 4] is one of the most famous techniques among them. The codematrix employed in ECOC algorithm is vital to its performance. Assume the number of rows and columns are n and m respectively. Each row of the codematrix is a codeword, representing a class. Each column indicates a scheme to split original classes into different groups, employing m corresponding base classifiers. All base classifiers make decisions for an unknown

© Springer International Publishing AG 2017
D. Liu et al. (Eds.): ICONIP 2017, Part VI, LNCS 10639, pp. 683–691, 2017.
https://doi.org/10.1007/978-3-319-70136-3_72

sample, and the outputs form a vector. The sample is assigned to the class whose corresponding row get the highest similarity with the output vector.

ECOC has been applied successfully in different fields [5, 6], but it is still a great challenge to design a robust ECOC algorithm for complex datasets. Some researchers have proposed genetic algorithm (GA) based ECOC algorithms to improve the generalization ability utilizing its global search capabilities. For example, in [7] researchers use GA to search optimal feature subsets for each column in codematrices, so as to enhance the independence and accuracy of binary classifiers. Some GA based works are implemented by transferring a codematrix to a linear individual in GA.

On the contrary, we propose a Genetic Programming (GP) based framework for developing ECOC coding matrices because its individual in tree structure provides more potentials in exploring data sets. Since individuals in GP take form of syntax trees, GP can directly solve binary classification problem, and has been applied in various fields. In our algorithm, each individual represents an ECOC codematrix, and a legality checking process is used to correct illegal matrices. At the end of evolutionary process, optimal ECOC codematrices are produced with great classification capability for multiclass microarray datasets.

In this paper, a detailed description about our algorithm is given in Sect. 2. In Sect. 3, experiments are deployed to verify the discriminant ability of our algorithm by comparing with other algorithms. And Sect. 4 concludes this paper.

2   The Algorithm of GP Based ECOC

2.1   The Design of Individual

GP is a well-known evolutionary algorithm. In the tree structure of its individual, a terminal node contains a primitive element, and a nonterminal node consists of an operator. By designing different operators and elements, for example, using important features as terminal nodes and arithmetic operators as nonterminal nodes, each individuals can act as a classification rule for a binary classification problem [8].

In our algorithm, each individual represents an ECOC codematrix. Each terminal node represents a class, and each nonterminal node represents the combination of a group of classes without duplicates. At the same time, a nonterminal node also represents a feature subset, filtered by a feature selection method.

An example is shown in Fig. 1(a), where the terminals are four classes, A, B, C and D. Nonterminal nodes represent different groups of classes, containing the classes passed by from their child nodes. Such an individual can directly be mapped as a coding matrix. Let the classes in the right/left child node be marked as $+1/-1$, and all absent or duplicated classes marked as 0, the individual in Fig. 1(a) is transferred into an ECOC codematrix, as shown in Fig. 1(b). And the black, white and grey cells color corresponds to $(+1, -1, 0)$. Besides, f1, f2, f3 marked in the nodes (d1, d2, d3, d4) represent three feature selection methods used in the four binary class problems. For example, for the first column represented by d1, only the subset obtained by f1 method is used. In this way, an individual can search for an optimal feature subset for each binary classification problem in the evolutionary process.

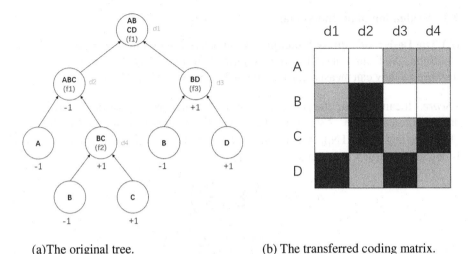

(a)The original tree.   (b) The transferred coding matrix.

Fig. 1. An example individual and the corresponding codematrix.

2.2 The Iteration Process of GP

(A) The GP Framework. The general settings for GP are adapted in our framework. That is, the first generation is randomly produced by the ramped half-and-half scheme. The crossover operator is the simple swapping operator, which swaps two subtrees from two parents randomly. And the mutation operator is the single mutation operator, replacing a subtree in the parents with a random subtree according to the mutation rate. Once the crossover and mutation process are completed, a new population is generated.

However, because each tree represents an ECOC coding matrix, and in the process of random initialization, crossover and mutation operation, some individuals would unavoidably conflict with the essential rules for ECOC codematrix generation. So the legality checking process is carried to guarantee only producing legal individuals. And the illegal individuals are re-built randomly so as to simplify our discussion.

(B) The Legality Checking Process. Legality checking process aims to covert illegal individuals to complying with the following six rules [7]. That is: For columns: (1) Any two columns could not be the same except they own different feature selection methods; (2) Any two columns could not be the opposite except they own different feature selection methods; (3) Each column should contain both 1 and −1 at the same time; (4) The number of columns m could not be greater than $2 \times n$ (n is the number of classes) [9]. For rows: (5) Any two rows could not be the same; (6) Each row's codeword could not only consist of 0. All these rules are used in validating the codematrices.

2.3   Evaluation of an Individual

(A) The Design of Fitness Function. An effective fitness function is key to our GP algorithm. And our fitness function is formed by two parts, Fscore and hamming distance, as they can measure each individual from two different aspects.

FScore. It can evaluate the performance of codematrix by considering the imbalance among different classes. Assume for the i-th class, measures are named as true positives (TP_i), true negatives (TN_i), false positives (FP_i) and false negatives (FN_i), then Fscore is defined as follows (β is generally set to 1):

$$recall = avg\left(\sum_{i=1}^{n} \frac{TP_i}{P_i}\right) \tag{1}$$

$$precision = avg\left(\sum_{i=1}^{n} \frac{TP_i}{TP_i + FP_i}\right) \tag{2}$$

$$Fscore = avg\left(\sum_{i=1}^{n} \frac{(\beta^2 + 1) * precision_i * recall_i}{\beta^2 * precision_i + recall_i}\right) \tag{3}$$

Average Hamming Distance. We define a new way to measure the Average Hamming Distance (AHD) of a codematrix. Assume d_{ij} be the hamming distance between the ith and j^{th} row, then AHD is calculated as follows:

$$C_n^2 = \frac{n!}{2!(n-2)!} \tag{4}$$

$$AHD = \frac{\sum_{i=1}^{n} \sum_{j=1}^{n} d_{ij}}{C_n^2 * m} \tag{5}$$

Here, both the value of AHD and Fscore range from 0 to 1, and the multiplication of Fscore and AHD is used as the fitness value for each individual, as shown in formula (6). In this way, GP evolves towards the exploration of accurate and diverse solutions with compact size.

$$Fitness = Fscore * AHD \tag{6}$$

(B) The Training Process of Multiclass Problems. *Feature Selection.* Feature selection process is of vital importance, because only genes with biological significance can provide enough information for classification in microarray dataset. As different feature selection methods are proposed based on different assumptions, we apply F-Test, Random Forest, SVM-REF and BSSWSS methods with keeping top 75 features respectively. Three-fold cross validation is applied, and the average value of three folds is used as the final fitness value for each individual.

Decoding Process. An ECOC algorithm tries to assign each unknown sample to a class according to the distance between each output vector and each row in the codematrix in the decoding process. In our algorithm, a distance measure, named as Corrected Euclidean Distance (*CED*), is used for distance evaluation. To the best of our knowledge, it is the first time this measure is proposed. Let *score* be the output vector of a sample, and *codeword$_i$* be the ith row in the codematrix. Then the *CED* between *score* and *codeword$_i$* is described as formula (7).

$$CED\left(score, codeword_i\right) = \sqrt{\frac{\sum_{j=1}^{m} \left|codeword_{ij}\right|\left(score_j - codeword_{ij}\right)^2}{\sum_{k=1}^{m} \left|codeword_{ik}\right|}} \tag{7}$$

where $\sum_{k=1}^{m}\left|codeword_{ik}\right|$ represents the length of nonzero codes in *codeword$_i$*. The decoding process use *CED* to assign the sample to a class obtaining the minimum *CED* value.

3   Experimental Results and Analysis

In our experiments, One-VS-One(OVO) and One-VS-All(OVA) are used for comparisons. Base classifier *KNN*(*k* = 3), OVO, OVA, and all feature selection methods are provided by Scikit-learn package. GP is based on the Pyevolve library(0.6rc1) [10]. The mutation rate and crossover rate are set to 0.25 and 1 respectively. As the maximum depth of the tree limits the number of nonterminal node, it is set to allows $2 \times n$ base classifiers at most by referring to the setting of ECOC-ONE [9], which can be calculated by (8). And default settings are deployed for all other required parameters.

$$depth_{max} = ceil\left(\log_2\left(2 \times N\right)\right) \tag{8}$$

3.1   Descriptions of Datasets

Five multiclass microarray datasets Cancers, Breast, DLBCL, Lung and SRBCT are used in our experiments. The detailed information is illustrated in Table 1. Before training, each feature is standardized to zero mean and unit variance, as described in [11].

Table 1. The information of multiclass microarray datasets used in experiments

Dataset	No. of classes	No. of genes	No. of training/test	Reference
Cancers	11	12533	100/74	[12]
Breast	5	9216	54/30	[13]
DLBCL	6	4026	58/30	[14]
Lung	5	5543	136/67	[15]
SRBCT	4	2308	63/20	[16]

3.2   Analysis of Evolutionary Process

Because the fitness value can't reflect the performance, the average class accuracy is used to judge the merits of our results, as shown in formula (9).

$$Accuracy = \frac{\sum_{i=1}^{n} TP_i}{\sum_{i=1}^{n} (TP_i + TN_i + FP_i + FN_i)} \tag{9}$$

Figure 2 illustrated the changes of best individuals from the first generation to the 100th on the Cancers dataset. TrainAccuracy/TestAccuracy is calculated using three-fold validation method based on training/test samples. And Columns means the ratio of required base classifiers by the best codematrix over those of OVO method. It is clear that Fitness, Accuracy, AHD increase continuously from 1st generation to 30th generation, which proves the evolutionary power of GP. And then they leveled off till the end because they reach an optimal value. Whereas, at the same time, it is obvious that our algorithm requires much fewer leaners than OVO. And in the evolution process, our algorithm can produce more effective results at lower and lower cost.

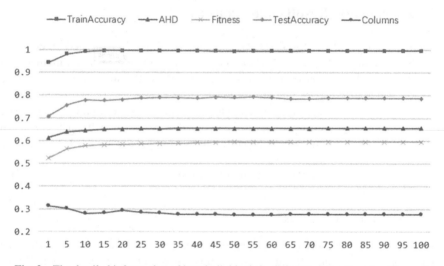

Fig. 2. The detailed information of best individuals in different generations (on Cancers)

Figure 3 shows the performances of our GP algorithm for these five datasets in different generation. It can be seen that the results are stable during 30 generations to 80 generations and some dataset even can reach an excellent accuracy such as Leukemia2 and DLBCL (0.99 for average, 1.00 for best). Moreover, it can be found that the performance of 50th generation is the best and stable relatively among all generations. Therefore, the number of generations in GP is set to 50 in our experiment.

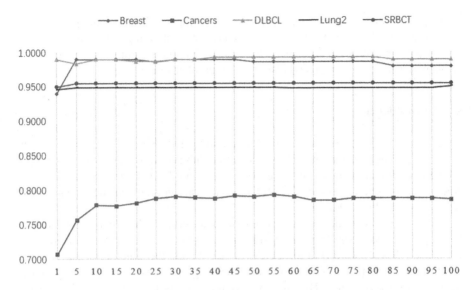

Fig. 3. The average accuracy of best individuals in different generations

3.3 Comparisons of GP with Other Methods

To reduce the influence of randomness on the result in each experiment, we run our algorithm for 10 rounds, and the best and average values are for each dataset. However, OVO and OVA are data independent coding strategies, so the results are constant for each feature selection method. To make fair comparisons among OVO, OVA and GP-ECOC, the best and average accuracy of four feature selection method are taken as the result of OVO and OVA.

As is shown in Table 2, for the best case, our algorithm can always get the highest results in SRBCT, Breast, DLBCL and Lung. In Cancers, it gets a second highest result, but it is much higher than OVO and OVA in average case (about 6 to 10% higher). In other datasets, our algorithm also has a great performance in average case. For example, the results in SRBCT, Breast and DLBCL are higher than OVO and OVA of about 2 to 4%, and it even reaches to 0.993 in DLBCL. In Lung, it is just a little lower than OVO and OVA (just 0.003), but it is obviously higher than OVO and OVA in the best case.

Table 2. The performance of GP, OVO and OVA

	Best case			Average case		
	OVA	OVO	GP	OVA	OVO	GP
SRBCT	0.950	0.950	**1.000**	0.925	0.938	**0.955**
Breast	**1.000**	**1.000**	**1.000**	0.858	0.875	**0.990**
DLBCL	**1.000**	**1.000**	**1.000**	0.958	0.958	**0.993**
Lung	0.955	0.955	**0.970**	**0.952**	**0.952**	0.949
Cancers	**0.851**	0.811	0.838	0.726	0.696	**0.792**

In general, we can safely conclude that our algorithm can lead to better performance compared with OVA and OVO. Overall, GP can always get the highest or second highest results in either average or best case, which means that this algorithm leads to good and stable performances in multiclass classification problems in most cases.

4   Conclusion

In this paper, we propose a Genetic Programming based ECOC algorithm. In this schema, each individual represents a codematrix with classifying different binary class problem in different feature subspace, which maintain diversity among codematrices. And the legality checking process is implemented to pick up all illegal individuals, which are re-produced by random settings.

In our experiment, the results in an evolutionary process show that the individuals become better and better. And our algorithm achieves better performance compared with OVO and OVA algorithms in most cases. What's more, the structure of our GP individual promises potential power for more complex problem as more information could be inject into the structure. Therefore, we would try to further improve the framework of the GP based ECOC algorithm, which is our future research direction.

Acknowledgment. This work is supported by National Key Technology Research and Development Program of the Ministry of Science and Technology of China (2015BAH55F05), and Natural Science Foundation of Fujian Province (No. 2016J01320), and XMU Training Program of Innovation and Enterpreneurship for Undergraduates (No. 2017X0331).

References

1. Jhajharia, S., Varshney, H.K., Verma, S., Kumar, R.: A neural network based breast cancer prognosis model with PCA processed features. In: 2016 International Conference on Advances in Computing, Communications and Informatics (ICACCI), pp. 1896–1901 (2016)
2. West, M.: Bayesian factor regression models in the "Large p, Small n" paradigm. Bayesian Stat. **7**, 733–742 (2003)
3. Allwein, E.L., Schapire, R.E., Singer, Y.: Reducing multiclass to binary: a unifying approach for margin classifiers. J. Mach. Learn. Res. **1**(2), 113–141 (2001)
4. Dietterich, T.G., Bakiri, G.: Solving multiclass learning problems via error-correcting output codes. J. Artif. Intell. Res. **2**, 263–286 (1995)
5. David, A., Lerner, B.: Support vector machine-based image classification for genetic syndrome diagnosis. Pattern Recogn. Lett. **26**(8), 1029–1038 (2005)
6. Kittler, J., Ghaderi, R., Windeatt, T., Matas, J.: Face verification via error correcting output codes. Image Vis. Comput. **21**(13), 1163–1169 (2003)
7. Bagheri, M.A., Gao, Q.G., Escalera, S.: A genetic-based subspace analysis method for improving Error-Correcting Output Coding. Pattern Recogn. **46**(10), 2830–2839 (2013)
8. Liu, K.-H., Xu, C.-G.: A genetic programming-based approach to the classification of multiclass microarray datasets. Bioinformatics **25**(3), 331–337 (2009)
9. Escalera, S., Pujol, O., Radeva, P.: ECOC-ONE: a novel coding and decoding strategy. In: 18th International Conference on Pattern Recognition, vol. 3, pp. 578–581 (2006)

10. Perone, C.S.: Pyevolve: a Python open-source framework for genetic algorithms. ACM SIGEVOlution **4**(1), 12–20 (2009)
11. Tong, M., Liu, K.-H., Xu, C., Ju, W.: An ensemble of SVM classifiers based on gene pairs. Comput. Biol. Med. **43**(6), 729–737 (2013)
12. Su, A.I., Welsh, J.B., Sapinoso, L.M., Kern, S.G., Dimitrov, P., Lapp, H., Schultz, P.G., Powell, S.M., Moskaluk, C.A., Frierson, H.F., Hampton, G.M.: Molecular classification of human carcinomas by use of gene expression signatures. Can. Res. **61**(20), 7388–7393 (2001)
13. Armstrong, S.A., Staunton, J.E., Silverman, L.B., Pieters, R., den Boer, M.L., Minden, M.D., Sallan, S.E., Lander, E.S., Golub, T.R., Korsmeyer, S.J.: MLL translocations specify a distinct gene expression profile that distinguishes a unique leukemia. Nat. Genet. **30**(1), 41 (2002)
14. Shipp, M.A., Ross, K.N., Tamayo, P., Weng, A.P., Kutok, J.L., Aguiar, R.C.T., Gaasenbeek, M., Angelo, M., Reich, M., Pinkus, G.S., Ray, T.S., Koval, M.A., Last, K.W., Norton, A., Lister, T.A., Mesirov, J., Neuberg, D.S., Lander, E.S., Aster, J.C., Golub, T.R.: Diffuse large B-cell lymphoma outcome prediction by gene-expression profiling and supervised machine learning. Nat. Med. **8**(1), 68–74 (2002)
15. Hong, Z.Q., Yang, J.Y.: Optimal discriminant plane for a small number of samples and design method of classifier on the plane. Pattern Recogn. **24**(4), 317–324 (1991)
16. Khan, J., Wei, J.S., Ringner, M., Saal, L.H., Ladanyi, M., Westermann, F., Berthold, F., Schwab, M., Antonescu, C.R., Peterson, C., Meltzer, P.S.: Classification and diagnostic prediction of cancers using gene expression profiling and artificial neural networks. Nat. Med. **7**(6), 673–679 (2001)

Co-evolutionary Multi-task Learning for Modular Pattern Classification

Rohitash Chandra[(⊠)]

Centre for Translational Data Science, The University of Sydney,
Sydney, NSW 2006, Australia
rohitash.chandra@sydney.edu.au

Abstract. Modularity in the learning process is a means by which effective decision making can be maintained when some of the input features are missing. In this paper, co-evolutionary multi-task learning algorithm is used for pattern classification which is robust to situations when some input features are unavailable during the deployment stage of decision support or control systems. The main feature of the algorithm is the ability to make decisions with some degree of error given misinformation. The results show that the method produces results comparable to non-modular methods while having modular features for dynamic and robust pattern classification.

Keywords: Cooperative coevolution · Neuroevolution · Multi-task learning · Modular pattern classification

1 Introduction

In biological neural systems, due to a certain level of modularity in knowledge representation, the absence of a sensory input does not completely hinder the decision making process [9]. The knowledge perceived through different senses can be seen as a modular input to biological neural systems [13]. For instance, we can identify a person just by listening to their voice when we do not see their face given sudden darkness due to malfunction of light in a room. This is through the presence of modularity of knowledge representation in learning that gives effective decision making when some parts or input features are missing. Therefore, a person can make an identification through sense of hearing when visual signal is missing. We can identify a person or objects to a high degree of certainty given information from the sense of sight and auditory information. However, we do not have complete loss of sight or hearing when we close an eye or have difficulty with one ear. This is possible through modular knowledge representation in the human brain [16].

Modular neural networks have been motivated from repeating structures in nature. They were introduced for visual recognition tasks that were trained by genetic algorithms [12]. More recently, a modular neural network was presented where the performance and connection costs were optimised through neuro-evolution which achieved better performance when compared to fully connected

© Springer International Publishing AG 2017
D. Liu et al. (Eds.): ICONIP 2017, Part VI, LNCS 10639, pp. 692–701, 2017.
https://doi.org/10.1007/978-3-319-70136-3_73

neural networks [7] and had the feature to learn new tasks without forgetting old ones [9]. Developmental learning is an approach for learning new tasks with competence as they are encountered [10,14] which differs from conventional learning algorithms. The goal is not only concerned with building task specific knowledge and models, but to support the growth of learning for continuous development. Multi-task learning exploits knowledge learned from related tasks through shared knowledge representation [2]. This can motivate the development of learning algorithms that can feature robust decision making given sudden misinformation from the input feature space.

Neuro-evolution refers to the use of evolutionary algorithms for training neural networks [1]. Cooperative coevolution [18] has been a prominent methodology for neuro-evolution where the neural network is decomposed into modules [19] that are implemented as sub-populations. This is also known as cooperative neuro-evolution [3]. The features of multi-task and ensemble learning have been incorporated to develop co-evolutionary multi-task learning algorithm to address dynamic time series problems [4] and multi-step ahead prediction [5].

In this paper, co-evolutionary multi-task learning is used for modular pattern classification where a group of features are used as building blocks of knowledge. This tackles dynamic and modular pattern classification using notions from multi-task and developmental learning. The effectiveness of the method is demonstrated using benchmark classification datasets.

The rest of the paper is organised as follows. Section 2 gives details of proposed method and problem formulation while Sect. 3 presents the results and discussion. Section 4 concludes the paper with directions for future research.

2   Modular Pattern Classification

We give an overview for the motivation for modular pattern classification using the case for a robot navigation task as shown in Fig. 1. Consider a robot navigation problem that depends on input sensors that are controlled through a neural network [17]. In this case, if the robot is moving forward, the two front sensors (S1 and S2 in Fig. 1) contributes the most. The goal is to develop a dynamic control system that can withstand malfunction or misinformation from the sensors at certain time. Howsoever, in a conventional classification-based control system, this could pose a serious problem if there is a sudden disruption of information from sensors. Therefore, a dynamic and robust control is needed that can guide the robot further given sudden misinformation from the respective sensors.

2.1   Co-evolutionary Multi-task Learning

We present modular pattern classification from the perspective of data that can be decomposed as feature groups with overlapping features, known as subtasks. A feature group, X_m, is a subset of features. The subtasks $\Omega_1, \ldots, \Omega_m$ are defined as the union of selected feature groups $X_1, \ldots X_m$, for $m = 1, \ldots, M$, where M

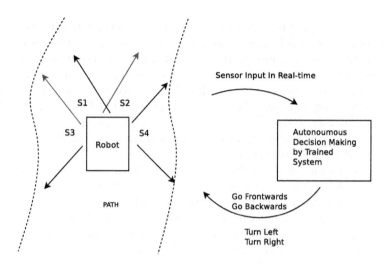

Fig. 1. Control problem for autonomous robots based on sensor input (S1, S2, S3, and S4). The decision making can be done through a control system that features modular pattern classification.

is the total number of feature groups, so that;

$$\Omega_1 = [X_1] \qquad (1)$$
$$\Omega_2 = [X_1, X_2]$$
$$\Omega_3 = [X_1, X_2, X_3]$$
$$\Omega_M = [X_1, X_2, ..., X_M]$$

In the example of the robot navigation problem in Fig. 1, the first feature group is defined to be $X_1 = \{S1, S2\}$ and the second to be $X_2 = \{S3, S4\}$. The overlapping subtasks are then $\Omega_1 = X_1$ and $\Omega_2 = \{X_1, X_2\}$. The input-hidden layer ω_m weights and the hidden-output layer υ_m weights are combined for the respective network module Φ_m as shown in Fig. 2. The base module is given as $\Phi_1 = [\omega_1, \upsilon_1]$. Let $\theta_1 = \Phi_1$ be the set of weights in the base network module Φ_1 which takes the features in Ω_1 as input. Note that the cascaded network module θ_m of subtask m is constructed by combining with current Φ_m and previous network module Φ_{m-1} as follows.

$$\Phi_1 = [\omega_1, \upsilon_1]; \quad \theta_1 = (\Phi_1)$$
$$\Phi_2 = [\omega_2, \upsilon_2]; \quad \theta_2 = [\theta_1, \Phi_2]$$
$$\vdots$$
$$\Phi_M = [\omega_M, \upsilon_M]; \quad \theta_M = [\theta_{M-1}, \Phi_M]$$

$$(2)$$

The list of network modules considered for training or optimisation is therefore $\mathbf{\Phi} = (\Phi_1, ..., \Phi_M)$.

Algorithm 1. Co-evolutionary multi-task learning

Data: Feature space X_m and response Y from data.
Result: Knowledge modules (weights) θ_m for the respective subtasks Ω_m.
initialization
for *each subtask Ω_m* **do**
    1. Define different sub-populations S_m using network module Φ_m

    2. Initialize the values in sub-populations S_m
end
while *each phase until termination* **do**
    for *each sub-population S_m* **do**
        for *each generation until depth β* **do**
            for *each i individual in sub-population $S_{m_{ij}}$* **do**
                for *each j in individual $S_{m_{ij}}$* **do**
                    Assign individual $V_m = S_{m_{ij}}$

                end
                if $m == 1$ **then**
                    1. $Z_m = [V_m]$
                    2. Fitness evaluation by encoding Z_m in cascaded network module θ_m given in Fig. 2

                end
                else
                    1. Append to best individual B_{m-1} of previous sub-population: $Z_m = [V_m, B_{m-1}]$
                    2. Fitness evaluation by encoding Z_m in cascaded network module θ_m given in Fig. 2

                end
            end
            for *each i individual in sub-population $S_{m_{ij}}$* **do**
                * Select and create new offspring via evolutionary operators:
                1. Selection, 2. Crossover, and 3. Mutation

            end
        end
    end
end
for *each subtask Ω_m* **do**
    1. Get best solution B_m from sub-population S_m
    2. Load test data for the respective cascaded network module θ_m
    3. Report classification performance for the subtask
end

The learning problem at hand is in optimising the respective knowledge modules for the given subtasks. Therefore, co-evolutionary multi-task learning (CMTL) initially proposed for dynamic time series is adapted for modular pattern classification [4]. The algorithm involves optimisation of sub-populations that feature a pool of solutions called individuals that consist of weights and biases for the respective modules. The decomposed modules in a cascaded network shown in Fig. 2 are implemented as sub-populations. Algorithm 1 gives further details of the co-evolutionary multi-task learning algorithm. Each sub-population is given as $S_1, S_2, ..S_N$, where N is number of sub-populations. The algorithm begins by creating sub-populations $S_{m_{ij}}$ that map the respective network modules Φ_m for optimisation. i refers to the individuals in the respective sub-population and j refers to each element in the individual. The algorithm initialises the sub-populations by drawing from uniform distribution $U(-\alpha, \alpha)$ where α defines the range. Afterwards, the algorithm moves into the evolution phase where each sub-population is evolved for a fixed number for generations defined by the depth of evolution β. Here, each individual from a sub-population is assigned to a vector $V_m = S_{m_{ij}}$, that is further concatenated by the best individual B_{m-1} from previous sub-population $Z_m = [V_m, B_{m-1}]$. Evaluation of Z_m is done by encoding it to the respective neural network module given the reference to the subtask m as shown in Fig. 2. Note that given base case (where $m == 1$), there is no concatenation from previous subtasks, therefore $Z_{m_j} = [V_{m_j}]$. Moving on, the loss is computed which is used as the fitness of the given individual. This is used further for creating new individuals with operators such as selection, crossover, and mutation that make the basis for co-evolutionary algorithms [6]. This procedure is done for every individual i in the sub-population, S_m. All the sub-populations are evaluated and evolved with evolutionary operators such as selection, crossover, and mutation. Note that a phase is complete when all the subtask modules have been evolved for n generations. This is repeated until the termination condition for evolution or optimisation is reached. The termination condition can be either the maximum number of function evaluations or a given fitness value (loss) from the training or validation dataset. Once the termination criteria has been reached, the algorithm moves into the testing phase where the best individuals from the respective sub-populations are mapped into the cascaded network. The classification performance for each subtask is then reported. The implementation code in Matlab has been given online[1].

3   Simulation and Analysis

In this section, CMTL is compared with conventional neuro-evolution methods such as cooperative neuro-evolution (CNE) and evolutionary algorithms (EA). The covariance matrix adaptation evolution strategies (CMAES) is used as the designated evolutionary algorithm in all the respective methods [11].

3.1   Experimental Design

The Wine, Iris, Ionosphere, Zoo, Cancer, Lenses problem are selected from the University of California, Irvine (UCI) Machine Learning Data repository [15].

---

[1] https://github.com/rohitash-chandra/CMTL-patternclassification.

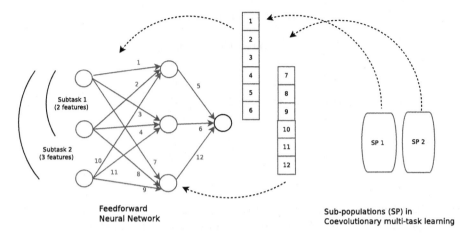

Fig. 2. This cascaded modular neural network which can also be viewed and implemented as an ensemble of neural networks. The colours associated with the synapses in the network are linked to their encoding that are given as different modules. Subtask 1 employs a network topology with 2 hidden neurons while the rest of the modules add extra input and hidden neurons. (Color figure online)

The subtasks in CMTL are defined by a set of features which must be defined beforehand. In these experiments, the features are selected consecutively in portions that are defined as follows. Subtask one Ω_1 contains first 50% of the features, while subtasks two and three (Ω_2 and Ω_3) contain 75% and 100%, respectively. Table 1 gives details of the respective problems used with details about the number of features, number of classes, and number of instances used. Sigmoid units in hidden and output layers are used for all the problems. The number of hidden neurons for foundation module that corresponds to Ω_1 is given by $\hat{h}$ in Table 1. The rest of hidden neurons in the respective network modules are incremented by $h_n = \hat{h} + h_{n-1} + \epsilon$, given that $h_1 = \hat{h}$. $\epsilon = 2$ is used in all the experiments. The termination condition is when a total of $120\,000 \times M$ function evaluations have been reached for the respective problems where M represents maximum number of subtasks. Note that all the sub-populations evolve for the same depth of search. The population size of the CMAES in all the respective methods is given by $P = 4 + floor(3 * log(\gamma))$, where γ is the total number of weights and biases in the cascaded network architecture. A fixed depth of evolution of 6 generations is used in CMTL that was obtained from trail experiments. Note that all the sub-populations in CMTL and CNE evolve for the same depth of search.

Table 2 shows the mean and confidence interval for classification performance given on the train and test datasets. A discussion is given about the comparison with non-modular pattern classification (EA and CNE) in terms of training and generalisation performance on the test dataset. The results show that the Ionosphere, Zoo and Cancer classification problems seem to have little effect on

Table 1. Configuration

Dataset	Features	Classes	Instances	$\hat{h}$
Wine	13	3	178	8
Iris	4	3	150	5
Ionosphere	34	2	351	8
Zoo	16	7	102	6
Cancer	9	2	699	6
Lenses	4	3	24	5

the performance of the different subtasks. This shows that the module from the first subtask Ω_1 contains all the relevant information to develop the basic knowledge modules where not much is addressed from the rest of the features. Hence, in a way, the rest of the features have little information for the classification problem and would be eliminated by feature selection algorithms. Moving on, for the rest of the problems, the knowledge from first subtask has been further improved by additional subtasks (Ω_2 and Ω_3) which is shown for the Wine, Iris and Lenses problems.

Overall, it is reasonable to compare Ω_3 with CNE and EA since they use all the features. Hence, Ω_3 gives the best generalisation (test) performance for Wine, Ionosphere, Zoo, and Lenses datasets. In the rest, i.e. Iris and Cancer datasets, CMTL performance is close to either CNE or EA. Note that in general, EA gives the weakest performance when compared to CNE and CMTL. Similar trend can also be observed for the training performance. Overall, the results show that CMTL can perform similar or better when compared to the non-modular pattern classification methods (EA and CNE).

Table 2. Comparison with related methods

Prob.		EA	CNE	Ω_1	Ω_2	Ω_3
Wine	Train	66.43 ± 10.10	75.00 ± 7.58	75.00 ± 5.66	87.33 ± 3.25	91.75 ± 2.19
	Test	74.92 ± 9.71	86.17 ± 3.55	74.88 ± 5.57	83.96 ± 4.54	93.99 ± 2.74
Iris	Train	69.79 ± 8.49	91.39 ± 2.91	54.83 ± 5.11	76.00 ± 4.17	88.17 ± 2.34
	Test	71.00 ± 8.08	90.00 ± 2.27	65.03 ± 3.88	78.36 ± 5.66	87.45 ± 5.02
Ionos.	Train	95.06 ± 0.60	90.44 ± 1.14	93.70 ± 0.52	94.74 ± 0.73	95.26 ± 0.73
	Test	94.65 ± 1.04	90.73 ± 1.80	98.23 ± 0.24	98.69 ± 0.23	99.01 ± 0.19
Zoo	Train	100.00 ± 0.00	100.00 ± 0.00	90.63 ± 0.00	90.31 ± 0.45	90.00 ± 0.45
	Test	90.42 ± 0.50	91.25 ± 0.80	100.00 ± 0.00	100.00 ± 0.00	100.00 ± 0.00
Cancer	Train	95.45 ± 0.29	91.60 ± 0.90	97.52 ± 0.13	97.83 ± 0.29	97.81 ± 0.33
	Test	97.13 ± 0.51	95.10 ± 0.63	95.30 ± 0.12	96.20 ± 0.23	96.41 ± 0.23
Lenses	Train	55.15 ± 3.62	52.62 ± 2.87	44.58 ± 9.37	39.58 ± 7.89	62.50 ± 6.43
	Test	67.67 ± 1.06	62.75 ± 2.26	2.92 ± 2.25	11.67 ± 4.65	79.17 ± 8.42

4   Discussion

The results have shown that the subtasks have important characteristics that contribute to overall decision making through the network modules. In some cases, the problem can be solved by the first subtask alone while in others, the other subtasks are needed. This highlights a further advantage of the proposed methodology which highlights strength or feature contribution during and at the end of the learning process. Apart from this, the main feature is the ability of the algorithm to make decision with some degree of error based on the base subtask in cases the features from the rest of the subtasks are missing.

CMTL differs from cooperative coevolutionary methods [3, 19] by the way the problem is decomposed and the way the fitness for each individual is calculated. In CMTL, the fitness of an individual from a sub-population generally depends on the knowledge from the modules. This is different for the case of cooperative coevolution as the fitness of an individual is calculated when it is concatenated with the best individuals from all the sub-populations. This difference makes CMTL particularly useful for developmental and multi-task learning.

The depth of evolution determines how much training is needed for the particular subtask before knowledge is utilised in the larger cascaded network module. Although a fixed depth of evolution was used for all the sub-populations, there needs to be an investigation between the depth of evolution and transfer of knowledge for different types of problems. Feature selection methods [8, 20] in a prior stage could help in depending better feature groups that consider inter-dependencies, relevance and importance for the constriction of various subtasks. This could be effective for real-world applications.

A limitation of the algorithm is timely convergence since it is based on neuro-evolution which is a black-box non-gradient based learning method. Hence, big data problems could not be considered in this work. Howsoever, there is scope for future work that will derive a gradient based learning method that will have much faster convergence.

5   Conclusions and Future Work

The application of co-evolutionary multi-task learning for modular pattern classification incorporated feature-based knowledge development. It provided information about contribution of the respective subtasks during and after the learning process. In results show that in some cases, the problem can be solved by the first subtask alone while in others, the other subtasks are needed. Moreover, the results comparable to non-modular methods while having modular features for dynamic and robust pattern classification. The main feature of the algorithm is the ability to make decisions with some degree of error given the base subtask is present and others are missing.

In future work, it would be worthwhile to study if and modular pattern classification can be a way for developing robust control systems. The proposed algorithm can be extended to datasets to address missing values or attributes in the test stage. Heterogeneous transfer learning that considers various streams of data is a major challenge of data science. This can be addressed by an extension of the proposed method where the modules identified could be seen as different sources of data with heterogeneous feature space. Moreover, development of gradient based learning can further speed up the learning process and the approach could be used for other neural network architectures such as recurrent neural networks.

References

1. Angeline, P., Saunders, G., Pollack, J.: An evolutionary algorithm that constructs recurrent neural networks. IEEE Trans. Neural Netw. **5**(1), 54–65 (1994)
2. Caruana, R.: Multitask learning. In: Thrun, S., Pratt, L. (eds.) Learning to Learn, pp. 95–133. Springer, Boston (1998)
3. Chandra, R., Frean, M., Zhang, M.: On the issue of separability for problem decomposition in cooperative neuro-evolution. Neurocomputing **87**, 33–40 (2012)
4. Chandra, R., Ong, Y.S., Goh, C.K.: Co-evolutionary multi-task learning for dynamic time series prediction. CoRR abs/1703.01887 (2017). http://arxiv.org/abs/1703.01887
5. Chandra, R., Ong, Y.S., Goh, C.K.: Co-evolutionary multi-task learning with predictive recurrence for multi-step chaotic time series prediction. Neurocomputing **243**, 21–34 (2017)
6. Chandra, R., Zhang, M.: Cooperative coevolution of Elman recurrent neural networks for chaotic time series prediction. Neurocomputing **186**, 116–123 (2012)
7. Clune, J., Mouret, J.B., Lipson, H.: The evolutionary origins of modularity. Proc. R. Soc. Lond. B Biol. Sci. **280**(1755), 20122863 (2013). doi:10.1098/rspb.2012.2863
8. Dash, M., Liu, H.: Feature selection for classification. Intell. Data Anal. **1**(3), 131–156 (1997)
9. Ellefsen, K.O., Mouret, J.B., Clune, J.: Neural modularity helps organisms evolve to learn new skills without forgetting old skills. PLoS Comput. Biol. **11**(4), 1–24 (2015)
10. Geschwind, N., Behan, P.: Left-handedness: association with immune disease, migraine, and developmental learning disorder. Proc. Natl. Acad. Sci. **79**(16), 5097–5100 (1982)
11. Hansen, N., Müller, S.D., Koumoutsakos, P.: Reducing the time complexity of the derandomized evolution strategy with covariance matrix adaptation (CMA-ES). Evol. Comput. **11**(1), 1–18 (2003)
12. Happel, B.L., Murre, J.M.: Design and evolution of modular neural network architectures. Neural Netw. **7**(6–7), 985–1004 (1994)
13. Johnson, M.K.: A multiple-entry, modular memory system. Psychol. Learn. Motiv. **17**, 81–123 (1983). Academic Press
14. Lee, M.H., Meng, Q., Chao, F.: Developmental learning for autonomous robots. Robot. Auton. Syst. **55**(9), 750–759 (2007)
15. Lichman, M.: UCI Machine Learning Repository. School of Information and Computer Science, University of California, Irvine (2013). http://archive.ics.uci.edu/ml
16. Meunier, D., Lambiotte, R., Bullmore, E.T.: Modular and hierarchically modular organization of brain networks. Front. Neurosci. **4**, 200 (2010). doi:10.3389/fnins.2010.00200

17. Miller, W.T.: Real-time application of neural networks for sensor-based control of robots with vision. IEEE Trans. Syst. Man Cybern. **19**(4), 825–831 (1989)
18. Potter, M.A., Jong, K.A.: A cooperative coevolutionary approach to function optimization. In: Davidor, Y., Schwefel, H.-P., Männer, R. (eds.) PPSN 1994. LNCS, vol. 866, pp. 249–257. Springer, Heidelberg (1994). doi:10.1007/3-540-58484-6_269
19. Potter, M.A., De Jong, K.A.: Cooperative coevolution: an architecture for evolving coadapted subcomponents. Evol. Comput. **8**(1), 1–29 (2000)
20. Saeys, Y., Inza, I., Larrañaga, P.: A review of feature selection techniques in bioinformatics. Bioinformatics **23**(19), 2507–2517 (2007)

CNN Based Transfer Learning for Scene Script Identification

Maroua Tounsi[1]([✉]), Ikram Moalla[1], Frank Lebourgeois[2], and Adel M. Alimi[1]

[1] REGIM-Laboratory: REsearch Groups in Intelligent Machines,
National Engineering School of Sfax (ENIS),
University of Sfax, BP 1173, 3038 Sfax, Tunisia
tounsi.maroua@ieee.org
[2] Laboratoire d'InfoRmatique en Images et Systmes d'information (LIRIS),
INSA of Lyon, Villeurbanne, France

Abstract. Identifying scripts in natural images is an important step in document analysis. Recently, Convolutional Neural Network (CNN) has achieved great success in image classification tasks, due to its strong capacity and invariance to translation and distortions. A problem with training a new CNN is that it requires a large amount of labelled images and extensive computation resources. Transfer learning from pre-trained models proves to ease the application of CNN and even boost the performance in some circumstances. In this paper, we use transfer learning and fine-tuning in document analysis. Indeed, we deal with the scene script identification quantitatively by comparing the performances of transfer learning and learning from scratch. We evaluate two CNN architectures trained on natural images: AlexNet and VGG-16. Experimental results on several benchmark datasets namely, SIW-13, MLe2e and CVSI2015, demonstrate that our approach outperforms previous approaches and full training.

Keywords: Transfer learning · Convolutional Neural Network · Deep learning · Script identification · Natural scenes

1 Introduction

Script identification is one of the key components in Optical Character Recognition (OCR), which has received much attention from the document analysis community. In multi-lingual and multi-script countries, the use of two or more scripts is quite common. So, as a first step of reading text in such images, we need to identify the script. In this area, script identification on documents [1] or videos, [2] is the focus of the community. In document script identification, many approaches have been proposed. A recent and detailed survey has been introduced in [3]. Contrary to the scanned and handwritten images, script identification in scene images is more challenging due to the huge variance in size, font, color, non-planar surface, perspective distortion, *etc.*

© Springer International Publishing AG 2017
D. Liu et al. (Eds.): ICONIP 2017, Part VI, LNCS 10639, pp. 702–711, 2017.
https://doi.org/10.1007/978-3-319-70136-3_74

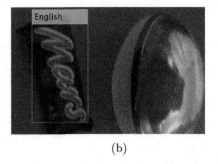

(a)   (b)

Fig. 1. End-to-end scene script identification of our method. In this work, we aim to localize the text and identify the script to facilitate the reading in scene images.

Most successful approaches for scene script identification include object recognition based methods. Using this approach means using methods for recognizing objects. The idea here is that text in natural scene is considered as object rather than text in documents (Fig. 1).

Recently, CNN has achieved great success in object Recognition, due to its strong capacity and invariance to translation and distortions [4,5]. A disadvantage of training a new CNN is that the training stage requires a large amount of labelled images and require extensive computation resources due to the estimation of millions of parameters. Although many deep neural networks are trained on natural images, features are learned hierarchically from the first layers to deeper layers.

On another hand, many recent works [6,7] have demonstrated that the intermediate activations learned with deep CNNs pre-trained on large datasets can be transferable to many other recognition problems with a few amount of training data.

Hence, our aim in this paper is to respond to this important question and which still remains unclear: Can we transfer the successfully pre-trained CNNs to address scene script identification, which is also a typical scene text recognition task with limited training data.

The main contributions of this paper are:

- We present a comparative study of various pre-trained CNN models and training CNN from sratch.
- We conduct a novel feature extraction method, where we encode the CNN activations from the convolutional layer to obtain image scene script.

The rest of the paper is organized as follows. Section 2 discusses related work and Sect. 3 presents a description of our method. Experimental results are then presented in Sect. 4. Concluding remarks and future work are finally presented in Sect. 5.

2   Related Work

2.1   CNN Based Transfer Learning

Transfer learning has been explored in many problems including generic object recognition [6,7], character recognition [8,9], medical image analysis [10–12]. Various studies have been interested on the adaptability of features and have demonstrated the success of transfer learning [7,13]. A popular strategy for transfer learning is fine-tuning, by training a linear classifier on top of the final layer of a CNN.

In [6], the authors described how they used the pre-training a CNN on ImageNet, and training a linear classifier on 3 target datasets (PASCAL VOC 2012, Caltech-101 and Caltech-256). They varied the target dataset size, as well as the layer from which the classifier is trained on and they proved the advantages of applying transfer learning. Using the same target datasets with transfer learning, good results were demonstrated in [14]. More precisely, in the document analysis domain, Cires et al. [9] demonstrate the efficiency of transfer learning for Printed Latin and Chinese characters by using Deep Neural Network (DNN) trained by Latin characters to initialize the weights of another DNN. In [8], the authors used a transfer learning method based on CNN for historical Chinese character recognition and achieved good results.

While this diversity of research proving the success of transfer learning on CNN in several domains, there is not any previous work that can prove the efficiency of transfer learning in scene text recognition domain especially for scene script identification task.

2.2   Scene Script Identification

There are many methods in the literature for scene script identification [15–20].

In 2015, the ICDAR Competition on Video Script Identification (CVSI-2015) [15] challenged the document analysis community with a new competitive benchmark dataset. In [20] the authors explored the use of Bag of Features(BoF) based techniques for word script identification in scene video text.

The most successful and recent methods are based on CNN [16,17,19,21,22]. While these methods achieve noticeable success on many benchmarks, they often require huge training data and computation resources.

3   Methodology

3.1   Transfer Learning

Transfer Learning is a technique in machine learning which consists on recycling the pre-trained model on large datasets to fit more specific data. This is done by refactoring a portion of the weights from the pre-trained model and reinitializing or altering weights at shallower layers.

3.2   Pre-trained Models

In this section, we briefly review some successful CNN architectures evaluated in our work.

3.2.1   AlexNet

The AlexNet architecture [4] outperforms the other non-deep learning methods for ImageNet Challenge in 2012. It contains 5 convolutional and pooling layers and 3 fully connected layers including local response normalization (ReLU) layers and dropouts.

3.2.2   VGG-16

Similar with AlexNet architecture, VGG-16 network has 13 convolutional layers followed by pooling and rectification layers, and 3 fully connected layers [23]. All convolutional layers use small 3 * 3 filters and the network performs only 2 * 2 pooling. VGG-16 has a receptive field of size 224 * 224. While VGG-16 outperforms the AlexNet, it has 3* more parameters which use more computation resources.

3.3   CNN Based Transfer Learning for Scene Script Identification

In this section, we illustrate in Fig. 2 the proposed scenario using transfer learning with CNN for generating global feature representations for scene script identification.

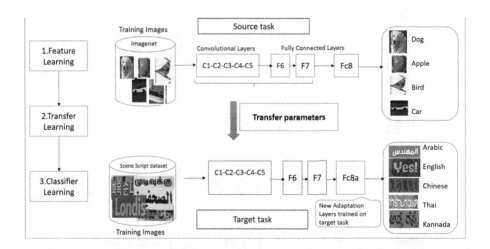

Fig. 2. Transferring parameters of CNN for scene script identification.

4   Experiments and Results

We evaluate our approach on common script identification dataset, including SIW-13 [16] and CVSI2015 [15] and MLe2e [21] which have standardized splits. We also compare our method with previous state-of-art methods on these datasets. We evaluate two CNN architectures trained on natural images: AlexNet and VGG-16.

4.1   Experimental Setup

In our experiments, all networks are fine-tuned using the minibatch stochastic gradient descent with a momentum factor of 0.9. Base learning rate is initialzed as 0.0001. Batch size is set to 80 images for AlexNet whereas VGG-16 and to 20 images for VGG-16 images. We resize all images to $227 * 227$ for AlexNet and to $224 * 224$ for VGG-16. We train Softmax on features from the last fully connected layer (fc8-2). All experiments are performed on a computer with i7-6700U (3.5 GHz), 16 GB RAM and NVIDIA GeFORCE GTX 950 M.

4.2   Datasets

4.2.1   SIW-13

The dataset contains a large number of cropped text images taken from natural scene images. As illustrated in Fig. 3a, SIW-13 dataset [16] contains text images from 13 different scripts: Arabic, Cambodian, Chinese, English, Greek, Hebrew, Japanese, Kannada, Korean, Mongolian, Russian, Thai and Tibetan.

4.2.2   MLe2e

The MLe2e was introduced in [21]. It has been harvested from various existing scene text datasets. It contains text images from different scripts namely, Latin, Chinese, Kannada and Hangul. Some examples of the collected dataset are shown in Fig. 3b.

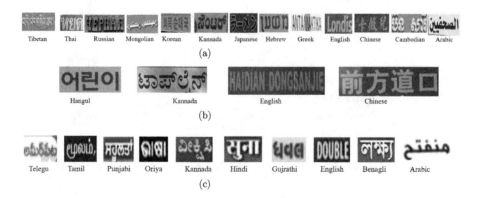

Fig. 3. Examples of cropped text images in the (a) SIW-13 dataset, (b) MLe2e dataset and (c) CVSI dataset.

4.2.3   CVSI

To prove the robustness of our method, we also evaluate our method on CVSI dataset which has been introduced in Video Script Identification Competition held at ICDAR 2015 [15]. The dataset contains images harvest from news videos. It contains text images from 10 scripts: English, Hindi, Bengali, Oriya, Gujarati, Punjabi, Kannada, Tamil, Telugu and Arabic. Some examples of the collected dataset are shown in Fig. 3c.

4.2.4   Experiments on SIW-13

In this section, we evaluate our method on SIW-13 dataset. As a comparison, we also show the results of the previous state-of-art. Compared to basic CNN trained from scratch, we attain an improvement about 1.1% on average using transfer learning with VGG-16 network. The best accuracy is achieved when fine-tuning with VGG-16 network. See Fig. 4 and Table 1 for final results.

Also, we vary the number of training images per class. The best accuracy is obtained with 600 training images (Fig. 5). Hence, we can see here that using transfer learning with a less amount of data, we achieved better results than previous works like in [16,19], in which the authors trained CNN from scratch.

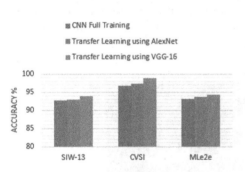

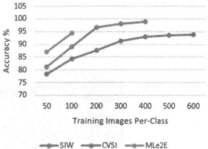

Fig. 4. Comparison of transfer learning with AlexNet, transfer learning with VGG-16, with and CNN full training.

Fig. 5. Varying the number of training images per class

As shown in the confusion matrix (Fig. 6), the performances of majority of these thirteen languages has been improved compared with state-of-the-art results. As shown in this confusion matrix the most obvious mistakes are the mis-classification between languages which share a subset of letters such as English, Russian and Greek.

4.2.5   Experiments on CVSI

We also evaluate our method on a common script identification dataset, namely CVSI215.

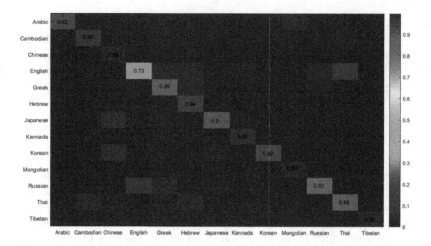

Fig. 6. Confusion Matrix on SIW-13 dataset.

Compared to basic CNN trained from scratch, we attain an improvement about 2.2% using transfer learning with VGG-16 network. See Fig. 4 and Table 1 for final results. The best accuracy is obtained with 400 training images (See Fig. 5). To study the script wise confusion we illustrate confusion matrix of our method for CVSI dataset in Fig. 7.

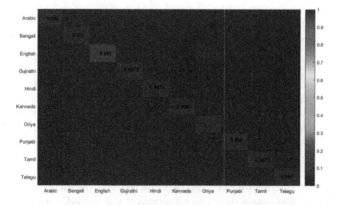

Fig. 7. Confusion Matrix on CVSI dataset.

4.2.6   Experiments on MLe2e

Experiments on MLe2e dataset also demonstrate that result are improved by 3.18% compared to previous works (See Table 1). The script wise confusion is illustrated in Fig. 8.

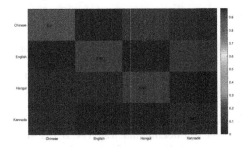

Fig. 8. Confusion Matrix on MLe2e dataset.

Table 1. The performance of our method compared to previously published results using other methods.

	SIW-13	MLe2e	CVSI
Shi et al. [16]	89.4	-	94.3
Hust [15,19]	88.4	-	96.69
Nicola [24]	83.7	-	98.18
Gomez et al. [21]	76.9	91.12	97.91
CVC-2 [15]	-	88.16	96.0
Sift + BoF + SVM	83.4	86.45	84.38
CNN	92.8	93.1	96.7
Proposed system	**93.9**	**94.3**	**98.9**

5   Conclusion

In this paper, we proposed and trained a new strategy for identifying scene script by exploring transfer learning from pre-trained models via fine-tuning. The obtained results demonstrate that transferring learning outperforms learning from scratch and it requires less training time and smaller amount of data. Besides, experimental results on several benchmark datasets demonstrate that our approach outperforms previous approaches. The best accuracy is achieved when fine-tuning with VGG-16 network.

In future studies, we aim to improve our strategies to encode the CNN features to improve the invariance of representations. We plan also to transfer CNN features to other scene text recognition, such as scene word spotting.

Acknowledgment. This work is performed in the framework of a thesis MOBIDOC financed by the EU under the program PASRI. The authors would like also to acknowledge the partial financial support of this work by grants from General Direction of Scientific Research (DGRT), Tunisia, under the ARUB program. The research leading to these results has received funding from the Ministry of Higher Education and Scientific Research of Tunisia under the grant agreement number LR11ES48.

References

1. Andrew, B., Wageeh, W., Sridha, S.: Texture for Script Identification. IEEE Trans. Pattern Anal. Mach. Intell. **27**(11), 1720–1732 (2005)
2. Palaiahnakote, S., Ze, H.Y., Danni, Z., Tong, L., Chew, L.T.: New gradient-spatial-structural features for video script identification. Comput. Vis. Image Underst. **130**, 35–53 (2015)
3. Ubul, K., Tursun, G., Aysa, A., Impedovo, D., Pirlo, G., Yibulayin, I.: Script identification of multi-script documents: a survey. IEEE Access **PP**(99), p. 1 (2017)
4. Alex, K., Ilya, S., Georey, E.H.: ImageNet classification with deep convolutional neural networks. In: Advances in Neural Information Processing Systems 25: 26th Annual Conference on Neural Information Processing Systems 2012. Proceedings of a Meeting Held 3–6 December 2012, Lake Tahoe, Nevada, United States, pp. 1106–1114 (2012)
5. Gil, L., Tal, H.: Age and gender classification using convolutional neural networks. In: 2015 IEEE Conference on Computer Vision and Pattern Recognition Workshops, CVPR Workshops 2012, Boston, MA, USA, 7–12 June, pp. 34–42 (2012)
6. Zeiler, M.D., Fergus, R.: Visualizing and understanding convolutional networks. In: Fleet, D., Pajdla, T., Schiele, B., Tuytelaars, T. (eds.) ECCV 2014. LNCS, vol. 8689, pp. 818–833. Springer, Cham (2014). doi:10.1007/978-3-319-10590-1_53
7. Maxime, O., Leon, B., Ivan, L., Josef, S.: Learning and transferring mid-level image representations using convolutional neural networks. In: 2014 IEEE Conference on Computer Vision and Pattern Recognition, CVPR 2014, Columbus, OH, USA, 23–28 June, pp. 1717–1724 (2014)
8. Dan, C.C., Ueli, M., Jurgen, S.: Transfer learning for Latin and Chinese characters with deep neural networks. In: The 2012 International Joint Conference on Neural Networks (IJCNN), Brisbane, Australia, 10–15 June, pp. 1–6 (2012)
9. Yejun T. Liangrui P., Qian X., Yanwei W., Akio F.: CNN based transfer learning for historical Chinese character recognition. In: 12th IAPR Workshop on Document Analysis Systems, DAS 2016, Santorini, Greece, 11–14 April, pp. 25–29 (2016)
10. Nima, T., Jae, Y.S., Suryakanth, R., Gurudu, R., Todd, H., Christopher, B.K., Michael, B.G., Jianming, L.: Convolutional neural networks for medical image analysis: full training or fine tuning? IEEE Trans. Med. Imaging **35**(5), 1299–1312 (2016)
11. Neslihan, B., Juho, K., Janne, H.: Human Epithelial Type 2 cell classification with convolutional neural networks. In: 15th IEEE International Conference on Bioinformatics and Bioengineering, BIBE, Belgrade, Serbia, 2–4 November, pp. 1–6 (2015)
12. Hoo, C.S., Holger, R.R., Mingchen, G., Le, L., Ziyue, X., Isabella, N., Jianhua, Y., Daniel, J.M., Ronald, M.S.: Deep convolutional neural networks for computer aided detection: CNN architectures, dataset characteristics and transfer learning. IEEE Trans. Med. Imaging **35**(5), 1285–1298 (2016)
13. Ross, B.G., Jeff, D., Trevor, D., Jitendra, M.: Rich feature hierarchies for accurate object detection and semantic segmentation. In: 2014 IEEE Conference on Computer Vision and Pattern Recognition, CVPR 2014, Columbus, OH, USA, 23–28 June, pp. 580–587 (2016)
14. Ali, S.R., Hossein, A., Josephine, S., Stefan, C.: CNN features off-the-shelf: an astounding baseline for recognition. In: IEEE Conference on Computer Vision and Pattern Recognition, CVPR Workshops 2014, Columbus, OH, USA, 23–28 June, pp. 512–519 (2014)

15. Nabin, S., Ranju, M., Rabi, S., Umapada, P., Michael, B.: ICDAR 2015 competition on video script identification (CVSI 2015). In: 13th International Conference on Document Analysis and Recognition, ICDAR 2015, Nancy, France, 23–26 August, pp. 1196–1200 (2015)
16. Shi, B., Cong, Y., Chengquan, Z., Xiaowei, G., Feiyue, H., Xiang, B.: Script identification in the wild via discriminative convolutional neural network. Pattern Recogn. **52**, 448–458 (2016)
17. Louis, G.B., Anguelos, N., Dimosthenis, K.: Boosting patch-based scene text script identification with ensembles of conjoined networks. CoRR abs/1602.07480. (2016)
18. Nabin, S., Sukalpa, C., Umapada, P., Michael, B.: Word-wise script identification from video frames. In: 2013 12th International Conference on Document Analysis and Recognition, Washington, DC, USA, 25–28 August 2013, pp. 867–871 (2013)
19. Baoguang, S., Cong, Y., Chengquan, Z., Xiaowei, G., Feiyue, H., Xiang, B.: Automatic script identification in the wild. In: 13th International Conference on Document Analysis and Recognition, ICDAR 2015, Nancy, France, 23–26 August 2015, pp. 531–535. (2013)
20. Nabin, S., Ranju, M., Rabi, S., Umapada, P., Michael, B.: Bag-of-Visual Words for word-wise video script identification: A study. In: 2015 International Joint Conference on Neural Networks, IJCNN 2015, Killarney, Ireland, 12–17 July 2015, pp. 1–7. (2015)
21. Lluis, G.B., Dimosthenis, K.: A fine-grained approach to scene text script identification. In: 12th IAPR Workshop on Document Analysis Systems, DAS 2016, Santorini, Greece, 11–14 April 2016, pp. 192–197 (2016)
22. Jieru, M., Luo, D., Baoguang, S., Xiang, B.: Scene text script identification with Convolutional Recurrent Neural Networks. In: 23rd International Conference on Pattern Recognition, ICPR 2016, Cancun, Mexico, 4–8 December 2016, pp. 4053–4058 (2016)
23. Karen, S., Andrew, Z.: Very Deep Convolutional Networks for Large-Scale Image Recognition. CoRR abs/1409.1556 (2014)
24. Nicolaou, A., Bagdanov, A.D., Louis, G., Karatzas, D.: Visual script and language identification. In: 2016 12th IAPR Workshop on Document Analysis Systems (DAS), pp. 393–398 (2016)

A Method of Pedestrian Re-identification Based on Multiple Saliency Features

Cailing Wang, Yechao Xu[($\boxtimes$)], Guangwei Gao, Song Tang,
and Xiaoyuan Jing

Nanjing University of Posts and Telecommunications,
Nanjing 210023, Jiangsu, China
xuyechao2014@outlook.com

Abstract. In the field of pedestrian re-identification, the appearance of pedestrians usually varies greatly in different cameras as the pedestrians in the sequences of surveillance video may be affected by the changes of the visual angles, the postures and the light. According to this, a method of pedestrian re-identification based on multiple salient features is proposed. The traditional method of pedestrian re-identification based on salient features characterizes the weight through the difference between different samples. However, the calculation result of the traditional way is not stable enough and may vary with the rich diversity of samples. Therefore, a method based on the cellular automata is used to calculate the inherently salient features of pedestrian images. In order to make full use of the advantages of the above methods, we introduce the multi-layer cellular automata to fuse them to achieve better results in the experiment. The experimental results show that the proposed algorithm has better performance on CAVIAR4REID and iLIDS databases than the existing algorithms.

Keywords: Pedestrian re-identification · Fusion of multiple salient features · Multi-layer cellular automata

1 Introduction

In the methods used by Bak et al. [1] and Schwartz et al. [2], all feature vectors of the pedestrian image to be matched have a consistent global weight at the time of matching. However, Liu et al. [3] firstly discussed the importance of different features under various situations. Experiments prove that not all the features are of the same importance to both cases of different pedestrians and the process of target recognition. Therefore, an algorithm based on the importance of vision has been proposed by some researchers in recent years. The literature [4] shows that some of the appearance features play a more important role in describing a particular target.

The method used by Gray et al. [5] and Tamar et al. [6] requires the use of a calibrated database for supervised learning and meanwhile collecting and marking large amounts of image data is a very heavy work. Zhao et al. [4] firstly proposed a method based on salient features to deal with this problem. This method characterizes the importance of sub-blocks according to the difference between sub-blocks and the

© Springer International Publishing AG 2017
D. Liu et al. (Eds.): ICONIP 2017, Part VI, LNCS 10639, pp. 712–721, 2017.
https://doi.org/10.1007/978-3-319-70136-3_75

matching blocks and similarity between two images is characterized by the grand total of the distance of all sub-blocks. But, there are some limitations in the method of calculating the salient features by using the difference of different samples, which are much more dependent on the training samples. The traditional fusion algorithm is often achieved by assigning different weights to the inter-class salient features and internal ones, but it is difficult to determine the appropriate proportions. In order to solve the above problems, we propose a multi-layer cellular automata saliency (MCAS) feature. By using the multi-layer cellular automata, inter-class salient features and internal salient features are fused together, and the ability to describe the image is further enhanced. Our main contribution is a method used to generate a special kind of feature representation (MCAS) by fusing inter-class salient features and internal salient features, which can efficiently improve the performance of the pedestrian re-identification algorithm.

2   Salient Features

2.1   Inter-class Salient Features

The method is divided into three steps: (1) Feature extraction. The algorithm Simple Linear Iterative Clustering (SLIC) is utilized to segment the image into several sub-blocks, then the features of color histogram and texture are extracted from each block. (2) Sub-block matching and (3) calculation of salient score will be discussed later.

Each image is equally divided into about 100 sub-blocks, and 3 * 3 * 32-dimensional color histograms and 64-dimensional SURF features are extracted from each sub-block. Thus each image is represented as a feature vector of 100 * (288 + 64) = 35200.

Sub-block matching. Suppose that $x_{m,n}^{A,p}$ represents the feature vector of each sub-block, (A, p) represents p-th image in camera A, (m, n) represents the location of the center of the sub-block, then the description of sub-blocks of m-th row of p-th image in camera A is:

$$T^{A,p}(m) = \{x_{m,n}^{A,p}|n = 1, 2, \cdots, N\}, \tag{1}$$

where N represents the total number of columns of the block. Considering that a small amount of jitter may occur in the vertical direction of blocks, the feature blocks within the distance d in vertical direction are added to the range of our searching:

$$\hat{S}\left(x_{m,n}^{A,p}, x^{B,q}\right) = \{T^{B,q}(b)|b = m - d, \cdots, m, \cdots, m+d\}, \tag{2}$$

where $m + d < M$, $m - d > 0$, m represents the number of the rows of the blocks. M represents the number of total rows of all feature blocks in the image and d represents the largest distance in the vertical direction during the search of neighborhood.

We use a simple nearest neighbor algorithm to search each feature sub-block of the image to be recognized in $T^{B,q}(m)$. Then, a most similar feature sub-block within the range of search is derived according to the Euclid Distance. To solve the problem of mistaken matching, we transform the problem of distance into a Gaussian function which can effectively suppress the influence that caused by individual sub-blocks to the result. Therefore, the similarity function of two feature sub-blocks is defined as:

$$s(x, y) = exp(-\frac{d(x, y)^2}{2\sigma^2}). \tag{3}$$

where $d(x, y) = ||x-y||_2$ represents the Euclidean Distance of two feature vectors, σ represents the bandwidth of the Gaussian function.

As shown in Fig. 1, (a) is the image to be tested, and four red boxes in this figure indicate the feature blocks of (a). (b) is the result of the neighborhood search of the feature blocks in various target images (the top five).

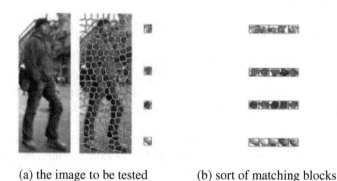

(a) the image to be tested   (b) sort of matching blocks

Fig. 1. Search of neighborhood (Color figure online)

Calculation of salient score. Each of the feature blocks in the image to be recognized captured by camera A has a corresponding matching block in each of the images obtained by camera B. Assuming that there were N_r pedestrian images obtained by camera B, then there are also N_r matching blocks for the sub-blocks to be measured $x_{m,n}^{A,p}$.

$$X_{nn}\left(x_{m,n}^{A,p}\right) = \left\{x \Big| \arg\max_{\hat{x} \in \hat{S}_{p,q}} x = s\left(x_{m,n}^{A,p}, \hat{x}\right), q = 1, 2, \cdots, N_r\right\} \quad \hat{S}_{p,q} = \hat{S}(x_{m,n}^{A,p}, x^{B,q}). \tag{4}$$

The score of saliency of $x_{m,n}^{A,p}$ can be expressed as:

$$score\left(x_{m,n}^{A,p}\right) = D_k(X_{nn}(x_{m,n}^{A,p})), \tag{5}$$

where D_k represents the distance of k-th nearest neighbor. If the test set can well reflect the distribution of the target image, then to a feature block, only part of the corresponding matching blocks in the target image are salient ($k = \alpha N_r$). Assuming that the number of pedestrians with this characteristic in the target image exceeds half of all the pedestrians, then the value k in the experiment can be set to $N_r/2$.

The probability of a feature block in the image being salient is calculated as:

$$P\left(l_{m,n}^{A,u} = 1 \mid x_{m,n}^{A,u}\right) = 1 - exp(-score(x_{m,n}^{A,u})^2 / \sigma_0^2). \tag{6}$$

2.2 Internal Salient Feature

In this paper, a method of single-layer cellular automata was used to characterize the internal salient features [7]. A color distance matrix and a spatial distance matrix are combined to obtain the map of i-th super pixel block that based on the background.

$$S_i^{bg} = \sum_{k=1}^{K} w_{k,i} \times s_{k,i}, \tag{7}$$

where k is the number of initial clustering centers, $w_{k,i}$ is the spatial distance between all super pixels within the interior of k-th cluster and super pixel block i, $s_{k,i}$ represents the salient value of block i reference to k-th global color difference (GCD) map.

Each block of super pixel in a pedestrian image represents a cell. The next state of the super pixel is determined by its own state and the state of the neighbor block. Neighbors with similar color features have a greater impact on the next state of the block. The similarity of all super pixel pairs is measured by the distance defined by the CIELAB color space. We define the influence factor f_{ij} of the super pixel pair i and j to construct the influence factor matrix $F = [f_{ij}]_{N*N}$.

$$f_{ij} = \left\{ \begin{array}{c} exp\left(\frac{\|c_i, c_j\|}{\sigma_3^2}\right), j \in NB(i) \\ 0, i = j \, or \, others \end{array} \right\}, \tag{8}$$

where $\|c_i, c_j\|$ represents the Euclidean Distance between the super pixel blocks i and j in CIELAB space. σ_3 is the parameter used to adjust the degree of similarity (by default, $\sigma_3^2 = 0.1$), NB (i) is the collection of the neighbor of cell i.

We establish a coherent matrix $C = diag\{c1, c2, \cdots, cN\}$ to better promote the evolution. The coherence of each super pixel block is calculated as follows:

$$c_i = \frac{1}{max(f_{ij})}, \tag{9}$$

In order to ensure that the range of ci is $[b, a + b]$, the coherence matrix $C^* = diag$ $\{c1^*, c2^*, \cdots, cN^*\}$ can be calculated by the following formula:

$$c_i = \frac{c_j - min(c_j)}{max(c_j) - min(c_j)} + b, \tag{10}$$

where $j = 1, \cdots, N$, $a = 0.6$, $b = 0.2$. If a is fixed at 0.6, b will be at the range [0.1, 0.3].

All units update their states based on the updating rules synchronously. Known as impact factor matrix and coherence matrix, the updating rule $S^{NB} \rightarrow S$ is:

$$S^{t+1} = C^* \cdot S^t + (I - C^*) \cdot F^* \cdot S^t. \tag{11}$$

where I represents the identity matrix, C^* and F^* respectively represent the coherence matrix and the influence factor matrix. When $t = 0$, the initial matrix S^t is S^{bg} in Eq. (7), and after NI time step (one time step is defined as the iteration of all cells iterations), the final super pixel block saliency map can be denoted as S^{NI}.

3   Fusion of the Inter-class Salient Feature and the Internal Salient Feature

In a multi-layer cellular automata (MCA), each cell represents a pixel and neighbors are pixels located in different layers but with the same coordinates. S_i represents the probability of it belonging to foreground F, denoted as $P(i \in F) = S_i$, and $1 - S_i$ represents its probability of belonging to background B, denoted as $P(i \in B) = 1 - S_i$. We usually use the adaptive thresholds generated by the OTSU method [8] to binarize each layer. The threshold for the m-th salient map is expressed as γ_m.

If pixel i is classified as foreground after segmentation, it can be expressed as $\eta_i = +1$, and in contrast $\eta_i = -1$. If pixel i belongs to the foreground, the probability its neighbor pixel j being foreground is $\lambda = P(\eta_j = +1|i \in F)$. Correspondingly, $\mu = P(\eta_j = -1|i \in B)$ represents the probability j belonging to the background under the same conditions (λ, μ are constant values). The posterior probability $P(i \in F|\eta_j = +1)$ is:

$$P(i \in F|\eta_j = +1) \propto P(i \in F)P(\eta_j = +1|i \in F) = S_i \cdot \lambda. \tag{12}$$

In order to eliminate the normalized constant, the priori ratio $\Lambda(i \in F)$ is defined as

$$\Lambda(i \in F) = \frac{P(i \in F)}{P(i \in B)} = \frac{S_i}{1 - S_i}, \tag{13}$$

The posteriori ratio $\Lambda(i \in F|\eta_j = +1)$ can be expressed as,

$$\Lambda(i \in F|\eta_j = +1) = \frac{P(i \in F|\eta_j = +1)}{P(i \in B|\eta_j = +1)} = \frac{S_i}{1 - S_i} \cdot \frac{\lambda}{1 - \mu}, \tag{14}$$

$\Lambda(i \in F)$ and $\Lambda(i \in F | \eta_j = +1)$ may also be defined as,

$$\Lambda(i \in F) = \frac{S_i^t}{1 - S_i^t}, \Lambda(i \in F | \eta_j = +1) = \frac{S_i^{t+1}}{1 - S_i^{t+1}}, \tag{15}$$

where S_i^t represents the salient value of pixel i at time t. The logarithmic representation and definition of the synchronous update rule $f : S^{M-1} \to S$ is

$$l(S_m^{t+1}) = l(S_m^t) + \sum_{k=1; k \neq m}^{m} sign(S_k^t - \gamma_k \cdot I) \cdot ln(\frac{\lambda}{1 - \lambda}), \tag{16}$$

where $S_m^t = [S_{m1}^t \ S_{m2}^t]^T$ represents the salient value of all cells at time k, and the matrix I has H elements ($I = [1, 1, \ldots, 1]^T$). Obviously, if a larger salient value is given to a neighbor of a pixel, the salient value of this pixel should also increase. Therefore, the above equation requires $\lambda > 0.5$, $ln (\lambda/(1 - \lambda)) > 0$. Let $ln (\lambda/(1 - \lambda)) = 0.15$, after N_2 iterations, the final comprehensive salient map S^{N_2} can be expressed as

$$S^{N_2} = \frac{1}{M} \sum_{m=1}^{M} S_m^{N_2}, \tag{17}$$

The fusion of two salient features can be expressed as

$$S_{MCA}^{N_2} = \frac{1}{2} \sum_{m=1}^{2} S_m^{N_2}. \tag{18}$$

where $S1 = Sal_{knn}$ (inter-class saliency score), $S_2 = S_{SCA}$ (internal saliency score).

4 Experimental Results and Analysis

In this section, the experiment is conducted on several standard databases and the experimental results are compared with existing algorithms. By single-layer cellular automata, the internal saliency of the image is calculated (Single cellular automata saliency, SCAS). In order to make better use of the advantages of the calculation based on difference (KNN), multi-layer cellular automata was used to fuse the inter-class saliency and internal saliency (Multiple cellular automata saliency, MCAS).

4.1 Experimental Data

Experiments are conducted on the standard databases CAVIAR4REID and iLIDS.

The CAVIAR4REID database was captured by two cameras at the shopping mall. A total of 72 pedestrians and 1220 images. The main difficulty lies in the great changes of resolution, light and pedestrian postures in the image (As is in Fig. 2).

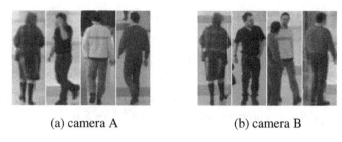

(a) camera A   (b) camera B

Fig. 2. CAVIAR4REID database

iLIDS was captured from two cameras in the airport, a total of 119 pedestrians and 476 images. Changes of pedestrian postures and the cover are obvious (As in Fig. 3).

(a)changes of the visual angels   (b)situations of cover

Fig. 3. iLIDS database

For comparison, the experimental process in this chapter is consistent with the literature [4]. Assuming that there are N pedestrians in the database $S = \{xi \mid I = 1, 2, ..., N\}$, we randomly selected p pedestrians ($p < N$) from the set S for testing. One of all the images of the same pedestrian is randomly selected to be a part of the set of candidates and the rest of the images are used as the set of searching. At this time, there are p images of pedestrians which are different in the set. Finally, images of the searching set are calculated with each pedestrian image in the set of the candidates. After that, images in the set of candidates are sorted according to the distance and the location of the correct target is recorded.

4.2   Experimental Results and Analysis

The analysis of the results based on the CAVIAR4REID database: with the comparison of the salient feature method (SDC) based on the block set, our proposed algorithm of fusion of multiple salient features is confirmed. It can be seen form Table 1 and Fig. 4 that on CAVIAR4REID database SDC [4] outperforms SCAS by 18.0% at time of Rank1 and MCAS outperforms SCAS by 15.6% at time of Rank1. From the whole perspective, performance of SCAS increases 4.4% on average while MCAS increases 5.9% on average. On the CAVIAR4REID database, the effect of using internal features

Table 1. Comparison of performance on CAVIAR4REID database

Rank	1	5	10	15	20
SDC [4]	21.22%	36.98%	46.27%	53.60%	59.12%
SCAS	25.04%	39.36%	48.46%	55.21%	61.19%
MCAS	24.55%	39.99%	49.09%	56.12%	61.91%

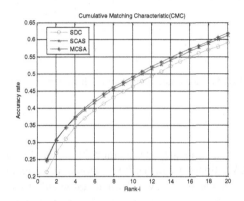

Fig. 4. Accumulated matching characteristic curve

alone is better than SDC. But using internal features alone, the difference between samples are lack of through consideration and with the knowledge of this the accuracy of MCAS is slightly improved.

Analysis of the results on the iLIDS database: As we can see in Table 2 and Fig. 5 that on iLIDS database. The performance of SCAS algorithm slightly goes down (4.5% on average) compared to SDC algorithm. This is due to the fact that the algorithm only takes the inherent saliency of the interior of the pedestrian image into consideration, but the difference between the samples is ignored. At the time of Rank1, performance of MCAS algorithm increases by 6.53% and on the whole the accuracy increases by 7.54% on average.

Table 2. Comparison of performance on iLIDS database

Rank	1	5	10	15	20
SDC [4]	30.76%	46.92%	54.71%	60.62%	66.78%
SCAS	26.47%	43.59%	51.76%	58.54%	64.12%
MCAS	32.77%	49.58%	58.82%	66.67%	72.16%

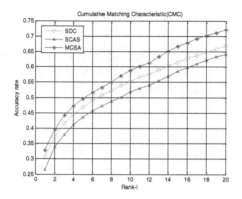

Fig. 5. Accumulated matching characteristic curve

5 Conclusion

According to the algorithm in [4], our method based on fusion of multiple salient features is proposed. We firstly use the cellular automata to calculate the salient features of the image. And then the multi-layer cellular automata is used to integrate above features with the inter-class salient features. Finally, the experimental results prove that the proposed algorithm of the fusion of multiple salient features can effectively improve the performance of the re-identification algorithm.

Acknowledgements. The authors would like to thank the providers for their open pedestrian datasets. This work is supported by Scientific Research Foundation of China (61402237).

References

1. Bąk, S., Corvee, E., Brémond, F., Thonnat, M.: Person re-identification using spatial covariance regions of human body parts. In: Proceedings of the 7th IEEE International Conference on Advanced Video and Signal Based Surveillance, pp. 435–440. IEEE, Washington DC (2010)
2. Schwartz, W.R., Davis, L.S.: Learning discriminative appearance-based models using partial least squares. In: Proceedings of the 2009 XXII Brazilian Symposium on Computer Graphics and Image Processing, pp. 322–329. IEEE, Washington DC (2009)
3. Liu, C., Gong, S., Chen, C.L.: On-the-fly feature importance mining for person re-identification. Pattern Recogn. **47**(4), 1602–1615 (2014)
4. Zhao, R., Ouyang, W., Wang, X.: Unsupervised salience learning for person re-identification. In: 2013 IEEE Conference on Computer Vision and Pattern Recognition, pp. 3586–3593. IEEE, Washington DC (2013)
5. Gray, D., Tao, H.: Viewpoint invariant pedestrian recognition with an ensemble of localized features. In: Forsyth, D., Torr, P., Zisserman, A. (eds.) ECCV 2008. LNCS, vol. 5302, pp. 262–275. Springer, Heidelberg (2008). doi:10.1007/978-3-540-88682-2_21

6. Avraham, T., Gurvich, I., Lindenbaum, M., Markovitch, S.: Learning implicit transfer for person re-identification. In: Fusiello, A., Murino, V., Cucchiara, R. (eds.) ECCV 2012. LNCS, vol. 7583, pp. 381–390. Springer, Heidelberg (2012). doi:10.1007/978-3-642-33863-2_38
7. Qin, Y., Lu, H., Xu, Y., Wang, H.: Saliency detection via cellular automata. In: IEEE Conference on Computer Vision and Pattern Recognition, pp. 110–119. IEEE, Boston (2015)
8. Ohtsu, N.: A threshold selection method from gray-level histograms. IEEE Trans. Syst. Man Cybern. **9**(1), 62–66 (1979)

Improvement of Texture Clustering Performance in Complex-Valued SOM by Using Complex-Valued Auto-encoder for Millimeter-Wave Coherent Imaging

Yuya Arima$^{(\boxtimes)}$ and Akira Hirose

Department of Electrical Engineering and Information Systems,
The University of Tokyo, 7-3-1 Hongo, Bunkyo-ku, Tokyo 113-8656, Japan
y_arima@eis.t.u-tokyo.ac.jp

Abstract. Interference in millimeter-wave active radar imaging causes harmful effects such as amplitude fluctuation and phase distortion, resulting in deterioration in visualization quality in a radar system employing complex-valued self-organizing map. We show that a complex-valued auto-encoder is capable of extracting features properly even under these influences, resulting in improvement of clustering performance effectively.

Keywords: Complex-valued neural network · Self-organizing map · Auto-encoder · Millimeter-wave imaging · Security

1 Introduction

There are many imaging methods to visualize physical information of objects. Improvement in their resolution and signal-to-noise ratio (SNR) is limited by increasing equipment cost and physical restriction in of the sensor structure and materials. A lot of attempts have been reported to improve the imaging system performance by neural networks that imitate the high generalization ability and noise resistance of human perception.

Our group has proposed various neural methods to utilize phase information obtained in coherent measurements in addition to amplitude information. We can obtain information on substance transfer characteristics in transmission measurement and/or local depth in reflection measurement by introducing phase information. We can obtain a three-dimensional local shape by combining the phase with the amplitude into complex-amplitude for evaluation in local windows. For pedestrian applications and on-vehicle use, we have developed an imaging system composed of millimeter-wave active radar for capturing moving objects that pass through in front of an array antenna in real time, and processing part to identify target by using complex-valued self-organizing map (CSOM). We have been evaluating its basic performance [1,2].

© Springer International Publishing AG 2017
D. Liu et al. (Eds.): ICONIP 2017, Part VI, LNCS 10639, pp. 722–730, 2017.
https://doi.org/10.1007/978-3-319-70136-3_76

In this paper, we report that the introduction of a complex-valued auto-encoder in the process to extract complex-texture features in local windows improves the performances of the CSOM clustering and of the segmentation of targets. This radar system performs coherent millimeter-wave imaging, where the phase information has a significant meaning. Therefore, we use a complex neural network. Since coherent imaging is susceptible to the harmful effects of interference in measurement, it often suffers from amplitude fluctuation and phase distortion. These effects are serious in measurements of moving objects. The auto-encoder is useful for extracting features appropriately under such influences. We find that the auto-encoder is extremely effective for millimeter-wave active imaging.

2   Local Texture Classification by Complex-Valued Self-organizing Map

We use a complex-valued neural network to handle phase and amplitude data obtained by coherent measurement method. In this system, we use a complex-valued self-organizing map (CSOM) which is a SOM extended into the complex domain. The CSOM is effective in visualizing plastic landmines buried under ground in our ground penetrating radar (GPR) system [3–5]. The flow of processing is shown in Fig. 1. First, feature vectors are extracted from measurement data. Next, in our conventional system, the extracted feature vector is fed to CSOM to perform self-organization and classification. Then, a segmented image is obtained by assigning colors corresponding to the CSOM classes to respective pixels. The feature extraction method and the CSOM processing will be described in detail below.

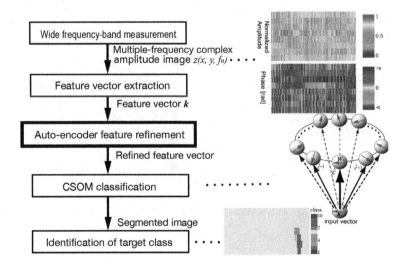

Fig. 1. Flowchart of image processing.

2.1 Complex Textural Feature Extraction of Local Region

We obtain a set of three-dimensional data, namely, spatial two dimensions and frequency one dimension, with high-speed frequency stepped observation. We extract feature vectors by calculating correlations among local pixels in a window as shown in Fig. 2. The extraction procedure is as follows.

(i) Cut out a local window of $L \times T$ size. $(L, T$: window size)

(ii) Calculate correlations in the real space $K_s(i, j)$ and the frequency space $K_f(f_n)$ in the local window as feature values as expressed in (3) and (4).

(iii) Combine these values and the average value in the local window M in (2) to make a feature vector $\boldsymbol{K}$ in (1).

$$\boldsymbol{K} = \left[M \ K_s(0,0) \ K_s(0,1) \ K_s(1,0) \ K_s(1,1) \ K_f(f_1) \dots K_f(f_{N_f-1}) \right]^\top \quad (1)$$

$$M = \frac{1}{LTN_f} \sum_{l=1}^{L} \sum_{t=1}^{T} \sum_{n=1}^{N_f} z(l, t, f_n) \quad (2)$$

$$K_s(i, j) = \frac{1}{(L-i)(T-j)N_f} \sum_{l=1}^{L-i} \sum_{t=1}^{T-j} \sum_{n=1}^{N_f} \left\{ z^*(l, t, f_n) z(l+i, t+j, f_n) \right\}$$

$$(i, j \in \{0, 1\}) \quad (3)$$

$$K_f(f_n) = \frac{1}{LT} \sum_{l=1}^{L} \sum_{t=1}^{T} z^*(l, t, f_n) z(l, t, f_{n+1}) \quad (4)$$

Since we have one average, 4 spatial correlations and $(N_f - 1)$ frequency correlations, we obtain a set of $(N_f + 4)$-dimensional feature vectors.

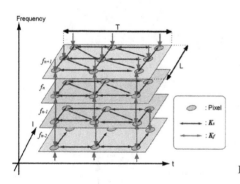

Fig. 2. Window of feature extraction.

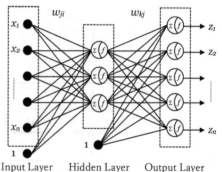

Input Layer   Hidden Layer   Output Layer

Fig. 3. Schematic diagram of auto-encoder.

2.2   Complex-Valued Self-organizing Map

We feed the feature vectors to the CSOM to perform classification. We use a CSOM whose network configuration is a ring to represent the feature-vector similarity in one-dimensional space. To determine the winner $\hat{c}$ out of the reference vectors, we use the metric based on the complex inner product $\boldsymbol{k}^*\boldsymbol{w}_c$ as

$$\hat{c} = \underset{c}{\operatorname{argmax}} \left(\left| \frac{\boldsymbol{k}^*\boldsymbol{w}_c}{\|\boldsymbol{k}\|\|\boldsymbol{w}_c\|} \right| \right) \quad (c : \text{class index}) \tag{5}$$

$$\boldsymbol{k} \equiv \begin{bmatrix} r_1 \exp(i\theta_1) \\ r_2 \exp(i\theta_2) \\ \vdots \end{bmatrix}, \quad \boldsymbol{w}_c \equiv \begin{bmatrix} q_{c1} \exp(i\psi_{c1}) \\ q_{c2} \exp(i\psi_{c2}) \\ \vdots \end{bmatrix} \tag{6}$$

The absolute value of the inner product is expressed as

$$|\boldsymbol{k}^*\boldsymbol{w}_c| = \left| \sum_{j=1}^{N} [r_j \exp(-i\theta_j)] [q_{cj} \exp(+i\psi_{cj})] \right| = \left| \sum_{j=1}^{N} r_j q_{cj} \exp(i(\psi_{cj} - \theta_j)) \right| \tag{7}$$

where N is the dimension of feature vectors and reference vectors. The use of a complex inner product makes it possible to perform clustering with more emphasis on phase information than the use of the Euclidean distance [6].

3   Refinement of Features by Complex-Valued Auto-Encoder

In the previous system, we have fed feature vectors extracted by the above-mentioned method directly to the CSOM for classification. However, in this paper, we interpose a feature refinement process using a complex-valued auto-encoder to improve the robustness of the system. Auto-encoder is a type of multi-layer feedforward neural network having hourglass type structure. The numbers of neurons in the input and output layers are the same while that in the hidden layer is smaller as shown in the schematic diagram in Fig. 3. The hidden layer acquires an expression form that effectively represents the signal features in smaller dimensions with a set of teacher signals fed to the input and output layers fed for the learning by backpropagation. This process refines the feature vectors, which are newly obtained in the hidden layer of the auto-encoder [7–9]. This process is similar to the denoising for general images [10–12]. In the present case, we use it to exclude harmful interference effects such as amplitude fluctuation and phase distortion arising in the coherent active imaging.

Since our system handles the complex features, we use an auto-encoder which is extended to complex domain. We use an amplitude-phase type activation function expressed as [13]

$$f(u) = \tanh(|u|) \exp(i\angle u) \tag{8}$$

which causes saturation in the amplitude, while it leaves the phase unchanged.

The output signals in each layer is expressed with the activation function $f(u)$, neural weight matrices $\mathbf{W}_{\text{hidden}}$, $\mathbf{W}_{\text{output}}$ and neural thresholds $\boldsymbol{w}_{0\ \text{hidden}}$, $\boldsymbol{w}_{0\ \text{output}}$ as

$$\boldsymbol{y} = f(\mathbf{W}_{\text{hidden}} \cdot \boldsymbol{x} + \boldsymbol{w}_{0\ \text{hidden}}) \tag{9}$$

$$\boldsymbol{z} = f(\mathbf{W}_{\text{output}} \cdot \boldsymbol{y} + \boldsymbol{w}_{0\ \text{output}}) \tag{10}$$

The matrices $\mathbf{W}_{\text{hidden}}$ and $\mathbf{W}_{\text{output}}$ changes through the learning process in such a manner that the outputs $\boldsymbol{z}$ approach the inputs $\boldsymbol{x}$ for a set of feature vectors extracted in Sect. 2.1. Then we use the output signals in the hidden layer $\boldsymbol{y}$ as a set of new feature vectors to be fed to the CSOM.

4   Experiment

4.1   Experimental Setup

We propose and construct a millimeter-wave active imaging system targeting pedestrians for security purpose as an application of local complex-texture classification imaging by CSOM. It employs a complex-valued auto-encoder.

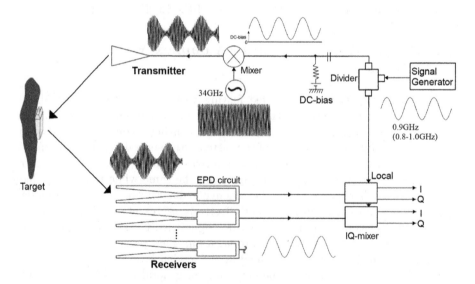

Fig. 4. Schematic diagram of amplitude modulation for active illumination and envelope phase detection (EPD).

Figure 4 shows a schematic diagram of the signal processing flow in the millimeter-wave active radar unit of our system. We use millimeter wave modulated in its amplitude with sine wave of around 900 MHz as an illuminating wave.

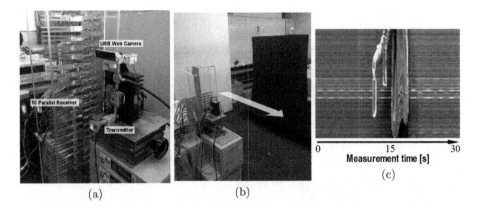

Fig. 5. (a) Photo of the transmitting unit and the 16-parallel antenna elements of the receiving unit, (b) measurement setup and (c) optical image of a pedestrian holding two PET bottles. Two horizontal red line shows the top and bottom height of observation. (Color figure online)

The wave scattered by targets is received by aligned antenna elements and envelope-detected in detection circuits directly connected to the antenna elements. Then the signal after envelope detection is homodyne-detected with the local oscillator, and digitally converted to be fed to a computer as phase and amplitude. Since this envelope phase detection (EPD) limits the circuit domain where we handled millimeter wave directly, and reduces the cost of circuit design. In addition, we can utilize the phase information corresponding to the modulation wavelength of about 30 cm. Photo of the front end of the measurement unit is shown in Fig. 5(a). Targets pass along the white arrow in Fig. 5(b). In the background of the targets, a 1 cm thick radio wave absorber is hung at approximately 90 cm from the antennas.

4.2   Measurement and Result

In this experiment, we target a pedestrian holding two 500 mL PET bottles filled with water, assuming a liquid bomb. The pedestrian passes through a position approximately 30 cm away from the antennas. Figure 5(c) shows the optical image taken synchronously with the millimeter-wave measurement by the web camera placed beside the receiving antennas. Two PET bottles are held one by one in both hands. The far PET bottle precedes the other in the traveling direction. The distances of the PET bottles from the antennas are 60 cm and 30 cm respectively, and the distance of the closer to the antennas is almost the same as that of side face of the torso. The walking speed is about 4 cm/s. We chose 10 frequency points in 855 MHz–945 MHz band with a 10 MHz interval. The measurement time is 30 s.

Figure 6 shows 10 pairs of phase and amplitude images at each modulation frequencies. The amplitude is normalized to the range from 0 to 1 after taking

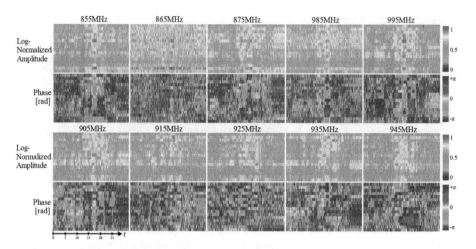

Fig. 6. Captured raw data showing log-normalized amplitude and phase in rad for 10 modulation frequency points with 34 GHz carrier wave.

the logarithm. The horizontal direction in each image corresponds to the measurement time, and the vertical direction corresponds to the position of a parallel antenna element. Looking at the amplitude, the value increases at the time when the pedestrian passes. The phase also fluctuates according to the fluctuation of the amplitude. However, since there is no large difference in reflectance between PET bottles and human body, it is difficult to distinguish them.

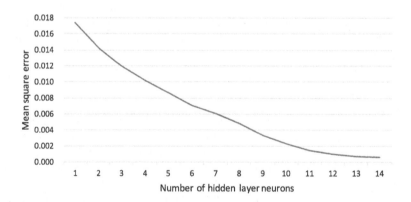

Fig. 7. Mean square error with number of hidden layer neurons of the auto-encoder.

We made auto-encoders having different numbers of hidden layer neurons using the measurement data for learning. Figure 7 shows a plot of the mean square error in the learning versus the number of neurons in the hidden layer of the auto-encoders. As the number of hidden layer neurons increases, the mean square error decreases. But the decrease rate reduces. Here, we selected the auto-encoder having 12 hidden layer neurons among the auto-encoders for classification process by CSOM.

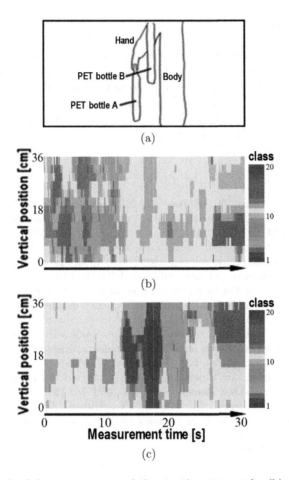

Fig. 8. (a) Sketch of the target area and the visualization results (b) without and (c) with the auto-encoder. (Color figure online)

Figure 8 shows the classification result by CSOM with and without feature refinement process using the auto-encoder. In the result without the auto-encoder shown in Fig. 8(b), many false images occur particularly in the part corresponding to the first half of the measurement (left-hand side), and it is impossible to discriminate the target. On the other hand, in the result with the auto-encoder shown in Fig. 8(c), the position corresponding to the two PET bottles is classified into dark blue classes, and the position corresponding to the arm having the PET bottle and the torso are classified into light blue to green classes. Thus, the parts having different characteristics can be distinguished.

In addition, the number of classes classified into the background area is smaller. This fact shows that the auto-encoder is capable of reducing harmful influences such as amplitude fluctuation and phase distortion due to interference.

5 Conclusion

We investigate millimeter-wave coherent active imaging for moving people and objects. In this paper, we introduced a complex-valued auto-encoder for this system. Since coherent imaging is susceptible to the harmful effects of interference in measurement, it often suffers from amplitude fluctuation and phase distortion. We showed that the auto-encoder is extremely useful in extracting features appropriately even under such influences.

References

1. Onojima, S., Arima, Y., Hirose, A.: Millimeter-wave security imaging using complex-valued self-organizing map for visualization of moving targets. Neurocomputing **134**, 247–253 (2014)
2. Arima, Y., Hirose, A.: Millimeter-wave active imaging using multiple frequencies with complex-valued self-organizing map image processing. In: Asia-Pacific Microwave Conference (APMC) 2014, pp. 1031–1033 (2014)
3. Hara, T., Hirose, A.: Plastic mine detecting radar system using complex-valued self-organizing map that deals with multiple-frequency interferometric images. Neural Netw. **17**(8–9), 1201–1210 (2004)
4. Masuyama, S., Yasuda, K., Hirose, A.: Multiple mode selection of walled-ltsa array elements for high resolution imaging to visualize antipersonnel plastic landmines. IEEE Geosci. Remote Sens. Lett. **5**(4), 745–749 (2008)
5. Nakano, Y., Hirose, A.: Taper-walled linearly tapered slot antenna. IEEE J. Sel. Topics Appl. Earth Obs. Remote Sens. **4**(4), 779–784 (2011)
6. Aoyagi, T., Radenamad, D., Nakano, Y., Hirose, A.: Complex-valued self-organizing map clustering using complex inner product in active mmillimeter-wave imaging. In: Proceedings of the International Joint Conference on Neural Networks (IJCNN) 2010 Barcelona, pp. 1346–1351. IEEE/INNS, Barcelona, July 2010
7. Cottrell, G.W., Munro, P., Zipser, D.: Image compression by back propagation: an example of extensional propagation. ICS report **8702**, 321 (1987)
8. Cottrell, G.W., Munro, P.: Principal components analysis of images via back propagation. Proc. SPIE **1001**, 1070–1077 (1988)
9. DeMers, D., Cottrell, G.W.: Non-linear dimensionality reduction. Adv. Neural Inf. Process. Syst. **5**, 580–587 (1993)
10. Vincent, P., Larochelle, H., Lajoie, I., Bengio, Y., Manzagol, P.A.: Stacked denoising autoencoders: learning useful representations in a deep network with a local denoising criterion. J. Mach. Learn. Res. **11**, 3371–3408 (2010)
11. Rifai, S., Vincent, P., Muller, X., Glorot, X., Bengio, Y.: Contractive auto-encoders: explicit invariance during feature extraction. In: Proceedings of the 28th International Conference on Machine Learning (ICML 2011), pp. 833–840 (2011)
12. Xie, J., Xu, L., Chen, E.: Image denoising and inpainting with deep neural networks. In: Advances in Neural Information Processing Systems, pp. 341–349 (2012)
13. Hirose, A.: Complex-Valued Neural Networks, 2nd edn. Springer, Heidelberg (2012)

A Radiomics Approach for Automated Identification of Aggressive Tumors on Combined PET and Multi-parametric MRI

Tao Wan[1]([✉]), Bixiao Cui[2], Yaping Wang[3], Zengchang Qin[3]([✉]), and Jie Lu[2]([✉])

[1] School of Biological Science and Medical Engineering,
Beihang University, Beijing, China
taowan@buaa.edu.cn
[2] Department of Radiology, Xuanwu Hospital Capital Medical University,
Beijing, China
imaginglu@hotmail.com
[3] Intelligent Computing and Machine Learning Lab,
School of ASEE, Beihang University, Beijing, China
zcqin@buaa.edu.cn

Abstract. We present a computerized image-based method to automatically identify aggressive tumors on combined positron emission tomography and magnetic resonance imaging (PET-MRI) using radiomics texture features from both PET and multi-parametric MRI (MP-MRI). The work aims at investigating the potential use of new composite textures from PET-MRI for the assessment of different biological properties present in cancer and non-cancer regions, and eventually for early detection of malignant tumors in real clinical practice. Towards this goal, a large number of radiomics features are extracted to characterize the intratumoural heterogeneity and microarchitectural morphologic differences within tumors. These image attributes are valuable for determining tumor aggressiveness. The radiomics model was evaluated on three types of cancers (pancreas, gallbladder, and liver). Compared to single image modality (PET or MRI), the fused PET and MP-MRI achieved the best classification performance in differentiating cancer and non-cancer regions with the area of under curve (AUC) of 0.87 for pancreas cancer, 0.89 for gallbladder cancer, and 0.82 for liver cancer. The results indicated that PET-MRI based imaging biomarkers could be useful in identifying aggressive tumors.

Keywords: Aggressive tumor · Radiomics · PET · Multi-parametric MRI

1 Introduction

Tumor, also referred as neoplasm, is a mass of abnormal tissue. According to the World Health Organization, tumors are classified into four main groups, and they

---

T. Wan and B. Cui are the co-first authors.

© Springer International Publishing AG 2017
D. Liu et al. (Eds.): ICONIP 2017, Part VI, LNCS 10639, pp. 731–739, 2017.
https://doi.org/10.1007/978-3-319-70136-3_77

are benign, in situ, malignant, and tumor of uncertain [13]. Malignant tumors are cancerous and aggressive because they are often resistant to treatment, may spread to other parts of the body, and sometimes recur after they are removed. Aggressive tumors are characterized with great differentiation from normal tissue, cellular heterogeneity, and high growth rates. Due to their strong ability to invade and damage healthy host tissue, thus early detection and treatment of malignant tumors are of great clinical value in improving patient survival [3]. Recently, combined positron emission tomography (PET) with magnetic resonance imaging (MRI) has become a promising and advanced new imaging tool for diagnosis, staging, and restaging of cancers [1]. PET-MRI allows simultaneous data acquisition of functional images (e.g., occupation of receptors and activity of glucose metabolism) with superior soft-tissue contrast resolution as well as valuable anatomic and morphological information. In addition, a multi-parametric MRI (MP-MRI) can provide multi-functional information of physiological processes in vivo [12].

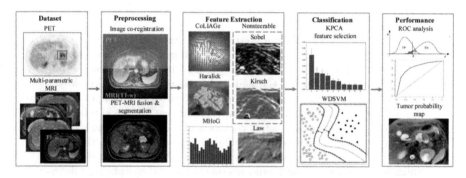

Fig. 1. The flowchart shows that the presented method comprises three main modules to identify aggressive tumors. Module I is to combine PET and MP-MRI to generate a hybrid image and segment region of interest (tumor) from the image background. Module II is to compute radiomics features from individual PEI, MP-MRI, and fused PET-MRI. Module III is to distinguish cancer and non-cancer regions using the extracted image features with the KPCA feature selection method and WDSVM classification.

Radiomics is a rapid emerging field in medical image analysis that evolves extraction of large amounts of features derived from routine radiologic imaging to improve cancer diagnosis, prognosis, prediction and response to therapy [6]. Recent studies on qualitative as well as quantitative assessments of tumor characteristics suggested that cancer imaging phenotypes captured by PET and MRI can reveal the underlying gene expression profiles in many cancer types [18]. For instance, Wan et al. [16] showed that computer extracted texture features of dynamic contrast enhanced MRI were highly correlated with the validated prognostic gene expression profiles of breast cancers. Lian et al. [9] presented a framework primarily using radiomics features for PET based treatment outcome prediction. Further, Vallières et al. [15] developed a radiomics model from

PET-MRI texture features for the early evaluation of lung metastasis risk in soft-tissue sarcomas, showing the prediction performance was significantly enhanced by integrating PET and MRI. The purpose of this work is to investigate if the creation of new composite textures from the combination of PET and MP-MRI information could better identify aggressive tumors.

We presented a radiomics approach for automatically identifying aggressive tumors using joint PET and MP-MRI texture features. The methodology consisted of three main modules as shown in Fig. 1. The method was evaluated using the routinely clinical PET-MRI cohort acquired for the diagnosis and screening of three types of cancers (pancreas, gallbladder, and liver). A total of 105 radiomics texture features were computed to capture spatially proximal textural changes and microarchitectural morphologic differences between the types of pathologies present in cancer and non-cancer regions. In this study, we explore the potential of the radiomics features from the PET-MRI information in assessing different biological properties present in cancer and non-cancer regions. The extracted features were scored and selected by a kernel principal components analysis (KPCA) based feature selection method before performing a distance-weighted support vector machine (DWSVM) classification [11]. The key contribution of this work is to develop a radiomics model from combined PET and MRI texture features for the assessment of different biological properties present in cancer and non-cancer regions.

The remainder of this paper is organized as follows. The data description and methods are presented in Sects. 2 and 3, respectively. The experimental results and discussion are demonstrated in Sect. 4. Section 5 concludes the paper.

2 Dataset Description

The image data were retrospectively collected from the Xuanwu Hospital Capital Medical University. A total of 30 patients were recruited to a trial study of PET-MRI in the diagnosis and screening of cancers before undergoing pre-treatment PET-MRI scans between September 2015 and January 2017. All PET-MRI scans were performed with a PET/MRI scanner (Signa; General Electric Healthcare, Milwaukee, WI). For the PET portion of the scans, a median of 410 MBq (range: 200–570 MBq) of FDG was injected intravenously. In our patient population, four types of MRI sequences (i.e., T1-weighted (T1-w), T2-weighted fat-saturated (T2-w), diffusion weighted imaging (DWI), short tau inversion recovery (STIR)) routinely used in clinical protocols were selected for the study. The patient cohort consisted 20 patients who diagnosed with pancreas cancer, 5 with gallbladder cancer, and 5 with liver cancer. All the case studies were proven through biopsy followed by the histopathologic examination. The tumor regions for each patient were drawn manually using a box on PET scans by an expert radiologist.

3 Methods

The presented cancer detection method comprised of image pre-processing (PET-MRI registration, fusion, and segmentation), image feature extraction, and classification in distinguishing cancer and non-cancer pixels on PET-MRI. We define a dataset $\mathcal{Z} = \{Z_1, Z_2, ..., Z_M\}$ of M patient studies. Each case study Z contains multi-modality images I_k, $k \in \{\text{PET}, \text{T1-w}, \text{T2-w}, \text{DWI}, \text{STIR}\}$. Each $I_{m,k}$, $m \in \{1, .., M\}$ is associated with a radiomics feature set $\mathcal{F}(I_{m,k})$.

3.1 Image Preprocessing

PET-MRI Registration and Fusion. The purpose of registration is to gain the spatial consistency and anatomical correspondence between PET and MRI. We utilized a newly introduced multi-modality registration approach to co-register PET and MP-MRI. The texture features were extracted to reveal similar underlying structural attributes between the images to be registered, in which similarities might not be discernible on the signal intensity representation alone [8]. The registration process can be formulated as an optimization problem: $\widehat{\psi} = \arg\min_\psi \zeta(T_\psi : (I_{\text{PET}} : \Omega_{\text{PET}}) \rightarrow (I_{\text{MRI}} : \Omega_{\text{MRI}}))$, with ψ being the vector of transformation parameters $(T_\psi : \Omega_{\text{PET}} \rightarrow \Omega_{\text{MRI}})$, and ζ a suitable cost function. T1-w was chosen as a reference image. In this work, only a single scale was used to accelerate the registration process. A fusion of the PET and MP-MRI scans was implemented using the wavelet transform in order to extract new composite textures from the joint PET and MP-MRI. The fused PET-MRI can be computed by: $I_{\text{PET-MRI}} = \xi^{-1}(W_{\text{PET}}\xi(I_{\text{PET}}) + (1 - W_{\text{PET}})\xi(I_{\text{MRI}}))$, where ξ and ξ^{-1} are the discrete wavelet transform (DWT) and inverse DWT. These features have showed good capability in identifying aggressive tumors [15].

Tumor Segmentation. We used a semi-automated image segmentation approach (i.e., the distance regularized level set evolution (DRLSE) segmentation method [7]) to segment tumor region on PET using the center of manually marked region as initialization point. The energy function was defined by: $\mathcal{E}(\phi) = \mu\mathcal{R}_p(\phi) + \lambda\mathcal{L}_g(\phi) + \alpha\mathcal{A}_g(\phi)$, where ϕ is a level set function. $\mathcal{R}_p(\phi)$ is the level set regularization term, and $\mu > 0$ is a constant. $\lambda > 0$ and α are the coefficients of the edge-based energy functions $\mathcal{L}_g(\phi)$ and $\mathcal{A}_g(\phi)$, which are defined as external energy functions to ensure that the zero level contour of ϕ is located at the object boundaries. In the segmentation model, the level set evolution was derived as the gradient flow which minimized an energy function with a distance regularization term and an external energy that drove the motion of the zero level set toward desired locations. The DRLSE method provided noticeable performance in segmenting small and irregularly-shaped regions, which is particularly useful for tumor segmentation on I_{PET}.

3.2 Feature Extraction

A total of 105 2D radiomics texture features were extracted from individual PET, T1-w, T2-w, apparent diffusion co-efficient (ADC) map of DWI, STIR, and fused PET-MRI on a per-voxel basis. These features were obtained by computing gray-level intensity co-occurrence statistics and calculating responses to various filtering operators, as follows:

Co-occurrence of local anisotropic gradient orientations (CoLlAGe) [10]: is a newly developed radiomics descriptor for capturing and exploiting local anisotropic differences in voxel-level gradient orientations to distinguish similar appearing on routine anatomic imaging. The computation of CoLlAGe involves calculation of gradient magnitudes $\partial I_x(g)$ and $\partial I_y(g)$ along X- and Y-axes for each pixel g. The dominant orientation $\theta(g)$ was computed through the singular value decomposition of matrix $[\partial I_x(g_i)\partial I_y(g_i)]$, $g_i \in N \times N$ neighborhood. Entropy measure ξ was computed from co-occurrence matrix on θ. The CoLlAGe features are obtained via aggregation of histogram of ξ across neighborhood. The entire histogram is binned in 30 bins to form a 30×1 feature vector.

Haralick features [5]: are based on quantifying the spatial gray-level co-occurrence within local neighborhoods around each pixel in an image, which can reflect texture heterogeneity within the tumor. A total of 13 Haralick texture descriptors are calculated in a voxel basis.

Multi-scale histogram of gradient orientations (MHoG) [16]: is able to capture the frequency of occurrence of different spatial textural patterns in a multi-scale way. The local texture in tumor is captured by the distribution over edge orientations within a small region, while the spatial contextual information is obtained by tiling the image into regions at multiple scales. The feature vector consists of binned histogram values in the form of vectors of 20×1 in length.

Nonsteerable gradient features [17]: are obtained via convolution with Sobel, Kirsch edge filters, and first-order spatial derivative operators from each image, generating a set of 17 features. These features are able to capture both local and global spatial variations present in PET-MRI.

Law texture feature [14]: is a texture energy measure to use local masks (size of 5×5), that are symmetric or antisymmetric to detect level, edge, spot, wave, and ripple patterns on an image. The convolution of these masks with image results in 25 distinct Law features for each image.

3.3   Feature Selection and Classification

Feature Selection. The computerized radiomics features $\mathcal{F}$ were selected and scored by a new kernel principal components analysis based feature selection method [4]. The KPCA based method was proven to be able to identify a stable set of features that provided good classification accuracy in digital pathology images, which involved extraction of hundreds of features. The feature importance was measured via a variable importance in projection (VIP) score S, which was computed for each feature as follows:

$$S_j = \sqrt{m \sum_{i=1}^{h} b_i^2 t_i^T t_i (\frac{p_{ji}}{\|P_i\|})^2 / \sum_{i=1}^{h} b_i^2 t_i^T t_i}, \tag{1}$$

where m is the number of features in the original, high-dimensional feature space, T is made up of the h principal component vector t_i, $i \in \{1, ..., h\}$, h denotes eigenvectors. The fraction $(\frac{p_{ji}}{\|P_i\|})^2$ represents the contribution of jth feature to the ith principal component in the low-dimensional embedding, and b_i is the regression coefficient. The VIP score allowed for feature weighting and ranking based on their contributions to classification within a linearly-derived embedding.

SVM Classification. To evaluate the capability of computerized radiomics features in discriminating cancer and non-cancer regions on PET-MRI, the DWSVM classification was performed on the individual features obtained from PET, MP-MRI, and fused PET-MRI. The DWSVM classifier is a linear classification method with a combination of SVM and the distance weighted discrimination (DWD) to overcome the data-piling and overfitting issues through simultaneously minimizing both the SVM and DWD loss functions. The DWSVM classifier was trained via an iterative 2-fold cross-validation scheme. A ranked minority over-sampling technique was utilized to reduce the classification bias due to the imbalanced dataset (the number of non-cancer pixels was much larger than the cancer pixels) [2]. In the classification, we used the best values of DWSVM parameters (C_{svm}, C_{dwd}, α) that were reported in [11].

4   Experimental Results and Discussion

4.1   Experimental Design

The SVM classification was performed via a stratified 2-fold cross-validation process, and the resulting mean μ and standard deviation σ of the classification accuracy (ACC), sensitivity (SN), specificity (SP), and an area under the curve (AUC) of receiver operating characteristic (ROC) analysis were computed to quantitatively measure the extracted features' ability in distinguishing cancer and non-cancer on PET-MRI. The non-cancer samples were automatically selected within the adjacent areas of tumor region and non-cancer regions with high metabolic tumor burden.

4.2   Classification Performance

We evaluated the presented PET-MRI based method on three datasets containing pancreas cancer, gallbladder cancer, and liver cancer. The quantitative results are listed in Table 1. For all the cancers, the PET outperformed MRI for accurately identifying tumor regions in terms of high SN because PET provided unparalleled sensitivity to molecular events, such as occupation of receptors, activity of glucose metabolism, inflammation, reflecting tumor malignancy. Due to the low resolution and single modality, the PET yielded lower values of specificity in detecting non-cancer regions, thus resulting in lower ACC and AUC for pancreas cancer and liver cancer, compared to the multi-parametric MRI.

Table 1. The classification performance ($\mu(\sigma)$) using individual PET or MRI and combined PET-MRI measured by ACC, SN, SP, and AUC. For each experiment, 15 radiomics features were selected by the KPCA based feature selection method.

Modality	ACC	SN	SP	AUC
Pancreas Cancer				
PET	0.70(0.07)	0.76(0.16)	0.71(0.12)	0.75(0.08)
MRI	0.76(0.08)	0.72(0.12)	0.81(0.11)	0.80(0.09)
PET-MRI	**0.84**(0.06)	**0.79**(0.08)	**0.86**(0.04)	**0.87**(0.06)
Gallbladder Cancer				
PET	0.73(0.14)	0.78(0.07)	0.72(0.09)	0.80(0.10)
MRI	0.71(0.18)	0.61(0.23)	0.80(0.13)	0.74(0.09)
PET-MRI	**0.85**(0.08)	**0.78**(0.03)	**0.88**(0.05)	**0.89**(0.04)
Liver Cancer				
PET	0.67(0.20)	0.76(0.08)	0.64(0.16)	0.69(0.10)
MRI	0.69(0.15)	0.71(0.12)	0.68(0.15)	0.72(0.17)
PET-MRI	**0.78**(0.05)	**0.82**(0.05)	**0.72**(0.08)	**0.82**(0.05)

For the case of gallbladder cancer, the PET achieved greater ACC and AUC than the MRI because of distinct metabolic differences between normal and cancerous regions. We noted that combined PET-MRI obtained the best classification performance for all three types of cancers. This suggested that the extracted computerized features from PET and MRI could generate a set of powerful and complementary descriptors for identifying aggressive tumors.

For all the experiments, we utilized an optimal set of 15 features ranked and chosen via the KPCA method. Table 2 shows the selected features from the hybrid PET-MRI for each cancer type. Three classes of features (i.e., CoLlAGe, Haralick, and nonsteerable gradient features) were scored as the most important image attributes for all three cancers. The CoLlAGe feature seeks to capture and exploit local anisotropic differences in voxel-level gradient orientations to

Table 2. The selected important features from PET-MRI. The number of features from each feature class that were selected by KPCA is given in brackets.

Cancer	Modality	Selected features
Pancreas	PET(5)	Nonsteerable(Kirsch(1)), CoLlAGe(3), Haralick(Entropy)
	MRI(10)	Law(2), Nonsteerable(Kirsch(3)), CoLlAGe(4), MHoG(1)
Gallbladder	PET(8)	Haralick(Contrast, Entropy), MHoG(4), CoLlAGe(2)
	MRI(7)	Haralick(Entropy), Nonsteerable(Kirsch(4), Sobel(2))
Liver	PET(5)	Haralick(Sum Average, Entropy), Law(3)
	MRI(10)	Nonsteerable(Kirsch(4), Sobel(2)), CoLlAGe(4)

distinguish cancerous and normal regions. Haralick features are able to describe regional heterogeneity in the tumor by capturing gray-level co-occurrence patterns. Nonsteerable gradient features, including Sobel, Kirsch, and first-order spatial derivative operators, allow for characterization of local, spatially proximal textural changes (i.e., microchanges). These features could be useful to form imaging biomarkers for distinguishing tumor and non-tumor regions on PET-MRI.

5   Concluding Remarks

Hybrid PET with MRI enables the acquisition of functional information by PET, and structural as well as functional information by MP-MRI, thus offering complementary information to reflect the heterogeneous sub-region characteristics of aggressive tumors. We devised a radiomics model for automated identification of aggressive tumors using fused PET and MP-MRI. The quantitative results showed that PET-MRI outperformed individual PET and MRI to distinguish cancerous and normal regions, suggesting that extracted features from PET-MRI could serve as useful imaging biomarkers to establish a computer-aided diagnosis system in detecting malignant tumors in daily clinic. Future work will involve validation on a large data cohort with more cancer types. In addition, more texture features will be computed on the fused PET and MP-MRI to identify important image attributes in discriminating different human cancers.

Acknowledgments. This work was supported in part by the National Natural Science Foundation of China under award No. 61401012.

References

1. Bashir, U., Mallia, A., Stirling, J., Joemon, J., MacKewn, J., Charles-Edwards, G., Goh, V., Cook, G.: PET/MRI in oncological imaging: state of the art. Diagnostics **21**(5), 333–357 (2015)
2. Chen, S., He, H., Garcia, E.: RAMOBoost: ranked minority oversampling in boosting. IEEE Trans. Neural Networks **21**(10), 1624–1642 (2010)
3. Edwards, B., Brown, M., Wingo, P., Howe, H., Ward, E., Ries, L., Schrag, D., Jamison, P., Jemal, A., Wu, X., Friedman, C., Harlan, L., Warren, J., Anderson, R., Pickle, L.: Annual report to the nation on the status of cancer, 1975–2002, featuring population-based trends in cancer treatment. J. Natl. Cancer Inst. **97**(19), 1407–1427 (2005)
4. Ginsburg, S., Lee, G., Ali, S., Madabhushi, A.: Feature importance in nonlinear embeddings (FINE): applications in digital pathology. IEEE Trans. Med. Imaging **35**(1), 76–88 (2016)
5. Haralick, R.: Statistical and structural approaches to texture. Proc. IEEE **67**(5), 786–804 (1979)
6. Lambin, P., Rios-Velazquez, E., Leijenaar, R., Carvalho, S., van Stiphout, R., Granton, P., Zegers, C., Gillies, R., Boellard, R., Dekker, A., Aerts, H.: Radiomics: extracting more information from medical images using advanced feature analysis. Eur. J. Cancer **48**(4), 441–446 (2012)

7. Li, C., Xu, C., Gui, C., Fox, M.: Distance regularized level set evolution and its application to image segmentation. IEEE Trans. Image Process. **19**, 3243–3254 (2010)
8. Li, L., Rusu, M., Viswanath, S., Penzias, G., Pahwa, S., Gollamudi, J., Madabhushi, A.: Multi-modality registration via multi-scale textural and spectral embedding representations. In: Proceedings of SPIE, p. 978446-1 (2016)
9. Lian, C., Ruan, S., Denaux, T., Jardin, F., Vera, P.: Selecting radiomic features from FDG-PET images for cancer treatment outcome prediction. Med. Image Anal. **32**, 257–267 (2016)
10. Prasanna, P., Tiwari, P., Madabhushi, A.: Co-occurrence of local anisotropic gradient orientations (CoLlAGe): a new radiomics descriptor. Sci. Rep. **22**(6), 37241 (2016)
11. Qiao, X., Zhang, L.: Distance-weighted support vector machine. Stat. Interface **8**, 331–345 (2015)
12. Riola-Parada, C., Garcia-Canamaque, L., Perez-Duenas, V., Garcerant-Tafur, M., Carreras-Delgado, J.: Simultaneous PET/MRI vs PET/CT in oncology. A systematic review. Rev. Esp. Med. Nucl. Imagen. Mol. **35**(5), 306–312 (2016)
13. Siegel, R., Miller, K., Jemal, A.: Cancer statistics. CA Cancer J. Clin. **66**(1), 7–30 (2016)
14. Tiwari, P., Prasanna, P., Wolansky, L., Pinho, M., Cohen, M., Nayate, A., Gupta, A., Singh, G., Hatanpaa, K., Sloan, A., Rogers, L., Madabhushi, A.: Computer-extracted texture features to distinguish cerebral radionecrosis from recurrent brain tumors on multiparametric MRI: a feasibility study. AJNR Am. J. Neuroradiol. **37**(12), 2231–2236 (2016)
15. Vallières, M., Freeman, C., Skamene, S., El Naqa, I.: A radiomics model from joint FDG-PET and MRI texture features for the prediction of lung metastases in soft-tissue sarcomas of the extremities. Phys. Med. Biol. **60**(14), 5471–5496 (2015)
16. Wan, T., Bloch, B., Plecha, D., Thompson, C., Gilmore, H., Jaffe, C., Harris, L., Madabhushi, A.: A radio-genomics approach for identifying high risk estrogen receptor-positive breast cancers on DCE-MRI: preliminary results in predicting Oncotypedx risk scores. Sci. Rep. **18**(6), 21394 (2016)
17. Wan, T., Madabhushi, A., Phinikaridou, A., Hamilton, J.A., Hua, N., Pham, T., Danagoulian, J., Kleiman, R., Buckler, A.: Spatio-temporal texture (SpTeT) for distinguishing vulnerable from stable atherosclerotic plaque on dynamic contrast enhancement (DCE) MRI in a rabbit model. Med. Phys. **41**(4), 042303 (2014)
18. Zhao, B., Tan, Y., Tsai, W., Qi, J., Xie, C., Lu, L., Schwartz, L.: Reproducibility of radiomics for deciphering tumor phenotype with imaging. Sci. Rep. **24**(6), 23428 (2016)

Image Recognition with Histogram of Oriented Gradient Feature and Pseudoinverse Learning AutoEncoders

Sibo Feng, Shijia Li, Ping Guo[✉], and Qian Yin[✉]

Image Processing and Pattern Recognition Laboratory,
Beijing Normal University, Beijing, China
{sibofeng,sjli}@mail.bnu.edu.cn, pguo@ieee.org, yinqian@bnu.edu.cn

Abstract. Neural network is an artificial intelligence technology which achieve good results in computer vision, natural language processing and other related fields. Currently the most used model for image recognition is convolutional neural networks, however, it has complex structure, there many group open sources of code but it is difficult to reuse. Moreover, most of training algorithm of the model is based on the gradient descent which takes a lot of time to adjust parameters. In order to solve these problems, this paper presents a model combining the histogram of oriented gradient and the pseudoinverse learning autoencoders. Our model does not require any iterative optimization, the number of the neurons and the number of hidden layers are automatically determined in the model. At the same time, our model has a simple structure, do not requires a huge amount of computing resources. Experimental results show that our model is superior to other baseline models.

Keywords: Pseudoinverse learning autoencoder · Feedforward neural network · Histogram of oriented gradient · Image recognition

1 Introduction

Machine learning algorithm attracted many researchers to study large data processing requirements. In 2006, Hinton et al. proposed an unsupervised learning algorithm for deep belief network (DBN) [1] to solve the difficult problem of deep neural network models, which is the beginning of deep learning. Recently, the improvement of computer hardware makes training deep neural networks possible. AlexNet [2] is proposed by Krizhevsky et al. in 2012, which is a deep neural network model firstly using convolutional neural network (CNN) to achieve Top5 error rate of 15.4% at ImageNet competition for the first time. AlexNet uses five convolution layers and three fully connected layers for classification. In 2015, He et al. proposes ResNet [3] model which reached 152 layers.

Many well performing neural network models extract features using convolution layers [2–4] and using fully connection layer for classification. However, it takes a lot of time to adjust the hyper parameters and most training algorithms

© Springer International Publishing AG 2017
D. Liu et al. (Eds.): ICONIP 2017, Part VI, LNCS 10639, pp. 740–749, 2017.
https://doi.org/10.1007/978-3-319-70136-3_78

are based on the gradient descent (GD) and its variations method [4,5] which can be realized nonlinear mapping. GD repeated to learn the parameters, it is easy to fall into the local minimum and result training failure. Although CNN achieves good results in image recognition, it has large workload that requires a huge amount of computing resources and difficult to reproduce because of optimal hyper parameter selection problem. Some research teams give the open source code about their work, but still need very professional knowledge to use the model, for most users it often can not get very good results.

In order to reduce the training time and improve the generalization of learned networks, we proposed a model which is the combination of histogram of oriented gradient (HOG) [6] and pseudoinverse learning autoencoders (PILAE) [7–10]. HOG is a hand-craft image feature, it can be computed easily, quickly and more efficient than that of CNN, and it is successfully applied to pedestrian detection as well as many other image feature related problems. First, since HOG computes on the squares of the image, it has a good invariance in geometrical and illumination deformations. Moreover, in the case of coarse airspace sampling, fine directional sampling, and strong localized optical normalization, it is possible to allow pedestrians to have some subtle movements, which can be ignored without affecting the detection effect. Because of its merits we select HOG to extract image features. In the work [8] of Wang et al., we know that PILAE do well in one-dimensional data classification like spectrum, but pixel spatial neighborhood relationship is not counted for two-dimensional image. Hence, we use HOG first to get oriented features, then apply PILAE to further extract feature and classification.

Unlike CNN, our model does not require repeated iterative optimization, the weight of the network can be computed with pseudoinverse learning algorithm. Training errors can be eliminated error by adding layers so learning accuracy is determined by the number of layers of the network. Our model is easy to use, though users may not have enough professional knowledge, it is our efforts to prompt democratized artificial intelligence development.

2   Related Work

2.1   Histogram of Oriented Gradient

Histogram of Oriented Gradient [6] was proposed by Navneet et al., it is a hand-craft feature descriptor with many applications in image processing. The main idea of HOG is to describe the local information of the image in a gradient and edge direction density. The main steps to calculate HOG are shown as Fig. 1.

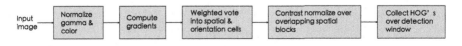

Fig. 1. The feature extraction procedure of histogram of oriented gradient.

The first step is the calculation of the gradient values by filtering the color or intensity data of the image with filter kernels. In order to reduce the impact of light factor, the entire image is normalized. For the texture feature of the image, the local surface gives large contribution, we use gamma compression in Eq. (1) to reduce influence of the local shadow and illumination.

$$H(x, y) = H(x, y)^{gamma}. \tag{1}$$

where $H(x, y)$ represent the pixel of the image at coordinate (x, y), *gamma* is the compression parameter.

We compute the oriented gradient of each pixel with Eqs. (2) and (3). Then the cell histograms are created, each pixel within the cell casts a weighted vote for orientation-based histogram channel based on the values found in the gradient computation.

$$G_x(x, y) = H(x + 1, y) - H(x - 1, y), \tag{2}$$

$$G_y(x, y) = H(x, y + 1) - H(x, y - 1). \tag{3}$$

where $G_x(x, y), G_y(x, y)$ are the horizontal gradient and the vertical gradient of pixel $H(x, y)$, respectively.

To account for change in illumination and contrast, the gradient strengths need locally normalized, which requires grouping the cells together into larger, spatially connected blocks. These blocks usually overlap which means that each cell contributes several times to the final descriptor. After feature is extracted, it will use norm for block normalization.

2.2   AutoEncoder

An autoencoder [11–13] was first proposed by Rumelhart et al. in 1986. An autoencoder neural network can be regarded as an unsupervised learning because it sets the target values be equal to the inputs. Autoencoder is used as building blocks for the construction of deep neural network model, as well as data dimension reduction for feature learning and data dimension increment for sparse coding. The single hidden layer autoencoder consists of an encoder and a decoder, which trend to learn a function that output approximately equal to input,

$$h_{W,b}(x) \approx x. \tag{4}$$

where W and b are the weight and bias of the model.

A stacked autoencoders (SAE) [14] is a neural network composed of multi-layers autoencoder in which the output of previous layer as input of the next layer. Greedy training network each layer, and then fine tune the whole neural network. Train process is as follows:

$$H^l = f(z^l), \tag{5}$$

$$z^{l+1} = W^{l+1}H^l + b^{l+1}, \tag{6}$$

where z^l is the input of l layer, H^l is the output of l layer and W^{l+1} and b^{l+1} are the parameters of the $l + 1$ layer.

3   Proposed Methodology

3.1   Proposed Classification Model

We proposed a model which uses the HOG to extract the image feature and the PILAE to further extract the feature and classification. We utilize the idea of SAE which used single hidden layer forward network learning algorithm. Proposed model training stacked autoencoders with pseudoinverse learning which extend the PIL algorithm to the depth learning framework. Compared to other multilayer neural network models, our model does not require iterative optimization, PIL can calculate the network weight, do not need to adjust those hyper parameters.

The framework of the model training is illustrated in Fig. 2. It consists of two parts. The first part, we use different cells and blocks to generate several feature maps, the second part is PILAE. The PILAE constructed by the n single-hidden layers feedforward neural network. After the training is completed, we remove each individual autoencoder's decoder to form a deep feedforward neural network.

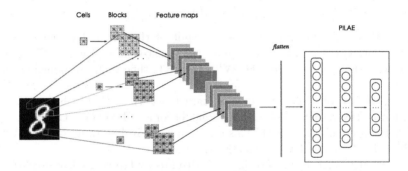

Fig. 2. The architecture of the proposed model. It is achieved by combining the histogram of oriented gradient feature and the PILAE.

3.2   Training Model

Pseudoinverse learning algorithm [15,16] was originally proposed by Guo et al., it is a supervised learning algorithm for feedforward neural network which based on generalized linear algebraic methods. Differ from back propagation algorithm and other GD based learning algorithms, PIL do not need to set related parameters such as step length, learning epochs and momentum these hyper parameters usually difficult selected by users.

Suppose we have a data set $\mathbf{D} = \left\{\mathbf{x}^i, \mathbf{o}^i\right\}_{i=1}^{N}$, where sample number is N, and output dimension is m, the task of training network is to find the weight matrix for each layer of the network via optimize the error function,

$$E = \frac{1}{2N} \sum_{i=1}^{N} \sum_{j=1}^{m} \left\| g_j \left(\mathbf{x}^i, \mathbf{\Theta}\right) - o_j^i \right\|^2, \tag{7}$$

where $g(\mathbf{x}, \Theta)$ is the neural network mapping function and Θ is the network parameter set includes weight $\mathbf{W}$ and bias parameter. The mapping function can be written as:

$$g_j(\mathbf{x}, \Theta) = \sum_{i=1}^{N} w_{i,j} \sigma_i (\sum_{l=1}^{n} w_{i,l} x_l + \theta_i). \tag{8}$$

where θ_i is a bias value for network input.

We assume only the input layer has a bias neuron, while others hidden layers and the output layer have no bias neuron, the input of the layer l is multiplied by the weight between the layer l and the layer $l+1$. and applying the nonlinear activate functions, we get:

$$\mathbf{H}^{l+1} = \sigma(\mathbf{H}^l \mathbf{W}^l). \tag{9}$$

and the output of the network is $\mathbf{G} = \mathbf{H}^L \mathbf{W}^L$. where L donate the output and the weight matrix of the last hidden layer.

According to the above reformulation, we can get the following optimization target

$$\text{minimize} \|\mathbf{H}^L \mathbf{W}^L - \mathbf{O}\|^2, \tag{10}$$

where $\mathbf{H}^L \mathbf{W}^L$ is the product of the output of the last hidden layer and the weight matrix, the problem become a linear least-square problem. The optimal solution to the problem is let $\|\mathbf{H}^L \mathbf{W}^L - \mathbf{O}\|^2 = 0$, then we have trained the input samples.

In order to solve the optimization target, let $\mathbf{W} = \mathbf{H}^+ \mathbf{O}$, the approximate solution of $\mathbf{H}\mathbf{W}$, then the learning target becomes $\|\mathbf{H}\mathbf{H}^+ \mathbf{O} - \mathbf{O}\|^2 = 0$, where $\mathbf{H}^+$ is the pseudoinverse of $\mathbf{H}$. This question is equivalent to find matrix $\mathbf{H}$ that $\mathbf{H}\mathbf{H}^+ - \mathbf{I} = 0$, where $\mathbf{I}$ is the identity matrix.

We use PIL algorithm to train SAE with greedy layer-wise learning strategy, PILAE is used as the building block of the SAE. The hidden neuron number is set with formula in [10]. To learn the feature of the data, hidden neuron number is usually smaller than that of the input vector dimension, and is a little greater than that of the rank of the input matrix. The rank can be calculated by decomposing the input matrix with singular value decomposition (SVD) method. The pseudoinverse of the input matrix, calculated by the truncated SVD, is used as the encoder weight matrix. The decoder weight matrix is calculated with PIL. In addition, in order to reduce the degree of freedom of parameter, we tie the weight of the encoder and the decoder, which let the encoder weight matrix equal to the transposed decoder weight.

Autoencoder can map the data to high-dimensional or low-dimensional space, we use the low rank approximation to map the data into low dimensions of the space.

We calculate the pseudoinverse of the input matrix with SVD method,

$$\mathbf{X} = \mathbf{U}\mathbf{\Sigma}\mathbf{V}^T. \tag{11}$$

From the result of SVD, the pseudoinverse of the input matrix is:

$$\mathbf{X}^+ = \mathbf{V}\mathbf{\Sigma}'\mathbf{U}^T. \tag{12}$$

where $\mathbf{\Sigma}'$ is the transposed diagonal matrix composed of the reciprocal of nonzero elements in matrix $\mathbf{\Sigma}$.

The number of first hidden layer neuron is set to equal to the rank of input matrix, for succeed hidden layer neuron number, we empirically assign with following formula,

$$p = \beta Dim(\mathbf{x}), \beta \in [0, 1], \tag{13}$$

where function Dim returns the dimension of the input matrix, and β is a empirical parameter which depend on the what kind degree of dimension should be reduced. This is to force dimension reduction.

The low rank approximation matrix $\hat{\mathbf{X}}^+$ is truncated SVD of the matrix $\mathbf{X}^+$:

$$\hat{\mathbf{X}}^+ = \hat{\mathbf{V}}\mathbf{\Sigma}'\mathbf{U}^T, \tag{14}$$

where $\hat{\mathbf{V}}$ is composed of the $p \times N$ consist of first p rows of matrix $\mathbf{V}$.

Since the input data of the autoencoder is approximately equal to the output, we add the constraint $\mathbf{O} = \mathbf{X}$, where $\mathbf{O}$ is the output matrix and $\mathbf{X}$ is the input matrix. $\mathbf{W}_e$ is the weight matrix of encoder and $\mathbf{W}_d$ is the weight matrix of decoder, here we assign $\mathbf{W}_e = \hat{\mathbf{X}}^+$. Hence, we rewrite the optimization objective function as follows:

$$\text{minimize} \|\mathbf{H}\mathbf{W} - \mathbf{X}\|^2. \tag{15}$$

To solve this optimization problem, we use the following pseudoinverse approximate solution:

$$\mathbf{W} = \mathbf{H}^+\mathbf{X}. \tag{16}$$

According the work of Horel et al. [17] that in the case of multiple linear regression $b = Ax + \varepsilon$, if $A^T A$ is not a unit matrix, the least squares estimation is sensitive to the error in A, and x is not meaningful. So we use the following formula to describe.

$$x = (A^T A + k)^{-1} A^T b, k > 0. \tag{17}$$

Where k is a regularization parameter. When the column rank of matrix is full, we use the orthogonal projection method to solve the pseudoinverse:

$$\mathbf{W}^L = (\mathbf{H}^T\mathbf{H})^{-1}\mathbf{H}^T\mathbf{X}. \tag{18}$$

To avoid ill-posed problem, a weight decay regularization term solution is:

$$\mathbf{W} = (\mathbf{H}^T\mathbf{H} + k\mathbf{I})^{-1}\mathbf{H}^T\mathbf{X}. \tag{19}$$

Where k is a regularization parameter setting by user, it is also can be estimated with formula in [18]. Therefore, we tune the k to find the tradeoff between the generalization and the accuracy.

4   Performance Evaluation

4.1   MNIST Dataset

We use the MNIST image data set to verify model performance. The input of the model is 28 × 28 pixels image. We use 8 kernels extract HOG feature maps and three layers for PILAE. We conduct all the experiments on the same computer with 6 Xeon 2.00 GHz processors.

Table 1. MNIST recognition performance comparison

Model	Training time (s)	Training accuracy (%)	Testing accuracy (%)
SAE	298.43	97.53	96.72
Lenet-5	523.43	100.00	98.33
SVM	2583.82	98.72	96.46
HOG	30.83	94.88	94.32
PILAE	62.32	97.32	96.39
HOG+PILAE	92.58	99.12	98.01

We compare the proposed model with several model including SAE, Lenet-5, support vector machine (SVM), PILAE. In Table 1 the results of classification on the MNIST data set are shown, including the training time, training accuracy and testing accuracy. We can observe through the form that the proposed model achieve comparable accuracy to other baseline models, whereas the training time of our model is far less than any other CNN model.

From Fig. 3(a) we can seen that recognition loss decrease with the number of feature maps increases. HOG feature varies from several to dozens of input dimensions features. In the experiments, we use different cells and orientations constitute several blocks to product feature maps, these maps flattened to one-dimension feature vectors. The effect of the number of hidden layers is analyzed by increasing the layer one by one. Figure 3(b) shows the relationship between the number of hidden layers and the recognition loss. It can be seen that the minimum value of training loss and testing loss is reached at third layers. After that, loss increase where we should stop our training, so early stop regularization is utilized in setting the number of hidden layers. It also can be seen from Fig. 3(c) that the decrease of the reconstruction error with layer number increase. The reconstruction error becomes smaller when the number of layer increases. The small reconstruction error cannot bring the better generalization performance for a model, sometimes, it means loss too many features, results to degrade model classification ability.

4.2   Cambridge-Gesture Dataset

Gesture recognition is an important part in computer vision, widely used in human-computer interaction gesture remote control and sifted language interpreting.

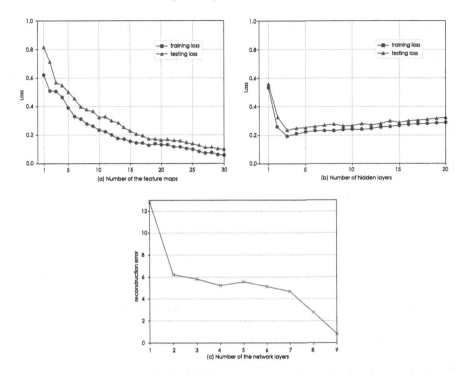

Fig. 3. (a) The loss with feature maps extract from HOG increasing. (b) The recognition loss with increasing the number of the model layers. (c) The reconstruction error with the increasing of the model layers.

The Cambridge-Gesture data set [19] consists of 900 images sequences of gesture with 9 classes.

The original images contains lots of noise and light effects in different directions. We use a filter to extract the image of the solid line contour and use binarization to weaken background and light. Since the images is a sequence, we combined one sequence images into one single fused images.

Table 2. Gesture recognition performance comparison

Method	SDA	H-ELM	HOG	PILAE	HOG+PILAE
Training time (s)	16035.79	57.70	20.45	52.96	77.13
Testing accuracy (%)	93.3	99.4	90.67	97.06	99.72

We use 4 kernels extract HOG feature maps to get more than one thousands dimensions of the features, then two hidden layers PILAE for further feature learning. It takes about 80 seconds to train the model, and achieves recognition performance with 99.72% testing accuracy. We also compared with stacked denoising autoencoders (SDA) [13] and so called H-ELM[1] model, shown as Table 2, our model combine handcrafted feature extractors with PILAE based neural network shows the best result over others. In addition, our model's training time is also on the same order comparative with those less training time models.

5   Conclusions

In this paper, we propose a model by combining HOG and PILAE for image recognition. HOG features are used for PILAE based neural network model input. Our model has an advantage in learning speed, meanwhile achieving a certain accuracy. It is no need to adjust hyper parameters, training model can be automatically stopped with early stop technique, the number of the neurons and the number of hidden layers are automatically determined by the strategy we provide. Our model is easy to use, it reduces the dependent of professional knowledge requirements for most users. We validate the performance of the network using some benchmark dataset such as the MNIST, Cambridge-Gesture. The results show that our model has a better performance on classification tasks. This is our effort to prompt the development of automatic machine learning and expect to democratize artificial intelligence.

Acknowledgments. This work is fully supported by National Natural Science Foundation of China (NSFC) (61472043, 61375045) and Joint Research Fund in Astronomy under cooperative agreement between the National Natural Science Foundation of China (NSFC) and Chinese Academy of Sciences (CAS) (U1531242).

References

1. Hinton, G.E., Osindero, S., Teh, Y.W.: A fast learning algorithm for deep belief nets. Neural Comput. **18**(7), 1527–1554 (2006)
2. Krizhevsky, A., Sutskever, I., Hinton, G.E.: Imagenet classification with deep convolutional neural networks. In: Advances in Neural Information Processing Systems, pp. 1097–1105 (2012)
3. He, K., Zhang, X., Ren, S., et al.: Deep residual learning for image recognition. In: Proceedings of the IEEE Conference on Computer Vision and Pattern Recognition, pp. 770–778 (2016)
4. LeCun, Y., Bottou, L., Bengio, Y., et al.: Gradient-based learning applied to document recognition. Proc. IEEE **86**(11), 2278–2324 (1998)
5. Simonyan, K., Zisserman, A.: Very deep convolutional networks for large-scale image recognition. arXiv preprint arXiv:1409.1556 (2014)
6. Dalal, N., Triggs, B.: Histograms of oriented gradients for human detection. In: IEEE Computer Society Conference on CVPR Computer Vision and Pattern Recognition, pp. 886–893. IEEE (2005)

---

[1] The structure of H-ELM consists of several hidden layers with noise (random value) output matrix and one lasso regression layer.

7. Wang, K., Guo, P., Yin, Q., et al.: A pseudoinverse incremental algorithm for fast training deep neural networks with application to spectra pattern recognition. In: 2016 International Joint Conference on Neural Networks (IJCNN), pp. 3453–3460. IEEE (2016)

8. Wang, K., Guo, P., Luo, A.L.: A new automated spectral feature extraction method and its application in spectral classification and defective spectra recovery. Mon. Not. Roy. Astron. Soc. **465**(4), 4311–4324 (2017)

9. Wang, K., Guo, P., Luo, A.L., et al.: Deep neural networks with local connectivity and its application to astronomical spectral data. In: 2016 IEEE International Conference on Systems, Man, and Cybernetics (SMC), pp. 002687–002692. IEEE (2016)

10. Wang, K., Guo, P., Xin, X., Ye, Z.: Autoencoder, low rank approximation and pseudoinverse learning algorithm. In: 2017 IEEE International Conference on Systems, Man, and Cybernetics (SMC), pp. 948–953. IEEE (2017)

11. Hinton, G.E., Salakhutdinov, R.R.: Reducing the dimensionality of data with neural networks. Science **313**(5786), 504–507 (2006)

12. Bengio, Y.: Learning deep architectures for AI. Found. Trends Mach. Learn. **2**(1), 1–127 (2009)

13. Vincent, P., Larochelle, H., Bengio, Y., et al.: Extracting and composing robust features with denoising autoencoders. In: Proceedings of the 25th International Conference on Machine Learning, pp. 1096–1103. ACM (2008)

14. Bengio, Y., Lamblin, P., Popovici, D., et al.: Greedy layer-wise training of deep networks. In: Advances in Neural Information Processing Systems, vol. 19, p. 153 (2007)

15. Guo, P., Lyu, M.R., Mastorakis, N.E.: Pseudoinverse learning algorithm for feedforward neural networks. In: Advances in Neural Networks and Applications, pp. 321–326 (2001)

16. Guo, P., Lyu, M.R.: A pseudoinverse learning algorithm for feedforward neural networks with stacked generalization applications to software reliability growth data. Neurocomputing **56**, 101–121 (2004)

17. Hoerl, A.E., Kennard, R.W.: Ridge regression: biased estimation for nonorthogonal problems. Technometrics **12**(1), 55–67 (1970)

18. Guo, P., Lyu, M.R., Chen, C.L.P.: Regularization parameter estimation for feedforward neural networks. IEEE trans Syst. Man Cybern. (B) **33**(1), 35–44 (2003)

19. Kim, T.K., Wong, S.F., Cipolla, R.: Tensor canonical correlation analysis for action classification. In: IEEE Conference on Computer Vision and Pattern Recognition (CVPR), pp. 1–8. IEEE (2007)

A New Vector Space Model
Based on the Deep Learning

Hanen Karamti[1]([✉]), Mohamed Tmar[2], and Faiez Gargouri[2]

[1] Princess Nourah bint Abdulrahman University, PO Box 84428,
Riyadh, Saudi Arabia
hmkaramti@pnu.edu.sa
[2] MIRACL-ISIMS, BP242, City Ons, 3021 Sfax, Tunisia
mohamed.tmar@isimsf.rnu.tn, faiez.gargouri@isims.usf.tn

Abstract. Deep learning has become one of the top performing methods for many computer vision tasks such as images retrieval. It has been deployed so far to bring improvements to learning feature representations and similarity measures.

In this article, we present a new search method to represent and to retrieve images based on the vector space method, called vectorization. This method transforms any matching model of images to a vector space model providing a score using the Convolutional Neural Networks (CNN). The results obtained by this model are illustrated through some experiments and compared with several state-of-art methods.

Keywords: Image · CNN · Deep learning · Logistic regression · Vector space model · Convolutional neural networks

1 Introduction

Researchers are interested in learning methods for image retrieval improvement. Images retrieval is a visual search task that aims at, given a query as image example, retrieving all images that contain the same object instance as the query within a database of images. Image retrieval and other related visual search tasks have range of applications, e.g., reverse image search on the web or organization of personal photo collections. Image retrieval applications were based on image representation as a set of extracted low-level features such as color, texture and shape. These features describe the global image information, the overall description describes the whole of the image taking into account its background. However, local image descriptors attracted more attention within the content-based image retrieval domain [2]. Features are extracted around interest points or interest areas detected in the images. Then, the region centered on a local feature is converted into descriptors.

Recently, a large amount of research is oriented towards deep learning techniques to improve the image representation. Deep learning includes supervised [3] feature learning and unsupervised feature learning [4]. Supervised feature

D. Liu et al. (Eds.): ICONIP 2017, Part VI, LNCS 10639, pp. 750–758, 2017.
https://doi.org/10.1007/978-3-319-70136-3_79

learning requires a large amount of accurately annotated data. Moreover, these algorithms generally require a large sparse matrix to describe the similarity between data points in the training set. Unsupervised feature learning [4] is based on unlabeled data, and therefore the properties emphasized in the representation might differ from the once perceived by humans. Deep learning, and particularly deep convolutional neural networks (CNN), have become an extremely powerful tool in computer vision [8] such as object detection, recognition and image classification. This has inspired many researchers to explore deep CNNs in order to solve a variety of problems. After Krizhevsky et al. [10] achieved the first place on the ImageNet classification and localization challenges using a convolutional neural network, deep learning-based methods have significantly improved the state of the art in other tasks such as object detection [11] and semantic segmentation. However, deep learning has been less successful so far in instance-level image retrieval. On most retrieval benchmarks, deep methods perform worse than conventional methods that rely on local descriptor matching and reranking with elaborate spatial verification [12].

The focus of this paper is image retrieval and in particular the transformation of the matching image model to vector space model providing scores. The remaining of the paper is organized as follows: we give our initial architecture in Sect. 2. Section 3 describes our images retrieve model based on the deep learning technique. Section 4 discusses the results obtained with our system on two benchmark datasets. Finally, Sect. 5 concludes and presents further research directions.

2   Initial System Description

The different component of our research system are feature extraction and retrieval. The feature extraction process, performed off-line, is responsible for extracting features from images and storing them into the index database. Each image is represented by a vector of global features. We used four global descriptors for feature extraction: Layout Color (CLD) [27], Scalabe Color (SCD) [9], Edge Histogram (EHD) [6] and the Color and Edge Directivity Descriptor (CEDD) [5]. To make the content-based image retrieval truly scalable to large size image collections, we merge these descriptors in two efficient manners: late fusion and early fusion. Early fusion is the fusion of different feature spaces before indexing. The different features extracted from images are concatenated into one single large vector. Normalization pre-processing is performed so that features are expressed on the same scale. To normalize the feature vectors, we use the Min-Max method [7].

Let $(I_1, I_2...I_n)$ the set n of images and $(C_{i,1}, C_{i,2}...C_{i,f}...C_{i,Z_p})$ their low-level features, where $C_{i,f}$ is the value of feature f in the image I_i using the descriptor p. Let Q is therefore a query features vector designed by $(C_{q,1}, C_{q,2}...C_{q,f}...C_{q,Z_p})$ features values, is the individual descriptor considered where $C_{q,f}$ is the value of feature f in the query and Z_p is the number of features. To compare two images I_i and I_j, we use the Euclidean distance [1]. Late fusion addresses the problem of combining multiple result lists obtained from each descriptor. In late fusion, the calculation of similarity between the images is done for each descriptor and then merged therefore in our case. For each descriptor, we look for the K nearest neighbor images, that will be stored in a result list. Concerning the late fusion of the results obtained by several features. If we have 4 result lists (each vector corresponds to the results found by a descriptor), we sort the list according to the frequency of image appearance. In fact, we count the number of appearance of one image in each result, then we will construct a new vector of images depending of the descending sort of its frequency [13].

3   A New Vector Space Model

In the previous works [13], we used the vectorization technique which makes it possible to transform the images matching model to a vector space model. We have seen several techniques, the best one was based on neural networks. We have used a neural network without hidden layers (logistic regression). The idea of this method is to multiply the features vector of the query Q by the matrix W to find the result score vector S ($Z \times n$), where n is the number of images and Z is the number of features.

This method attempts to estimate the weight matrix W over a set of queries and their associated score vectors S. We build a logistic regression containing 3 layers L_Q, L_H and L_S. L_Q (resp L_S) is relative to the image feature values I_i (resp image scores S_{I_i}). $L_Q = \{C_{I_i,1}, C_{I_i,2} \ldots C_{I_i,j} \ldots C_{I_i,Z}\}$ is the input layer of our network, where each neuron represents a feature $C_{I_i,j}$. $L_S = \{S_{I_i,1}, S_{I_i,2} \ldots S_{I_i,j'} \ldots S_{I_i,n}\}$ is the output layer, where each neuron represents a score $S_{I_i,j'}$.

In our case, Matrix W is estimated by a gradient propagation approach (with random initialization), where $w1_{jj'}$ is given respectively by Eq. 1:

$$W1[j,j'] = w1_{jj'} \quad \forall(j,j') \in \{1,2\ldots Z\} \times \{1,2\ldots n\} \tag{1}$$

$$W = \begin{pmatrix} w1_{11} & w1_{12} & w1_{1j'} & \ldots & w1_{1n} \\ w1_{21} & w1_{22} & w1_{2j'} & \ldots & w1_{2n} \\ & & \vdots & & \\ w1_{Z1} & w1_{Z2} & w1_{Zj'} & \ldots & w1_{Zn} \end{pmatrix}$$

Once the matrix W is constructed, each query Q can be calculated directly without applying an Euclidean metric but by applying the equation $Q * W = S$. Thus, the ranks (scores) of resulting images are obtained as a result of multiplication of query feature vector by the weight matrix W.

This process will be repeat for each descriptor p. That is to say for each descriptor p, a neuron network is constructed with the same treatment described in above. So the number of layers of entries for our CNN is four. Our object is to propose a new neural network to merge the results obtained from the heterogeneous features. By improving the fusion techniques used, we have thought of

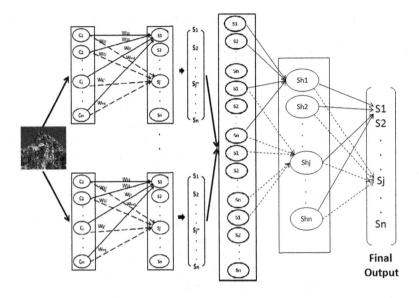

Fig. 1. Our new CNN architecture with deep learning.

a method that allows to find the scores of an image retrieval by several descriptors without going through the late fusion. The idea is based on deep learning. Indeed, we apply the logistic regression for each descriptor. Then, after network stabilization, we again apply another neural network based on the scores found by each descriptor to have the final scores found by the late merger. Figure 1 presents our architecture.

Our new system is composed of two parts: the first part is devoted to learning the network to retrieve the result list, or each list and represented by a score vector. Indeed, we have p logistic regression, each network is applied for a descriptor. The neuron number and the layer number is the same to the last section. The second part is devoted to the merge of the result lists. The lists found in the first part are trained to result in a single result list.

4 Experimental Comparison

We evaluate the performance of our model on two standard datasets:

- INRIA Holidays dataset (Holidays[1]) contains 1491 vacation snapshots corresponding to 500 groups each having the same scene or object. One image from each group serves as a query. The performance is reported as mean average precision over 500 queries.

---

[1] https://lear.inrialpes.fr/~jegou/data.php.

– Oxford Buildings dataset (Oxford5K[2]) contains 5062 photographs from Flickr associated with Oxford landmarks. 55 queries corresponding to 11 buildings/landmarks are fixed, and the ground truth relevance of the remaining dataset. These 11 classes is provided. The performance is measured using mean average precision (mAP) over the 55 queries.

We extract deep convolutional features using the very deep CNN trained by Simonyan and Zisserman [14]. Caffe [15] package for CNNs is used. For this architecture, the number of maps in the last convolutional layer is $C = 1000$. All images are resized to the size 520×520 prior to passing through the network.

4.1 Feature Extraction

In this section, we evaluate the feature combination. We compare the performances of the following three methods: early fusion (EF), late fusion according to frequency (LF_Freq) and late fusion according to rank (LF_Rank). In the first step, we evaluate each descriptor separately. In the second step, we try every possible combinations between descriptors. The results obtained on Holidays and Oxford5k datasets are given in Table 1.

Table 1. Results obtained on the both Holidays and Oxford5k dataset to compare the three fusion methods.

Database	Holidays			Oxford5k		
MAP/Method	EF	LF_Freq	LF_Rank	EF	LF_Freq	LF_Rank
SCD	20.4	–	–	19.2	–	–
CLD	28.8	–	–	21.3	–	–
EHD	35.5	–	–	30.2	–	–
CEDD	43.5	–	–	35.4	–	–
SCD + CLD	32.1	32.1	33.3	21.5	22.1	23.2
SCD + CEDD	34.3	34.6	34.8	30.1	31.5	32.2
SCD + EHD	34.4	36.7	36.9	32.8	33.1	33.3
CLD + CEDD	54.4	55.3	55.6	41.5	43.2	43.8
CLD + EHD	53.3	53.8	54.4	44.2	45.3	45.3
EHD + CEDD	55.2	57.4	57.6	44.8	44.9	45.1
CLD + SCD + EHD	46.6	48.4	50.2	46.1	47	47.2
CLD + SCD + CEDD	48.1	48.4	48.8	46.2	46.8	47
SCD + EHD + CEDD	46.5	48.6	50.6	46.8	47.2	47.3
CLD + EHD + CEDD	54.3	55.2	57.5	48.2	49.1	49.3
SCD + CLD + EHD + CEDD	56.5	57.8	58.4	49.2	50.4	51.5

---

[2] http://www.robots.ox.ac.uk/~vgg/data/oxbuildings/.

From Table 1 (results on Holidays dataset), we can see that considering for each descriptor separately is not sufficient to obtain good retrieval results ($SCD = 20, 6$, $CLD = 28, 8$, $EHD = 35, 5$ and $CEDD = 43, 5$). So, a fusion step is necessary to improve the results. Fusion by two or three descriptors prove the results. However, we can see that fusion of the 4 descriptors gives the best results. We also see that the best result is given by the fusion by rank.

Similar results are observed on oxford dataset, the MAP of retrieval results of different images are shown on Table 1. The MAP value is high with the last fusion method of descriptors compared to others. This is because fusion between descriptor retrieves ($MAP = 51.5$) the best number of relevant images after merging result lists. We found the combination of the fourth features is very important compared to other retrieve methods (that use one or two or three descriptors).

4.2   Evaluation of Our Method

Among various techniques, machine learning has been actively investigated as a possible direction to bridge the semantic gap in the long term. Inspired by recent successes of deep learning techniques for computer vision and other applications, we thought of using it to transform the image matching model to a vector model. In reality, our deep learning method allows to execute several neural networks at the same time to give a single result list with the CNN algorithm.

Table 2. Performance achieved by our model with deep learning.

Dataset name/MAP	EF of IS	LF_Freq of IS	LF_Rank of IS	New system
Holiday	56.5	57.8	58.4	**61.4**
Oxford	49.2	50.4	51.5	**53.3**

Table 2 shows the results obtained after improvement of the initial system method using the deep learning technique. The results illustrated show the efficiency of our method and above all the role of deep learning to improve the performance and to increase the values of MAP.

Now, we compare our method against the state of the art in Table 3. For these experiments, in addition to the two datasets introduced in the first part of this section, we also consider the Oxford 105k and Paris 6k datasets images [16]. In the first half of the table, we show results for other methods that employ global representations of images with a global descriptors.

In the Table 3, we compare our approach with others methods that also use global descriptors. We notice that our methods give the best results than other methods on the base oxford and than a few methods on the holidays dataset. But we have results less to an important number of methods because they have larger memory footprints and perform a costly spatial verification at test time. However, these methods require a lot of memory storage and a costly verification.

Table 3. Comparison with the state of the art.

Method	Dimension	Dataset Oxford5k	Paris6k	Oxford105k	Holidays
Jégou and Zisserman [17]	1024	56.0	–	50.2	72.0
Jégou and Zisserman [17]	128	43.3	–	35.3	61.7
Gordo et al. (2012) [18]	512	–	–	–	79.0
Babenko et al. (2014) [19]	128	55.7	–	52.3	75.9
Gong et al. (2014) [22]	2048	–	–	–	80.8
Babenko and Lempitsky (2015) [21]	256	53.1	–	50.1	80.2
Ng et al. (2015) [20]	128	59.3	59.0	–	83.6
Paulin et al. (2015) [23]	256	56.5	–	–	79.3
Tolias et al. (2016) [24]	512	66.9	83.0	61.6	85.2
Kalantidis et al. (2016) [25]	512	68.2	79.7	63.3	84.9
Radenovic et al. (2016) [26]	512	79.7	83.8	73.9	82.5
Ours	298	53.3	68.0	72.4	61.4

Radenovic et al. [26] give the best results for all the methods because it is scalable and perform some learning on the target dataset, while in our case we dont have the same configuration and conditions nor the materials to do the tests. We can see that our method outperforms existing approaches with similar feature dimensions, and even some methods with higher feature dimensions.

5 Conclusion

Given the great success enjoyed by the in-depth learning in recent years, we thought of integrating it into our research. In this paper, we can see that he deep learning allows to create a new vector space model. This model is constructed from the global features and score vectors. It relies on the same idea as the vector space model from text retrieval. This method is proposed and compared with state-of-the art methods of image retrieval on Holidays and Oxford5k, Paris6k and Oxford105k dataset. Future work focuses on the application of deep-learning with local characteristics.

References

1. Karamti, H.: Vectorisation du modèle d'appariement pour la recherche d'images par le contenu. In: CORIA, pp. 335–340 (2013)
2. David, G.L.: Object recognition from local scale-invariant features. In: ICCV, pp. 1150–1157 (1999)
3. Becker, C., Rigamonti, R., Lepetit, V., Fua, P.: Supervised feature learning for curvilinear structure segmentation. In: Mori, K., Sakuma, I., Sato, Y., Barillot, C., Navab, N. (eds.) MICCAI 2013. LNCS, vol. 8149, pp. 526–533. Springer, Heidelberg (2013). doi:10.1007/978-3-642-40811-3_66

4. Wang, D., Tan, X.: C-SVDDNet: an effective single-layer network for unsupervised feature learning (2014)
5. Chatzichristofis, S.A., Boutalis, Y.S.: CEDD: color and edge directivity descriptor: a compact descriptor for image indexing and retrieval. In: Gasteratos, A., Vincze, M., Tsotsos, J.K. (eds.) ICVS 2008. LNCS, vol. 5008, pp. 312–322. Springer, Heidelberg (2008). doi:10.1007/978-3-540-79547-6_30
6. Dong, K.P., Yoon, S.J., Chee, S.: Efficient use of local edge histogram descriptor. In: Proceedings of the ACM Multimedia 2000 Workshops, pp. 51–54 (2000)
7. Anil, K., Karthik, N., Arun, R.: Score normalization in multimodal biometric systems. Pattern Recogn. **38**, 2270–2285 (2005)
8. Donahue, J., Jia, Y., Vinyals, O., Hoffman, J., Zhang, N., Eric, T., Trevor, D.: DeCAF: a deep convolutional activation feature for generic visual recognition. In: ICML, pp. 647–655 (2014)
9. Salembier, T., Phillipe, S.: Introduction to MPEG-7: Multimedia Content Description Interface. Wiley, New York (2002)
10. Krizhevsky, A., Sutskever, I.H.: ImageNet classification with deep convolutional neural networks. In: NIPS (2012)
11. Girshick, R., Donahue, J., Darrell, T., Malik, J.: Rich feature hierarchies for accurate object detection and semantic segmentation. In: CVPR (2014)
12. Tolias, G., Avrithis, Y., Jégou, H.: Image search with selective match kernels: aggregation across single and multiple images. IJCV **116**, 247–261 (2015)
13. Karamti, H., Tmar, M., Visani, M., Urruty, T., Gargouri, F.: Vector space model adaptation and pseudo relevance feedback for content-based image retrieval. Multimedia Tools and Applications, pp. 1–27 (2017)
14. Simonyan, K., Zisserman, A.: Very deep convolutional networks for large-scale image recognition (2014)
15. Jia, Y., Shelhamer, E., Donahue, J., Karayev, S., Long, J., Girshick, R.B., Guadarrama, S., Darrell, T.: Caffe: convolutional architecture for fast feature embedding. In: Proceedings of the ACM International (2014)
16. Philbin, J., Chum, O., Isard, M., Sivic, J., Zisserman.: A object retrieval with large vocabularies and fast spatial matching. In: CVPR (2007)
17. Jégou, H., Zisserman, A.: Triangulation embedding and democratic aggregation for image search. In: CVPR (2014)
18. Gordo, A., Rodriguez-Serrano, J.A., Perronnin, F., Valveny, E.: Leveraging category-level labels for instance-level image retrieval. In: CVPR (2012)
19. Babenko, A., Slesarev, A., Chigorin, A., Lempitsky, V.: Neural codes for image retrieval. In: Fleet, D., Pajdla, T., Schiele, B., Tuytelaars, T. (eds.) ECCV 2014. LNCS, vol. 8689, pp. 584–599. Springer, Cham (2014). doi:10.1007/978-3-319-10590-1_38
20. Ng, J.Y.H., Yang.F, Davis, L.S.: Exploiting local features from deep networks for image retrieval. In: CVPR Workshops (2015)
21. Babenko, A., Lempitsky, V.S.: Aggregating deep convolutional features for image retrieval. In: ICCV (2015)
22. Gong, Y., Wang, L., Guo, R., Lazebnik, S.: Multi-scale orderless pooling of deep convolutional activation features. In: Fleet, D., Pajdla, T., Schiele, B., Tuytelaars, T. (eds.) ECCV 2014. LNCS, vol. 8695, pp. 392–407. Springer, Cham (2014). doi:10.1007/978-3-319-10584-0_26
23. Paulin, M., Douze, M., Harchaoui, Z., Mairal, J., Perronin, F., Schmid, C.: Local convolutional features with unsupervised training for image retrieval. In: ICCV (2015)

24. Tolias, G., Sicre, R., Jégou, H.: Particular object retrieval with integral max-pooling of CNN activations. In: ICLR (2016)
25. Kalantidis, Y., Mellina, C., Osindero, S.: Cross-dimensional weighting for aggregated deep convolutional features. In: Hua, G., Jégou, H. (eds.) ECCV 2016. LNCS, vol. 9913, pp. 685–701. Springer, Cham (2016). doi:10.1007/978-3-319-46604-0_48
26. Radenović, F., Tolias, G., Chum, O.: CNN image retrieval learns from BoW: unsupervised fine-tuning with hard examples. In: Leibe, B., Matas, J., Sebe, N., Welling, M. (eds.) ECCV 2016. LNCS, vol. 9905, pp. 3–20. Springer, Cham (2016). doi:10.1007/978-3-319-46448-0_1
27. Eiji, K., Akio, Y.: The MPEG-7 color layout descriptor: a compact image feature description for high-speed image/video segment retrieval. ICIP 1, 674–677 (2001)

Neuronal Classifier for both Rate and Timing-Based Spike Patterns

Qiang Yu[(✉)], Longbiao Wang, and Jianwu Dang

Tianjin Key Laboratory of Cognitive Computing and Application,
School of Computer Science and Technology, Tianjin University, Tianjin, China
yuqnus@gmail.com, longbiao_wang@tju.edu.cn, jdang@jaist.ac.jp

Abstract. Spikes play an essential role in information transmission and neural computation, but how neurons learn them remains unclear. Most learning rules depend on either the rate- or timing-based code, but rare one is suitable for both. In this paper, we present an efficient multi-spike learning rule which is suitable to train neurons to classify both rate- and timing-based spike patterns. With our learning rule, neurons can be trained to fire different numbers of output spikes in response to their input patterns, and therefore single neurons are capable for multi-category classification.

Keywords: Spiking neural network · Learning · Rate code · Timing code · Classification

1 Introduction

Spikes (or action potentials) play an essential role in information transmission and cognitive computation in biological nervous systems. Neurons communicate with each other by sending spikes forth and back. Therefore, information must be encoded by spikes with certain mechanisms. A sequence of spikes may contain information based on different coding schemes, among which rate and temporal code are the two most widely studied and dominating ones [1–5]. In a rate code, it is hypothesized that information is carried by the spike count within a time period. For example, in motor neurons, the strength at which innervated muscle is flexed depends solely on spike rate. At the other end, a temporal code utilizes the precise timing of single spikes to convey information. This timing-based code has been observed in visual [6], auditory [7] and olfactory [8] systems. The question of whether individual spikes matter or their firing rates has generated considerable debate in neuroscience, and is still unsettled [1,3]. Despite this debate, with what mechanisms of synaptic plasticity can neurons learn to process incoming spike patterns is an interesting and challenging question.

There has been a number of different learning algorithms proposed to train neurons to discriminate different spike patterns. In [9], a supervised and stochastic rule, the spike-driven synaptic plasticity, is introduced to process spike patterns encoded with mean firing rates. A teacher signal is used to steer the

© Springer International Publishing AG 2017
D. Liu et al. (Eds.): ICONIP 2017, Part VI, LNCS 10639, pp. 759–766, 2017.
https://doi.org/10.1007/978-3-319-70136-3_80

neuron's output to a desired rate. The coding basis of this rule is the rate code. In order to process patterns encoded with precise timings, other learning algorithms are developed. The tempotron [10] is an efficient learning rule that can be used to train neurons to discriminate two classes of patterns with a high capacity. Single neurons can only be applied to binary classification unless additional readout mechanisms are utilized such as grouping [11, 12]. In addition, the spike-or-not response of the tempotron limits its ability to transfer information to downstream neurons with precise timings. To overcome the inconsistency of coding schemes between neuron's input and output, other learning algorithms are introduced to train neurons to spike at desired times [13–16]. It is shown that single neurons with the precise-spike-driven (PSD) rule can learn multiple classes by associating different desired spike times to different categories [16, 17]. However, how to construct the supervisory signal of precise timings with an optimal performance is still unclear.

Most of the learning algorithms are designed with dependency on the hypotheses of a rate or timing-based code, but rare one is proposed being suitable for both. Recently, a new multi-spike tempotron rule [18] has been developed to train neurons to fire a number of spikes. This makes it a suitable candidate for processing both rate and timing-based spike patterns. In this paper, we introduce an alternative efficient learning rule to the multi-spike tempotron, and investigate its ability to process the two types of codes. In addition, we will examine the capability of our rule to train a single neuron to perform the challenging multi-category classification.

2 Methods

In this section, we present the neuron model and its dynamics, as well as the learning algorithms.

2.1 Neuron Model

We use the current-based leaky integrate-and-fire neuron model for investigation due to its simplicity and analytical tractability. In the neuron model, a reset dynamics will occur whenever a spike is elicited. Specifically, the neuron's membrane potential $V(t)$ is given by integrating its synaptic currents from N afferent inputs as follows:

$$V(t) = \sum_{i=1}^{N} w_i \sum_{t_i^j < t} K(t - t_i^j) - \vartheta \sum_{t_s^j < t} \exp\left(-\frac{t - t_s^j}{\tau_m}\right). \tag{1}$$

Here, t_i^j represents the j-th spike arriving at afferent i, and t_s^j is the j-th output spike time. Each afferent spike contributes a postsynaptic potential, whose peak amplitude and shape are determined by synaptic weight w_i and normalized kernel K, respectively. K is defined as

$$K(t - t_i^j) = V_0 \left[\exp\left(-\frac{t - t_i^j}{\tau_m} \right) - \exp\left(-\frac{t - t_i^j}{\tau_s} \right) \right]. \tag{2}$$

Here, τ_m and τ_s are the time constants of the membrane potential and synaptic currents, respectively. V_0 is a constant factor that is used to normalize the peak of K to unity. $K(t - t_i^j)$ is causal and thus is defined to vanish for $t < t_i^j$.

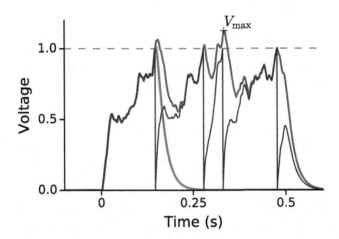

Fig. 1. Neuron's membrane potential dynamics with response to a spike pattern input. The green line is the dynamics of the neuron without considering threshold crossing and '+' denotes the global maximum V_{max} over the presence of the stimulus. In the red line, whenever the membrane potential crosses the threshold (dashed horizontal line), the neuron elicits an output spike and a reset dynamics will occur. In the blue line, the neuron shunts all the following input spikes after it fires. (Color figure online)

The last component of Eq. 1 denotes the reset dynamics after neuron fires. The neuron integrates its input spikes through synaptic efficacies and it will elicit an output spike whenever its membrane potential crosses the firing threshold from below (see Fig. 1). This continuous integrating-and-firing dynamics is different from the previous tempotron [10] where the neuron will shunt its input spikes after firing. The shunting will limit the neuron to have binary responses of firing or not, while it is free to fire as many as necessary with the reset dynamics.

2.2 Learning Algorithm

The learning target is to train neurons to fire a desired number of output spikes. A multi-spike neuron, in response to a spike pattern, can be characterized by the spike-threshold-surface (STS) [18], which is introduced to describe the relation between the number of output spikes n_{out} and the neuron's threshold ϑ (Fig. 2). n_{out} is monotonically decreasing with ϑ, i.e., a higher ϑ would result in a lower n_{out}. For a given ϑ, n_{out} can be determined from STS which is characterized by

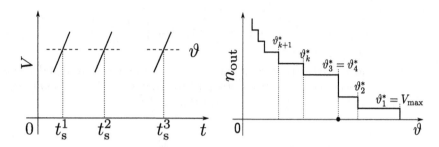

Fig. 2. Output spikes resulting from threshold crossing. Left, demonstration of threshold crossing. Whenever the membrane potential crosses the threshold from below, the neuron fires an output spike (e.g. t_s^1). Right, demonstration of spike-threshold-surface, i.e., the number of output spikes n_{out} versus threshold ϑ.

a sequence of critical threshold values ϑ_k^* ($k \in \mathbb{Z}^+$). n_{out} will jump from $k - 1$ to k at each critical point ϑ_k^*. Therefore, the learning task can be converted to shift ϑ_k^* values such that the given ϑ can result in a desired output spike number.

Each ϑ^* corresponds to a voltage value described by Eq. (1), and thus it is a function of the synaptic weights $\boldsymbol{w}$ and differentiable with respect to them. Therefore, a learning rule can be derived by evaluating the gradients of ϑ^* with respect to $\boldsymbol{w}$. Consider a given ϑ^* as the threshold, we assume there exists a t^* such that $V(t^*) = \vartheta^*$ is the continuous local maximum. Therefore, we have

$$\vartheta^* = V(t^*) = V_k(t^*) - \vartheta^* \sum_{j=1}^{m} \exp\left(-\frac{t^* - t_s^j}{\tau_m}\right), \tag{3}$$

where, $V_k(t) = \sum_{i=1}^{N} w_i \sum_{t_i^j < t} K(t - t_i^j)$, and m is the total number of output spikes that occur before t^*.

The derivative of ϑ^* with respect to w_i is denoted by $\vartheta_i^{*'}$ and given by

$$\vartheta_i^{*'} = \frac{\partial V(t^*)}{\partial w_i} + \sum_{j=1}^{m} \frac{\partial V(t^*)}{\partial t_s^j} \frac{\partial t_s^j}{\partial w_i}. \tag{4}$$

In [18], an analytical solution is used to calculate $\vartheta_i^{*'}$, while we develop a simple and efficient alternative in this paper. We denote our method and that of [18] as 'TDP' and 'MST' respectively in this paper. The difficulty of computing $\vartheta_i^{*'}$ is to get evaluations of $\partial t_s^j / \partial w_i$. According to the linear assumption of threshold crossing [15,19], the internal state of a neuron increases linearly in the infinitesimal time around occurrence of output spikes (see Fig. 2). Based on this assumption, one can get

$$\frac{\partial t_s^j}{\partial V(t_s^j)} = \frac{-1}{\partial V(t_s^j) / \partial t_s^j} = -\frac{1}{\dot{V}(t_s^j)}. \tag{5}$$

Applying the chain rule, we get

$$\frac{\partial t_s^j}{\partial w_i} = -\frac{1}{\dot{V}(t_s^j)}\frac{\partial V(t_s^j)}{\partial w_i}.$$

(6)

Equation (4) can thus be expressed as

$$\vartheta_i^{*'} = \frac{\partial V(t^*)}{\partial w_i} - \sum_{j=1}^{m}\frac{\partial V(t^*)}{\partial t_s^j}\frac{1}{\dot{V}(t_s^j)}\frac{\partial V(t_s^j)}{\partial w_i}.$$

(7)

Figure 3 illustrates learning curves of different methods. Each preceding output spike will have a contribution to the derivatives (determined by the last term of Eq. 7) and such contribution is reflected at non-differentiable points on the learning curves.

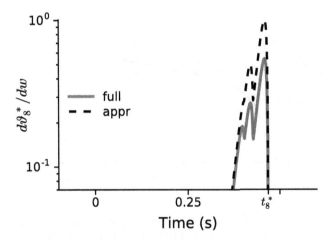

Fig. 3. Illustration of learning curves. The derivative of ϑ_8^* with respect to w is plotted for different methods.

With the derivatives in Eq. 7, the critical threshold values can thus be changed, and so as the resulting output spike number. One of the simplest objective function is to change the weights according to only a single ϑ_k^* after each error step. If the target output spike number is d, a direct training method is to consider ϑ_d^* in the learning as

$$\Delta w = \begin{cases} -\eta\frac{d\vartheta_{d+1}^*}{dw} & \text{if } o > d \\ \eta\frac{d\vartheta_d^*}{dw} & \text{if } o < d \end{cases}$$

(8)

where $\eta > 0$ is the learning rate that controls the step size of each individual update. The direct training method requires the supervisory signal to provide the exact number d. To simplify this, a relative training method can be developed based on the status of current output spike number o, yielding

$$\Delta w = \begin{cases} -\eta \frac{d\vartheta_o^*}{dw} & \text{if } o > d \\ \eta \frac{d\vartheta_{o+1}^*}{dw} & \text{if } o < d \end{cases}.$$ (9)

3   Experimental Results

Experimental results are presented in this section. The default parameters are as $N = 500$, $\tau_m = 20$ ms, $\tau_s = 5$ ms, $\eta = 10^{-4}$. The initial weights are drawn from a random Gaussian distribution with mean 0.01 and standard deviation 0.01. Input spike patterns are generated over a time window of $T = 500$ ms with each afferent neuron firing at a Poisson rate of $r_{in} = 4$ Hz over T.

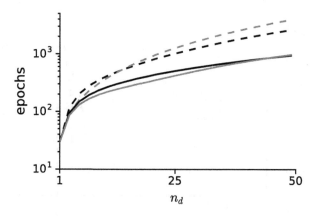

Fig. 4. Learning speed of different methods versus desired number of spikes n_d. Dashed and solid lines denote the 'MST' and 'TDP', respectively. The black and grey colors represent the relative and direct training methods, respectively. Data were averaged over 1000 runs.

Figure 4 shows that our method ('TDP') is generally faster than its alternative ('MST'). The training time will increase when the desired number of spikes increases. For small n_d, neurons trained with direct method (Eq. 8) is faster than that of relative one (Eq. 9). For a larger n_d, this relation will be reversed.

Next, we investigate the ability of our learning rule to perform classification task under two scenarios: timing- and rate-based spike patterns. We consider a 4-category task for both scenarios. In the timing-based scenario, 4 spike patterns are generated as before and then fixed as the template of each category. A new pattern is generated by adding a jitter noise of 3 ms and a random deletion probability of 0.3 to each spike of its corresponding template pattern. Neurons are trained to have n_d as: 1 (for C1), 2 (C2), 3 (C3) and 4 (C4). In the rate-based scenario, patterns are generated by specifying the firing rates where a random

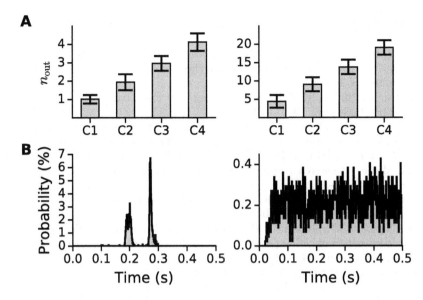

Fig. 5. Classification performance on timing-based (left column) and rate-based (right column) spike patterns. Row A, neuron's output response to different categories after training. Row B, distribution of output spike time in response to category C2 (left) and C1 (right).

half number of afferents have a low firing rate of 4 Hz while the other half have a high one of 10 Hz. 4 rate patterns are generated as the template. Each spike pattern is a new realization according to its rate template. n_d is set to 5, 10, 15 and 20 for different categories.

Figure 5 shows that our learning rule can be successfully used to train neurons to classify both timing- and rate-based spike patterns. A single neuron is capable to perform multi-category classifications by assigning different numbers of output spikes. Temporal features are used for timing-based patterns and neuron's output times are highly synchronized across trials. There is no significant temporal association found for rate-based patterns since information is carried by firing rates.

4   Conclusion

In this paper, we have proposed an efficient multi-spike learning rule which can be used to process both timing- and rate-based spike patterns. Neurons with the proposed rule can learn patterns much faster than its alternative. With our learning rule, single neurons are capable to perform multi-category classification.

Acknowledgments. This work was partly supported by the National Natural Science Foundation of China (No. 61233009).

References

1. Gütig, R.: To spike, or when to spike? Curr. Opin. Neurobiol. **25**, 134–139 (2014)
2. Borst, A., Theunissen, F.E.: Information theory and neural coding. Nat. Neurosci. **2**(11), 947–957 (1999)
3. Brette, R.: Philosophy of the spike: rate-based vs. spike-based theories of the brain. Front. Syst. Neurosci. **9**, 151 (2015)
4. Panzeri, S., Brunel, N., Logothetis, N.K., Kayser, C.: Sensory neural codes using multiplexed temporal scales. Trends Neurosci. **33**(3), 111–120 (2010)
5. Yu, Q., Tang, H., Hu, J., Tan, K.C.: Neuromorphic Cognitive Systems: A Learning and Memory Centered Approach, 1st edn. Springer, Cham (2017). doi:10.1007/978-3-319-55310-8
6. Reinagel, P., Reid, R.C.: Temporal coding of visual information in the thalamus. J. Neurosci. **20**(14), 5392–5400 (2000)
7. de Charms, R.C., Merzenich, M.M.: Primary cortical representation of sounds by the coordination of action-potential timing. Nature **381**(6583), 610 (1996)
8. Wehr, M., Laurent, G.: Odour encoding by temporal sequences of firing in oscillating neural assemblies. Nature **384**(6605), 162 (1996)
9. Brader, J.M., Senn, W., Fusi, S.: Learning real-world stimuli in a neural network with spike-driven synaptic dynamics. Neural Comput. **19**(11), 2881–2912 (2007)
10. Gütig, R., Sompolinsky, H.: The tempotron: a neuron that learns spike timing-based decisions. Nat. Neurosci. **9**(3), 420–428 (2006)
11. Yu, Q., Tang, H., Tan, K.C., Li, H.: Rapid feedforward computation by temporal encoding and learning with spiking neurons. IEEE Trans. Neural Netw. Learn. Syst. **24**(10), 1539–1552 (2013)
12. Yu, Q., Tang, H., Tan, K.C., Yu, H.: A brain-inspired spiking neural network model with temporal encoding and learning. Neurocomputing **138**, 3–13 (2014)
13. Ponulak, F., Kasinski, A.J.: Supervised learning in spiking neural networks with ReSuMe: sequence learning, classification, and spike shifting. Neural Comput. **22**(2), 467–510 (2010)
14. Florian, R.V.: The chronotron: a neuron that learns to fire temporally precise spike patterns. PLoS One **7**(8), e40233 (2012)
15. Bohte, S.M., Kok, J.N., Poutré, J.A.L.: Error-backpropagation in temporally encoded networks of spiking neurons. Neurocomputing **48**(1–4), 17–37 (2002)
16. Yu, Q., Tang, H., Tan, K.C., Li, H.: Precise-spike-driven synaptic plasticity: Learning hetero-association of spatiotemporal spike patterns. PLoS One **8**(11), e78318 (2013)
17. Yu, Q., Yan, R., Tang, H., Tan, K.C., Li, H.: A spiking neural network system for robust sequence recognition. IEEE Trans. Neural Netw. Learn. Syst. **27**(3), 621–635 (2016)
18. Gütig, R.: Spiking neurons can discover predictive features by aggregate-label learning. Science **351**(6277) (2016). doi:10.1126/science.aab4113
19. Ghosh-Dastidar, S., Adeli, H.: A new supervised learning algorithm for multiple spiking neural networks with application in epilepsy and seizure detection. Neural Netw. **22**(10), 1419–1431 (2009)

Neuromorphic Hardware and Speech Processing

Neuromorphic Hardware Using Simplified Elements and Thin-Film Semiconductor Devices as Synapse Elements - Simulation of Hopfield and Cellular Neural Network -

Tomoya Kameda[1], Mutsumi Kimura[1,2(✉)], and Yasuhiko Nakashima[1,2]

[1] Nara Institute of Science and Technology, Takayama, Ikoma 630-0192, Japan
[2] Ryukoku University, Seta, Otsu 520-2194, Japan
mutsu@rins.ryukoku.ac.jp

Abstract. Neuromorphic hardware using simplified elements and thin-film semiconductor devices as synapse elements is proposed. It is assumed that amorphous metal-oxide semiconductor devices are used for the synapse elements, and the characteristic degradation is utilized for the learning rule named modified Hebbian learning. First, we explain an architecture and operation of a Hopfield neural network. Next, we model the electrical characteristic of the thin-film semiconductor devices and simulate the letter recognition by the neural network. Particularly in this presentation, we show a degradation map. On the other hand, we also explain an architecture and operation of a cellular neural network, model the thin-film semiconductor devices, and simulate the letter recognition. Particularly in this presentation, we evaluate connection schemes. It is found that the cellular neural network has higher performance when it has diagonal connections. Moreover, we compare the Hopfield and cellular neural networks. It is found that the Hopfield neural network has higher performance, although the cellular neural network has a simple structure.

Keywords: Neuromorphic hardware · Thin-film semiconductor device · Synapse element · Hopfield neural network · Cellular neural network

1 Introduction

Artificial intelligences mimic biological brains and realize thinking machines as key technologies in future societies. Neural networks are promising architectures with many advantages, such as, self-organization, self-learning, parallel distributed computing, fault tolerance, etc. [1–4]. These advantages are obtained by connecting a large number of neuron elements with a much larger number of synapse elements. Actually, more than 10^{11} neuron elements and 10^{15} synapse elements exist in a human brain. However, the conventional neural networks are complicated software executed on high-spec hardware. Therefore, the machine size is very bulky and power consumption is unbelievably huge. Moreover, some of the aforementioned advantages, such as, parallel distributed computing and fault tolerance, are not acquired. This is because they are executed on conventional Neumann-type computers, which sequentially handle processes and stop by only one breakdown of a physical device.

© Springer International Publishing AG 2017
D. Liu et al. (Eds.): ICONIP 2017, Part VI, LNCS 10639, pp. 769–776, 2017.
https://doi.org/10.1007/978-3-319-70136-3_81

Currently, we are investigating neural networks built by actual hardware instead of virtual software. We name them "brain-type integrated system", which can be com-pact, low power, robust, and integrated on everything in future life [5–11]. In order to realize such system, it is necessary to simplify the processing elements, such as, neuron elements and synapse elements and fabricate them at low cost.

In this study, neuromorphic hardware using simplified elements and thin-film semi-conductor devices as synapse elements is proposed. It is assumed that amorphous metal-oxide semiconductor devices are used for the synapse elements, and the characteristic degradation is utilized for the learning rule named modified Hebbian learning. First, we will show an architecture, operation, model, and simulated results of a Hopfield neural network. Next, we will show those of a cellular neural network. Particularly in this presentation, we will compare the Hopfield and cellular neural networks.

2 Hopfield Neural Network

2.1 Architecture, Actual System, Operation, and Model

Architecture and actual system of the Hopfield neural network are shown in Fig. 1 [12]. Here, all neuron elements are connected to all neuron elements through synapse elements. The neuron elements are designed in an FPGA chip, and the synapse elements are fabricated using amorphous metal-oxide semiconductor devices. Amorphous metal-oxide semiconductor films are sandwiched between multiple upper electrode lines and multiple lower electrode lines, and all cross points work as synapse elements. A neuron element has a binary states of either fire or stable, which is decided by input signals from all neuron elements weighted by electric conductance as synaptic weights and outputted to all neuron elements.

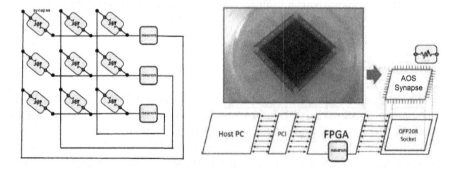

Fig. 1. Architecture and system of the Hopfield neural network.

Operation of the Hopfield neural network and model of the synapse elements are shown in Fig. 2. For example, when neuron 1 and 3 have stable states, GND = 0 V is applied to the corresponding upper and lower electrodes, whereas when neuron 2 and 4 have fire states, Vdd = 3.3 V is applied. At the cross points where the applied voltages are different, electric currents flow as shown by the red arrow in the left figure of Fig. 2, and the electric conductance is degraded, which realize the modified Hebbian learning. As shown in the right figure of Fig. 2, it is utilized that the electric conductance is gradually degraded as the time goes. This may be because trap states are generated in the amorphous metal-oxide semiconductor films or metal-semiconductor interfaces.

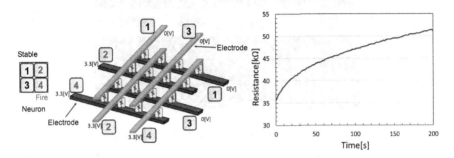

Fig. 2. Operation of the Hopfield neural network and model of the synapse elements (Color figure online).

2.2 Simulated Results

We assume the architecture, system, and operation of the Hopfield neural network, model the synapse elements, and simulate the letter recognition. Here, $9 \times 9 = 81$ neuron elements corresponds to the image pixels. Number letters, **0**, **1**, **2**, and **3**, are learned. The degradation map of the synapse elements is shown in Fig. 3. The red grayscale indicates the degradation degree of the electric conductance of the synapse elements.

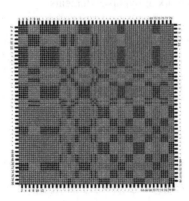

Fig. 3. Degradation map of the synapse elements (Color figure online).

The simulation results of the letter recognition are shown in Fig. 4. After a while of the learning, even if distorted letters are inputted, they are revised, and corrected letters are outputted. This is a part of procedure of the letter recognition with pattern matching. Namely, this Hopfield neural network can recognize hand-written letters.

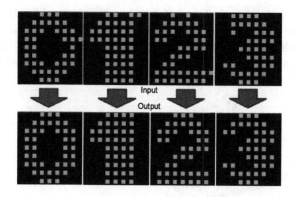

Fig. 4. Simulation results of the letter recognition.

3   Cellular Neural Network

3.1   Architecture, Actual Chip, and Operation

Architecture and actual chip of the cellular neural network are shown in Fig. 5 [13]. Here, neuron elements are aligned like an array matrix. They are connected only neighboring neuron elements orthogonally as shown in the left figure or orthogonally and diagonally as shown in the center figure. The neuron elements are fabricated in an LSI chip, and the synapse elements are fabricated using amorphous metal-oxide semiconductor devices. Amorphous metal-oxide semiconductor films are deposited on the LSI chip, and the planar films work as synapse elements.

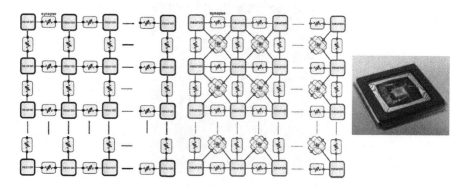

Fig. 5. Architecture and actual chip of the cellular neural network.

An operation the cellular neural network is shown in Fig. 6. Here, I/O neurons are assigned to every two neuron elements, and hidden neurons are assigned to the other neuron elements. For example, when **0** is learned, Vdd = 1.8 V, which is an internal voltage of the LSI chip, is applied to the corresponding I/O neurons, and GND = 0 V is applied to the other I/O neurons. All neuron elements dynamically become either fire or stable states. Through the synapse elements that are connected to the neuron elements with the different states, electric currents flow, and the electric conductance is degraded, which realize the modified Hebbian learning. As shown in the previous figure, it is utilized that the electric conductance is gradually degraded as the time goes.

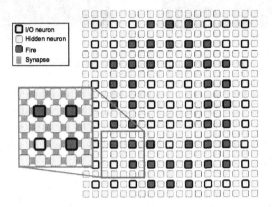

Fig. 6. Operation the cellular neural network.

3.2 Simulated Results

We assume the architecture, actual chip, and operation of the cellular neural network, model of the synapse elements, and simulate the letter recognition. Here, $9 \times 9 = 81$ I/O neuron elements corresponds to the image pixels. Number letters, **0** and **1** are learned. The degradation map of the synapse elements is shown in Fig. 7. The red grayscale indicates the degradation degree of the electric conductance of the synapse elements.

Fig. 7. Degradation map of the synapse elements (Color figure online).

The simulation results of the letter recognition are shown in Fig. 8. After a while of the learning, even if distorted letters are inputted, they are revised, and corrected letters are outputted. Similar to the Hopfield neural network, this is a part of procedure of the letter recognition with pattern matching. Namely, this cellular neural network can recognize hand-written letters.

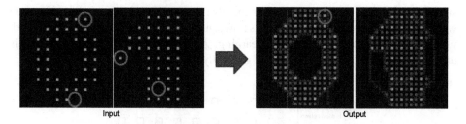

Input   Output

Fig. 8. Simulation results of the letter recognition.

The evaluation of the connection schemes between the orthogonal vs orthogonal and diagonal connections is shown in Fig. 9. It is found that the cellular neural network has higher performance when it has diagonal connections for all number of the distorted pixels and number letters of **0** and **1**. This is because it has more complexity.

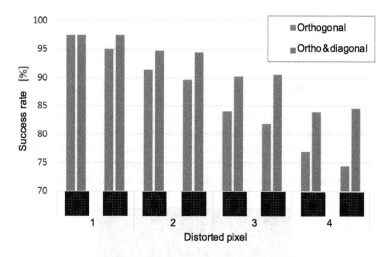

Fig. 9. Evaluation of the connection schemes between the orthogonal vs orthogonal and diagonal connections.

The comparison of the Hopfield and cellular neural networks is in Fig. 10. It is found that the Hopfield neural network has higher performance for all number of the distorted pixels and number letters of **0** and **1**. This is also because it has more complexity. However, the cellular neural network has a simple structure, We guess that the Hopfield neural network consumes more hardware, although the detailed discussion is difficult because many approximation is necessary. In any case, it can be concluded that there is a trade-off between the high performance and simple structure.

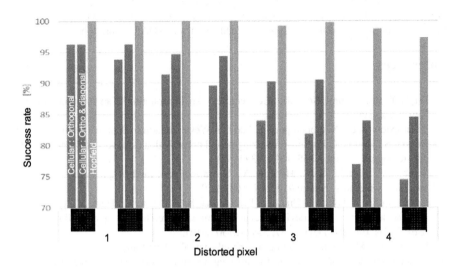

Fig. 10. Comparison of the Hopfield and cellular neural networks.

4 Conclusion

Neuromorphic hardware using simplified elements and thin-film semiconductor devices as synapse elements was proposed. It was assumed that amorphous metal-oxide semiconductor devices are used for the synapse elements, and the characteristic degradation is utilized for the learning rule named modified Hebbian learning. First, we explained architecture and operation of a Hopfield neural network, modeled the electrical characteristic of the thin-film semiconductor devices, and simulated the letter recognition by the neural network. Particularly in this presentation, we showed a degradation map. On the other hand, we also explained architecture and operation of a cellular neural network, modeled the thin-film semiconductor devices, and simulated the letter recognition. Particularly in this presentation, we evaluated connection schemes. It was found that the cellular neural network has higher performance when it has diagonal connections. Moreover, we compared the Hopfield and cellular neural networks. It was found that the Hopfield neural network has higher performance, although the cellular neural network has a simple structure. It can be concluded that there is a trade-off between the high performance and simple structure.

These results indicates potential possibilities that neuromorphic hardware will be key technologies to realize artificial intelligence that are compact and low power. In the next ICONIP, we believe that we can report the experimental results from the actual system and LSI chips with synapse elements.

Acknowledgement. We would like to thank Prof. Mamoru Furuta of Kochi University of Technology, Prof. Toshio Kamiya of Tokyo Institute of Technology, KAKENHI 16K06733, Laboratory for Materials and Structures of Tokyo Institute of Technology, ROHM Semiconductor,

Yazaki Memorial Foundation for Science and Technology, Support Center for Advanced Telecommunications Technology Research Foundation, and KOA Corporation.

References

1. Dayhoff, J.E.: Neural Network Architectures, An Introduction. Van Nostrand Reinhold, New York (1990)
2. Hecht-Nielsen, R.: Neurocomputing. Addison-Wesley Reading, Boston (1990)
3. Becker, S., Hinton, G.E.: Self-organizing neural network that discovers surfaces in random-dot stereograms. Nature **355**, 161–163 (1992)
4. Stone, J.V., Hunkin, N.M., Hornby, A.: Neural-network models: predicting spontaneous recovery of memory. Nature **414**, 167–168 (2001)
5. Kasakawa, T., Tabata, H., Onodera, R., Kojima, H., Kimura, M., Hara, H., Inoue, S.: An artificial neural network at device level using simplified architecture and thin-film transistors. IEEE Trans. Electron Devices **57**, 2744–2750 (2010)
6. Kimura, M., Miyatani, T., Fujita, Y., Kasakawa, T.: Apoptotic self-organized electronic device using thin-film transistors for artificial neural networks with unsupervised learning functions. Jpn. J. Appl. Phys. **54**, 03CB02 (2015)
7. Kimura, M., Fujita, Y., Kasakawa, T., Matsuda, T.: Novel architecture for cellular neural network suitable for high-density integration of electron devices-learning of multiple logics. In: Arik, S., Huang, T., Lai, W.K., Liu, Q. (eds.) ICONIP 2015. LNCS, vol. 9489, pp. 12–20. Springer, Cham (2015). doi:10.1007/978-3-319-26532-2_2
8. Kimura, M., Nakamura, N., Yokoyama, T., Matsuda, T., Kameda, T., Nakashima, Y.: Simplification of processing elements in cellular neural networks. In: Hirose, A., Ozawa, S., Doya, K., Ikeda, K., Lee, M., Liu, D. (eds.) ICONIP 2016. LNCS, vol. 9948, pp. 309–317. Springer, Cham (2016). doi:10.1007/978-3-319-46672-9_35
9. Kimura, M., Morita, R., Sugisaki, S., Matsuda, T., Kameda, T., Nakashima, Y.: Cellular neural network formed by simplified processing elements composed of thin-film transistors. Neurocomputing **248**, 112–119 (2017)
10. Kimura, M., Matsuda, T.: Neuromorphic application of oxide semiconductors. ECS Trans. **79**, 169–175 (2017)
11. Kimura, M., Nakanishi, H., Nakamura, N., Yokoyama, T., Matsuda, T., Kameda, T., Nakashima, Y.: Simplification of processing elements in cellular neural network. J. Electrical Engineering and Electronic Technology (to be published)
12. Kameda, T., Kimura, M., Nakashima, Y.: Letter reproduction simulator for hardware design of cellular neural network using thin-film synapses. In: Hirose, A., Ozawa, S., Doya, K., Ikeda, K., Lee, M., Liu, D. (eds.) ICONIP 2016. LNCS, vol. 9948, pp. 342–350. Springer, Cham (2016). doi:10.1007/978-3-319-46672-9_39
13. Kameda, T., Kimura, M., Nakashima, Y.: Letter reproduction simulator for hardware design of cellular neural network using thin-film synapses. In: 2016 International Symposium on Nonlinear Theory and its Applications (NOLTA 2016), pp. 40–43. NOLTA, IEICE, Tokyo (2016)

An Analog Probabilistic Spiking Neural Network with On-Chip Learning

Hung-Yi Hsieh, Pin-Yi Li, and Kea-Tiong Tang[✉]

Neuromorphic and Biomedical Engineering Lab, Department of Electrical Engineering,
National Tsing Hua University, Hsin-Chu, Taiwan
hyhsieh@larc.ee.nthu.edu.tw, pinyili@foxmail.com,
kttang@ee.nthu.edu.tw

Abstract. Portable or biomedical applications typically require signal processing, learning, and classification in conditions involving limited area and power consumption. Analog implementations of learning algorithms can satisfy these requirements and are thus attracting increasing attention. Probabilistic spiking neural network (PSNN) is a hardware friendly algorithm that is relax in weight resolution requirements and insensitive to noise and VLSI process variation. In this study, the probabilistic spiking neural network was implemented using analog very-large-scale integration (VLSI) to verify their hardware compatibility. The circuit was fabricated using 0.18 μm CMOS technology. The power consumption of the chip was less than 10 μW with a 1 V supply and the core area of chip was 0.43 mm^2. The chip can classify the electronic nose data with 92.3% accuracy and classify the electrocardiography data with 100% accuracy. The low power and high learning performance features make the chip suitable for portable or biomedical applications.

Keywords: Probabilistic spiking neural network (PSNN) · Analog implementation · On-Chip learning

1 Introduction

Pattern recognition and machine learning are applied extensively in daily life. The applications of machine learning include computer vision, data mining, and speech or written word recognition. Neural networks (NNs) are machine learning algorithms that mimic biology to provide effective learning capabilities for complex patterns. NNs provide advantages such as a simple and parallelizable computational structure and adaptive learning parameters [1]. They represent an effective method of learning and recognizing complex patterns.

To ensure mobility, long life, and bodily safety, battery-powered portable or implantable applications such as pacemakers [2], electronic noses [3], and cardiovascular disease detectors [1] require restrictions on power consumption and area. Variations in sensor fabrication, background noise, and human-dependent parameters complicate these requirements. Algorithms run using sequential processors; however, they struggle to simultaneously fulfill learning speed, learning performance, power consumption, and

© Springer International Publishing AG 2017
D. Liu et al. (Eds.): ICONIP 2017, Part VI, LNCS 10639, pp. 777–785, 2017.
https://doi.org/10.1007/978-3-319-70136-3_82

area requirements. Consequently, hardware-implemented NNs (HNNs) are applied extensively in these applications [2–4].

For an HNN designed for use in portable or implantable devices, compact and simple circuit blocks that occupy a small area and demonstrate low power consumption are the key requirement. In addition to a small area and low power consumption, achieving a high learning capability under nonideal conditions is challenging. Therefore, the algorithm is especially crucial for dealing with the aforementioned issues when the circuit is implemented using analog VLSI. One type of NN that comprises spiking neurons with probabilistic parameters is called the probabilistic spiking neural network (PSNN) [5]. PSNNs is hardware-friendly algorithm that compares with deterministic NNs in hardware compatibility [6].

In this study, the PSNN algorithm was implemented using analog VLSI. The remainder of this paper is organized as follows: Sect. 2 overviews the PSNN algorithm, Sect. 3 introduces the proposed network circuit implementation, Sect. 4 provides verification of the structure's learning performance, and Sect. 5 presents a discussion.

2   Probabilistic Spiking Neural Network

The network structure is shown in Fig. 1. The overall network included an input layer, a hidden layer, and an output layer. The input layer was fully connected to the hidden layer. The outputs of the hidden neurons converged at the output neuron. The synapse between each layers were plastic. The output of the output neuron was a spike train. The spiking probability of this spike train is $P(z)$. This output spike train was compared with the target spike train which spike with spiking probability Pd to produce error signals.

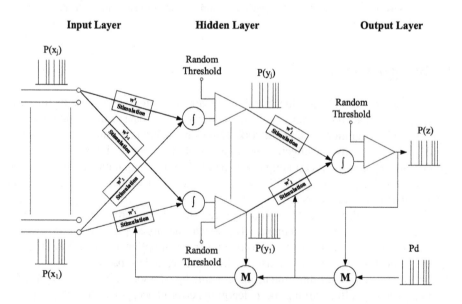

Fig. 1. Network structure of the PSNN

The error signal back propagated from the output layer to the encoding layer to modify the synaptic weights. The algorithm modified the weights to make the output spiking probability similar to the target spiking probability. As a result, after training, different input categories could be identified by the mean spiking probability of the output neuron.

PSNN algorithm [6] mainly focused on the hardware compatibility. As a result, several advantages are included. First, PSNNs do not suffer from multiplicative linearity. In the spiking neuron model, the presynaptic spike of a neuron can be viewed as a control signal, and the weight determines the postsynaptic current. When a neuron is stimulated by a presynaptic spike, the post synapse generates current. Therefore, the increase in membrane potential in the postsynaptic neuron is determined by multiplying the presynaptic spike and weight. Second, when the resolution is limited to less than 10 bits, the performance can be maintained by the algorithm, thereby making algorithm more easily realized through analog VLSI. Third, preliminary weights can be set to the same value rather than using random or dataset-specific initialization. Fifth, the weight distribution is not forced to be bimodal because the linearity and accuracy of a circuit are more difficult to maintain when the input and output values are close to the power rail or ground.

2.1 Neuron

The neuron model in the algorithm was chosen to be the IF model. Instead of setting a constant spiking threshold, the algorithm added uncorrelated Gaussian noise to the threshold to add probabilistic behavior to the neurons.

The neuron spiked only when the membrane potential was higher than the spiking threshold. Because the threshold was a Gaussian random value, the relation between spiking probability $P(z)$ and the membrane potential of output neuron V^z could be approximated to a sigmoid function (1).

$$P(z) = \frac{1}{1 + e^{-V^z}} \tag{1}$$

2.2 Synapse

The synapses transmit stimulation between neurons. When a presynaptic spike was generated, the synapse transfer charge to the membrane. The polarity and the magnitude were set by the synaptic weight.

The target signal was applied to the network as a spike train with a spiking probability Pd. The goal of the adaptation was making the output spiking probability of the network $P(z)$ similar to Pd. Therefore, after training, the categories of an input could be identified by the spiking probability on the network output.

The membrane potential of a postsynaptic neuron was related to the presynaptic neuron spiking probabilities and the synaptic weights. As measured by Pouille et al., the relative contribution of each input afferent to the membrane potential of a postsynaptic neuron is normalized by the number of active afferents [7]. The stimulation strength is indirectly proportional to the weight sum of each afferent. This phenomenon is quite different as in an ANN where the membrane potential is usually represented by the inner product of synaptic weight and the output of the presynaptic neuron. The proposed algorithm included this offset because this offset could release the requirement of weight range. Each synaptic weight, therefore, did not have to include the offset and could pay more attention (dynamic range of the weight) on distinguishing features of samples in different categories.

The membrane potential change ΔV^z of the output neuron was set by the spiking probability $P(y_i)$ of hidden neuron i, the synaptic weight w_i^y between hidden neuron i and the output neuron, and the stimulation offset w_o (2).

$$\Delta V^z = \left(1 - \prod_i \left(1 - P(y_i)\right)\right) \times w_0 + \sum_i w_i^y \times P(y_i) \tag{2}$$

At the beginning, the neuron was at rest and the membrane potential was zero. The membrane potential varied when stimulation began (3). The t is the time after the stimulation started and τ is the membrane time constant.

$$V^z = \frac{\Delta V^z \times (1 - e^{-\frac{t}{\tau}})}{1 - e^{-\frac{1}{\tau}}} \tag{3}$$

If t is large enough, the membrane potential reaches equilibrium. The representation can be approximated to (4).

$$V^z = \frac{\Delta V^z}{1 - e^{-\frac{1}{\tau}}} \tag{4}$$

The algorithm was a supervised learning algorithm thus has to define an error function from the difference of the output and target. This work chose relative entropy as the error function (5).

$$Error = (1 - Pd) \times ln\frac{1 - Pd}{1 - P(z)} + Pd \times ln\frac{Pd}{P(z)} \tag{5}$$

The purpose of the learning process is to reduce the difference between the spiking probability of the target and the output spike train. The amount of weight change is determined using (6)–(9), where w_i^y, w_{ji}^x, w_o, and w_{ij}^l are the weights between the hidden neuron i and the output neuron, input neuron j and hidden neuron i, the synaptic offset, and hidden neuron i and j, respectively. w^l is a short-term weight, meaning that it decreases gradually if no continuous potentiation signal $P(y_i,y_j)$ exists. The $P(y_i,y_j)$ is the probability that both hidden neurons i and j simultaneously produce spikes. Excepting w^l, all the other weights are long-term weights. The weight values are maintained as long as the power is on. The $P(y_i)$ and $P(x_i)$ are the spiking probabilities of hidden neuron i and input neuron i, respectively. The Pd and $P(z)$ are the spiking probabilities of the target and the output spike train, respectively. *Upd* is the update signal. w_{ji}^x is updated only when the hidden neuron i does not spike in the previous time unit but spikes in the current time unit or vice versa ($Upd_i = 1$), or all the Upd_i are 0.

$$\Delta w_i^y = P(y_i) \times (Pd - P(z)) \tag{6}$$

$$\Delta w_o = \left(1 - \prod_i \left(1 - P(y_i)\right)\right) \times (Pd - P(z)) \tag{7}$$

$$\Delta w_{ji}^x = \begin{cases} 2 \times P(x_j) \times (Pd - P(z)), \text{ if } Upd_i = 1 \\ P(x_j) \times (Pd - P(z)), \text{ if } \sum_i Upd_i = 0 \end{cases} \tag{8}$$

$$\tau_w \frac{dw_{ij}^l}{dt} = -w_{ij}^l + \eta_l P(y_i, y_j) \tag{9}$$

3   Network Structure

In this section, a method of implementing the PSNN algorithm by using analog VLSI is described. Figure 2 shows a block diagram of the PSNN circuit. The equivalent neural network structure is shown at the lower-right corner of the figure. A single PSNN chip contains 67 synapses (including a synapse for generating the synaptic offset), 32 input neurons, two hidden neurons, and one output neuron. Because the network size can be expanded by connecting multiple chips, the network size in a single chip was designed

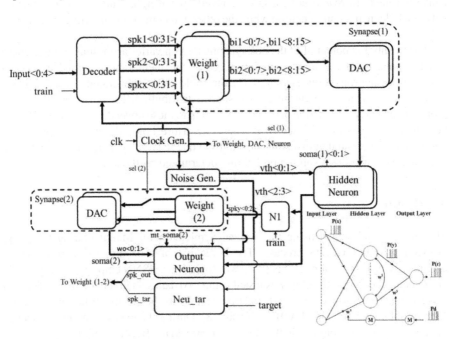

Fig. 2. Block diagram of the PSNN chip.

as small as possible to reduce the area and power of a single chip. Small network in a single chip can also prevent the learning from over-fitting. The input layer size should be at least the size of the dimension of the input pattern. As a result, this work designed a large input layer to make a single chip available for more problems.

The input patterns are represented by addresses that increase the digital circuit compatibility and reduce the number of input pads. The patterns are sequentially applied to the circuit, and are synchronized using the clock signal. Once an input pattern is applied to the chip, the Decoder decodes the address to the spike trains. These spike trains then stimulate neurons using synapses (*Synapse (1)*).

A synapse comprises a weight unit (Weight) and a stimulation unit (DAC). The weight unit is for weight adaptation and storage. The weight unit satisfy both the continuous value weight adaptation to ensure the convergence in training and the binary weight code storage to keep the weight value at least when the power is on.

After the weights are set, a presynaptic spike can stimulate the postsynaptic neuron with a strength specific to the weight value. Because the weights are digital weight codes, the stimulations are converted to analog values using low-power, charge-scaling DACs. To reduce the circuit area, four DACs are shared by 67 synapses (two DACs for the 64 synapses between the input and hidden layers, and two for the three synapses between the hidden and output layers).

Only the synapse with presynaptic stimulation can output its weight code (8 bits) to the corresponding DAC. In *Synapse(1)*, there are four weight codes waiting for conversion in a time unit. The selection signal *sel(1)* produced by the *ClockGen* decides which two among four weight codes are first converted by two DACs and which two are converted later. In *Synapse(2)*, a DAC converts the weight value from the synapse between hidden and output neuron while the other is specific for converting the synaptic offset.

The membrane potential of the postsynaptic neuron varies according to the strength and the polarity of the input stimulation. Once the membrane potential exceeds a threshold, the neuron produces a spike. The threshold voltage generated by the *NoiseGen* for each neuron is noisy, exhibiting a bell-shaped distribution. The noisy thresholds add probabilistic parameters to the neurons. In addition to these noisy thresholds that exhibit bell-shaped distributions, *NoiseGen* also generates a threshold exhibiting uniform distribution that is compared with an off-chip control voltage target, generating a target spike train that demonstrates a spiking probability determined by the target.

4   Result

The chip was fabricated using the Taiwan Semiconductor Manufacturing Company (TSMC) 0.18 μm CMOS process. The core area of the chip was approximately 0.43 mm^2. Because the aim of this study was to design a PSNN chip for use in portable or biomedical devices, the chip was tested using two data sets in related fields. The first was the electronic nose data set [3], and the second was the electrocardiography (ECG) data set obtained from the MIT-BIH website [8]. During the experiment, the frequency of the external controlling clock was set at 500 kHz. Because of this slow clock frequency, all of the transistors in analog circuits are operated in the subthreshold region to reduce the power consumption. The power consumption of a single chip was less than 10 μW.

4.1 Electronic Nose

The data were sampled using the commercially available Cyranose 320. This commercial e-nose possesses polymer carbon black composite resistive sensors. The data set included three fruity-odor groups: bananas, hami melons, and lemons. Each group comprised 10 training samples and 54 testing samples.

In the experiment, the same 8-dimensional data set used in the previous study was applied [3]. Each dimension represented the response of a gas sensor. The input dimension of this chip, however, was 32 rather than eight. Furthermore, the input representation was spikes rather than neural thresholds. Therefore, few further preprocessing is required. First, the 0.35 offset was removed. Second, the value of each dimension was multiplied by 16 and then rounded to the nearest integer. The final step was representing each dimension by a 4-bit binary code. Thus, the final testing patterns were binary patterns exhibiting 32 dimensions. A 32-dimensional sample from each group is shown in Fig. 3.

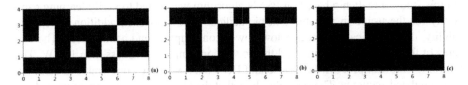

Fig. 3. One of the 32 dimensional samples for each fruit. Each column represents the response of a gas sensor. From top to bottom is (a) banana, (b) hami and (c) lemon.

To make a clear comparison between the result of this work and the result in the previous studies, the experimental procedure used was the same as that used in the previous study [3]. The overall accuracy of this chip in identifying the fruity odor was 92.3%. This measurement accuracy is similar to the simulated accuracy (93.1%) and significantly outperformed the result reported in [3] (87.6%).

4.2 Electrocardiography

The ECG data were obtained from the MIT-BIH website. The preprocessing method used was the same as that applied in [9]. The data were divided into training and testing data sets. The training set contained data for 500 heartbeats (six abnormal), and the testing set contained data for 1700 heartbeats (27 abnormal). After preprocessing, the final data comprised a 65-dimensional data set. To accommodate the dimensions of the input layer in a single chip, the data were further preprocessed by down-sampling the data to 32 dimensions and then linearly mapping the maximal and minimal value of each sample to one and zero. To generate graded samples, the values of each sample were multiplied by 10 and then the value in each dimension was rounded to the nearest integer. Examples of 32-dimensional graded samples of normal and abnormal heartbeats are shown in Fig. 4. The color on each dimension represents the spiking probability of the corresponding input neuron.

Fig. 4. Examples of 32 dimensional graded samples of normal and abnormal heartbeat.

The testing results indicate that the minimal spiking probability for the abnormal data was 0.92, and the maximal spiking probability for the normal data was 0.36. The spiking probability between the normal and abnormal data was distinct, proving that the network could perform precise on-chip learning and distinguish the ECG data. Furthermore, this result indicates that the PSNN chip can process both binary and graded patterns.

5   Conclusion

In this study, a real chip based on PSNN algorithm was tested to verify learning capability for the usage in portable and biomedical applications. In addition to learning ability, these applications require low power consumption and a small area. The core area of the chip was 0.43 mm^2 and the power consumption was less than 10 µW. This learning chip can process the e-nose and ECG data, yielding comparable accuracy to the simulated accuracy. These results show that the learning chip can be integrated into portable and implantable devices, facilitating convenient use and intelligence.

Acknowledgement. This work was supported in part by Ministry of Science and Technology, under Contract No. MOST 106-2221-E-007-119.

References

1. Sun, Y., Cheng, A.C.: Machine learning on-a-chip: A high-performance low-power reusable neuron architecture for artificial neural networks in ECG classifications. Comput. Biol. Med. **42**(7), 751–757 (2012)
2. Sun, Q., Schwartz, F., Michel, J., Herve, Y., Dalmolin, R.: Implementation study of an analog spiking neural network for assisting cardiac delay prediction in a cardiac resynchronization therapy device. IEEE Trans. Neural Networks **22**(6), 858–869 (2011)
3. Hsieh, H.Y., Tang, K.T.: VLSI implementation of a bio-inspired olfactory spiking neural network. IEEE Trans. Neural Netw. Learn. Syst. **23**(7), 1065–1073 (2012)
4. Misra, J., Saha, I.: Artificial neural networks in hardware: a survey of two decades of progress. Neurocomputing **74**(1), 239–255 (2010)
5. Kasabov, N.: To spike or not to spike: a probabilistic spiking neuron model. Neural Netw. Off. J. Int. Neural Netw. Soc. **23**(1), 16–19 (2010)

6. Hsieh, H.Y., Tang, K.T.: Hardware friendly probabilistic spiking neural network with long-term and short-term plasticity. IEEE Trans. Neural Netw. Learn. Syst. **24**(12), 2063–2074 (2013)
7. Pouille, F., Marin-Burgin, A., Adesnik, H., Atallah, B.V., Scanziani, M.: Input normalization by global feedforward inhibition expands cortical dynamic range. Nat. Neurosci. **12**(12), 1577–1585 (2009)
8. Goldberger, A.L., Amaral, L.A.N., Glass, L., Hausdorff, J.M., Ivanov, P.C., Mark, R.G., Mietus, J.E., Moody, G.B., Peng, C.K., Stanley, H.E.: PhysioBank, PhysioToolkit, and PhysioNet: components of a new research resource for complex physiologic signals. Circulation **101**(23), 215–220 (2000)
9. Tarassenko, L., Clifford, G., Townsend, N.: Detection of ectopic beats in the electrocardiogram using an auto-associative neural network. Neural Process. Lett. **14**(1), 15–25 (2001)

An Efficient Hardware Architecture for Multilayer Spiking Neural Networks

Yuling Luo[1], Lei Wan[1], Junxiu Liu[1(✉)], Jinlei Zhang[1], and Yi Cao[2]

[1] Guangxi Key Lab of Multi-source Information Mining and Security,
Faculty of Electronic Engineering, Guangxi Normal University, Guilin 541004, China
liujunxiu@mailbox.gxnu.edu.cn
[2] Department of Business Transformation and Sustainable Enterprise,
Surrey Business School, University of Surrey, Surrey GU2 7XH, UK

Abstract. Spiking Neural Network (SNN) is the most recent computational model that can emulate the behaviors of biological neuron system. This paper highlights and discusses an efficient hardware architecture for the hardware SNNs, which includes a layer-level tile architecture (LTA) for the neurons and synapses, and a novel routing architecture (NRA) for the interconnections between the neuron nodes. In addition, a visualization performance monitoring platform is designed, which is used as functional verification and performance monitoring for the SNN hardware system. Experimental results demonstrate that the proposed architecture is feasible and capable of scaling to large hardware multilayer SNNs.

Keywords: Spiking Neural Networks · Hardware architecture · FPGA

1 Introduction

Recently, Spiking Neural Network (SNN) is being studied due to its computational capabilities for solving problems. The researchers attempt to mimic this efficiency and build artificial neural systems in hardware device. However, one main challenge is that it is the computational complexity, area demanding, nonlinear operators and highly dense interconnection schemes, which limit the system scalability. For example, a SNN system normally includes a significant number of neurons and synapses and the complexity of inter-neuron connectivity increases significantly with the number of neurons and synapses. Recently, FPGA-based architectures are popular for the SNN implementations. For instance, a FPGA-based approach was proposed in [1] to provide biologically compatible neural networks and can simulate up to 100 neurons. Another 20×20 topology that used simplified Hodgkin-Huxley neuron model was proposed in [2]. Reducing the precision of the data helps to minimize the consumed hardware area, e.g. the approach of [3] can accommodate 64 K neurons. Its membrane potential value is updated by a synaptic weight with a 5-bit width. For the inter-neuron connections, the networks-on-chip (NoC) has been mostly used as an efficient SNN interconnect strategy. For example, a routing architecture

© Springer International Publishing AG 2017
D. Liu et al. (Eds.): ICONIP 2017, Part VI, LNCS 10639, pp. 786–795, 2017.
https://doi.org/10.1007/978-3-319-70136-3_83

based on two-dimensional (2D) mesh topology was proposed in the approach of [4]. The FACETS in the approach of [5] was based on a 2D torus which provided the connections of several FACETS wafers. A state-of-the-art hierarchical NoC architecture for SNN was proposed in the approach of [6], which combined the mesh and star topologies for different layers of the SNNs. Similar to the afore-mentioned approaches, most of current SNN hardware systems use the topologies with limited degree (e.g. mesh, torus etc.) to connect the neurons together, how-ever these topologies do not meet the fan-in/out requirement of layer-based SNN structures [7]. Therefore, it is necessary to explore a new hardware architecture to address these challenges.

This paper presents a FPGA-based LTA architecture for the SNN neurons and synapses. The LTA employs a two-level sharing mechanism of computing components at the synapse and neuron levels and achieves a trade-off between computational complexity and hardware resource costs. For the connection prob-lem between neurons, a compact and efficient routing architecture is proposed. It employs a traffic status weight-based arbitration and a traffic congestion-avoidance mechanism to provide traffic balance for the information transmission of multiple neurons. Further, a visualization performance monitoring platform is designed for the functional verification and performance monitoring of the hardware SNN.

2   SNN Hardware Architecture

The network topologies of the artificial neural networks can be divided into two categories, namely feed-forward and recurrent networks [8]. The feed-forward topology is mostly used and usually includes an input/output layer and one (or several) hidden layers. All the information is passed forward in one direction only. For example, a typical multilayer feed-forward network is shown in Fig. 1(a). Note that each neuron in a layer is connected to all neurons in the next layer by a weighted connection. The proposed LTA is illustrated in Fig. 1(b). Each LTA corresponds to a layer in the SNN system in Fig. 1(a), i.e., it is programmed

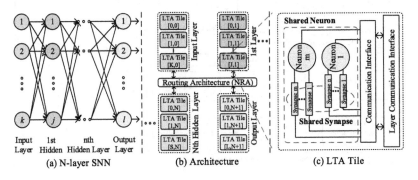

Fig. 1. An N-layer SNN and the overview of the SNN system using LTAs and NRA.

to realize a layer-level function of the SNNs. Inside the LTA, multiple neurons and synapses share computing components to provide a trade-off between computational complexity and the required hardware resources. For the LTAs in different layers, a novel routing architecture (NRA) is used as their communication infrastructure. The proposed LTA and NRA are presented in details in the following sections.

2.1 Compact Neuron Node

The micro-architecture of the proposed LTA is shown in Fig. 2. Based on the dynamic synapses model from the approach of [9], a digital synapse with sufficient resolution is developed and synthesized to an IP core as illustrated in the I/O block diagram of Fig. 2(a). It includes spike and configuration information inputs for the synapses (i.e., Spike_In and Config_In), the presynaptic and postsynaptic currents (i.e., I_In and I_Out), the variables (i.e., x, y, z_Excit_Inhib_In/Out, Use_In/Out) and the handshaking signals (i.e., hs_In and hs_Out). It uses floating-point data precision for the membrane potential value, weight etc. The digital synapse is used for synaptic computation and is shared by multiple synapses within a neuron cell. Using the digital synapse as the core component, the neuron architecture based on a typical Leaky Integrate-and-Fire (LIF) neuron model [10] is designed to model each neuron cell as shown in Fig. 2(b). The main components of a neuron (e.g., the soma, axon and synapse) are modularized, e.g. the Neuron Computing Core, the Cell Controller and the Communication Interface module implement the functions of the synapses, soma and axon, respectively. When packets are received from the Communication Interface, the Packet Decoder decodes them. For example, if the received data is

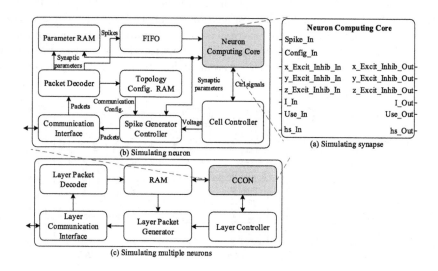

Fig. 2. LTA micro-architecture.

intended for configuration, then the parameters (e.g., the weight, decay, threshold value, lookup table and topology definitions) are saved in RAM for the synaptic computing and spike generation. When the spike packets arrive, the parameters and the initial membrane potential value are read from the Parameter RAM. Then, the NCC calculates the excitatory or inhibitory postsynaptic potentials of each synapse. The Cell Controller is used to manage the computation process. After completing all synapse computations, the Spike Generator Controller generates spike packets according to the communication parameters from the Topology Configuration RAM. In the final, it outputs the spike packets to the Communication Interface for the transmissions.

In this approach, in addition to the shared mechanism inside the neuron cell, neurons within the same layer (i.e., a single LTA) also share the computing component of one neuron (CCON) to further extend the efficiency of the design. Figure 2(c) shows the proposed LTA diagram. The sharing mechanism of the LTA at the neuron level is similar to the sharing achieved the single neuron cell in Fig. 2(b). The CCON is the core module. The different neurons within an LTA share a single CCON. The RAM module is used to store the variables of different neurons. The Layer Controller manages the working flow of the LTA at the layer level. The Layer Packet Generator module is used to manage the data generation of different neurons.

2.2   Efficient Routing Architecture for the Inter-neuron Connection

In this work, an efficient interconnection architecture, i.e. NRA, is proposed, which can efficiently forward the spike events for the communications of multilayer SNNs. An example of interconnection between the NRA and LTA neuron nodes is introduced in Fig. 3(a). The NRA is based on an all-to-all connection that takes the paired input and output nodes of multilayer SNNs as the

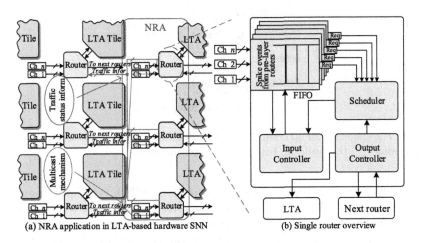

Fig. 3. The NRA application in multilayer SNN and its single router structure overview. (Color figure online)

source and destination. A novel multicast-based NoC router is developed as the fundamental work unit of NRA and its structure is shown by Fig. 3(b). Each router has n input channels that receive the outputs from previous layer. And it fully connects to all the routes of the next layer. The traffic status information (e.g. busy or congested) are transmitted through the red line between different routers. After the LTA generates spike packets, the associated router forwards these packets to the routers in next layer. Considering that the NRA applies to multiple similar routers, only the structure and functionality of a single router are presented in details in the following content.

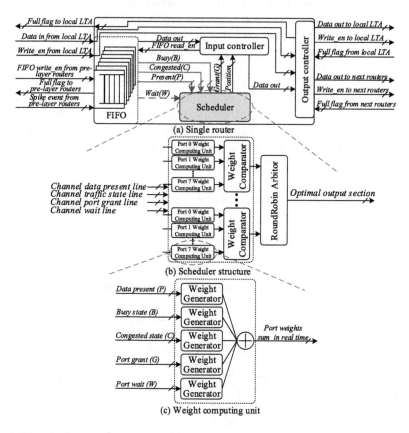

Fig. 4. The single router structure: (a) an overview of the single router; (b) the scheduler module; (c) the traffic status weight computing unit.

The single router diagram in Fig. 4(a) includes FIFO, Scheduler, Input controller, Output controller. Figure 4(b) illustrates the hardware structure of the Scheduler. The structure of one traffic status weight computing unit is shown in Fig. 4(c). Five traffic status weight generators calculate the corresponding traffic status weights in real-time according to the input channel traffic status, which can be achieved by reading the statuses of corresponding FIFOs and grant information. The five traffic status weight signals including Present (w_p), Busy (w_b), Congested (w_c), Grant (w_g) and Wait (w_w) are connected to the scheduler to aid making effective arbitration decisions and are calculated based on the following dynamic traffic status weight mechanism. If a channel has a data present, then the associated weight w_p is 3. Similarly, the weights for busy, congested, granted and waiting status are set to be 1, 2, −1 and 1, respectively. After all the traffic status weight values are generated, the total traffic status weight, w_{sum}, for each port i in each group, is calculated by $w_{sum}[i] = w_p[i] + w_b[i] + w_c[i] + w_g[i] + w_w[i]$ in real-time. The port with the largest traffic status weight in each group is selected to be granted by the round-robin arbiter. It can be noticed that the traffic status weight of each port is calculated in real-time. This allows the priorities of all ports are updated in real-time to access to the output channel [4].

2.3   A Visualization Performance Monitoring Platform for SNNs

Functional verification and performance monitoring of SNN hardware structure are challenges due to the SNN system complexity and large logic size. In this work, a visualization performance monitoring platform is designed. Figure 5 illustrates the structure of this platform. The monitoring target is the Xilinx Zynq 7000 device. Its internal structure is divided into two parts of processor system (PS) and programmable logic (PL), i.e. a single chip integrates FPGA devices and dual-core ARM Cortex-A9 processing system. The high-speed AXI bus is used as the intercommunication between ARM and FPGA. The SNN hardware system is implemented in the FPGA device (Fig. 5 shows a typical network based on a 2D mesh topology). Considering the system lightweight

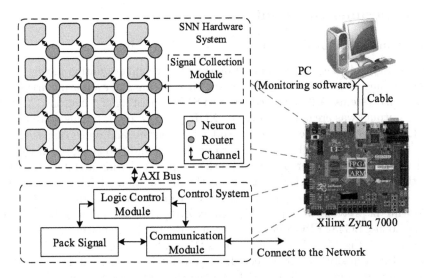

Fig. 5. The performance monitoring platform system overview.

design requirement, the monitoring platform uses the ARM processor to manage the workflow of the entire platform, signal statistics and communication. It connects to a computer via the high speed Ethernet communication. Only a compact signal collection unit is required for the PL side, which minimizes the resource overhead of the monitoring platform.

The computer software interface provides basic signal and data observation and control interfaces for each sub-module. It is divided into: (a) configuration module; (b) waveform display module; (c) frequency display module and (d) data display and storage module, which are shown by Fig. 6.

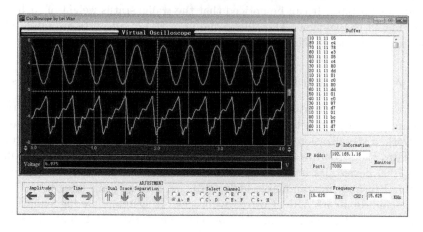

Fig. 6. The software interactive interface.

3   Experimental Results

3.1   Functional Evaluation

The XOR problem is used as a benchmark of functional evaluation in this experiment because it is a standard benchmark for verifying and evaluating artificially intelligent systems. A 2-layer feed-forward SNN consisting of 3 neurons (2 inputs and 1 output) was created to solve the XOR (see Fig. 7(a)). In this system, only 2 LTAs are required, one is used to model two neurons and four synapses in the first layer network, another is used for one neuron and two synapses in the second layer. They are interconnected by the proposed routing architecture NRA. All the LTAs use the packets to transmit the information [4]. The rate encoding scheme is used in this paper, and the SNN can be trained using the learning algorithm in previous work [11]. The Xilinx Zynq-7000 development board (with a XC7Z020-CLG484 FPGA device) is used as the hardware platform. The results are shown in Fig. 7(c). The logical values '1' and '0' are encoded as spikes of 60 and 15 Hz, respectively. As expected, the output is '1' (i.e., 60 Hz) when both inputs are different and '0' (i.e., 15 Hz) when the inputs are the same. The membrane potential for neuron #3 is also shown in Fig. 7(b).

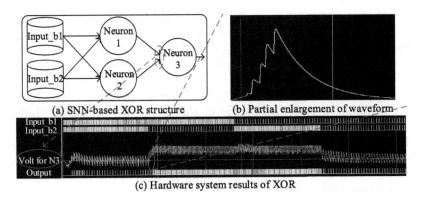

(a) SNN-based XOR structure   (b) Partial enlargement of waveform

(c) Hardware system results of XOR

Fig. 7. Simulation results of XOR using the proposed LTA and NRA.

For large size networks, the IRIS and Wisconsin breast cancer (WBC) classification tasks can be used to analyse the scalability. The former is a 16:208:3 (i.e.
16 input, 208 hidden, and 3 output neurons) three-layer network, and the latter
is 9:90:2 [6]. The IRIS or WBC requires only three LTAs and NRAs as each LTA
can contain multiple neurons and a single NRA can provide communications for
multiple LTAs. This demonstrates the scalability of the proposed architectures
in this paper.

3.2 Performance Analysis

Table 1 summarizes the recent approaches in terms of the network size, precision
etc. The approaches in [3,8] used simplified LIF and SRM models and simplified
routing architecture, which require relatively low hardware resources (e.g. the
approach in [3] used only adders and subtractors for the synaptic computation
and simplified 2D mesh-based NoC router for communication). Therefore, they
can accommodate more neurons and synapses. The GPU-based approach [12]
can simulate Izhikevich models by accelerating the computing process; however,
it has the drawback of high power consumption. Our work can accommodate a

Table 1. Performance comparison with other approaches.

Approach	Network size	Precision	Power	Architecture	Device
[3]	64 K neurons 1.5 M synapses	5 bit	N/A	Modular neural tile	Virtex-6 200 MHz
[8]	50 neurons 1000 synapses	16-bit FXP	N/A	Mixed serial- parallel	Spartan3 69 MHz
[12]	55,000 neurons	32-bit FLP	~7.35 W	Parallel	GPU 30 cores
[2]	400 neurons	32-bit FLP	N/A	20×20 topology	Virtex-4 100 MHz
[1]	100 neurons	32-bit FLP	N/A	Multiplexed neuron module	Virtex-6 100 MHz
This Work	1,728 neurons 43,200 synapses	32-bit FLP	56.3 mW	Two-level sharing mechanism	XC7Z020 200 MHz

larger number of neurons and synapses while keeping power consumption relatively low ($\sim$56.3 mW), which is an improvement over the approaches of [1,2] under similar conditions. The current high-performance FPGA is much larger than the one used in this work; therefore, using the proposed approach can accommodate more neurons and synapses.

For the proposed monitoring platform, the hardware overhead is an important metric of platform performance due to that the FPGA device hardware resources are limited. In this platform, only a signal collection module is needed in the FPGA device. The hardware resources used by the monitoring logic is shown in Table 2, which include 1,550 Slice LUTs and 1,109 Slice registers, respectively, i.e. only 2.91% and 1.04% of the resources of the FPGA devices in the Xilinx Zynq-7000 device.

Table 2. Hardware overhead for the performance monitoring platform

Logic	Available	Used	Utilization (%)
Slice LUTs	53,200	1,550	2.91%
Slice registers	106,400	1,109	1.04%

4 Conclusions

This paper proposes a compact layer-tile architecture for the neurons, and an efficient routing architecture for the interconnections between the neurons. The proposed architecture offers an efficient solution to address the problems of area demanding and dense interconnected requirements of the hardware SNNs. It has the capability of scaling to large scale hardware multilayer SNNs. In addition, the performance monitoring mechanism provides an auxiliary functional verification and performance analysis for the SNNs.

Acknowledgments. This research was supported by the National Natural Science Foundation of China under grants 61603104 and 61661008, the Guangxi Natural Science Foundation under grants 2015GXNSFBA139256 and 2016GXNSFCA380017, the funding of Overseas 100 Talents Program of Guangxi Higher Education, the Research Project of Guangxi University of China under grant KY2016YB059, Guangxi Key Lab of Multisource Information Mining & Security under grant MIMS15-07, the Doctoral Research Foundation of Guangxi Normal University, the Research Project of Guangxi Centre of Humanities & Social Sciences - Ecological Environment Forecast and Harnessing in Ecologically Vulnerable Region of Pearl River and Xijiang Economic Zone (ZX2016030), and the Innovation Project of Guangxi Graduate Education (YCSZ2016034).

References

1. Moctezuma, J.C., McGeehan, J.P., Nunez-Yanez, J.L.: Biologically compatible neural networks with reconfigurable hardware. Microprocessors Microsyst. **39**(8), 693–703 (2015)
2. Beuler, M., Tchaptchet, A., Bonath, W., Postnova, S., Braun, H.A.: Real-time simulations of synchronization in a conductance-based neuronal network with a digital FPGA hardware-core. Artif. Neural Netw. Mach. Learn. **7552**(6), 97–104 (2012)
3. Pande, S., Morgan, F., Cawley, S., Bruintjes, T., Smit, G., McGinley, B., Carrillo, S., Harkin, J., McDaid, L.: Modular neural tile architecture for compact embedded hardware spiking neural network. Neural Process. Lett. **38**(2), 131–153 (2013)
4. Carrillo, S., Harkin, J., Mcdaid, L., Pande, S., Cawley, S., Mcginley, B., Morgan, F.: Advancing interconnect density for spiking neural network hardware implementations using traffic-aware adaptive network-on-chip routers. Neural Netw. **33**(9), 42–57 (2012)
5. Schemmel, J., Fieres, J., Meier, K.: Wafer-scale integration of analog neural networks. In: Proceedings of the International Joint Conference on Neural Networks, pp. 431–438 (2008)
6. Carrillo, S., Harkin, J., McDaid, L.J., Morgan, F., Pande, S., Cawley, S., McGinley, B.: Scalable hierarchical network-on-chip architecture for spiking neural network hardware implementations. IEEE Trans. Parallel Distrib. Syst. **24**(12), 2451–2461 (2013)
7. Maguire, L.P., McGinnity, T.M., Glackin, B., Ghani, A., Belatreche, A., Harkin, J.: Challenges for large-scale implementations of spiking neural networks on FPGAs. Neurocomputing **71**(1–3), 13–29 (2007)
8. Iakymchuk, T., Rosado, A., Frances, J.V., Batallre, M.: Fast spiking neural network architecture for low-cost FPGA devices. In: 7th International Workshop on Reconfigurable and Communication-Centric Systems-on-Chip, pp. 1245–1248 (2012)
9. Tsodyks, M., Pawelzik, K., Markram, H.: Neural networks with dynamic synapses. Neural Comput. **10**(4), 821–835 (1998)
10. Stein, R.: A theoretical analysis of neuronal variability. Biophys. J. **5**(2), 173–194 (1965)
11. Wade, J.J., McDaid, L.J., Santos, J.A., Sayers, H.M.: SWAT: a spiking neural network training algorithm for classification problems. IEEE Trans. Neural Netw. **21**(11), 1817–1830 (2010)
12. Fidjeland, A.K., Shanahan, M.P.: Accelerated simulation of spiking neural networks using GPUs. In: Proceedings of the International Joint Conference on Neural Networks (IJCNN), pp. 1–8 (2010)

A Novel Design Method of Burst Mechanisms of a Piece-Wise Constant Neuron Model Based on Bifurcation Analysis

Chiaki Matsuda[✉] and Hiroyuki Torikai

Graduate School of Frontier Informatics, Kyoto Sangyo University, Motoyama, Kamigamo, Kita-Ku, Kyoto 603-8555, Japan
i1788214@cse.kyoto-su.ac.jp, hiroyuki.torikai@ieee.org

Abstract. A piece-wise constant (PWC) neuron model is an electronic circuit neuron model having a PWC vector field. In this paper, a PWC neuron model with a novel controlled voltage source is presented. Due to the nonlinearity of the voltage source, the presented model exhibits various bifurcations. Among such bifurcations, fundamental bifurcations related to burst behaviors are analyzed in this paper. Then, using the bifurcation analyses results, a novel design method of the vector field of the PWC neuron model is presented. It is shown that the presented design method enables the PWC neuron model to reproduce typical occurrence mechanisms of burst behaviors of neurons. Furthermore, the PWC neuron model is implemented as a breadboard prototype and occurrence of a typical burst behavior is validated by a real circuit experiment.

Keywords: Spiking neuron · Nonlinear circuit · Burst · Bifurcation

1 Introduction

Neurons exhibit a wide variety of nonlinear behaviors in response to stimulation inputs, where such behaviors can be classified mainly into two fundamental ones: spiking behavior (generation of relatively low-density spikes with simple spike patterns) and bursting behavior (repetition of high-density spikes and silent period like Fig. 1) [1]. In order to clarify occurrence mechanisms of such nonlinear behaviors, many mathematical models of neurons have been presented so far, e.g., [1–3]. Using such mathematical models, it has been pointed out that many nonlinear behaviors of neurons are caused by bifurcations of their nonlinear vector fields. For example, Fig. 1 summarizes the following four possible occurrence mechanisms of burst behaviors of neurons [1].

(a) A burst starts via a Hopf bifurcation and terminates via a Hopf bifurcation.
(b) A burst starts via a Hopf bifurcation and terminates via a fold bifurcation (fold of stable and unstable fast oscillations).
(c) A burst starts via a fold bifurcation and terminates via a Hopf bifurcation.

© Springer International Publishing AG 2017
D. Liu et al. (Eds.): ICONIP 2017, Part VI, LNCS 10639, pp. 796–803, 2017.
https://doi.org/10.1007/978-3-319-70136-3_84

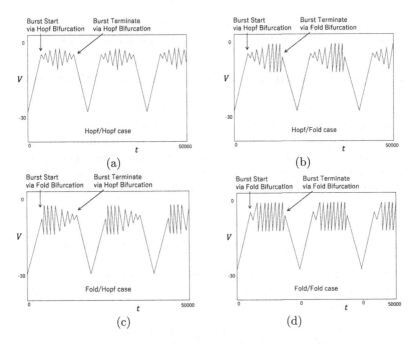

Fig. 1. Burst mechanisms of neurons [1]. (a) Hopf/Hopf case. Burst start via super-critical Hopf bifurcation and burst terminate via fold bifurcation. (b) Hopf/Fold case. Burst start via super-critical Hopf bifurcation and burst terminate via fold bifurcation. (c) Fold/Hopf case. Burst start via fold bifurcation and burst terminate via super-critical Hopf bifurcation. (d) Fold/Fold case. Burst start via fold bifurcation and burst terminate via fold bifurcation.

(d) A burst starts via a fold bifurcation and terminates via a fold bifurcation.

On the other hand, in order to develop brain-like hard/ware, many electron-ical circuit models of neurons have been also presented so far [4–8]. Among such electronical circuit neuron models, a piece-wise constant (PWC) neuron model [6–8] is focused on in this paper, where its advantages include: (i) the nonlinear vector field and related bifurcations can be analyzed theoretically (i.e., easy to analyze), and (ii) the PWC neuron model is relatively robust against parameter mismatch (i.e., easy to implement).

So, the purpose of this paper is to present a novel design method of the PWC neuron model, which can reproduce the occurrence mechanisms of the burst behaviors in Fig. 1. First, the PWC neuron model with a novel controlled voltage source is presented. Second, fundamental bifurcations related to burst behaviors are analyzed and the analyses results are summarized into bifurcation diagrams. Third, using the resulting bifurcation diagrams, a novel design method (parameter search algorithm) of the vector field of the PWC neuron model is presented. It is shown that the presented design method enables the PWC neuron model to reproduce the occurrence mechanisms of the burst behaviors. Finally, the PWC neuron model is implemented as a breadboard prototype and occurrence of a typical burst behavior is validated by a real circuit experiment.

2   PWC Neuron Model with a Novel Controlled Source

In this paper, a piece-wise constant (PWC) neuron model with a novel controlled voltage source is presented in order to reproduce the burst mechanisms of neurons summarized in Fig. 1. Figure 2(a) shows a circuit diagram of the PWC neuron model. The capacitor voltages v and u correspond to a membrane potential and a recovery variable of a neuron model, respectively. The current sources I_v and I_u are voltage-controlled and have the following PWC characteristics (see also Fig. 2(b)).

$$I_v(v_e) = \begin{cases} +I_v^+ & \text{if } v_e \geq 0, \\ -I_v^- & \text{if } v_e < 0, \end{cases} \quad I_u(v_e) = \begin{cases} +I_u^+ & \text{if } v_e \geq 0, \\ -I_u^- & \text{if } v_e < 0. \end{cases}$$

The switch SW in Fig. 2(a) is opened if the membrane potential v is less than a threshold value V_{th}. In this case, the PWC neuron model obeys the following sub-threshold dynamics.

$$\text{If } v(t) < V_{th}, \text{ then } \begin{cases} C\frac{dv}{dt} = I_v(|v| + V_{in} - u), \\ C\frac{du}{dt} = I_u(av - u). \end{cases} \tag{1}$$

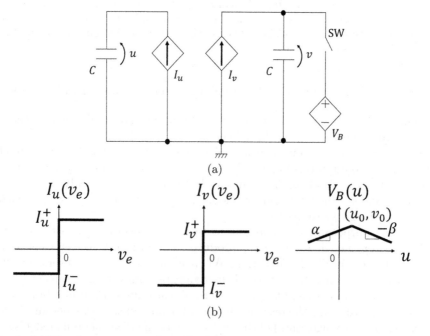

(a)

(b)

Fig. 2. (a) Piece-wise constant (PWC) neuron model. (b) Characteristics of voltage-controlled current sources I_v and I_u, and novel voltage-controlled voltage source V_B.

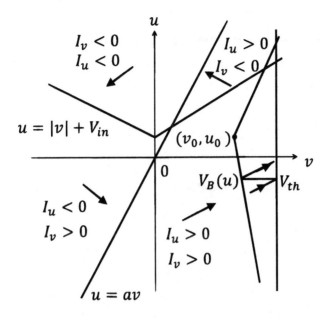

Fig. 3. PWC vector field of the PWC neuron model.

Under this sub-threshold dynamics, the vector field of the PWC neuron model has four PWC velocity vectors: $(Cdv/dt, Cdu/dt) = (I_v^+, I_u^+), (I_v^+, -I_u^-), (-I_v^-, I_u^+)$, and $(-I_v^-, -I_u^-)$ as shown in Fig. 3. On the other hand, the switch SW in Fig. 2(a) is closed instantaneously if the membrane potential v reaches the threshold value V_{th}. In this case, the PWC neuron model exhibits the following super-threshold firing.

$$\text{If } v(t) \geq V_{th}, \text{ then } v(t^+) = V_B(u), \tag{2}$$

where $t^+ = \lim_{\delta \to +0} t+\delta$ and $V_B(u)$ is a voltage source controlled by the recovery variable u. In this paper, we propose the following novel design of the voltage source $V_B(u)$ in order to reproduce the burst mechanisms of neurons summarized in Fig. 1.

$$V_B(u) = \begin{cases} \alpha(u - u_0) + v_0 & \text{if } u \geq u_0, \\ -\beta(u - u_0) + v_0 & \text{if } u < u_0. \end{cases}$$

The characteristics of $V_B(u)$ is shown in Fig. 2(b). As shown in Fig. 3, when the membrane potential v reaches the threshold value V_{th}, it is reset to $V_B(u)$. Figure 4 shows typical time waveforms and corresponding phase plane trajectories of the PWC neuron model.

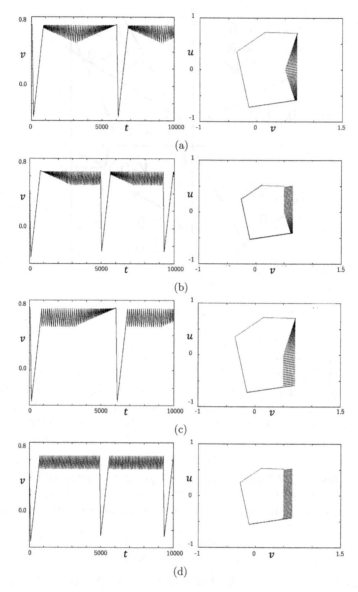

Fig. 4. Burst mechanisms of the PWC neuron model corresponding to those in Fig. 1. $(C, I_v^+, I_v^-, I_u^+, I_u^-, V_{in}, v_0, u_0) = (1.0, 0.3, 2, 0.05, 1.5, 3, 0.5, 0)$. (a) Hopf/Hopf case. Burst start via super-critical Hopf bifurcation and burst terminate via super-critical Hopf bifurcation. $(\alpha, \beta, V_{th}) = (0.3, 0.3, 0.7044)$. (b) Hopf/Fold case. Burst start via super-critical Hopf bifurcation and burst terminate via fold bifurcation. $(\alpha, \beta, V_{th}) = (0.3, 0, 0.7044)$. (c) Fold/Hopf case. Burst start via fold bifurcation and burst terminate via super-critical Hopf bifurcation. $(\alpha, \beta, V_{th}) = (0, 0.3, 0.65)$. (d) Fold/Fold case. Burst start via fold bifurcation and burst terminate via fold bifurcation. $(\alpha, \beta, V_{th}) = (0, 0, 0.65)$.

3   Bifurcation Analysis and Vector Field Design

Figure 5 shows bifurcation diagrams of the PWC neuron model corresponding to the four burst mechanisms of neurons summarized in Fig. 1. For example, in the black parameter region in Fig. 5(a), the PWC neuron model exhibits start of the burst via the super-critical Hopf bifurcation and terminate of the burst via the super-critical Hopf bifurcation. Then, using the bifurcation diagrams, we propose the following design method (parameter search algorithm) of the vector field of the PWC neuron model.

Parameter search algorithm utilizing the bifurcation analysis:

- A bursting time waveform of a membrane potential $v_{teacher}$ from an in vivo neuron, an in vitro neuron, or a mathematical model neuron is presented as a teacher signal to be reproduced by the PWC neuron model, where the corresponding bifurcation diagram is selected from Figs. 5(a)–(d).

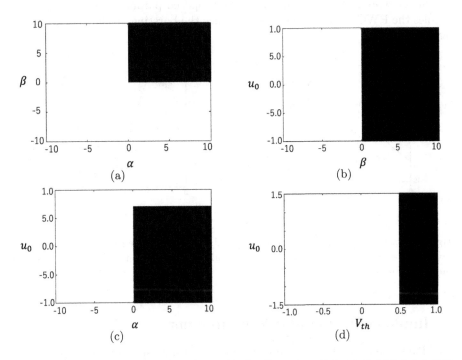

Fig. 5. Bifurcation diagrams. $(C, I_v^+, I_v^-, I_u^+, I_u^-, V_{in}, v_0) = (1.0, 0.3, 2, 0.05, 1.5, 3, 0.5)$. In the black parameter regions, the PWC neuron model exhibits the following burst mechanisms. (a) Hopf/Hopf case. Burst start via super-critical Hopf bifurcation and burst terminate via super-critical Hopf bifurcation. $(u_0, V_{th}) = (0, 0.7044)$. (b) Hopf/Fold case. Burst start via super-critical Hopf bifurcation and burst terminate via fold bifurcation. $(\alpha, V_{th}) = (0, 1.3)$. (c) Fold/Hopf case. Burst start via fold bifurcation and burst terminate via super-critical Hopf bifurcation. $(\beta, V_{th}) = (0, 0.7044)$. (d) Fold/Fold case. Burst start via fold bifurcation and burst terminate via fold bifurcation. $(\alpha, \beta) = (0, 0)$.

- The parameter values of the PWC neuron model are randomly set in the black region of the selected bifurcation diagram.
- The parameter values are slightly and randomly changed from the current values within the black region of the selected bifurcation diagram (mutation). The new parameter values and the original values are compared based on similarity between the time waveform of the membrane potential v of the PWC neuron model and the teacher signal $v_{teacher}$. The better parameter values are selected as the current values (selection). In addition, with a low probability, the parameter values are randomly changed within the black region of the selected bifurcation diagram (escape from local minimum).
- Repeat the above search until a given maximum search number.

Figure 6(a) shows a time waveform of an example of the teacher signal $v_{teacher}$ from a mathematical model neuron, where Fig. 5(c) (the Fold/Hopf case) is selected as the corresponding bifurcation diagram. Figure 6(b) shows a time waveforms of the membrane potential v of the PWC neuron model after the parameter search. It can be seen that the proposed parameter search algorithm enables the PWC neuron model to reproduce the bursting mechanism of teacher signal $v_{teacher}$.

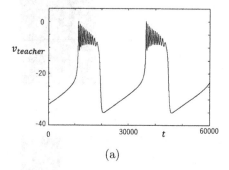
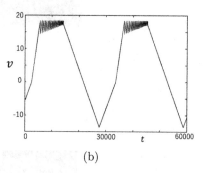

(a)   (b)

Fig. 6. Parameter search. (a) A teacher signal $v_{teacher}$ obtained from a mathematical model neuron [3]. (b) The membrane potential v of the PWC neuron model after the parameter search.

4   Implementation and Measurement

The PWC neuron model is implemented by using standard discrete circuit components: the voltage controlled current sources I_v and I_u are implemented by operational transconductance amplifiers (NJM13600), the voltage controlled voltage source V_B is implemented by operational amplifiers (TL074), and the switch SW is implemented by an analog switch (4066). The parameter values of the implemented circuit are adjusted by using the parameter search algorithm proposed in the previous section. Figure 7 shows a resulting experimental measurement. It can be seen that the implemented circuit of the PWC neuron model can reproduce the burst mechanism of the teacher signal x in Fig. 6(a).

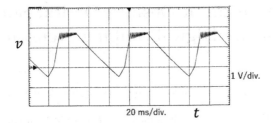

Fig. 7. Experimental measurement of the membrane potential $v_{teacher}$ of the PWC neuron model. The parameter values are designed by the parameter search algorithm.

5 Conclusions

It is shown that the PWC neuron model with the novel controlled voltage source can reproduce the four occurrence mechanisms of burst behaviors of neurons. The underlying bifurcation mechanisms of the burst behaviors were analyzed and summarized in the bifurcation diagrams. Then, using the bifurcation diagrams, the novel design method of the vector field of the PWC neuron model was presented. It was shown that the design method enables the PWC neuron model to reproduce the four occurrence mechanisms of the burst behaviors. Also, real circuit experiments validated occurrence of the typical burst behavior of the PWC neuron model. Future problems include: (a) comparison to other models, (b) more detailed analyses of bifurcations, and (c) development of a network of PWC neuron model with synaptic plasticity.

Acknowledgments. This work was partially supported by JSPS KAKENHI Grant Number 15K00352.

References

1. Izhikevich, E.: Dynamical Systems in Neuroscience: The Geometry of Excitability and Bursting. The MIT Press, Cambridge (2010)
2. Shilnikov, A., Cymbalyuk, G.: Transition between tonic spiking and bursting in a neuron model via the blue-sky catastrophe. Phys. Rev. Lett. **94**, 048101 (2005)
3. Duan, L., Zhai, D., Lu, Q.: Bifurcation and bursting in Morris-Lecar model for class I and class II excitability. Discr. Continuous Dyn. Syst. **3**, 391–399 (2011)
4. Wu, X., Saxena, V., Zhu, K.: Homogeneous spiking neuromorphic system for real-world pattern recognition. IEEE J. Emerg. Sel. Topics CAS **5**(2), 254–266 (2015)
5. Larras, B., Lahuec, C., Seguin, F., Arzel, M.: Ultra-low-energy mixed-signal IC implementing encoded neural networks. IEEE Trans. CAS-II **63**(11), 1974–1985 (2016)
6. Yamashita, Y., Torikai, H.: Theoretical analysis for efficient design of a piece-wise constant spiking neuron model. IEEE Trans. CAS-II **60**(1), 54–58 (2014)
7. Yamashita, Y., Torikai, H.: A novel PWC spiking neuron model: neuron-like bifurcation scenarios and responses. IEEE Trans. CAS-I **59**(11), 2678–2691 (2012)
8. Matsuda, C., Torikai, H.: Homoclinic bifurcations in a piece-wise constant neuron model. In: Proceedings of NOLTA, pp. 156–159 (2016)

Implementation of Desired Digital Spike Maps in the Digital Spiking Neurons

Hiroaki Uchida[✉] and Toshimichi Saito

Hosei University, Koganei, Tokyo 184-8584, Japan
`tsaito@hosei.ac.jp`

Abstract. This paper considers implementation of desired digital spike maps (DSmaps) in the digital spiking neurons (DSNs). The DSmap is defined on a set of points and can describe various spike-trains. The DSN is constructed by two shift registers and a wiring. Depending on the wiring pattern, the DSN can generate various spike-trains. We present a simple formula that clarifies relation between the DSmaps and DSNs. Using the formula, desired DSmaps can be implemented in DSNs. We then present a simple ring-coupled system of the DSNs and demonstrate multi-phase synchronization of periodic spike-trains in Verilog simulation. This coupled system will be developed into large-scale networks of DSNs.

Keywords: Spike-trains · Stability · Digital spiking neurons · Shift registers · Multi-phase synchronization

1 Introduction

A digital spike map (DSmap) is a simple digital dynamical system defined on a set of points [1–4]. The DSmap is regarded as a digital version of analog one-dimensional maps such as the logistic map [5] and is relevant to several digital systems such as cellular automata [6]. The DSmap can describe various periodic/transient spike-trains. Spike-trains have been used in many engineering applications including image processing [7], spike-based communication [8,9], and spike-based time series approximation [10]. In such applications, synchronization of multiple spike-trains plays a key role. Implementation/realization of desired spike-trains and their synchronization phenomena are important not only in fundamental study of nonlinear dynamics but also in engineering applications.

This paper studies implementation of the DSmaps in the digital spiking neurons (DSNs [9–11]). First, we show that the DSmap is represented by a characteristic vector and can describe various spike-trains. Based on the DSmap, we define super-stable periodic spike-train such that all the initial points fall rapidly into the spike-train. Such spike-trains are well suited for robust operation of engineering systems such as spike-based encoders [9]. Second, we consider the DSNs inspired by integrate-and-fire neuron models [12–14]. The DSN is constructed by

© Springer International Publishing AG 2017
D. Liu et al. (Eds.): ICONIP 2017, Part VI, LNCS 10639, pp. 804–811, 2017.
https://doi.org/10.1007/978-3-319-70136-3_85

two shift registers [15] connected by a wiring [10]. Depending on the wiring pattern and initial condition, the DSN can generate various periodic spike-trains. The dynamics of DSN is represented by a wiring vector. We give a simple formula that clarifies relation between wiring vectors of DSNs and characteristic vectors of DSmaps. Using the formula, desired DSmaps can be implemented in the DSNs. As a typical phenomenon, a super-stable periodic spike-train is demonstrated in Verilog simulation. Third, we present a simple ring-coupled system of the DSNs based on a digital delayed connection. As a typical phenomenon, multi-phase synchronization of periodic spike-trains is demonstrated in Verilog simulation.

The Verilog simulation and ring-coupled system will be developed into FPGA hardware implementation of large-scale networks of DSNs. It should be noted that the implementation of DSmaps in the DSNs and the ring-coupled system have not discussed in previous publications [1–4, 10, 11].

2   Digital Spike Maps and Periodic Spike-Trains

Figure 1(a) shows a digital spike-train where N denotes basic period and θ_n denotes the n-th spike-phase. Let such spike-trains be described by the DSmap

$$\theta_{n+1} = F(\theta_n), \ \theta_n \in \{1, \cdots, N\} \equiv L_N \tag{1}$$

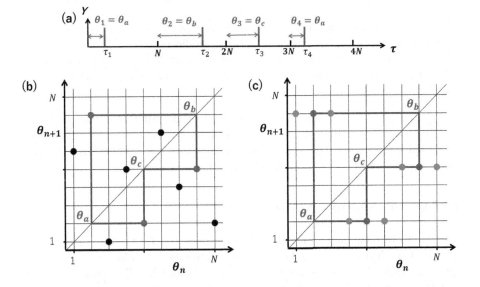

Fig. 1. Digital spike-train and digital spike map ($N = 9$). (a) Periodic spike-train with period $3N$. (b) DSmap of $d = (6, 8, 1, 5, 2, 7, 4, 5, 2)$ and complete-stable periodic orbit with period 3. (c) DSmap of $d = (8, 8, 8, 2, 2, 2, 5, 5, 5)$ and super-stable periodic orbit with period 3.

As an initial spike-phase $\theta_1 \in [0, N)$ is given, the DSmap outputs a sequence of spike-phases $\{\theta_n\}$. The sequence gives a spike-train

$$Y(\tau) = \begin{cases} 1 & \text{for } \tau = \tau_n \\ 0 & \text{for } \tau \neq \tau_n \end{cases} \quad \tau_n = \theta_n + N(n-1). \tag{2}$$

where τ_n denote the n-th spike-position. The n-th spike appears in the n-th interval: $\tau_n \in [(n-1)N, nN)$. The DSmap is represented by the characteristic vector

$$\boldsymbol{d} \equiv (d_1, \cdots, d_N), \quad F(i) = d_i \in \{1, \cdots, N\} \tag{3}$$

Since the domain L_N of the DSmap consists of a finite number of points, the steady state must be a periodic spike-rain. Here we give basic definitions.

Definition 1. A point $p \in L_N$ is said to be a periodic point with period k if $p = F^k(p)$ and $F(p)$ to $f^k(p)$ are all different where F^k is the k-fold composition of F. A sequence of the periodic points $\{F(p), \cdots, F^k(p)\}$ is said to be a periodic orbit. A periodic orbit with period k is equivalent to a periodic spike-train with period kN. For example, the periodic orbit with period 3 in Fig. 1 is equivalent to periodic spike-train with period 3×9.

Definition 2. A point $q \in L_N$ is said to be an eventually periodic point with step k if the q is not a periodic point but falls into some periodic point p after k steps: $F^k(q) = p$. The eventually periodic points represent transient phenomena.

Definition 3. A periodic orbit (and corresponding periodic spike-train) is said to be complete-stable if all the eventually periodic points fall into the periodic orbit. A periodic orbit (and corresponding periodic spike-train) is said to be a super-stable if all the eventually periodic points fall into the periodic orbit after 1 step.

Figure 1(c) shows a super-stable periodic orbit. All the initial points fall rapidly into the periodic orbit (and corresponding periodic spike-train). Super-stable spike-trains are well suited for robust operation of engineering systems such as spike-based encoders in multiplex communication [9].

3   Digital Spiking Neurons

In order to implement the DSmap, we introduce the DSN. Applying a wiring between two shift registers, a DSN is constructed as shown in Fig. 2(a) The left and right shift resistors are referred to as P-cells and X-cells, respectively. The P-cells consist of N_p elements and operate as a pacemaker. Only one element can be 1 (with period N_p) and all the other elements are 0:

$$P(\tau) = (P_1(\tau), \cdots, P_{N_p}(\tau)), \quad P_i = 1 \text{ iff } \tau \bmod N_p = i, \ i \in \{1, 2, \cdots, N_p\} \tag{4}$$

where τ denotes discrete time and is represented by a positive integer.

The X-cells consist of N_x elements and construct a state variable vector corresponding to the membrane potential in analog neuron models. Only one element can be 1 and all the other elements are 0.

$$X(\tau) = (X_1(\tau), \cdots, X_{N_x}(\tau)) \tag{5}$$

The P- and X-cells are connected by a wiring represented by the wiring vector

$$\boldsymbol{a} = (a_1, \cdots, a_{N_p}), \ a_i = j \text{ iff } P_i \text{ is connected to } X_j \tag{6}$$

For example, the DSN in Fig. 2 is represented by the wiring vector

$$\boldsymbol{a} = (4, 3, 11, 8, 12, 8, 12, 12, 16)$$

Each branch of the wiring activates either element of the X-cells. The activated elements construct a base signal where only one element can be 1 and all the other elements are 0:

$$B(\tau) = (B_1(\tau), \cdots, B_{N_x}(\tau)), \ B_j(\tau) = 1 \text{ iff } P_i(\tau) = 1 \text{ and } a_i = j \tag{7}$$

where $j \in \{1, 2, \cdots, N_x - 1\}$. In the DSN, X-cells are initialized such that $X_k(1) = 1$ at $\tau = 1$ for some k. For $\tau \geq 2$, the dynamics is defined as the following:

- If $X_j(\tau) = 1$ then $X_{j+1}(\tau + 1) = 1$ where $j \in \{1, 2, \cdots, N_x - 1\}$.
- If $X_{N_x}(\tau) = 1$ and $B_j(\tau) = 1$ then $Y(\tau) = 1$ and $X_j(\tau + 1) = 1$ where $j \in \{1, 2, \cdots, N_x - 1\}$.

As illustrated in Fig. 2, the DSN generates a spike-train:

$$Y(\tau) = \begin{cases} 1 & \text{if } X_{N_x}(\tau) = 1 \\ 0 & \text{otherwise} \end{cases} \tag{8}$$

Since the n-th spike determines the $(n + 1)$-th spike, a DSmap can be defined:

$$\theta_{n+1} = F(\theta_n), \ \theta_n \in \{1, 2, \cdots N_p\} \tag{9}$$

where θ_n is the n-th spike phase, τ_n is the n-th spike-position, and N_p is the basic period. For simplicity, we set

$$N_x = 2N_p - 1, \ 0 \leq a_i - i \leq N_p, \ i \in \{1, 2, \cdots, N_p\} \tag{10}$$

In this case, one spike appears once per one basic period N_p and the n-th spike appears in the n-th interval $\tau_n \in \{(n - 1)N_p, \cdots, nN_p\}$.

Here we show an important result. If a characteristic vector $\boldsymbol{d} = (d_1, \cdots, d_{N_p})$ of a DSmap is given, the corresponding wiring vector of a DSN is given by

$$\boldsymbol{a} = (a_1, \cdots, a_{N_p}), \ a_i = N_p - (d_i - i), \ i \in \{1, \cdots, N_p\} \tag{11}$$

Using Eq. (11), any DSmap can be implemented in the DSN. For example, the DSmap in Fig. 1(c) has super-stable periodic orbit and is implemented in the DSN of the wiring vector

$$\boldsymbol{a} = (2, 3, 4, 11, 12, 13, 11, 12, 13) \leftarrow \boldsymbol{d} = (8, 8, 8, 2, 2, 2, 5, 5, 5)$$

That is, the super-stable periodic orbit of the DSmap in Fig. 1(c) is realized by the super-stable spike-train of DSN in Fig. 3.

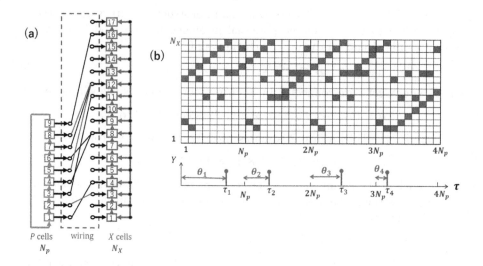

Fig. 2. Digital spiking neuron for $N_p = 9$ and $N_x = 17$. The wiring vector $a = (4, 3, 11, 8, 12, 8, 12, 12, 16)$. (a) P-cells, X-cells, and wiring. (b) Complete-stable periodic spike-train with period $3N_p$. It corresponds to complete-stable periodic orbit with period 3 of DSmap in Fig. 1(b)

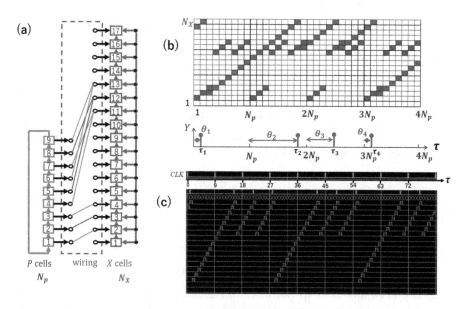

Fig. 3. Digital spiking neuron for $N_p = 9$ and $N_x = 17$. Wiring vector $a = (2, 3, 4, 11, 12, 13, 11, 12, 13)$. (a) P-cells, X-cells, and wiring. (b) Super-stable periodic spike-train with period $3N_p$. It corresponds to super-stable periodic orbit with period 3 of DSmap in Fig. 1(c). (c) Verilog simulation of super-stable periodic spike-train with period $3N_p$.

4   Ring-Coupled Digital Spiking Neurons and Multi-phase Synchronization

Here we present a ring-coupled system of DSNs. First, we prepare M pieces of DSNs with a common base signal as illustrated in Fig. 4:

$$X^1 \equiv (X_1^1, \cdots, X_{N_x}^1), \cdots, X^M \equiv (X_1^M, \cdots, X_{N_x}^M) \tag{12}$$

The ring-coupled-DSN is defined by the following two kinds of firing.

1. Self-firing. If $X_j^i(\tau) = 1$ then $X_{j+1}^i(\tau + 1) = 1$ for $j \in \{1, \cdots, N_x - 1\}$ and $i \in \{1, \cdots, M\}$. If $X_{N_x}^i(\tau) = 1$ and $B_j(\tau) = 1$ then $Y^i(\tau) = 1$ and $X_j^i(\tau + 1) = 1$. The common base signal is determined by Eq. (7).
2. Propagate-firing. If $X_{N_x}^i(\tau) = 1$ and $X_k^{i+1}(\tau) = 1$ for $k \in \{1, \cdots, N_x - N_p\}$ then $X_{N_x - N_p + 1}^{i+1}(\tau + 1) = 1$ where $i \in \{1, \cdots, M\}$ and $(X^{M+1} \equiv X^1)$.

For example, in the case $M = 3$, $N_x = 17$, and $N_p = 9$, the propagate-coupling is described by

If $X_{17}^1(\tau) = 1$ and $X_k^2(\tau) = 1$ for $k < 9$ then $X_9^2(\tau + 1) = 1$.
If $X_{17}^2(\tau) = 1$ and $X_k^3(\tau) = 1$ for $k < 9$ then $X_9^3(\tau + 1) = 1$.
If $X_{17}^3(\tau) = 1$ and $X_k^1(\tau) = 1$ for $k < 9$ then $X_9^1(\tau + 1) = 1$.

The firings are illustrated in Fig. 4. In the ring-coupled-DSN, the i-th DSN outputs a spike-train

$$Y^i(\tau) = \begin{cases} 1 \text{ if } X_{N_x}^i(\tau) = 1 \\ 0 \text{ otherwise} \end{cases} \quad i \in \{1, \cdots, M\} \tag{13}$$

We have constructed ring-coupled DSNs for $M = 3$, $N_x = 17$, and $N_p = 9$ as shown in Fig. 4. When each of the 3 DSNs outputs a periodic spike-train with period $3N_p$ before the ring-coupling, the ring-coupled DSN can exhibit 3-phase synchronization such that

$$\begin{aligned} Y^1(\tau) = Y^3(\tau - N_p), \ Y^2(\tau) = Y^1(\tau - N_p), \ Y^3(\tau) = Y^2(\tau - N_p) \\ X^1(\tau) = X^3(\tau - N_p), \ X^2(\tau) = X^1(\tau - N_p), \ X^3(\tau) = X^2(\tau - N_p) \end{aligned} \tag{14}$$

where $X^i(\tau - 3N_p) = X^i(\tau)$ for $i \in \{1, 2, 3\}$. Performing Verilog simulation, we have confirmed 3-phase synchronization phenomenon of periodic spike-trains with period $3N_p$ as shown in Fig. 5. The periodic spike-train is super-stable before the coupling as shown in Fig. 3 and the 3-phase synchronization is complete-stable. This ring-coupled-DSN and its Verilog simulations will be developed into FPGA hardware implementation of large-scale networks of DSNs and its applications.

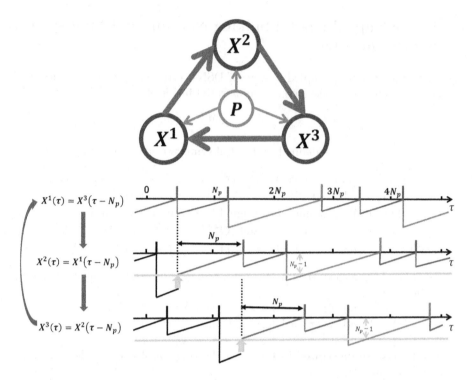

Fig. 4. Ring-coupled digital spiking neurons and M-phase synchronization for $M = 3$.

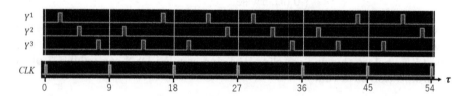

Fig. 5. M-phase synchronization with period $3N_p$ for $M = 3$, $N_p = 9$ and $N_x = 17$ in Verilog simulation. Before the coupling, each DSN outputs super-stable periodic spike-train with period 3×9 in Fig. 3. Parameters of the DSN are as in Fig. 3.

5   Conclusions

Realization of desired periodic spike-trains and multi-phase synchronization of them are studied in this paper. As a DSmap of desired spike-train dynamics is given, a suitable wiring vector is determined and the DSmap is implemented in the DSN. A simple ring-coupled system of DSNs is presented and multi-phase synchronization of periodic spike-trains is demonstrated.

Future problems include classification of various periodic spike-trains, stability analysis of the periodic spike-rains and synchronization phenomena, consideration of various coupling methods of DSNs, and hardware implementation for engineering applications.

Acknowledgements. The authors wish to thank Mr. Tomoki Hamaguchi of Hosei University for his valuable comments on the Verilog simulation. This work is supported in part by JSPS KAKENHI#15K00350.

References

1. Horimoto, N., Ogawa, T., Saito, T.: Basic analysis of digital spike maps. In: Villa, A.E.P., Duch, W., Érdi, P., Masulli, F., Palm, G. (eds.) ICANN 2012. LNCS, vol. 7552, pp. 161–168. Springer, Heidelberg (2012). doi:10.1007/978-3-642-33269-2_21
2. Horimoto, N., Saito, T.: Analysis of various transient phenomena and co-existing periodic spike-trains in simple digital spike maps. In: Proceedings of IJCNN, pp. 1751–1758 (2013)
3. Yamaoka, H., Saito, T.: Steady-versus-transient plot for analysis of digital maps. IEICE Trans. Fund. **E99–A**(10), 1806–1812 (2016)
4. Hamaguchi, T., Yamaoka, K., Saito, T.: Stability analysis of periodic orbits in digital spiking neurons. In: Hirose, A., Ozawa, S., Doya, K., Ikeda, K., Lee, M., Liu, D. (eds.) ICONIP 2016. LNCS, vol. 9948, pp. 334–341. Springer, Cham (2016). doi:10.1007/978-3-319-46672-9_38
5. Ott, E.: Chaos in Dynamical Systems. Cambridge University Press, Cambridge (1993)
6. Chua, L.O.: A Nonlinear Dynamics Perspective of Wolfram's New Kind of Science, I, II. World Scientific, Singapore (2005)
7. Campbell, S.R., Wang, D., Jayaprakash, C.: Synchrony and desynchrony in integrate-and-fire oscillators. Neural Comput. **11**, 1595–1619 (1999)
8. Rulkov, N.F., Sushchik, M.M., Tsimring, L.S., Volkovskii, A.R.: Digital communication using chaotic-pulse-position modulation. IEEE Trans. CAS-I **48**(12), 1436–1444 (2001)
9. Iguchi, T., Hirata, A., Torikai, H.: Theoretical and heuristic synthesis of digital spiking neurons for spike-pattern-division multiplexing. IEICE Trans. Fund. **E93–A**(8), 1486–1496 (2010)
10. Torikai, H., Funew, A., Saito, T.: Digital spiking neuron and its learning for approximation of various spike-trains. Neural Networks **21**, 140–149 (2008)
11. Yamaoka, K., Saito, T.: Realization of desired super-stable spike-trains based on digital spiking neurons. In: Proceedings of IJCNN, pp. 198–205 (2016)
12. Izhikevich, E.M.: Dynamical Systems in Neuroscience. MIT Press, Cambridge (2006)
13. Lee, G., Farhat, N.H.G.: The bifurcating neuron network 1. Neural Networks **14**, 115–131 (2001)
14. Torikai, H., Saito, T., Schwarz, W.: Synchronization via multiplex pulse-train. IEEE Trans. Circuits Syst. I **46**(9), 1072–1085 (1999)
15. Saravanan, S., Lavanya, M., Vijay Sai, R., Kumar, R.: Design and analysis of linear feedback shift register based on various tap connection. Procedia Eng. **38**, 640–646 (2012)

A Novel Hardware-Efficient CPG Model Based on Nonlinear Dynamics of Asynchronous Cellular Automaton

Kentaro Takeda$^{(\boxtimes)}$ and Hiroyuki Torikai

Kyoto Sangyo University, 1-3 Motoyama, Kamigamo, Kitaku, Kyoto 605-8555, Japan
takeda@mail.nsci.jp, torikai@cse.kyoto-su.ac.jp

Abstract. A novel hardware-efficient central pattern generator (CPG) model based on the nonlinear dynamics of an asynchronous cellular automaton is presented. It is shown that the presented model can generate multi-phase synchronized periodic signals, which are suitable for controlling a snake robot. Then, the presented model is implemented on a field programmable gate array (FPGA) and is connected to a snake robot hardware. It is shown by real machine experiments that the presented model can realize rhythmic spinal locomotions of the snake robot. Moreover, it is shown that the presented model consumes much fewer hardware resources (FPGA slices) than a standard simple CPG model.

Keywords: Central Pattern Generator · Nonlinear dynamics · Asynchronous Cellular automaton · Field-programmable gate array · Snake robot

1 Introduction

Central pattern generators (CPGs) are networks of neural oscillators, which generate rhythmic signals to control motor systems of animals [1]. Many mathematical models of CPGs have been presented so far and their nonlinear phenomena such as synchronizations and bifurcations have been analyzed intensively [2–6]. Also, CPG models have been used to control artificial robots of various kinds [2–6] including snake robots [4–6] like the one in Fig. 1. From a dynamical system theory viewpoint, biological system models including the CPG models can be classified into the following four classes based on continuousness and discontinuousness of state variables and times, where partial differential equation models are omitted for simplicity.

Class CTCS (Continuous Time and Continuous State): A nonlinear differential equation model of a biological system, which has a continuous time and continuous states. Such a model can be implemented by an analog nonlinear circuit.

Class DTCS (Discrete Time and Continuous State): A nonlinear difference equation model of a biological system, which has a discrete time and continuous states. Such a model can be implemented by a switched capacitor circuit.

© Springer International Publishing AG 2017
D. Liu et al. (Eds.): ICONIP 2017, Part VI, LNCS 10639, pp. 812–820, 2017.
https://doi.org/10.1007/978-3-319-70136-3_86

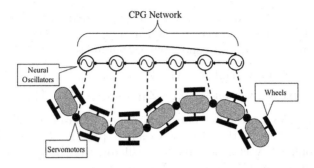

Fig. 1. Snake robot controlled by a network of neural oscillators called a central pattern generator (CPG).

Class DTDS (Discrete Time and Discrete State): A numerical integration model of a biological system, which has a discrete time and discrete states including fixed point numbers. Such a model can be implemented by a digital processor. A cellular automaton model of a biological system also belongs to this class, which has a discrete time and discrete states. Such a model can be implemented by a traditional synchronous sequential logic circuit.

Class CTDS (Continuous Time and Discrete State): An asynchronous cellular automaton model of a biological system, has a continuous (state transition) time and discrete states. Such a model can be implemented by an asynchronous sequential logic circuit.

Most conventional biological system models are belonging to the classes CTCS, DTCS, and DTDS. On the other hand, our group has been developing biological system models based on asynchronous cellular automata, which are belonging to the class CTDS [7–9]. It has been shown that biological system models based on the asynchronous cellular automata consume much fewer hardware resources (much fewer transistors) compared to conventional models [7–9].

So, the purpose of this paper is to present a novel hardware-efficient CPG model based on the nonlinear dynamics of the asynchronous cellular automaton. First, the novel CPG model is presented and it is shown that the presented model can generate multi-phase synchronized periodic signals, which are suitable for controlling a snake robot. Then, the presented model is implemented by a field programmable gate array (FPGA) and is connected to a snake robot hardware. It is shown by real machine experiments that the presented model can realize rhythmic spinal locomotion of the snake robot. Moreover, it is shown that the presented model consumes much fewer hardware resources than a standard simple CPG model.

2 Novel CPG Model Based on Asynchronous CA

2.1 Single Neural Oscillator

In this paper, a novel central pattern generator (CPG) model based on the nonlinear dynamics of an asynchronous cellular automaton is presented. Figure 1 shows a schematic of a snake robot controlled by the CPG model. As shown in the figure, the CPG model consists of a network of neural oscillators, where each oscillator has the following discrete states and auxiliary variables.

Discrete state variables : $X_i \in \mathbf{Z}_N = \{0, \cdots, N-1\}$, $\qquad Y_i \in \mathbf{Z}_N$,

Discrete auxiliary variables : $P_i \in \mathbf{Z}_M = \{0, \cdots, M-1\}$, $\qquad Q_i \in \mathbf{Z}_M$,

where i is the index for the oscillator, and N and M are natural numbers that determine resolutions of the discrete variables $\{X_i, Y_i, P_i, Q_i\}$. In order to design the nonlinear vector field of the oscillator, the following functions $g_x :$ $\mathbf{Z}_N \times \mathbf{Z}_N \to \mathbf{R}$ and $g_y : \mathbf{Z}_N \times \mathbf{Z}_N \to \mathbf{R}$ are prepared.

$$g_x(X_i, Y_i) = \delta l(X_i - \frac{N}{2}) - \omega l(Y_i - \frac{N}{2}) - l^3(X_i - \frac{N}{2})((X_i - \frac{N}{2})^2 + (Y_i - \frac{N}{2})^2),$$

$$g_y(X_i, Y_i) = \omega l(X_i - \frac{N}{2}) + \delta l(Y_i - \frac{N}{2}) - l^3(Y_i - \frac{N}{2})((X_i - \frac{N}{2})^2 + (Y_i - \frac{N}{2})^2),$$

where $l = m/N$, $\delta \in \mathbf{R}$, $\omega \in \mathbf{R}$, and $m \in \mathbf{R}$ are parameters. Note that the function g_x and g_y are not implemented as hardware but is used to design the following discrete functions $F_X : \mathbf{Z}_N \times \mathbf{Z}_N \to \mathbf{Z}_M^{\pm}$ and $F_Y : \mathbf{Z}_N \times \mathbf{Z}_N \to \mathbf{Z}_M^{\pm}$, where $\mathbf{Z}_M^{\pm} = \{-(M-1), \cdots, 0, \cdots, M-1\}$.

$$F_X(X_i, Y_i) = \begin{cases} M-1 & \text{if } \lfloor \dfrac{l}{g_x(X_i, Y_i)T_X} \rfloor \geq M-1, \\ -(M-1) & \text{if } \lfloor \dfrac{l}{g_x(X_i, Y_i)T_X} \rfloor \geq -(M-1), \\ \lfloor \dfrac{l}{g_x(X_i, Y_i)T_X} \rfloor & \text{otherwise,} \end{cases}$$

$$F_Y(X_i, Y_i) = \begin{cases} M-1 & \text{if } \lfloor \dfrac{l}{g_y(X_i, Y_i)T_Y} \rfloor \geq M-1, \\ -(M-1) & \text{if } \lfloor \dfrac{l}{g_y(X_i, Y_i)T_Y} \rfloor \geq -(M-1), \\ \lfloor \dfrac{l}{g_y(X_i, Y_i)T_Y} \rfloor & \text{otherwise,} \end{cases}$$

where $\lfloor . \rfloor$ denotes the floor function, and $T_X \in \mathbf{R}^+$ and $T_Y \in \mathbf{R}^+$ are periods of the following internal clocks $C_X(t)$ and $C_Y(t)$, respectively.

$$C_X(t) = \begin{cases} 1 & \text{if } t = 0, T_X, 2T_X, \cdots, \\ 0 & \text{if otherwise,} \end{cases} \qquad C_Y(t) = \begin{cases} 1 & \text{if } t = 0, T_Y, 2T_Y, \cdots, \\ 0 & \text{if otherwise.} \end{cases}$$

It is assumed that the ratio T_X/T_Y of the periods can be irrational, i.e., the internal clocks C_X and C_Y are generically asynchronous. These asynchronous internal clocks C_X and C_Y trigger the following asynchronous transitions of the discrete auxiliary variables P_i and Q_i, respectively.

$$\text{If } C_X(t) = 1, \text{ then } P_i(t_+) := \begin{cases} P_i(t) + 1 & \text{if } P_i(t) < |F_X|, \\ 0 & \text{if } P_i(t) \geq |F_X|, \end{cases} \qquad (1)$$

$$\text{If } C_Y(t) = 1, \text{ then } Q_i(t_+) := \begin{cases} Q_i(t) + 1 & \text{if } Q_i(t) < |F_Y|, \\ 0 & \text{if } Q_i(t) \geq |F_Y|, \end{cases} \qquad (2)$$

where the symbol "t_+" denotes "$\lim_{\epsilon \to +0} t + \epsilon$" and the symbol ":=" denotes an "instantaneous state transition" hereafter. In addition, the asynchronous internal clocks C_X and C_Y trigger the following asynchronous transitions of the discrete state variables X_i and Y_i, respectively.

If $C_X(t) = 1$ and $P_i(t) \geq |F_X|$, then

$$X_i(t_+) := \begin{cases} X_i(t) + 1 & \text{if } X_i(t) \neq N - 1 \text{ and } F_X \geq 0, \\ X_i(t) - 1 & \text{if } X_i(t) \neq 0 \text{ and } F_X < 0, \\ X_i(t) & \text{otherwise.} \end{cases} \qquad (3)$$

If $C_Y(t) = 1$ and $Q_i(t) \geq |F_Y|$, then

$$Y_i(t_+) := \begin{cases} Y_i(t) + 1 & \text{if } Y_i(t) \neq N - 1 \text{ and } F_Y \geq 0, \\ Y_i(t) - 1 & \text{if } Y_i(t) \neq 0 \text{ and } F_Y < 0, \\ Y_i(t) & \text{otherwise.} \end{cases} \qquad (4)$$

Figure 2 shows typical time waveforms and phase plane trajectories of the oscillator for different parameter values. Since the oscillator is used as a component of the pattern generator, the parameter values for Fig. 2(b) is used to design the CPG.

2.2 CPG

In this subsection, the novel CPG model (network of the oscillators) is presented, where the network has the ring topology as shown in Fig. 1. Let n denote the number of the oscillators and let the index i be modulo 1 (i.e., $i \in \{0, 1, \cdots, n-1\}$ (mod n)) to reflect the ring topology, e.g., $i = n$ is identical with $i = 0$ and $i = -1$ is identical with $i = n - 1$. In order to realize the coupling, let us introduce the following discrete signal s_i for the i-th oscillator.

$$s_i = Sat(Int(a_i X_{i+1} + b_i Y_{i+1} + c_i X_{i-1} + d_i Y_{i-1})),$$

where (a_i, b_i, c_i, d_i) are real parameters; $Int(r)$ gives the integer part of a real number r; and $Sat(p) = p$ for $-(N - 1) \leq p \leq N - 1$, $Sat(p) = -(N - 1)$ for $p < -(N - 1)$, and $Sat(p) = N - 1$ for $p > N - 1$. Using the signal s_i, the following spike-train (which is called a coupling spike-train) S_i is generated.

$$S_i(t) = \begin{cases} 1 & \text{if } t = \tau_i^p(1), \tau_i^p(2), \cdots, \\ -1 & \text{if } t = \tau_i^n(1), \tau_i^n(2), \cdots, \\ 0 & \text{otherwise,} \end{cases}$$

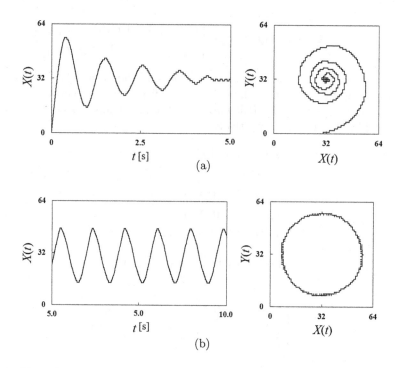

Fig. 2. Typical time waveforms and phase plane trajectories of the presented CPG model. The values of the parameters $(N, M, T_x, T_y, \delta, \omega, m)$ are (a) (64, 64, 0.000001, 0.0000011, -10, $2\pi \times 1000$, 64) and (b) (64, 64, 0.000001, 0.0000011, 625, $2\pi \times 1000$, 64). The time axes are rescaled (1000 times in (a) and 500 times in (b)).

where the instantaneous density of the spike positions $\{\tau_i^p(1), \tau_i^p(2), \cdots, \}$ is proportional to $s_i(t)$ for $s_i(t) > 0$ and the instantaneous density of the pulse positions $\{\tau_i^n(1), \tau_i^n(2), \cdots, \}$ is proportional to $-s_i(t)$ for $s_i(t) < 0$. Also, $\{\tau_i^p(1), \tau_i^p(2), \cdots, \}$ and $\{\tau_i^n(1), \tau_i^n(2), \cdots, \}$ are zeros for $s_i(t) \leq 0$ and $s_i(t) \geq 0$, respectively. The coupling spike-train $S_i(t)$ triggers the following transitions of the discrete auxiliary states P_i.

If $S_i(t) = 1$ and $F_X \geq 0$, then

$$P_i(t_+) := \begin{cases} P_i(t) + 1 & \text{if } P_i(t) < |F_X|, \\ 0 & \text{if } P_i(t) \geq |F_X|. \end{cases} \tag{5}$$

If $S_i(t) = -1$ and $F_X \geq 0$, then

$$P_i(t_+) := \begin{cases} P_i(t) - 1 & \text{if } P_i(t) > 0, \\ |F_X| & \text{if } P_i(t) = 0, \end{cases} \tag{6}$$

If $S_i(t) = 1$ and $F_X < 0$, then

$$P_i(t_+) := \begin{cases} P_i(t) - 1 & \text{if } P_i(t) > 0, \\ |F_X| & \text{if } P_i(t) = 0, \end{cases} \tag{7}$$

If $S_i(t) = -1$ and $F_X < 0$, then

$$P_i(t_+) := \begin{cases} P_i(t) + 1 & \text{if } P_i(t) < |F_X|, \\ 0 & \text{if } P_i(t) \geq |F_X|. \end{cases} \tag{8}$$

In addition, the coupling spike-train $S_i(t)$ triggers the following transitions of the discrete state variables X_i.

If $S_i(t) = 1$ and $F_X \geq 0$, then

$$X_i(t_+) := \begin{cases} X_i(t) + 1 & \text{if } X_i(t) \neq N - 1 \text{ and} P_i \geq F_X, \\ X_i(t) & \text{otherwise.} \end{cases} \tag{9}$$

If $S_i(t) = -1$ and $F_X \geq 0$, then

$$X_i(t_+) := \begin{cases} X_i(t) - 1 & \text{if } X_i(t) \neq 0 \text{ and} P_i = 0, \\ X_i(t) & \text{otherwise.} \end{cases} \tag{10}$$

If $S_i(t) = 1$ and $F_X < 0$, then

$$X_i(t_+) := \begin{cases} X_i(t) + 1 & \text{if } X_i(t) \neq N - 1 \text{ and} P_i \geq F_X, \\ X_i(t) & \text{otherwise.} \end{cases} \tag{11}$$

If $S_i(t) = -1$ and $F_X < 0$, then

$$X_i(t_+) := \begin{cases} X_i(t) - 1 & \text{if } X_i(t) \neq 0 \text{ and} P_i = 0, \\ X_i(t) & \text{otherwise.} \end{cases} \tag{12}$$

Figure 3 shows a typical time waveforms of the presented CPG model consisting of $n = 6$ oscillators. It can be seen that the CPG model can realize multi-phase synchronization of the discrete state variables $(X_0, X_1, \cdots, X_5)$.

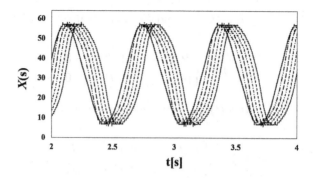

Fig. 3. Typical time waveforms of the presented CPG. $n = 6$. $(N, M, T_x, T_y, \delta, \omega, m) = (64, 64, 0.0001, 0.00011, 625, 2\pi \times 10, 64)$. $(a_0, b_0, c_0, d_0) = (-0.1, 0.5, -0.5, 0.1)$. $(a_{n-1}, b_{n-1}, c_{n-1}, d_{n-1}) = (0.1, 0.1, 3, 0.5)$. $(a_i, b_i, c_i, d_i) = (0.1, 0.1, 3, -0.5)$ for $i \neq 0, n-1$.

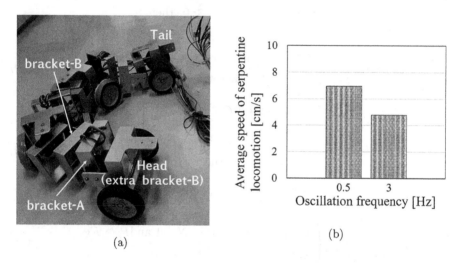

Fig. 4. (a) Picture of snake robot. (b) Characteristics of the snake robot controlled by the CPG model. The horizontal axis is the oscillation frequency of the oscillator and the vertical axis is the average speed of serpentine locomotion of the snake robot.

3   Hardware Implementation and Comparison

Recall that the dynamics of the presented CPG model is described by Eqs. (1)–(12). These equations are written in a VHDL code, which is compiled into a bitstream file by using Xilinx's design software environment Vivado 2016. 2. The resulting bitstream file is downloaded to Xilinx's field programmable gate array (FPGA) XC7K325T-2FFG900C. Figure 4 shows a picture of a snake robot controlled by the presented CPG model.

As show in the figure, the snake robot consists of $n = 6$ sections (with an extra bracket-B attached on the head of the snake) and each section consists of two brackets, bracket-A and bracket-B. Each i-th bracket-A has a servo motor (Tower Pro's SG92R), the target angle of which is indicated by the discrete state variable X_i of the CPG via a pulse width modulator. Figure 4(b) shows the characteristics of the implemented snake robot, where the vertical axis is the moving velocity of the robot and the horizontal axis is the oscillation frequency of the discrete state variable X_i.

It can be seen that the moving velocity can be controlled by adjusting the oscillation frequency. More detailed analysis of the moving velocity will be presented in a journal paper. Note that the vector field of the presented oscillator is designed to exhibit a Hopf bifurcation. So, for comparison, a CPG model using a simple Hopf-oscillator [5] is implemented by the same compiler and the same FPGA device. The bit-length of the Hopf-oscillator and the resolution (M, N) of the presented oscillator are decreased as short as possible under the condition that they properly reproduce the Hopf bifurcation. By real machine experiments, we have shown that the characteristics of the moving velocity of the Hopf-oscillator CPG model is almost identical with that of the presented CPG model. However, the FPGA slices of the presented CPG model is about 20% of those of the Hopf-oscillator CPG model. As a result, we can state the following.

- Both presented CPG model and Hopf-oscillator CPG model can control the snake robot with almost identical characteristics of the moving velocity.
- However, the presented model consumes much less fewer hardware resources.

4   Conclusions

In this paper, the novel CPG model based on the nonlinear dynamics of an asynchronous cellular automaton was presented. The presented CPG model was implemented by the FPGA and is used to control the snake robot. By real machine experiments, it was shown that the presented model can realize rhythmic spinal locomotions of the snake robot. Moreover, it was shown that the presented CPG model and the Hopf-oscillator CPG model (which is one of simple CPG models) realize almost identical characteristics of the moving speeds of the snake robot but the presented model consumes much fewer hardware resources. Future problems are including (a) comparison to other models, (b) more detailed analysis on the hardware cost, and (c) applications to other types robots. This work was partially supported by JSPS KAKENHI Grant Number 15K00352.

References

1. Kandel, E., et al.: Principles of Neural Science. McGraw-Hill, New York (2000)
2. Yu, J., Tan, M., Chen, J., Zhang, J.: Survey on CPG-inspired control models and system implementation. IEEE Trans. Neural Network Learn. Syst. **25**, 441–456 (2014)

3. Righetti, L., Ijspeert, A.: Pattern generators with sensory feedback for the control of quadruped locomotion. In: Proceedings of the IEEE International Conference on Robotics and Automation, pp. 819–824 (2008)
4. Hugo, J., Zambrano, B., Huitzil, C.: FPGA implementation of a configurable neuromorphic CPG-based locomotion controller. Neural Networks **45**, 50–61 (2013)
5. Wang, Z., Gao, Q., Zhao, H.: CPG-inspired locomotion control for a snake robot basing on nonlinear oscillators. J. Intell. Robot. Syst. **85**(2), 209–227 (2017)
6. Sato, T., Watanabe, W., Ishoguro, A.: An adaptive decentralized control of a serpentine robot based on the discrepancy between body, brain and environment. In: Proceedings of the IEEE International Conference on Robotics and Automation, pp. 709–714 (2010)
7. Takeda, K., Torikai, H.: A novel hardware-efficient cochlea model based on asynchronous cellular automaton dynamics: theoretical analysis and FPGA implementation. IEEE Trans. Circ. Syst. II Express Briefs **64**(9), 1107–1111 (2017)
8. Isobe, K., Torikai, H.: A novel hardware-efficient asynchronous cellular automaton model of spike-timing dependent synaptic plasticity. IEEE Trans. Circuits Syst. II Express Briefs **63**(6), 603–607 (2016)
9. Matsubara, T., Torikai, H.: Asynchronous cellular automaton based neuron: theoretical analysis and on-FPGA learning. IEEE Trans. Neural Networks Learn. Syst. **24**(5), 736–748 (2013)

A Hardware-Oriented Dropout Algorithm for Efficient FPGA Implementation

Yoeng Jye Yeoh[✉], Takashi Morie, and Hakaru Tamukoh

Graduate School of Life Science and Systems Engineering,
Kyushu Institute of Technology, Kitakyushu, Japan
yeoh-yoeng-jye@edu.brain.kyutech.ac.jp,
{morie,tamukoh}@brain.kyutech.ac.jp

Abstract. This paper proposes a hardware oriented dropout algorithm for an efficient field-programmable gate array (FPGA) implementation. Dropout is a regularization technique, which is commonly used in neural networks such as multilayer perceptrons (MLPs), convolutional neural networks (CNNs), among others. To generate a dropout mask to randomly drop neurons during training phase, random number generators (RNGs) are usually used in software implementations. However, RNGs consume considerable FPGA resources in hardware implementations. The proposed method is able to minimize the resources required for FPGA implementation of dropout by performing a simple rotation operation to a predefined dropout mask. We apply the proposed method to MLPs and CNNs and evaluate them on MNIST and CIFAR-10 classification. In addition, we employ the proposed method in GoogLeNet training using own dataset to develop a vision system for home service robots. The experimental results demonstrate that the proposed method achieves the same regularized effect as the ordinary dropout algorithm. Logic synthesis results show that the proposed method significantly reduces the consumption of FPGA resources in comparison to the ordinary RNG-based approaches.

Keywords: Neural networks · Dropout · Field programmable gate array

1 Introduction

In recent years, deep neural networks have caught the attention of researchers owing to their powerful performance in various fields such as image recognition, speech recognition, data mining, among others [1,2]. As the neural networks become deeper and deeper, more parameters can be learned and more features can be extracted, thereby, improving performance [3,4]. However, in such deep neural networks, overfitting is a serious problem. Dropout is a regularization technique to overcome the overfitting problem [5]. It is commonly used in Multi-Layer Perceptrons (MLPs), Convolutional Neural Networks (CNNs) and other deep neural networks [5]. Generally, random number generators (RNGs) are used

© Springer International Publishing AG 2017
D. Liu et al. (Eds.): ICONIP 2017, Part VI, LNCS 10639, pp. 821–829, 2017.
https://doi.org/10.1007/978-3-319-70136-3_87

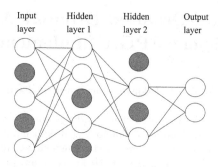

Fig. 1. Illustration of dropout in neural network

in software implementation to generate a dropout mask to randomly drop the neurons during training phase.

In practical application, high mobility, low power consumption and small size are the main criteria for embedded systems and are highly desired in many applications such as portable devices and robots. Graphics processing units (GPUs) enable training at very fast speed. However, GPUs consume a huge amount of power and lack mobility. Field-programmable gate arrays (FPGAs) are suitable for embedded systems and meet the aforementioned criteria; however, the resources of FPGAs are limited [6]. To realize the hardware implementation of the dropout algorithm in a massively parallel manner, each neuron should have an RNG occupying considerable FPGA resources.

In this paper, we propose a hardware-oriented dropout algorithm for efficient FPGA implementation. The contributions of this paper are as follows:

- A hardware-oriented dropout algorithm for efficient FPGA implementation.
- A software implementation of the proposed method, utilizing the C language and Chainer platform.
- Evaluation of the proposed method and conventional dropout methods in various neural networks and datasets.

2 Dropout

Dropout is a regularization technique, which randomly drops the neuron units in a neural network during training phase, temporarily removing them for forward propagation with a certain probability p (usually set to 0.5), as shown in Fig. 1 and Eqs. (1), (2) [5,7]. In Eq. (1), the mask is generated independently with Bernoulli distribution and is formed as a binary vector. The generated mask is multiplied with the input vector x, as shown in Eq. (2). Here, l indicates the arbitrary layer. The network is thinned into half by dropout and half of the parameters are omitted [5]. By omitting half of the feature detectors, the complex co-adaptations between neurons are prevented, forcing them to learn more robust features and solve the overfitting problem [3,5,7].

$$mask_i^{(l)} \sim Bernoulli(p) \tag{1}$$

$$y_j^{(l+1)} = f\{\, \boldsymbol{W}_j^{(l+1)} \cdot (\boldsymbol{mask}^{(l)} * \boldsymbol{x}^{(l)}) + b_j^{(l+1)}\} \tag{2}$$

The dropout algorithm has been widely used in neural networks; it has not only been restricted to feed-forward neural networks such as MLPs and CNNs but also can be applied to graphical models such as restricted Boltzmann machines (RBMs) [3,5,8]. The dropout algorithm can be extended to dropconnect. Instead of dropping out the neurons, dropconnect drops the connection between neurons [9]. In this paper, we only focus on dropout for MLPs and CNNs.

3   Proposed Method

In general, the dropout mask is generated by Eq. (3) in the software implementation.

$$mask[i] = \begin{cases} 1, & \text{random number} \geq \text{dropout ratio}, \\ 0, & \text{otherwise.} \end{cases} \tag{3}$$

Here, a random number is generated by an RNG with a uniform distribution from 0 to 1. If the random number is greater than the dropout ratio (usually set to 0.5 for the hidden layer and 0.2 for the input layer), $mask[i]$ is set to 1 and vice versa. Generally, as the generation of true random numbers are very costly and slow, they are replaced by pseudo random numbers, which are considered sufficient for most applications [10].

To calculate Eq. (3) on an FPGA, a hardware RNG and a comparator should be implemented. However, for hardware implementation, the biggest problem is that the RNGs in FPGA consume a large number of resources [10]. Another issue is parallelism. Equation (3) is repeated to generate the whole dropout mask for all i. This looping process is not favorable to the FPGA implementation because it is serial processing and slows down the process. Multiple RNGs are required for parallel processing, which massively increases the consumption of FPGA resources.

We hypothesized that true randomness in dropout is not very essential and can be replaced by a pseudo random number. Thus, we propose a method for eliminating both RNGs and comparators, by performing a simple rotation operation to generate a predefined mask as follows:

$$mask[0:n] = \{mask[r:n], mask[0:r-1]\} \tag{4}$$

The rotation bit r is introduced as a parameter and it controls the bit to be rotated. To further increase randomness, a split or XOR operation can be introduced by splitting the mask into several portions before performing rotation or XOR on the previous bits. In this paper, we only focus on the rotation operation to evaluate the performance of the proposed method.

4   Experimental Results

In this section, we show experimental results with different types of datasets and neural networks. First, we trained an MLP with the MNIST dataset [11], using the C language. Further in this section, we present the result of the CIFAR-10 dataset [12] with a CNN (LeNet) using the Chainer platform [13]. Next follows a custom dataset design, the @home dataset, trained with a deep CNN (GoogLeNet) [4]; this is also done using the Chainer platform. The last part of this section presents an estimation of resources saved with the proposed method, when implementing dropout on an FPGA.

4.1   MNIST Dataset

The MNIST dataset contains 60,000 training data and 10,000 test data, where each image data is a 28×28 pixels handwritten number in grayscale, with a total dataset of 10 classes (from 0 to 9) [11]. We trained a four-layer MLP (784-500-200-10). The mini-batch stochastic gradient descent (SGD), with a batch size of 100, was used as the optimizer, and softmax regression was used as the cost function.

In the proposed method, the rotate bit r was initialized as one. During the training phase, r was increased by one when the input batch was changed and was reset to one after r_{max}. The experiment was run five times to observe the robustness of the network, and r_{max} was changed to 14, 18, 22, 26 and 30 for each experiment.

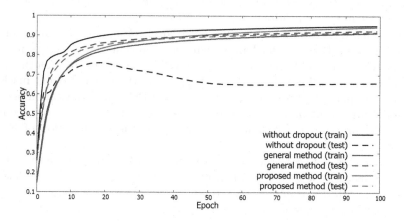

Fig. 2. Results of MLP trained with MNIST dataset.

Figure 2 shows the average results of five trials. In Fig. 2, an overfitting phenomenon can be observed when training without dropout. A sudden drop of accuracy ($\sim$65%) was observed during the inference, while the test accuracy remained high ($\sim$95%). This gap indicated that the MLP over fitted to the training data and failed to predict the new test data, which caused a drop in accuracy.

Both the general dropout method and the proposed method were able to solve the overfitting problem, thereby closing the gap between training and test accuracy and achieving a recognition accuracy of over 90%. The results demonstrated that the proposed method worked well in this experiment by achieving an similar effect to that of general dropout method.

4.2 CIFAR-10 Dataset

We evaluated the proposed method with a CNN trained by the CIFAR-10 dataset using the Chainer platform. In total, the CIFAR-10 dataset comprises 60,000 full color, 32 × 32 pixels images, where 50,000 images are training data and 10,000 images are test data [12]. It has 10 object classes, including airplane, automobile, bird, and others.

The LeNet architecture used in this experiment is shown in Fig. 3. Dropout was applied only at the fully-connected layer, because the number of parameters in the convolution layer was relatively small and did not cause an over fitting problem [3]. In this experiment, Adam optimization was used. In the proposed method, the rotate bit r was initially set to 8 and decreased by one for each input batch. When it reached to one, it reset back to 10.

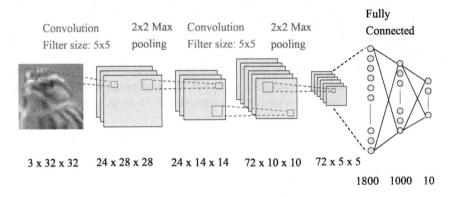

Fig. 3. Architecture of LeNet.

Similar to the MNIST dataset, we compared the average results as shown in Fig. 4. As the Cifar-10 dataset comprises color image data, the information contained is larger and the feature of objects is harder to classify. Thus, even though the accuracy achieved 98% and above during training phase, the test accuracy only reached approximately 70%. In this experiment, the same dropout effect was also achieved by the proposed method.

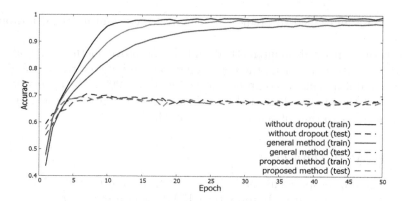

Fig. 4. Results of LeNet trained with Cifar-10 dataset.

4.3 @home Dataset

To further evaluate the proposed method, we applied it to a deeper neural network. An @home dataset was created from the object list used in the RoboCup Japan Open 2016 @Home competition [14]. We employed this dataset while developing a vision system for home service robots, i.e., @home service robots. The @home dataset contains 15 classes of objects as shown in Table 1. Each class contains 2,000 training and 700 test images in full color format, and all images were resized to 224 × 224 pixels before fetching into GoogLeNet. We trained a GoogLeNet, 22-layer CNN, by modifying the output from 1000 to 15 for the purpose of matching the dataset. We used the Chainer platform to train GoogLeNet.

As shown in Fig. 5, both approaches were able to achieve accuracy of almost 100% after 15 epochs. The results showed that in the deep neural networks, the proposed method worked as well as the conventional dropout method.

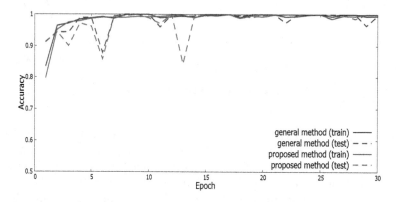

Fig. 5. Results of GoogLeNet trained with @home dataset.

Table 1. Object classes in @home dataset

Item Categories	Examples		
PET bottle	Iced-tea	Cafe-Au Lait	Green tea
Snack	Potato stick	Potato chips	Chocolate cookies
Fruit juice	Orange juice	Strawberry juice	
Fruit	Orange	Apple	
Instant soup	Egg soup	Potato soup	
Container	Tray	Bowl	Cup

4.4   FPGA Resources

To verify the effectiveness of the proposed method, we implemented two conventional methods and the proposed method on a Xilinx Virtex 6 FPGA. We described all methods using Verilog, a hardware description language (HDL). The Xilinx ISE Design Suite was used for logic synthesis. To simplify experiments, we generated an 8-bit dropout mask. For the RNG for conventional methods, we used an 8-bit linear feedback shift register (LFSR) as the reference.

In Table 2, we observe that with the proposed method, the number of required registers and look-up tables (LUTs) were much less in comparison to ordinary RNG-based methods. For the serial implementation, it took less resources; however, the number of clock cycles was increased, which caused the FPGA advantage to be lost. In contrast, for the parallel implementation of the conventional dropout method, only a single clock cycle was required to generate the mask; however, resource consumption increased significantly. The proposed method was able to achieve parallel processing by generating a dropout mask, in a single clock cycle, with a small number of resources required through the simple operation.

Table 2. Comparison of FPGA resources consumed for dropout implementation

Logic Utilization	Conventional dropout method in series	Conventional dropout method in parallel	Proposed method
Number of slice registers	32	7	8
Number of slice LUTs	44	80	7
Number of fully used LUT-FF pairs	27	72	0
Clock cycle required to generate a mask	8	1	1
RNG required	1	8	N/A

5   Conclusion

This paper proposed an alternative method for applying the dropout technique, which was shown to be efficient for hardware implementation. This method significantly minimized FPGA resource consumption by eliminating the use of RNGs and comparators. Experiments were conducted and the results were verified with different neural networks, MLPs and CNNs, trained using several datasets.

The experiments were conducted only with an 8-bit dropout mask. In general, for actual applications, the mask size is much larger than 8 bits and usually more than a few hundred, depending on batch size and number of hidden units. Thus, we expect that the proposed method can save a large number of FPGA resources in practical deep neural networks.

Acknowledgments. This research was supported by JSPS KAKENHI Grant Numbers 17H01798, 17K20010, 26330279, and 15H01706.

References

1. Schmidhuber, J.: Deep learning in neural networks: an overview. Neural Networks **61**, 85–117 (2015)
2. LeCun, Y., Bengio, Y., Hinton, G.: Deep learning. Nature **521**(7553), 436–444 (2015)
3. Krizhevsky, A., Sutskever, I., Hinton, G.E.: Imagenet classification with deep convolutional neural networks. In: Advances in Neural Information Processing Systems, pp. 1097–1105 (2012)
4. Szegedy, C., Liu, W., Jia, Y., Sermanet, P., Reed, S., Anguelov, D., Erhan, D., Vanhoucke, V., Rabinovich, A.: Going deeper with convolutions. In: Proceedings of the IEEE Conference on Computer Vision and Pattern Recognition, pp. 1–9 (2015)

5. Srivastava, N., Hinton, G.E., Krizhevsky, A., Sutskever, I., Salakhutdinov, R.: Dropout: a simple way to prevent neural networks from overfitting. J. Mach. Learn. Res. **15**(1), 1929–1958 (2014)

6. Omondi, A.R., Rajapakse, J.C. (eds.): FPGA Implementations of Neural Networks, vol. 365. Springer, New York (2006). doi:10.1007/0-387-28487-7

7. Hinton, G.E., Srivastava, N., Krizhevsky, A., Sutskever, I., Salakhutdinov, R.R.: Improving neural networks by preventing co-adaptation of feature detectors. arXiv preprint arXiv:1207.0580 (2012)

8. Wu, H., Gu, X.: Towards dropout training for convolutional neural networks. Neural Networks **71**, 1–10 (2015)

9. Wan, L., Zeiler, M., Zhang, S., Cun, Y.L., Fergus, R.: Regularization of neural networks using dropconnect. In: Proceedings of the 30th international conference on machine learning (ICML-2013), pp. 1058–1066 (2013)

10. Bonde, V.V., Kale, A.: Design and implementation of a random number generator on FPGA. Int. J. Sci. Res. **4**(5), 203–208 (2015)

11. LeCun, Y., Bottou, L., Bengio, Y., Haffner, P.: Gradient-based learning applied to document recognition. Proc. IEEE **86**(11), 2278–2324 (1998)

12. Krizhevsky, A., Hinton, G.: Learning multiple layers of features from tiny images (2009)

13. Tokui, S., Oono, K., Hido, S., Clayton, J.: Chainer: a next-generation open source framework for deep learning. In: Proceedings of Workshop on Machine Learning Systems (LearningSys) in the Twenty-Ninth Annual Conference on Neural Information Processing Systems (NIPS), vol. 5 (2015)

14. Robocup@home. http://www.robocupathome.org/

Complexity Reduction of Neural Network Model for Local Motion Detection in Motion Stereo Vision

Hisanao Akima[1]([✉]), Susumu Kawakami[1], Jordi Madrenas[2], Satoshi Moriya[1], Masafumi Yano[1], Koji Nakajima[1], Masao Sakuraba[1], and Shige Sato[1]

[1] Research Institute of Electrical Communication, Tohoku University,
2-1-1 Katahira, Aoba-ku, Sendai 980-8577, Japan
{akima,s-moriya,masafumi,hello,shigeo}@riec.tohoku.ac.jp,
RHC02471@nifty.com, sakuraba.masao@myad.jp
[2] Department of Electronic Engineering, Universitat Politècnica de Catalunya,
Jordi Girona 1-3, 08034 Barcelona, Catalunya, Spain
jordi.madrenas@upc.edu.com

Abstract. Spatial perception, in which objects' motion and positional relationship are recognized, is necessary for applications such as a walking robot and an autonomous car. One of the demanding features of spatial perception in real world applications is robustness. Neural network-based approaches, in which perception results are obtained by voting among a large number of neuronal activities, seem to be promising. We focused on a neural network model for motion stereo vision proposed by Kawakami et al. In this model, local motion in each small region of the visual field, which comprises optical flow, is detected by hierarchical neural network. Implementation of this model into a VLSI is required for real-time operation with low power consumption. In this study, we reduced the computational complexity of this model and showed cell responses of the reduced model by numerical simulation.

Keywords: Motion stereo vision · Local motion detection · Hough transform · VLSI

1 Introduction

Bio-inspired approaches for spatial perception have been considered attractive, because many animals recognize objects and move around the real world; these are essential and difficult tasks for applications, such as a walking robot and an autonomous car. For example, birds recognize rapid target motion in real-time to avoid collision with obstacles. The principle of the spatial perception adopted by birds is considered as motion stereo vision [1]. In psychological experiments, Gibson revealed that spatial perception by means of motion stereo vision is based on optical flow projected on retina [2]. Kawakami et al. proposed a neural network model, which we refer to as the "Kawakami model", describing the function of the visual cortex [3,4].

© Springer International Publishing AG 2017
D. Liu et al. (Eds.): ICONIP 2017, Part VI, LNCS 10639, pp. 830–839, 2017.
https://doi.org/10.1007/978-3-319-70136-3_88

In the Kawakami model, the local motion in each small region of the visual field is detected through a hierarchical neural network from the lateral geniculate nucleus (LGN) to the middle temporal (MT) area. The local motions detected in different small areas (receptive fields of LGN cells) are integrated in the medial superior temporal (MST) area and optical flow is estimated. Then, time-to-collision (TTC) and orientation of planar surface are detected from the optical flow by using cross-ratio transformation and polar transformation [4]. The TTC is useful information for avoiding collision with obstacles. The orientation of the planar surface is also used to decide on the avoidance direction.

We aim to implement the local motion detection by motion stereo vision on a very large-scale integration (VLSI) as a basis of a collision-avoidance system for an autonomous car or an unmanned aerial vehicle (UAV). First, we reduced the computational complexity and the memory capacity so as to fit in a VLSI chip. This paper is organized as follows. Section 2 explains the Kawakami model. Section 3 describes the reduction of computational complexity and memory capacity. The results of numerical simulation are given in Sect. 4. Finally, the conclusions of this work are summarized in Sect. 5.

2 Neural Network Model for Local Motion Detection in Motion Stereo Vision

The Kawakami model explains a two-stage hypothesis supported by a psychophysical observation by Adelson and Movshon [5]. In the first stage, one-dimensional (1-D) velocities perpendicular to oriented components, such as lines and edges, within the stimulus are measured in the primary visual cortex (V1). In the second stage, the 1-D velocities are combined with the two-dimensional (2-D) velocity in the MT area. In the Kawakami model, the V1 is composed of non-directionally selective (NDS) simple cells and directionally selective (DS) simple cells, while the MT area is composed of DS complex cells and motion-detection cells.

Let us consider, for example, a cross-bar stimulus moving across the receptive fields with the 2-D velocity of (V_{2D-x}, V_{2D-y}) (see Fig. 1). The cross-bar stimulus comprises two straight lines and the 1-D velocities V_{1D} of each line are detected by the neural network containing the LGN cells, NDS simple cells, DS simple cells, and the DS complex cells. The 2-D velocity is detected by integrating the 1-D velocities in the motion-detection cells. The details of the above are elaborated below.

First, the stimuli in the retinal cells are transmitted to the two types of LGN cells, lagged and non-lagged LGN cells. The lagged LGN cells have a longer temporal-latency t_d to the visual response than the non-lagged LGN cells. The responses of the lagged and non-lagged LGN cells are modeled as a convolution operation between retinal cell responses $I(x, y, t)$ and a function $DOG(u, v)$ [6]:

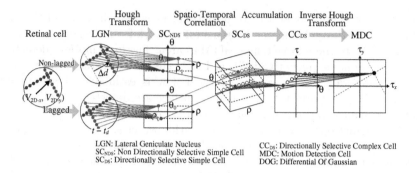

Fig. 1. Neural network model for local motion detection in motion stereo vision.

$$LGN_L(x, y) = \sum_u \sum_v I(x - u, y - v, t - t_d) DOG(u, v),$$

$$LGN_{NL}(x, y) = \sum_u \sum_v I(x - u, y - v, t) DOG(u, v), \tag{1}$$

where x and y are LGN cell addresses, t is time, and u and v are summed over all retinal cells in the receptive field. The DOG (Differential Of Gaussian) function is given by

$$DOG(u, v) = \exp\left(-\frac{u^2 + v^2}{s^2}\right) - 0.326 \exp\left(-\frac{u^2 + v^2}{(1.75s)^2}\right), \tag{2}$$

where s is the degree of broadness [3]. The DOG function represents a pair of excitatory and inhibitory concentric receptive fields in an LGN cell and the convolution operation, expressed as (1), enhances the edges of the retinal cell image.

Second, the LGN cell responses are accumulated to the NDS simple cell responses. The responses of the NDS simple cells in the lagged and non-lagged branches are expressed as a Hough transform [7]:

$$SC_{NDS-L}(\rho, \theta) = \sum_x \sum_y LGN_L(x, y)\delta(\rho - x\cos\theta - y\sin\theta),$$

$$SC_{NDS-NL}(\rho, \theta) = \sum_x \sum_y LGN_{NL}(x, y)\delta(\rho - x\cos\theta - y\sin\theta), \tag{3}$$

where ρ and θ are NDS simple cell addresses, and x and y are summed over all LGN cells within the receptive field. $\delta(\cdot)$ is the Dirac delta function, namely $\delta(\zeta) = 1$ for $\zeta = 0$ and $\delta(\zeta) = 0$ for $\zeta \neq 0$. Equation (3) shows that the group of LGN cells along a straight line, $\rho - x\cos\theta - y\sin\theta = 0$, in (x, y) LGN cell array are accumulated to an NDS simple cell at (ρ, θ). In Fig. 1, the parallel lines in the lagged and non-lagged LGN cell arrays are converted to two NDS simple cells activated at (ρ_0, θ_0) and (ρ_1, θ_0) with the same θ_0 orientation. Consequently, displacement Δd between lines in an (x, y) array is expressed as the difference between the NDS simple cells' ρ coordinates, i.e. $\rho_1 - \rho_0$.

Third, the responses of the lagged and non-lagged NDS simple cells are correlated in the DS simple cell. The response of the DS simple cell is modeled as the cross-correlation between the spatially-shifted lagged and non-lagged NDS simple cells whose ρ coordinates are shifted by τ:

$$SC_{DS}(\rho,\theta,\tau) = SC_{NDS-L}(\rho - \tau,\theta)SC_{NDS-NL}(\rho,\theta), \tag{4}$$

where ρ, θ, and τ are DS simple cell addresses. We assume that these cells are arranged three-dimensionally in the V1 area as a horizontal (ρ,θ) array with a depth arrangement of τ. The correlation formulated by (4) is called a "spatio-temporal correlation" because it contains the τ spatial shift and the t_d time delay. The spatio-temporal correlation is an application of the Reichardt detector initially proposed for a fly's visual system [8]. The DS simple cell at (ρ_2,θ_0,τ_2) will fire if activations of the lagged and non-lagged NDS simple cells at (ρ_0,θ_0) and (ρ_1,θ_0) coincide, where $\rho_1 = \rho_0 + \Delta d = \rho_0 + V_{1D}t_d$. This occurs when $\rho_2 = \rho_1$ and $\tau_2 = V_{1D}t_d$. From this τ_2 coordinate, the 1-D velocity of the line is determined by

$$V_{1D} = \tau_2/t_d. \tag{5}$$

Therefore, (4) indicates that a DS simple cell at (ρ,θ,τ) fires to detect a line with ρ location, θ orientation, and τ/t_d velocity. Hereafter, τ also denotes the 1-D velocity eliminating the coefficient t_d to simplify the description.

Then, the DS complex cell accumulates the responses of DS simple cells along the ρ coordinate:

$$CC_{DS}(\theta,\tau) = \sum_{\rho} SC_{DS}(\rho,\theta,\tau), \tag{6}$$

where θ and τ are DS complex cell addresses. Equation (6) indicates that a DS complex cell at (θ,τ) fires to detect a line with θ orientation and τ 1-D velocity, independent of the line's ρ location.

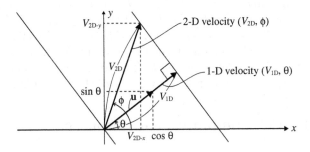

Fig. 2. Relation between 1-D velocity and 2-D velocity. The 1-D velocity of a line is the otrthogonal projection of its 2-D velocity in the perpendicular direction.

Before explaining the last stage for 2-D velocity detection in the motion-detection cells, let us consider the relationship between the 1-D velocity (V_{1D},θ)

and the 2-D velocity (V_{2D}, ϕ) (see Fig. 2):

$$V_{1D} = \mathbf{V_{2D}} \cdot \mathbf{u} = V_{2D} \cos(\phi - \theta) = V_{2D-x} \cos\theta + V_{2D-y} \sin\theta, \tag{7}$$

where,

$$\mathbf{V_{2D}} = (V_{2D-x}, V_{2D-y}) = V_{2D}(\cos\phi, \sin\phi) \tag{8}$$

and

$$\mathbf{u} = (\cos\theta, \sin\theta). \tag{9}$$

V_{1D}, θ, and $\mathbf{u}$ are the speed, direction, and unit vector of the 1-D velocity, respectively. V_{2D}, ϕ, V_{2D-x}, and V_{2D-y} are the speed, direction, and Cartesian coordinates of the 2-D velocity, respectively. Equation (7) represents the constraint line in the (V_x, V_y) velocity space [5], which indicates all 2-D velocities that can exist in a line moving with (V_{1D}, θ) 1-D velocity. The following equation is obtained by substituting (5) for (7):

$$\tau = t_d(V_{2D-x} \cos\theta + V_{2D-y} \sin\theta) = \tau_x \cos\theta + \tau_y \sin\theta. \tag{10}$$

The sine wave expressed as (10) is extracted by an inverse Hough transform in the motion-detection cells, and the Cartesian coordinates of the 2-D velocity (τ_x, τ_y) are determined.

The response of the motion-detection cell is given by

$$MDC(\tau_x, \tau_y) = \sum_\theta \sum_\tau CC_{DS}(\theta, \tau)\delta(\tau - \tau_x \cos\theta - \tau_y \sin\theta), \tag{11}$$

where τ_x and τ_y are motion-detection cell addresses, and θ and τ are summed over all DS complex cells. Equation (11) indicates that a motion-detection cell at (τ_x, τ_y) fires after accumulating the responses of a group of DS complex cells along a sine wave, $\tau - \tau_x \cos\theta - \tau_y \sin\theta = 0$, in the (θ, τ) array. From another point of view, a DS complex cell at (θ, τ) activates a group of motion-detection cells along a straight line, $\tau - \tau_x \cos\theta - \tau_y \sin\theta = 0$, in the (τ_x, τ_y) array. This line is equivalent to the constraint line, and the 2-D velocity are determined as the IOC (Intersection Of Constraints) solution [5] from more than two constraint lines caused by oriented components in the receptive field. Consequently, the coordinates of the motion-detection cell with the maximum response correspond to the Cartesian coordinates of the 2-D velocity of the moving lines.

3   Reduction of Computational Resources

Computational resources must be reduced to implement the neural network model mentioned above on a VLSI chip. Therefore, we examine the following: conversion of the cell responses from real to integer values, reduction from a 2-D DOG filter on (x, y) to a 1-D DOG skeleton filter on (ρ, θ) coordinates, and replacement of the multiplication in the spatio-temporal correlation with a multiplication-like function.

3.1 Conversion of Cell Responses from Real to Integer Values

Although the use of integer values for the cell responses saves memory capacity and reduces the size of the arithmetic circuit required as compared with the use of real values, the dynamic range of the cell responses should be of concern. Because the cell responses are accumulated hierarchically, a post-cell requires larger bits than a pre-cell, to prevent overflow of the accumulation. We limit the bit-width B_{LGN} assigned to the LGN cell response to 6, which seems to be sufficient to store edge information; the edge is more important than the texture detail in motion stereo vision. This limit is easily achieved, for example, by a 2-bit shift to the right of the output signal from an 8-bit camera. The bit-width assigned to an NDS simple cell is given by

$$B_{SC-NDS} = \text{ceil}(\log_2(NC_{LGN}(2^{B_{LGN}} - 1))) + 1, \tag{12}$$

where NC_{LGN} is the number of LGN cells accumulated to an NDS simple cell, and $\text{ceil}(\cdot)$ is the ceiling function; $\text{ceil}(x)$ is the smallest integer, not less than x. $B_{SC-NDS} = 14$ when $NC_{LGN} = 80$ with the parameters used in this study. The bit-widths assigned to other cells are calculated in the same manner and are shown in Table 1 in Sect. 4.

3.2 Reduction from a 2-D DOG Filter to a 1-D DOG Skeleton Filter

Kawakami et al. showed that the 1-D convolution of $DOG_{1D}(u)$,

$$DOG_{1D}(u) = \exp\left(-\frac{u^2}{s^2}\right) - 0.57 \exp\left(-\frac{u^2}{(1.75s)^2}\right), \tag{13}$$

along the ρ coordinate on the (ρ, θ) NDS simple cell array is equivalent to the 2-D convolution of $DOG(u, v)$ function on the (x, y) LGN cell array [9]. Figure 3(a) and (b) show the profiles of convolution kernels for the 2-D and 1-D DOG filter, respectively. It was also demonstrated that the simplified DOG filter, which we refer to as a "skeleton DOG filter", which has the main and sub peaks of $DOG_{1D}(u)$, yields almost the same effect, except that the response has slightly too sharp an edge. Therefore, a "skeleton Gaussian filter", which has the main (1.0) and half (0.5) peaks of the Gaussian function, as shown in Fig. 3(c), is convolved with the NDS simple cell array, in addition to the skeleton DOG filter. Furthermore, the values of the skeleton DOG filter are rounded to a power of two (2^0 and -2^{-1}) as shown in Fig. 3(d). As a result, the DOG filter is simply achieved with 1-bit shifter and sign-inverting (two's complement) circuits of the integer cell responses.

3.3 Replacement of Multiplication with a Multiplication-Like Function

The spatio-temporal correlation yields the DS simple cell response with bit-width B_{SC-DS}, which is two times as large as B_{SC-NDS} due to the multiplication

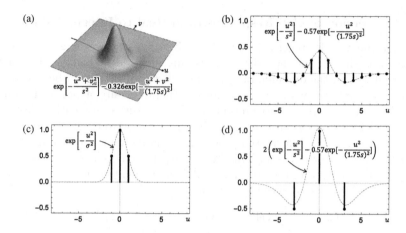

Fig. 3. Profiles of a convolution kernel for (a) a 2-D DOG filter, (b) a 1-D DOG filter, (c) a skeleton Gaussian filter, and (d) a skeleton DOG filter.

expressed as (4). By replacing the multiplication with the multiplication-like function proposed in [10], an approximate result with less bit-width is obtained. The multiplication-like function $\mathrm{MLF}(a, b)$ is defined as follows:

$$\mathrm{MLF}(a, b) = \begin{cases} |a| + |b| & (\mathrm{sign}(a) = \mathrm{sign}(b)) \\ -(|a| + |b|) & (\mathrm{sign}(a) \neq \mathrm{sign}(b)) \\ 0 & (a = 0 \quad \mathrm{or} \quad b = 0) \end{cases} \tag{14}$$

where $\mathrm{sign}(x)$ is a sign of x; $\mathrm{sign}(x) = 0$ if $x \geq 0$, 1 otherwise. The function formulated by (14) is achieved without a multiplier, which has large chip area and long latency in general, and reduces bit-width by 12 after the DS simple cell. Figure 4 shows a block diagram of the multiplication-like function implemented in a digital circuit design. The values of a and b are assumed to be two's complement numbers. A sign-inverting circuit is composed of a NOT gate and a half adder. The input a (b) or the output of the sign-inverting circuit $-a$ ($-b$) is selected by a multiplexer (MUX) in accordance with the sign of b (a). The coincidence with a (b) and 0 is detected with an XNOR gate. In addition to using the multiplication-like function, memory capacity of about 2 Mbit is saved by calculating the DS complex cell responses directory from the NDS simple cell responses using (4), (6), and (14).

4   Simulation Results

The numerical simulation result of local motion detection is shown in Fig. 5, and the cell parameters used in the simulation is shown in Table 1. Figure 5(a) shows the result for the original model in which the 1-D DOG filter and the spatio-temporal correlation by multiplication are applied to real value cell

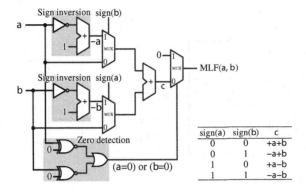

Fig. 4. Block diagram of multiplication-like function implemented in a digital design.

Table 1. Cell parameters

Cell type	Number of cells	Bit-width
LGN cell	3966	6
NDS simple cell	$N_\rho \times N_\theta = 53 \times 33 = 1749$	14
DS complex cell	$N_\theta \times N_\tau = 33 \times 45 = 1485$	21
Motion detection cell	$N_{\tau_x} \times N_{\tau_y} = 45 \times 45 = 2025$	27

responses, whereas Fig. 5(b) shows the result for the reduced model in which the 1-D DOG and Gaussian skeleton filters and the spatio-temporal correlation by multiplication-like function are applied to integer value cell responses. The plots other than for the LGN cells show contour plots of the cell responses normalized by the absolute maximum value of each cell array. The point at which the motion-detection cell has the maximum response corresponds to the detected local motion vector, and very similar local motion vectors are obtained in both cases. The inhibitory responses in Fig. 5(b) are emphasized in comparison to those in Fig. 5(a) because the intensity ratio of excitatory to inhibitory responses in the original model is about 8 times as large as the ratio in the reduced model. This means that the reduced model has relatively strong inhibitory responses. Therefore, the strong inhibitory responses in the reduced model emphasize the local motion by suppressing the cross-shaped excitatory responses shown in the original model; the reduced model has better S/N than the original model.

We also evaluated the circuit area except for wiring. A rough estimation indicates that the total circuit area of the reduced model is reduced by approximately 30% compared with that of the original model.

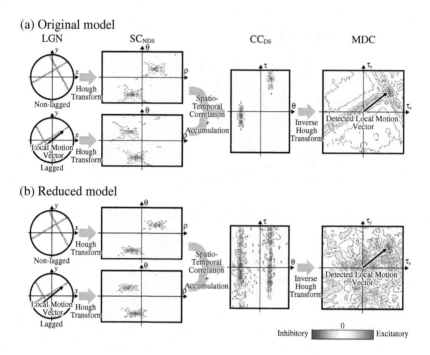

Fig. 5. Simulation results of local motion detection. (a) The original model in which a 1-D DOG filter and the spatio-temporal correlation by multiplication applied to real value cell responses. (b) The reduced model in which 1-D DOG and Gaussian skeleton filters and the spatio-temporal correlation by multiplication-like function applied to integer value cell responses.

5   Conclusions

In this study, we reduced the computational complexity and the memory capacity of the neural network model for motion stereo vision, the Kawakami model, by conversion of the cell responses from real to integer values, reduction from the 2-D DOG filter on (x, y) coordinates to the 1-D DOG skeleton filter on (ρ, θ) coordinates, and replacement of multiplication in the spatio-temporal correlation with a multiplication-like function. We also demonstrated, by numerical simulation, that virtually the same result is obtained even with the reduced model. This model, which is optimized for hardware implementation, will consume a smaller area on a VLSI chip than the original model and will be suitable for applications that require a large scale network.

Acknowledgments. This work was partly supported by JSPS KAKENHI Grant Number 15K18044. We would like to thank Editage (www.editage.jp) for English language editting.

References

1. Lee, D.N., Reddish, P.E.: Plummeting gannets: a paradigm of ecological optics. Nature **293**, 293–294 (1981)
2. Gibson, J.J.: The Perception of the Visual World. Houghton Mifflin, Boston (1950)
3. Kawakami, S., Okamoto, H.: A cell model for the detection of local image motion on the Magnocellular pathway of the visual cortex. Vision Res. **36**(1), 117–147 (1996)
4. Kawakami, S., Matsuoka, M., Okamoto, H., Hosogi, S.: A neural network model for detecting a planar surface spatially from the optical flow in area MST of the visual cortex. Syst. Comput. Jpn. **34**(4), 46–59 (2003)
5. Adelson, E.H., Movshon, J.A.: Phenomenal coherence of moving visual patterns. Nature **300**, 523–525 (1982)
6. Marr, D., Hildreth, E.: Theory of edge detection. Proc. R. Soc. London B **207**, 187–217 (1980)
7. Hough, P.V.C.: Method and means for recognizing complex patterns. U.S. Patent 3069654 (1962)
8. Reichart, W.: Autocorrelation. A Principle for the Evaluation of Sensory Information by the Central Nervous System. Sensory Communication, pp. 303–317. Wiley, New York (1961)
9. Kawakami, S., Morita, T., Okamoto, H., Hasegawa, F., Yasukawa, Y., Inamoto, Y.: A model for intracortical connections of hypercolumn. V. One dimensional filterings and Gabor functions. IEICE Technical report, NC 92, pp. 9–16 (1992)
10. Kawakami, S., Okamoto, H.: A neuronal circuit model for multiplication-like function performed by a combination of three synapse types. IEICE Technical report, NC 95, pp. 47–54 (1995)

Polymer Waveguide-Based Reservoir Computing

Jean Benoit Héroux$^{(\boxtimes)}$, Hidetoshi Numata, and Daiju Nakano

IBM Research, Tokyo, Kawasaki, Kanagawa 212-0032, Japan
{heroux,hnumata,dnakano}@jp.ibm.com

Abstract. Polymer waveguide optical interconnect technology, in which VCSEL and photodiode chip arrays are flip-mounted on an organic carrier to fabricate optical multi-chip modules, has been intensively developed over the last 15 years for data transfer applications in high performance computers. In that application, multiple-channel data signals transmitted to and from CPU and memory components in a system are converted into optical signals for short range, high density, high speed, low power and low cost digital communication. In this work we explore how these efforts could be leveraged to fabricate a compact, fully integrated photonic reservoir computing module with several devices potentially operating in parallel. We present experimental results of low optical loss in a crossing structure as well as good performance simulated with realistic parameters of a time-multiplexed reservoir performing a signal recovery task.

Keywords: Reservoir computing · Photonics · VCSEL · Waveguide · Array · Multi-chip module

1 Introduction

The design and implementation of novel brain-inspired computers based on non von Neumann architectures that have the capability to be trained to perform a variety of artificial intelligence tasks is a topic of great interest. Recently, several systems using an electronic spike processing platform such as IBM TrueNorth [1] or SpiNNaker [2] have been realized. Their low power consumption could respond to a critical need for edge computing near a sensor array, avoiding the wireless, power-hungry transfer of a large amount of data for analysis. Neuromorphic schemes with an architecture relying on photonics would offer important additional advantages, including high processing speed. The possibility to easily generate and process information spikes with a temporal width in the tens of picosecond timescale, as opposed to microsecond or millisecond timescales for electronic and true biological spikes respectively, would be advantageous [3].

One drawback of the above-mentioned systems is that a large amount of energy and computation resource is required for offline training of the high density connectivity between nodes. A potential solution to this issue is reservoir computing, a type of recurrent network in which only the output weights are trained, while the random connections inside the system and at the input,

© Springer International Publishing AG 2017
D. Liu et al. (Eds.): ICONIP 2017, Part VI, LNCS 10639, pp. 840–848, 2017.
https://doi.org/10.1007/978-3-319-70136-3_89

which is not spike-based but analog or defined by a sample-and-hold process, are fixed [4]. Whereas in the original implementation, referred as Echo State Network, real physical nodes are interconnected, an alternative approach recently proposed relies on time-division multiplexing, in which a single physical node with a feedback response input processes the information over time with virtual nodes [5]. This method is simpler for hardware implementation.

Photonic reservoir computers with a single physical node have been shown experimentally to be well-suited for time-dependent tasks, including series prediction, radar signal classification and speech classification up to a million words per second [6–9]. In parallel to these initial table-top demonstrations built with a meter-scale optical fiber and off-the-shelf discrete components for the telecommunication market, other teams have worked on the implementation of chip-integrated photonic reservoirs or neuromorphic spike processing units based on recent progress in Silicon Photonics technology. Initial results, however, have been hampered by a high optical loss of tens of dB in these single-mode circuits [10,11].

Surprisingly, no result has been reported so far in which the enormous effort put into the advancement of multi-mode, VCSEL-based optical interconnect technology for data transfer in high performance computers over the last 15 years is leveraged to create a compact, integrated neuromorphic computing platform that would be of a scale of a few centimeters, i.e., small enough for a wide range of edge computing applications such as drones and video surveillance cameras. The standard data rate for VCSEL-based optical links is now 25 Gb/s, and recent prototypes with record operating speed above 65 Gb/s as well as record low energy per bit below 1 pJ/bit for a full link have been shown. VCSEL operation for applications with four logical levels (PAM-4) has also been demonstrated [12], so that this technology may be adaptable to an analog implementation.

Our group has been a leader in the fabrication and optimization of optical multi-chip modules (MCM) in which a CPU socket along with laser diode driver, VCSEL, photodiode and trans-impedance amplifier chip arrays are integrated on a board including a polymer waveguide layer and micro-mirrors for optical data transfer. For example, a module with 18 channels operating above 30 Gb/s with a bandwidth density as high as 15 Gbps/mm^2 has been realized [13], as well as lens-free transmitter and receiver components with loss below 3 dB [14]. Moreover, and optical chip misalignment tolerance above ± 5 μm [15] and a low power, high modulation amplitude and extinction ratio cmos-driven optical link [16] have been reported. In this work, we present our very first results on the initial building blocks of a centimeter-scale, 25 Gb/s reservoir computer built with optical MCM technology and explain the potential of this platform for scaling up to a large number of physical nodes, or a large number of reservoir computers with virtual nodes operating in parallel.

2   Multi-chip Module Technology Concepts for Reservoir Computing

We present in Fig. 1(a) a typical optical MCM architecture for data transfer in a high performance computer. The substrate is a waveguide-integrated organic

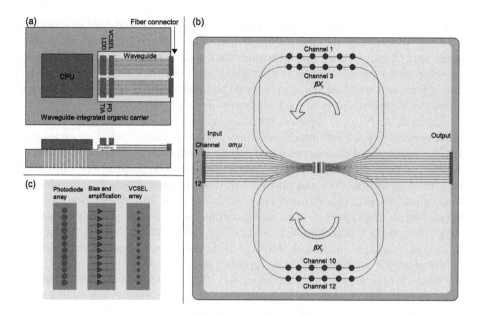

Fig. 1. (a) Typical optical multi-chip module (MCM) used for optical interconnect applications in future high performance computers. (b) New optical MCM scheme for reservoir computing. The center chip arrays contain 12 channels and have a 250 μm pitch, for a total length or the order of a few millimeters. Circles on the feedback loops are a representation of the virtual nodes. The drawing is for schematic illustration only and not exactly to scale. Arrows indicate light direction. (c) Enlarged view of the chip configuration, with a photodiode and laser array connected back-to-back with a passive amplifier.

carrier that contains several planes of electrical lines for connection between the different chips through vertical vias filled with metal. The laser diode driver LDD contains typically 12 or more channels and converts the binary logic data from the CPU to signals with a current bias and suitable amplitude to drive the VCSEL array, which is flip-chip bonded and emits light downward. As seen on the side view, light is reflected by a micro-mirror and sent to a polymer waveguide with a typical core size of 30 to 50 μm to another unit or computer rack. The photodiode array PD sends electrical signals to the trans-impedance amplifier TIA, which converts them back to binary logic values.

Figure 1(b) shows a concept of a reservoir computer built with the same technology. For this initial example design, we choose a time-division scheme in which four of the 12 channels are transformed into four reservoirs operating independently with waveguide optical feedback loops, while the remaining 8 channels could be used for other purposes. The inputs are optical signals that would typically come from an external VCSEL array not shown in the figure, or a fiber ribbon. At the center, photodiode and VCSEL arrays are connected back-to-back with suitable amplification to form an array of physical nodes with a standard pitch of 250 μm. For the reservoir channels (no. 1, 3, 10 and 12), light emitted from the VCSELs is split into a fraction going to the feedback loops and another going to the output optical signal for further processing. The loop part is fed back to the input channels to perform an optical sum by merging waveguide cores, an advantage of light signals being that a fan-in operation can be naturally performed. Away from the chips, the waveguides are shaped so that the pitch is larger to facilitate the design of the optical splitting and combining operation with minimum optical loss.

Figure 1(c) shows an enlarged view of the center chip arrays electrically linked by metal lines on the organic carrier. While the VCSEL and photodiode arrays are commercially available, the center chip will have to be realized but would not require technology not already widely available in a discrete form. It basically replaces the LDD and TIA chips shown in Fig. 1(a) into a simpler component that provides an equal operating bias (1–2 V) to the lasers and the photodiodes (bias tees) and passively amplifies the photocurrent signals to drive the lasers.

An important feature of the above design is that optical channels can physically cross each other on the same plane with very low loss so that time-coding features limiting data rate in an all-electrical platform are not required. As a first experimental result of a building block to realize the above prototype, we present in Fig. 2(a) a fabricated waveguide structure in which each of the 12 center channels undergoes two curves and six crossings. The average difference in optical loss between the straight and curved channels, which is due to the curve portions and the crossings, is 0.5 dB, which is low considering that the total loss budget in an optical link is more than 10 dB. In fact, it has been experimentally demonstrated that a loss lower than 0.01 dB per crossing is realizable even with incoming angles as small as 30°, which greatly enhances design flexibility [17].

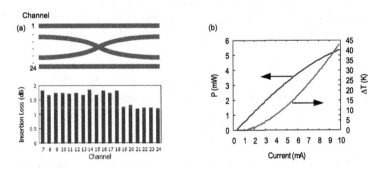

Fig. 2. (a) Fabricated multi-mode polymer waveguide structure to demonstrate optical core crossing. The bottom part shows the insertion loss at 850 nm for crossed (7–18) and straight (19–24) channels. The core size is 40 μm with a step-refractive index profile. The overall structure is 13 mm wide and 35 mm long. The crossing angle is 90° and the curve radius is 15 mm. (b) Simulated optical power and internal temperature curves as a function of the input bias for a 1060 nm VCSEL device based on experimental results that we previously published.

An essential requirement of a reservoir computer is a non-linearity of the signal in the processing nodes. Here, we must take a property that is undesired in an optical interconnect link for data transfer and enhance it for the present application. The VCSEL, photodiode and amplifier chips all exhibit some non-linearity, and for this first calculation we choose to use the curved shape of the output power as a function of the current in a VCSEL due to the internal temperature change, as shown in Fig. 2(b). The data presented are a fit of experimental results presented elsewhere [16] with low power, low noise VCSELs emitting at a 1060 nm wavelength designed and fabricated by Furukawa Electric Corp.

3   Simulation Method

To perform a preliminary evaluation of the potential of the architecture that we propose, we simulate the response of a single reservoir with a loop without crossing and bending loss. The formalism for a time-multiplexed reservoir is well-known, and the node response is given by

$$x_i(n+1) = \begin{cases} F_{NL}[\alpha x_{i-1}(n) + \beta m_i u(n+1)] & 2 \le i \le i_{max} \\ F_{NL}[\alpha x_{N+i-1}(n-1) + \beta m_i u(n+1)] & i = 1 \end{cases} \quad (1)$$

where $u(n)$ is the temporal sample-and-hold signal input, with a scaling step mask m_i that is randomly chosen and kept fixed for each virtual node. $x_i(n)$ is the physical node state for virtual node i at the input signal step n. Here we choose to use a physical node bitrate of 25 Gb/s with $i_{max} = 20$ virtual nodes for compactness, so that the input signal $u(n)$ is sampled at 1.25 GS/s. At 25 Gb/s with a polymer waveguide core refractive index near 1.5, each virtual node in the loop has a spatial dimension around 8 mm and the loop pattern must be designed accordingly. We relate the input attenuation and output gain factors β and α to remain close to the edge of the stability following the expression $\alpha = 0.9999(1 - \beta)$.

The non-linearity FNL comes from the light power vs current (L-I) curve presented above, and the slope efficiency of the curve η, which is around 0.8 W/A at low bias, is dependent on the internal temperature of the laser via the relation

$$\frac{\eta(T_1)}{\eta(T_2)} = e^{\frac{\Delta T}{T_\eta}} \quad (2)$$

where ΔT is the temperature increase due to the current in the device, found from experimental data and also shown in Fig. 2(b) ($T_\eta = 170\,K$).

The high speed response of the laser depends on the carrier and photon behavior in the cavity and is calculated with a large signal model that has been shown to accurately reproduce the bias dependence of eye patterns at high speed, using parameters extracted experimentally from detailed measurements [16]. The equations for our finite difference simulation model describing the photon and carrier dynamics in the cavity with a parameter choice solidly grounded in experimental results, are

$$\frac{dS_i}{dt} = \frac{-S_i}{\tau_{ph}} + \frac{\Gamma \beta N_i}{\tau_n} + \Gamma v_g G_i S_i \qquad (3)$$

$$\frac{dN_i}{dt} = \frac{\eta_i I_i}{qV} - \frac{N_i}{\tau_n} - v_g G_i S_i \qquad (4)$$

$$G_i = g_0 \left(\frac{N_i - N_{tr}}{1 + \epsilon S_i} \right). \qquad (5)$$

where S_i, N_i, G_i and I_i are the photon density, carrier density, gain and current in the cavity at time step i respectively, while the slope efficiency η_i depends on the current as explained above and brings the non-linearity. τ_{ph}, τ_n, v_g and ϵ are the photon and carrier lifetime, the group velocity and gain compression factor respectively, while g_0, N_{tr}, V and Γ are the cavity gain, transparent carrier density, cavity volume and confinement factor respectively. The light output power P_i is proportional to the photon density S_i according to a standard laser equation.

The bias of the laser, which corresponds to the minimum of the input signal u(n), is set to 1.5 mA, while the maximum current is set to 12 mA. An important parameter is the gain of the amplifier chip that is adjusted so that the maximum incoming optical power is regenerated without loss after going through the node. This situation corresponds to a photodiode gain of 140 V/W, a realistic and moderate value that could be further increased for more flexibility in a future design.

4   Task Performance Results

The chosen task for this first calculation is a classical one for a reservoir computer, namely channel equalization first introduced by Jaeger [18]. We generate a set of random integers d in the range {-3,-1,1,3} for each step n and compute a distorted signal $u(n)$ having non-linear and inter-symbol interference components according to the relation

$$\begin{aligned} q(n) = \ & 0.08d(n+2) - 0.12d(n+1) + d(n) + 0.18d(n-1) \\ & - 0.1d(n-2) + 0.091d(n-3) - 0.05d(n-4) + 0.04d(n-5) \\ & + 0.03d(n-6) + 0.01d(n-7) \end{aligned} \qquad (6)$$
$$u(n) = \ q(n) + 0.036q^2(n) - 0.011q^3(n) + \nu(n)$$

This signal is then normalized as an optical input into the photodiode so that the full amplitude of the laser emitting light out of the node is reached in the absence of feedback and attenuation. We take noise into account in the system via the randomly generated signal $\nu(n)$ that has a Gaussian distribution set to a given signal to noise ratio (SNR).

For the simulations, n = 5000 symbols were randomly generated for the training phase, while n = 1000 symbols were used for the test phase that was repeated 10 times for each condition. For each mask step, the signal was computed as the

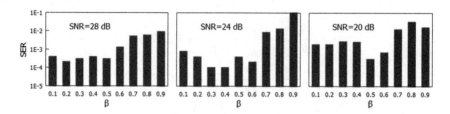

Fig. 3. Symbol Error Rate (SER) results for a channel equalization task with 20 virtual nodes.

average of 64 uniformly distributed data points (0.625 ps time interval) of the laser response. Figure 3 shows the symbol error rate for SNR of 28, 24 and 20 dB respectively as a function of the parameter β (and therefore α as well). A lower value corresponds to a stronger loop feedback, i.e., a higher attenuation of the input optical signal relative to the optical power in the loop. We note that performance is similar to that shown by other groups [8], and that the best results are obtained for $\beta \approx 0.5$, which is easier to implement experimentally that a higher value as it corresponds to roughly equal input and feedback optical signal amplitudes.

The input mask that we used for this experiment was limited to positive values between 0 and 1 (as opposed to a range of $[-1,1]$), so that the input signal is not completely random but oscillates around its true value u(n). The reason for this is that the thermal response time of the laser is expected to be in the tens of picoseconds, fast enough to follow a signal around 1 Gb/s but possibly too slow to follow a full current swing at 25 Gb/s. Other processes for which this is not a concern could be implemented in the future, as discrete amplifiers exhibiting non-linearity with a bandwidth over 40 GHz are commercially available. Using several non-linear processes with different time responses may also add to the reservoir richness, and this issue will need further investigation. Variability in the nodes has been shown to improve a reservoir computational performance [19].

5 Conclusion

To summarize, we have shown preliminary experimental and numerical results on the first building blocks for the realistic application of optical MCM technology for the realization of an optical reservoir computer with an architecture that could be straightforwardly and significantly scaled up for parallel processing. A 12-channel crossing polymer waveguide structure was fabricated and an average 0.5 dB optical loss due to the curved and crossing core sections was measured. An optical-electrical-optical configuration for the physical nodes that allows us to precisely tune parameters such as the gain and provides non-linearity was proposed. Simulation of a design in which the non-linearity comes from the temperature dependence of the light-current curve of a VCSEL was performed, and it was shown that a centimeter-scale device could be realized by using a

25 Gb/s processing speed with a relatively small number of nodes. A low symbol error rate was calculated for a signal recovery task with a typical signal-to-noise ratio.

With the approach we propose, we expect to be able to realize a fully integrated reservoir computer with state-of-the-art performance as obtained with benchtop setups, and avoid the drawbacks of a single mode-based platform such as high laser power consumption. Input and output signal weight encoding chips could eventually be integrated on the same platform for a true turn-key device without the need for offline processing. Ultimately, performance limits will depend on the attainable dynamic range with carefully designed chip array components, noise, and on the optical loss with an optimized waveguide refractive index profile. A large body of literature is already available on these topics. Other structures such as a waterfall with several VCSEL and photodiode arrays forming a network of physical nodes for high speed analog processing, or even a network of interacting real and physical nodes could also be considered, as well as an optical spike computer.

References

1. Merolla, P.A., et al.: A million spiking-neuron integrated circuit with a scalable communication network and interface. Science **345**, 668–673 (2014)
2. Furber, S., Galluppi, F., Temple, S., Plana, L.: The spinnaker project. Proc. IEEE **102**, 652–665 (2014)
3. Prucnal, P.R., Shastri, B.J., de Lima, T.F., Nahmias, M.A., Tait, A.N.: Recent progress in semiconductor excitable lasers for photonic spike processing. Adv. Optics Photonics **8**, 228–299 (2016)
4. Jaeger, H.: The 'echo state' approach to analyzing and training recurrent neural networks - with an erratum note, Technical report GMD Report Number 148, Fraunhofer Institute for Autonomous Intelligent Systems (2011)
5. Appeltant, L., Soriano, M.C., Van der Sande, G., Danckaert, J., Massar, S., Dambre, J., Schrauwen, B., Mirasso, C.R., Fischer, I.: Information processing using a single dynamical node as complex system. Nat. Commun. **2**, 468 (2011)
6. Duport, F., Schneider, B., Smerieri, A., Haelterman, M., Massar, S.: All-optical reservoir computing. Opt. Express **20**, 22783–22795 (2012)
7. Brunner, D., Soriano, M.C., Mirasso, C.R., Fischer, I.: Parallel photonic information processing at gigabyte per second data rates using transient states. Nat. Commun. **4**, 1364 (2013)
8. Dejonckheere, A., Duport, F., Smerieri, A., Fang, L., Oudar, J.-L., Haelterman, M., Massar, S.: All-optical reservoir computer based on saturation of absorption. Opt. Express **22**, 10868–10881 (2014)
9. Larger, L., Baylon-Fuentes, A., Martinenghi, R., Udaltsov, V.S., Chembo, Y.K., Jacquot, M.: High-speed photonic reservoir computing using a time-delay-based architecture: million words per second classification. Phys. Rev. X **7**, 011015 (2017)
10. Vandoorne, K., Mechet, P., Van Vaerenbergh, T., Fiers, M., Morthier, G., Verstraeten, D., Schrauwen, B., Dambre, J., Bienstman, P.: Experimental demonstration of reservoir computing on a silicon photonics chip. Nat. Commun. **5**, 3541 (2014)

11. Nahmias, M.A., Tait, A.N., Tolias, L., Chang, M.P., de Lima, T.F., Shastri, B.J., Prucnal, P.R.: An integrated analog O/E/O link for multi-channel laser neurons. Appl. Phys. Lett. **108**, 151106 (2016)

12. Chen, J., He, Z.S., Lengyel, T., Szczerba, K., Westbergh, P., Gustavsson, J.S., Zirath, H., Larsson, A.: An energy efficient 56 Gbps PAM-4 VCSEL transmitter enabled by a 100 Gbps driver in 0.25 um InP DHBT technology. J. Lightwave Technol. **34**, 4954–4964 (2016)

13. Tokunari, M., Hsu, H.H., Nakagawa, S.: Assembly and demonstration of high bandwidth-density optical MCM. In: 2015 IEEE 65th Electronic Components and Technology Conference, pp. 799–803. IEEE (2015)

14. Tokunari, M., Hsu, H.H., Masuda, K., Nakagawa, S., Assembly optimization for low power optical MCM link. In: Proc. IEEE CPMT Symposium Japan (ICSJ), Kyoto, 5 November 2015 (2015)

15. Tokunari, M., Hsu, H.H., Toriyama, K., Noma, H., Nakagawa, S.: High-bandwidth density and low-power optical MCM using waveguide-integrated organic substrate. J. Lightwave Technol. **32**, 1207–1212 (2014)

16. Heroux, J.B., Kise, T., Funabashi, M., Aoki, T., Schow, C.L., Rylyakov, A.V., Nakagawa, S.: Energy-efficient 1060-nm optical link operating up to 28 Gb/s. J. Lightwave Technol. **33**, 733–740 (2015)

17. Ishigure, T., Shitanda, K., Kudo, T., Takayama, S., Mori, T., Moriya, K., Choki, K., Low-loss design and fabrication of multimode polymer optical waveguide circuit with crossings for high-density optical PCB. In: 2013 IEEE 63rd Electronic Components and Technology Conference, pp. 297–304. IEEE (2013)

18. Jaeger, H., Haas, H.: Harnessing nonlinearity: predicting chaotic systems and saving energy in wireless communication. Science **304**, 78–80 (2004)

19. Tanaka, G., Nakane, R., Yamane, T., Nakano, D., Takeda, S., Nakagawa, S., Hirose, A.: Exploiting heterogeneous units for reservoir computing with simple architecture. In: Hirose, A., Ozawa, S., Doya, K., Ikeda, K., Lee, M., Liu, D. (eds.) ICONIP 2016. LNCS, vol. 9947, pp. 187–194. Springer, Cham (2016). doi:10.1007/978-3-319-46687-3_20

Weighted Robust Principal Component Analysis with Gammatone Auditory Filterbank for Singing Voice Separation

Feng Li[(✉)] and Masato Akagi

Japan Advanced Institute of Science and Technology,
1-1 Asahidai, Nomi, Ishikawa 923-1292, Japan
{lifeng,akagi}@jaist.ac.jp

Abstract. This paper presents a proposed extension of robust principal component analysis (RPCA) with weighting (WRPCA) based on gammatone auditory filterbank for singing voice separation. Although the conventional RPCA is an effective method to separate singing voice and music accompaniment, it makes some strong assumptions. For example, drums may lie in the sparse subspace instead of being low-rank, which decreases the separation performance in many real-world applications, especially for drums existing in the mixture music signal. Accordingly, the proposed WRPCA method utilizes different weighted values between sparse (singing voice) and low-rank matrices (music accompaniment). In addition, we developed an extended RPCA on cochleagram using an alternative time-frequency (T-F) representation based on gammatone auditory filterbank. We also applied IBM/IRM estimation to improve the separation results. Evaluation results show that WRPCA achieves better separation performance than the conventional RPCA, especially for the IBM estimation method.

Keywords: Singing voice separation · Robust principal component analysis (RPCA) · Weighted · Gammatone auditory filterbank · Cochleagram · IBM/IRM estimation

1 Introduction

In recent years, singing voice separation has attracted considerable interest and attention in many real-world applications. It attempts to separate singing voice and music accompaniment parts of a music recording, which is a very significant technology for music information retrieval (MIR) [1] and chord recognition [2]. However, current state-of-the-art results are still far behind human hearing capability. The existing problems of singing voice separation are challenging [3].

Many previous studied methods have been proposed with the goal of overcoming the difficulty in separation tasks. Most of them have attempted to use the distinctive characteristic of each source and rarely studied the human auditory system. Huang *et al.* [4] proposed a robust principal component analysis (RPCA)

© Springer International Publishing AG 2017
D. Liu et al. (Eds.): ICONIP 2017, Part VI, LNCS 10639, pp. 849–858, 2017.
https://doi.org/10.1007/978-3-319-70136-3_90

method for singing voice separation, which decomposed an input matrix into a sparse matrix plus a low-rank matrix. Inspired by a sparse and low-rank model, Yang [5] proposed new sparse and low-rank matrices that were based on the incorporation of harmonicity priors and a back-end drum removal procedure. He [6] also proposed a multiple low-rank representation (MLRR) to decompose a magnitude spectrogram into two low-rank matrices.

As stated above, RPCA is an effective method to separate singing voice from the mixture signal. It decomposes a given amplitude spectrogram (matrix) of a mixture signal into the sum of a low-rank matrix (music accompaniment) and a sparse matrix (singing voice). Since music instruments can reproduce the same sounds each time in the same music, so its magnitude spectrogram can be considered as a low-rank structure part. Singing voice, on the contrary, varies significantly and has a sparse distribution in the spectrogram domain owning to its harmonic structure part, resulting in a spectrogram with a sparse structure part. Although RPCA has been successfully applied to singing voice separation, it makes some strong assumptions. For example, drums may lie in the sparse subspace instead of being low-rank, which decreases the separation performance, especially for drums existing in the mixture music signal.

Even if all of the existing methods (e.g., RPCA and MLRR) can obtain acceptable separation results from mixture music signals, they ignore the features of the human auditory system, which plays a vital role in improving the quality of separation results. Recently a study was published hinting that cochleagram, as an alternative time-frequency (T-F) analysis based on gammatone filterbank, is more suitable than spectrogram for source separation [7]. This is because, cochleagram is derived from non-uniform T-F transform whereas T-F units in low-frequency regions have higher resolutions than in the high frequency regions, which closely resembles the functions of the human ear. Similarly, singing voice performances are quite different from music accompaniment on cochleagram. The spectral energy centralizes in a few T-F units for singing voice and thus can be assumed to be sparse. On the other hand, music accompaniment on the cochleagram has similar spectral patterns and structures that can be captured by a few basis vectors, so it can be hypothesized as a low-rank subspace. Therefore, it is promising to separate singing voice via sparse and low-rank decomposition on cochleagram instead of spectrogram.

To overcome the above-mentioned problems, we propose a weighted method to make sure different scale values are obtained to describe sparse and low-rank matrices. The method, which we call Weighted Robust Principal Component Analysis (WRPCA), chooses different weighted values between sparse and low-rank matrices. In addition, with the purpose of imitating the human auditory system, we adopt gammatone auditory filterbank as the first stage of WRPCA in cochleagram processing. Finally, in order to obtain better separation results, we further apply ideal binary mask (IBM) or ideal ratio mask (IRM) [8] to enforce the constraints between an input mixture signal and the output results.

The rest of this paper is organized as follows. In Sect. 2, we review the conventional RPCA and RPCA for singing voice separation. In Sect. 3, we describe the proposed WRPCA on cochleagram and its application to mask estimation. In Sect. 4, we evaluate WRPCA on the ccMixture and DSD100 datasets. Finally, we draw conclusions and describe future work in Sect. 5.

2 Background

In this section, we briefly review the conventional RPCA and RPCA method for singing voice separation.

2.1 Principle of RPCA

Candés *et al.* [9] presented a convex program RPCA, which decomposed an input matrix $M \in \mathbb{R}_{m \times n}$ into the sum of a low-rank matrix $L \in \mathbb{R}_{m \times n}$ plus a sparse matrix $S \in \mathbb{R}_{m \times n}$. The problem can be formulated as follows:

$$min \ |L|_* + \lambda |S|_1,$$
$$s.t. \ M = L + S. \tag{1}$$

where $|\cdot|_*$ denotes the nuclear norm (sum of singular values), $|\cdot|_1$ is the L_1-norm (sum of absolute values of matrix entries), and λ is a positive constant parameter between the low-rank matrix L and the sparsity matrix S. Candés *et al.* suggested $\lambda = 1/\sqrt{max(m, n)}$ [9]. Furthermore, this convex program can be solved by accelerated proximal gradient (APG) or augmented Lagrange multipliers (ALM) [10] (we used an inexact version of ALM in a baseline experiment).

2.2 RPCA for Singing Voice Separation

Huang *et al.* assumed that the RPCA method can be applied to the task of separating singing voice and music accompaniment from the mixture music signal [4]. On account of the music accompaniment part, music instruments can reproduce the same sounds each time in the same music, so its magnitude spectrogram can be considered as a low-rank matrix structure. Singing voice part, in contrast, varies significantly and has a sparse distribution in the spectrogram domain due to its harmonic structure part, resulting in a spectrogram with a sparse matrix structure. Therefore, we can use the RPCA method to decompose an input matrix into a sparse matrix (singing voice) and a low-rank matrix (music accompaniment). However, it makes some strong assumptions. For instance, drums may lie in the sparse subspace instead of being low-rank, which decreases the separation performance, especially for drums existing in the mixture signal.

3 Proposed Method

In this section, we first explain the proposed WRPCA method and then describe its application to IBM/IRM estimation. Finally, we give a block diagram of a singing voice separation system.

Algorithm 1. WRPCA for Singing Voice Separation

Input: Mixture signal $M \in \mathbb{R}_{m \times n}$, weight w.

1: **Initialization:** $\rho, \mu_0, L_0 = M, J_0 = 0, k = 0$.

2: While not convergence **do** :

3: **repeat**

4:     $S_{k+1} = \arg \min_S |S|_1 + \frac{\mu_k}{2} |M + \mu_k^{-1} J_k - L_k - S|_F^2$.

5:     $L_{k+1} = \arg \min_L |L|_{w,*} + \frac{\mu_k}{2} |M + \mu_k^{-1} J_k - S_{k+1} - L|_F^2$.

6:     $J_{k+1} = J_k + \mu_k (M - L_{k+1} - S_{k+1})$.

7:     $\mu_{k+1} = \rho * \mu_k$.

8: $k \leftarrow k + 1$.

9: **end while.**

Output: $S_{m \times n}$, $L_{m \times n}$.

3.1 Principle of WRPCA

WRPCA is an extension of RPCA, which has different scale values between sparse and low-rank matrices. The corresponding model can be defined as follows:

$$min \ |L|_{w,*} + \lambda |S|_1,$$
$$s.t. \ M = L + S. \tag{2}$$

where $|L|_{w,*}$ is the low-rank matrix with different weighted values, while S is the sparse matrix. $M \in \mathbb{R}_{m \times n}$ is an input matrix, which consists of $L \in \mathbb{R}_{m \times n}$ and $S \in \mathbb{R}_{m \times n}$, and $\lambda > 0$ is a trade-off constant parameter between the sparse matrix S and the low-rank matrix L. We used $\lambda = 1/\sqrt{max(m, n)}$ as suggested by Candés et al. [9]. We also adopted an efficient inexact version of the augmented Lagrange multiplier (ALM) [10] to solve this convex model. The corresponding augmented Lagrange function is defined as follows:

$$J(M, L, S, \mu) = |L|_{w,*} + \lambda |S|_1 + < J, M - L - S >$$
$$+ \frac{\mu}{2} |M - L - S|_F^2. \tag{3}$$

where J is the Lagrange multiplier and μ is a positive scaler. The process corresponding to mixture music signal separation can be seen in Algorithm 1 WRPCA for singing voice separation. The value of M is a mixture music signal from the observed data. After the separation by using WRPCA, we can obtain a sparse matrix S (singing voice) and a low-rank matrix L (music accompaniment).

3.2 Weighted Values

In this paper, we mainly focus on the fact that nuclear norm minimization and L_1-norm affect not only the sparsity and low-rankness of the two decomposed matrices, but also their relative scales. However, the RPCA method simply ignores the differences between the scales of the sparse and low-rank matrices. In order to solve this problem, and inspired by the success of weighted nuclear norm minimization [11], we adopted different weighted value strategies to trim the low-rank matrix during the singing voice separation processing. This enables the features of the separated matrices to be better represented.

Lemma 1. Set $M = U \sum V^T$ as the singular value decomposition (SVD) of $M \in \mathbb{R}_{m \times n}$, where

$$\sum = \begin{pmatrix} diag(\delta_1(M), \delta_2(M), ..., \delta_n(M)) \\ 0 \end{pmatrix}, \tag{4}$$

and $\delta_i(M)$ denotes the i-th singular value of M. If the positive regularization parameter C exists and the positive value $\varepsilon < min(\sqrt{C}, \frac{C}{\delta_1(M)})$ holds, by using the reweighting formula $W_i^l = \frac{C}{\delta_i(L_l) + \varepsilon}$ [12] with initial estimation $L_0 = M$, the reweighted problem has the closed-from solution:
$L^* = U \sum' V^T$, where

$$\sum' = \begin{pmatrix} diag(\delta_1(L^*), \delta_2(L^*), ..., \delta_n(L^*)) \\ 0 \end{pmatrix}, \tag{5}$$

and

$$\delta_i(L^*) = \begin{cases} 0 \\ \dfrac{c_1 + \sqrt{c_2}}{2} \end{cases} \tag{6}$$

where $c_1 = \delta_i(M) - \varepsilon$ and $c_2 = (\delta_i(M) + \varepsilon)^2 - 4C$. Gu *et al.* [11] described a more specific proof of Lemma 1. In our experiments, we empirically set the regularization parameter C as the maximum matrix size, which enabled us to obtain the best separation performance results, e.g., $C = max(m, n)$.

3.3   Application to Mask Estimation

After obtaining the separation results of sparse S and low-rank matrices L by using WRPCA, we applied IBM/IRM estimation to further improve the separation performance. A block diagram of the singing voice separation system is illustrated in Fig. 1. It consists of two stages: WRPCA on cochleagram and singing voice separation based on IBM/IRM estimation. The first stage performs the cochlear analysis with gammatone filter, calculates the cochleagram of the mixture music signal, and then decomposes matrixes into sparse and low-rank matrices by using WRPCA. The second stage applies IBM/IRM estimation to improve the separation results. The IBM and IRM are defined as [8]

$$M_{ibm} = \begin{cases} 1 & S_{ij} \geq L_{ij} \\ 0 & S_{ij} < L_{ij} \end{cases} \tag{7}$$

and

$$M_{irm} = \frac{S_{ij}}{S_{ij} + L_{ij}} \tag{8}$$

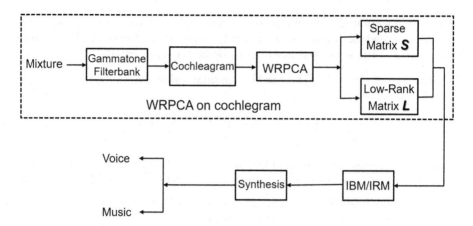

Fig. 1. Block diagram of singing voice separation system.

where M_{ibm} and M_{irm} are the values of IBM estimation and IRM estimation, respectively. S_{ij} and L_{ij} are the values of the sparse and low-rank matrices. The separated matrices can be synthesized as described by Wang *et al.* [13].

4   Experimental Evaluation

In this section, we show how evaluated WRPCA by using two different datasets: ccMixture[1] and DSD100[2], and how we compared it with the conventional RPCA.

4.1   Experimental Datasets

In our experiments, we used two different datasets to evaluate WRPCA. The first was the ccMixter dataset, for which we chose 43 full stereo songs with only 30-second fragments (from $0'30''$ to $1'00''$) at the same time of each song, which is the maximum period of all songs containing singing voice. Each audio contains three parts: singing voice, music accompaniment, and a mixture of them.

The second was the Demixing Secrets Dataset 100 (DSD100), which was also used in the 2016 Signal Separation Evaluation Campaign (SiSEC) [3]. To reduce computations, we adopted only 30-second fragments (from $1'45''$ to $2'15''$) at the same time for all songs, which comprised 36 development songs and 46 test songs. Because there are four sources (bass, drums, vocals and others) for each track, we considered the sum of bass, drums and others was the music accompaniment.

---

[1] http://www.ccmixter.org/.
[2] http://liutkus.net/DSD100.zip.

4.2 Experiment Conditions

We mainly focused on monaural source separation in our experiments. This is even more difficult than multichannel source separation since only a single channel is available. We downmixted the two-channel stereo mixtures into a single mono channel and obtained an average value for each channel. All experiment data were sampled at 44.1 kHz. We set parameters for cochleagram analysis: 128 channels, 40–11025 Hz frequency range, and 256 frequency length. To compare the results with those obtained with WRPCA, we calculated the input feature by using short-time Fourier transform (STFT) and inverse STFT (ISTFT), which is a part of contrast experiments that have been performed on spectrogram for conventional RPCA and WRPCA. We used a window size of 1024 samples, a hop size of 256 samples for the STFT and an FFT size of 1024.

To confirm the effectiveness of WRPCA, we assessed its quality of separation in terms of the source-to-distortion ratio (SDR) and the source-to-artifact ratio (SAR) by using the BSS-EVAL 3.0 metrics [14] and the normalized SDR (NSDR). The estimated signal $\hat{S}(t)$ is defined as

$$\hat{S}(t) = S_{target}(t) + S_{interf}(t) + S_{artif}(t). \tag{9}$$

where $S_{target}(t)$ is the allowable deformation of the target sound, $S_{interf}(t)$ is the allowable deformation of the sources that account for the interferences of the undesired sources, and $S_{artif}(t)$ is an artifact term that may correspond to the artifact of the separation method. The SDR, SAR and NSDR are defined as

$$SDR = 10log_{10} \frac{\sum_t S_{target}(t)^2}{\sum_t \{e_{interf}(t) + e_{artif}(t)\}^2}. \tag{10}$$

$$SAR = 10log_{10} \frac{\sum_t \{S_{target}(t) + e_{interf}(t)\}^2}{\sum_t e_{artif}(t)^2}. \tag{11}$$

$$NSDR(\hat{v}, v, x) = SDR(\hat{v}, v) - SDR(x, v). \tag{12}$$

where $\hat{v}$ is the separated voice part, v is the original clean signal, and x is the original mixture. The NSDR is used to estimate the overall improvement in the SDR between x and $\hat{v}$.

The higher values of the SDR, SAR and NSDR represent that the method exhibits better separation performance of source separation. The SDR represents the quality of the separated target sound signals. The SAR represents the absence of artificial distortion. All the metrics are expressed in dB.

4.3 Experiment Results

To examine WRPCA, we first evaluated it on the ccMixture dataset. Figure 2 shows the comparison results of conventional RPCA, RPCA with IRM, RPCA with IBM, WRPCA, WRPCA with IRM, and WRPCA with IBM, respectively. The first four methods (RPCA, RPCA with IRM, RPCA with IBM and WRPCA) are calculated on spectrogram (without gammatone filterbank), while WRPCA

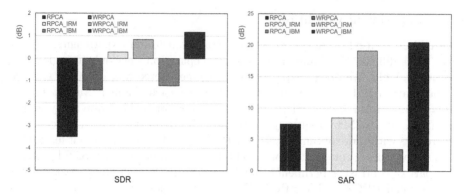

Fig. 2. Comparison of singing voice separation results on **ccMixture** dataset among conventional RPCA, RPCA with IRM, RPCA with IBM, WRPCA, WRPCA with IRM, and WRPCA with IBM, respectively.

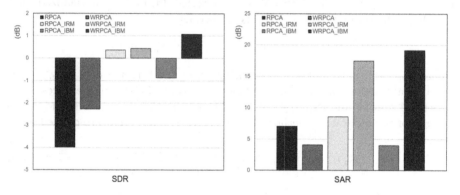

Fig. 3. Comparison of singing voice separation results on **DSD100** dataset among conventional RPCA, RPCA with IRM, RPCA with IBM, WRPCA, WRPCA with IRM, and WRPCA with IBM, respectively.

with IRM and WRPCA with IBM are calculated on cochleagram (with gamma-tone filterbank). From the experiment results obtained with the SDR and SAR, we can see that WRPCA gets better results on the ccMixture dataset, especially for the IBM estimation (with gammatone filterbank). In contrast, the conventional RPCA got worse results than the others. We also evaluated WRPCA on the DSD100 dataset. Figure 3 shows the comparison results obtained with the conventional RPCA, RPCA with IRM, RPCA with IBM, WRPCA, WRPCA with IRM, and WRPCA with IBM, respectively. The results clearly show that WRPCA obtains better separation results on the DSD100 dataset, especially for the IBM estimation (with gammatone filterbank). However, the opposite results were obtained with the conventional RPCA. In terms of the SAR in Figs. 2 and 3, WRPCA with IBM on cochleagram (with gammatone filterbank) attained higher values than others, while the RPCA with IBM (without gammatone filterbank) had the worst values among them.

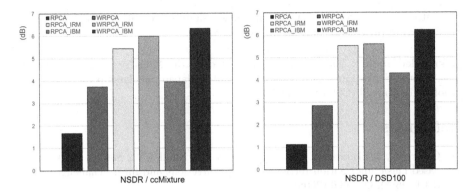

Fig. 4. Comparison of singing voice separation results between **ccMixture** and **DSD100** datasets among conventional RPCA, RPCA with IRM, RPCA with IBM, WRPCA, WRPCA with IRM, and WRPCA with IBM, respectively. Note that SDRs for the original datasets, ccMixture and DSD100, are −5.16 dB and −5.11 dB, respectively.

The NSDR provides overall improvement in the SDR; in other words, it provides better separation performance in singing voice separation. Figure 4 shows the NSDR results we obtained with WRPCA on the ccMixture and DSD100 datasets. The results show that the best performance was achieved by WRPCA with IBM (with gammatone filterbank).

Therefore, from the results of Figs. 2, 3 and 4, we can confirm that WRPCA on cochleagram provides better separation performance than RPCA on spectrogram under the same conditions with or without IBM or IRM. Moreover, WRPCA provided better results than RPCA without gammatone filterbank and IBM/IRM. We also can see that WRPCA on cochleagram with IBM (with gammatone filterbank) provides better separation results in all evaluation standard methods. However, RPCA with IBM does not provide values as good as those provided by RPCA with IRM.

5 Conclusions and Future Work

In this paper, we proposed an extension of RPCA with weighting on cochleagram (WRPCA). It is based on gammatone auditory filterbank and application to IBM/IRM estimation for singing voice separation. The cochleagram of the mixture signal was decomposed into sparse (singing voice) and low-rank matrices (music accompaniment) by using WRPCA, then IBM/IRM estimation was utilized to improve the separation results. Experimental results obtained on the ccMixture and DSD100 datasets confirmed that WRPCA outperforms the conventional RPCA method in singing voice separation tasks, especially for WRPCA on cochleagram based on gammatone auditory filterbank with IBM estimation. In future work, since prior information (e.g., melody annotations) and spatial information (e.g., localization and isolation) are very significant for separating singing voice from mixture music signals, we will attempt to fuse all of them to improve the separation performance.

Acknowledgments. This work was supported by the Ministry of Education, Culture, Sports, Science and Technology (MEXT) of Japan Scholarship and the China Scholarship Council (CSC) Scholarship.

References

1. Casey, M., Veltkamp, R., Goto, M., Leman, M., Rhodes, C., Slaney, M.: Content-based music information retrieval: current directions and future challenges. Proc. IEEE **96**(4), 668–696 (2008)
2. Fujishima, T.: Real-time chord recognition of musical sound: a system using common lisp music. In: Proceedings of the International Computer Music Conference (ICMC), pp. 464–467 (1999)
3. Liutkus, A., Stöter, F., Rafii, Z., Kitamura, D., Rivet, B., Ito, N., Ono, N., Fontecave, J.: The 2016 signal separation evaluation campaign. In: Proceedings of 13th International Conference on Latent Variable Analysis and Signal Separation (LVA/ICA 2017), Grenoble, France, pp. 323–332 (2017)
4. Huang, P.S., Chen, S.D., Smaragdis, P., Hasegawa-Johnson, M.: Singing-voice separation from monaural recordings using robust principal component analysis. In: Proceedings of the IEEE International Conference on Acoustics, Speech, Signal Processing (ICASSP), pp. 57–60 (2012)
5. Yang, Y.H.: On sparse and low-rank matrix decomposition for singing voice separation. In: Proceedings of the 20th ACM international conference on Multimedia, pp. 757–760. ACM (2012)
6. Yang, Y.H.: Low-rank representation of both singing voice and music accompaniment via learned dictionaries. In: Proceedings of the 13th International Society for Music Information Retrieval Conference (ISMIR), pp. 427–432 (2013)
7. Gao, B., Woo, W.L., Dlay, S.S.: Unsupervised single-channel separation of nonstationary signals using gammatone filterbank and itakura-saito nonnegative matrix two-dimensional factorizations. IEEE Trans. Circuits Syst. I Regul. Pap. **60**(3), 662–675 (2013)
8. Li, Y.P., Wang, D.L.: On the optimality of ideal binary time-frequency masks. Speech Commun. **51**(3), 230–239 (2009)
9. Candés, E., Li, X.D., Ma, Y., Wright, J.: Robust principal component analysis? J. ACM **58**(3), 11:1–11:37 (2011)
10. Lin, Z.C., Chen, M.M., Ma, Y.: The augmented Lagrange multiplier method for exact recovery of corrupted low-rank matrices. UIUC Technical report, UILU-ENG-09-2215 (2009)
11. Gu, S.H., Xie, Q., Meng, D.Y., Zuo, W.M., Feng, X.C., Zhang, L.: Weighted nuclear norm minimization and its applications to low level vision. Int. J. Comput. Vision **121**(2), 183–208 (2017)
12. Candés, E., Wakin, M., Boyd, S.: Enhancing sparsity by reweighted l_1 minimization. J. Fourier Anal. Appl. **14**(5–6), 877–905 (2008)
13. Wang, D.L., Brown, G.J.: Computational Auditory Scene Analysis: Principles, Algorithms, and Applications. Wiley-IEEE Press, Hoboken (2006)
14. Vincent, E., Gribonval, R., Févotte, C.: Performance measurement in blind audio source separation. IEEE Trans. Audio Speech Lang. Process. **14**(4), 1462–1469 (2006)

Word-Level Permutation and Improved Lower Frame Rate for RNN-Based Acoustic Modeling

Yuanyuan Zhao[1,2]($\boxtimes$), Shiyu Zhou[1,2], Shuang Xu[1], and Bo Xu[1]

[1] Institute of Automation, Chinese Academy of Sciences, Beijing, China
{yyzhao5231,zhoushiyu2013,shuang.xu,xubo}@ia.ac.cn
[2] University of Chinese Academy of Sciences, Beijing, China

Abstract. Recently, the RNN-based acoustic model has shown promising performance. However, its generalization ability to multiple scenarios is not powerful enough for two reasons. Firstly, it encodes inter-word dependency, which conflicts with the nature that an acoustic model should model the pronunciation of words only. Secondly, the RNN-based acoustic model depicting the inner-word acoustic trajectory frame-by-frame is too precise to tolerate small distortions. In this work, we propose two variants to address aforementioned two problems. One is the word-level permutation, i.e. the order of input features and corresponding labels is shuffled with a proper probability according to word boundaries. It aims to eliminate inter-word dependencies. The other one is the improved LFR (iLFR) model, which equidistantly splits the original sentence into N utterances to overcome the discarding data in LFR model. Results based on LSTM RNN demonstrate 7% relative performance improvement by jointing the word-level permutation and iLFR.

Keywords: RNN-based acoustic model · Acoustic trajectory · Lower frame rate · Word-level permutation

1 Introduction

Recently, acoustic models based on recurrent neural networks (RNNs), such as Long Short-Term Memory (LSTM), have been shown the state-of-art performance for large vocabulary speech recognition [1–5]. RNNs store the activations from the previous time step in the internal state, and provide indefinite temporal contextual information in contrast to the fixed contextual windows used as inputs in deep neural networks (DNNs). This capability of RNN makes it born to fit for sequence modeling.

For RNN based acoustic modeling, there are two alternative approaches. One uses the frame-level cross-entropy (CE) with conventional Hidden Markov Models (HMMs) hybrid architecture [1,2,5]. The other one uses sequence discriminative training criteria, such as connectionist temporal classification (CTC) criteria with end-to-end systems [3,4,6,7]. In both architectures, RNNs try to

© Springer International Publishing AG 2017
D. Liu et al. (Eds.): ICONIP 2017, Part VI, LNCS 10639, pp. 859–869, 2017.
https://doi.org/10.1007/978-3-319-70136-3_91

model long-span or even global dependencies regardless of being trained with standard BPTT [8] or truncated BPTT [9].

However, an ideal acoustic model should be devoted to only modeling the acoustic properties of words, while leaving iter-word dependencies to language model to learn. There are two main reasons account for this. On one hand, co-articulation effects mainly exist in adjacent phonetic units inside a word and are diminished considerably between words [10]. On the other hand, such acoustic models can be directly applied to different scenarios with the corresponding language model. Unfortunately, neither the standard BPTT nor the truncated BPTT could guarantee that dependencies only exist inside the word, since inter-word dependencies are variational but the optimization methods are invariable.

Based on the above observations, we proposed word-level permutation to eliminate the context dependency between words in RNN-based acoustic models. Before fed into RNN, the feature vectors and labels obtained by forced alignment are randomly shuffled according to the segment of words with a proper probability simultaneously. Since dependencies between words cannot be eliminated completely (e.g. clear the history at the begin of word in the training procedure, but boundaries of words are not known when testing), artificially disturbing the sequence order could uncouple the correlations of distant words substantially. For comparison, two other permutation granularities, called phone-level and character-level permutation are also explored.

Besides the problem of modeling inter-word dependencies, the inner-word acoustic trajectory is depicted frame-wisely so precise that it hampers generalization in RNN-based acoustic modeling. This has been verified by the observation that the lower frame rate (LFR) model [5] achieves best performance with the frame rate of 40 ms. The main reason given in [5] why the performance goes worse with the higher frame advance is the decrease of the amount of training data. We argue that the decrease also exists in the frame rate from 10 ms to 40 ms. It prevents the model from achieving better performance improvements. In order to overcome the defects of discarding data, we propose improved low frame rate (iLFR). iLFR equidistantly splits the original sentence into n utterances at a particular frame rate of n, rather than down-subsamples and drops the rest data as in LFR model. From the perspective of the total number of frames being trained, we make full use of all the data. And with regard to the total number of training utterances, iLFR expands n times than that of original training data at the frame rate of n.

Our methods are suitable for all types of RNN, and we take LSTM RNN [11] as an instance in following experiments. First of all, we demonstrate that the performance benefits most from shuffling utterances of appropriate proportion at word level than the phone level and the character level. Then, up to 5% relative character error rate (CER) reduction has been observed in our iLFR experiments compared with LFR model. What's more, we combine the two aforementioned proposed methods based on LSTM RNN, which shows approximate superimposed performance improvement. At last, we prove that models trained by our scheme are easier applying to new applications.

2   Related Work

RNN-based acoustic models learn both the acoustic and language characteristic also found in Paper [12]. It showed that modeling the language characteristic led systems to produce worse performance than the state-of-the-art DNN-HMM baseline. Though a new decoding framework, a subword LM (SLM) is subtracted from the output of RNN-based acoustic models to coordinate the AM score and the word-level LM score. By this, consistent improvements have been achieved over the conventional interpolation-based framework.

Paper [13] proposed a "pseudo-shuffling" procedure that does "augment the unexpectedness" of training samples by skipping successive training frames. This method achieves much better RNNs compared with the conventional training procedure. Paper [5] stacked the current feature with the past $l = 7$ frames and down-sampled to desired frame rate, and the best performance is obtained with lower frame rate up to 40 ms. In paper [14], the skip connection in the temporal dimension had been added to cope with the degradation problem, which can ensure information flowing across the time axis unimpededly. All these works are dedicated to address the precise dependency of adjacent frames in RNN-based acoustic modeling.

3   Word-Level Permutation and iLFR

In this section, we will firstly overview the RNN-HMM hybrid architecture briefly. The advantages and disadvantages are formulated in detail by comparing it with DNN-HMM method [15]. Then, word-level permutation and iLFR are introduced to address the weaknesses of the RNN-HMM approach.

3.1   Acoustic Modeling with RNNs

Let $\mathbf{X}_{1:T} = \mathbf{x}_1, \cdots, \mathbf{x}_T$ be the sequence of T acoustic feature vectors of an utterance, where $\mathbf{x}_t \in \mathbb{R}^N$ is a frame-level feature representation. In RNN-HMM hybrid architecture, the speech recognition task is formulated as follows:

$$\mathbf{w}^* = \arg\max_{\mathbf{w}} P\left(\mathbf{w} \,|\mathbf{X}_{1:T}\right) \tag{1}$$

$$= \arg\max_{\mathbf{w}} \sum_{\mathbf{l}} P\left(\mathbf{w} \,|\mathbf{l}_{1:T}, \mathbf{X}_{1:T}\right) P\left(\mathbf{l}_{1:T} \,|\mathbf{X}_{1:T}\right) \tag{2}$$

$$\simeq \arg\max_{\mathbf{w}} P\left(\mathbf{w} \,|\mathbf{l}_{1:T}^*\right) P\left(\mathbf{l}_{1:T}^* \,|\mathbf{X}_{1:T}\right) \tag{3}$$

$$= \arg\max_{\mathbf{w}} P\left(\mathbf{w}\right) P\left(\mathbf{l}_{1:T}^* \,|\mathbf{w}\right) \frac{P\left(\mathbf{l}_{1:T}^* \,|\mathbf{X}_{1:T}\right)}{P\left(\mathbf{l}_{1:T}^*\right)} \tag{4}$$

where $\mathbf{l}_{1:T} = l_1, \cdots, l_T$ denotes all possible labelings of input sequence (i.e. HMM states) and $\mathbf{l}_{1:T}^*$ is obtained by forced alignment with viterbi approximation. Implicit in above Eq. 3 is the assumption that probabilities of word sequences $\mathbf{w}$ and input feature sequences $\mathbf{X}$ are conditionally independent, given the label sequences $\mathbf{l}^*$, i.e. $\mathbf{w} \perp \mathbf{X} \,|\, \mathbf{l}^*$. This assumption is in principle true provided the language model and search algorithm are perfect enough. In Eq. 4, $P(\mathbf{l}^*_{1:T} \,|\, \mathbf{w})$ is computed by the transition model and the lexicon model, and $P(\mathbf{w})$ is estimated by a language model. $P(\mathbf{l}^*_{1:T} \,|\, \mathbf{X}_{1:T}) / P(\mathbf{l}^*_{1:T})$ is the acoustic likelihood required before fed to the decoder. Provided the training data is large enough, the probabilities of the labels at each timestep are conditionally independent given $\mathbf{X}$:

$$P(\mathbf{l}^*_{1:T} \,|\, \mathbf{X}_{1:T}) = \prod_{t=1}^{T} P(l^*_t \,|\, \mathbf{X}_{1:T}) \tag{5}$$

where the label posterior $P(l^*_t \,|\, \mathbf{X}_{1:T})$ is the standard form of all RNN-based acoustic models in principle. It's substantially different from traditional emission probability estimation based on short-time stationary within a state of HMM.

However, the posterior $P(\mathbf{w} \,|\, \mathbf{X}_{1:T})$ in DNN-HMM architecture is firstly transformed using Bayes' Rule [16], and then with the same assumption $\mathbf{w} \perp \mathbf{X} \,|\, \mathbf{l}^*$ and viterbi approximation it formulated as follows:

$$\mathbf{w}^* = \arg\max_{\mathbf{w}} P(\mathbf{w} \,|\, \mathbf{X}_{1:T}) \tag{6}$$

$$\simeq \arg\max_{\mathbf{w}} P(\mathbf{w}) \, P(\mathbf{l}^*_{1:T} \,|\, \mathbf{w}) \, P(\mathbf{X}_{1:T} \,|\, \mathbf{l}^*_{1:T}) \tag{7}$$

$$= \arg\max_{\mathbf{w}} P(\mathbf{w}) \, P(\mathbf{l}^*_{1:T} \,|\, \mathbf{w}) \prod_{t=1}^{T} \frac{P(l^*_t \,|\, \mathbf{x}_t)}{P(l^*_t)} \tag{8}$$

where $P(\mathbf{X}_{1:T})$ and $\prod_{t=1}^{T} P(\mathbf{x}_t)$ are ignored in Eqs. 7 and 8, since they are constant for each hypothesis. In Eq. 8, it is assumed that the current label l^*_t only depends on current frame $\mathbf{x}_t$:

$$l^*_t \perp (l^*_\alpha, \mathbf{x}_\beta) \,|\, \mathbf{x}_t \quad \forall \alpha, \beta \in [1 : t-1] \cup [t+1 : T] \tag{9}$$

This assumption is usually not true in practice. In contrast, the RNN-HMM architecture largely eliminates this unreasonable independence assumption by comparing Eqs. 4 and 8, which making it more suitable for speech recognition, a time-varying signal with complex multiple correlations at a range of different timescales. However, inter-word dependencies are encoded, which conflicts with the nature that an acoustic model should model the pronunciation of words only. Besides, the denominator $P(\mathbf{l}^*_{1:T})$ introduced in Eq. 4 is too hard to compute. Most works [2,14,17] coping with this problem are subtracting the prior $P(l^*_t)$ from the posterior by analogy with DNN-HMM. Recently, paper [12,18] proposed a high order estimating method of $P(\mathbf{l}^*_{1:T})$ to address this problem.

3.2   Word-Level Permutation

In Eq. 5, the label probability $P(l^*_t \,|\, \mathbf{X}_{1:T})$ is theoretically conditioned on the entire input sequence, and not just the part occurring before the label emitted, therefore bidirectional RNN are preferred. Even in low-latency applications with unidirectional RNN, the label probability is computed from the entire historical frames and a few future frames, and it's simplified as follow:

$$P\left(l_t^* \mid \mathbf{X}_{1:T}\right) \simeq P\left(l_t^* \mid \mathbf{X}_{1:t+R}\right) \tag{10}$$

where R is the length of target delay or the number of spliced right frames.

In fact, because of co-articulation effects, the acoustic realizations of phonetic units depend on the phonemes that precede and follow them. Furthermore, the strong correlations always exist inside the word and are considerably diminished between words [10]. Therefore, the acoustic model should focus on inner-word dependencies modeling instead of the whole sequence trajectory modeling. The probability $P\left(l_t^* \mid \mathbf{X}_{1:T}\right)$ of Eq. 5 should be exactly revised to the following form:

$$P\left(l_t^* \mid \mathbf{X}_{1:T}\right) \simeq P\left(l_t^* \mid \mathbf{X}_{t-n:t+m}\right) \tag{11}$$

where n and m are the number of frames counting from the current timestep to the beginning and the ending of the corresponding word respectively.

The gap between the perfect form $P\left(l_t^* \mid \mathbf{X}_{t-n:t+m}\right)$ characterized in Eq. 11 and the actual realizations $P\left(l_t^* \mid \mathbf{X}_{1:t+R}\right)$ in Eq. 10 or $P\left(l_t^* \mid \mathbf{X}_{1:T}\right)$ in Eq. 5 motivates this paper. In order to eliminate inter-word dependencies, word-level permutation method is proposed as illustrated in Fig. 1.

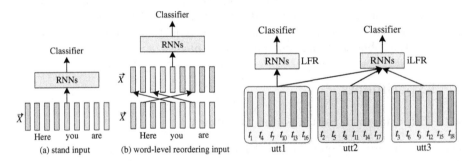

Fig. 1. Comparison of the standard input and word-level permutation. (a) the standard inputs. (b) the word-level permutation.

Fig. 2. Comparison of LFR model and iLFR model. The original sequence is splitted to n utterances. LFR model only uses one of them. iLFR model uses all the n utterances.

In proposed method, the word boundary can be extracted from the forced alignment of senones. And then the order of features and corresponding labels of words are randomly shuffled with a proper probability according to boundaries simultaneously before fed into networks.

Storing the activations from the previous time step in internal states gives rise to inner-word and inter-word dependencies. By changing the internal states in boundaries of words in clean training samples, we can considerably eliminate inter-word dependencies, making the following word appear uniformly. Getting rid of inter-word dependencies from acoustic model makes it easier to apply to desired applications with appropriate language model. Furthermore, from the perspective of data augmentation, the model are trained by more diverse data, which can improve the generalization and make it more robust.

3.3   Improved Lower Frame Rate

The label posterior $P(l_t^* | \mathbf{X}_{1:T})$ in Eq. 5 is calculated in RNN frame-by-frame from start timestep of t_0, which precisely depicts the utterance trajectory. However, it is too precise to tolerate small distortions, which is verified by performance improvement of LFR model [5].

The proposed iLFR model is introduced to address the decrease of the amount of training data. At a particular frame rate of n, the original sentence is equidistantly splitted into n utterances, rather than down subsampling and throwing the rest samples as in LFR model. The comparison of iLFR and LFR is illustrated in Fig. 2. Note that, n split utterances need to be shuffled across the whole training data. It is widely known that the neural networks can be trained much more efficiently by stochastic gradient decent if training samples are randomly shuffled [19].

Therefore, we make full use of the whole training frames, and the number of utterances becomes n times compared with original samples. Proposed approach not only fully exploits local dependencies by the reduction of frame rate, but also improves the robustness and generalization of models.

4   Experiments

4.1   Experimental Settings and Baselines

Our experiments are conducted on HKUST (LDC2005S15, LDC2005T32) [20] Mandarin Chinese conversational telephone speech, which contains 150-hour speech, and 873 calls in the training set and 24 calls in the test set, respectively. The standard Kaldi recipe s5 [21] is adopted for preparing features of 40-dimensional log-mel filterbank and 3-dimensional pitch with first and second order derivatives.

In experiments, a three layers LSTM RNN with 800 cells projected to 512 units is used. For training networks with CE loss using fixed alignments, the training utterances are force-aligned using a well-trained GMM-HMM systems with 2814 CD HMM states. Since the information of future frames helps making better decision for the current frame, a training strategy of 5 frames delayed target is adopted.

For computational efficiency, the model is trained on our asynchronous stochastic gradient descent (ASGD) training platform [22] with 4 GPUs after first layer-wise pre-training [23]. Each task processes 12 utterances at a time, using the truncated BPTT learning algorithm [9] to forward propagate and then back propagate for 20 consecutive frames. The learning rate is decreased exponentially with an initial value of 1.0e-04.

Baseline Systems. Two typical types of systems are established as baselines in our experiments: CE training of hybrid system with HMM and end-to-end system trained with CTC. In the hybrid architecture, traditional DNN and the popular LSTM RNNs are conducted. "DNN-6L-1024H" has 6 hidden layers with 1024 neurons in each layer and "LSTMP-3L-800C" has 3 layers with 800 cells projected to 512 units. "LSTMP-3L-Res" has 3 layers with spatial dimension residual learning and corresponding result is cited [14]. In the end-to-end system, unidirectional architecture "LSTMP-3L-800C" and bidirectional architecture "BiLSTMP-3L-800C" are conducted with 6,724 grapheme output units for Chinese characters set [24] for comparison (Table 1).

Table 1. Baselines of CER of hybrid and end-to-end systems with various configurations on HKUST tasks.

Type	Architecture	CER	Type	Architecture	CER
CE	DNN-6L-1024H	40.34	—	—	—
CE	LSTMP-3L-800C	34.30	CTC	LSTMP-3L-800C	35.63
CE	LSTMP-3L-Res [14]	33.64	CTC	BiLSTMP-3L-800C	34.22

4.2   Evaluation of Word-Level Permutation

Experiments of word-level permutation on the proportion of training data ranging from 0.1 to 0.9 are elaborated to explore the influence of inter-word dependencies. For comparison, the phone-level and character-level permutation are also experimented. The results are illustrated in Fig. 3. From the figure, it can be observed that with the permutation proportion increasing from 0.1 to 0.3, the performance has been improved, and the best performance is obtained at the proportion of 0.3. We argue that performance improvements mainly benefit from the elimination of inter-word dependencies, which exactly conforms to the nature of the ideal acoustic model. However, with the further increase of the proportion, the performance decreases. Besides, the word-level permutation mostly obtains the best performance in each proportion, followed by the character level, while the worst is the phone level. As is known that the CD-state adopted as the output unit also models dependencies between words. This inaccurate connections may affect the searching path and result in bad performance when decoding. Lastly, the best result of word-level permutation shows the 5% relative decrease of CER at the proportion of 0.3.

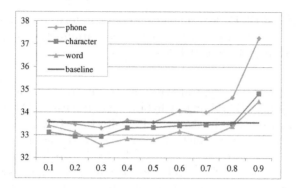

Fig. 3. Comparison of word-level, character-level and phone-level permutation scheme with different proportion of training data.

4.3   Evaluation of iLFR

In this section, we explore effects of lower frame rates of 20 ms, 30 ms and 40 ms in the iLFR model. For comparison, the best performance of the LFR model with 40 ms is experimented [5]. In addition, we also compared with the temporal dimension residual learning (TDRL) of 40 ms [14], which is a type of lower frame rate initially focusing on modeling the skip connections. Results of iLFR, LFR and TDRL are summarized in Table 2.

Table 2. Results of iLFR model with different lower frame rates and comparison with LFR and TDRL.

Model	LFR	TDRL	iLFR		
Frame rate	40 ms	40 ms	20 ms	30 ms	40 ms
CER	34.18	33.22	32.72	**32.43**	32.77

From the table, we can notice that the iLFR with different frame rates are all better than the baseline of 10 ms, and obtain the best performance of 5.5% relative decrease of CER at 30 ms. We argue that the toleration of small distortions and augmentation of training samples in lower frame rate lead to the initial performance improvement. But with further lower frame rate, the loss of information and the blurring of the trajectory become noticeable degrading the performance. The best trade-off occurs at 30 ms. What's more, the performance of iLFR is better than LFR and TDRL. On one hand, the augmented training data learned by iLFR gives rise to the improvement than LFR model.

On the other hand, the more efficient training strategy by the utterance level randomly shuffled brings the further improvement compared with TDRL.

4.4   Combination of Word-Level Permutation and iLFR

Due to the word-level permutation and the iLFR boosting the performance of LSTM based acoustic model from inter-word and inner-word aspects separately, it's reasonable to jointly utilize the two methods in one model. In this experiment, the best configure of the two methods are used and the results are shown in the first row of Table 3. We can find that combination of the word-level permutation and iLFR can get the further performance improvement and the best result achieves the 7.6% relative reduction of CER. Besides, consistent improvements are also observed in LFR and TDRL models trained with word-level permutation.

Table 3. The results of combination word-level permutation with iLFR, LFR and TDRL at the best configure of each are shown in the first row and the results of applying the combination models to heterogeneous data (ATHD) are listed in the second row.

Model	Standard-LSTM	LFR	TDRL	iLFR
combination-CER	34.30	32.95	32.67	**31.74**
ATHD-CER	54.00	49.88	49.13	**48.48**

In order to verify the assumption that models trained by proposed scheme are easier to apply to new applications with appropriate languages models, another heterogeneous testset is used to evaluate proposed methods. This testset consists of 20, 124 utterances from telephone conversations in real situation with multi-scenarios. The results are summarized in the second row of Table 3, up to 10% relative performance improvement is observed in iLFR models trained with word-level permutation. This demonstrates the effectiveness of the proposed methods applied to new applications.

5   Conclusion

Word-level permutation and iLFR model are proposed to address the defects of inter-word dependencies modeling and too precise inner-word modeling of RNN-based acoustic model separately. The results based on LSTM RNNs demonstrate 7% relative CER improvement by jointing the two methods. Besides, the evaluation of irrelevant test data shows separating the language model from the acoustic model can obtain 10% relative improvements.

Acknowledgments. This work was supported by 973 Program in China, grant No. 2013CB329302.

References

1. Graves, A., Jaitly, N., Mohamed, A.: Hybrid speech recognition with deep bidirectional LSTM. In: 2013 IEEE Workshop on Automatic Speech Recognition and Understanding (ASRU), pp. 273–278. IEEE (2013)
2. Sak, H., Senior, A., Beaufays, F.: Long short-term memory based recurrent neural network architectures for large vocabulary speech recognition. In: Interspeech (2014)
3. Sak, H., Senior, A., Rao, K., Beaufays, F.: Fast and accurate recurrent neural network acoustic models for speech recognition. arXiv preprint arXiv:1507.06947 (2015)
4. Sak, H., Senior, A., Rao, K., Irsoy, O., Graves, A., Beaufays, F., Schalkwyk, J.: Learning acoustic frame labeling for speech recognition with recurrent neural networks. In: Acoustics, Speech and Signal Processing (ICASSP), pp. 4280–4284 (2015)
5. Pundak, G., Sainath, T.N.: Lower frame rate neural network acoustic models. Interspeech **2016**, 22–26 (2016)
6. Graves, A.: Supervised Sequence Labelling with Recurrent Neural Networks. Springer, Heidelberg (2012). doi:10.1007/978-3-642-24797-2
7. Soltau, H., Liao, H., Sak, H.: Neural speech recognizer: acoustic-to-word LSTM model for large vocabulary speech recognition. arXiv preprint arXiv:1610.09975 (2016)
8. Rumelhart, D.E., Hinton, G.E., Williams, R.J.: Learning internal representations by error propagation. Technical report, DTIC Document (1985)
9. Williams, R.J., Peng, J.: An efficient gradient-based algorithm for on-line training of recurrent network trajectories. Neural Comput. **2**, 490–501 (1990)
10. Kühnert, B., Nolan, F.: The origin of coarticulation. In: Coarticulation: Theory, Data and Techniques, pp. 7–30 (1999)
11. Hochreiter, S., Schmidhuber, J.: Long short-term memory. Neural Comput. **9**(8), 1735–1780 (1997)
12. Kanda, N., Lu, X., Kawai, H.: Maximum a posteriori based decoding for CTC acoustic models. Interspeech **2016**, 1868–1872 (2016)
13. Kanda, N., Tachimori, M., Lu, X., Kawai, H.: Training data pseudo-shuffling and direct decoding framework for recurrent neural network based acoustic modeling. In: Automatic Speech Recognition and Understanding (ASRU), pp. 15–21 (2015)
14. Zhao, Y., Xu, S., Xu, B.: Multidimensional residual learning based on recurrent neural networks for acoustic modeling. Interspeech **2016**, 3419–3423 (2016)
15. Dahl, G.E., Yu, D., Deng, L., Acero, A.: Context-dependent pre-trained deep neural networks for large-vocabulary speech recognition. IEEE Trans. Audio Speech Lang. Process. **20**(1), 30–42 (2012)
16. Rabiner, L.R.: A tutorial on hidden Markov models and selected applications in speech recognition. Proc. IEEE **77**(2), 257–286 (1989)
17. Senior, A., Sak, H., Shafran, I.: Context dependent phone models for LSTM RNN acoustic modelling. In: 2015 IEEE International Conference on Acoustics, Speech and Signal Processing (ICASSP), pp. 4585–4589. IEEE (2015)
18. Miao, Y., Gowayyed, M., Metze, F.: EESEN: end-to-end speech recognition using deep RNN models and WFST-based decoding. In: 2015 IEEE Workshop on Automatic Speech Recognition and Understanding (ASRU), pp. 167–174. IEEE (2015)

19. LeCun, Y.A., Bottou, L., Orr, G.B., Müller, K.-R.: Efficient BackProp. In: Montavon, G., Orr, G.B., Müller, K.-R. (eds.) Neural Networks: Tricks of the Trade. LNCS, vol. 7700, pp. 9–48. Springer, Heidelberg (2012). doi:10.1007/978-3-642-35289-8_3
20. Liu, Y., Fung, P., Yang, Y., Cieri, C., Huang, S., Graff, D.: HKUST/MTS: a very large scale Mandarin telephone speech corpus. In: Huo, Q., Ma, B., Chng, E.-S., Li, H. (eds.) ISCSLP 2006. LNCS, vol. 4274, pp. 724–735. Springer, Heidelberg (2006). doi:10.1007/11939993_73
21. Seide, F., Li, G., Chen, X., Yu, D.: Feature engineering in context-dependent deep neural networks for conversational speech transcription. In: IEEE Workshop on Automatic Speech Recognition and Understanding (ASRU), pp. 24–29 (2011)
22. Zhang, S., Zhang, C., You, Z., Zheng, R., Xu, B.: Asynchronous stochastic gradient descent for DNN training. In: ICASSP, pp. 6660–6663. IEEE (2013)
23. Bengio, Y., Lamblin, P., Popovici, D., Larochelle, H., et al.: Greedy layer-wise training of deep networks. In: Advances in Neural Information Processing Systems, vol. 19, p. 153 (2007)
24. Li, J., Zhang, H., Cai, X., Xu, B.: Towards end-to-end speech recognition for Chinese Mandarin using long short-term memory recurrent neural networks. In: Sixteenth Annual Conference of the International Speech Communication Association (2015)

Phonemic Restoration Based on the Movement Continuity of Articulation

Cenxi Zhao[1], Longbiao Wang[1], and Jianwu Dang[1,2(✉)]

[1] Tianjin Key Laboratory of Cognitive Computing and Application,
Tianjin University, Tianjin, China
{zhaocenxi,longbiao_wang}@tju.edu.cn
[2] Japan Advanced Institute of Science and Technology, Ishikawa, Japan
jdang@jaist.ac.jp

Abstract. Phonemic restoration describes one of human capabilities that can retrieve the defective speech signal after adding a certain noise. It is believed that the movement continuity of articulation is one of main factors for realizing the phonemic restoration. This paper proposes an effective method based on this consideration to retrieve missing speech signal and makes the relevant hypothesis verified to some degree. For the proposed method, the mapping relationship between acoustic and articulatory features is established based on deep neural network (DNN), where a hierarchical DNN architecture with bottleneck feature is realized to improve the performance for acoustic-to-articulatory inversion, then missing articulatory feature obtained from missing speech signal is restored with cubic spline function. 25 sentences are selected from the database MNGU0 and short durations of the sentences are replaced by zeros and/or noise for evaluating. Experimental results show that the proposed method can effectively improve perceptual evaluation of speech quality (PESQ) of the speech with missing signal. And these experimental results provide preliminary experimental clues for verifying the first hypothesis of phonemic restoration—coarticulation.

Keywords: Phonemic restoration effect · Coarticulation · Movement continuity of articulation · Deep neural network · Spline interpolation

1 Introduction

Phonemic restoration effect is a perceptual phenomenon where under certain conditions, sounds actually missing from a speech signal can be synthesized by the brain and clearly heard [1]. This effect was first documented in 1970 [2] and since then, much research has been done to investigate about it. Most of these studies are from the view of neuroanatomy to investigate the auditory mechanism of human beings [3, 4] or conducting some behavioral experiments to focus on the influence factors of this effect [5–7]. Now there are two accepted hypotheses about how the brain fills up the speech

---

Cenxi Zhao and Longbiao Wang—Contributed equally to this work.

© Springer International Publishing AG 2017
D. Liu et al. (Eds.): ICONIP 2017, Part VI, LNCS 10639, pp. 870–879, 2017.
https://doi.org/10.1007/978-3-319-70136-3_92

signal, one is related to coarticulation and the other is according to semantic context provided by sentences [1]. These two hypotheses fight with each other and neither of them has been verified effectively.

Phonemic restoration effect is often encountered in noisy situations in dairy life, which reflects the reveals the sophisticated capability of the brain underlying robust speech perception. If the capability can be utilized through machine learning, it will contribute to many fields, such as speech enhancement [8], speech recognition [9], speech understanding [10] and so on. For example, the accuracy of automatic speech recognition (ASR) systems is still adversely affected by noise and other sources of acoustical variability. Restoring the speech signal masked by noise should improve the performance effectively.

To verify the hypotheses and take advantage of phonemic restoration effect, this paper focuses on the first hypothesis—coarticulation [1], which means that when the human being producing speech signal, the articulation organs such as lips, a tongue, and a jaw, cannot move freely and abruptly, instead, these organs move smoothly in a highly cooperative manner, resulting in the articulation of adjacent phonetic segments interacting with each other [11]. As a consequence of coarticulation, information for a phonetic segment distributes over time in the range of a few hundred milliseconds, overlapping with that for adjacent segments. The brain can exploit such acoustic redundancy of speech signal in the phonemic restoration [1].

As mentioned in the first hypothesis, under the influence of coarticulation, the trajectory of the articulatory organs is smooth and continuous. Therefore, a missing part of the articulatory trajectory which is small enough can be easily filled up based on its continuity. Meanwhile, the production of speech signals is closely related to the movement of the articulatory organs. As long as establishing a mapping model between them, it is probable to retrieve the missing speech signal according to the filled up articulatory trajectory. In recent years, deep neural network (DNN) based acoustic-to-articulatory inversion approaches have achieved the state-of-the-art performance [12]. Moreover, articulatory-to-acoustic conversion has been made a good progress [13]. Under these circumstances, this paper proposes a method utilizing DNN-based feature mapping and spline interpolation to do speech signal restoration. First, a mapping model between articulatory and acoustic is established. When doing acoustic-to-articulatory inversion, a hierarchical DNN architecture with bottleneck feature is proposed to improve the performance. Then, spline interpolation is adopted to fill up the missing articulatory feature thus retrieve the missing signal. And if the method achieves a good performance, we can think the first hypothesis be confirmed preliminarily.

The rest of the paper is organized as follows. Section 2 describes the proposed method how to verify and utilize the first hypothesis of phonemic restoration effect. The experimental setup, evaluation results and discussion are given in Sect. 3. Finally, we conclude the research and the future work in Sect. 4.

2   Missing Speech Signal Restoration with Proposed Method

The schematic diagram of proposed method for missing speech signal restoration based on the movement continuity of articulation is shown in Fig. 1. First, endpoint detection is conducted on the speech signal in which some parts are lost or damaged. Then, acoustic feature extracted from the existing parts is mapped to the corresponding articulatory feature. After arraying these articulatory feature parts in the order of time sequence, we can utilize the movement continuity of articulation to do interpolation on them to get the missing articulatory feature parts. At last, mapping the obtained articulatory feature parts to the corresponding acoustic feature and synthesizing speech to fill in, we can retrieve the missing speech signal. In this section, the major component of the schematic diagram is described in detail.

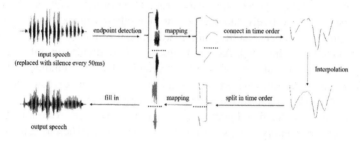

Fig. 1. The schematic diagram of proposed method

2.1   DNN-Based Articulatory-with-Acoustic Mapping

A DNN is a multi-layer perceptron with several hidden layers between the input layer and the output layer, as illustrated in Fig. 2. DNNs can be trained in a two-stage strategy: the pre-training stage and the fine-tuning stage [14]. DNN-based feature mapping approaches have been proposed for many speech signal processing fields [15–19]. For regression tasks, the fine-tuning stage adopts back-propagation (BP) algorithm to minimize the mean square error (MSE) on training set. In this paper, both articulatory-to-acoustic conversion and acoustic-to-articulatory inversion are based on DNN.

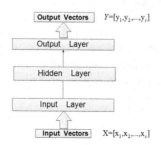

Fig. 2. Illustration of a DNN for regression

2.1.1 DNN-Based Articulatory to Acoustic Conversion

Consider a sequence of input feature vectors $X = [x_1, x_2, ..., x_t]$ and a parallel se-quence of output feature vectors $Y = [y_1, y_2, ..., y_t]$, where t is the number of frames. For articulatory-to-acoustic conversion, the input vector x denotes electro-magnetic midsagittal articulography (EMA) [20] features, and the output vector y includes 1-st to 40-th orders of mel-generlized cepstrum (MCCs), powers (0-th order of MCCs), U/V flags and logarithmic F0 values are extracted from the waveform using STRAIGHT vocoder [21]. STRAIGHT is also adopted as the vocoder for speech waveform reconstruction using the above acoustic features.

2.1.2 Hierarchical DNN-Based Acoustic-to-Articulatory Inversion

In recent years, DNN-based acoustic-to-articulatory inversion approaches have achieved the state-of-the-art performance. For these approaches, the mapping rela-tionship is established between the acoustic feature and all dimensions of EMA data during inversion [22–24]. Articulatory feature can be separated into several parts according to different organs, such as jaw, lip and tongue, which are represented for different dimensions of EMA. When the fine-tuning stage of DNN, BP algorithm is adopted to minimize the MSE on training set, but the obtained MSE is minimum for all the dimensions, not for each dimension. How can we get the MSE for each dimension and take into account the interaction of every articulator at the same time? In order to address this issue and improve the performance, this paper proposes an improved architecture hierarchically concatenating bottleneck feature and articulatory inversion component DNNs as shown in Fig. 3.

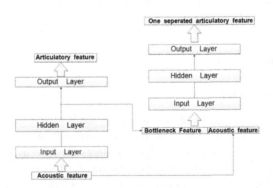

Fig. 3. Illustration of a hierarchical inversion DNN consisting of from left to right bottleneck features producing sub-network and a separated inversion sub-network

For hierarchical DNN-based acoustic-to-articulatory inversion, the input vector x denotes 1-st to 40-th orders of MCCs, and the output vector y denotes one dimension of EMA features. It consists of two sub-networks. The left sub-network taking acoustic feature as its inputs and at its outputs is articulatory feature used to produce bottleneck features. The resulting bottleneck features representing the underlying inter-acting information between acoustic feature and the articulatory feature and the information for coarticulation with all the articulators are then augmented to the acoustic features before being fed into the separated articulatory inversion DNN sub-network.

2.2 Missing Articulatory Feature Restoration Based on the Movement Continuity of Articulation

Spline interpolation is a form of interpolation where the interpolant is a special type of piecewise polynomial. Spline interpolation is often preferred over polynomial interpolation because the interpolation error can be made small even when using low degree polynomials for the spline [25]. Interpolation by means of splines, that is, the construction of an interpolation spline taking given values $f(x_i)$ at prescribed points x_i, $i = 1, 2,..., n$. Interpolation splines usually satisfy further conditions at the end points. E.g., for the cubic spline $S_3(\triangle n, x)$, where $\triangle n$ is the partition $a = x_0 \leqslant x_1 \leqslant \cdots \leqslant x_n = b$, which, on [a, b], consists of piecewise-cubic polynomials and has a continuous second-order derivative, one requires that $S_3(\triangle n, x_i) = f(x_i)$ and, in addition, one condition at each end point (e.g. $S_3'(\triangle n, a) = y_0'$ and $S_3'(\triangle n, b) = y_n'$, or $S_3'(\triangle n, a) = y_0''$ and $S_3'(\triangle n, b) = y_n''$). If the $f(x_i)$ are the values of a (b-a)-periodic function, then one requires the spline to be (b-a)-periodic also. For polynomial splines of degree $2k + 1$, the number of extra conditions at each end point a or b is increased by k. For interpolation splines of degree 2k, the knots of the spline (the points of discontinuity of the 2k-th derivative) are usually chosen halfway between the points xi, and a further k conditions are as-signed at a and b.

Cubic spline function is used for restoring the missing articulatory feature in this paper, because the movement of articulation and delta, delta-delta coefficients of articulatory data are all continuous.

3 Experiments

3.1 Experimental Setup

Experiments in this paper are conducted on the database MNGU0 [26], which consists of 1263 British English utterances from one male native British English speaker with parallel acoustic and EMA recordings. EMA features are used as articulatory feature, which are captured from 6 sensors located at tongue dorsum, tongue body, tongue lip, jaw, upper lip and lower lip with a sampling frequency of 200 Hz. For each sensor, the coordinates on the front-to-back axis and the bottom-to-top axis (relative to viewing the speakers head from the front) are used, making a total of 12 static EMA features at each frame. The waveforms are in 16 kHz PCM format with 16 bit precision.

For DNN-based articulatory-with-acoustic mapping, 1000 utterances are selected from the database to build the training set for our experiments. The validation set and test set contain 20 and 100 utterances respectively for the DNN-based articulatory-with-acoustic mapping model. After that, 25 utterances are selected from MNGU0 to test the proposed phonemic restoration method.

3.2   Experimental Results of Hierarchical DNN-Based Acoustic-to-Articulatory Inversion

In acoustic-to-articulatory inversion experiments, we compare the hierarchical DNN method and the conventional DNN method. The results on the 100-utterance test set are shown in Table 1 and root-mean-square error (RMSE) are chosen as the evaluation criterion. The structures of the two DNN models are both tuned to be one hidden layer and 512 hidden nodes for the layer, and the context windows are both set to 15 frames, which means that the previous 7 frames and the subsequent 7 frames along with the current frame are as inputs. As expected, hierarchical DNN method is found to generate consistently more precise articulatory movements than the conventional DNN on inversion, which is used in proposed phonemic restoration method eventually.

Table 1. Evaluation results of conventional DNN method and the Hierarchical-DNN

Method	RMSE
Conventional DNN	2.18
Hierarchical DNN	1.80

3.3   Experimental Results of Proposed Phonemic Restoration Method

For each sentence in the 25 selected sentences, 1 or 2 parts are replaced with silence manually and the duration is 50 ms and 100 ms respectively then retrieved with proposed method. To control the conditions of experiment, the starting point is set to be the same when replacing the speech with 50 ms and 100 ms silence, which means zeros, and the 1st part is set to be the same when replacing the speech with 1 part and 2 parts silence. As contrast, noise with the same duration is filled in the silence part because the relevance with natural speech signal of noise is more than silence. Perceptual Evaluation of Speech Quality (PESQ), a worldwide applied industry standard for objective voice quality testing used by phone manufacturers, network equipment vendors and telecom operators [27], is chosen as the evaluation criterion, which range is from 1 to 4.5 and a sentence with a better quality usually has higher PESQ. The results for replacing 1 part and 2 parts are illustrated in Tables 2 and 3 respectively, in which, the elements of the row 'sentence ID' are omitted the prefix 'mngu0_s1_', for example, '1003' stands for 'mngu0_s1_1003', and for others rows, 'S', 'N', 'F' stand for the sentence replaced with silence, noise and the sound filled up using proposed phonemic restoration method.

3.4   Discussion

From the two tables we can see almost all the PESQ of the sentences satisfy this law: $S < N < F$, which demonstrates that the proposed phonemic restoration method is effective for improving the PESQ of speech with missing signal. Also because the

Table 2. The PESQ of sentences which are missing 1 part

Sentence ID	Missing phoneme	Replaced content			Missing phoneme	Replaced content		
	50 ms	S	N	F	100 ms	S	N	F
1003	a /eɪ/	2.98	3.29	3.63	a /eɪ/	2.64	3.12	3.26
1006	c /k/	3.24	3.70	3.86	con /kən/	2.89	3.38	3.53
1010	a /æ/	3.21	3.84	3.93	an /æn/	3.00	3.75	4.04
1015	sh /ʃ/	3.19	3.70	3.88	sh /ʃ/	2.89	3.27	3.52
1021	l /l/	3.04	3.42	3.63	la /leɪ/	2.95	3.36	3.55
1023	f /f/	3.32	3.66	3.77	fron /frʌn/	3.13	3.57	3.21
1025	t /t/	3.36	3.77	3.95	t /t/	3.28	3.61	3.80
1026	tr /tr/	3.33	3.75	3.98	try /tra/	3.15	3.59	3.72
1027	j /dʒ/	3.19	3.32	3.73	ju /dʒʌ/	3.21	3.26	3.05
1029	re /rɪ/	2.76	3.35	3.40	re /rɪ/	2.85	2.78	3.09
1033	c /k/	3.50	3.77	3.91	cro /krɒ/	3.33	3.62	3.70
1034	d /d/	3.37	3.76	4.00	d /d/	3.10	3.68	3.80
1036	m /m/	3.21	3.45	3.80	m /m/	3.01	3.33	3.77
1043	a /ɒ/	3.11	3.64	3.73	at /ɒt/	2.98	3.43	3.14
1045	z /z/	3.77	3.76	3.95	z /z/	3.42	3.63	3.65
1047	w /w/	3.12	3.18	3.26	wan /wɒn/	2.67	2.92	3.26
1049	t /t/	3.83	3.76	4.11	to /tu/	3.49	3.56	3.87
1057	i /ɪ/	3.43	3.51	3.70	i /ɪ/	3.11	3.24	3.63
1060	ch /tʃ/	3.47	3.39	3.57	ch /tʃ/	3.21	3.15	3.61
1069	s /z/	3.53	3.67	3.99	s /z/	3.42	3.54	3.83
1086	ou /aʊ/	3.68	3.91	4.15	oun /aʊn/	3.27	3.58	3.66
1090	th /ð/	3.29	3.53	3.85	tha /ðæ/	3.08	3.45	3.50
1093	m /m/	3.39	3.64	3.73	me /miː/	3.10	3.53	3.67
1094	ir /əː/	3.82	4.05	4.31	ir /əː/	3.74	3.92	4.19
1095	r /r/	2.90	3.65	3.73	res /rɪ'z/	2.79	3.49	3.14
Mean	-	**3.32**	**3.62**	**3.82**	-	**3.11**	**3.43**	**3.57**

proposed phonemic restoration method is based on the movement continuity of articulation, which is a main basis of the hypothesis – coarticulation of phonemic restoration effect, we can consider that the proposed phonemic restoration method verifies this hypothesis to some degree.

When 1 is replaced part for 50 ms, the mean PESQ of 'F' increases 5.52% and 15.06% compared with 'N' and 'S', and for 100 ms, the percentages are 4.08% and 14.79%. When 2 parts are replaced each for 50 ms, the mean PESQ of 'F' increases 8.31% and 24.82% compared with 'N' and 'S', and for 100 ms, the percentages are 10.00% and 29.92%.

It seems that when replacing 1 part, the PESQ decreases slightly with the replaced part becomes longer, while when replacing 2 parts, the PESQ has an obviously increase with the replaced part becomes longer. And the more the number of replaced parts is,

Table 3. The PESQ of sentences which are missing 2 parts

Sentence ID	Missing phoneme		Replaced content			Missing phoneme		Replaced content		
	50 ms		S	N	F	100 ms		S	N	F
1003	a /eɪ/	ve /ve/	2.31	2.81	2.96	a /eɪ/	vel /vel/	1.78	2.41	2.86
1006	c /k/	sm /əm/	2.68	3.33	3.66	con /kən/	sm /əm/	2.29	3.06	3.49
1010	a /æ/	s /s/	2.99	3.50	3.76	an /æn/	so /soʊ/	2.69	3.38	3.63
1015	sh /ʃ/	ing /ɪŋ/	2.36	2.92	3.20	sh /ʃ/	ing /ɪŋ/	2.07	2.63	2.97
1021	l /l/	eu /ju/	2.74	3.01	3.51	la /leɪ/	eu /ju/	2.33	2.94	3.30
1023	f /f/	in /ɪn/	2.86	3.31	3.60	fron /frʌn/	in /ɪn/	2.60	3.21	3.46
1025	t /t/	s /s/	2.93	3.34	3.59	t /t/	sis /sɪs/	2.80	3.19	3.49
1026	tr /tr/	co /kɔ/	3.09	3.58	3.81	try /trɑ/	cot /kɔt/	2.73	3.32	3.52
1027	j /dʒ/	m /m/	2.46	2.89	3.28	ju /dʒʌ/	my /maɪ/	2.29	2.78	3.20
1029	re /rɪ/	ar /ɑː/	2.17	3.09	3.23	re /rɪ/	ar /ɑː/	1.90	2.50	3.35
1033	c /k/	te /te/	3.03	3.37	3.37	cro /krɒ/	te /te/	2.87	3.26	3.19
1034	d /d/	o /ɒ/	2.73	3.35	3.69	d /d/	og /ɒg/	2.56	3.25	3.05
1036	m /m/	co /kɒ/	3.00	3.27	3.64	m /m/	co /kɒ/	2.50	2.84	3.20
1043	a /ɒ/	do /duː/	2.70	3.21	3.42	at /ɒt/	do /duː/	2.65	2.91	3.25
1045	z /z/	ner /nɜː/	3.21	3.44	3.84	z /z/	ner /nɜː/	3.09	3.25	3.54
1047	w /w/	pa /pə/	2.78	2.85	3.16	wan /wɒn/	pa /pə/	2.07	2.44	2.92
1049	t /t/	ve /v/	3.02	3.34	3.76	to /tu/	ve /v/	2.78	3.03	3.51
1057	i /ɪ/	lu /lə/	2.81	3.22	3.49	i /ɪ/	lun /lən/	2.56	2.95	3.37
1060	ch /tʃ/	to /tʊ/	3.18	3.08	3.39	ch /tʃ/	to /tʊ/	2.86	2.84	3.26
1069	s /z/	a /æ/	2.76	3.35	3.60	s /z/	an /æn/	2.50	3.10	3.46
1086	ou /aʊ/	th /ð/	3.07	3.55	3.69	oun /aʊn/	the /ðə/	2.69	3.24	3.37
1090	th /ð/	j /dʒ/	3.07	3.24	3.58	tha /ðæ/	ja /dʒe/	2.74	3.11	3.42
1093	m /m/	f /f/	3.14	3.37	3.75	me /miː/	fore /fɔː/	2.87	3.00	3.40
1094	ir /əː/	r /r/	3.17	3.68	3.76	ir /əː/	ri /raɪ/	2.80	3.39	3.47
1095	r /r/	re /rɪ/	2.27	3.22	3.22	res /rɪ'z/	re /ri/	1.96	3.07	2.85
Mean	-	-	**2.82**	**3.25**	**3.52**	-	-	**2.54**	**3.00**	**3.30**

the more PESQ increases. The phenomenon indicates that the proposed phonemic restoration method becomes more effective when the missing speech signal become more within a limit duration. That's because when speech is replaced with silence, PESQ decreases sharply as the missing speech signal becomes more, then as long as filling up a relative signal, it will also rise a lot.

There are also several sentences that the PESQ of 'N' is larger than 'F', and in all of them the number of missing phonemes is more than one, in which situation the movement of articulation becomes too complex to be interpolated so the proposed phonemic restoration method may not behave well.

4 Conclusion and Future Work

In summary, the proposed phonemic restoration method based on the movement continuity of articulation in this paper has effectively improved perceptual evaluation of speech quality of the speech with short-duration missing signal. And these experimental results provide preliminary experimental clues for verifying the first hypothesis of phonemic restoration—coarticulation.

For the future work, more experiments will be conducted to study on the relation-ship between the number of replaced parts and the PESQ of the sentences with the proposed phonemic restoration method. Moreover, the problem of how missing phonemes affect the PESQ of the sentences will also be explored.

Acknowledgements. The research is partially supported by the National Basic Research Program of China (No. 2013CB329301), and the National Natural Science Foundation of China (No. 61233009). Besides, we are especially grateful to the partial support by JSPS KAKENHI Grant (16K00297).

References

1. Kashino, M.: Phonemic restoration: the brain creates missing speech sounds. Acoust. Sci. Technol. **27**(6), 318–321 (2006)
2. Warren, R.M.: Perceptual restoration of missing speech sounds. Science **167**(3917), 392–393 (1970)
3. Riecke, L., Vanbussel, M., Hausfeld, L.: Hearing an illusory vowel in noise: suppression of auditory cortical activity. J. Neurosci. Off. J. Soc. Neurosci. **32**(23), 8024–8034 (2012)
4. Başkent, D.: Effect of speech degradation on top-down repair: phonemic restoration with simulations of cochlear implants and combined electric-acoustic stimulation. J. Assoc. Res. Otolaryngol. **13**(5), 683 (2012)
5. Liederman, J., Gilbert, K., Fisher, J.M.: Are women more influenced than men by top-down semantic information when listening to disrupted speech? Lang. Speech **54**(1), 33–48 (2011)
6. Başkent, D., Eiler, C.L., Edwards, B.: Phonemic restoration by hearing-impaired listeners with mild to moderate sensorineural hearing loss. Hear. Res. **260**(1), 54–62 (2010)
7. Newman, R.S.: Perceptual restoration in children versus adults. Appl. Psycholinguist. **25**(4), 481–493 (2004)
8. Harding, P., Milner, B.: Speech enhancement by reconstruction from cleaned acoustic features. In: INTERSPEECH, Italy, pp. 1189–1192 (2011)
9. Kolossa, D., Häb-Umbach, R.: Robust Speech Recognition of Uncertain or Missing Data. Springer, Heidelberg (2011)
10. Devault, D., Sagae, K., Traum, D.R.: Detecting the status of a predictive incremental speech understanding model for real-time decision-making in a spoken dialogue system. In: Interspeech, Italy, pp. 1021–1024 (2011)
11. Cohen, M.M., Massaro, D.W.: Modeling coarticulation in synthetic visual speech. In: Thalmann, N.M., Thalmann, D. (eds.) Models and Techniques in Computer Animation. Springer, Tokyo (1993)
12. Liu, P., Yu, Q., Wu, Z.: A deep recurrent approach for acoustic-to-articulatory inversion. In: International Conference on Acoustics, Speech and Signal Processing, Australia, pp. 4450–4454 (2015)

13. Liu, Z.C., Ling, Z.H., Dai, L.R.: Articulatory-to-acoustic conversion with cascaded prediction of spectral and excitation features using neural networks. In: Interspeech, USA, pp. 1502-1506 (2016)
14. Hinton, G.E.: A Practical guide to training restricted Boltzmann machines. Momentum **9**(1), 599–619 (2012)
15. Ren, B., Wang, L., Lu, L., Ueda, Y., Kai, A.: Combination of bottleneck feature extraction and dereverberation for distant-talking speech recognition. Multimedia Tools Appl. **75**(9), 5093–5108 (2016)
16. Ueda, Y., Wang, L., Kai, A., Ren, B.: Environment-dependent denoising autoencoder for distant-talking speech recognition. EURASIP J. Adv. Sig. Process. **92**(1), 1–11 (2015)
17. Zhang, Z., Wang, L., Kai, A., Odani, K., Li, W., Iwahashi, M.: Deep neural network-based bottleneck feature and denoising autoencoder-based dereverberation for distant-talking speaker identification. EURASIP J. Audio Music Speech Process. **12**(1), 1–13 (2015)
18. Niwa, K., Koizumi, Y., Kawase, T.: Pinpoint extraction of distant sound source based on DNN mapping from multiple beamforming outputs to prior SNR. In: International Conference on Acoustics, Speech and Signal Processing, China, pp. 435–439 (2016)
19. Canevari, C., Badino, L., Fadiga, L.: Relevance weighted reconstruction of articulatory features in deep-neural-network-based acoustic-to-articulatory mapping. In: Interspeech, France (2013)
20. Schonle, P.W., Grabe, K., Wenig, P., Hohne, J., Schrader, J., Conrad, B.: Electromagnetic articulography: use of alternating magnetic fields for tracking movements of multiple points inside and outside the vocal tract. Brain Lang. **31**(1), 26–35 (1987)
21. Kawahara, H.: Speech representation and transformation using adaptive interpolation of weighted spectrum: VOCODER revisited. In: International Conference on Acoustics, Speech, and Signal Processing, Germany, p. 1303 (1997)
22. Atal, B.S., Rioul, O.: Neural networks for estimating articulatory positions from speech. J. Acoust. Soc. Am. **86**(S1), S67 (1989)
23. Rahim, A.M., Goodyear, C., Kleijn, B., Schroeter, J., Sondhi, M.: On the use of neural networks in articulatory speech synthesis. J. Acoust. Soc. Am. **93**(2), 1109–1121 (1993)
24. Kjellstom, H., Engwall, O.: Audiovisual-to-articulatory inversion. Speech Commun. **51**(3), 195–209 (2009)
25. Hazewinkel, M.: Spline Interpolation, Encyclopedia of Mathematics. Springer, Dordrecht (2001). (in Russian)
26. Richmond, K., Hoole, P., King, S.: Announcing the electromagnetic articulography (Day 1) subset of the mngu0 articulatory corpus. In: Conference on the International Speech Communication Association, INTERSPEECH 2011, Italy, pp. 1505–1508 (2011)
27. Pennock, S.: Accuracy of the perceptual evaluation of speech quality (PESQ) algorithm. In: Measurement of Speech and Audio Quality in Networks Line Workshop Mesaqin (2002)

Language Identification Using Deep Convolutional Recurrent Neural Networks

Christian Bartz[✉], Tom Herold, Haojin Yang, and Christoph Meinel

Hasso Plattner Institute, University of Potsdam, Potsdam, Germany
{christian.bartz,haojin.yang,meinel}@hpi.de, tom.herold@student.hpi.de

Abstract. *Language Identification (LID)* systems are used to classify the spoken language from a given audio sample and are typically the first step for many spoken language processing tasks, such as *Automatic Speech Recognition (ASR)* systems. Without automatic language detection, speech utterances cannot be parsed correctly and grammar rules cannot be applied, causing subsequent speech recognition steps to fail. We propose a LID system that solves the problem in the image domain, rather than the audio domain. We use a hybrid *Convolutional Recurrent Neural Network (CRNN)* that operates on spectrogram images of the provided audio snippets. In extensive experiments we show, that our model is applicable to a range of noisy scenarios and can easily be extended to previously unknown languages, while maintaining its classification accuracy. We release our code and a large scale training set for LID systems to the community.

1 Introduction

Intelligent assistants like Siri[1] or the Google Assistant[2] rely on ASR. Current ASR systems require users to manually specify the system's correct input language to work properly. However, as a sensible pre-processing step we can infer the spoken language using an automatic LID system. Traditional LID systems utilize domain-specific expert knowledge in the field of audio signal processing for extracting hand-crafted features from the audio samples. Lately, deep learning and artificial neural networks have become the state-of-the-art for many pattern recognition problems. *Deep Neural Networks (DNNs)* have become the best performing method for a range of computer vision tasks, such as image classification [17,18], or object detection and recognition [14,15].

In this paper, we address the problem of language identification from a computer vision perspective. We extract the target language of a given audio sample by utilizing a hybrid network constructed of a *Convolutional Neural Network (CNN)* combined with an *Recurrent Neural Network (RNN)*. Our contributions can be summarized as follows: (1) we propose a hybrid CRNN, combining the

---

C.Bartz and T. Herold—Equal contribution.

[1] https://www.apple.com/ios/siri/.
[2] https://assistant.google.com/.

© Springer International Publishing AG 2017
D. Liu et al. (Eds.): ICONIP 2017, Part VI, LNCS 10639, pp. 880–889, 2017.
https://doi.org/10.1007/978-3-319-70136-3_93

descriptive powers of CNNs with the ability to capture temporal features of RNNs. (2) We perform extensive experiments with our proposed network and show its applicability to a range of scenarios and its extensibility to new languages. (3) We release our code and a large scale training set for LID systems to the community[3].

The paper is structured in the following way: In Sect. 2 we introduce related work in the field of LID systems. We showcase our system in Sect. 3 and evaluate it on extensive experiments in Sect. 4. We conclude our work in Sect. 5.

2 Related Work

Traditional language identification systems are based on identity vector systems for spoken-language processing tasks [4,11,13,19]. In the recent years systems using feature extractors solely based on neural networks, especially *Long-Short Term Memory (LSTM)* networks, became more popular [5,10,19]. These neural networks based systems are better suited to LID tasks, since they are both simpler in design and provide a higher accuracy than traditional approaches.

2.1 Identity Vector Systems

Identity vector systems (i-vectors) have been introduced by Dehak et al. [4] for the purpose of speaker verification tasks. i-vectors are a special form of joined low-dimensional representations of speaker and channel factors, as found in earlier joint factor analysis supervectors.

Identity vectors are employed as a data representation in many systems and are fed as inputs to a classifier. Dehak et al. [4] used *Support Vector Machines (SVMs)* with cosine kernels. Other researchers used logistic regression [11] or neural networks with three to four layers [7,13]. Gelly et al. [6] proposed a complex system consisting of phonotactic components [20], identity vectors, a lexical system, and *Bidirectional Long-Short Term Memory (BLSTM)* networks for language identification. The extensive feature engineering with i-vectors results in very complex systems, with an increasing number of computational steps in their pipeline.

2.2 Neural Network Approaches

Approaches solely based on applying neural networks on input features like *Mel-Frequency Cepstral Coefficients (MFCC)* show that they reach state-of-the-art results, while being less complex.

Current research on language identification systems using DNN mainly focuses on using different forms of LSTMs, working on input sequences of transformed audio data. Zazo et al. [19] use *Mel Frequency Cepstral Coefficients with Shifted Delta Coefficients (MFCC-SDC)* features as input to their unidirectional

---

[3] https://github.com/HPI-DeepLearning/crnn-lid.

LSTM, which is directly connected to a softmax classifier. The last prediction of the softmax classifier contains the predicted language. Gelly et al. [5] use a BLSTM network to capture language information from the input (audio converted to *Perceptual Linear Prediction (PLP)* coefficients and their first and second order derivatives) in forward and backward direction. The resulting sequence features are fused together and used to classify the language of the input samples. Both approaches only consider sequences of features as input to their networks.

Lozano-Diez et al. [10] perform language identification with the help of CNNs. The authors transform the input data to an image containing MFCC-SDC features. The x-axis of that image represents the time-domain and the y-axis describes the individual frequency bins. Besides plain classification of the input languages with the CNN, they also use the CNN as feature extractor for identity vectors. The authors achieve better performance when combining both the CNN features and identity vectors.

Our research differs from the mentioned works in the following way: (1) We utilize a strong convolutional feature extractor based on the VGG [17] or Inception-v3 [18] architecture. (2) We use the extracted convolutional features as input to a BLSTM and generate our predictions solely based on a deep model.

3   Proposed System

In our work, we utilize the power of CNNs to capture spatial information, and the power of RNNs to capture information through a sequence of time steps for identifying the language from a given audio snippet. We developed a DNN based on a sequence recognition network presented by Shi et al. [16]. In this section, we present the datasets we used for training the network, the audio representation used for training our models, and the structure of our proposed network in detail.

3.1   Datasets

Since there are no large-scale, freely available datasets for LID tasks (datasets such as the NIST Language Recognition Evaluation are only available behind a paywall), we resorted to creating our own datasets for our experiments. We collected our datasets from two different sources: (1) we processed speeches, press conferences and statements from the European Parliament, and (2) we sourced data from news broadcast channels hosted on YouTube. We chose to collect data for 6 different languages, while making sure that we include languages with similar phonetics. Following this idea, we collected data for two Germanic languages (English and German), two Romance languages (French and Spanish), Russian, and Mandarin Chinese.

EU Speech Repository. The EU Speech Repository[4] is a collection of video resources for interpretation students. This dataset is provided for free and consists of debates of the European Parliament, as well as press conferences, interviews, and dedicated training materials from EU interpreters. Each audio clip

---

[4] https://webgate.ec.europa.eu/sr/.

is recorded in the speaker's native language and features only one speaker. The dataset consists of many different female and male speakers. From this dataset we collected 131 h of speech data in four languages: English, German, French and Spanish.

YouTube News Collection. We chose to use news broadcasts as a second data source to obtain audio snippets of similar quality to the EU Speech Repository (different speakers, mostly one speaker at a time and a single defined language). We gathered all data from YouTube channels such as the official BBC News[5] YouTube channel.

The obtained audio data has many desired properties. The quality of the audio recordings is very high and hundreds of hours are available online. News programs often feature guests or remote correspondents resulting in a good mix of different speakers. Further, news programs feature noise one would expect from a real-world situation: music jingles, nonspeech audio from video clips and transitions between reports. All in all, we were able to gather 1508 h of audio data for this dataset.

3.2   Audio Representation

To make our gathered data compatible with our LID system, we need to do some preprocessing. As a first step, we encode all audio files in the uncompressed, lossless WAVE format, as this format allows for future manipulations without any deterioration in signal quality. In order to treat our audio snippets as images, we need to transfer the data into the image domain. We convert our audio data to spectrogram representations for training our models. The spectrograms are discretized using a Hann [2] window and 129 frequency bins along the frequency axis (y-axis). As most phonemes in the English language do not exceed 3 kHz in conversational speech, we only included frequencies of up to 5 kHz in the spectrograms. The time axis (x-axis) is rendered at 50 pixels per second. We split each audio sequence into nonoverlapping ten-second segments and discard all segments shorter than ten seconds, as we did not want to introduce padding, which might resemble unnatural pauses or silence. The resulting images are saved as grayscale, lossless 500×129 PNG files, where frequency intensities are mapped to an eight-bit grayscale range.

3.3   Architecture

For our network architecture, we followed the overall structure of the network proposed by Shi et al. [16] in their work on scene text recognition. This network architecture consists of two parts. The first part is a convolutional feature extractor that takes a spectrogam image representation of the audio file as input (see Sect. 3.2). This feature extractor convolves the input image in several steps and produces a feature map with a height of one. This feature

---

[5] https://www.youtube.com/user/bbcnews.

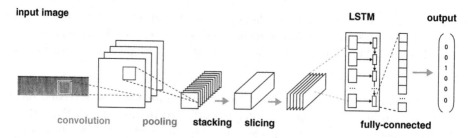

Fig. 1. Our proposed CRNN network architecture consists of two parts. A CNN extracts local visual features from our input images. The output of the final convolutional layer $t \times 1 \times c$ is sliced along the time axis into t time steps. Each time step represents the extracted frequency features, used as input to the LSTM. The final LSTM output is fed into a fully-connected layer for classification.

map is sliced along the x-axis and each slice is used as a time step for the subsequent BLSTM network. The design of the convolutional feature extractor is based on the well known VGG architecture [17]. Our network uses five convolutional layers, where each layer is followed by the ReLU activation function [12], BatchNormalization [8] and 2×2 max pooling with a stride of 2. The kernel sizes and number of filters for each convolutional layer are $(7 \times 7, 16), (5 \times 5, 32), (3 \times 3, 64), (3 \times 3, 128), (3 \times 3, 256)$, respectively. The BLSTM consists of two single LSTMs with 256 outputs units each. We concatenate both outputs to a vector of 512 dimensions and feed this into a fully-connected layer with 4/6 output units serving as the classifier. Figure 1 provides a schematic overview of the network architecture.

4   Experiments

Using our gathered dataset and the network architecture introduced in Sect. 3, we conducted several experiments, to assess the performance of our proposed network architecture on several kinds of input data. While performing our experiments we had a range of different questions in mind:

- Can we increase the classification accuracy with the help of a network, that combines a CNN with a LSTM, compared to a CNN-only approach?
- Is the network able to reliably discriminate between languages?
- Is the network robust against different forms of noise in the input data?
- Can the network easily be extended to handle other languages as well?

First, we shortly introduce our experimental environment and the metrics used. Then, we show our results on the EU Speech Repository and YouTube News dataset. Following this, we show the results of our experiments on noise robustness. We conclude this section with a discussion about the extensibility of our model to new languages.

4.1 Environment

We implemented our proposed model using Keras [3] with the Tensorflow [1] backend. We splitted the datasets into a training (70%), a validation (20%) and a testing set (10%), and all files were distributed equally between the languages. The European Speech dataset yields a total of about 19000 training images, which amounts to roughly 53 h of speech audio. The YouTube News dataset yields a total of about 194000 training images, or 540 h of speech audio. For training our networks, we used the Adam [9] optimizer and resorted to using stochastic gradient descent during fine-tuning. We observed the following metrics: accuracy, recall, precision and F1 score. We indicate the used networks in the following way: (1) CNN - A network only consisting of the proposed convolutional feature extractor without the recurrent part. (2) CRNN - The proposed hybrid CRNN model from Sect. 3.3.

4.2 EU Speech Dataset

In order to verify our idea of applying CNNs for classifying image representations of audio data, we established a baseline with the smaller EU Speech Repository dataset. Figure 2 shows the results for the two network architectures (CNN and CRNN). As can be seen, the CRNN architecture outperforms the plain network without the recurrent part significantly. This proves our assumption that combining a recurrent network with a convolutional feature extractor increases the accuracy for spoken language identification.

4.3 YouTube News

After achieving these promising results, we trained our networks on the considerably larger YouTube News dataset. We used only the same four languages

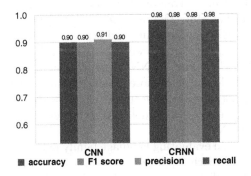

Fig. 2. Performance of the proposed network architectures on the EU Speech Repository dataset

	EN	DE	FR	ES
EN	6153	339	181	225
DE	426	6128	173	162
FR	200	145	6447	107
ES	214	170	115	6339

Fig. 3. Confusion matrix for our best performing CRNN, trained on the YouTube News dataset.

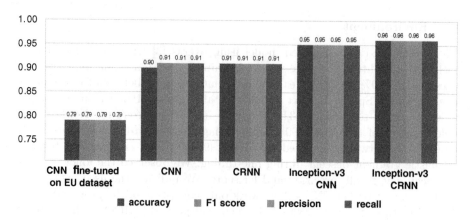

Fig. 4. Performance of the trained networks on the YouTube News dataset

that are available in both datasets in order to have comparable results between these. First, we took the pre-trained CNN from our experiments on the EU Speech Repository dataset and fine-tuned this model with the data from the YouTube dataset. However, with an accuracy of 79%, our CNN did not perform as accurately as expected. We argue that this is the case, because the EU dataset does not feature such a diverse range of situations, as the YouTube News dataset. Hence, we were unable to take advantage of the already trained convolutional features and the network did not converge on the new dataset (Fig. 4).

We trained the CNN again, this time from scratch, and were able to achieve an accuracy of 90% on this dataset. Our CRNN, using the trained CNN as feature extractor, is only able to increase the accuracy to 91%. We argue that the CNN already learns to capture some time-related information from the input images.

As a next step, we evaluate how our proposed model architecture compares to a model with a stronger convolutional feature extractor. Therefore, we trained a model using Google's Inception-v3 layout [18]. This network architecture is considerably deeper than our proposed CRNN architecture and hence should be able to extract more general features. With Inception-v3 we were able to achieve an accuracy of 95% and 96% using the CNN and CRNN, respectively. These results show that the deeper model is able to catch more general features on our large YouTube dataset. However, this increase in accuracy comes with an increase of computational cost, as the Inception-v3 model uses six times more parameters, than our initially proposed CNN.

Figure 3 shows the confusion matrix when evaluating language family pairs on our best-performing CRNN. Spanish and French separate very well with hardly any wrong classifications. German and English are more likely to be confused, but English has a slighty stronger bias towards French. All in all, the learned representations of the model are quite distinctive for each language.

Table 1. Accuracy and F1 Score measurements for our experiments on the YouTube News dataset with additional noise.

Dataset	CRNN		Inception-v3 CRNN	
	Accuracy	F1 Score	Accuracy	F1 Score
No noise	0.91	0.91	0.96	0.96
White noise	0.63	0.63	0.91	0.91
Crackling noise	0.82	0.83	0.93	0.93
Background music	0.70	0.70	0.89	0.89

4.4   Noise Robustness

In our next series of experiments, we added three different forms of noise to our test data. We evaluated our already trained models to judge their robustness to these changed conditions. First, we mixed the audio signal with randomly generated white noise, which has a strong audible presence, but still retains the identifiability of the language. Second, we added a periodic crackling noise, emulating analog telephony or a bad voice chat connection. For the last experiment, we added background music from different genres to our samples.

We performed all experiments using our initially proposed CRNN and the Inception-v3 CRNN architectures. As expected we observed a decrease in accuracy and F1 score for both models, across all experiments. The decrease in accuracy and F1 score is significantly higher for the initially proposed CRNN model, but relatively small for the Inception-v3 CRNN. We argue that this is the case because the Inception-v3 CRNN, with its deeper and more complex structure, is able to capture the frequency features in a more robust manner. Table 1 shows the results of our experiments with additional noise on the YouTube dataset.

4.5   Extensibility of the Network

In our last experiment, we evaluated how well our model is able to expand its capabilities to also include new languages, and how adding further languages affects the overall quality of the results produced by the network. We extended the existing set of four languages by two further languages spoken by millions around the globe: Mandarin Chinese and Russian. First, we fine-tuned our best performing CNN based on our proposed architecture. The resulting model served as the basis for training the CRNN as described earlier. Applied on the test set, we measure an accuracy of 92% and an F1 score of 0.92. Both measurements match our previous evaluation with four languages on the YouTube News dataset, proving that the proposed CRNN architecture can indeed easily be extended to cover more languages. Figure 5 shows individual performance measures for each language.

We note that Mandarin Chinese outperforms every other language with a top Accuracy of 96%, which is likely due to the fact that the sound of Mandarin Chinese is very distinct compared to western languages. We also find that English

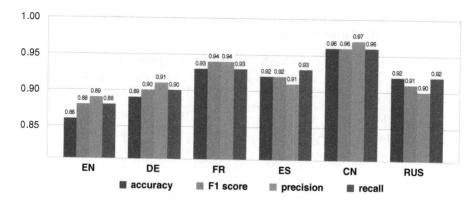

Fig. 5. Individual performance measurements for each of our six target languages. Chinese performs best, while English performs worst. Overall, the model performance is consistent with the results of earlier experiments reported in Sect. 4.3.

is now the worst performing language, which is in part due to a significant number of misclassifications as Russian samples.

In summary, we are content to find that the features learned by our model are universal in nature, as both new languages are rooted within their own language families and feature considerably different intonations. We believe that our proposed approach to language identification can be successfully applied to a wide variety of languages.

5   Conclusion

In this paper we proposed a language identification system, that solves the language identification problem in the image domain, rather than the audio domain. We proposed a hybrid CRNN that consists of a convolutional feature extractor and a RNN that combines the extracted features over time. Using this architecture, we performed several experiments on different datasets to show the wide applicability of our model to various scenarios and its extensibility to new languages. In order to compensate for the lack of freely available datasets for language identification, we gathered more than 1508 h of audio data from the EU Speech Repository and YouTube and offer them to the research community.

References

1. Abadi, M., Agarwal, A., Barham, P., Brevdo, E., et al.: Tensorflow: large-scale machine learning on heterogeneous distributed systems arXiv:1603.04467 (2016)
2. Blackman, R.B., Tukey, J.W.: The measurement of power spectra from the point of view of communications engineering-part I. Bell Labs Tech. J. **37**(1), 185–282 (1958)
3. Chollet, F.: keras: deep learning library for python. Runs on TensorFlow, Theano or CNTK (2017). https://github.com/fchollet/keras

4. Dehak, N., Kenny, P.J., Dehak, R., Dumouchel, P., Ouellet, P.: Front-end factor analysis for speaker verification. IEEE Trans. Audio Speech Lang. Process. **19**(4), 788–798 (2011)
5. Gelly, G., Gauvain, J.L., Le, V., Messaoudi, A.: A divide-and-conquer approach for language identification based on recurrent neural networks. In: INTERSPEECH 2016, pp. 3231–3235 (2016)
6. Gelly, G., Gauvain, J.L., Lamel, L., Laurent, A., Le, V.B., Messaoudi, A.: Language Recognition for Dialects and Closely Related Languages. Odyssey, Bilbao (2016)
7. Gonzalez-Dominguez, J., Lopez-Moreno, I., Moreno, P.J., Gonzalez-Rodriguez, J.: Frame-by-frame language identification in short utterances using deep neural networks. Neural Netw. **64**, 49–58 (2015)
8. Ioffe, S., Szegedy, C.: Batch normalization: accelerating deep network training by reducing internal covariate shift. In: Proceedings of the 32nd International Conference on Machine Learning, pp. 448–456 (2015)
9. Kingma, D.P., Ba, J.: Adam: a method for stochastic optimization. In: Proceedings of the 3rd International Conference on Learning Representations, San Diego (2015)
10. Lozano-Dez, A., Zazo Candil, R., Gonzlez Domnguez, J., Toledano, D.T., Gonzlez-Rodrguez, J.: An end-to-end approach to language identification in short utterances using convolutional neural networks. International Speech and Communication Association (2015)
11. Martnez, D., Plchot, O., Burget, L., Glembek, O., Matjka, P.: Language recognition in ivectors space. In: Twelfth Annual Conference of the International Speech Communication Association (2011)
12. Nair, V., Hinton, G.E.: Rectified linear units improve restricted Boltzmann machines. In: Proceedings of the 27th International Conference on Machine Learning (ICML 2010), pp. 807–814 (2010)
13. Plchot, O., Matejka, P., Glembek, O., Fer, R., Novotny, O., Pesan, J., Burget, L., Brummer, N., Cumani, S.: Bat system description for NIST LRE 2015. Odyssey 2016, pp. 166–173 (2016)
14. Redmon, J., Divvala, S., Girshick, R., Farhadi, A.: You only look once: unified, real-time object detection. In: Proceedings of the IEEE Conference on Computer Vision and Pattern Recognition, pp. 779–788 (2016)
15. Ren, S., He, K., Girshick, R., Sun, J.: Faster R-CNN: towards real-time object detection with region proposal networks. In: Cortes, C., Lawrence, N.D., Lee, D.D., Sugiyama, M., Garnett, R. (eds.) Advances in Neural Information Processing Systems 28, pp. 91–99. Curran Associates Inc., New York (2015)
16. Shi, B., Bai, X., Yao, C.: An end-to-end trainable neural network for image-based sequence recognition and its application to scene text recognition. IEEE Trans. Pattern Anal. Mach. Intell. **39**, 2298–2304 (2016)
17. Simonyan, K., Zisserman, A.: Very deep convolutional networks for large-scale image recognition. In: International Conference on Learning Representations (2015)
18. Szegedy, C., Vanhoucke, V., Ioffe, S., Shlens, J., Wojna, Z.: Rethinking the inception architecture for computer vision, pp. 2818–2826 (2016)
19. Zazo, R., Lozano-Diez, A., Gonzalez-Dominguez, J., Toledano, D.T., Gonzalez-Rodriguez, J.: Language identification in short utterances using long short-term memory (LSTM) recurrent neural networks. PLoS ONE **11**(1), e0146917 (2016)
20. Zissman, M.A., et al.: Comparison of four approaches to automatic language identification of telephone speech. IEEE Trans. Speech Audio Process. **4**(1), 31 (1996)

Underdetermined Mixture Matrix Estimation Based on Neural Network and Genetic Algorithm

Shuang Wei[1,2(✉)], Jian Peng[2], Feng Wang[2], Chungui Tao[2], and Defu Jiang[2]

[1] College of Information, Mechanical and Electrical Engineering,
Shanghai Normal University, Shanghai, China
wishuang@gmail.com
[2] Array and Information Processing Laboratory, College of Computer and Information,
Hohai University, Nanjing, China

Abstract. This paper proposes an improved approach to estimate the underdetermined mixture matrix to improve the performance of underdetermined blind source separation (UBSS) for speech sources. This approach only use two observed signals and consider a tangent value instead of each vector of the mixture matrix for estimation. An improved clustering method based on competitive neural network and genetic algorithm is then designed to estimate these tangent values. In the proposed method, those tangent values are designed as clustering centers. The competitive neural network is used first to obtain the initial clustering centers, and genetic algorithm is applied to search for the global optimum around the initial clustering centers. Experimental results show that the tangent values of the observed vectors have better clustering characteristics, which could reduce the computational complexity for mixture matrix estimation. The improved clustering algorithm based on neural network and genetic algorithm can estimate a better mixture matrix with high precision than the general neural network clustering algorithm, and it can improve the performance of underdetermined blind signal separation.

Keywords: Underdetermined blind source separation · Tangent value · Competitive neural network · Genetic algorithm

1 Introduction

Underdetermined blind source separation (UBSS) technology is widely concerned as an effective speech signals processing tool [1–3]. It can help to recovery the unknown source signals from the observed speech signal that is the mixture of the sound sources, in the case that the number of observed signals is much less than that of sources.

Generally, sparse component analysis (SCA) approach is used to solve the UBSS problem after transforming the unknown parameters into a sparse domain [4]. In the SCA approach, the underdetermined mixture matrix has to be estimated before recovering the unknown sources. Thus, the result of mixture matrix estimation plays an important effect on the performance of SCA approach. The task of this paper is to design

D. Liu et al. (Eds.): ICONIP 2017, Part VI, LNCS 10639, pp. 890–898, 2017.
https://doi.org/10.1007/978-3-319-70136-3_94

an improved algorithm for mixture matrix estimation with higher precision which benefits to improve the recovery of the speech signals.

To solve the underdetermined mixture matrix estimation problem, K-means clustering approach is a popular idea to solve the vectors of the mixture matrix as the clustering centers [5]. However, traditional K-means clustering methods perform poor for the exception data, and the convergence efficiency is still required to be improved. In order to improve the clustering performance, the optimization method is generally used to solve the K-means clustering problem. Thus, this paper proposes a clustering approach with the combination of neural network and genetic algorithm. In the proposed approach, neural network algorithm is used to generate the initial population for genetic algorithm, and genetic algorithm is designed to obtain the global optimum for clustering. Thus, the proposed approach can improve the global search ability and avoid falling into the local optimal.

In this paper, the UBSS problem model and the preprocessing of the observed signal are given in the Sect. 2. Section 3 introduces the proposed clustering algorithm, which is combined with the neural network algorithm [6] and genetic algorithm [7]. Simulation results of four speech source signals and two observed signals are presented in Sect. 4. Finally, conclusions and future work are summarized in Sect. 5.

2 Problem Statement

2.1 Model

Assume an underdetermined blind source separation model is given as

$$\mathbf{X}(t) = \mathbf{A}\mathbf{S}(t) \quad t = 1, 2, \cdots, T \tag{1}$$

where $\mathbf{X}(t) = \left[x_1(t), x_2(t), \cdots, x_m(t)\right]^T$ denotes the observed signals, $\mathbf{A}$ is the mixture matrix with the size of $m \times n$, and $\mathbf{S}(t) = \left[s_1(t), s_2(t), \cdots, s_n(t)\right]^T$ denotes the source signals. In the underdetermined system, the number of the source signals is larger than that of the observed signals, i.e., $n > m$. Among them, only $\mathbf{X}(t)$ is known, $\mathbf{A}$ and $\mathbf{S}(t)$ are unknown without any prior information. Our task is to estimate the mixture matrix $\mathbf{A}$ from the observed signals $\mathbf{X}(t)$.

When the sparsity of speech signals are poor in the time domain, the speech source signals should be transformed into a sparse domain as (2).

$$\wp\{\mathbf{X}(t)\} = \mathbf{A}\wp\{\mathbf{S}(t)\} \tag{2}$$

where $\wp\{\bullet\}$ denotes a method to transform the signals in the time-domain to a sparse domain, such as, Discrete Cosine Transform (DCT), Short Time Fourier Transform (STFT), etc. [8]. It depends on the characteristic of source signals $\mathbf{S}(t)$. For example, when voice signals are chosen as the sources, which are mostly unsteady in a long time but have stability in the short time, $\wp\{\bullet\}$ can be the STFT algorithm.

2.2 Preprocessing of Speech Signals

In the signal pre-processing, after signal transformation to the sparse domain, two sides of (1) are simultaneously transferred as (3).

$$\mathbf{X}(\omega) = \mathbf{A}\mathbf{S}(\omega) \tag{3}$$

where $\mathbf{X}(\omega) = \left[x_1(\omega), x_2(\omega), \cdots, x_m(\omega)\right]^T$ is the spectrum of the observed signals, and $\mathbf{S}(\omega) = \left[s_1(\omega), s_2(\omega), \cdots, s_n(\omega)\right]^T$ is the spectrum of the source signals. If only one item from the source $s_1(\omega)$ has a non-zero value and the items from other sources are zero at a slot ω, (3) can be abbreviated as:

$$\left[x_1(\omega) \ x_2(\omega) \ \cdots \ x_m(\omega)\right]^T = a_i \times s_i(\omega) \tag{4}$$

Then, we can get the model (5).

$$s_i(\omega) = \frac{x_1(\omega)}{a_{1i}} = \frac{x_2(\omega)}{a_{2i}} = \cdots = \frac{x_m(\omega)}{a_{mi}} \tag{5}$$

Obviously, when the source vector is sparse, the observed signal has the characteristics of linear clustering, and each clustering corresponds to each column of the mixture matrix. Based on this, n source signals will determine n straight lines, so that mixture matrix estimation problem is transformed into estimating the direction of the clustering line in the observation space. However, the observed points in (4) are distributed in the vicinity of the straight line of clustering, therefore a clustering algorithm has to be proposed to mining the underline clustering characteristics on these points.

In order to reduce the interference among data, absolution values of the observed signals are used instead of real or imaginary part. In addition, mirror processing is applied to improve the processing efficiency. Considering that the points near the origin have no obvious linear clustering characteristics, a specific radius can be selected according to the specific data, and data points inside the circle are filtered out. The selected data is then shown in Fig. 1.

The points in Fig. 1 shows the two-dimensional observation signals after short-time Fourier transform. It is found that the points in the same cluster have almost the same linear slope, and this conclusion is also proved by (5). Thus, the tangent value of every point is a good index for distinguishing the clusters. The closer the tangent values of two points are, the high possibility they belong to the same cluster. According to (5), it is known that the tangent value of all points in each cluster is the same as the tangent value of each column in the mixture matrix. Therefore, the problem of solving mixture matrix is converted to a clustering analysis of two-dimensional observation signals. In the clustering analysis, the one-dimensional tangent values are designed as the clustering centers instead of two-dimensional signals. It could simplify the calculation load. The tangent distribution is shown in Fig. 2.

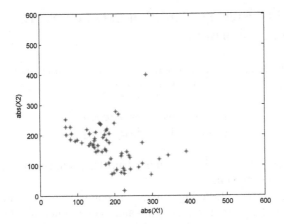

Fig. 1. Scatter distribution after filtrating

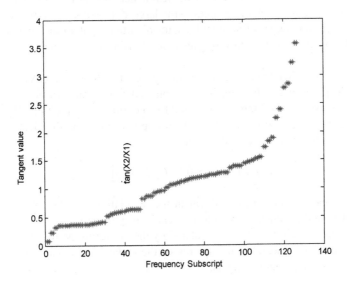

Fig. 2. Distribution of tangent value

From Fig. 2, it is seen that several values change slowly, it means that these values are concentrated in the vicinity of a classification value, which shows the clustering characteristic. Therefore, for two observed signals, it's feasible to use the tangent values of each column of mixture matrix corresponding to the two observed vectors as the input data of the cluster analysis.

At last, in order to reduce the clustering error, it is necessary to perform normalization to project the tangent values to the interval of $[-1,1]$.

3   Improved Clustering Algorithm Based on Neural Network and Genetic Algorithm

The number of the clustering centers is the same as the column values of mixture matrix. Assume n = 4, then the unknown mixture matrix can be calculated by:

$$\hat{A} = \begin{bmatrix} \cos \hat{\alpha}_1 & \cos \hat{\alpha}_2 & \cos \hat{\alpha}_3 & \cos \hat{\alpha}_4 \\ \sin \hat{\alpha}_1 & \sin \hat{\alpha}_2 & \sin \hat{\alpha}_3 & \sin \hat{\alpha}_4 \end{bmatrix} \tag{6}$$

where $\hat{\alpha}_i = \arctan C_i$, $i = 1, 2, 3, 4$. The input data of the neural network clustering algorithm are all the tangent values.

In order to solve four clustering centers, the output layer of neural network is set with four neurons. The normalized tangent value is one-dimensional input data, so the input layer of the neural network is set with one neuron.

The number of training iterations of neural network is initialized to ensure the applicability of clustering of samples with large data volumes. After finishing the training of neural network of all iterations, the distribution of all the tangent values are learned. Then we can do the clustering analysis with the normalized tangent values after training.

In order to improve the clustering accuracy, genetic algorithm (GA) is then used to optimize the preliminary clustering results obtained by the competitive neural networks above. The clustering problem is converted to an optimization problem [9].

We use the coding approach of the floating point to present the clustering centers. The genetic individuals are coded as below.

$$pop(k).gene = \begin{bmatrix} C_1 & C_2 & C_3 & C_4 \end{bmatrix} \tag{7}$$

Where $pop(k)$ is the k-th individual in the population and the four floating-point numbers denote the values of four cluster centers respectively.

The optimization objective is calculated by the clustering performance, which can be evaluated by the mean of the squares of the distance of clustering points to the respective clustering centers, that is,

$$pop(k).value = \sum_{i=1}^{4} (\sum_{j=1}^{S_i} (x_{ij} - C_i)^2)/S_i \tag{8}$$

Where x_{ij} is marked as the j-th data in class i, C_i is a cluster center of class i, S_i is the total number of data points in class i. Then the individuals are sorted in ascending order, and the number of each individual is represented as $pop(k)$.index. The *fitness* is calculated as:

$$pop(k).fitness = a(1 - a)^{pop(k).index-1} \tag{9}$$

where parameter a is commonly set as $a = 0.6$.

In the selection step, a selection array *cFitness[popSize]* is built based on the calculated fitness value *pop(k).fitness* of the individual. The formula is as follows:

$$cFitness[k] = \frac{\sum_{u=1}^{k} pop(u).fitness}{S} \qquad (10)$$

where $S = \sum_{k=1}^{popSize} pop(k).fitness$. Then a random number *randn* is generated on interval (0,1), and the *k*-th individual is copied into the population in the next generation if *rand < cFitness(k)*.

In the crossover step, the clustering centers of two individuals are sorted in ascending before crossover. The calculation of the new individual is as follows:

$$pop(k_{new}).gene = a_1 \times pop(k_1).gene + a_2 \times pop(k_2).gene \qquad (11)$$

where parameters a_1 and a_2 are 0.6 and 0.4, respectively.

When a mutation is made, a random number is generated on the interval (0,1) for each gene of all individuals in the population. When the random number is less than the mutation probability, −10% to 10% of its own floating value is added randomly.

The flow chart of the above proposed algorithm based on neural network and genetic algorithm is shown in Fig. 3. After that, mixture matrix is calculated by (6) using the tangent values that are the optimum result of the clustering center.

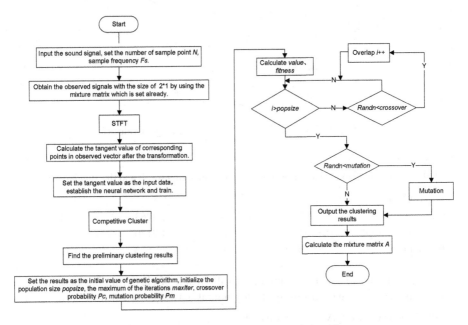

Fig. 3. The flow chart of the proposed algorithm

4   Simulation Results

The experiments of four voice signals are carried out in Matlab 2010b. The speech examples are available on-line in [10]. The signal format is .wav, the coding method is PCM and the sampling point is selected as 65365. The mixture matrix is defined which mix the four source signals into two observation signals as follows:

$$\mathbf{A} = \begin{bmatrix} a_1 & a_2 & a_3 & a_4 \end{bmatrix} = \begin{bmatrix} \cos 18° & \cos 36° & \cos 54° & \cos 72° \\ \sin 18° & \sin 36° & \sin 54° & \sin 72° \end{bmatrix} \tag{12}$$

Figure 4 shows the classification result of the tangent values by neural network clustering, where the number of iterations is set to 400, the adjustment step length of weight is initialized to 0.2. It is seen that four classes are clearly separated. In order to illustrate the performance, the clustering center obtained by neural network (NN) is compared with the standard setting shown in Table 1.

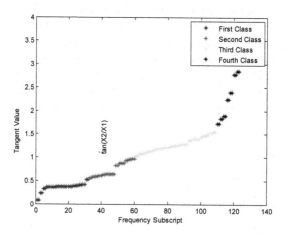

Fig. 4. The classification result of the tangent values

Table 1. Comparison between Neural Network clustering result and the standard setting

Clustering center	C1	C2	C3	C4
Standard setting	0.3249	0.7266	1.3763	3.0780
NN clustering result	0.3538	0.7774	1.2170	2.1417
Error ratio	8.91%	6.99%	11.57%	30.42%

According to Table 1, it is founded that the result of clustering has certain errors compared with the standard setting if only neural network is used for clustering. The result of the estimation $\hat{\mathbf{A}}_{NN}$ is obtained as

$$\hat{A}_{NN} = \begin{bmatrix} 0.9427 & 0.7895 & 0.6349 & 0.4231 \\ 0.3335 & 0.6138 & 0.7726 & 0.9061 \end{bmatrix} \tag{13}$$

In the general neural network, the optimal strategy uses gradient descent method, which tends to let the solution fall into the local optimum. So, in the proposed method, genetic algorithm and neural network are combined to reduce the probability of falling into the local optimum. Considering that the clustering solution of neural network is stable and convergent, it can be considered that the error range of the result is valid. Thus, it proved that the clustering results of the neural network can be used as the initial solution, genetic algorithm (GA) is then used to search for the better optimum near the results obtained by neural network algorithm. In addition, GA can simultaneously optimize multiple interval regions near the local optimum, which can improve the convergence efficiency. Therefore, the proposed method can obtain better solutions with less error ratio than those of the single neural network method. The results of the proposed method are shown in Table 2.

Table 2. Comparison between Neural-Genetic clustering result and the standard setting

Clustering center	C1	C2	C3	C4
Standard setting	0.3249	0.7266	1.3763	3.0780
NN-GA clustering result	0.3427	0.7340	1.2743	2.4994
Error ratio	5.46%	1.02%	7.41%	18.81%

In contrast to Tables 1 and 2, it is found that the error ratio of C1, C2, C3, and C4 are improved by the proposed algorithm. The estimation result by the proposed algorithm based on neural network and genetic algorithm is obtained as

$$\hat{A}_{NN\text{-}GA} = \begin{bmatrix} 0.9460 & 0.8061 & 0.6173 & 0.3715 \\ 0.3242 & 0.5917 & 0.7867 & 0.9284 \end{bmatrix} \tag{14}$$

5 Conclusion

This article mainly researches on an improved algorithm of mixture matrix estimation to solve the problem of underdetermined blind speech separation. In the preprocessing section, the two-dimensional observation is converted into one-dimensional tangent value, it is found to have clustering characteristics from the figure of scatter points. The clustering analysis is carried out by the neural network algorithm to obtain the initial clustering center. Then genetic algorithm is used to optimize the result of neural network algorithm, which improves the stability and convergence of clustering. Experimental results of four speech signals prove that the proposed algorithm can achieve the mixture matrix with better accuracy than neural network, and adoption of the tangent value is useful in the process of clustering analysis. In the future, we will improve the proposed algorithm in different cases, such as, it could be applied to separate the power signals to improve the power quality.

Acknowledgments. This work was supported by the National Natural Science Foundation of China (Grant No. 61401145), the Natural Science Foundation of Jiangsu Province (Grant No. BK20140858, BK20151501), and the Priority Academic Program Development of Jiangsu Higher Education Institutions (PAPD).

References

1. Bel, A.J., Sejnowski, T.J.: An information-maximization approach to blind separation and blind deconvolution. Neural Comput. **7**(6), 1129–1159 (1995)
2. Zou, L., Chen, X., Ji, X., Wang, Z.J.: Underdetermined joint blind source separation of multiple datasets. IEEE Access **5**, 7474–7487 (2017)
3. Zhen, L., Peng, D., Yi, Z., Xiang, Y., Chen, P.: Underdetermined blind source separation using sparse coding. IEEE Trans. Neural Netw. Learn. Syst. **PP**(99), 1–7 (2015)
4. Li, Y., Cichocki, A., Amari, S.I.: Sparse component analysis for blind source separation with less sensors than sources. In: Independent Component Analysis (2010)
5. Huang, X., Ye, Y., Zhang, H.: Extensions of Kmeans-type algorithms: a new clustering framework by integrating intracluster compactness and intercluster separation. IEEE Trans. Neural Netw. Learn. Syst. **25**(8), 1433–1446 (2014)
6. Cichock, A., Kasprzak, W., Amari, S.I.: Neural network approach to blind separation and enhancement of images. In: 1996 8th European Signal Processing Conference (EUSIPCO 1996), Trieste, Italy, pp. 1–4 (1996)
7. Pradhan, D., Wang, S., Ali, S., Yue, T., Liaaen, M.: CBGA-ES: a cluster-based genetic algorithm with elitist selection for supporting multi-objective test optimization. In: 2017 IEEE International Conference on Software Testing, Verification and Validation (ICST), Tokyo, Japan, pp. 367–378 (2017)
8. Aissa-El-Bey, A., Linh-Trung, N., Abed-Meraim, K., Belouchrani, A., Grenier, Y.: Underdetermined blind separation of nondisjoint sources in the time-frequency domain. IEEE Trans. Signal Process. **55**(3), 897–907 (2007)
9. Zhang, M., Li, X., Peng, J.: Blind source separation using joint canonical decomposition of two higher order tensors. In: 2017 51st Annual Conference on Information Sciences and Systems (CISS), Baltimore, MD, pp. 1–6 (2017)
10. Bofill, P., Zibulevsky, M.: Sound examples. http://www.ac.upc.es/homes/pau/

Bio-inspired Multi-layer Spiking Neural Network Extracts Discriminative Features from Speech Signals

Amirhossein Tavanaei[✉] and Anthony Maida

The Center for Advanced Computer Studies, Bio-inspired AI Lab,
University of Louisiana at Lafayette, Lafayette, LA 70503, USA
{tavanaei,maida}@louisiana.edu

Abstract. Spiking neural networks (SNNs) enable power-efficient implementations due to their sparse, spike-based coding scheme. This paper develops a bio-inspired SNN that uses unsupervised learning to extract discriminative features from speech signals, which can subsequently be used in a classifier. The architecture consists of a spiking convolutional/pooling layer followed by a fully connected spiking layer for feature discovery. The convolutional layer of leaky, integrate-and-fire (LIF) neurons represents primary acoustic features. The fully connected layer is equipped with a probabilistic spike-timing-dependent plasticity learning rule. This layer represents the discriminative features through probabilistic, LIF neurons. To assess the discriminative power of the learned features, they are used in a hidden Markov model (HMM) for spoken digit recognition. The experimental results show performance above 96% that compares favorably with popular statistical feature extraction methods. Our results provide a novel demonstration of unsupervised feature acquisition in an SNN.

Keywords: Bio-inspired multi-layer framework · Spiking network · Speech recognition · Unsupervised feature extraction

1 Introduction

Multi-layer neural network (NN) learning extracts signal features by using a hierarchy of non-linear elements [1]. Such networks extract increasingly complex, discriminative, and independent features and serve as the basis for deep learning architectures [2,3]. The power of a multi-layer neural architecture can be used for a challenging problem like automatic speech recognition (ASR). Speech signal characteristics are highly variable in time and frequency. The feature extraction method must convert the speech signal to discriminative features to support the recognition task. Recently, multi-layer neural architectures have outperformed previous ASR models. Examples are convolutional neural networks (CNNs) [4], deep CNNs [5], deep NNs [6], and deep recurrent NNs [7]. Despite the high performance of these architectures, training and then using them is expensive from

© Springer International Publishing AG 2017
D. Liu et al. (Eds.): ICONIP 2017, Part VI, LNCS 10639, pp. 899–908, 2017.
https://doi.org/10.1007/978-3-319-70136-3_95

a power consumption viewpoint. The quest to meet a power-efficient framework can be accomplished by a spike-based neuromorphic platform. Spiking neural networks (SNNs) [8–10] provide an appropriate starting point for this. After introducing the power of SNNs as a third generation neural network [8], a number of studies have concentrated on biologically motivated approaches for pattern recognition [11–13]. An SNN architecture consists of spiking neurons and interconnecting synapses undergoing spatio-temporally local learning in response to the stimulus presentation.

Word recognition functionality in the auditory ventral stream of the human brain is enabled by a multi-layer, biological SNN. Multi-layer SNNs have performed comparably with conventional NNs in visual pattern recognition tasks [14–16]. Also, SNNs have been employed for the spoken word recognition tasks such as using synaptic weight association training [17], extracting spike signatures from speech signals [18], and Gaussian mixture model (GMM) implementation using SNNs [19]. Representing speech signal features through temporal spike trains has attracted much interest. Verstraeten et al. developed a high performance reservoir-based SNN for spoken digit recognition problem [20]. The reservoir is not trained and it maps the inputs to a higher dimensional space to be linearly separable. Dibazar et al. proposed a feature extraction method using a dynamic synaptic neural network for isolated word recognition [21]. In another study, Loiselle et al. utilized the cochlear Gammatone filter bank to generate spike trains in French spoken word recognition based on rank-order coding with an SNN [22]. However, these studies did not develop a multi-layer SNN to extract discriminative speech characteristics in a hierarchy of feature discovery neural layers.

This paper develops a multi-layer spiking neural network consisting of a convolutional layer, a pooling layer, and an unsupervised feature-discovery layer. The convolutional layer extracts primary acoustic features through the spike trains emitted from the feature map neurons. The pooling layer reduces size of the feature maps by a novel max-pooling operation based on Mel-scaled patch sizes. The feature discovery layer receives presynaptic spikes from the pooling layer and undergoes learning via a probabilistic spike-timing-dependent plasticity (STDP) rule. Neurons in this layer represent the final features extracted from a speech signal. During the training phase, weights connecting the pooling layer and the feature discovery layer are adjusted based on the speech signal characteristics. The features extracted by the SNN are used for training and evaluating a hidden Markov model (HMM) [23] to handle temporal behavior of the speech signal. The proposed network offers a novel way to discover discriminative features for spoken digits while implementing a bio-inspired model, potentially enabling low-power consumption on appropriate hardware [24].

2   Network Architecture

Our multi-layer SNN, shown in Fig. 1a, consists of two spiking neural layers which follow an input layer. The input layer's stimulus is the magnitude Fourier

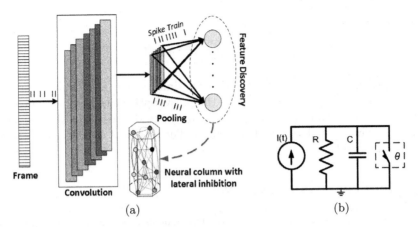

Fig. 1. (a): Multi-layer SNN architecture. Each rectangle shows a frame's feature vector in each layer. The convolutional layer produces seven 1-D feature maps of spiking neurons. (b): RC circuit implementing the LIF neuron with $R = 1\,\Omega$, $C = 1\,\text{mF}$, and threshold, $\theta = \theta^{\text{conv}}$.

transform of a speech frame (M values). This layer converts the stimuli to spike trains using a Poisson process over $T = 40\,\text{ms}$. The convolutional layer maps the presynaptic spike trains to a higher dimensional feature space using convolutional filters. The pooling layer reduces the feature map dimension, according to Mel-scaled frequencies, and then transfers the new spike trains to the fully connected feature discovery layer for unsupervised training. After training, the neuronal activities in the feature discovery layer represent the frame's feature vector that may be input to a classifier (e.g., an HMM classifier).

3   Spiking Convolutional Layer

The convolutional layer receives presynaptic spike trains from the input layer and generates D independent feature maps. Each feature map contributes to a convolutional filter acquired by shifted p-point difference-of-Gaussian (DoG) ($p = 7$ in this network) filters. Therefore, seven shifted DoG filters are convolved with the presynaptic spike trains to generate $D = 7$ feature maps. An LIF neuron in a feature map integrates the convolution results for a particular signal patch ($p = 7$ points) over $T = 40$ time steps and fires a spike when reaching threshold. The neuron's membrane potential, $U(t)$, is reset to the resting potential (zero) upon firing. Equation 1 calculates the membrane potential of neuron m in feature map k at time t.

$$\frac{dU_m^k(t)}{dt} + U_m^k(t) = I_m^k(t) \tag{1a}$$

$$\text{if } U_m^k(t) \geq \theta^{\text{conv}}, \text{then } U_m^k(t) = 0 \tag{1b}$$

I_m^k is computed by

$$I_m^k(t) = \sum_{i=1}^{p} W_i^k \cdot s_{m,i}(t) \tag{2}$$

The threshold, θ^{conv}, is set to 0.4 in the experiments. The $I_m^k(t)$ value determines the convolution of the filter, W^k, and the presynaptic spike train, s_m, in $T = 40$ time steps. This value is considered as an injected current in the RC circuit (Fig. 1b), which simulates the LIF neuron. The length of a feature map is same as the input vector.

4   Mel-Scaled Pooling Layer

The human hearing mechanism resolves frequencies non-linearly with higher resolution at lower frequencies. The Mel scale makes the features close to the hearing model. In the pooling layer, the stride value (pooling window size) is computed based on the Mel-scaled bandwidths. Equation 3 converts the frequency scale to the Mel scale. Same stride value $l = 2$ is used for the frequencies in the range 0 to 1000 Hz. Then, the stride values increase corresponding to the feature frequency. The number of pooling windows (N) is analogous to the number of Mel-spaced filter banks (20–40) selected for computing the Mel-scaled frequency cepstral coefficients (MFCCs). The pooling layer selects a neuron with the highest activity in a pooling window (max pooling). Activities of the neurons in a feature map can be characterized by their spike rate. This layer summarizes and extracts effective signal characteristics.

$$f_{mel} = 1125 \ln \left(1 + \frac{f}{700}\right) \tag{3}$$

The new pooling strategy and the Mel-scaled bandwidths can also be employed by conventional CNNs for extracting acoustic features.

5   Feature Discovery Layer

The feature discovery layer, containing H neurons and equipped with lateral inhibition, is fully connected to the pooling layer. It learns and extracts the signal features based on the provided Mel-scaled pooling features. This layer conveys $D \times N$ spike trains emitted from the pooling layer to H probabilistic LIF neurons. The feature discovery layer is shown in the last layer of Fig. 1a.

5.1   Neuron Model

The stochastic LIF neurons in the feature discovery layer fire based on both their membrane potential and their firing posterior probability (imposed by a softmax function). A neuron fires if its membrane potential reaches the threshold, θ^h, (following Eq. 1) and its posterior probability is greater than 0.5. In the experiments, θ^h is set to 3. The posterior probability of neuron h firing at time t given input spike vector $\mathbf{y}_t$ and weights W is given by Eq. 4. The posterior probability determines a softmax function in which the mutual exclusivity is not enforced. This neuron model implements a winners-take-all competition (inhibition) in the feature discovery layer. Although there are no direct inhibitory connections between neurons, the softmax function imposes an overall inhibition upon the neural column extracting independent features. The neural column shown in Fig. 1a illustrates that because of the lateral inhibitions, only a small subset of the neurons can fire at the same time. The inhibition constrains the model to extract independent features in response to the input.

$$P(z_h = 1 | W, \mathbf{y}_t) = \frac{e^{W_h^T \cdot \mathbf{y}_t}}{\sum_{j=1}^{H} e^{W_j^T \cdot \mathbf{y}_t}} \tag{4}$$

5.2 Learning

Spike-timing-dependent plasticity (STDP) is a learning rule used in SNNs that increases the weight of a synapse if the presynaptic spike occurs briefly before the postsynaptic spike (LTP) and decreases the synaptic weight otherwise (LTD) [25]. We use a probabilistic version of the STDP rule provided by Tavanaei et al. [26] (Eq. 5) to learn the final acoustic features.

$$\Delta w_{hi} = \begin{cases} a^+ e^{-w_{hi}}, & \text{if } i \text{ fires in } [t - \epsilon, t] \\ -a^-, & \text{otherwise.} \end{cases} \tag{5}$$

In the above, $a^+ = 10^{-3}$ and $a^- = 0.75 \times 10^{-3}$ are, respectively, LTP and LTD learning rates. When a postsynaptic neuron h fires, STDP is triggered for the incoming weights. LTP occurs if the presynaptic neuron i fires briefly (e.g. within $\epsilon = 5$ ms) before h fires, while the weight change magnitude is controlled by the current weight. Weights remain in the range $(0, 1)$. The probability derivations and justifications are given in [26]. Weights are initialized by sampling uniformly in the range $(0, 1)$.

5.3 Final Feature Representation

A speech frame is built from H neurons in the feature discovery layer. The elements of the vector are the neurons' activities in response to received spike trains via trained weights, W. More specifically, the accumulated membrane potentials of the neurons are used for the feature values. Samples with H attributes obtained by the feature discovery layer are then used to train the HMM classifier.

6 Experiments and Results

This investigation uses the proposed SNN to discover and extract discriminative features from the spoken digits 0 to 9 selected in the Aurora dataset [27] that is recorded at the sampling rate of 8000 Hz. Each speech signal (spoken digit) is divided into 25 ms frames with 50% temporal overlap, resulting in about 60 frames per digit. The frames are converted to the frequency domain by using the magnitude of the Fourier transform. Each frame is represented by 100 sample values (0 to 4000 Hz).

DoG convolutional filters are obtained by the difference of two Gaussian functions with variances $\sigma^2 = 1$ and $\sigma^2 = 6$ (Eq. 6). Seven filters produce $D = 7$ feature maps containing 100 spiking neurons. Each map is converted to a pooled map by the max-operation over the Mel-scaled pooling windows. The pooling windows are shown in Fig. 2a with the stride values 2 through 10. In the experiments, we use 28 values to represent each speech frame. The stride values for the sample points 1 to 26 (0 to 1040 Hz) are set to 2 (13 feature values). The last stride value is 10. Figure 2b shows neural spike rates of three selected pooled maps extracted from the spoken digit 'one'. The pooled layer conveys the speech frame characteristics with only $7 \times 28 = 196$ values.

$$\text{DoG} = \mathcal{N}(x, \mu = 0, \sigma^2 = 1) - \mathcal{N}(x, \mu = 0, \sigma^2 = 6),$$
$$x = \{-3, -2, ..., 3\} \tag{6}$$

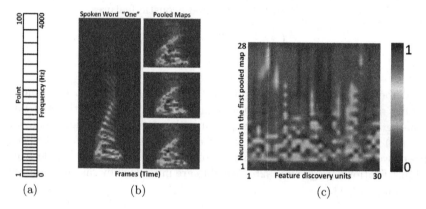

Fig. 2. (a): Mel-scaled stride values spanning 0–4000 Hz. (b): Neural spike rates of three selected pooled maps extracted from the spoken digit 'one'. Neurons emit zero (dark blue) to 39 (dark red) spikes. (c): Synaptic weights of the feature discovery layer connecting the neurons in a pooled map to 30 LIF neurons. (Color figure online)

The feature discovery layer extracts the final feature vectors for the speech frames using its trained synaptic weights. Training the network involved cycling through a dataset of 1000 spoken digits for 10 iterations. Figure 2c shows an example synaptic weight set connecting a pooled map and the feature discovery neurons. Most neurons show higher resolution at lower frequencies. The feature vectors extracted from the temporal frames are used to train and evaluate the HMM. In the first experiment, $H = 30$ feature discovery neurons (as feature vector dimension) were used to train 12 HMMs with $\{5, 10, 15\}$ states and

$\{4, 8, 16, 32\}$ GMMs embedded in each state. The testing set was sampled from the spoken digits that were not used for the training. Table 1 shows the accuracy rates reported for the spoken digit recognition task. Performances higher than 95% were achieved by the HMMs with 10 and 15 states and 32 GMMs. These accuracy rates show that the SNN, which uses unsupervised learning, has extracted discriminative features from the speech signals.

Table 1. Accuracy rates of the HMMs trained and evaluated by the features extracted by the multi-layer SNN. S: number of states. G: number of GMMs.

HMM variations	$G = 4$	$G = 8$	$G = 16$	$G = 32$
$S = 5$	62.88	75.59	85.95	90.97
$S = 10$	71.91	87.63	92.31	**95.32**
$S = 15$	84.95	91.30	**95.32**	**96.32**

The next experiment evaluates: (1) the number of extracted features, H, (number of neurons in the feature discovery layer); and, (2) applying Δ (differential, **D**) and $\Delta\Delta$ (acceleration, **A**) features to use more dynamic information. The HMM with ten states and 32 GMMs is selected for this experiment. Figure 3 shows that the model with $H = 30$ probabilistic neurons in the feature discovery layer outperforms the other architectures. Additionally, the Δ features improved the accuracy rate. However, the $\Delta\Delta$ features did not improve performance in the networks with more than $H = 20$ output neurons. This could happen because the HMM might be overtrained by the high dimensional feature vectors.

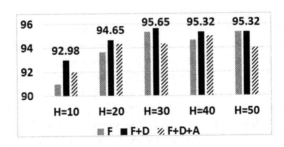

Fig. 3. Performance of the networks with 10 through 50 spiking neurons in the feature discovery layer for different sets of features. Δ (D) and $\Delta\Delta$ (A) features are concatenated to the extracted features (F).

Our SNN extracted discriminative features that were classified at 96% accuracy. This accuracy rate is comparable with [17] (95.25% accuracy) that uses synaptic weight association training in a neural layer. Although the reservoir approach [20] has performed better (near perfect) on spoken digit recognition,

Table 2. Spoken digit recognition models using SNNs (Top) and non-SNN (Bottom) architectures evaluated on the Aurora [27], TIDigits [28], and TI46 [29] spoken digit datasets. Aurora is based on a version of the TIDigits dataset, but downsampled at 8 kHz, and is roughly comparable to the TI46 dataset.

Model	Method	Dataset	Acc. (%)
Wade et al. [17]	Synaptic weight association (SNN)	TI46	95.25
Tavanaei et al. [18]	Single layer SNN and SVM classifier	Aurora	91
Verstraeten et al. [20]	Reservoir computing (LSM)	TI46	>97.5
Our Model	Spiking CNN and HMM classifier	Aurora	96
Dao et al. [30]	Structured sparse representation	Aurora	95
Van Doremalen et al. [31]	Hierarchical Temporal Memory	TIDigits	91.6
Neil et al. [32]	MFCC and Deep RNN	TIDigits	96.1
Groenland et al. [33]	CNN and deep shifting methods	TI46	>99

the question of training a reservoir to scale to larger problems remains unresolved. Additionally, our multi-layer SNN provides an environment to support a deep learning architecture in a spiking platform that compares with conventional deep networks. Table 2 shows the performance of spoken digit recognition models using spiking neural networks and recent conventional approaches. The proposed model compares favorably with the high performance methods, such as conventional CNN (with >99% accuracy), while using a power-efficient, biologically plausible framework.

7   Conclusion

A multi-layer SNN was developed to give a novel demonstration of unsupervised feature extraction and discovery for speech processing. The SNN receives input in the form of spike trains from incoming speech signals, extracts Mel-scaled convolutional features, and then extracts higher-level discriminative features. The convolutional layer extracts primary acoustic features to make the network layer stack-admissible for the next layers. The pooling layer summarizes the primary features such that the lower frequencies had higher resolution using Mel-scaled pooling windows. As far as we know, this is a novel feature of the network. The last layer is the feature discovery layer equipped with the probabilistic STDP learning rule. It is trained to discover more complex, independent features using stochastic LIF neurons. The classification results reported by the HMM (with 96% accuracy for the spoken digit recognition problem) showed that the network architecture can discover effective, discriminative acoustic features. Furthermore, the multi-layer network uses sparse, spike-based coding which can be implemented by appropriate, power-efficient VLSI chips.

The initial promising results obtained by unsupervised learning in this model offer promise of scaling to larger problems, such as developing a deep spiking network for the large vocabulary speech recognition (LVSR) problem. Our future work concentrates on a multi-layer SNN for feature extraction followed by a spike-based sequential feature classifier.

References

1. LeCun, Y.: Learning invariant feature hierarchies. In: Fusiello, A., Murino, V., Cucchiara, R. (eds.) ECCV 2012. LNCS, vol. 7583, pp. 496–505. Springer, Heidelberg (2012). doi:10.1007/978-3-642-33863-2_51
2. Bengio, Y.: Learning deep architectures for AI. Found. Trends Mach. Learn. $2(1)$, 1–127 (2009)
3. LeCun, Y., Bengio, Y., Hinton, G.: Deep learning. Nature $521(7553)$, 436–444 (2015)
4. Abdel-Hamid, O., Mohamed, A.R., Jiang, H., Deng, L., Penn, G., Yu, D.: Convolutional neural networks for speech recognition. IEEE/ACM Trans. Audio Speech Lang. Process. $22(10)$, 1533–1545 (2014)
5. Sainath, T.N., Mohamed, A., Kingsbury, B., Ramabhadran, B.: Deep convolutional neural networks for LVCSR. In: 2013 IEEE International Conference on Acoustics, Speech and Signal Processing, pp. 8614–8618. IEEE (2013)
6. Hinton, G., Deng, L., Yu, D., et al.: Deep neural networks for acoustic modeling in speech recognition: the shared views of four research groups. IEEE Signal Process. Mag. $29(6)$, 82–97 (2012)
7. Graves, A., Mohamed, A., Hinton, G.: Speech recognition with deep recurrent neural networks. In: 2013 IEEE International Conference on Acoustics, Speech and Signal Processing, pp. 6645–6649. IEEE (2013)
8. Maass, W.: Networks of spiking neurons: the third generation of neural network models. Neural Netw. $10(9)$, 1659–1671 (1997)
9. Ghosh-Dastidar, S., Adeli, H.: Spiking neural networks. Int. J. Neural Syst. $19(04)$, 295–308 (2009)
10. Kasabov, N., Dhoble, K., Nuntalid, N., Indiveri, G.: Dynamic evolving spiking neural networks for on-line spatio-and spectro-temporal pattern recognition. Neural Netw. 41, 188–201 (2013)
11. Diehl, P.U., Cook, M.: Unsupervised learning of digit recognition using spike-timing-dependent plasticity. Front. Comput. Neurosci. 9 (2015)
12. Kheradpisheh, S.R., Ganjtabesh, M., Masquelier, T.: Bio-inspired unsupervised learning of visual features leads to robust invariant object recognition. Neurocomputing 205, 382–392 (2016)
13. Bengio, Y., Mesnard, T., Fischer, A., Zhang, S., Wu, Y.: STDP-compatible approximation of backpropagation in an energy-based model. Neural Comput. $29(3)$, 555–577 (2017)
14. Masquelier, T., Thorpe, S.J.: Unsupervised learning of visual features through spike timing dependent plasticity. PLoS Comput. Biol. $3(2)$, e31 (2007)
15. Wysoski, S.G., Benuskova, L., Kasabov, N.: Fast and adaptive network of spiking neurons for multi-view visual pattern recognition. Neurocomputing $71(13)$, 2563–2575 (2008)
16. Beyeler, M., Dutt, N.D., Krichmar, J.L.: Categorization and decision-making in a neurobiologically plausible spiking network using a STDP-like learning rule. Neural Netw. 48, 109–124 (2013)

17. Wade, J.J., McDaid, L.J., Santos, J.A., Sayers, H.M.: SWAT: a spiking neural network training algorithm for classification problems. IEEE Trans. Neural Netw. **21**(11), 1817–1830 (2010)

18. Tavanaei, A., Maida, A.S.: A spiking network that learns to extract spike signatures from speech signals. Neurocomputing **240**, 191–199 (2017)

19. Tavanaei, A., Maida, A.S.: Training a hidden Markov model with a Bayesian spiking neural network. J. Signal Process. Syst. 1–10 (2016)

20. Verstraeten, D., Schrauwen, B., Stroobandt, D.: Reservoir-based techniques for speech recognition. In: The 2006 IEEE International Joint Conference on Neural Network Proceedings, pp. 1050–1053. IEEE (2006)

21. Dibazar, A.A., Song, D., Yamada, W., Berger, T.W.: Speech recognition based on fundamental functional principles of the brain. In: IEEE International Joint Conference on Neural Networks, vol. 4, pp. 3071–3075 (2004)

22. Loiselle, S., Rouat, J., Pressnitzer, D., Thorpe, S.: Exploration of rank order coding with spiking neural networks for speech recognition. In: Proceedings of the 2005 IEEE International Joint Conference on Neural Networks, vol. 4, pp. 2076–2080. IEEE (2005)

23. Rabiner, L.R.: A tutorial on hidden Markov models and selected applications in speech recognition. Proc. IEEE **77**(2), 257–286 (1989)

24. Cao, Y., Chen, Y., Khosla, D.: Spiking deep convolutional neural networks for energy-efficient object recognition. Int. J. Comput. Vision **113**(1), 54–66 (2015)

25. Dan, Y., Poo, M.M.: Spike timing-dependent plasticity: from synapse to perception. Physiol. Rev. **86**(3), 1033–1048 (2006)

26. Tavanaei, A., Masquelier, T., Maida, A.S.: Acquisition of visual features through probabilistic spike-timing-dependent plasticity. In: Proceedings of the IEEE International Joint Conference on Neural Networks, pp. 307–314 (2016)

27. Hirsch, H.G., Pearce, D.: The Aurora experimental framework for the performance evaluation of speech recognition systems under noisy conditions. In: ASR2000-Automatic Speech Recognition: Challenges for the New Millenium ISCA Tutorial and Research Workshop (ITRW) (2000)

28. Leonard, R.: A database for speaker-independent digit recognition. In: IEEE International Conference on Acoustics, Speech, and Signal Processing, ICASSP 1984, vol. 9, pp. 328–331. IEEE (1984)

29. Doddington, G.R., Schalk, T.B.: Computers: speech recognition: turning theory to practice: new ICs have brought the requisite computer power to speech technology; an evaluation of equipment shows where it stands today. IEEE Spectr. **18**(9), 26–32 (1981)

30. Dao, M., Suo, Y., Chin, S.P., Tran, T.D.: Structured sparse representation with low-rank interference. In: 2014 48th Asilomar Conference on Signals, Systems and Computers, pp. 106–110. IEEE (2014)

31. Van Doremalen, J., Boves, L.: Spoken digit recognition using a hierarchical temporal memory. In: INTERSPEECH, pp. 2566–2569 (2008)

32. Neil, D., Liu, S.C.: Effective sensor fusion with event-based sensors and deep network architectures. In: 2016 IEEE International Symposium on Circuits and Systems (ISCAS), pp. 2282–2285. IEEE (2016)

33. Groenland, K., Bohte, S.: Efficient forward propagation of time-sequences in convolutional neural networks using deep shifting. arXiv preprint arXiv:1603.03657 (2016)

Author Index

Printed in the United States
By Bookmasters